New
Perspectives

21st Edition

Computer Concepts

Comprehensive

Cengage

Australia • Brazil • Canada • Mexico • Singapore • United Kingdom • United States

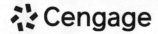

New Perspectives on Computer Concepts:
Comprehensive 21st edition
June Jamrich Parsons

SVP, Product: Erin Joyner

VP, Product: Thais Alencar

Product Director: Mark Santee

Senior Product Manager: Amy Savino

Product Assistant: Ciara Horne

Learning Designer: Zenya Molnar

Content Manager: Christina Nyren

Digital Delivery Quality Partner: Jim Vaughey

Developmental Editor: Dan Seiter

VP, Product Marketing: Jason Sakos

Director, Product Marketing: Danaë April

Executive Product Marketing Manager: Jill Staut

IP Analyst: Ann Hoffman

IP Project Manager: Nick Barrows

Production Service: Lumina Datamatics, Inc.

Designer: Erin Griffin

Cover Credit: Kaveex/Shutterstock.com

Notice to the Reader

Publisher does not warrant or guarantee any of the products described herein or perform any independent analysis in connection with any of the product information contained herein. Publisher does not assume, and expressly disclaims, any obligation to obtain and include information other than that provided to it by the manufacturer. The reader is expressly warned to consider and adopt all safety precautions that might be indicated by the activities described herein and to avoid all potential hazards. By following the instructions contained herein, the reader willingly assumes all risks in connection with such instructions. The publisher makes no representations or warranties of any kind, including but not limited to, the warranties of fitness for particular purpose or merchantability, nor are any such representations implied with respect to the material set forth herein, and the publisher takes no responsibility with respect to such material. The publisher shall not be liable for any special, consequential, or exemplary damages resulting, in whole or part, from the readers' use of, or reliance upon, this material.

For product information and technology assistance, contact us at
Cengage Customer & Sales Support, 1-800-354-9706 or support.cengage.com.

For permission to use material from this text or product, submit all requests online at **www.cengage.com.**

Library of Congress Control Number: 2022934626

Student Edition: ISBN: 978-0-357-67461-1

Loose-leaf Edition: ISBN: 978-0-357-67463-5

Cengage
200 Pier 4 Boulevard
Boston, MA 02210
USA

Cengage is a leading provider of customized learning solutions with employees residing in nearly 40 different countries and sales in more than 125 countries around the world. Find your local representative at **www.cengage.com**.

To learn more about Cengage platforms and services, register or access your online learning solution, or purchase materials for your course, visit **www.cengage.com**.

Printed in the United States of America
Print Number: 01   Print Year: 2022

Table of Contents

Contents at a Glance

Introduction

Module 1

Module 2

Module 3

Module 4

Module 5

Module 6

Module 7

Module 8

Module 9

Module 10

Module 11

Module PY

New Perspectives on Computer Concepts

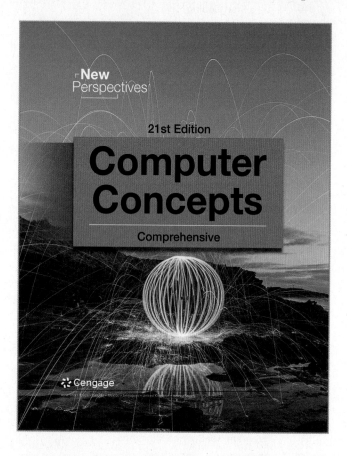

College graduates of the 21st century are expected to have a **broad base of knowledge** to intelligently address social, political, economic, and legal issues associated with rapidly evolving digital technology.

Today's students have a patchwork of knowledge, acquired from using various digital devices. *New Perspectives on Computer Concepts,* 21st edition, helps students build a cohesive framework that organizes this acquired knowledge and serves as a foundation for assimilating new concepts **essential to careers and lifestyles** in our digital world. This course is geared toward introductory students who are first learning about digital literacy and fundamentals of technology.

Updated. This edition has been newly **revised and updated** to increase learning effectiveness and to reflect the wide scope of digital devices in use today, with an enhanced focus on the connectivity that pervades modern life and the security necessary to protect it. Notable updates include the addition of digital assistants in the Introduction module, extensive revisions to the social network lab in Module 5, a new Issue feature in Module 6 about banned apps, updates to the Module 7 Issue and Lab features, a new Issue feature in Module 8 (Is Big Tech Too Big?), coverage of blockchain in Module 10, updates to the Technology in Context feature about politics in Module 10, and revised objectives for the Python programming module.

Targeted Learning Support. This award-winning textbook contains layers of targeted learning support for **active learning** that keeps students engaged and helps them succeed. Using the **MindTap digital platform**, students benefit from interactive feedback and collaborative opportunities.

Reading in the Discipline. Short paragraphs and a clear narrative style help students grasp concepts and learn **how to read technical material**.

Retention. What's the most effective study technique: Taking notes? Reviewing? According to researchers, students study most effectively by simply trying to recall the material they've read, seen, or heard. That's why this edition offers **continuous assessment**. Embedded QuickChecks on just about every page help students recall key concepts while reading and later while reviewing. QuickQuizzes and end-of-module reinforcement promote **successful learning outcomes**.

Hands-On. This edition contains plenty of practical information about how to use apps, manage files, create content, configure security software, and more. Try It! activities throughout the book show students how to **immediately apply concepts in real-world contexts**.

Flipped Classrooms. Flipping a course is easy with this textbook, which includes flipped class projects for **critical thinking**, cyberclassroom exploration, **collaborative group work**, multimedia integration, career building, and **globalization**. End-of-module features, such as Issues and Information Tools, offer additional topics for hands-on in-class activities.

A Fresh Approach to Social Media. Sure, students use social media, but are they familiar with underlying concepts, such as the **Social Media Honeycomb, geolocation, and sociograms**? Are they up to speed with Creative Commons and intellectual property concepts? Do they recognize **fake news**? And do they understand the relevance of **online identity, privacy, and reputation management**? Module 5 offers a fresh approach to social media that delves into concepts while also providing practical how-to tips.

Imaging Technologies. In an increasingly visual world, graphical imaging is becoming ever more sophisticated. Module 1 is packed with information about 360-degree video, stereoscopic graphics, and spherical imaging popularized by **GoPro cameras, YouTube 360, and virtual reality**.

The Latest Technology. Digital technology evolves at a fast pace. This edition keeps students up to date with **Raspberry Pi**, 3D printers, smart appliances, Lightning ports, USB-C, accelerometers, gyro sensors, magnetometers, macOS, **Windows 11**, virtual reality headsets, Microsoft Edge, **two-factor authentication**, ransomware, and more!

Hands-On Programming Module. Using Python provides highly interactive programming activities that **introduce students to the world of programming** without requiring any prior experience. Python is an easy-to-learn language that supports procedural and object-oriented programs.

Infographic Illustrations. Illustrations based on popular infographic visuals are carefully integrated into the learning path to provide **visual scaffolding** that is so important to understanding technical concepts.

Infographic-style illustrations

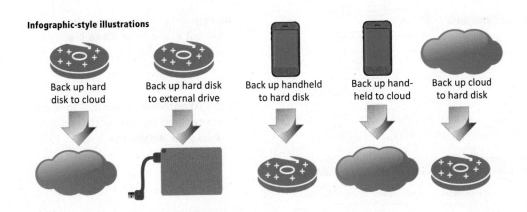

Back up hard disk to cloud

Back up hard disk to external drive

Back up handheld to hard disk

Back up handheld to cloud

Back up cloud to hard disk

Student Resources: The Book

Whether you use the printed book or digital versions, New Perspectives learning materials give you the straight story on today's technology.

Easy to Read. Each module is divided into five **sections**, beginning with a **concept map** that provides a visual overview of topics. **FAQs** answer commonly asked questions about technology and help you follow the flow of the presentation.

Keeps You on Track. As you read each page, watch for **QuickChecks**. They'll help you gauge if you comprehend key concepts. And take some time to complete the **Try It! activities**. They bring concepts to the real world and help you hone your digital skills. **QuickQuizzes** at the end of each section provide a chance to find out if you remember the most important concepts. **End-of-module review** activities such as Key Terms, Interactive Situation Questions, and Interactive Summary questions are great for test prep.

Helps You Explore. The **Issue** section in each module highlights controversial aspects of technology. In the **Technology in Context** section, you'll discover how technology plays a role in careers such as film-making, architecture, banking, and fashion design. The **Information Tools** section helps you sharpen your digital research techniques. Check out the **labs** at the end of each module for some step-by-step exploration into your digital devices.

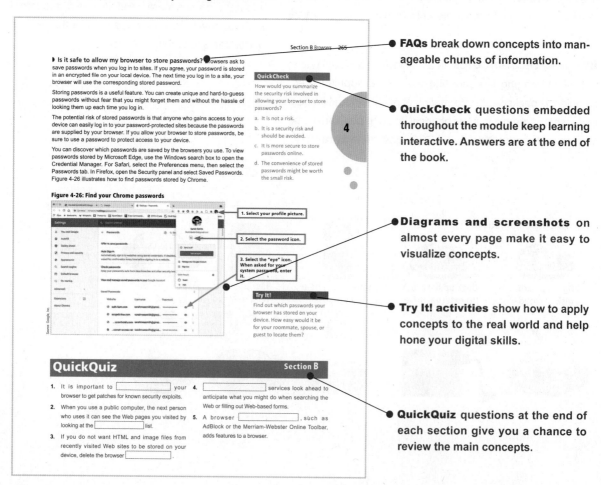

FAQs break down concepts into manageable chunks of information.

QuickCheck questions embedded throughout the module keep learning interactive. Answers are at the end of the book.

Diagrams and screenshots on almost every page make it easy to visualize concepts.

Try It! activities show how to apply concepts to the real world and help hone your digital skills.

QuickQuiz questions at the end of each section give you a chance to review the main concepts.

Student Resources: Online

Digital versions of your textbook include multimedia and hands-on activities designed to enhance your learning experience.

MindTap. The digital version of this book is available in **MindTap**, a personalized online learning platform. In addition to the full text contained in the printed book, the digital version includes activities based on a learning path designed by your instructor that **guides you through the course**.

MindTap is a cost-effective alternative to a printed textbook. You can purchase access to MindTap from *www.cengagebrain.com*.

Jaimie Duplass /Shutterstock.com

Student Resources: Hone Your Technical Reading Skills

If you would like to improve the way you comprehend and retain the information found in technical books and documentation, read on.

Prepare. Your goal is to complete one section of a module. That's a sufficient amount of material for one session. **Look at the concept map** at the beginning of the section. It is designed to help you connect concepts in a Web of relationships, so they become more than random facts.

Divide and Conquer. Don't expect to read technical material in the same way you'd read a novel. Trying to read without stopping from the beginning to the end of a module, chapter, or section is likely to produce more confusion than confidence. Instead, **take it one page at a time**. Read the page and then pause. Imagine that you are going to teach that material to someone else. Then summarize the main points in your own words.

Take Notes. When you come across a fact that you want to remember, make a note. A study conducted by researchers at UCLA and Princeton University revealed that students who take lecture notes using a pen or pencil scored better on tests than students who took notes on their laptops. The same effect may come into play when taking notes as you read. Whether you make notes on screen or on paper, make sure to **use your own words**. That will help you understand the essence of a concept and retain it for future use.

Highlight. Use highlights to **mark passages you do not understand**. This advice may seem contrary to the idea of highlighting key concepts, but simply marking something in the book—or worse, copying and pasting passages from a digital book—does little to help you internalize a concept. Highlighting passages that you do not understand allows you to return to them after you've completed a section. You may find that the passage now makes sense. If not, you've marked a concept that will be a great question for your instructor.

Read the Pictures. The figures in this book are included to reinforce, explain, and **expand the information presented in the written narrative**. Concepts that may seem complex when explained in words can be much easier to understand when you see an illustration, screenshot, or photo. So, take some time with each figure to make sure you understand how it is related to the text that precedes it.

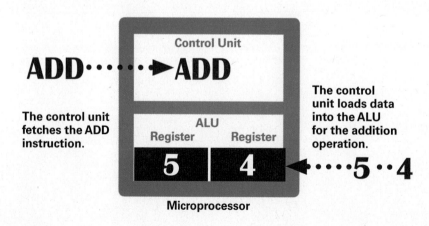

The control unit fetches the ADD instruction.

The control unit loads data into the ALU for the addition operation.

Test Yourself. Researchers at Purdue University discovered that "practicing retrieval" through self-testing is one of the **most effective techniques for learning**. New Perspectives learning materials supply you with lots of opportunities to retrieve material. Make sure to use the QuickChecks, QuickQuizzes, Interactive Summaries, and Interactive Situation Questions. Additional resources, such as flashcards and module quizzes, are available with MindTap.

Be an Active Learner. The concepts you'll learn are not abstract theories. Most have practical applications for today's digital lifestyles. You'll find that concepts are much easier to remember if you can apply them and understand how they are relevant. The **Try It! activities** throughout every module show you how to apply concepts. The best learning strategy is to complete these activities as you encounter them. They'll give you a break from reading and help you to understand how all the practical and conceptual pieces fit together.

Get the Connections. The bubble diagrams supplied at the beginning of each section provide an overview of concepts and their linkages. After reading a section, you might want to **extend the concept maps** by adding more details. You can add another level of concepts. Also, think of additional relationships between the existing concepts and mark them with dotted lines.

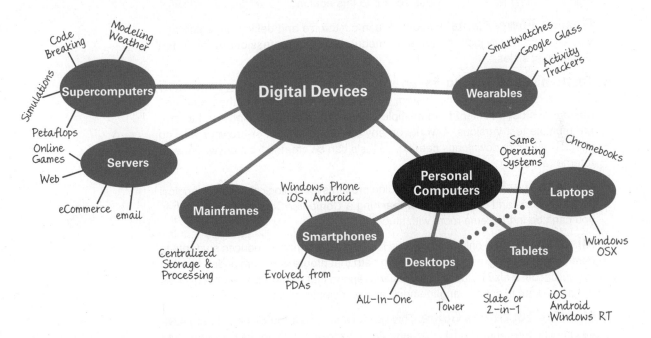

Corrections. Despite intensive attention to quality, occasional typos and other errata slip into the book. Corrections are posted to your student companion site, which you can access by logging in to your account at *login.cengage.com*.

Cengage Instructor Center

Additional instructor resources for this product are available online. Instructor assets include an Instructor's Manual, Educator's Guide, PowerPoint® slides, Solution and Answer Guide, and a testbank powered by Cognero®. Sign up or sign in at *www.cengage.com* to search for and access this product and its online resources.

Instructor's Manual. The Instructor's Manual offers the following comprehensive instructional materials:

- Module objectives
- Purpose and perspective of the module
- What's new in each module
- Module Outline
- Discussion questions and activities

Solution and Answer Guide. Your password-protected instructor resources provide answers to all the QuickChecks, Lab Assignments, Interactive Summaries, Interactive Situation Questions, Issue Try It! activities, and Information Tools Try It! activities.

Transition Guide. This guide highlights all of the changes in the text and in the digital offerings from the previous edition to this edition.

Flexible PowerPoints. Instructors can customize and deliver engaging and visually impressive lectures for each module with the professionally designed PowerPoint slides.

Testbanks and Testing Software. Cengage Learning Testing powered by Cognero is a flexible, online system that allows instructors to author, edit, and manage testbank content from multiple Cengage Learning solutions and to create multiple test versions. It works on any operating system or browser with no special installs or downloads needed, so tests can be created from anywhere with Internet access.

Guide to Teaching Online. This guide presents technological and pedagogical considerations and suggestions for teaching a Computer Concepts course when you can't be in the same room with students.

MindTap. This fully online, interactive learning experience introduces students to core concepts using a simplified learning path that progresses from understanding to application. It also includes analytics and reports that provide a snapshot of class progress, time in course, engagement, and completion rates.

MindTap Educator's Guide. This guide walks you through the unique activities in MindTap, where you'll find them, and how they're built for easier curriculum integration.

From the Author

So much has changed since the first edition of *Computer Concepts* was published in 1994! From year to year, the changes have been subtle, but looking back, it is clear that technology, students, and even education has progressed in amazing and sometimes unexpected directions. As digital technology continues to evolve, New Perspectives continues to keep pace, providing students with up-to-date content and cognitive tools that engage and ensure successful learning outcomes.

Many of today's students have substantially more practical experience with digital devices than their counterparts of twenty years ago, but even these experienced students may lack a cohesive framework for their knowledge.

The goal of *New Perspectives on Computer Concepts* is to bring every student up to speed with computer basics, and then go beyond basic computer literacy to provide students with technical and practical information that every college-educated person would be expected to know.

Whether you are an instructor or a student, we hope that you enjoy the learning experience provided by our text-based and technology-based materials.

Acknowledgments

The book would not exist—and certainly wouldn't arrive on schedule—were it not for the efforts of our media, editorial, and production teams. Grateful thanks to Dan Seiter for his developmental edit and tireless work on every detail of the project; Amy Savino and Christina Nyren for their leadership; Flora Emanuel and the team at Lumina for managing production; and our brilliant sales reps for encouraging instructors to adopt this book to enhance their introductory courses.

A special shout-out in this edition goes to my father, John X. Jamrich, who as a lifelong educator and president of Northern Michigan University showed me the value of helping students achieve their goals through education.

Additional acknowledgements go to the New Perspectives Advisory Committee members, reviewers, and students who have made a tremendous contribution to every edition of *Computer Concepts*. Thank you all!

June Jamrich Parsons

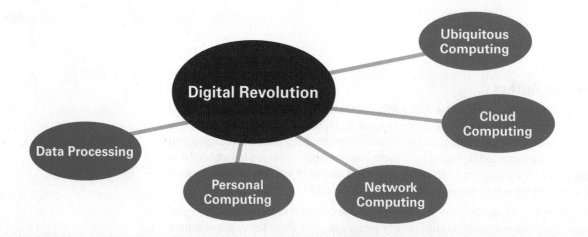

Introduction

Objectives

▶ Name the five phases of the digital revolution and place each on a timeline.

▶ Describe the digital devices that were popular during each phase of the digital revolution.

▶ List at least five characteristics of each phase of the digital revolution.

▶ Find two similarities and two differences between technology in the data processing era and technology in the cloud computing era.

▶ Explain the concept of convergence as it pertains to digital devices.

▶ Distinguish between virtual reality and augmented reality.

▶ Explain the relationship between the Internet of Things and ubiquitous computing.

You live in the information age:

a period in history when information is accessible and technology affects many aspects of everyday life, from the economy to politics and social relationships. The importance of information is not new. It has always been a powerful tool. Scrolls treasured by monks during the Middle Ages, scientific knowledge collected during the Renaissance, and intelligence data collected during the Cold War were all critical in shaping world events. The Information Age is unique because of its underlying technology, which is based on digital electronics. This introduction will help you put the technology that you use into the context of the digital revolution that continues to reinvent the Information Age.

Terminology

digital revolution	data processing	cloud computing	ubiquitous computing
digital	personal computing	convergence	augmented reality
digital content	local software	Web 2.0	Internet of Things
user interface	computer network	social media	virtual assistant
computer terminal	Internet	sharing economy	voice as a user interface
centralized computing	Web	virtual reality	autonomous vehicles

The Digital Revolution

The **digital revolution** is an ongoing process of social, political, and economic change brought about by digital technology, such as microchips, computers, and the Internet.

▶ **What is digital?** **Digital** is a type of technology that represents written, visual, audio, and quantitative data as numbers, such as 1s and 0s. The word *digital* comes from the root *digit*. In the language of mathematics, a digit is the symbol used to write the numerals 0, 1, 2, 3, 4, 5, 6, 7, 8, and 9.

Like the agricultural revolution and the industrial revolution, the digital revolution offers advantages but requires adaptations. Digital innovations challenge the status quo and require societies to make adjustments to traditions, lifestyles, and legislation.

Digital devices were originally called *computer hardware* or *computing machines*. The programs and data they contain were referred to as *computer software*. The software that runs on today's smartphones and tablet devices has come to be known as *apps*.

The technology driving the digital revolution is based on digital electronics and the idea that electrical signals can represent data, such as numbers, words, pictures, and music. We often call this data **digital content**.

▶ **What is the significance of digital content?** An interesting characteristic of digital content is that it can be easily duplicated with no loss of quality. Before digital technology, photocopies of paper documents usually looked blurred. Copying a movie on videotape reduced its quality, and every subsequent copy became progressively worse. Now, digital copies are essentially indistinguishable from originals, which has created new possibilities for content distribution on platforms such as Apple Music and Netflix.

Digital devices, including computers and smartphones, transformed our world. Without them, your favorite form of entertainment would probably be foosball, and you'd be listening to a bulky old Victrola instead of your sleek smartphone (Figure 1).

Figure 1: Is music cheaper today?

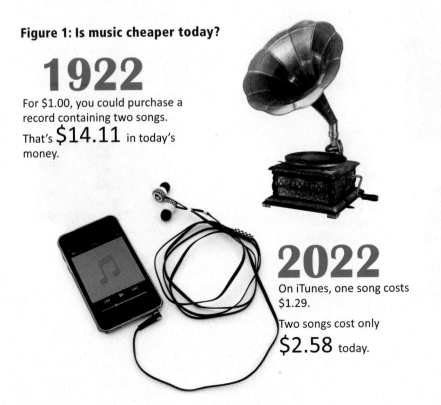

1922
For $1.00, you could purchase a record containing two songs.
That's **$14.11** in today's money.

2022
On iTunes, one song costs $1.29.
Two songs cost only **$2.58** today.

Try It!

Music is less expensive today than it was back in 1922, but what about books? Can you find the price of a book during the 1920s and the price of an equivalent Kindle book today? Don't forget to convert the cost into today's dollars. (Search online for *inflation calculator*.)

Intro

Data Processing

Some historians mark the 1980s as the beginning of the digital revolution, but engineers built the first digital computers during World War II for breaking codes and calculating missile trajectories. In the 1950s, computers were marketed for business applications, such as payroll and inventory management.

▶ **What was computing like back then?** In the first phase of the digital revolution, computers were huge, complex, and expensive devices that stored data on reels of magnetic tape. They existed in limited numbers and were primarily housed in big corporations and government agencies. Computers were operated by trained technicians. Each computer installation required specialized software. The thought that computers might someday be used by millions of people in their homes was only a glimmer of an idea in the minds of science fiction writers.

One drawback to computer use was the **user interface**, the mechanism for entering and viewing data. Back then, processing components for computers were housed in closet-sized cabinets. The main computer unit was separate from the devices used for input and output. Initially, data was entered on punched cards and results were printed on continuous form paper. Later, computers were accessed using the keyboard and display screen of a terminal. A **computer terminal** has little processing capability of its own, so it was simply used to enter data and view results produced by software that ran on the main computer (Figure 2).

This method of computing, in which a main computer holds all of the data and performs all of the processing, is called **centralized computing**. It was the main technology model used during the data processing era. Devices such as terminals and printers were connected to a centralized computer with cables, as shown in Figure 2.

Figure 2: Centralized computing

100%
processing performed
on central computer

Enter
data that will be
processed by central
computer

0%
processing
performed on
terminals

View
data received from
central computer

▶ **Who had access to computers?** During the antiestablishment era of the 1960s, the digital revolution was beginning to transform organizations, but ordinary people had little direct contact with computers.

As with many new technologies, computers were initially viewed with suspicion by consumers. IBM's corporate slogan "THINK" conveyed to some people a disturbing image of giant machine brains.

Computers seemed remote. They were housed out of sight in special facilities and were inaccessible to ordinary people. Computers also seemed impersonal. To uniquely identify an individual, computers used a sequence of numbers such as a Social Security number. The fact that computers tracked people by numbers, rather than by their names, alienated many students and workers.

In the 1960s, computers and punched cards became a symbol of the establishment. Students were uncomfortable with the use of punched cards for storing academic records (Figure 3). The leader of a protest on the University of California, Berkeley campus complained, "You're processed. You become a number on a set of file cards that go through an IBM machine."

▶ **What is data processing?** Throughout the first phase of the digital revolution, businesses adopted computers with increasing enthusiasm based on benefits such as cutting costs and managing mountains of data. Computers and data processing became crucial tools for effective business operations. **Data processing** is based on an input-processing-output cycle. Data goes into a computer, it is processed, and then it is output (Figure 4).

The data processing era lasted from the 1940s through the 1970s. Data processing installations still exist today, but other technologies emerged, making computing available to a more diverse group of users.

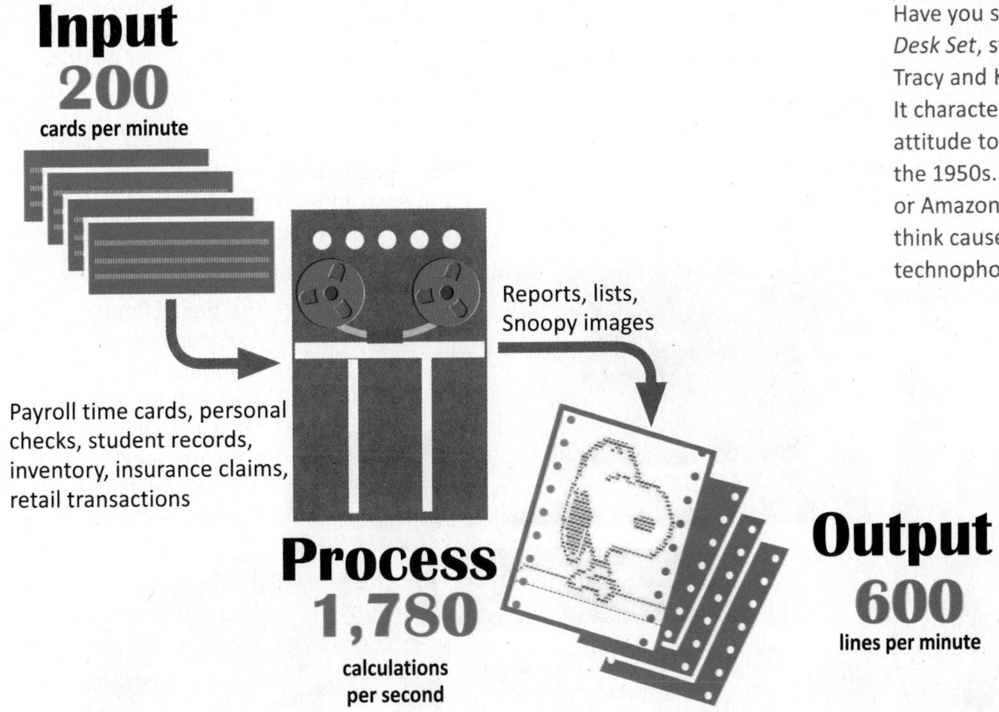

Figure 3: Antiestablishment protests
In the 1950s and 1960s, data used by government and business computers was coded onto punched cards that contained the warning "Do not fold, tear, or mutilate this card." Similar slogans were used by protesters who were concerned that computers would have a dehumanizing effect on society.

Intro

I AM A STUDENT. DO NOT FOLD, SPINDLE, OR MUTILATE.

Try It!

Have you seen the classic film *Desk Set*, starring Spencer Tracy and Katharine Hepburn? It characterizes the public's attitude toward computers in the 1950s. Look for it on Netflix or Amazon Prime. What do you think caused such widespread technophobia?

Figure 4: Data processing

Input
200
cards per minute

Payroll time cards, personal checks, student records, inventory, insurance claims, retail transactions

Reports, lists, Snoopy images

Process
1,780
calculations per second

Output
600
lines per minute

Personal Computing

Digital devices were first available to consumers in the 1970s, when handheld calculators and digital watches hit store shelves. The first personal computers made their debut in 1976, but sales got off to a slow start. Without compelling software applications, personal computers, such as the Apple II and IBM PC, seemed to offer little for their $3,000 price tag. As the variety of software increased, however, consumer interest grew.

▶ **What is personal computing?** The second phase of the digital revolution, **personal computing**, is characterized by standalone computers powered by local software. **Local software** refers to any software that is installed on a computer's storage device. Today, local software resides on hard disks, solid state drives, and flash drives. In the personal computing era, local software was often stored on floppy disks.

During this phase of the digital revolution, computers were used to enhance productivity. Writing, gathering numbers into uncomplicated charts, and scheduling were popular computer-based activities. Computers and videogame machines emerged as entertainment devices, and the game industry drove the development of ever faster and more sophisticated digital components.

During the personal computing phase of the digital revolution, computers were not connected to networks, so they were essentially self-contained units that allowed users to interact only with installed software. On the business front, centralized computer systems continued to run payroll, inventory, and financial software. Some managers used personal computers and spreadsheet software to crunch numbers for business planning.

If you had owned a computer back in the second phase of the digital revolution, it was probably a standalone machine with primitive sound capabilities. The display device looked like an old-fashioned television (Figure 5).

QuickCheck

Personal computing was characterized by _____.

a. software housed on a centralized computer

b. sophisticated software applications

c. storing data in the cloud

d. local software and data storage

Try It!

Imagine that there is no Internet. Take a look at your computer and make a quick list of programs that you'd be able to use in a world without the Internet.

Figure 5: Personal computing circa 1985

Don't expect a color display.

This computer's keyboard weighs more than a modern laptop.

Software was sold in boxes with printed manuals.

You need two disk drives so you can copy data from one disk to another.

This box of floppy disks contains all your data. A disk doesn't have the capacity to hold even one song from your digital music collection.

▶ How extensive was computer use? In contrast to the corporate focus of the data processing phase, personal computing promised to put the power of digital devices in the hands of ordinary people. Computers were no longer a symbol of the corporate establishment. As a new generation of computing devices evolved, IBM's "THINK" slogan was upstaged by Apple's message: "Think Different."

The promise of populist computing, however, was not backed up with compelling reasons to invest in a computer. In 1982, fewer than 10% of U.S. households had a computer. Working on a standalone computer wasn't for everyone. People without an interest in typing up corporate reports or school papers, crunching numbers for accounting, or playing computer games weren't tempted to become active in the digital revolution.

Social scientists even worried that if personal computing became widespread, people would become increasingly isolated as they focused on computer activities rather than social ones. Although rudimentary email systems existed on centralized corporate computers, home computers were not connected, so there was no way to transmit email messages among them.

▶ How long was the second phase of the digital revolution? Computer ownership increased at a gradual pace until the mid-1990s, and then it accelerated into the third phase of the digital revolution (Figure 6).

Intro

QuickCheck

What problem arising from personal computing worried social scientists?

a. Big corporations spying on customer behavior

b. Increasing isolation as people spent more and more time using a computer

c. Privacy

d. Piracy

Figure 6: Personal computer ownership (percent of U.S. households)

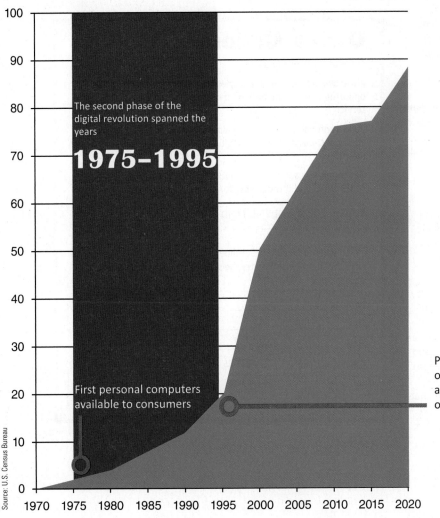

The second phase of the digital revolution spanned the years

1975–1995

First personal computers available to consumers

Personal computer ownership took off after the Internet opened to public use

Source: U.S. Census Bureau

QuickCheck

During the second phase of the digital revolution, which one of the following was making news headlines?

a. A new band called The Beatles

b. The first space flights

c. Think Different

d. WikiLeaks

Network Computing

The third phase of the digital revolution materialized as computers became networked and when the Internet was opened to public use. A **computer network** is a group of computers linked together to share data and resources.

❱ **What kinds of networks were available?** Network technology existed before the Internet became popular, but these networks were mainly deployed to connect computers within a school or business. For the most part, these networks connected devices using cables; wireless networks were not available.

During this era, networks were complicated to set up and were often unreliable. Before the Internet opened to public use, online services such as CompuServe and America Online operated centralized computer networks that could be accessed by the public from dial-up modems.

❱ **What role did the Internet play?** The Internet is a global computer network that was originally developed as a military project and was later handed over to the National Science Foundation for research and academic use. When restrictions on commercial use of the Internet were lifted in the early 1990s, newly emerged ISPs offered fee-based Internet access. America Online, CompuServe, and other online services expanded to offer Internet-based chat and Web access. Excerpts from the AOL ad in Figure 7 may help you to appreciate the digital environment during this phase of the digital revolution.

Try It!

Internet connections were initially made over telephone lines with a device called an acoustic modem. You'll be surprised to see how these modems work. Search for a photo of one online. Could you use this type of modem with your smartphone?

Figure 7: Using an online service in the 1990s

Step 1: Mail in your application and wait to receive your software.

Step 2: Your software arrives on a floppy disk. Insert it in the disk drive and install it.

Step 3: Fire up the software and your modem to make a connection. If you have an acoustic modem, put your telephone handset into it.

Step 4: Download software, send email, post messages, and mingle with people from all over the world in online chat rooms.

Own a Modem?

Try America Online for FREE

If you own a computer and modem, we invite you to take this opportunity to **try the nation's most exciting online service**.

Build a software library by downloading selected files from a library of thousands—productivity software, games, and more!

Get computing support from industry experts at online conferences and through easy-to-use message boards.

DETACH AND MAIL TODAY

YES, I want to try America Online! Send me FREE software and a FREE trial membership to try the service.

Name: _____

Address: _____

City: _____

State: _____ Zip: _____

Disk type and size: ❑ 5.25   ❑ 3.5

                           ❑ High Density   ❑ Double Density

Source: *Wired*, May 1993

▶ What about the Web? When historians look back on the digital revolution, they are certain to identify the Web as a major transformative influence. The **Web** (short for *World Wide Web*) is a collection of linked documents, graphics, and audio that can be accessed over the Internet.

A key aspect of the Web is that it adds content and substance to the Internet. Without the Web, the Internet would be like a library without any books or a railroad without any trains. Online storefronts, auction sites, news, sports, travel reservations, and music downloads made the Web a compelling digital technology for just about everyone.

▶ So what was computing like during this phase? From 1995 to 2010, computing was characterized by the increasing use of laptops (Figure 8) and the following elements:

Sophisticated software. The network computing phase may have been the peak for productivity software. Computer owners amassed large collections of software, purchased in boxes containing multiple distribution CDs. Software such as Microsoft Office, Norton's Internet Security suite, and Corel Digital Studio required local installation and provided more features than most people had any desire to use. This trend reverses during the next phase of the digital revolution, when applications become simpler and more focused on specific tasks.

Stationary Internet access. Even as laptop computers began to displace desktop models, connecting to the Internet required a cable that effectively tethered computers to a nearby phone jack or cable outlet. In the next phase of the digital revolution, Internet access breaks free from cables and goes mobile.

Online communication. Email was the first widespread technology used to communicate over the Internet. Online services such as CompuServe and AOL pioneered chat rooms, which were primitive versions of Google Hangouts. Early forums and message boards were similar to Facebook timelines. A technology called Voice over IP allowed participants to bypass the telephone company to make phone calls over the Internet. That technology eventually developed into Skype and similar video chat services.

Multiplayer games. Sophisticated computer games reached a peak during the network phase of the digital revolution. Audio and visual hardware components improved to support video-realistic game environments, artificial intelligence opponents, and multiple players logging in remotely and chatting with other players over headsets. In the next phase, mobile devices become popular gaming platforms, but hardware limitations restrict the feature set.

Music downloads. During the network computing phase, an online business called Napster pioneered the concept of sharing and downloading music. Subscribers exchanged millions of music files, which they played through the speakers of their computers. The music was protected by copyright, however, making sharing and distribution illegal. This type of file sharing activity and rampant software piracy became one of the defining problems associated with the network phase of the digital revolution.

iTunes and other services for legally downloading music soon appeared, along with dedicated playback devices, such as the iPod. Video distribution over the Internet lagged behind until connection speeds increased in the next phase of the digital revolution.

Intro

Figure 8: Laptops
Laptop computers were the primary devices for accessing the Internet prior to 2010. User interfaces evolved to include color, graphics, and mice.

Cloud Computing

Around 2010, the digital revolution eased into a fourth phase called **cloud computing**, which provided access to information, applications, communications, and storage over the Internet.

◗ **What did cloud computing change?** Before cloud computing, most computers ran software based locally. For example, to use a word processor, you might fire up the latest edition of Microsoft Word, which you'd installed on your computer's hard disk. Prior to the cloud, you stored data locally, too. Email, documents, photos, and music all resided on your computer's hard disk or flash drive.

With cloud computing, all that changed. In the cloud, you can use your browser to access word processing applications that run from the Internet instead of software that you have installed on your local hard disk. You can use online applications to manage your email, create floor plans, produce presentations, and carry out a host of other activities. You can store your data in the cloud, too, making it available on any of your digital devices that connect to the Internet.

The cloud gets its name from diagrams like the one in Figure 9, which shows Internet-based applications, storage, and other services outlined by a cloud-like shape designed to help you visualize the idea that cloud services are "out there" somewhere on the Internet.

QuickCheck

Which characteristic of cloud computing most sets it apart from network computing?

a. Internet access

b. Sophisticated software

c. The migration of applications and data off local devices

d. File sharing

Figure 9: The cloud hosts applications, content, and services

◗ **Wait, this sounds familiar!** If cloud computing sounds a bit like centralized computing, you're paying attention. The concept of applications and data residing somewhere other than on a local device is common to both centralized and cloud computing. The cloud concept reawakens the idea of monolithic computing facilities, as opposed to distributed architectures of the network era. The fact that your cloud-based data is not stored on devices under your direct control is a potential privacy and security concern, which is a topic for later modules.

▶ **Are smartphones the signature device of the cloud computing era?**
The cloud itself is populated by commercial-grade high-speed computers and high-capacity storage devices. The consumer side is dominated by smartphones (Figure 10) and tablet computers. These handheld devices—a product of convergence—were the driving force for many cloud innovations.

▶ **What is convergence?** The expansion of cloud computing is due in part to convergence, a process by which several technologies with distinct functionalities evolve to form a single product. Convergence was important to the digital revolution because it created sophisticated mobile devices whose owners demanded access to the same services available from a full-size desktop computer. Those services became available in the cloud.

Your computer plays movies. Your cell phone has a camera. Your clock has a radio. Your watch functions as a communications device. You can store data on your iPod Touch. All these are examples of technological convergence.

Convergence worked its magic on cell phones, computers, portable media players, televisions, digital cameras, GPSs, watches, and ebook readers. Now you get features from all of them by purchasing a single digital device, such as a smartphone or tablet computer (Figure 11).

Figure 10: Smartphones
Cloud computing caters to smartphones and other mobile devices that are a product of convergence. They access and share data from the cloud using apps.

Intro

Figure 11: Smartphones are a prime example of convergence

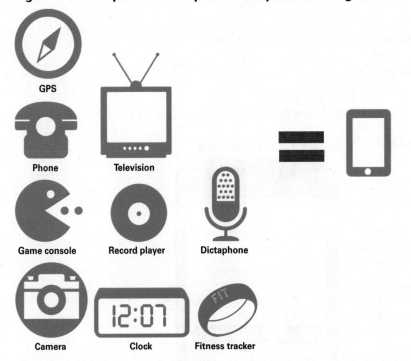

▶ **Why do these devices need the cloud?** Smartphones are portable. Compared to desktop and laptop computers, smartphones have small screens, lack a proper keyboard, and have limited space for storing apps and data. The cloud offers a convenient place to store data and applications. Think of the cloud as a repository for streaming videos, music, photos, and apps. With that concept in mind, you will begin to understand the cloud's importance to today's consumers.

QuickCheck

Which of the following instigated the move to cloud computing?

a. Social media

b. Mobile devices

c. Touchscreens

d. Music downloads

▶ **Did the cloud kill the Web?** A 2010 *Wired* magazine cover announced "The Web Is Dead." That pronouncement was premature. The cloud consumed the Web but did not kill it. As a legacy technology from the networking era, the Web continues to be a global marketplace where Amazon, Alibaba, and other retailers sell directly to consumers.

That said, Facebook, Twitter, and Google Apps sent the Web in new directions. Once a collection of storefronts run exclusively by businesses and corporations, the Web expanded into a global hub where content was created by individuals, shared on social media sites, and uploaded to content sharing platforms. This grassroots Web of user-created content is sometimes referred to as **Web 2.0**.

▶ **What role do social media play in the cloud era?** Facebook, Twitter, and other social media turned the worry of social isolation on its head; instead of computers decreasing human interaction, social media encourage interpersonal communications and relationships. **Social media** are digitally mediated applications designed for communication, social interaction, and consumer-generated content.

Many factors influenced the popularity of these sites, but one important factor is their ease of use. Initially offered as Web sites, there was no software to install and no updates to worry about. Getting started was as simple as registering your name and creating a password. Now, access to social media is also available from mobile apps, which can be installed on a smartphone or tablet with a single touch.

The connections that social media offer come at a price, and that price is not just monetary. Today's digital citizens surrender a substantial amount of privacy, exposing information that can be used by predators. Privacy, or the lack of it, may be the defining challenge of cloud computing.

Another challenge is the growing pervasiveness of advertising. Where social media was once a platform for exchanging information between friends and colleagues, intrusive advertising is now found on virtually every Web page, Facebook timeline, and Twitter stream.

▶ **Cloud-enabled apps?** A key characteristic of the cloud computing era is globe-spanning sharing services. Cloud-based services such as Uber, Airbnb, and Etsy are part of the **sharing economy** in which consumers offer goods and services to other consumers through a shared digital platform.

These sharing services use the cloud to communicate and process data. The apps used by consumers may look simple (Figure 12), but behind the scenes an amazing amount of computer power handles the necessary data and logistics.

Try It!

In 2011, the United Nations declared that the Internet "is an indispensable tool for realizing a range of human rights...." Visit the Internet World Stats site to find out what percentage of the world's population has Internet access.

Figure 12: The Uber app

2017 Uber Technologies Inc.

Ubiquitous Computing

Many computing technologies use data to represent things in the real world. Photos represent people. Maps show the location of places. Videos give us a glimpse of events. Game-based fantasy worlds and characters entertain us. **Virtual reality** (VR) creates a simulated three-dimensional world that's experienced with a headset (Figure 13).

Figure 13: Virtual reality simulates the real world

Photos, videos, and games are all conjured from data. None of it is tangible reality. Augmented reality, the Internet of Things, digital assistants, and automated vehicles are shaping a new digital era in which technologies bring computing beyond the screen and into the world of tangible objects. This fifth stage of the digital revolution, **ubiquitous computing**, is characterized by a focus on controlling and manipulating real-world objects instead of data.

▶ **What is augmented reality?** **Augmented reality** (AR) superimposes data over the real world. AR applications can help you navigate through a city by displaying your route over a live view of surrounding streets and buildings. It is the technology that "paints" the first-down line on the field as you watch an NFL game.

Pokémon GO popularized augmented reality and provides a great example of how it works. It shows the real world in your vicinity as a pass-through image from your cell phone camera. Pokémon augments this reality with game characters that are superimposed on the camera image (Figure 14).

Figure 14: Pokémon Go is augmented reality

▶ **What is the Internet of Things?** The **Internet of Things** (IoT) connects sensors embedded in machines, clothing, and other objects to the Internet, where they can report data and receive commands. It provides a clear example of digital technology controlling objects in the real world.

You're probably familiar with smartphone-controlled IoT devices such as digital locks, smart LED lights, smoke alarms, and doorbell cameras. These devices send and receive signals to and from your phone using a Wi-Fi network, the Internet, or a cellular network.

Terminology

Ubiquitous computing is sometimes referred to as *pervasive computing*. The idea is not new. In the 1990s, Mark Weiser predicted that computers will "weave themselves into the fabric of everyday life until they are indistinguishable from it."

Intro

A smart smoke alarm is an IoT device that not only contains sensors but also contains circuitry that connects to a home Wi-Fi network. That Wi-Fi network can establish communication with a smartphone to report its status and accept commands. If the device senses smoke when you are away from home, it sends an alarm to your phone. The phone can be used to remotely silence a false alarm—such as when your roommate burns a bagel in the toaster.

IoT devices can also be controlled by using a **virtual assistant**, such as Alexa, Cortana, Google Assistant, or Siri. This technology's **voice as a user interface** (VUI) lets you issue voice commands to turn on lights, play music, lock doors, search for answers, and monitor your home security system.

However, the Internet of Things also connects multiple devices so that they can communicate with each other. A smart thermostat is designed to control a home's heating and cooling systems. For example, if a faulty furnace outputs dangerous carbon monoxide (CO), an IoT smoke detector can sense a high level of CO and send a message to a compatible IoT thermostat to turn off the furnace (Figure 15).

Figure 15: The Internet of Things links devices with embedded sensors

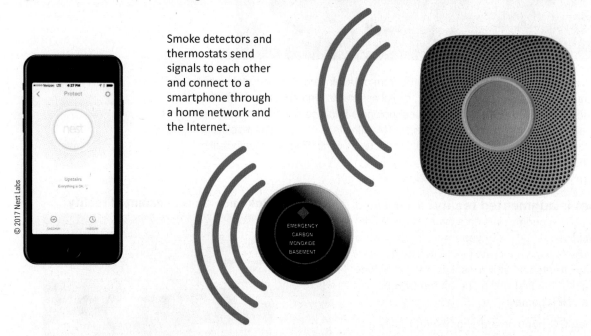

Smoke detectors and thermostats send signals to each other and connect to a smartphone through a home network and the Internet.

© 2017 Nest Labs

▶ **What about autonomous vehicles?** Self-driving cars and robots are related to the Internet of Things because they require sensor-equipped parts to communicate with each other. **Autonomous vehicles**, for example, navigate without human intervention using sensors to detect the surrounding environment, physical location, speed, and other parameters. They send data and receive commands from an onboard computer running sophisticated artificial intelligence software.

Autonomous vehicles are clear examples of ubiquitous computing—the use of digital technology to manipulate objects in the real world, instead of abstract data. You'll delve into some of these ubiquitous technologies in future modules. For now, try to guess the year in which you take your first ride in a self-driving car (Figure 16).

Figure 16: Autonomous vehicles exemplify ubiquitous computing

No hands!

Intro

▶ **Are there more changes to come?** If we can learn one thing from the evolving Information Age, it is this: Change is inevitable. Where savvy consumers once gave up on slow GEO satellite Internet service, new LEO satellites may offer speedy access from remote areas. (GEO stands for "geosynchronous equatorial orbit"; LEO stands for "low Earth orbit.") Today, your favorite social media platform is Facebook; in the future, Facebook may go the way of CompuServe. Figure 17 summarizes changes through each era of the digital revolution.

Figure 17: The Information Age evolves

Expired	Tired	Uninspired	Desired	Admired
Data processing	Personal computing	Network computing	Cloud computing	Ubiquitous IoT
Big corporate and government computers	Desktop computers	Laptop computers	Smartphones and tablets	Digital assistants
Custom applications	Standalone applications	Software suites	Mobile apps and cloud-based apps	Embedded apps
CB radios	Dial-up Internet access	Cable and GEO satellite Internet	4G and Wi-Fi Internet access	5G and LEO satellite Internet
ARPANET	AOL and CompuServe	The Web and email	Social media	Augmented reality
Arcade games	2D action games	3D multiplayer games	Touchscreen microgames	Virtual reality
Printers	Keyboards	Mice	Touchscreens	Voice as a user interface

▶ **So what's the point?** Learning about digital technology is not just about circuits and electronics, nor is it only about digital gadgets, such as computers and portable music players. Digital technology permeates the very core of modern life.

Understanding how this technology works and thinking about its potential can help you comprehend many issues related to privacy, security, freedom of speech, and intellectual property. It will help you become a better consumer and give you insights into local and world events.

As you continue to read this textbook, don't lose sight of the big picture. On one level, you might be simply learning about how to use a computer and software in this course. On a more profound level, however, you are accumulating knowledge about how digital technology applies to broader cultural and legal issues that are certain to affect your life far into the future.

QuickCheck

According to Figure 17, AOL and CompuServe were popular when _____.

a. data processing was the main digital technology

b. most people had dial-up Internet access and used desktop computers

c. smartphones and tablets were introduced

d. people stopped using cloud computing

QuickQuiz

Introduction

1. Data processing is based on an [_____]-processing-output cycle.

2. In the personal computing phase of the digital revolution, data and software were stored on [_____] devices, such as hard drives.

3. The idea that several technologies evolve into a single device is called [_____].

4. Two major technologies that defined the network computing era were the [_____] and the Web.

5. [_____] computing provides access to information, applications, communications, and storage over the Internet.

1 Digital Content

So many aspects of life today are digital: music, photos, movies, news, and communications. How can all this diverse "stuff" be accessed through one device, such as a laptop or a smartphone? It's all about digitization.

●Try It!   Apply what you learn.

- Compress files containing various types of data, including text, photos, music, and videos.
- Record audio files.
- Select an audio sampling rate and file format for high-quality sound in files that won't use up all your storage space.
- Convert audio files from one format to another.
- Use voice commands to control your digital devices.
- Select the best file format for digital images, such as photos and scans, taking into account which formats reduce image quality with lossy compression.
- Convert a paper document into a digital file that can be edited using word processing software.
- Work with RGB colors in decimal, hexadecimal, or binary notation.
- Use resolution to gauge the maximum size for an image.
- Use "photoshopping" techniques to enhance, colorize, clone, inpaint, clip, and merge photo images.
- Capture 360-degree images on your smartphone.
- Draw vector images for logos and infographics.
- Convert vector images into bitmaps.
- Render a 3D image from a wireframe.
- Use video editing software to combine video footage with a soundtrack.
- Select output settings for a video, including aspect ratio, resolution, bit rate, compression level, and file format.
- Transcode a video from one file format to another.
- View vector and bitmap images in a VR headset.

● Pre-Check

Gauge your level of expertise. The answers are in the module.

6

How do you write it in binary?

How do you write it in ASCII?

A sound wave is digitized by _____ its height thousands of times per second.

Which type of compression makes files smaller without any data loss?

LOSSY

LOSSLESS

List **FIVE** bitmap graphics formats:

_____

_____

_____

_____

_____

What is the basic unit of sound in speech synthesis?

#EE82EE

is the hexadecimal number for what color?

BLACK

GREEN

VIOLET

WHITE

Bike.svg

Bitmap or vector?

List two popular video codecs:

_____

_____

Adding light and shadows is part of what process that creates an image from a wireframe?

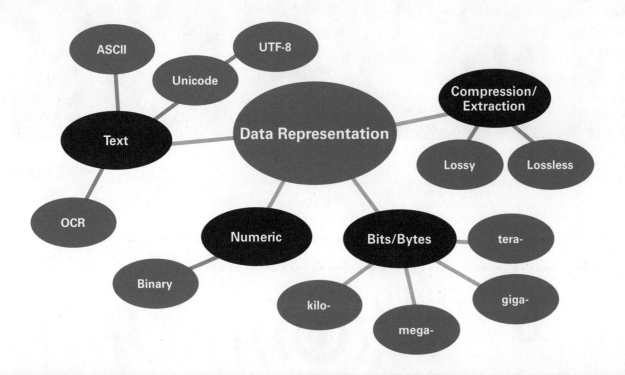

Objectives

▶ List three technologies that digital devices use to physically store or transmit 1s and 0s.

▶ Write the numbers 1 through 10 in binary.

▶ Decipher ASCII text.

▶ Demonstrate how to use the terms *bit, byte, megabyte, megabit,* and *gigabyte* in the context of data storage and digital devices.

▶ Distinguish between data that would be represented by binary numbers and data that would be represented by ASCII or Unicode.

▶ Explain how OCR relates to ASCII and Unicode.

▶ Describe the difference between lossy and lossless compression.

▶ Demonstrate how to compress a file.

Text, numbers, music, videos, images, and speech; all of this "stuff" is digital content. The amazing aspect of digital technology is that it distills such diverse content into 0s and 1s and stores them as pulses of electricity. Understanding the data representation concepts presented in Section A will help you grasp the essence of the digital world and get a handle on all the jargon pertaining to bits, bytes, megahertz, and gigabytes.

Terminology

data	file name extension	UTF-8	megabyte
data representation	file format	ASCII text	gigabit
digital data	numeric data	delimiter	gigabyte
analog data	binary number system	OCR	data compression
binary	character data	byte	lossless compression
digitization	ASCII	kilobit	lossy compression
bit	Extended ASCII	kilobyte	
file	Unicode	megabit	

Data Representation Basics

Digital content, such as an ebook, document, image, music, or video, is a compilation of data. **Data** refers to the symbols that represent people, events, things, and ideas. Data can be a name, a number, the colors in a photograph, or the notes in a musical composition.

▶ **Is there a difference between data and information?** In everyday conversation, people use the terms *data* and *information* interchangeably. However, some technology professionals make a distinction between the two terms. They define data as the symbols that represent people, events, things, and ideas. Data becomes information when it is presented in a format that people can understand and use. As a general rule, remember that (technically speaking) data is used by machines, such as computers; information is used by humans.

▶ **What is data representation?** **Data representation** refers to the form in which data is stored, processed, and transmitted. Devices such as smartphones, portable media players, and computers store data in digital formats that can be handled by electronic circuitry. Today, digital data representation has replaced the analog methods previously used for storing and transmitting photos, videos, music, and text.

▶ **What's the difference between analog and digital?** **Digital data** is text, numbers, graphics, sound, and video that have been converted into discrete digits such as 0s and 1s. In contrast, **analog data** is represented using an infinite scale of values. For a simple illustration of the difference between analog and digital, consider the way you can control the lights in a room using a traditional light switch or a dimmer switch.

A dimmer switch has a rotating dial that controls a continuous range of brightness. It is, therefore, analog. A traditional light switch, on the other hand, has two discrete states: on and off. There are no inbetween states, so this type of light switch is digital.

A traditional light switch is also **binary** because there are only two possible states. Technically, a digital device could represent data using more than two states. Some of the earliest computers represented numbers using the decimal system. Today, however, most digital devices represent numbers and other data using the binary system.

Terminology

The word *data* can be correctly treated either as a plural noun or as an abstract mass noun, so the phrases "The data are being processed" and "The data is being processed" are both correct usage. In this textbook, the word *data* is paired with singular verbs and modifiers.

1

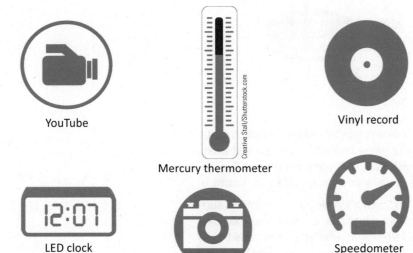

YouTube

Mercury thermometer

Creative Stall/Shutterstock.com

Vinyl record

LED clock

Film camera

Speedometer

QuickCheck

Which of the devices on the left illustrate analog data representation?

a. The speedometer and YouTube

b. The thermometer and the vinyl record

c. All but the speedometer

d. All but YouTube and the clock

How does digital data work? The process of converting information, such as text, numbers, photos, videos, or music, into digital data that can be manipulated by electronic devices is called **digitization**.

Imagine that you want to send a message by flashing a light. Your light switch offers two states: on and off. You can use sequences of ons and offs to represent various letters of the alphabet. To write down the representation for each letter, you can use 0s and 1s. The 0s represent the off state of your light switch; the 1s indicate the on state. For example, the sequence *on on off off* would be written as 1100, and you might decide that sequence represents the letter *A*.

The 0s and 1s used to represent digital data are referred to as binary digits. It is from this term that we get the word *bit—binary digit*. A **bit** is a 0 or 1 used in the digital representation of data.

Digital devices are electronic, so you can envision bits flowing within these devices as pulses of light. But digital signals can take many forms, as shown in Figure 1-1.

QuickCheck

Digital devices work with bits in all of the following ways except:

a. voltage variations

b. light and dark spots

c. analog values

d. orientation of magnetized particles

Figure 1-1: Many ways to represent digital data

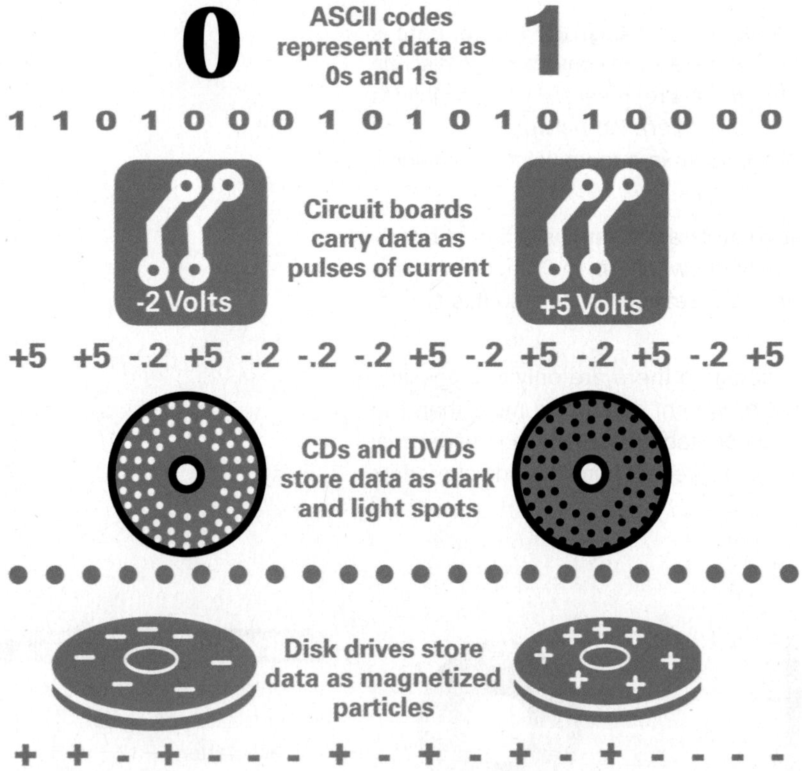
0
ASCII codes represent data as 0s and 1s
1
1 1 0 1 0 0 0 1 0 1 0 1 0 1 0 0 0 0
Circuit boards carry data as pulses of current
-2 Volts
+5 Volts
+5 +5 -.2 +5 -.2 -.2 -.2 +5 -.2 +5 -.2 +5 -.2 +5
CDs and DVDs store data as dark and light spots
Disk drives store data as magnetized particles
+ + - + - - - + - + - + - + - - - -

How is digital data stored? Digital data is typically stored in files. A digital file, usually referred to simply as a **file**, is a named collection of data that exists on a storage medium, such as a hard disk, CD, DVD, or flash drive. A file can contain data for a term paper, Web page, email message, or video, for example.

Every file has a unique name, such as MyPodCast.mp3. A **file name extension**, such as .mp3, can be appended to the end of the file name after a period. This extension indicates the **file format**—the type of data in the file and the way it is encoded. Let's take a look at how numbers, text, images, sound, and video are encoded into digital formats that become computer files.

Representing Numbers

Numeric data consists of numbers that can be used in arithmetic operations. For example, your annual income is numeric data, as is your age. That concept seems clear, but some data that looks numeric is represented differently. Social Security numbers, telephone numbers, street numbers, and similar data are not represented by numeric data. These "numerals" are not considered numeric data because they are never used in mathematical calculations. This numeric quirk is a key concept in the digital world and turns up when you work with spreadsheets, databases, and computer programming.

▶ How do digital devices represent numbers? Digital devices represent numeric data using the binary number system, also called base 2. The **binary number system** has only two digits: 0 and 1. No numeral like 2 exists in this system, so the number "two" is represented in binary as 10 (pronounced "one zero"). You'll understand why if you think about what happens when you're counting from 1 to 10 in the familiar decimal system. After reaching 9, you run out of digits. For ten, you have to use the digits 10—zero is a placeholder and the 1 indicates one group of tens.

In binary, you just run out of digits sooner—right after you count to 1. To get to the next number, you use 0 as a placeholder and 1 indicates one group of twos. In binary, then, you count 0 (zero), 1 (one), 10 (one zero), instead of counting 0, 1, 2 in decimal. If you need to brush up on binary numbers, refer to Figure 1-2.

QuickCheck

Which one of the following is considered numeric data?

a. Driver license number J522-67-20-200-5

b. Telephone number 906-222-3450

c. The $28,995.00 cost of a car

d. The address 22 E. Main Street

1

Figure 1-2: Binary equivalent of decimal numbers

Decimal (Base 10)	Binary (Base 2)
0	0
1	1
2	10
3	11
4	100
5	101
6	110
7	111
8	1000
9	1001
10	1010
11	1011
1000	1111101000

QuickCheck

Figure 1-2 shows the binary equivalent for numbers 0 through 11 and 1000. What is the binary equivalent for the number 12?

a. 10111

b. 1100

c. 10000

d. 1111

The important point to understand is that the binary number system allows digital devices to represent virtually any number simply by using 0s and 1s. Digital devices can then perform calculations using these numbers. The ability to perform rapid and accurate calculations was the key feature of the first computers, and it now provides the foundation for online banking, ecommerce, and many other number-crunching applications.

Representing Text

Character data is composed of letters, symbols, and numerals that are not used in calculations. Examples of character data include your name, address, and hair color. Character data is commonly referred to as "text."

❱ How do digital devices represent text? Digital devices employ several types of codes to represent character data, including ASCII, Unicode, and their variants. **ASCII** (American Standard Code for Information Interchange, pronounced "ASK ee") requires seven bits for each character. For example, the ASCII code for an uppercase *A* is 1000001. ASCII provides codes for 128 characters, including uppercase letters, lowercase letters, punctuation symbols, and numerals.

Extended ASCII is a superset of ASCII that uses eight bits for each character. For example, Extended ASCII represents the uppercase letter *A* as 01000001. Using eight bits instead of seven bits allows Extended ASCII to provide codes for 256 characters. The additional Extended ASCII characters include boxes and other graphical symbols.

Unicode (pronounced "YOU ni code") uses 8, 16, 24, or 32 bits and provides codes for representing the alphabets of 154 modern and historical languages, as well as a variety of symbols and emojis.

UTF-8 is a variable-length Unicode standard that uses eight bits for common ASCII characters, but can use 16, 24, or 32 bits as necessary to represent the alphabets for Cyrillic, Greek, Hebrew, and other languages.

Take a look at the ASCII codes in Figure 1-3. Notice there is a code for the space character in addition to codes for symbols, numerals, uppercase letters, and lowercase letters.

QuickCheck

Write out **Hi!** in Extended ASCII code. (Hint: Use an uppercase *H*, but a lowercase *i*.)

H   [   ]

i   [   ]

!   [   ]

Figure 1-3: ASCII codes

00100000	Space	00110011	3	01000110	F	01011001	Y	01101100	l
00100001	!	00110100	4	01000111	G	01011010	Z	01101101	m
00100010	"	00110101	5	01001000	H	01011011	[	01101110	n
00100011	#	00110110	6	01001001	I	01011100	\	01101111	o
00100100	$	00110111	7	01001010	J	01011101	]	01110000	p
00100101	%	00111000	8	01001011	K	01011110	^	01110001	q
00100110	&	00111001	9	01001100	L	01011111	_	01110010	r
00100111	'	00111010	:	01001101	M	01100000	`	01110011	s
00101000	(	00111011	;	01001110	N	01100001	a	01110100	t
00101001	)	00111100	<	01001111	O	01100010	b	01110101	u
00101010	*	00111101	=	01010000	P	01100011	c	01110110	v
00101011	+	00111110	>	01010001	Q	01100100	d	01110111	w
00101100	,	00111111	?	01010010	R	01100101	e	01111000	x
00101101	-	01000000	@	01010011	S	01100110	f	01111001	y
00101110	.	01000001	A	01010100	T	01100111	g	01111010	z
00101111	/	01000010	B	01010101	U	01101000	h	01111011	{
00110000	0	01000011	C	01010110	V	01101001	i	01111100		
00110001	1	01000100	D	01010111	W	01101010	j	01111101	}
00110010	2	01000101	E	01011000	X	01101011	k	01111110	~

▶ **Why are there ASCII codes for numbers?** While glancing at the table of ASCII codes in Figure 1-3, you might have wondered why the table contains codes for 0, 1, 2, 3, and so on. Aren't these numbers represented by the binary number system? Yes, the binary number system is used for representing numeric data, but these ASCII codes are used for numerals, such as Social Security numbers and phone numbers that are not used for calculations. For example, 475-6677 is a phone number; it is not a formula that means subtract 6677 from 475.

▶ **Where is digital text used?** Digital text is everywhere. It is the foundation for all kinds of digital documents, Web sites, social media sites, games, and email. It is also the basis for ebooks designed for Kindles and other ebook readers.

Documents produced on a digital device are stored as a string of 1s and 0s and generally encoded as ASCII or UTF-8. Some kinds of documents simply contain this plain text, whereas other documents contain formatting codes to produce bold fonts, columns, and other effects.

▶ **What is plain text?** Plain, unformatted text is sometimes called **ASCII text** and is stored in a so-called text file with a name ending in .txt. On Apple devices, these files are labeled "Plain Text." In Windows, these files are labeled "Text Document," like this:

 Roller Coasters.txt   Text   Document   2   KB

ASCII text files can be created with text editors, such as TextEdit and Notepad. They are typically used for writing computer programs because executable program code cannot include formatting such as underlining and special fonts. They can also be used for creating Web pages.

Text files can usually be opened by any word processing software, regardless of the type of device. In that sense, they are universal. Figure 1-4 illustrates an ASCII text file and the actual binary code that is stored for it.

Figure 1-4: ASCII text files contain no formatting codes

```
01010010 01101111 01101100 01101100 01100101 01110010 00100000
01000011 01101111 01100001 01110011 01110100 01100101 01110010
01110011 00100000 01010111 01101000 01101111 00100000 01110111
01100001 01101110 01110100 01110011 00100000 01110100 01101111
00100000 01110011 01100001 01110110 01100101 00100000 01100001
01101110 00100000 01101111 01101100 01100100 00100000 01110010
01101111 01101100 01101
01101111 01100001 01
00100000 01001100 01100
01101000 01100101 00101
00100000 01101001 01110
00100000 01110111 01101
00100111 01110011 00100
01110011 01110100 00100
01100101 01110010 00100
01110100 01100101 01110
00101100 00100000 01100001 01100011 01100011 01101111 01110010
01100100 01101001 01101110 01100111 00100000 01110100 01101111
```

```
Untitled - Notepad                                  —  □  ✕
File  Edit  Format  View  Help
Roller Coasters Who wants to save an old roller
coaster? Leap-the-Dips is the world's oldest
roller coaster and, according to a spokesperson
for the Leap-the-Dips Preservation Foundation,
one of the most historically significant. Built
in 1902, Leap-the-Dips is "the sole survivor of
a style and technology that was represented in
more than 250 parks in North America alone in
the early years of the amusement industry."
```

▶ **How does formatting get added to documents?** ASCII text files contain no formatting. They have no bold, italics, underlining, or font colors. There are no margins, columns, bullets, headers, or page numbers.

Suppose you want the title of the Roller Coasters document to be centered and shown in a large, bold font, like this:

To create documents with styles and formats, formatting codes have to be embedded in the text. There are many techniques for doing so, and each one produces a unique file format. These formats can be opened by the software that produced them. Opening those files with other kinds of software requires conversion.

Microsoft Word produces formatted text and creates documents in DOCX format, whereas Apple Pages produces documents in PAGES format. Adobe Acrobat produces documents in PDF format. The HTML markup language used for Web pages produces documents in HTML format. Many ebooks are created using the EPUB format.

Formatting codes can be added to documents directly within the text stream, using some sort of **delimiter** to signal the beginning and end of the formatting command. When the document is displayed, the formatting codes are hidden. What do those hidden codes look like? Figure 1-5 gives you a behind-the-scenes look at the Roller Coasters document with all the embedded formatting codes revealed.

Terminology

A *delimiter* is a special character used to separate commands or formatting characters from the rest of the text in a file. Slashes // and angle brackets < > are commonly used delimiters.

Figure 1-5: Formatting codes within a document

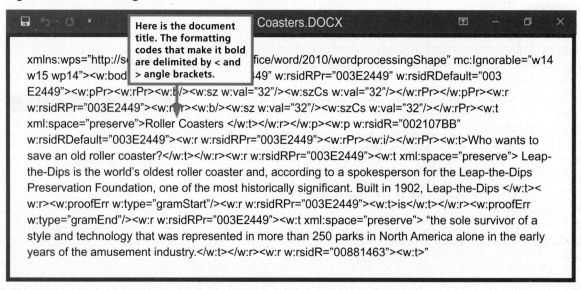

▶ **What happens when I scan a document?** When using a scanner to digitize a document, you may have a choice between graphics formats and OCR. Graphics formats, presented later in the module, essentially capture a photo of the document. Individual letters and punctuation marks are not encoded as ASCII. A document scanned into a graphics format cannot be edited using a word processor.

OCR (optical character recognition) is a process that interprets individual characters during or after a scan. It assigns the appropriate ASCII code to each letter and outputs the document in a format that can be edited using word processing software. OCR software is available for most scanners and is handy when you have a printed copy of a document that you want to modify, but would prefer not to retype.

Bits and Bytes

All of the text and numeric data stored and transmitted by digital devices is encoded as bits. Terminology related to bits and bytes is extensively used to describe storage capacity and network access speed. As a digital-goods consumer, you'll want to have this terminology handy.

▶ **What is the difference between bits and bytes?** Even though the word *bit* is an abbreviation for *binary digit*, it can be further abbreviated, usually as a lowercase *b*. A group of eight bits is called a **byte** and is usually abbreviated as an uppercase *B*.

Transmission speeds are expressed in bits, whereas storage space is expressed in bytes. For example, a cable Internet connection might transfer data from the Internet to your computer at 50 mega*bits* per second. In an iPad ad, you might notice that it can store up to 128 giga*bytes* of music, video, photos, and games.

▶ **What do the prefixes kilo-, mega-, giga-, and tera- mean?** When reading about digital devices, you'll frequently encounter references such as 90 kilobits per second, 1.44 megabytes, 2.4 gigahertz, and 2 terabytes. *Kilo*, *mega*, *giga*, *tera*, and similar terms are used to quantify digital data, as shown in Figure 1-6.

Figure 1-6: Digital quantities

Bit	One binary digit	Gigabit	2^{30} bits
Byte	8 bits	Gigabyte	2^{30} bytes
Kilobit	1,024 or 2^{10} bits	Terabyte	2^{40} bytes
Kilobyte	1,024 or 2^{10} bytes	Petabyte	2^{50} bytes
Megabit	1,048,576 or 2^{20} bits	Exabyte	2^{60} bytes
Megabyte	1,048,576 or 2^{20} bytes		

▶ **Why such odd numbers?** In common usage, kilo, abbreviated as K, means a thousand. For example, $50K means $50,000. In the context of computers, however, 50K means 51,200. Why the difference? In the decimal number system we use on a daily basis, the number 1,000 is 10 to the third power, or 10^3. For digital devices where base 2 is the norm, a kilo is precisely 1,024, or 2^{10}. Mega is derived from 2^{20} and giga from 2^{30}.

QuickCheck

Which one of the following would most likely require OCR?

a. A two-page bibliography of award-winning books from 1945 that you would like to annotate

b. An excerpt from a magazine article that you want to include in a term paper

c. A football poster containing the home game schedule

d. A page from a handwritten diary that you want to include in a historical biography

1

Try It!

Scan a one-page document using a scanner or a multifunction printer. The default format for the scan is probably a JPEG or PNG graphic. Try using your scanner's OCR feature or a free online OCR service to convert the scan into a document that can be edited using word processing software.

Terminology

What's a *kibibyte*? Some computer scientists have proposed alternative terminology to dispel the ambiguity in terms such as *kilo* that can mean 1,000 or 1,024. They suggest the following prefixes:

Kibi = 1,024

Mebi = 1,048,576

Gibi = 1,073,741,824

> **When do I use bits and when do I use bytes?** As a general rule, use bits for data rates, such as Internet connection speeds and movie download speeds. Use bytes for file sizes and storage capacities. Figure 1-7 provides some examples.

Figure 1-7: Bits or bytes?

56 Kbps

104 KB

50 Mbps

Kilobit (Kb or Kbit) can be used for slow data rates, such as a 56 Kbps (kilobits per second) dial-up connection.

Kilobyte (KB or Kbyte) is often used when referring to the size of small text files.

Megabit (Mb or Mbit) is used for faster data rates, such as a 50 Mbps (megabits per second) Internet connection.

3.2 MB

100 Gbit

16 GB

Megabyte (MB or MByte) is typically used when referring to the size of files containing photos and videos.

Gigabit (Gb or Gbit) is used for really fast network speeds.

Gigabyte (GB or GByte) is commonly used to refer to storage capacity.

Compression

All those 1s and 0s can quickly expand the size of digital files. Whereas a "€" is simply one character in a printed document, it requires 16 bits when represented as ASCII and 16 bits when represented as Unicode. That "1" in "1st place" seems like it could be represented by a simple 1 bit, but it requires multiple bits when encoded. Numeric data also requires lots of bits. The number 10 is 1010 in binary and requires four bits.

To reduce file size and transmission times, digital data can be compressed. **Data compression** refers to any technique that recodes the data in a file so that it contains fewer bits. Compression is commonly referred to as "zipping." Many compression techniques exist. They can be divided into two categories: lossless and lossy.

> **What is the difference between lossless and lossy compression?** **Lossless compression** provides a way to compress data and reconstitute it into its original state. Character data and numeric data in documents and spreadsheets are compressed using lossless techniques so that the uncompressed data is exactly the same as the original data.

Lossy compression throws away some of the original data during the compression process. After the data is uncompressed, it is not exactly the same as the original. This type of compression is typically used for music, images, and videos because the human ear or eye cannot discern minor changes. Later in the module, you'll learn more about the compression techniques used to shrink the size of music, image, and video files.

▶ **How do I compress data?** The software for compressing data is sometimes referred to as a compression utility or a zip tool. Most computers include software for compressing data, but tablets and smartphones may require a third-party app for working with compressed data.

On laptops and desktop computers, the compression utility is accessed from the same screen used to manage files. You can compress the data in a single file or you can combine multiple files to create a single zipped file that is reconstituted to the original files when unzipped (Figure 1-8).

1

Figure 1-8: Compressing files

1. Open Finder by selecting this icon.

2. Select one or more files, right-click, then select the Compress option.

Source: Apple Inc.

Compressing files using Finder on a Mac

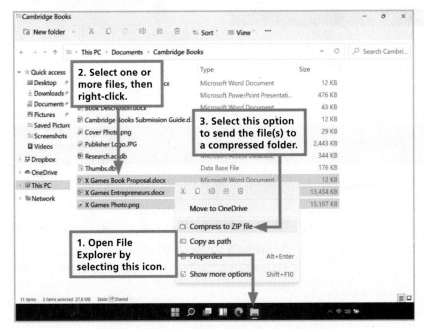

2. Select one or more files, then right-click.

3. Select this option to send the file(s) to a compressed folder.

1. Open File Explorer by selecting this icon.

Compressing files using File Explorer on a PC

❯ **How do I return files to their uncompressed state?** The process of reconstituting files is called extracting or unzipping. As with compression, most laptops and desktop computers include extraction and unzipping software; tablets and smartphones may require a third-party app.

Compressed files usually have .zip at the end of the file name and are represented with specialty icons. Compressed files may also end with .gz, .pkg, or .tar.gz. These files have to be extracted or unzipped before you can view the data they contain. The process is easy. To extract a file on a Mac, simply double-click the zipped folder. With Windows (Figure 1-9), use the Extract All option.

Figure 1-9: Extracting files in Windows

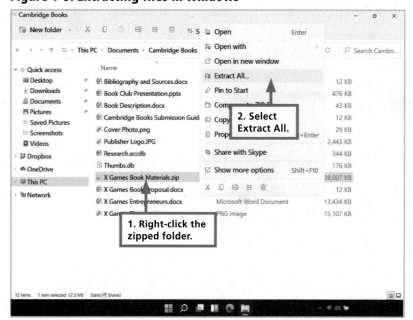

1. Right-click the zipped folder.

2. Select Extract All.

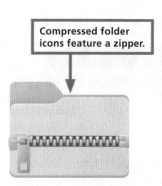

Compressed folder icons feature a zipper.

QuickQuiz   Section A

1. A(n) [_____] is a 0 or 1 used in the digital representation of data.

2. Most computer data is encoded as UTF-8 or Extended [_____] code to represent character data. (Hint: Use the acronym.)

3. Formatting codes can be added to documents using a(n) [_____] , such as slashes // and angle brackets< >.

4. In the computer world, TB is the abbreviation for [_____] .

5. The data files containing photos, videos, and music are typically compressed using [_____] compression that throws away some of the original data.

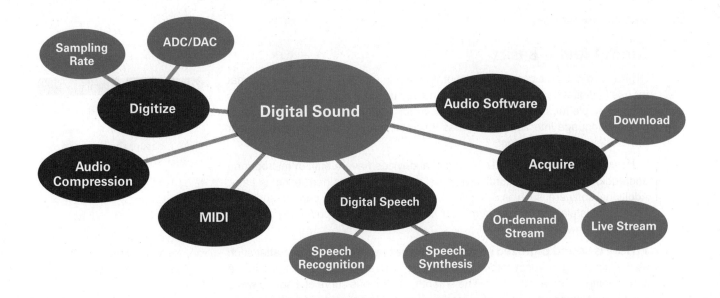

Digital Sound

Objectives

▶ Describe the process of digital sampling.

▶ Select the appropriate sampling rate for a digital audio recording.

▶ Identify digital audio files by their file name extensions.

▶ Convert digital audio files from one format to another.

▶ Explain why most audio files are compressed and how this affects sound quality.

▶ Decide when to download, live stream, or stream music on demand.

▶ Describe the difference between digital audio and MIDI.

▶ Explain how Siri and similar services work.

Music downloads were one of the first massively popular types of digital content, but audio technology plays a key role in other interesting applications. This section covers a wide-ranging selection of digital audio concepts and technologies that you're likely to find handy for personal and professional use.

Terminology

digital audio	MP3	live stream	speech synthesis
analog-to-digital	Ogg Vorbis	on-demand stream	speech recognition
converter	WAV	copy protection	phoneme
digital-to-analog	AAX	digital rights	text-to-speech software
converter	WMA	management	
sampling rate	audio interface	synthesized sound	
audio compression	digital audio extraction	MIDI	
AAC	download	MIDI messages	

Digital Audio Basics

Digital audio is music, speech, and other sounds represented in binary format for use in digital devices. It is a key technology used by popular music services such as Apple Music and Spotify. It is used for audiobooks and plays a role in natural language interactions, such as voice messaging and speaking to your Siri or Alexa virtual assistant.

▶ **How do I record sound?** Most digital devices have a built-in microphone and audio software, so recording external sounds, such as narrations, is easy. Additional software, such as Soundflower, might be required to capture and save sound that is playing on your computer from Internet radio, podcasts, or online television shows.

▶ **How is sound digitized?** Sound is produced by the vibration of matter such as a violin string or vocal cords. This vibration causes pressure changes in the surrounding air, creating waves. The smooth, continuous curve of a sound wave can be directly recorded on analog media, such as vinyl records or cassette tape, but digital recordings are based on samples of a sound wave.

To digitally record sound, samples of a sound wave are collected at periodic intervals and stored as numeric data in an audio file. For example, when recording a voice message on your phone, the sound waves of your voice are sampled many times per second by an **analog-to-digital converter** (ADC). Those samples are converted into binary 1s and 0s, which are stored in an audio file. When the audio file is played, a **digital-to-analog converter** (DAC) transforms the digital bits into analog sound waves and outputs them through speakers. Figure 1-10 shows how a sound wave is digitally sampled.

QuickCheck

What is the purpose of sampling?

a. To measure the height of each sound wave

b. To take multiple height measurements of a wave and convert them into binary

c. To determine the type of instrument that makes each sound

d. To record a sound at the highest fidelity

Figure 1-10: Digitizing a sound wave

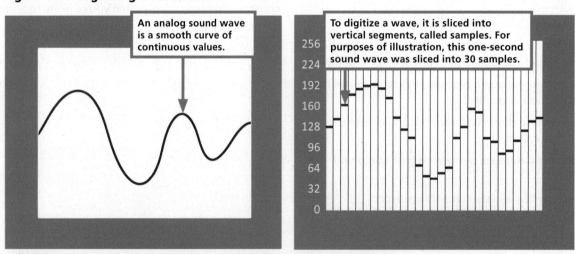

An analog sound wave is a smooth curve of continuous values.

To digitize a wave, it is sliced into vertical segments, called samples. For purposes of illustration, this one-second sound wave was sliced into 30 samples.

Sample	Sample Height (Decimal)	Sample Height (Binary)
1	130	10000010
2	140	1000110
3	160	10100000
4	175	10101111

The height of each sample is converted into a binary number and stored. The height of sample 3 is 160 (decimal), so it is stored as its binary equivalent—10100000.

▶ **Does sampling rate affect sound quality?** Sampling rate refers to the number of times per second that a sound is measured during the recording process. It is expressed in hertz (Hz). One thousand samples per second is expressed as 1,000 Hz or 1 kHz (kilohertz). Higher sampling rates increase the quality of the recording but require more storage space than lower sampling rates.

The standard sampling rate for most consumer audio is 44.1 kHz. To conserve space, voice-overs and narrations that do not require high-quality sound can be recorded with sampling rates of 11 kHz (11,000 samples per second). This rate results in lower-quality sound, but the file is about one-fourth the size of a file for the same sound recorded at 44.1 kHz (44,100 samples per second). Figure 1-11 illustrates how sampling rate affects sound quality and file size.

Try It!

Try recording a short narration. Does your digital device have a built-in microphone and recording software?

Figure 1-11: Sampling rate, sound quality, and file size

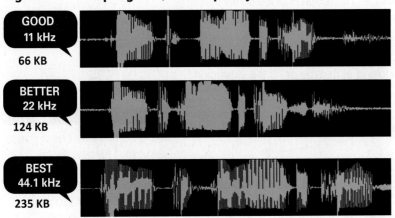

GOOD
11 kHz
66 KB

BETTER
22 kHz
124 KB

BEST
44.1 kHz
235 KB

▶ **How much space is required to store an audio file?** When sampling stereo high-fidelity music at 44.1 kHz, one second of music requires about 0.176 MB of storage space. Forty-five minutes of music—the length of a typical album—requires about 475 MB. You might wonder how audio files rack up so much space.

The height of each sound sample is saved as a 16-bit number for high-fidelity recordings. To achieve stereo effects, you must take two of these 16-bit samples. Therefore, each sample requires 32 bits of storage space. A sampling rate of 44.1 kHz records 44,100 32-bit samples per second. Here is the calculation:

$$32 \times 44{,}100 = 1{,}411{,}200$$

bits in one stereo sample	samples per second	bits (176,400 bytes) for each second of music

QuickCheck

In this calculation, the sampling rate is _____.

a. 32 bits

b. 44.1 kHz

c. 1.4 Mbps

d. 2.8 Mbps

▶ **Is there any way to compress audio files?** Regardless of sampling rate, digital audio file size can be reduced using audio compression techniques. Audio compression reduces the size of a sound file by removing bits that represent extraneous noise and sounds that are beyond the frequencies of normal hearing.

Most music for portable media players is stored in compressed audio file formats. These lossy formats reduce the size of audio files, but also reduce their quality. Sophisticated listeners can tell the difference, but most casual listeners are content with the quality produced by compressed files streaming from an iPod or a similar device. Files in compressed formats, such as MP3, don't get much smaller if you subsequently use general compression tools provided by Finder and File Explorer.

Files containing "raw" noncompressed audio can be compressed using the same general compression tools used for text and numeric data. For example, using lossless tools provided by Finder and File Explorer, you can compress a large audio file before attaching it to an email message. The recipient of the compressed files will have to unzip the file before listening to it, however.

Digital Audio File Formats

You can recognize a digital audio file by looking at its type or its file extension. For example, Thriller.mp3 is an audio file, not a music video.

Thriller.mp3 ── File extension   Michael Jackson   MP3 Format Sound ── File type

▶ **Which audio formats are most popular?** Digital audio is stored in a variety of file formats. The table in Figure 1-12 provides an overview of the most popular digital audio formats, which include AAC, MP3, Ogg Vorbis, WAV, AAX, and WMA.

Figure 1-12: Popular audio file formats

Audio Format	Extension	Advantages	Disadvantages
AAC (Advanced Audio Coding)	.aac, .m4p, or .mp4	Very good sound quality based on MPEG-4; lossy compression; used for streaming Apple Music	Files can be copy protected so that use is limited to approved devices
MP3 (also called MPEG-1 Layer 3)	.mp3	Good sound quality; lossy compression; can be streamed over the Web	Might require a standalone player or browser plugin
Ogg Vorbis	.ogg	Free, open standard; lossy compression; used by Spotify; part of Google's WebM format	Slow to catch on as a popular standard
WAV	.wav	Good sound quality; supported in browsers without a plugin	Audio data is stored in raw, noncompressed format, so files are very large
AAX (Audible Enhanced Audio)	.aa, .aax	Used by Amazon to distribute audio books	.aa is lower quality than .aax; copying may be limited
WMA (Windows Media Audio)	.wma	Lossy or lossless compression; very good sound quality; used on several music download sites	Files can be copy protected; requires an add-on player for some devices

❱ **What are the best sources for digital music?** There are several options for obtaining audio content, such as music, soundtracks, narrations, and sound effects.

Live recording is an option for obtaining digital sound files from concerts or lectures. For casual recording, Voice Memos and similar apps work well. Professional recordings require more sophisticated software and hardware tools. A device called an **audio interface** accepts input from a standalone microphone and feeds it into a computer.

Ripping CD tracks is handy for someone who inherits a stack of old CDs and wants to convert the music into a format that plays on a smartphone or other mobile device. *Ripping* is a slang term that refers to the process of importing tracks from a CD or DVD to your computer's hard disk. The technical term for ripping music tracks is **digital audio extraction**.

Downloading is popular for saving audio files on local devices. A **download** copies a file from a private network or Internet server to a local device. The file is transferred as a unit and cannot be played until the entire file has arrived.

Streaming offers yet another way of obtaining audio content. Unlike some digital content, such as photos, that must be accessed as a whole piece, audio content plays back over a period of time. Audio files can be acquired as a **live stream** or **on-demand stream** in addition to downloads (Figure 1-13).

1

Figure 1-13: Downloading and streaming

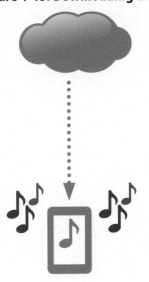

Download

A download transfers an audio file from a server to your local device.

You can play back the file even when your device is not online.

The file can be played with any compatible software or player.

Live stream

A live stream sends media from a server to your local device, where it is played, but not stored.

This method is also known as Webcasting.

You have to be online while listening.

The content stream cannot be paused, stored, or rewound.

On-demand stream

An on-demand stream sends the media to your local device, where it is stored temporarily, or "buffered," until there is enough data to begin playback.

You can fast-forward to any point in the stream without waiting for the entire file to download.

❱ What type of software is required to work with digital audio files?

To play a digital audio file, you must use some type of audio software that works with the file's audio format.

General-purpose audio software and apps provide tools for recording, playing, and modifying audio files. They also provide tools for converting audio files from one format to another. Popular audio software includes Apple GarageBand, Windows Media Player, and Audacity (Figure 1-14).

Figure 1-14: Audacity audio software

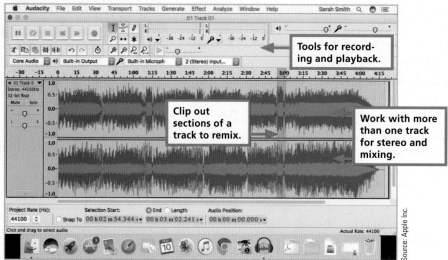

Source: Apple Inc.

❱ **Why can't I copy some music files?** Music and video distributors may use various technologies to curtail unauthorized copying, a process called **copy protection** or **digital rights management** (DRM). When implemented, DRM technologies may prevent you from copying a file or may limit the number of copies you can make. These technologies could prevent you from converting files from one format to another. DRM may also prevent you from playing files on certain hardware or in certain geographical locations.

MIDI

Digital audio is a recording of real analog sound signals. In contrast, **synthesized sound** is an artificially created, or synthetic, sound. The first music synthesizers were analog. When digital synthesizers became popular, MIDI was developed as a way to control them.

❱ **What is MIDI music?** MIDI (Musical Instrument Digital Interface) specifies a standard way to store music data for synthesizers, electronic MIDI instruments, and computers. Unlike digital audio files, which contain digitized recordings of real performances, MIDI files contain instructions, called **MIDI messages**, specifying the pitch of a note, the point at which the note begins, the instrument that plays the note, the volume of the note, and the point at which the note ends. MIDI music is usually stored in .mid files.

▶ **What is the data representation for a MIDI message?** As with all digital data, MIDI messages are distilled into a series of bits represented by 1s and 0s. A MIDI message might look like this:

1001
Play note

0001
Channel 1
designates piano

01010100
Note number 84
designates high C

0111000
Velocity 112 designates
loud volume

▶ **What are the advantages and disadvantages of MIDI?** MIDI files are much more compact than digital audio files. Depending on the exact piece of music, three minutes of MIDI music might require only 10 KB of storage space, whereas the same piece of music stored in a high-quality, noncompressed digital audio file might require 30,000 KB of storage space.

One of the main disadvantages of MIDI is that it cannot produce vocals. Another disadvantage is that the quality of MIDI music depends on the playback device, which stores a collection of synthesized sounds. MIDI music might sound great on a computer equipped with high-end MIDI equipment, but the same MIDI sequence might sound artificial on a handheld device.

▶ **Who uses MIDI?** Today, MIDI is primarily a tool used by studio musicians, performers, and composers. Musicians can input notes for several instrumental parts directly from a MIDI keyboard and create backup instrumentation for performances. One or two musicians with MIDI gear can sound like a large band.

Music composition software with MIDI support makes it easy to place notes on a screen-based music staff, then play back the composition on a MIDI keyboard or through the speakers of a digital device (Figure 1-15).

QuickCheck

Which of the following files is likely to contain synthesized music?

a. Bongos.mp3

b. Screech.wav

c. Waltz.ogg

d. Sugar.mid

Figure 1-15: MIDI music composition

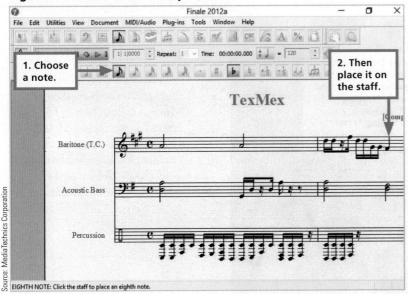

Source: MediaTechnics Corporation

Digitized Speech

Speech technologies are used to collect information from callers using telephone-based services such as Directory Assistance. They are the foundation for interactive voice response systems such as Google Voice Search, Siri, Alexa, and Cortana. Speech recognition enables people to control software with spoken commands, as well as dictate text into a word processing document. Speech technologies can also read a computer screen aloud, which unlocks access to computers and the Internet for individuals with visual disabilities.

▶ **What's the difference between speech synthesis and speech recognition?** Speech synthesis is the process by which machines produce sound that resembles spoken words. Speech recognition (or voice recognition) refers to the ability of a machine to understand spoken words.

▶ **How does speech synthesis work?** A basic sound unit, such as "reh" or "gay," is called a phoneme. Most speech synthesizers string together phonemes to form words. For example, the phonemes "reh" and "gay" produce the word *reggae*. Phonemes are usually derived from recordings of human voices reading specially prepared passages of text. Text-to-speech software analyzes the words in a section of text, finds corresponding phonemes, and combines them into sentences for output.

▶ **How does speech recognition work?** On a personal computer or smartphone, a speech recognition system collects words spoken into a microphone that's connected to sound processing circuitry. This circuitry's analog-to-digital converter transforms the analog sound of your voice into digital data. This data is then processed by speech recognition software.

Speech recognition software analyzes the sounds of your voice and converts each word into groups of phonemes. Next, the software compares the groups of phonemes to the words in a digital dictionary that lists phoneme combinations along with their corresponding words. When a match is found, the software can display the word on the screen or use it to carry out a command. Most digital devices offer a way to use spoken commands (Figure 1-16).

Figure 1-16: Windows speech recognition

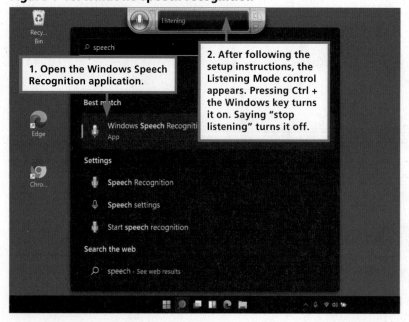

▶ **How does Siri work?** Devices of the Speak & Spell generation had robotic voices and were not responsive to a wide variety of commands and queries. What makes modern technologies like Siri so much more versatile and lifelike? Figure 1-17 provides an overview.

Figure 1-17: How Siri works

The voices of Siri were created by live actors, but they couldn't record every possible response to user queries.

Instead they recorded the words and sentences from a script. Although the script may appear nonsensical, the sentences are rich in phonemes.

When the recordings are complete, a team of linguists analyzes and tags various speech components and loads them into a database. The process is called concatenative speech synthesis.

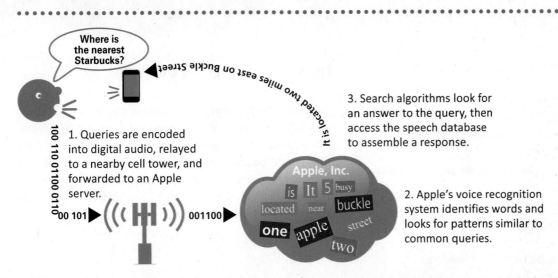

1. Queries are encoded into digital audio, relayed to a nearby cell tower, and forwarded to an Apple server.

2. Apple's voice recognition system identifies words and looks for patterns similar to common queries.

3. Search algorithms look for an answer to the query, then access the speech database to assemble a response.

QuickQuiz   Section B

1. [_____] rate refers to the number of times per second that a sound is measured during the recording process.

2. Audio formats such as MP3, Ogg Vorbis, and AAC have good sound quality even though they use [_____] compression.

3. The process of ripping tracks from an audio CD to a digital format is called digital audio [_____].

4. [_____] files store a series of instructions that specify which notes to play, their duration, and their volume.

5. The audio components for virtual assistants such as Siri are obtained by recording real voices and then applying [_____] speech synthesis.

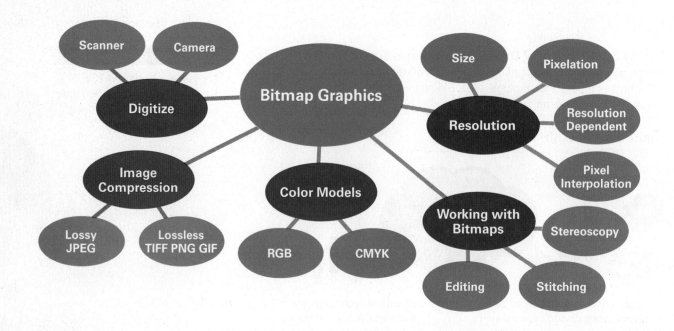

Objectives

▶ Describe the differences between bitmap and vector graphics.

▶ Explain how pixel color is represented in decimal, hexadecimal, and binary.

▶ Describe how cameras and scanners produce digital images.

▶ List six popular bitmap file formats.

▶ Decide which graphics format to use for school, work, or personal projects.

▶ Describe the RGB and CMYK color models.

▶ Calculate the size of a bitmap file given its resolution.

▶ List the bitmap file formats that use lossless compression.

▶ Explain what a color histogram represents and how to use one.

▶ Explain how 3D images are created.

▶ Provide examples of image stitching.

▶ Describe two types of stereoscopic imaging.

Terminology

computer graphics	RAW	resolution dependent	clipping path
still images	TIFF	pixelation	alpha blending
motion graphics	JPEG	pixel interpolation	image stitching
bitmap graphic	GIF	image compression	stereoscopic imaging
pixel	PNG	run-length encoding	stereo pair
scanner	RGB color model	image histogram	stereogram
CCD	color depth	cloning	anaglyph
photosites	True Color	inpainting	
BMP	image resolution	digital compositing	

Images are everywhere. Photos plaster Pinterest boards like so many posters on a Paris kiosk. Facebook feeds offer a continuous stream of vacation pics. Colorful icons dot the screens of every digital device. Infographics use images to convey information, and Web sites would be much less interesting if not for the colorful graphics they display. Section C explains the technology that powers this point-and-shoot world to help you harness the power of digital graphics.

Bitmap Basics

As digital devices gained the ability to display images, two types of **computer graphics** evolved: bitmap and vector. These graphics can produce **still images**, such as photographs and diagrams, or **motion graphics**, such as videos and animations.

Computer graphics can produce two-dimensional flat images and stereoscopic images with visual depth that makes close-up objects appear near enough to grasp.

Despite their similarities, bitmap and vector images are quite different. Bitmap graphics may be the most common, but they are less flexible than vector graphics and cannot be used to model three-dimensional objects. To find out why, let's take a look at the characteristics of bitmaps.

▶ **What is a bitmap graphic?** A **bitmap graphic**, also called a raster graphic or simply a bitmap, is composed of a grid of tiny rectangular cells. Each cell is a picture element, commonly called a **pixel**. Each pixel is assigned a color, which is stored as a binary number. Figure 1-18 illustrates these basic characteristics of a bitmap graphic.

Terminology

The term *3D* is used today to refer to a variety of commercial products that should be called stereoscopic. For example, those so-called 3D glasses with blue and red lenses are technically stereoscopic, not 3D. As you continue in this module, pay attention to the difference between 3D and stereoscopic.

1

Figure 1-18: Bitmap graphics are pixel based

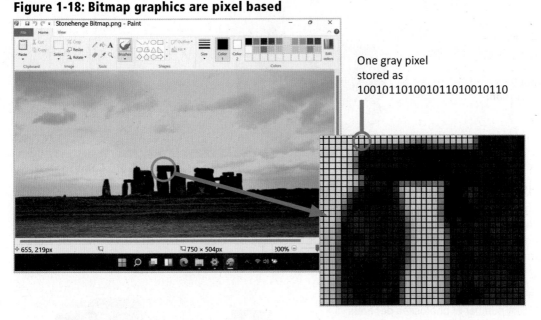

One gray pixel stored as 10010110100101101010010110

▶ **Where would I encounter bitmap graphics?** Bitmap graphics are used to create realistic images, such as photographs. You might also encounter bitmaps in the form of cartoons, images that appear in computer games, the desktop images displayed by your computer or smartphone, and photorealistic images derived from 3D graphical objects.

When you use a digital camera or camera-enabled cell phone, your photos are stored as bitmaps. A scanner also produces bitmaps. The photos you send or receive as email attachments are bitmaps, as are most Web page graphics.

QuickCheck

Bitmap graphics are based on:

a. codecs

b. pixels

c. rasters

d. vectors

❱ How do I create bitmap images? You can create a bitmap graphic from scratch using the tools provided by graphics software—specifically a category of graphics software referred to as paint software. You might be familiar with paint software such as Adobe Photoshop, Apple Photos (included with Apple computers), and Microsoft Paint (included with Windows). Other alternatives, such as AutoDesk SketchBook, are available online and as downloads for smartphones and laptops.

❱ How do I convert a printed image into a bitmap? When you have a printed image, such as a photograph, a page from a magazine, or a picture from a book, you can use a **scanner** to convert the printed image into a bitmap graphic.

A scanner essentially divides an image into a fine grid of cells and assigns a digital value for the color of each cell. As the scan progresses, these values are transferred to your digital device and stored as a bitmap graphics file. Scanners, such as the one pictured in Figure 1-19, are inexpensive and easy to use.

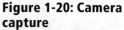

Try It!

Check the features of the photo app on your smartphone. Which of the following does it provide?

Retouch

Crop

Special effects

Exposure adjustment

Figure 1-19: Scan images
To scan an image, turn on the scanner and start your scanner software. Place the image face down on the scanner glass, then use the scanner software to initiate the scan. The scanned image is saved in memory and can then be saved on your computer's hard disk or in another storage location.

Figure 1-20: Camera capture
A digital camera's CCD converts the image captured by the camera lens into a grid of colored pixels, which are stored as bits.

❱ How does a digital camera capture bitmap images? The lens of a film camera captures the light from an image onto a light-sensitive roll of film, which is developed to produce a photographic print. In a digital camera, the lens focuses light from the image onto a small image sensor called a **CCD** (charge-coupled device). This technology is used in standalone digital cameras and smartphone cameras.

A CCD contains a grid of tiny light-sensitive diodes called **photosites**. The number of photosites depends on the size of the CCD. A one-half-inch square CCD can contain more than 500,000 photosites. Each photosite detects the brightness and color for its tiny piece of the image (Figure 1-20).

A CCD's photosites correspond to pixels. The more pixels used to capture an image, the higher its resolution, and the better the resulting picture. Cameras with larger CCDs produce higher-quality images. Some cameras contain multiple CCDs, which enhance the color quality of a camera's output.

1

▶ **What are the most common bitmap file formats?** Cameras, scanners, and graphics software may offer a choice of bitmap formats, such as BMP, RAW, TIFF, JPEG, GIF, and PNG. Selecting the best graphics file format to use depends on what you intend to do with the image. Figure 1-21 summarizes popular bitmap formats and their uses.

Figure 1-21: Bitmap formats

	Bitmap Format	Use
	BMP, pronounced "bee-em-pee" or "bump," is the native bitmap graphics file format of the Microsoft Windows environment. Microsoft Paint, included as part of Microsoft Windows, creates BMP graphics files, as well as PNGs and JPEGs. The BMP format supports True Color and can be used for a wide variety of graphics applications, such as photographs, illustrations, and graphs. BMP files are often too large for email attachments. Their size makes BMPs undesirable for use on Web pages.	Graphical elements, such as buttons and other controls for graphical user interfaces
	RAW image formats contain the unprocessed pixel data generated directly by a digital camera's sensor. Up to 12 bits of data can be stored for each of the red, blue, and green values for a pixel, so RAW files are very large. Cameras that offer a RAW format usually supply software to convert RAW data to smaller JPEG or TIFF files.	Photographic images before they are stored in other formats
	TIFF (Tagged Image File Format), or TIF, is a flexible and platform-independent graphics file format supported by most photoediting software packages. Scanners and digital cameras commonly store bitmaps in TIFF format because it supports True Color and can be easily converted into other graphics file formats.	Desktop publishing and any projects that require high-resolution graphics; not supported by browsers
	JPEG (pronounced "JAY-peg"), which stands for Joint Photographic Experts Group, is a graphics format with built-in compression that stores True Color bitmap data very efficiently in a small file. The JPEG format is popular for Web graphics, smartphone photos, and for photos attached to email messages. When creating a JPEG or converting an image to JPEG format, you can control the level of compression and the resulting file size. The compression process eliminates some image data, however, so highly compressed files suffer some quality deterioration.	General use, such as desktop publishing or Web pages, where flexibility in file size is important
	GIF (Graphics Interchange Format), pronounced "gif" or "jiff," was specifically designed to create images that can be displayed on multiple platforms, such as PCs and Macs. GIF graphics are limited to 256 colors, but the format supports simple animations. Once a popular format for Web pages, GIF is being replaced by JPEG and PNG.	Web graphics and simple animations
	PNG (Portable Network Graphics), pronounced "ping," is a graphics format designed to improve on the GIF format. A PNG graphic can display up to 48-bit True Color (trillions of colors). Unlike JPEG, PNG compresses bitmap files without losing any data, so compressed images retain the same high quality as the originals. PNG was developed as a public domain format without any restrictions on its use.	Web graphics and other general uses

Bitmap Data Representation

The fact that bitmap images are formed by a grid of pixels controls not only how those images are stored, but also how they can be modified. Color and resolution are key elements in bitmap data representation.

▶ **How does each pixel get a color number?** Today's color display devices represent color using the **RGB color model**. The color displayed for a pixel is based on the intensity of red, green, and blue signals received by the screen's color elements.

Each red, green, and blue signal is assigned a value ranging from 0 to 255: 0 represents the absence of color, and 255 represents the highest intensity level for that color. A pixel appears white if the red, green, and blue signals are set to maximum intensity. If red, green, and blue signals are equal but at a lower intensity, the pixel displays a shade of gray. A pixel appears violet if it receives high red and blue signals and just a bit of green (Figure 1-22).

Terminology

The *CMYK* color model defines four color values: cyan, magenta, yellow, and black. It is a subtractive system, whereas RGB is an additive system. In CMYK, white is 00000000; but in RGB, 11111111 is white. CMYK is typically used for projects that require color printing.

Figure 1-22: RGB color

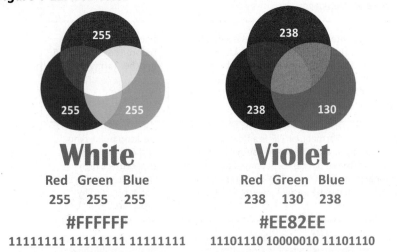

Look at the center where the circles intersect to see the color that is generated. Color numbers are shown in decimal, hexadecimal, and binary.

▶ **How are colors specified?** Color values can be specified in decimal (base 10), hexadecimal (base 16), or binary (base 2). Even artists need to know their way around number systems! Decimal notation tends to be used within graphics software, and hexadecimal (hex) notation is common on the Web. Whichever notation is used, however, color data is ultimately represented as binary digits when it is stored and transmitted.

In decimal, a pixel color is specified with values such as Red 238, Green 130, and Blue 238. In hexadecimal, each pair of digits refers to a color value. For example, the hexadecimal number for violet is #EE82EE. That means EE(hex) = 238 Red, 82(hex) = 130 Green, and EE(hex) = 238 Blue. You can find lists of colors and their hexadecimal triplets on the Web. In binary, eight bits are used to represent the red value, another eight bits are used for the green value, and eight more bits are used for blue.

▶ **How much data is required for each pixel color?** With eight bits used to represent each color value, one pixel requires 24 bits. Because each R, G, and B can have 256 values, the number of possible colors is 16.7 million (256 x 256 x 256). The number of colors available in a graphic is referred to as **color depth**. Images that use 24 bits for each pixel have a color depth of 24, which is also called **True Color**.

QuickCheck

To represent the color violet in Figure 1-22, the decimal value for green is 130. What are the equivalent hexadecimal and binary values for green?

a. 82 and 10000010

b. 255 and 11111111

c. EE and 11101110

▶ **How does resolution relate to image quality?** The dimensions of the grid that forms a bitmap graphic are referred to as image resolution. The resolution of a bitmap is usually expressed as the number of horizontal and vertical pixels it contains. For example, a small graphic for a Web page might have a resolution of 150 x 100 pixels—150 pixels across and 100 pixels high.

High-resolution graphics contain more data than low-resolution graphics. With more data, it is possible to display and print high-quality images that are sharper and clearer than images produced using less data.

▶ **Can I shrink and enlarge bitmaps?** Bitmap graphics are resolution dependent because each element is a discrete pixel. Imagine that a bitmap image and its grid come on a surface that you can stretch or shrink. As you stretch the surface, the grid maintains the same number of horizontal and vertical cells, but each cell becomes larger, the grid becomes more visible, and the image develops an undesirable jagged appearance referred to as pixelation. Simply stretching a bitmap to enlarge it doesn't produce high-quality results (Figure 1-23).

▶ **Can I change a bitmap's resolution?** Graphics software offers options for changing the resolution of bitmap images. Suppose you reduce the resolution from 2160 x 1440 to 1080 x 720. The image grid becomes a quarter of its original size, but every fourth pixel was removed from the image, which typically reduces image quality.

If you attempt to enlarge a bitmap by increasing its resolution, your computer must somehow add pixels because no additional picture data exists. But what colors should these additional pixels become? Most graphics software uses a process called pixel interpolation to create new pixels by averaging the colors of nearby pixels.

For some images, pixel interpolation produces an enlargement that appears very similar to the original. Other images—particularly those with strong curved or diagonal lines—may appear pixelated.

▶ **So how much resolution does a bitmap need to be printed as a poster?** Graphics software, such as Adobe Photoshop, can help you gauge how large an image can be printed before the quality begins to deteriorate. The minimum resolution for printed output is 72 pixels per inch (ppi). Suppose that a photo taken with a smartphone has a resolution of 1936 x 2592. At 72 ppi, the photo can be printed up to a size of 26" x 36".

To print the same photo but with a better resolution of 150 ppi, the poster would be much smaller: about 12" x 17" as shown in Figure 1-24.

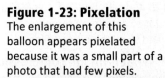

Figure 1-23: Pixelation
The enlargement of this balloon appears pixelated because it was a small part of a photo that had few pixels.

1

Try It!

Open an image with Photoshop or similar graphics software. Check its size and its ppi. At 300 ppi, how large can the image be printed before its quality begins to deteriorate?

Figure 1-24: Image size
Check these specifications to determine maximum print size.

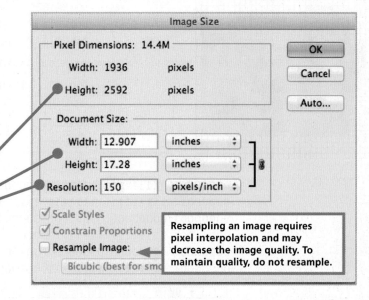

Image Size

Pixel Dimensions: 14.4M

Width: 1936   pixels

Height: 2592   pixels

Document Size:

Width: 12.907   inches ⇕

Height: 17.28   inches ⇕

Resolution: 150   pixels/inch ⇕

☑ Scale Styles
☑ Constrain Proportions
☐ Resample Image:
   Bicubic (best for sm

OK

Cancel

Auto...

Resampling an image requires pixel interpolation and may decrease the image quality. To maintain quality, do not resample.

Image Compression

Bitmap files are big. An image with a resolution of 1936 x 2592 contains 5,018,112 pixels. Each pixel requires 24 bits, so the RAW image file could be as large as 120,434,688 bits (12,434,696 bytes or 12 megabytes). By any measure, that's a lot of data to store and move. Various image compression techniques can be used to shrink bitmap files.

▶ **What is image compression?** Image compression refers to any technique that recodes the data in an image file so that it contains fewer bits. Many bitmap file formats automatically apply compression to an image when it is saved.

▶ **Which formats apply lossless compression?** TIFF, PNG, and GIF graphics formats offer lossless compression. Images stored in these formats do not lose any quality when compressed.

▶ **How does lossless compression shrink a file without throwing away data?** Various techniques exist for lossless image compression. As a simple example, consider a type of lossless compression called run-length encoding. **Run-length encoding** (RLE) replaces a series of similarly colored pixels with a binary code that indicates the number of pixels and their colors.

Suppose that a section of a picture has 167 consecutive white pixels, and each pixel is described by three bytes of data. RLE compresses this series of 167 bytes into as few as four bytes, as shown in Figure 1-25.

Figure 1-25: Run-length encoding

The data for the first 167 white pixels can be compressed as **10100111 11111111 11111111 11111111**. The first byte is the binary representation of 167. The next three bytes are the code for white.

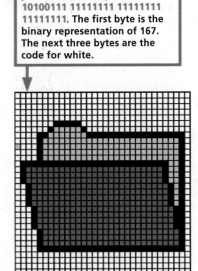

Number of Pixels (Decimal)	Number of Pixels (Binary)	Pixel Color	Pixel Color (Binary)
167	10100111	White	11111111 11111111 11111111
5	00000101	Black	00000000 00000000 00000000
26	00011010	White	11111111 11111111 11111111
1	00000001	Black	00000000 00000000 00000000
5	00000101	Yellow	11111111 11111111 00000000
1	00000001	Black	00000000 00000000 00000000
23	00010111	White	11111111 11111111 11111111
2	00000010	Black	00000000 00000000 00000000
7	00000111	Yellow	11111111 11111111 00000000
18	00010010	Black	00000000 00000000 00000000
5	00000101	White	11111111 11111111 11111111
1	00000001	Black	00000000 00000000 00000000
25	00011001	Yellow	11111111 11111111 00000000
1	00000001	Black	00000000 00000000 00000000
1	00000001	White	11111111 11111111 11111111

00000001 11111111 11111111 00000000
00000011 11111111 11111111 11111111
00000001 00000000 00000000 00000000
00011001 11111111 11111111 00000000
00000001 00000000 00000000 00000000
00000001 11111111 11111111 00000000

▶ **Which formats apply lossless compression?** JPEG files are compressed using lossy compression, so some quality is lost when the file is saved. When saving an image as a JPEG, you may be able to select a compression level. Take care with lossy compression to ensure that your image is not further compressed every time you save it (Figure 1-26).

Figure 1-26: JPEG compression

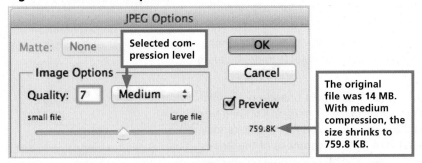

▶ **What happens during lossy compression?** Lossy compression techniques discard some data from an image to shrink its file size. JPEG is a lossy version of run-length encoding that can be applied to images, such as photographs, that don't have large areas of solid color.

A True Color photograph might not have any adjoining pixels of the same color. Applying RLE to such a photo would not result in any compression whatsoever. JPEG preprocesses an image by tweaking the colors in adjoining pixels so that they are the same color whenever possible. After this preprocessing is complete, run-length encoding can be applied with more success.

For many images, lossy compression results in only a minor reduction in the sharpness of the image. The reduction in quality can be unnoticeable in many circumstances. Figure 1-27 illustrates a section of a noncompressed image and a section of that same image after JPEG compression has been applied. Can you see any difference?

Figure 1-27: Compressed image quality

Noncompressed JPEG image   JPEG image with 35% compression

▶ **Can I compress images using general compression tools?** The same compression tools used to shrink text and numeric data can be used with bitmaps. Images stored in file formats such as JPEG and PNG, which are automatically compressed, may not shrink much, whereas RAW files, BMPs, and noncompressed TIFFs may shrink quite a bit.

Modifying Bitmap Images

"Photoshopping" has become an everyday term for fixing up photos that are underexposed, are marred by red eye effects, or display an awkward object in the background. Photoshop software and a host of local and online apps make it easy to modify digital images.

▶ **What characteristics of a bitmap can I modify?** Because bitmap graphics are coded as a series of bits that represent pixels, you can use graphics software to modify or edit this type of graphic by changing the color of pixels.

In the early days of digital imaging, primitive photoediting was limited to changing the color of individual pixels, or roughly cropping out objects to delete them or paste them elsewhere.

Today, photoediting software includes sophisticated tools based on graphics algorithms that produce amazing transformations of digital images. Knowing how to use the available toolset can improve the images you produce. Understanding the extent to which photos can be edited also builds awareness of the "tricks" that can be used to alter images in news stories and other information sources.

Noise reduction. In an image, "noise" refers to artifacts such as spots, dust, and scratches that may be produced when old photos are scanned. Some images have undesirable speckles resulting from low light conditions. Noise reduction tools can remove these noisy artifacts.

Image enhancement. A mediocre photo can benefit from image enhancement techniques that correct brightness, improve color saturation, and sharpen the focus. Beyond one-click enhancement tools, image editors provide an **image histogram** that can be used to adjust the brightness values for various ranges of dark, mid-range, or light pixels (Figure 1-28).

Figure 1-28: How image histograms work

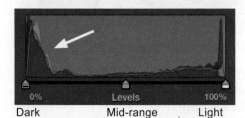
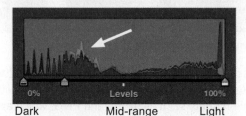

The histogram for the original photo shows lots of dark pixels (the buildings) and a few light ones (the sunset).

By sliding the Levels bar, more pixels become mid-range and the details of the buildings begin to emerge.

Selective color change. The mannequin at an online store displays a red dress, which is also available in other colors. How would it look in blue? The photographer did not have to take a photo of the dress in every color. Photoediting software can outline the dress in the original photo and then apply the new color. Similar algorithms are used to colorize black-and-white photos.

Correcting image distortion. The human eye compensates for perspective, but the camera does not. When a rectangular object in a photo appears distorted, reconstructing the straight edges is easy with photo editing software (Figure 1-29).

Figure 1-29: Correcting image distortion

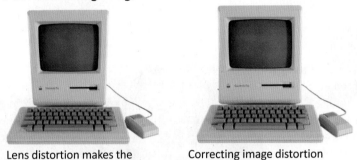

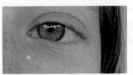 Lens distortion makes the computer unit appear angled.

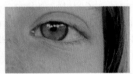 Correcting image distortion straightens the sides.

Cloning. Cloning employs algorithms that pull pixels from one area of an image and then apply them to another area. Cloning can be used to remove small blemishes, as shown in Figure 1-30.

Figure 1-30: Erasing artifacts with cloning

Cloning works well to remove natural blemishes and photo artifacts, such as the white spot under the subject's eye.

Inpainting. Reconstructing lost, unwanted, or deteriorated areas in a photo is called **inpainting**. Using information from nearby pixels, and taking into account the overall structure of the image, inpainting algorithms essentially scrub out designated areas and miraculously replace the missing pixels with a background or an object that fits with the rest of the image (Figure 1-31).

Figure 1-31: Inpainting with content-aware fill

The original photo includes a man in the foreground. Removing the man leaves a blank area.

Photoshop's Content-Aware Fill algorithm creates a background to fill the blank area.

Digital compositing. Have you seen the photo of a great white shark attacking a U.S. Air Force helicopter? That image and many more bizarre photos are a product of **digital compositing**, which assembles several images into one. Compositing is achieved using two tools: clipping paths and alpha blending.

A **clipping path** essentially cuts an object out of an image and knocks out the background to make it transparent. This object can then be superimposed on a different background. **Alpha blending** alters the pixel colors where the edges of the object and the background meet, so that the object appears to merge with the background (Figure 1-32).

Try It!

You can see digital compositing in action by going to YouTube and searching for **Content-Aware Fill**. If you have access to Photoshop, open a few of your own photos and see what kind of crazy composite you can create.

Figure 1-32: Digital compositing

A clipping path cuts out an object from the background.

The object is straightened and resized before being merged into the photo.

Panoramic and 360 Images

Photos are no longer limited to flat rectangles. They've gone beyond the box to become panoramic views, 360-degree images, and immersive photo spheres. These image formats are made possible by a technology called image stitching.

▶ **What is image stitching?** Image stitching (or photo stitching) creates a panoramic image by combining two or more separate photographs that have overlapping edges. The photos are captured from a fixed location. The photographer stands in one place and may rotate, but cannot step forward, back, or to the sides.

▶ **What kinds of images does stitching produce?** Stitching uses photos in standard bitmap formats, such as JPEG and PNG. The stitching process is based on sophisticated algorithms that match pixels near the edges of each image to determine how they fit together. Stitching connects the photos and produces various kinds of images called projections (Figure 1-33) that can be viewed on flat screens or with VR headsets.

QuickCheck

Image stitching knits photos into panoramic, cylindrical, and spherical images, but what technique is used to insert parts of one image into another image?

a. Cloning

b. Inpainting

c. Compression

d. Compositing

Figure 1-33: Image stitching

Rectilinear projections are viewed in a two-dimensional plane, typically as a long horizontal photo. These images can be produced using the panoramic feature of a digital camera.

Cylindrical projections produce a 360-degree image similar to the view from a merry-go-round. Images are captured from the front, back, and sides, and then stitched together.

Spherical projections include images from the 360-degree vertical view as well as the 360-degree horizontal panorama.

◗ **Are special software and equipment required to capture photos for stitched images?** A series of photos can be manually stitched together using software such as Autopano, PTGui, and AutoStitch, but many digital cameras take care of stitching automatically. Most smartphones include a camera app with a panoramic function for capturing a rectilinear projection. Panoramic functions are also available on most standalone digital cameras.

For producing 360-degree cylindrical projections with a smartphone, a third-party app might be required. Apps, such as Google Street View and Photo Sphere, guide photographers through the rotational process to capture a 360-degree view, which is then stitched together into a continuous image.

Special cameras are also available for capturing and stitching photos for cylindrical and spherical projections. These cameras typically use a fish-eye lens to capture a half-sphere (think of an upside-down cereal bowl) of images. Two of these fish-eye lenses can be linked to capture a full sphere of images.

Stereoscopy

Cylindrical and spherical projections can give viewers the sense of being immersed in a scene, but elements within the image remain flat and two-dimensional. Computer graphics technology can produce images with the illusion of depth that make some objects seem close enough to touch. These images are sometimes referred to as 3D, but technically they are stereoscopic.

◗ **What is stereoscopic imaging?** Stereoscopic imaging (or stereoscopy) is a graphical technique used to produce an illusion of spatial depth from flat, two-dimensional images. The technique dates back to the 1800s and the use of simple stereoscopes (Figure 1-34).

Figure 1-34: Stereoscopic imaging

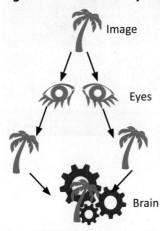

Because human eyes are spaced apart, they project two slightly different images onto the retinas. Those images are processed by the brain, which constructs an image of the world that corresponds to a three-dimensional environment with spatial depth.

Most cameras capture a photo using only one lens, so the image does not convey spatial depth. Two cameras, or a camera with two front-facing lenses, can produce two photos called a **stereo pair** that mimic the dual images captured by human eyes. Two images from a stereo pair displayed side by side are called a **stereogram**.

Simply looking at two similar photographs does not produce a 3D experience. Each image must be viewed with only one eye. A stereoscopic viewer, or stereoscope, provides this differentiation using lenses. Old-fashioned stereoscopic viewers placed images 5–11" away from the eyes and required a partition between the lenses to separate overlapping views.

▶ **What's the modern version of stereoscopic imaging?** Modern stereoscopic imaging uses digital images and viewers. Apps for capturing a stereo pair with a single lens camera are available, but somewhat tricky to use. As more cell phones sport dual front-facing cameras, creating stereo pairs becomes easier.

Some virtual reality headsets display images generated by mobile devices. A smartphone simply slides into the device where an app displays a digital stereogram (Figure 1-35).

Figure 1-35: Digital stereoscopy

MsMaria/Shutterstock.com

VR headset stereoscope   Digital stereogram

▶ **What about those red and blue stereo glasses?** An **anaglyph** is a graphic composed of two images, one that is tinted red and the other that is tinted blue. The two images are printed on top of each other to produce a stereoscopic effect (Figure 1-36).

Viewing anaglyph images requires red-green or red-blue glasses. Usually, the red lens on the left filters out blue and green, while the blue- or green-colored lens on the right filters out red. As a result each eye sees a slightly different image. The two images are processed in the brain to give the impression of three dimensions.

Figure 1-36: Anaglyphic image

QuickQuiz   Section C

1. A digital camera captures images on the photosites of a(n) [_____] . (Hint: Use the acronym.)

2. A characteristic of bitmap graphics is that they are resolution [_____] , so that reducing the resolution also reduces the image quality.

3. Graphics stored in True Color format require [_____] bits for each pixel.

4. Two images from a stereo pair displayed side by side are called a(n) [_____] .

5. The most popular True Color formats for Web graphics include [_____] and JPEG. (Hint: Use the acronym.)

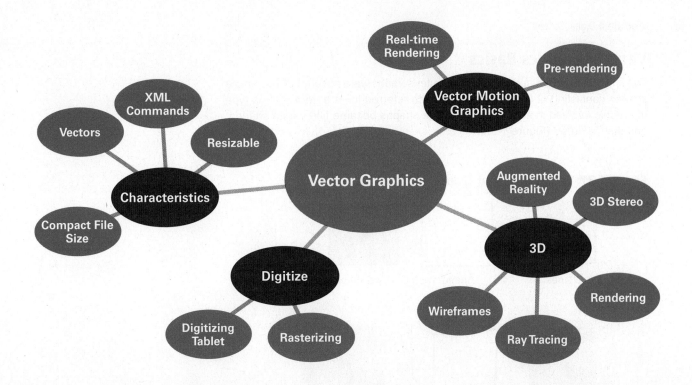

Objectives

▸ Identify vector graphics used on Web sites and social media.

▸ Based on the characteristics of vector graphics, determine when they are more suitable for a project than bitmaps.

▸ Draw simple vector shapes and outlines using drawing software.

▸ Convert a vector drawing into a bitmap.

▸ Explain the process of rendering a 3D wireframe into an image.

▸ Explain the process of animating vector graphics.

▸ Differentiate the roles CGI and VFX play in today's blockbuster films.

▸ Identify the key difference between rendering 3D graphics for computer games and creating special effects for movies.

If you've played any computer games recently or watched an animated movie, you've seen computer-generated graphics. This section begins with two-dimensional vector graphics. You'll find out how they differ from bitmaps and why you might want to use them. After covering the basics for two-dimensional graphics, the section progresses to static 3D graphics and concludes with a look at vector motion graphics for virtual reality videogames and instructional modules.

Terminology

vector	3D graphics	vector animation	CGI
vector graphic	wireframe	frame	VFX
SVG	rendering	keyframe	real-time rendering
rasterization	ray tracing	pre-rendering	game engine

Vector Graphics Basics

The first graphics that appeared on computer screens were not photos, but simple shapes consisting of lines and curves, each referred to as a **vector**. This type of graphic evolved in sophistication as the shapes became filled, then shaded, and then textured (Figure 1-37).

Figure 1-37: Vector lines and shapes

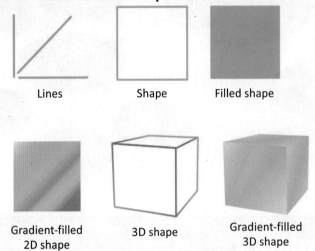

Lines   Shape   Filled shape

Gradient-filled   3D shape   Gradient-filled
2D shape   3D shape

▶ **What is a vector graphic?** A **vector graphic** consists of a set of instructions for creating a picture. Instead of storing the color value for each pixel, a vector graphics file contains instructions that a computer uses to create the shape, size, position, and color for each object in an image.

Vector drawing instructions are similar to those a drafting teacher might give students: "Draw a line of width 3 beginning at coordinates 20, 20 and extend the line to coordinates 20, 60. Color the line with #00BF00 (green)."

The command in "computerese" using an XML script would be:

```
<line x1 = "20" y1 = "20" x2 = "20" y2 = "60" stroke
= "#00BF00" stroke-width = "3"/>
```

Vector graphics include standard shapes such as circles and rectangles, so they don't have to be built from scratch. The green square in Figure 1-37 was created by specifying a rectangle beginning at coordinates 100,100 with a width of 400 and a height of 400, filled with #00BF00, like this:

```
<rect x = "100" y = "100" width = "400" height
= "400" fill = "#00BF00"/>
```

QuickCheck

What kind of shape would the following vector command create?

```
<circle cx = "100" cy = "100" r = "80" fill = "#FFFFFF" stroke =
"#00BF00" stroke-width = "10"/>
```

a. A green circle that's 100 wide with a black border

b. A white circle that has a radius of 80 and a green border

c. A white circle located at 100, 100 that has a black border

d. A green circle located at 100, 80 with a white border

❭ **How do vector graphics compare with bitmap images?** Because vector graphics are based on commands, they have different characteristics than bitmap images, which are stored as a collection of colored pixels. The differences between the two are important when considering which is best for specific projects.

Vector graphics resize better than bitmaps. When you change the size of a vector graphic, the objects change proportionally and maintain their smooth edges. In contrast, bitmap graphics might appear to have jagged edges after they are enlarged, as shown in Figure 1-38.

Figure 1-38: Vector images do not pixelate when enlarged

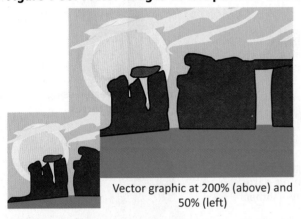

Vector graphic at 200% (above) and 50% (left)

Bitmap graphic at 200% (above) and 50% (right)

Vector graphics usually require less storage space than bitmaps. The storage space required for a vector graphic reflects the complexity of the image. Each instruction requires storage space; the more lines, shapes, and fill patterns in the graphic, the more storage space it requires. The Stonehenge vector graphic used as an example in this module requires less than 4 KB of storage space. A True Color photograph of the same image requires 1,109 KB.

Vector graphics have a different visual quality than bitmap images. Many 2D vector images have a flat, cartoon-like appearance instead of the realistic appearance you expect from a photograph. This cartoon-like characteristic of vector images results from the use of objects filled with blocks of color.

It is easier to edit an object in a vector graphic than an object in a bitmap graphic. A vector graphic is like a collage of objects that can be layered over each other, but moved and edited independently. Figure 1-39 illustrates the difference between vector and bitmap graphics when you try to edit out parts of the Stonehenge image.

Figure 1-39: Vector objects are layered

Stones in this vector image are in a separate layer that can easily be removed.

A bitmap graphic is not layered, so without an inpainting algorithm, removing the stones leaves a hole.

▶ **Where are vector graphics used?** Vector graphics are suitable for most line art, logos, simple illustrations, infographic elements, and diagrams that might be displayed and printed at various sizes. Vector graphics can include text, which is easily editable and scalable. Most modern fonts are created from vectors because they can scale smoothly to large sizes. Font effects for WordArt are based on vectors. Vector graphics are also used for floor plans, engineering diagrams, and spreadsheet charts because they are constructed from simple lines and shapes (Figure 1-40).

Figure 1-40: Vector images

Vector images created by combining shapes can look primitive.

More sophisticated vector images are created by outlining paths drawn from one point to another.

Fonts are also created using outlines and curves.

Combining circles and other simple shapes with outlined shapes produces clip art images.

Gradients can be added to vector objects to create the illusion of three dimensions.

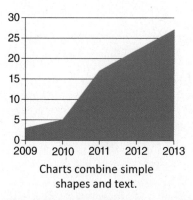

Charts combine simple shapes and text.

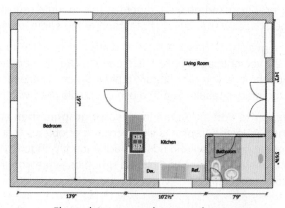

Floor plans merge shapes and text.

▶ **How can I identify vector graphics?** It can be tricky to accurately identify a vector graphic just by looking at an on-screen image. Some have a flat, cartoon-like quality, but others can look fairly realistic. Also remember that not all bitmap graphics are photos. Bitmaps are used for on-screen icons, and a bitmap could consist of simple blocks of color that look like vector shapes.

For a more definitive identification, check the file type or extension. Vector graphics files have file extensions such as .wmf, .ai, .dxf, .eps, .swf, and .svg. **SVG** (scalable vector graphics) stores the commands for vector images as XML text files. It is the most popular format for Web-based vector graphics.

QuickCheck

Which format tends to require the least storage space?

a. Bitmap

b. Vector

c. Compressed bitmap

d. MIDI

Vector Tools

Neither scanners nor digital cameras produce vector graphics. Architects and engineers might use a digitizing tablet to turn a paper-based line drawing into a vector graphic. A digitizing tablet (sometimes called a 2D digitizer) is a device that provides a flat surface for a paper-based drawing and a pen or mouse-like puck that you can use to click the endpoints of each line on the drawing. The endpoints are converted into vectors and stored.

❱ What tools do I need to create vector graphics? Vector graphics are created from scratch with vector graphics software, referred to as drawing software. Popular drawing software includes Adobe Illustrator, LibreOffice Draw, and open source Inkscape. There are also numerous online vector drawing apps; just search for "vector drawing."

Vector graphics software provides an array of drawing tools that you can use to create objects, position them, and fill them with colors, gradients, or patterns. The software converts the items you draw into instructions that are stored, which can be later used to re-create your drawing. Figure 1-41 illustrates how to use drawing tools to create a vector graphic.

Figure 1-41: Drawing vector shapes

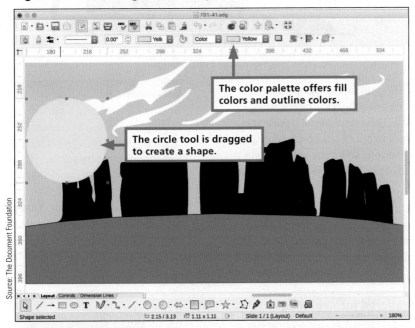

The color palette offers fill colors and outline colors.

The circle tool is dragged to create a shape.

Source: The Document Foundation

The clouds are created as a series of short line segments and filled with color.

The stones are created as a series of short line segments and filled with black.

The sun is two circles, each filled with a slightly different shade of yellow.

❱ Is it possible to convert a vector graphic into a bitmap? A vector graphic can be converted quite easily into a bitmap graphic through a process called rasterizing. **Rasterization** works by superimposing a grid over a vector image and determining the color for each pixel. This process can be carried out by graphics software, which allows you to specify the output size for the final bitmap image.

On a PC, you can rasterize a vector graphic by using the Print Screen (PrtSc) key to take a screenshot of a vector image. On a Mac, the Command-Shift-3 key combination takes a screenshot. It is important to rasterize images at the size you ultimately need. If you rasterize a vector image at a small size and then try to enlarge the resulting bitmap image, you will likely get a poor-quality pixelated image, such as the one in Figure 1-42.

After a vector graphic is converted to a bitmap, the resulting graphic no longer has the qualities of a vector graphic. For example, if you convert the Stonehenge vector graphic into a bitmap, the sun is no longer an object that you can easily move or assign a different color.

Figure 1-42: Enlarged rasterized vector

3D Graphics

❱ How do vector graphics relate to 3D graphics? 3D graphics are based on vectors stored as a set of instructions describing the coordinates for lines and shapes in a three-dimensional space. The vectors form a **wireframe** that acts in much the same way as the framework of a pop-up tent. Just as you would construct the framework for the tent and then cover it with a nylon tent cover, a 3D wireframe can be covered with surface texture and color to create a graphic of a 3D object.

The process of covering a wireframe with surface color and texture is called **rendering**. The rendering process requires a computer to perform intensive calculations to determine the surface dimensions between vectors. Rendering outputs a bitmap image that can be displayed on the screen or printed (Figure 1-43).

Try It!

Turning a vector into a bitmap is as simple as taking a screenshot. Open your Stonehenge vector and then take a screenshot (PrtSc on a PC; Command-Shift-3 on a Mac). Next, try to move the sun on the screenshot. That simple task now requires digital compositing tools!

Figure 1-43: 3D wireframe partially rendered into an image

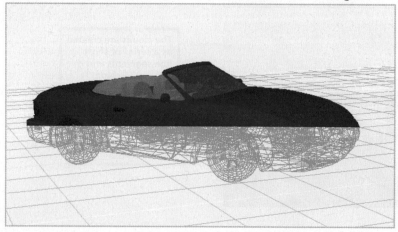

QuickCheck

Rasterization and rendering both produce a _____.

a. bitmap

b. vector

c. 3D graphic

d. wireframe

For added realism, the rendering process can take into account the way that light shines on surfaces and creates shadows. The technique for adding light and shadows to a 3D image is called **ray tracing**.

Before an image is rendered, the artist selects a location for one or more light sources. The computer applies a complex mathematical algorithm to determine how the light source affects the color of each pixel in the final rendered image. Figure 1-44 shows the image from the previous figure rendered with an additional light source and ray tracing.

Figure 1-44: Ray tracing adds highlights and shadows

Software for creating 3D graphics includes Autodesk AutoCAD, open source Blender, and Trimble SketchUp. This software provides tools for drawing a wireframe and rotating it to any angle. It provides rendering and ray tracing tools, along with an assortment of surface textures that can be applied to individual objects.

▶ **Can 3D images go stereo?** A 3D vector image may have a three-dimensional appearance, but as a single image, it cannot convey visual depth. As with bitmap photos, 3D renderings require two images for a stereoscopic effect.

A 3D rendered image can be modified to create a second rendering slightly offset from the original. When viewed with a VR headset, the two images converge into one.

Anaglyph techniques can also be applied to rendered images by tinting one image red, tinting the other image blue, and then combining both images (Figure 1-45).

Figure 1-45: 3D anaglyphs

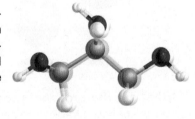

▶ **What about augmented reality?** Augmented reality adds computer-generated vector objects to a view of the real world. For example, in smartphone-based games such as Pokémon GO, game characters are computer-generated 3D graphics. A smartphone camera captures an image of the real world, and then a game character is rendered onto that image. The composite image is output to the smartphone screen (Figure 1-46).

Figure 1-46: Vectors augment reality

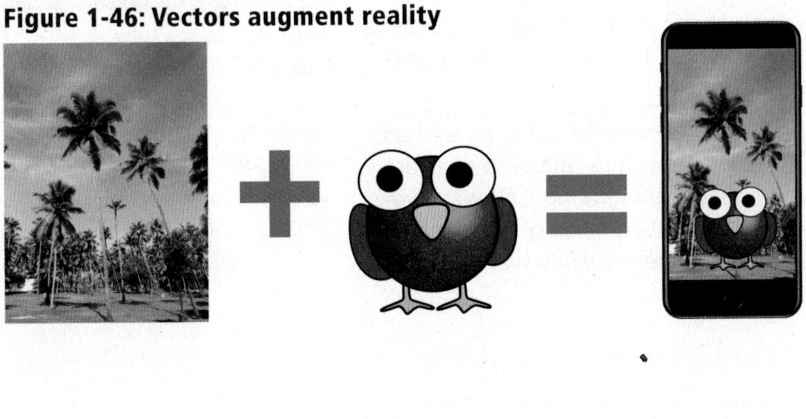

Animated Vector Graphics

From simplistic bouncing Web page icons to sophisticated interactive virtual reality, vector graphics can be set in motion. The key characteristic of vector graphics is that they are rendered from wireframes into solid objects. For animated sequences, the rendering process can occur ahead of time. Other applications, such as videogames and virtual reality, require rendering to occur in real time. Let's find out why this is the case.

▶ **How are vector animations created?** A **vector animation** is a type of motion graphic in which a series of vector images is displayed sequentially to convey the illusion of movement. Each image is called a **frame**. The process of assembling frames for a vector animation is based on techniques pioneered for hand-drawn animations in classic cartoons.

In traditional hand-drawn animation, a chief artist draws each **keyframe** that marks the beginning and end points of action. For an animation of a bouncing ball, the first keyframe depicts the ball in its original position. A second keyframe shows the ball as it reaches the floor. Once keyframes are complete, a team of assistants creates a series of inbetween images—24 of these images for each second of animation.

For vector-based computer animation, the animation artist creates keyframes of vector objects. Graphics software creates inbetween images by moving the objects along paths specified by the artist. The software then renders each image to give it substance, color, and texture. After rendering, each frame has become a bitmap image. All the images are combined into a single file, creating essentially a digital movie (Figure 1-47).

Figure 1-47: Vector objects are animated and rendered into bitmaps

QuickCheck

How many keyframes are needed to create the bouncing ball animation shown at left?

a. 1

b. 2

c. 3

d. 6

▶ **What are the pros and cons of pre-rendering?** The process of rendering vector-based frames and packaging them into a digital video file is called **pre-rendering**. The advantage of pre-rendering is that the time-consuming process of rendering and assembly can be done ahead of time using a computer with a fast processor. The resulting file can be distributed and viewed on less powerful devices, such as smartphones.

Pre-rendering is used to create special effect sequences for films, as well as full-length animated movies. In the film business, these pre-rendered clips are referred to as **CGI** (computer-generated imagery). Integrating CGI with live-action footage is called **VFX** (visual effects). Notable examples of VFX include the realistic but totally CG Thanos character in *Avengers: Infinity War* and all of the backgrounds and animals in *The Jungle Book*.

Try It!

Head over to YouTube and search for "The Jungle Book VFX Breakdown" and "Avengers: Infinity War VFX Breakdown" to see the way that incredible VFX footage was created for these films.

▶ **How do vector animations handle interaction?** Pre-rendered files are not interactive. They play sequentially from beginning to end. Creating videogames and interactive educational modules that allow viewers to manipulate objects requires a different rendering technique.

Real-time rendering fills in wireframe objects and generates a bitmap image as the action unfolds. Rendering happens in real time as the computer turns the vector instructions into points of light on the screen.

For videogames, each frame is rendered while the game is played (Figure 1-48). When manipulating an instructional 3D model, rendering takes place as students point, click, and swipe displayed objects.

Real-time rendering deals with an incredible number of bits. To give you a handle on the immensity of the processing power required to render the real-time images for computer games, consider a classic game like *Doom* that is displayed on a screen set at 1,600 x 900 resolution. At this resolution, the screen contains 1,440,000 pixels (1,600 multiplied by 900). If the game is presented in 24-bit color, each frame of the animation requires 34,560,000 bits.

To display 60 frames per second, the computer must handle 2,073,600,000 bits of data every second just to render the image frames. Additional data is processed to control character movement and game play.

▶ **How does real-time rendering relate to virtual reality?** Most interactive virtual reality visuals are generated from 3D vector graphics and displayed on VR headsets. Stereoscopic rendering produces the sense that some objects are closer than others. Each object in a vector scene can have defined properties that allow it to be manipulated by players within a game engine.

▶ **What's a game engine?** A **game engine** is graphics software that allows developers to create interactive videogames and educational modules. One of the most popular motion graphics tools is the Unity game engine. Introduced in 2005, its popularity continues to grow because it produces games and educational modules for multiple platforms, including mobile devices, Web browsers, and desktop computers. Additional tools include the Unreal Engine, developed by Epic Games for the Unreal action game, and Godot, a development environment for non-programmers.

Figure 1-48: 3D real-time rendering

Source: OpenArena

Try It!

Can you find at least three popular games that were created using the Unity game engine?

QuickQuiz   Section D

1. Vector graphics require more storage space than bitmaps, but vectors can be enlarged without becoming pixelated. True or false? [ ]

2. A process called [ ] converts vector graphics into bitmap images.

3. Based on XML, [ ] is a popular format for vector graphics on the Web.

4. A 3D image is based on an assemblage of vectors called a(n) [ ].

5. The technique of adding light and shadows to a 3D image is called ray [ ].

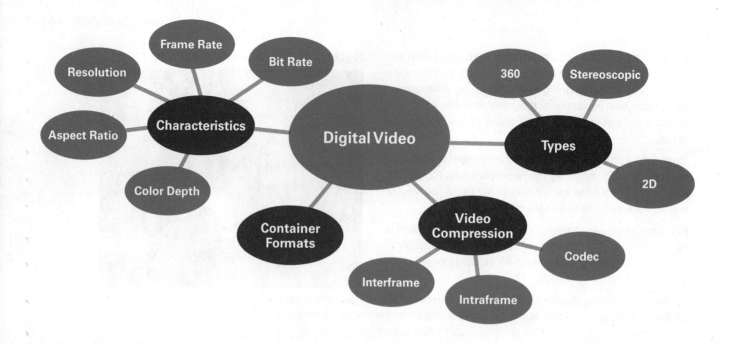

Objectives

▶ List devices and other sources that are commonly used to capture video footage.

▶ Describe the characteristics of five access options for digital video.

▶ List five factors that affect the size and quality of digital videos.

▶ Differentiate between interlaced and progressive scans.

▶ State the most commonly used aspect ratios on the following: iPhone screen, iPad screen, YouTube, and Windows laptop computer screen.

▶ Explain the purpose of a codec.

▶ Recognize digital video files by their file name extensions.

▶ List the video formats that are commonly used on the following: YouTube, iPhone, Android phone, television, and Web browsers.

▶ Explain the contents of a video container.

▶ List the variety of videos that originate as bitmap graphics.

Digital video is everywhere. It

encompasses several technologies, including those that produce theater-quality movies, Snapchat shorts, and YouTube videos. In this section, you'll take a look at what you can do with affordable, easy-to-use video tools.

Terminology

digital video	aspect ratio	codec	WebM
frame rate	bit rate	container formats	ASF
upconverting	intraframe compression	AVI	VOB
progressive scan	interframe compression	MOV	Ogg Theora
interlaced scan	compression ratio	MPEG	transcoding

Digital Video Basics

A video is a series of still images projected at a rate fast enough to fool the human eye into perceiving continuous motion. Video technology for movies and television was exclusively analog until 1986, when Sony introduced a digital video format stored on videocassette tapes. In 1991, Apple introduced a digital video format for computers. Microsoft followed with a competing digital video format in 1992.

▶ **What is digital video?** Digital video is a type of motion graphics that uses bits to store color and brightness data for each video frame. The process is similar to storing the data for a series of bitmap images in which the color for each pixel is represented by a binary number.

▶ **Where does digital video footage originate?** Today, the most common source of digital video is smartphone cameras, but footage can be recorded with a webcam or camcorder, and it can be acquired from a DVD or a digital video recording device. Analog footage from Super 8 home movies, VHS videotapes, and other legacy sources can be digitized using video capture equipment.

Professional filmmakers in the motion picture industry use digital cinematography to capture moving images as bits, rather than on film. Digital video is a core technology for digital television, videoconferencing systems, and video messaging. Real-time video even allows people with hearing loss to use sign language over cell phones.

▶ **What are the access options?** YouTube, Snapchat, Instagram, Facebook, Comcast, Netflix, and Apple Music: the list of digital video suppliers goes on and on. These suppliers provide consumers with several options for accessing digital videos. Figure 1-49 explains these options.

QuickCheck

A digital video is essentially:

a. a series of bitmap images

b. a sequence of vector graphic frames

c. an on-demand pixel stream

d. an analog capture device

1

Figure 1-49: Accessing digital video

Broadcast	Download	On-Demand Stream	Short Live Stream	Real Live Stream
Pre-recorded	Pre-recorded	Pre-recorded	Pre-recorded	Live, real-time
Delivered at a set time; Internet not required	Obtained at any time; stored on consumer devices; Internet not required for viewing	Obtained at any time; not stored on consumer devices; requires Internet connection	Obtained only within a short time frame of recording; requires Internet connection	Delivered at a set time; requires Internet connection
Broadcast and cable television; movie theaters	Netflix movie download service	YouTube, Instagram, Facebook, Netflix, Amazon Prime Video	Snapchat	Periscope

hugolacasse/Shutterstock.com

▶ What are the key properties of digital video? Most people can point a smartphone, shoot a few seconds of video, and upload it to YouTube, Facebook, or Snapchat. The quality of those videos, however, might be less than stellar. Achieving better quality and creating video for more widespread use requires a bit of background information.

The quality of digital video is based on several factors, including frame rate, resolution, color depth, bit depth, bit rate, compression technique, and file format.

▶ What should I know about frame rate? Digital video displays bitmap images in rapid succession. Each bitmap image is referred to as a frame. The number of frames that are displayed per second is the frame rate (fps). Higher frame rates produce video that more smoothly simulates real motion. The standard frame rate for motion pictures was set in the 1930s before digital formats. Digital video can produce higher frame rates (Figure 1-50).

Figure 1-50: Video frame rates

6 Frame rate for the first 3D videogame

24 Standard frame rate for motion pictures

24 Standard frame rate for YouTube videos

48 Frame rate for *The Hobbit: An Unexpected Journey*

60 Frame rate for broadcast television

30–60 Acceptable frame rates for modern videogames

60 Maximum frame rate for YouTube videos

▶ How does resolution affect video quality? Each frame is essentially a bitmap image with a resolution determined by the frame's width and height. A frame with 640 x 480 resolution contains 307,200 bits (multiply 640 by 480).

A video with a frame size of 640 x 480 will fill the screen of a device that has a similar screen size, mapping each pixel in the video frame to each pixel on the screen. Stretching the video to fit a larger screen requires pixel interpolation, which tends to reduce the quality of the image.

Modern projection devices and video playback software do an admirable job of **upconverting**, which is the digital video term for interpolation. As a rule, however, videos look sharpest when they are displayed at a resolution that is the same as the frame size.

QuickCheck

Suppose your computer screen has a resolution of 1920 x 1080, but you want to play a video with a resolution of 640 x 480. What happens?

a. The video won't play.

b. The video plays in a 640 x 480 window.

c. The video is upconverted to 640 x 480 resolution.

1

▶ **How is resolution expressed?** Video resolutions can be expressed as width x height, as the horizontal resolution, or as the vertical resolution. Digital cinematography cameras capture video with a minimum resolution of 2048 x 1536. That resolution is also referred to as 2K because the horizontal resolution is about 2,000 pixels.

A resolution of 1920 x 1080 can also be expressed using its vertical resolution as 1080p. The "p" means **progressive scan**, in which the frame is drawn line by line in sequence from the top of the image to the bottom. An **interlaced scan** is a contrasting scanning technique that produces an image by drawing every other line, then going back and filling in the in-between lines. Digital video for computers typically uses progressive scanning, whereas digital television uses interlaced scanning (Figure 1-51).

Figure 1-51: Progressive or interlaced

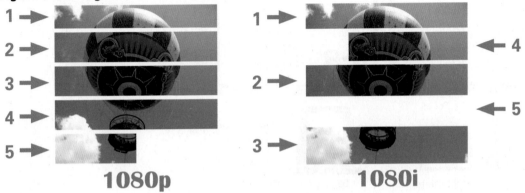

▶ **What about aspect ratio?** **Aspect ratio** is the proportional relation between the width and height of an image or video frame. A 1:1 aspect ratio is a square. A 4:3 aspect ratio is slightly wider than high. Before widescreen cinema became popular in the 1960s, 4:3 was the standard aspect ratio for television and old movies. It was also the aspect ratio of early digital videos produced for 4:3 screens on the first generation of personal computers. iPads currently use the 4:3 aspect ratio.

Today's widescreen devices, such as laptops and smartphones, are designed for the 16:9 aspect ratio, which is recommended for most modern videos, including those uploaded to YouTube.

When 4:3 videos are displayed in a widescreen player, they are bordered by the black bars of a letterbox (Figure 1-52).

Figure 1-52: Letterboxes

The video on the left has a 16:9 aspect ratio that fits into the YouTube player window. The video on the right has a 4:3 aspect ratio. A letterbox creates black bars to fill the playback window.

Letterbox

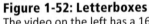

▶ **How does resolution relate to aspect ratio?** As long as the proportion of horizontal and vertical pixels remains the same, the aspect ratio is consistent. For example, a video frame with 1280 x 720 resolution has an aspect ratio of 16:9, as does a video with a resolution of 3840 x 2160. Both videos fit in a widescreen playback window, but the video with higher resolution offers a sharper, higher-quality image.

The math: Divide the horizontal by the vertical resolution. If the result is 1.7, then the aspect ratio is 16:9. If the result is 1.3, then the aspect ratio is 4:3. Try it yourself with the resolutions in Figure 1-53.

Figure 1-53: Aspect ratios for popular devices

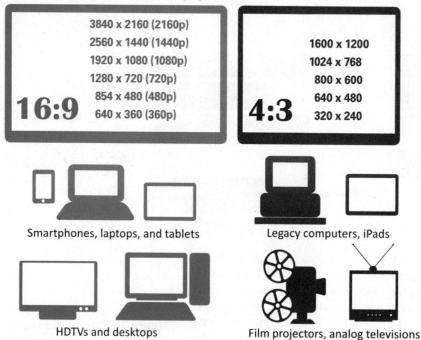

▶ **How does color depth affect video quality?** Recall from earlier in the module that color depth refers to the number and variety of colors that can be used in an image. 24-bit color depth offers a palette of 16.7 million colors. A wide selection of colors produces realistic digital videos, but requires lots of space to store all the bits for every frame.

Let's use 1920 x 1080 as a typical resolution. The number of pixels in the frame is 2,073,600 (multiply 1920 x 1080). When each pixel requires 24 bits to define its color, 49,766,400 bits are required for the data in one frame.

Now take into consideration the video frame rate of 24 fps. How much data is required for one second of video? 1,194,393,600 bits! And for one minute of video? 71,663,616,000. That's more than 71 billion bits! You can see how the bits stack up for a two-hour movie by multiplying 71 billion by 120 minutes. A feature-length video requires an astounding 8,599,633,920,000 bits. Yes, more than eight trillion bits, or one trillion bytes.

QuickCheck

How big is the file that holds a two-hour noncompressed video?

a. 8 MB

b. 1 GB

c. 8 GB

d. 1 TB

▶ **Are digital devices powerful enough to handle all those bits?** When working with digital video, you can't escape bit rates. You might have to specify a bit rate when you save a video, or when you convert a video from one format to another.

Bit rate is the number of bits that are processed during a specific unit of time, usually during one second. Bit rate can be expressed as bits per second (b/sec or bps), kilobits per second (Kbit/s or Kbps), and so on.

Bit rate becomes more important than file size for streaming video because it indicates how many bits must be transferred per second for the video to play smoothly without pausing to refill the buffer. To determine the bit rate for our 1920 x 1080 video, we have to find out how many bits are required for one second of video. We did that on the previous page, but here is the math:

$$1920 \times 1080 \times 24 \ \times 24 = 1{,}194{,}393{,}600$$

resolution x color depth x fps = bits per second

1,194,393,600 bits per second would usually be expressed as 1.19 Gbps. That bit rate is far too high for today's network connections. A fast cable Internet connection maxes out at 50 Mbps, so it can handle megabytes of data each second, but not gigabytes of data.

The bit rate for this video must decrease or it will stutter and pause frequently as it is watched. To reduce the bit rate, digital videos can be compressed.

Video Compression

Okay, so video files are big. They can easily get too big to send as email attachments, post on Facebook, or stream without pauses. The size of a video file can be scaled down by reducing the resolution, specifying a destination, selecting a maximum file size, or choosing a bit rate (Figure 1-54).

Try It!

Open a video that you've captured with a smartphone, camera, or other source. Can you use compression and other techniques to whittle the video to a file that is less than 1 MB?

Figure 1-54: Making video files smaller and faster

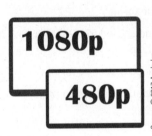

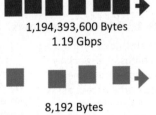

Source: © 2017 Apple Inc

Reduce Resolution	Specify Destination	Select File Size	Choose Bit Rate
Lower resolutions produce smaller file sizes and bit rates.	Choosing a video service produces files sized appropriately for use.	Smaller file sizes are achieved through compression that may reduce video quality.	Compression can produce videos with lower bit rates that stream quickly, but quality might degrade.

▶ How does video compression work? Compression removes some of the data from a video through techniques such as image compression and interframe compression.

Image compression. Earlier in the module, you found out how still images are compressed using lossy and lossless compression. This type of **intraframe compression** can be applied to each frame of a video. Suppose the data for each frame of a 1920 x 1080 video can be compressed by a factor of 10 from 49,766,400 bits to 50,000 bits. The resulting bit rate is 1.2 Mbps, which is suitable for most Internet connections.

Interframe compression. Two frames in a sequence often contain many similarly colored pixels, especially if the background remains unchanged. **Interframe compression** stores only the pixels that change color from one frame to the next. More sophisticated interframe compression uses motion compensation to track along with the camera, essentially following the camera movement to gain additional similarities between frames.

Video compression can be expressed as a **compression ratio**, which indicates the ratio of compressed data to noncompressed data. A video file with a high compression ratio, such as 35:1, has more compression, a smaller file size, and lower image quality than a file with a smaller compression ratio, such as 5:1.

▶ Where does the compression come from? A **codec** (compressor/decompressor) is the software that compresses a video stream when a video is stored, and decompresses the file when the video is played.

Each codec uses a unique algorithm to shrink the size of a video file, so codecs are not interchangeable. A file compressed using one codec cannot be extracted and played using a different codec.

When creating videos, you should use one of the codecs included in popular video players. Popular codecs include MPEG, DivX, H.264, Theora, and Windows Media Video.

Video File Formats

Video files are stored in **container formats** that hold the compressed video stream and an audio stream. For example, the popular MP4 container format holds a video stream that was produced with the H.264 codec and an AAC audio stream (Figure 1-55).

QuickCheck

Which compression ratio produces the best-quality video?

a. 2:1

b. 5:1

c. 10:1

d. 35:1

QuickCheck

When people say they have H.264 video, they are referring to the:

a. file format

b. codec used to compress the video

c. video container format

d. video compression ratio

Figure 1-55: Video containers

Codecs and video formats are easily confused, especially because some containers have the same names as codecs. A codec, such as H.264, is software that compresses the video stream, whereas a container format, such as MP4, stores the video and audio streams.

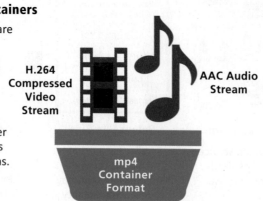

H.264 Compressed Video Stream

AAC Audio Stream

mp4 Container Format

❱ What are popular video container formats? Figure 1-56 describes some popular video container formats: AVI, MOV, MPEG, WebM, ASF, VOB, and Ogg Theora.

Figure 1-56: Video container formats

Format	Extension	Description and Use
MPEG (Moving Picture Experts Group)	.mpg, .mp4, .mpeg	Versions include MPEG-1, MPEG-2, and MPEG-4; used for downloaded and streaming Web video
WebM	.webm	Royalty-free, high-quality open format for use with HTML5
AVI (Audio Video Interleave)	.avi	A format sometimes used for storing digital clips from video cameras; used for legacy video on the PC platform
MOV (QuickTime Movie)	.mov	A legacy format for downloaded and streaming Web videos
ASF (Advanced Systems Format)	.asf, .wmv	Container format for Microsoft's Windows Media Video (WMV); supports downloads and streaming
VOB (Video Object)	.vob	Industry-standard format for standalone DVD players
Ogg Theora	.ogg	A non-proprietary container (Ogg) and video codec (Theora)

❱ Can I change videos from one format to another? Digital videos can be converted from one file format to another through a process called **transcoding**. If you want to move a video into a different file format, you can check to see if your video editing software offers a conversion, export, or transcoding option. If not, you can find transcoding software on the Web. Transcoding can cause loss of quality, so avoid transcoding an already transcoded video file.

❱ What tools are provided by video editing software? Basic video editing tools are used to arrange video clips, add a soundtrack, insert captions, select special effects such as fades between clips, and choose an output format (Figure 1-57).

Figure 1-57: Create a video

The storyboard is an area where you can arrange audio and video clips for your movie.

Preview your movie to see how the video segments, transitions, and soundtrack all work together.

Try It!

Apply the skills you picked up from this module to combine video footage, music clips, narrations, and a still photo into a video that is about ten seconds in length. How can you share it with your classmates?

Digital Video Variations

Car chases, space battles, and marauding monsters can be exciting, but somehow a flat screen prevents viewers from making a closer connection to the action. Filmmakers, game developers, and educational technology specialists have a basket of techniques for going beyond 2D video to create immersive visuals. Technologies for 360-degree videos and stereoscopic movies are here today, along with tools aimed at consumers who want to experience, create, and share the adventure.

▶ **What is a 360-degree video?** Movies are simply multiframe bitmaps that build on techniques used to create basic bitmap still images. Think back to the cylindrical projections of a 360-degree view or a spherical projection that can be constructed by stitching together a series of images filmed from a single pivot point. Those images were all stills—single frame photos.

Now imagine that instead of still frames, a photographer uses multiple video cameras to simultaneously film footage from all angles (Figure 1-58). A 360-degree video is a motion graphic that depicts continuous events happening within a 360-degree radius or sphere of a single pivot point.

Try It!

You can view examples of 360-degree videos on Facebook and YouTube. When watching on a flat screen, try dragging the mouse or swiping to scroll the video around the fixed pivot point. You can also watch these videos with a VR headset, and as you rotate in place, the scene will shift.

Figure 1-58: A multi-camera rig to capture 360-degree videos

betto rodrigues/Shutterstock.com

▶ **How about 3D movies?** Movies that appear to have visual depth are commonly called "3D," but technically, they are stereoscopic. These movies create the illusion of visual depth using anaglyphs or stereograms.

When movies are constructed with anaglyphs, each frame contains a blue and red stereo pair. Viewers wear glasses with red and blue lenses to experience the effect of visual depth. Anaglyph movies like the one in Figure 1-59 can be projected on movie theater screens, but despite popular movies being available in this format, some moviegoers complain of headaches and eye strain.

Figure 1-59: Anaglyph movies

WARNER BROS / Ronald Grant Archive / Alamy Stock Photo

▶ **Can movies be created with stereograms?** Displaying a pair of images side by side on a movie theater screen will not produce a stereoscopic experience. However, when projected in a VR headset, stereograms produce an amazingly realistic three-dimensional world.

Each frame of the video is divided vertically into two halves. The left half contains the image for the left eye. The right half contains the image for the right eye. When projected on the screens of a VR headset, these video frames produce the sensation of being within an unfolding three-dimensional movie (Figure 1-60).

Try It!

Enter your address in Google Maps, and then select Street View. Now that you understand graphics technology, how would you classify the type of graphics used for this app?

1

Figure 1-60: Stereographic video for VR headsets

▶ **Are stereoscopic movies virtual reality?** Computer scientists define virtual reality as a computer-generated three-dimensional world that provides participants with seemingly real, direct, or physical interaction. Based on that definition, the underlying technology for virtual reality requires 3D motion vectors rendered in real time because the three-dimensional objects it produces can be moved and manipulated.

Today, however, the term *virtual reality* is applied to just about any motion graphics that are viewed through a VR headset, including vector-based pre-rendered animations, 360-degree videos, and stereoscopic movies. How this terminology sorts itself out in the future will depend on consumer awareness, marketing integrity, and technology development.

QuickQuiz   Section E

1. The process of converting analog video signals into digital format is referred to as video [_____].

2. A(n) [_____] is the software that compresses a video stream when a video is stored, and decompresses the file when the video is played.

3. The "p" in 1080p stands for [_____] scan.

4. MP4 is an example of a video [_____] format.

5. Digital videos can be converted from one file format to another through a process called [_____].

Issue: What is Fair Use?

Fair use is the right to use portions of copyrighted material without the permission of the copyright holder for purposes such as review, criticism, or parody. Under certain circumstances, fair use is also a successful defense for practices such as time shifting, place shifting, and format shifting.

Exactly what constitutes fair use, however, is only sketched out in copyright law. The precise nature of fair use is shaped by court decisions covering situations and devices as diverse as vinyl records, printer toner cartridges, videotape recorders, and file sharing networks.

It seems incredible, but there once were no restrictions on copying sound recordings. "Record pirates" could legally copy and distribute, say, an Elvis Presley recording.

In 1971, the U.S. Congress passed the Sound Recording Act that prohibited copying music for commercial use. The law was not, however, aimed at prohibiting consumers from making copies for their own use.

Time shifting is the practice of recording music, videos, or other works for playback at another time. The legal precedent that gave consumers permission for time shifting was the landmark 1984 Betamax case in which Universal Studios attempted to hold Sony Corp. of America liable for copyright infringement by people who used video recorders to tape movies from their televisions. The U.S. Supreme Court sided with Sony and concluded that some instances of time shifting were legal.

The court's decision, however, was based on a definition of time shifting as "the practice of recording a program to view it once at a later time." Note the word *once*. The Betamax case did not offer legal precedent for copying and saving content for viewing multiple times.

The proliferation of computer networks and streaming media has made place shifting possible. Place shifting is the prac-

> **"Specifically, it is not the intention of Congress to restrain the home recording, from broadcasts or from tapes or records, of recorded performances, where the home recording is for private use and with no purpose of reproducing or otherwise capitalizing commercially on it."**
>
> U.S. Judiciary Committee statement regarding the Sound Recording Act of 1971

tice of transmitting a copy of a song or video to another device for playback. For example, you can view a cable television broadcast sent from your Wi-Fi equipped set-top box in your living room to your Wi-Fi equipped laptop out on the deck. Your network is transmitting a copy of the broadcast, a practice that is not explicitly allowed by copyright law in most countries. Therefore, unless a user agreement extends the basic rights granted by copyright law, place shifting would be considered a questionable practice.

So how about format shifting? Surely, it must be legal to rip tracks from a CD that you own and save them as an MP3 file that you can play on a digital device. Many consumers believe that they have a right to use a legally purchased song or video in any manner they please, short of redistributing it for profit.

Consumers are familiar with copyright restrictions on printed books and have an expectation that digital media can be legally used in parallel ways.

Readers expect to be able to carry a book with them to any location, read it at any time, use any type of reading light or reading glasses, loan the book to friends, and sell the book when they have finished using it.

Although it is convenient to focus on the "once I buy it, I can use it as I like" rationale, we tend to ignore situations in which our expectations about content use are more limited. For example, we do not expect that after attending a Justin Timberlake concert, we are entitled to a free MP3 of the performance. If we pay to see a movie at a theater, we don't then expect to download the movie or soundtrack for free when they are released.

Content suppliers, such as Apple Music and Netflix, allow their customers to stream music and videos to various devices. But even those services have restrictions. Savvy consumers always check the supplier's usage policy before subscribing to download and streaming services.

Try It! Do you know how to legally use music, movies, ebooks, and other media? Here's a chance for you to explore fair use and content usage policies.

1 Fair use is defined in Section 107 of U.S. copyright law. It includes four factors designed to determine whether a use is fair. Look up Section 107 of the U.S. Copyright Law. In your own words, what are those four factors?

2 The book *Grateful Dead: The Illustrated Trip* included concert posters and ticket images used without approval of the copyright holder. In a subsequent suit, courts decided the use was fair and transformative, based on a four-factor analysis. Look up the results of this case by searching for the article *Grateful Dead Posters' Re-publication Held to Be a Transformative, Fair Use* by Martine Courant Rife. In your own words, what did the court say about each of the four factors?

3 "Transformative use" means that you change a work enough to make it your own. Collages, music remixes, and video parodies can fall into this category. Find an example of a transformative work on YouTube and list the original works from which it is derived. In your opinion, what makes this a transformative work?

4 Digital content providers such as Netflix, Amazon, and YouTube each have their own rules about how you can use the content you purchase, rent, or subscribe to. To get an idea of a typical usage policy, search for *Amazon Prime Video Usage Rules*, and then answer the following questions:

    a. Are you allowed to stream more than one video at a time?

    b. Are you allowed to stream the same video to two devices at the same time?

    c. Are you allowed to stream videos to any digital device?

    d. Are you allowed to save rented content to a hand-held device so that you can watch it after the viewing period has ended?

5 Because digital music is so accessible, it can be easily added to video footage as a soundtrack. Suppose you've purchased a Beyoncé song on iTunes. You want to use the song as a soundtrack for a video that you plan to post on YouTube. Would using the song in that situation be considered fair use? Would it be transformative? To find out, check YouTube's Web pages about using music in YouTube videos.

Charlie Gillett/Redferns/Getty Images

What Do You Think?

1. What would you change about the Fair Use Doctrine to make it more fair?

2. In your opinion, do services such as Amazon Prime Video provide consumers with enough flexibility for accessing content?

3. Have you heard of situations in which someone appeared to follow fair use guidelines, but was still charged with copyright infringement?

Information Tools: Photo Forensics

Digital tools make it easy to manipulate images. Many of the photos we see in magazines, in newspapers, and online have been adjusted to improve color and contrast. But they can also be altered in ways that are intended to deceive viewers.

Some images are obviously fake. Just about everyone is familiar with tabloid cover photos with a celebrity's head pasted onto another person's body, and cosmetic ads airbrushed beyond believability.

A photo of a family in the war-torn city of Aleppo, Syria, was altered to make the background appear more dramatic. The altered photo is shown at left above.

According to researchers, most people can identify clumsy photo fakes by looking for body parts that seem out of proportion and cloned areas that repeat themselves within the image.

Savvy consumers understand that the faces and bodies depicted in ads are not always realistic, but they have different expectations about photojournalism and the photos published about world events.

Photos in mainstream news outlets affect our views and opinions of real events. Yet photographs that record these events are sometimes manipulated to improve composition or convey a message.

Although detailed photographic analysis is beyond the ability of most readers, many photo fakes are eventually unmasked. Before you base opinions on a dramatic photo or use an image to substantiate your own research, check Internet resources to make sure the photo is not a known fake.

Oprah's head on Ann-Margret's body

Airbrushed skin

Before   **After**

To spot a fake photo, look for:

▶ Body parts that seem out of proportion

▶ Remnants of body parts, scenery, or objects removed from a photo

▶ Areas of lighting that seem brighter or darker than they should be

▶ Light and shadow that are not consistent for all objects in the photo

▶ Parts of the background or crowd that seem to be cloned duplicates

Try It!

"If you can change photographs, you can change history." That quote from Hany Farid, a computer scientist specializing in digital forensics, contains a warning about the perils of digital photo manipulation. Here's your chance to find out how to uncover photo forgeries.

1 Search for "photo tampering throughout history" to see some surprising examples about doctored photos, beginning with an iconic image of Abraham Lincoln. Look through the photo gallery and select the five photos you think are the most misleading, then explain why.

2 It is surprisingly easy to edit digital photos using today's sophisticated graphics software. To see how it works, check out the YouTube video "How to Remove Anything from a Photo on a Smartphone." Summarize the tools and processes used in the demonstration.

3 A Web site called TinEye bills itself as a reverse image search engine. Given any image, TinEye can find out where it came from and how it is being used. TinEye even finds modified versions of the image. Click the link for "How to use TinEye" and look at the examples to see the results that TinEye can produce. Then, upload an image of your own (or use an image that you select from the Web) to see what TinEye finds. Take a screenshot of your results. (Use the PrtSc or Print Screen key on a PC; use Command-Shift-3 on a Mac.)

4 Exif (Exchangeable image file format) data can reveal information that helps to verify or unveil a photo's ori-gins. Specialized software is needed to view all the Exif data, but operating system utilities display some of the data. Select a photo stored in JPEG format and view its tags. On a PC, right-click the image, select Properties, then select the Details tab. On a Mac, click File, click Get Info, then expand the More Info section. Which of the following are revealed?

a. Date taken

b. Date modified

c. Camera brand and model

d. Photographer

e. Place taken

5 When the eye cannot discern whether a photo is real or fake, photo detectives turn to computer science, mathematics, and physics to find answers. The same equations that are used to create light and shadows in 3D rendered images can also be used to analyze the shadows in a suspicious photograph. Dartmouth College researcher Hany Farid conducted an analysis of a suspicious shadow in a frame of the 1963 Zapruder film of President Kennedy's assassination. Locate his research paper. What did he conclude? Was the film a fake or real?

Technology in Context: Film

In 1895, eager Parisians crowded into a busy cafe to watch the first public presentation of an exciting new invention—the Cinematograph. The 10-minute film, mostly scenes of everyday life, was a smashing success and ushered in the motion picture era. Early films were short, grainy, grayscale, and silent, but technology quickly improved. In the New York debut of *The Jazz Singer* (1927), Al Jolson spoke the first words in a feature film: "Wait a minute, wait a minute. You ain't heard nothin' yet!"

Even before "talkies" and Technicolor, filmmakers sought ways to escape the bounds of reality through special effects. As early as 1925, directors such as Willis O'Brien used stop-motion photography to animate dinosaurs, giant gorillas, and sword-wielding skeletons. Special-effects technologies—miniatures, blue screens, puppets, Claymation, 3D, and composite shots—were used with varying degrees of skill over the next 50 years. Films such as Stanley Kubrick's masterpiece, *2001: A Space Odyssey* (1968), and George Lucas's original *Star Wars* (1977) stretched these technologies to their limits, but audiences demanded even more spectacular, yet "realistic," effects.

In 1982, Disney released *TRON*, a movie about a programmer who becomes trapped in the depths of a computer where programs are human-like creatures that serve every whim of an evil Master Control Program. The movie included the first primitive attempts at computer-generated footage—30 minutes of computer-generated imagery (CGI) created by two Cray X-MP supercomputers.

CGI uses rendering techniques to create a 3D scene from a 2D image, a camera angle, and a light source. Sophisticated algorithms determine how textures, colors, and shadows appear in the rendered scene. Camera angles can be changed at will, and fantastic effects can be created by bending or stretching the image, manipulating light, creating textures, and adding movement to the scene.

Rendered scenes can be set in motion with computer animation techniques. Manual animation requires a painstaking process called inbetweening, in which an artist draws a series of incrementally different images to produce the illusion of movement. Computers can easily generate inbetween images and free up human animators for more challenging work.

A captivating animation special effect called morphing was first seen on the big screen in James Cameron's *The Abyss* (1989), and was later used in *Terminator 2* (1991) and other movies. Like inbetweening, morphing starts out with animators defining the morph's start and end points—for example, in *Terminator 2*, the liquid metal face of the T-1000 robot and actor Robert Patrick's face. The start and end points are rendered into digital images, and then the computer generates the inbetween images. Human animators tweak the images by inserting small discrepancies for a touch of less-than-perfect realism in the final footage.

Although the process might sound simple, morphing complex objects realistically and believably takes a tremendous amount of time and computer power. The five minutes of morphing sequences in *Terminator 2* took special-effects company Industrial Light & Magic a year to create.

© Disney/Pixar/Photofest

Memorable computer-generated scenes from classic blockbusters include the breathtaking aerial scenes in *Spiderman*, a furry blue monster called Sully careening downhill in *Monsters, Inc.*, the endless army of Uruk-hai marching down the valley toward Helm's Deep in *The Lord of the Rings: The Two Towers*, and Princess Merida unfurling her wildly curly locks in *Brave*.

Spiderman's acrobatic swing through Manhattan was generated with three professional rendering products: Maya, Houdini, and RenderMan. The Uruk-hai were created with MASSIVE, a custom program that gave each computer-generated warrior a unique sequence of actions. To individually animate each of Sully's 2,320,413 blue hairs, animators developed software called Fizt, a dynamic simulator.

Animation took another leap forward when Pixar's team of artists and engineers developed a computer program called Taz to realistically depict Princess Merida's flowing, curly hair.

Rendering, morphing, and other special effects require sophisticated computer systems. Pixar Animation Studios, the company that provided the technology behind *Toy Story*, *Up*, *Ratatouille*, *WALL-E*, and many other feature-length animated films, uses a cluster of computers called a renderfarm.

The film *Toy Story* took more than 800,000 computer hours to produce using the renderfarm. That might seem like a long time; but if Pixar animators had used a single-processor computer, it would have taken 43 years to finish the job!

Other CGI variations are being used for increasingly sophisticated effects. Special-effects guru John Gaeta developed "bullet time" and image-based rendering for *The Matrix* (1999). Bullet time produces reality-defying action sequences that slow time to a tantalizing crawl and then crank it back up to normal speed as the camera pivots rapidly around the scene. The effect requires a computer to meticulously trigger a circular array of more than 100 still cameras.

Films such as *Sky Captain and the World of Tomorrow* (2004) and *Sin City* (2005) took green screen special effects to a new level. Filmed entirely indoors on a sound stage, these movies used a technique called compositing that layers two or more video clips over each other and merges them into one image. Actors were filmed against a green background screen. During post-production, video editing software removed the background and layered in scenery created with CGI or from real footage on location.

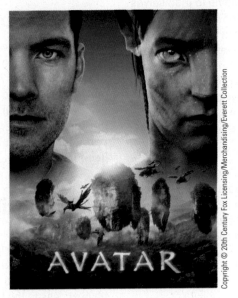

Copyright © 20th Century Fox Licensing/Merchandising/Everett Collection

Sin City is also notable as one of the first fully digital live-action motion pictures. It was filmed in full color with high-definition digital cameras. The footage was converted to black and white, and then color was reintroduced digitally with the use of a DLP Cinema projector.

Until 2013, movies were distributed on film, but Paramount Pictures led the switch to digital. Now studios deliver most films on hard drives or through an Internet download. For the dwindling number of theaters without digital projection equipment, digital footage can be output to film and reproduced using legacy techniques.

Motion capture suits were put to award-winning use for Peter Jackson's *The Lord of the Rings*. The actor who played Gollum was outfitted with sensors that tracked the position of his head, arms, and legs. The collected data was later used by animators to create the 3D animated Gollum seen on the screen. Motion capture was further refined for *Avatar*, which used digital technology to capture the actors' facial expressions.

Sophisticated animation and rendering techniques now come close to producing realistic human figures. Animations were once clearly two-dimensional and far from lifelike, but CGI renderings are becoming more difficult to distinguish from real actors.

What might happen in the future is the subject of *Simone* (2002), starring Al Pacino as a washed-up director who is given a hard disk containing code for a computer-generated movie star. Pacino uses her as the leading lady in a string of hits, all the while keeping her identity secret. According to reviewer Leigh Johnson, it becomes clear that Simone, a virtual computer-generated image, is more authentic than the people watching her. It is one of the film's main themes, expressed by Pacino's character: "Our ability to manufacture fraud now exceeds our ability to detect it."

The issues surrounding computer-generated actors are just emerging. Not only do they blur the line between reality and fiction, but they also raise puzzling questions for actors and their agents, directors, and programmers. It is possible to create CGI doubles for long-dead actors, such as Marilyn Monroe and James Dean, but who controls their use and profits from their work? Can aging actors sign contracts for use of their "young" CGI counterparts? Would it be legal and ethical for programmers to create and market virtual characters based on real actors or a compilation of the best traits of popular stars? As is often the case, new technologies present issues along with their benefits—issues you might want to consider the next time you watch a movie.

Flipped Class Projects

Critical Thinking

Copyright laws are changing as digital sound, image, and video technologies evolve and become easier to use. Although the courts seem to clearly hold that it is illegal to copy media for profit, they are not as clear about the acceptability of modifications. For example, video editing software makes it relatively simple for people to clip out parts of movies they find to be objectionable to themselves or their children. Should it be legal to do so for personal use? What if an organization wanted to rent out such edited copies? What if a specialized video player was set up so that it would edit and display the revised version on the fly? After you consider your own opinion, you might check the Web to see the latest information about this issue.

Group Project

Work with a group of four students to research three Web-based music download or streaming sites. Create one PowerPoint slide for each site. The slide should give a basic overview of the site, including its name, URL, music file format, price, pros, and cons. For the final slide in the presentation, create a table comparing the features and prices of each site.

Cyberclassroom

Each person on your team should email a photo in JPEG format to the other members of the group. The photo can be one you've taken or one you find on the Web. If you get your photo from the Web, make sure there are no restrictions on using it for a personal project, and note the Web site's URL so you have a record of your source. When you receive the photos from your teammates, be creative and use Photoshop or similar photo editing software to create a composite image that contains elements from all the photos. Submit your original photo and your composite photo to your instructor.

Multimedia Project

Use Windows Voice Recorder or similar software to record an original 15-second radio ad for your favorite music or video streaming service. Be sure to use an efficient sampling rate. Submit the text of your script along with the audio file containing your ad.

Resume Builder

Artists routinely create a portfolio containing examples of their best work. How can you apply the portfolio concept to your job search? Suppose you've decided to create a multimedia portfolio that showcases your talents. Describe what you'd like your portfolio to contain, indicating which of the items you currently have and which you'd like to create and add in the future. Also, describe the format for each item: photo, document, scan, audio, or video.

Globalization

The United States has been accused of exporting its culture and values through films and television. Sometimes referred to as "Coca-Colonization," the mass exportation of American culture is expected to increase as more and more people have access to the Internet. But is digital distribution a two-way street? What can you find out about the importation of cultures to the United States (or your country)? Incorporate your findings into a two-page paper. Make sure you cite specific examples and offer your ideas on how technology aids or discourages cross-cultural interchanges. Include a list of references on a third page.

Key Terms

3D graphics 56
AAC 32
AAX 32
alpha blending 48
anaglyph 50
analog data 19
analog-to-digital converter 30
ASCII 22
ASCII text 23
ASF 67
aspect ratio 63
audio compression 32
audio interface 33
AVI 67
binary 19
binary number system 21
bit 20
bit rate 65
bitmap graphic 39
BMP 41
byte 25
CCD 40
CGI 58
character data 22
clipping path 48
cloning 47
codec 66
color depth 42
compression ratio 66
computer graphics 39
container formats 66
copy protection 34
data 19
data compression 26
data representation 19
delimiter 24
digital audio 30
digital audio extraction 33
digital compositing 48
digital data 19
digital rights management 34
digital video 61

digital-to-analog converter 30
digitization 20
download 33
Extended ASCII 22
file 20
file format 20
file name extension 20
frame 58
frame rate 62
game engine 59
GIF 41
gigabit 26
gigabyte 26
image compression 44
image histogram 46
image resolution 43
image stitching 48
inpainting 47
interframe compression 66
interlaced scan 63
intraframe compression 66
JPEG 41
keyframe 58
kilobit 26
kilobyte 26
live stream 33
lossless compression 26
lossy compression 26
megabit 26
megabyte 26
MIDI 34
MIDI messages 34
motion graphics 39
MOV 67
MP3 32
MPEG 67
numeric data 21
OCR 25
Ogg Theora 67
Ogg Vorbis 32
on-demand stream 33
phoneme 36

photosites 40
pixel 39
pixel interpolation 43
pixelation 43
PNG 41
pre-rendering 58
progressive scan 63
rasterization 56
RAW 41
ray tracing 57
real-time rendering 59
rendering 56
resolution dependent 43
RGB color model 42
run-length encoding 44
sampling rate 31
scanner 40
speech recognition 36
speech synthesis 36
stereo pair 49
stereogram 49
stereoscopic imaging 49
still images 39
SVG 54
synthesized sound 34
text-to-speech software 36
TIFF 41
transcoding 67
True Color 42
Unicode 22
upconverting 62
UTF-8 22
vector 52
vector animation 58
vector graphic 52
VFX 58
VOB 67
WAV 32
WebM 67
wireframe 56
WMA 32

Interactive Summary

Section A: [_____] data is processed, stored, and transmitted as a series of 1s and 0s. Each 1 or 0 is called a(n) [_____]. A series of eight 0s and 1s, called a(n) [_____], represents one character—a letter, number, or punctuation mark. Data becomes [_____] when it is presented in a format that people can understand and use. Digital signals are represented by two different [_____], such as +5 volts and +.2 volts. Digital data can also take the form of light and dark spots etched onto the surface of a CD or the positive and negative orientation of [_____] particles on the surface of a hard disk. [_____] data consists of numbers that might be used in arithmetic operations. It can be represented digitally using the [_____] number system. [_____] data is composed of letters, symbols, and numerals that are not used in arithmetic operations. Computers represent this type of data using [_____], Unicode, or UTF-8. Data is quantified using terms such as [_____] or kibibyte (1024 bytes), and prefixes such as [_____] or mebi (1,048,576), and giga or [_____] (1,073,741,824). To reduce file size and transmission times, digital data can be compressed. [_____] compression provides the means to compress data and reconstitute it into its original state. [_____] compression throws away some of the original data during the compression process. Files created with a compression utility usually have [_____] at the end of the file name and are represented with special icons. These files have to be [_____] or unzipped before you can view the data they contain.

Section B: Music, voice, and sound effects can all be recorded and stored on a computer as [_____] audio. To digitally record sound, [_____] of the sound are collected at periodic intervals and stored as numeric data. High-quality sound is usually sampled at 44.1 [_____], and each stereo sample requires 32 bits of storage space. To conserve space, radio-quality recordings of speaking voices are often recorded at lower sampling rates. Digital audio file formats include WAV, AAC, WMA, AAX, Ogg, and MP3. Most portable media players work with MP3 format or with the [_____] format, used for streaming Apple Music. These media files can be acquired as a download, [_____] stream, or on-demand stream. MIDI music is [_____] sound that is artificially created. A series of MIDI [_____] specify the pitch, volume, and duration of notes that sound like various musical instruments. MIDI files are typically much smaller than digital audio files for similar musical passages. However, MIDI music tends to lack the full resonance of symphony-quality sound that can be achieved with digital audio. Speech [_____] is the process by which machines, such as computers, produce sound that resembles spoken words. Speech [_____] refers to the ability of machines to "understand" spoken words.

Section C: A bitmap graphic is composed of a grid of tiny rectangular cells called [_____]. The color of each cell is stored as a(n) [_____] number. Popular bitmap graphics formats include BMP, TIFF, GIF, JPEG, RAW, and PNG. Both scanners and cameras produce images in bitmap format. Digital display devices represent colors using the [_____] color model. Although colors are ultimately represented as bits when a graphic is stored or transmitted, color values can be specified in binary, [_____], or decimal. Color [_____] refers to the number of colors available for use in an image. The dimensions of the grid that forms a bitmap graphic are referred to as its [_____]. It is possible to change the resolution and/or the file size of a bitmap graphic; but because bitmaps are resolution [_____], these changes can reduce image quality. For example, enlarging a bitmap requires your computer to fill in missing pixels, which often results in a jagged or [_____] image. Image compression shrinks the size of a graphics file. [_____] compression is used for images stored in JPEG format, but [_____] compression is used for PNG, GIF, and TIFF files. Photoediting software includes tools, such as an image [_____], that adjusts brightness values for various ranges of pixels. Algorithms for [_____] scrub out designated areas of an image and replace the missing pixels. Clipping paths and alpha blending are useful for digital [_____] when you want to assemble parts of several photos into one image. Panoramic and 360-degree images can be assembled using image [_____] to match the edges of a sequence of photos. Stereoscopic effects can be achieved with a photo pair or by creating a(n) [_____] with red and blue coloration.

Section D: Unlike a bitmap graphic, created by superimposing a grid of pixels over an image, a vector graphic consists of a set of instructions for creating a picture. Vector graphics are stored as a collection of [_____] and their corresponding sizes, colors, and positions. The big advantage of vector graphics is that they can be enlarged without becoming [_____]. Vector graphics are created by using [_____] software. A vector graphic can be converted into a bitmap by a process called [_____]. Once converted, however, the resulting graphic loses the object-editing qualities it had in its vector state. The most common vector graphics format for the Web is [_____]. 3D graphics are stored as a set of instructions that contain the locations and lengths of lines that form a(n) [_____] for a 3D object. This framework then can be covered by colored, patterned, and textured surfaces. This process, called [_____], produces a bitmap image of the 3D object. [_____] tracing adds highlights and shadows to the image. 3D graphics can be [_____] to produce animated special effects for movies. Real-time [_____] is required for 3D computer games and virtual reality.

Section E: Footage for digital videos can be supplied from a digital source, or from a(n) [_____] source that requires conversion. In addition to standalone digital cameras, digital footage can also be obtained from cameras embedded in handheld devices and from [_____] built in above a computer screen. Video resolution varies, but 1080p is common. The "p" stands for [_____] scan. Most videos today have a widescreen aspect ratio of [_____]. Most videos are output in a compressed format using intraframe and [_____] compression. Software, such as MPEG, DivX, Theora, and H.264, that compresses the video stream is referred to as a(n) [_____]. A compression [_____], such as 5:1, indicates the degree of compression. Video and audio streams are combined into the final video file and stored using a(n) [_____] format, such as AVI, MOV, or WebM. So-called 3D movies are technically [_____] in their use of anaglyphs or stereograms.

Interactive Situation Questions

1. At work, no one can find the digital version of a 20-page document that needs to be revised. You save the day by using a scanner and ⬚ software to digitize the paper document.

2. Suppose you are creating an English-as-a-Second-Language Web page and you want to add links to sound files that pronounce English phrases. Would it be better to store the files in MP3 or MIDI format? ⬚

3. Imagine that you're a musician and you are asked to synthesize some upbeat music for a modern ballet. For this project, you would most likely work with ⬚ music.

4. Suppose you visit a Web site that allows you to enter sentences, and then it reads the sentences back to you. The site even gives you a choice of a female or male voice. You assume that this site uses speech ⬚ technology.

5. You have an old photograph that you want to incorporate in a brochure for your antiques business. To convert the photo into digital format, you use a(n) ⬚ .

6. Imagine that you are preparing a series of bitmap graphics for a Web site. To decrease the download time for each graphic, you can use a compressed format such as GIF, PNG, TIFF, or ⬚ .

7. You've taken a photo with a high-resolution digital camera and you want to send it as an email attachment. You decide to ⬚ it to reduce the image to a more manageable size.

8. Suppose you are designing a logo for a client. You know the design will undergo several revisions, and you understand that the logo will be used at various sizes. You decide it would be best to use drawing software to create the logo as a(n) ⬚ graphic.

9. After you finish arranging video clips and adding a soundtrack, you can select a video file format and a compression technique. For example, you might store the video in WebM container format and use the H.264 ⬚ to compress the file.

10. You uploaded a video to YouTube, but it's got black bars on the side. If you want to get rid of them, you'll have to re-output your video and change its ⬚ .

Lab: The Digital World with Eyes Shut

The digital world is very visual. Email demands to be read. Web sites are full of text. Social media feeds are constantly changing. Pinterest and Flickr are all about photos. And a lifetime is not long enough to view all the videos on YouTube. But what would this digital world be like if you could not see it? Can speech synthesizers and voice recognition tools change the visual experience into an auditory one? In this lab, you'll have an opportunity to set up a screen reader, activate voice recognition, and experience the digital world with your eyes closed.

Requirements:

For this lab, you'll need a Windows computer, an Apple computer, an iPhone 4s or newer, or an Android phone. The instructions are generalized; they provide helpful guidelines, but not specific steps. You may have to explore a bit to find all the tools needed to complete the assignment, but that is all part of the learning experience. You might find this lab goes more smoothly if you work with a partner.

Assignment:

1 Activate voice commands on your device.

On a Mac, select the Apple menu, then choose System Preferences, Accessibility, and Voice Control. Enable Voice Control. Click the Commands button to see a list of voice commands that you can use.

On a PC with Windows, locate the Speech Recognition utility. If setup is required, select a microphone, then continue with the setup (choosing Disable document review). You can access a tutorial by searching online for "Windows Speech recognition."

On an iPhone, access Settings, then select Siri. Make sure Siri is on. Hold the Home button to open Siri (or hold your iPhone up to your ear if you've enabled Raise to Speak).

On an Android phone, access the Settings menu, select My device, then choose Voice control. Turn voice control on, then select it to find out what kinds of commands you can say.

2 Try these activities and make notes on the results:

Does your device respond when you ask "What time is it?"

Can you launch the camera app and take a photo using voice commands?

Can you issue a voice command to get to the desktop, Start screen, or Home screen?

Can you dictate an email message or text message using only voice commands?

3 Activate the screen reader for your device.

On a Mac, select the Apple icon, then choose System Preferences, Accessibility, and VoiceOver. Enable VoiceOver. (Leave the Accessibility window open so that you can disable VoiceOver when you complete the lab.) Take a few minutes to step through the VoiceOver training.

On a PC with Windows, enter Narrator in the Windows search box. Start the Narrator.

On an iPhone, select Settings, then select Accessibility. Turn on VoiceOver.

On an Android phone, select Applications, Accessibility, and TalkBack. Turn TalkBack on. Listen carefully to the instructions; you have to tap twice to select any screen options.

4 Close your eyes and try a very simple activity, such as starting a browser, going to Wikipedia, or searching for information about wolves. Describe your experience.

5 With your eyes open, explore the Web to locate any additional information or settings that might make navigation with eyes shut easier. Describe what you find.

6 Reset your device to its usual speech mode.

Hint: On Windows, hold down the Windows key, Ctrl, and Enter to turn off the narration.

2 Digital Devices

Module Contents

The availability of digital devices is mind-boggling. How do you know which devices are right for your lifestyle and career? The first step is making sense of digital hardware.

●Try It! Apply what you learn.

- Identify chips on the system board of any digital device.
- Identify components of a digital device, such as display, system unit, storage devices, input devices, output devices, and expansion ports.
- Safely clean and maintain a digital device.
- Operate portable devices using best practices to prolong battery life and battery lifespan.
- Take stock of your digital devices and maintain a list of their serial numbers.
- Shop for digital devices based on a usage plan.
- Interpret computer ads and specifications in order to make smart purchasing decisions.
- Find the processor specifications for digital devices that you own.
- Determine the RAM capacity of your digital devices.
- Understand when you might need to flash ROM and how to do it safely.
- Select the most effective storage devices for transporting, archiving, and backing up files.
- Use cloud storage safely and securely.
- Back up important data files.
- Use backup tools such as recovery drives, the Copy command, File History, Time Machine, and disk images so that you can restore a digital device after an incident that wipes out main storage.
- Use expansion ports to connect peripheral devices.
- Determine the resolution settings of your screen display.
- Correctly follow procedures to unplug devices such as USB drives.
- Determine if a digital device is equipped for Bluetooth connectivity.
- Describe the role of various sensors used in digital devices, the Internet of Things, and autonomous vehicles.

● Pre-Check

Gauge your level of expertise. The answers are in the module.

IPOS

This acronym stands for:

_____ _____

_____ _____

What's the most popular type of battery in today's digital devices?

What two components are crucial if you play lots of computer games?

Smith1979/Shutterstock.com

Which device uses iOS?

3.2

Processor speed is measured in

_____.

GB

GHz

Gigaflops

Gbps

What's the name of the set of instructions that loads the operating system into RAM?

What kind of processing is like a pizza oven conveyor belt?

Identify this port.

A bit-for-bit backup of every sector on a hard disk is called a disk _____.

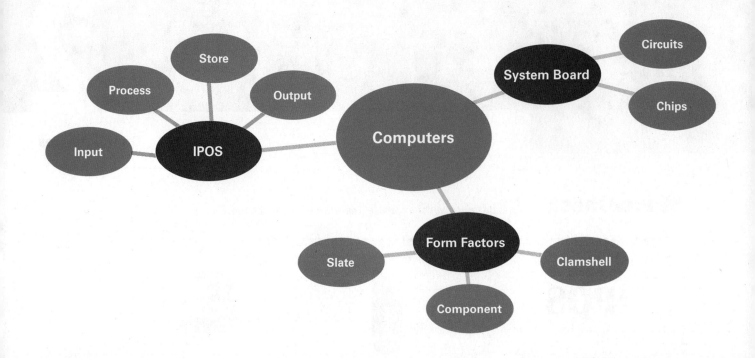

Objectives

▶ Draw a diagram showing the IPOS model of activities characteristic of computers.

▶ Describe the stored program concept and why it distinguishes computers from other simpler and less versatile digital devices.

▶ State which of the following are application software and which are system software: iOS, Windows, Microsoft Word, Android, PowerPoint.

▶ List three terms that are commonly used alternatives for "integrated circuits."

▶ Explain why semiconductors are the materials used for integrated circuits.

▶ Identify the microprocessor on a system board.

▶ Identify the components of a typical device that has a component, clamshell, or slate form factor.

▶ List four mistakes to avoid when cleaning a digital device.

▶ Describe what to do if liquid is spilled on a device.

▶ Explain how to care for a touchscreen.

▶ List six steps to take to increase battery life and lifespan.

What's inside all these digital devices that we use?
Whether you're operating your trusty laptop or figuring out how to safely clean your smartphone screen, it is useful to have some background about the components of digital devices and how they work. Section A looks at digital devices from the outside in, first focusing on characteristics common to all digital devices, and then drilling down to circuits and chips.

Terminology

computer	memory	app	system board
input	storage	system software	form factor
output	computer program	operating system	system unit
process data	software	development tools	oleophobic
central processing unit	stored program	integrated circuit	lithium ion
microprocessor	application software	semiconductors	discharge rate

Computers

Pixar's huge server array that renders 3D animated movies and the tiny iPhone you can hold in your hand have more in common than you might think. These devices, along with mainframes, desktops, tablets, ebook readers, and game consoles, are all based on computer technology. Understanding the classical definition of a computer provides a useful picture of what all these devices have in common.

▶ **What is a computer?** Most people can formulate a mental picture of a computer, but computers do so many things and come in such a variety of shapes and sizes that it might seem difficult to distill their common characteristics into an all-purpose definition. At its core, a **computer** is a multipurpose device that accepts input, processes data, stores data, and produces output, all according to a series of stored instructions.

Input is whatever is typed, submitted, or transmitted to a computer. **Output** is the result produced by a computer. Input and output can be handled by components contained within the computer or by add-ons, such as keyboards and printers, that are attached to the computer with cables or connected wirelessly.

Computers **process data** by performing calculations, modifying documents and pictures, drawing graphs, and sorting lists of words or numbers. Processing is handled by the computer's **central processing unit** (CPU). The CPU of most modern computers is a **microprocessor**, which is an electronic component that can be programmed to process data.

Computers store data and the software that processes data. Most computers have temporary holding areas called **memory** in addition to long-term **storage** housed on hard disks or flash drives. Figure 2-1 illustrates the IPOS (input, process, output, store) activities characteristic of computers.

Terminology

The word *computer* has been part of the English language since 1613; but if you look in a dictionary printed before 1940, you might be surprised to find a computer defined as a person who performs calculations. Prior to 1940, machines designed to perform calculations were usually referred to as calculators and tabulators, not computers. The modern definition and use of the term *computer* emerged in the 1940s, when the first electronic computing devices were developed.

2

Figure 2-1: The IPOS model defines computers

calculate
sort
draw
manipulate words
generate sound

Process

Input

words and symbols
numbers
dates
photos
temperatures
locations
audio recordings
video footage

Store

data files
software

Output

documents
music
graphs
images
movies
schedules
maps
text messages

▶ What's so significant about a computer's ability to store instructions? The instructions that tell a digital device how to carry out processing tasks are referred to as a **computer program**, or simply a program. These programs form the **software** that sets up a computer to do a specific task. When a computer "runs" software, it performs the instructions to carry out the task.

The first computers were "programmed" to perform a specific task by connecting wire circuitry in a certain way. Changing tasks meant rewiring the circuits. The term **stored program** means that a series of instructions for a computing task can be loaded into a computer's memory. These instructions can be replaced easily by a different set of instructions when it is time for the computer to perform another task. This ability to switch programs makes computers multipurpose devices (Figure 2-2).

Figure 2-2: Stored programs make computers versatile machines

Word processing software

Music software

The stored program concept allows you to use a computer for one task, such as word processing, and then easily switch to a different type of computing task, such as editing a photo or playing music. It is the single most important characteristic that distinguishes computers from other simpler and less versatile digital devices, such as digital clocks, calculators, and cameras.

▶ What kinds of software do computers run? Computers run three main types of software: application software, system software, and development tools (Figure 2-3). A computer can be *applied* to many tasks, such as writing, number crunching, video editing, and online shopping. **Application software** is a set of computer programs that helps a person carry out a task. Application software for mobile devices is usually referred to as an **app**.

Whereas application software is designed to help a person carry out a task, the primary purpose of **system software** is to help the computer system monitor itself in order to function efficiently. An example of system software is a computer **operating system** (OS), which is essentially the primary controller for all the activities that take place within a computer.

Development tools are used for creating software applications, Web sites, operating systems, and utilities. Examples of development tools include computer programming languages, such as C++, and scripting languages, such as HTML.

Figure 2-3: Software categories

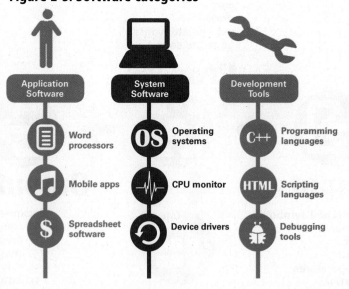

Application Software
- Word processors
- Mobile apps
- Spreadsheet software

System Software
- Operating systems
- CPU monitor
- Device drivers

Development Tools
- Programming languages
- Scripting languages
- Debugging tools

Circuits and Chips

The first computers were closet-sized devices filled with wires, vacuum tubes, transistors, and other bulky components. As digital electronics evolved, components became smaller and smaller. Open up a digital device. You won't see clumps of wires and gears. Instead, you'll see small circuit boards and integrated circuits. These tiny components are the essence of digital electronics.

▶ **What are digital electronics?** Digital electronics represent data bits as electrical signals that travel over circuits in much the same way that electricity flows over a wire when you turn on a light switch. To represent data, such as 01101100, high-voltage signals are used for 1 bits, and low-voltage signals are used for 0 bits. All the calculations performed by digital devices take place in a maze of electronic circuitry (Figure 2-4).

QuickCheck

In Figure 2-4, the fiery bit _____.

a. represents an electrical fault

b. is heading toward a resistor

c. is a low-voltage signal

d. represents a 0

2

Figure 2-4: A simple circuit

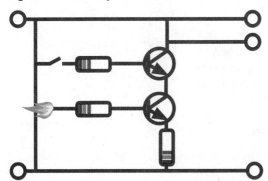

This little circuit is composed of electrical pathways (lines), transistors (circles), and resistors (rectangles). The electronics for digital devices require millions of similar circuits. Today, this circuitry is condensed into integrated circuits.

▶ **What's an integrated circuit?** An **integrated circuit** (IC) is a set of microscopic electronic components etched onto a thin slice of semiconducting material. The terms *computer chip*, *microchip*, and *chip* are commonly used to refer to integrated circuits. Some integrated circuits are devoted to collecting input, while others might be devoted to processing tasks, output, or storage. The first computer chips contained fewer than 100 miniaturized components, such as resistors and transistors. The chips for today's digital devices contain billions of transistors.

Semiconductors, such as silicon and germanium, are substances with properties between those of a conductor (like copper) and an insulator (like wood). To fabricate a chip, the conductive properties of selective parts of the semiconductor can be enhanced to essentially create miniature electronic pathways and components, such as transistors, as shown in Figure 2-5.

QuickCheck

There is an abundant supply of materials for fabricating semiconductors because:

a. They are made from purified silicon (sand).

b. They are basically insulators made from wood.

Figure 2-5: Computer chips are made from semiconductors

Source: Intel Corporation

Blank semiconductor chip

Chip etched with circuits

Chip ready for packaging

▶ **Aren't chips black?** Integrated circuits are packaged in protective carriers that vary in shape and size. Figure 2-6 illustrates some chip carriers, including small rectangular DIPs (dual in-line packages) with caterpillar-like legs protruding from a black, rectangular body, and pincushion-like LGAs (land-grid arrays).

Figure 2-6: Chips are housed in ceramic packages

DIPs have two rows of pins that connect the chip to a circuit board.

An LGA is a square chip package, typically used for microprocessors, with pins arranged in concentric squares.

▶ **How do chips fit together?** The electronic components of most digital devices are mounted on a circuit board called a system board, motherboard, or main board. The **system board** houses all essential chips and provides connecting circuitry between them. Figure 2-7 illustrates the main chips on the front and back sides of a laptop system board.

Figure 2-7: A system board holds chips and other components

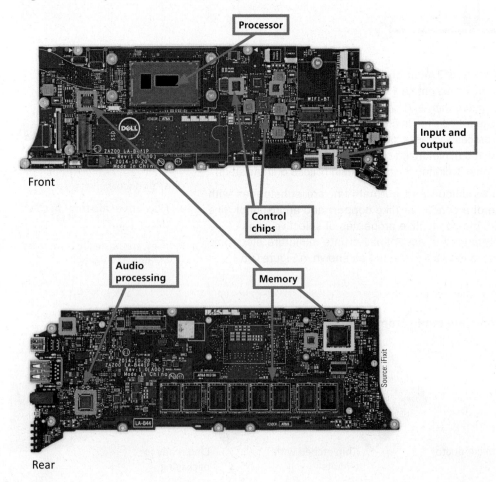

Front

Rear

Try It!

The chips on a circuit board have identifying numbers that you can look up online. Suppose you've opened the system unit of a Microsoft Surface tablet and you're looking at a chip labeled Samsung LPDDR4X. Can you find out what it does?

Components

When you acquire a new digital device, your first step is to locate the power button and all the other hardware components. The devices you use today have a fairly predictable collection of features, depending on the device's form factor.

▶ **What is a form factor?** In the computer industry, the term **form factor** refers to the size and dimensions of a device or components, such as circuit boards and system units. The term **system unit** is tech-speak for the part of a digital device that holds the system board. It can apply to the body of a smartphone or laptop, as well as to the tower unit of a desktop computer. Digital devices are available in all sorts of form factors; some of the most popular include component, clamshell, and slate.

▶ **What are the features of a component system?** A component device is composed of various standalone parts, such as a display unit, system unit, and keyboard. Components can be connected using cables or wireless signals. Most of the first personal computers were component systems. Today, this form factor is much less popular because of the effort required to assemble the components. Figure 2-8 illustrates the hardware features of a vintage component system.

Figure 2-8: A vintage component system

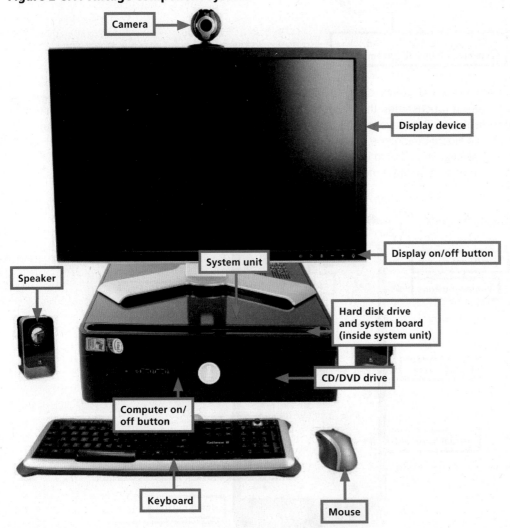

▶ **What are the features of a clamshell device?** Clamshell devices have a keyboard as the base and a screen on the hinged cover. The system unit on these devices contains all of the basic components required for input, processing, storage, and output (Figure 2-9).

Figure 2-9: A typical clamshell device

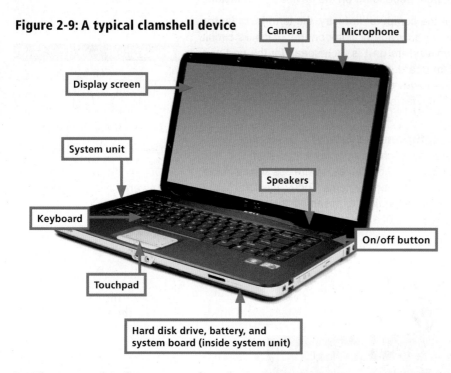

QuickCheck

How many components are housed on the top half of the clamshell device in Figure 2-9?

a. One

b. Two

c. Three

d. Four

▶ **What are the features of a slate device?** Devices configured in the slate form factor feature a touchscreen that covers most of the device's surface. The screen can display a virtual keyboard for text and numeric input. An additional control, such as a Home button or a circular control pad, is featured on some slate devices. The system unit also includes controls for commonly used features, such as volume and airplane mode (Figure 2-10).

Try It!

Check out the devices that you own. Can you find all of the components listed in the figures?

Figure 2-10: A typical slate device

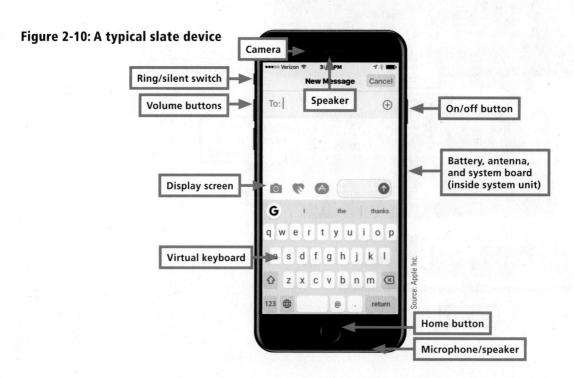

Source: Apple Inc.

Maintenance

Digital devices can be costly. You can extend their life with a bit of regular maintenance. There are four components of digital devices that require maintenance: the system unit, keyboard, screen, and battery.

▶ **How do I start?** Before you undertake any maintenance, turn the device off—that's *off*, not just asleep—and disconnect any power cables. Doing so will prevent random screen swipes or key presses from altering your device settings.

▶ **Which cleaning products are safe to use?** The products you can use depend on the component you are cleaning. What might work well to scrub out stubborn stains on the system unit case could permanently cloud or scratch your touchscreen. Always follow the manufacturer's advice for cleaning procedures and products (Figure 2-11).

2

Figure 2-11: Cleaning guidelines

Don't use harsh cleaning products; follow manufacturer recommendations.

Never immerse a device in liquid; water and electronics don't mix.

Do not allow cleaning agents to drip on keyboards or touchpads.

Do not spray cleaning agents directly on the device; spray them onto a cleaning cloth.

▶ **What kind of maintenance does the system unit require?** Basic system unit maintenance is simple. You want to keep the unit clean, prevent it from overheating, shield it from damage, and protect it from electrical surges (Figure 2-12).

Figure 2-12: Basic system unit maintenance

Dust with a clean microfiber cloth and disinfect with antibacterial wipes.

Use a low vacuum setting to remove dust from fan vents.

Use a protective case or carrying bag.

Only plug into a surge-protected outlet.

▶ **How can I safely clean and disinfect a touchscreen?** Touchscreens collect fingerprints and are a breeding ground for bacteria, so it is a good idea to clean them periodically. Many touchscreens are made from Gorilla Glass, which is designed to resist scratching and cracking. Damaged screens can be replaced, but that can cost close to $100, so a few preventive measures may help you avoid costly repairs.

A plastic screen protector is the first line of defense against scratches and cracks. These films can be cleaned using water and a soft cloth, or a disinfecting wipe. When the screen protector gets grubby, simply peel it off and replace it with a new one.

Without a screen protector, you will have to carefully clean the screen itself. Many touchscreens have an **oleophobic** coating designed to repel the oils deposited by fingertips. When alcohol is used to clean these screens, each application degrades the coating. Non-alcohol wipes are available, or use eyeglass cleaner.

▶ **What about my keyboard?** Keyboards quickly build up grime, gather dust, and collect crumbs. To start the cleaning process, turn the keyboard upside down and shake it gently to dislodge debris. Most manufacturers suggest using an antibacterial wipe to clean key surfaces. Take a moment to test the cleaning product on a small unnoticeable spot, just to make sure it will not discolor the keys or leave a residue. Use cotton swabs to clean between the keys.

▶ **What is the best way to clean up spills?** Liquids and electronics don't mix. If you spill liquid on a device, turn it off immediately. With luck, that step will prevent electrical shorts that would permanently damage circuit boards. Once the device is off, you can assess the damage. If the spill is water, dry off the device, shake out the moisture, and set it in a warm, dry place where there is good air circulation. A fan or hair dryer *set on low* can help drive out moisture. Allow the device to dry for at least 72 hours.

Sticky spills are another matter. If the goo has penetrated the interior of the device, it is best to leave the cleanup to a professional. If you think the spill only affected the surface, you can wipe the device with clean water and allow it to dry for 24 hours (Figure 2-13).

Figure 2-13: Do not set liquids near a keyboard

QuickCheck

When liquid spills on a digital device, what should you do?

a. Shut off the device immediately.

b. Back up all your data before turning off the device.

c. Rinse the device with clear water.

d. Call *611.

▶ **How do I maintain the battery for a device?** You know how it goes. It happens to everyone. The battery on your device dies just when you really need it. Battery life is the time your device operates before it must be recharged. Battery lifespan is the amount of time a battery lasts until it must be replaced. Good maintenance extends the life of your battery and a device's lifetime, so your digital devices are ready when you need them.

Most of today's battery-powered digital devices contain a **lithium ion** (Li-ion) battery. Unlike batteries of the past, Li-ion batteries contain no toxic compounds and operate efficiently, but they are sensitive to heat.

Li-ion batteries can occasionally overheat, and in the worst case, they can explode. Most devices today contain circuitry to prevent heat-triggered damage, but smart consumers don't operate devices that are hot to the touch.

Batteries have a **discharge rate** at which they lose charge even when not in use. The discharge rate for Li-ion batteries is quite low—about 1.5% per month—so the batteries in your devices basically discharge only as they are used.

Device manufacturers often advertise battery watts per hour (Wh). A 60 Wh battery will last 60 hours if it expends 1 watt per hour. A typical laptop uses about 30 watts per hour, however, so a 60 Wh battery can power the device for two hours (60 Wh ÷ 30 watts = 2 hours).

Some applications require more battery power than others. Location-based apps that keep track of your whereabouts are constantly using extra power to check cell towers or Wi-Fi networks. Push applications, such as autoretrieving email, make your device continually check for new messages. To extend battery life, disable these kinds of apps when you are not using them. Figure 2-14 summarizes good practices for charging and using Li-ion batteries.

2

Figure 2-14: Extend the life of the batteries in your devices

1 Charge when the low battery indicator comes on.

2 Avoid totally discharging the battery.

3 Remove the device from the charger when it's fully charged.

4 If your device becomes hot while in use, turn it off.

5 Disable unused apps that constantly connect to the Internet.

6 Switch to airplane mode when in an area with no cell coverage.

QuickCheck

Suppose your smartphone has a battery rated at 5.2 Wh. When you use map guidance, the phone draws 1.3 watts per hour. How long can you travel before your phone runs out of juice?

a. One hour

b. Four hours

c. Eight hours

d. Ten hours

QuickQuiz   Section A

1. A computer is a multipurpose device that accepts input, processes [_____], stores data, and produces output, all according to the instructions of a stored program.

2. An operating system is an example of [_____] software.

3. A(n) [_____] circuit is a set of microscopic electronic components etched onto a thin slice of semiconducting material.

4. Three form factors for digital devices are component, [_____], and slate.

5. Touchscreens on many digital devices have a(n) [_____] coating that resists fingerprints.

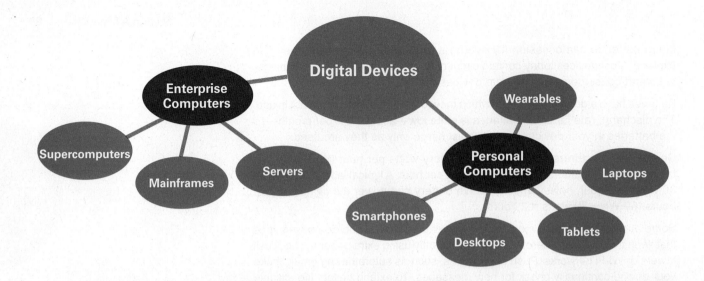

Objectives

▶ List three types of computers that are commonly used in businesses, serve multiple simultaneous users, and offer very fast processing speeds.

▶ Draw a hierarchy chart showing the classifications of personal computers.

▶ Identify seven digital niche devices.

▶ List five activities that are important for consumers who are shopping for digital devices.

▶ List three pros and three cons that influence purchase decisions for each of the following: desktop, laptop, tablet, smartphone.

▶ Specify the operating systems that are common in each of the three major families of operating systems.

When shopping for a new device, the choices may seem overwhelming. Section B helps you sort out the devices that are on the market by function and price. It addresses the tricky issue of compatibility and other factors important to consumers.

Terminology

supercomputer	desktop computer	tablet computer	PDA
mainframe	portable computer	slate tablet	wearable computers
server	laptop computer	2-in-1	microcontrollers
personal computer	Chromebook	smartphones	compatible

Enterprise Computers

At one time, it was possible to define three distinct categories of computers. Mainframes were housed in large, closet-sized metal frames. Minicomputers were smaller, less expensive, and less powerful, but they could support multiple users and run business software. Microcomputers were clearly differentiated from computers in other categories because they were dedicated to a single user and their CPUs consisted of a single microprocessor chip.

Today, microprocessors are no longer a distinction between computer categories because just about every computer uses one or more microprocessors as its CPU. The term *minicomputer* has fallen into disuse, and the terms *microcomputer* and *mainframe* are used with less and less frequency.

Figure 2-15: "Big" computers

Supercomputer

Mainframe

Servers

▶ What are the most powerful computers? Today's most powerful computers include supercomputers, mainframes, and servers. These devices are generally used in businesses and government agencies. They have the ability to service many simultaneous users and process data at very fast speeds (Figure 2-15).

Supercomputers. A computer falls into the **supercomputer** category if it is, at the time of construction, one of the fastest computers in the world. Because of their speed, supercomputers can tackle complex tasks that just would not be practical for other computers. Typical uses for supercomputers include breaking codes, modeling worldwide weather systems, and simulating nuclear explosions.

Computer manufacturers such as IBM, Nvidia, and Fujitsu have in recent years held top honors for the world's fastest computer. Supercomputer speeds are measured in petaflops (PFLOPS). One petaflop is an astounding 1,000,000,000,000,000 (quadrillion) calculations per second. That's about 20,000 times faster than your laptop computer.

Mainframes. A **mainframe** computer (or simply a mainframe) is a large and expensive computer capable of simultaneously processing data for hundreds or thousands of users. Its main processing circuitry is housed in a closet-sized cabinet like the one shown at left; but after large components are added for storage and output, a mainframe installation can fill a good-sized room.

Mainframes are generally used by businesses and government agencies to provide centralized storage, processing, and management for large amounts of data. For example, banks depend on mainframes as their computer of choice to ensure reliability, data security, and centralized control. The price of a mainframe computer typically starts at several hundred thousand dollars and can easily exceed $1 million.

Servers. The purpose of a **server** is to "serve" data to computers connected to a network. When you search Google or access a Web site, the information you obtain is provided by servers. At ecommerce sites, the store's merchandise information is housed in database servers. Email, chat, Skype, and online multiplayer games are all operated by servers.

Technically, just about any computer can be configured to perform the work of a server. However, computer manufacturers such as IBM and Dell offer devices classified as servers that are especially suited for storing and distributing data on networks. These devices are about the size of a desk drawer and are often mounted in racks of multiple servers.

Figure 2-16: Personal computers

Source: Apple Inc.

Desktop

Laptop

Slate tablet

2-in-1 tablet

Personal Computers

A **personal computer** is designed to meet the computing needs of an individual. These computers were originally referred to as microcomputers. Personal computers provide access to a wide variety of computing applications, such as word processing, photo editing, email, and Internet access.

The term *personal computer* is sometimes abbreviated as PC. However, *PC* can also refer to a specific type of personal computer that descended from the original IBM PC and runs Windows software. In this book, *PC* refers to IBM PC descendants. It is not used as an abbreviation for personal computer.

▶**What are the options for personal computers?** Personal computers can be classified as desktop, portable, or mobile devices. The lines that delineate these categories are sometimes a bit blurry, but the general characteristics of each category are described below and common configurations are shown in Figure 2-16.

Desktops. A **desktop computer** fits on a desk and runs on power from an electrical wall outlet. The keyboard is typically a separate component. A desktop computer can be housed in a vertical case or in a horizontal case. In some modern desktops, called all-in-one units, the system board is incorporated into the display device.

Desktop computers are popular for offices and schools where portability is not important. Their operating systems include Microsoft Windows, macOS, and Linux. The price of an entry-level desktop computer starts at $500 or a bit less.

Portables. A **portable computer** runs on battery power. Its screen, keyboard, camera, storage devices, and speakers are fully contained in a single case so that the device can be easily transported from one place to another. Portable computers include laptops, tablets, and smartphones.

Laptops. A **laptop computer** (also referred to as a notebook computer) is a small, lightweight personal computer designed like a clamshell with a keyboard as the base and a screen on the hinged cover. Most laptops use the same operating systems as desktop computers, with the exception of Chromebooks, which use Google's Chrome OS as their operating system.

A **Chromebook** is a special category of laptop, designed to be connected to the Internet for most routine computing activities. Chromebook owners use Web-based software and store all their data in the cloud rather than on a local hard disk. Chromebooks use a standard clamshell form factor, so they look very much like a laptop. Their sub-$300 price tags are attractive to consumers who primarily browse the Web and use Web-based apps.

Tablets. A **tablet computer** is a portable computing device featuring a touch-sensitive screen that can be used for input as well as for output. Popular tablet computers use specialized operating systems, such as iOS and Android. Some models support cell phone network data plans but require apps such as FaceTime or Skype for voice calls.

A **slate tablet** configuration is basically a screen in a narrow frame that lacks a physical keyboard (although one can be attached). The Apple iPad and Samsung Galaxy Tab are popular slate tablets. A **2-in-1** (or convertible tablet) can be operated using its touch-sensitive screen or with a physical keyboard that can be folded out of the way or removed.

Smartphones. **Smartphones** are mobile devices that have features similar to those of tablet computers, but they also provide telecommunications capabilities over cell phone networks. They can make voice calls, send text messages, and access the Internet. Unlike a basic mobile phone, smartphones are programmable, so they can download, store, and run software.

Smartphones are the most commonly used digital device in the world. A smartphone features a small keyboard or touchscreen and is designed to fit into a pocket, run on batteries, and be used while you are holding it in your hands (Figure 2-17).

Try It!

How many digital devices do you own? Which do you use most often? Make a list of your devices and their serial numbers, and tuck it away in a safe place in case one of your devices is lost or stolen.

Figure 2-17: Smartphones accept input from a touchscreen or microphone

Source: Amazon.com, Inc.   Source: Apple Inc.   Source: Apple Inc.

Smartphones are equipped with built-in speech recognition that allows you to ask questions and control the device using spoken commands. Smartphones also include GPS capability so that apps are able to provide location-based services such as a route navigation map or a list of nearby restaurants.

Smartphones evolved from basic cell phones and PDAs. A **PDA** (personal digital assistant) was a handheld device used as an electronic appointment book, calculator, and notepad. Modern smartphones include a similar suite of applications, but they also have access to a huge variety of mobile apps that help you calculate tips, listen to your favorite music, and play entertaining games.

The operating systems for smartphones are similar to those used for tablet computers. iOS is used on the iPad and iPhone. The Android operating system used on Samsung tablets is also used for smartphones such as the Samsung Galaxy and Google Pixel.

Figure 2-18: Specialized devices

Raspberry Pi

Videogame console

Portable media player

Smartwatch

Fitness tracker

Smart appliances

Niche Devices

The list of digital devices is long. Many devices, such as fitness trackers, cameras, and handheld GPSs, are dedicated to specific tasks. Other devices perform a wider variety of tasks.

▶ **What about other digital devices?** Niche devices all have one thing in common: They contain a microprocessor. Some of these devices, such as smartwatches and fitness trackers, can be classified as **wearable computers**. Which of the devices in Figure 2-18 do you own?

Raspberry Pi. A full computer system unit that is just a tad larger than a deck of cards, the Raspberry Pi can be connected to a keyboard and screen for a full computer experience. These little powerhouses cost less than $50 and provide an inexpensive platform for experimenting with programming, robotics, and just about any creative computer application you can imagine.

Game consoles. Devices for playing computer games include Sony's PlayStation, Nintendo's Switch, and Microsoft's Xbox. They feature powerful processing capability and excellent graphics, but they are generally used for dedicated game playing and streaming videos rather than running application software.

Portable media players. Media players, such as the iPod Touch, revolutionized the music industry by providing consumers with a handheld device that can store and play thousands of songs. These devices are controlled by touchscreens or simple click-wheel mechanisms.

Smartwatches. Watches and clocks were some of the first devices to go digital. Mass produced in the 1970s with a price as low as $10, these watches were limited to time and date functions. Today's multifunction smartwatches can include a camera, thermometer, compass, calculator, cell phone, GPS, media player, and fitness tracker. Some smartwatch functions are onboard the device, whereas other functions require access to the Internet or to the wearer's smartphone.

Activity trackers. To monitor activity throughout the day, you can wear a fitness tracker. These devices, worn on the wrist or clipped to a pocket, monitor your steps and heart rate. They can calculate calories, graph your fitness achievements, and share information with your Facebook friends.

Smart speakers. Saying "Hey Alexa" activates an Amazon Echo smart speaker's virtual assistant that can carry out your verbal commands to control various devices or search the Internet. Apple's HomePod and Google's Nest are other examples of smart speakers that listen for your voice commands.

Smart appliances. Modern refrigerators, washing machines, and other appliances are controlled by integrated circuits called **microcontrollers** that combine sensors with processing circuitry. Microcontrollers can monitor energy efficiency, offer programmed start times, and may be controlled remotely from a smartphone or laptop.

Choosing a Digital Device

The process of selecting a digital device is all about choices, and there can be an overwhelming number of them. Do you want a tablet or a laptop? Do you need a super-light device? What size screen? Mac or Windows? Is the most powerful and most expensive processor necessary? Understanding the choices is the key to getting the right device at the right price.

▶ **How do I get started?** Whether you are replacing an outdated device or adding to your digital collection, the following activities can get you started:

Consider how you plan to use your device.

Choose the type of device.

Decide on a budget and stick to it.

Select a platform.

Check out the device's specifications.

▶ **Why is it important to figure out how I'm going to use my new device?** Some digital tasks require specific devices, processing power, storage capacity, and connectivity. Therefore, if you consider the usage guidelines in Figure 2-19, you're more likely to buy the right device and not have to purchase expensive upgrades later.

QuickCheck

Which tasks tend to require the fastest processor?

a. Email and photo editing

b. Social media and Web browsing

c. Desktop publishing and video editing

d. Accounting and budgeting

2

Figure 2-19: Usage guidelines

	Usage Plan	Purchase Recommendation
✉	You plan to use your computer for email and Facebook, browsing the Web, playing games, managing finances, downloading digital music, and writing school papers.	A mid-priced laptop with standard features might meet your needs.
💻	You're buying a new computer to replace an old one.	If you have a big investment in software, you should select a new computer that's compatible with the old one.
📈	You plan to work on accounting and budgeting for a small business.	Consider one of the business systems offered by a local or online computer vendor.
🟡	You spend lots of time playing computer games.	Buy a computer with the fastest processor and graphics card you can afford, or consider a dedicated game console.
🎥	You plan to work extensively with video editing or desktop publishing.	Select a computer system with a fast processor, lots of hard disk capacity, a large screen, and a graphics card loaded with memory.
♿	Someone who will use the computer has special needs.	Consider purchasing appropriate adaptive equipment, such as a voice synthesizer or one-handed keyboard.
⚙	You plan to use specialized peripheral devices.	Make sure the computer you purchase can accommodate the devices you plan to use.
🎓	Your work at home overlaps your work at school or on the job.	Shop for a computer that's compatible with the computers you use at school or work.
🔲	You want to work with specific software, such as a 3D graphics tool.	Select a computer that meets the specifications listed on the software box or Web site.

▶ **What are the pros and cons of the most popular consumer devices?**
The most popular digital devices are desktops, laptops, tablets, and smartphones.
Figure 2-20 can help you choose the one that best meets your needs.

Figure 2-20: Choose the right device

 **Desktop**

Most power per dollar

Can make repairs and upgrade
components yourself (except for
all-in-one units)

Full-size keyboard with numeric
keypad for data entry

Large screen for multiple
windows and detail work

Adjustable placement of
components means less strain on
eyes, back, and wrists

Bottom line ◄ ·······

**The choice for dedicated
gamers, serious designers,
desktop publishers, and video
editors**

 **Laptop** ·······

All components in one unit

Easier to move

Battery powered for portability

Energy efficient means low
operating cost

Connects to Wi-Fi networks for
Internet access

Lightweight models have higher
price tags

Bottom line ◄ ·······

**Adequate for most digital tasks
that are not dependent on cellular
connections**

**The choice for students and
on-the-go professionals who want
to create content and be productive,
in addition to consuming content**

 **Tablet** ······

Small and easier to carry

Battery powered

Connects to Wi-Fi networks

Cellular data plans available for
mobile Internet access

Convertible units with keyboards
available for writing long
documents and creating other
content

Might not use software designed
for desktop and laptops

Small screen limits multitasking

Bottom line ◄ ·······

**Great for consuming content,
such as ebooks, music, and
videos**

**Adequate for browsing the Web
and managing social media**

**Works for some specialized
tasks, such as business
presentations**

Smartphone ···

Cellular connection for voice and
texting

Add a cellular data connection for
Internet access

Connects to Wi-Fi networks

Longer battery life than tablets and
laptops

Larger sizes offer bigger, easier-to-
read screens

Bottom line ◄ ·········

**Great for communications and
mobile apps**

**Adequate for watching occasional
videos and for mobile access to
social media**

**Not optimal for creating text-based
content, but excellent for voice
calls, texting, and Web browsing**

▶ **How important is compatibility?** Suppose that you want to work on some assignments at home using the same software provided by your school lab. Maybe you want to transport data back and forth between your job and home. Or, perhaps your children want to use a computer at home that is similar to those they use at school.

Computers that operate in essentially the same way and use the same software are said to be **compatible**. They can also be described as having the same "platform." To assess whether two computers are compatible, check their operating systems. Computers with the same operating systems can typically use the same software and peripheral devices. Figure 2-21 provides an overview of popular platforms. You'll learn more about operating systems in a later module.

Figure 2-21: Compatibility is related to operating systems

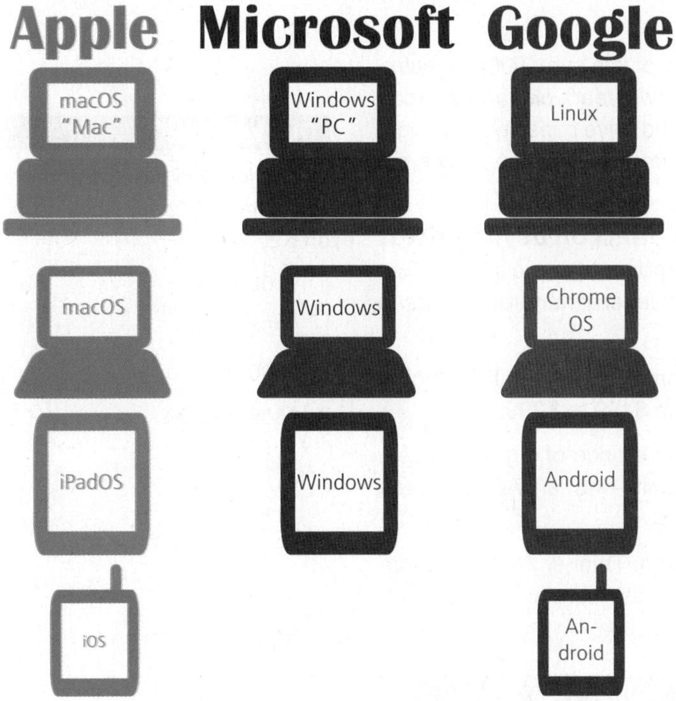

QuickCheck

Do Apple and Android tablets use the same software and apps as laptops?

a. Yes

b. No

▶ **Should I stick to one family of devices?** As you can see from Figure 2-21, operating systems and the devices that use them are grouped into families. Apple produces macOS and iOS. The open source community produces Linux for desktops and servers; with the support of Google, it also produces Chrome OS and Android.

The operating systems within a family have similarities in the way they look and function. So if you are familiar with macOS on your laptop, then you might find it easier to work with an iPhone rather than an Android phone.

Working within an operating system family can have other benefits. For example, if you are storing your photos, documents, and other data in Apple's iCloud, you'll have easier access to them from devices running iOS, iPadOS, and macOS than from a device running Windows.

Finally, you might find that synching and backing up data between devices is easier if they have operating systems from the same family.

Terminology

Desktops and laptops that run Windows are sometimes referred to as *PCs*. Computers that run macOS are referred to as *Macs*.

◗ **What can I expect to pay for a personal device?** The price tag for a smartphone is $200–$900, whereas tablet computer prices range from $200 to $1,500. Desktop and laptop computers usually cost a bit more, with price points roughly grouped into three categories: above $1,200, $500–$1,200, and under $500.

Computers priced above $1,200 contain one or more fast processors, a generous amount of RAM, and a copious amount of disk space. These computers contain state-of-the-art components and should not have to be replaced as quickly as less expensive computers. Computer game enthusiasts and anyone planning to work extensively with video editing, graphics, and desktop publishing are likely to require a high-end computer.

A majority of buyers select desktops and laptops that retail for between $500 and $1,200. These popular computers lack the flashy specifications of their state-of-the-art cousins but provide ample computing power to meet the needs of an average user.

In the computer industry, the equivalent of a compact car is a sub-$500 computer. The technology in these computers is usually one or two years old, and you can expect reduced processor speed, memory capacity, and drive capacity. You might have to replace a budget computer sooner than a more expensive computer, but it should be serviceable for typical applications.

◗ **What are the factors that have the biggest effect on device prices?** A microprocessor is one of the most expensive components in a digital device. The newest, fastest microprocessor is likely to add several hundred dollars to the price tag.

Memory is another factor that affects price. For example, doubling the amount of memory in a smartphone could raise the cost from $199 to $299.

Large screens cost more to manufacture and raise the price of digital devices. An iMac—Apple's version of an all-in-one desktop unit—with a 27-inch screen costs $800 more than the 21-inch version.

For laptops, size and weight make a difference in price. Thinner and lighter laptops are priced higher, not necessarily because they cost more to manufacture, but because they are more desirable to consumers.

QuickCheck

Which one of the following statements is correct about computer classifications?

a. The speed of supercomputers is measured in petaflops, which makes them the ideal platform for ecommerce stores that are accessed by millions of people.

b. The fact that features of small tablets overlap with features of large smartphones is an example of how the lines between categories of computers can be a bit blurry.

c. The main distinction between desktop computers and laptops is the inclusion of processing circuitry in the display device.

d. Portable computers and desktops have similar characteristics when it comes to accessing cellular voice and data.

Try It!

Visit the Dell Web site. What is the price of the least expensive desktop computer?

QuickCheck

The majority of desktop and laptop buyers spend how much on a computer?

a. $100–$250

b. $250–$500

c. $500–$1,200

d. $800–$1,500

▶ **How can I make sense of all the jargon in computer ads?** Computer ads are loaded with jargon and acronyms, such as RAM, ROM, GHz, GB, and USB. You're sure to spot lots of this computer lingo in ads like the one in Figure 2-22.

The remaining sections of Module 2 delve into specifications for digital components. You'll see how these components work and how they affect the way you work. By the end of Module 2, you should be able to understand the terminology in computer ads and use your knowledge to evaluate various digital devices.

Figure 2-22: Computer ads are full of jargon

Powerfully Light
Do everything you love.

- 11th Generation Intel Core i7 4.7 GHz processor
- 12 MB cache
- 16 GB DDR4 2666 MHz RAM
- 512 GB solid state drive
- 17.3" LCD display screen
- Intel integrated graphics
- Integrated speakers
- Integrated 1080p megapixel webcam
- 2 USB 3.2 Gen 1 USB ports
- 1 USB Type C port
- HDMI port
- MicroSD card reader
- Wi-Fi 802.11 ax, Bluetooth
- 53 Wh, 4-cell battery
- Windows 64-bit operating system
- Home/small business software bundle
- 2.7 pounds
- 1-year limited warranty

QuickQuiz   Section B

1. Google and other Web service providers use banks of [_____] to process and manage data.

2. Windows is the operating system used on desktop and laptop PCs. What is the equivalent operating system for Apple computers? [_____]

3. A(n) [_____] computer is the only type of personal computer that must remain plugged into an electrical source during operation.

4. [_____] are the most popular digital devices worldwide.

5. Compatibility is primarily controlled by a device's [_____] system.

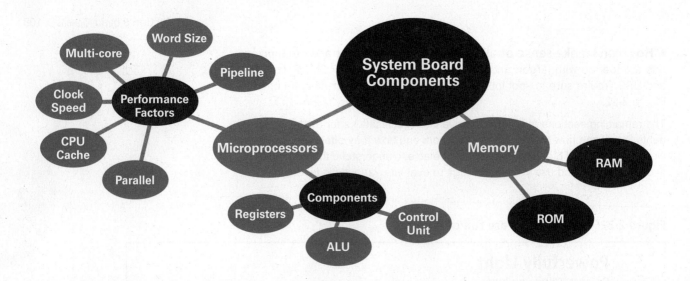

Objectives

▶ Distinguish between the x86 and ARM processor standards.

▶ Describe the significance of microprocessor instruction sets.

▶ Trace an instruction through RAM, the control unit, and ALU as it is processed.

▶ List seven factors that affect microprocessor performance.

▶ Use the pizza analogy to explain serial, pipeline, and parallel processing.

▶ Identify the terminology that pertains to RAM in consumer literature and technical specifications.

▶ List at least three items that would be found in RAM while you are using a digital device.

▶ List three events that occur during the boot process.

▶ Explain why digital devices have ROM in addition to RAM.

▶ List four reasons for flashing ROM.

Architecture.
That's how techies refer to the inner workings of digital devices. Sure, you can use a digital device without understanding its architecture. But to intelligently discuss the opportunities and controversies of your digital world, you need more than a vague notion about microprocessors. Section C will help you keep your head above water when the talk gets technical.

Terminology

x86	control unit	pipeline processing	capacitors
ARM	instruction cycle	parallel processing	volatile
instruction set	instruction pointer	CPU cache	dynamic RAM
programming language	microprocessor clock	word size	virtual memory
machine language	gigahertz	CISC	ROM
ALU	multi-core processor	RISC	boot loader
registers	serial processing	RAM	

Microprocessors

A microprocessor is an integrated circuit designed to process instructions. It is the most important, and usually the most expensive, component of a digital device. The digital devices you use today likely include x86 or ARM microprocessors.

▶ **Which devices use x86 microprocessors?** Intel Corporation is one of the world's largest chipmakers and supplies a sizeable percentage of the microprocessors that power desktops and laptops. In 1971, Intel introduced the world's first microprocessor—the 4004. Intel's 8088 processor powered the original IBM PC, and chips in Intel's 8086 family powered subsequent models of PCs manufactured by IBM and other companies.

The 8086 chip family set the standard for processors used in many of today's desktop and laptop computers, as well as servers. This standard is sometimes referred to as **x86** because it includes chip models that originally ended in 86, such as the 8086, 80286, and 80386.

Chipmakers no longer follow Intel's original numbering sequence, but x86 is still used when referring to the modern descendants of the 8086. These modern processors include Intel's Core i3, i5, and i7 microprocessors (Figure 2-23), as well as AMD's Radeon and Ryzen microprocessors. You'll find these chips in desktop and laptop computers that run Microsoft's Windows operating system.

Figure 2-23: Intel processors for desktops and laptops

Source: Intel Corporation

▶ **Which devices use ARM microprocessors?** Whereas processors based on x86 technology are inside just about all desktop and laptop computers that run Windows, processors based on **ARM** technology dominate in Apple's ecosystem. You'll also find them in most tablet computers and smartphones from other manufacturers.

ARM technology was originally designed by ARM Holdings, a British technology company founded by Acorn Computers, Apple Inc., and VLSI Technology. Today, ARM processors are designed and manufactured by companies that include NVIDIA, Samsung, Qualcomm, and Apple.

ARM-based processors are energy efficient—an important characteristic for devices that run primarily on battery power. Most Android smartphones contain ARM processors. ARM processors are found in Apple's iPads and iPhones. As of 2021, Apple began using M1 ARM processors for its Mac laptops and desktops, too. Apple's M-class processors integrate a CPU, RAM, graphics, and input/output circuitry into a single chip.

2

QuickCheck

What does x86 mean?

a. It is the model of an Intel chip.

b. It designates low-power chips suitable for tablets and smartphones.

c. It is used to refer to a standard family of processors used in most Windows-based desktop and laptop computers.

d. It means the chip was manufactured by Intel.

QuickCheck

Which processor would you be likely to find in an iPhone?

a. Intel x86

b. ARM

c. Intel Core M3

d. 8088

▶ **Which microprocessor is best?** The microprocessor that's best for you depends on your budget and the type of work and play you plan to do. The microprocessors marketed with the current crop of desktops and laptops can handle most business, educational, and entertainment applications. You'll want to consider the fastest processor offerings if you engage in processing-hungry activities, such as 3D animated computer games, desktop publishing, multitrack sound recording, and video editing.

▶ **What microprocessor is in my favorite device?** If you know the make and model of a digital device, you can generally find processor specifications by searching online. For example, searching for *processor specifications iPhone 12* reveals that the phone contains an A14 Bionic processor. Although an online search might be required to find processor specifications for phones and tablets, desktops and laptops offer an easier way to discover what's inside (Figure 2-24).

Figure 2-24: Find the processor specifications for a desktop or laptop

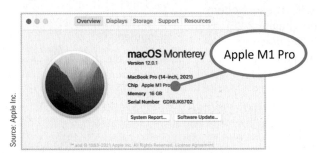

Source: Apple Inc.

On a Mac desktop or laptop, selecting the Apple icon and then choosing About This Mac displays processor specifications, along with memory capacity.

Try It!

Find the processor specifications for your favorite desktop computer, laptop, or smartphone. How are the specs similar to or different from the processor specifications shown in Figure 2-24?

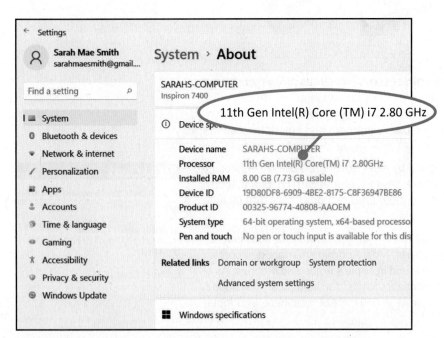

Windows 11 displays processor specs when you type "PC Info" in the Windows search box and then choose the option "About your PC."

How Processors Work

To appreciate the microprocessor specifications in your digital devices, it is handy to have a little background on how processors work. This key technology is quite fascinating in its ability to perform an astounding variety of tasks based on a set of really simple instructions.

▶ **What is the significance of microprocessor instruction sets?** Microprocessors are hard-wired to perform a limited set of activities. This collection of preprogrammed activities is called an instruction set. Instruction sets are unique to processor families. x86 processors use a different instruction set than ARM processors. That is one reason why a game designed to run on a smartphone with an ARM processor cannot directly run on your laptop with its Intel i7 processor.

▶ **What is in an instruction set?** An instruction set contains a collection of instructions for actions that the circuitry in a microprocessor can perform. The ARM instruction set contains about 35 instructions, whereas the x86 set includes more than 100 instructions. Each instruction carries out a seemingly insignificant task, such as moving a number from computer memory into the processor or comparing two numbers to see if they are the same. Only when millions of these instructions are executed by the processor does a digital device seem to carry out any useful actions.

▶ **Are you talking about a computer program?** Not exactly. Let's use a game like Fruit Ninja as an example. This game is written by programmers using a programming language such as C++, BASIC, COBOL, or Java. When we think of a computer program, we think of the long list of statements written in one of these programming languages.

Surprisingly, microprocessors can't directly understand these programming languages, so programs like Fruit Ninja have to be converted into machine language that corresponds to the microprocessor's instruction set. These machine language instructions are binary strings of 0s and 1s that can be processed by a digital device.

▶ **What are machine language instructions like?** Machine language instructions are like baby steps. Take a look at the commonly used machine language instructions in Figure 2-25. It seems incredible that digital devices can carry out such a wide variety of tasks using such limited instructions.

QuickCheck

An instruction set is _____.

a. a set of commands, such as Print and Get, that programmers use to create software

b. the collection of pre-programmed activities that a microprocessor can perform

c. a command that is in binary format

d. the options that appear on a software application's main menu

2

Figure 2-25: Common commands from the x86 instruction set

Add	0000 0000
Input	0110 0011
Compare	0011 1100
Move	1010 0000
Multiply	1111 0110
Output	1110 1110
Subtract	0010 1100
Halt	1111 0100

What happens inside a computer chip? A microprocessor contains miles of microscopic circuitry and millions of miniature components divided into different kinds of operational units, such as the ALU and the control unit.

The **ALU** (arithmetic logic unit) is the part of the microprocessor that performs arithmetic operations, such as addition and subtraction. It also performs logical operations, such as comparing two numbers to see if they are the same. The ALU uses **registers** to hold data that is being processed. As an analogy, registers are similar to a mixing bowl you might use to hold the ingredients for a batch of cookies.

The microprocessor's **control unit** fetches each instruction, in the same way you might get ingredients for cookies out of a cupboard or the refrigerator. Data is loaded into the ALU's registers, just like you add all the cookie ingredients to the mixing bowl. Finally, the control unit gives the ALU the green light to begin processing, just the way you flip the switch on your electric mixer to blend the cookie ingredients. Figure 2-26 illustrates a microprocessor control unit and its ALU preparing to add 5 + 4.

QuickCheck

When the control unit swings into action, which step comes first?

a. Perform arithmetic operations.

b. Load data into the ALU.

c. Fetch an instruction.

d. Execute the instruction.

Figure 2-26: The microprocessor's control unit and ALU

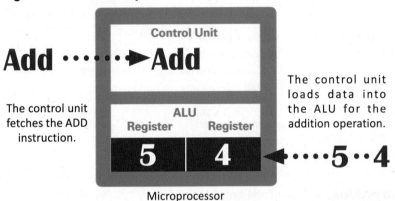

The control unit fetches the ADD instruction.

The control unit loads data into the ALU for the addition operation.

Microprocessor

QuickCheck

The processor in Figure 2-26 would use binary for the instruction and data. What is the binary machine language instruction for ADD? (Hint: Look back at Figure 2-25.)

a. 0000 0000

b. 0101 0100

c. 1110 1110

d. 1111 1111

What happens when a computer executes an instruction? The term **instruction cycle** refers to the process in which a computer executes a single instruction. Some parts of the instruction cycle are performed by the microprocessor's control unit; other parts of the cycle are performed by the ALU. The steps in this cycle are summarized in Figure 2-27.

Figure 2-27: The instruction cycle

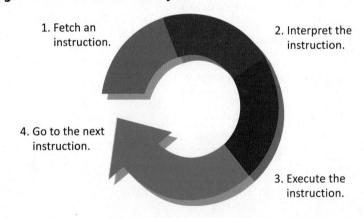

1. Fetch an instruction.

2. Interpret the instruction.

4. Go to the next instruction.

3. Execute the instruction.

▶ **What role does the control unit play?** The machine language instructions for a particular program are held in memory. When the program begins, the memory address of the first instruction is placed in a part of the microprocessor's control unit called an **instruction pointer**.

Figure 2-28 shows how the control unit can then go to the memory address (A) and fetch the instruction by copying data from that address into its instruction register (B). Next, the control unit interprets the instruction and executes it (C).

Figure 2-28: Processing an instruction

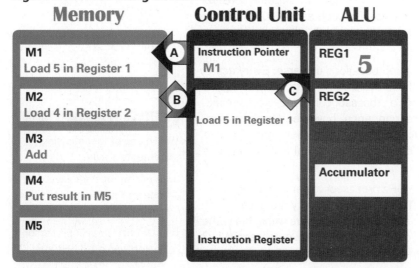

▶ **When does the ALU swing into action?** The ALU is responsible for performing arithmetic and logical operations. As shown in Figure 2-29, the ALU uses registers to hold data that is ready to be processed. When it gets the go-ahead signal from the control unit (A), the ALU processes the data and places the result in an accumulator (B). From the accumulator, the data can be sent to memory or used for further processing. When the computer completes an instruction, the control unit increments the instruction pointer to the memory address of the next instruction, and the instruction cycle begins again.

Figure 2-29: The ALU adds, subtracts, and compares

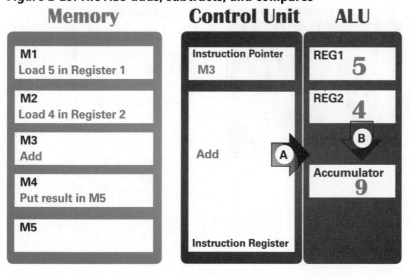

Performance

Now that you have some background on how microprocessors work, you can begin to appreciate what makes some microprocessors perform better than others. A microprocessor's performance is affected by several factors, including clock speed, number of cores, processing techniques, cache size, word size, and instruction set.

▶ **What does GHz have to do with processor performance?** A processor specification, such as 3.4 GHz, indicates the speed of the **microprocessor clock**—a timing device that sets the pace for executing instructions. Most computer ads specify the speed of a microprocessor in gigahertz. **Gigahertz** (GHz) means a billion cycles per second. A specification such as 2.13 GHz means that the microprocessor's clock operates at a speed of 2.13 billion cycles per second.

A cycle is the smallest unit of time in a microprocessor's universe. Every action a processor performs is measured by these cycles. It is customary to equate clock cycles with the number of instructions a processor can execute per second. There is not always a one-to-one correspondence, however. Some instructions are processed within one clock cycle, but other instructions might require multiple cycles. Some processors can even execute several instructions in a single clock cycle.

You might expect a computer with a 2.13 GHz processor to perform slower than a computer with a 3.4 GHz processor. This is not necessarily the case. Clock speed comparisons are only valid when comparing processors within the same chip family. A 2.13 GHz processor could outperform a 3.4 GHz processor. Why? Because factors other than clock speed contribute to the overall performance of a microprocessor.

▶ **What's a multi-core processor?** The "core" of a microprocessor consists of the control unit and ALU. A microprocessor that contains circuitry for more than one processing unit is called a **multi-core processor**. Having more cores usually equates to faster performance. A 2.4 GHz processor with two cores has the equivalent of 4.8 GHz performance (2.4 x 2). A 1.6 GHz processor with four cores has the equivalent of 6.4 GHz performance (1.6 x 4). Figure 2-30 illustrates a microscopic view of a processor with multiple cores.

QuickCheck

Which one of the following statements is true?

a. A microprocessor executes one instruction for each clock cycle.

b. A 2.4 GHz Intel i5 processor is faster than a 1.6 GHz Intel i7 processor.

c. Clock speed is the most important factor that affects processor performance.

d. A multi-core processor can outperform a single-core processor that has a faster clock speed.

Figure 2-30: Four cores of an Intel fourth-generation microprocessor

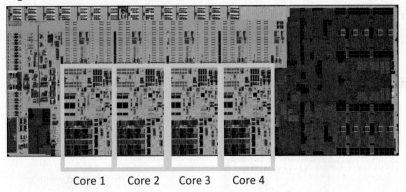

Core 1   Core 2   Core 3   Core 4

Terminology

The thin wafer of silicon and the microscopic circuitry it contains is called a *die*. Figure 2-30 illustrates a microprocessor die with four cores.

❱ Can a microprocessor execute more than one instruction at a time?

Some processors execute instructions "serially"—that is, one instruction at a time. With **serial processing**, the processor must complete all steps in the instruction cycle before it begins to execute the next instruction. To use an analogy, visualize a pizzeria with one small oven. The pizzas are instructions; the oven is the microprocessor. Pizzas (instructions) are processed one at a time.

Now, what if the pizzeria rigs up a conveyor belt through the oven? A pizza (instruction) starts moving along the conveyor belt into the oven; but before it reaches the end, another pizza starts moving along the belt. When a processor begins to execute an instruction before it completes the previous instruction, it is using **pipeline processing**.

A pizzeria might also have large ovens that hold multiple pizzas. Just as these ovens can bake more than one pizza at a time, **parallel processing** executes more than one instruction at a time. This efficient processing technology is possible with today's multi-core microprocessors.

Pipeline and parallel processing offer better performance than serial processing (Figure 2-31).

QuickCheck

Many of today's digital devices are capable of parallel processing because:

a. Their processors have multiple cores.

b. They have pipelining.

c. They can run more than one program at a time.

d. They have high GHz specifications.

2

Figure 2-31: Serial, pipeline, and parallel processing

Instruction 3
01001100100101111

Instruction 2
01001010100101111

Instruction 1
01001100100101111

CPU

Serial Processing
The execution cycle for each instruction must be completed before the next instruction is executed.

Instruction 3
01001100100101111

Instruction 2
01001010100101111

CPU

Instruction 1
01001100100101111

Pipeline Processing
Before all four stages of the execution cycle for Instruction 1 are complete, the CPU begins to execute Instruction 2.

Instruction 3
01001100100101111

Instruction 4
0010111010101010

Instruction 2
01001010100101111

CPU

Instruction 1
01001100100101111

Parallel Processing
The CPU executes multiple instructions at the same time.

▶ **How does cache size affect performance?** CPU cache (pronounced "cash") is special high-speed memory that allows a microprocessor to access data more rapidly than from memory located elsewhere on the system board. A large cache can increase processing performance.

CPU cache is structured into several levels. Level 1 cache (L1) is the fastest, whereas Level 2 (L2) and Level 3 (L3) are slightly slower but still faster than accessing main memory or disk storage. Cache capacity is usually measured in megabytes.

▶ **What impact does word size have on performance?** Word size refers to the number of bits that a microprocessor can manipulate at one time. It corresponds to the size of the registers used by the control unit and ALU. A processor with a 64-bit word size, for example, has registers that can process 64 bits at a time.

Word size controls the amount of memory that the processor can access. Processors with a 32-bit word size can access a maximum of 4 GB of memory, whereas processors with a 64-bit word size can potentially access many terabytes of memory.

A large word size gives processors the ability to handle more data during each processing cycle—a factor that leads to increased performance. Today's digital devices typically contain 32-bit processors or 64-bit processors. In a computer with a 32-bit word size, registers that hold data and those that hold instructions all have capacity for 32 bits (Figure 2-32).

Figure 2-32: A register holds a 32-bit word

`0110010110010010101111000010110101`

The bits in this 32-bit register could be an instruction or an item of data that is waiting to be processed.

▶ **How does an instruction set affect performance?** As chip designers developed various instruction sets for microprocessors, they added increasingly complex instructions, each requiring several clock cycles for execution. A microprocessor with such an instruction set uses CISC (complex instruction set computer) technology. A microprocessor with a limited set of simple instructions uses RISC (reduced instruction set computer) technology.

A RISC processor performs most instructions faster than a CISC processor. It might, however, require more of these simple instructions to complete a task than a CISC processor requires for the same task.

CISC technology is the basis for most x86 processors. RISC technology is the basis for ARM processors. With that information, you can now understand why ARM was originally an acronym for Advanced RISC Machines.

Try It!

Take another look at the processor specifications for your favorite desktop or laptop computer. Can you tell if its processor has a 32-bit or 64-bit word size?

QuickCheck

x86 processors use

_____.

a. RISC technology

b. CISC technology

c. ARM technology

Random Access Memory

RAM (random access memory) is a temporary holding area for data, application program instructions, and the operating system. RAM can be packaged in a chip carrier that is wired to the system board or it can be located on small circuit boards that plug into the system board.

▶ **How much RAM does a device need?** When purchasing a digital device, you may have a choice of RAM capacity. Higher RAM capacity adds to the expense of a device. RAM capacity is expressed in gigabytes. Today's desktop and laptop computers typically feature 8 to 32 GB of RAM. Handheld devices usually have 2 to 12 GB of RAM.

▶ **But my smartphone has 64 GB, right?** Your smartphone has RAM, but not 64 GB. The specifications for smartphones that describe "memory" capacity are not referring to RAM, but to another kind of storage that is more permanent. You'll learn more about this type of storage in the next section. For now, let's focus on RAM and why it is such an essential component of your favorite digital devices.

▶ **Why is RAM so important?** RAM is the "waiting room" for the microprocessor. It holds raw data waiting to be processed as well as the program instructions for processing that data. RAM also holds the results of processing until they can be moved to a more permanent location such as an internal drive, flash drive, or cloud storage.

In addition to data and application software instructions, RAM holds operating system instructions that control the basic functions of a computer system. These instructions are loaded into RAM every time you turn on a digital device, and they remain there until you turn off the device (Figure 2-33).

Figure 2-33: RAM holds the elements for current tasks

▶ **How does RAM work?** In RAM, microscopic electronic parts called **capacitors** hold the bits that represent data. You can visualize the capacitors as microscopic lights that can be turned on or off. A charged capacitor is "turned on" and represents a "1" bit. A discharged capacitor is "turned off" and represents a "0" bit. A RAM address on each bank helps the computer locate data, as needed, for processing.

Unlike disk storage, most RAM is **volatile**, which means it requires electrical power to hold data. If the device is turned off, if the battery runs out of juice, or if a desktop computer is accidentally unplugged or experiences a power failure, all data stored in RAM instantly and permanently disappears. This type of RAM is technically classified as **dynamic RAM** (DRAM), but it is commonly referred to simply as RAM. A technical specification such as DDR4 refers to double data rate fourth generation dynamic random access memory.

2

❱ **Can a device run out of memory?** Suppose that you want to work with several programs and large graphics at the same time. Will your device eventually run out of memory? The answer is probably not. If a program exceeds its allocated space, the operating system uses an area of the hard disk or other storage medium as **virtual memory** to store parts of programs or data files until they are needed.

By selectively exchanging the data in RAM with the data in virtual memory, your computer effectively gains almost unlimited memory capacity. Too much dependence on virtual memory can decrease performance, however, especially if virtual memory is located on a relatively slow mechanical device, such as a hard disk drive.

Read-only Memory

ROM (read-only memory) is a type of memory circuitry that is housed in a single integrated circuit on the system board. Whereas RAM is temporary and volatile, ROM is more permanent and non-volatile. The contents of ROM remain in place even when the device is turned off.

❱ **Why do digital devices have ROM?** When you switch on a digital device, there is a waiting period while the device gets ready for use. While you are waiting, ROM is performing its role to "boot" the device. The boot process varies from one kind of device to another; but in general, it begins when you press the power button and ends when the device is ready to use.

ROM contains a small set of instructions and data called the **boot loader**. The boot loader instructions tell a digital device how to start. Typically, the boot loader performs self-tests to find out if the hardware is operating properly and may also verify that essential programs have not been corrupted. It then loads the operating system into RAM.

❱ **Why isn't the boot loader stored in RAM?** RAM requires power to hold data. When a device is off, RAM is empty. When you turn on the device, RAM is still empty and doesn't contain any instructions for the microprocessor to execute. ROM, on the other hand, holds data even when the power is off. As Figure 2-34 shows, when you press the power button (A), your device can immediately access the instructions in ROM and proceed with the startup routine (B). Only when the startup is complete can you access apps and data (C).

Terminology

A ROM chip, along with its instructions, is commonly referred to as *firmware* because it is a combination of hardware and software.

QuickCheck

While you are waiting for a digital device to boot, all of the following occur except:

a. The microprocessor fetches data from the ALU.

b. The boot loader checks hardware functions.

c. Instructions in ROM verify that essential programs have not been corrupted.

d. The operating system is loaded into RAM.

Figure 2-34: Why the wait?

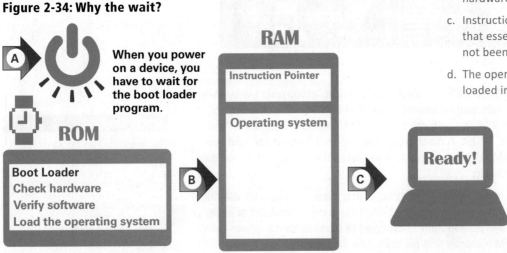

▶ Can I change the contents of ROM? The process of changing the contents of ROM is sometimes called "flashing" because it is similar to the way a camera flash helps the camera capture an image. There are several reasons that you might want to change the contents of ROM and boot loader instructions.

Repair. Electrical surges and other hardware problems might corrupt the contents of ROM, which would prevent the device from powering on properly. Flashing the ROM to restore the boot loader instructions might correct the problem.

User modification. The boot loader may limit the programs that can be downloaded and run on a device. Flashing the ROM with a modified boot loader can bypass these limitations. The process is sometimes called "jailbreaking" on iOS devices and "rooting" on Android devices. These ROM modifications may cause more problems than they solve and may void the device's warranty.

Forensics. Tricky criminals may hide incriminating data in ROM, or they may alter the boot loader so that it deletes incriminating files when the device is powered on by an unauthorized person. Investigators may want to examine the BIOS for hidden data, and they may have to flash the BIOS to restore it to a non-destructive state.

Updates. Device manufacturers offer updates to the boot loader as necessary to patch security weaknesses. Such updates are performed by running a program supplied by the manufacturer. Be sure to back up your device before flashing, and carefully follow instructions for this procedure. If the flash fails, your device will not start until you get the ROM chip replaced. After a successful update (Figure 2-35), your device should boot normally.

Terminology

There are many types of non-volatile memory, such as EEPROM and NAND, but for convenience the term ROM is used for all of them. Technically, the contents of ROM cannot be changed. The EEPROM and NAND chips that hold the boot loader programs for modern computers can be changed by flashing.

2

Try It!

What does Apple have to say about jailbreaking iPhones and iPads? You can find out by conducting an online search for *support apple jailbreak*.

Figure 2-35: ROM update

Boot Instructions v 2.0

The ROM chip containing the boot loader is located on the system board.

The process of flashing erases the contents of ROM and replaces it with a new set of instructions.

QuickQuiz   Section C

1. A laptop with an Intel Core i7 microprocessor operates at a speed of 3.4 [   ]. (Hint: Use the abbreviation.)

2. ARM and [   ] are two distinct families of microprocessors.

3. The two main parts of a microprocessor include the [   ] and the control unit.

4. Because RAM is [   ], it cannot retain data in a device that is turned off.

5. The instructions for loading the operating system into RAM when a device is first turned on originate in [   ]. (Hint: Use the acronym.)

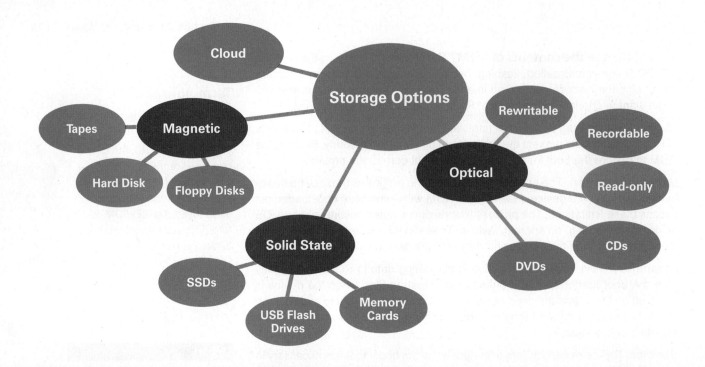

Objectives

▶ List five criteria for comparing storage options.

▶ Describe the relationship between storage and memory.

▶ Identify the technology used for hard disk drives, DVDs, USB drives, and other storage accessories.

▶ Interpret the storage specifications given for digital devices.

▶ State the advantages and disadvantages of devices that use magnetic storage technology.

▶ Name two types of optical storage media.

▶ Explain the significance of ROM, R, and RW for optical storage.

▶ List three commonly used solid state storage devices.

▶ Evaluate whether to use local or cloud storage for various projects.

▶ List at least four common backup pairings.

▶ List four backup tools available to Windows users.

▶ Explain the process of restoring a Windows computer after a hard drive failure.

▶ Describe the backup options for macOS and iOS devices.

Hard drives, flash drives, SSDs, CDs,

DVDs, and memory cards. What's the point of having so many storage options? As it turns out, none of today's storage technologies are perfect. In this section, you'll find guidelines that can make you a smart storage technology buyer and owner. The storage technologies you'll learn about are used in a variety of devices—from digital cameras to player pianos—so an understanding of storage technology can be useful even outside the boundaries of personal computing.

Terminology

local storage	SATA	rewritable	remote storage
magnetic storage	data transfer rate	solid state storage	cloud storage
hard disk drive	CDs	non-volatile	backup
hard disk platter	DVDs	memory card	recovery drive
read-write head	optical storage	card reader	file synchronization
head crash	read-only	solid state drive	disk image
access time	recordable	USB flash drive	

Storage Basics

Storage is the term used for the components of a digital device designed to hold data permanently. Unlike RAM, storage is non-volatile and retains data even when the device is powered down. Storage is used to save documents, photos, and playlists. It also houses software and the operating system.

Today's digital devices may use local storage and remote storage, but they are not interchangeable. To find out what gets stored where, let's look at local storage first, then expand into remote storage.

▶ **Which local storage technology is best?** Local storage refers to storage devices and media that can be directly attached to a computer, smartphone, or appliance. Local storage options include hard drives, CDs, DVDs, flash drives, solid state drives, and memory cards.

Most digital devices have some type of local storage that is permanently available as you use the device. Built-in storage can be supplemented by removable storage, such as flash drives and memory cards.

Each of these local storage options has its advantages and disadvantages. If one storage system were perfect, we wouldn't need so many storage devices for our digital gear! To compare local storage options, it is useful to review their durability, dependability, speed, capacity, and cost (Figure 2-36).

Figure 2-36: Evaluating storage options

Durability

Resistance to damage from handling and environmental factors such as dust, humidity, heat, and cold. Can be measured in lifespan or in write cycles (the number of times data can be written and revised).

Dependability

Available when needed; not subject to breakdown, malfunction, network outages, or service interruptions. Can be measured by mean time between failures (MTBF is the time a device is expected to function before failing).

Speed

The rate at which data can be stored or accessed. Faster is better. Can be measured by data transfer rate (the number of megabytes per second that are read or written by the storage device).

Capacity

The amount of data that can be stored, usually measured in gigabytes (GB) or terabytes (TB).

Cost

The price of the storage device and media, usually expressed per gigabyte (GB).

▶ **How much storage do I have?** The amount of local storage available on a digital device depends on the capacity of each storage device and the amount of data that is currently stored. Available storage space is sometimes referred to as "free space." The process of finding the amount of free space depends on the device. Figure 2-37 can get you started.

Figure 2-37: Are you running out of storage space?

macOS (Macs)

1. Right-click the Macintosh HD icon.

2. Select Get Info.

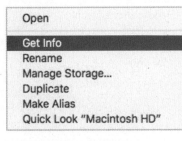

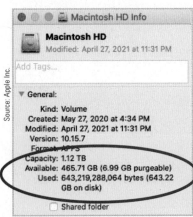

Windows (PCs)

1. Enter **storage** in the Windows search box, then select the "Storage settings" option.

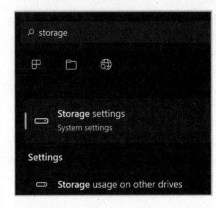

2. Select a storage device, such as C:.

Try It!

How close are you to running out of storage space on your favorite digital device? Check now to find out. For laptops and desktops, follow the steps in Figure 2-37. For iOS tablets and phones, select Settings→General→About. For Android devices, select Settings→More→Storage.

Source: Apple Inc.

▶ **How do storage technologies work?** You can think of your computer's storage devices as having a direct pipeline to RAM. Data gets copied from a storage device into RAM, where it waits to be processed. After data is processed, it is held temporarily in RAM, but it is usually copied to a storage medium for more permanent safekeeping.

As you know, a computer's processor works with data that has been coded into bits that can be represented by 1s and 0s. When data is stored, these 1s and 0s must be converted into some kind of signal or mark that's fairly permanent but can be changed when necessary.

Obviously, the data is not literally written as "1" or "0." Instead, the 1s and 0s must be transformed into something that can remain on a storage medium. Exactly how this transformation happens depends on the storage technology. For example, hard disks store data in a different way than CDs. Three types of storage technologies are commonly used for personal computers: magnetic, optical, and solid state.

Terminology

The process of storing data is often referred to as *writing data* or *saving a file* because the storage device writes the data on the storage medium to save it for later use.

The process of retrieving data is often referred to as *reading data, loading data,* or *opening a file.*

Magnetic Storage Technology

Those big reels of tape that you see on computers in classic science fiction movies are an example of magnetic storage technology used on data-processing era mainframe computers. The first personal computers used cassette tapes for storage, though floppy disk storage was soon available. Today, magnetic storage technology is the foundation for the hard disk drives in desktop computers, laptops, and enterprise servers.

◗ What is magnetic storage technology? Magnetic storage represents data by magnetizing microscopic particles on a disk or tape surface. The particles retain their magnetic orientation until that orientation is changed, providing permanent but modifiable storage for data.

Data stored magnetically can be easily changed or deleted simply by changing the magnetic orientation of particles on the disk surface. This feature of magnetic storage provides lots of flexibility for editing data and reusing areas of a storage medium containing unneeded data.

◗ How does a hard disk drive work? A hard disk drive (often abbreviated as HDD) contains one or more platters and their associated read-write heads. A hard disk platter is a flat, rigid disk made of aluminum or glass and coated with magnetic iron oxide particles.

The platters rotate as a unit on a spindle, making thousands of rotations per minute. Each platter has a read-write head that hovers just a few microinches above the surface. A read-write head mechanism in the disk drive magnetizes particles to write data, and senses the particles' polarities to read data (Figure 2-38).

Terminology

You might hear the term *fixed disk* used to refer to hard disks. You often see the terms *hard disk* and *hard disk drive* used interchangeably, though technically *hard disk* refers to the platters sealed inside the hard disk drive.

Figure 2-38: Orienting particles on a hard disk

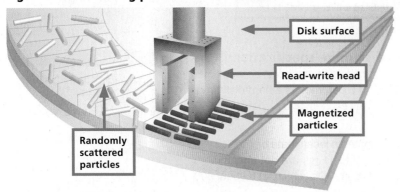

Before data is stored on a hard disk, particles on the disk surface are scattered in random patterns. The disk drive's read-write head orients them in a positive (north) or negative (south) direction to represent 0 and 1 bits, respectively.

◗ What are the advantages of hard disk drives? Hard disk drives can be installed inside a device or attached externally for additional storage capacity or backup. Hard disk technology has three advantages. First, it provides lots of storage, with capacities ranging from 40 GB to 8 TB. Second, it provides fast access to files. Third, hard disk drives are economical. The cost of storing 1 gigabyte of data is about two cents.

QuickCheck

What is the purpose of a read-write head?

a. It pulls particles up as data is read.

b. It etches a track on the disk surface.

c. It orients particles north or south depending on if they represent 0s or 1s.

❱ What's the downside of hard disk storage? Data stored on magnetic media can be unintentionally altered by magnetic fields, dust, mold, smoke particles, heat, and mechanical problems with a storage device. Over time, magnetic media gradually lose their magnetic charge. Some experts estimate that the reliable lifespan of data stored on magnetic media is about three years. They recommend that you refresh your data every two years by recopying it.

The read-write heads in a hard disk drive hover a microscopic distance above each platter. If a read-write head comes into contact with the platter, the **head crash** is likely to damage the platter and corrupt the data contained on it. The causes of a head crash are explained in Figure 2-39.

Figure 2-39: What causes a head crash?

Dropping a device may cause the read-write head to bounce off the surface of the platter, scraping off particles that represent data.

If dust particles or other contaminants seep into the drive case, they may come to rest on a platter where the read-write head will crash into them.

❱ What should I know about hard disk drive specifications? The specifications for a hard disk drive commonly include its capacity, access time, and speed. For example, "2 TB 8 ms 7200 RPM HDD" means a hard disk drive with a 2 terabyte capacity, an access time of 8 milliseconds, and a speed of 7,200 revolutions per minute.

Access time is the average time it takes a computer to locate data on the storage medium and read it. Hard disk access times of 6 to 11 ms are not uncommon. Hard disk drives have much faster access times than CDs, which take about 500 ms to spin up to speed and find data.

Hard disk drive speed is sometimes measured in revolutions per minute (rpm). The faster a drive spins, the more rapidly it can position the read-write head over specific data. For example, a 7,200 rpm drive is able to access data faster than a 5,400 rpm drive.

You might see the term *SATA* included in technical specifications for hard disk drives. **SATA** refers to Serial Advanced Technology Attachment, which is the interface that transfers data from the drive to the main circuit board.

When comparing hard disk drives to other storage technologies, data transfer rates can be useful. **Data transfer rate** is the amount of data a storage device can move per second from the storage medium to RAM. Higher numbers indicate faster transfer rates. Hard disk drive transfer rates are typically 100-200 megabytes per second (expressed as MBps or MB/s).

QuickCheck

If you see an ad for a computer with a 6 ms hard drive, you can assume that 6 ms refers to the drive's _____.

a. access time

b. capacity

c. rotational speed

d. data transfer rate

Try It!

Check online. What's the average price for a 2 TB hard drive?

Optical Storage Technology

CDs (compact discs) and DVDs (digital video discs) may seem outdated, yet they remain useful for archival storage because they can provide a permanent home for collections of documents, music, and photos that you might not trust to less robust storage technologies.

▶ **How does optical technology work?** CDs and DVDs are classified as **optical storage**, which represents data as microscopic light and dark spots on the disc surface. An optical drive contains a laser that directs a beam of light toward the underside of the disc. Reflected light is collected by a lens and converted into 0s and 1s that represent data.

▶ **How do CD and DVD technologies differ?** A single optical drive typically handles CDs and DVDs, but the costs and capacities of these discs vary (Figure 2-40).

Figure 2-40: Optical storage options

CD
650 MB 15¢

DVD
4.7 GB 25¢

CD (compact disc): Designed to hold 74 minutes of recorded music, then adapted for computer storage with capacity for 650 MB of data. Later improvements in CD standards increased the capacity to 80 minutes of music or 700 MB of data.

DVD (digital video disc): Designed with the capacity to hold a feature-length film. A single-sided DVD offers 4.7 GB (4,700 MB) of data storage. A double-layer DVD has two recordable layers on the same side and can store 8.5 GB of data.

▶ **What's the significance of ROM, R, and RW?** Optical technologies are grouped into three categories:

Read-only (ROM). CD-ROMs and DVD-ROMs are mass produced. Their contents cannot be changed; their lifespan is estimated to be 100 years.

Recordable (R). Data can be written on a recordable disc by consumer devices, but once written, the data cannot be changed. Lifespan: 100 years.

Rewritable (RW). Data can be written on the disc and later changed. The estimated lifespan of data is about 30 years.

▶ **How durable are optical discs?** Optical discs are not disrupted by humidity, fingerprints, dust, magnets, or spilled soft drinks. Some optical discs have an estimated lifespan of at least 30 years, while other types of optical discs can probably hold data securely for up to 100 years. When using optical technology for archival purposes, the archive should include an optical drive as well as the media containing data. The drive that recorded the data will have the best chance of reading it as the years go by.

Solid State Storage Technology

If you're a typical digital device owner, you use solid state storage every day. You carry a flash drive and you might swap memory cards in a camera or tablet. The main storage for your smartphone is also based on solid state technology, as is the storage for many of today's laptops.

▶ **What is solid state storage?** **Solid state storage** (sometimes called flash memory) stores data in erasable, rewritable circuitry, rather than on spinning disks or streaming tape. Each data bit is held in a gate-like circuit that can be open or shut.

Very little power is required to open or close the gates, which makes solid state storage ideal for battery-operated devices, such as digital cameras and media players. Once the data is stored, it is **non-volatile**—the circuits retain data without the need for an external power source.

Solid state storage provides fast access to data because it includes no moving parts. This storage technology is very durable—it is virtually impervious to vibration, magnetic fields, or extreme temperature fluctuations. It is also dependable. With no mechanical parts, it is less likely to fail than a hard disk drive.

▶ **When should I use memory cards?** A **memory card** is a flat, solid state storage medium commonly used to transfer files from digital cameras and media players to computers. The term *memory card* might lead you to believe that it is similar to random access memory (RAM). However, these cards are non-volatile and classified as storage because they retain data even when they are disconnected from computers and other devices.

A **card reader** is a device that reads and writes data on memory cards. Common memory card formats include SD cards and microSD cards, which come in a variety of capacities and speeds. Those specifications are displayed on the card's casing, as shown in Figure 2-41.

Figure 2-41: Solid state memory cards

Memory cards are available in several speeds and capacities.

Many digital devices are equipped with a card reader for transferring data to and from solid state memory cards.

Card reader

▶ **Do I need a solid state drive?** A **solid state drive** (SSD) is a package of flash memory that can be used as a substitute for a hard disk drive. An SSD is installed inside the system unit and is not meant to be removed except for servicing. Some solid state drives are about the same size as a microprocessor chip; others are about the size of a small deck of cards (Figure 2-42).

Figure 2-42: Solid state drives

15¢ cost per GB

SSDs are widely used as the main storage device in smartphones and tablet computers. Many laptops and some desktop computers also include an SSD instead of a hard disk drive.

▶ **What should I know about USB flash drives?** A **USB flash drive** is a portable storage device that plugs directly into a computer's system unit using a built-in USB connector. Also called thumb drives, pen drives, jump drives, keychain drives, or UFDs, USB flash drives are small and so durable that you can literally carry them on your key ring. USB flash drives have capacities ranging from 128 MB to 2 TB.

The data transfer rate of a USB flash drive depends on the USB version. USB 3.1 Gen 1 rates can reach 5 Gbps, rivaling hard disk drive speed. USB 3.2 Gen 2x2 speeds are four times faster.

Cloud Storage

You probably use several digital devices. Suppose you stored class notes on your laptop, but you've left it at home. Imagine if you could access those notes from your phone. Cloud storage can make that happen.

▶ **What is cloud storage?** Storage that is built into a digital device or that can be plugged directly into a device is classified as local storage. In contrast, **remote storage** is housed on an external device that can be accessed from a network. Remote storage may be available on a home, school, or work network. It can also be available as an Internet service, in which case it is called **cloud storage**.

Cloud storage is provided to individuals by services such as Apple iCloud, Microsoft OneDrive, Google Drive, and Dropbox. The basic concept is that files can be stored in a subscriber's cloud-based storage area and accessed by logging in from any device. In a simple implementation, cloud storage functions just like a local drive (Figure 2-43).

Figure 2-43: Dropbox is in the cloud but accessed like a local drive

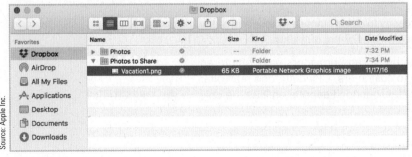

Source: Apple Inc.

2

Some cloud implementations offer a synchronization feature that automatically duplicates files stored on a local device by also saving them in the cloud (Figure 2-44).

Figure 2-44: Cloud synchronization

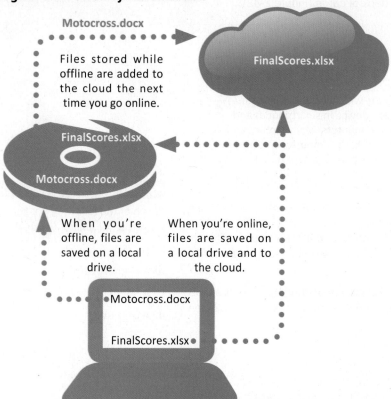

▶ **What should I know about cloud storage?** The term *cloud storage* refers to a set of technologies for transporting, synchronizing, and managing data stored on banks of high-performance hard disk drives housed in the service provider's data center.

Most cloud services offer a generous amount of free storage space, so the price is right. If you regularly use several digital devices and want to access your files from all of them, then cloud storage is an excellent solution. Also, if you procrastinate about backing up your devices, files stored in the cloud remain there even if a local device malfunctions. That being said, cloud storage has several drawbacks.

Security and privacy risks. The more places your data is stored and the more networks on which it travels, the more susceptible it becomes to intercepts from hackers and government spying agencies. Carefully consider what you store in the cloud.

Service outages. When a cloud storage site has an outage, all the data stored there becomes temporarily inaccessible. If you have a term paper due in two days, it would be best not to trust the only copy to cloud storage, where a two-day outage could make your files inaccessible until after the due date.

Discontinuation of service. Some cloud storage providers have shuttered their storage services with little warning to customers. Cloud storage may offer a convenient option for backing up your files, but don't depend on it as the only backup.

QuickCheck

Cloud services generally use what type of storage devices?

a. Magnetic

b. Optical

c. Flash

d. Cloud circuits

Backup

Storage devices fail. Cloud storage services go dark. When they do, the data they contain might not be recoverable. To protect your data, you need backups. Do you have them? Do they contain the files you'll need to resume work without a hitch?

❱ **What do I really need to back up?** A **backup** is a copy of one or more files that is made in case the originals become damaged. Although the best practice might seem to be "back up everything," that is not always practical.

Your files are often scattered—some on a local hard disk, others on USB drives, some on your phone, and even others on cloud storage. Simply copying all of your files from one device to another or to the cloud requires lots of space and lots of time. Plus, there are some sticky technical issues that make it difficult to actually get a complete backup. To understand the problem, consider what a typical hard disk contains (Figure 2-45).

Try It!

How many GB of data would be stored in a backup of the entire contents of your desktop or laptop computer? (Hint: Figure 2-37 showed you how to check the amount of space that is used on a local hard disk.)

2

Figure 2-45: What can you afford to lose?

 **Operating system:** The operating system is required to start your device, but a backup copy might not run if it is unauthorized.

 **Software:** Most devices are populated with preinstalled software, and you've probably downloaded and installed many additional apps. If these are wiped out when a storage device fails, the process of downloading and reinstalling them can be time consuming.

 **Data files:** Your documents, photos, music, videos—all the goodies that you've created and gathered—can be difficult or impossible to reconstruct from scratch.

Settings, accounts, and profiles: How much time did you spend customizing your home screen, entering contacts, choosing passwords, and setting preferences for your favorite apps? No one wants to have to do that all over again!

❱ **Then what should I do?** The best advice is this: Know what's important and ensure that current versions exist on more than one storage device. The easiest pairings of devices for backups are illustrated in Figure 2-46.

Figure 2-46: Backup pairings

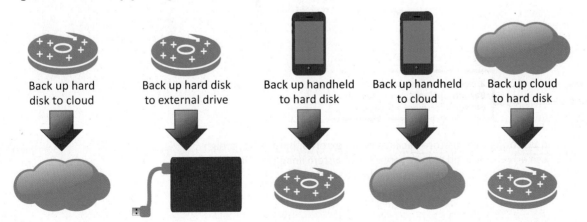

Back up hard disk to cloud   Back up hard disk to external drive   Back up handheld to hard disk   Back up handheld to cloud   Back up cloud to hard disk

▶ What tools do I need for backups? The tools you'll need depend on what you are backing up and where you are putting the backups. If you are a typical consumer with a laptop and a smartphone, you will need a cloud storage account, an external hard disk drive, synchronization software, a blank USB flash drive, and backup or disk imaging software.

▶ I've got a Windows PC. What should I do? Windows users have access to several backup tools and will need to use more than one of them.

Recovery drive. A **recovery drive** (or system repair disc) contains parts of the operating system necessary to boot your computer and diagnose system problems after a hard drive failure or software malfunction. Files for creating a recovery drive are usually preinstalled on the hard disk drive, but they won't do you any good there when the hard disk fails. Follow the manufacturer's instructions to move the recovery files to a blank USB flash drive, which you can store until it is needed.

Copy command. As you are working on important projects, make copies of essential files. You can store the copies on the same device as the originals using versioning techniques, such as adding "v2" and "v3" to the file names of versions. And for safety, periodically copy a version to a USB drive or to cloud storage. You can manually create copies of your data files using the Copy option in Windows File Explorer.

File History. Data file backup can be automated using File History, which is included with Windows 8.0 and subsequent versions. File History uses **file synchronization** to make copies of files from your Documents, Music, Pictures, and Videos folders, along with any files that were created or modified while OneDrive was offline. File History is useful if a data file goes missing, but it requires the System Image Backup option for system files, software, and settings. File History is relatively easy to set up (Figure 2-47).

QuickCheck

Which backup tool can be used to boot a Windows computer after a hard drive malfunction?

a. A recovery drive

b. The Copy command

c. File History

d. A cloud drive

Figure 2-47: Activate File History

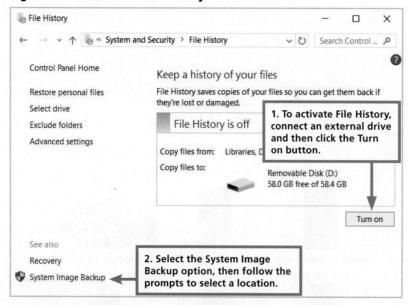

File History can be configured to store backups on an external hard drive, a high-capacity USB flash drive, or a cloud storage service. The system image requires more space than is available on most USB flash drives.

System image. A **disk image** is a bit-for-bit copy of the data from all sectors of a hard disk. Windows includes a disk imaging option called System Image that creates an exact clone of the original disk, including the operating system, your software, and all your settings. Be sure to select the System Image Backup option in the File History window to activate it.

▶ **If my computer's hard drive fails, how do I proceed?** First, a new hard drive has to be installed. Then, as shown in Figure 2-48, (A) use the recovery drive to boot the computer. Then, (B) attach the backup drive containing your system image. Respond to the prompts displayed on the screen to copy the system image to the new hard disk. After the system image is installed, recover your files by using the File History utility.

Figure 2-48: Restoring Windows after a hard disk crash

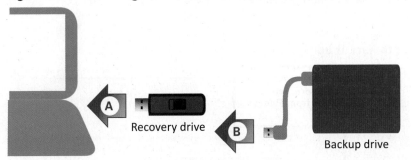

Recovery drive

Backup drive

▶ **I have a Mac. What's my best backup option?** macOS offers a comprehensive file synchronization utility called Time Machine, which backs up the entire hard disk, including system files, applications, accounts, preferences, email messages, music, photos, movies, and documents. Make sure that Time Machine is set to run in the background at all times while your computer is turned on.

If you need to restore a single file, you can open Time Machine, choose a file, and then select the Restore option. To restore an entire backup, make sure the backup drive is connected and hold down the Command and R keys as the computer starts. Figure 2-49 illustrates Time Machine.

Figure 2-49: Time Machine backups

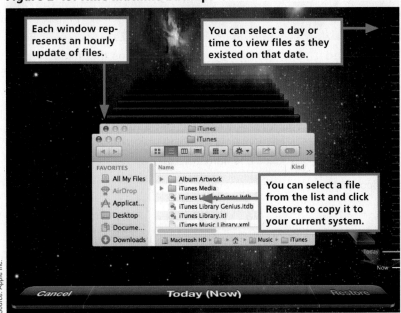

Source: Apple Inc.

▶ What about backing up my smartphone and tablet? Many Android devices include backup software, which is usually accessible from the Settings icon. Generally, backups from Android devices are stored in the cloud on Google servers. If your Android device accepts SD cards, you may also be able to make backups of individual files.

Owners of iOS devices can back up to a local computer using Finder, iTunes, or iCloud. The process is usually referred to as synchronization because it updates the files on the backup device with newer versions of files found on the smartphone or tablet.

To activate iCloud backup, you can access Settings for your iOS device, tap your account name, tap iCloud, and then select iCloud Backup. Slide the iCloud Backup button to On. To sync to a local drive using Finder, simply connect the device to a desktop or laptop using a USB cable and then choose the iPhone icon (Figure 2-50).

Figure 2-50: Sync your iPhone or iPad to back it up

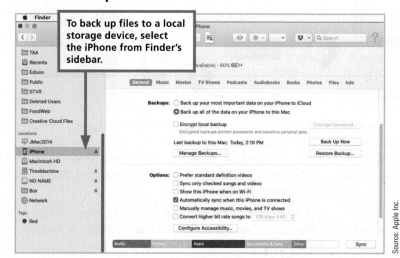

To back up files to a local storage device, select the iPhone from Finder's sidebar.

Source: Apple Inc.

Synching is usually initiated by tethering your handheld device to a desktop or laptop computer using a USB cable.

QuickQuiz   Section D

1. A magnetic storage device uses a read-[_____] head to magnetize particles that represent data.

2. Today, [_____] storage technology, such as CDs and DVDs, is used for archiving data.

3. Cloud storage, such as OneDrive and iCloud, is classified as [_____] storage as opposed to local storage.

4. A(n) [_____] uses the same storage technology as a USB flash drive but is not designed to be removable. (Hint: Use the acronym.)

5. A disk [_____] is a bit-for-bit copy of the contents of a hard disk, created as a backup in case of a hard drive failure.

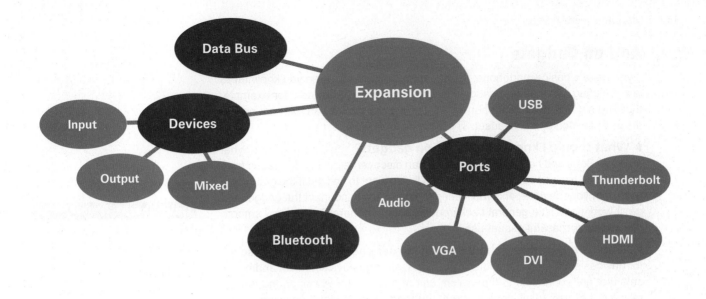

Objectives

▶ Categorize devices as input, output, or mixed.

▶ Diagram the path of data from external devices to the CPU.

▶ Identify common expansion ports and connectors, such as USB, VGA, HDMI, DVI, DisplayPort, Thunderbolt, and Ethernet.

▶ State which types of devices should not be unplugged without notification.

▶ List at least three examples of devices that might be connected using Bluetooth.

▶ Explain the purpose of a device driver and why one might have to be installed or updated manually.

▶ List four factors that affect display quality.

▶ Explain the role of a GPU and list the applications for which one is most useful.

▶ Explain how resolution settings affect the size of objects and text on the screen.

▶ Identify which printing tasks are best fulfilled by a dot matrix, laser, or 3D printer.

▶ Describe the function of the three most popular IMU sensors used by the Internet of Things.

▶ List five types of sensors that provide input to autonomous vehicles.

Gadgets.
Those fitness trackers, VR headsets, credit card readers, and other gadgets are basically input and output devices. Section E focuses on the technology that makes it possible to expand a host device by connecting input and output devices, such as displays and printers. The section winds up with a look at the amazing array of sensors that collect data for the Internet of Things and self-driving vehicles.

Terminology

peripheral device	LCD	capacitive technology	smart sensors
expansion ports	response rate	integrated graphics	sense-plan-act
data bus	dot pitch	dedicated graphics	algorithms
hot-plugging	screen resolution	graphics processing unit	accelerometer
USB hub	touchscreen	ink jet printer	gyro sensor
Bluetooth	virtual keyboard	laser printer	magnetometer
device driver	resistive technology	additive manufacturing	lidar

Add-on Gadgets

If you have a basic smartphone, tablet, laptop, or desktop, then you know there is a tempting list of add-on gadgets to accompany these devices: for example, that fine set of AirPod headphones, a Fitbit activity tracker, an external optical drive, or an Oculus VR headset. There are lots of options.

▶ **What should I know about add-on gadgets?** You'll want to know what a gadget does and how well it works. You can discover relevant information from product reviews and customer ratings. You'll also want to find out if the gadget will work with your devices, and you'll need to know how to connect the gadget and get it working. A little general background about peripheral devices will smooth the way to successful gadget use.

▶ **What is a peripheral device?** The term **peripheral device** is tech-speak for devices such as printers, display devices, storage devices, mice, and head-sets that are connected to the system unit of a computer. Although the term is falling out of use, it still pops up here and there, so it is worth knowing. Some modern nontechnical terms for peripheral devices include *gadgets*, *add-ons*, and *accessories*. Peripheral devices are classified as input, output, or mixed devices, as shown in Figure 2-51.

QuickCheck

Which of the following are not considered peripheral devices?

a. RAM and CPU

b. Speakers and headsets

c. Hard disk drive and memory cards

d. Touchscreen and keyboard

Figure 2-51: Peripheral devices

Keyboards	Fitness trackers	Printers
Mice	Touchscreens	Headphones
Touchpads	Home security systems	Speakers
Game controllers	MIDI instruments	Projectors
Scanners	Home control systems	Monitors
Microphones	Audio headsets	Robots
Credit card scanners	VR headsets	
Barcode readers	Haptic gloves	
Biometric scanners		

▶ **What can I connect to my devices?** Many gadgets, such as earbuds, work with a wide variety of devices, including smartphones, smartwatches, tablets, laptops, and desktops. Other gadgets are designed to work only with iPhones, for example. When shopping for gadgets, read the specifications and make sure they include your device.

▶ **What about connections?** Add-on gadgets can connect to laptops, desktops, and handhelds using a cable or a wireless connection. Let's take a look at commonly used connectors so that you can identify them on your devices.

Expansion Ports

Like an ocean liner's portholes, many digital devices have ports in the system unit that can be opened or closed. A computer port can be opened to allow data to flow to and from various add-on devices. Because these ports expand the options for input, output, and storage, they are commonly called **expansion ports**. When you plug in a USB flash drive or insert a memory card, you are using an expansion port.

▶ **How do expansion ports relate to the rest of the circuitry in a device?** All of the components on the system board are connected by circuitry. The main circuits that carry data are called the **data bus**. These circuits carry data at lightning speeds as pulses of electrical voltages.

The part of the data bus that runs between the microprocessor and RAM is called the local bus or internal bus. This is the fastest part of the data bus because it has to keep up with the data demands of the microprocessor.

The part of the data bus that stretches from RAM to various expansion ports is called the expansion bus. This part of the bus has several branches to accommodate data traveling to and from various ports (Figure 2-52).

Figure 2-52: The expansion bus

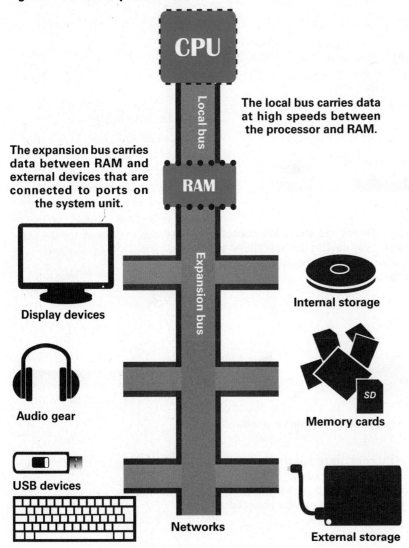

The local bus carries data at high speeds between the processor and RAM.

The expansion bus carries data between RAM and external devices that are connected to ports on the system unit.

CPU

Local bus

RAM

Expansion bus

Display devices

Audio gear

USB devices

Networks

Internal storage

Memory cards

External storage

QuickCheck

How does data flow from an external storage device to the processor?

a. Data first travels on the expansion bus, and then switches to the data bus.

b. Data begins on the internal bus, and then ends up on the local bus.

c. Data from the expansion bus reaches RAM, and then it is transferred to the processor.

d. Data starts on the network bus, is processed in the CPU, and then is sent to RAM.

2

▶ **What should I know about expansion ports?** When making a connection between a peripheral device and a computer, the cable must connect to the proper expansion port. Ports are sometimes marked by tiny symbols that are difficult to see. You'll want to be able to identify ports by their size and shape.

From Section D, you are already familiar with the storage ports used for memory cards. You'll also want to be able to identify general-purpose, video, audio, and network ports (Figure 2-53).

Try It!

Take a look at your laptop or desktop computer. Can you make a list of all its ports?

Figure 2-53: Expansion ports

Thunderbolt   USB   Mini USB   Lightning

USB 3.0   USB-C

Suleyman Delil Karakurt/Shutterstock.com

General-purpose ports are used to connect a variety of gadgets. Small devices, such as smartphones, might use a single Lightning connector that does double duty as a recharging cable and a connector for peripheral devices. Lightning ports resemble USB-C ports, but their cables are not interchangeable.

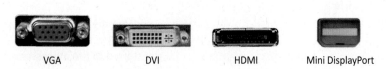

VGA   DVI   HDMI   Mini DisplayPort

Some display devices, such as external display screens and projection devices, are designed to connect to USB ports, but other display devices use specialized video ports, such as HDMI, DVI, VGA, and DisplayPort. Using a specialized video port leaves USB ports free for other gadgets.

Terminology

An *adapter* converts one type of connector to another. For example, a projector might have a DVI connector; but if your laptop has only a Mini DisplayPort, you can use an adapter to change the DVI plug to a Mini DisplayPort plug.

Audio In   Audio Out

Most devices have at least one Audio Out port for a headset or earbuds. There may be an additional Audio In port for connecting a microphone.

Ethernet   Wireless antenna

An Ethernet port handles wired network connections. Wireless network connections are usually built in, but an antenna can be inserted in a USB port.

QuickCheck

Which port would be the first choice for connecting a display device?

a. HDMI

b. USB

c. Lightning

d. Ethernet

What is hot-plugging? When a peripheral device is connected or disconnected while the host device is operating, it is called **hot-plugging**. Although it is unnecessary to turn devices off before disconnecting them, some devices should not be disconnected while in the middle of data transfers. Before unplugging a device, such as a USB flash drive, your computer might require notification. Figure 2-54 shows how to safely remove a USB drive.

Figure 2-54: How to safely eject USB flash drives

With Windows, use the File Explorer folder icon to view the flash drive icon. Right-click it, then select Eject. You can remove the flash drive when its name disappears from the list or the Safe to Remove Hardware message appears.

Safe To Remove Hardware
The 'USB DRIVE (D:)' device can now be safely removed from the computer.
Windows host process (Rundll32)

With macOS, use Finder to view the flash drive icon. Select the round Eject icon. It is safe to remove the flash drive when its listing disappears.

Source: Apple Inc.

What if I run out of USB ports? If you want to connect more devices than the available number of USB ports, you can use a USB hub. A **USB hub** is an inexpensive device that turns one USB port into multiple ports. It also saves wear and tear on USB ports caused by repeatedly inserting and removing USB devices (Figure 2-55).

Figure 2-55: A USB hub is handy for connecting lots of gadgets

USB hub

QuickCheck

When you're ready to put your laptop in your backpack, which of the following do you need to eject?

a. A printer that's connected with a USB cable

b. A USB flash drive

c. The mouse

d. The DVI port

Try It!

Do you have any devices connected to your computer that require notification before they are removed? (Hint: Use one of the methods in Figure 2-54 to find out.)

Bluetooth

Increasingly, gadgets are going wireless. Instead of exchanging data through a cable, devices can send signals through the air—no cable required. A common wireless technology for connecting peripherals is **Bluetooth**.

▶ **What kinds of devices use Bluetooth?** You'll find Bluetooth options for connecting wireless keyboards and mice to laptops and desktops. The connection between your phone and your car uses Bluetooth.

Bluetooth is a low-power technology, so it is ideal for mobile devices that don't have big batteries. Bluetooth is used to connect wireless headsets to smartphones. And if you're into fitness, then your fitness tracker may transmit data to your phone or computer using Bluetooth technology.

▶ **What are the range and speed of Bluetooth?** Bluetooth devices must be within 30 feet of each other. The peak data transmission rate is 3 Mbps, which is suitable for sending small bursts of data rather than large files. Compared to wired connections, Bluetooth is quite slow (Figure 2-56).

Figure 2-56: Data transfer rates of popular connection technologies

Thunderbolt 40 Gbps

USB 3 10 Gbps

Bluetooth 3 Mbps

▶ **Can I tell if a device is equipped with Bluetooth?** Bluetooth is built into many smartphones, tablets, laptops, and desktops, but there is no corresponding physical port on the system unit. Look for the Bluetooth logo on the Windows taskbar or the Mac menu bar (Figure 2-57). For handheld devices, check Settings. If a device is not equipped with Bluetooth, you can plug a Bluetooth antenna into a USB port.

Figure 2-57: Does this device have Bluetooth?

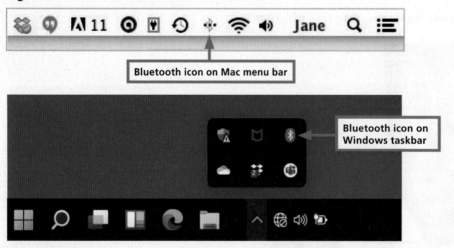

Bluetooth icon on Mac menu bar

Bluetooth icon on Windows taskbar

QuickCheck

Which of the following would be least likely to connect through a Bluetooth port?

a. A wireless headset

b. An external hard drive

c. A keyboard

d. A game controller

Try It!

Does your favorite device have Bluetooth? Look for the Bluetooth icon or settings to find out.

Device Drivers

Many gadgets have associated software. For example, there's an iPhone app for your fitness wristband that graphs your progress and shares it with your training buddies. These applications help you get the most out of your gadgets. In addition to application software, devices also require a type of software called a device driver.

▶ **What's a device driver?** A **device driver** is software that helps a peripheral device establish communication with its host device. For example, the device driver for an HP printer sets up data streams from RAM to the printer and makes sure that the data is formatted in a way that the printer can work with.

▶ **When do I have to install device drivers?** Operating systems include built-in drivers for standard expansion ports. This feature, sometimes called Plug and Play, makes it relatively easy to connect devices without manually installing device drivers. When you connect a new peripheral device, the operating system looks for an appropriate driver. If the device is unable to use a standard driver, you'll be prompted to install the device driver supplied by the peripheral device manufacturer.

▶ **Where do I get device drivers?** Device drivers, updates, and instructions for installing them can be downloaded from the manufacturer's Web site.

▶ **When do I need a device driver update?** Device drivers work directly with the host device's operating system. A printer or other connected gadgets might work perfectly—until the operating system gets an update. Then some device drivers might stop working correctly and the devices they control could malfunction.

In addition to checking cables, trying a different port, and rebooting, one of the first steps in troubleshooting a malfunctioning peripheral device is to access the manufacturer's Web site and look for a driver update. Updated driver downloads are usually available from the Support link (Figure 2-58).

QuickCheck

Suppose that the printer connected to your computer's USB port stopped working right after an operating system update. Which of the following would most likely fix the problem?

a. Install a new ink cartridge.

b. Plug the printer into a surge protector.

c. Connect the printer to a Bluetooth port.

d. Update the printer driver.

Figure 2-58: Device driver updates are available online

© 2015 Hewlett-Packard Development Company, L.P.

At most device manufacturers' sites, you'll find a support link where you can look for updated device drivers.

Display Devices

A computer display device that simply displays text and images is classified as an output device. Touchscreens, however, can be classified as both input and output devices because they accept input and display output.

❱ What are my options for display devices? Standalone display devices, sometimes called monitors, are popular for desktop computers. Display devices for laptops, tablets, and handheld devices are built into the system units, but these devices may also accept an external monitor. Most of today's display devices are based on LCD technology.

LCD (liquid crystal display) technology produces an image by filtering light through a layer of liquid crystal cells (Figure 2-59). The advantages of LCD screens include display clarity, low radiation emission, portability, and compactness. The source of the light that filters through the LCD is referred to as backlighting.

Figure 2-59: LCD displays

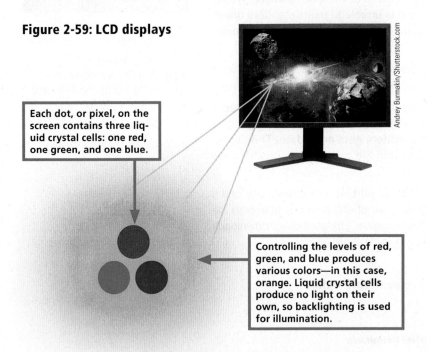

Each dot, or pixel, on the screen contains three liquid crystal cells: one red, one green, and one blue.

Controlling the levels of red, green, and blue produces various colors—in this case, orange. Liquid crystal cells produce no light on their own, so backlighting is used for illumination.

Andrey Burmakin/Shutterstock.com

❱ What factors affect image quality? Image quality is a factor of screen size, response rate, dot pitch, and screen resolution.

Screen size. Screen size is the measurement in inches from one corner of the screen diagonally across to the opposite corner. Screen sizes range from 1" for smartwatches to 60" or more for home entertainment systems.

Response rate. Response rate is the time it takes for one pixel to change from black to white and then back to black. Display devices with fast response rates display a crisp image with minimal blurring or "ghosting" of moving objects. Response rate is measured in milliseconds (ms). For gaming systems, a response rate of 5 ms or less is desirable.

Dot pitch. The crystals that form an image on the screen are spaced in a grid. **Dot pitch** (dp) is the distance in millimeters between like-colored crystals (Figure 2-60).

Figure 2-60: Dot pitch

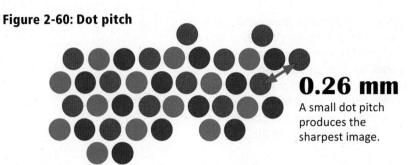

0.26 mm

A small dot pitch produces the sharpest image.

2

Screen resolution. The number of horizontal and vertical pixels that a device displays on the screen is referred to as **screen resolution**. Your smartphone, for example, might have a resolution of 2532 x 1170. Another way to express resolution is pixels per inch (ppi). Your smartphone's 6.1-inch screen would have a resolution of 460 ppi.

▶ Should I set my computer on its highest resolution? Most displays have a recommended resolution at which images are clearest and text is crispest. On laptops and desktops, however, you can change the resolution. In Windows, you can right-click the desktop and select Display settings. In macOS, use the Apple icon to open System Preferences and choose Displays.

At higher resolutions, text and objects may appear smaller, but the desktop appears more spacious. The two screens in Figure 2-61 help you compare the same display set at two different resolutions.

Figure 2-61: Screen resolution and window size

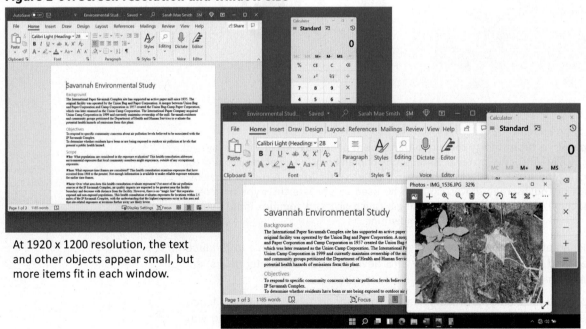

At 1920 x 1200 resolution, the text and other objects appear small, but more items fit in each window.

At 1280 x 768 resolution, the text and other objects appear large, but less text appears in the document window.

▶ **How does a touchscreen work?** Tablet computers, handheld devices, retail store self-checkouts, and ATMs display output and collect input from a **touchscreen**. Touchscreens display menus, scroll bars, and other controls. They can also display a **virtual keyboard** for devices that are not connected to a physical keyboard.

Touch events, such as taps, drags, and pinches, are sometimes called gestures. The coordinates for a touch event are processed in essentially the same way as a mouse click. For example, if you touch your iPad screen at the location of a button labeled Calendar, the area you touch generates coordinates and sends them to the processor. The processor compares the coordinates to the image displayed on the screen to find out what is at the coordinates, and then responds—in this case, by opening your appointment calendar. The two most commonly used touchscreen technologies are resistive and capacitive (Figure 2-62).

Figure 2-62: Touchscreens

Screens built with **resistive technology** contain a base panel and a flexible top layer separated by a small space. Pressing slightly on the top layer brings it into contact with the base layer, and the point of contact is collected and passed to the processor. Resistive technology is not susceptible to dust or water, but it can be damaged by sharp objects.

Capacitive technology contains a transparent panel coated with a thin layer of electrically conductive material. Because the human body is an electrical conductor, touching the screen produces a change in the electrical current. A special capacitive stylus or touchscreen gloves can also be used to operate this type of screen. Capacitive screens can interpret a single touch or more complex input such as handwriting.

Touchscreens based on resistive technology are less expensive to produce. They tend to be used for handheld GPS devices, point of sale terminals, and digital camera displays.

Capacitive technology is predominant on smartphone, tablet, and laptop touchscreens. That's why you can't operate your smartphone when wearing your woolen mittens or when your fingers are wet.

▶ **What is a GPU?** Display devices require graphics circuitry to generate and transport the signals for displaying an image on the screen. One type of graphics circuitry, referred to as **integrated graphics**, is built into a computer's system board. A second option, called **dedicated graphics**, is graphics circuitry mounted on a small circuit board called a graphics card (or video card) like the one in Figure 2-63.

Figure 2-63: Graphics card

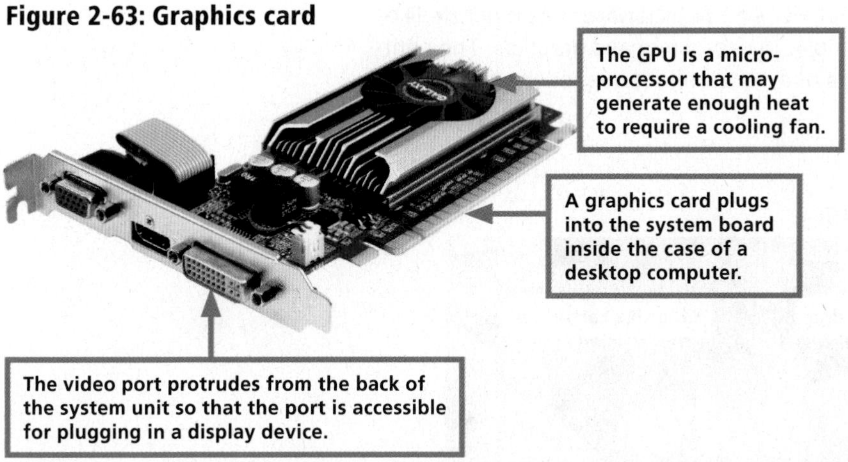

The GPU is a micro-processor that may generate enough heat to require a cooling fan.

A graphics card plugs into the system board inside the case of a desktop computer.

The video port protrudes from the back of the system unit so that the port is accessible for plugging in a display device.

A **graphics processing unit** (GPU) is an integrated circuit that contains processing circuitry and video memory. A GPU stores screen images as they are processed but before they are displayed. A fast GPU and lots of video memory are the keys to lightning-fast screen updating for fast action games, 3D modeling, and graphics-intensive desktop publishing (Figure 2-64).

Figure 2-64: Integrated vs. dedicated graphics

In a device with integrated graphics, image data is processed by the main CPU, then sent to the graphics circuits that stream the image to the display device.

In a device with dedicated graphics, image data is processed by the GPU, freeing the CPU for other tasks.

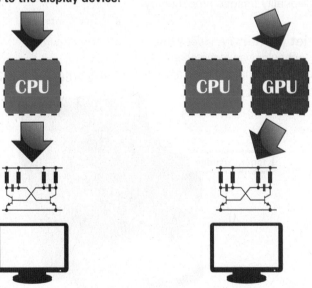

Printers

The importance of printers has declined as digital distribution becomes more prevalent and cloud-based print services become more popular. Yet a printer can come in handy for creating printed documents, handouts, posters, and photos. Today's best-selling multifunction printers use ink jet or laser technology and can also serve as scanners, copiers, and fax machines.

▶ **How does an ink jet printer work?** An **ink jet printer** has a nozzle-like print head that sprays ink onto paper to form characters and graphics. The print head in a color ink jet printer consists of a series of nozzles, each with its own ink cartridge (Figure 2-65).

Figure 2-65: Ink jet CMYK cartridges

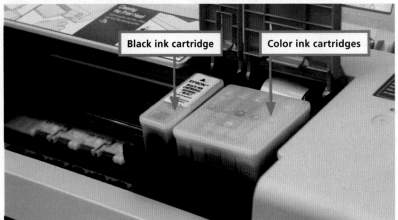

Black ink cartridge   Color ink cartridges

Most ink jet printers use CMYK color, which requires only cyan (blue), magenta (pink), yellow, and black inks to create a printout that appears to contain thousands of colors.

Ink jet printers outsell all other types of printers because they are inexpensive and produce both color and black-and-white printouts. They work well for most home and small business applications. Ink jet technology also powers many photo printers, which are optimized to print high-quality images produced by digital cameras and scanners.

▶ **How do laser printers compare to ink jet printers?** A **laser printer** like the one shown in Figure 2-66 uses the same technology as a photocopier to paint dots of light on a light-sensitive drum. Electrostatically charged ink is applied to the drum and then transferred to paper. A laser printer prints faster than an ink jet printer, but laser technology is more complex than ink jet technology, which accounts for the higher price of laser printers.

A basic laser printer produces only black-and-white printouts. Color laser printers are available, but they are somewhat more costly than basic black-and-white models. Laser printers are often the choice for business printers, particularly for applications that produce a high volume of printed material.

Figure 2-66: Laser printer

Toner cartridge

▶ **What about 3D printers?** The technology that deposits ink on paper is the foundation for 3D printers that deposit layers of plastic, resin, or metal to build a three-dimensional object. 3D printing is technically called **additive manufacturing**.

Consumers can use 3D printers to produce small toys, ornaments, and even simple electronic devices. These printers have been used to create wearable items, such as shoes, and replacement parts for household appliances.

An important industrial use for 3D printers is prototyping new products, such as automobile headlights, smartphone cases, firearms, and even full-scale bicycles.

Additive manufacturing is used to produce hearing aids and other medical devices that are custom fit or in other ways unique. Dental laboratories use 3D printing to produce crowns, bridges, and other dental appliances.

▶ **How do 3D printers work?** There are several additive manufacturing technologies, but most consumer-grade 3D printers use a technology called filament deposit modeling (FDM) that melts a coiled filament and deposits it in layers that harden and form an object (Figure 2-67).

Figure 2-67: 3D printing

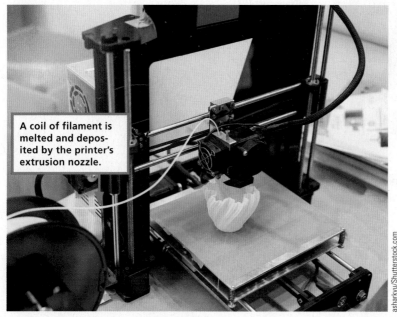

A coil of filament is melted and deposited by the printer's extrusion nozzle.

asharkyu/Shutterstock.com

▶ **What are the filaments made from?** Several types of filament are available. Polylactic acid (PLA) filament is versatile, and biodegradable because it is made from corn starch. Acrylonitrile butadiene styrene (ABS) filament is more durable and heat-resistant, making it suitable for printing objects that need to withstand some wear and tear. Polycarbonate (PC) filament is even sturdier and is used primarily for items that will be needed in high-impact situations. Filaments cost about $10 per pound.

▶ **What controls the printout?** A 3D printed object is based on a 3D model that is essentially a 3D vector graphic. The model can be created using graphics software or it can be derived from a 3D scan of a real object. Models are often stored in the STL file format. Several Web sites offer collections of STL files for 3D printing.

The Internet of Things

The utopian vision for the Internet of Things (IoT) is a busy hive of **smart sensors** that work behind the scenes to collect data and use it to improve just about everything. All types of "things" equipped with smart sensors can monitor our homes, cars, and workplaces. They can also monitor our habits and physical fitness and communicate with each other while doing so.

▶ **What are the basic features required for IoT devices?** IoT devices require some way to communicate with other sensors and devices. That communication is handled by network technology, which is covered in the next module.

IoT devices may include a microprocessor and memory if the device must process data, make decisions, or initiate an activity. A basic IoT circuit board contains one or more sensors, a power source, a transmitter, and an antenna (Figure 2-68).

Figure 2-68: Anatomy of an IoT device

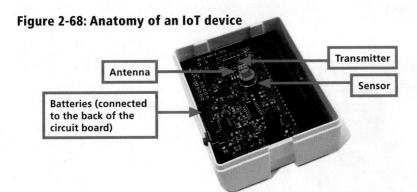

▶ **What types of smart sensors are available?** The most popular IoT sensors send alerts based on data they collect (Figure 2-69).

Figure 2-69: Sensors

Sound

"A window on your house just broke."
"Your dog is barking."
"The club is busy (noisy)."

Water

"Your basement floor seems to be wet."
"Your swimming pool needs more chlorine."
"Your plant needs water."

GPS

"Your dog is out of your yard."
"Your car is not in your driveway."
"You hiked a 2.5-mile circuit."

Contact

"Your front door isn't locked."
"Your doorbell just rang."
"Your child just got home from school."

Motion

"A person or animal approached your
  cabin last night."
"Your cat is at the litter box."

Accelerometer

"You've walked 10,000 steps today."
"The baggage handlers just dropped your
  suitcase."

Light

"It's 10 pm; your porch light isn't on."
"Do you want to dim the lights?"
"Your UV exposure has reached the limit."

Temperature

"Your oven is on."
"Your apartment is unusually hot."
"It's below zero; remote start your car."

▶ **What are the most popular sensors?** Many smartphones, VR headsets, and automobile internal navigation systems incorporate three sensors: an accelerometer, a gyroscope, and a magnetometer. Figure 2-70 illustrates an IMU (inertial measurement unit) that packages these sensors into a single unit.

Figure 2-70: IMU sensors

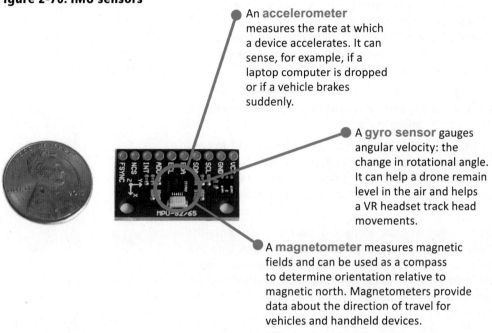

An **accelerometer** measures the rate at which a device accelerates. It can sense, for example, if a laptop computer is dropped or if a vehicle brakes suddenly.

A **gyro sensor** gauges angular velocity: the change in rotational angle. It can help a drone remain level in the air and helps a VR headset track head movements.

A **magnetometer** measures magnetic fields and can be used as a compass to determine orientation relative to magnetic north. Magnetometers provide data about the direction of travel for vehicles and handheld devices.

▶ **Where can I get IoT devices?** Smart sensors are available in electronics stores, hardware stores, and online. Sensors can be purchased individually or in packages. Popular home monitoring packages, such as Apple's HomeKit, include cameras, thermostats, light bulbs, water sensors, door locks, and air quality sensors.

▶ **Do sensors have security risks?** Sensors themselves are not generally a security risk, but the data they collect can be used for unauthorized purposes.

A smart thermostat can be used legitimately by a homeowner to remotely track and adjust the temperature of a house or apartment. With approval, data from the thermostat might even be collected by the local power company and used to gauge usage levels.

Because the thermostat communicates using a wireless network, the signal is subject to interception. An unauthorized person might monitor the signal to determine when a homeowner leaves the house (heat is turned down), arrives home (heat is turned up), or goes on vacation (heat remains down for several days).

When considering smart sensors, take care to understand where their data can be stored, who can access the data, and who can control the device. To maximize security, select sensors that store data locally or on a secure site. In addition, confirm that all data is encrypted before it is transmitted and stored, and ensure it can be controlled only by you.

QuickCheck

Which one of the following aspects of smart sensors on the IoT would be the least likely to pose a security risk?

a. Anonymized data

b. Data transmitted without encryption

c. Data stored on a Web site

d. Temperature sensors supplied by your electric service provider

Autonomous Vehicles

There are drones in the sky, Roombas crisscrossing the floor, and cars speeding down the highway in Supercruise mode. The technology that allows these vehicles to operate autonomously or semi-autonomously requires an array of sensors communicating with an onboard computer.

▶ **Exactly what is an autonomous vehicle?** Cars, trucks, trains, drones, planes, and machines that are usually piloted by humans become autonomous as the vehicles, rather than the humans, take over control of speed, braking, and steering. Fully autonomous vehicles operate without a person at the controls. Semi-autonomous vehicles provide assistance to a human operator.

Features available in semi-autonomous automobiles include adaptive cruise control, in-lane steering control, automatic parking, and collision avoidance systems, which take over some, but not all, driving tasks.

▶ **How do autonomous vehicles make control decisions?** In general, autonomous vehicles use sense-plan-act algorithms that emerged with the development of robotic systems. These algorithms may be classified as artificial intelligence (AI) because they make decisions and carry out activities without human intervention.

Sense-plan-act algorithms gather data, analyze it, and then carry out the required actions. Multiple sense-plan-act loops operate simultaneously. For example, in a self-driving car one loop may be sensing lane markings, while another loop is monitoring the distance to the vehicle ahead, and yet another loop is watching for suddenly appearing objects. Figure 2-71 provides additional details pertaining to sense-plan-act.

Try It!

Autonomous vehicles, such as self-driving cars, have limitations. Can you discover what type of pre-mapping is required before a Google car takes to the road?

Figure 2-71: Sense-plan-act algorithms for self-driving cars

Brake?

Reduce Speed?

Honk?

Change Lanes?

Sense. Sensors on the vehicle gather raw data about the nearby environment and the status of the vehicle itself. Environmental data comes from sensing nearby vehicles, people, animals, and other objects, as well as the roadway itself. Vehicle status data includes speed, direction, angle, and altitude.

Sensor data is delivered to an onboard computer, where software quickly processes the input to identify road hazards and navigational points.

Plan. Based on its interpretation of sensor data, the onboard computer applies a series of rules to determine the best course of action. For example, if radar data indicates that the vehicle ahead is slowing down, the computer must decide whether to adjust the speed or change lanes. The decision is based on rules such as "If the vehicle ahead slows down gradually, and the left lane is clear, then move to the left lane."

Act. After the computer determines a course of action, it sends signals to the vehicle's control systems. A signal to the car's steering system can initiate a lane change. Signals could also be sent to the car's throttle or braking system to achieve a change in speed.

▶ What kinds of sensors keep an autonomous vehicle on the road?

Lidar (light detection and radar) is a key input for the computer algorithms that steer an autonomous vehicle, but radar, sonar, infrared, GPS, cameras, and internal navigation systems also supply essential data (Figure 2-72).

Figure 2-72: Autonomous vehicle sensors

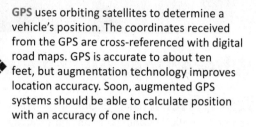

Lidar systems determine distance to obstacles using laser range finders. This device calculates the distance to objects based on the time it takes for the laser beam to reach an object and return. The range for this device is about 650 feet (200 meters), and 360-degree Lidar arrays can gather millions of data points per second to map objects in a 65-foot radius of the vehicle.

GPS uses orbiting satellites to determine a vehicle's position. The coordinates received from the GPS are cross-referenced with digital road maps. GPS is accurate to about ten feet, but augmentation technology improves location accuracy. Soon, augmented GPS systems should be able to calculate position with an accuracy of one inch.

Infrared sensors can be used to sense the heat signatures of pedestrians and animals, particularly when it is dark.

Radar adds more data about the nearby environment. Radar, which uses sound waves, does a good job of sensing metallic objects, but does not sense pedestrians and other non-metallic objects. It is primarily used to track nearby vehicles. Radar is currently used in adaptive cruise control systems to maintain a safe distance to the car in front.

DETOUR AHEAD

Internal navigation systems (INS) include gyroscopes and accelerometers that continuously calculate position, orientation, and speed of the vehicle. These systems can monitor position if GPS signals are temporarily blocked by the structures in a dense urban area.

Cameras collect images of road signs and traffic signals, which are analyzed by image recognition software.

QuickQuiz   Section E

1. The _____ bus carries data from an external device to RAM.

2. _____ is a slow wireless technology used to connect devices within a radius of about 30 feet.

3. A(n) _____ handles image data, freeing the CPU for other processing tasks. (Hint: Use the acronym.)

4. The two most common technologies used for touchscreen displays are resistive and _____.

5. The most commonly used general-purpose technology for connecting gadgets to laptop and desktop computers is a(n) _____ port. (Hint: Use the acronym.)

Issue: Where Does All the Ewaste Go?

In the West African nation of Ghana, smoldering piles of discarded computers and monitors ring a mucky river, polluted beyond recovery. Teenage boys play soccer in a toxic haze. When their break is over, they get back to work smashing monitors, ripping out the innards, and tossing the plastic cases onto a smoking pyre of oozing plastic.

In Guiyu, China, thousands of women huddle over primitive stoves "cooking" circuit boards to retrieve trace amounts of gold. Toxic fumes from the cooking process cloud the air; a toddler showing symptoms of lead poisoning plays listlessly with the carcasses of discarded mice and cell phones.

It is called ewaste, e-garbage, or technotrash—all unwanted and outdated computers, monitors, printers, cell phones, disk drives, disks, CDs, and DVDs. According to the Global E-waste Monitor, more than 50 million metric tons of ewaste are discarded worldwide every year. About 7 million tons of that total are discarded by U.S. consumers. More than 10 million tons are discarded in China.

Computers and other electronic gear contain toxic substances such as lead, cadmium, and mercury. When discarded equipment is buried in landfills, these substances can leach into groundwater and streams. When burned, electronic components can emit toxic dioxin.

Ewaste is a global problem. As countries struggle to deal with discarded electronic components, an alarming amount of ewaste is shipped to developing countries where villagers, working for pennies a day, are exposed to toxic chemicals as they attempt to reclaim resalable metals from discarded equipment. Throughout the emerging world, ugly ewaste dumps defile the landscape and have yet unknown health effects.

Where does all this ewaste originate? Every country generates ewaste, but the bulk of it comes from prosperous, technology-forward countries such as the United States, Great Britain, Germany, Japan, France, and China. Despite laws that ban ewaste transhipping, loopholes allow discarded but working electronics to be shipped as "donations." Tons of donations arrive every day in port cities, such as Hong Kong, where they follow a shadowy route to unregulated workshops and dump sites.

Some illegal ewaste originates in legitimate recycling centers, where consumers assume electronic components will be handled in environmentally friendly ways. Many recycling centers do not process materials on site. Instead, they ship the ewaste to third parties. Without careful monitoring, that ewaste can be diverted to offshore locations where it piles up, waiting to be disassembled by backstreet laborers ungoverned by environmental protection regulations.

Developed countries have strict environmental regulations designed to prevent toxic substances from polluting air, land, and water. Proper disposal is expensive, however. In countries with high labor costs and stringent environmental regulations, the value of compounds retrieved from ewaste does not cover the cost of extraction.

Some illegal ewaste originates in legitimate recycling centers...

The high cost of properly processing ewaste makes gray market options attractive. Ewaste can be handled more cost-effectively in emerging countries where environmental regulations are ignored, wages are pitiful, and workers are not covered by health and safety laws.

So, who is responsible for ewaste sweatshops and pollution? Is it consumers in developed countries who deposit unwanted gear at recycling stations that don't carry out the recycling process in-house, or is it the recycling firms that ship ewaste to third parties? Is it the firms that ship ewaste to emerging countries or the governments that can't close the loopholes on ewaste transhipping?

Perhaps the responsibility lies with emerging countries that are unable to control ewaste sweatshops and ignore the resulting environmental and human casualties.

Wherever the blame lies, consumers who are aware of the problem can become more responsible in the way they dispose of unwanted gear to keep it out of landfills at home and offshore.

Try It!

Delve into the ewaste issue and explore the steps you can take to minimize the number of electronic components that end up in landfills and toxic waste dumps.

1 Which countries are taking steps to properly manage ewaste? Select five countries of your choice, and then use resources such as the Global E-waste Statistics Partnership to discover how much ewaste is generated per capita, how much ewaste is formally collected, and whether the country has national legislation governing the disposal of ewaste.

2 An environmental advocacy group, Basel Action Network, secretly planted tracking devices in electronic items donated to recycling centers in the EU. The project is summarized in a report called "Holes in the Circular Economy: WEEE Leakage from Europe." Read the key findings of the report and watch the video on YouTube. What is the circular economy and how is it related to ewaste?

3 Many computers, mobile phones, and other electronic components pile up in landfills because their owners are unaware of potential environmental hazards and simply toss them in the garbage. Use Web sites such as Earth911.com, or search for *recycling computers* and add your city name, as in *recycling computers Chicago*. Where is the nearest drop-off location for old laptop computers? Would you be charged a fee, and if so, how much?

4 Before donating or discarding a computer, you should erase all the data it contains. Simply deleting files is not sufficient to prevent data from being recovered. Search online for information about deleting or "wiping" the data from a hard drive. What are three ways you can securely prevent access to the data on a hard disk?

5 You might wonder if your digital devices are environmentally friendly. The Global Electronics Council rates specific digital devices as bronze, silver, or gold. Connect to the EPEAT site (*www.epeat.net*), select a product category, and then fill in the fields to find the rating for at least one digital device. Hint: Choose Select All for the EPEAT Tier.

Source: epeat.net.

What Do You Think?

1. Have you ever thrown away an old computer or other electronic device?

2. Do you research products before purchasing them to find out if they are environmentally friendly throughout their life cycle?

3. Would it be fair for consumers to pay a recycling tax on electronic equipment that they purchase?

Information Tools: Finding the Right Stuff

You're looking for information. Where you start depends on how you plan to use the information. The sources you need for a class research paper often differ from information sources for personal use.

Information sources can be roughly divided into two categories: those that serve academic audiences and those that serve consumers.

> **Use these sources for class papers, theses, essays, and dissertations.**

Scholarly and Academic Sources

- ○ Written by experts
- ○ Intended for academic or professional readers
- ○ Peer-reviewed by other experts before publication
- ○ Contain original research, theoretical analysis, or best practices
- ○ Carefully documented by footnotes or endnotes
- ○ Published by academic publishers, professional associations, or university presses
- ○ Include academic books, academic journals, papers, conference proceedings, dissertations, textbooks, and monographs in printed or digital format

> **Find these sources using Google Scholar and academic databases/directories such as DOAJ.**

> **Use these sources for product information, troubleshooting, news, and topic overviews.**

Consumer-Level Sources

- ○ Written by reporters, bloggers, or practitioners
- ○ Intended for the general public
- ○ Possibly reviewed by an editor before publication
- ○ Sometimes open to public comment after publication 👍 Like
- ○ Printed or displayed in color with included photos
- ○ Often published in for-profit publications that include advertising
- ○ Include trade books, magazines, encyclopedias, press releases, trade journals, blogs, news sites, and online forums

> **Find these sources using Google, Google News, and commercial Web sites.**

Help!

Can't access what you need for a research project? Here are some common problems encountered by students, and solutions that help you find the resources you need for a paper that earns you an A.

Problem: Web search engines, such as Google, sometimes miss many of the articles most relevant for a college-level research project because articles are often locked behind paywalls or firewalls that don't allow search engine access. **Solution:** Go directly to a journal's Web site and search there.

Problem: Many scholarly journals display only abstracts to the general public; viewing the full text of articles requires a subscription or download fee.

Solution: Use your library's online database to locate articles that are included in the physical collection. You might have to go to the library to read the articles or ask for the full article from inter-library loan.

Problem: Access to academic search engines and databases, such as LexisNexis, requires subscriptions.

Solution: Your school might provide registered students with free access to journal databases if you log in from a computer on the school network or from within the library.

Try It!

Try It! Research about computers and technology relies on information from a broad base of sources. Let's explore these sources by comparing what they offer. Some searches will produce information suitable for academic projects, such as term papers, while other searches tend to produce information suitable for personal use, such as how to troubleshoot your smart thermostat.

To record the results of this comparison, write down (or screen capture) one example that you get from each source, and then describe an academic project or personal use for which that information would be suitable. As an example, suppose that you search for *Internet of Things or IoT* using Google Scholar and one of the results is:

Internet of Things: Evolution and technologies from a security perspective
R Ande, B Adebisi, M Hammoudeh, J Saleem - Sustainable Cities and ..., 2020 - Elsevier
In recent years, IoT has developed into many areas of life, including smart homes, smart cities, agriculture, offices, and workplaces. Everyday physical items such as lights, locks, and industrial machineries can now be part of the IoT ecosystem. IoT has redefined the. ...
Cited by 27 - Related articles - All 5 versions

This information is academic and could be a suitable source for a term paper about Internet of Things security in a computer science course. Okay, now see what you can do with the following sources.

1. Check Wikipedia for general information about IoT.

2. Search for a book about IoT at Amazon Books.

3. Search for conference proceedings about IoT at the ACM Digital Library.

4. Search an open access database such as DOAJ (see sidebar) for a recent paper about the Internet of Things.

5. Search an academic database (see sidebar) for an abstract about the Internet of Things.

6. Search Science.gov for a full text article about the Internet of Things.

7. Search an online computer magazine, such as *Wired*, for a recent article about IoT.

8. Use a search engine, such as Google or Bing, to locate a recent press release about IoT.

9. Search Amazon Electronics for IoT sensors and customer reviews.

10. Search a technology news site (see sidebar) for the latest industry news about the Internet of Things.

Technology in Context: Military

In *Engines of the Mind,* Joel Shurkin writes, "If necessity is the mother of invention, then war can be said to be its grandmother." The military, an early pioneer in computer and communication technologies, continues to be the driving force behind technologies that have revolutionized everyday life.

During World War II, the U.S. military initiated a classified research program called Project PX to develop an electronic device to calculate artillery firing tables; by hand, each table required weeks of grueling calculations.

Project PX produced ENIAC (Electronic Numerical Integrator And Computer), one of the first general-purpose electronic computers. When ENIAC was completed in 1946, the war was over, but ENIAC's versatile architecture could be used for other calculations, such as designing hydrogen bombs, predicting weather, and engineering wind tunnels. ENIAC's technology evolved into the computers used today.

After Project PX, the military continued to support computer research. Like most large corporations, the military used mainframe computers to maintain personnel, inventory, supply, and facilities records. This data was distributed to terminals at other locations through rudimentary networks.

Because all data communication flowed through the mainframe, a single point of failure for the entire system was a possible risk. A malfunction or an enemy "hit" could disrupt command and control, sending the military into chaos. Therefore, the armed forces created the Advanced Research Projects Agency (ARPA) to design a distributed communications system that could continue operating without a centralized computer.

The result was ARPANET, which paved the way for the data communications system we know today as the Internet. ARPANET was activated in 1967, but the .mil domain that designates U.S. military Web sites was not implemented until 1984.

The U.S. Department of Defense (DoD) currently maintains several data communications networks, including SIPRNet, a classified (secret-level) network, and NIPRNet, which provides unclassified services. The DoD's public Web site provides official information about defense policies, organizations, budgets, and operations.

Computers and communications technology have also become an integral part of high-tech flight operations. U.S. Apache helicopters, for example, are equipped with computer-based Target Acquisition Designation Sights, laser range finder/designators, and Pilot Night Vision Sensors.

Networks are also crucial for combat operations, and a new generation of communication tools is evolving for soldiers deployed to battlefields. Networked communication devices offer immediate situational awareness by providing critical information such as orders, imagery, graphics, and maps. The U.S. Army's Nett Warrior program is essentially a secure smartphone carried by a soldier that displays the locations of friendly troops and facilitates text messaging when spoken communication is not possible.

An enhancement to the Nett Warrior handheld device is a head-mounted Integrated Visual Augmentation System (IVAS) based on Microsoft's HoloLens technology. Like a virtual/augmented reality headset, IVAS goggles and a head-mounted camera provide infrared and night-vision displays of surrounding territory as well as GPS mapping with overlays of routes and troop locations.

IVAS goggles can display information on how to repair combat vehicles and how to apply first aid to injured personnel. IVAS also acts as a weapons site, enabling soldiers to literally "shoot from the hip" instead of targeting through the site of a shoulder-mounted weapon.

IVAS goggles are used for combat training as well as on the battlefield. Using a combination of virtual and augmented reality, the goggles display scenarios similar to those in first-person shooter games, placing virtual enemy fighters around corners in settings based on real-world locations. IVAS training is a major step beyond previous arcade-style simulations. Intertwined evolution of civilian computer games and military training simulations is likely to continue.

"Live" military training is dangerous—weapons are deadly and equipment costs millions of dollars. With computer-generated simulations, however, troops can train in a true-to-life environment without physical harm or equipment damage.

Flying an F-16 fighter, for example, costs thousands of dollars an hour, but flying an F-16 simulator costs only a few hundred dollars per hour. The military uses simulators to teach Air Force pilots to fly fighter jets, Navy submarine officers to navigate in harbors, and Marine infantry squads to handle urban combat.

Photo Courtesy of U.S. Army

The U.S. Navy also seeks help from civilian developers—even college students. In the annual International RoboBoat competition, a $20,000 prize is awarded for the best-designed ships that can operate without crews in harsh environments or dangerous situations.

The Internet of Things has not escaped notice by the military. The Internet of Military Things (IoMT) is a concept that integrates environmental sensors, robots, drones, vehicles, munitions, armor, and biosensors to collect data from surrounding terrain, control equipment, and monitor soldiers' biometrics.

The next time you see a small drone swooping over a park or hovering for a bird's-eye view of a real estate listing, you can trace the technology to military research. Military optionally manned vehicles (OMVs) are used for air and underwater reconnaissance—situations that are often dangerous for on-platform troops.

Today, a growing cadre of computer and communications specialists is needed to create and maintain increasingly complex military systems such as the Defense Department's Distributed Common Ground System (DCGS) for sharing surveillance imagery and intelligence.

In the past, armies depended primarily on their infantry divisions, but today's high-tech armies also depend on database designers, computer programmers, and network specialists. Even previously low-tech military jobs, such as mechanics and dietitians, require some computer expertise. Happily, new recruits are finding military computer systems easier to learn based on their knowledge of civilian technologies, such as the Internet and computer games.

Although most citizens recognize that an adequate national defense is necessary, the cost of defense-related equipment, personnel, and cutting-edge research remains controversial. In a 1961 speech, President Dwight Eisenhower warned, "We must guard against the acquisition of unwarranted influence, whether sought or unsought, by the military-industrial complex."

Some socially motivated citizens and pacifists tried to withhold tax dollars from the military-industrial complex that Eisenhower cautioned against. In retrospect, however, military funding contributed to many technologies we depend on today.

For example, detractors tried to convince the government that Project PX was doomed to failure; but without ENIAC research, computers might not exist today. Skeptics saw no future for the fruits of ARPANET research; but it led to the Internet, which has changed our lives significantly.

Critical Thinking

For many years, personal computers were desktop models designed around four main components: system unit, monitor, keyboard, and mouse. Today, more than half the devices we use are slate form factors without physical keyboards. Some industry analysts speculate that the move away from physical keyboards signals a fundamental change in the use of digital devices. Whereas computers were once seen as tools for producing, they are now becoming tools for consuming. How significant is a physical keyboard to the creative and productive use of digital devices? What kinds of evidence would help to support your opinion?

Group Project

For this project, work in groups of three or four. The group should select a trending digital device, such as a fitness wristband, a smartwatch, a home security system, or a just-released smartphone. If a member of your group owns the device, that's a plus. Create promotional materials for a tradeshow booth featuring your device. You might include a product photo, a list of specifications, and a short instruction manual. If time permits, your instructor might ask your group to present your sales pitch or a demonstration to the rest of the class.

Cyberclassroom

Work in pairs to set up a cloud-based storage location where you can share files. Experiment with the following scenarios to find out what happens:

1) Two people access the same file at approximately the same time; neither person changes the file contents.

2) While one person is modifying a file, another person tries to access the file but does not try to modify it.

3) While one person is modifying a file, a second person attempts to access it and change it.

Multimedia Project

Imagine that you are a high school teacher and you have to design materials to teach a unit on how microprocessors work. To kick off the unit, create a 30- to 60-second video showing the control unit, registers, and ALU and how an instruction like ADD 9 + 2 would be processed. Be creative and make it interesting!

Resume Builder

Use the Web and other resources to learn about the digital devices and other technologies used in your career field. Format the information you find in a style similar to the Technology in Context section of each module in this textbook. Be sure to select two photos to accompany your narrative and include a list of relevant citations for your sources.

Globalization

Digital device ownership is growing worldwide and providing access to productivity tools and a global communications infrastructure. For this project, look for statistics and graphs showing the increase in device ownership around the world over time. How does it compare to telephone, television, and radio ownership? Are any aspects of this data unexpected or surprising? Gather your graphs and analysis into a two- to three-page executive summary.

Key Terms

2-in-1 97
accelerometer 143
access time 120
additive manufacturing 141
ALU 108
app 86
application software 86
ARM 105
backup 125
Bluetooth 134
boot loader 114
capacitive technology 138
capacitors 113
card reader 122
CDs 121
central processing unit 85
Chromebook 96
CISC 112
cloud storage 123
compatible 101
computer 85
computer program 86
control unit 108
CPU cache 112
data bus 131
data transfer rate 120
dedicated graphics 139
desktop computer 96
development tools 86
device driver 135
discharge rate 93
disk image 127
dot pitch 137
DVDs 121
dynamic RAM 113
expansion ports 131
file synchronization 126
form factor 89
gigahertz 110
graphics processing unit 139
gyro sensor 143

hard disk drive 119
hard disk platter 119
head crash 120
hot-plugging 133
ink jet printer 140
input 85
instruction cycle 108
instruction pointer 109
instruction set 107
integrated circuit 87
integrated graphics 139
laptop computer 96
laser printer 140
LCD 136
lidar 145
lithium ion 92
local storage 117
machine language 107
magnetic storage 119
magnetometer 143
mainframe 95
memory 85
memory card 122
microcontrollers 98
microprocessor 85
microprocessor clock 110
multi-core processor 110
non-volatile 122
oleophobic 92
operating system 86
optical storage 121
output 85
parallel processing 111
PDA 97
peripheral device 130
personal computer 96
pipeline processing 111
portable computer 96
process data 85
programming language 107
RAM 113

read-only 121
read-write head 119
recordable 121
recovery drive 126
registers 108
remote storage 123
resistive technology 138
response rate 136
rewritable 121
RISC 112
ROM 114
SATA 120
screen resolution 137
semiconductors 87
sense-plan-act algorithms 144
serial processing 111
server 95
slate tablet 97
smart sensors 142
smartphones 97
software 86
solid state drive 123
solid state storage 122
storage 85
stored program 86
supercomputer 95
system board 88
system software 86
system unit 89
tablet computer 97
touchscreen 138
USB flash drive 123
USB hub 133
virtual keyboard 138
virtual memory 114
volatile 113
wearable computers 98
word size 112
x86 105

Interactive Summary

Section A: A computer is a multipurpose device that accepts input, processes data, stores data, and produces output, all according to a series of stored [_____] . The [_____] processing unit of most modern computers is a(n) [_____] . The instructions that tell a computer how to carry out a task are referred to as computer [_____] , which are distributed as software. Computers run three main types of software: [_____] software, system software, and development tools. An example of system software is a computer [_____] system, which is essentially the primary controller for all the activities that a digital device performs. Digital devices are constructed using tiny electronic components that represent data bits as electrical signals. The system unit houses the system board, which contains several [_____] circuits made from semiconducting materials. Computers come in three popular form factors: component, [_____] , and slate. Many of today's digital devices operate on battery power supplied by [_____] ion batteries. Battery life and lifespan can be extended by following good battery management practices.

Section B: Today, there are many computer categories. A(n) [_____] is the category for the world's fastest computers. [_____] computers are large, expensive devices capable of simultaneously processing data for thousands of users. Computers used by Google and Web service providers are classified as [_____] . Personal computers come in several varieties. A(n) [_____] computer fits on a desk, runs on power from an electrical wall outlet, and can be housed in a horizontal case or vertical case. Three categories of portable computers include tablets, smartphones, and clamshell style [_____] computers. Selecting a digital device requires consumers to select a platform based on form factor and operating system. macOS is the operating system that runs on Apple laptops and [_____] computers. The operating system for iPhones is [_____] . The [_____] operating system from Microsoft runs on laptop and desktop PCs. The open source community produces Linux for desktops and servers. This family of operating systems also includes Chrome OS, and [_____] , which is popular for tablets and smartphones.

Section C: The microprocessor is a(n) [_____] circuit, which is designed to process data based on a set of instructions. Desktop computers running Windows contain a microprocessor based on the [_____] standard. Most tablets and smartphones contain processors based on [_____] technology. A microprocessor's circuitry is designed to perform a limited number of tasks contained in its [_____] set. During processing, an instruction is loaded into the processor's [_____] unit. Data is loaded into registers in the processor's [_____] where arithmetic and logic operations are performed. Microprocessor performance can be measured by its [_____] speed. Other factors affecting overall processing performance include word size, cache size, and instruction set complexity. Most digital devices contain only one microprocessor chip, but today's multi-[_____] processors contain circuitry that supports parallel processing. Computers contain various kinds of memory.

Random [ ] memory is a special holding area for data, program instructions, and the [ ] system. It stores data on a temporary basis until the processor makes a data request. RAM is different from disk storage because it is [ ], which means that it can hold data only when the computer power is turned on. Computers also contain read- [ ] memory, which is a type of non-volatile memory that provides a set of "hard-wired" instructions, called the [ ] loader, that a computer uses to boot up.

Section D:

Today's digital devices use a variety of storage technologies. [ ] storage technologies, such as hard disks, store data as particles oriented north or south. A hard disk drive provides multiple [ ] for data storage that are sealed inside the drive case to prevent airborne contaminants from interfering with the read-write heads. Hard disks are less durable than many other types of storage, so it is important to make a copy of the data they contain. [ ] storage technologies store data as a series of dark spots and light spots on the surface of CDs and DVDs. Storage technologies, such as CD- [ ], are used for distributing software and music, but you cannot alter the disc's contents. [ ] technology allows you to write data on a CD or DVD, but you cannot delete or change that data. Rerecordable or [ ] technology allows you to write and erase data on a CD or DVD. [ ] state storage technologies, such as USB flash drives, store data by activating electrons in a microscopic grid of circuitry. A backup is a copy of one or more files that have been made in case the original files become damaged. A good backup plan allows you to restore a device's operating system, software, data files, settings, accounts, and profiles in case of a massive hardware failure or virus infection. Personal computer backups are typically recorded on [ ] hard drives, USB flash drives, network servers, and online storage services. An easier way to get a backup of important data files is to use the [ ] command to make duplicates and store them on a USB drive. Backup utilities such as File History and Time Machine use a technique called file [ ] to make sure that files on two devices are the same. A disk [ ] is a bit-for-bit copy of the data from all sectors of a hard disk.

Section E:

Inside a digital device, a data [ ] connects the processor to RAM, and connects RAM to a series of expansion [ ]. There are three technologies commonly used for general-purpose ports: Thunderbolt, Lightning, and [ ]. For video devices, the most common ports are VGA, DVI, [ ], and Mini DisplayPort. Peripherals can be inserted or removed while the host device is on, but storage devices should not be removed without notification. To connect additional peripherals when all USB ports are full, it is possible to use a USB [ ]. Some peripherals can be connected wirelessly using [ ] technology. The software that helps a peripheral device establish communication with its host device is called a device [ ]. Most devices include a(n) [ ] crystal display. Image quality for a display device is a factor of screen size, response rate, dot [ ], and resolution. Touchscreens use either [ ] or capacitive technology to process gestures. Display devices receive images from graphics circuitry. A(n) [ ] and special video memory can enhance graphics processing and free the main processor for other tasks. For printed output, most personal computer owners select [ ] jet printers, though [ ] printers are a popular option when low operating costs at high volume are important. The Internet of [ ] is a technology that links smart sensors. Some of these sensors can also be found in smartphones and autonomous vehicles. A(n) [ ] can sense if a laptop computer is dropped or if a car brakes suddenly. A(n) [ ] sensor measures angular velocity. A(n) [ ] can be used as a compass for navigation and map displays. Autonomous vehicles use sensor data as input to sense-plan- [ ] algorithms processed on an onboard computer.

Interactive Situation Questions

1. Suppose you're reading a computer magazine and you come across the ad pictured to the right. By looking at the specs, you can tell that the microprocessor was manufactured by which company? [＿＿＿＿＿＿]

2. The capacity of the hard disk drive in the ad is [＿＿＿＿＿＿] GB and the memory capacity is [＿＿＿＿＿＿] GB.

3. Your friends are chatting about a low-cost laptop that "runs Google." You figure that they are actually talking about a device called a(n) [＿＿＿＿＿＿] that runs Google's Chrome OS as its operating system.

4. Looking over the specs for a new tablet device, would you expect it to have a RISC or CISC processor? [＿＿＿＿＿]

5. At the beginning of an update for your smartphone, you notice a warning: "Make sure your device is connected to a wall outlet and do not turn the device off until the update is complete." You suspect that the update is going to [＿＿＿＿＿＿] the ROM boot loader to fix a security vulnerability.

6. You've decided to archive your vast photo collection on DVDs. You want the longest possible lifespan. When you go to purchase blank DVDs, you see that some are marked DVD-R, whereas others are DVD-RW. Which should you choose? [＿＿＿＿＿＿]

7. You're working on a group project. Each person has to access a dataset for creating several graphs. You'll be compiling the graphs into a final report. Rather than emailing graphs back and forth, you suggest using Dropbox, a(n) [＿＿＿＿＿＿] storage service where members of the group can access a shared folder.

Sup-R Game Desktop Model EEXL

- Intel® Core™ i7
- 6 GB Tri-Channel DDR4
- 500 GB SATA (7200 rpm)
- 21.5" HD widescreen monitor
- NVIDIA® GeForce™
- Creative Sound Blaster® X-Fi Titanium
- Altec Lansing speakers
- Gigabit Ethernet port
- 3-year limited warranty
- Windows 11

$549

8. After purchasing a new Windows computer, your first step is to get all your backup tools in order, beginning with a(n) [＿＿＿＿＿＿] drive that you can use to boot your computer in case of a hard drive failure.

9. One of the ports on your laptop is rectangular and the inside of it is blue. It is a(n) [＿＿＿＿＿＿] port.

10. You need an external keyboard for your Android device, and thankfully you can add a wireless one because it has [＿＿＿＿＿＿] capability.

11. Suppose that you volunteer to produce a large quantity of black-and-white leaflets for a charity organization. It is fortunate that you have access to a(n) [＿＿＿＿＿＿] printer with low operating costs.

Lab: What's Going on in There?

The microprocessor clock is ticking. Data bits are flying in and out of RAM and zooming over the data bus to a storage device. All that seems invisible, but wait! You can get an idea of what's going on inside the system unit. Who needs to know? You might. If you suspect your computer has a virus. If you think your computer might have been compromised by a botnet. If your computer seems sluggish. Windows and macOS include monitoring utilities that provide all kinds of information about your computer's status.

Requirements:

For this lab, you'll need a desktop or laptop computer running either Windows or macOS. The instructions are generalized; they provide helpful guidelines, but not specific steps. As you complete the assignment, answer each question. Submit your answers in the format specified by your instructor.

Assignment:

1 Open your computer's monitoring utility.

On a Mac, select the Applications folder from the dock. Select the Utilities folder, then select Activity Monitor. Use the View menu to select All Processes.

On a PC with Windows, launch Task Manager. It might be necessary to select More Details.

2 Examine your computer's CPU usage.

On a Mac, select the CPU button; on Windows, select the Performance tab.

CPU utilization is expressed as a percentage of total processing capability. If CPU utilization exceeds 10% when you are not using software, it might signal a security breach. Temporary spikes are normal; when you are playing 3D games or using compute-intensive software, the usage could remain above 70%.

What is the current CPU utilization on your device?

3 Check processes.

On a Mac, processes are listed on the CPU tab; on Windows, select the Processes tab.

A process corresponds to a program. Any programs that are currently running put a load on the CPU.

What is the process with the highest CPU usage? Do you recognize the program associated with this process? If not, look it up online.

4 Check for malware.

Some processes are launched by the operating system rather than application software. If you don't recognize a process, you can find out if it is legitimate by checking online.

Select a process with an unusual name and search for it online. What is its name, and what does it do?

5 Check memory.

On a Mac, select the Memory tab; on Windows, remain on the Processes tab.

As you know, RAM holds the operating system, programs, and data, but the amount of stuff that's actually in RAM is pretty surprising.

Find the listing for Kernel_task (Mac) or System (Windows). That process is part of the operating system. How much memory is it using?

What is the name of the software application that uses the most memory?

6 Check storage.

On a Mac, choose the Disk tab; on Windows, remain on the Processes tab.

Programs send data to storage even when you are not in the process of manually saving files. Some programs create autorecovery files as temporary backups, and Web pages write cookies.

Find a process that is writing data to disk even when you are not actively using it. What is the name of that process and what is its purpose?

3 Networks

Module Contents

Networks let us reach out to the world. But they also let the world into our personal space. In this module you'll explore how to create and use networks that don't expose your darkest secrets.

 Try It! Apply what you learn.

- Choose when to use wired connections and when to use wireless connections.
- Check the signal strength of a wireless connection.
- Find your router's IP address.
- Find the private IP address for your device.
- Differentiate between IPv4 and IPv6 addresses.
- Obtain a domain name.
- Find the owners of domain names and IP addresses.
- Find the address of your DNS server and change it if necessary.
- Check the speed of your Internet connection and compare it to the speed advertised by your ISP.
- Determine the latency, jitter, and packet loss on your Internet connection and gauge whether it affects the quality of streaming services.
- Use Traceroute to troubleshoot a slow Internet connection.
- Select an Internet service provider.
- Reduce your security risks when connecting to Wi-Fi hotspots.
- Construct a local area network that allows devices to share files and an Internet connection.
- Configure and secure a router for a local area network.
- Piece together a small IoT network for home monitoring.
- Access files from other devices on a LAN.
- Activate file sharing and use permissions to limit how your files can be used.
- Obtain files from Internet-based services, such as FTP, Dropbox, and BitTorrent.

● **Pre-Check** Gauge your level of expertise. The answers are in the text.

What type of network topology does the diagram above illustrate?

_____

Before speeding over the Internet, files are divided into:

_____

The major problem with GEO satellite Internet access is excessive:

_____.

List five types of fixed Internet access:

_____

_____

_____

_____

_____

Which is more secure:

WEP or WPA

LTE

Broadband or narrowband?

www.course.com

What's the top-level domain?

TCP **WPA2**
IP   **WEP**

Which one is the Internet protocol stack?

To protect the files on your computer when connecting to a Wi-Fi hotspot, what should you turn off?

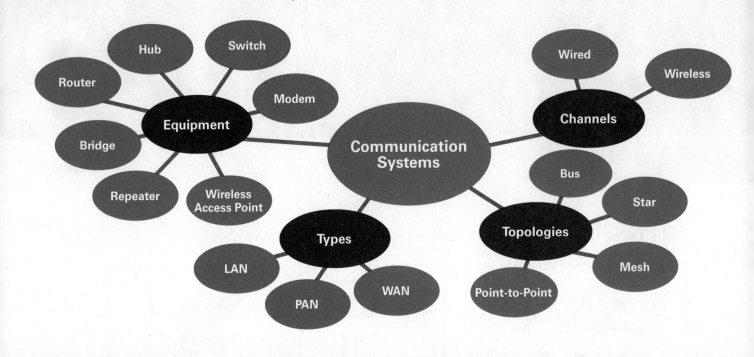

Objectives

▶ Replicate Shannon's diagram of a general communication system, including all nine labels.

▶ Give two examples of PANs, LANs, and WANs.

▶ List four examples of wired channels used for networks.

▶ State the two wireless channels most commonly used for communication networks.

▶ List two advantages and four disadvantages of wireless channels.

▶ State what differentiates broadband from narrowband.

▶ Draw a diagram showing how data from a smart thermostat could travel over several networks with different topologies.

▶ Compare and contrast mesh and star topologies based on dependability, security, capacity, expandability, control, and monitoring.

▶ List two examples of DTEs and two examples of DCEs.

▶ Explain the difference between a modem and a router.

▶ List five tasks that are handled by communication protocols.

Networks are everywhere. They are an indispensable part of our lives. When there are outages, things go haywire. When there are slowdowns, we get frustrated. What do you need to know about networks? The building blocks in Section A will get you started.

Terminology

communication network	RF signals	point-to-point topology	router
PAN	transceiver	star topology	modem
LAN	microwaves	mesh topology	communication protocol
WAN	bandwidth	bus topology	handshaking
communication channel	broadband	node	protocol stack
wired channels	narrowband	DTE	error correction
wireless channels	topology	DCE	

Communication Systems

You use many networks for communication, research, and entertainment. Some networks are large and some are small. The largest networks offer little control to consumers. Smaller networks that you set up can be completely under your control, but they are also your responsibility. Networks can be classified in many ways; as a network user, you'll want to keep in mind the idea of control and how it affects your privacy and security.

❱ **What is a network?** A network links things together. A **communication network** (or communication system) links together devices so that data and information can be shared among them.

In 1948, Claude Shannon, an engineer at Bell Labs, published an article describing a communication system model applicable to networks of all types. His diagram illustrates the essence of a network, so it is a good place to begin this module. Shannon's model (Figure 3-1) is relatively easy to understand.

QuickCheck

In Shannon's model, signals traveling along a communication channel can be disrupted by _____.

a. a source

b. a transmitter

c. a receiver

d. noise

3

Figure 3-1: Components of a basic communication system

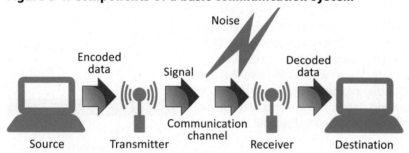

❱ **How are computer networks classified?** Networks can be classified according to their size and geographic scope, as shown in Figure 3-2.

Figure 3-2: Network classifications

PAN (personal area network)	LAN (local area network)	WAN (wide area network)
PANs connect smart devices or consumer electronics within a range of about 30 feet (10 meters) and usually without the use of wires or cables. The reference to *personal* indicates that the network serves a single individual, rather than multiple users. A PAN could be used to sync data from a handheld device to a desktop computer, ship data wirelessly to a printer, or transmit data from a smartphone to a wireless headset.	LANs are data communication networks that connect personal computers within a very limited geographical area—usually a single building. School computer labs and home networks are examples of LANs. Wi-Fi networks that you can access in airports, coffee shops, and other public places are LANs. The in-house networks operated by most businesses are also LANs.	WANs cover a large geographical area and usually consist of several smaller networks, which might use different computer platforms and network technologies. The Internet is the world's largest WAN. Other public WANs include telephone systems, cable television systems, and satellite-based communication systems.

▶ **Why is geographic scope important?** Localized networks normally include a small number of computers, which can be connected using basic equipment. As the area of network coverage expands, the number of devices grows, specialized devices are sometimes required to boost signals, and the diversity of devices requires sophisticated management tools and strategies.

▶ **What about the Internet of Things?** The Internet of Things (IoT) is an evolving concept that may be difficult to classify as a PAN, LAN, or WAN. The IoT has the potential to become a global collection of smart devices transmitting to other devices over the Internet. Today, smart devices are more often grouped into small local pods that report to a centralized device, which in turn exchanges data with local networks and the Internet.

Communication Channels

Do you suppose it is easier for a snooper to secretly access your computer when your device is connected to a Wi-Fi hotspot or cabled to a LAN? Some connections are more secure and more dependable than others, so it pays to understand the ins and outs of communication channels.

▶ **What is a communication channel?** A **communication channel** is the medium used to transport information from one network device to another. Data transmitted over a communication channel usually takes the form of an electromagnetic signal—waves of light, electricity, or sound. These waves can travel through the air or through cables, so channels are divided into two general classifications: wired and wireless. **Wired channels** transport data through wires and cables. **Wireless channels** transport data from one device to another without the use of cables or wires.

▶ **What are the options for wired channels?** Wired channels include twisted pair wires used for telephone landlines, coaxial cables used for cable television networks, Category 6 cables used for LANs, and fiber-optic cables used for high-capacity trunk lines that provide main routes for telephone, cable, and Internet communications (Figure 3-3).

Figure 3-3: Network cables

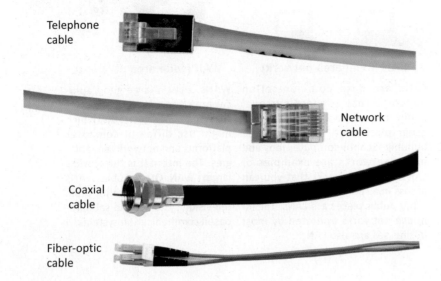

Telephone cable

Network cable

Coaxial cable

Fiber-optic cable

▶ **What are the advantages of wired channels?** Before wireless technologies became available, local area networks were exclusively wired. Today, wired connections are used less frequently for home, school, and business networks. They remain the network technology of choice, however, for segments of the Internet and local area networks that require fast and secure connectivity.

When you set up a wired connection, you don't have to worry about hackers intercepting your data from the sidewalk outside your house, or your neighbor stumbling across personal files when your wireless signal reaches past your property line. Yes, there are ways to tap into a wired network, but they require physical access to the cable or fairly sophisticated snooping equipment. The advantages of wired channels are summarized in Figure 3-4.

Figure 3-4: Advantages of wired channels

Cables can be shielded against interference and encased in protective casings for installations that are outdoors and underground.

Wired connections are dependable. Their carrying capacity and speed are not affected by airborne interference from rain, snow, or electrical devices.

Wired connections are more secure than their wireless counterparts because a device can join a wired network only if it is physically connected by a cable.

▶ **What are the disadvantages of wired connections?** The cables that offer speed and security for a wired connection are also the main weakness of this type of connection. The disadvantages of wired channels include cost, lack of mobility, and installation hassles. Figure 3-5 provides more details.

Figure 3-5: Disadvantages of wired channels

In WANs, wired installation can be costly because cables have to be suspended from poles or buried underground. They can be damaged by weather events and digging in the wrong place. Repairs to underground cables require heavy equipment to locate, access, and fix the break.

LAN devices connected by cables have limited mobility. Desktop computers tend to be better candidates for wired connections, whereas laptops, tablets, and handheld devices can retain their mobility when they are not tethered to a cable.

Cables are unsightly, tend to get tangled, and collect dust. Running cables through ceilings, walls, and floors can be challenging. Cables can also carry electrical surges that have the potential to damage network equipment.

▶ What are the options for wireless channels? The most widespread wireless channels for communication networks are radio signals and microwaves.

▶ How do radio signals transport data? Most wireless channels transport data as **RF signals**, commonly called radio waves. RF channels are typically used for Bluetooth connections and Wi-Fi networks. It is also the technology used to carry voice and data between a smartphone and a cell tower. RF signals are sent and received by a **transceiver** (a combination of a transmitter and a receiver) that is equipped with an antenna (Figure 3-6).

Terminology

RF stands for radio frequency.

Figure 3-6: Transceiver-equipped devices

Devices used with wireless connections are equipped with transceivers that include a transmitter for sending data and a receiver for collecting data. A transceiver has an antenna, which may be visible or may be housed out of sight within a device's system unit.

Terminology

Although we use the term *wireless connection*, there is no physical connection between wireless devices in a network. Their connection is conceptual in the sense that data can travel between "connected" devices.

▶ How do microwaves transport data? **Microwaves** (the waves themselves, not your oven!) provide another option for transporting data wirelessly. Like radio waves, microwaves are electromagnetic signals, but they behave differently. Microwaves can be aimed in a single direction and have more carrying capacity than radio waves. However, microwaves cannot penetrate metal objects and work best for line-of-sight transmission when a clear path exists between the transmitter and receiver.

Microwave installations usually provide data transport for large corporate networks. They are also used to transmit signals between towers in cellular and wide area wireless installations.

▶ What are the advantages and disadvantages of wireless? The main advantage of wireless connections is mobility. Wireless devices are not tethered to network cables, so battery-operated laptops, tablets, and smartphones can be easily moved from room to room, or even outdoors. With wireless networks, there are no unsightly cables, and power spikes are much less likely to run through cables to damage equipment. The main disadvantages of wireless channels are speed, range, security, and licensing.

▶ Why is wireless slower than wired? Wireless signals are susceptible to interference from devices such as microwave ovens, cordless telephones, and baby monitors. When interference affects a wireless signal, data must be retransmitted, and that takes extra time.

▶ What limits the range of a wireless connection? The range of a wireless signal can be limited by the type of signal, the transmitter strength, and the physical environment. Just as radio stations fade as you move away from their broadcasting towers, data signals fade as the distance between network devices increases. Signal range can also be limited by thick walls, floors, or ceilings.

QuickCheck

What type of wireless channels are most typically used for networks in homes and coffee shops?

a. RF

b. Coax

c. Microwave

d. WiMAX

As signal strength decreases, so can speed. A weak signal usually means slow data transfers. You can get a rough idea of signal strength for your desktop, laptop, tablet, or smartphone by checking the network signal strength meter (Figure 3-7).

Figure 3-7: Wireless network signal strength meter

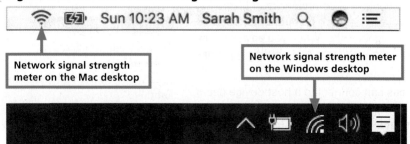

Network signal strength meter on the Mac desktop

Network signal strength meter on the Windows desktop

▶ **What's the problem with wireless security?** Wireless signals float through the air and penetrate walls. The signals that carry your wireless data can be accessed from outside your premises. Someone outside of your house, for example, could secretly join your network, access files, and piggyback on your Internet connection. To make wireless data useless to intruders, it should be encrypted. Later in this module, you'll learn how to use encryption to secure data sent over wireless connections.

▶ **How does licensing affect wireless connections?** Government agencies, such as the Federal Communications Commission (FCC), regulate signals that are sent through the air. To broadcast at most frequencies, including those used by radio and television stations, a license is required.

Wireless connections use unlicensed frequencies that are available for public use. These frequencies include 2.4 GHz and parts of the 5 GHz and 6 GHz spectrums. 2.4 GHz signals are subject to more interference from other devices, but have a wider range than 5 GHz or 6 GHz signals.

▶ **What's bandwidth?** Network channels must move data and move it quickly. Bandwidth is the transmission capacity of a communication channel. Just as a four-lane freeway can carry more traffic than a two-lane street, a high-bandwidth communication channel can carry more data than a low-bandwidth channel. For example, the coaxial cable that brings you more than 100 channels of cable TV has a higher bandwidth than your home telephone line.

The bandwidth of a channel that carries digital data is usually measured in bits per second (bps). For example, your wireless LAN might be rated for an average speed of 27 Mbps. The bandwidth of a channel carrying analog data is typically measured in hertz (Hz). For instance, the copper wires that carry voice-grade telephone signals are often described as having a bandwidth of 3,000 Hz.

In 2004, the FCC defined broadband as networks that are capable of downloading at least 25 megabits of data per second (25 Mbps) and uploading at least 3 megabits per second (3 Mbps). Channels slower than 25 Mbps are classified as narrowband. Broadband capacity is essential for networks that support many users and those that carry lots of audio and video data, such as streaming music and movies.

Terminology

Hz is an abbreviation for hertz, which refers to the number of times a wave oscillates, or peaks, per second. Telephone signals are transmitted in the 1,200 Hz range. A wireless network that transmits at 2.4 GHz has a wave that peaks 2.4 billion times per second.

QuickCheck

You have a choice of network connections. Which one of the following is broadband?

a. A 56 Kbps phone link

b. A 1,200 Hz landline

c. A 50 Mbps cable connection

d. A 1.2 Mbps satellite link

Network Topology

A spider weaves a web by making silky connections between leaves, branches, and other surfaces. Most spiderwebs have a structure, and the same can be said for communication networks. The topologies of the networks you use have an effect on their dependability, security, and scope.

▶ **What is network topology?** In the context of communication networks, **topology** refers to the structure and layout of network components, such as computers, connecting cables, and wireless signal paths. When you envision how devices are connected by communication channels, you are creating a picture of the network's topology.

Module 2 explained how peripheral devices can connect to a host device using expansion ports, USB cables, or Bluetooth. These connections are an example of **point-to-point topology**. When connecting several devices, two network topologies are popular. **Star topology** connects multiple devices to a central device. **Mesh topology** connects multiple devices to each other, either as a full mesh or as a partial mesh. The less popular **bus topology** connects devices in a linear sequence. Figure 3-8 illustrates these network topologies.

QuickCheck

In Figure 3-8, which topology offers the greatest number of possible paths from one node to another?

a. Star

b. Full mesh

c. Partial mesh

d. Bus

Figure 3-8: Network topologies

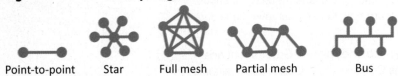

Point-to-point   Star   Full mesh   Partial mesh   Bus

▶ **Can a network use more than one topology?** Data can flow over multiple networks that have different topologies. As shown in Figure 3-9, data from a fitness wristband connects to a laptop via a point-to-point connection (A). The laptop is part of a home network configured as a star (B). The home network connects to an Internet service provider, so it is part of a larger star network (C). Finally, the data is passed to the Internet, which has a mesh topology (D).

Figure 3-9: Multiple topologies

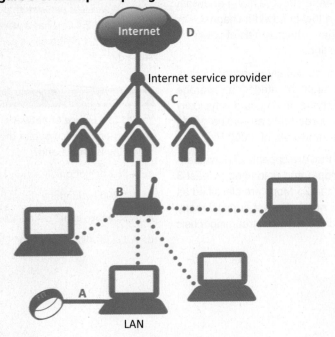

Internet   D

Internet service provider

C

B

A

LAN

▶ **Which topology is best?** Every topology has strengths and weaknesses, so there is no best network topology. Figure 3-10 compares strengths and weaknesses of the two most popular network topologies based on dependability, security, capacity, expandability, control, and monitoring.

Figure 3-10: Star or mesh?

Dependability

If the central point fails, data cannot flow anywhere on the network. If one of the other devices fails, however, the rest of the network remains operational.

There is no central point of failure; redundant paths between devices can be used to bypass failed devices.

Security

Data that travels on a star pathway makes only one intermediate hop between the sender and destination. The threat area for any transmission encompasses only three devices and two channels.

Within a mesh, data might travel through several devices and over multiple channels. Each leg presents a potential security risk. The chance of a security breach rises as the number of devices and channels increases.

Capacity

Star topologies are limited by the amount of data that can be handled by the central device.

Mesh topologies offer higher capacities because data can be transmitted from different devices simultaneously.

Expandability

Expandability is limited by the number of devices that can be attached to the central device within its immediate area of wireless coverage or maximum cable length.

The network can be expanded infinitely. As new devices are added, the network continues to repeat the signal as necessary until it reaches the farthest devices.

Control

Setup and updates are primarily done on the central device, which also can be used to shut down the entire network.

Setup is more complex, as each device must be configured to send, receive, and forward network data. There is no central point at which the network can be shut down.

Monitoring

All data passes through a central point, which is relatively easy to monitor for legitimate or illicit purposes.

Data does not pass through a central point, making data more challenging to monitor.

3

Network Nodes

Communication networks connect all kinds of devices: from smartphones to satellite dishes, from computers to cell towers, and even between tiny sensors and RFID tags. Any device in a network is called a **node**. You are familiar with network nodes such as laptops, smartphones, tablets, desktops, and peripheral devices. There are many other nodes that you don't interact with directly, yet they ultimately control how smoothly your Netflix movie streams and whether your email arrives at its destination.

▶ **What should I know about network nodes?** Devices on a network are classified as DTEs or DCEs. **DTE** stands for data terminal equipment. A DTE can be any device that stores or generates data. When connected to a network, your laptop is a DTE, as are your smartphone, tablet, and fitness tracker. The servers that house Web sites, handle email, offer cloud storage, and stream videos are also DTEs. Your own DTEs are under your control, and some servers are open to public access.

DCE stands for data communication equipment. These devices control the speed of data over networks, convert signals as they jump from cables to wireless, check for corrupted data, and route data from its origin to its destination. The most well-known DCEs are routers and modems.

▶ **How does a router work?** You probably have a DCE in your home network. A **router** is a device that controls the flow of data within a network and acts as a gateway to pass data from one network to another. Routers are used to direct traffic over major Internet trunk lines, and they are commonly used to route data from home networks to the Internet (Figure 3-11).

QuickCheck

When you connect a cell phone to a network, it is considered a(n)_____.

a. DTE

b. DCE

c. SPT

d. TCP

Figure 3-11: Routers

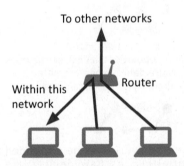

To other networks

Router

Within this network

▶ **How does a modem work?** A **modem** contains circuitry that converts the data-carrying signals from a digital device to signals that can travel over various communication channels. The kind of modem you use depends on whether you are connecting to a dial-up, wireless, cable, satellite, or DSL Internet service. A modem is usually supplied by your Internet service provider (Figure 3-12).

QuickCheck

A typical home network with Internet access would have _____.

a. a single DTE

b. multiple DCEs, but no DTEs

c. a modem and a router

d. multiple routers

Figure 3-12: Modems

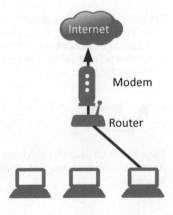

Internet

Modem

Router

pryzmat/Shutterstock.com

▶ **What about other DCEs?** DCEs perform all sorts of tasks. Suppose you want to extend the range of your home network out onto your balcony. What if your Internet provider wants to streamline network traffic in a neighborhood where lots of subscribers stream HD movies? DCEs such as repeaters, switches, and hubs can get the job done (Figure 3-13). These functions can sometimes be combined into a single device, such as a cable modem that also functions as a router.

Figure 3-13: Network devices

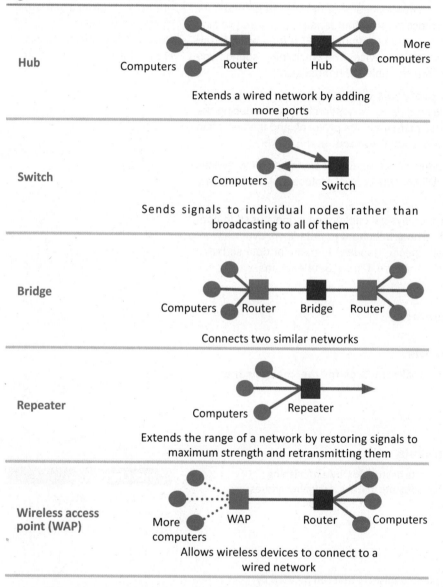

Hub — Extends a wired network by adding more ports

Switch — Sends signals to individual nodes rather than broadcasting to all of them

Bridge — Connects two similar networks

Repeater — Extends the range of a network by restoring signals to maximum strength and retransmitting them

Wireless access point (WAP) — Allows wireless devices to connect to a wired network

QuickCheck

To extend the reach of your wireless network out onto your balcony, which of the following devices would be best?

a. A hub

b. A router

c. A repeater

d. A gateway

Communication Protocols

A protocol is a set of rules for interacting and negotiating. In some respects, it is like the hand signals used by pitchers and catchers during baseball games. Before the ball is thrown, the pitcher and catcher use hand signals to negotiate the speed and style of the pitch. Similar to the way pitchers and catchers use signals, networks use communication protocols to coordinate data transfer.

▶ **What is a communication protocol?** In the context of networks, a **communication protocol** refers to a set of rules for efficiently transmitting data from one network node to another. Two devices on a network negotiate their communication protocols through a process called **handshaking**. The transmitting device sends a signal that means "I want to communicate." It then waits for an acknowledgment signal from the receiving device. The whooshing sounds you hear as two fax machines connect are examples of handshaking.

▶ **What can communication protocols do?** Protocols set standards for encoding and decoding data, guiding data to its destination, and reducing the effects of interference. Networks use more than one protocol, and the collection of protocols for a network is referred to as a **protocol stack**.

Communication protocols are provided by the circuitry of communicating devices and by communications software. Without the correct protocols, devices cannot communicate over a network.

Some protocols set standards for the physical cables and signals used to connect network nodes. Other protocols deal with the way data flows over network channels. And even more protocols specify standard formats for data so that it can be accessed by communication software. Figure 3-14 explains.

Try It!

People use many verbal and nonverbal communication protocols. Think of a nonverbal signal that you might use in a restaurant to indicate that you'd like the bill. How does the server acknowledge your request?

Figure 3-14: Communication protocols

Physical protocols

Specify cable and signal standards for the channels that carry data

Transport protocols

Make sure data gets to its destination by establishing standards for dividing data into chunks, assigning addresses, and correcting errors

Arrival protocols

Convert data into standard formats that can be used by applications, such as email, Web browsers, and Skype

QuickCheck

Which protocol category is responsible for the standards that attempt to block junk mail?

a. Physical

b. Transport

c. Arrival

▶ How can a network detect if a signal has been corrupted? Error correction is one of the responsibilities of communication protocols. Remember from Module 1 that text, numbers, sound, images, and video all are represented by bits. Suppose that some of those bits are garbled in transmission. Did that email say to meet at 29:00? Did your music track stop halfway through? Without error checking, the data you receive may not be reliable or complete.

Digital networks—those that transmit digital signals—can be easily monitored to determine if interference has corrupted any signals. At its most primitive level, digital equipment is sensitive to only two frequencies—one that represents 1s and one that represents 0s.

Suppose that a 0 is sent as −5 volts and a 1 is sent as +5 volts. What if, during transmission, some interference changes the voltage of a 1 bit from +5 volts to +3 volts?

To correct the corrupted bit, the receiving device realizes that +3 volts is not one of the two valid voltages. It guesses that a 1 bit (+5 volts) was actually transmitted and cleans the signal by reestablishing its voltage to +5 (Figure 3-15).

Figure 3-15: Error correction

QuickQuiz   Section A

1. A(n) [_____] area network connects smart sensors and digital devices within a range of about 30 feet.

2. The communication [_____] used for networks include copper cables, coaxial cables, radio signals, and microwaves.

3. Networks that upload at least 25 Mbps are classified by the FCC as [_____].

4. Modems and routers are examples of [_____] that control the flow of data within a network and act as a gateway from one network to another. Hint: Use the acronym.

5. Communication [_____] set standards for physical channels, transporting data, and correcting errors.

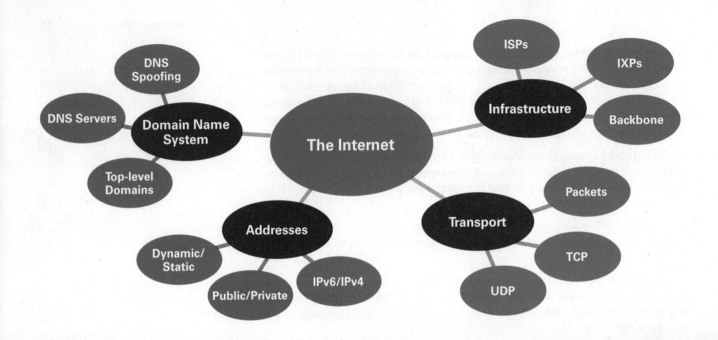

Objectives

▶ Briefly describe how the Internet developed from the ARPANET.

▶ Explain the state of Internet governance and funding.

▶ Draw a diagram showing the interrelationship among the three tiers of Internet service providers.

▶ Describe how packets are created and how they are carried on packet-switching networks.

▶ State the roles of TCP, IP, and UDP.

▶ Identify IPv4 and IPv6 addresses.

▶ Explain the differences between static addresses and dynamic addresses.

▶ Draw a diagram illustrating how a router deals with private and public IP addresses.

▶ List at least five top-level domains.

▶ Explain the role of the domain name system and why it is one of the Internet's vulnerabilities.

The Internet was once a cozy community run by nonprofit organizations and volunteer system operators called sysops. Connection speeds were slow, but the biggest security challenge was avoiding virus-infected downloads. Today, the Internet is essentially controlled by huge telecommunications conglomerates, government agencies tap into every stream of data, and real information is difficult to sort out from a hailstorm of ads. How did the Internet evolve into what it is today, and what makes it "tick"? Section B gives you a glimpse of what happens on the Net.

Terminology

ARPANET	packet	IPv6	domain name system
exabyte	circuit switching	static addresses	(DNS)
Internet governance	packet switching	dynamic addresses	top-level domain
ICANN	TCP	DHCP	domain name servers
Internet infrastructure	UDP	private IP address	DNS spoofing
Internet backbone	communication port	public IP address	
Internet service providers	IP	NAT	
Internet exchange points	IPv4	domain name	

Background

The Internet has its roots in a U.S. Department of Defense project that transitioned first into a nonprofit civilian operation, and then to a burgeoning commercial enterprise. We use the Internet without a second thought to communicate, create, and consume content. Yet the Internet also offers profound ethical, security, privacy, and legal challenges. To understand these challenges and the controversies surrounding them, you need a good understanding of basic Internet technology.

▶ **How did the Internet get started?** The history of the Internet begins in 1957 when the Soviet Union launched Sputnik, the first artificial satellite. In response to this display of Soviet expertise, the U.S. government resolved to improve its scientific and technical infrastructure. One of the resulting initiatives was the Advanced Research Projects Agency (ARPA).

ARPA swung into action with a project designed to help scientists communicate and share valuable computer resources. The **ARPANET**, created in 1969, connected computers at UCLA, the Stanford Research Institute, the University of Utah, and the University of California at Santa Barbara (Figure 3-16).

Figure 3-16: The ARPANET, 1969

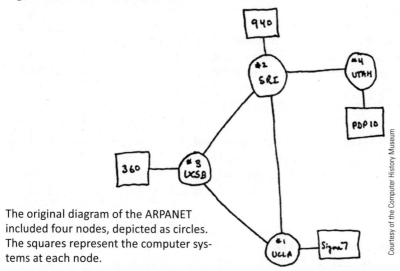

Courtesy of the Computer History Museum

The original diagram of the ARPANET included four nodes, depicted as circles. The squares represent the computer systems at each node.

In 1985, the National Science Foundation (NSF) used ARPANET technology to create a larger network, linking not just a few mainframe computers but entire LANs at each site. Connecting two or more networks creates an internetwork, or internet. The NSF network was an internet (with a lowercase *i*). As this network grew throughout the world, it became known as the Internet (with an uppercase I).

▶ **How did the Internet become so popular?** Early Internet pioneers used primitive command-line user interfaces to send email, transfer files, and run scientific calculations on Internet supercomputers. Finding information was not easy, and access was limited to a fairly small group of educators and scientists.

In the early 1990s, software developers created new user-friendly Internet access tools, and Internet accounts became available to anyone willing to pay a monthly subscription fee.

QuickCheck

The ARPANET was _____.

a. a network used by the Soviet Union's space program

b. essentially a pilot program for what later became the Internet

c. created by the National Science Foundation

▶ How big is the Internet? Connecting an estimated 50 billion devices and more than 4 billion users, the Internet is huge. Although exact figures cannot be determined, it is estimated that the Internet handles many exabytes of data every day. An **exabyte** is 1.074 billion gigabytes, and that's a nearly unimaginable amount of data. Visualizing such a vast network is difficult. Visualizations like the one in Figure 3-17 highlight locations with the most Internet activity.

Figure 3-17: There are many ways to visualize the Internet

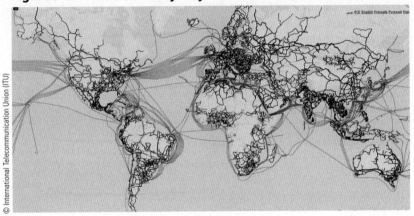

© International Telecommunication Union (ITU)

Try It!

How can you visualize the vast scope of the Internet? Do a Web search for *Internet visualizations* to see how scientists and artists have depicted the scope of the Internet throughout time.

▶ Who operates the Internet? Although the Internet is such a vast entity, in theory no single person, organization, company, or government runs it. At one time, the Internet was composed of many regional networks, established in countries throughout the world. Gradually, these networks have fallen under the control of large telecommunications companies, such as Verizon, AT&T, and NTT Communications.

The glue that holds the Internet together and makes it possible for data to travel across borders is a set of standard protocols that were developed for the original ARPANET. In this respect, **Internet governance** is just a set of shared protocols, procedures, and technologies that evolve through common agreement among network providers.

▶ Who supervises Internet standards? Although each country can develop laws, policies, and regulations for the networks within their jurisdiction, there is one crucial administrative task necessary to keep the Internet from sinking into chaos. Every Internet node—each server, each computer, and each piece of data communication equipment—must have a unique address in order to send and receive data.

The organization that supervises Internet addressing is **ICANN**, the Internet Corporation for Assigned Names and Numbers. ICANN is a not-for-profit private sector organization operated by an international board of directors. Its advisory committee has representatives from more than 100 nations, and public comments pertaining to ICANN policies are accepted at its Web site.

Control of Internet address assignments is a powerful tool. It provides the means to block users from accessing specific network nodes. Local governments exercise this power within their jurisdictions to shut down servers that violate copyrights and distribute inappropriate content. The power to globally shut down access to a server, however, only rests with ICANN. You will discover more about the key role of Internet addresses later in this section.

QuickCheck

The primary role of ICANN is to

_____.

a. run the Internet

b. provide funding for the Internet

c. supervise Internet address assignments

d. make sure that every country in the world gets equal access to the Internet

Internet Infrastructure

The Internet is not one huge communication network, but rather a network of networks. The way these networks fit together is referred to as the **Internet infrastructure**. Internet networks are organized into tiers. As a consumer, you are subject to the fees, policies, and technologies of the tiers that provide your Internet service.

❱ **What are the components of the Internet?** The Internet is structured as a hierarchy of networks. Tier 1 networks are at the top of the hierarchy, followed by Tier 2 and Tier 3 networks. Across the globe, approximately 15 Tier 1 networks, such as AT&T, Tata Communications, Verizon, and NTT Communications, form the **Internet backbone**, a system of high-capacity routers and fiber-optic communication links providing the main routes for data speeding across the Internet. Routers on the Internet backbone store routing tables that calculate and track the most efficient routes for data to travel from point A to point B.

The Internet backbone is configured as a mesh network that offers redundant routes for data transport. The backbone's mesh infrastructure is probably the basis for the myth that the Internet originated as a Department of Defense project to create a network that could survive nuclear attacks.

Networks that form the Internet are maintained by **Internet service providers** (ISPs) that supply routers and other data communication equipment, as well as physical and wireless channels to carry data. ISPs exchange data at **Internet exchange points** (IXPs).

Consumers generally connect to Tier 2 or Tier 3 networks. Use the infographic in Figure 3-18 to become familiar with the Internet's infrastructure and its terminology; pay attention to the arrangement of network tiers and points where data moves between them.

Figure 3-18: Internet infrastructure

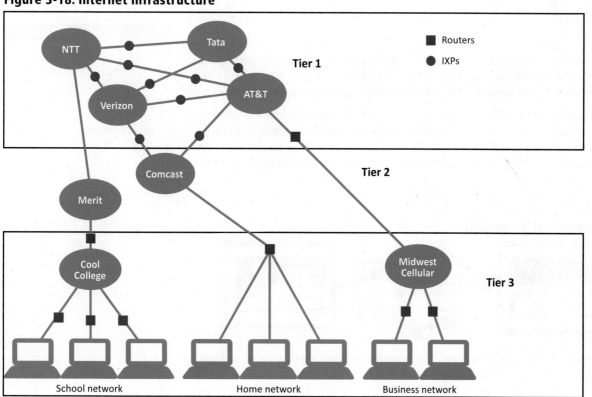

▶ **Who pays for the Internet?** The Internet is not free. ISPs make a substantial investment in equipment infrastructure. The largest providers each have close to 200,000 miles of cables installed across continents and under the ocean floor. ISPs also own and maintain millions of dollars' worth of data communication equipment.

In addition to infrastructure expenses, ISPs are subject to data transport fees, especially when shipping data up through higher tiers. To offset expenses, ISPs charge consumers for access. Figure 3-19 explains the Internet fee structure.

Figure 3-19: Internet fee structure

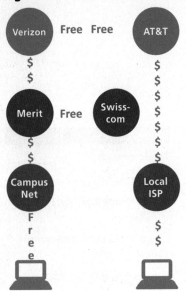

Tier 1 service providers exchange data with other Tier 1 providers on a no-cost basis.

Tier 2 service providers exchange data on a no-cost basis with other Tier 2 providers, but they pay fees to connect to the backbone through Tier 1 providers.

Tier 3 service providers connect to Tier 2 or Tier 1 providers and pay transit fees for the data exchanged.

Consumers either pay fees directly or their access is subsidized by an organization or government.

QuickCheck

Which ISP tier is not subject to transport fees from other tiers?

a. Tier 1

b. Tier 2

c. Tier 3

Packets

Most people envision their files, email, and other data flying through the Internet as a continuous stream of bits. This is not the case. Files are chopped up into small pieces called packets. The technology that breaks a file into packets and routes them to any location on Earth in the blink of an eye is absolutely amazing.

▶ **What's a packet?** A **packet** is a parcel of data that is sent across a computer network. Each packet contains the address of its sender, the destination address, a sequence number, and some data. When packets reach their destination, they are reassembled into the original message according to the sequence numbers (Figure 3-20).

QuickCheck

Files are divided into _____ before being shipped over the Internet.

a. packets

b. email messages

c. bits

d. tiers

Figure 3-20: Data packets

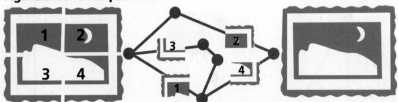

Messages divided into equal-size packets are easier to handle than an assortment of small, medium, large, and extra large files.

▶ **Why not just send an entire message?** Some communication networks use a technology called circuit switching, which essentially establishes a dedicated, private link between one device and another. Landline telephone systems use circuit switching technology to link two callers. Unfortunately, circuit switching is rather inefficient. For example, when someone is on hold during a phone call, no communication is taking place, yet the circuit is reserved and cannot be used for other communication.

A more efficient alternative to circuit switching is packet switching, which divides a message into several packets that can be routed independently to their destination. Packets from many different messages can share a single communication channel or circuit.

Packets are shipped over the circuit on a first-come, first-served basis. If some packets from a message are not available, the system does not need to wait for them. Instead, the system moves on to send packets from other messages. The end result is a steady stream of data (Figure 3-21).

Terminology

The telephone network is sometimes referred to as the *public switched telephone network (PSTN)*.

3

Figure 3-21: Circuit-switching and packet-switching networks

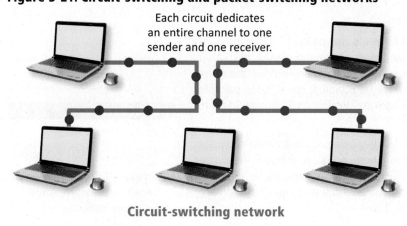

Each circuit dedicates an entire channel to one sender and one receiver.

Circuit-switching network

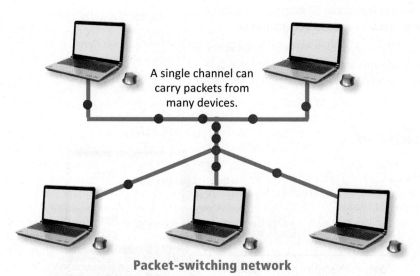

A single channel can carry packets from many devices.

Packet-switching network

Packet-switching networks (bottom) provide a more efficient communication system than circuit-switching networks (top).

Internet Protocols

▶ **How are packets created?** One of the core Internet protocols, **TCP** (Transmission Control Protocol) is responsible for dividing files into chunks, adding headers containing information for reassembling packets in their original order, and verifying that the data was not corrupted while in transit (a process called error checking). When data is sent over the Internet using TCP, it will reliably reach its destination. TCP is built into applications that transmit data from one digital device to another.

▶ **How are packets transported?** TCP is also responsible for establishing a connection, transferring packets, and closing the connection when the transmission is complete. Most of the data that flows over the Internet is under the control of TCP.

An alternative transport protocol, **UDP** (User Datagram Protocol) is faster than TCP but does not perform error checking and cannot reorder packets if they are received out of order. UDP, therefore, is suitable for applications in which a bit of lost data is not critical, such as streaming video and music, and Internet-based multiplayer games and voice calls. UDP and TCP both use communications ports to shuttle data into and out of a network device.

▶ **What is a communications port?** Here's the problem: On a packet-switching network, packets for Web pages, email, streaming videos, and other downloads may arrive at your digital device in the same stream and over the same channel. The packets may not arrive in neat little bundles; some video packets could arrive interspersed with Web page packets. Which packets should go to the browser and which to the Netflix player?

A **communication port** (usually referred to simply as a *port*) is a virtual end point for data entering and leaving a digital device. These ports are virtual in the sense that they are not physical ports, as are USB ports, for example. A communication port is not a physical circuit, but rather an abstract concept of a doorway, an opening, or a portal through which data flows.

Ports work in conjunction with Internet addresses. Computers can have up to 65,535 ports. Typically about 10–20 ports are in use and open for various types of data. Data originating from the Web, for instance, uses port 80, whereas streaming video uses port 554. When ports are open, data is allowed to flow freely. Closing ports can block data, and that strategy is used by firewalls to prevent unauthorized intrusions.

Ports create simulated end-to-end connections on packet-switching networks. So although the devices on two ends of a communication channel are not connected by a single dedicated circuit, ports create a conceptual circuit for each type of data, as shown in Figure 3-22.

Figure 3-22: How communications ports work

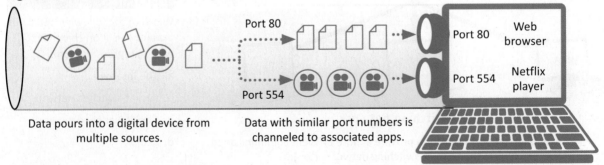

Data pours into a digital device from multiple sources.   Data with similar port numbers is channeled to associated apps.

Internet Addresses

You might have heard that Internet addresses are running out. Does that mean some people will be unable to get online? Will people have to share addresses? Networks use several kinds of addresses to determine where packets originate and where they are headed. To find out how Internet addresses might affect your online access, read on.

▶ **Exactly what is an Internet address?** Although most people are accustomed to entering something such as *www.wikipedia.org* to access Internet locations, those "www" addresses are not the underlying address used to transport data to its destination. Internet addresses are controlled by **IP** (Internet Protocol), which—along with TCP—is part of the Internet protocol suite. IP defines two sets of addresses: IPv4 and IPv6.

▶ **What is the difference between IPv4 and IPv6?** **IPv4**, which stands for Internet Protocol version 4, is the Internet address standard that has been used since the early 1980s. IPv4 uses 32-bit addresses to uniquely identify devices connected to the Internet. In binary, IPv4 addresses are written as:

11001111 01001011 01110101 00011010

For convenience, 32-bit binary addresses are usually written in decimal as four sets of digits separated by periods:

207.75.117.26

Using 32 bits, IPv4 offers about 4 billion unique addresses. In 2011, that supply of addresses was completely allocated. Yes, IP addresses can be recycled when the original assignees no longer want them, but the demand far outstrips the number of addresses coming up for recycling. Another set of addresses was needed.

IPv6 (Internet Protocol version 6) uses 128 bits for each address, producing billions and billions of unique Internet addresses. An IPv6 address is usually written as eight groups of hexadecimal digits, like this:

2001:48a8:800:1192:198:110:192:54

Don't worry, there are enough IPv6 addresses for the foreseeable future, even with the anticipated influx of 2 billion new Internet users and the Internet of Things adding hundreds of devices each second.

▶ **Does every Internet user need an IP address?** It is more accurate to say that every *device* on the Internet needs an IP address. Many, but not all, devices on the Internet have permanently assigned IP addresses, called **static IP addresses**. As a general rule, routers and computers on the Internet that act as servers use static IP addresses.

ISPs, Web sites, Web hosting services, and email servers that always need to be found at the same address also require static IP addresses. There is an emerging trend for individuals to request static IP addresses for their home networks, and a static address might be useful for remotely communicating with sensors and other devices in the Internet of Things.

Terminology

Internet Protocol is often referred to as *TCP/IP* (pronounced "T-C-P-I-P").

3

QuickCheck

An IP address that contains 84a3 would be a(n)

_____.

a. IPv4 address

b. IPv6 address

c. corrupted address

d. static address

▶ What happens when a device doesn't have a static IP address? IP addresses can be temporarily allocated so that a device uses an address only while it is actively online. When the device is turned off or its Internet connection is disabled, the address can be recycled to another device. The next time the device is turned on, it will be assigned a different IP address. Internet addresses that are temporarily assigned are called **dynamic IP addresses**.

In practice, dynamic IP addresses do not change very often. Today, most consumers have always-on Internet connections that remain active as long as the router that connects to the Internet remains powered on. Turning a computer off or on does not affect the IP address stored in the router. Customers who access the Internet using Comcast XFINITY or AT&T Internet, for example, could have the same IP address for weeks or months.

▶ How do devices get IP addresses? IP addresses can be assigned by a network administrator, but more commonly they are automatically assigned by **DHCP** (Dynamic Host Configuration Protocol). Most devices are preconfigured to receive an IP address by sending a query to the network device acting as the DHCP server. That device could be a router for a local area network or a DHCP server from your ISP. IP addresses get a bit tricky because a device can have a public IP address and a private IP address.

▶ What is a private IP address? Let's suppose that your laptop is connected to your school network. The DHCP server for the school assigns a dynamic IP address to your laptop when you log in. That address, which probably begins with 10, 172, 192, FD, or Fc00, is classified as a private IP address because it works only within the school network.

A **private IP address** can be allocated by any network without supervision from ICANN. However, the address cannot be used to send data over the Internet; it is not routable. Figure 3-23 demonstrates how to find your private IP address.

QuickCheck

When connected to a network, your computer can receive an address from _____.

a. DHCP

b. packets

c. IPv4

d. the CPU

Try It!

Find your IP address. Is it in the range of private addresses listed in Figure 3-23?

Figure 3-23: Find your private IP address on a Windows computer

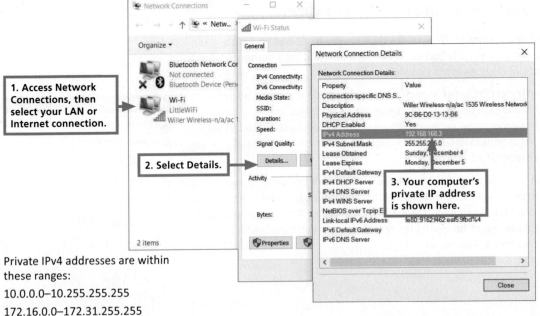

Private IPv4 addresses are within these ranges:

10.0.0.0–10.255.255.255

172.16.0.0–172.31.255.255

192.168.0.0–192.168.255.255

▶ If my private IP address can't be routed over the Internet, how does my data get anywhere? Here is where your local router plays a crucial role. Any network you use to access the Internet—a campus network, your home network, or a Wi-Fi hotspot—has a router that connects to the Internet. The router has a **public IP address** that is routable over the Internet. Figure 3-24 explains how public and private IP addresses work.

3

Figure 3-24: Routing data using private and public IP addresses

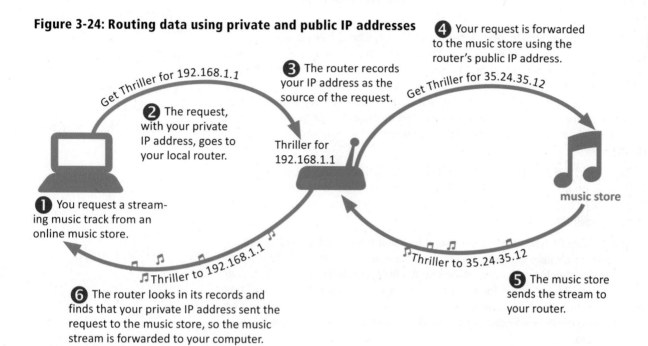

❶ You request a streaming music track from an online music store.

Get Thriller for 192.168.1.1

❷ The request, with your private IP address, goes to your local router.

❸ The router records your IP address as the source of the request.

Thriller for 192.168.1.1

❹ Your request is forwarded to the music store using the router's public IP address.

Get Thriller for 35.24.35.12

music store

❺ The music store sends the stream to your router.

Thriller to 35.24.35.12

❻ The router looks in its records and finds that your private IP address sent the request to the music store, so the music stream is forwarded to your computer.

Thriller to 192.168.1.1

▶ Does using a private IP address make me anonymous? No, the router's network address translation table keeps track of your activities, so your footprint across the Internet can be traced back to you. However, a private IP address can protect you from some threats. For example, a hacker who randomly enters IP addresses looking for unauthorized access will never find your private IP address because the only address that is visible to the public is the address of your local router. This security technique is usually referred to as **NAT** (network address translation).

That being said, private IP addresses cannot protect your devices from many other attacks. Clicking corrupted links or downloading infected files sends packets and makes a path in the network address translation table that can allow malware into your device.

Domain Names

If the Internet has an Achilles' heel, it is the domain name system. When a wide swath of the Internet goes dark, when you hear about massive outages, or when you struggle to get to a Web site that seems to have disappeared, the domain name system is probably at fault. The ability of governments to censor information by blocking sites is also made possible by the domain name system. And if there is an Internet kill switch, you can bet that the domain name system will be involved.

▶ **What is the domain name system?** People find it difficult to remember the string of numbers in an IP address. Therefore, most Internet destinations also have an easy-to-remember **domain name**, such as nike.com. A domain name is a key component of Web page addresses and email addresses. You can easily recognize the domain name in a Web site address such as *www.nike.com* or an email address such as *ceo@nike.com*. The mechanism for tracking domain names and their corresponding IP addresses is called the **domain name system (DNS)**.

▶ **Do I need a domain name?** For client-style Internet activities, such as Web browsing, email, and downloading, you do not need your own domain name. Today, social networking sites give ample opportunity for making your presence known on the Internet.

However, domain names are quite useful for businesses and individual artists, musicians, or crafters who want to engage in online commerce. The fees associated with obtaining a domain name might initially seem small. The first year may cost only $1, but prices for subsequent years are typically around $15. Then there is the question of how many domain names you need; one might not be enough. You might need domain names with more than one extension, such as .com or .club.

ICANN is the top-level authority for supervising domain name requests. Rather than going directly to ICANN, domain names can be obtained from several domain registrars and hosting services that provide Internet-based server space for Web sites (Figure 3-25).

QuickCheck

What's the purpose of the domain name system?

a. Hand out IP private addresses.

b. Translate domain names into IP addresses.

c. Route packets to their destinations.

d. Encrypt data that is sent over the Internet.

Figure 3-25: Choose your own domain name

Source: Register.com

▶ **What is a top-level domain?** A domain name ends with an extension that indicates its **top-level domain** (TLD). For example, in the domain name msu.edu, the top-level domain .edu indicates that the computer is maintained by an educational institution. Country codes also serve as top-level domains. Canada's top-level domain is .ca, the United Kingdom's is .uk, Australia's is .au, and the European Union uses .eu as a top-level domain.

Historically, businesses used the .com domain, while nonprofit organizations used .org. Educational institutions used .edu. The .net domain was usually used by communication companies.

Businesses generally obtained domain names with all applicable top-level domains (e.g., nike.com, nike.org, and nike.net) to prevent their use by competitors or fake businesses. Businesses also tried to acquire domain names with similar sounding names or those that are common misspellings of their corporate names.

Today, there are hundreds of additional top-level domains, such as .biz, .co, and .fit. Obtaining all the TLDs for a business name is not practical. Even within a sector such as education, .edu has been joined by .academy, .education, .guru, .institute, .training, and .university.

▶ **How does the domain name system work?** Scattered around the world are several **domain name servers** that maintain lists of all domain names and their corresponding IP addresses. In addition, frequently used domain names are stored by ISPs, educational institutions, organizations, and Internet companies such as Google.

When new domain names are added, these lists are updated. New domain names may take several days to propagate to all of the lists, which is why new Web sites can be accessed only by their IP addresses for the first few days they are in operation. A Web site can be accessed by its domain name once the name is added to the domain name server lists.

Suppose you want to look at the newest selection of Nike athletic shoes. You enter *nike.com* in your browser's address bar. Your browser must find the IP address that corresponds to nike.com before it can connect you to the site. Your browser queries a domain name server to get the IP address, a process that generally happens without noticeable delay (Figure 3-26).

QuickCheck

What is the top-level domain in *www.nike.com*?

a. www

b. nike

c. .com

d. "dot"

3

Figure 3-26: How does the domain name system work?

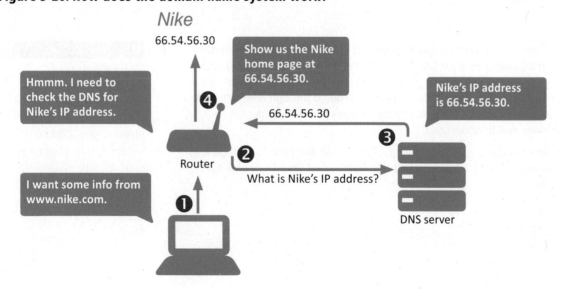

▶ **Can I discover the IP address and owner of a domain name?** You might want to vet a Web site to assess the legitimacy of its owner. Access to information in the domain name database is provided by ICANN and various online apps. You can use a WHOIS lookup to find the IP address that corresponds to a domain name. Or you can look up an IP address to find its domain name and owner.

There are limitations, however. Large corporations tend to use a hosting service such as Akamai Technologies, which essentially operates its own DNS system with IP addresses and domains sheltered under its domain. A WHOIS lookup for Nike.com, for example, produces the IP address for Akamai Technologies and the address for Nike remains hidden. For smaller firms, WHOIS lookups continue to work, though ICANN is considering eliminating these lookups because they can be a potential security risk.

▶ **So what makes the DNS one of the Internet's weaknesses?** Altering the DNS records can change the destination of email, browser connections, and download requests. Unauthorized changes to the DNS are called **DNS spoofing**.

Hackers use DNS spoofing so that queries for legitimate sites are directed to fake sites. Some governments use DNS spoofing to redirect searches from culturally or politically inappropriate sites to government-approved sites. Figure 3-27 illustrates what happens when unauthorized changes are made in the DNS.

Figure 3-27: DNS spoofing

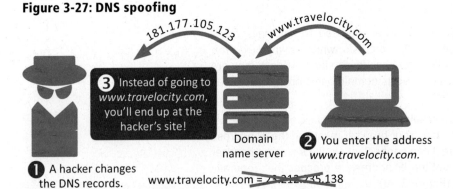

▶ **Can domain name servers be turned off?** Yes, though more commonly a DNS server operated by your ISP will go offline as a result of an equipment failure. When the DNS you're using goes down, the process of accessing the Internet can get very slow while DNS requests are routed through alternate servers. It is even possible that a DNS outage can leave you without Internet access unless you enter raw IP addresses.

It is a good idea to know how to find your DNS server and how to change it in case of an outage. Figure 3-28 demonstrates how to find your DNS settings.

Figure 3-28: Find your DNS settings

Windows

1. Use the Windows search box to open Network Connections.

2. Right-click your network, then select Properties.

3. Select Internet Protocol Version 4 (TCP/IPv4).

4. Select Properties. If the DNS server address is obtained automatically, your device is likely using your ISP's DNS. You can override the automatic settings as shown at right.

macOS

1. Click the Apple menu and select System Preferences.

2. Select Network. Select the Advanced button, then select DNS. The DNS server is listed in the DNS Servers window.

3. To add an alternative DNS server, select the + button, then enter the IP address of the server.

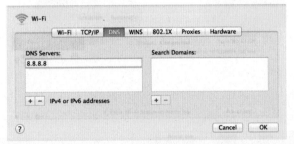

Source: Apple Inc.

▶ **What can I use as an alternative DNS server?** Surprisingly, you might be able to bypass DNS outages, blocks, and hacks by changing your DNS server. Errors in the domain name tables may be limited to the domain name server that you are using. Connecting to a different domain name server might restore full access. In addition, when you are traveling—especially overseas—a local DNS server might be closer and quicker.

Keep the numbers in Figure 3-29 handy in case you need to change your domain name server. Write them down, or store them locally on your device. Remember, if your domain name server has an outage, you won't be able to use domain names to search the Internet for a solution.

Figure 3-29: Public domain name servers

Google's public DNS
8.8.8.8   2001:4860:4860::8888
8.8.4.4   2001:4860:4860::8844

OpenDNS
208.67.222.222
208.67.220.220

QuickQuiz   Section B

1. The Internet [_____] is a system of high-capacity routers and fiber-optic communication links.

2. The Internet uses [_____] switching technology to route data from many different messages over a single communication channel.

3. [_____] and UDP are two of the main protocols used to transport data over the Internet.

4. The Internet's supply of [_____] addresses ran out in 2011.

5. [_____] IP addresses are not routable over the Internet.

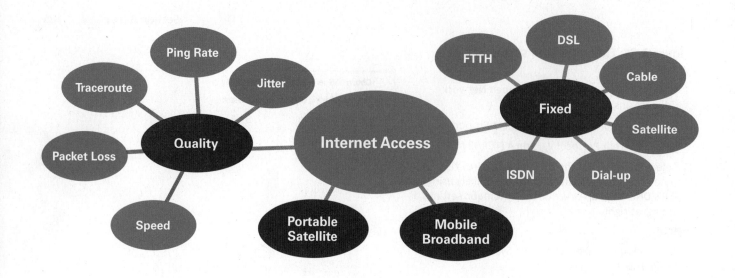

Section C Internet Access

Objectives

▶ List acceptable speeds for the following: basic Skype video calls, streaming standard-definition movies, and viewing YouTube videos.

▶ Explain the significance of asymmetric Internet connections.

▶ Define latency and state the type of Internet service that it affects most negatively.

▶ List online activities that are most affected by jitter and packet loss.

▶ Name three tools that you can use to troubleshoot an Internet connection.

▶ Explain the pros and cons of fixed, portable, and mobile Internet access.

▶ Rank each type of Internet service according to speed, then rank them according to dependability.

▶ Draw diagrams of the infrastructures for cable, dial-up, DSL, satellite, mobile broadband, and Wi-Fi hotspot Internet services.

▶ Discuss why mobile Internet access is globally the most popular way to connect to the Internet.

A human rights violation. That's what the
United Nations had to say about laws in France and England that penalize copyright violators by banning them from the Internet. Whether or not you agree that Internet access is a human right, there is little doubt that global network access is increasingly required to participate in activities ranging from politics to education to dating. As you read Section C, consider which of the access technologies are likely to be available in various regions of the globe.

Terminology

connection speed	latency	mobile Internet access	FTTH
bandwidth cap	jitter	cable Internet service	satellite Internet service
bandwidth throttling	packet loss	dial-up	mobile broadband
asymmetric connection	Traceroute	voiceband modem	tethering
symmetric connection	fixed Internet access	ISDN	mobile hotspot
Ping	portable Internet access	DSL	Wi-Fi hotspot

Connection Basics

With online access becoming an essential component in our daily lives, sociologists have been tracking Internet "haves" and "have-nots." According to the Statista Global Consumer Survey, an estimated 99% of American adults have Internet access. Worldwide, about 50% of the population has Internet access. Not all of these connections are fast and dependable. Let's take a look at what makes a good Internet connection.

▶ **How fast is the Internet?** Data travels over the Internet at an incredible speed, but that speed varies. Some Internet services are faster than others. Speed is affected by the amount of traffic flowing over the connection. It slows down when usage is heavy. Slowdowns also occur as a result of faulty routers and when hackers launch denial-of-service attacks that overwhelm server capacity.

It is relatively easy to check the speed of your Internet connection by running a few online tests. Figure 3-30 shows results from testing speed in a metropolitan area. Is this connection suitable for streaming movies, playing online games, and conducting video chats?

Figure 3-30: Is your connection fast enough?

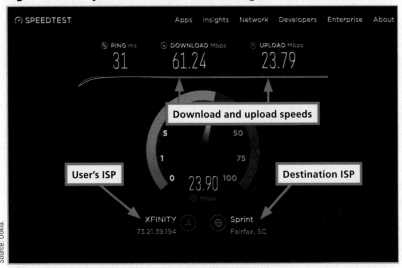

This speed test measured the rate of data flowing between an Xfinity customer in Columbia, SC and a Sprint server in Fairfax, SC.

▶ **What does connection speed measure?** Speed is the distance something travels in a specified amount of time. The speed of a car, for example, is measured in miles (distance) per hour (time). What we casually refer to as "connection speed" has little to do with distance. The most common measurement of **connection speed** is the amount of data that can be transmitted in a specified time. Technically, it is a measure of capacity. But let's use nontechnical terms and call it speed.

The speed test in Figure 3-30 produced a download speed of 61.24 Mbps because it was able to move 61 megabits of data down from a server to the user's computer in one second. The upload speed at which data is transferred from the computer to a server was only 23.79 Mbps. With this connection, downloading a two-hour SD-quality movie would take about 2 minutes. Uploading a 4 MB photo would take less than 1 second.

Try It!

What is the speed of your Internet connection right now? Connect to a Web site such as *Ookla's Speedtest* or *the Bandwidth Place* and run a speed test to find out.

QuickCheck

Would the connection used for the speed test in Figure 3-30 be classified as broadband?

a. Yes, it is synchronous.

b. Yes, the upload and download speeds qualify as broadband.

c. No, its upload speed of 23.79 Mbps is not fast enough.

d. No, its average speed is only 9.79 Mbps.

❱ **How much speed do I need?** For email, browsing the Web, and streaming videos, 0.5 Mbps (500 Kbps) speeds are adequate. However, other activities require higher speeds, as shown in Figure 3-31.

Figure 3-31: Connection speeds required for popular Internet activities

Service	Recommended Download	Recommended Upload
Skype video calling and screen sharing	300 Kbps	300 Kbps
Skype video calls (HD)	1.5 Mbps	1.5 Mbps
Skype three-person group calling	2 Mbps	512 Kbps
Netflix minimum required speed	.5 Mbps	—
Netflix SD-quality movie	3 Mbps	—
Netflix HD-quality movie	5 Mbps	—
Netflix Ultra HD-quality movie	25 Mbps	—
YouTube basic videos	500 Kbps	—
YouTube movies, TV shows, and live events	1 Mbps	—
Amazon Prime Video (SD)	8 Mbps	—
Amazon Prime Video (HD)	5 Mbps	—
Netflix and Amazon 4K Streaming Video	15–25 Mbps	—

❱ **Why are upload and download speeds different?** ISPs control connection speeds based on the service plan you've selected. Your **bandwidth cap** is the top speed allowed by your plan. During peak times, ISPs can place further limits on speed, a process called **bandwidth throttling**.

When Internet upload speed differs from download speed, you have an **asymmetric connection**. When upload and download speeds are the same, you have a **symmetric connection**.

Most Internet connections are asymmetrical, with upload speeds considerably less than download speeds. Asymmetric connections discourage subscribers from setting up Web and email servers that would transmit lots of outgoing data. For most users, however, an asymmetric connection is sufficient, but download speeds of less than 1.5 Mbps may not provide the full Internet experience.

❱ **What is Ping?** **Ping** is utility software designed to measure responsiveness. Ping rate indicates how quickly data can reach a server and bounce back to you. Ping was named after the sound that a submarine's sonar makes when it bounces off an undersea object.

Technically, Ping measures latency. **Latency** is the elapsed time for data to make a round trip from point A to point B and back to point A. Latency is measured in milliseconds (ms). A millisecond is a thousandth of a second, so data transmitted on an Internet connection with 100 ms latency makes a round trip in one-tenth of a second.

QuickCheck

In the table at left, why are there recommended upload speeds only for Skype?

a. Skype doesn't use uploads.

b. Skype requires two-way communication, whereas the other services use most of the bandwidth only for downloads.

c. Skype is the slowest service of those listed.

d. Amazon, YouTube, and Netflix offer different levels of service, so the upload speed cannot be specified.

Terminology

Download and upload speeds are sometimes referred to as *downstream speeds* and *upstream speeds*, respectively.

▶ **What is an acceptable ping rate?** Latency generally averages less than 30 ms (milliseconds) within North America, but increases to about 70 ms for transatlantic transmissions. If you want to play online multiplayer games, it is best to have less than 100 ms latency. Good-quality video streaming and videoconferencing require latency rates of 200 ms or less.

Speed and latency are not the only factors that affect your Internet experience. Even if your connection gets good marks on speed tests, jitter and packet loss can degrade the quality of online activities.

▶ **What are jitter and packet loss?** Jitter measures the variability of packet latency. Network traffic and interference can delay some packets and create erratic data flow. If the variation between packets exceeds 5 ms, Internet voice and video call quality is likely to be poor.

Packet loss refers to data that never reaches its destination or gets discarded because it arrives too late to be of any use. Packet loss of less than 2% is required for acceptable streaming, gaming, Skype, and voice calls. Too many lost packets during an online gaming session can cause the game to stutter or stall. And if packets don't arrive in the correct order, your game character might seem to act randomly for a few seconds. An Internet quality test can measure jitter and packet loss, producing results similar to those shown in Figure 3-32.

Figure 3-32: Check the jitter and packet loss on your connection

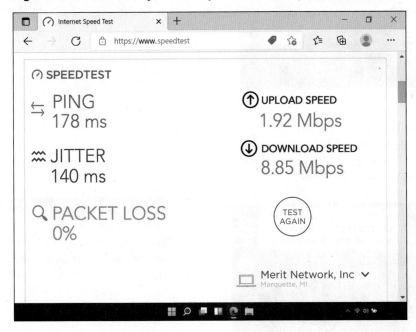

QuickCheck

The connection in Figure 3-32 gets a grade of D for bad performance. What are the problems?

a. The speed is too low and packet loss is too high.

b. The ping rate is too low and packet loss is too high.

c. The ping rate and the jitter rate are too high.

d. The ping rate is too high, but the jitter rate is too low.

▶ Can I troubleshoot an Internet connection? Suppose your Internet connection seems unusually slow one day. Or, perhaps you cannot access a favorite Web site. You wonder, "Is the problem on my computer, with my ISP, or somewhere else on the Internet?" To find out, you can use Traceroute, a network diagnostic tool that lists each router and server your data encounters as it travels over the Internet.

Traceroute sends three packets of data to a specified destination. It records the address of each router along the way and the elapsed time for each "hop." When a connection is inoperable, the packets will not reach their destination and they will become lost. Figure 3-33 illustrates how to use Traceroute and how to interpret its results.

Figure 3-33: Where does your data travel?

On a Mac, open the Utilities folder, then select Terminal. Enter the command traceroute followed by any domain name, like this:

```
●●●              🏠 sarahsmith — bash — 65×24

Last login: Sun Dec 14 18:47:00 on console
sarahiMac:~ sarahsmith$ traceroute msu.edu ▮
```

Source: © 2017 Apple Inc

On a PC, enter cmd in the Windows search box to open the Command Prompt window. Enter the command tracert followed by any domain name, like this:

```
▩ Command Prompt
Microsoft Windows [Version 10.0.19042.1052]
(c) Microsoft Corporation. All rights reserved.

C:\Users\sarah>tracert msu.edu
```

Traceroute results appear as a list, showing each router, the router's IP address, and the elapsed time for each hop. Traceroute may produce a "Request timed out message" if a Web site is not operational or has defensive security measures in place.

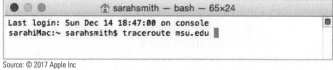

A list of routers indicates the path of the packet as it traveled over the Internet.

```
▩ Command Prompt                                        —  □  ×
Microsoft Windows [Version 10.0.19042.1052]
(c) Microsoft Corporation. All rights reserved.

C:\Users\sarah>tracert msu.edu

Tracing route to msu.edu [45.60.63.246]
over a maximum of 30 hops:

  1    1 ms    <1 ms     2 ms  Linksys09 [192.168.1.1]
  2    3 ms     4 ms     4 ms  10.0.0.1
  3   14 ms    13 ms    15 ms  96.120.85.29
  4   14 ms    14 ms    14 ms  96.110.16.181
  5   19 ms    21 ms    21 ms  ae-112-ar06.savannah.ga.savannah.comcast.net [162.151.19.225]
  6   20 ms    20 ms    19 ms  ae-25-ar02.westside.fl.jacksvil.comcast.net [68.86.168.49]
  7   37 ms    37 ms    36 ms  be-33642-cs04.56marietta.ga.ibone.comcast.net [96.110.43.125]
  8   28 ms    41 ms    50 ms  be-2403-pe03.56marietta.ga.ibone.comcast.net [96.110.37.94]
  9   31 ms    29 ms    30 ms  173.167.57.234
 10   31 ms    30 ms    29 ms  45.60.63.246

Trace complete.

C:\Users\sarah>
```

Travel times for this connection are quick, indicating a fast Internet connection.

Try It!

Find out how many hops your data makes before it arrives at *www.wired.com*. What was the slowest leg of the trip? (Hint: Mac users may need to add -I after the traceroute command word.)

QuickCheck

How many Comcast routers did each packet pass through when this Traceroute report was generated?

a. 1

b. 4

c. 10

d. 16

▶ **What else affects the speed of my connection?** Your Internet connection can be affected by outages and traffic. In Section B, you found out what can happen when a DNS server goes down. Service disruptions can also occur at ISPs, cloud storage sites, email servers, and other Internet-based services. You can use online tools such as downdetector.com and downrightnow.com to check the status of various Internet services.

▶ **What are my Internet connection options?** Although public Internet access is available in many locations, such as coffee shops and libraries, most consumers like the convenience of having their own Internet connection. Depending on your geographical location, you may have several options for connecting to the Internet. Before we look at the most popular Internet access options such as cable Internet service and cellular broadband, consider the pros and cons of the three classifications of Internet connections in Figure 3-34.

3

Figure 3-34: Internet connection options

Fixed Internet Access

Fixed Internet access links your computer to an ISP from a stationary point, such as a wall socket or roof-mounted antenna. This service is dependable and relatively cost effective. You can't take it with you, so when you're away from home, you must depend on public access points.

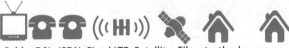

Cable, DSL, ISDN, Fixed LTE, Satellite, Fiber-to-the-home

Portable Internet Access

Portable Internet access allows you to easily move your access device, as in the case of vehicle-mounted satellite dishes that can be deployed when the vehicle is parked. This service is primarily used in situations where mobile and fixed access are not available.

Mobile satellite

Mobile Internet Access

Mobile Internet access allows you to use the Internet while you are on the go, such as using a cell phone to collect your email while you are traveling by train or querying Siri while riding in a car. These services usually require a data plan.

Mobile broadband

Cable Internet Service

The gold standard of fixed Internet access is **cable Internet service**, which is offered by the same companies that supply cable television. Cable service is a luxury enjoyed by developed countries; emerging nations cannot afford its expensive infrastructure, and device owners may not be able to afford the high cost of monthly subscriptions.

▶ **How does cable Internet service work?** The cable television system was originally designed for remote areas where TV broadcast signals could not be received with a roof-mounted antenna. These systems were called community antenna television, or CATV. The CATV concept was to install one or more large, expensive satellite dishes in a community, catch TV signals with these dishes, and then send the signals over a system of cables to individual homes.

With cables branching out from a central location, the topology of a CATV system happened to also work as the infrastructure for a digital data network. Now, in addition to carrying signals for cable television, the CATV infrastructure also carries Internet data. When your cable TV company becomes your Internet provider, your computer becomes part of a neighborhood network linked together by the cable company's wiring (Figure 3-35).

Figure 3-35: Cable television infrastructure

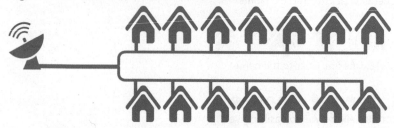

▶ **How does the system transport data?** The cable modem supplied with your subscription converts signals from your computer to signals that can travel over the cable infrastructure. CATV coaxial and fiber-optic cables have plenty of bandwidth to carry television signals for hundreds of channels in addition to digital data. CATV cables provide bandwidth for television signals, incoming data signals, and outgoing data signals (Figure 3-36).

Figure 3-36: TV and data streams on one cable

TV CHANNELS
Downstream Data
Upstream Data

▶ **How fast is cable Internet service?** Most cable Internet service is asymmetric, with upload speeds considerably slower than download speeds to discourage subscribers from setting up public Web servers. Service plans range from economy packages offering speeds of 25 Mbps to an expensive 400 Mbps package. Your actual speed may be less than the advertised speed due to traffic from other subscribers in your neighborhood.

Telephone Network Internet Service

Some people limp along with narrowband access to the Internet, which is frustratingly slow. Telephone companies offer four types of service: dial-up, ISDN, DSL, and FTTH. Only one of these technologies is considered broadband. Are the other three of any use at all?

▶ **What is a dial-up connection?** A **dial-up** connection is a fixed Internet connection that uses a voiceband modem and the telephone company's circuit-switched network to transport data between a computer and an ISP. A **voiceband modem** converts digital signals from a computer into audible analog signals that can travel over telephone landlines. A modem transmits a 1070 Hz tone for a 0 data bit and a 1270 Hz tone for a 1 data bit (Figure 3-37).

Figure 3-37: A voiceband modem changes voltages to audio tones

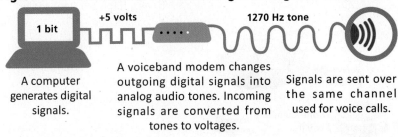

A computer generates digital signals.

A voiceband modem changes outgoing digital signals into analog audio tones. Incoming signals are converted from tones to voltages.

Signals are sent over the same channel used for voice calls.

▶ **How does a dial-up connection work?** The dial-up voiceband modem places a regular telephone call to the ISP. When the ISP's computer answers the call, a dedicated circuit is established between the modem and the ISP. The procedure is similar to placing a voice call and someone at the ISP answering the phone.

The circuit remains connected for the duration of the call to carry data between the computer and the ISP. As data arrives at the ISP, a router sends it out over the Internet (Figure 3-38).

Figure 3-38: Dial-up infrastructure

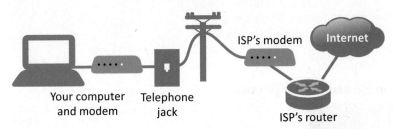

Your computer and modem   Telephone jack   ISP's modem   Internet   ISP's router

▶ **How fast is dial-up service?** The maximum speed of a dial-up connection is 56 Kbps, so it is not classified as broadband. Actual data transfer speeds are affected by factors such as the quality of your phone line and connection. In practice, the top speed for downloads is about 44 Kbps. For uploads, the data rate drops to 33 Kbps or less—that's kilobytes, not megabytes!

Dial-up service is the Internet connection of last resort for people who live in remote areas where landlines are the only communication services.

QuickCheck

Dial-up connections use a voiceband modem to convert signals from _____.

a. analog to digital

b. tones to pulses for outgoing signals, and voltages to binary digits for incoming signals

c. digital to analog

d. digital to analog for outgoing signals, and analog to digital for incoming signals

3

▶ **How about ISDN?** ISDN stands for Integrated Services Digital Network. It essentially divides a telephone line into two channels: one for data and one for voice. The data channel uses packet switching and sends data in digital format, unlike dial-up, which uses analog tones to carry data. With data rates of 128 Kbps, ISDN was only briefly popular in the United States, though in Europe it still has an active base of users.

▶ **What is DSL?** DSL (digital subscriber line) is a high-speed, digital, always-on, Internet access technology that runs over standard phone lines at speeds that range from 5 to 25 Mbps.

▶ **How does DSL work?** A DSL modem converts computer signals into high-frequency data signals. Voice and data signals travel over telephone lines to the telephone company's local switching station. There, voice signals are routed to the regular telephone system and data signals are routed to the Internet (Figure 3-39).

Figure 3-39: DSL data path

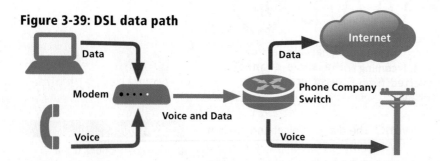

▶ **What about a fiber Internet connection?** As communication companies install more and more fiber-optic cables, an increasing number of consumers have this high-speed Internet option. FTTH stands for fiber-to-the-home. It is the use of high-capacity fiber-optic cables, rather than coaxial cables or twisted pair wires, to connect homes to broader municipal networks.

As telephone companies upgrade their infrastructure with fiber-optic cables, they are able to offer access speeds ranging from 100 Mbps to 1,000 Mbps. These speeds are available only in areas where fiber runs to homes. If you see a crew laying orange cable carriers like the one in Figure 3-40, fiber-optic Internet service might soon be available in your neighborhood.

Figure 3-40: Fiber-optic cables are often housed in orange carriers

Satellite Internet Service

Communications satellites seem so retro. They settled into orbit during an era when your grandparents watched *The Jetsons* and the United States rushed to catch up to the Soviet Union's spaceflight program. Yet, at one point in time, satellites used for continent-to-continent telephone communications appeared to be a natural fit with the emerging Internet. Unfortunately, those satellites had a fatal flaw that reduced their suitability for today's Internet. Has that problem been solved? Read on to find out.

▶ **What is satellite Internet service?** Satellite Internet service is a means of distributing broadband asymmetric Internet access by broadcasting signals to a satellite. In many rural areas, satellite Internet service is the only alternative to a slow dial-up connection.

Prior to 2020, the communications satellites providing Internet service were in geosynchronous equatorial orbit (GEO) 22,000 miles above the Earth's surface. Signals traveling from Earth to a satellite have a latency of 1,000 to 1,400 ms. That's a delay of about 1 second or more.

Geosynchronous latency might not pose much of a problem for general Web surfing and downloading files, but it can become a showstopper for interactive gaming, and for video chat, automated stock trading, and similar services that require quick response.

▶ **Is there faster satellite Internet service?** Yes. Low Earth orbit (LEO) satellites circle 2,000 miles above the Earth. Because they are much closer than GEO satellites, latency is reduced to about 40 ms—similar to a cable Internet connection.

▶ **How does satellite Internet service work?** Figure 3-41 illustrates how data from a customer's computer (1) is converted into signals by the customer's modem (2) that are carried by cable to a personal satellite dish (3) and broadcast to a communication satellite (4). Signals are rebroadcast from the satellite to a groundstation (5) that forwards them to the Internet (6).

Figure 3-41: Your data travels into space and back

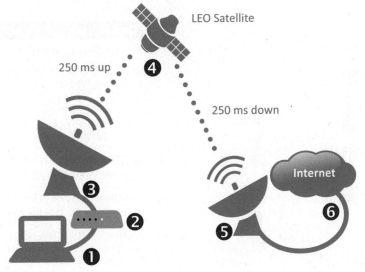

LEO Satellite

250 ms up   ❹

250 ms down

Internet

❸
❷
❶
❺
❻

3

Mobile Broadband Service

Mobile broadband delivers voice, data, and text messages by means of a cellular tower that transmits and receives signals. The defining characteristic of mobile broadband is that you can use it while in motion. As you reach the edge of a cellular tower's range, your signal is seamlessly handed off to the next tower within range.

Mobile broadband is available on smartphones, cellular-equipped tablets and laptop computers, cellular smartwatches, and even some IoT devices. The most popular device for accessing mobile broadband is a smartphone.

◗ **What's the difference between a mobile connection and Wi-Fi?** Smartphones support both cellular and Wi-Fi connections. Cellular connections require a service plan from a cell phone carrier, such as Verizon. Those service plans may distinguish between voice, data, and text for billing purposes.

When using a cellular connection, voice calls, texts, and data travel through a cellular tower. The minutes you use for voice calls, the number of texts you send, and the amount of data you transfer are tracked as part of your cellular plan. Fees may apply depending on the type of cellular plan you've selected. The upside is that you have mobile broadband coverage, so you can be a passenger in a moving car and carry out a phone conversation or stream music without interruption.

Wi-Fi connections can be supplied through a home network or a network located in a coffee shop, airport, or other business. When using a Wi-Fi connection, voice calls, texts, and data travel from a local area network to the Internet. Using Wi-Fi, voice calls do not count as minutes in your cellular plan, text messages are not tracked by your cellular carrier, and data transfers do not count against your cellular data limit. Wi-Fi is not mobile broadband, however, because you must remain within range of the Wi-Fi network for the duration of your call or streaming activity. Wi-Fi signals have a range of about 150 feet indoors and 300 feet outdoors. Unlike the cellular system, Wi-Fi has no standard for handing off signals when you move out of range (Figure 3-42).

Figure 3-42: The difference between cellular and Wi-Fi

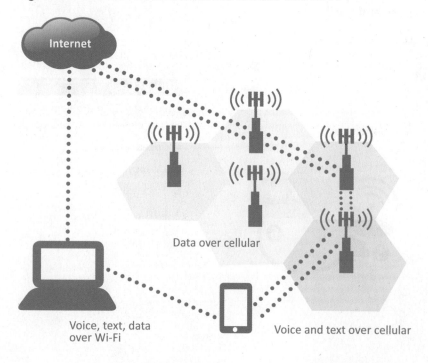

Data over cellular

Voice, text, data over Wi-Fi

Voice and text over cellular

▶ **How fast is mobile broadband service?** Mobile broadband has evolved through several generations. The most recent of these generations is 5G.

3G (third generation) service was available in the United States beginning in 2001. Common protocols included CDMA, which reached maximum download speeds of 4.9 Mbps, and GSM EDGE, with 1.6 Mbps speeds.

4G (fourth generation) technologies include LTE, which has typical download rates of 150 Mbps and upload rates of 50 Mbps. The range of 4G signals is about 10 miles.

5G (fifth generation) networks can carry data at ten times the speed of a 4G network and with much lower latency. 5G signals have a very short unobstructed range of about 1,500 feet. Instead of massive cell towers beaming signals over a broad area, 5G uses localized small cells with discreet transceivers mounted on nearby buildings and utility poles. For the near future, 4G and 5G will work together to provide coverage in cities, towns, and rural areas.

Mobile broadband speed decreases at the edges of coverage. It can be reduced by obstacles such as trees, hills, walls, and even metal roofs. Electromagnetic interference from speakers, microwave ovens, and other electrical devices can reduce speeds, too. Rain, snow, and high humidity can also reduce speeds.

▶ **Can I access mobile broadband with my laptop?** A mobile broadband device can provide Internet access from a laptop or desktop computer. Most of today's smartphones include a **tethering** feature that connects wirelessly with other digital devices. Figure 3-43 demonstrates how to set up tethering to create a **mobile hotspot**. Just remember that data sent over the tethered connection accumulates toward your monthly data usage total.

QuickCheck

Which of the following is true about LTE?

a. It is 3G technology.

b. It is not affected by weather like earlier mobile technologies were.

c. It is slower than a 5G network.

d. It uses circuit-switched networks for data.

Figure 3-43: Create a network with your cell phone

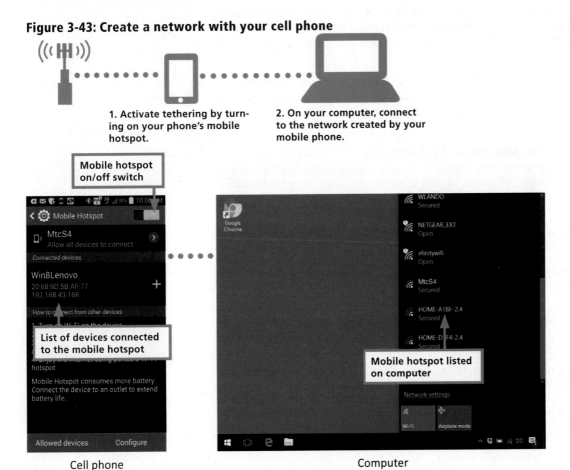

1. Activate tethering by turning on your phone's mobile hotspot.

2. On your computer, connect to the network created by your mobile phone.

Mobile hotspot on/off switch

List of devices connected to the mobile hotspot

Mobile hotspot listed on computer

Cell phone   Computer

Wi-Fi Hotspots

Wi-Fi hotspots are everywhere. Pull out your smartphone in any coffee shop, airport, hotel lobby, or university building and you'll likely find more than one network that serves as an Internet on-ramp. But public Wi-Fi hotspots are fraught with security risks, so it pays to know how they work.

▶ **How do Wi-Fi hotspots work?** A **Wi-Fi hotspot** is a wireless local area network, usually operated by a business, that offers Internet access to the public. The network has an Internet connection and a device called an access point that broadcasts Wi-Fi signals within a range of about 150 feet. Any and all devices with Wi-Fi capability can detect the signal (Figure 3-44).

Figure 3-44: Behind the scenes of a coffee shop Wi-Fi hotspot

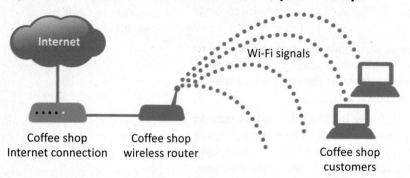

▶ **How fast is hotspot access?** The speed of a hotspot is related to the speed of the Wi-Fi network and the service that connects it to the Internet. A hotspot that goes through a 1 Mbps DSL line will be slower than a hotspot that goes through a 50 Mbps cable Internet connection. Hotspot speed can vary depending on your distance from the access point, the number of people logged in, and interference from other networks.

▶ **Is hotspot access secure?** The data that travels over unsecured hotspots is not encrypted, so eavesdroppers can easily tap into data that flows over the network. Figure 3-45 summarizes hotspot risk levels.

Figure 3-45: Gauge your risk at Wi-Fi hotspots

 Browsing. When using a Wi-Fi hotspot for simple browsing activities such as checking sports scores, reading Google news, and looking for directions, your security risk is fairly low if you have antivirus software running on the device you use to access the hotspot.

 Using secure sites. Your security risk is low when you are accessing secured Web sites that have addresses beginning with HTTPS. These secured sites, which are used for activities such as online banking, accessing medical records, and making credit card purchases, encrypt the data that you enter to keep it safe from eavesdroppers.

 File sharing. Eavesdroppers might be able to access the files on your computer if you have file sharing turned on. When using public networks, you should turn file sharing off. You can do so manually if your operating system does not offer that option when you connect.

 Using unsecured sites. When you log in to unsecured sites while using public Wi-Fi hotspots, a wireless eavesdropper could potentially snag your user ID and password information, then use it later to access your accounts. Logging in to your Webmail account, for example, could be risky if your user ID and password are transmitted over an unsecured connection.

QuickCheck

Which of the following is most likely to affect the maximum speed of a Wi-Fi hotspot?

a. The hotspot's Internet service provider

b. Your Internet service provider

c. The number of people who are using the hotspot

d. Whether the hotspot is secured or not

▶ **How do I access a Wi-Fi hotspot?** The network utility on your computer or phone automatically senses a Wi-Fi network and adds it to the list of available connections. You can then connect using your network utility. Some Wi-Fi hotspots can be accessed simply by starting your browser and accepting the license. Other networks require you to enter a password, which you can obtain from the hotspot manager.

Select public networks with care. Hackers create networks that have names similar to those of legitimate hotspots. Those networks are not usually secured. Network utilities indicate unsecured hotspots in various ways. Microsoft Windows displays a shield icon for hotspots that are not secured.

If you mistakenly connect to a non-secured network, any passwords you enter or data you transmit could fall into the hands of a hacker. You can view a list of available networks and connect to one, as shown in Figure 3-46.

QuickCheck

In Figure 3-46, what tells you that the HolidayInn-FREE! network is not secured?

a. The misspelled SSID

b. The word *FREE!*

c. The shield icon

d. The number of bars

Figure 3-46: Access Wi-Fi hotspots securely

Look for a list of nearby Wi-Fi hotspots using the Wireless icon on the desktop or home screen.

Source: IHG 2015

Some Wi-Fi hotspots display an access screen when you start a browser while within range of the hotspot.

QuickQuiz   Section C

1. A specification such as 10 Mbps that we commonly refer to as "connection speed" is technically a measurement of [_____] .

2. An Internet connection can be fast and have an acceptable ping rate but still have poor quality due to excessive [_____] and packet loss.

3. A utility called [_____] reports the path of packets over the Internet.

4. The problem with GEO satellite Internet service is excessive [_____] .

5. The defining characteristic of mobile broadband is that you can use it while in [_____] .

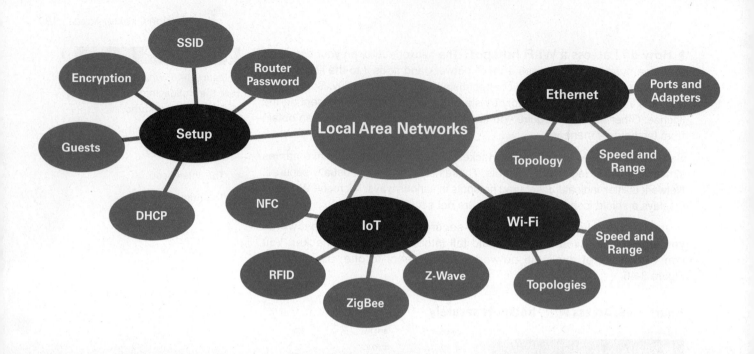

Objectives

▶ Diagram the components and connections in a typical home LAN.

▶ Explain the roles of MAC addresses and IP addresses in local area networks.

▶ List five advantages of Ethernet wired network standards.

▶ Explain the pros and cons of wireless mesh networks as compared to centralized wireless networks.

▶ Compare the speeds and ranges of Ethernet and Wi-Fi.

▶ List five steps for securely configuring a wireless router.

▶ State the purpose of an SSID.

▶ List four types of wireless encryption.

▶ Identify tools that can be used to monitor network activity

▶ Provide two example scenarios for using RFID tags and NFC tags.

▶ List three low-power wireless standards used for IoT networks.

▶ Evaluate potential security exposure for data that is collected by IoT networks.

A network of your own. What was once a
technology enjoyed only by huge corporations and government agencies can now be yours. Although the cloud offers apps, storage, and connectivity, keeping some of your data local offers security that is not available at remote sites. For passing data between your own devices and collecting data from wearables and home monitoring systems, your own network can become a safe little data fortress. Section D guides you through the basics of local area networks, including how to set them up.

Terminology

AirDrop	Wi-Fi	wireless encryption	NFC
network interface	IEEE 802.11	WEP	Bluetooth LE
controller	Wi-Fi adapter	WPA	ZigBee
MAC address	dual-band	WPS	Z-Wave
Ethernet	MU-MIMO	wireless encryption key	
IEEE 802.3	WAN port	Guest network	
Ethernet adapter	SSID	RFID	

LAN Basics

In the early years of personal computers, networks were scarce. Most personal computers functioned as standalone units, and computing was essentially a solitary activity in which one person interacted with one computer. Some computer engineers, however, had the foresight to anticipate that personal computers could be networked to provide advantages not available with standalone computers.

▶ **What are the characteristics of LANs?** Local area networks are often referred to as LANs. They are designed to provide connectivity for devices within a limited area, typically within the premises of a home, office building, business, or school.

LANs use many of the same network technologies as the Internet, just on a smaller scale. They have a topology. They use communication protocols to ship packets. They require communication channels such as cables or wireless signals. They also include data communication equipment such as routers and modems. Figure 3-47 illustrates a LAN that you can easily build.

Figure 3-47: Build this LAN

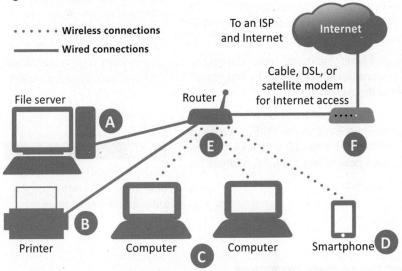

The plan for your network hinges on a centralized router that supports wired and wireless connections.

A Connect a computer to a wired connection for maximum speed. Use it for online games or as a file server where you store and back up your data.

B Connect a printer to a wired or wireless connection so that all devices on the network can access it.

C Connect computers wirelessly so you can use them in various rooms.

D Connect your smartphone and you'll be able to use the LAN's Internet connection instead of your expensive data plan.

E The router is the centerpiece of your network. Most wireless routers support five wired devices and a maximum of 255 wireless devices.

F All the devices in your LAN can access the Internet if you connect the router to a modem supplied by an ISP.

QuickCheck

In the LAN depicted in Figure 3-47, all the network data goes through the _____.

a. modem

b. printer

c. router

d. Internet

▶ **Do I need a LAN to share files?** Not necessarily. If you have two devices within about 30 feet of each other, you might be able to transfer files using Bluetooth. The Windows operating system has a Share feature that uses a Bluetooth connection to transmit files between two nearby computers. macOS provides a tool called **AirDrop** for making a point-to-point connection between two computers.

Bluetooth is generally used to connect only two devices that are quite close to each other. To connect multiple devices, you'll want to use a LAN.

▶ **Are LANs regulated by the government?** LANs can use wired or wireless connections. Wired connections are unregulated because the signals traveling through a wire are unlikely to interfere with broadcasts to radios, televisions, or other networks.

Most wireless LANs use the 2.4 GHz, 5.0 GHz, and 6.0 GHz unlicensed frequencies so that they can be set up without applying to the FCC for permission. The few unlicensed frequencies are crowded, however, and neighboring networks that are forced to use the same frequencies pose security risks.

▶ **Are my devices equipped to access LANs?** The circuitry that enables a device to access a LAN is called a **network interface controller** (NIC). NICs are built into the circuit boards of most digital devices. NICs are also available as add-on circuit boards and USB devices.

NICs contain a **MAC address** (media access control address) used to uniquely identify devices on LANs. MAC addresses are usually assigned by the manufacturer of digital devices and embedded in the hardware.

A MAC address functions in conjunction with an IP address on a LAN. Each device on a LAN has a MAC address (sometimes listed as the Wi-Fi address or physical address). DHCP assigns an IP address to a device and links it to the device's MAC address. Figure 3-48 illustrates how to find the MAC address on various devices.

QuickCheck

Which frequencies are unlicensed?

a. Wireless frequencies

b. Radio frequencies

c. Internet frequencies

d. 2.4, 5.0, and 6.0 GHz

Terminology

The term *MAC address* has nothing to do with Apple's Mac computers. Both PCs and Macs have MAC addresses, as do smartphones, routers, and other data communication equipment.

Try It!

Find the MAC address for the device you're currently using. Does it look similar to an IP address?

Figure 3-48: Find the MAC address

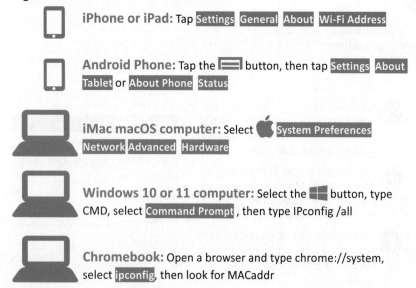

iPhone or iPad: Tap Settings General About Wi-Fi Address

Android Phone: Tap the ▤ button, then tap Settings About Tablet or About Phone Status

iMac macOS computer: Select System Preferences Network Advanced Hardware

Windows 10 or 11 computer: Select the ⊞ button, type CMD, select Command Prompt , then type IPconfig /all

Chromebook: Open a browser and type chrome://system, select ipconfig, then look for MACaddr

Ethernet

The first computer networks were configured with wired connections. These networks used a variety of topologies and protocols, but a technology called Ethernet emerged as the dominant standard and became a key element in large and small computer networks.

▶ **What is Ethernet?** Ethernet is a wired network technology that is defined by IEEE 802.3 standards. It was first deployed in 1976 and is now used for wired connections in just about every local area network.

▶ **Why is Ethernet so popular?** Ethernet's success is attributable to several factors:

Easy. Ethernet is relatively easy to understand, implement, manage, and maintain.

Secure. The wired connections in an Ethernet LAN are more secure than wireless LAN technologies.

Inexpensive. As a nonproprietary technology, Ethernet equipment is available from a variety of vendors, and market competition keeps prices low.

Flexible. Current Ethernet standards allow extensive flexibility in network configurations to meet the needs of small and large installations.

Compatible. Ethernet is compatible with popular Wi-Fi wireless technology, so it is possible to mix wired and wireless devices on a single network.

▶ **How does Ethernet work?** Ethernet was originally a bus topology in which computers were all strung along a cable like birds on a power line. Today's Ethernet LANs are usually arranged in a star topology with computers wired to central switching circuitry that is incorporated in modern routers. Data sent from a computer on the network is transmitted to the router, which then sends the data to the network nodes (Figure 3-49).

Terminology

IEEE is the Institute of Electrical and Electronics Engineers, a professional organization that develops technical standards in areas such as electronics and networking. These standards are grouped and numbered. Many IEEE LAN standards begin with the number 802.

QuickCheck

Ethernet and Wi-Fi are compatible network standards.

a. True

b. False

3

Figure 3-49: Ethernet topology

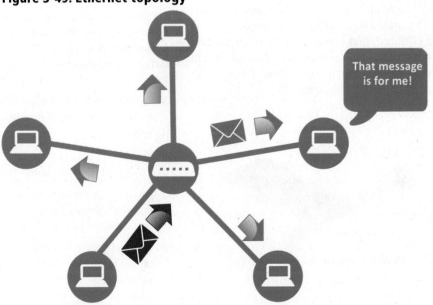

The central router handles all the traffic within the Ethernet. The router receives data and then broadcasts it to all of the nodes. The data is accepted only by the device to which it was addressed.

▶ **How fast is Ethernet?** The original Ethernet standard carried data over a coaxial cable at 10 Mbps. Ethernet encompasses a family of LAN technologies that offer various data transmission rates, as shown in Figure 3-50. Today, most personal computers and LAN equipment work with Gigabit Ethernet.

Figure 3-50 Ethernet standards

Ethernet Standard	IEEE Designation	Speed
10BaseT Ethernet	IEEE 802.3i	10 Mbps
Fast Ethernet	IEEE 802.3u	100 Mbps
Gigabit Ethernet	IEEE 802.3z	1,000 Mbps
10 Gigabit Ethernet	IEEE 802.3ae	10 Gbps
40/100 Gigabit Ethernet	IEEE 802.3ba	40 or 100 Gbps

▶ **How can I tell if a device is Ethernet ready?** Many computers have a built-in Ethernet port located on the system case. The port looks very similar to an oversized telephone jack (Figure 3-51).

Figure 3-51: Does your computer have an Ethernet port?

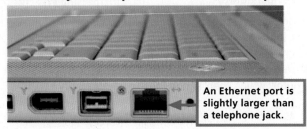

An Ethernet port is slightly larger than a telephone jack.

▶ **What if a computer doesn't have an Ethernet port?** If you want a wired network connection but your computer has no Ethernet port, you can purchase and install an **Ethernet adapter** (also called an Ethernet card). A USB Ethernet adapter plugs into a USB port and can be used with laptop and desktop computers. You also have the option of installing an Ethernet card in an expansion slot inside the system unit of a desktop computer. Figure 3-52 illustrates two types of adapters for adding Ethernet ports.

Figure 3-52: Ethernet adapters

Ethernet adapter for USB port   Ethernet adapter for expansion slot

Try It!

Check your computer. Does it have an Ethernet port for wired network connections?

QuickCheck

Suppose you have a Fast Ethernet connection to your LAN. Will it keep up with the data you exchange with the Internet?

a. Yes, Fast Ethernet is faster than my Internet connection speed.

b. Yes, my ISP uses Fast Ethernet for my modem.

c. No, my Internet connection is faster than my Ethernet connection.

d. No, Fast Ethernet makes streaming video pause occasionally.

Wi-Fi

Wi-Fi refers to a set of wireless networking technologies defined by **IEEE 802.11** standards. A Wi-Fi device transmits data as radio waves and is compatible with Ethernet, so you can use the two technologies in a single network.

◗ **How does Wi-Fi work?** You can set up Wi-Fi in two ways. One option is to use wireless mesh topology in which devices broadcast directly to each other (Figure 3-53).

Figure 3-53: Wireless mesh configuration

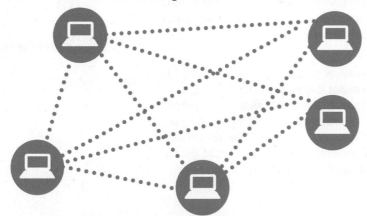

Wireless mesh networks are conceptually simple but provide few security safeguards. This type of connection is best limited to occasional use when you want to temporarily connect two computers to share a few files.

A second option for Wi-Fi networks is a star topology in which a centralized broadcasting device—a wireless access point—coordinates communication among network devices. Technically, the centralized device is a wireless access point, but that function is built into most routers (Figure 3-54).

Figure 3-54: Wireless star configuration

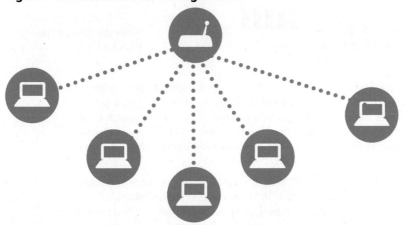

The most common wireless network technology uses a centralized device to handle data that travels from one device to another.

Terminology

Wireless mesh networks are sometimes called *peer networks* or *ad-hoc networks*. Wireless networks that depend on a router are sometimes called *wireless infrastructure networks* or *managed networks*.

3

QuickCheck

Which Wi-Fi infrastructure is more similar to Ethernet?

a. Wireless mesh

b. Wireless star

▶ **How can I tell if a device is Wi-Fi ready?** Today, Wi-Fi capability is included with just about every desktop, laptop, tablet, and smartphone. Don't worry if your device has no visible antenna for transmitting and receiving data; the antenna is likely integrated into the case. Older equipment without Wi-Fi can be outfitted with a **Wi-Fi adapter** that plugs into a USB port or an internal expansion slot.

▶ **What is the range of a Wi-Fi network?** Wi-Fi signals may reach up to 300 feet (90 meters) from the router. Thick cement walls, steel beams, and other environmental obstacles can drastically reduce this range.

▶ **How fast is Wi-Fi?** Wi-Fi speed depends on the Wi-Fi standards of your router and your network devices. Current Wi-Fi standards include 802.11ac (Wi-Fi 5) and 802.11ax (Wi-Fi 6). When setting up a Wi-Fi network, check your devices. The router you select should support the fastest device you want to use on the network.

Routers can transmit data over different frequency bands and simultaneously to multiple devices. The advertised speed of a router is typically its total throughput capacity on all frequencies and to all devices. It is not necessarily the speed available for a single device. For example, a router capable of transmitting at 600 Mbps at 2.4 GHz frequency and 1300 Mbps at 5 GHz might be advertised as having a speed of 1900 Mbps, but the maximum speed you would get is 1300 Mbps. Figure 3-55 can help you make sense of advertised router speeds.

QuickCheck

Are Wi-Fi actual speeds faster than Ethernet actual speeds?

a. Yes.

b. No.

c. Some Wi-Fi speeds are faster than 10BaseT Ethernet.

d. Only 802.11ac Wi-Fi is slower than Ethernet.

QuickCheck

In Figure 3-55, how many of the routers are dual-band?

a. 0

b. 1

c. 2

d. 3

Figure 3-55: Wireless router options

Advertised speed	Max speed per user	Bands	Range	MU-MIMO	Uses
600 Mbps	600 Mbps	600 Mbps at 2.4 GHz		None	Browsing, email, voice chat
1900 Mbps 2x2	1300 Mbps	600 Mbps at 2.4 GHz 1300 Mbps at 5 GHz		2x2	Online gaming, simultaneous music downloads
1900 Mbps 4x4	1300 Mbps	600 Mbps at 2.4 GHz 1300 Mbps at 5 GHz		4x4	Video streaming, multiple-story buildings

Speed: Router speed can be designated by a single number or a combination of numbers. A router specification such as 600+1300 Mbps indicates the speed for each frequency. This router would be able to supply 1300 Mbps to a single user, not 1900 Mbps.

Bands: Wi-Fi can be transmitted over 2.4 GHz, 5 GHz, or 6 GHz frequencies. When a router uses two frequencies, it is referred to as **dual-band**. Dual-band offers flexibility to support various network devices and can overcome interference on either of the bands.

MU-MIMO: Devices with one or more antennas use **MU-MIMO** (multi-user multiple-input multiple-output) technology that transmits signals simultaneously to multiple devices. A router with two channels is designated as 2x2. A 4x4 router can broadcast simultaneously to four devices using two frequency bands. Adding channels does not increase the speed to each device.

Set Up Your Own Network

Having your own network is great. You can access the Internet from multiple devices, share files, and download apps to your smartphone without maxing out your data plan. But LANs can be a security risk. Here's how to set up your own safe and secure LAN.

▶ **What's the general procedure for setting up a network?** The basic steps for setting up a LAN are:

1 Plug in the router and connect it to your Internet modem.

2 Configure the router.

3 Connect wired and wireless devices.

▶ **How do I connect the router to my Internet modem?** Use a cable to connect the router's **WAN port** to the Internet modem's Ethernet port (Figure 3-56).

Figure 3-56: Connect the router to the Internet modem

Connect the router's WAN or Internet port to the modem provided by your ISP.

▶ **How do I set up a router?** A router has no screen or keyboard of its own; to access the router's configuration software, you'll use a computer and connect to the router using a browser. Instructions are included with the router.

Change the password. The first step is to change the router password. All routers are shipped with a standard password. Your router can be accessed and controlled by anyone who enters that password until you've created a secure password, as shown in Figure 3-57.

Figure 3-57: Change your router's password

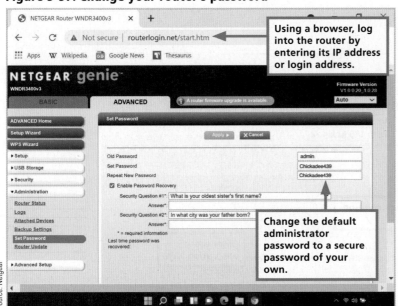

Using a browser, log into the router by entering its IP address or login address.

Change the default administrator password to a secure password of your own.

Create an SSID. After changing the router password, you can create an SSID for your network. An **SSID** (service set identifier) is the name of a wireless network. In areas where there are overlapping wireless networks, such as in a city or on a college campus, SSIDs help you log in to the right network, rather than a network run by a hacker who will try to suck important information off your computer as soon as you connect.

At the same time you change the router password, you can decide whether or not you want to broadcast the SSID. When SSID broadcasting is turned on, any wireless device passing by can see that a network exists. Go ahead and broadcast the SSID, as shown in Figure 3-58. You can use encryption to secure the network.

Try It!

Check your computer. What is the SSID for the network you're currently using? (Hint: Click the Wi-Fi icon to see a list of networks.)

Figure 3-58: Create an SSID

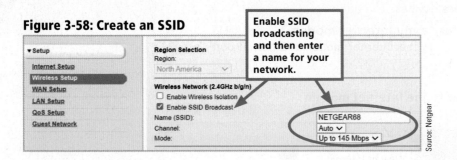

Source: Netgear

Activate encryption. **Wireless encryption** scrambles the data transmitted between wireless devices and then unscrambles the data only on devices that have a valid encryption key. **WEP** (**Wired Equivalent Privacy**) is the oldest and weakest wireless encryption protocol. **WPA** (Wi-Fi Protected Access) and related protocols, WPA2 and PSK, offer more security. Use the strongest encryption that is available.

When setting up encryption, you'll create a **wireless encryption key** (sometimes referred to as a network security key or password). The key is similar to a password. Any devices that connect to your secure LAN must have this key unless you've configured your router for **WPS** (Wi-Fi Protected Setup). With WPS on the router, devices can connect using an autoconnect feature. Figure 3-59 illustrates how to activate wireless encryption.

QuickCheck

What is the most effective encryption technology?

a. SSID

b. WEP

c. WPA

Figure 3-59: Activate encryption

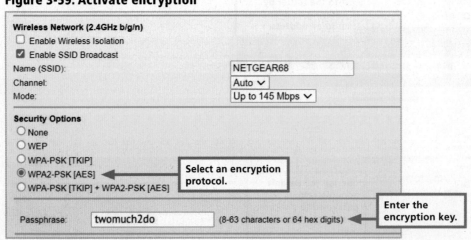

Source: Netgear

Configure the Guest network. A **Guest network** is essentially a second network that you can configure on your LAN's router. Guest networks allow visitors to access the Internet through your LAN, but don't allow them to access other resources on your network, such as your data files. Some routers come preconfigured with a Guest network. You should be sure to check your router's settings to verify that they meet your security requirements.

You can view Guest network settings using your router's configuration software. Your Guest network will have its own SSID and security settings. You may be allowed to change these settings, or the router manufacturer may have designated permanent settings.

If the Guest network is secured, it should have its own unique encryption key or password, which you'll have to supply to your visitors. Leaving the Guest network unsecured makes access open to anyone—not a good idea. Even when secured, a Guest network offers a potential security risk, so it should be disabled when you are not expecting visitors.

Activate DHCP. Each workstation requires a unique address for sending and receiving data. When you configure your router to act as a DHCP server, it will automatically assign an address to each device that joins your network. Figure 3-60 illustrates how to set up DHCP.

Try It!

Does the network you usually use have a Guest network? How can you tell?

3

Figure 3-60: Activate DHCP

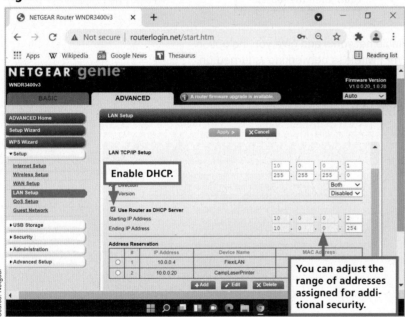

Source: Netgear

QuickCheck

If you have four wireless devices connected to your network and you do not want any interlopers to join, you can configure _____ to assign only four IP addresses.

a. SSID

b. WEP

c. DHCP

d. the Guest network

❱ **How do I connect devices to a LAN?** Simply connect wired devices to the router using a network cable. Routers automatically sense wired devices and allow them to initiate a connection. A password is not needed for wired devices because the signals do not travel through the air where they are easy to intercept.

A wireless router is constantly broadcasting its SSID. Wireless devices, such as smartphones, laptops, and tablets, sense the router's signal and add the SSID to a list of nearby networks. The first time you connect to a secured network, you must enter the encryption key. Your device remembers the key for future logins.

Laptops and tablets running Windows display a list of nearby networks and their security status. Figure 3-61 illustrates the process of connecting to a secured network from a device using Windows 11.

Figure 3-61: Connecting to a LAN with Windows 11

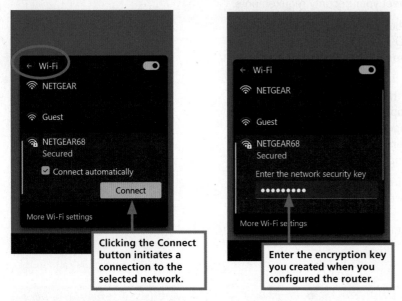

Clicking the Connect button initiates a connection to the selected network.

Enter the encryption key you created when you configured the router.

Like PCs, Macs automatically sense available networks and give you the option of connecting to them. Make sure that Wi-Fi wireless networking is turned on, then enter the encryption key when asked for the password (Figure 3-62).

Figure 3-62: Connecting to a LAN with macOS

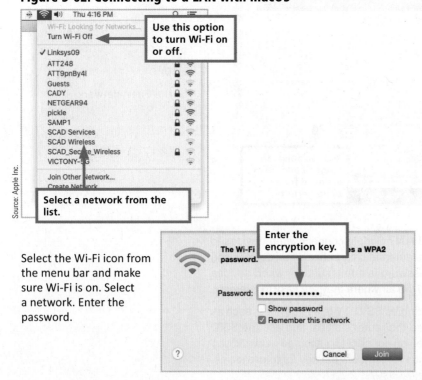

Source: Apple Inc.

Use this option to turn Wi-Fi on or off.

Select a network from the list.

Enter the encryption key.

Select the Wi-Fi icon from the menu bar and make sure Wi-Fi is on. Select a network. Enter the password.

Network Monitoring

If your data isn't moving and you have no Internet access, the problem could be on your LAN. When your network has stopped sending and receiving packets, you might be able to correct the problem by turning off your router and Internet modem, waiting a few seconds, and then turning them on again.

▶ **How do I monitor network activity?** On Macs, you can view the number of incoming and outgoing packets using the Activity Monitor (Figure 3-63).

3

Figure 3-63: Mac network monitoring

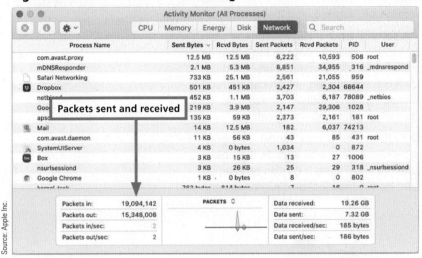

Source: Apple Inc.

On a PC, the Resource Monitor provides information about incoming and outgoing packets. It shows the incoming and outgoing activity for each connection, but does not offer a summarized total (Figure 3-64).

Figure 3-64: Windows Resource Monitor

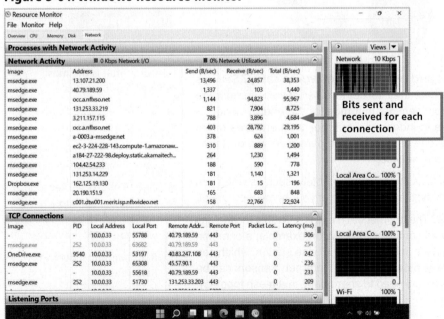

IoT Networks

Those plants you're growing indoors need constant attention. Would you like a text message when they need water? The Internet of Things connects active sensors and passive tags to communication networks, making it easier to remotely monitor places and things.

▶ **Do IoT networks use Wi-Fi technology?** Most sensors use battery power to collect data and to transmit it. Extended battery life is possible only if these activities consume small amounts of power. Wi-Fi is fairly power hungry, so it is not an optimal IoT technology. Existing wireless technologies such as **RFID** and **NFC** offer potential solutions. Additional low-power, short-range technologies developed specifically for IoT networks include **Bluetooth LE**, **ZigBee**, and **Z-Wave**.

▶ **What's the difference between a sensor and a tag?** A sensor, such as a thermometer or heart rate monitor, actively collects data. A tag contains passive data. An RFID tag in a passport, for example, contains personal data, such as the name and birth date that are stored on the tag, which can be read electronically. An NFC tag might be attached to merchandise, for example, so that you can tap it with your cell phone to see its price and specifications.

Tags can be battery powered, but many RFID and NFC tags contain no power source of their own and depend on the receiving device to provide the power for data exchange. Data from tags like the ones in Figure 3-65 can be read by network devices and used for identification, for making electronic payments, and for tracking things or people.

Figure 3-65: RFID and NFC tags

▶ **What kinds of sensor input and output do networks carry?** Sensors can use networks to transmit the data they collect to other devices for storage and output. For example, data from sensors that monitor the energy usage of your air conditioning unit relative to indoor and outdoor temperatures might be stored on your home network, on your electric company's server, or on the sensor manufacturer's cloud storage service.

Networks also provide a way to access the sensors remotely, such as when you use your smartphone at work to adjust the temperature of your home thermostat.

▶ **How do IoT networks work?** The Internet of Things is a flexible technology with many different applications and configurations. As an example, a common configuration for home monitoring is to link sensors to a base station, which can then ship data to routers in local area networks and the Internet. Sensors can be linked in a star topology or, if the sensors need to share data, in a mesh topology.

Terminology

RFID stands for radio-frequency identification. RFID tags have a range of about 300 feet (100 meters). *NFC* stands for near field communication. NFC tags have a range of just four inches (10 cm).

QuickCheck

If you are putting together an IoT network of home control sensors, what is the most efficient configuration?

a. Sensors equipped with Wi-Fi to transmit data to a Web site

b. Sensors with IP addresses to communicate with your LAN

c. ZigBee or Z-Wave sensors that send results to a base station, which communicates with your LAN's router

d. RFID tags and a dedicated RFID reader

▶ **How do sensors communicate with an IoT network?** IoT sensors can be wired to a base station, but more typically they are equipped with some type of communication device that allows them to wirelessly send and receive signals. Digi XBee chips use radio signals to transport data wirelessly. Devices like the one shown in Figure 3-66 can easily pair with sensors in small form factor packages.

Figure 3-66: XBee transmitter

▶ **Are IoT networks secure?** Data passing over IoT networks can seem trivial, but is it? Do you care if anyone else knows that your fitness wristband recorded lots of activity between midnight and 3:00 am last Saturday? As the IoT collects more and more data about our personal lives and the machines that run factory and power-grid infrastructures, security becomes crucial.

Secure IoT networks encrypt data transmissions, store data in encrypted format, password-protect access to base stations, and expose the least possible amount of data to the public Internet. As you begin to collect wearable devices and home monitoring sensors, think carefully about the security of the data they collect, transport, and store.

QuickCheck

Suppose you want to collect data from your fitness wristband. What is the most secure way to get that data to your laptop?

a. Use a USB cable to plug the band directly into your laptop.

b. Collect the data at a ZigBee base station, which will relay it to your LAN, where you can access it from your laptop.

c. Transmit the signal to your laptop using unencrypted Wi-Fi.

3

QuickQuiz   Section D

1. The key device at the center of a LAN is a(n) [　　　　].

2. In addition to an IP address, devices on a LAN have a physical [　　　　] address that uniquely identifies them.

3. The dominant standard for wired LANs is [　　　　].

4. Technologies such as WEP, WPA, and PSK are examples of [　　　　] that can be used on wireless networks.

5. ZigBee, Z-Wave, and RFID are low-power wireless technologies that transport data on [　　　　] networks.

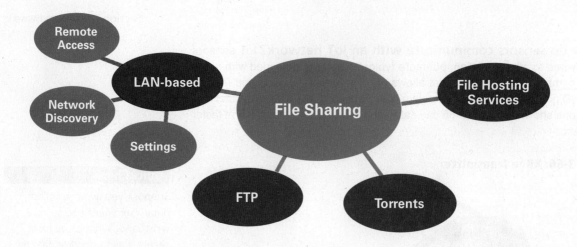

Objectives

▶ List seven factors that control your ability to share files.

▶ State the names of the utilities you use to view a list of files on Macs and on Windows.

▶ Explain the purpose of network discovery.

▶ List three precautions you can take when working with shared files.

▶ Define the three types of permissions that can be assigned to shared files.

▶ Describe at least two situations in which FTP would be a useful technology.

▶ List two factors that have a negative effect on files stored in the cloud.

▶ Draw a diagram that explains how torrents work.

▶ Discuss the legal issues that pertain to file sharing technologies, such as Napster and BitTorrent.

Digital defenses? One of the ways we invite trouble into our digital lives is by careless file sharing. This convenient technology for exchanging photos, documents, music, and videos can be the weak link in our chain of digital defenses. When was the last time you checked your file sharing settings?

Terminology

file sharing   permissions   file hosting services   BitTorrent
network discovery   FTP

File Sharing Basics

Networks provide access to all types of files. From Snapchats to feature-length movies, from magazine articles to full-length novels, and from sound effects to symphonies, a wide variety of files exist on local networks and on the Internet.

You may spend lots of time downloading files to your local devices, but there are also times when you want to provide access to files you have stored locally or in the cloud. File sharing makes this magic happen.

▶ **What is file sharing?** File sharing allows files containing documents, photos, music, and more to be accessed from devices other than the ones on which they are stored. Sharing can take place within a LAN or across multiple networks, including the Internet.

File sharing is a limited version of remote access that allows access to files, but it does not provide access to commands that launch programs or change settings on the remote computer.

▶ **How does file sharing work?** Given permission, you may open, view, edit, copy, and delete files stored on a remote device. The remote file will open with software that is running on your device, but will remain stored on the remote computer.

Your ability to share files with other devices on a network depends on several factors, which are listed in Figure 3-67.

Figure 3-67: File sharing depends on these factors

Which devices your computer can discover

Whether other network devices can discover your computer

Whether you are allowed to access files on other computers

Whether you allow other computers to access files on your computer

Which files you allow others to access

What you are allowed to do with files on other computers

What you allow others to do with the files they can access

Accessing LAN Files

Let's begin with a simple scenario. You've set up a home network and want to use one computer on the network to access files from another connected computer.

❱ How can I see all of the devices that are connected to my network?

To see a list of devices on your network, you can use your operating system's file management utility, such as Finder or File Explorer (Figure 3-68).

Figure 3-68: Find other computers on a LAN

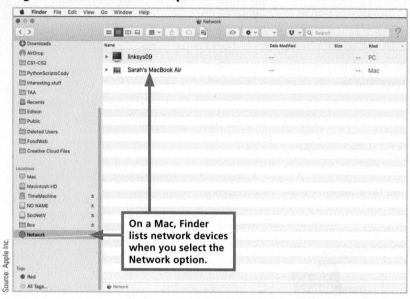

macOS Finder

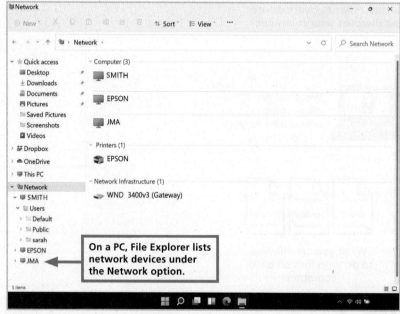

Windows File Explorer

Source: Apple Inc.

QuickCheck

How many devices are set to discovery mode on the Windows network shown in Figure 3-68? (Hint: EPSON is a printer!)

a. 0

b. 1

c. 2

d. 3

Try It!

Check your computer. Are any network devices visible?

▶ **What if other network devices aren't listed?** The network utilities provided by operating systems such as Windows and macOS automatically detect other devices when network discovery is turned on. **Network discovery** is a setting that affects whether your computer can see other devices on a network, and whether your computer can be seen by others.

When network discovery is turned on, your computer can see other computers on a LAN and those computers can see yours. When network discovery is off, the name of your computer will not appear in the list of network devices displayed on other computers. Network discovery works in different ways on different devices.

Mobile devices. The operating systems on mobile devices may not offer a way to see other devices on a network or to broadcast their presence on a network.

Macs. macOS devices, such as iMacs, have no user-modifiable network discovery settings, but offer file sharing settings instead. If file sharing is on, then network discovery is enabled.

Windows. PCs running Microsoft Windows offer a network discovery setting that allows users to turn network discovery off or on. When using public networks, this setting should be off (Figure 3-69).

3

Figure 3-69: Network discovery settings in Windows

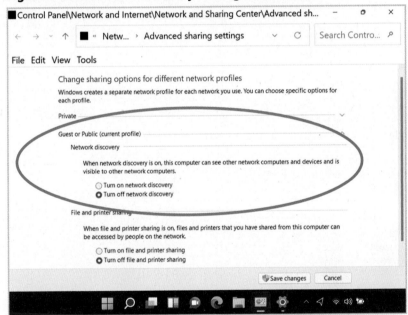

When using a public network, such as a Wi-Fi hotspot, turning network discovery off hides your computer from other users connected to the network. One caveat: The network administrator can see your device using router utilities even when network discovery is off.

▶ **How do I access files located on other computers?** Folders on some computers require a valid password for access. Your file sharing user ID and password are usually the same as the password you use to log in to your computer.

Assuming that you have permission to access files on a network device, you can access files just as if they were on your own computer. Select the device that holds the files. Open the folder that contains the file, then select the file you'd like to access (Figure 3-70).

QuickCheck

One way to ensure that only valid users can access shared files is to _____.

a. require a password

b. check the MAC address

c. only accept IP addresses

d. require encryption

Figure 3-70: Accessing files stored on other computers

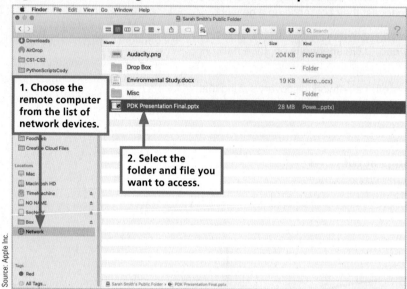

macOS Finder

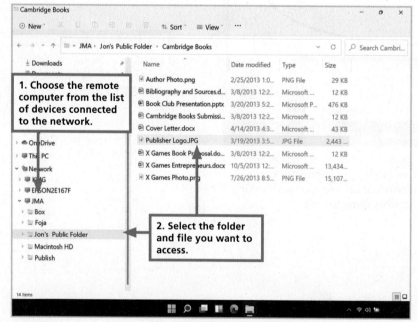

Windows File Explorer

Sharing Your Files

There are occasions when you'd like to share files stored on your computer with other people who are using your network. You may have guests who want to copy some of your sports photos, or you might want to transfer files from an old computer to a new one. Once computers can see each other on a network, sharing files can be easy—but take care to do it securely.

▶ **How secure is file sharing?** File sharing poses security risks that have several dimensions. Shared files are subject to misuse, inadvertent modifications, and intentional alterations by those who have access to them. In addition, security holes in file sharing routines are notorious for providing Internet-based hackers with unauthorized access to computers.

If you don't need to share files, turn off file sharing globally. If you want the convenience of sharing files, limit what you share and who you share it with by following the tips in Figure 3-71.

Figure 3-71: Get smart about file sharing

Assign permissions to files.

Limit sharing to specific people.

Remove sharing from files you no longer want to share.

▶ **What are permissions?** Permissions specify how shared files can be used.

Read and write permission (full control) allows access for opening, viewing, modifying, and deleting files.

Read permission (also known as view-only) allows authorized people to open a file and view it, but they are not allowed to modify or delete it.

▶ **Can I control how files are modified?** You can control who modifies a file, but not what they do to it. Once a shared file is bestowed with read and write permission, it can be modified so much that it is unrecognizable. If you are not checking shared files frequently, you may be surprised by what some of those files contain. You can see the potential problem. Read and write permission is not to be given without considerable thought.

One important consideration about file sharing is whether to provide access to the original file or to a copy of it. Your decision depends on the reason for sharing the file.

As a general guideline, do not offer read and write access to the original version of a file. Instead, make a copy of the file and designate the copy as shared with read and write permissions. If the file gets modified in some bizarre way, you will have a version of the original file that was not shared or modified.

Terminology

Permissions are also referred to as *user rights* or *privileges*.

QuickCheck

Suppose you would like to allow friends to access some photos, but you don't want them to make changes. What permissions would you assign?

a. Read

b. Read and write

c. Write

d. Admin

▶ **How do I share files from a Mac?** The first step is to turn on file sharing, then select the folders you'd like to share. You can designate an entire folder or a single file for sharing. To share one file, right-click it and select Get Info to access the Sharing & Permissions options. Use System Preferences to turn on file sharing and designate folders to share, as shown in Figure 3-72.

Figure 3-72: Sharing files from a Mac

1 Access System Preferences from the Apple menu. There, you can select Sharing to turn on file sharing.

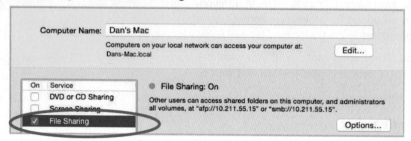

2 Add folders to the Shared Folders list, then specify who can have access and the permissions they are allowed.

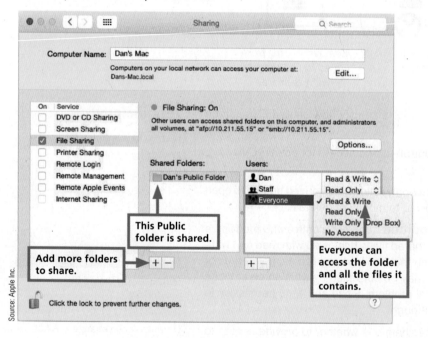

Source: Apple Inc.

QuickCheck

What kind of files should Dan store in his Public folder?

a. Original files

b. Files he would prefer not to share

c. Copies of files that he doesn't mind being altered

d. Files that he doesn't want deleted

Try It!

If you're using a Mac, check to see if file sharing is turned on. Which folders are shared?

❭ **How do I share files from a PC?** On a PC using Windows, the first step is to use the Control Panel's Network and Sharing utility to make sure that network discovery is on and then turn on file sharing.

Windows File Explorer includes a Share tab that's used to select folders or files you want to share. The Share tab also lets you specify permissions (Figure 3-73).

Figure 3-73: Sharing files from Windows

1 Access Windows Advanced Sharing Settings. Turn on network discovery and then turn on file and printer sharing.

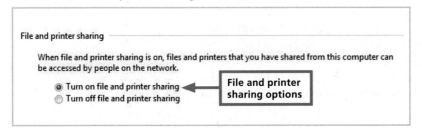

2 In File Explorer, you can select a folder or file that you want to share. Right-click the file and use the "Give access to" option to specify users and permissions.

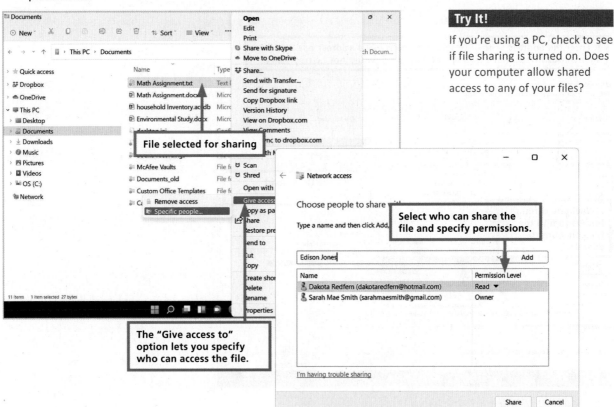

3

Internet-Based Sharing

As more and more activity moves to the cloud, companies that provide cloud services have increased their interest in encouraging consumers to use those services. Cloud storage and sharing services are commonly hyped as being more convenient and more secure than local options, but many consumers are wary of cloud security, not to mention the rampant advertising that accompanies many of the free cloud storage services.

The concept of pulling files from remote servers traces back to a protocol called FTP. Newer technologies now power Dropbox and similar services. So what are they all about?

▶ **What is FTP?** FTP (File Transfer Protocol) provides a way to transfer files from one computer to another over any TCP/IP network, such as a LAN or the Internet. The purpose of FTP is to make it easy to upload and download computer files without having to deal directly with the operating system or file management system of a remote computer. FTP also allows authorized remote users to change file names and delete files.

▶ **How can I access FTP servers?** You can access FTP servers with FTP client software, such as FileZilla. Addresses of FTP servers usually begin with ftp://. To use FileZilla to download a file, enter the address of the FTP server, then select folders and files, as shown in Figure 3-74.

QuickCheck

FTP is _____.

a. a cloud hosting service

b. a file sharing protocol

c. LAN-based secure file sharing

d. a permission-free file sharing service

Figure 3-74: FTP using FileZilla

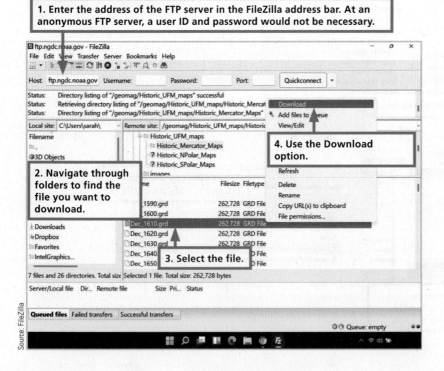

1. Enter the address of the FTP server in the FileZilla address bar. At an anonymous FTP server, a user ID and password would not be necessary.

2. Navigate through folders to find the file you want to download.

3. Select the file.

4. Use the Download option.

Source: FileZilla

▶ **What about Dropbox?** Dropbox and similar **file hosting services** store files in the cloud. Those files can be shared when multiple users are allowed access to the same folders (Figure 3-75).

Figure 3-75: Dropbox file sharing

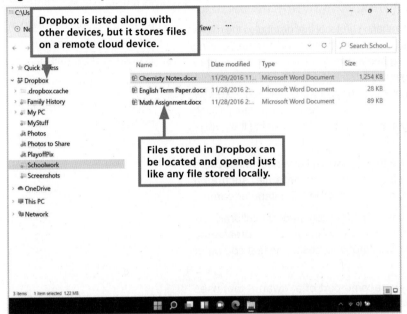

Dropbox is listed along with other devices, but it stores files on a remote cloud device.

Files stored in Dropbox can be located and opened just like any file stored locally.

Dropbox can be installed as an app on a local device, but can be configured to store your files in the cloud. Those files can be accessed just as if they were stored locally.

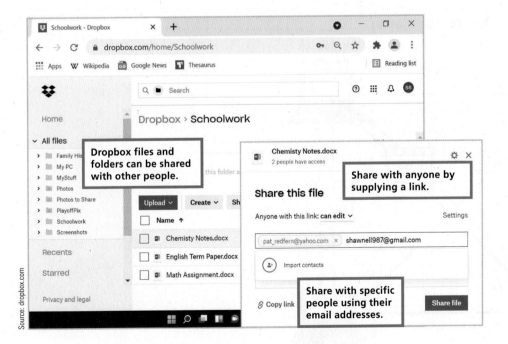

Dropbox files and folders can be shared with other people.

Share with anyone by supplying a link.

Share with specific people using their email addresses.

Source: dropbox.com

You can also access and share your Dropbox files using a browser.

Torrents

In the late 1990s, an online service called Napster burst onto the national scene when college students became aware that it provided free access to thousands of music downloads. Napster ran into some copyright infringement difficulties, but the concept of sharing files over the Internet spurred development of sophisticated, distributed protocols such as BitTorrent.

▶ **What is BitTorrent?** BitTorrent is a file sharing protocol that distributes the role of a file server across a collection of dispersed computers. If you envision data traveling over a mesh rather than a star, you'll have a general idea of the difference between a distributed file sharing system and a centralized distribution system such as Netflix Downloads. However, BitTorrent's mesh topology is logical, not physical. Your computer is still physically a part of a LAN with a star topology that accesses BitTorrent through a router. BitTorrent's logical mesh topology is simply a way of envisioning the path of data.

A BitTorrent network is designed to reduce the bandwidth bottleneck that occurs when many people attempt to download the same very large file, such as a feature-length film, application software, or an interactive 3D computer game.

▶ **How does BitTorrent work?** Suppose that 1,000 computers simultaneously request the newly released sequel to the film *Star Wars*. A server breaks the movie file into pieces and begins to download those pieces to the first computer that requested the movie.

As more computers request the file, they become part of a "swarm" that uses peer-to-peer technology to exchange movie segments with each other. After the server has downloaded all the segments to the swarm, its job is complete and it can service other requests. The swarm continues to exchange movie segments until every computer in the swarm has the entire movie (Figure 3-76).

Figure 3-76: Torrent peering for file sharing

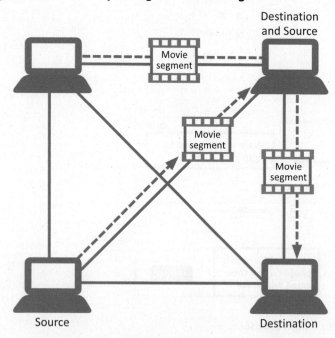

Every user who downloads from a torrent is automatically uploading to other users.

▶ **How do I use BitTorrent?** When you want to download a musical album, movie, software, or ebook rather than stream it, BitTorrent may be able to provide the necessary content and technology.

BitTorrent client software is currently available from several Web sites. After installing the client, you can use it to download from any BitTorrent-enabled site by clicking the file you want. The BitTorrent client handles the entire file swapping procedure. After getting the entire file, good etiquette requires clients to remain connected to the swarm so that they can "seed" file pieces to others.

▶ **Are BitTorrent and similar file swapping networks legal?** File sharing originated on Internet-based file servers, which held huge collections of popular music stored as digital MP3 files that could be easily downloaded and played on a computer or transferred to CDs. Free distribution of music without the copyright holder's permission is illegal, and file sharing server operators quickly encountered the legal ramifications of their computers' shady dealings.

Peer-to-peer file sharing networks and distributed technologies such as BitTorrent have legitimate uses for distributing music, images, videos, and software with the approval of copyright holders. For example, a bundle of ten *Doctor Who* episodes is available via BitTorrent with the approval of the BBC. The technology itself is not illegal; it is the use of the technology that is subject to legal scrutiny.

▶ **Is BitTorrent safe?** Because BitTorrent files are assembled from little segments that come from a jumble of computers, they would seem to be bad candidates for distributing malware. Intelligent hackers would realize that their malicious code could easily be chopped up, too, and that pieces of it might not be delivered. Yet, BitTorrent files have become a source of adware and spyware. If you use BitTorrent, make sure your computer is protected with a security software suite that offers good spyware protection.

3

QuickCheck

BitTorrent would not be classified as a(n) _____.

a. distributed network

b. peer-to-peer network

c. file sharing network

d. secure network

QuickQuiz   Section E

1. When network [_____] is on, your computer can see other devices that are connected to a LAN.

2. Read and [_____] permission allows a shared file to be opened, viewed, modified, and deleted.

3. File [_____] has to be turned on before any files on your computer can be accessed by other devices on a network.

4. [_____] client software, such as FileZilla, provides a way to upload and download files from an Internet-based server to a computer on a LAN.

5. Torrents exchange segments of files over a distributed network using a logical [_____] topology.

Issue: Do We Want Net Neutrality?

It all started in October 2007, when the FCC accused Comcast of slowing and in some cases blocking Internet traffic from BitTorrent. Comcast claimed that it was attempting to even the playing field for the average Internet user, whose online speeds were languishing due to file sharing traffic from a minority of its customers.

Comcast's ability to adjust some users' bandwidth for the benefit of other users might seem beneficial until you consider that ISPs could manipulate Internet speeds to give preferential access to certain sites and services while slowing access to others. That practice could essentially give ISPs the power to deny access to sites based on business, political, or other values.

> **Today's action at the FCC could begin the dismantling of the open Internet as we know it...**
>
> Senator Edward J. Markey

What if your ISP institutes a system whereby you have to pay extra for high-bandwidth data, such as movie downloads? You might be thinking, "There ought to be a law against that!" That is exactly the opinion of net neutrality supporters.

The term *net neutrality* was created by Columbia media law professor Tim Wu in a 2003 paper *Network Neutrality, Broadband Discrimination*. Although the term *net neutrality* is relatively new, its roots can be traced to pre-1860 telegram technology. Back then, standard telegrams were routed equally, without discrimination, and without regard to their contents, source, or recipient. Telegraphs were end-to-end neutral networks. Because telegraph and—later—telephone networks were considered to be public utilities, or common carriers, they were not allowed to give preferential treatment to one customer over another. The Federal Communications Commission (FCC) was formed to regulate common carriers and ensure equal access and fair prices.

As the Internet evolved into a massive communication network, the FCC began to regard it as a common carrier that should fall under the FCC's umbrella of influence. The first step would be to ban ISPs from slowing or blocking traffic indiscriminately. In 2010, under the banner of net neutrality, the FCC issued the Open Internet Order, a set of regulations designed to "preserve the Internet as an open platform enabling consumer choice, freedom of expression, end-user control, competition, and the freedom to innovate without permission."

Shortly after the Open Internet Order, Comcast was back in court again to contest the FCC's right to regulate the Internet. The court ruled in favor of Comcast, based on the fact that the FCC's jurisdiction did not extend to the Internet.

Yet the FCC persisted. In 2014, FCC chairman Tom Wheeler proposed a compromise form of net neutrality that would allow ISPs to offer "faster lane" options at a premium rate to content providers such as Netflix, Facebook, and Amazon. That proposal absolutely confused the issue; the FCC's proposed version of net neutrality was not neutral at all.

Opponents of this new non-neutral neutrality pointed out that, considering the finite amount of bandwidth available on the Internet, users outside the proposed "faster lanes" would have their bandwidth squeezed while the added cost of fast-lane services would be passed directly on to the consumers of such services.

In 2015, Wheeler changed tactics and the FCC passed a net neutrality order. That order was reversed in 2017 under then FCC chair Ajit Pai. In 2018, more than 20 states sued the FCC in an attempt to reinstate the 2015 net neutrality policies. The court did not reinstate the 2015 net neutrality order, but ruled that states could implement their own net neutrality laws. As you can see, this issue has bounced back and forth between regulation and deregulation.

The net neutrality controversy boils down to simple ideology: Should the government regulate the Internet or not? On the one hand, regulation could prevent abusive business practices on the part of ISPs. On the other hand, if the Internet were to fall under the regulatory control of the FCC, where would the regulation end? The FCC currently regulates telephone and cellular service. It imposes a variety of taxes and fees that add to your monthly bill. Would similar taxes and fees be added to your monthly Internet service? And would FCC Internet monitoring add yet more points where the government can collect data on the activities of its citizens?

Try It!

Net neutrality has become a political issue, and organizations with vested interests add to the confusion with misleading information. Here's a chance for you to explore the current status of net neutrality and to read arguments both for and against regulating ISPs.

1 Search online to find recent articles about net neutrality. What is its current status?

2 The Communications Act of 1934 was passed before there were computers or the Internet. Search online to find the full text version of the 1934 act and read the first two paragraphs. Explain why this act could be interpreted to apply to the Internet.

3 Shortly after the Internet went public, the U.S. Congress passed the Telecommunications Act of 1996. It defined two different but complementary services: "information services" and "telecommunications services." Explain the difference between these two services. How do these definitions relate to Title I and Title II of the Telecommunications Act? Classify the following as an information service or a telecommunications service: Amazon, Facebook, Comcast, Verizon, Twitter, Google.

4 Many ISPs and media companies have published written statements about their stance on net neutrality. What do you guess are the positions of Amazon, Mozilla, Netflix, Comcast, and the Electronic Frontier Foundation? Find the net neutrality statements of these companies online. Do they take the positions you expected? Why, or why not?

5 Search online for one article that supports net neutrality and one article that opposes it. Summarize the two positions.

Source: politicalLoudMouth.com 2015

What Do You Think?

Issue

1. Do you support the idea that Internet traffic should flow freely?

2. Do you believe that the U.S. government should regulate the Internet as a common carrier?

3. Were you aware of the net neutrality controversy?

Information Tools: Fact Checking

These days, you have to be a skeptic. Bloggers have opinions that are not always based on facts. Scam artists say anything to get your money. Fake news sites are proliferating. Just because an article shows up in Google results doesn't mean its contents are factual. Even reputable journalists sometimes make mistakes.

Before you form an opinion, make a decision, or take action based on what you read, see, or hear, you can easily use your computer or smartphone to verify facts and look up background information.

Search Google. You can use Google or a similar search engine to find information from all corners of the Web. You can search for information in specific formats, such as videos, images, and news reports. Check out Google Scholar for links to authoritative information in peer-reviewed journals, theses, and other professional publications. Remember that you can formulate searches such as *Define DNS spoofing* to learn the meaning of technical terms and find the meaning of acronyms.

Search within sites. Rather than conducting a wide-ranging Google search, you can go to a specific Web site and search within it. Search Wikipedia for definitions and topic overviews. Search news sites for articles and video footage about current events. Start at *www.snopes.com* or *www.factcheck.org* to identify email scams.

When you check facts or use them in your own research papers, primary sources tend to be more reliable than secondary or tertiary sources. How can you tell the difference?

Primary Sources

Original material such as speeches, interviews, letters, photos, email messages, tweets, artwork, diaries, laws, database reports, and accounting records

Example: A video of Apple's CEO announcing a new music product for the iPhone and iPad

Secondary Sources

Reviews, critiques, panel discussions, biographies, and other sources that analyze, summarize, or otherwise repackage information from primary sources

Example: An article on Google News that describes Apple's new music product

Tertiary Sources

A list or compilation of material that pertains to a topic; from sources that include bibliographies, dictionaries, almanacs, indexes, timelines, and inventory lists

Example: A Wikipedia article that presents a timeline of Apple products

Fact-Checking Tips

▶ **Two sources are better than one.** Cross-check facts between two or more sites.

▶ **Use common sense.** Claims that seem outlandish require extra verification.

▶ **Understand your priorities.** For example, you can go to YouTube and view the trailer for *Live Free or Die Hard*. That might be fun, but it might not be relevant for a term paper on cyberterrorism.

▶ **Use primary sources when possible.** Go to the original text of a speech, check the product manufacturer's Web site, or watch the video clip.

▶ **Use reputable sources.** The Web contains billions of documents; few of them follow strict journalistic standards for accuracy. Check the author's credentials, look at the general quality of the Web site, and make sure the information is up to date.

▶ **Maintain a list of the sites you frequently use for fact checking.** You can create a Fact Check folder in your browser's Bookmarks or Favorites list.

▶ **Nail down your search terms.** When using voice search on your mobile phone, think about an exact set of keywords before you launch Speak Now.

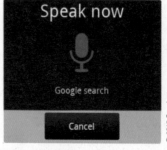

Try It!
Fact checking can be fun and it can lead you to all sorts of intriguing factoids as well as to substantive information. Practice your fact-checking skills by completing the following activities:

1 In any given time period, there are controversies that tend to generate false or misleading information that is spread on social media, on news media, and by word of mouth. Identify a controversy that is currently trending. Summarize the opposing viewpoints that underlie the controversy. Specify the major stakeholders on each side of the controversy. Provide an example of a statement made by each of these stakeholders.

2 Fact-checking Web sites operated by Snopes, The Washington Post, PolitiFact, and FactCheck.org provide analyses of controversial statements. Find a statement that is analyzed by four fact-checking sites. Do they all come to the same conclusion about the truth or falsehood of the claim?

3 As controversies escalate, stakeholders sometimes misrepresent their opponents by taking quotations out of context or providing incomplete quotations. Find an example of this kind of misrepresentation. Summarize the example by providing the misleading quotation, its source, the actual quotation, and its source. Explain how you found the example.

4 Fact-checking organizations have been accused of bias in the stories they choose to fact-check and in the way they present conclusions about the veracity of information. This bias is often very subtle. A fact-checking organization may choose to fact-check only one side of an issue, for example, by only checking false claims made by liberals. Another sign of bias is editorializing within the analysis—for example, by using exaggerated wording such as "liar," "whopper," and "bizarre" to describe people or the statements that they make. Examine an analysis from your favorite fact-checking organization. Can you find evidence of bias? Explain why or why not.

5 Suppose you're gathering information for a term paper about the emergence of the Internet, and you come across the following short article posted on Facebook. Internaut Day could be an interesting addition to your report; but before you include material from this article, you should do a fact check. Go online and find answers to the questions in the diagram below.

Happy Internaut Day!

skaljac/Shutterstock.com

a. Was the Internet invented on August 23rd?

This year's calendar will feature a new U.S. national holiday recognizing the day the Internet was invented. Circle August 23rd. That is the date when then Vice President Al Gore threw the switch that opened the Internet to public use.

The Internet has become an indispensable part of everyday life. In declaring this new national holiday, the President stated, "The Internet is not a luxury, it is a necessity."

b. Is this an accurate quote from a U.S. president?

Few people would disagree, especially those who call themselves internauts. An "internaut" is a person who possesses a thorough knowledge of how to use the Internet and its history. The word, a combination of Internet and astronaut, first appeared in a 1999 article about response rates to information posted on the Web. A group of hardy internauts has been petitioning presidents, from Nixon to Obama, for national recognition of this special day.

The hashtag #internautday has become a rallying point for Internet enthusiasts and was instrumental in garnering more than five million digital signatures on the petition to institute a national Internet Day.

c. Is there such a thing as an internaut?

d. What's wrong with including Nixon here?

e. Is Internaut Day a U.S. national holiday?

Technology in Context: Education

The first educational application of computers emerged in the 1960s, when huge mainframes with clunky interfaces introduced students to computer-aided instruction (CAI). Based on operant conditioning research by B. F. Skinner and Ivan Pavlov—remember dogs salivating when a bell rings?—CAI uses basic drill and practice: The computer presents a problem, the student responds, and the computer evaluates the response.

Studies in the 1970s indicated that programmed instruction systems, such as Programmed Logic for Automated Teaching Operations (PLATO), improved test scores, but students soon became bored with the monochrome display and found the regimented drill format boring.

Courtesy of the University of Illinois at Urbana-Champaign Archive

Educators know that students have diverse learning styles and are equipped with varying degrees of background knowledge about a topic. Computers, with all their processing power, should be able to provide individualized instruction.

With promising breakthroughs in artificial intelligence during the 1980s, deploying computers for individualized instruction seemed within easy grasp. The problem, however, was more complex than first expected. Forty-some years later, individualized instruction in the form of adaptive learning has yet to mature.

Simulations have become a popular educational tool. There are educational simulations that mimic real-world situations through narrative descriptions, 2D graphics, or virtual reality. There are also game simulations that educate within an entertaining environment. Flight simulators are an example of real-world simulations, whereas Battlefield 1942 is a first-person shooter game based on historic World War II battles. The line between the two types of simulations is blurred. Is Guts and Bolts an anatomy simulation or a game for designing bizarre organisms?

In the 1990s, when laptops began appearing in classrooms, most educators assumed that equipping every student with a computer would lead to easy gains in academic achievement. The validity of this assumption is nuanced and research does not provide a clear answer. Technology seems to help some students with some subjects and some skills, but it also seems to provide distractions that may affect students' ability to focus.

In elementary schools with laptops or tablet devices in the hands of every child, students may spend up to 50% of class time on their digital devices. Students use their devices to interact with computer-scored workbooks, learn from educational apps, research topics on the Internet, and take standardized tests. The amount of time spent with digital devices has some parents concerned that their children are missing out on valuable in-person interactions with other students and their teachers.

Classroom technology has had a significant influence on K-12 teaching. Learning management systems (LMSs) provide teachers with handy tools for tracking student progress and grading. These tools have also become instrumental in standardizing curricula by providing lesson plans and learning content.

The U.S. Department of Defense Education Activity (DoDEA) operates K-12 schools in U.S. military bases throughout the world. It is important that the curricula for all schools are synchronized so that students in families who are transferred or deployed arrive at a new school where instruction picks up seamlessly at the same place it left off in the previous school. Using a standard LMS-based curriculum provides this continuity.

In higher education, computer use by both students and instructors is widespread. Colleges offer campus-wide Wi-Fi service with Internet access so that laptop-toting students can easily take notes in class, contact instructors via email, use the Internet as a research resource, and run educational software.

Another educational use of computers can be seen in distance education (DE), which is also referred to as remote learning, distance learning, elearning, and virtual learning. Historically, distance education meant correspondence study or courses delivered by radio or television, but the meaning has been broadened to encompass any educational situation in which students and instructors aren't in the same place.

Most DE courses today require students to have access to a computer and an Internet connection. DE courses are offered to K-12 students, college students, military personnel, businesspeople, and the general public.

Many students who choose DE courses do so because they want to learn at their own pace, at a convenient time, and in a location close to home. Parents who deal with the realities of child care, working professionals who cannot relocate to a college town, and students with physical disabilities find distance education handy.

Perimeter and Area Basics
Definitions of perimeter and area.

Source: Khan Academy

Distance education has the potential of increasing the pool of students for a by making it financially feasible; for example, an advanced Kanji course could be offered at a Midwestern university with only ten on-campus Japanese majors if enough distance education students can boost enrollment.

The Internet hosts a wide variety of DE courses, both credit-earning and noncredit. Online courses can be presented to a small group of enrollees or to huge numbers of students. The trend toward massive open online courses (MOOCs) gained momentum in 2011 when 160,000 students enrolled in an online course in artificial intelligence offered by Stanford-based Sebastian Thrun and Peter Norvig. MOOCs are currently offered by Udacity, edX, and Coursera. They are "open" to enrollments by almost anyone; students do not have to be formally admitted to a university to participate. Courses are offered by instructors from Stanford, MIT, and other prestigious schools, so they attract students from all over the world.

Some DE courses are offered in real time, whereas other online courses are posted on the Web and can be accessed at any time. Khan Academy, with its distinctively colorful instructional "chalkboard," is representative of this type of any-time access online course. Its video lessons (below) cover a wide range of topics.

The 2020 COVID-19 pandemic tested the limits of distance education. As schools and colleges shut down in-person instruction, online instruction appeared to offer a solution that would allow learning to continue.

School districts quickly cobbled together resources for virtual learning, using videoconferencing, online learning platforms, and educational apps. Teachers who were not trained on digital platforms struggled to quickly learn how to use them. Students were unprepared for the responsibility of directing their own learning. As the pandemic came to an end, there was consensus that for most younger students, the experience with virtual learning was a failure. However, the experience has provided new insight into the effective use of technology at all levels of in-person and virtual learning.

Computers and the Internet have opened opportunities for lifelong learning. Prospective students can use a search engine to find non-credit courses and tutorials for a wide range of topics, including pottery, dog grooming, radio astronomy, desktop publishing, and drumming. Some tutorials are free, and others charge a small fee.

In a society that promotes learning as a lifelong endeavor, the Internet has certainly made it possible for students of all ages to pursue knowledge and skills just by using a computer and an Internet connection.

Flipped Class Projects

Critical Thinking

After completing this module, you should have a comprehensive view of how the Internet works. Based on this knowledge, does it seem possible that there is some sort of "kill switch" that could turn off large swaths of the Internet? Suppose there was a period of extreme political unrest in your country. Would it be conceivable that your country's leader, or perhaps a group of technologically savvy insurgents, could shut down the Internet? Think about the question on your own for a bit, then check online for additional opinions. Does your government have an official statement on this issue?

Group Project

The purpose of this project is to explore file sharing within your school network. Work in groups of three or four, with at least two computers equipped with Wi-Fi in your group. Begin by checking which files and folders are designated as shareable. Make only one folder shareable on each computer, and be sure that it contains no files that would reveal personal information. Next, turn on network discovery (PCs only) and file sharing. Can the computers see each other? Why, or why not? Are the computers able to share files? Discuss why file sharing is or is not possible within the network you are using.

Cyberclassroom

Students sometimes hesitate to state their opinions or ask questions in class. Can network technology offer more opportunities for interaction? For this project, work in groups of five to research three technologies that can be used as classroom response systems, also known as "clickers." Set up one of these systems and try it among the five people in your group. How would you rate it for increasing the quality of your classroom experience?

Multimedia Project

Run Traceroute from your computer to various domains until you get a report that contains 10–15 hops. You might have to try several destinations to obtain a trace that is not too long. Next, use an online WHOIS search to find the location of each router in the trace. To find the location, copy the IP address into the WHOIS search box. Finally, use a Google map to create a visual track of the packets from your computer to their destination.

Resume Builder

Bluetooth technology can be used to exchange electronic business cards. Suppose you're working in the technology department of a corporation and your boss asks you to research the value of this concept for the company's sales representatives. After completing your research, write a one-page memo that summarizes your findings about cost and usefulness.

Globalization

The model for telecommunications in most technologically advanced countries depends on large telecommunication corporations for telephone and Internet access. The infrastructure costs are huge. Can you envision ways in which people in technologically underdeveloped countries could benefit from inexpensive network technologies? Jot down your initial thoughts, then search the Web for additional ideas. Write a one-page executive summary that describes your opinion.

Key Terms

Interactive Summary

Section A: Networks can be classified by geographical scope as PANs, [   ], and WANs. The cables and signals used to transport data from one network device to another are a communication [   ]. Wired channels include twisted pair wires, [   ] cables used for cable television, and [   ] -optic cables used for high-capacity trunk lines. Wireless channels use [   ] signals and micro-waves. Government agencies regulate some wireless [   ]. The transmission capacity of a channel is referred to as [   ]. Channels that are capable of downloading at least 25 Mbps are classified as [   ]. Networks can be configured in various [   ], such as star, mesh, point to point, or bus. Any device in a network is referred to as a(n) [   ]. Data [   ] equipment includes computers. Data [   ] equipment includes modems and routers. Additional DCEs include hubs, switches, bridges, repeaters, and [   ] access points. Networks use physical, transport, and arrival communication [   ] to set the rules for efficiently transmitting data and handling errors.

Section B: The Internet is based on a U.S. government project called [   ]. Today, the Internet is a collection of networks, tied together by common [   ]. Tier 1 networks form the Internet [   ], a system of high-capacity routers and fiber-optic communication links arranged in a(n) [   ] topology. Networks that form the Internet are maintained by [   ] that offer access to consumers. Before data travels over the Internet, it is divided into [   ] by a protocol called [   ], which also reassembles the data when it reaches its destination. Every device on the Internet uses an IP address. [   ] addresses are 32 bits long, whereas [   ] addresses are 128 bits long, providing billions and billions of possible addresses. Addresses are assigned by [   ] servers. IP addresses that are temporarily assigned are called [   ] addresses, whereas perma-nent ones are called [   ] addresses. [   ] IP addresses cannot be routed over the Internet and are usually assigned to devices within LANs. Because it is difficult to remember IP addresses, the [   ] name system allocates easy-to-remember names, such as nike.com. [   ] -level domains include .com and .edu. The servers that track these names are a vulnerable point in Internet security.

Section C:
The speed and quality of Internet connections vary. For email and browsing the Web, speeds of [_____] Mbps are acceptable, whereas Skype video calls require 1.5 Mbps connections. Your bandwidth [_____] is the top speed allowed by your Internet access plan. You can use [_____] to check the latency of an Internet connection. You can use online tools to check for packet loss and [_____], which is the variability in packet latency. Another utility called [_____] reports the path that your data takes to reach its destination. Options for [_____] Internet access include cable, DSL, ISDN, satellite, and fiber-to-the-home. [_____] access options include mobile satellite. [_____] Internet access is available from cellular services. [_____] Internet service offers dependable connections over coaxial and fiber cables. The fastest offering that uses the telephone network is [_____]. GEO satellite Internet service suffers from high rates of [_____]. Mobile broadband service is offered by cell phone companies. Public Wi-Fi [_____] offer yet another Internet access option, though users have to be vigilant about security.

Section D:
Local area networks use many of the same network technologies as the Internet, only on a smaller scale. Devices that access LANs are equipped with a network interface [_____] that contains circuitry for wireless or wired connections. Devices also have a physical [_____] address, in addition to the IP addresses acquired from a DHCP server. The most popular wired technology is [_____]. The most popular wireless technology is [_____], which can be configured as a(n) [_____] or star topology. Setting up a LAN and configuring its router is uncomplicated. The first step is to change the standard [_____] to one that is secure. Next, create a(n) [_____] that uniquely identifies the network by name. It is also important to activate wireless [_____] to prevent wireless signals from being intercepted during transmission. A limited-access [_____] network can be created for visitors to use. By activating [_____], the router will be able to assign IP addresses to each device that joins the network. To connect to a secure LAN that is protected by encryption, an encryption [_____], or password, is required. LANs can be used to access data collected by IoT devices and the networks that tie these devices together. Technologies such as RFID, NFC, Bluetooth LE, ZigBee, and Z-Wave offer [_____]-power links, essential for battery-powered devices that can't expend excess amounts of energy transmitting data.

Section E:
File sharing allows files containing documents, photos, music, and other data to be accessed from computers other than the one on which they are stored. To access files on a LAN, network [_____] allows your computer to see other devices and permits other devices to see your computer. Sharing the files on your computer poses a security risk, but it is possible to specify [_____] for how your shared files can be used. File sharing is also possible across networks, as when you download files from Internet servers. One technology used for this purpose is [_____], which provides a way to transfer files over any TCP/IP network. Another file sharing protocol called [_____] distributes the role of a file server across a collection of dispersed computers.

Interactive Situation Questions

1. You're setting up an Ethernet wired network using a router. To access the router and its configuration software, you open your ⬚ and type the router's IP address.

2. You're trying to figure out if your computer has a built-in Ethernet port. You see the port pictured to the right. Is that the port you should use for your Ethernet plug? Yes or no? ⬚

3. You're shopping for a new router and are attracted by the advertising for a 600N model. Upon examining the specifications, you see that the router transmits 300+300, so you know it is using ⬚ broadcast channels.

4. You arrive at work and one of your co-workers tells you that the router is down. Is it correct to surmise that your workstation will not be able to access other workstations, but will be able to access the Internet? Yes or no? ⬚

5. You have a small network in your house that uses a wireless router. For the past week, you've seen an SUV parked outside, and its occupant seems to be using a laptop computer. The first step you should take to discover if this person has hacked into your network is: a) knock on the car window and ask; b) call the police; or c) use your router utilities to check who is connected to your network. ⬚

6. You've set up a network using some new equipment and a few old Wi-Fi adapters given to you by your roommates. One of the adapters is equipped only for WEP, whereas all the other adapters support WPA2. Your roommate tells you that in order to use all the adapters, you'll have to disable wireless encryption. Is your roommate right? ⬚

7. You're accustomed to using Dropbox to share files over the Internet; but at your new job, files are stored on an FTP server. This is not a problem. You know that you can access work files using FTP ⬚ software such as FileZilla.

8. You've got class notes and you don't mind sharing them with your roommates, but you'd prefer that they don't change the files. You can keep your notes intact if you assign ⬚ permission to those files.

9. Suppose you're connected to a Wi-Fi hotspot. When you use File Explorer, you see the names of other computers listed under Network. Oops! You must have network ⬚ turned on.

10. You're expecting visitors who will be demanding Internet access. Before they arrive, you can activate a Guest network that has its own ⬚ and a different password from the one used with the network where you store all your files.

Lab: Hack Your Net

Hackers and government snoopers love networks. Data flows freely. Most of it is not encrypted. Networks are a paradise for anyone who wants to peer into our private lives. But what do these snoopers actually find, and how much data must they sort through to find anything valuable? Let's take a look at the data flowing on your LAN and the data that's exchanged over the Internet.

Requirements:

For this lab, you'll need a computer running macOS or Microsoft Windows. Your computer should be connected to a Wi-Fi network. The instructions are generalized; they provide helpful guidelines, but not specific steps. You may have to explore a bit to find all the tools needed to complete the assignment, but that is all part of the learning experience.

There are two versions of this assignment: one for computers running Windows and one for computers running macOS. The Windows version begins on this page. The macOS version begins on the next page.

Windows Assignment:

1 Open Task Manager's Performance tab to view Wi-Fi activity.

The easiest way to open Task Manager is by typing its name into a search box on the Start menu or Home screen. You can also open Control Panel and access Task Manager from there.

Once open, select the Performance tab and use the More Details link, if necessary, to display the graph and network statistics.

Arrange your desktop into two windows: one with Task Manager and one with a browser. Now navigate to several Web sites and note what happens in Task Manager.

What are typical speeds for sending and receiving data on your network?

2 Monitor Wi-Fi throughput.

Continue watching the Wi-Fi graph when you are not using the browser. Why do you think there is Wi-Fi activity even when you are not actively using network services?

3 Switch to the Processes tab.

The Network column of the Processes tab displays the applications that are active. Can you determine which applications are sending and receiving data over the network even when you are not actively using network services?

4 Return to the Performance tab and select the Open Resource Monitor link. Select the Network link.

This set of monitoring tools gives you another view of the data that's traveling to and from your computer. Look at the list for Processes with Network Activity.

Do the active processes here match the processes you identified in Step 3?

5 Monitor TCP connections.

Expand the list of TCP connections, if necessary, by selecting the ⊙ button. The Remote Address column displays the IP addresses of servers that have sent packets to your computer.

Type a few of these IP addresses into a browser address bar. Where do they lead?

6 Open the Command Prompt window and enter the command netstat -e.

To open the Command Prompt window, you can enter cmd in the Windows search box. When the window opens, enter netstat -e.

The netstat command displays the number of bytes sent and received. It also displays the number of packets you've sent and received.

Unicast packets are simple TCP packets of data. Non-unicast packets are broadcast or multicast to multiple network nodes—typically from DHCP queries and Windows services.

You can see that snoopers have to examine lots of packets to find specific data. Record the number of unicast packets your computer has sent and received.

Lab: Hack Your Net

macOS Assignment:

1 Open Activity Monitor's Network tab to view network activity.

The easiest way to open Activity Monitor is to select the Applications folder from the dock, select the Utilities folder, then select Activity Monitor.

Once the Activity Monitor window is open, select the Network button.

Arrange your desktop into two windows: one with Activity Monitor and one with a browser. Now navigate to several Web sites and note what happens in Activity Monitor.

The graph uses red for sent packets and blue for received packets. Data transport speeds are listed as "Data received/ sec" and "Data sent/sec."

What are typical speeds for sending and receiving data on your network?

2 Monitor network activity.

Continue watching the graph when you are not using the browser. Why do you think there is activity even when you are not actively using network services?

3 Look at the process chart above the graph.

The Sent Bytes and Rcvd Bytes columns of the chart list active processes and show when they send or receive data.

Can you determine which applications are sending and receiving data over the network even when you are not actively using network services?

4 Get ready to use the Netstat command by selecting the Applications folder and then selecting Terminal. At the prompt, type netstat -lb | head. (Be sure to use the | key, not the ! mark.)

Look at the beginning of the report. The columns contain the following data:

- Proto: The protocol, which is TCP or UDP.
- Rec-Q and Send-Q: Data that is queued up for sending or receiving.
- Local Address: The origin of outgoing packets.
- Foreign Address: The source of incoming packets. The address ends with its protocol; https indicates a secure Web protocol.
- (state): ESTABLISHED is an active connection. A socket is CLOSED. A CLOSE-WAIT socket is in the process of closing.
- rxbytes and txbytes: The number of bytes received by or transmitted from the foreign server.

For three of the foreign addresses, use an IP address lookup to see if you can associate them with your recent online activity.

Answer the following questions:

1. How many foreign addresses are listed?

2. What is the IP address of the server that is sending the most bytes?

3. What is the protocol of the server you identified in item 2?

4. Can you identify the domain name of the most active foreign server using an IP lookup? If so, what is it?

```
Mac2014:~ jns$ netstat -lb | head
Active Internet connections
Proto Recv-Q Send-Q  Local Address          Foreign Address       (state)         rxbytes    txbytes
tcp4      0      0   mac2014.hsd1.ga.5633   ec2-113-24-211-1.https  ESTABLISHED       189       2548
tcp4      0      0   mac2014.hsd1.ga.5633   ec2-52-72-138-96.https  ESTABLISHED      6117       6924
tcp4      0      0   mac2014.hsd1.ga.5633   107.152.26.202.https    ESTABLISHED      3602       1052
tcp4      0      0   mac2014.hsd1.ga.5632   162.125.5.17.https      ESTABLISHED      4597      74877
tcp4      0      0   mac2014.hsd1.ga.5632   162.125.19.131.https    ESTABLISHED       558       6945
tcp4      0      0   mac2014.hsd1.ga.5632   192.184.68.188.https    ESTABLISHED       786       2362
tcp4      0      0   mac2014.hsd1.ga.5632   stackoverflow.co.https  ESTABLISHED      4048       2552
tcp4      0      0   mac2014.hsd1.ga.5632   server-13-226-51.https  ESTABLISHED      8034       2657
Mac2014:~ jns$
```

Source: Apple, Inc.

Extra Credit Lab: Hack Your Net Part II

But what's in those packets? You were able to use utilities to see the number of packets flowing into and out of your computer. But what is a packet, exactly? What would a hacker see by using a packet sniffer to tap into your wireless communications? What do those government snoopers gather with their sophisticated surveillance? In this extra credit lab, you'll get a glimpse of the packet landscape.

Requirements:

For this lab, you'll need a computer running macOS or Microsoft Windows. Your computer should be connected to a Wi-Fi network. This part of the lab requires you to download and install software; make sure that you have permission to do so. You will need administrative privileges, so you must be logged in as an administrator.

Assignment:

❶ Download and install the free Wireshark packet sniffer application.

Make sure you obtain the download from a trusted site!

The official Wireshark site is *www.wireshark.org*.

There are versions of Wireshark for Windows and for macOS. Be sure to download the correct version.

❷ Verify that you are logged in using an administrator account, then start Wireshark.

❸ Set up a capture.

When the Welcome screen appears, use the "interface" pull-down menu to select Wired or Wireless, depending on the type of network connection you are using.

Click the Start option by selecting the blue fin icon on the menu bar.

❹ View the capture report.

The capture report is displayed in three sections, as shown in the figure below.

Selecting one of the packets in the Packet List displays details in the Packet Details and Packet Bytes sections.

The Packet Bytes section contains a capture of what is contained in your packets. That's what snoopers see!

❺ Take a screenshot of your Wireshark window.

If you're using Windows, press the PrtSc key, then start Paint and paste the screenshot into the Paint window. On a Mac, use Command-Shift-3 to capture the screen to your desktop. Save your screenshot with the file name *Module3XtraLab* followed by your name.

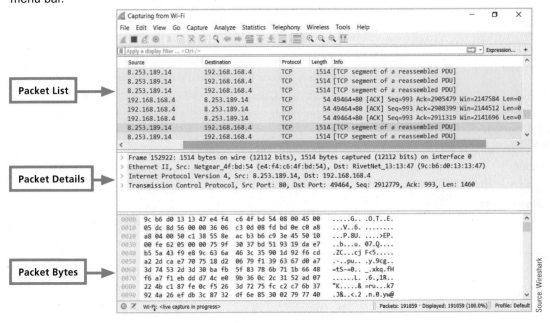

Source: Wireshark

4 The Web

Module Contents

The Web is a platform for free speech, if you don't mind it being tracked by advertisers, recorded by government snoopers, and stored indefinitely by search engines. Learn how to navigate the Web without leaving a trail.

● Try It! Apply what you learn.

- Identify text and graphics links on Web pages.
- Manipulate URLs in the address box to recover from bad links.
- Shorten URLs for use in social media posts and short messages.
- Expand short URLs to see where they originate before clicking them.
- Designate a default browser.
- Choose a home page for your browser.
- Customize your browser's predictive services and tabs.
- Set bookmarks on the browser toolbar.
- Determine if your browser is storing passwords.
- View and clear your browser cache.
- Use private browsing to avoid accumulating evidence of Web sites visited.
- Select and install browser extensions.
- View the source code and HTML tags for a Web page.
- Create a Cascading Style Sheet for a Web site.
- Use HTML to create, test, and post a basic Web page.
- View cookies stored on your digital devices.
- Block third-party cookies.
- Identify secure HTTPS connections.
- Use a search engine's advanced search options to formulate queries.
- Manage your search history to maintain privacy.
- Use appropriate citations for Web content incorporated in your own work.

● **Pre-Check**   Gauge your level of expertise. The answers are in the module.

On a Web page, this pointer indicates a(n)

_____

This browser icon means

_____

http://www.dig.com/banner

This is an example of a(n)

_____

Third parties use these to display targeted ads based on your browsing activity.

_____

Google uses this icon for

_____

Web source documents end with one of these extensions.

_____

List three search operators:

_____

_____

_____

When you see this icon in the browser address box, what protocol is being used?

_____

What type of Web encryption uses two keys?

_____

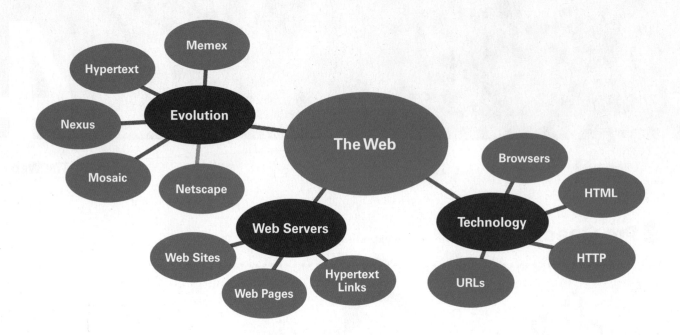

Objectives

▶ List six essential technologies that are the foundation of the World Wide Web.

▶ Summarize the key events in the emergence of the modern Web.

▶ Draw a diagram showing the hierarchy of the following: Web server, Web sites, Web pages, hypertext links.

▶ Describe a situation in which bidirectional hypertext links would improve your online research experience.

▶ Give an example of the URL for a Web site home page, one for a Web page that is stored in a folder, and one for a Web page that is produced based on a query.

▶ State four rules for correctly typing URLs.

▶ Define the term *linkrot*.

▶ Describe a situation in which you might use a short URL service.

▶ Explain the difference between a URL and a domain name.

There were visionaries who dreamed of some way to link libraries of knowledge and navigate through them with the ease of floating down a lazy river. Those visionaries never imagined the tsunami of information that's awash on today's Web. To help you navigate all that the Web has to offer, this module begins with the basics: hypertext, Web content, and URLs.

Terminology

World Wide Web	Web site	hypertext links	URL
Web browser	Web server	unidirectional links	linkrot
hypertext	Web page	bidirectional links	short URLs

Web Overview

The Web is not the Internet. Just as cellular towers are different from the text messages you send over them, the Internet is different from the Web. The Internet is a global data communications network. The Web is just one of the many technologies that use the Internet to distribute data.

▶ **What are the key elements of Web technology?** The **World Wide Web** (usually referred to simply as *the Web*) is a collection of HTML documents, images, videos, and sound files that can be linked to each other and accessed over the Internet using a protocol called HTTP.

The Web is accessed from desktop computers, laptops, tablets, and smartphones using software commonly called a browser. A **Web browser** is client software that displays Web page elements and handles links between those pages. Popular browsers include Microsoft Edge, open source Mozilla Firefox, Google Chrome, and Apple Safari. Figure 4-1 lists the essential Web technologies that you'll explore in this module.

Terminology

The process of accessing a Web site is sometimes referred to as *surfing the Web* and visitors are called *Web surfers*.

4

Figure 4-1: Essential Web technologies

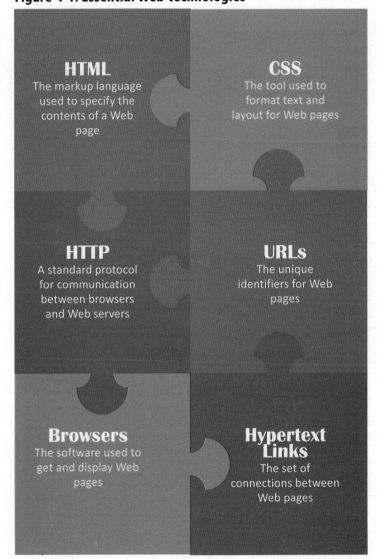

HTML
The markup language used to specify the contents of a Web page

CSS
The tool used to format text and layout for Web pages

HTTP
A standard protocol for communication between browsers and Web servers

URLs
The unique identifiers for Web pages

Browsers
The software used to get and display Web pages

Hypertext Links
The set of connections between Web pages

QuickCheck

Content is the main emphasis for which of the following?

a. The Internet

b. The Web

c. CSS

d. URLs

Evolution

According to MIT researcher Matthew Gray, in June 1993 there were a total of 130 Web sites containing linked documents. By January 1996, there were 100,000 Web sites. Today, there are more than a hundred million active Web sites and new sites appear every day. The remarkable story of such explosive growth began more than half a century ago.

▶ **How did the Web evolve?** In 1945, an engineer named Vannevar Bush described a microfilm-based machine called the Memex that linked associated information or ideas through "trails." By following trails from one document to another, readers could track down ideas from within an extensive library of information. Bush's Memex was hypothetical, however; the microfilm readers and analog computers of the time were not suitable for such a complex task.

The idea of linked documents resurfaced in the mid-1960s when Harvard graduate Ted Nelson coined the term **hypertext** to describe a computer system that could store literary documents, link them according to logical relationships, and allow readers to comment on and annotate what they read. Nelson sketched the diagram in Figure 4-2 to explain his idea of a computer-based "web" of "links."

Figure 4-2: Ted Nelson's sketch of Project Xanadu

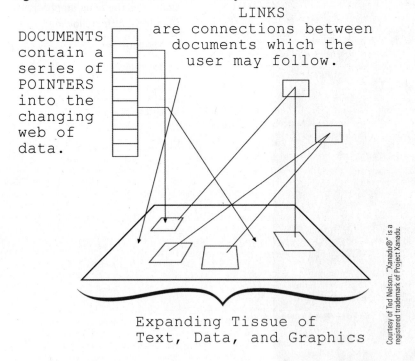

DOCUMENTS contain a series of POINTERS into the changing web of data.

LINKS are connections between documents which the user may follow.

Expanding Tissue of Text, Data, and Graphics

Courtesy of Ted Nelson. "Xanadu®" is a registered trademark of Project Xanadu.

Ted Nelson sketched his vision for Project Xanadu in the 1960s. Notice his use of the terms *web* and *links*, which are now familiar to everyone who uses the World Wide Web.

Fast-forward to 1990 when a British scientist named Tim Berners-Lee developed specifications for URLs, HTML, and HTTP—the foundation technologies of today's Web. Berners-Lee also created Web browser software originally called WorldWideWeb but later renamed Nexus (Figure 4-3).

Figure 4-3: The first Web browser

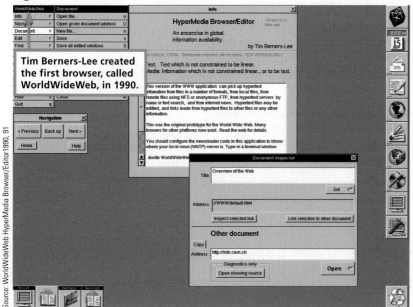

> Tim Berners-Lee created the first browser, called WorldWideWeb, in 1990.

Nexus ran on NeXT computers and was not available to the huge installed base of IBM PCs. In 1993, Marc Andreessen and his colleagues at the University of Illinois created Mosaic, a browser that ran on several computing platforms, including Windows. Andreessen later formed his own company and produced a browser called Netscape (Figure 4-4), which put the Web into the hands of millions of consumers.

Figure 4-4: The browser that popularized the Web

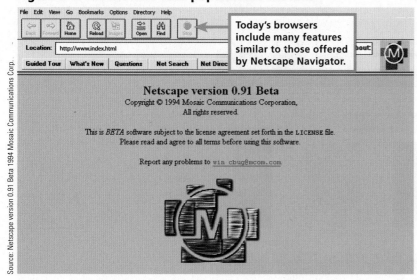

> Today's browsers include many features similar to those offered by Netscape Navigator.

Netscape Navigator was the first browser in widespread use. Can you recognize elements of the Netscape window that are similar to elements of the browser you use today?

Web Sites

Web sites are the cyberspace equivalent of shops and offices in a city's commercial district. A home page serves as the Web site's doorway and links to all the Web pages that the site offers.

▶ **What is a Web site?** A **Web site** typically contains a collection of related information organized and formatted so it can be accessed using a browser.

You are probably familiar with informational Web sites such as HowStuffWorks.com, CNN.com, ESPN.com, and Wikipedia.org. Web sites can also offer Web-based applications, such as Google Docs, and social networking, such as Facebook. Another popular category of Web sites includes ecommerce stores such as Amazon, eBay, and Etsy.

The activities that take place at Web sites are under the control of Web servers. A **Web server** is an Internet-based computer that stores Web site content and accepts requests from browsers. One server can host multiple Web sites, and some Web sites are spread across multiple servers.

▶ **What is a Web page?** A **Web page** is based on an HTML source document that is stored as a file on a Web server. The source document contains the text for a Web page interspersed with coding for how to display text and any additional visual or auditory elements.

The content of Web pages can incorporate text, images, videos, and sound files, as well as elements pulled on the fly from databases (Figure 4-5).

Figure 4-5: Web servers collect Web page content from many sources

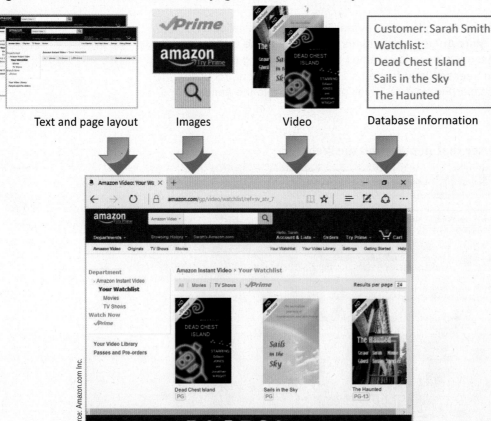

Text and page layout   Images   Video   Database information

Source: Amazon.com Inc.

Hypertext Links

Most of us have used the Web so much that we've become conditioned to the way it works. We rarely stop to consider how it might be improved. But the way hypertext links function might have been quite different if Ted Nelson's vision of the Web had come to fruition.

▶ **What are hypertext links?** Web pages are connected by **hypertext links** (commonly referred to simply as *links*). For example, a syllabus can contain links to other documents, such as lecture notes or an assigned reading.

Links are commonly indicated by underlined or colored text, but a photo, button, tab, or other object on a Web page can act as the source of a link. On conventional screens, the mouse pointer changes to a hand when it rolls over a link (Figure 4-6). On touchscreens, users often have to experiment with tapping and swiping to discover links.

QuickCheck

Where did the term *hypertext* originate?

a. From Ted Nelson

b. From Microsoft

c. From IBM

d. From a science fiction novel

4

Figure 4-6: Finding the links

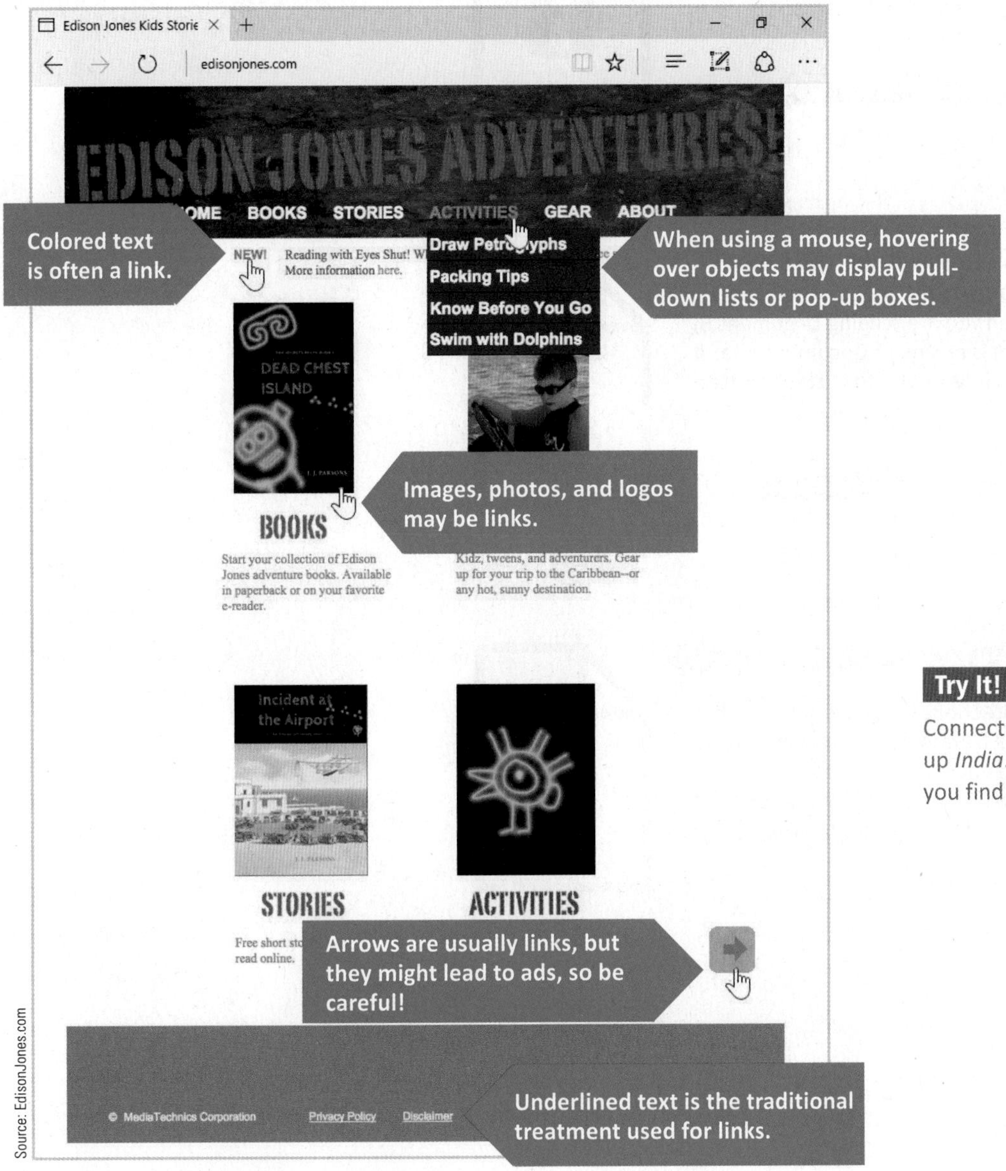

Colored text is often a link.

When using a mouse, hovering over objects may display pull-down lists or pop-up boxes.

Images, photos, and logos may be links.

Arrows are usually links, but they might lead to ads, so be careful!

Underlined text is the traditional treatment used for links.

Source: EdisonJones.com

Try It!

Connect to Wikipedia and look up *India*. What kinds of links do you find on that page?

▶ **How do links work?** In today's Web, Web pages have **unidirectional links**—so Document A links to Document B, but not vice versa. Unidirectional links were a key factor in simplifying early Web prototypes so that they could be feasibly implemented. However, this type of link limits the ability to trace back to related material.

Bidirectional links connect two documents using a two-way link that can be followed from either document. A Web with bidirectional links, such as that envisioned by Ted Nelson's Project Xanadu, was too complex to successfully construct. Figure 4-7 illustrates the difference between unidirectional links and bidirectional links.

Figure 4-7: Unidirectional and bidirectional links

Document A contains a link to Document B. When reading Document A, you can easily follow the link to the related material in Document B.

But the link from Document A to Document B is unidirectional. When you are reading Document B, there is no link to Document A, and you may never find that related material.

Bidirectional links would establish links from A to B and from B to A. Regardless of which document you viewed first, a link would exist to the other document.

URLs

URLs identify Web sites and Web pages. They offer clues about what pages contain. Or do they? URLs can be long and complex. They can also be shortened to disguise what they contain. The security of your digital devices may depend on your understanding of URLs and their components.

▶ **What are the components of a URL?** Every Web page has a unique address called a **URL** (Uniform Resource Locator, pronounced "you are ELL"). For example, the URL for the Cable News Network (CNN) Web site is *https://www.cnn.com*. Most URLs begin with http:// or https://.

The pages for a Web site are stored in folders on the Web server. The names of folders and subfolders that hold a Web page are reflected in the URL. For example, the CNN site might store entertainment news stories in a folder called Showbiz. The URL for that folder would be *https://www.cnn.com/showbiz/*.

The file name of a specific Web page always appears last in the URL. Web page files usually have an .htm or .html extension, indicating that the page was created with Hypertext Markup Language. The main page for a Web site is usually called Index.html. Figure 4-8 identifies the parts of a URL.

4

Figure 4-8: URL components

https://www.cnn.com/showbiz/movies.htm

| Web protocol | Web server name | Folder name | File name and extension |

▶ **Do all URLs reference pages?** Some URLs contain a search string rather than the name of an HTML document. Suppose you are at the CNN site and want to find the latest music news. Entering *music* in the search box produces an address that includes a question mark and a query string. The Web page that's displayed is a result of the search (Figure 4-9).

Figure 4-9: A URL can contain a query string

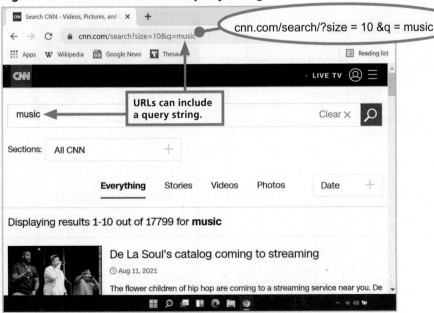

Source: 2021 Cable News Network Turner Broadcasting System, Inc.

❱ What are the rules for correctly typing a URL? When typing URLs in the browser address box, there are a few rules to remember:

- A URL never contains spaces, even after a punctuation mark, so do not type any spaces within a URL. An underline symbol is sometimes used to give the appearance of a space between words in a file name—for example, *www .detroit.com/top_10.html*.

- When typing a URL, the http:// or https:// can be omitted, so *www.cnn.com* works just as well as *https://www.cnn.com*.

- Be sure to use the correct type of slash—always a forward slash (/).

- Duplicate the URL's capitalization exactly. Some Web servers are case sensitive. On these servers, typing *www.cmu.edu/Info.html* (with an uppercase *I*) will not locate the Web page that's stored on the Web server as *www.cmu.edu/info.html* (with a lowercase *i*).

❱ Are links URLs? No, but a link contains the URL that points to another Web page. Before linking to a page, for security reasons, you might want to preview the URL for the page. Figure 4-10 shows how.

Try It!

Can you connect to the CNN Web site without using https:// in the address? Can you connect without using www?

Figure 4-10: Look before you click

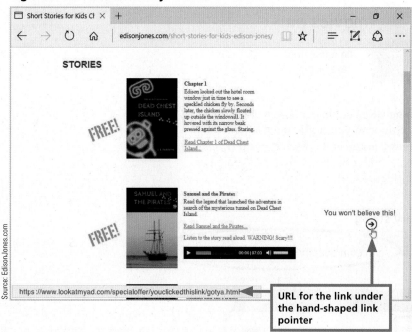

When using a mouse, hovering over a link displays a link preview that indicates where the link leads.

On a touchscreen device, pressing and holding a link may display the URL.

▶ **How are URLs related to domain names?** URLs contain a domain name. For example, the URL *https://www.nike.com/fitness* contains the domain name nike.com. Some domain names are based on the name of the business or organization that operates the Web site. But many domain names and Web site URLs provide no indication of a site's real owner. To discover that information, you can use a WHOIS search, as explained in Module 3.

▶ **Can I manipulate URLs?** When you click a link, your browser links to the URL and displays the associated Web page. Sometimes links lead to pages that are no longer available, a situation known as **linkrot**. Links that no longer work are called broken links or dead links. If you reach a dead link, you can sometimes manipulate the URL to locate similar material that remains on the Web site. Figure 4-11 illustrates the technique.

Figure 4-11: Getting past linkrot

www.bleacherreport.com/articles/nfl/injuries/new-helmets.htm

www.bleacherreport.com/articles/nfl/injuries/

When a Web page no longer exists at the specified URL, edit the link in the address box by backtracking to the first slash. Press the Enter key. The modified link may take you to a list of content similar to the original link.

www.SavannahBookFestival.com/events/2023/calendar.htm

www.SavannahBookFestival.com/events/2024/calendar.htm

You can also experiment with changing words or numbers in a URL—a technique that often works for locating materials for a different date or page number.

QuickCheck

Bikes.com is an example of a

_____.

a. URL

b. hypertext link

c. domain name

d. Web page

4

Try It!

Can you connect to *https://www.sec.gov/news/pressrelease/2016-500.html*? What happens if you change the URL in the address bar to end with 50, instead of 500?

▶ **Why are URLs so long?** When visiting Web sites, glance at the address bar from time to time. Many of the URLs are long and complex. Here's a long URL that's the Web page for a short article about UV clothing:

http://www.edisonjones.com/kid-gear-swim-shop/sun-safety-uv-clothing-kids.html

▶ **Is there any way to shorten URLs?** Long URLs can be a problem. The longer they are, the easier it is to make a typing error. Also, long URLs consume too many characters in short messaging applications such as Twitter.

Several services, such as Bitly and TinyURL, create **short URLs**. You can request a short URL by entering the normal URL at one of these services. The service will generate a short URL. The original URL and the short URL are stored in a translation table on the service's server. Figure 4-12 illustrates how short URLs work.

Figure 4-12: Shorten that URL

❶ Copy and paste the full URL into the box provided by a short URL service such as TinyURL.

❷ The service produces a short URL.

❸ The short URL is stored on the server along with the full URL.

❹ Links to the short URL are directed to the server, which forwards the link to the full URL.

▶ **Why use a short URL?** Suppose you want to share an article or video with your friends on Twitter. Just find the Twitter icon and click it, right? Twitter automatically shortens the URL to 22 characters.

Sure, that works on Twitter and a few other social media sites, but what if you want to share something from a site without Share links to social media sites? You can copy the link and obtain a short URL before pasting it into an email message or social media post.

Posting a short URL takes up less space in a Tweet or post. Also, if you expect that recipients might manually type the URL, they will make fewer mistakes when typing a short one.

Try It!

Use TinyURL or Bitly to create a short URL for an article or video you've found on the Web. Mail the link to yourself. Test the link. Does it produce the article or video you specified?

▶ **Do short URLs expire?** Short URL services may lead consumers to believe that all short URLs will last forever, but they last only as long as the service maintains its servers. If a service ceases operations, the short URLs maintained on its servers will no longer work.

Short URLs are sometimes used to disguise the real address of a Web site that is illegitimate. This practice has resulted in short URL services being blocked by Web hosts and ISPs. When URL services are blocked, the short URLs on their servers will not work.

You should be aware that short URLs may lead to questionable Web sites and scams. Never click a short URL link in an email message if you are not certain it leads to a legitimate site. As shown in Figure 4-13, several sites, such as checkshorturl.com and getlinkinfo.com, provide ways to check the actual destination of a shortened URL before you click it.

4

Figure 4-13: Expand that URL

Online services such as checkshorturl expand short URLs and display the original, full URL.

Try It!

Can you discover where the short URL *https://tinyurl.com/y7rvussm* goes without actually visiting the site?

QuickQuiz   Section A

1. The World Wide Web is one of the many technologies that uses the [_____] infrastructure to distribute data.

2. The basis for Ted Nelson's original idea for [_____] was to use bidirectional links to navigate between digital documents.

3. A(n) [_____] symbol in a URL indicates a query.

4. In the URL *https://www.musicwire.com/bit.htm*, the [_____] name is musicwire.com.

5. *Https://bit.ly/MY67dd93B* is an example of a(n) [_____] URL.

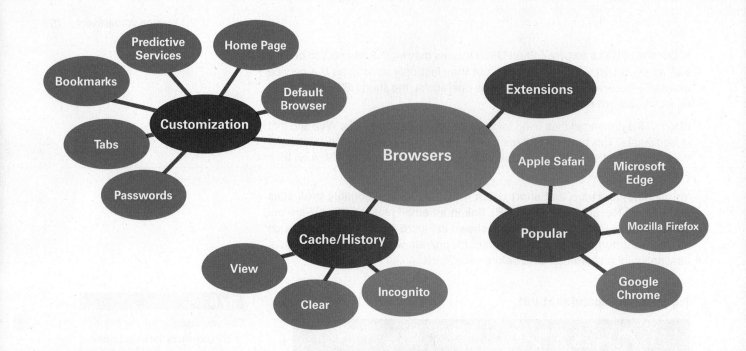

Objectives

▶ Identify the following elements of a browser window: address box, refresh and home buttons, back and forward buttons, tabs, and settings menu.

▶ List four popular browsers.

▶ State the difference between the default browser and the browser home page.

▶ Explain the purpose of predictive services.

▶ Provide an example of a browser extension.

▶ Describe what is in a browser cache and how it can affect your privacy.

▶ Describe what is in a browser's History list.

▶ Explain how private browsing works.

▶ Summarize the potential problem with allowing your browser to store passwords.

Go incognito. After you read Section B, you might want to put dark glasses on your browser so you can navigate the Web in private without accumulating a trail of Web sites, images, and ads that trace your Web activity.

Terminology

default browser
browser home page
predictive services

bookmarks
browser tabs
browser extension

browser cache
History list

private browsing

Browser Basics

Web browsers are the all-purpose tool for accessing the Web and everything it has to offer. They are used on all personal computer platforms. What's surprising is that the essential elements of browsers for small-screen devices, such as smartphones, are so similar to those for large-screen devices, such as desktops and laptops.

▶ **What's in the standard browser window?** The essential elements of a browser include an entry area for URLs and searches, navigation controls to move from one page to another, a refresh button, a home button, a settings menu, and a display area for Web page content. Additional elements, such as tabs, facilitate the browsing experience. Figure 4-14 illustrates essential browser elements and several additional features common to browsers on full-screen and mobile devices.

Terminology

The address box originally was used only for entering URLs. Today, the trend is to also use it for entering search terms. The address box is sometimes called an *Omnibox* to reflect its dual use.

4

Figure 4-14: Essential browser elements

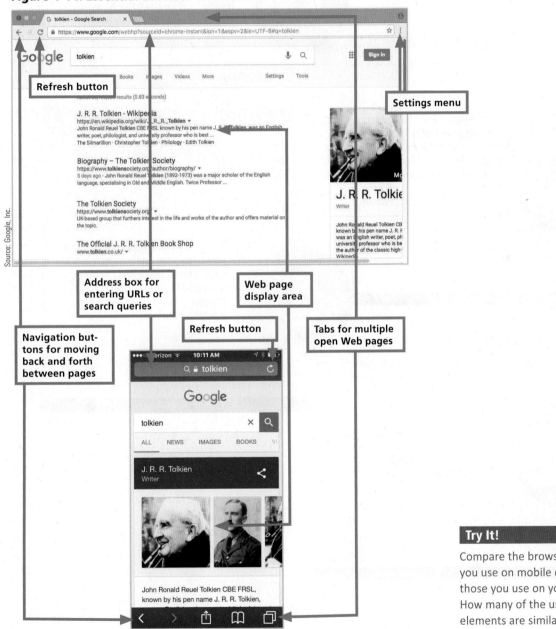

Source: Google, Inc.

Refresh button

Settings menu

Address box for entering URLs or search queries

Web page display area

Navigation buttons for moving back and forth between pages

Refresh button

Tabs for multiple open Web pages

▶ **What are the most popular browsers?** Today's popular browsers are Apple Safari, Google Chrome, Microsoft Edge, and Mozilla Firefox. In Figure 4-15, compare the placement and design of the address bars and navigation controls of these popular browsers.

Figure 4-15: Popular browsers

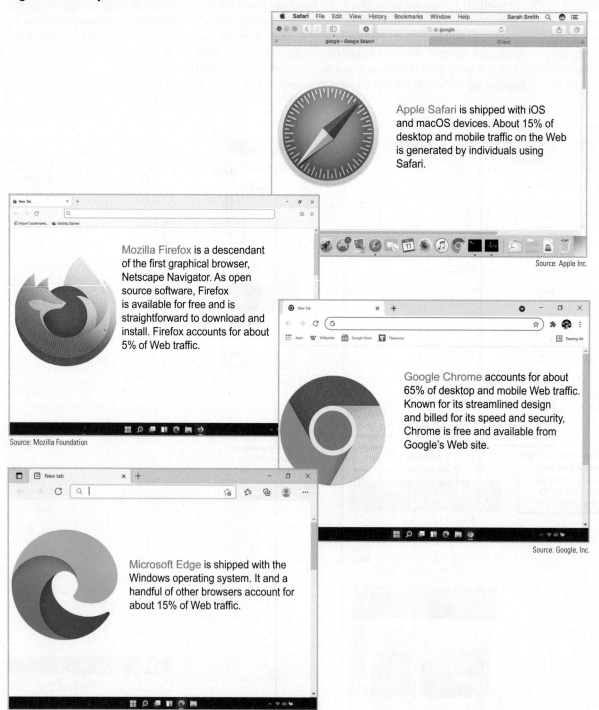

Apple Safari is shipped with iOS and macOS devices. About 15% of desktop and mobile traffic on the Web is generated by individuals using Safari.

Source: Apple Inc.

Mozilla Firefox is a descendant of the first graphical browser, Netscape Navigator. As open source software, Firefox is available for free and is straightforward to download and install. Firefox accounts for about 5% of Web traffic.

Source: Mozilla Foundation

Google Chrome accounts for about 65% of desktop and mobile Web traffic. Known for its streamlined design and billed for its speed and security, Chrome is free and available from Google's Web site.

Source: Google, Inc.

Microsoft Edge is shipped with the Windows operating system. It and a handful of other browsers account for about 15% of Web traffic.

▶ **When should I upgrade my browser?** It is a good idea to upgrade when a new version of your browser becomes available. Because most browser updates are free, you can get up-to-date functionality simply by spending a few minutes downloading and installing an update.

The most important reason to upgrade is for increased security. As hackers discover and take advantage of security holes, browser publishers try to patch the holes. Upgrades normally contain patches for known security exploits, although new features might sometimes open new holes.

New versions of browsers also reflect changes in operating systems and specifications for the HTML used to create Web pages. To take advantage of the latest innovations and to experience Web pages with all the bells and whistles intended by their designers, an updated browser is recommended.

▶ **Is it possible to use multiple browsers?** It is allowable to have more than one browser installed on a device, and you can open any installed browser and use it to surf the Web. Only one browser can be designated as the **default browser**, which is automatically used when you click a link in an email message or PDF file, for example.

You can add browsers and change which browser is used as the default. Suppose that your device is equipped with Microsoft Edge, but you'd prefer to use Chrome or Firefox. There is no need to delete Microsoft Edge. After you download and install an additional browser, you can set it as your default browser using the browser's Settings menu, as shown in Figure 4-16.

QuickCheck

Which of the following is not a reason to upgrade your browser?

a. To improve security

b. To keep up with new Web technologies

c. To get a free one

4

Try It!

How many browsers are installed on the device you use most frequently? What is the default browser?

Figure 4-16: Make Chrome your default browser

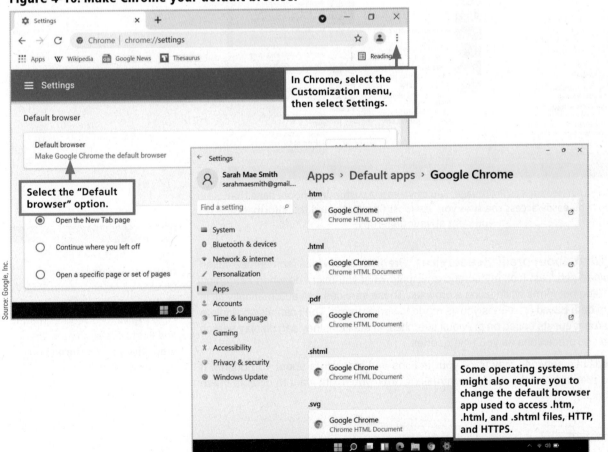

Source: Google, Inc.

Customization

Stop for a moment and think about how many hours a day you spend using a browser for research, entertainment, and communication. Why settle for a plain vanilla interface when you can streamline your Web experience by customizing your browser? You can change your home page, customize bookmarks and favorites, control tab behavior, select predictive services, adjust password settings, and more.

▶ **What should I set as my home page?** The browser home page is the first page displayed when the browser starts. Set the home page to a site that works as a doorway to your Web world. If your primary use of the Web is seeking information, then a search engine site, such as Google, makes a good home page. If you prefer to land amidst your online friends, then Facebook makes a good home page. If you're a newshound, point your home page to Google News, CNN, or Fox News. You can also use services such as Protopage, My Yahoo, or uStart to design your own start page, like the one in Figure 4-17.

Try It!

Which Web site is designated as your browser's home page? Would you prefer a different one?

Figure 4-17: Create your own home page

Source: Protopage.com

Using a service such as Protopage, you can create a customized home page that helps you easily access the sites you use most frequently and the information you want at your fingertips.

▶ **What about predictive services?** Predictive services (sometimes called *preload services*) look ahead and anticipate what you might do when searching or filling out forms while using a browser. These services can automatically fill in form data based on entries you've made to earlier forms. They can also complete search requests based on previous searches. In addition, they can display search and site predictions as you type queries.

Predictive services may track your actions and store data about you online. If you are nervous about privacy intrusions, then you might want to disable these services.

Try It!

You can adjust the behavior of predictive services from Chrome's Settings menu, Safari's Preferences menu, Microsoft Edge's Advanced Settings menu, and Firefox's search box. Are predictive services turned on in your browser?

▶ **How do I customize bookmarks and favorites?** **Bookmarks** (or Favorites, as they are called in some browsers) link to pages that you use frequently. When the browser is configured to show bookmarks, they appear on the browser toolbar and are fairly easy to access.

Consider creating bookmarks to your favorite social networking and informational sites. Set a bookmark to your favorite music service, or create a bookmark to quickly check the caloric content of the food you eat. Perhaps a bookmark to an online thesaurus can help improve your writing (Figure 4-18). One caution: Create bookmarks for sites that help, not hinder. That addictive cat video site? Don't bookmark it if the site becomes a distraction.

4

Figure 4-18: Customize your Favorites toolbar

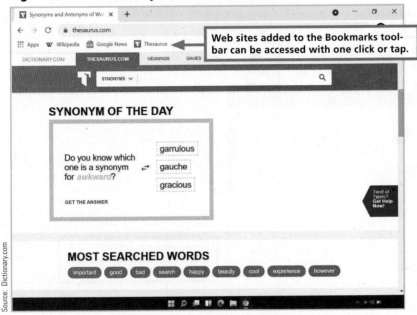

Web sites added to the Bookmarks tool-bar can be accessed with one click or tap.

Source: Dictionary.com

▶ **Can I control tabs?** **Browser tabs** allow your browser to queue up multiple Web pages so that you can easily switch between them. Your browser's Settings menu allows you to specify whether to use tabs or a new browser window. Each tab holds a Web page, and simply clicking the tab displays the corresponding page.

An alternative to tabs is opening new pages in separate browser windows—a process that allows you to see multiple pages at the same time, rather than switching among them (Figure 4-19).

Figure 4-19: Display multiple sites as tabs or separate windows

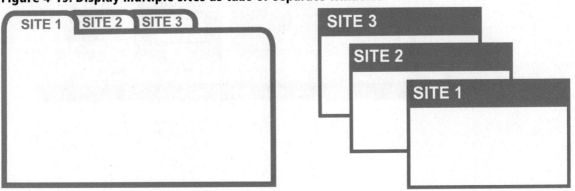

▶ **What is an extension?** A **browser extension** adds features to a browser. For example, one very popular extension called AdBlock removes advertisements from Web pages. Extensions are similar to apps because they provide you with a tool to accomplish a task. Unlike apps, which are accessed from a desktop or home screen, extensions are available only when using your browser.

Extensions for work, play, security, and accessibility are available online. To find them, search for the name of your browser followed by the word "extensions," like this: *Chrome extensions*.

▶ **How do I manage extensions?** Browsers provide a list of installed extensions and provide tools for disabling, enabling, or deleting them, as shown in Figure 4-20.

Try It!

Search online for a list of extensions that are available for your browser. If you don't have AdBlock, you might consider downloading it from a reputable source, such as the Chrome Web Store.

Figure 4-20: Find your browser's extensions

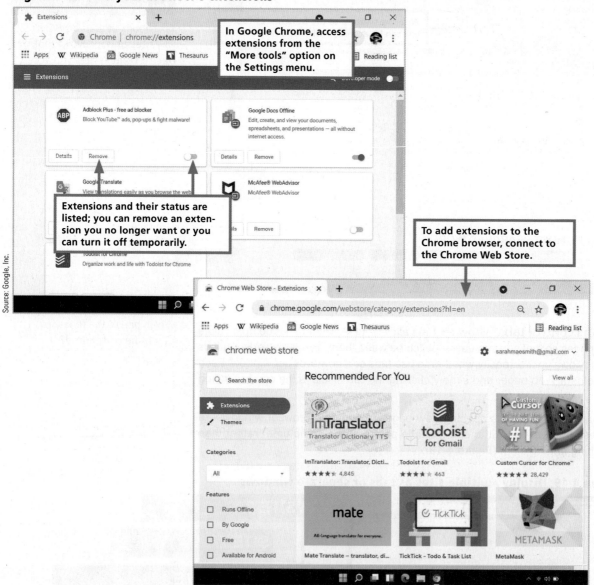

In Google Chrome, access extensions from the "More tools" option on the Settings menu.

Extensions and their status are listed; you can remove an extension you no longer want or you can turn it off temporarily.

To add extensions to the Chrome browser, connect to the Chrome Web Store.

Source: Google, Inc.

❱ What else can I customize on my browser? Your browser provides lots of built-in customization tools. Here are some handy options that might be available with your browser:

- Change the color of the tabs, address bar, and Favorites or Bookmarks bar.

- Select a different font or font size.

- Adjust the zoom level.

- Specify whether to display the Favorites or Bookmarks bar.

- Show or hide the status bar that shows the destination URL for Web page links.

- Set what happens when you open your browser: open a specific page, open a set of pages, or continue where you left off the last time you closed the browser.

- Control the browser tabs by specifying if new tabs should become active, selecting shortcut keys for switching between tabs, and showing or hiding Web site icons in tabs.

- Select your default language and indicate if you'd like an automatic translation for material that is not in your selected language.

- Spell check your queries.

- Specify the destination for downloaded files.

- Select accessibility options, such as providing live captions for audio and video.

- Tighten security by identifying fraudulent Web sites and preventing automatic use of your computer's camera and microphone.

- Ensure your privacy by reducing the ability of sites to track your footprints as you navigate the Web.

Figure 4-21 highlights some of the customization settings for the Google Chrome browser.

4

Try It!

Access the customization settings for your browser to make sure they reflect the way you access the Web.

Figure 4-21: Browser customization settings

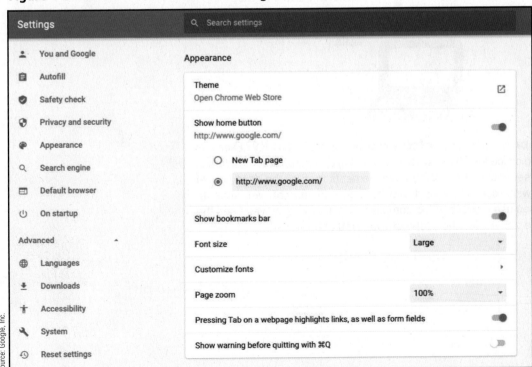

Source: Google, Inc.

Browser Cache

Browsers pull HTML documents, images, and other Web page elements to your local device—and not just the main elements of a page. All those funky ads are pulled down, too. It is somewhat troubling that these elements may remain in a Web cache on your device, leaving a trail of digital bread crumbs to the Web sites you've visited.

▶ **What is a browser cache?** When your browser fetches pages and graphics to form a Web page, it stores that material on your device in temporary files referred to as a **browser cache**, Web cache, or browser data.

A browser cache comes in handy if you switch back and forth between pages or sites. Rather than fetch the entire page and all its graphics again, your browser can simply load them from the local cache (Figure 4-22).

> **QuickCheck**
>
> Which of the following would you not expect to find in a browser cache?
>
> a. Passwords
>
> b. Image files from Web pages
>
> c. Images from ads
>
> d. HTML documents

Figure 4-22: Your browser cache in action

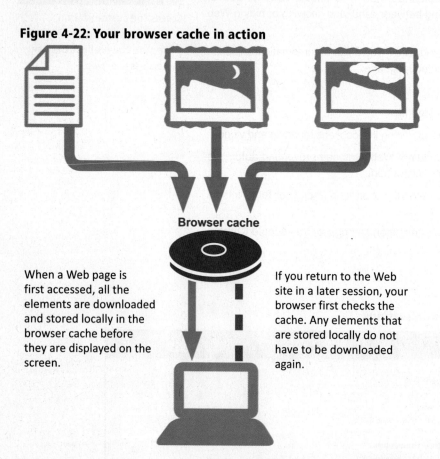

Browser cache

When a Web page is first accessed, all the elements are downloaded and stored locally in the browser cache before they are displayed on the screen.

If you return to the Web site in a later session, your browser first checks the cache. Any elements that are stored locally do not have to be downloaded again.

▶ **How does a browser cache affect my privacy and security?** Files can remain in the Web cache for days or weeks, depending on your browser's settings. Because a browser cache stores Web page elements from all the sites you've visited, anyone with access to your device can view this trail of Web sites. In addition, when you use a public or lab computer, the next person who uses the computer may be able to see the cache of your Web activity.

▶ **Can I see what's in a browser cache?** Your browser maintains a **History list** of the Web sites you've visited. This list displays Web pages, but not the video, audio, or link components that form the page. Those components are stored in a folder somewhere on a local storage device.

If you use more than one browser, each one has its own cache. With modern browsers, the files in the cache are likely to be stored in a compressed format, making it difficult to view their contents.

Although you may not be able to view the actual cache files, you can remove them by deleting the contents of the History list.

Figure 4-23 illustrates options for clearing the Safari browser cache.

Figure 4-23: Clear the Safari browser cache

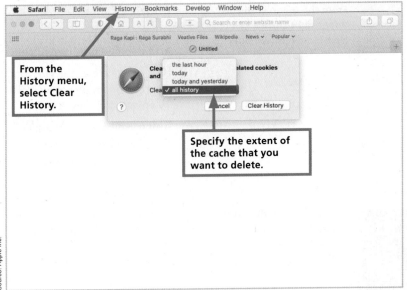

Source: Apple Inc.

The Chrome browser provides more options for clearing items in the cache. Figure 4-24 illustrates.

Figure 4-24: Clear the Chrome browser cache

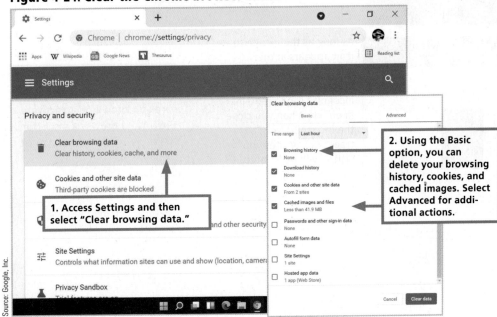

Source: Google, Inc.

▶ **Is there a way to browse without using the cache?** Today's browsers offer **private browsing** modes, in which traces of your activity are not maintained in the History list or browser cache. Microsoft browsers call this mode InPrivate Browsing. Google Chrome calls it incognito mode. In Safari and Firefox, it is called Private Browsing.

Although private browsing accumulates no trail of Web activity on your local device, it does not prevent external sources, such as advertisers and government snoopers, from tracking your activity. Use private browsing when you prefer not to leave a trail that can be seen by others who gain access to a device that you have recently used. Figure 4-25 demonstrates how to enter incognito mode in Google Chrome.

Figure 4-25: Go incognito!

From the menu in the upper-right corner, select New Incognito Window.

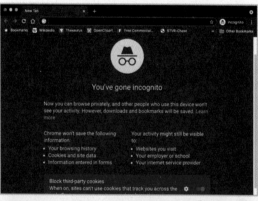

Google Chrome displays the incognito home screen.

Incognito icon

As long as the incognito icon appears in the address bar of the browser window, incognito mode remains in effect. When you close the incognito tabs, all traces of the sites you visited will be deleted.

Source: Google, Inc.

▶ **Is it safe to allow my browser to store passwords?** Browsers ask to save passwords when you log in to sites. If you agree, your password is stored in an encrypted file on your local device. The next time you log in to a site, your browser will use the corresponding stored password.

Storing passwords is a useful feature. You can create unique and hard-to-guess passwords without fear that you might forget them and without the hassle of looking them up each time you log in.

The potential risk of stored passwords is that anyone who gains access to your device can easily log in to your password-protected sites because the passwords are supplied by your browser. If you allow your browser to store passwords, be sure to use a password to protect access to your device.

You can discover which passwords are saved by the browsers you use. To view passwords stored by Microsoft Edge, use the Windows search box to open the Credential Manager. For Safari, select the Preferences menu, then select the Passwords tab. In Firefox, open the Security panel and select Saved Passwords. Figure 4-26 illustrates how to find passwords stored by Chrome.

QuickCheck

How would you summarize the security risk involved in allowing your browser to store passwords?

a. It is not a risk.

b. It is a security risk and should be avoided.

c. It is more secure to store passwords online.

d. The convenience of stored passwords might be worth the small risk.

4

Figure 4-26: Find your Chrome passwords

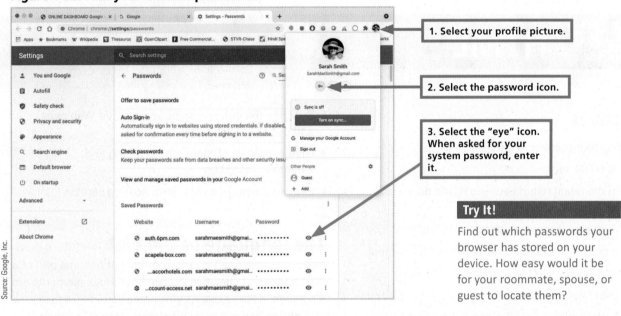

1. Select your profile picture.

2. Select the password icon.

3. Select the "eye" icon. When asked for your system password, enter it.

Source: Google, Inc.

Try It!

Find out which passwords your browser has stored on your device. How easy would it be for your roommate, spouse, or guest to locate them?

QuickQuiz   Section B

1. It is important to [_____] your browser to get patches for known security exploits.

2. When you use a public computer, the next person who uses it can see the Web pages you visited by looking at the [_____] list.

3. If you do not want HTML and image files from recently visited Web sites to be stored on your device, delete the browser [_____].

4. [_____] services look ahead to anticipate what you might do when searching the Web or filling out Web-based forms.

5. A browser [_____], such as AdBlock or the Merriam-Webster Online Toolbar, adds features to a browser.

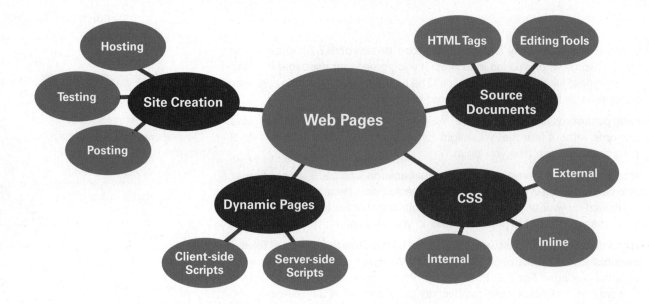

Objectives

▶ Describe four markup languages.

▶ Identify HTML tags.

▶ Explain the relationship between HTML documents and Web pages.

▶ List four types of tools for creating Web pages.

▶ Sketch out the template for a basic HTML document.

▶ Correctly use basic HTML tags.

▶ Describe the purpose of CSS.

▶ Differentiate inline CSS from internal and external CSS.

▶ Describe the differences between static Web pages and dynamic Web pages.

▶ Give examples of client-side scripting and server-side scripting.

▶ Explain the purpose of a Web hosting service.

The language of the Web is HTML. It determines the text, images, and sounds that become part of a Web page, and specifies exactly how those elements are displayed. It also explains why some Web pages look kind of funky in one browser but picture perfect in others. The language of the Web, it seems, is open to interpretation.

Terminology

HTML5	HTML conversion utility	inline CSS	client-side scripts
markup language	online HTML editor	internal CSS	server-side scripts
HTML tags	local HTML editors	external CSS	Web hosting service
HTML document	CSS	static Web page	
source document	style rules	dynamic Web page	

HTML Basics

HTML is the foundation for professionally designed corporate Web sites, but a little knowledge of HTML can come in handy for your everyday interactions online. You can use HTML tags to enhance blog posts, and some Web sites allow HTML for reader comments.

▶ **What should I know about HTML?** Tim Berners-Lee developed the original HTML specifications in 1990. These specifications have been revised several times by the World Wide Web Consortium (W3C). The current version, HTML5, was introduced in 2010.

HTML is a set of elements for creating documents that a browser can display as a Web page. It is called a markup language because authors "mark up" documents by inserting special instructions called HTML tags that specify how the document should appear when displayed in a browser.

HTML is a member of a family of markup languages. You may see references to these languages as you work with Web site design. Figure 4-27 summarizes the markup language family tree.

Figure 4-27: Markup language family tree

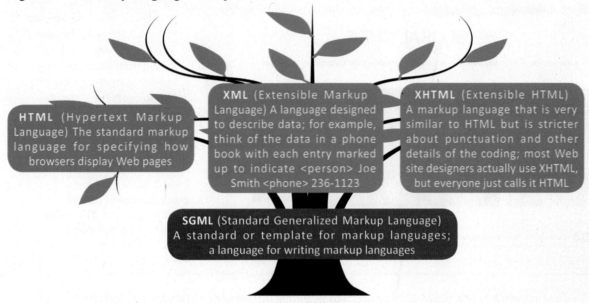

HTML (Hypertext Markup Language) The standard markup language for specifying how browsers display Web pages

XML (Extensible Markup Language) A language designed to describe data; for example, think of the data in a phone book with each entry marked up to indicate <person> Joe Smith <phone> 236-1123

XHTML (Extensible HTML) A markup language that is very similar to HTML but is stricter about punctuation and other details of the coding; most Web site designers actually use XHTML, but everyone just calls it HTML

SGML (Standard Generalized Markup Language) A standard or template for markup languages; a language for writing markup languages

▶ **How do HTML tags work?** HTML tags are incorporated into an HTML document, which is similar to a word processing file but has an .htm or .html extension. HTML tags such as <h1> and <p> are enclosed in angle brackets and embedded in the document. The <h1> tag specifies a heading; the <p> indicates a new paragraph.

Most tags are inserted as pairs. The start tag and end tag enclose the content like this:

<h1> THE GLOBAL CHEF </h1>

HTML tags are instructions for the browser. When your browser displays a Web page on your computer screen, it does not show the tags or angle brackets. Instead, it attempts to follow the tags' instructions. When displayed in a browser, the <h1> tag for THE GLOBAL CHEF might produce this:

THE GLOBAL CHEF

QuickCheck

The HTML tag <h1> specifies the _____.

a. style of text used as headings

b. title of an HTML page

c. beginning of an HTML document

d. format for images

▶ **So HTML documents look a lot different from Web pages, right?**

Exactly. An HTML document is like a screenplay, and your browser is like a director who makes a screenplay come to life by assembling cast members and making sure they deliver their lines correctly.

As the HTML "screenplay" unfolds, your browser follows the instructions in an HTML document to display lines of text on the screen in the right color, size, and position.

If the screenplay calls for a graphic, your browser collects it from the Web server and displays it. Although the HTML screenplay exists as a permanent file, the Web page you see on the screen exists only for the duration of the "performance."

An HTML document is sometimes referred to as a **source document** because it is the source of the HTML tags used to construct a Web page. Figure 4-28 illustrates the difference between an HTML source document (bottom) and the Web page it produces (top).

Figure 4-28: HTML source document

A source document contains text but no graphics. The <img> tag links to the graphic and displays it in the browser.

```
<div style="margin: 4.32px 2.16px 4.32px 2.16px;"><p style="line-height:54px;margin-top:0px;margin-bottom:11.25px;" class="Style1">THE GLOBAL CHEF</p></div></div></div>

<div style="margin: 2.16px 2.16px 2.16px 2.16px;"><p style="line-height:17px;margin-top:0px;margin-bottom:14.58333px;" class="Style2">Travel around the world. A delectable feast for the eyes. Food served with brilliance and imagination.</p></div></div></div>

<div style="position:relative"><img src="London.jpg" style="left:56px;top:236px;height:232px;width:174px;z-index: 3;position: absolute;"></div></div>

<div style="position:relative"><img src="Paris.jpg" style="left:248px;top:236px;height:232px;width:309px;z-index: 4;position: absolute;"></div></div>

<div style="position:relative"><img src="Tokyo.jpg" style="left:576px;top:236px;height:232px;width:175px;z-index: 5;position: absolute;"></div></div>

<div style="position:relative"><div class="shape_6" style="left:371px;top:487px;height:32px;width:48px;z-index: 6;position: absolute;"><div style="margin: 4.32px 2.16px 4.32px 2.16px;"><p style="line-height:14px;margin-top:0px;margin-bottom:11.25px;" class="linkStyle_3"><a href="choose-the-course.html" class="linkStyle_6">Enter</a></p></div></div></div>
```

HTML Editing Tools

There is an extensive toolset available for creating Web pages. Once you're aware of the options, you can select the tools that best suit your project and your ability as a designer.

▶ **What tools are available for creating Web pages?** You can create files for Web pages with an HTML conversion utility, online HTML editor, local HTML editor, or text editor.

HTML conversion utility. An **HTML conversion utility** creates an HTML document from a conventional document, spreadsheet, or other text-based file. For example, you can work with Microsoft Word to create a standard DOCX file, and then use Word's Save As Web Page option or the Transform option to convert the document into HTML format. The HTML conversion process occasionally produces an unusual result, however, because some of the features and formatting in your original document might not be possible within the world of HTML.

Online HTML editor. A second option for Web page authors is to use an **online HTML editor**, such as WordPress or Google Sites. Working with these tools is straightforward—select a template, choose a color scheme, enter titles and other text, upload graphics, and add links to other pages (Figure 4-29).

Figure 4-29: Using Google sites to create Web pages

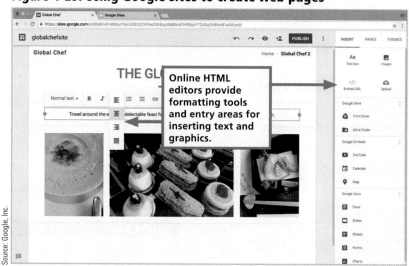

Source: Google, Inc.

Locally installed HTML editor. Two more options for creating Web pages include **local HTML editors** and comprehensive Web development software. Some of these tools offer professional features for managing extensive corporate Web sites, while others are geared toward creating smaller personal sites. Popular Web development products include Adobe Dreamweaver CC and open source Atom.

Text editor. HTML documents can be created with a basic ASCII text editor, such as Windows Notepad or TextEdit. With these tools, you start from scratch, with a blank page, and enter HTML codes along with the text that you want to include in the Web page. Although Web designers rarely use these tools to create entire Web sites, text editors can be useful for troubleshooting HTML documents. Text editors also offer a great way to learn HTML basics that you may be able to use for formatting online comments and posts.

QuickCheck

Documents created with word processing software _____.

a. can be posted to the Web as DOCX files

b. cannot be used on the Web

c. can be converted to HTML files for the Web

d. contain HTML tags

▶ **What are the parts of an HTML document?** The framework for an HTML document consists of two sections: the head and the body. The head section begins with <!DOCTYPE html> and <head> tags. It may also include information that defines global properties, including the Web page title that appears in the browser title bar and information about the page that can be used by search engines.

The body section of an HTML document begins with the <body> HTML tag. This section of the document contains text, HTML tags that format the text, plus a variety of links to graphics, sounds, and videos. Figure 4-30 contains basic HTML for a Web page. You can use it as a template for creating your own pages.

Figure 4-30: HTML document template

① An HTML document begins with the DOCTYPE and html declarations.

② The <head> tag contains the page title.

③ The body section contains text and links to images.

④ Headings are formatted with the <h1> tag and can be set off with the <p> tag.

⑤ Images are linked to pages with the <img> tag.

⑥ Links to other Web pages are coded using the <a href> tag.

▶ **How do I specify the text and graphics for a Web page?** In the body section of your HTML document, you can enter text and HTML tags to mark sections of text that should appear in different styles. You can also specify the images you want to appear on the page, and you can create clickable links to other Web pages. The table in Figure 4-31 provides a list of basic tags that you can use to create your own HTML documents.

Figure 4-31: Basic HTML tags

HTML Tag	Use	Example
\<b> \<i>	Bold or italicize text	\<b> Hello \</b>
\<h1> \<h2> ... \<h6>	Change font size; h1 is largest	\<h1> Chapter 1 \</h1>
\<h1 style="color: ">	Change font color	\<h1 style="color:green"> Fir Trees \</h1>
\<hr/>	Include a horizontal line (no end tag)	Section 2 \<hr/>
**\ **	Line break (no end tag)	This is line one. \ This is line two.
\<p>	Paragraph break	\<p>It was the best of times, it...of comparison only. \</p>
\<ol> \<ul> \<li>	Numbered list \<ol>; bulleted list \<ul>; list items \<li>	\<ol> \<li> First item\</li> \<li> Second item\</li> \</ol>
\<a href="URL">	Link to another Web page	\<a href="www.news.com/today.htm"> Click here \</a>
\<img src="File">	Include an image	\<img src="Photo.jpg">
\<table>, \<tr>, \<td>	Create tables, table rows, and cells	\<table>

▶ **Which HTML tags can be used in blog posts and comments?** Most blogging platforms allow authors to insert HTML tags to format blog posts. Some social media sites also allow readers to insert basic HTML tags, such as \<b> and \<i>, in comments.

To discover if HTML tags are allowed in a specific online venue, check its Help link or perform a Web search such as *Goodreads HTML*, as shown in Figure 4-32.

Figure 4-32: Using HTML on social media

Help Topic

How do I format text into HTML?

Goodreads supports a set list of html tags that you can use to format your comments, reviews, and stories & writing. They are posted on the right side of most pages, and are also below:

formatting tips

- link: \<a href="http://www.goodreads.com">my link text\</a>
- link to book: [book: Harry Potter and the Sorcerer's Stone]
- link to author: [author: J.K. Rowling]
- **bold text**: \<b>...\</b>
- *italic text*: \<i>...\</i>
- underline text: \<u>...\</u>
- format text: \<pre>...\</pre>

CSS

A Web page displayed in a browser may look simple. The page might contain some blocks of text, a handful of photos, some text links, and a few navigation buttons. With your knowledge of HTML, you can probably envision the source document for such a page. But that document is usually accompanied by CSS. What's that all about?

▶ **What is CSS?** CSS, which stands for Cascading Style Sheets, is a set of detailed style specifications for an HTML document. These specifications are called style rules, which include settings for font colors, font sizes, background colors, borders, text alignment, link formats, and margins. There are three types of style sheets:

Inline. Style sheets can be intermixed within an HTML document, but the use of an inline CSS is avoided by professional designers.

Internal. An internal CSS is included within the header of an HTML document. It places all the formatting elements where they can be edited without hunting through the entire document.

External. With an external CSS, style rules are placed in a separate file with a .css extension. CSS files can be manually created with a text editor. HTML editors generally create external CSSs automatically. For Web sites with more than one page, an external CSS is the recommended approach.

The advantage of external CSS is that all of the pages for a Web site can be controlled by a single style sheet. If you decide, for example, to change the color of the heading font, you make only one change to the style sheet and it will be applied to every page on the site.

▶ **What does a style rule look like?** CSS style rules have a selector and a declaration block. The selector indicates an HTML element to which you want to apply a style rule. The declaration specifies the styles. Here is a style rule for displaying Heading 1 text in purple 10-point font.

> `h1 {color: purple; font-size: 10 px;}`

A CSS containing several styles for a Web site might look like Figure 4-33.

Figure 4-33: Use a CSS to set font colors

```
body
{
font-family: arial; } ❶
h1 {
    color: purple; text-align: center;} ❷
a:link {
    color: purple; } ❸
a:visited {
    color: blue; } ❹
```

❶ Set the font to Arial for the entire Web page.

❷ Set the Heading 1 font color to purple and the alignment to centered.

❸ Set the font color of text links to purple.

❹ Set the font color of visited text links to blue.

QuickCheck

Professional Web designers should avoid using _____ CSS.

a. inline

b. internal

c. external

QuickCheck

Based on the CSS in Figure 4-33, what is the color for visited links?

a. Purple

b. White

c. Blue

d. Black

▶ **How does external CSS work?** Let's suppose you have a Web site containing five pages. You have five HTML documents—one for each page. At the top of each page is the heading "THE GLOBAL CHEF." You want the browser to display that text in purple and centered in the browser window. Figure 4-34 illustrates how to link the CSS to the five Web pages.

Figure 4-34: Use one CSS for multiple Web pages

❶ Create a CSS called SiteStyle.css and define the h1 style like this:

h1 {color: purple; text-align: center;}

❷ Link each of the HTML documents to the CSS by placing a <link> tag within the <head> area of the HTML document like this:

<head> <link rel="stylesheet" type="text/css" href="SiteStyle.css">

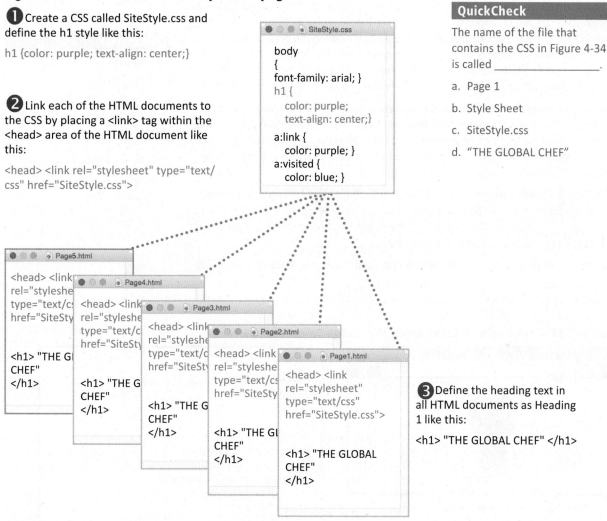

SiteStyle.css

```
body
{
font-family: arial; }
h1 {
    color: purple;
    text-align: center;}
a:link {
    color: purple; }
a:visited {
    color: blue; }
```

Page5.html

<head> <link rel="styleshe type="text/cs href="SiteSty

<h1> "THE GL CHEF" </h1>

Page4.html

<head> <link rel="styleshe type="text/c href="SiteSty

<h1> "THE GL CHEF" </h1>

Page3.html

<head> <link rel="styleshe type="text/c href="SiteSty

<h1> "THE GL CHEF" </h1>

Page2.html

<head> <link rel="styleshe type="text/cs href="SiteSty

<h1> "THE GL CHEF" </h1>

Page1.html

<head> <link rel="stylesheet" type="text/css" href="SiteStyle.css">

<h1> "THE GLOBAL CHEF" </h1>

❸ Define the heading text in all HTML documents as Heading 1 like this:

<h1> "THE GLOBAL CHEF" </h1>

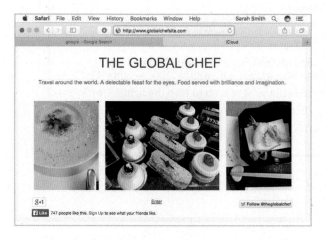

❹ When any of the five Web pages are displayed in a browser, the Heading 1 font will be purple and centered.

Dynamic Web Pages

Using HTML and CSS, Web designers can create a **static Web page** that displays the same information, regardless of who accesses it. The page will have the same content and format for all visitors. In your experience, however, Web sites can display customized pages that show products you're shopping for, tunes from your favorite musicians, and driving directions for your next road trip. These dynamic Web pages require an additional layer of technology.

▶ **How do Web pages become dynamic?** A **dynamic Web page** displays customized content in response to keyboard or mouse actions, or based on information supplied directly or indirectly by the person viewing the page. Information is supplied directly when a Web site visitor searches for a product, for example, or asks for driving directions. Information is supplied indirectly when a Web page can autonomously grab data based on the visitor's location or browsing history.

Dynamic elements can be incorporated in Web pages with the addition of instructions, called scripts, written with scripting languages such as JavaScript, PHP, and Python. These scripts can be incorporated into the <head> or <body> sections of an HTML document or in a separate document. There are two ways to script dynamic Web pages: client-side and server-side.

▶ **When do Web designers use client-side dynamics?** **Client-side scripts** are embedded in an HTML document and run locally when a Web page is displayed by a browser. Client-side dynamics are used to customize aspects of the user interface and for simple interactions.

A classic example of a client-side script is changing the appearance of a graphical object displayed on a Web page (Figure 4-35).

Figure 4-35: Client-side script changes the image when clicked

Clicking or tapping the lightbulb image...

...runs the script to change the image.

```
<!DOCTYPE html>
<html>
<body>
<script>
function changeImage() {
    var image=document.
    getElementById('myImage');
    if (image.src.match("bulbon")) {
        image.src="pic_bulboff.gif"; }
    else {
        image.src="pic_bulbon.gif";   }}
</script>
<img id="myImage" onclick="changeImage()"
src="pic_bulboff.gif" width="100" height="180">
<p>Click the light bulb to turn the light on/off.</p>
</body>
</html>
```

▶ **When do Web designers use server-side dynamics?** Server-side scripts run on Web servers rather than on your local device. The server typically accesses information from a database and uses that information to create customized Web pages on the fly.

A common use of server-side scripting is online shopping. Figure 4-36 illustrates how an online store uses server-side scripts to display a customized list of products when you search for *Mountain Bikes*.

Figure 4-36: Server-side scripts can create Web pages on the fly

The site initially displays a generic home page.

Entering a search initiates a server-side script.

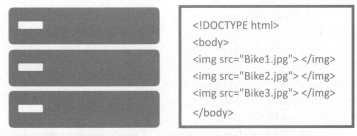

The script looks for mountain bikes and generates an HTML page, which is sent to the local browser.

The browser displays the page that was created on the fly by the server-side script.

QuickCheck

In Figure 4-36, what generated the Web page?

a. A database

b. An HTML document

c. A query

d. A server-side script

4

Site Creation

Whether you work with a text editor or another authoring tool, HTML documents should be saved in files with .htm or .html extensions. Creating a Web page is not the end of the publishing process. The steps for establishing a Web site include selecting a hosting service, choosing a domain, posting Web pages, and testing pages in various browsers.

What is a hosting service? Getting a Web site up and running is uncomplicated and inexpensive. You need a hosting service, a URL, and a set of Web pages for your site.

A **Web hosting service** is a company that provides space on a server to house Web pages. Web hosting services such as GoDaddy, Amazon Web Services, HostGator, and Google offer a variety of hosting plans. Figure 4-37 illustrates the types of plans available from a typical hosting service.

Figure 4-37: Plan options from a typical hosting service

Starter	Standard
1 GB storage space	Your own domain
Site management tools	100 MB Web space
Supported by ads selected by the hosting service	Site management tools
	Ads
Free	$5.95/month

Enhanced	Ecommerce
Your own domain	Merchandise database
No ads	Credit card processing
1 GB Web space	Secure connection
Site management tools	Site management tools
$10.95/month	$19.95/month

What are the choices for URLs? The URL for your Web site depends on its domain. You can obtain your own domain name, such as MyOwnWebSite.com, and then your site can be accessed using the URL *www.MyOwnWebSite.com*. Once you have your own domain name, you can use it with any hosting service. Another option is to use a subdomain of your hosting service. For example, a Web site created with Google Sites could use Google's domain name combined with a name that you choose for your site—for example, *sites.google.com/site/MyOwnWebSite*.

How do I post pages? When pages are created locally using a text editor or local HTML editor, those pages must be uploaded to your hosting service. A mechanism for doing so is usually provided by your hosting service. If not, you can use FTP to upload files.

Pages that are created online using tools from your hosting service just need to be "published," which specifies that they become publicly accessible.

QuickCheck

What is the purpose of a Web hosting service?

a. Storing documents offline

b. Supplying a server platform for Web sites

c. Providing Internet service

d. Providing access to the Web

▶ **What does testing involve?** Basic Web page testing involves trying every text link to make sure that it leads to the intended destination. In addition, it is important to test every navigation link to ensure that visitors can easily reach every page of your site.

It is an unfortunate fact that today's browsers are not completely standardized. They render some HTML tags differently. Effects that work on some browsers may look odd and behave very differently on others.

An additional problem involving fonts can affect how pages are displayed. A browser generally uses the fonts installed on the local device when displaying Web pages. Suppose our example Web site, The Global Chef, uses an unusual font such as American Typewriter. When its pages are displayed on devices without the American Typewriter font, a substitute font will be used; that font might make the page look quite different from the intended design (Figure 4-38).

To uncover problems that might be caused by browser compatibility, careful designers test new and revised sites using each one of the popular browsers.

Try It!

Connect to the same Web page using two different browsers; one can be on a mobile device, such as a smartphone. What are the major differences in the way the page is displayed?

4

Figure 4-38: Available fonts may affect Web page appearance

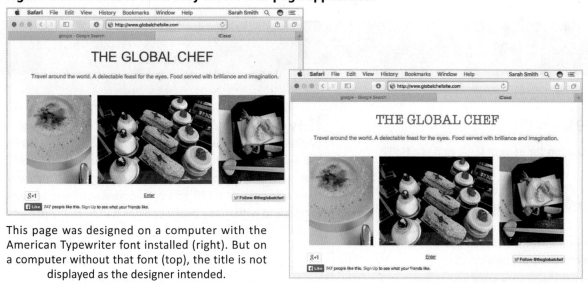

This page was designed on a computer with the American Typewriter font installed (right). But on a computer without that font (top), the title is not displayed as the designer intended.

QuickQuiz   Section C

1. A Web server sends a(n) [_____] document to a browser, which then displays it as a Web page.

2. Notepad and TextEdit can be used to manually enter HTML [_____] into a document.

3. <a href> is used to create [_____] in an HTML document.

4. CSS stands for Cascading [_____] Sheets.

5. Dynamic Web pages are created with [_____] written in languages such as PHP and JavaScript.

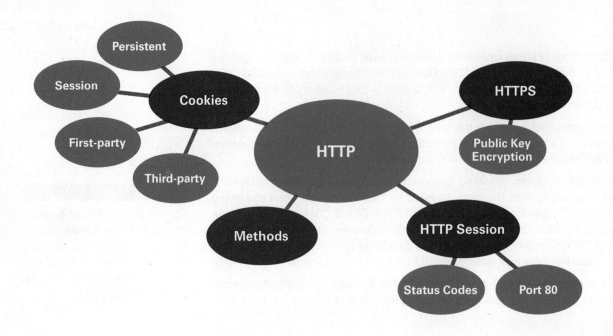

Objectives

▶ State the function for each of the five basic HTTP methods.

▶ Identify the HTTP status codes for requests that are fulfilled and for requests that ask for a nonexistent URL.

▶ Explain the relationship between cookies, sessions, and HTTP's stateless protocol.

▶ List four reasons that Web sites use cookies.

▶ Describe the difference between session cookies and persistent cookies.

▶ Summarize the reasons for blocking third-party cookies but not blocking first-party cookies.

▶ Identify when your browser is displaying a secure site where it is safe to enter passwords, financial information, and other personal data.

▶ Explain how public key encryption works.

Have you ever wondered why your digital devices are littered with cookies from every Web site you've visited? Blame it on HTTP, the protocol that handles communications between browsers and Web servers. Once you have a handle on HTTP, you can understand your options for dealing with those pesky cookies that push bizarre ads to your screen.

Terminology

HTTP	HTTP status code	first-party cookie	public key encryption
HTTP methods	cookie	third-party cookie	
HTTP session	session cookies	cross-site tracking	
stateless protocol	persistent cookies	HTTPS	

HTTP Basics

You can think of HTTP as the system that browsers use to communicate with a Web server and ask for HTML documents. HTTP is responsible for transporting Web pages, whereas HTML is responsible for the way Web pages look when displayed by a browser.

▶ **How does HTTP work?** HTTP is a communication protocol that works with TCP/IP to get the elements for Web pages to a local browser. A set of commands called **HTTP methods** helps your browser communicate with Web servers.

GET is the most frequently used HTTP method. GET is used to retrieve text and image files necessary for displaying a Web page. GET can also be used to pass a search query to a Web server (Figure 4-39).

QuickCheck

One of the key transport technologies for Web pages is

_____.

a. HTML

b. HTTP

c. BitTorrent

d. Chrome

4

Figure 4-39: How GET requests data from a Web server

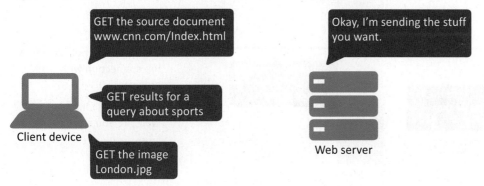

The set of methods for HTTP is not very large. As with many aspects of the digital world, amazingly complex activities are carried out by seemingly simple elements. The most commonly used HTTP methods are listed in Figure 4-40.

Figure 4-40: HTTP methods

Method	Function
GET	Requests data from a specified source
POST	Submits data to a specified source
HEAD	Requests the HTTP header only for requested data
PUT	Uploads data to a specific Web address
DELETE	Removes a specified resource
OPTIONS	Fetches a list of methods supported by the server

QuickCheck

Which HTTP method does a browser use to request an HTML source document?

a. GET

b. POST

c. HEAD

d. OPTIONS

▶ **What is an HTTP session?** HTTP uses port 80 for communications between a client device and a server. The exchange takes place within a session. An **HTTP session** is a sequence of transactions most commonly used to request data from a Web server and fetch the files needed to display a Web page in a browser window.

At the end of a session, the connection is closed. Because the server does not "remember" its state from one session to the next, HTTP is called a **stateless protocol**. Figure 4-41 illustrates typical HTTP sessions.

Figure 4-41: HTTP sessions

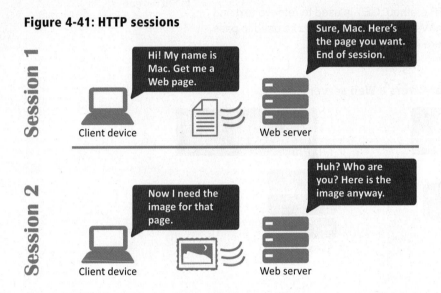

▶ **What if an element cannot be found?** A Web server's response to a browser's request includes an **HTTP status code** that indicates whether the browser's request could be fulfilled. The status code 200 means that the request was fulfilled—the requested HTML document, graphic, or other resource was sent.

While surfing the Web, you might have encountered the "404 Not Found" message. Your browser displays this message when a Web server sends a 404 status code to indicate that the requested resource does not exist (Figure 4-42).

Figure 4-42: An HTTP 404 status code

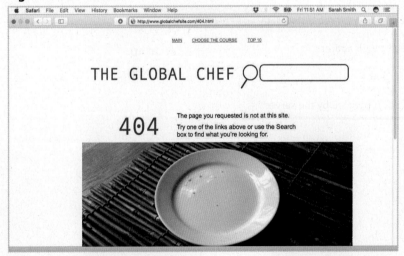

Cookies

Cookies—the kind associated with the Web—have a bad reputation. They are affiliated with marketing exploits that track your browsing behavior by recording products you've viewed, merchandise you've purchased, and Web sites you've visited. You can take control of cookies once you understand why they are used and how they work.

▶ **What is a cookie?** A **cookie** (technically an HTTP cookie) is a small chunk of data generated by a Web server and stored as a text file in memory or on disk. Cookies can be stored on any devices—desktop computers, laptops, tablets, or smartphones—on which you use a browser.

Cookies provide a way for Web sites to store information on a client device for later retrieval. Web sites use cookies to:

- Monitor your path through a site to keep track of the pages you viewed or the items you purchased.

- Gather information that allows a Web server to present ads targeted to products you previously purchased at that Web site.

- Collect personal information you submit to a Web page, and retain it for the next time you visit the Web site.

- Verify that you have logged in to a site using a valid user ID and password, if necessary.

▶ **Why do Web sites need to use cookies?** In many respects, cookies are the solution for problems caused by HTTP's stateless protocol, which maintains no record of the pages you visit at a Web site.

Suppose that you use your browser to visit a popular online music store. You search for your favorite bands, listen to some sample tracks, and put a few albums in your shopping cart. Because HTTP is a stateless protocol, each time you connect to a different Web page at the site, the server regards it as a new visit. Therefore, HTTP by itself cannot record your path through a Web site. Cookies, however, enable the server to keep track of your activity and compile a list of your purchases.

▶ **What's in a cookie?** A cookie can contain any information that's collected by the host site, such as a customer number, Web page URL, shopping cart number, or access date. It may also contain an ID number that is assigned by the server or by a JavaScript. Figure 4-43 illustrates the contents of a typical cookie.

Terminology

HTTP cookies are also referred to as *Web cookies* and *browser cookies*.

4

QuickCheck

When a Web server cannot determine if a series of requests comes from the same browser, the protocol is _____.

a. stateless

b. a 404 error

c. HTML

Figure 4-43: Cookie contents

"domain": ".amazon.com",

"expirationDate": 2043165173.969223,

"hostOnly": false,

"httpOnly": false,

"name": "session-token",

"path": "/",

"secure": false,

"session": false,

"storeId": "0",

"value": "oH3JSTye7MX5OYLxKPdZCxY-RPLOj3GAb42bWfdUPv8f-nXBwSIG6rFt7RVY/uWxPUB453CMBR2d65uoEjJ-kA1HcqBYbmRhJ1perKUghJF/dYLU2Ylv3HqYBrasNH8Yvsjj-tjwWysyGvLvWW7U9pFcauCs-0GYjSC4V9ugYNJ4UOsryW7+iEK+H0AuAg3A/zctXp00Ysodb203NvgdY72obobXhgio4vMxVjoiPlnoucjzOWRZa+iJXas2JjLj",

"id": 3

QuickCheck

Why does the cookie in Figure 4-43 refer to Amazon.com?

a. The cookie is stored on the Amazon.com Web server.

b. The cookie was set by Amazon.com.

c. The cookie transfers a Web page to Amazon.com.

▶ **How long do cookies remain on a device?** There are two kinds of cookies: session cookies and persistent cookies.

Session cookies. Some cookies are stored in memory and are deleted when the browser is closed. These session cookies are never stored on a disk or other permanent storage medium.

Persistent cookies. Cookies that are stored on a device after a session ends are referred to as persistent cookies. These cookies remain on a device until they expire or are deleted. Some persistent cookies are programmed to time out after a designated date. When one of these cookies reaches the end of its predefined lifetime, your Web browser simply erases it. Some persistent cookies have no expiration date or expire on a date far into the future, so they tend to accumulate in the main storage area of digital devices.

▶ **What's the problem with cookies?** A **first-party cookie** is set by the domain that hosts a Web page. A **third-party cookie** is set by a site other than the one you connected to. Third-party cookies are often set by Web sites that have affiliations with wide-ranging ad-serving companies able to combine cookie data from multiple sites, a practice called **cross-site tracking**. This tracking can be used to create profiles of your browsing habits. These profiles are used to generate targeted ads for products that might appeal to your interests.

Profiles compiled by ad aggregators are not always accurate. But regardless of their accuracy, those profiles generate ads and other offers that pop up in your browser window with maddening frequency. Figure 4-44 explains how third-party cookies are used to create profiles.

Terminology

Persistent cookies are also called *permanent cookies* or *stored cookies*.

Try It!

Connect to an informational Web site, such as *www.huffpost.com*, and look at the ads that are displayed. Do the ads seem to be generic, or do they seem to be based on personal data about you?

QuickCheck

The cookies in Figure 4-44 are _____.

a. stateless

b. session

c. persistent

d. second-party

Figure 4-44: Third-party cookies track and profile

❶ Suppose you connect to GlobalChef.com. It sets a cookie that's called a first-party cookie because it came from a site that you deliberately accessed.

❸ Next, you visit Sports.com, where there is an ad for SlimSlurp, another member of the WeSeeU ad network. Now your device is accumulating WeSeeU cookies.

❷ GlobalChef.com also displays an ad from FatBusters.com. FatBusters is part of an ad network called WeSeeU. The ad sets a cookie for WeSeeU.com. That cookie might seem innocent, but just wait.

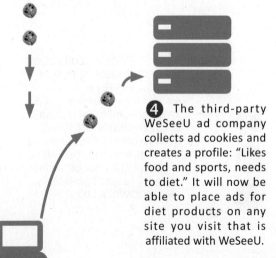

❹ The third-party WeSeeU ad company collects ad cookies and creates a profile: "Likes food and sports, needs to diet." It will now be able to place ads for diet products on any site you visit that is affiliated with WeSeeU.

❱ **Is it possible to see the cookies stored on a device?** You can view a list of cookies stored on your device. Some parts of cookies are generally encrypted, so you cannot tell exactly what they contain. You can, however, see where the cookies are from. Cookies from domains such as adnxs.com, doubleclick.com, fetchback .com, 33across, and ad.360yield.com are likely to contain tracking information that is shared with advertisers.

Periodically, you can take a look at your accumulated cookies to gauge the amount of tracking information that is building up. For instructions about locating cookies, refer to your browser documentation. Figure 4-45 shows how to find cookies stored by Google Chrome.

Try It!

Look at the cookies stored on your device. Can you identify any that appear to be set by advertisers?

4

Figure 4-45: How to view cookies

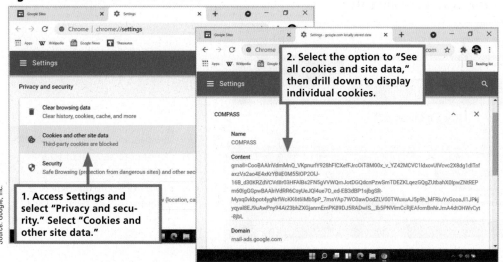

Source: Google, Inc.

❱ **Can I block cookies?** Blocking all cookies drastically changes your Web experience. When you don't allow sites to set cookies on your device, those sites cannot keep track of your preferences or purchases.

Rather than turning off all cookies, you may prefer to turn off third-party cookies. Doing so should eliminate much of the profiling that is produced by cookies. Blocking cookies does not eliminate ads, however. You'll still see ads in your browser window, but they will be more generalized. Figure 4-46 illustrates the procedure for blocking third-party cookies in Google Chrome.

QuickCheck

Blocking first-party cookies _____.

a. prevents profiling

b. makes it difficult to use online shopping carts

c. secures your device from fraud

d. prevents snoopers from discovering the Web sites you've visited

Figure 4-46: How to block third-party cookies

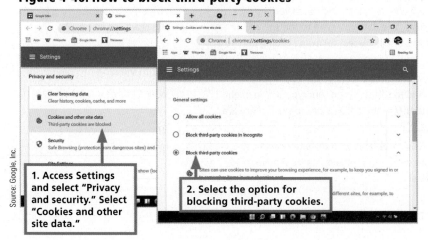

Source: Google, Inc.

HTTPS

When you see https:// in the address box, pay attention. It is important.

❯ **Is HTTP secure?** No. HTTP transports unencrypted data between your device and a Web server. Your login passwords, credit card numbers, and other personal data are not secure on an HTTP connection. The data you transmit to a Web server can be secured, however, if it is sent over an **HTTPS** (HTTP Secure) connection, which encrypts the data stream between client devices and servers.

Currently, most Web sites use HTTPS, but when submitting personal data, you can verify that it will be transmitted by HTTPS if the URL in the address box begins with https:// or displays a lock icon (Figure 4-47).

Figure 4-47: How to verify a secure connection

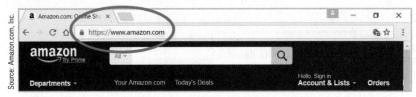

Google Chrome

Microsoft Edge

Try It!

Connect to several of your favorite Web sites. Do they use HTTPS only for login and purchase pages, or are other pages on the site transmitted as HTTPS?

❯ **How does HTTPS work?** Sites that use HTTPS are required to present an SSL certificate to the browser. This certificate helps the browser verify that the site is not pretending to be another site. Your browser may indicate the status of the SSL certificate. Figure 4-48 shows the SSL certificate icons Google Chrome displays to help you decide if a connection is secure and if it is safe to enter personal data.

Figure 4-48: SSL certificate icons

Icon	What It Means
🔒	The site's certificate is valid and its identity has been verified by a trusted third-party authority. The data you send to the site will be encrypted. Confirm that the URL is correct to avoid sending data to a fake site.
ⓘ	The site is using HTTP, not HTTPS, to exchange data with your browser. Data that you send to this site is not encrypted. You might try changing http:// to https:// in the address bar to see if there is a secure version of the site.
⚠	Google Chrome has detected problems with the site's certificate. Avoid using the site. If you decide to proceed, realize that your private information is at risk.

QuickCheck

For which of the following is HTTPS least important?

a. When logging in

b. When viewing merchandise

c. When providing credit card details

d. When signing up for an online service

▶ How does HTTPS encryption work? HTTPS is based on HTTP and a public key encryption technology called SSL/TLS. **Public key encryption** is a very clever process that requires one key to encrypt data, but a different key to decrypt it. The encryption key can't be used to decrypt the message, so if that key falls into the hands of a third party, it cannot decrypt the data. Figure 4-49 explains how it works.

Figure 4-49: Public key encryption

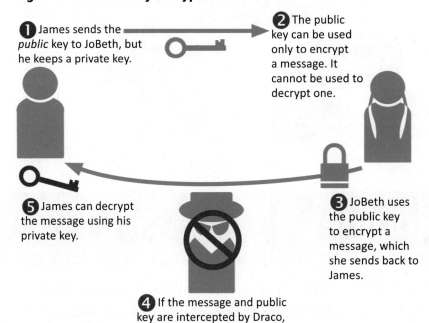

① James sends the *public* key to JoBeth, but he keeps a private key.

② The public key can be used only to encrypt a message. It cannot be used to decrypt one.

⑤ James can decrypt the message using his private key.

③ JoBeth uses the public key to encrypt a message, which she sends back to James.

④ If the message and public key are intercepted by Draco, he cannot decrypt the message because he does not have the private key.

QuickCheck

How does HTTPS protect data transmitted from Web pages to Web servers?

a. Public key encryption

b. Ad blocking

c. Setting cookies

d. Switching to a stateless protocol

4

QuickQuiz   Section D

1. HTTP is a(n) [＿＿＿＿＿＿＿] protocol, so it cannot tell if a series of sessions were initiated by a single source or multiple sources.

2. A(n) [＿＿＿＿＿＿＿]-party cookie is not set by the domain that houses the Web page displayed by the browser.

3. A(n) [＿＿＿＿＿＿＿] cookie is deleted when you close your browser.

4. When a browser request is fulfilled, the Web server sends an HTTP [＿＿＿＿＿＿＿] code, such as 200.

5. HTTPS uses [＿＿＿＿＿＿＿] key encryption, which requires two keys: one to encrypt data and the other to decrypt it.

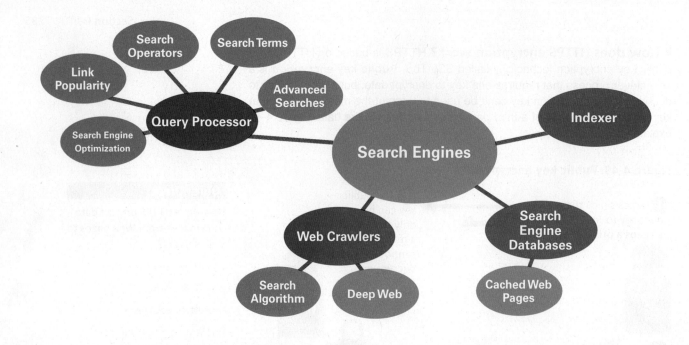

Objectives

▶ List three popular search engine Web sites.

▶ List the four components of a search engine.

▶ Explain how Web crawlers traverse the Web to collect pages for search engines.

▶ Provide at least three examples of the deep Web.

▶ Explain the difference between cached pages and live pages.

▶ Explain the function of a search engine indexer.

▶ List the steps executed by a query processor to respond to a query.

▶ State five techniques that can be used for search engine optimization.

▶ Give examples of queries using search operators such as AND, OR, NOT, quotation marks, asterisks, and range dots.

▶ Explain the significance of search history to privacy.

▶ Explain the difference between search history and browser history.

▶ Describe general guidelines for when fair use applies to content that you might incorporate in your own work.

The Web encompasses hundreds of millions

of pages stored on servers scattered all over the globe. To use this information, you have to find it. Like most people, you probably depend on search engines to wade through the tsunami of information stored on the Web. In Section E, you'll find out how Web search engines work so that you can use them more efficiently.

Terminology

Web search engine	search engine indexer	sponsored links	search history
Web crawler	query processor	search terms	
deep Web	link popularity	search operator	
dark Web	search engine optimization		

Search Engine Basics

According to Google, the Web has billions of unique pages and it continues to grow. We depend on search sites, such as *www.google.com*, to quickly locate specific pages. But behind the fairly straightforward act of entering a search query, there is mind-boggling technology. Let's see how it works.

▶ **What is a Web search engine?** A Web search engine (commonly referred to simply as a search engine) is a computer program designed to help people locate information on the Web by formulating queries consisting of one or more words called keywords or search terms.

In response to a query, the search engine displays results, or "hits," as a list of relevant Web sites, accompanied by links to source pages and short excerpts containing the keywords (Figure 4-50).

Figure 4-50: Search engine results

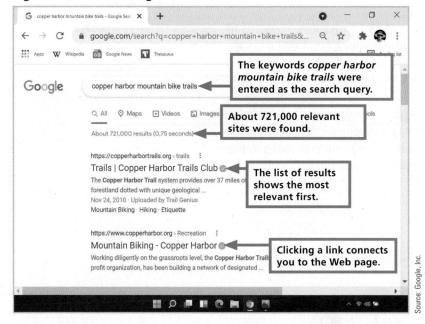

Source: Google, Inc.

The keywords *copper harbor mountain bike trails* were entered as the search query.

About 721,000 relevant sites were found.

The list of results shows the most relevant first.

Clicking a link connects you to the Web page.

Try It!

The Web is constantly changing. Search for *copper harbor mountain bike trails* and compare the results of your search to the results in Figure 4-50.

▶ **What is the difference between a search engine and a search engine site?** Search engines are found at Web sites, such as *www.google.com*, *www.yahoo.com*, and *www.bing.com*. Search engines can also be accessed from mobile apps on a tablet device or smartphone.

It is easy to think of *www.google.com* as a search engine; but to be precise, it is a Web site that offers access to a search engine. A search engine is the program that works behind the scenes to gather, index, find, and rank information from the Web.

Some sites, including Google, use their own proprietary search engines, but other sites use third-party search technology. For example, Microsoft's Bing search engine is the underlying technology used for Yahoo! searches.

▶ **How do search engines work?** A search engine contains four components:

Web crawler: Combs the Web to gather data that's representative of the contents of Web pages

Indexer: Processes the information gathered by the crawler into a list of keywords and URLs stored in a database

Database: Stores billions of index references to Web pages

Query processor: Allows you to access the database by entering search terms, and then produces a list of Web pages that contain content relevant to your query

Let's take a look at each of these components to find out how they affect your ability to mine information from the Web.

▶ **What is a Web crawler?** A Web crawler (also referred to as a Web spider) is a computer program that is automated to methodically visit Web sites. Web crawlers can be programmed to perform various activities as they visit sites, but in the context of search engines, Web crawlers download Web pages and submit them to an indexing utility for processing.

▶ **How does a Web crawler know where to go?** A Web crawler uses a search algorithm to traverse the Web. It begins with a list of URLs to visit. The URLs on this list may have been submitted by Web site owners, but more commonly they are collected from the links that exist on previously crawled Web pages.

After copying the material at a specified URL, the Web crawler looks for hypertext links and adds them to the list of URLs to visit next. To cover the Web as efficiently as possible, a Web crawler can run multiple processes in parallel. Sophisticated algorithms keep processes from overlapping or getting stuck in loops (Figure 4-51).

Figure 4-51: Crawling the Web

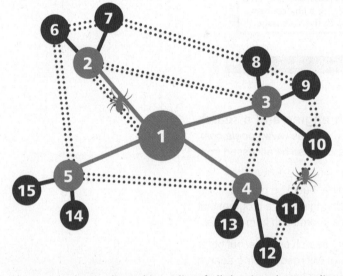

The crawler begins by making a list of all the sites that are directly connected to site 1. It crawls to each of those sites and adds links from those sites to its list of sites to crawl.

▶ **How much of the Web does a Web crawler cover?** High-performance Web crawlers can visit hundreds of millions of Web pages a day. Those pages, however, only constitute a fraction of the Web. Researchers estimate that the most extensive search engines cover no more than 70% of the Web. Each search engine seems to focus on a slightly different collection of Web sites. The same search entered into different search engines can produce different results, so it is sometimes worthwhile to try alternative search engines.

Web crawlers generally do not gather material from the **deep Web** (also called the "invisible Web"), which encompasses pages that require password-protected logins and pages that are dynamically generated with server-side scripts.

The potential volume of dynamically generated pages, such as all the possible pages that Amazon.com could generate from its inventory database, is just too great to feasibly index. To access information related to online merchandise or library catalogs, you might have to go directly to the merchant's or library's Web site and use its local search tools.

Search engines also do not index the **dark Web** (or darknet), which is a part of the deep Web accessible with special software that encrypts searches and anonymizes users. The dark Web has a reputation for illicit content and activities.

▶ **How frequently do Web crawlers revisit sites?** When you query a search engine, you want the results to be up to date so that you don't waste time trying to link to pages that have changed or have been deleted. Search engines use various algorithms to refresh their indexes.

The number of times a search engine's crawler visits a Web page varies, depending on several factors such as how often the page tends to change and its popularity. Obscure pages might be visited only once a month, whereas the pages at a news site would be visited daily.

Search engine results are based on the material on a Web page when the crawler last visited it. Content can change by the time you link to a page, but you can look at the cached page to see the exact page indexed by the crawler (Figure 4-52).

Figure 4-52: Cached pages

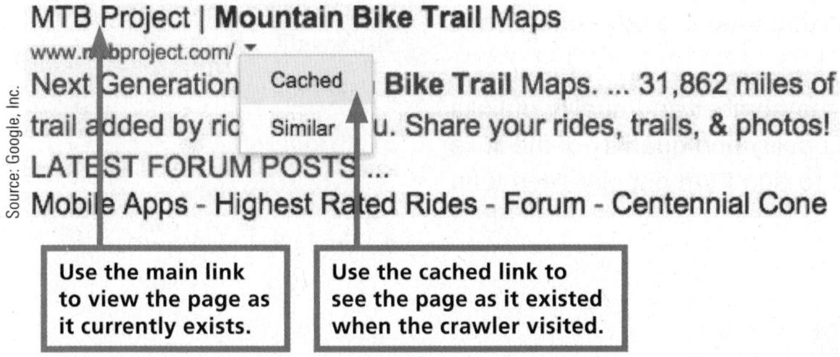

Source: Google, Inc.

MTB Project | **Mountain Bike Trail** Maps
www.mtbproject.com/ ▾
Next Generation [Cached] Bike Trail Maps. ... 31,862 miles of
trail added by ri[Similar   ]u. Share your rides, trails, & photos!
LATEST FORUM POSTS ...
Mobile Apps - Highest Rated Rides - Forum - Centennial Cone

Use the main link to view the page as it currently exists.

Use the cached link to see the page as it existed when the crawler visited.

▶ **How do search engine indexers work?** A **search engine indexer** is software that pulls keywords from a Web page and stores them in an index database. The purpose of the indexer is to make pages easier to find based on their contents. For example, a Web page at a mountain biking site might contain information about bikes, gear, riding, and trail maps. Keywords that might help catalog this page for future access include *mountain*, *bike*, *trail*, *directions*, *gear*, *Michigan*, *bikepacking*, and *bunny hop*.

QuickCheck

Which of the following would not be considered part of the deep Web?

a. Library of Congress catalog record for a book

b. Facebook posts

c. A syllabus in the Blackboard learning management system

d. An article on CNN entertainment news

Try It!

Use Google to search for *Noquemanon Trail*. Are there any differences between the current page and the cached page?

▶ What does a query processor do? A search engine's **query processor** looks for your search terms in the search engine's indexed database and returns a list of relevant Web sites. Google's query processor handles more than 60,000 queries per second. On some days, the total number of Google queries exceeds 6 billion! Each query is processed in less than a second. What happens in that second is summarized in Figure 4-53.

Figure 4-53: Query processing

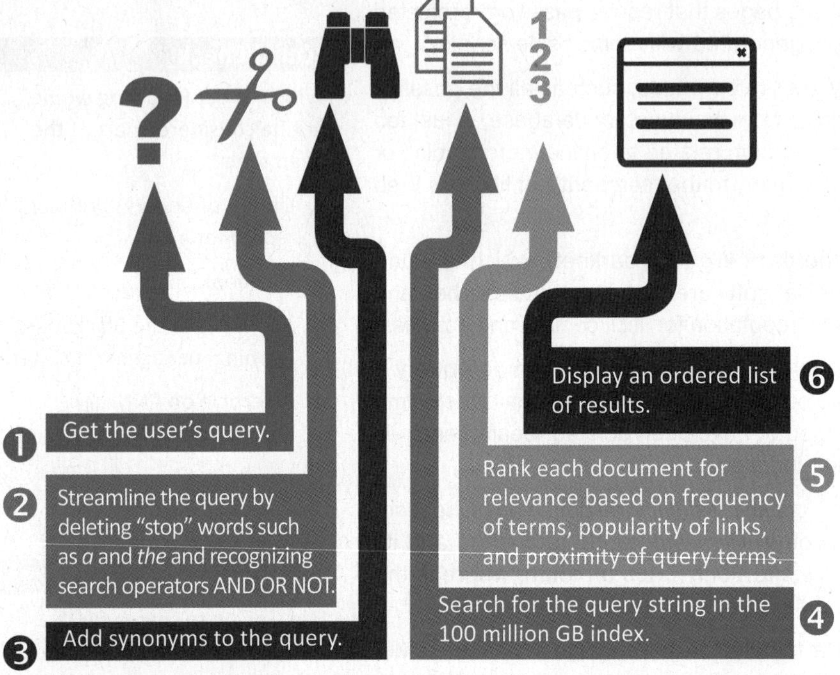

① Get the user's query.

② Streamline the query by deleting "stop" words such as *a* and *the* and recognizing search operators AND OR NOT.

③ Add synonyms to the query.

④ Search for the query string in the 100 million GB index.

⑤ Rank each document for relevance based on frequency of terms, popularity of links, and proximity of query terms.

⑥ Display an ordered list of results.

▶ What determines the order of results? A query processor is likely to find millions of pages that contain words matching the query. The order in which those pages are listed depends on the search engine's ranking algorithm. Google keeps this algorithm a closely guarded secret so that Web site developers can't manipulate pages to get better placement.

The underlying ranking algorithm is based on the number and quality of links to a page. **Link popularity** is a measure of the quality and quantity of the links from one Web page to others. Pages with links to and from popular sites tend to get high relevancy ratings (Figure 4-54).

Figure 4-54: Which sites rank first?

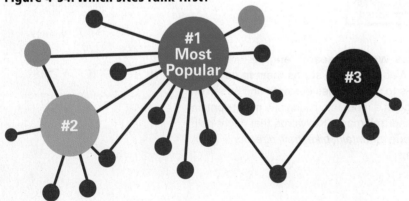

QuickCheck

What does a search engine use to rank pages before they are displayed?

a. An algorithm

b. An indexer

c. A Web crawler

d. The links to keywords

Try It!

Can you find the popularity ranking and other metrics for your favorite Web sites? Go to Alexa Site Info (*www.alexa.com/siteinfo*) and paste the URL for bicycling. com in the search box. What do the metrics tell you about this site's popularity?

◗ **Can a search engine be manipulated to give a high ranking to a page?** A series of techniques called **search engine optimization** (SEO) can affect the ranking and visibility of Web pages. Search engine companies, such as Google, Yahoo!, and Bing, provide guidelines for optimizing Web sites and the pages they contain. Figure 4-55 summarizes some of these SEO techniques.

Figure 4-55: SEO techniques

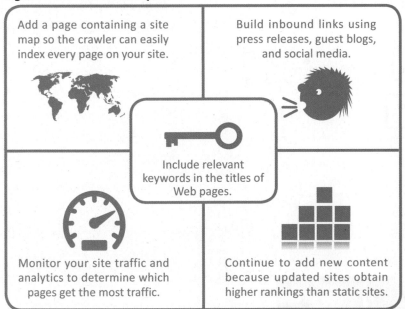

Add a page containing a site map so the crawler can easily index every page on your site.

Build inbound links using press releases, guest blogs, and social media.

Include relevant keywords in the titles of Web pages.

Monitor your site traffic and analytics to determine which pages get the most traffic.

Continue to add new content because updated sites obtain higher rankings than static sites.

4

◗ **What are sponsored links?** Some search engines accept paid ads, sometimes called **sponsored links**, which are bumped to the top positions on the results list. Other search engines also accept paid ads but place them in a clearly marked area (Figure 4-56).

Figure 4-56: Sponsored links

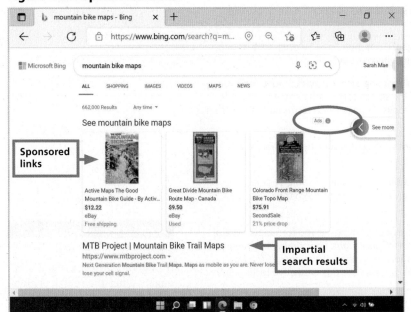

Formulating Searches

Basic queries consist of a few keywords. When these basic queries don't produce useful results, you can try advanced query techniques.

▶ **How do I formulate a basic search?** Most search engines work with keyword queries in which you enter one or more words, called **search terms**, related to the information you want to find. For example, if you're interested in Batman comics, you can type *Batman* (Figure 4-57).

Terminology

The words you enter for your search can be referred to as *queries, search criteria, search terms,* and *keywords.*

Figure 4-57: Basic queries

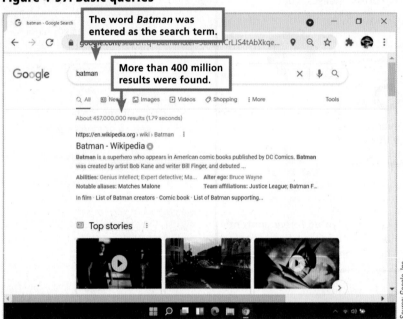

The word *Batman* was entered as the search term.

More than 400 million results were found.

When formulating queries, keep the guidelines from Figure 4-58 in mind.

Figure 4-58: Tips for effective queries

Case. Most search engines are not case sensitive, so you don't have to use the Shift key when entering proper nouns.

Stop words. Search engines generally ignore common "stop" words, such as *and, a,* and *the,* so don't bother to include them in your query.

Stemming. The top search engines use stemming technology that automatically looks for plurals and other variations of the search terms you enter. For example, if you enter *diet,* the search engine also looks for pages with terms such as *diets, dietary,* and *dietician.*

Order. A search for *time machine* produces different results than a search for *machine time.*

Location. If your search engine is able to determine your location, your results might be affected. Most search engines give you an option to change your location or hide it.

Context. Search engines build on your previous searches. If you formulate several Batman-related searches and then search for *dark night,* your search engine might assume that you are looking for information about the Batman movie *The Dark Knight* instead of astronomy information. Google uses this predictive technology unless you clear your Web history.

Try It!

Enter the query *nearby restaurants* into any search engine. Does the search engine seem to know your location?

◗ **How do I get more targeted results?** Narrowing a search can reduce the number of results and produce a more targeted list. It may seem counterintuitive, but entering more words in a query produces fewer, more targeted results.

Whereas the short query *Batman* produces more than 400 million results, a query for *Orson Welles Batman hoax* produces a few thousand results.

◗ **What are search operators?** A **search operator** is a word or symbol that describes a relationship between search terms and helps you create a more focused query. Figure 4-59 provides a quick overview of how to use search operators when formulating searches.

Figure 4-59: Search operators

AND	When two search terms are joined by AND, both terms must appear on a Web page before it can be included in the search results. *Batman AND movies* Result: Pages about Batman movies
OR	When two search terms are joined by OR, either one or both of the search words could appear on a page. *Batman OR Catwoman* Result: Pages about Batman and pages about Catwoman
NOT	The search term following NOT must not appear on any of the pages found by the search engine. *Batman NOT Catwoman* Result: Pages about Batman, but no pages about Catwoman
" "	To search for an exact phrase, enter it in quotes. *"Dynamic Duo"* Result: Pages that contain the exact phrase *Dynamic Duo*
*	The asterisk (*) is sometimes referred to as a wildcard character. It allows a search engine to find pages with any derivation of a basic word. *Bat** Result: Pages about bats, batters, Batman, batteries, etc.
..	Google lets you use two dots to specify a range of numbers, dates, episodes, or prices. *Batman episodes 5..8* Result: Pages about Batman episodes 5, 6, 7, and 8

Try It!

Which one of the following searches returns the most targeted (fewest) results?

racing shell gear

"racing shell" gear

racing shell -gear

racing OR shell OR gear

4

▶ **Is it possible to filter results by file type?** Some search engine sites offer separate searches for academic works, images, videos, news, maps, and blogs. Look for links to these specialized searches at your favorite search engine sites (Figure 4-60).

Figure 4-60: Filter searches for images, videos, or other criteria

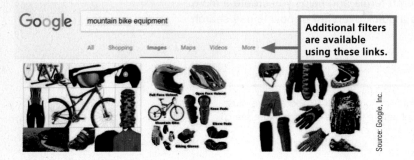

▶ **What is an advanced search?** Many search engines provide ways to make your searches more precise and obtain more useful results. You might be able to use advanced search options to limit your search to material written in a specific language or stored in a specific file format. You might be able to specify a date and stipulate whether to look for your search terms in the title, URL, or body of the Web page (Figure 4-61).

Figure 4-61: Google advanced search

Try It!

What results would you expect based on the advanced search in Figure 4-61? Try the query to find out if you guessed correctly.

4

Search Privacy

It is troubling that browsers store a list of sites you've visited and cache the files for those sites. And then there are cookies that can be used to profile your browsing activities. Yet another intrusion into your privacy is the data stored in query logs maintained by search engines.

▶ **Do search engines keep records of queries?** Considering that a major search engine can receive billions of queries every day, the surprising answer to this question is "yes." Search engines at major sites such as Google, Bing, and Yahoo! save massive numbers of searches made by site visitors. Industry analysts believe that some sites retain user queries for at least 30 days and that at least one search engine site has retained every search ever made at the site.

In 2006, AOL provided researchers with a database of 20 million queries made by site visitors. Figure 4-62 illustrates a small section of this database for queries made by users interested in Batman.

Figure 4-62: Should search engines retain users' queries?

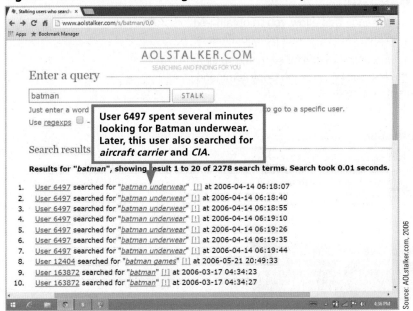

Source: AOLstalker.com, 2006

▶ **What kind of information does a search engine store?** Your **search history** contains a list of queries that you've made in a specific search engine. It is not the same as your browser history, which is a list of Web sites you've visited and is maintained by your browser. Search history is stored in server logs on the search engines' computers. In its Privacy Policy, Google provides the example of a server log shown in Figure 4-63.

Figure 4-63: What's in a search engine server log?

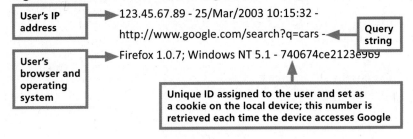

QuickCheck

Which one of the following is stored on search engine computers?

a. Browsing history

b. Browser cache

c. Search history

d. Search settings

▶ **Can I access my search history?** Check your search engine's privacy policy to find out if it offers access to your search history. Your Google search history can be viewed and deleted by entering *Google My Activity* in the search bar of any browser. Your search history is accessible only if you have a Google account and are logged in.

▶ **What can I do to keep my searches confidential?** For Google users, go to *Google My Activity* and turn Web & App Activity off. Yahoo! users can control search history settings from the Search History option on the Settings menu. Bing users can find settings on the History page at *www.bing.com/profile/history*.

Anonymizer sites, such as *www.torproject.org*, act as relay stations to forward your searches to Google or other search engines without leaving a trail back to a cookie or an IP address. Tor also offers a browser that runs on a distributed network to cloak queries. Although law-abiding citizens may have nothing to hide, the increasingly invasive tracking and advertising at many Web sites is leading many Web surfers to use anonymizer tools that offer privacy.

Using Web-based Source Material

Most browsers provide Copy and Save commands that allow you to obtain text and images from a Web page, which you can then paste into your own documents.

▶ **How do I save the source?** To keep track of the source for each text section, you can highlight the Web page's URL in the Address box, use the Copy command, and then paste the URL into your document (Figure 4-64).

Figure 4-64: Copy the URL along with source material

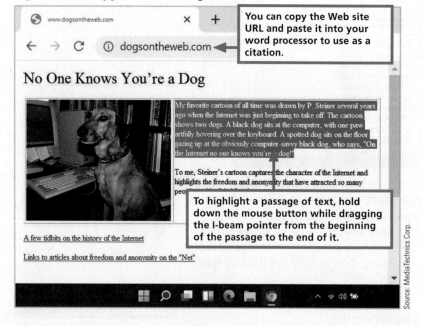

You can copy the Web site URL and paste it into your word processor to use as a citation.

To highlight a passage of text, hold down the mouse button while dragging the I-beam pointer from the beginning of the passage to the end of it.

Source: MediaTechnics Corp.

Try It!

Are your search queries being tracked? Use the information supplied on this page and additional online resources to find out.

▶ How do I cite sources? Presenting someone else's work as your own is plagiarism. If you copy text, pictures, or other works from a Web page, be sure to credit the original author. Information that identifies the source of a quotation or excerpted work is called a citation. Written documents, such as reports and projects, generally include footnotes, endnotes, or in-line citations formatted according to a standard style, such as MLA, APA, or Chicago.

When compiling the citation for online sources, be sure to provide sufficient information so readers can locate the source. Also, include the date when you accessed the source and the full URL. According to APA style, a citation to a Web-based source should provide a document title or description; the author's name, if available; the date of publication, update, or retrieval; and a URL.

▶ Do I need permission to use material? In the United States, the Fair Use Doctrine allows limited use of copyrighted material for scholarship and review without obtaining permission. For scholarly reports and projects, for example, you can use a sentence or paragraph of text without obtaining permission if you include a citation to the original source.

Photos and excerpts from music and videos can be used within the context of critique, but their use purely as decorative elements for a document or Web page would, in most cases, not be considered fair use.

Some Web sites clearly state allowable uses for material. Look for a link to Terms of Use. For example, the YouTube Web site contains a collection of videos submitted by amateurs and semi-professionals, who retain the copyright to their materials. The Terms of Use section of the site allows the public to access, use, reproduce, distribute, create derivatives of, display, and perform user-submitted works within the YouTube platform. Even with such broad terms of use, however, it is essential to cite the original source of the material if you incorporate it in your own work.

▶ How do I get permission? To obtain permission to use text, photos, music, videos, and other elements you find on the Web, contact the copyright holder by email, and explain what you want to use and how you plan to use it. You can often find contact information on the Web site—if not for the copyright holder, at least for a Web site administrator who can direct you to the copyright holder.

4

QuickCheck

When you incorporate Web-based material in research papers, why is it not necessary to get permission from the source?

a. Because the Fair Use Doctrine allows it.

b. Because the material is not copyrighted.

c. Because it is on the Web.

d. Because your school library has a deal with the content owner.

QuickQuiz   Section E

1. A search engine's _____ pulls keywords from a Web page and stores them in a database.

2. When you enter search terms, the search engine's _____ processor looks for the terms in the search engine's database.

3. *AND*, *OR*, and *NOT* are examples of search _____ .

4. Most search engines keep track of users by assigning a unique ID number, which is stored in a(n) _____ on the hard disk of the user's device.

5. To keep track of the Web pages where you obtained information or images, you can highlight the Web page's _____ , copy it, and then paste it into a list of sources. (Hint: Use the acronym.)

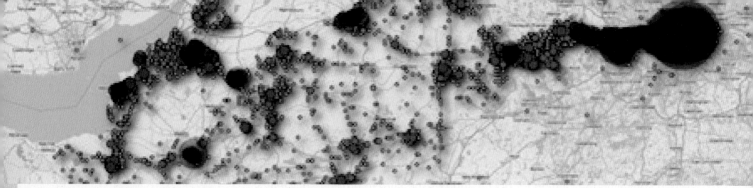

Issue: Who Is Tracking You?

In the movie *Harry Potter and the Prisoner of Azkaban*, Harry acquires a magical item called the Marauder's Map, which shows the location of every teacher and student at the Hogwarts School of Witchcraft and Wizardry.

In the context of Harry Potter, tracking technology seems fun, but real-life tracking technologies have a dark side, which privacy advocates fear might be misused by governments, corporations, and possibly criminals to monitor the daily activities of ordinary people.

According to the EFF (Electronic Frontier Foundation), "Tracking is the retention of information that can be used to connect records of a person's actions or reading habits across space, cyberspace, or time."

Two broad categories of tracking are behavioral tracking and locational tracking. Behavioral tracking accumulates information about what you do: the Web sites you visit, the merchandise you purchase online, and the people with whom you correspond. Locational tracking records your physical location: where you live and work, where and when you shop, and the route you take to get to school.

Tracking made headlines in 2011 when security experts Pete Warden and Alasdair Allan discovered that iPhones collected and stored date-stamped information that triangulated the phone's location. A simple software application called iPhone Tracker could retrieve this data and display it on a map.

The iPhone tracking story spread like wildfire over the mainstream media, blogs, and social networks. Privacy advocates pointed out that government agencies, disgruntled spouses, parents, and criminals could easily trace a person's whereabouts.

In 2020, location tracking hit the headlines again when tracking apps were considered as a possible way of controlling the COVID-19 pandemic. Privacy organizations such as Human Rights Watch questioned the efficacy, equity, and even the constitutionality of government-mandated location tracking.

The technology that makes it easy for a cell phone to track your movements can be incorporated into other handheld devices and tucked into vehicles, identification badges, pet collars, clothing, and even tiny chips that can be implanted under the skin. Tracking is controversial, especially when it occurs without the consent or control of the trackee.

Privacy advocates want strict protocols for collecting, using, storing, and distributing location information. They face opposition, however, from government officials who would like to explore ways that location technology can be used to track criminals, prevent terrorism, and control the spread of diseases.

Commercial interest in tracking technology for marketing and advertising is also high, and consumers seem willing to give up some privacy for the convenience offered by location-based services, such as Yelp and Foursquare.

The outcome of conflicting interests will determine if location-tracking technology can be implemented in such a way that the rights and privacy of individuals are protected.

© Warner Bros/Everett Collection

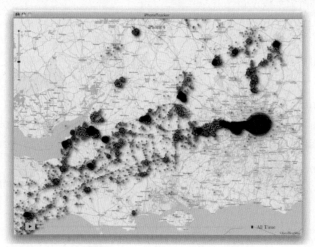

Try It!

Locational tracking is kind of creepy. The idea that someone can pinpoint where you regularly use your digital devices is a little unsettling, but knowing that someone might be tracking your movements as you travel from home to school, to the mall, to the doctor, and to the movies might give you more than a moment of concern. Explore tracking technologies to arm yourself with knowledge that can help protect your privacy.

1 As an experiment, make sure that location services are turned on for one of your digital devices, and track your activities for one day. If possible, print out a map. After you collect your tracking data, write a short summary describing how this data could be used to your benefit, or how it might infringe on your privacy. The following instructions will help you turn tracking on for various devices:

Android smartphones. Go to Settings and make sure Location service is on. Turn on Google Location Reporting and Location History. After you've tracked for a day, view your location history on a map by connecting your device to *maps.google.com/locationhistory*.

iPhones. Go to Settings, Privacy, Location Services, and turn Location Services on. Then, scroll down to System Services, turn on all settings, and select Significant Locations to turn it on. After you've tracked for a day, view the track by accessing Significant Locations and looking at its History options.

Laptops. You can install free tracking software such as FollowMee GPS Tracker (*www.followmee.com*) and Prey (*preyproject.com*). Or, sign up for iCloud and install the FindMyiPhone app on any macOS or Windows device.

2 Your smartphone might be tracking your location. In addition, some apps might be storing data related to your whereabouts. Review the settings on one of your digital devices to ensure that they reflect the level of location privacy you prefer. Describe what you think is an ideal level of privacy for people with a lifestyle similar to yours.

3 The location of digital devices can be pinpointed using three different, but complementary, technologies: GPS, cell-tower triangulation, and WPS. Use Wikipedia and other online resources to explore these technologies. How would you describe each technology?

4 Tracking usually happens behind the scenes, often without a user's knowledge or approval. However, information that people intentionally post online can also be used to track their locations. Think about the information that you post on your social networking and media sharing sites. How might that information be used to determine your location or track your movements?

What Do You Think?

Issue

1. Do you worry about behavioral tracking based on your Internet use?

2. Do you have a device that can track your physical location?

3. Under what circumstances do you think tracking is justified?

Information Tools: Citations

You can use other people's ideas in your own research papers and presentations, but you must cite the source for any information that is not common knowledge. A citation is a formal reference to a published work, like this:

"It Can't Happen Here." *Encyclopædia Britannica. Encyclopædia Britannica Online.* Encyclopædia Britannica, 2011. Web. 13 Sep. 2014. <http://www.britannica.com/EBchecked/topic/297133/It-Cant-Happen-Here>.

A collection of citations is called a bibliography.

Use an approved citation style, such as MLA, APA, or Chicago. Several Web sites, such as the Purdue University Online Writing Lab, include detailed style guides.

Papers on technology topics frequently contain material from books, magazines, journals, news reports, press releases, and court decisions. Make sure you understand the citation data that you need to collect for each of these formats, both in print and online.

Articles from Print Sources

Author, article title, periodical title, date of publication, page numbers

Books

Author, book title, edition, publisher, place and date of publication, ISBN

(If referencing a section of a book, note page numbers, chapter title, and chapter author, if applicable.)

Journals

Same information as a periodical with the addition of the volume and issue numbers

Legal Decisions

Case name; the volume, abbreviation, and page reference for the legal reporter where the case was reported; the date of the case

Web Pages

Author, title of Web page, title of Web site, complete URL, date of publication (sometimes there will not be a publication date; some citation styles use "n.d." in this case), sponsoring organization (look for it on the copyright line at the bottom of the page), date visited

A publication might have several unique identifying numbers. Stay alert so that you use the correct one.

ISBN (International Standard Book Number): A unique number given to a book or monograph

DOI (Digital Object Identifier): A unique number assigned to journal articles and other online documents

LCCN (Library of Congress Control Number): A unique number assigned to each publication in the Library of Congress

Desktop software such as EndNote, RefWorks, Cite This For Me, and Zotero can help you create and manage all the citations for your bibliographies.

Mobile apps such as Cite It Now and Bookends read bar codes on book covers and accept manual entries to automatically create citations on the go.

Try It! Let's go beyond the basics and work with some advanced citation tools. Use any word processor and create a document called Citation Project [Your Name], then complete the following steps:

1 Suppose that you'd like to include information from press releases in a research paper. How should you format the citations? Use a search engine to look for *How do I cite a press release*. Next, search for a recent press release from Apple. Create a citation for the press release and save it in your Citation Project document.

2 Some academic directories/databases provide citation information for the resources they list. BibTeX, illustrated at right, is a common format. Open an academic directory of technology articles, such as Microsoft Academic, ACM Digital Library, or Google Scholar. Search for "privacy" and select a recent article related to mobile phone privacy. Look for the Cite, Bib, or BibTeX icon, and then click it. Notice that each element of the reference is clearly labeled. Copy the BibTeX data and paste it into your Citation Project document; you'll find out how to format this citation data in the next steps.

> Be sure to collect data for the article itself, not simply the directory that lists the article.

3 Microsoft Word includes a built-in bibliography manager that helps you format citations. To access the citation feature, select References, choose the MLA style, then click Insert Citation. Fill in the form to create an MLA citation for the BibTeX data you found in Step 2.

4 You can use free Web-based citation formatters, such as BibMe, Citation Machine, Cite This For Me, or EasyBib, to format citations in MLA, APA, or other approved styles. Connect to a Web-based citation formatter, choose Online Journal as the source, select the MLA citation style, then enter the BibTeX data you collected in Step 2. Paste the formatted citation into your Citation Project document.

> When using automated citation formatters based on ISBNs or DOIs, look carefully at the citation that is produced to ensure that it contains all required citation information.

5 For some books, Web sites, and journal articles, you can use their ISBN, URL, or DOI instead of manually entering the citation data. Connect to a Web-based citation formatter, such as one of those listed in Step 4. Enter the ISBN 978-0316380508 to search for the citation. Produce the MLA citation, copy it, then paste it into your Citation Project document.

6 DOIs are an alternative to ISBNs for identifying academic articles. Enter the DOI 10.1145/2818717 in any browser to connect to the source document. Add the citation to your Citation Project document.

BibTeX Citation

@article{Aditya15,

title = {Brave New World: Privacy Risks for Mobile Users},

author = {Paarijaat Aditya and Bobby Bhattacharjee and Peter Druschel and Viktor Erdelyi and Matthew Lentz},

journal = {ACM SIGMOBILE Mobile Computing and Communications Review},

volume = {18},

number = {3},

pages = {49-54},

issn = {1559-1662},

month = {1},

year = {2015},

note = {http://www.odysci. com/artcle/ 1010113021738527},

url = {http://portal.acm.org/ citation.cfm ?id=2721896.2721907},

doi = {10.1145/2721896.2721907},

Technology in Context: Fashion Industry

Fashion is big business. Worldwide, this industry generates more than $1 trillion in annual revenue. Competition is tough as designers, manufacturers, and retailers compete for customer dollars.

In the fashion industry, trends change quickly. As the saying goes, "Today's style is tomorrow's markdown." Fashion industry players look for every competitive advantage. It is no surprise that technology plays a major role in this glitzy industry.

Fashion begins with designers, such as Miuccia Prada, John Galliano, and Marc Jacobs. Their runway extravaganzas set off fashion trends that eventually work their way to retail stores. Fashion runways went high-tech in 1999 when lingerie manufacturer Victoria's Secret produced a Webcast watched by over 1 million viewers. Bravo television's *Project Runway* show has been one of the top iPod downloads. Fashion podcasts and blogs abound on the Web, as do fashion sites packed with news about the latest trends.

Although runway fashions are often conceived with a sketch and stitched by hand, designs are adapted for the ready-to-wear market by using computer-aided design (CAD) tools, such as pattern-making software.

Garments are constructed by sewing together sections of fabric that form arms, fronts, backs, collars, and so forth. The set of templates used to cut fabric sections is called a pattern. Pattern-making is a tricky 3D challenge because flat pieces of fabric eventually become garments shaped to conform to curved body contours. Pattern-making software helps designers visualize how flat pieces fit together and drape when sewn. Once a pattern is complete, pattern-making software automatically generates a set of patterns for each garment size.

Fashion requires fabric, and computers play a major role in fabric design and manufacturing. Computer software, such as ArahWeave, lets fabric designers experiment with colors, yarns, and weaves while viewing detailed, realistic on-screen samples.

Most of today's weaving mills use computerized machinery that directly accepts digital input to control threads and patterns. Networks tie looms to CAD stations and to the Internet. Fabric designs can be stored in XML format, transmitted to a fabric

manufacturer over the Internet, and used directly by computerized weaving machines.

Fabrics that can alert the wearer to conditions in their surroundings are currently being developed. Two students at the Tisch School of the Arts designed a shirt that can detect carbon monoxide. Microcontrollers change the color of the shirt's thermochromatic fabric to alert wearers of harmful pollutants in their vicinity.

Clothing production, warehousing, and shipping are also highly automated. Benetton's high-tech facility in Castrette, Italy, can produce over 110 million garments per year. Its automated distribution center handles 120,000 boxes of merchandise daily. RFID tags—sometimes called smart labels—can be attached to individual garments or to packing boxes as an important tool for controlling inventory.

RFID technology uses an inexpensive, tiny computer chip with a built-in antenna and the capacity to store between 64 and 128 bits of data about a garment—its SKU number, size, model, dye lot, manufacturing date, and so on. Tags can be attached to a garment or its label. An RFID reader that can retrieve data from tags is used to track merchandise from the manufacturing plant through the distribution chain to the retailer.

RFID tags have become popular for all types of merchandise. Businesses that use them can save time and money. For example, RFID tags can reduce the time it takes to do a physical inventory by a factor of 10. Privacy advocates, however, are worried because these tags remain active even after you bring your merchandise home. Could a thief circle your house with an RFID scanner to find out what's inside? Could a stalker follow your movements by tracking the RFID tag embedded in your sweater?

Next time you buy a garment, check to see if an RFID tag is attached. It would normally be sewn into a seam and may carry a warning such as "Remove before wearing."

Online shopping has become routine, but one drawback of catalog and online ordering is the cost associated with restocking returned merchandise. Can an online customer find out how a garment will fit and look before ordering it?

A company called TrueFit has accumulated a database containing millions of detailed garment specifications that help consumers select the correct garment size based on their body measurements, actual garment measurements, and customer reviews. Some fashion brands offer digital showrooms where shoppers can photographically try on apparel to see how it looks.

No discussion of fashion and technology would be complete without highlighting wearable technology. MIT's Media Lab has been a hub of wearable technology development. One student project integrated a webcam, a battery-powered projector, and an Internet-enabled mobile phone so that wearers could use hand gestures in 3D space to conjure up information from the phone and project it on any surface.

Some wearables have even emerged from the laboratory and onto store shelves.

Originally popular with Secret Service agents, jackets produced by SCOTTeVEST include pockets for a cell phone, MP3 player, and iPad, along with built-in wiring to connect

© Lynn Barry/MIT Media Lab

these devices into a personal area network (PAN). Available in both men's and women's sizes, the jackets can now be purchased by civilians.

At the more extreme end of the wearable technology spectrum and sometimes reminiscent of technology found in science-fiction books and movies, solar panels that can be used for charging smartphones and other mobile devices are starting to illuminate the more fashionable side of wearables. Designer Pauline van Dongen's Wearable Solar clothing incorporates traditional fabrics and materials such as wool and leather with high-technology solar cells strategically hidden in the garment to create an aesthetically pleasing and functional high-tech fashion statement.

And then there is Nadi X, yoga clothing containing sensors that assess your body position and produce subtle pulses to guide you into the correct yoga poses.

Even more extreme and futuristic, invisibility cloaks made from smart fabrics and metamaterials are beginning to blur the line between camouflage and invisibility. Using technologies that bend light around a special fabric, companies such as HyperStealth Biotechnology Corp. have developed products that they call "active camouflage." One promising camouflage technology uses fractals to create repeated patterns with the ability to change color. Whether this technology becomes more popular on the runway or in the military is yet to be determined.

With a growing emphasis on the use of technology in fashion design and manufacturing, fashion degree programs at colleges and technical schools have added courses such as computer-aided fashion design, computer-based pattern drafting, pattern grading and computer-aided drafting, and wearable computers.

Flipped Class Projects

Critical Thinking

Your browser can track the Web sites you've visited and save Web page files in its cache. The search engine you use can store a record of your search queries. The U.S. government seems to be recording all of the data that flows over the Internet. Advertisers track your Web activities using cookies. How much do these privacy intrusions bother you? Which seem the most disturbing? Have you taken steps to curb these intrusions, or in your opinion is tracking no big deal?

Group Project

The purpose of this project is to hone your search skills. Work in groups to develop a set of five questions for a Web scavenger hunt. The questions should have concrete answers and should not be easy to locate with a basic Wikipedia query. Exchange your group's question set with another group, then see which group finds all the answers first.

Cyberclassroom

The use of digital devices in the classroom is controversial. In some classrooms, digital devices are welcomed and incorporated into activities. In other classrooms, digital devices are seen as a distraction. Compile a list of your personal observations about the way digital devices are used in classes by you and the students around you. Be prepared to share your observations in a class discussion.

Multimedia Project

Surf the Web to select a home page that needs improvement. Take a screenshot of the original page. Use an online Web page authoring tool, such as Simbla, Webflow, or Google Sites, to create an improved home page. Consider a design that works both on a full-size screen and on the screens of mobile devices. Also consider how the design works with a mouse or touchscreen. Take a screenshot of your makeover and save it as Home Page Makeover [Your Name]. Make a list of the changes you made. Submit the original page, the makeover page, and the list of changes to your instructor.

Resume Builder

Many companies have a Web site that provides information on their products and services. Use a search engine to locate a company in your career field. Suppose you are a recruiter for that company and you'll be attending a series of college career fairs. Create a one-page information flyer that you can hand out to prospective recruits. The flyer should include:

- The company's name, URL, and physical location(s)
- A brief description of the company's mission, products, and services
- Instructions on how to submit a resume electronically

Globalization

We're accustomed to seeing Web pages in English. But for many people, English is not their native language. Explore online resources to find the current percentage of Web pages that are published in languages other than English. Also explore to find the number of Web users who are not English-language natives. As a supplemental activity, use Advanced search to find a Web page in a language such as Arabic or Chinese, and use Google Translate to view the same page in English. Record your impressions about Web access across the spectrum of human languages.

Key Terms

Interactive Summary

Section A: The Web, one of the Internet's hottest attractions, is a collection of document, image, video, and sound files that can be linked and accessed over the Internet via the [_____] protocol. The Web is an interlinked collection of information, whereas the [_____] is the communications system used to transport Web information. The Web evolved from a concept called [_____], which describes a collection of literary documents linked according to logical relationships. In 1990, Tim Berners-Lee developed the technologies used for today's Web. An Internet-based computer that stores and distributes Web files is called a Web [_____]. It can host one or more Web [_____] such as *www.wikipedia.org* or *www.facebook.com* containing HTML [_____] documents, which can be accessed and displayed using client software called a Web [_____]. Each Web page has a unique address called a(n) [_____].

Section B: Today's popular browsers include Microsoft Edge, Google [_____], Apple Safari, and Mozilla Firefox. The browser that starts automatically when clicking links in email messages is called the [_____] browser. Browsers can be customized in many ways—for example, by adding [_____] for pages you use frequently. Browser [_____] such as AdBlock and toolbars add functionality to browsers. Browsers can also store user IDs and [_____] to make logging in to Web sites more convenient. Browser users can decide whether or not to turn this feature on even though it is a slight security risk. When browsers download HTML documents, images, and links for a Web page, they are stored in a browser [_____]. Browsers also store a list of the Web sites you've visited in the [_____] list. Turning on [_____] browsing stores these items only temporarily and deletes them when the browser is closed.

Section C: The current version of HTML is [____], which was introduced in 2010. HTML is an example of a(n) [____] language that uses HTML [____], such as <h1> and <p>, to specify the format for text and images. A similar language, called [____], is used to describe data by inserting tags that represent database fields. An HTML document is also called a(n) [____] document, which can be viewed from within a browser. Several online and local tools are available for creating HTML documents. An HTML document consists of two parts: the head and the [____]. The specifications for text styles in Web pages can be included in [____] style sheets. These can be [____],

internal, or external. A link to an external CSS document can be inserted in the [____] section of an HTML document. Using HTML and CSS, Web designers can create a(n) [____] Web page that displays the same information regardless of who accesses it. Designers can also use client-side and server-side scripting to create [____] Web pages featuring animations or content that is customized for a specific user. Web sites can be posted on Web [____] services, where they can be thoroughly tested before being open for public access.

Section D: HTTP is the Web's communications [____] that works with TCP/IP to deliver elements of Web pages to a local browser. A browser communicates with a Web server using HTTP [____] such as GET and POST. An HTTP [____] is a sequence of transactions that typically include a browser request and the server's response. HTTP [____] codes such as 200 and 404 indicate whether the server was able to fulfill the browser's request. HTTP is a(n) [____] protocol, which cannot detect if a sequence of sessions originate from the same source. To compensate, Web servers use cookies, which store a small file of data on the user's device. Cookies

can be collected during subsequent sessions to keep track of pages viewed and items purchased. [____] cookies remain on the local device after a session ends. Cookies can be set by the domain that hosts a Web site. Additional cookies can be set by advertisers that have a presence on the site. These [____]-party cookies can be blocked using browser settings. HTTP is not a secure transport protocol, so financial transactions and personal data should be submitted to Web servers using a more secure protocol that displays [____] in the browser address bar. This technology uses [____] key encryption to scramble the data while it is in transit.

Section E: To sift through the massive amounts of information available on the Web and locate pertinent information about a topic, Web surfers utilize programs called search [____]. These special programs have four major components. A Web [____], also called a Web spider, is automated to methodically visit Web sites and gather Web pages. A search engine [____] culls keywords from the gathered pages and stores them in a(n) [____]. The search engine's query [____] accepts one or

more words called search [____], looks them up in the database, and produces a list of relevant Web sites. There are a number of ways to narrow searches and produce more targeted results, such as using [____] operators or putting exact phrases in [____]. The order in which Web sites are returned in response to your query is dependent on relevancy criteria, such as keyword matches and [____] popularity.

1. You are mentoring two elementary school students who are creating their first Web page. They've asked you to recommend some tools for the task. Which one requires less knowledge of HTML tags: Notepad or Microsoft Word? [_____]

2. Suppose you visit a Web site that has eye-catching pages. You want to know how these pages were formatted, so you use one of the options on your browser's menu to take a look at the HTML [_____] document.

3. Embedded in an email message is a link to *https://bit.ly/40Lm3320*. You can assume that this is a [_____] URL.

4. You'd prefer not to have the search engine you use maintain accumulative records of your searches. You can block [_____] from a specific search engine site, and that setting will force the search engine to assign a different ID number to you for each session.

5. Some of your relatives are afraid that their credit card numbers might get stolen from a merchant's server by a hacker. Is it correct to tell them that they can best avoid these potential rip-offs by using a secure connection, such as HTTPS? Yes or no? [_____]

6. You're conducting a research project that requires you to visit sites that include lots of pop-up ads and other junk that you don't want accumulating in your browser cache. You remember that you can turn on [_____] browsing to delete all that junk when you end your session.

7. You think that your browser is secured so your Web activity won't be tracked, but now you discover that you can't check out at Zappos.com. Ooops! Looks like you have blocked all [_____].

THE GLOBAL CHEF

Travel around the world. A delectable feast for the eyes. Food served with brilliance and imagination.

Enter   Follow @theglobalchef

8. You've designed your first Web site and it looks great. But you know that the design is only the beginning of the process of developing a Web site. To make sure that your pages get the best ranking and most visibility, it is important to consider techniques for search engine [_____].

9. Your Web pages should all have a similar design based on heading styles, fonts, and colors. Using an external [_____] keeps the design consistent for all the pages on your site.

10. Suppose that you want to add some simple interaction to your site by changing the color of buttons when they are clicked. You can accomplish this goal using [_____] -side scripting.

Lab: Design Your Home Page

HTML can be fun. Really! The basics of HTML and CSS are not complicated, and this lab will give you an opportunity to design a customized Web page.

Requirements:

For this lab, you'll need a computer running macOS or Windows. Your computer should be connected to the Internet. The instructions are generalized; they provide helpful guidelines but not specific steps. You may have to explore a bit to find all the tools needed to complete the assignment, but that is all part of the learning experience.

Assignment:

1 Connect to an online HTML editor, from a site such as *www.jsfiddle.net* or the *W3Schools Online Code Editor*.

You might be happiest with an HTML editor that allows you to save your work, so look for a Save button before you begin. When this book was published, both jsFiddle and W3Schools offered great tools for HTML and CSS.

2 Enter the outline for a basic HTML document using the template in Figure 4-30.

3 Modify the template to add your name as an h1 heading at the beginning of the body section of the document.

The HTML code will look something like this:

`<p><h1> Sarah Smith </h1></p>`

4 Make sure the editor is able to show you what your Web page will look like when displayed in a browser.

If you are using jsFiddle, click the Run button and look for your results on the right side of the screen. If you are using W3Schools, select the Run button.

5 Next, locate a photo that you like on the Wikimedia site and copy its URL.

To copy the URL, right-click the photo and select Copy Image URL.

6 Return to the HTML editor and enter the tags to insert the image. Make sure you include the quotation marks. The HTML should look something like this:

`<img src="http://name_of_photo.jpeg" style="left:56px;top:236px;height:232px;width:174px;position: absolute;> </img>`

You can play around with the numbers for left, top, height, and width until the image is positioned where you want it to be.

Add two more images positioned artistically on the page.

7 Add a hypertext link under the photos that leads to your favorite Wikipedia page. Your link should look something like this:

`<p> <a href="https://en.wikipedia.org/wiki/Astronomy"> I love Astronomy! </a> </p>`

8 Next, turn to the CSS tab or work area and enter the code to center the h1 style for your name and display it in the color and size of your choice. Here is a sample:

`body`
`{ font-family: arial; }`
`h1 { color: purple; text-align: center; font-size: xx-large}`

9 Finally, select colors for the link and add the code to the CSS, like this:

`a:link { color: green; }`

`a:visited { color: blue; }`

10 Save your work in a format that you can submit to your instructor. Depending on the HTML editor you used, you may:

- Take a screenshot using the PrtSc key (Windows) or Command-Shift-4 (Mac).
- Save a file locally and email it to your instructor.
- Save the URL and submit it to your instructor.
- Copy the text of your HTML and CSS, then paste it into a text editor, such as Notepad or TextEdit. Submit that document to your instructor.

5 Social Media

Module Contents

They're personal, global, and disruptive. Social media are a unique part of 21st-century life. Have you mastered them, or are you struggling to find your social media niche?

⬤ Try It!   Apply what you learn.

- Create effective social media profiles that reflect your identity and uniqueness.
- Use social networking tools to convey your personal "brand."
- Enable or disable location services as necessary for geosocial networking.
- Interpret a sociogram or adjacency matrix to evaluate connections in a social network.
- Use tools provided by your social media services to discover if you've been tagged in photos or videos.
- Assign a Creative Commons license to your original work before posting it.
- Evaluate whether your use of copyrighted media would be considered fair use, a derivative use, or a transformative use.
- Identify and use basic blogging tools to create blogs and interact with bloggers.
- Evaluate a blog to determine if its information is accurate and reliable.
- Use Twitter to tweet, retweet, and read messages using @ mentions and # hashtags.
- Use tabs on Wikipedia articles to access Talk pages, edits, and revision history.
- Use Wikipedia information appropriately in your academic setting.
- Set up forwarding between Webmail and local mail accounts.
- Use online chat, VoIP services, and mobile communication apps.
- Manage your online reputation to ensure that it is not hijacked by impersonators, identity thieves, or cyberbullies.
- Monitor third-party social media apps to limit the amount of your social data that is gathered by off-site entities.

● Pre-Check

Gauge your level of expertise. The answers are in the module.

This image is a generic _____ for a social media account.

In the context of social media, this symbol is called a(n)

_____

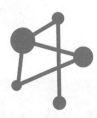

What is the name of this analytical tool that depicts social networking connections?

_____

List **3** email protocols

_____

_____

_____

What does this symbol mean?

_____

NPOV

What social media platform requires editors to adhere to this standard?

_____

What can't you create if you see this icon?

_____

Your online twin is called a(n)

_____

What is the meaning of this Creative Commons license icon?

_____

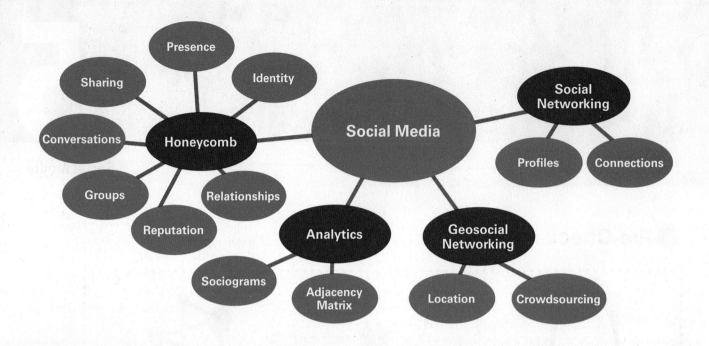

Section A Social Networking

Objectives

- Use the Social Media Honeycomb to differentiate among various social media.

- Provide at least two examples of social networking, geosocial networking, content communities, and online communication.

- Trace the history of social networking services.

- List the three elements of a social media profile.

- Provide three examples of crowdsourcing.

- Describe four technologies that can be used to locate mobile and stationary devices.

- Interpret the analytics displayed by a sociogram.

- Explain how Six Degrees of Separation applies to social networking.

- Provide examples of the inferences that might be drawn from an adjacency matrix.

The social media landscape is vast. From
megasites such as Facebook to emerging niche services such as Caffeine, social media have spread across the globe. They now soak up hours of screen time and spill over into other media outlets such as news, television, and movies. Section A offers some structures for selecting and categorizing social media services, and then focuses on social networking and surprising linkages that put the concept of Six Degrees of Separation to the test.

Terminology

social media	geosocial networking	IP address lookup	two-way edges
Social Media Honeycomb	social discovery	geocoding	one-way edges
social networking service	crowdsourcing	geotagging	binary adjacency matrix
online services	GPS trilateration	sociograms	
online identity	cell tower triangulation	sociogram nodes	
social media profile	hotspot triangulation	sociogram edges	

The Social Media Mix

Across the globe, billions of people participate in social media, using services such as Facebook, Twitter, Snapchat, Pinterest, YouTube, Wikipedia, Yelp, and Flickr. The variety of social media offerings is immense, and trying to take part in all of them would be a daunting task. So choices have to be made. Let's look at the social media mix available to you.

▶ **What are social media?** Social media are online services that facilitate communication and interaction among people who want to share information about their lives, issues, and events using a multimedia mix of text, pictures, video, and audio.

Classifying social media provides a general structure for comparisons and helps you to understand their benefits. Various classification schemes have been proposed for social media. For example, one way to classify social media is by their focus. In such a classification, a professional social media service such as LinkedIn would be placed in a different category from friends-and-family services such as Facebook and TikTok.

Social media are sometimes categorized by the type of content that they support. Text-based services, such as Blogger and WordPress, would be classified differently from image and video services, such as Flickr and YouTube.

The Social Media Honeycomb provides a visual model for classifying and comparing various social media services. Each hexagon in the honeycomb represents a social media building block. Look at the honeycomb in Figure 5-1 and think about how strongly the characteristics in each hexagon apply to your favorite social media site.

Figure 5-1: The Social Media Honeycomb

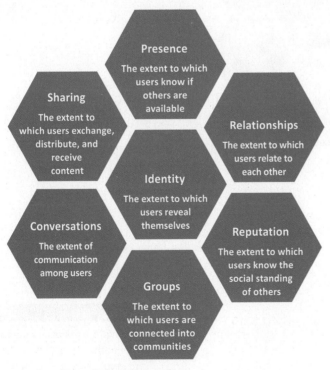

Source: Kietzmann, Hermkens, McCarthy, and Silvestre

5

QuickCheck

Which hexagon in the Social Media Honeycomb characterizes Facebook "Likes"?

a. Relationships

b. Sharing

c. Reputation

d. Conversations

❱ How does the honeycomb help me compare social media services?

Each social media service emphasizes a different set of social interactions. Services such as LinkedIn emphasize identity but do not encourage conversations among users. Facebook and similar services tend to emphasize relationships among users, with a secondary emphasis on conversations, identity, presence, and reputation. In the social media honeycombs shown in Figure 5-2, darker hexagons indicate factors with more emphasis.

Figure 5-2: Social media services emphasize different social factors

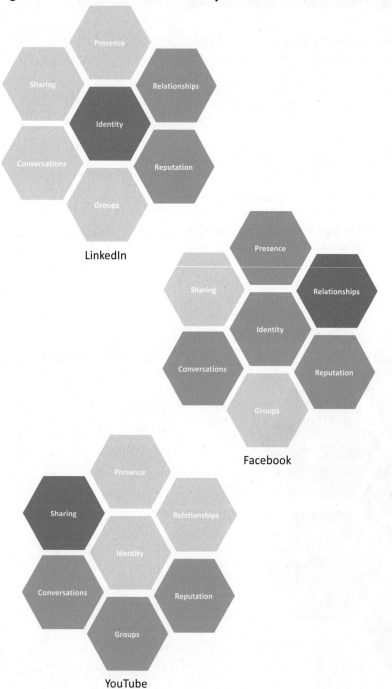

LinkedIn

Facebook

YouTube

QuickCheck

Which of the Social Media Honeycombs in Figure 5-2 would be most similar to the honeycomb for Flickr?

a. LinkedIn

b. Facebook

c. YouTube

Try It!

Sketch out a honeycomb and color in the social factors that are emphasized by Twitter.

◗ **What are the most popular social media services?** New social media services pop up every day, or so it seems. Some are in the spotlight briefly, while others have more staying power. In this module, social media are categorized into four groups: social networking, geosocial networking, content communities, and online communications. Figure 5-3 offers a brief overview of these categories and lists some of the most popular services in each one.

Figure 5-3: Popular social media services

Social Networking	Geosocial Networking	Content Communities	Online Communication
Good for:	**Good for:**	**Good for:**	**Good for:**
Creating an online presence Connecting with friends and family	Locating places, people, and events	Sharing user-generated media and topical information Ratings Spreading a message	One-to-one, real-time communication Asynchronous messaging
Examples:	**Examples:**	**Examples:**	**Examples:**
Facebook	Yelp	YouTube	Email
Classmates.com	Foursquare Swarm	Flickr	Snapchat
LinkedIn	Nearby	Pinterest	Skype
Twitter	Zillow	Instagram	Chat
Tumblr	Google Maps	Wikipedia	WhatsApp
Nextdoor	OpenTable	Reddit	Zoom
	Meetup	Blogger	
		WordPress	
		TikTok	

5

Social Networking Evolution

Let's turn our focus from the broad spectrum of social media to the specific category of social networking. Today's social networking landscape is dominated by Facebook, but social media were born in a rapidly changing environment, and they are likely to continue to evolve as consumer preferences change. It may seem as if social networking sprang up overnight when Facebook went online, but that is not the case.

▶ **What are social networking services?** A **social networking service** revolves around personal profiles and interconnections among subscribers who want to share information about themselves.

▶ **What was the first social networking service?** Social networking can be traced back to **online services**, such as CompuServe, Prodigy, and America Online (AOL), that were not part of the Internet. The popularity of those services decreased as a new generation of Internet-based services emerged. The timeline in Figure 5-4 traces the evolution of social networking services.

Figure 5-4: Social networking services timeline

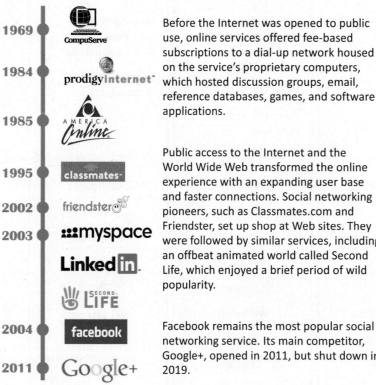

1969 — CompuServe
1984 — prodigy internet
1985 — AMERICA Online

Before the Internet was opened to public use, online services offered fee-based subscriptions to a dial-up network housed on the service's proprietary computers, which hosted discussion groups, email, reference databases, games, and software applications.

1995 — classmates
2002 — friendster
2003 — myspace / Linked in / SECOND LIFE

Public access to the Internet and the World Wide Web transformed the online experience with an expanding user base and faster connections. Social networking pioneers, such as Classmates.com and Friendster, set up shop at Web sites. They were followed by similar services, including an offbeat animated world called Second Life, which enjoyed a brief period of wild popularity.

2004 — facebook
2011 — Google+

Facebook remains the most popular social networking service. Its main competitor, Google+, opened in 2011, but shut down in 2019.

▶ **How are social networking services likely to evolve?** When it comes to the online social scene, history tells us that nothing lasts forever. Consumer tastes change, and a site with billions of users today can all too quickly become old news. A report from the research division of the asset firm Piper Jaffray indicates that the popularity of Facebook among teens decreases every year.

Teen preferences for simpler social media platforms such as Instagram, TikTok, and Snapchat may be a glimpse of the future in which a young demographic seeks easy-to-use, smartphone-based communication platforms, while career-minded individuals maintain LinkedIn profiles.

Try It!

Social networks come and go. Are the ones listed in the first column of Figure 5-3 still popular? Which social networking services are your favorites?

QuickCheck

The first generation of social networking services _____.

a. offered free access

b. was not part of the Internet

c. was launched by Facebook

d. became popular with the launch of mobile devices

Social Networking Basics

Each social networking service has its own focus and terminology. "Friends" on one service are called "followers" or "connections" on other services. "Likes" might be called "endorsements." When joining a social network, one of your first steps should be to get a handle on its terminology, which will help you learn how to use its features.

❱ What should I know about social network profiles? A person's presence on a social media service is referred to as an **online identity**. Each online identity is encapsulated in a profile. A **social media profile** is the set of information provided to friends, contacts, and the public. A basic profile generally includes a user name, an image, and a few lines of descriptive text. Figure 5-5 illustrates profiles from several popular social networking services.

Figure 5-5: Social media profile elements

A Twitter profile can include a photo and a tagline. Bill Gates sets a good example, using his tagline to provide potential followers with information about the topics he tweets about.

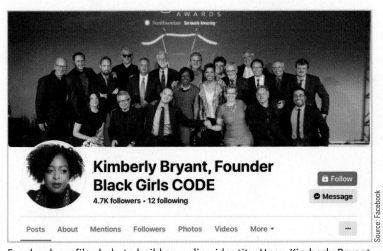

Facebook profiles help to build an online identity. Here, Kimberly Bryant highlights her organization, Black Girls CODE.

Terminology

Online identities are also called *personas* and *avatars*.

5

Try It!

Visit your favorite social networking service and look at the profiles for at least three people. Which of those profiles seems most effective?

▶ **What are the common elements of social networks?** Reflect back on the social media characteristics presented in the honeycomb diagram in Figure 5-1. Social networking services tend to emphasize identity and relationships. Most social networking sites offer elements similar to those in Figure 5-6.

Figure 5-6: Anatomy of a social network account

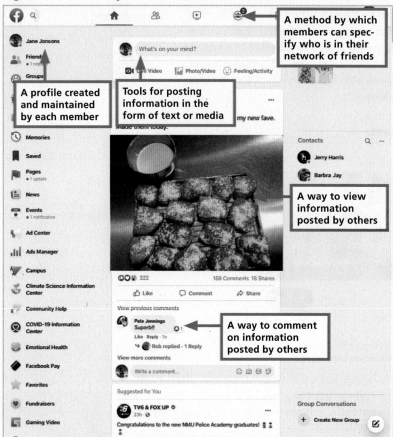

Source: Facebook

A method by which members can specify who is in their network of friends

A profile created and maintained by each member

Tools for posting information in the form of text or media

A way to view information posted by others

A way to comment on information posted by others

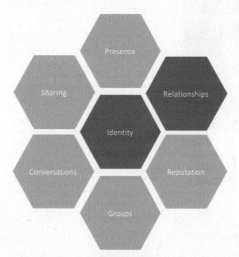

Social networking sites focus on identity (the user's profile) and relationships (friends and connections).

Geosocial Networking

Your smartphone's GPS can pinpoint your location. Although it presents some security and privacy issues, judicious use of location-based services can expand your social circle.

▶ **What is geosocial networking?** Geosocial networking provides a platform for users to carry out interactions based on their current locations. Some of the most popular and well-designed geosocial networking services include Yelp, Foursquare Swarm, and Google Maps. Social networking services, such as Facebook and Twitter, also offer geosocial features.

Geosocial networking services can help you find the nearest popular restaurant, pinpoint the location of your friends' favorite biking trails, get special deals from nearby merchants, and leave feedback about business services and products. An emerging subset of geosocial networking called social discovery uses geolocation to locate people who are nearby and have similar interests. The basic activities offered by geosocial networking are summarized in Figure 5-7.

5

Figure 5-7: Geosocial network activities

Check in	**Locate**	**Search**	**Recommend**	**Map**
Registered users open the app or otherwise sign in to indicate they want to interact.	Using automatic geolocation technology or manually initiated location tracking, the user's current location is determined.	Depending on the service, users can search for geotagged places, people, or events that are nearby.	Crowdsourced ratings and recommendations are offered.	Maps and directions to selected places, people, or events are provided.

▶ **What is crowdsourcing?** When individuals contribute computer time, expertise, opinions, or money to a defined project, they are participating in crowdsourcing. For example, Yelp provides restaurant ratings compiled from user reviews. Amazon, Zappos, and other online merchants also collect and display customer reviews. Waze is a crowdsourcing app that collects real-time traffic information from subscribers and then uses that information to provide drivers with the optimal route to their destinations.

Crowdsourcing is often associated with geosocial networking because the focus of many crowdsourcing apps is on user reviews of places. Not all crowdsourcing apps are geosocial, however. As an example, Kickstarter is a crowdsourcing app that provides consumers with a platform for donating money to creative projects.

Crowdsourcing is based on contributions from groups of individuals, but it differs from collaborative work. For collaborative work, participants interact with each other to achieve a goal. Crowdsourcing does not require collaboration among participants. Contributions from each crowd participant are aggregated by the crowdsourcing platform. For example, the rating for Cathy's Cafe is not created by Yelp users chatting with each other until they agree on a three-star rating. Instead, reviewers submit independent reviews, which are consolidated by algorithms on the Yelp platform.

❱ How does geolocation work? Most people are aware that mobile devices, such as smartphones, send out location signals that can be used to track the device. Desktop computers, laptops, and tablets without GPS or cellular service can also be located, though not with dependable accuracy. Figure 5-8 lists four ways that the location of a device can be determined.

Figure 5-8: Location technologies

GPS trilateration
This technology locates smartphones and other devices containing GPS chips. It is accurate to within a 16-foot radius.

Cell tower triangulation
Cellular telephone companies monitor the position of mobile phones relative to nearby cell towers. If a phone is turned on and within range of three towers, a process called cell tower triangulation can determine the position of a device to an area of about three-quarters of a mile.

Hotspot triangulation
This technique can gauge the location of a Wi-Fi router based on its signal strength relative to nearby routers. Desktop and laptop computers connected to the router can be assumed to be operating within a circle of about 50 feet.

IP address lookup
IP addresses can provide a rough estimate of a device's location based on information in the WHOIS database. The country in which a device is located can be determined with 99% accuracy. However, the accuracy of pinpointing the region or city dwindles to about 50%.

❱ What should I keep in mind about geolocation? Location-aware apps may use more than one type of location service. The location services settings for a digital device can be used to enable or disable location tracking for each individual app.

Geosocial networking depends on geolocation, so your participation requires an accurate assessment of your location. If you want to be found, activate all available location services by making sure GPS, cellular, and Wi-Fi are turned on. If you don't want to be found, make sure that all of those location services are turned off.

❱ What is geotagging? Presenting information about what's nearby requires places and landmarks to be tagged with their location. Restaurants featured on Yelp, for example, must have a street address or longitude and latitude available in a machine-readable format that can be interpreted by the geosocial networking service's search engines. Geotagging and geocoding provide the necessary geographical information.

Geocoding is the process of determining the coordinates of a specific place, such as the street address or the longitude and latitude of Cathy's Cafe. **Geotagging** is the process of adding location data to photos, Web sites, HTML documents, audio files, blog posts, and text messages. Standard formats for geotagging and geocoding ensure that location data can be read by the computer programs operated by geosocial networking services.

Try It!

Check the location settings on any handy digital device. Are they set to allow geosocial networking?

QuickCheck

A service that displays the location of a post office on a map is using _____ data.

a. geotagged

b. geocoded

c. social media

d. crowdsourced

Social Network Analytics

The now infamous game Six Degrees of Kevin Bacon is based on a notion that any Hollywood actor can be linked to Kevin Bacon in six steps through the actors' roles in various films. The Six Degrees of Separation concept originated in a 1929 short story by author Frigyes Karinthy, whose characters devised a game of figuring how to most quickly relay a letter between any two people on Earth based on links between their personal acquaintances. Today, tools let us map and analyze social networks. What do they tell us?

▶ **How are social networks mapped?** Social networks are not exclusively online. Everyone has face-to-face networks of family, friends, and acquaintances, who in turn have their own networks of social connections. You may envision these networks as points connected by lines. Sociologists use social network diagrams called **sociograms** to depict connections between people.

The circles in these diagrams are referred to as **sociogram nodes**. The lines connecting nodes are referred to as **sociogram edges. Two-way edges** exist when two people consider each other to be friends. **One-way edges** exist when a relationship is not reciprocal, such as a Twitter follower who does not follow back. What do the connections in Figure 5-9 tell you about the relationships between characters in *The Lord of the Rings*?

5

Figure 5-9: Anatomy of social networking

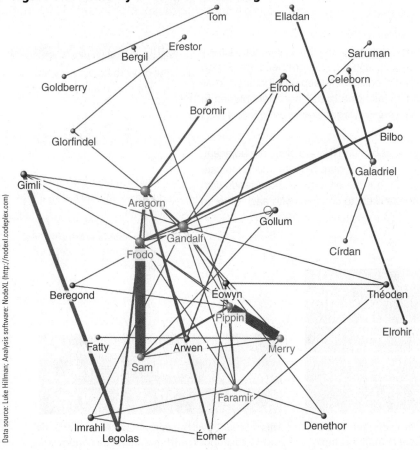

Data source: Luke Hillman; Analysis software: NodeXL (http://nodexl.codeplex.com)

The thickness of connecting lines (edges) indicates connection strength.
Node colors indicate which characters are most important.

QuickCheck

In a sociogram, edges indicate
_____.

a. connections

b. the boundaries of relationships

c. individuals with few friends

d. 3D connections

Try It!

Do the most important characters in Figure 5-9 appear to have the most "friends"?

▶ Is it possible to sort through the complexity? Sociograms can get extremely complex, which makes connections difficult to trace and analyze. An alternative method for depicting social connections is with an adjacency matrix.

A **binary adjacency matrix** is simply a set of cells containing a 0 if there is no connection between two people and a 1 if there is a connection. The adjacency matrix in Figure 5-10 depicts the relationships between some of the elves and hobbits of Middle Earth as a sociogram and as an adjacency matrix.

Figure 5-10: Hobbits and elves

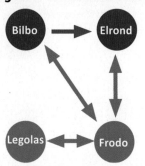

	Bilbo	Elrond	Frodo	Legolas
Bilbo	—	1	1	0
Elrond	0	—	1	0
Frodo	1	1	—	1
Legolas	0	0	1	—

In this sociogram, Bilbo considers Elrond his friend, but Elrond does not consider Bilbo to be his friend.

The intersection of dark blue cells in the adjacency matrix contains a 1 to show that Bilbo considers Elrond his friend. Can you find the cell that indicates Elrond does not consider Bilbo to be his friend?

▶ What else does the matrix reveal? Matrices can be manipulated visually and mathematically to reveal more information about social connections. These manipulations can expose pathways, connections, and groupings that lead to all sorts of revelations. Law enforcement agencies hope to use such techniques to uncover criminal organizations, and national security agencies hope to follow links to identify members of terrorist groups.

Suppose we rearrange the matrix so the two hobbits and the two elves are adjacent. The results are interesting. The rearranged matrix in Figure 5-11 seems to indicate that the hobbits chose each other as friends, but the elves were not friends with other elves. Therefore, the elves would not be likely to conspire with each other to overthrow Middle Earth or to save it.

Figure 5-11: Inferred connections

	Bilbo	Frodo	Elrond	Legolas
Bilbo	—	1	1	0
Frodo	1	—	1	1
Elrond	0	1	—	0
Legolas	0	1	0	—

In the rearranged matrix, the two hobbits are adjacent, as are the two elves. Color blocks illustrate the general relationships between hobbits (red) and between elves (green).

	Hobbits	Elves
Hobbits	100%	75%
Elves	50%	0%

This matrix shows the percentage of connections within each block, with hobbits well connected, but elves not connected to each other.

QuickCheck

How does the adjacency matrix indicate that the elves are not friends?

a. It has a zero (0) where the elf rows intersect with elf columns.

b. It has a dash (-) where the elf rows intersect with elf columns.

c. It has a one (1) where the elf rows intersect with elf columns.

▶ **How do analytic tools apply to online social networks?** Sociograms and other analytic tools help us understand the quality and quantity of our personal social networks. The concept of one-way edges is important, for example, in understanding that although you may receive status updates directly from the President of the United States and the First Lady, you are not likely to enjoy a similar link in the other direction—they are probably not going to read your Facebook posts.

Social network analytic tools also uncovered a very odd phenomenon. Does it seem like most of your friends have more friends than you have? It turns out that is the case with more than 80% of Facebook users. This phenomenon is referred to as the class size paradox because it is related to the reason students feel that they are always in larger than average classes. The explanation is that people tend to choose popular classes and friends, and such popularity does indeed mean that the classes are larger and your friends have more friends than you have. Figure 5-12 offers additional interesting facts about Facebook friends.

Figure 5-12: Facebook friend facts

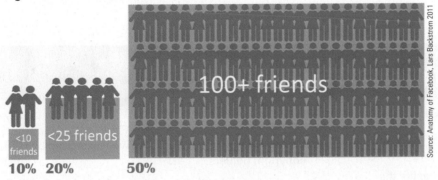

▶ **So how many degrees of separation are there on social networks?**
In 2001, a professor at Columbia University set out to track the path of more than 50,000 email messages forwarded from senders to intermediaries. The messages finally wended their way to one of 19 designated people with undisclosed email addresses. The average number of intermediaries turned out to be six—an amazing confirmation of the Six Degrees of Separation theory.

Researchers studying Twitter connections, however, found the average degree of separation was less than 4. The majority of Facebook users have between 2.9 and 4.2 degrees of separation.

QuickCheck

If you are a typical Facebook user, your friends have _____ you have.

a. more friends than

b. fewer friends than

c. the same number of friends as

QuickQuiz   Section A

1. The Social Media [_____] uses hexagons to depict characteristics of social media.

2. Algorithms at Yelp, Amazon, and Zappos depend upon [_____] to produce ratings based on user reviews.

3. Cellular services can determine the location of a mobile device using cell tower [_____].

4. A(n) [_____] depicts connections between people as nodes and edges.

5. A(n) [_____] matrix is a social media analytic tool arranged as a table.

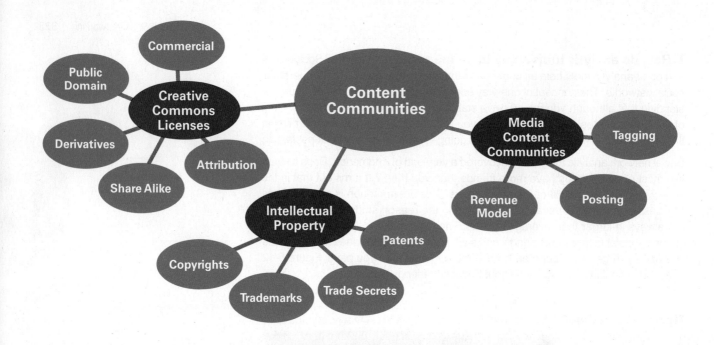

Content Communities

Objectives

▶ Use the Social Media Honeycomb to identify the primary characteristics of content communities.

▶ Draw a timeline of the emergence of content communities, including significant dates.

▶ Explain the concept of viral media.

▶ Explain where content is stored and how that may affect privacy.

▶ Describe the financial model for most content communities and how that model may affect the future of these communities.

▶ State the difference between formal tagging and informal tagging.

▶ List four types of intellectual property.

▶ Identify which types of intellectual property are typically encountered in content communities.

▶ List the six rights that are exclusively exercised by copyright holders.

▶ List the five rights that can be granted under a Creative Commons license.

▶ List the four factors that characterize fair use.

▶ State the difference between a derivative work and a transformative work.

Content communities struggle with the

divide between what is shared and what is owned. One side champions shared ownership; the other side believes that personal property is associated with ownership rights. Bridging the gap is an organization called Creative Commons. If you have not yet used its services, the information at the end of this section can get you started.

Terminology

content communities	formal tagging	public domain	fair use
bulletin board systems	intellectual property	Creative Commons	derivative work
viral	trademark	license	transformative work
metadata tag	copyright	copyleft	

Evolution

Back before the Internet, the creative world was controlled by a small set of gatekeepers who influenced popular culture. Music moguls decided which bands to promote. Hollywood studios selected the films that were produced. The editors at publishing houses filtered the books and magazines that went to print.

Today, those gatekeepers can be bypassed because online content communities so effortlessly distribute books, photos, videos, and music. Popularity no longer depends on endorsement by an elite band of critics, but instead by a democratic vote of "Likes" from everyday folks. Where this democratization of culture leads is anyone's guess. The availability of tools to create and distribute digital media removed the old gates but erected new barriers to talent based on the sheer volume of media that competes for screen time.

▶ **What is a content community?** Many social media sites, such as Wikipedia, YouTube, and Flickr, were designed as repositories for user-generated content. These social media sites are sometimes called **content communities**. Although it can be said that just about every social media site is populated with user-generated content, content communities emphasize the content itself, unlike social networking sites that revolve around user identities.

Content communities may focus on text-based information, or their focus may be on other media, such as photos, music, or video. Content communities typically have the characteristics listed in Figure 5-13.

Figure 5-13: Content community characteristics

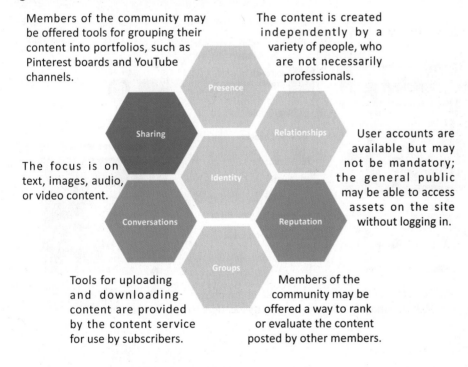

Members of the community may be offered tools for grouping their content into portfolios, such as Pinterest boards and YouTube channels.

The content is created independently by a variety of people, who are not necessarily professionals.

The focus is on text, images, audio, or video content.

User accounts are available but may not be mandatory; the general public may be able to access assets on the site without logging in.

Tools for uploading and downloading content are provided by the content service for use by subscribers.

Members of the community may be offered a way to rank or evaluate the content posted by other members.

▶ **When did content communities originate?** The bulletin board systems (BBSs) of the 1970s contained user-generated content and could be considered forerunners of today's content communities as well as today's social networks. Bulletin boards were popular for about 20 years before other efforts to gather and archive meaningful collections of online content emerged.

One of the first online content communities was Project Gutenberg. Started in 1991 by Michael S. Hart and now supervised by a nonprofit organization, Project Gutenberg's mission is to preserve literary works, particularly those with expired copyrights. Initially, volunteers manually entered the text from printed books; however, today, books are digitally scanned.

In 2001, another text-based collaborative appeared. An online encyclopedia called Wikipedia was launched, and a community of contributors quickly formed around it.

In 1999, the Webshots community became one of the first social media sites for sharing photos online. Competing communities such as Flickr and Photobucket soon followed. Video content communities launched with the founding of YouTube in 2005, and that same year the world saw the first instance of an online video that went viral. SlideShare opened in 2006, offering an archive of PowerPoint-style slide presentations.

Pinterest, founded in 2010, revived interest in photo sharing communities, with its use of "boards" containing a collection of related items, such as photos of fashions, home decor, or book covers. Mobile photo sharing became popular in 2010, when Instagram made it simpler to snap, modify, tag, and share photos taken with the smartphone app shown in Figure 5-14.

Terminology

In the context of social media, *viral* refers to videos, music tracks, blog posts, and other media elements that quickly infiltrate popular culture via social media.

Figure 5-14: Instagram snap, modify, tag, and share

Source © 2017 INSTAGRAM

| Start the Instagram app and snap the photo. | Use tools to edit and retouch the image. | Tag people in the photo and map its location. | Share the photo with friends and followers. |

Media Content Communities

Media content communities are so popular that almost everyone with an Internet connection has logged in to take a look at videos from YouTube and images from sites such as Flickr. Many people participate in these communities by posting media. Others become unknowing participants when they are the subject of photos and videos posted by others.

▶ How do media content communities work? Media content communities specialize in user-generated images, videos, animations, and audio. Posted content can be accessed using a general search engine, such as Google, or an internal search engine provided by the community site. Community members who post content can specify whether it is available to the public or to a limited list of members. Unlike wikis, where editing the source content is encouraged, the media in content communities are not usually modified by other members.

The technological core of media content communities is server-based content management software and an associated database, which stores content and information about that content. Once media are posted to a server, they may remain there indefinitely.

Some media communities incorporate advertising as a source of revenue both for content creators and for operational income. The fact that content communities have few options for generating revenue may lead to their eventual demise if advertising revenue cannot sustain operational costs for server space and administrative personnel.

▶ How do I post content to a media community? Although many content communities allow open access to media, most require registration before files can be uploaded. Content communities offer basic tools for uploading media files from a computer, and most offer apps that handle uploads from mobile devices. Figure 5-15 illustrates how to upload a photo to Flickr from a computer.

5

Figure 5-15: How to upload a photo to Flickr

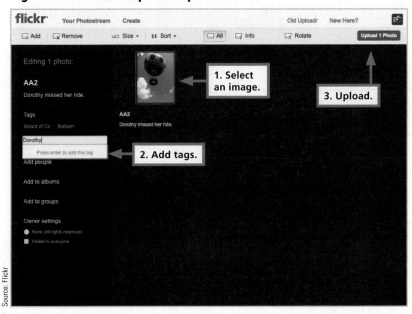

Source: Flickr

▶ **What should I know about tagging media?** A **metadata tag** is a keyword that describes information, such as the content of a media element. In the context of content communities, tags are used to describe people and places in photos and videos.

Unlike documents and other text-based information, media elements contain no text that can be used for indexing, identification, or searching. Tags make it possible to search for photos or videos using keywords, such as *dogs*, *beach*, *sun*, *water*, and *driftwood*. Audio file tags help to locate tracks based on musicians' names, record labels, recording dates, and so on.

Informal tagging simply requires content creators to assign one or more keywords to a media element. The format for entering tags depends on the community. Some require a comma between tags, whereas others separate tags with a space.

Formal tagging methods add information to a tag according to a set of tagging standards. These standards make it possible to create generalized media search engines that can locate media from multiple locations.

Dublin Core schema is an example of a formal tagging standard. It can be used for digital resources as well as for physical media such as CDs, books, and phonograph records.

▶ **Have I been tagged?** Suppose that an acquaintance takes an unflattering photo of you and posts it on Facebook with your name as one of the tags. If you are not friends with the poster, you may never see the post, but wouldn't you want to know about it?

Facebook and several other social media services provide ways to discover if you've been tagged. On Facebook, you can access your activity log and look at the activities that you are tagged in. If you find a photo in which you'd rather not be identified, you can choose to remove the tag yourself or ask the poster to remove the entire photo (Figure 5-16).

Figure 5-16: How to remove your name from a Facebook tag

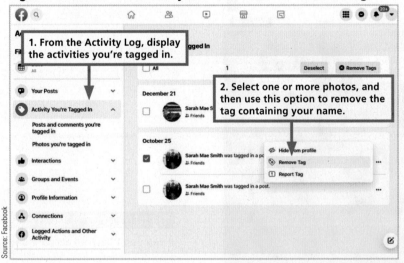

Source: Facebook

1. From the Activity Log, display the activities you're tagged in.

2. Select one or more photos, and then use this option to remove the tag containing your name.

Intellectual Property

Content communities put all types of media at your fingertips. You have access to photos, stories, reports, videos, animations, and music, all in digital formats that you can copy, modify, and incorporate into your own works. But just because you can access this media doesn't necessarily mean that it is legal or ethical to use it. Conscientious citizens of content communities know how, when, and where it is okay to use the media created by other community members.

▶ **What is intellectual property?** People are creative. They produce beautiful art. They invent useful machines. They write captivating novels. All of the creations that materialize from the mind or intellect are considered **intellectual property**. Inventors, artists, writers, and other creative individuals are the owners of their intellectual property. Like other property, intellectual property is protected by various laws and regulations.

There are four categories of intellectual property: patents, trademarks, copyrights, and trade secrets. Some of the media in content communities can be classified as trademarks, but most of it is copyrighted material.

▶ **What should I know about trademarks?** A **trademark** is any word, name, symbol, or design used in commerce to identify and distinguish the goods of one company from those of another. Twitter's little blue bird is a trademark, as is Facebook's stylized "f" logo. Trademarks occasionally display a ® or TM, but those marks are sometimes not visible. You should assume that all company logos are trademarks that are legally protected from misuse by law.

Many companies with an online presence, such as a Web site, provide information about the acceptable use of their trademarks. Before including a company's logo on your Web site, in a blog, or as part of a Pinterest board, check the company's policy on the use of its trademark. You may find, for example, that it is acceptable to use Facebook's Like button on your Web site, but that it is not permissible to mash up a banner image for your site that combines your name with the Facebook logo (Figure 5-17).

QuickCheck

The works in most content communities are classified as what types of intellectual property?

a. Trademark and patent

b. Copyright and trademark

c. Patent and trade secret

d. Copyright and patent

5

Figure 5-17: Use trademarks according to policy

Source: Facebook

Acceptable use   Unacceptable use

❱ How much stuff is copyrighted? Copyright is a form of legal protection that grants the author of an original work an exclusive right to copy, distribute, sell, and modify that work. Copyright applies to "works" such as photos, books, articles, plays, dance performances, videos, animations, sound effects, musical compositions, and audio recordings.

Just about everything available on content communities is protected by copyright. It is not necessary for the work to carry a copyright notice, nor is it required that the work's creator register the work to obtain copyright protection. Any original work automatically becomes copyrighted as soon as it is created, and the rights in Figure 5-18 can only be exercised by the copyright holder.

Figure 5-18: Copyright holder exclusive rights

 Reproduce the Work

 Prepare Derivative Works

 Distribute Copies of the Work

 Perform the Work

 Display the Work Publicly

 Transfer Ownership of the Work

❱ Is it legal to use copyrighted works? The copyright holder has total control over how a work may be used. The default protections make it illegal for anyone else to copy, distribute, perform, display, or license the work, or to prepare derivatives of it. That means it would be illegal, for example, to copy a photo from a content community and publish it as a Facebook post or as an illustration for a magazine article without the copyright holder's permission.

Copyright holders can give permission for the use of their work. They can agree to the content community's Terms of Use that allow works to be reposted within that community. They can place a work in the public domain, or they can license the work.

❱ When does a work become part of the public domain? Public domain refers to the status of works with expired copyrights or whose creators have forfeited their copyright. The works of Shakespeare, for example, are in the public domain. You can perform one of Shakespeare's plays or publish an anthology of his works. However, the 1996 film *Hamlet* directed by Kenneth Branagh is a new instance of the work and is protected by copyright.

In the United States, copyrights do not expire until 70 years after the author's death, and various loopholes allow for extensions. Legal specialists sometimes have difficulty determining if a work has reverted to the public domain. Even when a work seems very old, it is best not to assume that it is in the public domain.

Creative Commons

A nonprofit organization called Creative Commons (CC) has done content communities a welcomed service by providing a set of standardized licenses that copyright holders can use to extend the rights to use their works to others.

▶ **What is a Creative Commons license?** A Creative Commons license is based on five rights that copyright holders can grant or deny to others (Figure 5-19).

5

Figure 5-19: Creative Commons license rights

 Attribution. When the work is used, the copyright holder must be given credit for the work in a citation or another appropriate manner.

 Share Alike. New works based on the original must be distributed under the same license as the original work.

 No Derivatives. The work must not be changed when it is redistributed or shared.

  Public Domain. All rights are granted for reuse or the work has been placed in the public domain.

   Noncommercial. The work may not be used for commercial purposes.

Creative Commons rights can be combined for a variety of licenses.

▶ **How do CC licenses work?** Copyright holders can assign any combination of CC rights to create a license. For example, a photographer who posts a photo on Flickr might offer a CC BY-ND license, which means it has a Creative Commons license allowing the photo to be used as long as there is a credit line attributing the photographer (BY) and the photo is not modified to create a derivative work (ND).

The Share Alike right is sometimes referred to as copyleft. The term *copyleft* was chosen to convey the idea that it is the opposite of copyright. Whereas copyright is designed to limit the use of a work, **copyleft** is designed to make a work freely available for distribution and modification under the condition that all derivative works use the same license. Works and their derivatives with a copyleft license cannot be later licensed in a way that would restrict their use.

Before using any work that you find at a content community, check for a Creative Commons license. You'll usually find it in the tags for a photo.

▶ **Can I assign a CC license to my own work?** When you create a work, it is automatically protected by copyright and you have exclusive rights to its distribution, modification, and sale. If you would like to release some of those rights to make the work easier for others to use and share, you can assign a Creative Commons license. Figure 5-20 explains how to assign CC licenses to various types of media.

QuickCheck

Look back at the CC licenses in Figure 5-19. Which one would be considered a copyleft license?

a. BY NC SA

b. BY ND

c. BY

d. BY NC

Figure 5-20: How to assign CC rights

1 Connect to the Creative Commons license chooser at *creativecommons.org/choose.*

2 Choose the rights you want to grant to others.

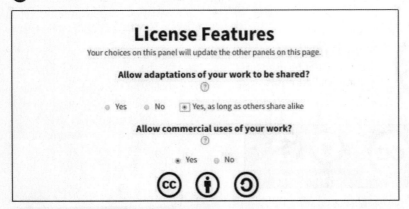

3 Place the license where it can be easily accessed.

Type of Work	Where to Place License
Web page, Web site, or blog	At the Creative Commons site *creativecommons.org/choose/*, select a license, copy the HTML code provided, then paste it onto a Web page or blog.
Image	Reference the CC license you've selected in the image caption or in the image tag.
Presentation	Reference the CC license you've selected on the title slide or the last slide. Add a link, if possible, to the license.

❱ **What about fair use?** Earlier modules touched on the concept of **fair use**, which allows for the limited use of copyrighted material without obtaining permission from the copyright holder. United States copyright regulations include four factors that characterize fair use:

1 **The purpose and character of the use.** The use of copyrighted materials without permission is more likely to be "fair" when the materials are transformed and used for a purpose different from that of the original work.

2 **The nature of the copyrighted work.** Guidelines for fair use of photos may differ from guidelines for music, videos, or written works.

3 **The amount of the copyrighted work that is used.** Quoting a paragraph from a book is more likely to be fair use than reproducing an entire chapter.

4 **The effect on the value of the copyrighted work.** Uses that deprive the copyright holder of income are not generally considered fair use.

❱ **Is a transformative work different from a derivative work?** Yes. A **derivative work** modifies a copyrighted work but does not substantially change its content or purpose. Translations, adaptations, musical arrangements, dramatizations, reproductions, condensations, and similar modifications would all be considered derivative.

Mashups that combine two or more music tracks into a single recording are usually regarded as derivative works because they are intended for the same uses as the original recordings. Derivative works are not fair use, and they require permission directly from the copyright holder or from an applicable license, such as CC BY.

A **transformative work** repackages a copyrighted work to add new meaning or produce a work that is used for a purpose different from the original work. Parodies, for example, are considered transformative. Cutting up magazine covers to create a collage to hang on a wall would also be considered a transformative use.

Transformative works are considered fair use; they can be produced and distributed without the copyright holder's permission.

Although the differences between derivative and transformative works may seem clear, in practice copyright holders are free to sue anyone who produces a work that is based on their copyrighted works. The courts are the ultimate decision makers in copyright infringement cases. If you want to safely incorporate the works of others into your own work, use only works that have a CC BY or CCØ license.

5

QuickCheck

Suppose that you create a YouTube video and add a music track from a recent hit film. Would your work be considered transformative?

a. Yes, I've created a new, original work.

b. Yes, the copyrighted sound track is just part of the new work.

c. No, I'm not going to make any money from it.

d. No, the sound track is used in my work for the same purpose as in the original work.

QuickQuiz   Section B

1. A media element goes ☐ when it quickly infiltrates popular culture and is accessed by millions of people around the globe.

2. Content communities form around user-☐ content.

3. Dublin Core is an example of a formal ☐ standard.

4. The Twitter bird logo is an example of a company ☐ that is protected from misuse by law.

5. A Creative Commons license designated as CC BY ☐ does not allow derivative works.

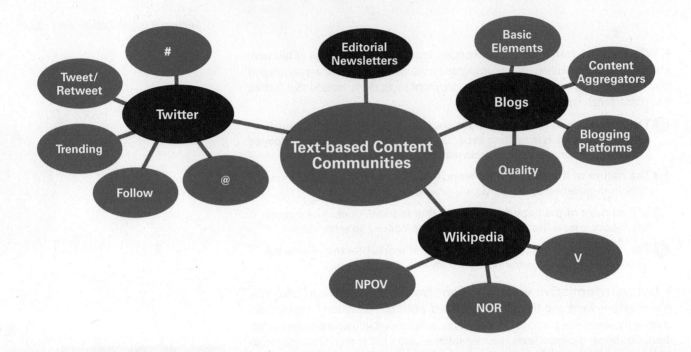

Objectives

▶ Identify the major elements of a blog page.

▶ List examples of at least two blogging platforms.

▶ Discuss why blogs could be considered a disruptive technology.

▶ List five questions that help to evaluate the quality of information presented in a blog.

▶ Give examples of six ways in which Twitter has expanded its focus to go beyond personal status updates.

▶ Identify the major elements of a Twitter page.

▶ Describe the characteristics of a wiki.

▶ Explain how Wikipedia articles are written and edited.

▶ Explain the meaning of NPOV, NOR, and V in the context of Wikipedia.

▶ Identify the elements of a Wikipedia article.

▶ Identify the purpose of each Wikipedia tab.

Blogs, newsletters, tweets, and wikis. The major text-based content communities offer up a mountain of content. Some of it is accurate and dependable; some of it is downright false. Even more of it is misleading in subtle ways. In this section, you'll explore the origins of this text-based content and how to tell the good from the bad.

Terminology

blog	tweets	follow	trending
blogging platform	microblogging service	follower	wiki
content aggregator	@username	follow back	NPOV
blogosphere	retweet	@mention	NOR
editorial newsletter	promoted tweet	#hashtag	V
platforms	Twitter stream/timeline	DM	

Blogs

The democratization of culture is not limited to art; it spills over into the mainstream news media. Today, blogs provide alternative news sources that offer a greater diversity of topics and opinions than pre-Internet gatekeepers such as Reuters, Associated Press, and CNN. The ease of broadcasting information has become a major disruptive force with no clear outcome in sight.

▶ **What is a blog?** A **blog** (short for Web log) is a sequence of informational articles posted in reverse chronological order and displayed on a scrollable Web page. Blogs are generally maintained by a person, a company, or an organization.

▶ **What are the basic elements of a blog?** Blog entries are text based, but they can get visually fancy with lots of photos and videos. Basic blogs have a standard set of elements illustrated in Figure 5-21.

5

Figure 5-21: Anatomy of a blog

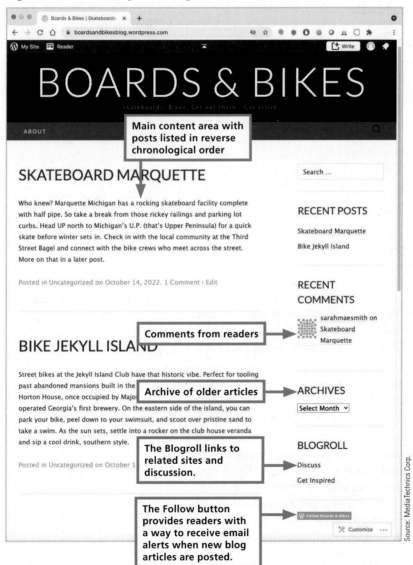

Source: MediaTechnics Corp.

▶ **How can I become a blogger?** Popular blogging platforms include Blogger, WordPress, Wix, and Medium. A **blogging platform** provides tools for creating blogs. It may also provide a Web site where blogs can be posted for access by the public.

Bloggers may post to a subdomain, such as *https://medium.com/@sarah*, offered by the blogging platform. Bloggers who want a dedicated domain name, such as *www.edisonjones.com*, can use a Web hosting service, such as HostGator or GoDaddy. These hosting services offer blogging plug-ins for authoring and managing blog posts.

▶ **How can I find and access blogs?** You can find blogs by going to Blogger, WordPress, and Medium or by simply launching an online search such as *Skateboard Blogs*. You can use a **content aggregator** to set up a "feed" that monitors your favorite blogs, collects the latest posts, and displays them (Figure 5-22).

Figure 5-22: Setting up a "feed" using Feedly

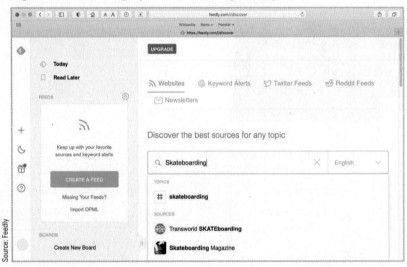

Source: Feedly

Try It!

How would you discover if there are any skateboarding blogs on WordPress?

Terminology

Blogger (uppercase *B*) is the name of Google's blogging platform. A *blogger* (lowercase *b*) is a person who blogs. Bloggers are sometimes referred to as *influencers*.

▶ **How significant are blogs?** The **blogosphere**—all the blogs and their interconnections—is influential. Some bloggers have been tapped to be commentators for headline news shows on CNN and FOX News. Top blog sites have millions of monthly readers.

Many blogs are open to the public, so blogging has become a form of personal journalism. Bloggers can chase down facts, write commentary, post photos, and offer opinions. Blogs have been used extensively for political commentary, celebrity publicity, and technology news.

Blogs and other Internet-based news outlets have the potential to reach mass audiences. Totalitarian governments, which can control mainstream media, find it more difficult to silence a multitude of freelance bloggers than a small group of professional journalists. In that respect, blogs support democratic free speech values and have the potential to disrupt oppressive governments.

Blogging also offers an alternative source of news and information, reducing the audience for mainstream news outlets. The fact that blogs and many Internet-based news outlets offer free access has disrupted print-based news media by reducing sales and forcing major newspapers to shutter operations. Industry analysts are concerned that if this trend continues in the years ahead, few reliable mainstream news outlets will remain.

But blogs themselves may be on the endangered list. Some readers find it inconvenient to periodically connect to their favorite blogs. Many bloggers offer subscriptions to their blog content in the form of a newsletter that is sent directly to a subscriber's email address. As a spin-off, **editorial newsletter platforms** such as Substack and Review offer tools for creating and sending content directly to subscribers' inboxes.

▶ **Who is responsible for blog content?** Professional journalists and the media companies they represent are guided by a code of ethics that encourages seeking truth, reporting it, minimizing harm, resisting outside influences, and maintaining accountability. It is true that not all professional journalists live up to these standards, but the standards do exist.

Bloggers, who may not have journalistic training or the supervision of responsible corporations, may have a less rigorous approach to accuracy and accountability. They might not take steps to verify information, and they might not understand the significance of intellectual property.

Overall, the information provided by blogs tends to be less reliable than information from the mainstream media. However, many reliable and professional blogs exist. As with other online and offline materials, readers are ultimately responsible for evaluating the quality of information in a blog. Figure 5-23 offers some tips for evaluating blogs.

Figure 5-23: How to evaluate blogs

 Who is the blogger? Look for information about the blogger's expertise at sites other than the blog.

 What are the blog's readership and Alexa rating? Popular blogs tend to be more reliable because they are subject to scrutiny by many readers.

 Are comments substantive and supportive? Blogs that generate negative comments and corrections may not contain accurate information.

 How extensive is the blog's archive? Well-established blogs may remain active for many years, so look at the blog's track record and make sure it contains recent posts.

5

Microblogs

Michael Brown's death, the Hudson River plane crash, the Osama bin Laden raid, and the Boston Marathon bombings are some of the breaking news stories that appeared first on Twitter, a social media service that relays information from the mundane to the extraordinary.

▶ **What was the original idea behind Twitter?** Twitter was modeled as a Web-based version of the text messaging services offered on mobile phones. Just as those services were limited to 140 characters, Twitter messages, called **tweets**, initially carried such a limit. Now expanded to 280 characters and associated videos, Twitter is an example of a **microblogging service** because a Twitter message is basically a short blog post.

Twitter originated as a social networking service where participants could keep track of what their friends were doing based on trivial status updates such as "I'm heading to my bio class" or "Just saw Peter at the Laundromat." As the service evolved and the participants' circles of influence mushroomed, Twitter's focus expanded to include topics of more substance, in addition to a continuing stream of personal updates. Some examples of Twitter's expanding influence include the following:

A platform for breaking news. In 2008, NASA researchers used Twitter to announce an exciting discovery from the Phoenix Mars mission: "Are you ready to celebrate? Well, get ready: We have ICE!!!!! Yes, ICE, *WATER ICE* on Mars! w00t!!! Best day ever!!" Tweets have since evolved into one of the main sources for news.

Citizen journalism. In 2021, Taliban fighters seized control of Afghanistan, throwing the country into chaos. Citizen journalists chronicled the throngs of desperate people crowding the road to the airport and futile protests staged against the Taliban's treatment of women, journalists, and those who refused to recognize the new, fundamentalist government.

Celebrity watching. Twitter illustrates and reinforces the power of celebrity. Oprah Winfrey had more than 100,000 followers on the day she opened her Twitter account. Ellen DeGeneres's selfie at the 2014 Oscars became one of the most popular tweets of all time.

Online presence. Companies from McDonald's to Starbucks have established corporate Twitter accounts where product information can be quickly disseminated to customers. Corporate presence on social media sites is a requirement of doing business in the digital age.

Public opinion. Twitter users can be quick to comment about breaking events and controversies, though their opinions may be based on information gleaned from a mere 280 characters of information. Principles of justice, such as being innocent until proven guilty, can be forgotten as Twitter users rush to tweet reactions to trending controversies.

Social organizing. Twitter's ability to quickly disseminate information makes it a desirable platform for social organizing. Hashtags such as #blacklivesmatter, #metoo, #prolife, and #bluelivesmatter have been instrumental in organizing protests, rallies, and virtual meetups. Twitter and other social media have also been used, however, by government authorities to identify protesters.

Try It!

Access Twitter and look at the list of trending topics. How many of these would you classify as substantive? Next, try conducting an online search for *Most popular Twitter handles.* Examine the list and guess how many are not self-promotional.

QuickCheck

Technically, Twitter is most similar to _____.

a. blogs

b. Flickr

c. email

d. crowdsourcing

▶ **What's the basic Twitter vocabulary?** Twitter has a vocabulary all its own, and some of its terminology has spilled over to other social media. Figure 5-24 presents Twitter jargon in the context of a Twitter page.

Figure 5-24: Twitter terminology

Source: 2015 Twitter

Try It!

Access Twitter and make sure that you can identify examples of each term in Figure 5-24.

5

@username: A unique identifier for each Twitter account holder

Tweet: A message consisting of 280 or fewer characters of text plus optional photos/videos

Retweet: A tweet that is forwarded from one Twitter user to others

Promoted tweet: Tweets that contain paid advertising and are labeled to distinguish them from noncommercial tweets

Twitter stream/timeline: A list of tweets; a user's Home timeline shows the user's own tweets and tweets from anyone the user is following

Follow: Specifying a Twitter user whose tweets you want to receive

Follower: A Twitter user who follows your tweets

Follow back: When Twitter users mutually follow each other (e.g., Keysha follows Joe, and then Joe follows Keysha back)

@mention: A person who is referred to in a tweet with a Twitter username preceded by an @ symbol (e.g., mentioning @BillGates in a tweet broadcasts it to your followers and places it in Bill Gates' Mentions tab)

Reply: A message sent in reply to a tweet; automatically addressed to the source of the original tweet preceded by the @ symbol

#hashtag: A hashtag, such as #ipadgames, specifies a keyword that can be used to find and group tweets by topic, both in Twitter and across other social media; clicking a hashtag in a tweet displays other tweets with that hashtag (a directory of hashtags can be found at *www.hashtags.org*)

DM: Direct, private email-like messages sent by Twitter users to any of their followers

Trending: Twitter hashtags that are popular for a period of time

▶ **How substantive is the information on Twitter?** There is no doubt that tweets shape the social dialogue. Mainstream news organizations use tweets as a source of breaking news and as indicators of public opinion. Although socially significant discussions occasionally appear in the list of trending topics, a casual review of trending topics and popular Twitter handles seems to reveal a breathtaking number of tweets that have little social relevance.

Researchers have found Twitter to be a fascinating topic of study. Notable efforts include a study of trending topic classifications conducted by Northwestern University, and a project called Truthy that traced the spread of memes. There was also a University of Pennsylvania study of cardiovascular disease commentary, and a study conducted by the Pew Research Center that examined Americans' use of social media for political activism.

QuickCheck

Twitter pioneered the use of the _____ symbol to group messages pertaining to a topic.

a. @

b. !

c. RT

d. #

Wikis

The content communities that attract attention today serve up user-generated videos and images. However, some of the oldest and most productive content communities are built upon text-based wikis.

▶ **What is a wiki?** A **wiki** is a collaborative Web application that provides tools for contributors to post, read, and modify content. For example, one contributor might write and post an article about wolves. That article can be read and modified by others. Changes to an article are tracked, allowing the community to view changes, leave changes in place, or revert back to earlier content.

Wiki software runs on a wiki server and provides a set of tools for creating and editing content. Content is stored in a database on the wiki server, along with a list of changes to the content. Popular wiki software, such as MediaWiki, is open source, so all users are free to create and host a public or private wiki. The world's most popular wiki is Wikipedia.

▶ **How does Wikipedia work?** Wikipedia is an online encyclopedia. It uses MediaWiki software to manage millions of articles in 285 languages. Wikipedia receives about a billion page views per day as people from all over the world seek factual information about the arts, geography, history, science, society, and technology. Wikipedia is organized by topics, such as Wolves, Egypt, Origami, Tolkien, London, American Revolution, and Skateboards.

Wikipedia pages can be accessed, viewed, and edited anonymously by the general public without subscription or registration. Participants are encouraged to register with the Wikipedia community and become "Wikipedians." These editors not only contribute new material and updates but also monitor pages to ensure that they retain high-quality contents, adhere to Wikipedia standards, and are not subject to vandalism.

▶ **What are Wikipedia standards?** Wikipedia endeavors to provide non-biased, accurate, and verifiable information. Content creators and editors are encouraged to filter material through a sieve of strict standards known to insiders as **NPOV**, **NOR**, and **V**. Figure 5-25 explains these standards.

Figure 5-25: Wikipedia content policies

 Neutral point of view: Content for Wikipedia articles should be phrased and presented in neutral language and with unbiased intent.

 No original research: Articles should be based on existing recognized knowledge. Personal views and original research are not appropriate.

 Verifiability: Readers must be able to verify all content against reliable external sources based on citations included within the text and listed at the conclusion.

QuickCheck

In an attempt to keep articles unbiased, Wikipedia has a(n) _____ policy.

a. NPOV

b. NOR

c. RS

d. V

◗ **What are the elements of a Wikipedia article?** Wikipedia articles vary in length but contain the set of standard elements that are shown in Figure 5-26.

Figure 5-26: Wikipedia page elements

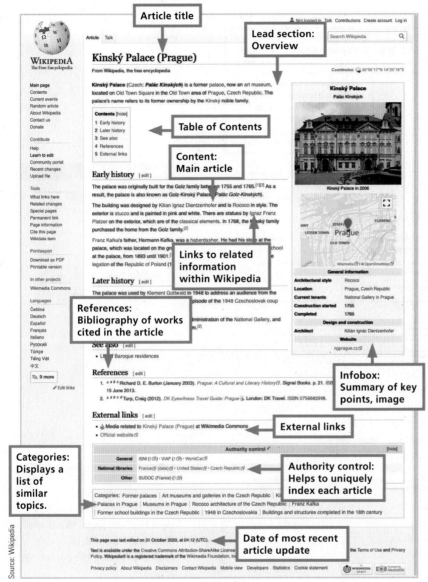

Source: Wikipedia

▶ **What's on the other Wikipedia tabs?** Most Wikipedia users focus on the main topic page displayed on the Article tab; however, valuable information can be found on other tabs. For example, it is possible to edit the text of an article from the Edit tab using wiki markup or HTML, as shown in Figure 5-27.

Figure 5-27: Wikipedia tabs

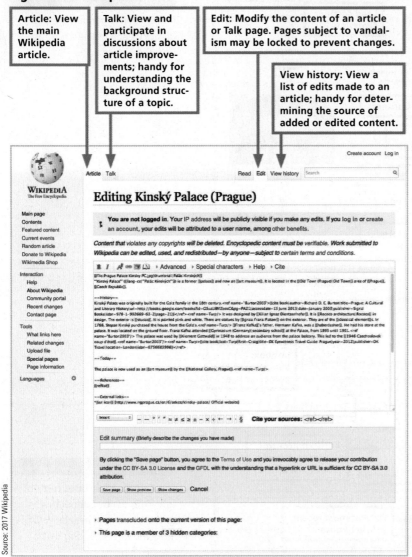

> **Article: View the main Wikipedia article.**

> **Talk: View and participate in discussions about article improvements; handy for understanding the background structure of a topic.**

> **Edit: Modify the content of an article or Talk page. Pages subject to vandalism may be locked to prevent changes.**

> **View history: View a list of edits made to an article; handy for determining the source of added or edited content.**

Source: 2017 Wikipedia

▶ What should I know about using Wikipedia information? Because Wikipedia articles can be edited by anyone at any time, the accuracy and reliability of Wikipedia information are controversial. Some articles contain errors and omit important data. Occasionally, articles are deliberately falsified. Older Wikipedia articles tend to be more accurate than new articles because they have been through more editing cycles. Older articles, however, may not be up to date.

In some academic settings, Wikipedia is not regarded as a reliable source of information. Figure 5-28 lists some guidelines for its use in academia.

Figure 5-28: Wikipedia academic usage guidelines

 Do not quote Wikipedia directly; do not list Wikipedia articles in bibliographies; work with original sources.

 Cross-check before using facts from Wikipedia articles.

 Follow links in citations or use Google to locate original sources before including information in research papers.

 Never "lift" citations from the references section of a Wikipedia article; use citations only if you have examined the source document.

 Be sure to use sources beyond Wikipedia to research topics in sufficient depth.

 Before submitting papers, articles, and other academic work, check the sourcing guidelines provided by instructors or editors who will review your work.

QuickQuiz   Section C

1. WordPress and Blogger are examples of blogging _____ .

2. A(n) _____ aggregator sets up a feed that monitors your favorite blogs, collects the most recent posts, and displays them.

3. The _____ symbol specifies a Twitter topic.

4. A collaborative Web application that provides tools for contributors to post and modify content is called a(n) _____ .

5. Wikipedia articles are not supposed to refer to original _____ (NOR).

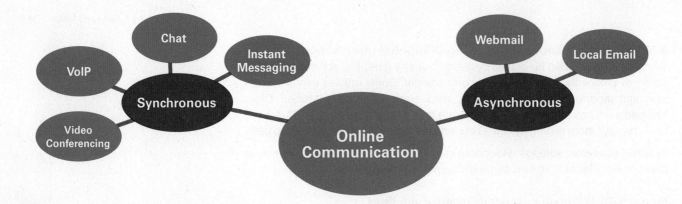

Section D Online Communication

Objectives

▶ Classify communications technologies as synchronous, asynchronous, public, or private.

▶ Interpret the information in an email header.

▶ List the pros and cons of Webmail and local mail.

▶ Explain how the term *store-and-forward* relates to email.

▶ Differentiate between IMAP and POP.

▶ List four steps that help to reduce the security risk of accessing email on a public computer.

▶ Explain the circumstances under which a person might want to forward email between a Webmail account and a local account.

▶ Describe the evolution of online chat.

▶ Name four services that use VoIP technologies.

▶ List some of the security and privacy problems associated with videoconferencing systems.

When you think of social media, email and Skype might not immediately come to mind. And yet, what could be more social than corresponding with friends or chatting with them in real time? Social media offer plenty of choices for communicating. Section D presents communication technologies in a handy, purpose-oriented structure.

Terminology

synchronous	email system	local email	SMTP
asynchronous	email server	store-and-forward	instant messaging
email	message header	POP3	VoIP
email message	Webmail	IMAP	

Communication Matrix

The Internet offers many tools for communicating and collaborating; more are appearing every day. These tools can be classified into a four-cell matrix, as shown in Figure 5-29.

Figure 5-29: Communication matrix

Public Asynchronous	Public Synchronous
Blogs	Chat rooms
Microblogs (Twitter)	Live streaming video
Forums and discussion groups	
Public social media posts	
Private Asynchronous	**Private Synchronous**
Email	Voice over IP (Skype)
Text messaging service (SMS)	Videoconferencing (Zoom)
Multimedia messaging service (MMS)	Instant messaging (ICQ, AIM)
Private social media posts	

▶ How are synchronous and asynchronous communications different? Think about email and Skype. You use them differently because one is synchronous and the other is asynchronous.

Synchronous. When communication is **synchronous**, interchanges happen in real time while all parties are online. Synchronous communications have the advantage of immediacy. They can convey your thoughts as you speak and events as they happen. Telephone calls are synchronous, as are video conferences and live streaming video.

Asynchronous. When communication is **asynchronous**, messages are held until the recipient is ready to view them. Asynchronous communication offers convenience because information can be gathered whenever you want it. That information can, however, be out of date by the time you obtain it. Email is an example of asynchronous communication.

▶ What is significant about public or private communications? There are times when you want to communicate with certain people, and there are times when you want to reach a wider audience. Networks offer opportunities for both public and private communications.

Public. Public communications can be accessed by individuals unknown to the person who created a message. The word *posting* is associated with this type of communication because it is similar to posting a billboard, sign, or poster. Public communication platforms, such as Twitter and blogs, are useful for disseminating information to a wide audience.

Private. Communications for which you specify one or more recipients would be classified as private. Text messaging is a popular type of private communication. A limited audience can be an advantage or a disadvantage, depending on what you hope to accomplish with your message. Be aware, however, that private messages can be forwarded by recipients, so they do not necessarily remain private.

QuickCheck

Email is an example of _____ communication.

a. synchronous

b. asynchronous

c. mediated

d. public

Email

An estimated 300 billion email messages speed over the Internet each day. You can access email using Webmail, local mail, or both. Which system you use has implications for your security and privacy.

▶ **Exactly what is email?** The term **email** can refer to a single message or to the entire system of computers and software that transmits, receives, and stores email messages. An **email message** is an electronic document transmitted over a computer network to a specific recipient

The computers and software that provide email services form an **email system**. At the heart of a typical email system is an **email server**—a computer that essentially acts as a central post office for a group of people. Email servers run special email server software, which provides an electronic mailbox for each person, sorts incoming messages into these mailboxes, and routes outgoing mail over the Internet to other email servers.

Email messages have a standard format that consists of a message header and the message body. The **message header** contains the sender and recipient addresses, date, and subject line. When you view an email message, this information is a simplified version of a more complex header that contains a huge amount of routing information, which traces the path of the message and reveals how it was treated by various servers. If you want to know exactly where a message originated or why a message was returned to sender, check the header (Figure 5-30).

QuickCheck

The message header in Figure 5-30 indicates that the message originated _____.

a. from a Yahoo! account

b. from a Facebook user

c. from a Hotmail account

d. from a POP mail server

Try It!

Open one of your own email messages and take a look at the header. Can you locate any information indicating security checks on the sender?

Figure 5-30: Email message headers

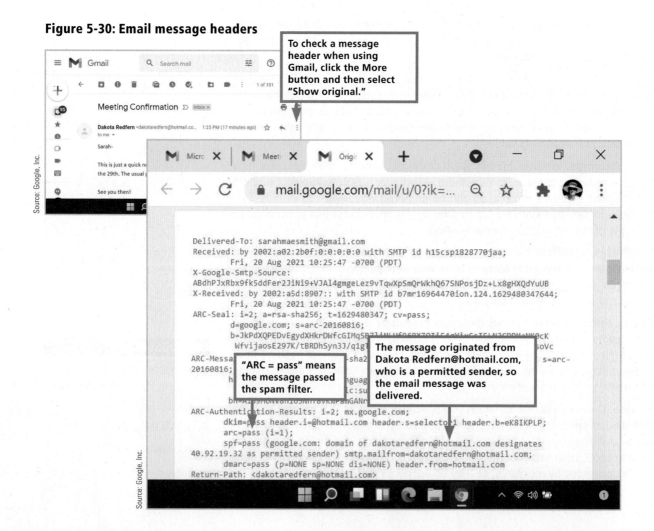

To check a message header when using Gmail, click the More button and then select "Show original."

"ARC = pass" means the message passed the spam filter.

The message originated from Dakota Redfern@hotmail.com, who is a permitted sender, so the email message was delivered.

Source: Google, Inc.

▶ **How does Webmail work?** Webmail is typically a free service accessed using a browser. In a classic Webmail configuration, incoming messages are stored in an inbox on the Web. When you want to read or send mail, use a browser to go to your email provider's Web site and log in. The controls for reading, composing, and managing messages are all presented in the browser window. While reading and composing mail, you generally must remain online (Figure 5-31).

Figure 5-31: Webmail

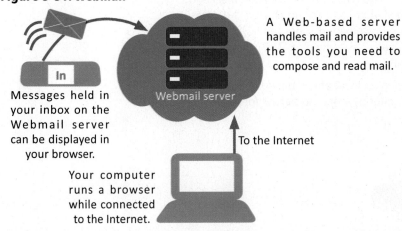

A Web-based server handles mail and provides the tools you need to compose and read mail.

Messages held in your inbox on the Webmail server can be displayed in your browser.

To the Internet

Your computer runs a browser while connected to the Internet.

▶ **What are the pros and cons of Webmail?** Webmail accounts are handy. They offer several advantages, but they also have a few disadvantages that require consumer awareness.

Affordable. Most Webmail is free. In addition to your primary account, you can establish additional accounts to use as throwaways for online activities that require registration, but that you don't intend to continue using.

Access from any device. Webmail can be accessed from any device that has a browser. With smartphones and tablets, as well as laptops and desktops, just open a browser and log in to your Webmail account.

Access anywhere. Webmail is ideal for people who travel, because messages can be accessed from any computer connected to the Internet.

Security risks. Your email messages are stored on Web servers that can be targets for hackers and are monitored by government agencies. Accessing email from a public computer is handy when traveling, but it can be a security risk. To reduce the risk, you should:

- Reboot the computer before logging in to your email account.

- Avoid entering sensitive information, such as your credit card number, in case your keystrokes are being monitored by malicious software lurking on the public computer.

- Be sure to log off when your session is finished.

- Log out and shut down the computer.

Advertising. Free Webmail is supported by advertising, so expect to see advertisements. Today's sophisticated ad servers can search the contents of an incoming message looking for keywords and then use them to display targeted ads in your browser window.

5

How does local email work? When you use local email, an Internet-based email server stores your incoming messages until you launch your email client and get your mail. Messages are then downloaded to a folder on a local storage device that serves as your email inbox. This telecommunications technique is sometimes referred to as store-and-forward.

Using your email client, you can read your mail at your leisure. You can also compose new mail and reply to messages. This outgoing mail can be temporarily stored in an outbox or it can be sent immediately.

The protocols POP3 (Post Office Protocol version 3) and IMAP (Internet Message Access Protocol) can be used to manage your incoming mail. POP3 deletes messages from the server after they are downloaded, whereas IMAP leaves messages on the server until you specifically delete them. SMTP (Simple Mail Transfer Protocol) handles outgoing mail.

Keep these protocols in mind when setting up local email, because the server you specify for outgoing mail might be different from the server for incoming mail (Figure 5-32).

Figure 5-32: Local email

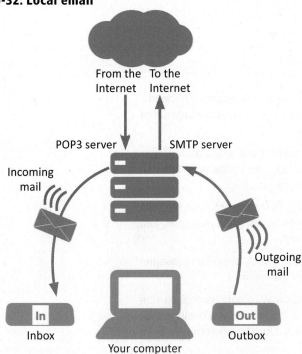

From the Internet   To the Internet

POP3 server   SMTP server

Incoming mail

Outgoing mail

In — Inbox

Your computer

Out — Outbox

What are the advantages of local email? Local email has the following advantages:

Offline access. Because local email stores your inbox and outbox on your computer, you can compose and read mail offline. You are required to go online only to transfer outgoing mail from your outbox to the email server, and to receive incoming messages. This feature is useful if you have a very slow connection or sporadic Internet access.

Control. When you use POP3 to collect your mail, your messages are transferred to your computer's hard disk, where you can control who has access to them. With this control, however, comes the responsibility for maintaining backups of your important email messages.

❱ **How do I set up local email?** To set up local email, the first step is selecting a local email client. Macs include an email client called Mail. Microsoft Outlook is one of the most popular email clients for Windows.

After installing an email client, you can configure it for the email service you're using. Your email provider can supply the information needed for this task. That information can include the following:

- Your email user ID, which is the first part of your email address (e.g., in LiuChan@gsu.edu, the user ID is LiuChan)

- Your email password, if required to access the email server

- An address for the outgoing (SMTP) server, such as mail.viserver.net or smtp.charter.com

- An address for the incoming (POP3 or IMAP) server, such as mail.gsu.edu or pop.media.net

- Port numbers for incoming and outgoing servers, which are usually Port 110 (incoming) and Port 25 or 587 (outgoing)

- Whether the connection uses SSL security

Figure 5-33 displays basic information needed to set up a local email account.

QuickCheck

What happens on the server when mail is downloaded for the account in Figure 5-33?

a. The messages in Sarah's inbox are deleted.

b. Sarah's outgoing mail is blocked.

c. The messages are forwarded to an online account.

d. The messages remain on the server.

5

Figure 5-33: How to set up local mail

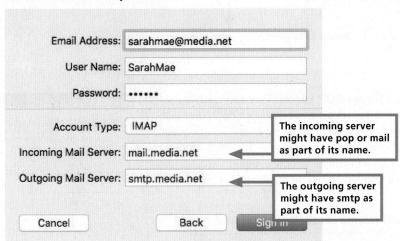

❱ **What about email apps for mobile devices?** Webmail and local email services, such as Gmail, Apple Mail, Windows Mail, and Microsoft Outlook, are available as mobile apps. Downloading an email app to a mobile device places the necessary client software on your smartphone or tablet.

When an email app opens, it collects the most recent messages from your inbox on the email server. These messages are temporarily copied to your device so that you can read them. The original copy of the message is retained on the email server.

When you delete messages and mark them as read while using a mobile app, IMAP protocols generally perform the same actions on the email server. Deleting a message using a mobile app deletes the message from the server. Some email apps provide menu options for customizing this synchronization. Be sure to understand the synchronization settings for your mobile app so you don't mistakenly delete messages you might later want to access from another device.

▶ **Can I use both local email and Webmail?** Yes. You can mix and match Webmail and local mail in various ways.

Use local email software to access messages sent to your Webmail account. This approach is useful if you want to compose mail offline or if you prefer the interface of a local email client such as Outlook compared to the interface offered by Webmail services, such as Gmail.

Once you've created a Gmail account, for example, you can access Settings to enable POP/IMAP mail and then forward your mail to your local client (Figure 5-34).

Figure 5-34: How to forward mail from Gmail to a local client

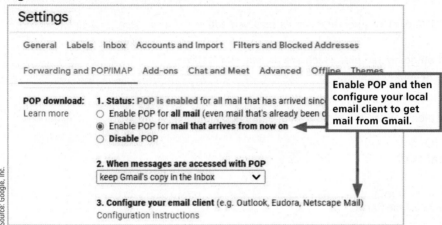

Source: Google, Inc.

Use Webmail to collect messages from a POP server. This approach is useful if you have a local email account but don't always have your computer with you. Your local mail is copied to your Webmail account so it can be accessed when you log in to any computer with an Internet connection. Figure 5-35 demonstrates how to forward local mail to a Webmail account, using Gmail again as an example of a Webmail service and Media.net as the local POP3 account.

Figure 5-35: How to forward mail from a local client to Gmail

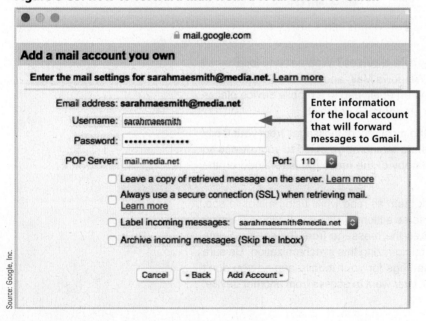

Source: Google, Inc.

Online Chat

When email might take too long, and when you want to establish two-way communication, online chat services offer just the technology you need. The concept of shipping synchronous text, voice, or video over the Internet has its roots in instant messaging.

▶ **What is instant messaging?** Instant messaging (IM) is a synchronous, real-time technology for two or more people to type messages back and forth while online. It has the vibe of a phone call except that instead of talking, the parties are typing. With some IM systems, both parties can see messages character by character as they are typed. More typically, however, the recipient does not see the message as it is typed but must wait until it is completed.

Instant messaging technologies were available on local area networks even before the Internet was open to the public. As the Internet grew, online services, such as Yahoo!, MSN, AOL, and Excite, developed IM systems. Initially, all these systems were proprietary. This meant that messages could not be sent from one service's IM client to a different service's client. Eventually, some IM systems were able to interoperate.

IM technology offers a degree of anonymity because typed messages have no associated voice or video. This anonymity led to the popularity of chat rooms, where individuals could discuss a variety of topics without fear of being identified and without necessarily taking responsibility for their statements.

Today, consumer preferences have shifted to audio and video communications platforms, but IM is still quite popular for customer service at ecommerce sites, where customers can ask questions about merchandise and services as well as get help and support (Figure 5-36).

Figure 5-36: Online chat

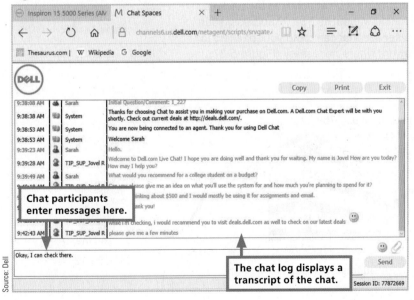

Chat participants enter messages here.

The chat log displays a transcript of the chat.

Source: Dell

Voice and Video Over IP

A soldier Skypes home from a faraway country to spend a few precious moments talking with his spouse. Proud parents use FaceTime to give the grandparents a first peek at a newborn baby. College students keep in touch from all over the globe without incurring long-distance charges. Communication today is far different from the handwritten letters and expensive long-distance telephone calls of 20th century technology.

▶ **What is Voice over IP?** VoIP (Voice over Internet Protocol) is a technology that uses a broadband Internet connection instead of telephone landlines to place voice and video calls. Today's VoIP systems use a variety of communication protocols. Some of these protocols are open standards, while others, such as those used by Skype, Google Hangouts, Zoom, and FaceTime, are proprietary. Therefore, consumers have several options when choosing a system to install and use.

VoIP technologies are ideal for instant, synchronous communications, and video calls are currently "the next best thing to being there," to borrow the tagline from old Bell telephone ads. VoIP is also the underlying technology for business tele-conferencing applications such as GoToMeeting and WebEx.

Voice and video calls can be made between various devices, including laptops, desktops, tablets, and smartphones. On mobile devices, VoIP uses the data stream, not the voice stream. Communications are easiest when the person initiating a call and the person receiving a call use the same VoIP software and service. Callers are generally online, but some services can route calls to landlines.

▶ **How do today's VoIP systems work?** Software converts voice communications and video images into data packets using digitizing techniques similar to those presented in Module 1.

An IP address is attached to each packet. If you are calling a friend with computer-based VoIP, for example, your friend's IP address will be attached to the packets. If you are calling a landline or other destination without its own IP address, your VoIP packets will carry an IP address of a service that can route your packets to their destination using landlines or cell towers where necessary (Figure 5-37).

Terminology

VoIP is also referred to as *Internet telephony*.

Figure 5-37: VoIP to landlines

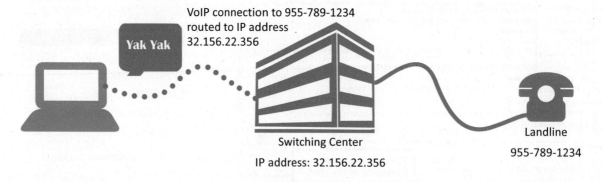

VoIP connection to 955-789-1234 routed to IP address 32.156.22.356

Yak Yak

Switching Center
IP address: 32.156.22.356

Landline
955-789-1234

▶ **What about videoconferencing?** During the COVID-19 pandemic, video-conferencing went mainstream. In response to stay-at-home lockdowns around the world, many segments of society turned to online videoconferencing. Schools held virtual classes. Doctors held telemedicine consultations. Businesses embraced teleworking. Families reached out using Zoom and FaceTime. Politicians held virtual legislative sessions, and charitable organizations held online fundraisers.

The need to use this virtual lifeline, however, has not been without controversy. A government investigation of one videoconferencing service revealed that promised end-to-end encryption had not been implemented. Thousands of videoconferences that were thought to be private were found freely viewable and unsecured on the Web.

More than 500,000 accounts from one videoconferencing service were harvested by hackers and posted on the dark Web. Meetings have been disrupted by "zoombombing," a phenomenon perpetrated by agitators who join a meeting and harass legitimate participants with hateful messages and indecent images.

When privacy risks and security breaches are revealed, the companies that provide videoconferencing services typically respond with program patches and updates.

Videoconferencing systems have become essential tools, but the controversies surrounding security and privacy illustrate the need to exercise caution when using them (Figure 5-38).

Figure 5-38: Exercise caution when videoconferencing

Source: Zoom Video Communications, Inc.

QuickQuiz   Section D

1. In the communication matrix, email is an example of private, _____ communication.

2. Information in an email _____ tracks the path of a message from the sender to the recipient.

3. Local email uses protocols such as POP3 and _____ to manage incoming mail.

4. The concept of shipping synchronous text, voice, or video over the Internet has its roots in _____ . (Hint: Use the acronym.)

5. VoIP, Skype, and FaceTime are examples of _____ communications because both parties are online at the same time.

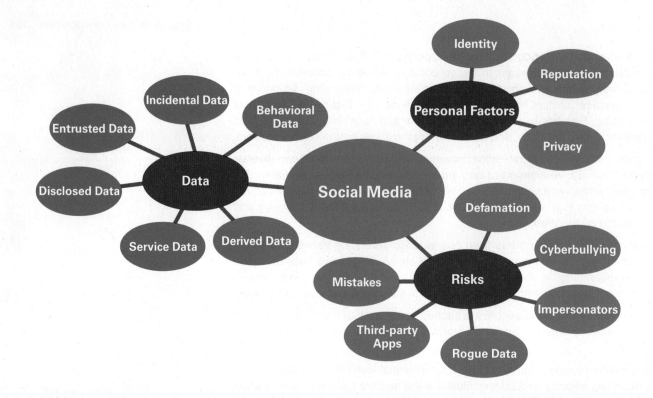

Social Media Values

Objectives

- List the elements that constitute an online identity.

- Describe four ways in which sockpuppets are used for purposes of deception.

- List three situations in which the use of an online pseudonym is justified if allowed by the social media service.

- Explain why using a generic profile image should be avoided.

- Differentiate between an online identity and an online reputation.

- List five factors that can ruin an online reputation.

- List four techniques for dealing with cyberbullies.

- State the difference between an impersonator and a doppelganger.

- List at least five reputation management practices.

- Explain how an online presence can become a threat to an individual's privacy.

- Define each of the six types of social media data.

- List four potential problems with third-party social media apps.

Social media offer a sea of content that ranges from commonplace to momentous. Much of the information that floats through these communities is light entertainment, but some of it profoundly affects people's lives. Although laws and regulations influence online behavior, there is also a set of evolving ethics regarding online self-governance. You'll find out more about this topic in this section.

Terminology

sockpuppets	online reputation	impersonation	personally identifiable
generic profile image	defamation	doppelgangers	information
tagline	cyberbullying	privacy	privacy policy

Identity

Self-identity is the way we view and define ourselves as unique individuals. That identity, however, may not be the one we strive to project in our social media profiles. Some scholars worry that social media encourage individuals to construct facades that depict identities they hope are acceptable to others, rather than identities that reflect who they really are. You should exercise caution when constructing an online identity, because social media personas are globally public. Creating an online profile that reflects your identity requires careful attention.

❱ What constitutes a social media identity? An online identity consists of far more than a photo and a brief autobiographical sketch. The elements that constitute a social media identity include a biographical profile, the set of people who form connections, and the information supplied as posts. All these elements create a social media identity and offer clues to an individual's offline identity.

❱ How important are first impressions? Whether you're connecting with former classmates, collaborating with colleagues, or climbing the career ladder, people looking for you online first encounter your social media profile—and the impression it conveys influences subsequent interactions. For example, a user name carries lots of information. A familiar name can convey a favorable first impression, whereas a wacky pseudonym might be a turnoff.

❱ How prevalent are pseudonyms? The terms of use policies for some social media services require participants to use their real names, whereas other services permit pseudonyms. Regardless of the terms of service, online identities are not always genuine, and it is important to remain aware of that fact. User names such as BumbleBee532 and CrossWalkTrekker are obviously pseudonyms. But user names such as BillGWillis or ShenikaLouisaEspinosa that seem legitimate also could be fakes.

Some fake identities are created by people who prefer not to use their real names. Spammers control armies of fake avatars that want to be your friends so they can carry out a variety of identity exploits. False identities are used for nefarious purposes by cyberbullies, criminals, and stalkers. The use of **sockpuppets**—any online identity created and used for purposes of deception— is widespread (Figure 5-39).

Figure 5-39: Sockpuppet primer

Photka/Shutterstock.com

Sockpuppet: A false identity used for purposes of deception such as:

- To circumvent a suspension or ban from an online group
- For surreptitious self-promotion
- For criminal identity theft
- To stuff online ballot boxes

▶ **What about anonymity?** The principle of anonymity was expressed by former Supreme Court Justice John Paul Stevens: "Anonymity is a shield from the tyranny of the majority. It thus exemplifies the purpose behind the Bill of Rights, and of the First Amendment in particular: to protect unpopular individuals from retaliation—and their ideas from suppression—at the hand of an intolerant society."

There are legitimate reasons for people to conceal their identities. Political dissidents, victims of abuse, and corporate whistleblowers, for example, may not be able to safely interact online under their real names. However, with a little detective work on the contents of posts, photo locations, and IP addresses, real identities can be uncovered.

If you decide to conceal your offline identity by using an online pseudonym, be careful not to tread on someone else's legitimate identity.

▶ **How significant is a profile photo?** Most social media sites provide a **generic profile image** for users who do not upload a personal photo. Users who retain the generic image tend to be newcomers or spammers. Members of online communities may ignore friend requests and comments that come from accounts without a custom image. Figure 5-40 lists some things to consider when selecting a profile image.

Figure 5-40: Image guidelines

What are you wearing?

What is your facial expression?

What are you holding?

What are you doing?

Who are you with?

▶ **What does a tagline reveal?** Most social media profiles include a short, publicly viewable **tagline**. In LinkedIn, this tagline is called a Headline; on Facebook, it is called a Bio. Along with the profile photo, a tagline establishes the first impression of an online persona. Taglines not only reveal biographical information but also can offer insights into a person's personality. Taglines are not dependable, however. They can be total fiction.

When creating a tagline, be aware that it is part of your public first impression. Consider your wording carefully. Tailor it to the site and to your audience, but give it some personality to convey your uniqueness.

▶ **What about detailed biographical information?** Detailed biographical information is generally viewable only by designated connections, depending on the user's privacy settings. Biographical information can include details about a person's education, work experience, residences, family, skills, expertise, and volunteer work. Providing these details helps the social media service to recommend groups or individuals with similar interests. This information can also be abused by advertisers and identity thieves, so be cautious about the information you reveal.

Reputation

When a prospective employer asks for access to your social media accounts, is it time to panic, or do you have a well-managed set of sites that you don't hesitate to share with the world? "Starting today you are a brand." That is the advice of Tom Peters, author of *In Search of Excellence*. Nowhere is this statement more true than online. Your online identity requires careful nurturing and constant vigilance. Maintaining your online reputation ensures that it is an accurate reflection of your offline identity as well as your online presence.

▶ **How important are online reputations?** An **online reputation** is the impression that is generated by an online persona. It relates to the way a person perceives the online identities of others, as opposed to the way those people define themselves.

An individual's online reputation may be used to evaluate whether to accept friend requests and whether a person's tweets are worth following. It can also help to gauge the authority of a person's comments, ratings, and posts.

Online reputations can affect real life. A good online reputation can lead to job offers, collaborative projects, and other opportunities. A bad online reputation can have disastrous consequences. Examples are scattered across the digital landscape. A job applicant's embarrassing vacation photos on Classmates.com. A high school student's Facebook page defaced by cyberbullies. An offensive tweet made by a high-profile athlete. Inappropriate photos sent as text messages by a prominent politician.

▶ **What can ruin an online reputation?** According to executive coach Steve Tobak, "Everything you do on the Internet is like a tattoo you get late at night that can never ever be erased." Many factors can have a negative effect on an individual's online reputation.

Mistakes. An individual may inadvertently post messages, comments, photos, or personal details that are incorrect or unwise, or that can be misinterpreted. Such posts can affect public opinion by damaging the poster's reputation.

Defamation. Communicating false statements that damage the reputation of another individual is referred to as **defamation**. In most countries, defamation is illegal.

Cyberbullying. Using information technology, such as the Internet, to deliberately harm or harass someone is called **cyberbullying**. The intent of cyberbullying is often to damage the reputation of the targeted person. Recommended techniques for dealing with cyberbullying include not responding, deleting posts, blocking the perpetrator, and saving screenshots in case you decide to notify authorities.

Impersonation. Deliberately using the name or avatar of another person without consent and with the intent to harm, defraud, or intimidate is called **impersonation**. Impersonators can be prosecuted for carrying out reputation-damaging activities, such as posting inflammatory comments.

Doppelgangers. Online **doppelgangers** are two or more online personas with the same name or user name. The personas of doppelgangers are sometimes mistaken for each other, and their reputations may become intertwined.

5

Try It!

Use Google to search for your name. Try entering your first and last names, then enter your first, middle, and last names. Do you have any doppelgangers?

❱ What factors contribute to a person's online reputation? Online reputation encompasses many factors that affect the perception of an online identity. It includes the user profile, list of friends, list of followers, posts, comments, mentions, photo tags, and blog entries at social media sites. It also includes personal Web sites, Web pages, publications, and other original works that may exist online. Further, it may include data that tracks online activity, such as purchases and downloads.

Some of the data that contributes to an online reputation is created and managed by the person who controls the online persona. Other data is posted by friends and connections. Yet other data, such as credit scores and shopping activity, is compiled by third parties. Figure 5-41 summarizes the elements of an online reputation.

Figure 5-41: Anatomy of an online reputation

User Profile
Profiles may explicitly state a reputation, such as "avid skier" or "award-winning author."

Media Presence
Elements of an online reputation are derived from multiple sources, so it includes social media accounts, blogs, and Web sites.

Comments
The comments that individuals append to other peoples' posts, tweets, and blogs contribute to building a reputation within the group of participants.

Contacts
People tend to interact with those who share their interests. An individual's contacts and group associations contribute to the way that individual is regarded by others.

Google Results
When someone uses Google to search for an individual, the first page of search results forms an impression that may be perceived as the individual's reputation.

Popularity
The popularity of blogs and Web sites as measured by Alexa and other rating services indicate a person's relevancy.

Expertise
Many reputations are built on knowledge and expertise that are displayed in various online forums, social media, and offline sources.

Images
Whether posted by you or by others, images provide clues about a person's age, ethnicity, personality, and lifestyle. Viewers form opinions based on those images.

Posts
Words, pictures, and videos that individuals post about themselves are evaluated by others to form an impression that becomes an online reputation.

QuickCheck

How does an online identity differ from an online reputation?

a. Your online identity is how you see yourself, but your online reputation is how others see you.

b. Your online identity is more extensive than your online reputation.

c. Your online reputation is established at social networking sites, whereas your online identity is produced offline.

d. They are both the same.

▶ **What are best practices for managing online reputations?** The key to managing your online reputation is vigilance. Just as you learn to use social media tools for connecting to friends and colleagues, it is important to learn how to use the evolving set of tools for understanding and managing your online reputation. Figure 5-42 explains the basic tools and techniques for reputation management.

Figure 5-42: Reputation management best practices

Cultivate your roster of friends. Don't be tempted to bump up your numbers by accepting invitations from random avatars operated by spammers.

Search for your name and make note of any results that might damage your reputation.

Use Google Alerts to keep informed of information that is posted about you.

Adjust settings within your social media accounts so that you are notified when you are tagged in photos and videos.

Don't let your online identities languish. Add posts regularly.

Check all your social media sites periodically to make sure they have not been compromised by identity thieves.

Maintain a consistent user name and identity across sites—especially those that are open to the public.

Remove posts, comments, photos, and blog entries that don't portray your desired online image.

Push enough positive information to the top of your Google search results to obscure any negative content that relates to you.

Separate your professional sites from your personal sites and keep posts appropriate to each.

Consider buying domain names that contain your real name.

Establish accounts on all the popular social media sites so that others cannot impersonate you there.

Maintain civil discourse. Democracies promote free speech, but there are legal and cultural limits. You must be alert, within all of your networking circles, for the norms regarding speech that is acceptable and speech that is not.

Try It!

Which of the items listed in Figure 5-42 are most likely to help improve your online reputation?

Privacy

It was 1890, and journalists using a new technology called photography were snapping sensationalistic photos and publishing them without the consent of the photo subjects. This breach of ethics prompted two young attorneys to call for laws that would keep pace with new technology. One of these attorneys was appointed to the Supreme Court in 1916. Justice Louis Brandeis became a staunch defender of privacy rights and defined the legal precedents for today's privacy laws.

▶ **Exactly what is the right to privacy?** In the words of Justice Brandeis, **privacy** is the "right to be let alone." Commonly held expectations of privacy include freedom from intrusive surveillance and the expectation that individuals can control their own **personally identifiable information** (PII) to limit when they can be identified, tracked, or contacted.

Privacy is different from security, though the two overlap. Security refers to the way we protect ourselves and our property. Privacy is our ability to control access to our personal information and activities. Security is the lock on your front door. Privacy is the curtains on your bedroom window.

▶ **Why is privacy important?** You may think that you have nothing to hide and so privacy rights are unimportant. You may be happy to share the details of your life with friends and even with the general public. But ask yourself this: Would you be willing to give your social media passwords to any stranger who asked for them? If you answered no, then privacy is important to you.

It is somewhat ironic that you need a password to access your social media accounts, even though the information they hold can be accessed without passwords by marketing agencies, third-party app developers, government agencies, and various data collection programs.

Although the United States Constitution does not explicitly define privacy as a right, wording in that document infers the importance of privacy. According to many legal scholars, the importance of privacy goes beyond individual rights and is a foundational concept of freedom and democracy.

In the *Harvard Law Review* article "What Privacy Is For," Julie E. Cohen states: "... privacy is an indispensable structural feature of liberal democratic political systems. Freedom from surveillance, whether public or private, is foundational to the capacity for critical self-reflection and informed citizenship. Second, privacy is also foundational to the capacity for innovation.... A society that values innovation ignores privacy at its peril, for privacy also shelters the processes of play and experimentation from which innovation emerges."

▶ **What is a privacy policy?** Most social media services have a written **privacy policy** that states how PII data is handled, including how it is accessed and how long it is stored. Privacy policies can be several pages long, and they are worth reading to discover if your expectations of privacy correspond to the privacy protections offered by the service. Even if you don't read the entire policy, try to determine how your data may be used by third parties such as advertisers. Also check to see if your posts, photos, and other media remain your own, or if they become the property of the social media service.

Privacy policies change, and the changes usually offer fewer privacy protections. When you receive a privacy policy change notification, check your account settings. As a result of changes, data that was previously private may have become public.

QuickCheck

The right to privacy is _____.

a. explicitly guaranteed by the U.S. Constitution

b. the same as personal security

c. a commonly held expectation

d. described by the privacy policies of online communities

Where can users access privacy settings? Privacy settings are usually included along with general account settings and accessed from the menu bar or account icon. Figure 5-43 illustrates privacy settings available for Facebook users.

Figure 5-43: Check your privacy settings regularly

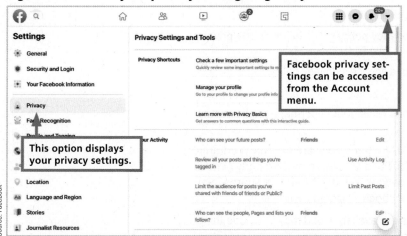

Source: Facebook

Are there levels of privacy? Some data is suitable for general publication, while other data is suitable for colleagues. Yet another set of data may be suitable for friends, while some data is confidential. Key steps in maintaining online privacy include awareness of the different types of data collected by social media services and the level of privacy appropriate for each type. Computer security expert Bruce Schneier devised the taxonomy of social media data in Figure 5-44.

Figure 5-44: Taxonomy of social media data

Service data	The data you give to a social media service when registering to use it. Such data might include your legal name, your age, and your credit card number.
Disclosed data	Information that you post on your own pages. Such information can include blog entries, photos, messages, and comments.
Entrusted data	Information that you post on other people's pages. This information includes the same items as disclosed data, but you don't have control over the data once you post it.
Incidental data	Information that other people post about you. As with entrusted data, you do not have control over it.
Behavioral data	Data about you that is collected by the social media service based on your habits, site usage, post contents, and connections.
Derived data	Data about you that is derived from all the other data. For example, if lots of your friends self-identify as gay, your derived data might profile you as gay, too.

QuickCheck

According to the table in Figure 5-44, the information that other people post about you is ________.

a. service data

b. disclosed data

c. entrusted data

d. incidental data

Try It!

For each type of data in the table in Figure 5-44, consider whether you have the means to control it through privacy settings or other methods.

▶ How does personal information go rogue? Data "gone rogue" escapes its appropriate privacy setting and somehow goes public. An item of PII such as a photograph or a Facebook post can become publicly accessible when users explicitly make it so, either by choice or by mistake. PII can also become public through the actions of others. The most common causes of rogue data include:

- A user changes the global privacy setting to Public.

- A user designates an item as public when it is posted.

- Changes in the social media service's privacy policy result in previously private information becoming public.

- A user ignores changes in the social media service's privacy policy.

- Posted information is reposted publicly.

- Third-party social networking applications redistribute information collected as the user works with an app.

▶ How risky are social media apps? Third-party apps are external programs that interact with social networking services. For example, some third-party games allow you to share your winnings with Facebook friends. WhatsApp shares user phone numbers and activity data with Facebook-affiliated companies.

Hundreds of third-party social media apps are available, and they have one thing in common: All of them collect information from social media profiles, including personal data and contact lists.

The following aspects of third-party apps may affect your privacy:

- Collected data might not be transmitted over secure channels.

- An excessive amount of personal data could be collected.

- Data about your contacts might be collected.

- The collected data may not be subject to the same privacy policies as the social networking service it accesses.

The amount of information accessed by third-party apps depends on your privacy settings and the access you grant when signing up to use the app (Figure 5-45).

Figure 5-45: Apps may require access to your social media profiles

Before installing a third-party app, be aware of the information that it will collect from your social media accounts.

5

▶ **Can I monitor social media apps?** Once permission to use a third-party app has been granted, that permission remains in effect until you cancel it. Major social networking services with associated third-party apps provide information about the apps that are permitted to access a user's account. Be sure to check this setting for your social media accounts and disable any apps that you are no longer using (Figure 5-46).

Figure 5-46: Manage your third-party apps

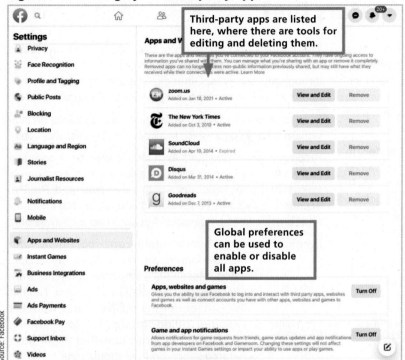

Access Facebook's third-party app settings from the Account menu located in the upper-right corner of the Facebook toolbar.

QuickQuiz   Section E

1. A(n) [_____] is a false identity used for purposes of deception.

2. Online [_____] are the way in which people define themselves on social media sites and other Internet-based venues.

3. The intent of [_____] is usually to damage a person's online reputation through harassment.

4. Personally [_____] information consists of details that can be used to find, track, or contact an individual.

5. Data that a subscriber gives to a social media service when registering is called [_____] data.

Issue: When Do Online Avatars Die?

30 million. That's the number of Facebook users who died during the service's first eight years in operation. The number of deceased Facebook members is projected to outnumber the service's living avatars by 2030. Have you ever wondered what happens to online avatars when their owners pass away?

Consider the case of a 15-year-old high school student in Virginia who tragically committed suicide. His parents wanted to access their son's social media accounts to look for clues that might explain his motivation. Their request for access was denied. Facebook's denial was based on state statutes, federal laws, and language in the 1986 Electronic Communications Privacy Act that protects the privacy of minors.

As a result of the ensuing controversy, the Virginia Legislature passed HB 1752, or the Virginia Digital Assets Law. This law allows parents or legal guardians of minors to access their children's social media accounts. According to the official summary, this bill "Provides that the personal representative of a deceased minor has the power to assume the deceased minor's terms of service agreement with an Internet service provider, communications service provider, or other online account service provider for the purposes of consenting to and obtaining the disclosure of the minor's digital assets."

The Virginia law focuses on the rights of minors and their parents, but who has rights to an adult's digital data after death?

The estate of a deceased person includes personal effects such as clothing and household implements. It may also include financial assets and real estate. An executor is an individual whose responsibility is to dispose of these personal effects. The ability of an executor to access the digital assets of a deceased person depends on a myriad of state and federal laws as well as the policies of various social media services. The terms of use for most social media sites are nontransferable, which means that account access and use cannot be transferred from a deceased person to an executor.

"Do you want to live forever?"

Valeria asks Conan in the movie *Conan the Barbarian* (1982)

The images and posts on social media sites are just a fraction of the many digital assets that people accumulate throughout their lives. Other digital assets include accounts for email, online banking, bill paying, and medical records.

Each category of assets has different implications for an individual's privacy rights, which legally remain in effect after death.

Processes and procedures exist for releasing bank accounts and similar financial assets to an executor. However, purely online financial holdings such as Bitcoin and PayPal accounts may be more difficult to access, as the executor must provide valid credentials digitally rather than in person.

Email accounts, which contain correspondence with multiple individuals, are even further complicated. Messages from correspondents were sent with an expectation of privacy. Neither the sender nor the recipient may want the executor rifling through old love letters, complaints, or messages that might have repercussions on their reputations.

As with other aspects surrounding estate planning, a fully executed will is the key to ensuring that real and digital assets are handled in a specific way and by specified people. Some people may wish their online avatars to live forever, whereas others may wish to exercise their right to be forgotten.

Facebook will memorialize deceased members' accounts when provided with proof of death. A memorialized account cannot be modified and logins are not allowed. The account can, however, accept messages, and content that was posted before the account holder's demise continues to be accessible.

Individuals may not live forever, but their social media avatars can continue to exist in cyberspace. Online identities can be frozen in time, surrounded by posts and images accumulated over a lifetime and now set as a permanent, unalterable record of a person's activities, friends, and accomplishments. It makes you think: What kind of digital legacy are you leaving behind?

Try It! Who can go through your digital belongings after you die? There's never a good time to think about your demise, but no one is immortal. Keeping an eye on your digital reputation includes specifying your wishes for the disposition of your digital assets even after you are no longer around to manage them.

① Visit one of the social networking sites that you frequently use. Search for its policy about access to the accounts of deceased members. Briefly describe the policy and explain if you are satisfied with its terms. If the site offers user-modifiable settings, are the default settings appropriate or would you choose to change the settings?

② The afterlife has not been ignored by resourceful developers. Projects such as Replika, LifeNaut, and Eterni.me have attempted to create immortal digital avatars based on real people. Use online resources to explore this "immortality technology." Report your findings by summarizing the current state of the art and describing some of the platforms that are currently available.

③ Search online for *state laws on digital passing*. Find your state in the list, and read its associated laws and proposals. Read about your state's policy regarding digital property in the event of death. Write a brief summary of the laws and/or proposals in your state.

④ One of the first things that you can do when creating your own digital legacy is to compile a list of your digital assets and accounts. Visit a Web page such as "How to Safeguard Your Digital Legacy" at *Deathwithdignity.org* to get some tips on how to accurately compile an inventory of your digital assets. Then, make your own list. You don't need to be specific—for security, do not include bank names, account numbers, or passwords. Instead, refer to these confidential items generically as "my bank account," "my computer password," and so on.

⑤ Document how you want your online accounts handled in the event of your own death, and decide who will handle your accounts. Also think about and determine a place where you would store your list of digital accounts and assets, including by whom and how your accounts should be handled.

Frenzel/Shutterstock.com

What Do You Think?

1. Have you ever thought about what happens to the social media accounts of people who are deceased?

2. Do you know who might have access to your social media accounts if you meet an untimely death?

3. Are memorialized accounts a good idea?

Information Tools: Media Attribution

You can copy music, photos, and video clips for use in reports, on your blog, on YouTube, and on your Facebook page. If you are not creating a transformative work or a critical work that would be covered by fair use, what steps must you take to use "borrowed" content correctly?

As a general rule, assume that all images and media are copyrighted. Media elements on the Web are covered by the same copyrights as works in print and in other formats. When using copyrighted media, you should seek permission and provide attribution that identifies the copyright holder. Permission and attribution are not the same:

- **Permission** means obtaining rights for a specific use, such as on a Web site.
- **Attribution** means acknowledging the person who holds the copyright, usually by including a tagline under a media element or a citation in a bibliography.

You can obtain permission by asking the copyright holder. Most media sharing sites provide links to copyright holders. Supply the copyright holder with information about the item you want to use and how you intend to use it.

You might not have to contact the copyright holder for permission if the media element is covered by a license. Look for a license or rights link near the media element or a site-use policy near the bottom of a Web page.

You can place your photo attribution in a small font directly under the photo or on its side, or you can include it in the bibliography. Video and music attributions should be placed near the "Play" link or in a bibliography.

The copyright holder might specify the text you should use for the attribution (e.g., "Courtesy of IBM" or "Jerry Harris Photography").

If the wording for an attribution is not specified, then you should include the following:

- Copyright holder's name
- License type, such as "with permission" or "Creative Commons"
- URL (optional)

The easiest media elements to use legally have a Creative Commons license for Attribution (BY).

These licenses specify whether the element can be used for personal or commercial use, and they only require you to provide an attribution crediting the source.

For academic work, such as term papers and theses, you must include attributions for any media elements that you use, even though academic work falls under the umbrella of fair use. As with citations for quoted and paraphrased material, media attribution helps to establish the legitimacy of your work.

Courtesy of NASA

Courtesy of Creative Commons

Try It!

The more you learn about copyright, citations, and attributions, the more complex these topics seem. Here's your chance to track down a few more concepts pertaining to media citations and then summarize what you've learned. For this project, create a document called Module 5 Media Project.

1 Photographers occasionally give permission to use images that are not free from other copyright and legal restrictions. For example, if a photographer takes a photo of a painting, it is considered a derivative work and it is subject to the painting's copyright. Link to the Shutterstock photo site and search for photos of the Mona Lisa. Can you find any photos of the actual painting? Why do you think this is the case?

2 Some museums and libraries allow personal, educational, and noncommercial use of digital images and other media. What is the policy for personal and educational use of digital versions of works from the Smithsonian American Art Museum's collection?

3 Media elements that include images of identifiable people are open to complex legal issues, depending on the subject, the subject's age, and the element's intended use. To be on the safe side, photos or videos that contain images of identifiable people should be used only if the license includes a model release. Link to Shutterstock and Flickr and search for images of businesspeople. Which site provides clear information about model releases?

4 Go to Flickr and enter *pyramids* in the search field, then select the options for "Creative Commons–commercial use allowed." Select an image with a BY attribution license that can be used commercially. Download the smallest resolution and paste the image into your Media Project document. Add the appropriate attribution under the pyramids photo in your Media Project document.

5 Fill in the following table to summarize what you've learned about media attributions and citations.

Situation	Is This Use Correct? Why or Why Not?
You use a photo from an online magazine in a research paper without seeking permission, and you do not attribute the source.	
You use a photo from an online magazine in a research paper without seeking permission, but you do attribute the source.	
You use a photo from an online magazine in a poster for an event without seeking permission, but you do attribute the source.	
You use a photo from an online magazine in a poster for an event after getting permission to do so, and you follow the photographer's instructions for attribution.	
A photo from Shutterstock is royalty free, so you use it on your Facebook page.	
You use a photo from the Smithsonian American Art Museum for a background in an app that you sell on iTunes.	

Eddie Gerald/Alamy Stock photo

Technology in Context: Journalism

In the ancient world, news spread by word of mouth, relayed by bards and merchants who traveled from town to town—in essence, they were the first reporters to broadcast the news. The news business is all about gathering and disseminating information quickly. Technology has played a major role in news reporting's evolution from its bardic roots to modern 24-hour news networks and Web sites.

Johann Gutenberg's printing press (ca. 1450), the first technological breakthrough in the news business, made it feasible to publish news as printed notices tacked to walls in the town square. As paper became more economical, resourceful entrepreneurs sold broadsheets to people eager for news, and the concept of a newspaper was born. The first regularly published newspapers appeared in Germany and Holland in 1609, and the first English newspaper, the *Weekly News*, was published in 1622.

But the news spread slowly. In the early 1800s, it took four weeks for newspapers in New York to receive and publish reports from London. With the advent of the telegraph in 1844, however, reporters from far-flung regions could wire stories to their newspapers for publication the next day. The first radio reporters in the 1920s offered live broadcasts of sports events, church services, and variety shows. Before the 1950s, black-and-white newsreels shown in movie theaters provided the only visual imagery of news events, but within a few years, viewers could watch the news at home on their televisions.

Technology has benefited print journalism, too. For decades, typesetters transferred reporters' handwritten stories into neatly set columns of type. Today, reporters use computers and word processing software to tap out their stories and run a preliminary check of spelling and grammar.

Stories are submitted by computer network to editors, who also use word processing software to edit stories to fit time and space constraints. The typesetting process has been replaced by desktop publishing software and computer to plate (CTP) technology. Digital pages produced with desktop publishing software are sent to a raster image processor (RIP), which converts the pages into dots that form words and images. After a page has been RIPed, a platesetter uses lasers to etch the dots onto a physical plate, which is then mounted on the printing press to produce printed pages. CTP is much faster and more flexible than typesetting, so publishers can make last-minute changes to accommodate late-breaking stories.

Personal computers also added new dimensions to the news-gathering process. Reporters were once limited to personal interviews, observation, and fact gathering at libraries, but they can now make extensive use of Internet resources and email. Web sites and online databases provide background information on all sorts of topics. Other resources include social media, where reporters can monitor public opinion on current events and identify potential sources.

Erik S. Lesser/The New York Times/Redux Pictures

Most major networks maintain interactive Web sites and social media accounts that offer online polls designed to collect viewers' opinions. Although online poll respondents are not a representative sample of the population, they can help news organizations gauge viewer opinions and determine whether news coverage is comprehensive and effective.

A 2019 Muck Rack study identified Twitter as the most popular type of social media used by journalists. Watching Twitter trends helps journalists stay on top of breaking events, supplies information on the competition's reporting, and provides journalists with ideas for news stories.

Email has changed the way reporters communicate with colleagues and sources. It is often the only practical method for contacting people in remote locations or distant time zones, and it is useful for communicating with reluctant sources, who feel more comfortable providing information under the cloak of anonymous Gmail or Yahoo! accounts. Vetting email sources—verifying credentials such as name, location, and occupation—can be difficult, however, so reporters tend not to rely on these sources without substantial corroboration.

For broadcast journalism, digital communications play a major role in today's live, "on the scene" television reporting. Most news organizations maintain remote production vans, sometimes called satellite news gathering (SNG) trucks, that travel to the site of breaking news, raise their antennas, and begin to broadcast. These complete mobile production facilities include camera control units, audio and video recording equipment, and satellite or microwave transmitters.

Eddie Gerald/Alamy Stock photo

A memorable tour de force in SNG was the brainchild of David Bloom, an NBC reporter embedded with the U.S. Army 3rd Infantry Division during Operation Iraqi Freedom. In 2002, he helped modify an M-88 tank recovery vehicle into a high-tech, armored SNG vehicle. The $500,000 Bloommobile featured a gyrostabilized camera that could produce jiggle-free video as the tank blasted over sand dunes at 50 mph. Tragically, Bloom died while covering the conflict. However, viewers vividly remember his exhilarating reports as the Bloommobile raced down desert roads, trundled along with Army supply convoys, and narrowly escaped enemy fire.

On-the-scene reporting no longer requires a truck full of equipment, however. Citizen journalists who are on the spot during news-making events simply use their smartphones to shoot and email footage to media Web sites, such as CNN.com and FOXNews.com. During the tragic

2008 terrorist attacks in Mumbai, eyewitness accounts and updates flooded social networking sites such as Facebook and Twitter. The first images of the attacks spread through social networking sites minutes before they appeared on mainstream news channels.

One drawback of point-and-shoot journalism is that the video quality usually isn't as crisp as images filmed with studio cameras. News organizations with high standards were once hesitant to use this lower-quality video, but they have found that viewers would rather see a low-quality image now than a high-quality image later. To many viewers, a few rough edges just make the footage seem more compelling—more like you are there.

Social media have radically altered the financial models that support news organizations. Newspaper readership is in steep decline while revenue from advertising is also dropping. News organizations attempting to move online are forced to compete with free news gathered by automated aggregators such as Google News and online news sites including *HuffPost* and *Reuters*.

The availability of free news on the Internet has had a devastating effect on newsroom jobs. Journalism graduates face a tough job market as news organizations scramble to restructure their business models. Today, many journalism graduates are finding employment at online startups and in related industries that require research and intelligence-gathering skills.

Computers, the Internet, and communications technology make it possible to instantly broadcast live reports across the globe, but live reporting is not without controversy. Reporters and amateur journalists who arrive at the scene of a disaster with microphones, cameras, or smartphones in hand have little time for reflection, vetting, and cross-checking, so grievous errors, libelous images, and distasteful video footage sometimes find their way into news reports.

According to Jeff Gralnick, former executive producer for ABC News, "In the old days, we had time to think before we spoke. We had time to write, time to research, and time to say, 'Hey, wait a minute.' Now we don't even have the time to say, 'Hey, wait a nanosecond.' Just because we can say it or do it, should we?"

Technology has given journalists a powerful arsenal of tools for gathering and reporting the news, but it has also increased their accountability for accurate, socially responsible reporting.

Critical Thinking

There's a cartoon that has become a social media meme. Two pigs are chatting. The first pig says, "Isn't it great? We have to pay nothing for the barn." The second pig replies, "Yeah! And even the food is free." This cartoon is frequently linked to a quote that goes something like this: "If you're not paying for it, you're not the customer; you're the product being sold." What do these statements imply about social media? What are specific ways that social media users become a product that is being sold?

Group Project

Work with a group of three or four students to research a new social media service. If possible, install it on your devices and try it out. On the basis of your trial run, make a list of the service's advantages and where there is room for improvement. Discuss the target audience for the service and how easy or difficult the service is to use. Also consider if use of the site poses privacy concerns. Collaborate with your group to write a review of the service that you can present to the rest of the class.

Cyberclassroom

In a small group, discuss the use of social media as a tool in education, specifically thinking about how it can be used effectively for on-campus students. Is its best use for communication or instruction? Can you share personal experiences of when social media have been used effectively for education or examples of attempts to use them that have fallen short?

Multimedia Project

Create an original work, such as a photo, video, or audio track. Select a Creative Commons license for the work using the license chooser located at *creativecommons.org/choose*. Post the work along with its license on a social media site.

Resume Builder

LinkedIn is the leading social media service for building a professional online image. If you don't have a LinkedIn account, sign up for one and begin building a profile. If you already have a LinkedIn account, revisit it, consider the information you've collected from this module, and revise your profile as necessary.

Globalization

Social media are used across cultures, but the specific sites that rank highest differ by country and region. Search the Web for usage statistics for social networking sites. For example, Alexa (*www.alexa.com/topsites/countries*) provides data that ranks Web sites by country. What are the most popular services in the United States, England, and Australia? Which services are most popular in Japan, China, South Korea, and India? Can you find the services that are most popular in Russia and in Middle Eastern countries? What about African countries, such as Botswana and Kenya? Are similar services popular in Mexico, Brazil, and Colombia? Based on the information you find, what can you conclude about social media usage differences around the world? Gather statistics and create a graph to support your conclusions.

Key Terms

@mention 339
@username 339
#hashtag 339
asynchronous 345
binary adjacency matrix 322
blog 335
blogging platform 336
blogosphere 336
bulletin board systems 326
cell tower triangulation 320
content aggregator 336
content communities 325
copyleft 332
copyright 330
Creative Commons license 331
crowdsourcing 319
cyberbullying 357
defamation 357
derivative work 333
DM 339
doppelgangers 357
editorial newsletter platforms 337
email 346
email message 346
email server 346
email system 346
fair use 333
follow 339
follow back 339
follower 339

formal tagging 328
generic profile image 356
geocoding 320
geosocial networking 319
geotagging 320
GPS trilateration 320
hotspot triangulation 320
IMAP (Internet Message Access
   Protocol) 348
impersonation 357
instant messaging (IM) 351
intellectual property 329
IP address lookup 320
local email 348
message header 346
metadata tag 328
microblogging service 338
NOR 340
NPOV 340
one-way edges 321
online identity 317
online reputation 357
online services 316
personally identifiable information
   (PII) 360
POP3 (Post Office Protocol
   version 3) 348
privacy 360
privacy policy 360
promoted tweet 339

public domain 330
retweet 339
SMTP (Simple Mail
   Transfer Protocol) 348
social discovery 319
social media 313
Social Media Honeycomb 313
social media profile 317
social networking service 316
sociogram edges 321
sociogram nodes 321
sociograms 321
sockpuppets 355
store-and-forward 348
synchronous 345
tagline 356
trademark 329
transformative work 333
trending 339
tweets 338
Twitter stream/timeline 339
two-way edges 321
V 340
viral 326
VoIP (Voice over Internet
   Protocol) 352
Webmail 347
wiki 340

Interactive Summary

Section A: Social media are online services that facilitate communication and [   ] among people who want to share information about their lives, issues, and events. Social media can be characterized using the Social Media [   ], which contains elements such as identity and presence. Social networking is a type of social media that revolves around personal [   ] and interconnections among contacts, friends, and followers. Social networks evolved from online [   ] such as CompuServe and America Online. A person's presence on a social media service is referred to as an online identity. [   ] networking services provide a platform for users to carry out interactions based on their current locations. Many of these services incorporate [   ] features for reviews and ratings. User locations can be determined by [   ] trilateration, cell tower triangulation, hotspot triangulation, and IP address lookup. Destination locations are identified by [   ] or geocoding. Social networks can be mapped using tools such as [   ] that depict relationships as nodes and edges. Another useful tool called an adjacency [   ] depicts social relationships in table format.

Section B: Content communities are social media sites that focus on sharing user-[   ] content. These communities originated as pre-Internet [   ] board systems. Media content communities specialize in images, videos, animations, and audio rather than text-based content. The technological core of content communities is server-based content [   ] software and an associated database. Once media are posted to a server, they may remain in the database indefinitely. To facilitate indexing, identification, and searching, content can be assigned [   ] tags. Media elements are the [   ] property of their creators. Some media, such as corporate logos, are protected by [   ], but most of the media at content communities are protected by copyright. Copyright is a form of legal protection that grants the author of an original work a(n) [   ] right to copy, distribute, sell, and modify that work. A copyright holder can forfeit the copyright and place the work in the public [   ]. A copyright holder can also choose to license the work. A Creative [   ] license allows a work to be used by others under specified conditions that include attribution (BY), [   ] (SA), no derivatives (ND), and noncommercial (NC). A(n) [   ] work modifies a copyrighted work but does not substantially change its content or purpose. A(n) [   ] work repackages a work to add new meaning or produce a work that is used for a purpose different from the original work.

Section C:

Text-based content communities form around blogging and wiki platforms. A(n) [_____] created on a platform such as WordPress or Medium contains a series of entries on one or more topics and may include photos or other media. Subscription services make it easy to follow specific blogs. The information published on blogs may not be as reliable as mainstream information sources. [_____] services, such as Twitter, offer a platform for messages similar to those in blogs but with limited length. Tweets, for example, are limited to 280 characters. Twitter jargon has infiltrated into other social media platforms. For example, the [_____]

symbol is universally used to identify and tag topics, whereas the [_____] symbol is used to indicate user names in mentions and replies. A(n) [_____] is a collaborative Web application that provides tools that contributors can use to post, read, and modify content. The best-known example is Wikipedia, an online [_____] that can be accessed, viewed, and edited anonymously by the general public. To maintain quality standards, Wikipedia is supervised by volunteer editors who encourage [_____] point of view, no original research, and verifiability.

Section D:

Online communications tools can be classified as [_____], in which all parties are online at the same time, and [_____], in which messages are held until the recipient is ready to view them. Communication can also be characterized as public or private. Email is a communication service provided by email servers that provide an electronic [_____] for each subscriber, sort incoming messages, and route outgoing messages to recipients. [_____] is a type of email service that stores messages on a server and requires a browser to access those messages. Using a browser to access mail is handy, but doing so may pose security risks when mail is accessed from public computers. Local email is a store-and-[_____] technology that

holds messages on a server until they are downloaded by email client software such as Microsoft Outlook. Local mail uses IMAP or [_____] protocols to manage incoming mail and [_____] to manage outgoing mail. Mobile email apps use a locally installed client to temporarily download messages to the local device and use [_____] protocols to synchronize the local and server-based mailboxes. Local mail and Webmail can be used interchangeably when appropriate forwarding settings are enabled. Synchronous text-based communication characterizes instant [_____] and online chat. Synchronous voice and video communications are handled by [_____] technologies on platforms such as Skype, Google Hangouts, Zoom, and FaceTime.

Section E:

An online [_____] is a collection of elements that reflect an individual's self-perception. The core of that identity is an online [_____] that commonly consists of a user name, image, and short biographical tagline. The use of [_____] as user names is widespread, though it is banned on some social media sites. An online [_____] is the impression that is generated by an online persona. It relates to the way that others perceive an online identity. Factors such as mistakes, defamation, cyberbullying, impersonation, and the existence of doppelgangers have the potential to damage an online reputation. Best practices for

monitoring and managing online reputations include setting up Google [_____], removing detrimental posts and photos, creating separate personal and professional sites, and maintaining civil discourse. [_____] is freedom from intrusive surveillance and the expectation that individuals can control their personally [_____] information. Most social media services provide settings that can limit the extent to which personal information is disseminated. There are six types of social media data: service, [_____], entrusted, incidental, behavioral, and derived.

Interactive Situation Questions

1. Your friend complains that a lot of her Facebook friend requests are refused. To help her find out why, the first step is to check her [ ] and make sure she's replaced the generic photo with one of her own.

2. When you prefer not to be tracked by a geosocial networking app, use the [ ] services setting to turn off the tracking feature for the app.

3. If you want your social media contacts to know when they are included in photos that you've posted, you can add their names to the photo [ ].

4. You've found the perfect photo on Flickr to include in a paper you're writing about recycling. The photo has a CC BY-ND license, which means that you can use the photo if you credit the photographer, but you cannot make [ ].

5. Your friend wants to create a [ ], so you recommend a platform such as WordPress or Wix.

6. You're composing a tweet about politics and Barack Obama. To include a mention of Obama's name in the tweet, you need to use a(n) [ ] symbol.

7. The Wikipedia article about the Tea Party movement contains a statement that doesn't seem correct. To find the origin of the statement, you might use the [ ] tab.

8. Suppose that you have a local email account, but you want to switch to Webmail. You're worried that some people might continue to use your old email address, so you set up mail [ ] from your local account to your Webmail account.

9. When it's time to look for your next job, having a good online reputation will be important. To keep tabs on information that might pertain to your online identity, you set up a Google [ ].

10. When registering to use a new social media site, you hesitate because it collects [ ] data including your name, phone number, and Apple account ID.

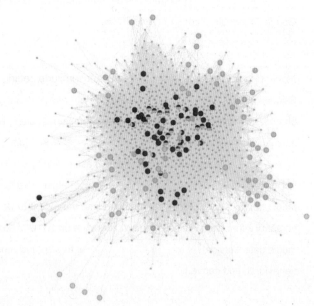

Facebook friends network graphed using Wolfram|Alpha Facebook Report

Lab: Social Network Analysis

Social analytics rock. They provide statistics about friends and contacts, connections, and links. They are used for contact tracing, literary analysis, and business analytics. Professor Robin Banerjee and colleagues at the University of Sussex developed an analytical tool for understanding patterns of acceptance and rejection among student groups.

Requirements:

For this lab, you'll need a computer with access to the Internet.

Assignment:

1 Connect to the Web site for Robin Banerjee's Sociogram Tools. Follow the link for "Sociogram Creator."

code	name	ml1	ml2	ml3	ll1	ll2	ll3
1	Jack						
3	Sonia						
4	Mei						
5	Dakota						
6	Shakir						
7	Eloise						
8	Fatima						

ENTER DATA   NOMINATION COUNTS   SOCIOGRAM   HELP

GET ANALYSIS

Source: Robin Banerjee, *https://users.sussex.ac.uk/~robinb/socio.html.*

2 Use the matrix to enter 1 as the code for a student named Jack.

3 Enter the codes and names of the remaining seven students.

4 In the matrix, the headings ml1, ml2, and ml3 refer to the individuals that each student most likes. The headings ll1, ll2, and ll3 refer to the individuals that each student least likes. Jack most likes Eloise, whose code number is 7. Enter 7 in the ml1 column in Jack's row.

5 Complete the matrix as shown below.

ENTER DATA   NOMINATION COUNTS   SOCIOGRAM   HELP

GET ANALYSIS

code	name	ml1	ml2	ml3	ll1	ll2	ll3
1	Jack	7	5	4	3	2	6
3	Sonia	5	7	4	2	1	6
4	Mei	7	2	3	8	5	6
5	Dakota	7	4	3	2	1	6
6	Shakir	7	4	3	1	2	5
7	Eloise	6	2	3	1	4	5
8	Fatima	7	4	3	1	2	6

Source: Robin Banerjee, *https://users.sussex.ac.uk/~robinb/socio.html.*

6 Who do you think is the most popular student? The least popular? To find out, select the GET ANALYSIS button to view the sociogram.

7 Notice how the color coding indicates the most popular, rejected, and ignored students. Drag the ovals to position the most popular student in the center of the sociogram. Download the image and save it.

8 Use the matrix to create a sociogram for a group of real or fictional students. Download and save your final sociogram and write a short paragraph explaining what it indicates about the social interactions within the group.

Optional: Your instructor might specify that you create a sociometric survey to collect actual data for a sociogram. Your survey might collect data about friends, students, celebrities, or historic figures. The survey would consist of two questions:

Which three people would you most like to associate with?

Which three people would you least like to associate with?

6

Software

In the digital world, anything that is not hardware is software. The realm of software "stuff" includes apps, applications, operating systems, and files. Module 6 explores these diverse software elements.

● Try It! Apply what you learn.

- Determine if a software app or application can run on a specific digital device.
- Understand the terms of a software license before accepting them.
- Identify the operating system that is installed on a digital device.
- Identify the key desktop elements in Windows, macOS, iOS, Android, and Chrome OS.
- Use a computer that has one or more virtual machines.
- Access and use Web apps.
- Find, download, and install mobile apps.
- Download and install local applications on PCs.
- Download and install local applications on Macs.
- Uninstall software.
- Use features of word processing software to enter text, improve your writing, and produce appropriately formatted output.
- Use spreadsheet software to create what-if analyses using formulas, functions, and relative or absolute references.
- Identify fields and records in a database table.
- Create a basic presentation that includes speaker notes.
- Select valid and meaningful names for files.
- Identify storage devices based on their names or device letters.
- Follow best practices for file management by organizing files into a sensible structure of folders.
- Send files to the trash, permanently delete them, and shred them.

● Pre-Check

Gauge your level of expertise. The answers are in the module.

The operating system _____ remains in RAM while a device is in use.

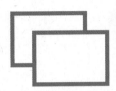

Two or more applications running simultaneously is an example of _____ .

Chrome OS is an example of a(n) _____ client.

A computer running more than one operating system is using a(n) _____ machine.

Software downloads for Macs are packaged as _____ files.

$B$6

In a spreadsheet, this is a(n) _____ reference.

| 1 | 2 | 3 | 4 | 5 |

What is the maximum length of a file name in macOS or Windows?

_____

C:

In Windows, this is the prompt for the _____ directory.

Name two file management utilities.

_____

_____

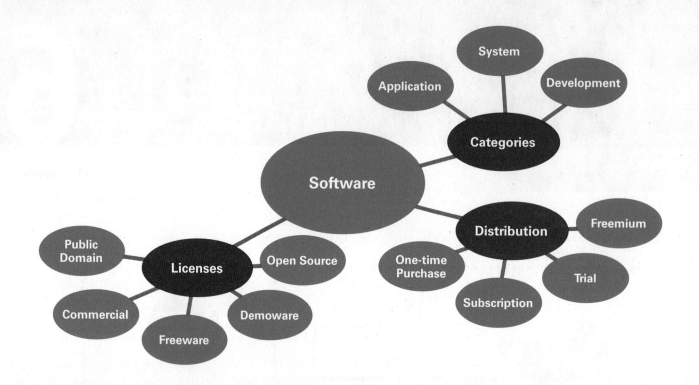

Software Basics

Objectives

▶ Draw a hierarchical diagram that illustrates the three main categories of software and their subcategories.

▶ List the software that is considered essential for desktop, laptop, and mobile devices.

▶ Distinguish between software updates and upgrades.

▶ List five pricing models commonly used in the software industry.

▶ Explain why most software is licensed.

▶ Describe the difference between proprietary software and public domain software.

▶ Describe three types of commercial software licenses.

▶ Identify the key differences in licenses for freeware, demoware, and open source software.

▶ Name two popular open source software licenses.

▶ List four ways to avoid fake mobile apps.

You never actually buy software. Instead, you receive a license to use it. So how does that work? Section A begins with an overview of software essentials, and then it focuses on the way software is distributed and licensed.

Terminology

executable file	EULAs	site license	hash value
system requirements	public domain software	multiple-user license	open source software
software upgrade	proprietary software	freeware	BSD license
software update	commercial software	demoware	GPL
software license	single-user license	product activation	pirated software

Essentials

In the broadest meaning of the term, *software* refers to all the nonhardware components of a digital device. Those components include data files as well as files that contain program code. In common use, however, the term *software* is used for computer programs, such as operating systems, applications, and apps. Let's begin by looking at the software products that give digital devices such a diverse repertoire of functions.

▶ **What are the main software categories?** There are millions of software titles. When searching through this overabundance of choices for new software, it helps to have a framework of categories, such as the one in Figure 6-1.

6

Figure 6-1: Software categories

System Software

Operating Systems

For controlling a digital device's internal operations

Windows macOS iOS Linux Android UNIX Chrome OS

Device Drivers

For digital devices to communicate with each other

Printer Drivers
Video Drivers

Utilities

For file management, security, communications, backup, network management, and system monitoring

Development Software

Programming Languages

For writing programs

C Basic Java Fortran C++ C# Scheme Objective-C Python

Scripting Languages

For writing scripts, creating Web pages, and querying databases

HTML JavaScript PHP Python Ruby SQL

Quality Assurance Tools

For testing software

Debuggers
Load Testing
Security Testing

Application Software

Professional Tools

For automating professional activities at work and in the home office

Desktop Publishing Graphic Design Special Effects

Educational Software

For students and teachers engaged in the process of learning in classrooms and at a distance

Tutorials Courseware Learning Management Systems

Personal Finance Software

For managing bank accounts, preparing taxes, retirement planning, and other financial matters

Tax Preparation Banking Apps Loan Calculators

Entertainment Software

For accessing media and playing games

Ebook Readers
Games Media Players
Media Editors

Reference Software

For accessing information in specific topic areas

Travel Sports Medical Hobbies Lifestyle Maps News Weather Shopping

Social Media Software

For accessing and working with social media services, such as Facebook and WordPress

Social Analytics Dashboards Marketing

Business Software

For automating core business functions

Accounting
Inventory Management
Billing Databases
Point of Sale
Salesforce Management
Estimating

Productivity Software

For automating tasks formerly carried out with legacy technologies, such as pen and paper, typewriters, calculators, and slide projectors

Word Processors
Spreadsheets
Presentations
Calendars
Contact Managers

▶ **Are software categories universal?** No. There is no universal standard for categorizing software, but various categorization schemes have many similarities. For example, Google Play uses a different set of categories from Apple's App Store and Amazon, and yet there are similarities. Look for similarities and differences in the software categories shown for the online merchants in Figure 6-2.

Figure 6-2: Software categories are not standardized

amazon

Accounting & Finance

Antivirus & Security

Business & Office

Children's

Education & Reference

Lifestyle & Hobbies

Music

Networking & Servers

Operating Systems

Photography & Graphic Design

Programming & Web Development

Tax Preparation

Utilities

Video

 App Store

Business

Developer Tools

Education

Entertainment

Finance

Games

Graphics & Design

Health & Fitness

Lifestyle

Medical

Music

News

Photo & Video

Productivity

Reference

Safari Extensions

Social Networking

Sports

Travel

Utilities

Weather

Google play

Art & Design

Auto & Vehicles

Beauty

Books & Reference

Business

Comics

Communication

Dating

Education

Entertainment

Events

Finance

Food & Drink

Games

Health & Fitness

House & Home

Libraries & Demo

Lifestyle

Maps & Navigation

Medical

Music & Audio

News & Magazines

Parenting

Personalization

Photography

Productivity

Shopping

Social

Sports

Tools

Travel and Local

Video Players & Editors

Weather

▶ **What are the most essential applications for desktop and laptop computers?** Most digital devices come loaded with preinstalled applications. Some of these software applications are included because the software developer has made a deal with the device vendor; other applications are more essential.

Desktop and laptop computers require an operating system with a file manager that allows users to view and manipulate data files. A basic set of system utilities includes security and antivirus software, network management tools, a browser, and device drivers for the mouse, keyboard, display device, printer, and other peripheral devices. For application software, most desktop and laptop owners require an office suite containing productivity software for word processing, spreadsheet manipulation, slide show presentations, and scheduling.

▶ **What are the essential applications for mobile devices?** Mobile devices tend to be used somewhat differently from desktop and laptop computers, so the configuration of their software is slightly different.

Mobile devices require an operating system and utilities for adjusting system settings and accessing networks. Additional basic utilities include a browser, camera controls, and voice integration. Files tend to be stored and retrieved by each app, so users have little need for a utility that allows access to the file management system. Also, because mobile devices are used primarily to consume content rather than create it, an office suite is not at the top of the must-have list. Instead, mobile devices tend to be populated by entertainment apps, games, and social media services.

Figure 6-3 lists the core sets of software for desktops and laptops as well as for mobile devices.

6

QuickCheck

Which of the following would not be considered essential software for mobile devices, desktops, and laptops?

a. An operating system

b. An office suite

c. Network utilities

d. A browser

Figure 6-3: Essential applications

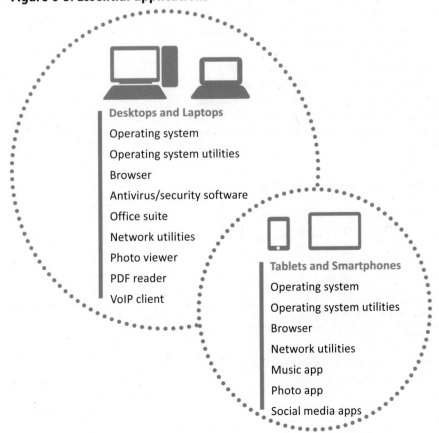

Desktops and Laptops

Operating system

Operating system utilities

Browser

Antivirus/security software

Office suite

Network utilities

Photo viewer

PDF reader

VoIP client

Tablets and Smartphones

Operating system

Operating system utilities

Browser

Network utilities

Music app

Photo app

Social media apps

Distribution

Although there are offline sources for software, most consumers obtain software online, where it can be downloaded directly from the developer or from a software aggregator, such as an app store.

▶ **What are the components of a typical software application?** A software application may contain a single executable file or it may be composed of many separate files that work together. An **executable file** contains a computer program that is carried out step by step within the microprocessor. Executable files designed for PCs usually have an .exe file name extension, whereas executable files for Macs have .app extensions.

To prepare software for distribution, the distribution files are usually "zipped" or packaged into a single unit that can be easily downloaded over the Internet.

▶ **What are the best sources for software?** Software can contain viruses and other malware, so consumers should download new applications only from trusted sources. Although there is never a guarantee that an application is malware-free, the major app stores, such as Google Play and the Apple App Store, have policies in place that discourage harmful programming. Checking user comments and ratings at these sites is always a good practice that can help consumers avoid downloading risky apps and those that are not well designed.

Software download sites, such as CNET Downloads and FileHippo, offer applications from multiple developers. The focus of these software outlets is applications for desktop and laptop computers. A Google search for *free software* yields many sites, but be careful. Some of these sites are riddled with ads and spyware that will infect your device even if you do not download anything.

Software developers usually have a Web site for distributing software. Well-established developers tend to offer trustworthy products. Be careful when dealing with smaller vendors. Always confirm that payment transactions are processed over a secure HTTPS connection, and consider using PayPal rather than a credit card if you doubt the integrity of the site operators.

▶ **How important are system requirements?** **System requirements** specify the operating system and minimum hardware capacities necessary for a software product to work correctly. These requirements are listed at the download site and are worth reviewing. They will help you to determine if the software is compatible with your device and how much storage space it requires (Figure 6-4).

QuickCheck

Which of the following is not an executable file?

a. *Notepad.exe*

b. *Textedit.app*

c. *Spreadsheet.dat*

d. *Virus.exe*

Figure 6-4: Review system requirements before downloading

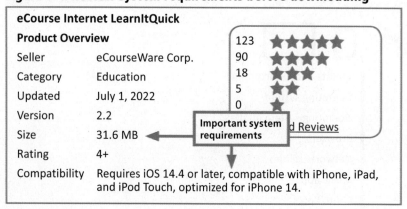

▶ What payment options are available? Software can be obtained under a variety of pricing models. The availability of one or more of these pricing plans depends on the software vendor.

Free. Some software and apps are free to use without payment. Users of free products might be subjected to ads or in-app purchases, however.

One-time payment. Some software can be obtained through a one-time payment in which the consumer pays a set amount to license and use the software without an expiration date. The advantage of the one-time payment model is that there are no additional fees, and with the exception of a few updates, the software remains basically the same as when it was initially installed. There are no surprise changes to the way the software looks or works during its lifetime.

Subscription. The subscription pricing model is an established distribution method in which consumers pay a monthly or annual fee to use the software. Consumers benefit because updates and upgrades are usually included in the pricing. Consumers must remain alert while using subscription services. When a subscription lapses, the software may cease to function. Some vendors allow former customers to launch the software and view files but do not allow those files to be further modified. Credit card information is stored on the vendor's site and may be vulnerable to hacking.

Trial. A third type of pricing model offers consumers the use of a software product during a free trial period. The trial version may be fully functional or it may be limited in functionality. When the trial period ends, a one-time payment or paid subscription is required. This pricing model is common for software applications, such as antivirus utilities and productivity applications, that are preinstalled on new devices.

Freemium. Another popular pricing model for software provides free use of a stripped-down or basic version of the product but requires payment for upgraded features (Figure 6-5).

Terminology

An *in-app purchase* refers to buying goods or services from inside a mobile app. These purchases could be for a clue in a game, for a subscription, or for extra content. In-app purchases allow developers to make a profit while distributing a basic app for free.

6

Figure 6-5: The freemium model

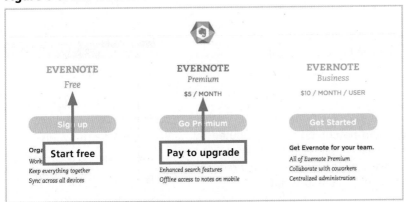

▶ What are updates and upgrades? Periodically, some software publishers release a new version or edition of a software product that is referred to as a **software upgrade**. An upgrade entirely replaces an older edition with a new one. Each edition carries a version number, such as 1.0 or 2.0. Upgrading software obtained with a one-time payment may involve a fee.

A **software update** (sometimes called a software patch) is a small section of program code that replaces part of the software currently installed. Updates are designed to correct problems and address security vulnerabilities. They are distinguished by revision numbers to the right of the decimal, such as 2.101. Software updates are usually free.

Try It!

Visit Microsoft's Web site to find out which pricing models are available for Microsoft Office.

Software Licenses

Obtaining software is not the same as buying tangible goods, such as mittens, chairs, and shoes, that can be bought outright by consumers. Once they've been purchased, tangible goods can be used, altered, loaned to friends, resold, or given away. In contrast, a software "purchase" is actually a license agreement that may include certain restrictions. Some licenses are less restrictive than others, so their terms are factors to consider when selecting software.

▶ **Why is software licensed?** A **software license**, or license agreement, is a legal contract that defines the ways in which a computer program may be used. These licenses are sometimes referred to as **EULAs** (End User License Agreements). The reason software is licensed has to do with copyrights.

Like books and movies, software is a type of intellectual property. Software copyrights protect the rights of the person or corporation that developed the intellectual property. Most software displays a copyright notice, such as © *2023 eCourse Corporation*, on one of its screens. This notice is not required by law, however, so programs without a copyright notice are still protected by copyright law.

A copyright grants the author of a software product an exclusive right to copy, distribute, sell, and modify that work. Purchasers do not have this right except under the circumstances listed in Figure 6-6.

Figure 6-6: When can software be legally copied?

 DOWNLOAD   The purchaser has the right to copy software from distribution media or a Web site to a device's internal storage medium in order to install it.

 BACKUP   The purchaser can make an extra, or backup, copy of the software in case the original copy becomes erased or damaged—unless the process of making the backup requires the purchaser to defeat a copy protection mechanism designed to prohibit copying.

 EDUCATION   The purchaser is allowed to copy and distribute sections of a software program for use in critical reviews and teaching.

Without copyright protection, software would be copied and distributed by unauthorized parties without compensation to its authors. Although that situation might sound like it benefits consumers, it discourages innovation and reduces the incentives for technical support and upgrades in the long run.

Copyright protects a software product by imposing a set of restrictions on its use. The copyright holder may want to add or remove some of those restrictions, and a software license provides the means to do so.

6

▶ **Where can I find the license for a software product?** Most legal contracts require signatures before the terms of the contract can take effect. This requirement becomes hard to manage with software—imagine having to sign a license agreement and return it before you can use a new app. To circumvent the signature requirement, software publishers use screen-based license agreements.

License agreements are displayed during the installation process. By clicking the I Agree button, you consent to the terms of the license agreement (Figure 6-7).

Figure 6-7: Viewing the license agreement

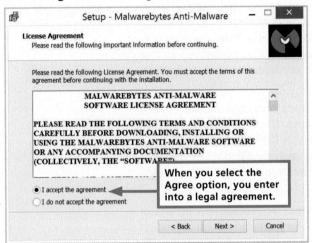

▶ **What are the most common types of software licenses?** From a legal perspective, there are two categories of software: public domain and proprietary. **Public domain software** is not protected by copyright because the copyright has expired or the author has placed the program in the public domain, making it available without restriction. Public domain software may be freely copied, distributed, and even resold. The primary restriction on public domain software is that you are not allowed to apply for a copyright on it.

Proprietary software has restrictions on its use that are delineated by copyright, patents, or license agreements. Some proprietary software is distributed commercially, whereas some of it is free. Based on licensing rights, proprietary software is distributed as commercial software, freeware, demoware, or open source software.

▶ **What is commercial software?** **Commercial software** is usually distributed from the software publisher's Web site or from an app store. Most licenses for commercial software adhere closely to the limitations provided by copyright law, although they might permit the software to be installed on multiple devices. A further restriction could permit the software to be used on only one device at a time.

Most commercial software is distributed under a **single-user license** that limits use to one person at a time. However, some software publishers offer volume licenses, such as site licenses and multiple-user licenses, to households, schools, organizations, and businesses.

A **site license** is generally priced at a flat rate and allows software to be used on all computers at a specific location. A **multiple-user license** is priced per copy and allows the allocated number of copies to be used simultaneously.

▶ What about freeware? Freeware is copyrighted software that—as you might expect—is available for free. It is fully functional and requires no payment for its use. A freeware license permits you to use the software, copy it, and give it away, but the license does not permit you to alter or sell the software. Many utility programs, most device drivers, many mobile apps, and some games are available as freeware.

▶ What is demoware? Some proprietary software is available as a trial version, sometimes called demoware. Demoware is distributed for free and often comes preinstalled on new devices, but it is limited in some way until you pay for it.

Demoware publishers can use a variety of techniques to limit the use of the software. It might remain functional for a set number of days before expiring and requiring payment. It might run for a limited amount of time—for example, 60 minutes—each time you launch it. Demoware could be configured so that you can run it only a limited number of times. Or key features, such as printing, might be disabled.

Demoware publishers usually take steps to prevent users from uninstalling and reinstalling the demo to circumvent time limitations. Users who want to unlock the full version of a demo can do so by following links to the software publisher's Web site and using a credit card to purchase an activation code. The software can then be restarted and used without further interruption after the activation code is entered.

▶ How do activation codes work? Product activation is a means of protecting software from illegal copying by requiring users to enter a product key or an activation code before the software can be used. Activation is usually part of the software installation process, but it can also occur when demoware times out. Failure to enter a valid code prohibits the program from launching. A software publisher can validate a user's activation code by checking it against an online database or a hash value.

Checking an activation code against an online database ensures that the code you've entered has not been used before. If the code is a duplicate, then the license for that copy of the software is being used by someone else and you will have to call customer service to straighten out the problem.

A hash value is a unique number derived from encoding one or more data sets, such as names, serial numbers, and validation codes. Product validation can create a hash value based on your validation code and your device's internal serial number, effectively tying the software and its use to one specific device.

◗ What is open source software? Open source software makes uncompiled program instructions—the source code—available to programmers who want to modify and improve the software. Open source software may be distributed free of charge or for payment in a compiled form, but it must always include the source code.

Linux is an example of open source software, as are programs such as Blender and FileZilla. LibreOffice—a full-featured productivity suite—is another popular example of open source software. You can search for open source applications at the SourceForge Web site.

Despite the lack of restrictions on distribution and use, open source software is copyrighted and is not in the public domain. It is not the same as freeware, which you are not supposed to modify or resell.

Two of the most common open source and free software licenses are BSD and GPL. The **BSD license** originated as the Berkeley Software Distribution license for a server operating system (Figure 6-8).

Figure 6-8: The BSD license

Copyright (c) 2022, [Publisher] All rights reserved.

Redistribution and use in source and binary forms, with or without modification, are permitted provided that the following conditions are met:

- Redistributions of source code must retain the above copyright notice, this list of conditions, and the following disclaimer.

- Redistributions in binary form must reproduce the above copyright notice, this list of conditions, and the following disclaimer in the documentation and/or other materials provided with the distribution.

- Neither the name of the Publisher nor the names of its contributors may be used to endorse or promote products derived from this software without specific prior written permission.

THIS SOFTWARE IS PROVIDED BY THE PUBLISHER AND CONTRIBUTORS "AS IS" AND ANY EXPRESS OR IMPLIED WARRANTIES, INCLUDING, BUT NOT LIMITED TO, THE IMPLIED WARRANTIES OF MERCHANTABILITY AND FITNESS FOR A PARTICULAR PURPOSE ARE DISCLAIMED. IN NO EVENT SHALL THE PUBLISHER AND CONTRIBUTORS BE LIABLE FOR ANY DIRECT, INDIRECT, INCIDENTAL, SPECIAL, EXEMPLARY, OR CONSEQUENTIAL DAMAGES (INCLUDING, BUT NOT LIMITED TO, PROCUREMENT OF SUBSTITUTE GOODS OR SERVICES; LOSS OF USE, DATA, OR PROFITS; OR BUSINESS INTERRUPTION) HOWEVER CAUSED AND ON ANY THEORY OF LIABILITY, WHETHER IN CONTRACT, STRICT LIABILITY, OR TORT (INCLUDING NEGLIGENCE OR OTHERWISE) ARISING IN ANY WAY OUT OF THE USE OF THIS SOFTWARE, EVEN IF ADVISED OF THE POSSIBILITY OF SUCH DAMAGE.

QuickCheck

The first clause of the BSD license permits what?

a. Breaking copy protection

b. Distributing the source code

c. Pirating

d. Modifying the copyright

◗ What is unique about GPL licenses? The **GPL** (General Public License) was developed for a free operating system called GNU. The GPL is slightly more restrictive than the BSD license because it requires derivative works to be licensed. That means if you get a really cool computer game that's licensed under a GPL and you modify the game to create a new level, you have to distribute your modification under the GPL. You cannot legally market your modification under a commercial software license. There are currently three versions of the GPL. Their differences are of interest primarily to software developers.

▶ When I accept a software license, what am I agreeing to?

Software licenses are often lengthy and written in legalese, but your legal right to use the software continues only as long as you abide by the terms of the software license. Therefore, you should understand the software license for any software you use (Figure 6-9).

Figure 6-9: Elements of a software license

Software License Agreement

Important - Read Carefully: This License Agreement ("Agreement") is a legal agreement between you and eCourse Corporation for the software product, eCourse GraphWare ("The SOFTWARE"). By installing, copying, or otherwise using the SOFTWARE, you agree to be bound by the terms of this Agreement. The SOFTWARE is protected by copyright laws and international copyright treaties. The SOFTWARE is licensed, not sold.

Grant of License. This Agreement gives you the right to install and use one copy of the SOFTWARE on a single digital device. The primary user of the device on which the SOFTWARE is installed may make a second copy for use on a portable device.

Other Rights and Limitations. You may not reverse engineer, decompile, or disassemble the SOFTWARE except and only to the extent that such activity is expressly permitted by applicable law.

The SOFTWARE is licensed as a single product; its components may not be separated for use on more than one device. You may not rent, lease, or lend the SOFTWARE.

You may permanently transfer all of your rights under this Agreement, provided you retain no copies, you transfer all of the SOFTWARE, and the recipient agrees to the terms of this Agreement. If the software product is an upgrade, any transfer must include all prior versions of the SOFTWARE.

You may receive the SOFTWARE in more than one medium. Regardless of the type of medium you receive, you may use only one medium that is appropriate for your single device. You may not use or install the other medium on another device.

Warranty. eCourse warrants that the SOFTWARE will perform substantially in accordance with the accompanying written documentation for a period of ninety (90) days from the date of receipt. TO THE MAXIMUM EXTENT PERMITTED BY APPLICABLE LAW, eCourse AND ITS SUPPLIERS DISCLAIM ALL OTHER WARRANTIES AND CONDITIONS EITHER EXPRESS OR IMPLIED, INCLUDING, BUT NOT LIMITED TO, IMPLIED WARRANTIES OF MERCHANTABILITY, FITNESS FOR A PARTICULAR PURPOSE, TITLE, AND NON-INFRINGEMENT, WITH REGARD TO THE SOFTWARE PRODUCT.

Try It!

Read the EULA in Figure 6-9 and answer the following questions:

Is the consumer buying the software or licensing it?

When does the license go into effect?

Under what circumstances is it legal to make copies?

Is it permissible to loan the software?

Is it permissible to sell the software?

Does the software publisher provide a warranty?

Fake and Pirated Software

Not all software is legitimate. *New York Times* investigators discovered hundreds of fake shopping apps in Apple's App Store, and similar apps lurk in the Google Play Store. Illegal copies of software are also sold. Consumers should be cautious when selecting apps to make sure they are legitimate.

▶ **What is a fake app?** Fake apps masquerade as something they are not. For example, the Overstock Inc app is designed to fool consumers who are looking for the Overstock.com app. Fake apps may steal passwords, spread malware, and access personal social media data. Here are some tips to help you avoid fake apps:

- Carefully compare the name of the app publisher with the company that produces the company's legitimate Web site.

- Check reviews of the app. Legitimate apps have hundreds of reviews, and most of them should be favorable.

- Watch for spelling and grammar errors in the description of the app. Most fake apps are not professionally reviewed for spelling and grammar errors.

- Check the date. Apps for established companies rarely have recent publication dates, though they may have recent "updated on" dates.

▶ **What's the problem with illegal copies?** Software that is illegally copied and sold is referred to as **pirated software**. It is not always easy to identify pirated software. Some unsuspecting consumers have inadvertently obtained pirated software, even when paying full price from a reputable source. Pirated software may not update properly and is not eligible for authenticated upgrades. The following characteristics could be signs of pirated software:

- Software sold at Web sites for prices well below retail

- Commercial software offered as a free download from a third-party Web site or Tor server

- Software sold in a clear CD-ROM jewel case with no accompanying documentation, license, registration card, or Certificate of Authenticity

- Software marked as "Academic" that requires no proof of eligibility

- Software marked as "OEM" or "For Distribution Only with New PC Hardware"

QuickQuiz   Section A

1. Device drivers and utilities are classified as [_____] software.

2. Most executable files for a PC have a(n) .[_____] extension, whereas executable files for Macs have an .app extension.

3. Software is a type of [_____] property and is therefore protected by copyright.

4. The [_____] pricing model provides free use of a basic version of the product, but upgraded features require payment.

5. A hash value can be created during the [_____] process to tie a software product to a specific device.

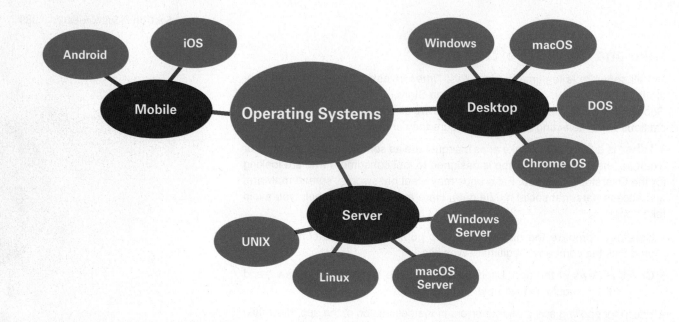

Objectives

▶ Describe three categories of operating systems.

▶ Explain the purpose of an operating system kernel.

▶ Name the operating system kernels that were used to develop Windows and macOS.

▶ List five digital device resources that are managed by the operating system.

▶ Define the terms *multitasking*, *multiprocessing*, and *multithreading*.

▶ Explain how memory leaks develop and why they are a problem.

▶ Give an example of a buffer that is managed by the operating system.

▶ Summarize the strengths and weaknesses of the Windows operating system.

▶ Summarize the strengths and weaknesses of macOS.

▶ List three ways in which iOS and Android are the same and two ways in which they differ.

▶ Explain why Chrome OS is considered a thin client.

▶ Give an example of a situation in which Linux would be a desirable operating system.

▶ Provide an example of a situation that would benefit from the use of a virtual machine.

An operating system is an integral part of
virtually every digital device. It fundamentally affects how you can use a desktop, laptop, tablet, or smartphone. Can you run two programs at the same time? Can you connect the device to a network? Does the device run dependably? Does it accept touch input? To answer questions like these, it is helpful to have a clear idea about what an operating system is and what it does.

Terminology

user interface	resource	Microsoft Windows	forked
desktop operating system	processes	DOS	thin client
mobile operating systems	multitasking	macOS	Linux distribution
	multithreading	iOS	virtual machine
server operating system	multiprocessing	Android	
kernel	memory leak	Chrome OS	
	buffers	Linux	

Operating System Basics

An operating system gives your digital device a personality. It controls key elements of the **user interface**, which includes the visual experience as well as the keyboard, mouse, microphone, or touchscreen that collects user commands. Behind the scenes, the operating system is busy supervising critical operations that take place within a device.

▶ **Are there different categories of operating systems?** Consumers are familiar with operating systems such as Windows and iOS, but there are several others in widespread use. Operating systems can be categorized by the devices on which they are used (Figure 6-10).

6

Figure 6-10: Operating system categories

Desktop operating systems. A **desktop operating system** is designed for a desktop or laptop computer. The computer you use at home, at school, or at work is most likely configured with a desktop operating system, such as Microsoft Windows, macOS, or Chrome OS. Key characteristics of desktop operating systems include the following:

● Accommodate one user at a time, but allow multiple accounts

● Provide local area networking capability

● Include file management tools

● Run more than one application at a time

● Offer a graphical user interface designed for keyboard, mouse, and optional touchscreen or voice input

Mobile operating systems. Operating systems such as iOS and Android are classified as **mobile operating systems** because they are designed for use on smartphones, tablet computers, and ebook readers. Key characteristics of mobile operating systems include the following:

● Accommodate one user at a time

● Provide connectivity to wireless local area networks

● Offer a graphical user interface designed for touchscreen input

● Support voice input

● Include integrated cellular communications

Server operating systems. Computers that are deployed as Web servers, or as servers for files, applications, databases, or email, generally use a **server operating system** designed for distributed networks accessed by many simultaneous users. Linux, UNIX, Windows Server, and macOS Server are examples of popular server operating systems with the following characteristics:

● Accommodate multiple simultaneous users

● Include sophisticated network management and security tools

● Provide a utilitarian user interface

▶ **Where is the operating system?** In some digital devices, such as smartphones and ebook readers, the entire operating system is small enough to be stored in ROM. For most other computers, the operating system program is quite large, so most of it is stored on a hard disk or SSD.

During the boot process, the operating system kernel is loaded into RAM. A **kernel** provides essential operating system services, such as memory management and file access. The kernel stays in RAM the entire time your computer is on. Other parts of the operating system, such as customization utilities, are loaded into RAM as they are needed.

QuickCheck

The operating system kernel provides essential services and remains _____ while the computer is on.

a. inactive

b. in RAM

c. off

d. mobile

▶ **What does an operating system do?** An operating system interacts with application software, device drivers, and hardware to manage a set of resources. In the context of digital devices, the term **resource** refers to any component that is required to perform work.

The processor is a device's main resource. RAM, storage space, and peripheral devices are also resources. While you interact with application software, the operating system is busy behind the scenes performing resource management tasks such as those listed in Figure 6-11.

Figure 6-11: Operating system resource management tasks

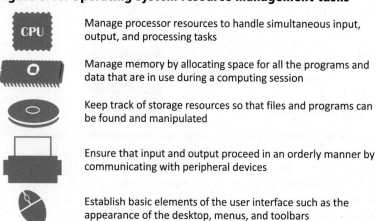

Manage processor resources to handle simultaneous input, output, and processing tasks

Manage memory by allocating space for all the programs and data that are in use during a computing session

Keep track of storage resources so that files and programs can be found and manipulated

Ensure that input and output proceed in an orderly manner by communicating with peripheral devices

Establish basic elements of the user interface such as the appearance of the desktop, menus, and toolbars

▶ **How do operating systems manage processor resources?** Every microprocessor cycle is a resource for accomplishing a task, such as executing a program instruction. Many activities—called **processes**—compete for the attention of a device's microprocessor. The microprocessor receives commands as software carries out tasks and while input arrives from the keyboard, mouse, and other devices. At the same time, data is being sent to output devices or over network connections.

To manage all these competing processes, an operating system must ensure that each process receives its share of attention from the microprocessor. You can check the processes that are being executed by using system utilities such as Task Manager (Figure 6-12).

Figure 6-12: View active processes

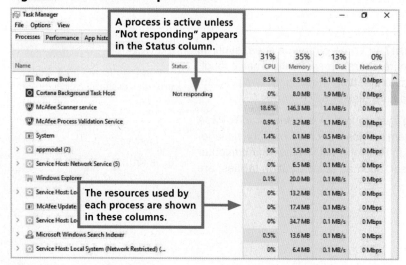

QuickCheck

In Figure 6-12, which process seems to be using the most memory resources?

a. Runtime Broker

b. McAfee Scanner service

c. Windows Explorer

d. Microsoft Windows Search Indexer

6

▶ **How do operating systems handle so many processes?** During a typical session, a laptop computer might run an average of 50 processes. Ideally, the operating system should be able to help the microprocessor switch seamlessly from one process to another. Depending on the capabilities of the operating system and computer hardware, processes can be managed by multitasking, multithreading, and multiprocessing.

Multitasking. Most of today's popular operating systems offer multitasking services. **Multitasking** provides process and memory management services that allow two or more tasks, jobs, or programs to run simultaneously.

Multithreading. Within a single program, **multithreading** allows multiple commands, or threads, to run simultaneously. For example, one thread for a spreadsheet program might be waiting for input from you, while other threads perform a long calculation in the background. Multithreading can speed up performance on single- or multiple-processor devices.

Multiprocessing. Many digital devices include multi-core processors or multiple processors. An operating system's **multiprocessing** capability supports a division of labor among all the processing units.

▶ **How does an operating system manage memory?** A microprocessor works with data and executes instructions stored in RAM—one of the most important resources for a digital device. When you want to run more than one application at a time, the operating system has to allocate specific areas of memory for each application.

Sometimes an application requests memory but never releases it—a condition called a **memory leak**. These leaks slowly drain available memory, eventually preventing other applications from accessing enough memory to function properly (Figure 6-13). Applications affected by memory leaks can crash, and the operating system might display error messages, such as "General Protection Fault" or "Program Not Responding." A device can sometimes recover from a memory leak if you access Task Manager (PC) or Activity Monitor (Mac) to close the non-responding application.

Figure 6-13: During a memory leak, a program overruns its memory space

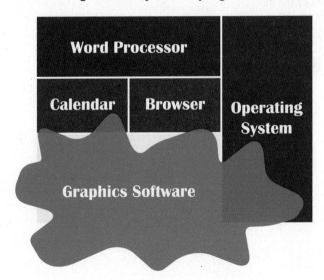

Word Processor

Calendar   Browser   Operating System

Graphics Software

▶ **How does the OS keep track of storage resources?** Behind the scenes, an operating system acts as a filing clerk that stores and retrieves files from various storage devices. It remembers the names and locations of all your files and keeps track of empty spaces where new files can be stored. Later in this module, you'll explore file storage in more depth and learn how the operating system affects the way you create, name, save, and retrieve files.

▶ **Why does the operating system get involved with peripheral devices?** Every peripheral device connected to a computer is regarded as an input or output resource. Your computer's operating system communicates with device driver software so that data can travel smoothly between the computer and peripheral resources. If a peripheral device or driver is not performing correctly, the operating system makes a decision about what to do—usually it displays an on-screen message to warn you of the problem.

An operating system ensures that input and output proceed in an orderly manner, using **buffers** to collect and hold data while the device is busy with other tasks. By using a keyboard buffer, for example, your computer never misses one of your keystrokes, regardless of how fast you type or what else is happening in your computer at the same time (Figure 6-14).

Try It!

Open any word processing software or email client and type as fast as you can. Can you type fast enough to overrun the keyboard buffer so that some of the characters you type are lost and not displayed on the screen?

Figure 6-14: How buffers work

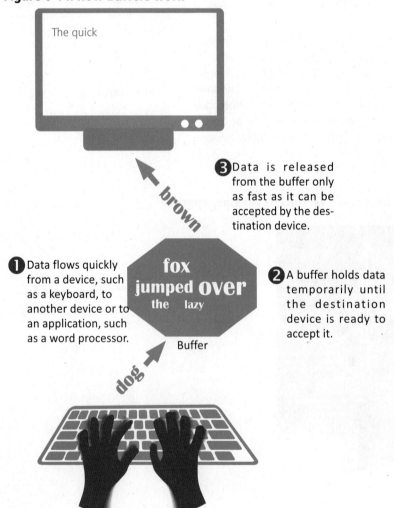

The quick

❸ Data is released from the buffer only as fast as it can be accepted by the destination device.

brown

❶ Data flows quickly from a device, such as a keyboard, to another device or to an application, such as a word processor.

fox jumped over the lazy

Buffer

❷ A buffer holds data temporarily until the destination device is ready to accept it.

dog

Microsoft Windows

Microsoft Windows is installed on about 75% of the world's personal computers. Its screen-based desktop is populated with colorful icons used to launch applications, connect to Web sites, and organize files.

❱ **Why "Windows"?** The Windows operating system got its name from the rectangular work areas displayed on its screen-based desktop. Each window can display a different document or application, which provides a visual model of the operating system's multitasking capabilities. Figure 6-15 illustrates the characteristics of the Windows desktop.

6

Figure 6-15: Windows 11 desktop elements

Try It!

Make sure that you can use the correct terminology to identify all of the elements on the Windows desktop.

❶ Desktop **icons** represent programs, folders, and data files.

❷ **Pinned icons** provide quick access to apps.

❸ An **application window** displays a program.

❹ Another application window displays a calculator.

❺ The Windows **Start button** opens the Start menu.

❻ The **Start menu** provides access to frequently used applications and utilities.

❼ Application icons are "pinned" to the taskbar.

❽ The desktop **taskbar** contains the Start button, pinned icons, and the notification area.

❾ The **notification area** displays status icons.

QuickCheck

How many application windows are displayed on the Windows desktop in Figure 6-15?

a. 1

b. 2

c. 3

d. 4

❱ What do I need to know about the evolution of Windows?

Windows evolved from a Microsoft operating system called **DOS** (Disk Operating System) that was designed to run on early PCs with Intel or Intel-compatible microprocessors.

To create Microsoft Windows, developers used the DOS kernel but added a point-and-click graphical user interface. DOS was eventually dropped in favor of the NT kernel. Since its introduction in 1985, Windows has evolved through several versions. Although Windows 11, shown on the previous page, was the most recent version when this book was published, you might encounter some older computers that run Windows 7, Windows 8, or Windows 10 (Figure 6-16).

Figure 6-16: Windows 7, 8, and 10

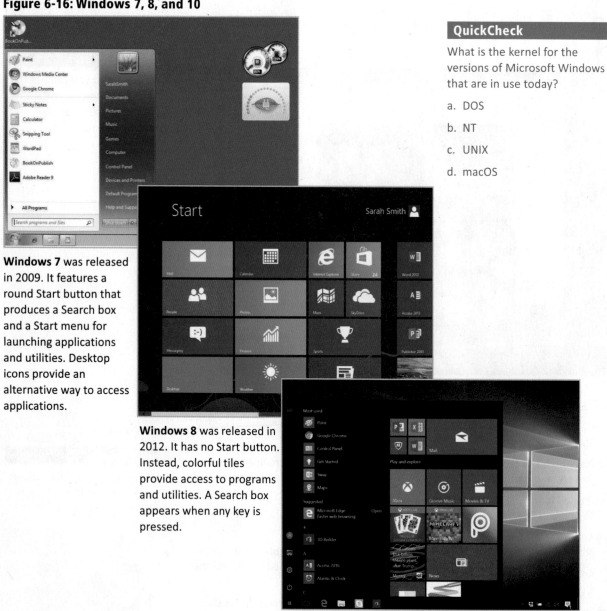

Windows 7 was released in 2009. It features a round Start button that produces a Search box and a Start menu for launching applications and utilities. Desktop icons provide an alternative way to access applications.

Windows 8 was released in 2012. It has no Start button. Instead, colorful tiles provide access to programs and utilities. A Search box appears when any key is pressed.

Windows 10 was released in 2015 after Microsoft decided to skip Windows 9. The Start button is again a prominent element of the taskbar. The desktop includes a Search box, a list of frequently used applications, and a set of tiles for accessing applications.

▶ **Does Windows run on tablets and phones, too?** Microsoft offers several editions of Windows. The Home edition is designed for desktop, laptop, and tablet computers. Windows Pro and Windows Enterprise offer built-in tools for power users and businesses, such as encrypting the data on local drives, accessing a computer remotely, and managing networks.

Microsoft does not offer an operating system for mobile phones. Windows 11 can, however, be installed on tablet computers that are equipped with a SIM slot for cellular calling (Figure 6-17).

Figure 6-17: Windows 11 on a tablet with SIM card for cellular calls

▶ **What are the strengths of Windows?** The number and variety of programs that run on Windows are unmatched by any other operating system. For the best selection of software, especially for games and business software, Windows is the operating system of choice.

The Windows user community is also a strength. Comprehensive tutorials and troubleshooting guides can be found online, including a vast array of YouTube instructional videos. Microsoft's official site, *www.microsoft.com*, includes thousands of pages of searchable information.

Windows runs on third-party hardware from vendors such as Dell and Lenovo. Shoppers have lots of options for configuring a Windows device that meets their needs.

▶ **What are Windows' weaknesses?** Windows has been criticized for two major weaknesses: reliability and security. The reliability of an operating system is usually gauged by the length of time it operates without glitches. Windows tends to become unstable with more frequency than other operating systems.

Slow system response, programs that stop working, and error messages can be symptoms of a Windows malfunction. Rebooting usually clears the error condition and returns a computer to normal functionality, but the time wasted shutting down and waiting for a reboot adds unnecessary frustration to the computing experience.

Of the major desktop operating systems, Windows has the reputation for being the most vulnerable to viruses, worms, and other attacks. One reason for Windows' vulnerability is its huge user base, which makes it the biggest target for hackers. Although Microsoft is diligent in its efforts to patch security holes, its programmers are often one step behind the hackers; while users wait for patches, their computers are vulnerable.

macOS

In 1984, Apple Inc. introduced a computer "for the rest of us," designed for nonbusiness, non-IBM-PC users. The first Macintosh computers featured a desktop dotted with graphical icons that could be launched by clicking a mouse. That desktop evolved into the macOS that powers today's Macs.

▶ **What's unique about macOS?** As a desktop operating system, **macOS** features beautifully designed icons and multiple rectangular work areas to reflect multitasking capabilities. Characteristic features of the Mac desktop are shown in Figure 6-18.

Figure 6-18: macOS desktop elements

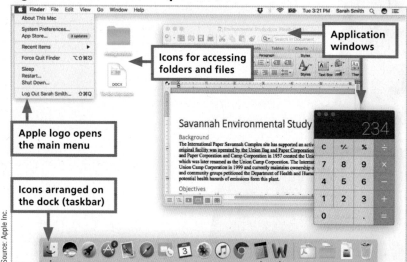

Application windows

Icons for accessing folders and files

Apple logo opens the main menu

Icons arranged on the dock (taskbar)

Source: Apple Inc.

▶ **What do I need to know about the evolution of macOS?** Like Windows, macOS has been through a number of revisions. The original Classic Mac OS was introduced in 1984 and designed for a line of Macintosh computers based on the Motorola 68000 microprocessor.

In 2001, Classic Mac OS was rewritten to run on Macintosh computers containing PowerPC microprocessors produced by IBM. The new Mac OS was designated Mac OS X. It was commonly called Cheetah, starting a tradition for easy-to-remember nicknames that continues today.

In 2006, Macintosh computers changed significantly with the switch from PowerPC to Intel processors and Mac OS X 10.4.4. In 2012, Apple released OS X 10.8 and officially dropped "Mac" from the operating system's name. With the release of Sierra in 2016, the operating system was renamed macOS. In 2020, Apple announced that Macs would use M-class processors with the Big Sur operating system (Figure 6-19).

Terminology

OS X is pronounced "oh es ten."

Figure 6-19: macOS evolution

2001	2006	2007	2009	2011	2012	2014	2015	2016	2017	2018	2019	2020	2021
Mac OS X 10.0 10.4 (Cheetah)	Mac OS X 10.4.4 (Tiger Intel)	Mac OS X 10.5 (Leopard)	Mac OS X 10.6 (Snow Leopard)	Mac OS X 10.7 (Lion)	OS X 10.8 (Mountain Lion)	OS X 10.9 (Mavericks)	OS X 10.10 (Yosemite)	macOS 10.12 (Sierra)	macOS 10.13 (High Sierra)	macOS 10.14 (Mojave)	macOS 10.15 (Catalina)	macOS 11 (Big Sur)	macOS 12 (Monterey)

▶ **What are the strengths of macOS?** macOS has a reputation for being an easy-to-use, reliable, and secure operating system. According to industry observers, Macintosh developers have always been in the lead when it comes to intuitive user interface design.

The operating system kernel of macOS is based on UNIX, a server operating system that includes industrial-strength memory protection features that contribute to a low incidence of errors and glitches. macOS inherited a strong security foundation from UNIX that tends to limit the number of security holes and the damage that can be done by hackers who manage to slip in.

Another factor that contributes to the security of computers running macOS is that fewer viruses are designed to target Macs because the user base is smaller than the Windows user base. Regardless of the relative security of computers running macOS, Mac owners should practice safe computing by applying software updates and OS patches as they become available, running security software, activating wireless network encryption, not opening suspicious email attachments, and not clicking links embedded in email messages.

The Apple ecosystem is yet another advantage of macOS. In the context of technology, an ecosystem is a family of devices, software, and services that work with one another. The Apple ecosystem includes computers running macOS and other devices such as iPhones, iPads, Apple Watches, and Apple TV.

Using devices in the Apple ecosystem, you can seamlessly share content. For example, an appointment made on an iMac computer automatically updates the calendar on your iPhone. With Apple's Handoff you can start an email message on your laptop and then complete it later on your iPhone (Figure 6-20).

Figure 6-20: Handoff in the Apple ecosystem

Use Handoff to continue tasks on your other devices

With Handoff, you can start work on one device, then switch to another nearby device and pick up where you left off.

Source: Apple Inc.

▶ **What are the weaknesses of macOS?** A decent collection of software is available for computers that run macOS, although the selection is not as vast as the Windows collection. Many of the most prolific software publishers produce one version of their software for Windows and another, similar version for macOS.

In contrast to the Windows platform, macOS runs only on devices from Apple. Shoppers are limited to the hardware devices offered by Apple, such as iMacs, Macbooks, and iPads. Hardware and configuration options are much more limited than those available for the Windows platform.

iOS

macOS is for desktop computers, but its cousin, iOS, powers mobile devices, such as iPhones, iPads, and iPods.

▶**How is iOS related to macOS?** iOS is a mobile operating system derived from the same UNIX code that is the basis for macOS. Both operating systems feature icons with a similar design aesthetic.

▶**How does iOS work?** iOS displays a home screen containing application icons. At the bottom of the screen, a dock holds icons for frequently used apps. Touching an icon launches its app. Pressing the physical or virtual Home button returns you to the home screen. The Settings icon leads to a variety of system utilities (Figure 6-21).

Figure 6-21: iOS is designed for mobile devices

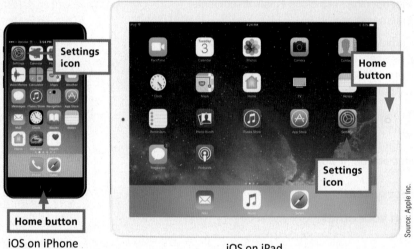

Settings icon

Home button

Home button

Settings icon

Source: Apple Inc.

iOS on iPhone   iOS on iPad

Apps can be grouped into folders to save space on the Home screen. Touching and holding an app icon produces "Jiggle mode" in which icons vibrate to indicate they are in a modifiable state. From Jiggle mode, icons can be deleted or dragged on top of each other to put them into a folder.

iOS was the first operating system to offer routines to manage touchscreen gesture inputs, such as using your fingers to "squeeze" an on-screen graphic into a smaller size.

As a mobile operating system, iOS provides connectivity options, such as cell phone connections, as well as local networking. Although all iOS devices have Wi-Fi and Bluetooth capability, only iPhones and some iPads have cellular capabilities.

▶**What are the limitations of iOS?** iOS limits your selection of apps to those provided by the online Apple App Store, unless you make unauthorized modifications to the phone. Those modifications can also overcome other limitations, such as lack of access to the file system. Unlike full desktop operating systems, iOS does not include a file manager. The only way to access a data file is through the app that was used to create it.

You won't find a desktop with application windows on an iOS device. Each app fills the entire screen. Background processes, such as music, voice calls, and notifications, provide very limited multitasking capabilities.

QuickCheck

Which device does not use iOS?

a. iPhone

b. MacBook Air

c. iPad

d. iPod Touch

Android

Words such as *marshmallow, jellybean*, and *lollipop* might bring to mind sugary sweets, but they were also the nicknames for versions of the Android operating system.

▶**What is Android?** Android is a mobile operating system that is a popular platform for tablet computers, smartphones, and ebook readers. Android was developed by a consortium of technology companies and unveiled in 2007. It is an open source operating system under the project leadership of Google. As with other popular mobile operating systems, Android is designed for ARM processors.

▶**How does the Android interface work?** Android displays a home screen containing icons that represent software applications. Touching an icon launches the app.

Android devices have a screen-based home button that displays the home screen (Figure 6-22). In addition to touchscreen input, the Android OS supports voice input for Google searching, voice dialing, navigation, and other applications.

Figure 6-22: Android runs on smartphones and tablets

Source: Google, Inc.

▶**What are the key features of Android?** The Android OS contains basic network and routing routines that allow Android devices to become Wi-Fi hotspots. For example, activating the Network utility on an Android-based smartphone transforms the phone into a router, and the phone's data connection can be used by a nearby desktop, laptop, or tablet computer to access the Internet.

Android provides access to the file system and provides a utility for viewing files stored internally or on external SD cards. A third-party file manager utility is required to manipulate files.

QuickCheck

Where can you find the home button on an Android device?

a. On the Start menu

b. On the system unit

c. Next to the Apple icon

d. At the bottom of the screen

Chrome OS

For consumers whose digital footprints rarely leave the cloud, there is an operating system that provides a secure platform. Sometimes described as a browser-based operating system, Chrome OS has limitations, but those limitations are not necessarily negative.

▶**What is Chrome OS?** Google launched an operating system called Chrome OS in 2009. Its kernel is based on an open source operating system called Linux, but Chrome OS itself is distributed under a proprietary license. This situation is common in the open source community where a product with an open source license is forked—meaning that the source code is developed and updated on two different paths by separate organizations. In the case of Chrome OS, the source code from a project called Chromium was appropriated by Google, modified with proprietary code, and then distributed under the Chrome OS license, which does not allow copying, modifications, or redistribution.

▶**What are the pros and cons of Chrome OS?** Chrome OS is an example of a thin client because it depends substantially on processing and storage provided by a remote computer—in this case, cloud-based servers. To get a sense of the Chrome OS world, visualize a browser as your desktop and imagine that your digital world is limited to only those online applications, communications, and storage locations that the browser can access.

As cloud services become more extensive, Chrome OS becomes less and less limiting. Unlike iPads, Chromebooks support multiple users. They provide very limited local storage space, however. Google claims that Chrome OS is very secure, but consumers understand that the security is equivalent to that provided by a browser and by cloud storage services.

▶**Who uses Chrome OS?** Currently, Chrome OS powers inexpensive clamshell-style devices called Chromebooks that are popular in educational settings and for light business use. Chromebooks boot very quickly to a basic desktop where apps are displayed in the Chrome browser (Figure 6-23).

QuickCheck

Why is Chrome OS considered a thin client?

a. Because it doesn't have many applications

b. Because it includes a browser

c. Because it depends on programs that run on remote Web servers

d. Because it runs on laptop computers called Chromebooks

Figure 6-23: Elements of Chrome OS

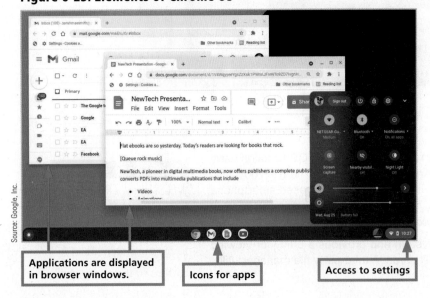

Source: Google, Inc.

Applications are displayed in browser windows.

Icons for apps

Access to settings

Linux

When technology experts are in need of an operating system that is dependable, expandable, and versatile, they frequently turn to Linux. The Linux landscape offers a multitude of choices that might seem daunting to the uninitiated, but are prized by experts.

▶ **What is the origin of Linux?** In 1991, a young Finnish student named Linus Torvalds developed the **Linux** (pronounced "LIH nucks") operating system. Linux was inspired by and loosely based on a UNIX derivative called MINIX, created by Andrew Tanenbaum. Linux is frequently used as an operating system for servers. It is not as popular for desktop applications as Windows or macOS.

▶ **What are the strengths of Linux?** As an operating system, Linux is unique because it is distributed along with its source code under the terms of a GPL (General Public License), which allows everyone to make copies for their own use, to give to others, or to sell. This licensing policy has encouraged programmers to develop Linux utilities, software, and enhancements. Linux is primarily distributed over the Web.

One of the strongest aspects of Linux is the abundance of tools it provides for customization. Linux users can select from a long list of system utilities for file management, packaged to meet the needs of various businesses and industries. In addition to system utilities, Linux users can choose from a variety of desktops, each with its own set of icons and menus that create a unique user interface.

▶ **What are the weaknesses of Linux?** Linux requires more tinkering than the Windows and macOS operating systems. The comparatively limited number of programs that run under Linux also discourages many nontechnical users. A collection of high-quality open source software is available for the Linux platform, but many of these applications are targeted toward business and technical users.

▶ **How do I get Linux?** A **Linux distribution** (or "distro") is a download that contains the Linux kernel, system utilities, desktop user interface, applications, and an installation routine. Beginner-friendly Linux distributions include Arch, Fedora, Ubuntu, Debian, openSUSE, and Mint (Figure 6-24).

QuickCheck

The user interface for Linux is supplied as part of a(n)

_____.

a. MINIX

b. device driver

c. kernel

d. distro

Figure 6-24: Linux Mint

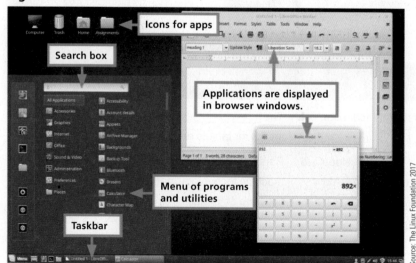

Source: The Linux Foundation 2017

Icons for apps

Search box

Applications are displayed in browser windows.

Menu of programs and utilities

Taskbar

Virtual Machines

We tend to think of an operating system as an immutable part of each digital device. PCs always run Windows, Macs always run macOS, and Samsung phones run Android. Is it possible to run Windows on a Mac and emulate an Android device on a desktop computer? Yes, it is possible using virtual machines.

▶ **What is a virtual machine?** A **virtual machine** (VM) allows one computer to simulate the hardware and software of another. Each virtual machine has its own simulated processor, RAM, video card, input and output ports, and operating system. Each machine can run most software that's compatible with the virtual OS platform.

Popular virtual machine software such as VMware Fusion and Parallels Desktop create platforms where, for example, an iMac computer can run Windows. The iMac boots using its native macOS, but you can then launch a virtual machine that runs guest operating systems, such as Windows and Linux. The virtual machine's desktop appears in a window on the host desktop (Figure 6-25).

Terminology

Virtual machine software is also called a *hypervisor*.

Figure 6-25: A virtual machine simulates one or more digital devices

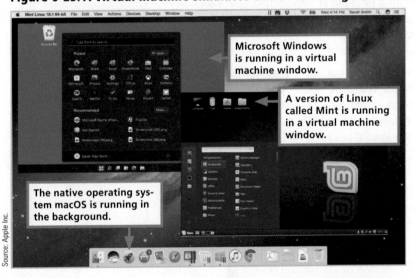

Microsoft Windows is running in a virtual machine window.

A version of Linux called Mint is running in a virtual machine window.

The native operating system macOS is running in the background.

Source: Apple Inc.

QuickCheck

_____ machine technology can be used to run two different operating systems on a single computer.

a. OS

b. Dedicated

c. Virtual

d. Windows

QuickQuiz   Section B

1. Microsoft Windows featured the first graphical user interface. True or false? [_____]

2. The operating system [_____] provides essential system programming and remains in RAM while the computer is on.

3. The operating system for iPads and iPhones is called [_____] .

4. The [_____] operating system is an alternative to iOS for tablets and smartphones.

5. Parallels Desktop is an example of [_____] machine technology that can be used to run Windows software on a Mac.

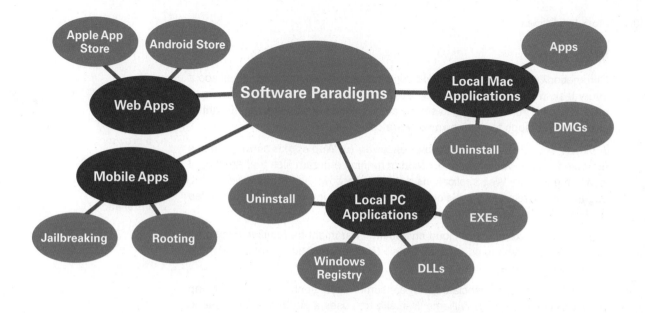

Apps and Applications

Objectives

- Describe two ways in which Web apps differ from mobile apps.
- List four advantages and three disadvantages of Web apps.
- Describe the installation process for mobile apps.
- Explain why iPhone owners might want to jailbreak their devices.
- State whether the following file extensions are associated with PCs or Macs: .exe, .app, .dll, .dmg.
- List the seven activities that take place during the installation process for PC software.
- Describe the process for installing software on Macs.
- Summarize the different procedures necessary to uninstall software on PCs and Macs.

It is surprising how quickly you outgrow the standard set of apps that are preinstalled on your digital devices. When shopping for new apps and applications, you'll have your choice of software paradigms, which determine whether the software gets installed and takes up space on an internal storage device. Knowing the ins and outs of each paradigm will help you make the right software choices.

Terminology

Web application	rooting	setup program	uninstall utility
mobile app	local application	DMG	
jailbreak	application extensions		

Web Apps

Chromebook owners depend on Web apps for the software they use for just about every task in the digital world. Web apps also have advantages for owners of other devices, from desktops to smartwatches. Find out why you might want to seek out Web apps for your own software collection.

▶ **What are Web apps?** A **Web application** (or Web app) is software that is accessed with a Web browser. Instead of running program files that are stored locally, the code for Web applications is temporarily downloaded along with HTML pages and is executed client-side by the browser. Program code for some Web applications may also run on a remote server.

Web apps are examples of cloud computing. You might be familiar with some frequently used Web apps, such as Gmail, Google Docs, and Turnitin, but there are thousands more.

Many Web apps are associated with consumer sites, such as the Color Snap visualizer at the Sherwin-Williams Web site that uses a photo of your house to help you select paint colors. Other Web apps, such as the XE Currency Converter, have dedicated sites.

▶ **Do I have to install Web apps?** Most Web apps require no installation at all on your local computer or handheld device. Your device must, however, have a Web browser and an Internet connection.

To access a Web app, go to its Web site. You might have to register before your first use, and then log in using your registered user name and password for subsequent visits. Your browser will remain open while the app is in use (Figure 6-26).

Figure 6-26: Web apps run in a browser

2. The Web app runs within a browser window.

1. Connect to the Web site and launch the Web app.

Source: Pixlr.

Source: Pixlr.

▶ **Who uses Web apps?** Just about everyone. Web apps are particularly suited for consumer-level activities, such as basic word processing, spreadsheet creation, photo editing, audio recording, video editing, presentation design, and personal finance management. Although they may not yet provide features required by professionals, the sophistication of Web apps continues to increase.

As an extra bonus, many Web apps allow several people to collaborate on projects because the project files are stored on the Web and can be easily shared (Figure 6-27).

Figure 6-27: Web apps facilitate collaboration

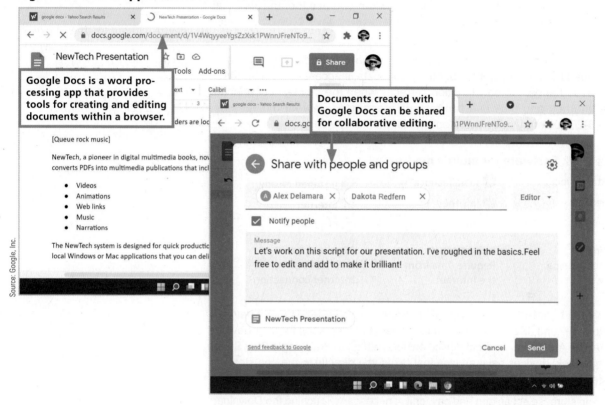

▶ **What are the advantages and disadvantages of Web apps?** Web apps are truly handy, but consider their advantages and disadvantages before entrusting them with your work:

➕ You can access Web apps from any device that has a browser and an Internet connection, including full-size computers, smartphones, tablet computers, and enhanced media players.

➕ Your data is usually stored on the app's Web site, so you can access data even when you are away from your main computer.

➕ Web apps are always up to date; you don't have to install updates because the latest version is the one posted at the Web site where you access the app.

➕ Web apps don't require local storage space, so you don't have to worry about them accumulating on your hard disk or SSD.

➖ Web apps tend to have fewer features than applications that require installation.

➖ If the site hosting the app shuts down, you will not be able to access the application or your data.

➖ Your data might be more vulnerable to exposure or loss because it is out of your control. If possible, back up data to a local device or to an auxiliary cloud storage site.

Mobile Apps

Although just about every mobile device includes a browser, the current trend is not to use Web apps on mobile devices. Following Apple's lead, most mobile developers offer apps that are installed locally on a smartphone or tablet.

▶ **What are mobile apps?** A **mobile app** is designed for a handheld device, such as a smartphone, tablet computer, or enhanced media player. They are generally small, focused applications sold through an online app store.

▶ **How do mobile apps differ from Web apps?** Most handheld devices can use both Web apps and mobile apps. The difference between the two is that the program code for Web apps arrives only when you use the app, whereas mobile apps are stored on the handheld device, so they have to be downloaded and installed.

Some mobile apps, such as Yelp and Pandora, are hybrids. A thin client is downloaded from an app store, but during use, data is accessed from the Web. These hybrid apps can only function correctly when the device is connected to the Internet, and their use can rack up megabytes on your mobile plan. Figure 6-28 summarizes software options for mobile devices.

Try It!

What happens when you try to use a hybrid app on a mobile device without Internet service? Turn on Airplane mode to switch off your cellular and Wi-Fi service. Then try to launch an app, such as Yelp, to find out how the hybrid app reacts.

Figure 6-28: Software for mobile devices

⊗ Installed locally	⊕ Installed locally	⊕ Installed locally
⊕ Internet	⊕ Internet	⊗ Internet
⊕ Browser	⊗ Browser	⊗ Browser
Web apps	**Hybrid apps**	**Mobile apps**
Accessed using a mobile browser	Require data from the Internet	Operate without an Internet connection

▶ **How do I install mobile apps?** The first step is to head to your device's app store. iPhone, iPad, and iPod Touch owners can find apps for their devices at the Apple App Store; Android device owners can go to the Google Play Store. Most handheld devices have an icon that takes you directly to the app store for your device's platform.

At the app store, select an app and pay for it, if necessary. Touching the Download button retrieves the file and installs it automatically. The installation process places the app's program file on the storage device and creates an icon that you can use to launch the app.

▶ **What is jailbreaking?** iPads, iPhones, and iPods are only allowed to download apps from the official Apple App Store. Apps are available from other sources, but using them requires an unauthorized change called a **jailbreak** to the device's software. After downloading and installing the jailbreak software, your device will be able to install apps from a variety of sources other than the Apple App Store. The jailbreak lasts until you accept a software update from Apple. Updates wipe out the jailbreak software, forcing you to reinstall it.

▶ **Can I jailbreak an Android device?** Android phones are not limited to a single app store, so there is no need to jailbreak them to access more apps. There are various ways to make unauthorized modifications to any mobile device to overcome limitations imposed by mobile service providers. The process is called **rooting**, but most consumers have no need to root their mobile devices.

QuickCheck

Apps such as Yelp and Pandora are hybrids that use a _____ and Web-based data.

a. browser

b. thin client

c. mobile OS

d. smartphone

Local Applications

A **local application** is installed on a computer's hard disk. When it runs, the program code is copied into RAM, where it can be accessed by the microprocessor. Office suites, games, and professional software tools are common examples of local applications for desktop and laptop computers. Local applications do not require an Internet connection to run.

▶ **What's included in a typical software package?** Software for Macs is usually stored in a single executable file with an .app extension. That file, however, is actually a package that contains other files and folders. The contents of an application's package can be viewed by right-clicking the .app file and selecting Show Package Contents.

Software designed for computers that run Microsoft Windows is commonly composed of multiple files. The main executable file has an .exe extension—for example, *Inkscape.exe*. Additional files required for Windows application software contain support modules called **application extensions** with file names that end in .dll, as shown in Figure 6-29.

6

Figure 6-29: PC software can be composed of many files

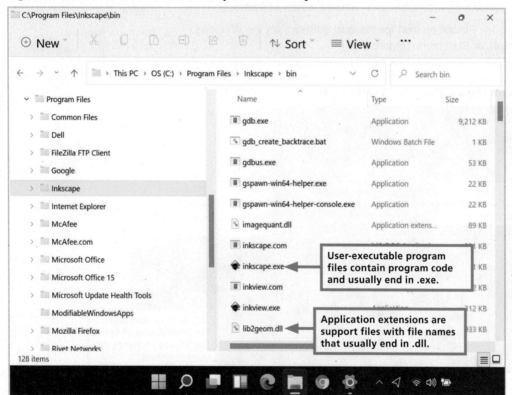

▶ **What is the process for installing software on PCs?** Software for PCs contains a **setup program** that guides you through the installation process. The setup program simplifies installation because it handles a variety of behind-the-scenes technical details. During the installation process, the setup program usually performs the following activities:

- **Copy files.** Copies application files from distribution media (CDs or DVDs) or downloads files to specified folders on the hard disk or SSD.

- **Unzip files.** Reconstitutes files that have been distributed in compressed format.

- **Check resources.** Analyzes the computer's resources, such as processor speed, RAM capacity, and hard disk capacity, to verify that they meet or exceed the minimum system requirements.

- **Select device drivers.** Analyzes hardware components and peripheral devices to select appropriate device drivers.

- **Find players.** Looks for any system files and players, such as Microsoft Edge or Windows Media Player, that are required to run the program but are not supplied on the distribution media or download.

- **Update the Registry.** Updates necessary system files, such as the Windows Registry and the Start menu, with information about the new software.

- **Update the desktop.** Places an icon for the new software on the Windows desktop, Start screen, or Start menu (Figure 6-30).

Terminology

The *Windows Registry* is a database that keeps track of a PC's peripheral devices, software, preferences, and settings. When you install software on a computer running the Windows operating system, information about the software is recorded in the Registry.

QuickCheck

When an application is installed on a PC, the application's name is added to the _____.

a. EXE file

b. operating system

c. ZIP file

d. Windows Registry

Figure 6-30: Icons on the desktop and Start menu

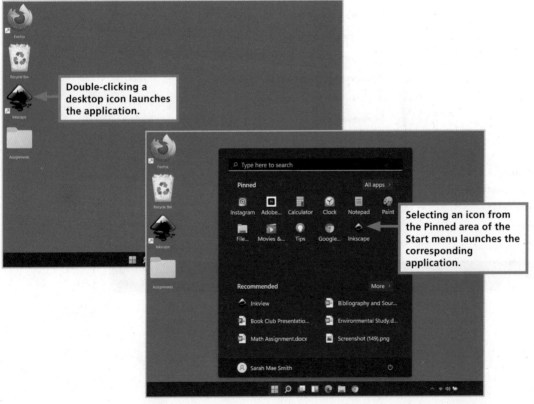

Double-clicking a desktop icon launches the application.

Selecting an icon from the Pinned area of the Start menu launches the corresponding application.

❱ **How do I download and install software on a PC?** The EXE and DLL files for Windows application software are zipped to consolidate them into one large file, which is compressed to decrease its size and reduce the download time. As part of the installation process, this downloaded file must be reconstituted, or unzipped, into the original collection of files.

Downloaded files are generally stored in the Downloads folder. You can back up this folder periodically. If your computer's hard drive malfunctions, you can use these files to rebuild your software collection without having to download all of it again. Figure 6-31 maps out the process of downloading and installing local apps on a PC.

Try It!

If you are using a PC, open File Explorer by clicking the folder icon on the taskbar, then search for *.exe*. Can you identify the software applications that these EXE files launch?

6

Figure 6-31: Download and install software on a PC

1. At the distribution Web site, read the installation instructions, then select the Download link.

2. If you are downloading from a trusted site and have antivirus software running, select the Run button.

3. Wait for the download to finish. The setup program included in the download starts automatically.

4. Read the license agreement and accept its terms to continue with the installation.

5. Select a folder to hold the new application. You can use the default folder specified by the setup program or a folder of your own choosing. You can also create a new folder during the setup process.

6. Wait for the setup program to uncompress the downloaded file and install the software in the selected directory. When the installation is complete, launch the software to make sure it works.

Source: Inkscape

QuickCheck

When downloading software, why should you select Run only at trusted sites?

a. Because the download doesn't have to check for viruses

b. Because the setup program is going to run automatically; if it contains a virus, it could be transmitted

c. Because if you select Save, you might forget where the program is stored

d. Because the download is then transmitted over an HTTPS connection

▶ **How do I install software on a Mac?** Mac software is straightforward to install. Downloads are ordinarily supplied as a **DMG** package commonly referred to as a "disk image." The DMG package has a .dmg extension. It contains the main APP file for the software, and it may also contain a Read Me file or other data files used by the application. Once the download is complete, open the DMG file from the Downloads folder and then drag the APP file to your Applications folder, as shown in Figure 6-32.

Figure 6-32: Install Mac software

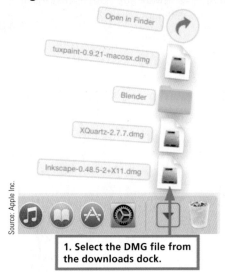
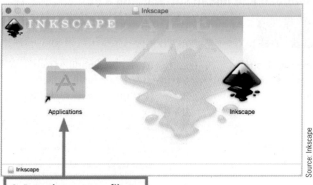

1. Select the DMG file from the downloads dock.

2. Drag the program file to the Applications folder.

▶ **How do I access Mac software after it is installed?** On a Mac, you can access most software from the Launchpad at the bottom of the screen. Clicking an icon tells the computer to start the APP executable file. You can drag an icon from the Launchpad to the Dock if you use it frequently (Figure 6-33).

Figure 6-33: Launch an application

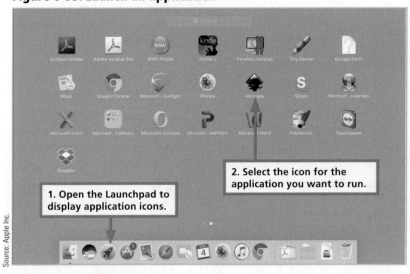

1. Open the Launchpad to display application icons.

2. Select the icon for the application you want to run.

Uninstalling Software

When your smartphone or computer gets cluttered with unneeded demoware, unused applications, or outdated mobile apps, you can clean house.

▶ **How do I remove mobile apps?** On an iPhone, press and hold the app icon until a menu appears, then select Remove App. On an Android device, go to Settings, and find the Applications Manager. Tap the program name, then select Uninstall.

▶ **How do I remove Mac software?** Most Mac users simply use Finder to locate the program's APP file or folder and move it to the trash. Some Mac programs, such as those in the Adobe Creative Suite, include a more thorough uninstall routine, which is usually listed in the Utilities folder.

▶ **How do I get rid of PC software?** Removing software from a PC is complicated by two factors. First, the process of installing software often sprinkles files into various folders, including the System folder, where they can be shared with other programs. Second, the Windows Registry must be updated when an application is removed.

Windows includes an **uninstall utility**, which deletes the software's files from various folders on your computer's hard disk. The uninstall routine helps you decide what to do with shared files that are used by more than one program. As a rule, you should leave the shared files in place. The uninstall utility provides access to the uninstall routine (Figure 6-34).

Figure 6-34: The uninstall utility removes software on a Windows PC

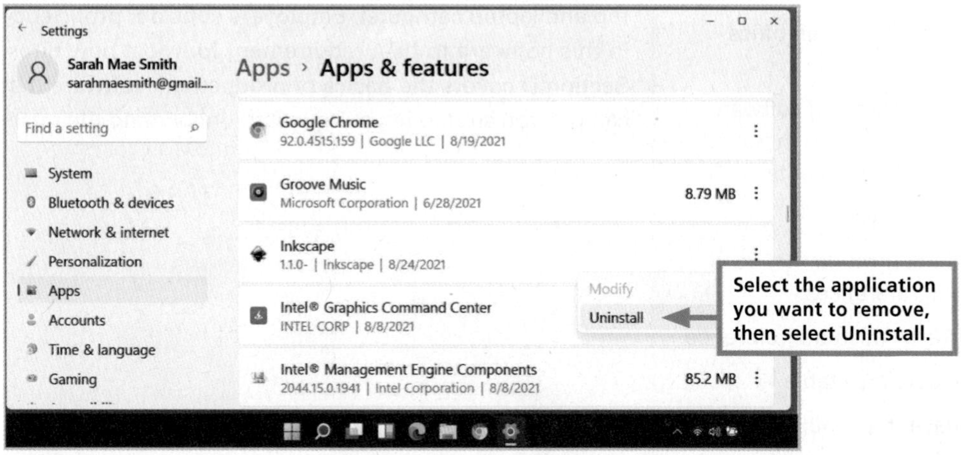

QuickQuiz   Section C

1. Most _____ applications require no installation and are accessed through a browser.

2. On a PC, a(n) _____ program guides you through the installation process.

3. Installing or removing a program from a computer running Windows requires an update to the Windows _____ .

4. Software applications for Macs are usually distributed as files with _____ extensions.

5. To remove files from a PC, it is important to use the _____ utility to make sure the application's files are deleted from various folders where they were placed during installation.

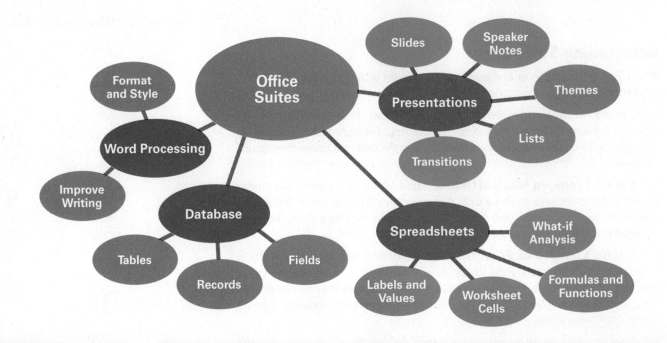

Section D Productivity Software

Objectives

▶ List three applications that are the core of an office suite.

▶ Describe three features of word processing software that help improve the quality of writing and three features that improve the format of documents.

▶ Provide an example of a what-if analysis.

▶ Give an example of a spreadsheet formula that uses mathematical operators and cell references.

▶ Describe a formula that requires an absolute reference.

▶ Identify fields and records in a database table.

▶ Provide an example of a database that would have two or more related tables.

▶ List five commonly used features of presentation software.

It's an essential set of applications for every desktop and laptop computer. Employers consider proficiency in this software to be a requirement for most new hires. Section D covers the basics of productivity software that can get you started in your quest to understand their use.

Terminology

productivity software
office suite
module
word processing
   software
word wrap
search and replace
thesaurus
grammar checker
readability formula
spelling checker

spelling dictionary
document formatting
page layout
header
footer
paragraph style
leading
paragraph alignment
fully justified
font
point size

style
spreadsheet
spreadsheet software
what-if analysis
worksheet
cell
value
label
formula
cell references
function

automatic recalculation
relative reference
absolute reference
database
database software
record
field
presentation software

Office Suite Basics

Office suites, such as Microsoft Office and Google Docs Editors, are popular with individuals and in business environments. They are sometimes referred to as productivity software because they offer features that really help get work done.

▶ **What is an office suite?** An office suite is a collection of programs that typically include word processing, spreadsheet, and presentation modules. Suites may also include email and contact managers, calendars, and project management, database management, and drawing modules.

In the context of office suites, the term module refers to a component, such as a word processing module. Modules can be run as individual programs, but all of the modules in an office suite have a standard set of controls, enabling you to transfer your expertise on one module to the others.

▶ **What are the most popular office suites?** Popular office suites include Google Docs Editors, iWork, LibreOffice, Microsoft Office, and Zoho Office Suite (Figure 6-35).

6

Figure 6-35: Office suites

Name	Modules	Platform
Google Docs Editors	Word processing, spreadsheet, presentation, drawing, forms	Online (Free)
iWork	Word processing, spreadsheet, presentation	macOS ($$)
LibreOffice	Word processing, spreadsheet, presentation, database, drawing	Windows, macOS, Linux (Free)
Microsoft Office	Word processing, spreadsheet, presentation, database, mail/calendar	Windows, macOS, Linux, iOS, Android ($$)
Zoho Office Suite	Word processing, spreadsheet, presentation, calendar, and more	Online (Free)

Word Processing

Whether you are writing a ten-page paper, generating software documentation, designing a brochure, or writing a dissertation, you will probably use the word processing module of an office suite.

▶ **How can software help me with my writing?** Word processing software replaced typewriters for producing many types of documents, including reports, letters, memos, papers, and book manuscripts. Word processing packages, such as Microsoft Word, iWork Pages, and LibreOffice Writer, give you the ability to create, spell-check, edit, and format a document on the screen before it is finalized.

A typical word processor window displays a work area, called a workspace, that represents a blank piece of paper. The window also includes controls for viewing and formatting the document (Figure 6-36).

Figure 6-36: Microsoft Word basics

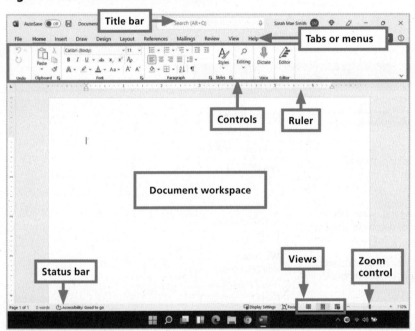

▶ **How does word processing software help me turn my ideas into sentences and paragraphs?** Word processing software facilitates the flow of ideas because it automatically handles many tasks that might otherwise be distractions. For example, you don't need to worry about fitting words within the margins. A feature called **word wrap** determines how your text flows from line to line by automatically moving words down to the next line as you reach the right margin.

Imagine that the sentences in your document are ribbons of text; word wrap bends the ribbons. Changing the margin size just means bending the ribbon in different places. Even after you type an entire document, adjusting the size of the right, left, top, and bottom margins is straightforward.

▶ **Can word processing software help me break bad writing habits?** You can use the **search and replace** feature to hunt down mistakes that you habitually make in your writing. For example, if you tend to overuse the word *typically,* you can use search and replace to find each occurrence of *typically* and then decide whether you should substitute a different word, such as *usually* or *ordinarily.*

QuickCheck

When using word processing software, it is not necessary to press Enter at the end of each line because _____.

a. you might want to go back and make edits

b. word wrap automatically moves text to the next line

c. doing so activates search and replace

d. doing so would create double spacing

▶ **Can word processing software improve my writing?** Because word processing software is geared toward the writing process, it offers several features that can improve the quality of your writing.

Word processing software is likely to include a **thesaurus**, which can help you find a synonym for a word so that you can make your writing more varied and interesting. A **grammar checker** reads through your document and points out potential grammatical trouble spots, such as incomplete sentences, run-on sentences, and verbs that don't agree with nouns.

Your word processing software might also be able to analyze the reading level of your document using a standard **readability formula**, such as the Flesch-Kincaid reading level. You can use this analysis to find out if your writing level is appropriate for your target audience based on sentence length and vocabulary.

Most word processing software includes a **spelling checker** that marks misspelled words in a document. You can easily correct a misspelled word as you type, or you can run the spelling checker when you finish entering all the text. Some software even has autocorrecting capability; as you type, it automatically changes a typo (such as *teh*) to the correct spelling (*the*).

Although your software's spelling checker helps you correct misspellings, it cannot guarantee an error-free document. A spelling checker works by comparing each word from your document to a list of correctly spelled words stored in a data file called a **spelling dictionary**. If the word from your document is in the dictionary, the spelling checker considers the word correctly spelled. If the word is not in the dictionary, the word is counted as misspelled.

Spelling checkers can't tell if you misuse a word, such as if you use the phrase *pear of shoes* instead of *pair of shoes*. Also, spelling checkers flag many proper nouns and scientific, medical, and technical words because they are not included in the spelling checker's dictionary. Make sure you proofread, even after using a spelling checker (Figure 6-37).

Try It!

What is the reading level of a document that you've recently written? Use reading level analytics from your word processing software or use a Web app such as the Readability Test Tool.

6

QuickCheck

You can depend on your word processor's spelling checker to _____.

a. flag words that are not in its dictionary

b. catch all your misspellings

c. identify words that you misuse

d. correct grammar errors

Figure 6-37: Check spelling and grammar

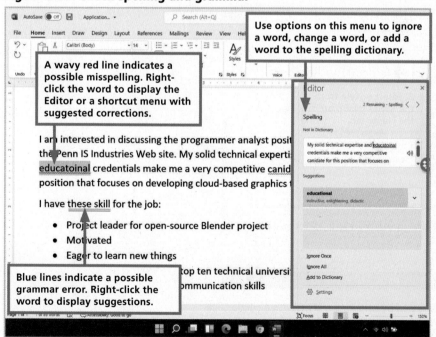

A wavy red line indicates a possible misspelling. Right-click the word to display the Editor or a shortcut menu with suggested corrections.

Use options on this menu to ignore a word, change a word, or add a word to the spelling dictionary.

Blue lines indicate a possible grammar error. Right-click the word to display suggestions.

▶ How do I get my documents to look good? The term **document formatting** refers to the way that all the elements of a document—text, pictures, titles, and page numbers—are arranged on the page.

The final format of a document depends on how and where you intend to use it. A school paper, for example, simply needs to be produced in standard paragraph format—perhaps double spaced and with numbered pages. A brochure, newsletter, or corporate report, on the other hand, might require more ambitious formatting, such as columns, headers, and graphics.

The look of your final document depends on several formatting factors, such as page layout, paragraph style, and font.

- **Layout and headers. Page layout** refers to the physical position of each element on a page. In addition to paragraphs of text, these elements might include margins, page numbers, **header** text that you specify to automatically appear in the top margin of every page, and **footer** text that you specify to automatically appear in the bottom margin of every page.

- **Styles and alignment. Paragraph style** includes the alignment of text within the margins and the space between each line of text. The vertical spacing between lines of text is called **leading** (pronounced "LED ding"). Most documents are single spaced or double spaced, but you can adjust line spacing in 1 pt. increments. **Paragraph alignment** refers to the horizontal position of text—whether it is aligned at the left margin, aligned at the right margin, or **fully justified** so that the text is aligned evenly on both the right and left margins.

- **Fonts.** A **font** is a set of letters that share a unified design. Font size is measured as **point size**, which is abbreviated as pt. One point is about 1/72 of an inch.

Instead of individually selecting font and paragraph style elements, word processing software allows you to select a **style** that lets you apply several font and paragraph characteristics with a single click (Figure 6-38).

QuickCheck

In the context of word processing, the term *leading* refers to _____.

a. text that automatically appears at the top of each page

b. the feature that automatically moves text down when you reach the margin

c. the size of a font

d. the space between lines of text

Figure 6-38: Use styles for professional formatting

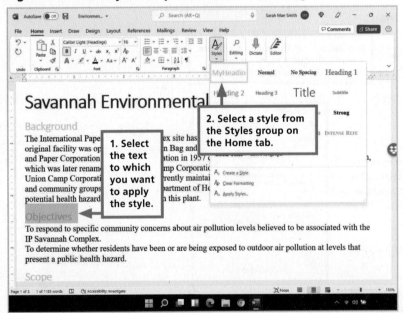

In this document, headings were formatted by selecting a style with a single click instead of individually selecting a font color, font size, and font style. Now if the heading style is changed to red, all the headings will automatically change color.

Spreadsheets

Spreadsheet software was initially popular with accountants who dealt with paper-based spreadsheets; they found the electronic version far easier to use and less prone to errors than manual calculations. Other people soon discovered the benefits of spreadsheets for projects that require repetitive calculations, such as budgeting, computing grades, tracking investments, calculating loan payments, and estimating project costs.

▶ **What is a spreadsheet?** A spreadsheet uses rows and columns of numbers to create a model or representation of a real situation. For example, your bank statement is a type of spreadsheet because it is a numerical representation of cash flowing into and out of your bank account.

▶ **When do I need spreadsheet software?** Spreadsheet software, such as Microsoft Excel, iWork Numbers, Google Sheets, and LibreOffice Calc, provides tools to create electronic spreadsheets. It is like a smart piece of paper that automatically adds up columns of numbers written on it.

Spreadsheet calculations are based on equations that you create or more complex built-in formulas. Spreadsheet software can turn data into colorful graphs. It also includes special data-handling features that sort data, search for data that meets specific criteria, and print reports.

Because you can experiment with different numbers, spreadsheet software is particularly useful for what-if analysis. You can use what-if analyses to answer questions such as "What if I get an A on my next two economics exams? But what if I get only Bs?" or "What if I invest $100 a month in my retirement plan? But what if I invest $200 a month?"

▶ **What does a computerized spreadsheet look like?** Spreadsheet software can be used to create an on-screen worksheet. A worksheet is based on a grid of columns and rows. Each cell in the grid can contain a value, label, or formula. A value is a number that you want to use in a calculation. A label is any text used to describe data (Figure 6-39).

6

Figure 6-39: Microsoft Excel basics

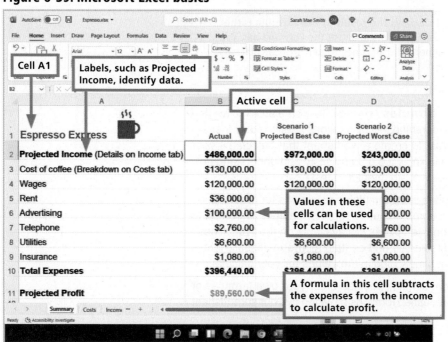

▶ **Are there formatting options?** The labels and values on a worksheet can be formatted in much the same way as you would format text in a word processing document. You can change fonts and font size, select a font color, and select font styles, such as bold, italics, and underline.

▶ **How does spreadsheet software work?** The values contained in a cell can be manipulated by formulas placed in other cells. A **formula** works behind the scenes to tell the microprocessor how to use the contents of cells in calculations. You can enter a formula into a cell to add, subtract, multiply, or divide numbers. More complex formulas can be designed to perform just about any calculation you can imagine. Figure 6-40 illustrates how a formula might be used in a spreadsheet to calculate savings.

Figure 6-40: How spreadsheet formulas work behind the scenes

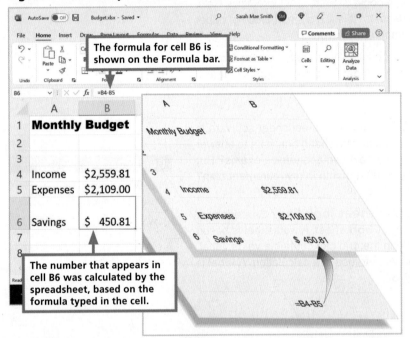

QuickCheck

Where is the formula in Figure 6-40?

a. In cell A1

b. In cell A4

c. In cell B4

d. In cell B6

When a cell contains a formula, it displays the result of the formula rather than the formula itself. To view and edit the formula, use the Formula bar. You can think of the formula as working behind the scenes to perform calculations and then display the result.

▶ **How will I know which formulas to use?** To create an effective and accurate worksheet, you must understand the calculations and formulas that are involved. If, for example, you want to create a worksheet that calculates your final grade in a course, you need to know the grading scale and understand how your instructor plans to weight each assignment and test.

Most spreadsheet software includes a few templates or wizards for predesigned worksheets, such as invoices, income–expense reports, balance sheets, and loan payment schedules. Additional templates are available on the Web. These templates are designed by professionals and contain all the necessary labels and formulas. To use a template, simply plug in the values for your calculation.

When creating spreadsheets from scratch, you can enter your own formulas or you can select from a series of predefined formulas provided by your spreadsheet software.

6

❱ **What is the format for formulas?** A formula, such as =A6-(B6*2), can contain **cell references** (such as A6 and B6), numbers (such as 2), and mathematical operators (such as the multiplication symbol [*], the division symbol [/], the addition symbol, and the subtraction symbol). Parts of a formula can be enclosed in parentheses to indicate the order in which the mathematical operations should be performed. The operation enclosed in parentheses—in this case, (B6*2)—should be performed first.

You can type the entire formula, or you can use pointer math, which adds cell references to the formula as you point to them. Figure 6-41 illustrates how to enter a formula into a cell.

Figure 6-41: Entering a formula

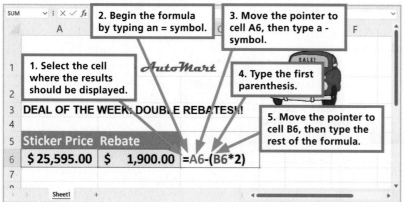

❱ **What is the process for entering functions?** Spreadsheet software provides functions that are set up to perform common calculations, such as averages, loan payments, and comparisons. A **function** is a built-in preset formula. To use a function, select one from a list, as shown in Figure 6-42, and then indicate the cell references of any values you want to include in the calculation.

Figure 6-42: Using built-in functions

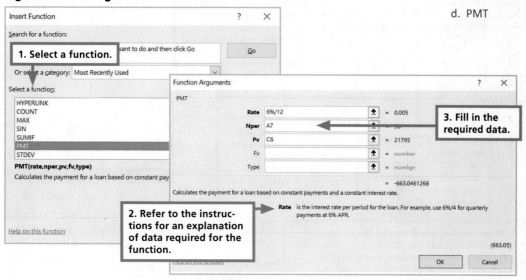

QuickCheck

In Figure 6-42, what information is entered for the Rate?

a. 5

b. The interest rate divided by number of annual payments

c. The Nper

d. PMT

▶ **What happens when I modify a worksheet?** When you change the contents of any cell in a worksheet, all the formulas are recalculated. This automatic recalculation feature ensures that the results in every cell are accurate for the information currently entered in the worksheet.

Your worksheet is also automatically updated to reflect any rows or columns that you add, delete, or copy within the worksheet. Unless you specify otherwise, a cell reference is a relative reference—that is, a reference that can change from B4 to B3, for example, if row 3 is deleted and all the data moves up one row.

If you don't want a cell reference to change, you can use an absolute reference. An absolute reference never changes when you insert rows or copy or move formulas. Understanding when to use absolute references is one of the key aspects of developing spreadsheet design expertise. Figure 6-43 provides additional information about relative and absolute references.

Figure 6-43: Absolute and relative references

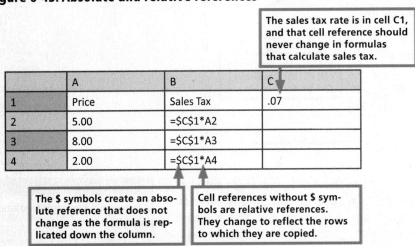

The sales tax rate is in cell C1, and that cell reference should never change in formulas that calculate sales tax.

	A	B	C
1	Price	Sales Tax	.07
2	5.00	=$C$1*A2	
3	8.00	=$C$1*A3	
4	2.00	=$C$1*A4	

The $ symbols create an absolute reference that does not change as the formula is replicated down the column.

Cell references without $ symbols are relative references. They change to reflect the rows to which they are copied.

What happens when a formula is not set up with the correct absolute references, and it is then copied or moved?

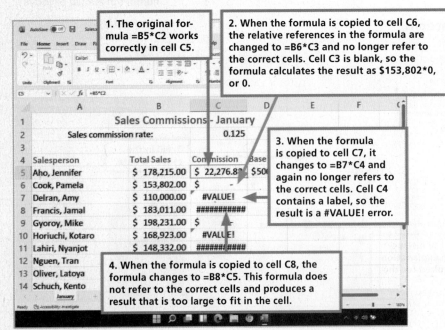

1. The original formula =B5*C2 works correctly in cell C5.

2. When the formula is copied to cell C6, the relative references in the formula are changed to =B6*C3 and no longer refer to the correct cells. Cell C3 is blank, so the formula calculates the result as $153,802*0, or 0.

3. When the formula is copied to cell C7, it changes to =B7*C4 and again no longer refers to the correct cells. Cell C4 contains a label, so the result is a #VALUE! error.

4. When the formula is copied to cell C8, the formula changes to =B8*C5. This formula does not refer to the correct cells and produces a result that is too large to fit in the cell.

QuickCheck

In Figure 6-43, the formula in cell C5 is =B5*C2. Are B5 and C2 relative references or absolute references?

a. Relative

b. Absolute

Databases

A database can contain any sort of data, such as a university's student records, a library's card catalog, a store's inventory, an individual's address book, or a utility company's customers. Databases can be stored on personal computers, network servers, Web servers, mainframes, and even mobile devices.

▶ **What is a database?** The term *database* has evolved from a specialized technical term into a part of our everyday vocabulary. In the context of modern usage, a **database** is simply a collection of data that may be stored on one or more digital devices.

▶ **What is database software?** Database software provides tools for entering, finding, organizing, updating, and reporting information stored in a database. Microsoft Access, Claris FileMaker, and LibreOffice Base are three examples of popular database software for personal computers. Oracle and MySQL are popular server database software packages.

▶ **How does a database store data?** Database software stores data as a series of records, which are composed of fields that hold data. A **record** holds data for a single entity—a person, place, thing, or event. A **field** holds one item of data relevant to a record. You can envision a record as a Rolodex card or an index card. A series of records is often presented as a table arranged in rows and columns (Figure 6-44).

6

QuickCheck

In Figure 6-44, how many fields are in the database table?

a. 5

b. 7

c. 9

d. 11

Figure 6-44: Database elements

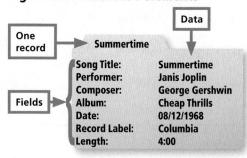

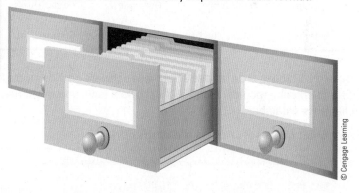

A single database record is similar to a Rolodex card or an index card. A series of records is usually depicted in table format.

© Cengage Learning

A series of records in table format

Song Title	Performer	Composer	Album	Date	Label	Length
Take It Back	Norah Jones	Jones	Little Broken Hearts	05/01/2012	Blue Note	4:05
Even Though	Norah Jones	Jones and Harris	The Fall	11/17/2009	Blue Note	3:52
Summertime	Janis Joplin	Gershwin	Cheap Thrills	08/12/1968	Columbia	4:00
Summertime	Sarah Vaughan	Gershwin	Compact Jazz	06/22/1987	PolyGram	4:34

▶ **Can a database hold different kinds of records?** Some database software provides tools to work with more than one collection of records, as long as the records are somehow related to each other. For example, suppose MTV maintains a database pertaining to classic jazz music. One series of database records might contain data about jazz songs. It could contain fields such as song title, performer, and length.

Another series of records might contain biographical data about jazz performers, including the performer's name, birth date, and hometown. It might even include a field for the performer's photo. These two sets of records can be related by the name of the performing artist, as shown in Figure 6-45.

QuickCheck

Figure 6-45 shows a table of jazz performers and a table of jazz songs. How many databases do these tables represent?

a. 1

b. 2

c. 4

d. 8

Figure 6-45: Database records can be related based on common fields

Jazz Performers

Performer	Birth Date	Hometown
Ella Fitzgerald	04/25/1917	Newport News, VA
Norah Jones	03/30/1979	New York, NY
Billie Holiday	04/07/1915	Baltimore, MD
Lena Horne	06/30/1917	Brooklyn, NY

These two records are related by the Performer field. The relationship allows you to select Norah Jones from the Jazz Performers table and locate two of her songs in the Jazz Songs table.

Jazz Songs

Song Title	Performer	Composer	Album	Date	Label	Length
Take It Back	Norah Jones	Jones	Little Broken Hearts	05/01/2012	Blue Note	4:05
Even Though	Norah Jones	Jones and Harris	The Fall	11/17/2009	Blue Note	3:52
Summertime	Janis Joplin	Gershwin	Cheap Thrills	08/12/1968	Columbia	4:00
Summertime	Sarah Vaughan	Gershwin	Compact Jazz	06/22/1987	PolyGram	4:34

▶ **How do I create a database?** Database software provides tools for defining fields and entering records. Figure 6-46 shows a table you might use to specify the fields for a database.

Figure 6-46: Microsoft Access elements

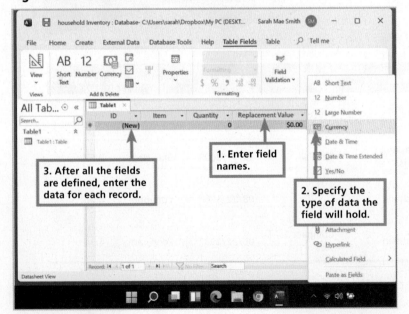

1. Enter field names.

2. Specify the type of data the field will hold.

3. After all the fields are defined, enter the data for each record.

QuickCheck

How many fields are shown in Figure 6-46?

a. 0

b. 1

c. 4

d. 8

Presentations

Presentation software supplies the tools for combining text, photos, clip art, graphs, animations, and sound into a series of electronic slides that can be shown on a screen or projector (Figure 6-47).

Popular presentation software products include Microsoft PowerPoint, iWork Keynote, LibreOffice Impress, and Google Slides.

▶ What are the best features of presentation software? Presentation software highlights include:

- Bulleted lists to summarize the points in your presentation
- Graphics to make your presentation visually interesting
- Transitions between slides to keep your audience's attention
- Speaker notes to help you remember what to say

- Themes and templates to give your slides a professional appearance
- Conversion routines to package presentations as PDF files and YouTube videos

Figure 6-47: Microsoft PowerPoint basics

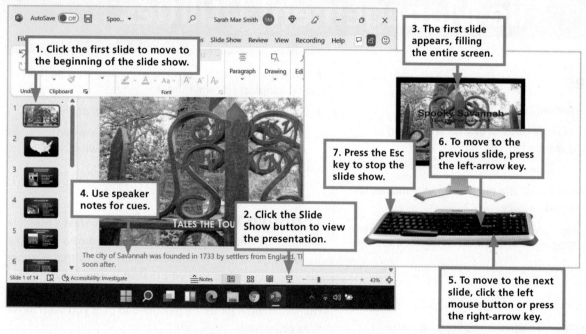

QuickQuiz   Section D

1. Word processing applications generally offer _____ style options including margins, leading, and alignment.

2. _____ software is useful for performing "what-if" analyses.

3. When entering formulas, you can use relative references and _____ references.

4. The information in a database is often represented as a(n) _____ with each row representing a record.

5. Each database record is composed of many _____.

Objectives

▶ List five file-naming conventions.

▶ Explain how storage devices on PCs are named or designated by device letters.

▶ Identify disk partitions.

▶ Write out the complete file path for any file that exists on a digital storage device.

▶ Identify the basic elements of Windows File Explorer and macOS Finder.

▶ Explain how operating systems use default applications.

▶ List at least ten file management best practices.

▶ Describe the file management options typically provided by application software.

▶ State the difference between a physical storage model and a logical storage model.

▶ Describe why an operating system uses an index file.

▶ Explain what the operating system does when you move a file to the Recycle Bin and when you permanently delete a file.

It doesn't take long to accumulate a massive
number of files. Your photo collection alone probably includes more than a thousand files. Add to that number all the documents you've created. Consider how that collection of files might grow over the next five years. File management utilities are designed to help you keep those files organized!

Terminology

file-naming
   conventions
device letter
disk partition
directory

root directory
subdirectory
folder
file path
file management utilities

default application
logical storage model
physical storage model
formatting
tracks

sectors
file system
cluster
file shredder software

File Basics

Computer files in digital format offer a compact and convenient way to store documents, photos, videos, and music. Computer files have several characteristics, such as a name, format, location, size, and date. To make effective use of computer files, you'll need a good understanding of these file basics.

▶ **What's important about a file name?** File names are the foundation for keeping files organized so that they can be easily located and so that old versions don't get mixed up with new versions. File names should be descriptive, and versioning must be clear. For example, if you anticipate several revisions to a report, add a version number, such as *Report v1.docx*, to the file name. Save the next version of the report as *Report v2.docx*. You then have the original version in case you want to retrieve some of the material it contains.

▶ **Are there rules for naming files?** As you learned in Module 1, a computer file—or simply a file—is defined as a named collection of data that exists on a storage medium, such as a hard disk, cloud drive, or USB flash drive. When saving a file, you must provide a valid file name that adheres to specific rules, referred to as **file-naming conventions**. The conventions vary slightly from one operating system to another. However, because file sharing is so prevalent, the conventions in Figure 6-48 represent best practices for naming files on any platform.

Figure 6-48: File-naming conventions

 Maximum length is 255 characters. Current versions of Windows and macOS support file names up to 255 characters long. In practice, some of the 255 characters are used for the file's drive letter, folder designation, and extension, so the name you assign to a file should be much shorter. A file name limitation of 255 characters gives you the flexibility to use descriptive file names, such as *Job Search Cover Letter Pixar*, so that you can easily identify what a file contains.

 Avoid using symbols. If an operating system attaches special significance to a symbol, you cannot use it in a file name. For example, Windows uses the colon (:) character to separate the device letter from a file name or folder, as in C:Music. A file name that contains a colon, such as *Report:Summary*, is not valid because the operating system would become confused about how to interpret the colon. Avoid using the symbols * \ < > | " / : and ? in file names.

 Do not use reserved words. Some operating systems also contain a list of reserved words that are used as commands or special identifiers. You cannot use these words alone as a file name. You can, however, use these words as part of a longer file name. For example, in Windows, the file name *Nul* would not be valid, but you could name a file something like *Null Set.exe*. The following words should not be used as file names: Aux, Com1, Com2, Com3, Com4, Con, Lpt1, Lpt2, Lpt3, Prn, and Nul.

Case is disregarded. Some operating systems are case sensitive, but those that you regularly work with on personal computers are not. A file named *Final Report* is the same as *FINAL REPORT* or *final report*.

Aa

Spaces are allowed. You can use spaces in file names. That's a different rule than for email addresses, where spaces are not allowed. You've probably noticed that people often use underscores or periods instead of spaces in email addresses such as Madi_Jones@msu.edu. That convention is not necessary in file names, so a file name such as *Letter to Edison Jones* is valid.

File 1

▶ **What are storage device designations?** Files can be saved on internal storage devices as well as on external devices and in the cloud. Knowing the location of a file is the key to retrieving it. Every storage location has a name, such as C:, JacksHD, DropBox, Macintosh HD, or SanDiskUSB. The storage location name may identify the location of the device, its type, or its owner.

When working with Windows, storage devices can be identified by a **device letter**. The main hard disk drive is referred to as drive C. A device letter is usually followed by a colon, so C: is typically the designation for a hard disk drive. Removable storage devices are assigned drive letters when they are inserted. For example, Removable Disk (E:) might be the designation for a USB drive.

Drive letters are a legacy of DOS, which is why they remain in use in Windows but not on Macs. Macs do not use drive letters. Every storage device on Macs has a name. The main hard disk is called Macintosh HD. Figure 6-49 illustrates how devices might be designated on a PC.

Terminology

Storage locations are sometimes referred to as *storage volumes*. A volume can be an entire storage device, a storage medium, or a portion of a storage medium, such as a partition.

Figure 6-49: Storage device designations

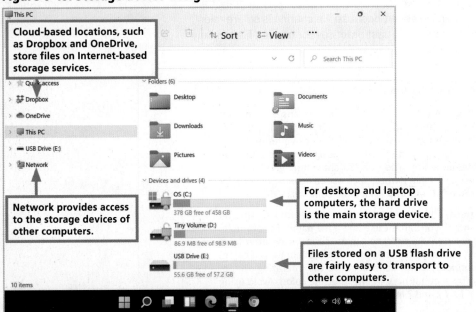

▶ **What is a disk partition?** A **disk partition** is a section of a hard disk drive that is treated as a separate storage unit. Most hard drives are configured with a single partition that contains the operating system, programs, and data. However, it is possible to create more than one hard disk partition, each with a separate name and device letter. Partitions are created, modified, and deleted using Disk Utility on Macs and Disk Management on PCs.

Based on the screenshot in Figure 6-49, the computer might appear to have two hard disk drives: C: and D:. However, in reality, it has one drive divided into two partitions. In such an arrangement, backing up files from C: to D: wouldn't offer protection in case of a hard disk failure because C: and D: are the same physical storage device.

Disk partitions help to separate programs from data files. For example, a PC might have one partition for operating system files and another partition for programs and data. This arrangement can speed up the process of disinfecting a computer that has been attacked by malicious software.

QuickCheck

Disk partitions C: and D: are generally used for

_____.

a. two USB drives

b. one hard drive

c. cloud storage locations

d. iOS devices

❱ **What is a folder?** Every storage device has a **directory** containing a list of its files. The main directory is referred to as the **root directory**. A root directory can be subdivided into smaller lists. Each list is called a **subdirectory**. Each subdirectory is depicted as a **folder**.

Folders help you envision files as if they were stored in a filing cabinet. Each folder can hold related items—for example, a set of documents, sound clips, financial data, or photos for a school project. Windows provides a folder called Documents that you might use to hold reports, letters, and so on. You can also create and name folders to meet your needs, such as a folder called QuickBooks to hold personal finance data.

Folders can be created within other folders. You might, for example, create a Graduation folder within your Pictures folder to hold a collection of graduation photos and another folder named Fido to hold photos of your faithful canine companion.

A folder name is separated from a drive letter and other folder names by a special symbol. In Microsoft Windows, this symbol is the backslash (\). For example, the folder for your dog pics (within the Pictures folder on drive C) would be written as C:\Pictures\Fido. Other operating systems use a forward slash (/) to separate folders.

❱ **What is a file path?** A computer file's location is defined by a **file path**, which on a PC includes the drive letter, folder(s), file name, and extension. Suppose that you have stored a JPEG file called *Yappy Hour* in the Fido folder on your hard disk. Its file specification is shown in Figure 6-50, along with a table of common file extensions.

6

Terminology

Modern operating systems may not display the slashes for a file path and instead use an alternative symbol, such as an arrow, triangle, or > symbol.

Figure 6-50: File paths

| Drive letter | Primary folder | Secondary folder | File name | File extension |

C:\Pictures\Fido\Yappy Hour.jpg

Type of File	Extensions
Text	.txt .dat .rtf .docx (Microsoft Word) .doc (Microsoft Word 2003) .odt (OpenDocument text) .wpd (WordPerfect) .pages (iWork)
Sound	.wav .mid .mp3 .m4p .aac
Graphics	.bmp .tif .wmf .gif .jpg .png .eps .ai (Adobe Illustrator)
Animation/video	.flc .swf .avi .mpg .mp4 .mov (QuickTime) .wmv (Windows Media Player)
Web page	.htm .html .asp .vrml .php
Spreadsheet	.xlsx (Microsoft Excel) .xls (Microsoft Excel 2003) .ods (OpenDocument spreadsheet) .numbers (iWork)
Database	.accdb (Microsoft Access) .odb (OpenDocument database)
Miscellaneous	.pdf (Adobe Acrobat) .pptx (Microsoft PowerPoint) .odp (OpenDocument presentations) .zip (WinZip) .pub (Microsoft Publisher)

File Management Tools

Operating systems provide file organization tools called **file management utilities**. Windows offers a utility called File Explorer, which is launched from the ![icon] icon on the taskbar. macOS offers a utility called Finder, which is launched from the ![icon] icon on the dock.

▶ **What's in the file management utility window?** File Explorer and Finder have many similarities. Although the icons are different, the general functions, features, and layouts are comparable. The examples in Figure 6-51 illustrate the components of File Explorer and Finder.

Figure 6-51: File management utility elements

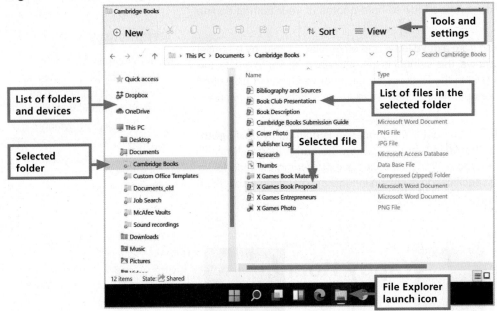

Windows File Explorer

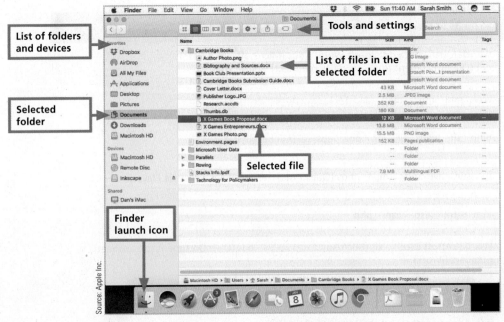

macOS Finder

▶ **Can I see file paths?** Proficient computer users are adept at using file extensions and paths to keep files organized. To apply these tools, settings that display extensions and paths must be enabled in File Explorer and Finder, as shown in Figure 6-52.

Figure 6-52: Set file managers to display extensions and paths

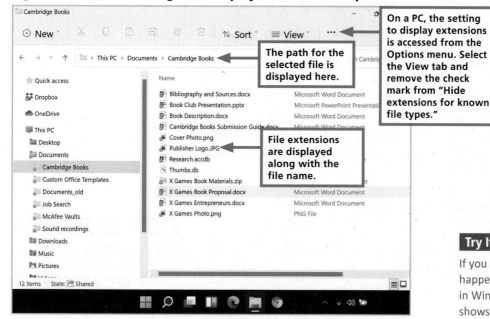

Windows File Explorer

> On a PC, the setting to display extensions is accessed from the Options menu. Select the View tab and remove the check mark from "Hide extensions for known file types."

> The path for the selected file is displayed here.

> File extensions are displayed along with the file name.

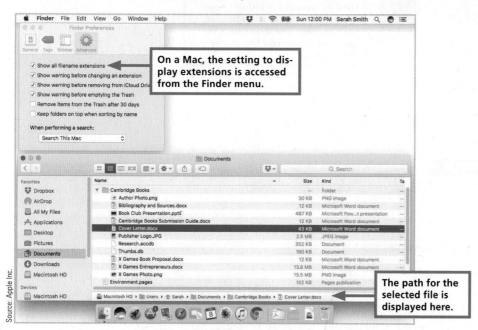

macOS Finder

> On a Mac, the setting to display extensions is accessed from the Finder menu.

> The path for the selected file is displayed here.

Source: Apple Inc.

▶ **What can I do with folders and files?** File management utilities are useful for locating files and for viewing their contents. Selecting a data file by double-clicking it or tapping it opens the file and its corresponding software application. The software application associated with a specific file type is called a **default application**. For example, the Paint application might be the default application for all PNG files, so when you select a file such as *Sunset. png*, the operating system automatically opens it using Paint.

But what if the operating system opens a file using an application that is not the one you want to use? Suppose that Windows opens a photo in Paint but you want to view it in Photoshop. Or what if macOS opens a photo in Viewer instead of Photoshop? You can select the application that you want to use by right-clicking the file and then selecting the application from a list.

You can also tell the operating system that you'd like to make a permanent change in the application that is used to open files of a specific type. For example, suppose you'd like to open all PNG files with Paint (on a PC) or Paintbrush (on a Mac). Follow the procedure in Figure 6-53.

Figure 6-53: Changing the default application

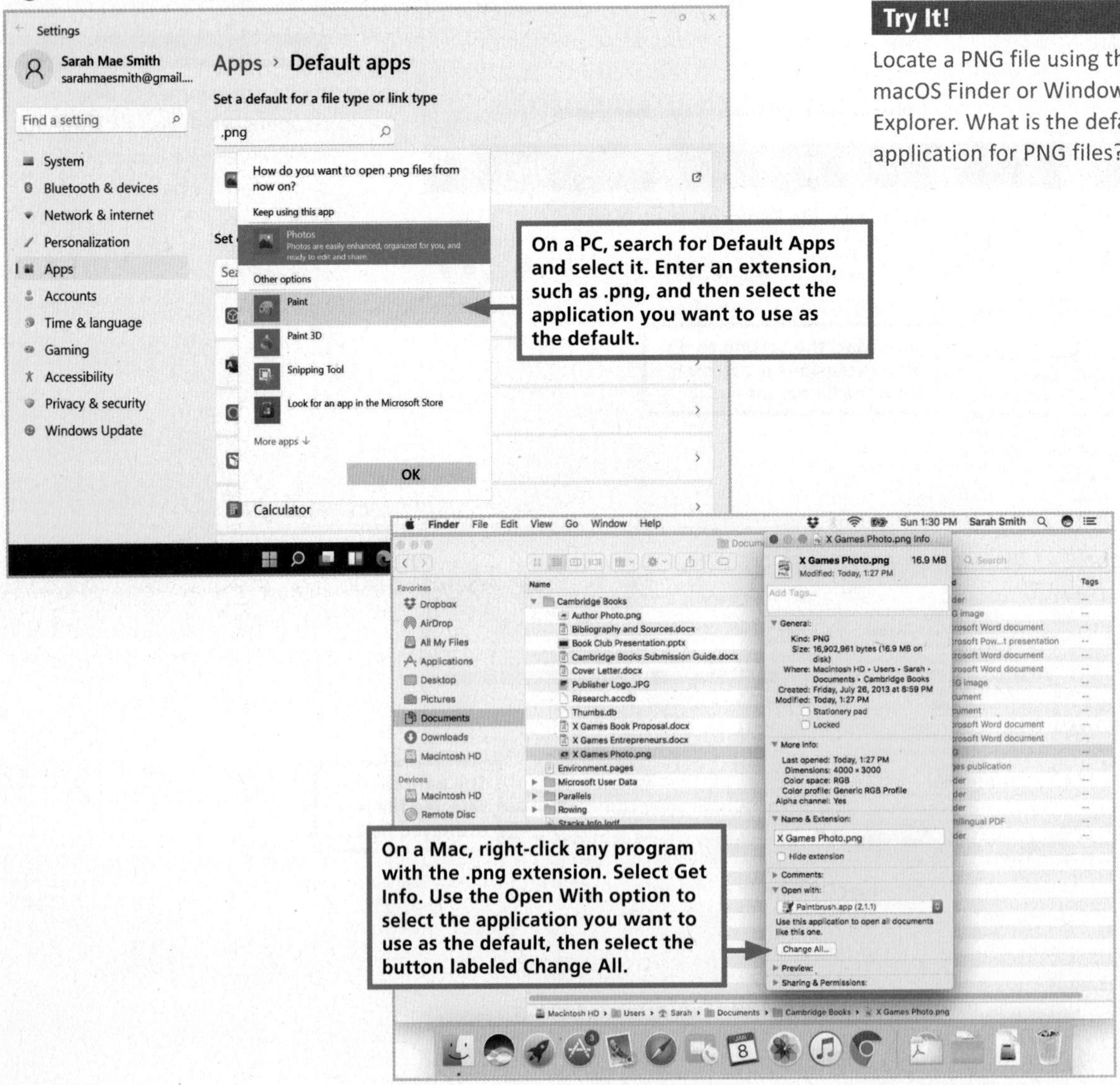

On a PC, search for Default Apps and select it. Enter an extension, such as .png, and then select the application you want to use as the default.

On a Mac, right-click any program with the .png extension. Select Get Info. Use the Open With option to select the application you want to use as the default, then select the button labeled Change All.

Try It!

Locate a PNG file using the macOS Finder or Windows File Explorer. What is the default application for PNG files?

▶ What else can I do with file management utilities? In addition to locating files and folders, file management utilities help you manipulate files and folders in the following ways:

- **Rename.** You can change the name of a file or folder to better describe its contents.

- **Copy.** You can copy a file from one device to another—for example, from a USB drive to the hard disk drive. You can also make a copy of a document so that you can revise the copy and leave the original intact.

- **Move.** You can move a file from one folder to another or from one storage device to another. When you move a file, it is erased from its original location, so make sure to remember the new location of the file. You can also move an entire folder and its contents from one storage device to another storage device or to a different folder.

- **Delete.** You can delete a file when you no longer need it. You can also delete a folder. Be careful when you delete a folder, because most file management utilities also delete all the files within a folder.

▶ Can I work with more than one file or folder at a time? To work with a group of files or folders, you must first select them. You can accomplish this task in several ways. You can hold down the Ctrl key (Command key on the Mac) as you click each item. This method works well if you are selecting files or folders that are not listed consecutively.

As an alternative, you can hold down the Shift key while you click the first item and the last item you want to select. By using the Shift key method, you select the two items that you clicked and all the items in between. After a group of items is selected, you can use the same copy, move, or delete procedure that you would use for a single item.

▶ What are personal folders? Windows and macOS offer a set of preconfigured personal folders, such as Documents and Music, for storing your personal data files. These folders may also appear in the Quick access list (PCs) or Favorites list (Macs). You can drag other folders to this list so that they can be accessed without clicking through several levels of folders (Figure 6-54).

Try It!

Use the macOS Finder or Windows File Explorer to experiment with selecting files using the Shift or Ctrl (Command) key.

Figure 6-54: Personalize your list of frequently used folders

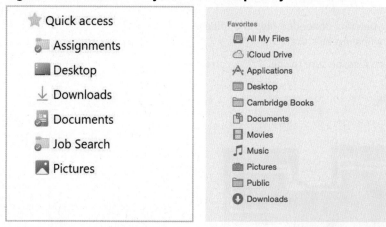

Source: Apple Inc.

On a PC, you can drag folders to the Quick access area of File Manager. To remove a folder without deleting it, right-click it and then select Unpin from Quick access.

On a Mac, you can drag folders to the Favorites area of Finder. To remove a folder without deleting it, right-click it and select Remove from Sidebar.

▶ **What are file management best practices?** A file management utility provides tools and procedures to help you keep track of your program and data files. However, these tools are most useful when you have a plan for organizing your files and when you follow some basic file management guidelines. Consider the tips in Figure 6-55 for managing files on your own computer. When working with files on lab computers, follow the guidelines from your instructor or lab manager.

Figure 6-55: File management best practices

- **Use descriptive names.** Give your files and folders descriptive names, and avoid using cryptic abbreviations.

- **Maintain file extensions.** When renaming a file, keep the original file extension so that the file can be opened with the correct application software.

- **Group similar files.** Separate files into folders based on subject matter. For example, store your creative writing assignments in one folder and your art history notes in another folder.

- **Organize your folders from the top down.** When devising a hierarchy of folders, consider how you want to access files and back them up. For example, you can specify one folder and its subfolders for a backup. If your important data is scattered in a variety of folders, however, making backups is more time-consuming.

- **Consider using default folders.** You should use preconfigured personal folders, such as Documents and Music, as your main data folders. Add subfolders to these personal folders as necessary to organize your files.

- **Use public folders for files you want to share.** Use the public folders for files that you want to share with other network users.

- **Don't mix data files and program files.** Do not store data files in the folders that hold your software. Most software is stored in subfolders of the Program Files folder on Windows systems and in the Applications folder on Macs.

- **Don't store files in the root directory.** Although it is acceptable to create folders in the root directory, it's not a good practice to store programs or data files in the root directory of your computer's hard disk.

- **Access files from the hard disk.** For best performance, copy files from USB drives to your computer's hard disk before accessing them.

- **Follow copyright rules.** When copying files, make sure you adhere to copyright and license restrictions.

- **Delete or archive files you no longer need.** Deleting unneeded files and folders helps keep your list of files from growing to an unmanageable size.

- **Be aware of storage locations.** When you save files, be sure to specify the correct storage device and folder.

- **Back up!** Back up your folders and files regularly.

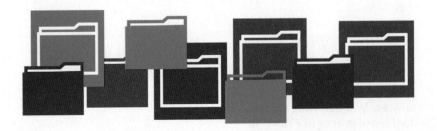

QuickCheck

When following best practices, whether you're using a PC or a Mac, you should not store files _____.

a. on the hard drive

b. in the root directory

c. with spaces in the name

d. in personal folders

Saving Files

Applications include menu options for opening and saving files. In fact, applications call the operating system's file management routines to get the job done. That is the reason the Save window provided by an application might look similar to the file management utility window.

▶ **What should I know about saving files?** Applications generally provide a way to open files and save them in a specific folder on a designated storage device. Some applications also allow you to delete and rename files. To save a file, use the Save option provided by your application, specify a location for the file, and give it a name. Most applications allow you to create a new folder and add tags to a file during the save process (Figure 6-56).

Try It!

Use an application, such as Word, to save a file. Examine the Save window and compare it to the window for the file management utility (File Explorer or Finder) on your computer. Are they similar?

6

Figure 6-56: Creating folders and saving files with Microsoft Word

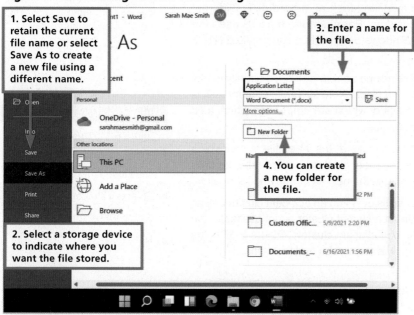

1. Select Save to retain the current file name or select Save As to create a new file using a different name.

3. Enter a name for the file.

4. You can create a new folder for the file.

2. Select a storage device to indicate where you want the file stored.

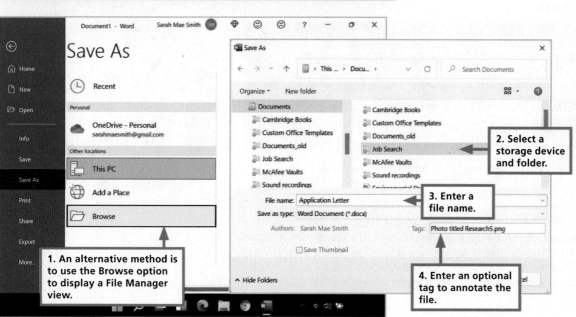

1. An alternative method is to use the Browse option to display a File Manager view.

2. Select a storage device and folder.

3. Enter a file name.

4. Enter an optional tag to annotate the file.

Physical File Storage

The structure of files and folders displayed in a file manager window is called a **logical storage model** because it helps you create a mental picture of the way files are organized in a hierarchy of folders. A **physical storage model** describes what actually happens on the disks and in the circuits. As you will see, the physical model is quite different from the logical model.

▶ **How is data stored?** Before a computer can store a file, the storage medium must be formatted. The **formatting** process creates the equivalent of electronic storage bins. Magnetic and optical media are divided into circular **tracks** and then further divided into pie-shaped **sectors**. Solid state storage media are divided into units.

▶ **How does the operating system keep track of a file's location?** The operating system uses a **file system** to keep track of the names and locations of files that reside on a storage medium, such as a hard disk. Different operating systems use different file systems. For example, macOS uses the Apple File System (APFS). Microsoft Windows uses a file system called NTFS (New Technology File System).

To speed up the process of storing and retrieving data, a disk drive usually works with a group of sectors called a **cluster** or a block. A file system's primary task is to maintain a list of clusters and keep track of which are empty and which hold data. This information is stored in an index file.

When you save a file, the operating system looks at the index file to see which clusters are empty. It selects one of these empty clusters, records the file data there, and then revises the index file to include the new file name and its location.

A file that does not fit into a single cluster spills over into an adjacent cluster unless that cluster already contains data. When an adjacent cluster is not available, the operating system stores parts of a file in nonadjacent clusters. Figure 6-57 helps you visualize how an index file keeps track of file names and locations.

Terminology

In NTFS, the index file containing metadata for all files is stored in the *Master File Table* (MFT).

QuickCheck

In Figure 6-57, the beige clusters illustrate _____.

a. the clusters for *Jordan.docx*

b. adjacent clusters

c. *Pick.bmp* sectors

d. NTFS

Figure 6-57: How an index file works

Index File

File	Cluster	Comment
MFT	1	Reserved for MFT files
DISK USE	2	Part of MFT that contains a list of empty sectors
Bio.txt	3, 4	*Bio.txt* file stored in clusters 3 and 4
Jordan.docx	7, 8, 10	*Jordan.docx* file stored noncontiguously in clusters 7, 8, and 10
Pick.bmp	9	*Pick.bmp* file stored in cluster 9

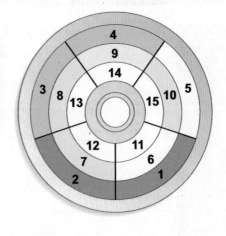

Each colored cluster on the disk contains part of a file. *Bio.txt* is stored in adjacent clusters (green). *Jordan.docx* is stored in nonadjacent clusters (beige). A computer locates and displays the *Jordan.docx* file by looking for its name in the index file to find the location of the first cluster.

6

▶ **What happens when a file is deleted?** When you click a file's icon and then select the Delete option, you might have visions of the read-write head somehow scrubbing out the clusters that contain data. That doesn't happen. Instead, the operating system changes the status of the file's clusters to "empty" and removes the file name from the index file. The file name no longer appears in a directory listing, but the file's data remains in the clusters until a new file is stored there.

▶ **Can deleted files be undeleted?** The Windows Recycle Bin and similar utilities in other operating systems are designed to protect you from accidentally deleting hard disk files you actually need. Instead of marking a file's clusters as empty, the operating system moves the file to the Recycle Bin folder. The deleted file still takes up space on the disk but does not appear in the usual directory listing.

Files in the Recycle Bin folder can be undeleted so that they again appear in the regular directory. In addition, the Recycle Bin can be emptied to permanently delete any files it contains.

▶ **What happens when I empty the Recycle Bin?** When the Recycle Bin is emptied, the index file marks the clusters containing deleted files as "empty" and the file name is removed from all directory listings. The old data remains in the clusters, however, until it is overwritten by other files. Various third-party utilities can recover a lot of this supposedly deleted data. Law enforcement agents, for example, use these utilities to gather evidence from deleted files on the computer disks of suspected criminals.

To delete data from a disk in such a way that no one can ever read it, you can use special **file shredder software** that overwrites supposedly empty sectors with random 1s and 0s. This software is handy if you plan to donate your computer to a charitable organization and you want to make sure your personal data no longer remains on the hard disk.

QuickCheck

What happens when you delete a file and then empty the Trash (Mac) or Recycle Bin (PC)?

a. The clusters containing the file data are scrubbed clean.

b. The file is stuffed with 1s and 0s.

c. The file's clusters are marked "empty" but the data remains in them until it is overwritten.

d. The file is shredded.

QuickQuiz   Section E

1. File-naming [_____] are a list of rules for creating valid file names.

2. A disk [_____] divides a hard disk into two or more storage units.

3. Drive C:\ is also called the [_____] directory.

4. A group of tracks and sectors used as a storage unit is called a(n) [_____].

5. NTFS and APFS are examples of Windows and macOS file [_____].

Issue: What Happened to That App?

That app got banned. iPhone owners head to the Apple App Store to download apps for their phones. Samsung phone owners connect to the Google Play Store or the Galaxy Store for apps to enhance their devices.

These app stores offer millions of apps that generate billions of downloads. The apps also generate substantial profits for the stores, which take a percentage cut of all sales.

The companies that operate these app stores have good intentions. Here's what Apple has to say: "The guiding principle of the App Store is simple—we want to provide a safe experience for users to get apps and a great opportunity for all developers to be successful. We do this by offering a highly curated App Store where every app is reviewed by experts and an editorial team helps users discover new apps every day."

> **"We want to provide a safe experience for users..."**
>
> Apple App Developer Guidelines

Consumers have an expectation that apps marketed at app stores will be functional and secure. They expect the app to work as described. They expect the app to be free of creepy or offensive content. They do not want apps that sell personal data to marketers, contain malware, exploit minors, or promote unscientific medical practices.

Ensuring that millions of apps meet consumer expectations is not easy. Third-party developers from all over the world create apps and submit them to the app store's review process. During the review process, professional reviewers test the apps to make sure they comply with the app store's policy guidelines. The task is daunting. In a typical month, thousands of apps are submitted by developers hoping for approval.

According to Apple, about 40% of developer submissions are rejected, though many are subsequently approved after developers implement modifications required by the review process. But some apps are permanently rejected. Apps are banned if they contain objectionable content, if they collect or share personal data without permission, or if they are copycats of other apps.

The list of no-nos that are detailed in app review guidelines is long. Some of the criteria are subjective. The guidelines give app stores a lot of power over the apps that are published and those that are banned.

During the early days of the Apple App Store, its review process rejected the Google Voice app and banned several related apps that had previously been approved. Google appealed to the Federal Communications Commission, asking it to investigate whether Apple was colluding with its exclusive carrier, AT&T, to restrict user choice for wireless voice and text services. The issue was resolved in favor of Google, so now consumers are able to download Google Voice and similar VoIP apps.

More recently, Apple banned an app that was used by Hong Kong protesters to crowdsource the location of police forces. Regardless of its legitimate use to avoid streets on which conflicts might be taking place, authorities claimed that the app was being used to victimize people and property where there was no nearby police presence.

And then there was the Fortnite controversy. The popular game published by Epic Games was released on the Apple App Store and Google Play Store in 2018. Epic Games CEO Tim Sweeney was at the time an outspoken critic of the 30% revenue cut required by the stores. He also maintained that Apple's App Store was essentially a monopoly and anticompetitive.

In 2020, a new version of Fortnite was released. It included a 20% discount to gamers who used the in-game V-bucks currency. The discount was not made available to Fortnite users who purchased through the Apple or Google stores. Fortnite was immediately banned by Apple and Google. Lawsuits followed.

The controversies surrounding banned apps prompted companies such as Spotify and Blockchain to join Epic Games in forming the Coalition for App Fairness, which urges app stores to "recognize that every app developer, regardless of size or the nature of the developer's business, is entitled to fair treatment."

Try It!

Are app developers and consumers being exploited by the companies that operate app stores? Explore the issue by completing the Try It! activities. Your instructor can specify how to submit your findings.

1 To discover current information about your favorite app store, look online for answers to the following questions:

a. Approximately how many apps are currently offered by the app store?

b. What was the app store's revenue for the previous year?

c. What percentage of a sale does the app store retain?

d. How long does it take to approve or reject an app once it has been submitted for review?

e. How many apps actually make money for the developer?

2 Take a look at an app store's review guidelines for developers to discover what is considered objectionable or inappropriate content. Describe the types of content that fall into this category. Provide examples of guidelines for this category that are subjective and could be the basis for banning apps that might not be harmful to consumers.

3 How successful is your app store at rejecting apps that contain malware? Search online to see if there have been recent warnings about apps that contain malware that was not discovered during the review process. Summarize what you find.

4 There is a YouTube video called *Fortnite 1984 Apple Parody Video*. Watch the original *Apple-1984* video and then watch the parody. Summarize the message of each video.

5 What is the current status of the Fortnite controversy? Explore online to find information about the original case, *Epic Games Inc. v. Apple Inc.* Explain how "in-app purchases" are relevant to the case. If the case has been resolved, what was the verdict? If the case has not yet been resolved, explain its current status.

6 The Fortnite case is representative of a growing sense that big tech companies are getting too big and wielding too much power over developers and consumers. In 2021, the European Commission found Apple in breach of EU antitrust law on the basis that the Apple App Store charged high commission fees and prohibited developers from informing consumers of alternative subscription and purchase options. What is the meaning of "antitrust"? How does that term relate to controversies about tech companies' app stores?

What Do You Think?

Issue

1. Have you downloaded an app that has later been banned?

2. Do you think that app stores are doing a good job of reviewing apps before publicly posting them?

3. Do you think that devices should be limited to obtaining apps from only one source?

Information Tools: Documentation Literacy

It wasn't too long ago that software arrived in a box that contained a CD and a lengthy printed manual. This documentation included a detailed description of every feature as well as tutorials and troubleshooting guides. Today, printed manuals have been replaced by a variety of online documentation. Finding and using it is a skill that is sometimes referred to as documentation literacy. You can use documentation like a pro by following a few easy guidelines.

Know what you are using. Make sure you know the name of the software that you are using, the software publisher, and the software version. To find this information on Macs, look at the About option on the software menu. On PCs, use the About option on the Help menu.

Use the Help menu. The Help menu is a great tool for learning how to use specific features of the software. From the Help menu you can expect to find:

- A searchable list or an index of help topics
- Links to online tutorials and help resources provided by the software publisher

Find the publisher's online documentation. An online user manual can include an overview of the software, information about system requirements, technical information about the software, and instructions for using each feature. Some documentation is very extensive; use the table of contents, index, and Search box to quickly find the information you seek. Don't spend too much time paging through a lengthy user manual. Your time might be spent more efficiently by looking elsewhere.

Check YouTube. When looking for a "getting started" tutorial or a walkthrough of how to use a specific software feature, YouTube is a good resource. You may also find software reviews that are helpful when deciding whether the software is worth downloading. Some software videos on YouTube are created by the software publisher, whereas others are created by unaffiliated users. Video tutorials tend to be accurate because they are recorded using the actual software. Their quality can vary, however. If multiple videos on the same topic are available, don't hesitate to bail out of a low-quality production. Product reviews posted on YouTube may be biased, so cross-check with other user reviews.

Use a search engine. For troubleshooting, a search engine may be your best resource. Entering a general search that includes the software product name, such as *LibreOffice help* or *Photoshop help*, usually yields results from the software publisher's online help resources.

Visit online forums. Popular software spawns user forums. Some are independent, whereas others are sponsored by the software's publisher. Independent forums are a good source of troubleshooting information—especially for problems that the software publisher would prefer to ignore.

You can find forums by entering a query such as *LibreOffice user group* or *Photoshop discussion forum*.

Keep notes. Write down error messages. Enter the text of the error message in a search engine along with the name of the troublesome software product and your device's operating system. When you find a solution, pay it forward and post the fix on an appropriate online forum.

Evaluate before you implement. Not all of the information you find in user forums is accurate or up to date. Be especially careful when troubleshooting malware because some malware "fixes" introduce even more malware. Before implementing instructions for fixing a problem, cross-check the solution by searching further. Look for users who have successfully implemented the instructions. Also, make sure the instructions pertain to the software and operating system versions you are using. The information from moderated or software publishers' forums is more likely to be accurate than information from non-moderated forums.

Try It!

As the amount of online information grows, more and more of it becomes outdated. When troubleshooting software, outdated information can be useless. Let's take a look at the assortment of software documentation available online.

1 Suppose that you are curious about Chromebooks. Would one be a useful addition to your digital device collection? Use a search engine to browse the Chrome OS discussion group on Reddit. Then browse the Community link of Google's Chromebook Help site. How would you characterize the discussion topics at each of these sites? How would you characterize the expertise of participants?

2 Suppose you are using a Chromebook and need to find its IP address. Watch at least three YouTube videos on the topic. For each video, record its URL and evaluate its quality.

3 What if you want to use your Chromebook offline to compose documents and spreadsheets? Is it possible to do so? What do you need to consider if you plan to edit documents using Google Docs and Google Drive offline? What is the most frequent problem that other people seem to have when attempting this? Use a search engine to locate information on this topic. Record what you find and where you find it.

4 A dynamic dashboard collects data from a spreadsheet and displays it in chart format, updating the charts on the fly as new data arrives. Locate an online tutorial about dynamic dashboards and attempt to follow the instructions to create one with graphs or tables from more than one data set. Record the URL for the tutorial. Submit your completed dashboard file along with a short rating and review of the tutorial. In your review, include information about the clarity and completeness of the tutorial.

5 Find the software publisher's documentation for an open source program called GIMP. What does the GIMP application do? Does the publisher's documentation include a tutorial or FAQs? Are there help groups?

6 Find tutorials and help resources for GIMP other than those supplied by the GIMP Web site. Give examples of at least three additional online GIMP resources. Can you locate instructions at any one of these sites for isolating an image from its background so that the "cut out" image could be overlaid on a different background? Write out the steps for doing so.

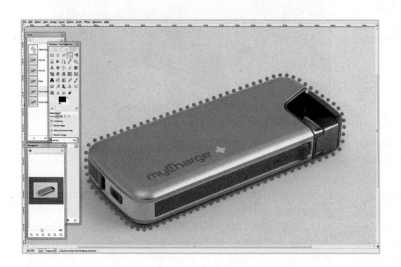

Source: MIDASoft Inc.

Technology in Context: Architecture and Construction

A cluster of workers in hardhats study a blueprint. Sun-bronzed laborers perch on a makeshift bench, munching sandwiches and waving to a group of carpenters hauling 2x4s onto a foundation. The sounds of hammers, shovels, and power tools fill the air from early morning through late afternoon. It is a typical construction site: an anthill of activity where a structure of some sort is eventually assembled—a house, a shopping mall, or a skyscraper.

Behind the scenes of this busy site, digital technology has added a high-tech flavor to construction projects with real-time interactive graphics, broadband wireless communications, distributed database management systems, wearable and vehicle-mounted computers, global positioning satellites, and laser-guided surveying systems.

Architects use computers to create blueprints. Contractors use computers for cost estimates and scheduling. Computers also appear on the job site, carried as handheld devices and embedded in construction equipment.

In the past, architects drew construction plans by hand on semitransparent film called vellum. To create a blueprint, they overlaid the vellum on special blue paper and then ran it through a machine that exposed it to intensified light and ammonia. Minor changes to a design were possible; but for major changes, architects often needed to create a new set of vellum drawings.

With the advent of computers and computer-aided design (CAD) software, architects realized they could be more productive—and make design changes more easily—by replacing their drafting tables with computers running CAD software. Using plotters with wide print beds, architects are able to produce computer-generated blueprints similar to those they created at a drafting table.

Initially, architects used CAD software to create 2D floor plans and elevations. Today, architects use 3D CAD software that offers a greatly expanded toolset. The HGTV series *The Property Brothers* works with a 3D rendering and animation company called Neezo Renders to create spiffy visualizations for home remodeling projects.

Architects begin with a 2D floor plan and then use CAD tools to draw interior and exterior walls, ceilings, and roofs. Standard building materials, such as doors and windows, can be selected from a list of clip-art objects and dragged into position with a mouse. Electrical, plumbing, and framing schematics can also be added.

Any elements of the drawing can be displayed or hidden. For example, when discussing the design with an electrical contractor, an architect can hide the plumbing details. These 3D wireframe drawings with building, electrical, and plumbing elements included can be rotated and viewed from any angle.

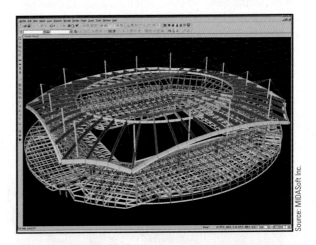

Source: MIDASoft Inc.

Inexpensive ink jet printers have replaced expensive first-generation plotters and give architects the option of printing in realistic color. Using 3D CAD software, they can also apply textures and colors to convert wireframes into 3D models that can be viewed from the inside or outside. Architects sometimes use an animated version of a 3D model for virtual reality walkthroughs.

After an architect has completed the building plans, a contractor estimates the project's price tag by calculating the cost of materials and labor. Computerized spreadsheets, such as Excel, are a popular tool for cost estimates. Large contracting firms often use commercial software specifically designed for construction estimates.

Contractors are also responsible for scheduling the tasks in a construction project, such as excavating the building site, erecting the foundation, constructing the frame, assembling the roof, adding wiring and plumbing, and doing interior finish work. Large construction projects, such as malls and government buildings, can involve thousands of tasks and many subcontractors.

Computerized scheduling tools, such as Gantt charts, PERT diagrams, and work breakdown scheduling software, make it possible to plan and track each construction phase and break a project down into a series of tasks. For each task, planners enter its estimated duration and how it relates to other tasks. For example, drywall work that requires eight days depends on interior framing, electrical work, and plumbing being finished first. Given information about all the tasks in a project, planning software can create a schedule showing both best-case and worst-case completion dates, and contractors can update the schedule based on actual construction progress.

At a high-tech construction site, computers can play several additional roles. A site supervisor can use a wireless handheld computer to view and update the construction schedule stored on a desktop computer at the contractor's main office. Rather than referring to a set of printed—and possibly outdated—plans, the supervisor can refer to up-to-date plans transmitted from the home office. A supervisor might even wear a hardhat-mounted computer that collects multimedia data, such as video and sound, to document site inspections. A voice-activated microphone records the supervisor's comments and adds them to the digital video, which can be uploaded to a database in the contractor's main office.

Digital devices also play a role in guiding bulldozers during site preparation by using construction software developed at Ohio State University that works with a global positioning system (GPS). A GPS receiver is mounted on a vehicle that traverses the site. GPS signals are collected and entered in the software program, which creates a map and a plan for site preparation. A wireless device mounted in each bulldozer's cab receives data from the software and displays it to the operator. The system allows construction crews to stake and grade a site with to-the-centimeter accuracy.

Computers embedded in robots are used extensively on large construction projects in Japan. These single-task robots perform specific jobs. For example, a concrete-task robot might lay forms, bend rebar for reinforcement, pour concrete, and screed the surface to a smooth finish. Other robots weld steel components, apply paint, or install tile. Single-task robots have been successful because they shield human workers from dangerous and difficult jobs, and tend to work faster and more consistently than humans. However, trained technicians are required to set up and monitor robot work.

It was once a summer tradition for college students to work in construction. Today, however, fewer students are attracted to those jobs, creating a labor shortage.

Construction robots might help fill the labor gap. For example, a robot that finishes drywall can be cost-effectively deployed at commercial construction sites. The robot, created by a construction robotics company, uses laser-light measuring devices to scan the walls and then activates a robotic arm to smooth the surface and apply drywall compound.

Potential barriers, such as union regulations, could discourage the use of construction robots. Some observers question how building trade union agreements might affect construction site robots. According to one supervisor's worst-case scenario, "Millwrights will want to set up the device, electricians will want to fix the electronic controls, equipment operators will want to run it, cement finishers will want to adjust it, and laborers will be expected to clean it."

The future of computer-powered robots at construction sites is still unclear, which illustrates the controversies that sometimes surround technology as it filters into society and the workplace.

Flipped Class Projects

Critical Thinking

Free content. Free software. Freemium pricing models. Viral popularity. Disappearing gatekeepers. These are the disrupters of the digital age. They affect software as well as digital content. But what is the endgame? Will these disrupters lead to a cultural renaissance or to a cultural dark age? Watch the Vimeo video titled "PressPausePlay." What are the two opposing viewpoints it presents? What is your perspective on the issue?

Group Project

Form a group with at least two of your classmates. Now imagine that your college (or business) has decided to negotiate with software publishers to offer students (or employees) a bundled software package at a greatly discounted price. Your group's job is to select the 15 software products for the bundle. Your group must make sure the software effectively meets the major needs of the students at your school (or employees in your workplace). Use Internet resources to look at the range of software available and make your selections. Make sure you take advantage of group members' expertise and experience with software products.

Cyberclassroom

Mobile apps used for educational activities are called mLearning apps. Do you use mobile flashcards? Have you downloaded a periodic table to your Android phone? Do you have a link to a reference portal or academic journal handy? Is your mobile device helping you to learn a second language? Do you have a stash of articles pertaining to your major field? Does your phone hold a list of assignments and due dates? Work in groups of two or three to share the mLearning apps that you use. Brainstorm ways you can use generic apps, such as Notes, Reminders, and Calendar, for mLearning.

Multimedia Project

Create an infographic that offers ten best practices for computer file management. You can base your infographic on the tips in Figure 6-55. To get started, browse the Web for some examples and ideas. You'll also find several free apps for creating infographics online, or use your favorite graphics software.

Resume Builder

Use the Web and other resources to compile a list of the software used in your current or future career field. Are there standard software products that job applicants need to know how to use? If so, what can you find out about those products on the Web? If your career field does not use any standard software products, explain why you think that is the case. Also, make a list of the software products you're familiar with. As you consider your school and career goals for the next year, list at least five additional software applications you would like to learn. Explain why they would be helpful.

Globalization

Computer games are big business. They are exported worldwide and accessed by communities of online players around the globe. For this project, gather information about the most internationally popular computer games. Try some of them yourself to see what they're all about. What effect, if any, would you expect these games to have on individual players living in the cultures of 1) industrialized countries, 2) Middle Eastern countries, and 3) developing countries? Summarize your ideas in one or two pages.

Key Terms

absolute reference 422
Android 401
application extensions 409
automatic recalculation 422
BSD license 387
buffers 394
cell 419
cell references 421
Chrome OS 402
cluster 436
commercial software 385
database 423
database software 423
default application 432
demoware 386
desktop operating system 391
device letter 428
directory 429
disk partition 428
DMG 412
document formatting 418
DOS (Disk Operating System) 396
EULAs 384
executable file 382
field 423
file management utilities 430
file path 429
file shredder software 437
file system 436
file-naming conventions 427
folder 429
font 418
footer 418
forked 402
formatting 436
formula 420
freeware 386

fully justified 418
function 421
GPL 387
grammar checker 417
hash value 386
header 418
iOS 400
jailbreak 408
kernel 391
label 419
leading 418
Linux 403
Linux distribution 403
local application 409
logical storage model 436
macOS 398
memory leak 393
Microsoft Windows 395
mobile app 408
mobile operating systems 391
module 415
multiple-user license 385
multiprocessing 393
multitasking 393
multithreading 393
office suite 415
open source software 387
page layout 418
paragraph alignment 418
paragraph style 418
physical storage model 436
pirated software 389
point size 418
presentation software 425
processes 392
product activation 386
productivity software 415

proprietary software 385
public domain software 385
readability formula 417
record 423
relative reference 422
resource 392
root directory 429
rooting 408
search and replace 416
sectors 436
server operating system 391
setup program 410
single-user license 385
site license 385
software license 384
software update 383
software upgrade 383
spelling checker 417
spelling dictionary 417
spreadsheet 419
spreadsheet software 419
style 418
subdirectory 429
system requirements 382
thesaurus 417
thin client 402
tracks 436
uninstall utility 413
user interface 391
value 419
virtual machine 404
Web application 406
what-if analysis 419
word processing software 416
word wrap 416
worksheet 419

Interactive Summary

Section A: Both [ ] software and application software are essential for accomplishing tasks with a digital device. Today, most application software is distributed online or through app stores. The main executable file for PC software has a(n) [ ] extension, whereas executable files for Macs have a(n) [ ] extension. New versions of software are called [ ] and are indicated by version numbers such as 1.0 and 2.0. A software [ ] or patch is a small section of program code designed to correct problems and address security vulnerabilities. Software payment models include free, one-time purchase, [ ], trial, and freemium. Software licenses, referred to by the acronym [ ], can be divided into two main categories: public [ ] and proprietary. [ ] software is typically available directly from the publisher or an app store and may have options for site licenses as well as single-user licenses. Freeware is copyrighted software that is available free of charge. [ ] is also available free of charge, but is limited in some way until you pay for it. Open [ ] software may be sold or distributed free of charge, but the distribution must include the source code.

Section B: [ ] operating systems—such as Windows, Chrome OS, and macOS—accommodate one user at a time, are capable of multitasking, and include a graphical user interface designed for keyboard and mouse input. Chrome OS is considered a thin [ ] because it depends substantially on processing supplied by a remote computer. [ ] operating systems, such as iOS and Android, are designed for smartphones and tablet computers. [ ] operating systems, such as UNIX and Linux, are designed for hosting distributed networks. A single device can run more than one operating system as a(n) [ ] machine. The operating system [ ] remains in RAM while a device is in operation and manages the device's resources. Most operating systems have [ ] capabilities that allow two or more processes to run simultaneously. [ ] capabilities allow an operating system to run multiple simultaneous operations for a single program. [ ] supports a division of labor among several processing units. Operating systems manage resources by monitoring processor cycles, allocating [ ] space to programs, tracking stored files, and supervising data exchanges with peripheral devices. When an operating system fails to correctly track the allocation of RAM space to applications, a memory [ ] may produce "Program Not Responding" error messages. Operating systems also manage [ ] that collect and hold data from peripheral devices until a device is ready to accept it.

Section C: Software is available in several paradigms that affect how it is installed and used. [_____] apps run in a browser and require no installation. Mobile apps are designed for smartphones and tablets. They are typically downloaded and [_____] from an app store or Web sites, though owners with [_____] devices must [_____] the device to obtain apps from third-party sources. Local applications for PCs are installed using a(n) [_____] program that copies files, checks resources, and updates the Windows [_____]. Software for Macs is distributed as [_____] packages that are dragged to the Applications folder to complete the installation. To remove software that has been installed on a PC, Windows supplies a(n) [_____] utility. To remove most applications from a Mac, the [_____] file or folder can simply be dragged to the trash.

Section D: Office suites are sometimes referred to as [_____] software because they offer features that really help get work done. Word [_____] software assists you with composing, editing, designing, printing, and electronically publishing documents. When you want to change margins, headers, and footers, you can use [_____] layout tools. To change the spacing between lines or the alignment of text, you can use tools to adjust [_____] style. [_____] software is like a smart piece of paper that automatically adds up the columns of numbers you write on it. You can use it to make other calculations, too, based on basic equations that you write or more complex, built-in formulas. Because you can experiment with different numbers, this type of software is particularly useful for [_____] analyses. [_____] software helps you store, find, organize, update, and report information located in one or more tables. Data is stored in [_____], which form records. When two sets of records are [_____], database software allows you to access data from both tables at the same time. [_____] software supplies tools for creating a series of electronic slides that can be shown on a computer screen or projector.

Section E: Every file has a name and might also have a file extension. The rules that specify valid file names are called file-naming [_____]. These rules typically do not allow you to use certain characters or [_____] words in a file name. A file's location is defined by a file [_____], which includes the storage device, folder(s), file name, and extension. In Windows, storage devices are identified by a drive letter, followed by a(n) [_____]. Every storage device has a(n) [_____] containing a list of files stored on the device. The top-level list of a device is referred to as the [_____] directory, which can be subdivided into several smaller lists called subdirectories that are depicted as [_____]. Windows File Explorer and the macOS [_____] are examples of file management utilities provided by operating systems. These utilities allow you to find, rename, copy, move, and delete files and folders. In addition, they allow you to perform file management activities with more than one file at a time. The way that data is actually stored is referred to as the [_____] storage model. Before a computer stores data on a disk, CD, or DVD, it creates the equivalent of electronic storage bins by dividing the disk into [_____] and then further dividing the disk into [_____]. This dividing process is referred to as [_____]. Each sector of a disk is numbered, providing a storage address that the operating system can track. Many computers work with a group of sectors, called a(n) [_____], to increase the efficiency of file storage operations. When a file is deleted from a PC, the operating system changes the status of the file to "empty" and removes the file name from the [_____] listing.

1. Imagine that you've just paid for a year's subscription to highly rated antivirus software. You've installed the software, but it requires a(n) [_____] code before it begins scanning for viruses.

2. Every time you want to edit a photo, your PC pulls up a Viewer application that has no editing capabilities. To avoid this frustration in the future, you have to change the [_____] application that is associated with the JPEG and PNG file extensions.

3. Your friend has an iPhone that's loaded with all kinds of applications. But every time there's a software update, your friend grumbles about "redoing stuff." You guess that your friend's iPhone is [_____].

4. Suppose that you've been hired to organize a professional skateboard competition. When you consider how you'll need to use digital devices, you realize that you must collect information on each competitor and keep track of every competitive event. With at least two types of related records, you'll probably need to use [_____] software.

5. The screen below is likely to appear during the process of [_____] a software application.

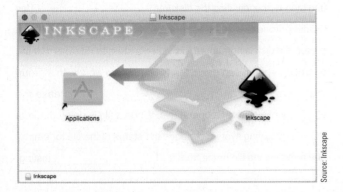

Source: Inkscape

6. While using several Windows programs at the same time, your computer displays an error message that refers to a program that is not responding. You recognize this message as one that might result from a(n) [_____] leak and decide to close the nonresponding program using Task Manager.

7. Your friend wants to open a window on a Mac computer in order to run Microsoft Windows and play some games designed for the Windows platform. You tell your friend to create a(n) [_____] machine using software such as Parallels Desktop.

8. Can you use a Windows application, create a document, and store it using the file name *I L*ve NY*? Yes or no? [_____]

9. When specifying a location for a data file on your hard disk, you should avoid saving it in the [_____] directory.

10. You have an old computer that you will donate to a school, but you want to make sure its hard disk contains no trace of your data. To do so, you use file [_____] software that overwrites empty sectors with random 1s and 0s.

Lab: Organize Your Files Today!

Some day you have to get organized. That day is here. This lab is designed to help you evaluate your current file organization and make improvements that will increase your productivity and reduce the frustration of rifling through a jumble of unorganized files and folders.

Requirements:

For this lab, you'll need a desktop or laptop computer running Windows or macOS. The instructions are generalized; they provide helpful guidelines but not specific steps. You may have to do some exploring to find all the tools needed to complete the assignment, but that is all part of the learning experience.

Assignment:

1 Examine your desktop computer, laptop, or cloud drive and total up your organizational points as described below:

Count the icons on your desktop. If you have fewer than 20, award yourself 1 point.

Check the root directory (Macintosh HD or Windows C:). Award yourself 1 point if there are only folders and no files there.

Examine the folders listed under your user name. Give yourself 1 point if you can identify the kinds of files that each one contains.

Open each of the folders listed under your user name. Award yourself 1 point if none of the folders is empty.

Open the Documents folder. Award yourself 1 point if you have fewer than 100 files (not counting folders) listed there.

If you use one set of folders for your personal data and another set of folders for school or work data, award yourself 1 point.

Open the folder that contains most of your photos. Give yourself 1 point if the photos are organized into subfolders according to date, subject, or other criteria.

Browse files on your storage device. If you don't seem to have unnecessary duplicates, give yourself 1 point.

If you can launch any program in fewer than 5 seconds, award yourself 1 point.

If files and folders that you use frequently are in your Quick Access or Favorites list, add another point to your score.

2 Evaluate your score.

8–10 points: You're organized!

5–7 points: You're on the right track.

0–4 points: It is not too late to get organized.

3 Make a backup of your data files. Do it.

If you have a backup, make sure it is current. If you have no backup, at least copy your data files to a USB flash drive. How much space does your backup require?

4 Switch to Details view (PC) or List view (Macs).

For organizing files, the Details and List views provide the best visual picture of the folder hierarchy. After your files are in order, you may want to use a different view for everyday file access.

Use the View menu to experiment with various views. You may also explore the Sort options to see how they affect the arrangement of folders and files.

When you are finished exploring, return to the List view.

On a PC, select View and then select Details. Also use the Sort by option to select Type and Ascending, which lists all of the subfolders, followed by files.

On a Mac, select the List view and sort by Kind, which groups all of the subfolders together. Don't worry if the subfolders are not at the top of the list.

5 Organize your Quick Access or Favorites list.

On PCs running Windows 10 and 11, the Quick Access list is a handy location for the folders that you use most frequently. On earlier versions of Windows and on Macs, the Favorites list is the recommended location for preconfigured personal folders titled Desktop, Documents, Music, Pictures, Videos, and Downloads.

If the Quick Access or Favorites folder already contains the preconfigured personal folders, skip this step. Otherwise, locate your preconfigured folders and drag them to the Quick Access or Favorites list.

On a Mac, you'll find the preconfigured personal folders listed under Macintosh HD/Users/YourUserName. On a PC, you'll find these folders on drive C: under Users\YourUserName.

6 Add project subfolders to the Quick Access or Favorites list.

Folders in the Quick Access or Favorites area can be accessed with a single click. Consider the projects that you are currently working on and the folders that you access

most frequently. Are there any additional folders that you would like to add to the Quick Access or Favorites list?

Drag additional folders to the Quick Access or Favorites list as necessary.

Tip: Don't let the Quick Access or Favorites list get too long or it will no longer be a quick way to access folders. When the number of folders in the list exceeds 20, it is time to remove folders that are less frequently used. To remove a folder, right-click it and select the Remove option or the Unpin option. Do not select the Delete option unless you want to move the folder and its contents to the trash.

7 Clean up your desktop.

The desktop should be reserved for files that you access on a daily basis. For example, the desktop is a good place for a To-Do list. You may also store frequently used programs there, though the Start menu and taskbar are preferable locations because they are always visible.

Remove any icons that are cluttering up your desktop.

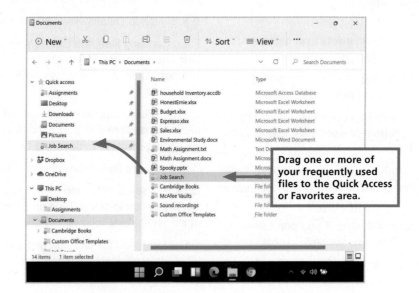

Drag one or more of your frequently used files to the Quick Access or Favorites area.

8 Deal with shortcuts.

A shortcut (PC) or alias (Mac) is a link to a file, folder, or application. Shortcuts and aliases are useful for items that you want to access from multiple places but don't want to save as actual copies. For example, if you use the same photo for two projects, you might not want to duplicate the photo, but you might want a link for the photo to exist in more than one folder.

As another example, you might want to be able to launch an application from the desktop as well as from the taskbar or dock. You don't want two copies of the application, but a shortcut or alias will provide an icon that you can use.

Deleting a shortcut or alias only deletes the shortcut icon, not the file, folder, or application that it represents. You can identify shortcuts because their icons include an arrow.

Check your desktop and file listings for shortcuts or aliases by looking for icons, folders, and files that display arrows. If you do not need the shortcuts, remove them by right-clicking and selecting the Delete option (PC) or the Move to Trash option (Mac).

9 Organize your Documents folder.

A well-organized set of folders has a logical hierarchical structure. For example, in the Documents folder, there can be subfolders for various types of documents. These folders can reflect various projects, assignments, classes, or jobs. The arrangement should reflect your work patterns.

To organize the files and subfolders in your Documents folder, do the following:

- Make sure that subfolders are clearly named. Rename folders if necessary.

- For folders that contain an excessive number of files, create additional subfolders and move files into them.

- Delete unneeded folders and files.

10 Take a screenshot showing the subfolders in your newly organized Documents folder.

On a PC, press the Windows and PrtSc keys to capture the screen in memory. Next, launch the Paint program. When Paint is open, hold down the Ctrl key and press the V key to paste the image into Paint. Save the image using the File menu.

On a Mac, press Command-Shift-3 to capture the screen image on the desktop. Locate the image on the desktop, rename the image, and move it to an appropriate folder.

The Firefox shortcut on the desktop can be identified by its arrow. If it is removed from the desktop, the Chrome software will not be deleted.

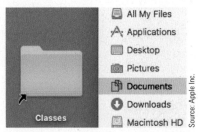

The blue Classes folder on the desktop is an alias for the actual folder. Deleting the alias does not delete the actual folder or its contents.

7 Digital Security

Module Contents

As the rate of malicious attacks on digital devices expands, our level of privacy and security dwindles. What can you do to reinforce your digital defenses? Read on.

● Try It! Apply what you learn.

- Encrypt an individual file or an entire storage volume.
- Adjust the login options on your digital devices to enhance security.
- Use two-factor authentication to enhance the security of your devices.
- Devise a personal strategy for creating strong passwords and maintaining them securely.
- Select, install, and configure antivirus software.
- Verify that antivirus software is actively scanning, and deal with virus alerts.
- Identify virus hoaxes.
- Close remote access features that might pose security risks.
- Take steps to be prepared if your device is infected with ransomware.
- Use an on-demand virus scanner as necessary to find and remove zero-day attacks.
- Discover which ports are open on your digital devices.
- Install, activate, and configure a personal firewall.
- Avoid Evil Twin exploits when using Wi-Fi hotspots.
- Watch for the signs of digital certificate hacks.
- Take steps to reduce the amount of spam you receive.
- Use spam filters to block unwanted email messages.
- Identify and avoid phishing, pharming, rogue antivirus, and PUA exploits.

● Pre-Check

Gauge your level of expertise. The answers are in the module.

Current encryption standard:

_____

$$\log_2 10^4$$

This formula calculates

_____

Viruses have a unique

_____

Malware that masquerades as a legitimate application:

_____

One of the first cyberwar exploits:

_____

0

An attack that exploits previously unknown hardware or software vulnerabilities:

_____

A firewall is designed to defend against exploits entering a device through open

_____

What kind of attack is this?

_____

Computers under the secret control of a hacker form a(n)

_____

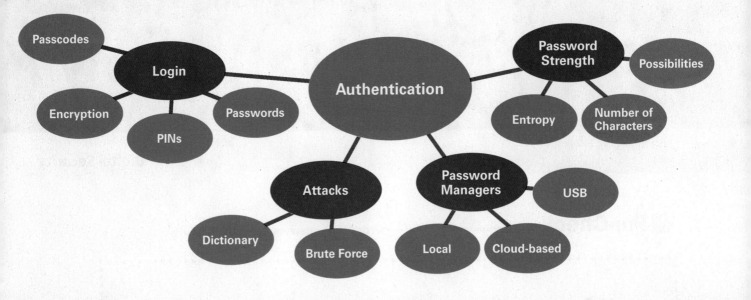

Objectives

▶ List five examples in which digital data is encrypted for security purposes.

▶ Compare and contrast PINs, passcodes, and passwords.

▶ Describe how two-factor authentication works when you log in to an account from a device you have never used before.

▶ Explain how encryption is linked to passcodes in some digital devices.

▶ Describe the advantages of encrypting an entire storage volume.

▶ Recite the basic rules for creating a strong password.

▶ List at least five characteristics of weak passwords.

▶ Recite the formula for calculating the number of possible passwords that can be generated using a four-digit PIN.

▶ Explain the concept of password entropy.

▶ Describe the advantages and disadvantages of local, cloud-based, and USB password managers.

Your smartphone is stolen. Your roommate is a busybody. A law enforcement agent wants to look at your files. Today, digital devices contain important and personal information. In the wrong hands, that information can compromise your privacy, ruin your credit rating, or even make you the target of legal action. Protecting physical devices and the data they contain is an important safeguard against identity theft and other security assaults.

Terminology

encryption	cryptographic algorithm	two-factor authentication	password entropy
plaintext	cryptographic key	strong password	password manager
ciphertext	AES	brute force attack	strength meter
decryption	user authentication	dictionary attack	

Encryption

Basic digital security depends on two techniques: encryption and authentication. These techniques are often combined to protect data from unauthorized access and to make data unintelligible if it is somehow hacked.

▶ **How does encryption work?** **Encryption** transforms a message or data file in such a way that its contents are hidden from unauthorized readers. An original message or file that has not yet been encrypted is referred to as **plaintext** or cleartext. An encrypted message or file is referred to as **ciphertext**. The process of converting plaintext into ciphertext is called encryption. The reverse process—converting ciphertext into plaintext—is called **decryption**.

Data is encrypted by using a cryptographic algorithm and a key. A **cryptographic algorithm** is a procedure for encryption or decryption. A **cryptographic key** (usually just called a key) is a word, number, or phrase that must be known to encrypt or decrypt data. A password, PIN, or passcode is typically used as the key to encrypt and decrypt data.

▶ **What can be encrypted?** Encryption is commonly applied to data packets sent over wired or wireless networks, bank card numbers and other personal data sent to ecommerce sites, email messages that contain confidential information, entire storage volumes for a digital device, and individual files that contain sensitive information.

▶ **How well does encryption protect files?** There are various encryption methods, and some are more secure than others. **AES** (Advanced Encryption Standard) is the encryption standard currently used worldwide. It is possible to crack AES, but the process is difficult and requires lots of computer power.

▶ **How can I encrypt files?** Methods for encrypting storage volumes are described later in this section. Individual files can be encrypted using encryption features built into applications such as word processing, spreadsheet, and database software. Encryption options, if available, can usually be found on the File menu. Figure 7-1 illustrates how to encrypt a file using Microsoft Word.

Terminology

A *password* is a series of characters that can contain letters, numbers, and symbols. A PIN (personal identification number) is typically four to six numeric digits, but it can be as long as 12 digits. *Passcode* is another term for a PIN because, technically speaking, PINs and passcodes contain only numbers. In common usage, however, the terms "passcode" and "password" are used interchangeably. When asked to create a PIN, passcode, or password, check the instructions to see if you need to include letters, numbers, or special characters.

Try It!

Use Microsoft Word or Apple iWork Pages to open a document. Find the encryption option on the application's menu and encrypt the document. Close the document, and then make sure that it can be opened only by providing the password.

7

Figure 7-1: How to encrypt individual files with Microsoft Word

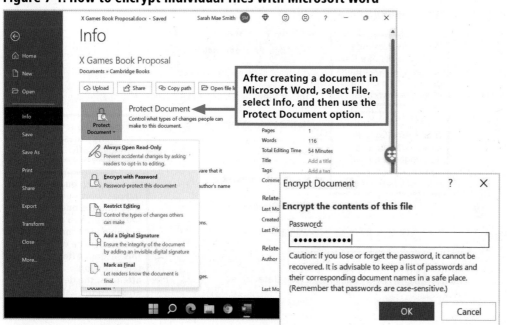

Authentication

In the context of digital security, **user authentication** is any technique used to verify or confirm a person's identity. Authentication techniques such as passwords, PINs, fingerprint scans, and facial recognition can prevent unauthorized access to the data on Web sites or stolen devices.

Two-factor authentication increases security by verifying identity based on two components, such as a password and a verification code. It is most useful for verifying logins initiated from a device that was not used previously to log in. After a valid password is entered, a verification code is sent to a secondary device, such as a mobile phone, known to belong to the user. The verification code is then entered, in addition to the password, as the second authentication component.

▶ **What are the authentication options for iOS devices?** iPhones and iPads can be "locked" to require a login password, PIN, or some other form of authentication each time the device is used. When an iOS device is locked, the contents of its storage volume are automatically encrypted. A hacker who manages to gain possession of a locked device cannot access its files without the proper authentication credentials. Even if the storage device is removed, the data it contains is meaningless because it is encrypted.

Authentication options for iOS devices include short passcodes, long alphanumeric passwords, facial recognition, and fingerprint scans. Refer to Apple Support for information about how exercising, swimming, cooking, and other activities might affect the ability of a device to reliably recognize fingerprints.

The standard iOS security setting establishes a six-digit numeric passcode. Short passcodes are not very secure. With six digits, 1 million passcodes are possible. Password hacking utilities can quickly try all of them in a matter of seconds. iOS can be set to erase a device after ten unsuccessful login attempts. When using a short passcode, the erase option offers much-needed protection.

Long alphanumeric codes are more difficult to hack than six-digit passcodes. To configure a longer code for an iOS device, use the Settings icon and select the Passcode option, as shown in Figure 7-2.

QuickCheck

Which one of the following would offer the most login security?

a. A 4-digit PIN.

b. An 8-letter password.

c. A 6-digit numeric passcode.

d. An 8-character alphanumeric code.

Try It!

If you have an iPhone, look at the password settings and consider whether you would like to secure your device with more than a basic passcode.

Figure 7-2: Login password management on iOS devices

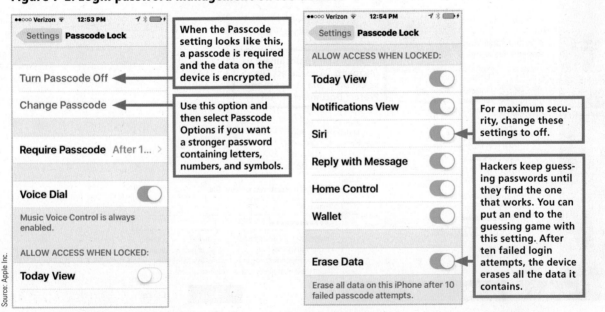

Source: Apple Inc.

What are the authentication options for Android devices? Android devices have an overwhelming number of security settings, including PINs, passwords, facial recognition, voice recognition, and drawing a pattern on the screen. Setting a strong password provides the highest level of security.

Unlike iOS devices, Android devices do not automatically encrypt stored data. Configuring a password and activating encryption are two separate steps, as shown in Figure 7-3.

Figure 7-3: Login password management on Android devices

1 Android password options are accessed from the Settings menu by selecting the Lock Screen option and then selecting Screen lock. A strong password provides the best security.

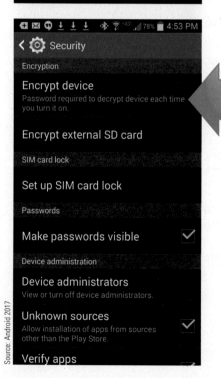

2 To encrypt the files on an Android device, use the Security setting and select Encrypt device. When first activated, the encryption process may require up to an hour. Make sure your device is fully charged and plugged in during the process.

Source: Android 2017

Try It!

If you have an Android phone, look at the password settings and consider whether you would like to secure your device with a longer password.

❱ What are the authentication options for Windows? Windows offers several sign-in options that can be configured using the Accounts option on the Settings screen. Figure 7-4 explains the authentication options and points out the critical security settings.

Try It!

If you have a laptop or desktop PC, look at the password settings and consider whether you should enhance the login security.

Figure 7-4: Login password management on Windows devices

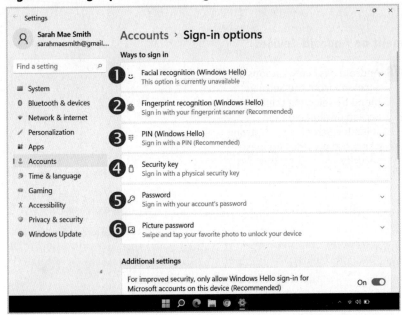

❶ Facial recognition is possible with a computer equipped with a camera.

❷ Fingerprint recognition requires a built-in or add-on fingerprint scanning device.

❸ The Windows Hello PIN is a four-digit number that gives you a quick way to log in. For the best security, however, do not use a PIN instead of a longer password.

❹ A security key is a device that connects to a USB port. This device provides an extra layer of security, but you must be careful not to lose it.

❺ Windows password login uses the same password as for your Microsoft account, typically consisting of letters, numbers, and special characters.

❻ You can set up a picture password on a touchscreen device by selecting an image and then drawing three gestures over it. Those three gestures allow you to log in.

❱ Is it possible to encrypt a Windows hard drive volume? Devices with Windows Pro and Enterprise editions can be encrypted using Microsoft's BitLocker or third-party utilities.

For Windows users who are working with the Home edition, Windows provides a Device Encryption option. As an alternative, individual file encryption can be used for critical files, as explained earlier in this module. Third-party software utilities that offer more comprehensive volume encryption capabilities include Symantec Encryption and GNU Privacy Guard.

❱ **What are the authentication options for macOS?** Macs offer several password settings, which are accessed from the Security & Privacy preferences. A feature called Automatic Login allows access to a device without a password. For security, this feature should be disabled, as shown in Figure 7-5.

Figure 7-5: Login password management on Macs

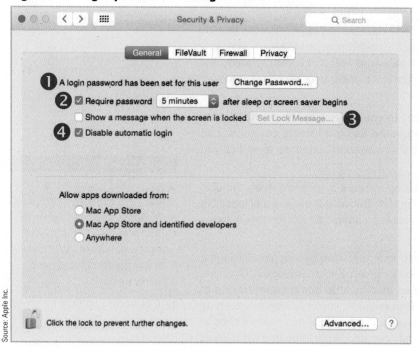

QuickCheck

Based on the settings in Figure 7-5, what happens when the device is awakened after it has been asleep for three minutes?

a. The device asks for a login password.

b. The device displays the "If found" message.

c. The display resumes without asking for a password.

d. The computer shuts down with a security warning.

7

❶ Use this option to change the password or disable the login password. If a password has not been set, check the option labeled *Disable automatic login*, and then create a password.

❷ Users typically leave their digital devices in sleep mode rather than shutting them down, so devices that are lost or stolen are likely to be in sleep mode. Configuring a device to require a password when waking from sleep adds an important layer of security. For convenience, allow the device to awaken from short sleep periods without requiring a password.

❸ Showing a message when the screen is locked can be useful if a device is lost. You can create a message to display your contact information so that the device can be returned if found.

❹ When this option is not checked, no password is required to access the device. For security, make sure this setting is checked.

❱ **Is password authentication required before a macOS file volume can be encrypted?** macOS devices include a utility called FileVault that automatically encrypts data stored locally. FileVault settings are accessed from the same Security & Privacy window used for password settings.

Try It!

If you have a Mac laptop or desktop computer, look at the password settings and consider whether you should enhance the login security.

Passwords

Passwords protect digital devices from unauthorized access, and they protect user accounts at online banks, Web sites, and app stores. A **strong password** is difficult to hack. Conventional wisdom tells us that strong passwords are at least eight characters in length and include one or more uppercase letters, numbers, and symbols. These conventions create passwords that may be fairly difficult to crack, but they are also impossible to remember. What to do?

▶ **How can hackers get my password?** Hackers and identity thieves employ a whole range of ways to steal passwords. In public places, a hacker might simply look over your shoulder as you type in your password. Identity thieves can easily find your password if you write it down on a note stuck under your keyboard or tucked inside your mobile phone case.

If a hacker doesn't have physical access to your device but it is connected to a network, your password can be discovered using a remote computer and software tools that systematically guess your password, intercept it, or trick you into revealing it.

A **brute force attack** uses password-cracking software to generate every possible combination of letters, numerals, and symbols. Because it exhausts all possible combinations to discover a password, a brute force attack can run for days before a password is cracked.

A **dictionary attack** helps hackers guess your password by stepping through a dictionary containing word lists in common languages such as English, Spanish, French, and German. These dictionaries also include common mutations of words, such as p@ssw0rd, and hundreds of frequently used passwords, such as qwerty and 12345. Dictionary attacks are effective because many users choose passwords that are easy for them to remember and likely to be in a list of most commonly used passwords (Figure 7-6).

QuickCheck

Suppose that you've lost a digital device that has a@rdvark as the login password. Will the hacker who found your device crack the password more quickly with a brute force attack or a dictionary attack?

a. A brute force attack

b. A dictionary attack

Figure 7-6: Commonly used passwords

12345	000000	buster	coffee	eeyore
abc123	money	dragon	dave	fishing
password	carmen	jordan	falcon	football
p@ssw0rd	mickey	michael	freedom	george
Pa55word	secret	michelle	gandalf	happy
password1	summer	mindy	green	iloveyou
!qaz2wsx	internet	patrick	helpme	jennifer
computer	service	123abc	linda	jonathan
123456	canada	andrew	magic	love
111111	hello	calvin	merlin	marina
a1b2c3	ranger	changeme	molson	missy
qwerty	shadow	diamond	newyork	monday
adobe123	baseball	matthew	soccer	monkey
123123	donald	miller	thomas	natasha
admin	harley	ou812	wizard	ncc1701
1234567890	hockey	tiger	Monday	newpass
photoshop	letmein	12345678	asdfgh	pamela
1234	maggie	apple	bandit	
sunshine	mike	avalon	batman	
azerty	mustang	brandy	boris	
trustno1	snoopy	chelsea	dorothy	

▶ **What makes a password susceptible to a dictionary attack?** Many of the clever schemes users devise to create passwords are obvious to hackers and the programmers who create password-cracking tools. Weak passwords include the following:

- Words from a dictionary, including words that are in languages other than English
- Doubled words such as passpass or computercomputer
- Default passwords such as password, admin, system, and guest
- Words with a sequence of numbers at the end, such as Secret123 and Dolphins2022
- Words with symbol or numeric mutations, such as p@ssw0rd and V01dem0rt
- Sequences of numbers formatted as dates or telephone numbers, such as 01/01/2000 and 888-5566
- Any sequence that includes a user name, such as BillMurray12345
- Any sequence that uses conventional capitalization, such as Book34 and Savannah912

QuickCheck

Which password for Dave Meyers is most secure?

a. DaveBMeyers

b. Dave12345

c. Ih2gtg8pw

d. D@veMeyer$

7

▶ **What makes a password susceptible to a brute force attack?** Brute force attacks methodically try every possible password until the correct one is found. Consider a simple guess-the-number game. You have a much better chance of guessing a number between 1 and 10 than guessing the correct number between 1 and 10,000. In the same way, a password selected from a universe of 10,000 possibilities is easier to crack than a password selected from a universe of 100 million possibilities.

The number of possible passwords depends on factors that include the size of the character set and the length of the password. Longer passwords and those consisting of a mixture of letters, numbers, and symbols are more difficult to crack. The general formula for calculating the number of possible passwords is:

$$\textbf{NumberOfCharacters}^{\text{PasswordLength}}$$

For example, suppose you are creating a four-digit numeric password for an iPhone. The character set consists of ten numerals on the keypad: 0, 1, 2, 3, etc. The password length is four digits. The number of possible passwords is:

$$10^4$$

NumberOfCharacters   PasswordLength

10^4 is 10 x 10 x 10 x 10, which is equal to 10,000. Password-cracking software, with its ability to try more than a billion passwords per second, can run through all those possibilities within milliseconds.

How much safer is a five-digit password? The number of possibilities is 10^5, which is 100,000. That's a big increase over the possibilities for a four-digit password, but those possibilities are still easily handled by password-cracking software.

An eight-character password using uppercase letters, lowercase letters, numerals, and symbols has 6,095,689,385,410,816 possibilities. Running through all those possibilities would take a considerable amount of time. The difficulty of cracking such a password is a good start in providing enough entropy for a secure password.

Try It!

To make sure that you understand how to find the number of possibilities for a password, calculate how many possibilities exist for a password that is four characters long and uses only lowercase letters from the English alphabet.

▶ **What is password entropy?** The number of possible passwords quickly becomes very large. Rather than discuss such huge numbers, security experts express password strength in terms of entropy. **Password entropy** is a measure in bits of a password's unpredictability. For example, the entropy of a four-digit iPhone passcode is 14 bits. For those of you interested in the math, entropy is calculated like this:

$$\log_2 10^4$$

$10^4 = 10,000$. $\log_2$ of $10,000 = 13.2877$

Notice that the number of bits does not refer to the length of the password. An iPhone's passcode is four digits in length, but its entropy is rounded up to 14. The number 14 enumerates how many bits are needed to represent the number of possible passcodes in binary. For a four-digit passcode, the number of possible codes is 10,000. That's 10011100010000 in binary. Count the number of bits. There are 14, and that is the entropy (Figure 7-7).

Figure 7-7: Entropy for common password sizes

	Number of Characters	Length	Possibilities	Entropy
PIN	10	4	10,000	14-bit
Lowercase alphabetic password	26	8	208,827,064,576	38-bit
Lower and uppercase alphabetic password	52	8	53,459,728,531,456	46-bit
Alphanumeric-symbol password	94	8	6,095,689,385,410,816	53-bit
Long alphanumeric-symbol password	94	12	4.75920314814253E23	79-bit

▶ **Is all that math important?** That math illustrates the principles underlying secure passwords. The takeaway about entropy is that passwords with higher entropy are more secure than passwords with low entropy. A 46-bit password, therefore, is far more secure than a 13-bit password.

Also, entropy is a theoretical concept. In the real world, security measures may be in place to prevent hacking tools from trying a continuous stream of passwords. Login routines at Web sites often restrict the speed at which passwords can be entered and the number of consecutive passwords that can be tried before the account is temporarily frozen and alternative authentication is required. Adjusting device settings to limit the number of login attempts is a wise security step.

QuickCheck

In Figure 7-7, why is the entropy for PINs 14 bits?

a. It is the number of possibilities.

b. It is the number of digits in the possibilities.

c. It is the number of bits when the possibilities are in binary.

d. It is 4 + 10.

▶ What is the recommended method for creating secure passwords?
The sophistication of password-cracking software and the processor speeds of today's computers pose challenges for consumers. Long, random passwords are most secure, but they are difficult to remember. It is possible to devise and remember a secure password for one or two sites, but the average consumer may have passwords for more than 50 devices and Web sites. Devising 50 unique, strong passwords and remembering which passwords correspond to which sites is just about impossible, or is it? Figure 7-8 offers some advice for creating passwords.

Try It!

Using the guidelines in Figure 7-8, create a secure multi-use password.

7

Figure 7-8: Password advice

Start with a phrase. Base your high-security password on the first letters of a phrase that generates a password containing numbers and proper nouns.

- Aim for a length of 8 to 12 characters because some sites limit password length.

- Use uppercase letters somewhere other than at the beginning of the password.

- Use numbers somewhere other than at the end of the password.

- Some sites do not allow symbols, so you may not want to use them in a password that will be modified for use on many sites.

Here is an example of a phrase that produces a fairly secure password:

I went to Detroit Michigan when I was 23 years old

IwtDMwiw23yo

Add the site name. By inserting the name of the site, every password will be unique and you will be able to remember the site on which it is used, like this:

I went to PayPal when I was 23 years old

IwtPayPalwiw23yo

Make a low-security password. A password achieves pretty good entropy when it is composed of four or more words. Create an everyday password using this method. Here is an example:

SpaBraidAmazonNuit

Be careful what you write. If you have to write down your passwords to remember them, keep them in a safe place that is not connected to your digital device. If your device is stolen, the passwords should not be located where they would also be stolen.

Use encryption. If you want to store passwords on your device, make sure to encrypt the file in which they are stored.

Use a password manager. If you feel more secure with a totally random and unique password for each of your logins, a password manager is an excellent option.

Password Managers

You hated memorizing facts in elementary school, and memorizing passwords is even less fun. Digital tools for managing passwords promise to shoulder the burden, but nothing is perfect, and password managers are not hacker-proof.

▶ **How does a password manager work?** The core function of a **password manager** (sometimes called a keychain) is to keep track of passwords so users don't have to memorize them. Some password managers also have the ability to fill in forms with stored address and credit card data. Password managers are available as operating system utilities, browser extensions, and standalone utilities.

Most password managers can generate unique passwords composed of random letters, numbers, and symbols. These passwords have very good entropy and do not have to be memorized because they are stored and automatically retrieved by the password manager as needed.

When you initially register for an account with a Web site or app, the password manager may display the user ID you typically use; usually it is your email address. You are then asked if you would like to create a password or use an auto-generated password.

Password managers may display a **strength meter** that indicates password security—a feature that is useful if you create a custom password rather than using one generated by the password manager (Figure 7-9).

Figure 7-9: Password managers can generate strong passwords

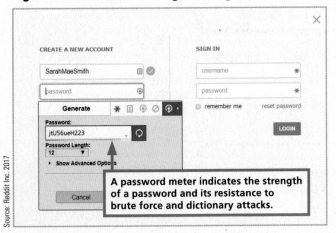

Source: Reddit Inc. 2017

A password meter indicates the strength of a password and its resistance to brute force and dictionary attacks.

▶ **Does a password manager save time?** A password manager stores a list of Web sites with corresponding user IDs and passwords in an encrypted file. Any time you reach a login screen for a known app or Web site, the password manager automatically supplies your user ID and password, saving you the time required to look them up.

The encrypted file that stores user IDs and passwords is protected by a primary password. That password has to be entered manually only once each time a device is turned on. The data stored by a password manager is secure unless the primary password is cracked. In that unfortunate situation, all of the passwords in the file are compromised and can be used by a hacker. In addition, if you forget the primary password, then you are locked out of all your password-protected accounts.

▶ Is the data stored by a password manager secure? The vulnerability of a file protected by a single primary password is the security tradeoff for the convenience of delegating password security to password management software. The security of passwords created and preserved by a password manager also depends on where the password file is stored.

Local Storage. Passwords stored locally are tied to the device on which they are created. When a password manager is installed on a laptop, for example, the passwords are available only when using that device. The password file is encrypted, but if the device is stolen, hackers can take their time trying to crack the primary password.

Passwords stored locally are not available when using other devices. Suppose that you usually work with the Safari browser on your MacBook Air, and it stores your passwords; but if you use a public computer in a coffee shop, your passwords are not accessible from that device. This disadvantage of local storage encourages many consumers to try cloud-based password managers.

Cloud Storage. Some password managers can store the encrypted password file in the cloud. That file can be accessed from any device as long as the primary password is provided. Storing a file full of passwords in the cloud can be a security risk, however. Web-based password managers can be attractive targets for password thieves. By breaking into a single site, a password thief could harvest millions of passwords. When considering cloud-based password management tools, evaluate them carefully before trusting them with your valuable login data.

USB Storage. There are a few password managers available that store your passwords in an encrypted file on a USB drive. The passwords are available on any device with a USB port. For extra protection against intruders who might search your device for passwords, a flash drive that contains a password manager can be unplugged when you are not planning to visit password-protected sites. You can also remove the flash drive from your device when you're out so that your nosy roommate can't snoop through your digital files. When you remove the USB drive, your portable password manager leaves behind no traces of passwords. Losing the USB drive puts your digital life at risk, however, so consider connecting it to your key ring.

7

Try It!

If you were to use a password manager, would you store passwords locally, in the cloud, or on a USB drive? Why?

QuickQuiz   Section A

1. PINs and passwords protect logins, but they can also be used to [_____] storage volumes.

2. User [_____] techniques include PINs, passwords, fingerprint scans, and facial recognition.

3. A(n) [_____] attack usually cracks passwords in less time than a brute force attack.

4. A term such as *46-bit* is used to indicate the strength, or [_____], of a password.

5. Password managers are available as operating system utilities, [_____] extensions, and standalone utilities.

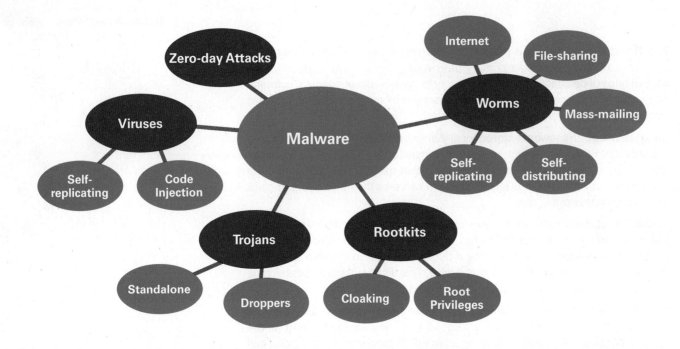

Objectives

▶ List at least five examples of malware payloads.

▶ Describe the characteristics that differentiate computer viruses from other types of malware.

▶ Explain the purpose of a rootkit.

▶ Describe the characteristics of computer worms, including three common infection vectors.

▶ Explain the purpose of malware trojans and how they relate to droppers.

▶ List the two ways that antivirus software is able to detect viruses.

▶ Explain the three possible actions that antivirus software can take when a virus is detected.

▶ Explain the significance of false positives in the context of virus detection.

▶ Describe how to determine if an email warning about a virus is real or a hoax.

The days when viruses were the greatest threat to computers are long gone. Today, there are many other types of malicious software, or malware, that can wreak havoc on computer systems, networks, and even handheld devices. Windows computers have the highest risk of malware infections, but any digital device that receives email, accesses the Web, and runs apps is potentially vulnerable.

Terminology

malware	rootkit	trojan	false positives
malware exploit	computer worm	dropper	quarantined file
computer virus	mass-mailing worm	antivirus software	virus hoax
code injection	Internet worm	virus signature	
side-loading	file-sharing worm	heuristic analysis	

Malware Threats

Exploits against digital devices began as harmless stunts but quickly turned nasty. Simple pranks evolved into attacks that wiped out data on hard drives, wormed into networks, stole massive numbers of personal records, and hijacked access to segments of the Web. Malware is also a component of cyberwarfare attacks that pose a threat to national security.

▶ **What are malware threats?** **Malware** refers to any computer program designed to secretly enter a digital device. Malware can be classified by the way in which it enters a device or by the type of activity it carries out. Common classifications of malware include viruses, worms, and trojans.

Malware is created and unleashed by individuals referred to as hackers, crackers, or cybercriminals. Some malware is released as a prank. Other malware is designed to distribute political messages or disrupt operations at specific companies. In an increasing number of cases, malware is exploited for monetary gain. Malware designed for identity theft or extortion has become a very real threat to individuals and corporations.

Once malware infiltrates a device, its behavior depends on how it is programmed. The action carried out by malware code is referred to as a **malware exploit** or a "payload." Malware can be used for many types of exploits, such as deleting files, recording login keystrokes, opening access for intruders, and allowing remote control of a device. Figure 7-10 lists some malware exploits that affect consumers.

Figure 7-10: Malware exploits

- Display irritating messages and pop-up ads
- Delete or modify your data
- Encrypt data and demand ransom for the encryption key
- Upload or download files
- Record keystrokes to steal passwords and credit card numbers
- Send messages containing malware and spam to everyone in an email address book or instant messaging buddy list
- Disable antivirus and firewall software
- Block access to specific Web sites and redirect a browser to infected Web sites
- Cause response time slowdowns
- Allow hackers to remotely access data stored on a device
- Allow hackers to take remote control of a device
- Link a device to others in a botnet that can send millions of spam emails or wage denial-of-service attacks against Web sites
- Cause network traffic jams

7

Computer Viruses

The first computer virus designed to affect personal computers appeared in 1982 when the Apple II was at the height of its popularity. This virus, called Elk Cloner, was relatively harmless. It blanked the screen and displayed a short poem. From such innocent beginnings, viruses developed into a major threat, launching nasty attacks such as wiping out all the data stored on hard disks and overwriting the BIOS to make a computer unbootable.

▶ **What is a virus?** A **computer virus** is a set of self-replicating program instructions that surreptitiously attaches itself to a legitimate executable file on a host device. When the infected file is run, the virus code is loaded into RAM with the rest of the program. Once in RAM, the virus code is executed. When executed, the virus can replicate itself by injecting malicious code into other files. A common misconception is that viruses spread themselves from one device to another; they don't. Viruses can only replicate themselves on the host device.

In addition to replicating itself, a virus usually delivers a payload, which can be as harmless as displaying an annoying message or as devastating as trashing the data on your computer's storage device. It can corrupt files, destroy data, or otherwise disrupt operations. A trigger event, such as a specific date, can unleash some viruses. Viruses that deliver their payloads on a specific date are sometimes referred to as time bombs. Viruses that deliver their payloads in response to some other system event are referred to as logic bombs.

Today, viruses are a mild threat. They do not spread rapidly, and they are easily filtered out by antivirus software. They are interesting, however, because they illustrate the beginning of hacker culture and reveal the basic techniques that are still used to inject third-party code into legitimate data streams. **Code injection** is the process of modifying an executable file or data stream by adding commands, as shown in Figure 7-11.

QuickCheck

Computer viruses are characterized by their

_____.

a. ability to spread themselves to various devices

b. ability to self-replicate

c. severe level of threat

d. size

Figure 7-11: Code injection

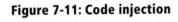

Code for a virus or other malware can be injected into a legitimate file. When that file is executed, the virus code is executed, too.

Malicious code can also be injected into a data stream as it travels from one device to another. After the altered data arrives, it is typically stored and eventually executed.

▶ **How does a virus spread?** Viruses spread when people exchange infected files on disks and CDs, as email attachments, and on file sharing networks, social networking sites, and download sites. They can also be inadvertently obtained from unauthorized app stores. Through a process called **side-loading**, an app from a source other than an official app store is installed on a device. Often these apps are altered versions of popular apps, which are placed on unofficial download sites. The app appears to be the same as the original legitimate app, but when downloaded, it may install a virus or other malware.

A key characteristic of viruses is their ability to lurk in a device for days or months, while quietly replicating themselves to other files on the device. As this replication takes place, you might not even know that your device has contracted a virus; therefore, it is possible to inadvertently spread infected files to other people's devices. Although viruses are no longer a top malware threat, virus-cloaking technology has become very sophisticated and is a key element of today's most serious security exploits. Viruses and other malware can cloak themselves using various techniques, such as rootkits.

▶ **What is a rootkit?** Any code that is designed to hide the existence of processes and privileges is referred to as a **rootkit**. Rootkits were originally designed to allow "root" or administrative access to digital devices and computer systems. By changing system settings and then hiding those changes, hackers were able to become shadow administrators with access to all data on a device or network.

Modern rootkits are used to hide malicious code by replacing parts of the operating system with modified code. For example, a rootkit might subvert the operating system's master file table to hide evidence of the sectors in which a virus is stored. Some rootkits are even able to disable antivirus software to prevent it from detecting the existence of malware (Figure 7-12).

Figure 7-12: Rootkits cloak malware

On this hard disk, a rootkit conceals a track that contains malware, so it is not visible to the file system.

Computer Worms

Initially, the spread of malware from computer to computer depended on humans to physically exchange infected floppy disks. In 1996, the distribution vector began to change as hackers devised malware that could spread on its own from one device to another. The first self-distributing malware infiltrated email address books to essentially mail copies of its code to other devices. By 2000, hackers were able to create malware that sent itself to huge numbers of IP addresses.

▶ **What is a worm?** A **computer worm** is a small, self-replicating, self-distributing program designed to carry out unauthorized activity on a victim's device. Worms are usually standalone executable programs that can spread themselves from one device to another without any assistance from victims.

Worms can enter a device through security holes in browsers and operating systems, as email attachments, and when victims click infected pop-up ads or links contained in email messages. There are several common types of computer worms.

A **mass-mailing worm** spreads by sending itself to every address in the contacts list of an infected device. If a mass-mailing worm infects one of your devices, for example, your friends receive infected messages sent from your mail account. Thinking that the message is from a trusted source, your friends are likely to open the infected attachment, spreading the worm to their devices and then passing it on to their friends.

An **Internet worm** looks for vulnerabilities in operating systems, open communications ports, and JavaScripts on Web pages. These worms travel over communications networks as small bootstrap files that infiltrate digital devices. When a worm finds a host, it connects to a remote computer to download more comprehensive malware.

A **file-sharing worm** copies itself into a shared folder under an innocuous name. When the folder is distributed over a file sharing network or BitTorrent, the worm tags along and spreads to all the devices that participate in the share. Figure 7-13 illustrates how computer worms spread.

QuickCheck

What is the key difference between computer viruses and worms?

a. Viruses deliver more damaging payloads than worms.

b. Worms replicate themselves, but viruses do not.

c. Viruses are self-distributing, whereas worms are not.

d. Worms are standalone executable programs, whereas viruses have to piggyback on other executable files.

Figure 7-13: How a computer worm spreads

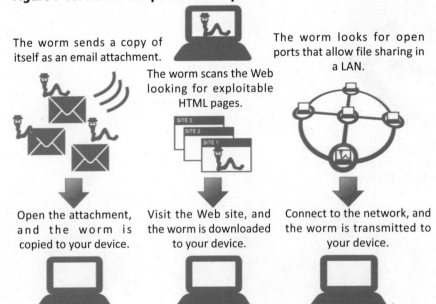

The worm sends a copy of itself as an email attachment.

The worm scans the Web looking for exploitable HTML pages.

The worm looks for open ports that allow file sharing in a LAN.

Open the attachment, and the worm is copied to your device.

Visit the Web site, and the worm is downloaded to your device.

Connect to the network, and the worm is transmitted to your device.

Trojans

Stuxnet is a notorious computer worm that damaged devices used in Iran's nuclear program. It is often identified as one of the first cyberwarfare tools. A file called Stuxnet.exe is unlikely to be downloaded, so malware developers depend on trojans to disguise malware as innocuous utility software and popular applications. Today, more than 80% of malware infections are trojans.

▶ **How do trojans differ from viruses and worms?** A **trojan** (sometimes called a "Trojan Horse") is a computer program that seems to perform one function while actually doing something else. Unlike a worm, a trojan is not designed to spread itself to other devices. Also differing from viruses and worms, most trojans are not designed to replicate themselves.

Trojans are standalone programs that masquerade as useful utilities or applications, which victims download and install while unaware of their destructive nature. Trojans depend on social engineering—fooling users—to spread. Social engineering exploits are covered in detail in a later section of this module.

Trojans can contain viruses, code to take control of a device, or routines called droppers.

▶ **What is a dropper?** A **dropper** is designed to deliver or "drop" malicious code into a device. It is similar to a setup program that unzips and installs software applications on Windows devices, except that droppers secretly install malware rather than legitimate software.

Droppers are commonly the first phase of a sophisticated malware attack. Most droppers contain compressed or encrypted malware files. When delivered, these files are uncompressed in memory to avoid detection. The uncompressed files are executed, sometimes to carry out a payload or to collect and install other malware components. Stuxnet famously used a dropper to initiate its attack (Figure 7-14).

QuickCheck

In the context of malware, a trojan's main purpose is to

_____.

a. disguise malware as legitimate software

b. replicate on a host machine

c. spread as quickly as possible

d. load additional malicious code

7

Terminology

There is a difference between a dropper and code injection. A *dropper* installs a malicious program on a device, and it works with an entire program. *Code injection* inserts a segment of malicious code into another program. It carries only a short segment of code rather than an entire program.

Figure 7-14: Stuxnet attacks nuclear centrifuges

❶ A USB drive containing the Stuxnet dropper in disguise is inserted into a computer at a nuclear facility.

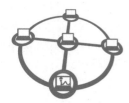

❷ A security hole in Windows runs the dropper when the USB directory is viewed.

❸ The dropper executes a second file containing a worm.

❹ The worm spreads through the LAN, looking for a specific type of hardware device that Stuxnet is designed to destroy.

❺ When the worm arrives at a target device, in this case a centrifuge, it downloads a more comprehensive file containing instructions for the payload.

❻ The malware payload causes the nuclear centrifuges to fail.

Antivirus Software

Any data entering a digital device could be malware. Users have little hope of identifying files that contain malicious code. Avoiding known sources of malware, such as free file sharing services and offshore download sites, may reduce the risk of encountering malware; however, malicious code exists at legitimate Web sites, lurks in official app stores, and infiltrates trusted networks. The best defense against malware is antivirus software.

▶ **What are the most popular antivirus products?** Antivirus software is a type of utility software that looks for and eliminates viruses, trojans, worms, and other malware. It is available for all types of computers and data storage devices, including smartphones, tablets, personal computers, USB flash drives, servers, PCs, and Macs. Popular antivirus software includes Norton AntiVirus, Kaspersky Anti-Virus, Bitdefender Antivirus, Windows Defender, and Avast.

▶ **How does antivirus software work?** Modern antivirus software runs as a background process and attempts to identify malware that exists on a device or is entering a device as a download, email message, attachment, or Web page. The process of searching for malware is sometimes referred to as scanning or performing a virus scan. To identify malware, antivirus software can look for a virus signature or perform heuristic analyses.

▶ **What is a virus signature?** A **virus signature** is a section of program code that contains a unique series of instructions known to be part of a malware exploit. Although they are called virus signatures, the unique code may identify a virus, worm, trojan, or other type of malware.

Virus signatures are discovered by security experts who examine the bit sequences contained in malware program code (Figure 7-15). When discovered, virus signatures are added to a collection of virus definitions, which form a database that is used by antivirus software as it works to scan files that may harbor malware.

Figure 7-15: A virus signature

Virus
Michelangelo

Signature
bb00508ec3cd13730432

Payload
Erase hard drive boot sectors on March 6, Michelangelo's birthday

▶ **What is heuristic analysis?** Antivirus software can use techniques called **heuristic analysis** to detect malware by analyzing the characteristics and behavior of suspicious files. These techniques are especially useful for detecting new malware for which signatures have yet to be collected and added to the virus database.

One method of heuristic analysis allows the suspicious file to run in a guarded environment called a sandbox. If the file exhibits malicious behavior, it is treated like a virus and quarantined or deleted.

A second method of heuristic analysis involves inspecting the contents of a suspicious file for commands that carry out destructive or surveillance activities.

◗ How well does heuristic analysis work? Heuristic analysis requires time and system resources to examine files that arrive as downloads and email attachments. The process can slightly affect performance while the analysis is in progress.

Heuristics may produce **false positives** that mistakenly identify a legitimate file as malware. For example, a legitimate disk utility that contains routines for enhancing disk drive performance by deleting redundant files might be mistaken for a virus and prevented from being installed. Such a situation could be perplexing for users who download software, only for it to disappear upon arrival. Users who understand how antivirus software works should be able to quickly conclude that the legitimate application was mistakenly flagged as malware.

◗ What happens when malware is detected? When antivirus software detects malware, it can try to remove the infection, put the file into quarantine, or simply delete the file (Figure 7-16).

Figure 7-16: Malware detected

Repair. Antivirus software can sometimes remove the malware code from infected files. This strategy is beneficial for files containing important documents that have become infected. Many of today's malware exploits are embedded in executable files and are difficult to remove. When malware cannot be removed, the file should not be used.

Quarantine. In the context of antivirus software, a **quarantined file** contains code that is suspected of being part of a virus. For your protection, most antivirus software encrypts the file's contents and isolates it in a quarantine folder so it can't be inadvertently opened or accessed by a hacker. Quarantined files cannot be run, but they can be moved out of quarantine if they are later found to have been falsely identified as malware.

Delete. Quarantined files should eventually be deleted. Most antivirus software allows users to specify how long an infected file should remain in quarantine before it is deleted. Most users rarely retrieve files from quarantine because it is risky to work with files that are suspected of harboring malicious code. There is no need, therefore, to delay deletion for more than a few days.

7

▶ How dependable is antivirus software? Today's antivirus software is quite dependable but not infallible. A fast-spreading worm can reach your digital device before a virus definition update arrives, and cloaking software can hide some viral exploits.

Despite occasional misses, however, antivirus software and other security software modules are constantly weeding out malware that would otherwise infect your device. It is essential to use security software, but it is also important to take additional precautions, such as making regular backups of your data and avoiding untrustworthy software distribution outlets.

▶ How do I ensure that my antivirus software is running? Antivirus software is an aspect of our digital lives that we tend to take for granted. We assume that it is installed and carrying out its work. However, antivirus software can be inadvertently disabled. Its configuration can be changed by malware that manages to infiltrate a device. It can expire at the end of a trial period or subscription. Ensuring that antivirus software is performing correctly may require periodic intervention from users.

Many antivirus products display an icon in the taskbar or notification area. The icon may offer a visual clue to indicate when the antivirus utility is active, scanning, or updating. Glancing at the icon can assure you that the software is running properly.

Some targeted malware attacks may alter the icons, however, leading you to believe that the antivirus software is active when, in fact, it has been disabled by a malware attack. As shown in Figure 7-17, opening antivirus software periodically to view its status is a good practice.

Try It!

Is your antivirus software actively scanning and up to date? Check it right now to find out.

Figure 7-17: Antivirus software is actively scanning

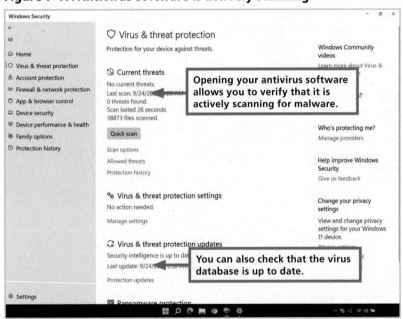

❱ **What configuration options are available?** Once you have installed antivirus software, the best and safest practice is to keep it running full time in the background so that it checks every email message as it arrives and scans all files that attempt to install themselves or run. For the most extensive protection from malware, you should look for and enable the following features of your antivirus software:

- Start scanning when the device boots.
- Scan all programs when they are launched, and scan document files when they are opened.
- Scan other types of files, such as graphics, if you engage in some risky computing behaviors and are not concerned with the extra time required to open files as they are scanned.
- Scan incoming email and attachments.
- Scan incoming instant message attachments.
- Scan outgoing email for worm activity such as mass-mailing worms.
- Scan zipped (compressed) files.
- Scan for spyware and PUAs (potentially unwanted applications).
- Scan all files on the device's storage volume at least once a week.

❱ **Where are the configuration settings?** The location for configuration settings depends on the antivirus software. Usually, there is a Settings menu or a Preferences option. It is important to examine the settings after installing new antivirus software and after getting updates to make sure the desired level of protection is in place.

Also check for exclusions. If files, processes, and locations are excluded, they will not be scanned for malware. This feature is available to enhance performance from trusted sites, but it can be a doorway for malware exploits. For maximum protection, make sure that there are no exclusions listed in your antivirus software settings. Settings for Windows Security are accessed from the "Virus and threat protection" option (Figure 7-18).

Figure 7-18: Be sure to eliminate all exclusions

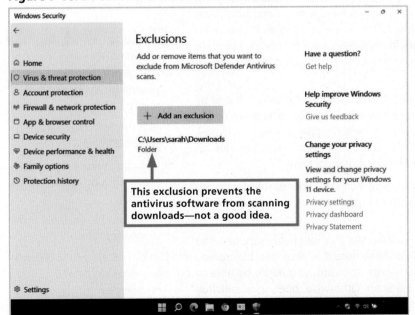

◗ Do I need to take any action when a virus is detected? Most antivirus software displays an alert when malware is detected. Antivirus software automatically takes action to protect your device by attempting to repair the file, place it in quarantine, or delete it.

You do not have to take any action. However, the alert message is an important piece of information that may indicate you are connected to a malicious site or receiving email from an unreliable source that would be best avoided in the future (Figure 7-19).

Figure 7-19: Malware security warning

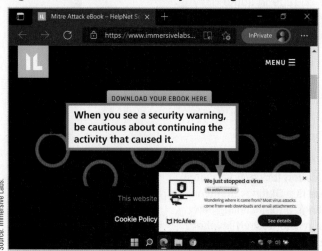

Source: Immersive Labs.

◗ What is the best way to handle updates? Two aspects of your antivirus software periodically need to be updated. First, the antivirus program itself might need a patch or an update to fix bugs or improve features. Second, the list of virus signatures must be updated to keep up with the latest malware developments.

Antivirus program updates and revised virus definitions are packaged into a file that can be manually or automatically downloaded. Most antivirus products are preconfigured to regularly check for updates, download them, and install them without user intervention. If you would rather control the download and installation process yourself, you can configure your antivirus software to alert you when updates are ready. In any case, you should manually check for updates periodically just in case the auto-update function has become disabled by malware or if your subscription has expired.

◗ What is the purpose of a manual scan? A manual scan is initiated by a user for the purpose of scanning one or more files. Manual scans are useful if you suspect that a virus has slipped into a device despite security measures. For example, a previously unknown attack might arrive undetected, but after an antivirus update, it can be detected by running a manual scan.

Manually scanning all the files stored on a device can slow performance, so schedule the scan for a time when you are not usually using your device, but it is turned on.

You can also run a manual scan of a specific file. For example, suppose you download an application and you want to make sure it is virus free before you install and run it. Depending on your antivirus software, you might be able to simply right-click the file name to start the scan. Otherwise, open your antivirus software and select the manual scan option.

▶ **What's a virus hoax?** Some virus threats are very real, but you're also likely to get email messages about so-called viruses that don't really exist. A **virus hoax** usually arrives as an email message containing dire warnings about a supposedly new virus on the loose. It typically provides a link to download some type of detection and protection software. It may include removal instructions that actually delete parts of the operating system. And, of course, you are encouraged to forward this "crucial" information to your friends.

When you receive an email message about a virus or any other type of malware, don't panic. It could be a hoax. You can check one of the many hoaxbuster or antivirus software Web sites to determine whether you've received a hoax or information about a real threat.

These Web sites also provide security or virus alerts, which list the most recent legitimate malware threats. If the virus is a real threat, the Web site can provide information to help determine whether your device has been infected. You can also find instructions for eradicating the virus. If the virus threat is a hoax like the one in Figure 7-20, by no means should you forward the email message to others.

Figure 7-20: A typical virus hoax

Source: Google, Inc.

QuickQuiz
Section B

1. A(n) _____ is self-replicating, self-distributing malware.

2. Malware trojans often contain code that is called a(n) _____ , which secretly installs malware.

3. Antivirus software can detect viruses by looking for signatures or by _____ analysis.

4. Antivirus software produces what is referred to as a false _____ when a legitimate program is mistakenly identified as a virus.

5. A virus _____ usually arrives as an email alert that warns against an imminent virus attack.

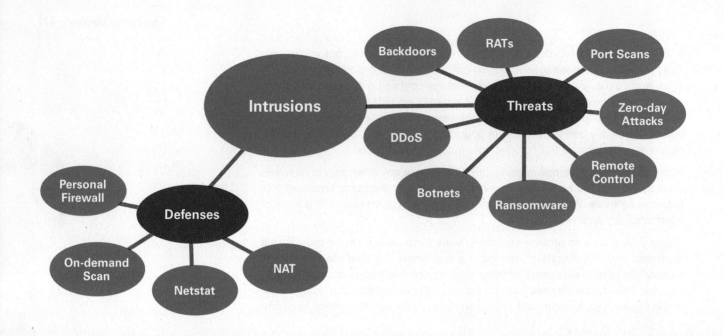

Online Intrusions

Objectives

▶ Provide an overview that describes how an online intrusion takes place.

▶ Describe how RATs use backdoors to access remote devices.

▶ Describe the security vulnerabilities associated with legitimate remote access utilities.

▶ Summarize the types of threats posed by ransomware.

▶ Explain how a DDoS attack takes place.

▶ Describe the difference between an on-demand scan and on-access scanning.

▶ Summarize the significance of communications ports in online intrusions.

▶ Describe how a personal firewall works.

▶ Explain how NAT works in conjunction with a router to provide a hardware firewall.

▶ Explain why security experts recommend using both NAT and a personal firewall.

Your webcam light flickers, but you aren't using it. Who could be at the controls? An unauthorized person operating your digital devices by remote control constitutes a serious breach of privacy and security. Although a webcam's light signals its use, many other remote intrusions take place without any warning signs. Your digital device could be sending out thousands of spam emails without your knowledge. Section C explains how to defend against online intrusions.

Terminology

online intrusion	ransomware	zero-day attack	port scan
RAT	botnet	on-access scan	firewall
backdoor	DDoS	on-demand scan	personal firewall

Intrusion Threats

Unleashing viruses, worms, and trojans kept hackers busy for many years, and they gleefully watched their creations spread to devices throughout the world. But viruses and worms were ultimately unsatisfying because once an exploit was released, hackers had no way to interact with it or take control of infected devices. Inevitably, someone came up with the concept of malware that could connect back to a hacker's command and control center.

▶ **What is the risk of online intrusions?** An **online intrusion** takes place when an unauthorized person gains access to a digital device by using an Internet connection and exploiting vulnerabilities in hardware or software. Across the globe, millions of devices have been surreptitiously infiltrated by online intruders.

Every day, thousands of people discover that they are the victims of identity theft resulting from an intruder gaining access to their digital files. Thousands more realize that cameras on their devices are controlled by an unknown hacker. A growing number of devices are being remotely locked by extortionists who demand payment to supply an unlock code. All of these exploits are likely to have been carried out by online intrusions.

An infiltrated device can be used as a launching platform for viruses and spam. Infiltrated devices can become part of a pornography network or an extortion ring. Hackers have even found ways to turn thousands of infiltrated computers into remote-controlled "zombies," link them together, and carry out coordinated attacks to disrupt online access to Microsoft, Bank of America, and other Internet businesses.

▶ **What are the characteristics of online intrusions?** Most online intrusions begin with malware. A worm or trojan infiltrates a device and sets up a backdoor that can be used for future access. That access can be used directly by a human to log in to the victim's device over the Internet. It can be used as a gateway for additional malware to infect a device. It can also be used as a conduit for commands issued from a hacker to a group of infected devices (Figure 7-21).

QuickCheck

How does an online intrusion usually begin?

a. With a virus alert

b. With a backdoor

c. With a worm or trojan

d. With a remote-controlled camera

Figure 7-21: Anatomy of an online intrusion

① Malware, such as a worm or trojan, enters a digital device.

② The malware runs and creates a backdoor.

③ The backdoor surreptitiously opens a communications link to a hacker.

④ The hacker sends commands that run programs, search for confidential data, and remotely control devices.

❱ **Are there different types of intrusions?** Yes. RATs, ransomware, and botnets are the most common types of online intrusions.

❱ **What is a RAT?** A RAT (Remote Access Trojan) is malware that arrives in a trojan disguised as legitimate software and sets up a secret communication link to a hacker. RATs are the underlying technology for most online intrusions.

❱ **How do hackers take remote control of digital devices?** A backdoor is an undocumented method of accessing a digital device. RATs create a backdoor to a victim's device that can be used by a hacker to send commands that take control of the device's camera, activate the microphone, or launch screen captures. Images and audio acquired by hackers are commonly posted on social media sites and used to extort money from victims who do not want their private activities made public.

❱ **Are legitimate remote access utilities a vulnerability?** Features such as Windows Remote Desktop, TeamViewer, and macOS Screen Sharing are legitimate software utilities that allow users to access their computers from a remote location. These utilities are handy for travelers who want to read, modify, or copy files stored on a computer that was left at home or at work. Remote access utilities open a communication port—on Windows computers, it is TCP port 3389—that is ready to accept remote data and commands.

In theory, remote commands are accepted only from someone who has logged in with valid credentials. However, a poorly configured remote access utility might not request a login password, or it may allow access through a standard guest account.

To block unauthorized use of remote access utilities, they should be disabled when they are not needed. Unless you are traveling and expect to access files on a computer that you've left at home, make sure Screen Sharing (macOS) or Remote Desktop (Windows Pro) is turned off. Figure 7-22 shows how to configure the Screen Sharing setting on a Mac.

Figure 7-22: Disable screen sharing in macOS

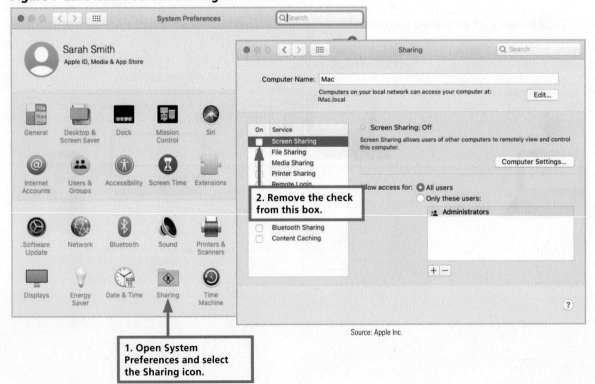

Source: Apple Inc.

◗ **What is ransomware?** Ransomware locks a device and then requests payment for an unlocking code. You'll want to defend against ransomware attacks such as these:

Nemty: Arrives as an email love letter and threatens to publish personal data if the ransom is not paid.

Maze: Spreads by exploits that target security holes in commonly used software. Threatens to steal files.

Snatch: Forces Windows computers to boot into safe mode and then encrypts the user's hard drive.

VegaLocker: Disables login access and removes crucial data, such as backup files and restore points, before asking for a ransom payment.

Ransomware attacks tend to target businesses rather than individuals, but these exploits can target Android, Windows, and macOS devices as well as smart TVs. iPhones are not typically at risk from ransomware unless the phone was jailbroken and contains side-loaded apps.

Victims who pay the ransom don't always obtain the unlocking code. Once the scammers have their money, they may not bother to unlock the files. The FBI recommends that victims ignore the ransom demand, scrub the device, and restore files from a backup.

Ransomware is one of the fastest-growing threats to digital devices. Hackers launch new variants that may not be blocked by antivirus software until the virus database is updated. Anti-ransomware software that runs in addition to antivirus software may offer further defenses against files being encrypted and held for ransom.

Consumers can expect ransomware exploits of increasing sophistication. Attacks not only affect files on a device's main storage volume, they can affect USB drives, external hard drives, and any other storage devices connected at the time of the attack.

To prepare for a possible ransomware exploit, be sure to maintain current backups of your important data and disconnect the backup device when backups are not in progress. Taking these steps will help ensure that you'll be prepared if you ever encounter a ransomware exploit such as the one in Figure 7-23.

Figure 7-23: Ransomware demands

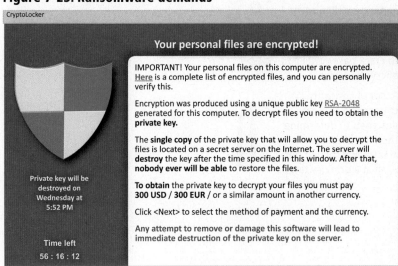

▶ **What is a botnet?** Hackers who gain control over several computers can organize them into a client-server network known as a **botnet**. This network is hidden from the victims, who continue to use their devices as usual and are unaware of botnet activities that may be taking place behind the scenes. In addition to computers, botnets can contain just about any device that connects to the Internet, including smartphones, baby cams, DVRs, and IoT sensors.

A botnet has a command and control server that is operated by hackers. Infiltrated devices become network nodes, which carry out a variety of activities as directed by the server. Small botnets contain a few hundred devices. However, the world's largest botnets are estimated to contain more than 450,000 devices!

Botnets have been used to carry out massive **DDoS** (distributed denial-of-service) attacks designed to flood a legitimate Web site or an Internet router with so much traffic that it can no longer provide its intended service. DDoS traffic is generated by hundreds, thousands, or millions of botnet nodes harnessed to do the bidding of a botmaster.

In addition to their role in DDoS attacks, botnets are commonly used to generate email spam, carry out click fraud, generate Bitcoin digital currency, and crack encryption. Some DDoS attacks appear to be proof-of-concept exercises to test security measures of government agencies, financial institutions, and key infrastructure systems. Figure 7-24 provides more information about botnets.

Try It!

In 2020, a massive DDoS attack targeted cloud-based Amazon Web Services (AWS). Look for information about this attack online. What was the magnitude of the attack? What was the name of the malware?

QuickCheck

Botnets might carry out all of the following exploits, except
_____.

a. RATs

b. DDoS

c. generating spam

d. cracking encryption

Figure 7-24: Anatomy of a botnet

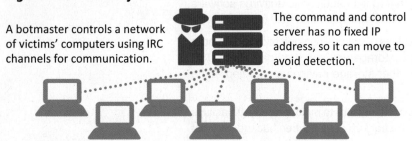

A botmaster controls a network of victims' computers using IRC channels for communication.

The command and control server has no fixed IP address, so it can move to avoid detection.

Victims' computers receive commands from the botmaster to carry out various nefarious tasks.

 Click fraud: Automated ad-clicking generates per-click revenue for botmasters.

 DDoS: Floods an IP address with massive amounts of traffic.

 Spam: Sends billions of spam emails per day.

Mine Bitcoins: Runs algorithms required to generate online cash.

Crack encryption: Runs brute force algorithms to crack passwords and encryption keys.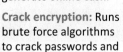

Proof of concept: Launches a test run designed to determine the effectiveness of an attack if carried out against a primary target.

Zero-Day Attacks

Consumers are justifiably concerned that their digital devices are vulnerable to intrusions. Even with antivirus software in place, each year millions of consumers are victims of intrusions and ransomware. Consumers have to establish additional defenses.

▶ **Does antivirus software protect devices from intrusions?** Antivirus software can prevent some, but not all, intrusions. It has a good track record for blocking exploits that attempt to gain access using a trojan or worm, especially if a signature of the exploit exists in the virus database. New exploits, such as zero-day attacks, may not be caught by antivirus software, however.

▶ **What is a zero-day attack?** A **zero-day attack** exploits previously unknown vulnerabilities in software applications, hardware, and operating system program code. The name "zero-day" implies that the software developer has zero days notification of the vulnerability before it is used as the basis for a security exploit.

When a zero-day attack first appears, its signature does not exist in virus databases, and if the exploit is designed to also bypass heuristic filters, these attacks can infiltrate computers guarded by antivirus software.

▶ **Is there any defense against zero-day attacks?** Zero-day attacks are usually discovered rapidly by security experts who attempt to correct the vulnerabilities by issuing updates and security patches. Configuring applications for automatic updates ensures that security patches are applied as soon as they are available. Adobe Reader, Microsoft Windows, and Android OS account for a large portion of all zero-day attacks. It is vital that consumers promptly apply security updates to this software.

For zero-day exploits that slip through the antivirus net, an on-demand scan can be an effective remedy. Standard antivirus software is set for an **on-access scan**, which takes place in the background as Web sites are accessed and as files are opened. An **on-demand scan** can be launched manually at any time and examines every segment of code on a storage volume. On-demand scans with products such as Malwarebytes (Figure 7-25) can be used in addition to antivirus software as a second line of defense.

QuickCheck

What is the significance of zero-day attacks?

a. They infect a device immediately upon arrival.

b. They take advantage of previously unknown vulnerabilities.

c. They have zero chance of being detected.

d. They make updates and patches unnecessary.

7

Terminology

On-access scans are also called real-time protection, background scanning, and autoprotect.

Figure 7-25: On-demand virus scan

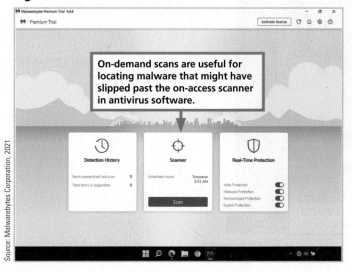

On-demand scans are useful for locating malware that might have slipped past the on-access scanner in antivirus software.

Source: Malwarebytes Corporation, 2021

Try It!

Make sure automatic updates are enabled for your operating system and software such as Microsoft Office.

Netstat

Digital devices use communication ports for all kinds of tasks, such as connecting to networks, sending and receiving email, exchanging data with peripheral devices, and accessing the Web. These ports are exploited by hackers to access devices and plant malware. Hackers also use ports to communicate with devices in botnets. Preventing unauthorized communication to and from a digital device is an essential security precaution.

▶ **How do hackers exploit communication ports?** Hackers use a technique called port scanning to discover which ports are open on a device. A **port scan** pings a packet of data to the port. If a reply is received, the port is open.

Open ports correspond to various services. For example, suppose you've installed an online game—let's call it Warcraft Legends—that uses TCP port 6112 for the game client to communicate with the game server. A hacker pinging port 6112 would learn that the port is open. An exploit to penetrate a vulnerability of Warcraft Legends would likely be successful if directed through port 6112. In this way, open ports can be used to deliver malware.

Open ports are also used for communications between botnets and their controllers. Botnet malware opens ports on victims' computers. To communicate with the botnet commander, client bots might use port 6667, for example. Data collected by the bot's keylogger could be sent via port 6667 to the botmaster, and commands from the botmaster might be relayed to infected devices using the same port. Ports that exhibit unusual activity could be a sign of a botnet intrusion.

▶ **Can I detect which ports are open?** Network utilities such as Netstat produce a detailed list of open ports on a device. Although these utilities are useful diagnostic tools, their reports are lengthy and do not clearly separate ports needed by legitimate services from those used for nefarious purposes (Figure 7-26).

Figure 7-26: Netstat detects open ports

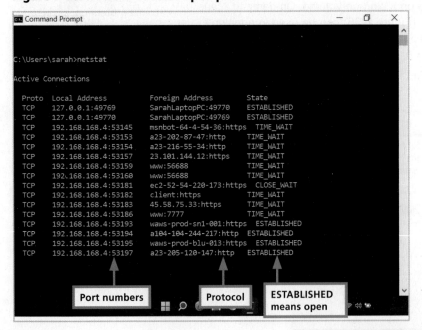

QuickCheck

In Figure 7-26, how many HTTP ports are not using a secure connection?

a. None

b. 2

c. 9

d. 16

Firewalls

Suppose that you could erect a digital wall that would block communication between your digital devices and the outside world. Although it would prevent unauthorized intrusions, it would also block email, and it would prevent access to the Web and a host of online communications services. What if you could drill holes through the wall for communications that you know are legitimate? That is the theory behind digital firewalls.

▶ **What is a firewall?** A firewall is a device or software that is designed to block unauthorized access while allowing authorized communications. A personal firewall is a software-based deterrent against unauthorized port access. A network router can be deployed as a hardware-based firewall.

▶ **How does a personal firewall work?** A personal firewall uses a set of rules to block data or allow it to enter a digital device. Because firewalls offer a good level of defense against unauthorized intrusions, they should be installed and correctly configured on all digital devices that have network connections.

Firewalls are included in most security software products, and it is possible that more than one firewall might be available for use. Only one software-based firewall should be active, however, because firewalls have a tendency to conflict with each other.

Most personal firewalls are configured to block all communication unless an app and its corresponding communication port are on a list of allowed exceptions. When a new app attempts to establish a connection, users are notified and given a chance to allow or block the app. The recommended configuration for Windows Defender Firewall is shown in Figure 7-27.

QuickCheck

Which of the following is true about multiple firewalls?

a. Multiple software-based firewalls tend to conflict with each other.

b. Activating multiple software-based firewalls provides added security.

c. A software-based firewall and a hardware-based firewall will reduce security.

d. Hardware firewalls should be disabled when a software-based firewall is installed.

7

Figure 7-27: Firewall configuration

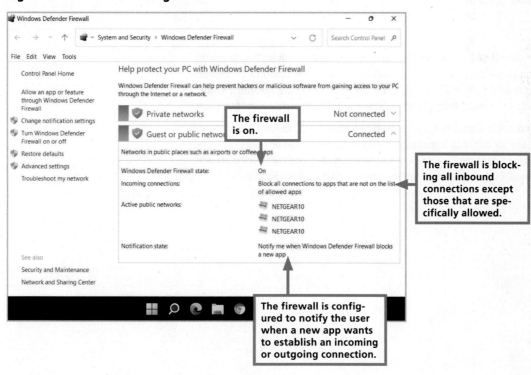

The firewall is on.

The firewall is blocking all inbound connections except those that are specifically allowed.

The firewall is configured to notify the user when a new app wants to establish an incoming or outgoing connection.

▶ **Which apps are allowed through a firewall?** Firewalls contain a list of allowed apps. Users can view this list and modify it by adding or blocking apps. For example, Windows Firewall allows users to specify which apps are allowed on private networks and which are allowed on public networks (Figure 7-28).

Figure 7-28: Apps allowed through the Windows firewall

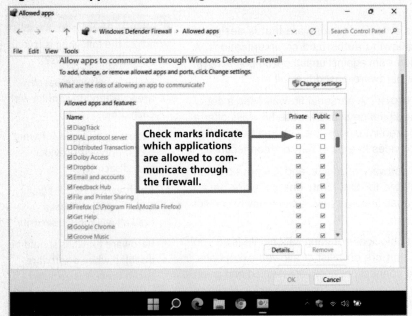

Applications that access the Internet require permission to communicate through the firewall. With permission, an app can open a port and use it to send and receive data.

Try It!

It is worth viewing the list of connections allowed by your firewall from time to time just to make sure there aren't any suspicious activities. Open the personal firewall on your digital device and check the configuration.

▶ **Are there firewall settings for ports?** Yes, most firewall software allows users to open and close specific communications ports. With Windows Firewall, this process requires multiple steps. Apparently, Microsoft developers would prefer that consumers steer clear of this potentially risky security configuration.

▶ **How does a router become a firewall?** Module 3 introduced the concept that routers use network address translation (NAT) to convert local IP addresses into routable IP addresses that can travel over the Internet. A router acts as a firewall to block connections that are not initiated inside a local network (Figure 7-29).

Figure 7-29: A router with NAT provides a hardware firewall

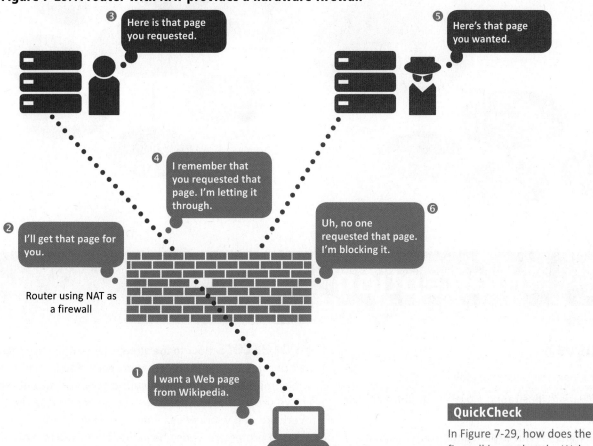

7

> ❶ I want a Web page from Wikipedia.

> ❷ I'll get that page for you.

> ❸ Here is that page you requested.

> ❹ I remember that you requested that page. I'm letting it through.

> ❺ Here's that page you wanted.

> ❻ Uh, no one requested that page. I'm blocking it.

Router using NAT as a firewall

▶ **Do I need NAT in addition to a personal firewall?** Yes. NAT is a good line of defense against attacks that originate from the Internet, but it does not protect against threats that originate inside a network. Suppose that your laptop gets infected with a worm while you are using the laptop at a Wi-Fi hotspot. You then take your laptop home and connect it to your LAN. The NAT running on your LAN's router will not prevent the worm from spreading to other devices within your LAN, because NAT shields communications to and from the Internet, not between the devices connected within the local network.

QuickCheck

In Figure 7-29, how does the firewall know that the Web page from the blue server is legitimate?

a. It is using an open port.

b. It has the correct IP address.

c. It was requested by a computer within the LAN.

d. The browser marked it as "safe."

QuickQuiz   Section C

1. A(n) [_____] access trojan is the underlying technology for most online intrusions.

2. Botnets are commonly used to carry out distributed [_____]-of-service attacks.

3. A(n) [_____]-day attack exploits previously unknown vulnerabilities in software applications, hardware, and operating systems.

4. A(n) [_____] scan is used by hackers to discover which applications are using online communications.

5. A personal [_____] uses a set of rules to block unauthorized access through open communications ports.

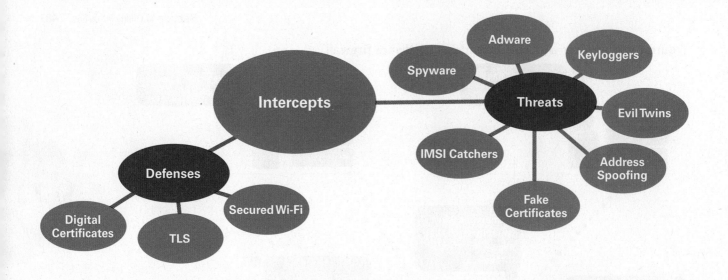

Interception

Objectives

▶ List four types of intercept exploits.

▶ Draw a diagram illustrating a basic man-in-the-middle exploit.

▶ Describe the Evil Twin exploit and how to avoid it.

▶ List four types of address spoofs.

▶ List the three important security components of a digital certificate.

▶ Describe or diagram how a digital certificate encrypts the connection between a client and a server.

▶ Explain how a fake digital certificate can defeat encryption.

▶ Describe how an IMSI catcher works.

Protesters flock to the streets. Organizers use their cell phones to communicate with each other. They use social media to gather more supporters. The size of the crowd grows, but law enforcement helicopters are flying overhead and windowless vans are moving close to the massed protesters. Those helicopters and vans might be deploying stingray devices to intercept cell phone communications, identify the protest leaders, and track their movements. This modern version of wiretapping is just one example of intercepts that can threaten your privacy and security.

Terminology

spyware	man-in-the-middle	TLS	IMSI
adware	Evil Twin	digital certificate	
keylogger	address spoofing		

Interception Basics

Networks are an integral part of our digital lives. Important information flows over Internet connections and mobile phone services. Consumers cannot, however, assume that those connections are secure, because a variety of exploits allow eavesdroppers to intercept data, email, text messages, and voice conversations that flow over communication infrastructures.

▶ **What types of interception exploits are threats?** Interception exploits that are current threats to consumers include the following:

Spyware. Any software that secretly gathers personal information without the victim's knowledge is classified as **spyware**. Some spyware is designed for advertising and similar commercial purposes, whereas other spyware is designed with criminal intent to steal identities or take remote control of a victim's digital device.

Adware. A type of spyware called **adware** monitors Web browsing activity to supply ad-serving sites with data used to generate targeted ads. More than a nuisance, the data compiled by adware has the potential to become a record of an individual's habits and lifestyle.

Keyloggers. A common type of spyware called a **keylogger** records keystrokes and sends them to a hacker who sifts out user passwords to access the victim's accounts. Keyloggers are a common tool of identity thieves and industrial spies.

Man-in-the-Middle. In the context of cyber security, an eavesdropping exploit is referred to as a **man-in-the-middle** (MITM or MIM) attack. MITM attacks include Evil Twins, address spoofing, digital certificate hacks, and IMSI catchers.

▶ **How do MITM attacks work?** The objective of an MITM attack is for a third party to intercept communications between two entities without their knowledge. The third party may passively monitor the communication or may actively modify the data before it reaches its destination. The person in the middle impersonates the other two entities to give the illusion that the two entities are communicating with each other, when in reality they are communicating with an intruder (Figure 7-30).

Figure 7-30: A basic MITM attack

In an MITM attack, two parties believe they are communicating directly with each other when they are actually communicating with a third party. Sue now thinks she should meet Joe at 1:00.

QuickCheck

The objective of most MITM attacks is to _____.

a. monitor or alter communications

b. remotely control a victim's device

c. install unwanted data on a victim's computer

d. gather marketing data

Evil Twins

Public Wi-Fi hotspots are everywhere. They are operated by coffee shops, colleges, airports, hotels…and hackers. The next time you access a Wi-Fi hotspot, your activities could be monitored, intercepted, and altered by unauthorized third parties using an exploit called an Evil Twin.

▶ **What is an Evil Twin?** An **Evil Twin** is a LAN server that is designed to look like a legitimate Wi-Fi hotspot. Module 3 explained the basic security issues with Wi-Fi hotspots. Many hotspots are unsecured, require no login passwords, and carry data over unencrypted connections. When connecting to an unsecured Wi-Fi hotspot, you are blindly trusting that it is what it appears to be. The hotspot might be fraudulent, however. Hackers are skilled at creating fraudulent sites, referred to as Evil Twins, that resemble legitimate sites.

▶ **How does the Evil Twin exploit work?** To establish an Evil Twin, hackers set up a Wi-Fi hotspot complete with an Internet connection. The network is unsecured, so data that travels over the network is not encrypted, which allows the hacker to capture any information that users enter as they surf the Web, make purchases from online stores, log in to online banking services, and enter passwords at social media sites. Users may never suspect that their activities are monitored if hackers pass the data on to its legitimate destination after it is captured.

Evil Twins are difficult to detect. To avoid this exploit, refrain from entering sensitive data while using any questionable network, and avoid using unsecured networks. For example, when looking for Internet access at the Los Angeles airport, your digital device might list several networks that appear to be operated by the LAX Airport authority. In Figure 7-31, which of the Wi-Fi networks is most likely to be an Evil Twin?

QuickCheck

The attack vector for an Evil Twin exploit is a(n) _____.

a. Wi-Fi hotspot

b. email message

c. software download

d. PUP or PUA

Figure 7-31: Which network is the Evil Twin?

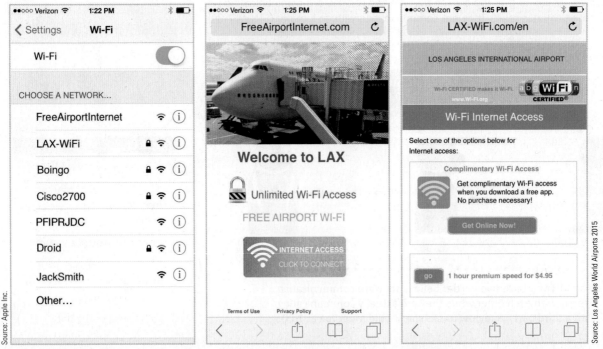

Three public Wi-Fi services appear to be offered at the LAX airport: FreeAirportInternet, LAX-WiFi, and Boingo. The remaining Wi-Fi hotspots are operated by individuals using their phones as a tethering device. Of the three public Wi-Fi services, FreeAirportInternet is not secured; therefore, it is most likely to be an Evil Twin.

Address Spoofing

As the 25th anniversary of the Tiananmen Square protest approached, the Chinese government worried that online queries about the event might incite further unrest. The solution: tighten Internet censorship. For ordinary citizens using government-controlled ISPs, access to Google from within China was totally blocked. For academics using a privileged research and education network, Chinese censors deployed address spoofing exploits to route data through an intermediary site that allowed only politically correct queries to proceed.

▶ **What is address spoofing?** Broadly speaking, address spoofing changes an originating address or a destination address to redirect the flow of data between two parties. In the context of security exploits, address spoofing can take place on various levels of communication (Figure 7-32).

7

Figure 7-32: Address spoofing is used for several black hat exploits

 Email Address Spoof

Changes the sender's address. The spoofed address masks the source of spam.

IP Address Spoof

Modifies the source IP address of data packets used in a denial-of-service attack.

 DNS Address Spoof

Changes the IP address that corresponds to a URL. The spoofed URL directs victims to a fraudulent Web site.

ARP Address Spoof

Changes the ARP (Address Resolution Protocol) routing table on a local area network. The spoofed address redirects traffic through a secondary, potentially malicious device.

▶ **How does address spoofing affect browsing?** Just about every exchange of data on the Internet takes place between a client and a server. When using a Web app, for example, your browser connects to a server, such as *www.zoho.com*. When collecting Webmail, your browser might access *www.gmail.com*. When you want to enter a Google query, you connect to *www.google.com*.

On the Web, URLs correspond to IP addresses. When you use a browser to access *www.google.com*, it should connect you to a Google server with a valid IPv6 address such as 2607:f8b0:4007:804::1013. By spoofing Google's IP address, however, Chinese authorities were able to send users to a fake Google site. The fake site examined queries and blocked those that were destined for banned sites or contained controversial keywords.

QuickCheck

DNS spoofing changes the

_____.

a. ARP address

b. IP address for a URL

c. sender's address

d. the URL

Digital Certificate Hacks

You can envision how an MITM attack can redirect data packets from a user's client device to a fake Web server. To make intercepted data useless to hackers, it would seem reasonable to encrypt it. Google offers end-to-end HTTPS encryption, for example, to scramble the text of queries made by users and the content of search results. Encryption should hide content from prying MITM attacks, but as Chinese users discovered, that is not always what happens.

▶ **Why is encryption vulnerable?** The current method of encrypting communication between a client and a server depends on a security protocol called **TLS** (Transport Layer Security) that checks a **digital certificate** to verify a server's identity and pass a public key to the client. The client then uses the public key to encrypt data that is sent to the server, as shown in Figure 7-33.

Figure 7-33: How digital certificates work

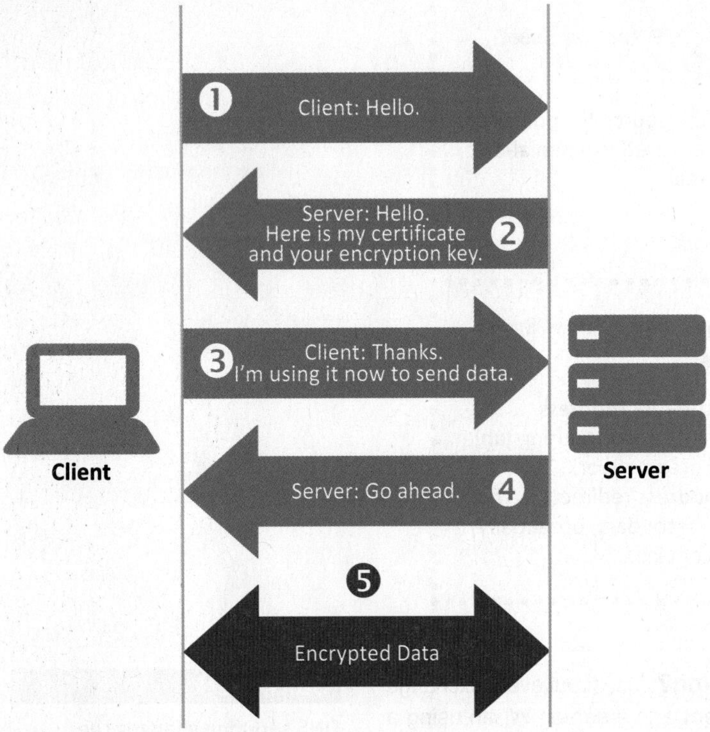

① Client: Hello.

② Server: Hello. Here is my certificate and your encryption key.

③ Client: Thanks. I'm using it now to send data.

④ Server: Go ahead.

⑤ Encrypted Data

Client

Server

▶ **So what is the problem with TLS?** Digital certificates can be faked. Valid digital certificates are issued by official security authorities. These certificates are validated or "signed" by the certificate authority. A fake digital certificate contains the server's credentials and an encryption key, but it might not have a valid signature. Chinese censors, hackers, and government security agencies use fake certificates to snoop on supposedly secure communications.

▶ **How does a digital certificate hack work?** Consider what you know about MITM attacks, and imagine that by using DNS address spoofing, all the data from Chinese Internet users gets funneled through a government server.

QuickCheck

Digital certificates do not contain _____.

a. server identification

b. a public key

c. a certificate authority's signature

d. an ARP routing table

To screen the data and block out queries about the Tiananmen Square protest, for example, users are sent fake digital certificates. These certificates encrypt data, but the key is known to the government server. Encrypted Google queries and other data can then be decrypted by the government server, and only those queries that are politically correct are passed along to the real destination. Figure 7-34 illustrates how this works.

Figure 7-34: How fake digital certificates defeat encryption

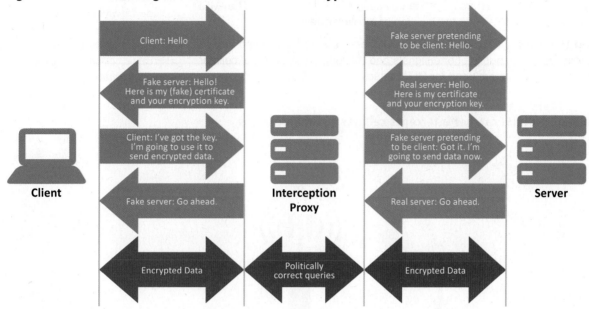

▶ **Is there a way to stop MITM attacks that use fake digital certificates?**
Although most fake digital certificates contain the server's credentials and an encryption key, they may not contain a valid signature from a certificate authority. Most modern browsers flag Web sites that do not have a valid digital certificate. Users who pay attention to invalid certificate notifications, similar to those in Figure 7-35, should be aware that the server may be part of an MITM exploit.

Figure 7-35: Invalid certificate alert

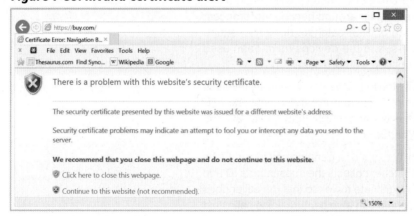

IMSI Catchers

While you drive through the streets of any city, your cell phone conversations, text messages, and Internet activity could be intercepted by fake cell towers. IMSI catchers are yet another MITM exploit.

▶ **What is IMSI?** IMSI is an acronym for International Mobile Subscriber Identity. It is a 64-bit number that uniquely identifies a cellular device. When a device connects to a cellular network, the IMSI is sent from the device to the tower. The tower uses the IMSI to determine if the device is a valid subscriber. The IMSI can also be used to determine the location of a cellular device.

▶ **What is an IMSI catcher?** An IMSI catcher is an eavesdropping device used for intercepting mobile phone signals and tracking the location of cellular devices. IMSI catchers are used for MITM attacks (Figure 7-36).

Terminology

IMSI catchers are sometimes called *stingrays* after the brand name of a well-known cellular surveillance device. They are also called *cell-site simulators* or *rogue base stations*.

Figure 7-36: An IMSI catcher intercepts cellular communications

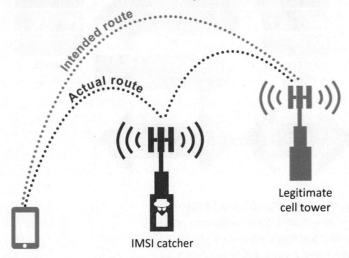

Legitimate cell tower

IMSI catcher

▶ **Who operates IMSI catchers?** IMSI catchers are operated by law enforcement agencies, criminals, and hackers. IMSI catchers are portable. They can be moved and quickly deployed, for example, during civil unrest when law enforcement agents want to intercept calls among protest organizers. Not surprisingly, IMSI catchers seem to spring up around hacker conferences, such as DEF CON and Black Hat. The use of IMSI catchers does not require cooperation from cellular service providers, and the devices have been used in some jurisdictions without a warrant or court authorization.

▶ **How does an IMSI catcher work?** Mobile phones have various levels of security, depending on the sophistication of the communications network. LTE and 5G cellular networks and devices offer better security than earlier 2G and 3G networks, but are not immune to IMSI attacks.

Sophisticated IMSI catchers have the ability to spoof a genuine cell tower. Once a mobile device has connected, the IMSI catcher collects the subscriber's ID and location before forwarding the signals to a legitimate tower so that the caller does not notice a disruption in service. IMSI catchers can also capture voice calls, text messages, and data streams that emanate from hijacked devices.

To bypass security, attackers can simply block the legitimate 3G, LTE, and 5G signals, forcing the target device to switch to a less secure 2G network. Once accomplished, the exploit proceeds to collect personal information before forwarding the call to a legitimate tower (Figure 7-37).

Figure 7-37: Anatomy of a basic IMSI catcher exploit

① Disable 3G, LTE, and 5G service so that phones cannot authenticate the tower.

② Broadcast a 2G signal, which phones are forced to use when no other service is available.

③ Connect phones to an IMSI catcher using unauthenticated 2G.

④ Collect a copy of the caller's ID, location, texts, and other data.

⑤ Pass the signal to a valid service provider so the caller does not notice a disruption in service.

▶ **Are there warning signs that an IMSI catcher is intercepting calls?** Callers are rarely aware of IMSI catchers because calls and other services appear to proceed as normal. If you notice that the network indicator on a device switches to 2G, that could signify a connection controlled by an IMSI catcher. However, some of these interception devices spoof the indicator to make it display 3G, LTE, or 5G when the connection is actually 2G.

Savvy criminals and terrorists tend not to use mobile phones for illegal activities. Law-abiding citizens, too, should be mindful that their conversations may be intercepted.

QuickCheck

IMSI catchers can force phones to use _____ in order to carry out an MITM attack.

a. a 2G connection

b. DNS spoofing

c. a fake digital certificate

d. a zero-day exploit

7

QuickQuiz   Section D

1. An Evil Twin exploit usually takes place on an unsecured [_____] network.

2. Hackers and government agencies sometimes use [_____] address spoofing to set up an intermediary server to capture Web traffic.

3. A digital certificate depends on a security protocol called [_____].

4. Encryption is the best defense against MITM attacks. True or false? [_____]

5. Mobile phones are susceptible to an interception exploit that uses [_____] catchers.

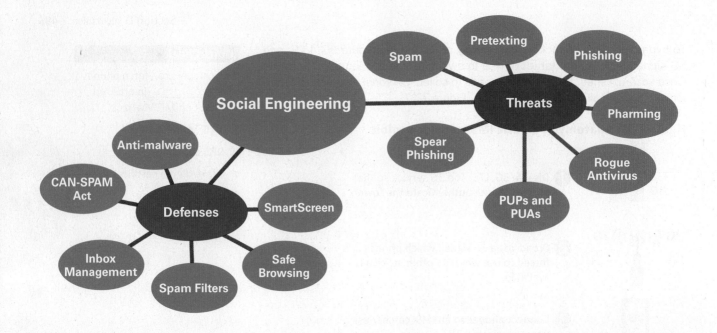

Social Engineering

Objectives

- Create a diagram that illustrates the six elements of a social engineering attack.
- Describe advance fee fraud and the stranded traveler scam.
- List the three limitations placed on spam by the CAN-SPAM Act of 2003.
- List at least six best practices for avoiding spam.
- Describe the four types of spam filters.
- Explain the difference between phishing and pharming attacks.
- Explain the purpose of Safe Browsing.
- Describe how a rogue antivirus exploit works.
- Give two examples of PUAs.

Malware, intrusions, and interceptions. How do all these exploits end up on digital devices? Human psychology is an open book to scammers, who use it to prey on victims. No one—not even the most savvy consumer—is immune to the clever scams that arrive in email or lie dormant on the Web. Section E delves into the shady world of scammers and spammers to uncover their exploits and their weaknesses.

Terminology

social engineering	spam	phishing	SmartScreen
social engineer	CAN-SPAM Act	spear phishing	rogue antivirus exploit
clickbait	pretexting	pharming	PUP
advance fee fraud	spam filter	Safe Browsing	PUA

Social Engineering Basics

One of the most enterprising con artists of all time was a man named George Parker, who managed to sell the Brooklyn Bridge not once but several times to a succession of gullible buyers. Today, con artists have moved into cyberspace, where they devise a continuous barrage of scams to trick consumers into parting with passwords, cash, and control of their digital devices. As these scams become more sophisticated, they also become more difficult to detect. Avoiding them requires a set of security tools and constant vigilance on the part of consumers.

▶ **What is social engineering?** In the context of cyber security, **social engineering** (SE) is a deceptive practice that exploits human psychology by inducing victims to interact with a digital device in a way that is not in their best interest. **Social engineer** is a judgment-neutral term for a person who devises and carries out a scam in order to accomplish a goal, such as financial gain, unauthorized access, or service disruption. The target of a social engineering exploit is an individual or organization that may be tricked into participating in the scam.

A relatively harmless example of SE is **clickbait**, an eye-catching image with a teaser headline designed to entice people to click a provided link and satisfy their curiosity. Many clickbait links lead to harmless Web sites, but some lead to sites that contain malware.

SE attacks can be carried out using a variety of technologies, such as email, malware, fraudulent Web sites, SMS, and IRC. For each of these technologies, social engineers have developed effective techniques for tricking victims, including phishing, pretexting, and pharming. Social engineering attacks are multifaceted. Figure 7-38 offers an overview to help you visualize the elements of a social engineering attack.

QuickCheck

Email scammers promise to deposit a large sum of money into your bank account if you pay them a small processing fee. Based on Figure 7-38, which of the following incentives are the scammers using?

a. Authority

b. Friendship

c. Scarcity

d. Reciprocity

7

Figure 7-38: Elements of a social engineering attack

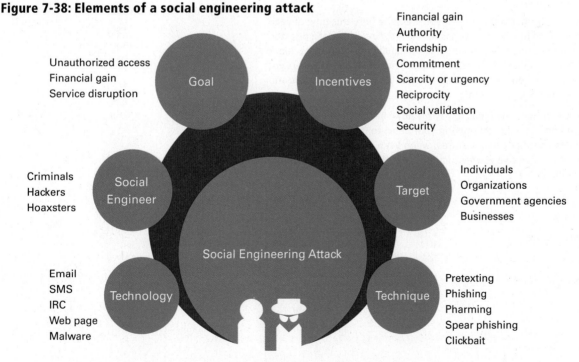

Diagram adapted from F. Mouton et al. Towards an Ontological Model Defining the Social Engineering Domain.

▶ **Why are people fooled by SE?** Social engineering attacks prey on human vulnerabilities, such as gullibility, ignorance, curiosity, greed, courtesy, indifference, and carelessness. The "bait" that is set forth in various social engineering scams is based on one or more incentives designed to compel individuals to participate in the scam.

One of the first examples of a social engineering email scam was **advance fee fraud**, in which a victim is promised a large sum of money in exchange for a bank account number from which a small advance fee is withdrawn. These scams prey on human greed and the hope that it is possible to "get rich quick" without any hard work. According to the FBI, a surprising number of people continue to be duped by these scams, which now often involve Bitcoin and other cryptocurrencies.

Most email-savvy consumers simply laugh at these preposterous messages and delete them, but other scams are much more insidious. For example, one widespread scam arrives as an "urgent" email message from a respected community member, such as a teacher, priest, or rabbi, who is traveling abroad, has been robbed, and needs a quick loan to return home. The message may, in fact, originate from a trusted person's account—one that has been hijacked by a hacker. Scams such as this one prey upon human kindness and the desire to help people who are in need (Figure 7-39).

Figure 7-39: Don't be fooled by the stranded traveler scam

FROM: **dbrownpastor@stmatthews.org**

TO: ManuellaAroyo@gmail.com

Need Assistance

Dear Manuella,

So sorry to bother you as I know you are quite busy this time of year. But my trip to the Philippines has turned into something of a disaster. Last night I was attacked and robbed. Thankfully, my injuries are minor and the hospital saw fit to release me this morning. The attackers got my wallet and phone, but I am glad that I locked my passport and airline ticket in the hotel safe.

I am left without any funds to pay my hotel bill or meet expenses to return home. Could you see it in your heart to loan me $2,000 just until I can get back to the States, when I can immediately pay you back? If so, I can give you instructions for wiring the money. It should not be difficult.

Sincerely,

Donald Brown

Spam

Spam is a nuisance and it accounts for approximately 50% of all email. Not only does spam clog up Internet bandwidth that could be put to better use, but it reduces individual productivity as users spend time separating useless and sometimes offensive messages from legitimate messages sent by friends, family, and colleagues. Some spam contains malicious attachments and links that lead to fake Web sites.

▶ **Where does spam originate?** Spam is defined as unsolicited messages that are usually sent in massive numbers using electronic mail systems. It is junk mail that recipients do not request or want. Spam includes advertisements from legitimate companies and from scammers attempting to trick victims into parting with their money or their personal information. Spam sent by scammers often uses spoofed email addresses or addresses of unfortunate victims whose computers are part of a botnet used to mass-mail spam.

▶ **Who gets spam?** Everyone. Mass-mailing databases are quite inexpensive. Obtaining a million email addresses for a mass mailing costs less than $200. Databases used by spammers contain millions of email addresses. Some of these addresses are legitimately compiled from customer lists, but many more are harvested from social media sites, discussion forums, Web sites, and other online locations using email extractor software. Malware also harvests addresses for mass-mailing databases. Even more email addresses can be generated by appending the domain of a popular email service to names from a telephone directory (Figure 7-40).

Figure 7-40: Generating email addresses for a mass-mailing database

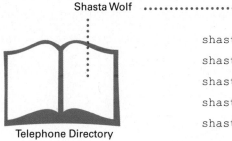

Shasta Wolf

Telephone Directory

shastawolf@gmail.com

shastawolf@yahoo.com

shastawolf@outlook.com

shastawolf@icloud.com

shastawolf@aol.com

Mass-Mailing Database

▶ **Isn't spam illegal?** Most countries have laws that regulate spam, but legal measures seem to have little effect on the volume of unsolicited email messages. In 2003, the United States Congress passed an anti-spam law, the **CAN-SPAM Act** (Controlling the Assault of Non-Solicited Pornography And Marketing Act of 2003). Ironically, this act confirmed the legality of sending unsolicited email messages. The act attempted to regulate bulk email by requiring senders to do the following:

- Provide a visible means for recipients to opt out of further messages.

- Include accurate information in the "From" line, a relevant subject line, and a legitimate physical address of the sender.

- Avoid using harvested email addresses or false email headers.

The effectiveness of this law can be evaluated by looking at the content of your inbox and examining a few of the many unsolicited messages that continue to pile up in your email trash and junk mail folders.

7

▶ **What are the most common email scams?** A high percentage of illegitimate spam contains stock market frauds, pretexting scams, advance fee fraud,
phishing attacks, and ads for dubious products. **Pretexting** is a term describing
spam that uses a false pretext to trick victims into participating. Spam messages
like those in Figure 7-41 are examples of common pretexting exploits.

Figure 7-41: Lots of spam uses pretexting exploits

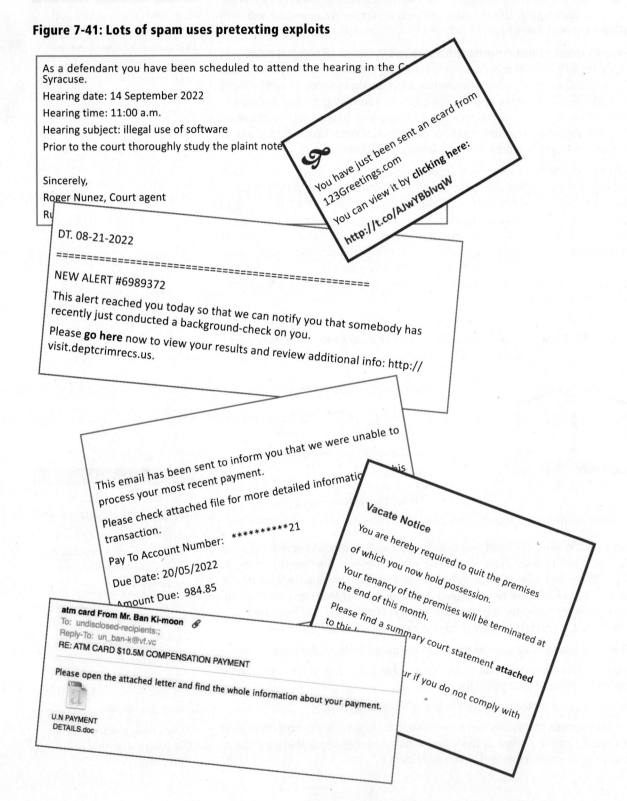

▶ **Is it possible to block spam?** Most ISPs and email services use filtering techniques to block spam coming from IP addresses and senders that are known to generate spam. These services also block messages sent in bulk that all contain the same wording. Spammers have developed techniques to bypass these barriers, and spam continues to make its way into consumer mailboxes.

Defending against spam requires careful inbox management. To reduce the amount of spam that lands in your online mailbox, consider the following recommendations:

✉ Share your primary email address only with people or businesses that you trust not to distribute it to others. Businesses sometimes share mailing lists with affiliates, and lists may fall into the hands of illegitimate spammers. Keeping your email address off one list can keep it from propagating to multiple lists.

✉ Never reply to spam. Mailing lists contain a high percentage of invalid addresses. Replying to a spam message marks your email address as valid, which only generates more unwanted mail.

✉ Do not click links in spam messages. If you are curious about where a link might lead, hover over it with the pointer and look at the destination URL. Links in spam often are designed to direct victims to fake sites where malware is waiting.

✉ Do not open attachments in email messages unless you are certain that the sender is trusted and the attached file is expected.

✉ Use a complex email address with a user name that would not be found in a telephone directory. For example, add a number or symbol to your name.

✉ Use a disposable email address in situations where an email address is required but you don't want to receive solicitations. Disposable email addresses are useful when registering to use Web apps and when signing up for merchant loyalty programs.

✉ When displaying your real email address—for example, on your Web site—disguise it by posting it as a graphic. You can create a graphic containing your email address by using graphics software such as Paint and saving it as a PNG file.

✉ Use an opt-out link only if the email originated from a reputable national company. Before clicking the opt-out link, hover over it to make sure it leads to a legitimate URL.

✉ Remember that if a deal seems too good to be true, it is probably a scam.

✉ Be suspicious of shortened URLs that do not reveal the genuine domain.

✉ Be wary of email messages addressed to "undisclosed recipients" or addressed to numerous recipients that you don't know.

✉ Be cautious of email messages addressed to your email user name rather than your real name.

✉ Use the spam filters provided by your email client.

7

Try It!

The next time you receive an outlandish spam email on your desktop or laptop, hover the mouse pointer over one of the links. DON'T CLICK THE LINK. Look at the destination address. Does it have any relationship to the organization that sent the message?

QuickCheck

A disposable email address is most useful for _____.

a. detecting infected email attachments

b. reducing the amount of spam that arrives at your main email account

c. evading mail extractors

d. opting out of legitimate URLs

How do spam filters work? A **spam filter** uses a set of rules to examine email messages and determine which are spam. Messages that are identified as spam can be blocked, deleted, or moved to a junk mail folder. There are four common types of spam filters:

- **Content filters** examine the content within a message for certain words or phrases commonly used in spam emails.

- **Header filters** review the email header for falsified information, such as spoofed IP addresses.

- **Blacklist filters** block mail that originates from IP addresses of known spammers.

- **Permission filters** block or allow mail based on the sender's address.

Blacklist and header filtering is usually performed by ISPs and email services, such as Google and Yahoo!. Email clients and Webmail services provide consumers with permission filters and content filters. Knowing how to use these filters is handy for blocking spam that can slip through filters operating upstream at your ISP or email service (Figure 7-42).

Figure 7-42: Gmail spam filters

The simplest spam filter blocks a specific sender based on that sender's email address. That technique works on unwanted mail from creepy individuals, but most spammers send mail from a spoofed address that is fraudulent. The spammer will never use the same address twice, so blocking it does little to curtail spam.

Suppose you're receiving a barrage of spam about "unbelievable stock deals." If the messages contain similar wording, you may be able to devise a content filter to block similar spam in the future. The trick is to create a specific filter rather than one that is general enough to block legitimate messages.

Some spam filters can be set up to allow email only from people who are included in your contacts list or address book. This technique introduces a problem, however, because email from new acquaintances who are not yet in your address book is blocked. When using a permission filter, it is important to periodically check the junk mail folder in case legitimate messages are there.

You can also use email filters to create "ham." In the world of email, ham is like a password that verifies the validity of a sender. For example, suppose you expect email from visitors to your Web site or blog. Tell your visitors to include a ham password, such as "BlogVisitor," in the subject line of their messages. Set your spam filter to require the password for any messages that don't originate from people who are in your contacts list.

Phishing

Phishing exploits are responsible for some of the most effective social engineering scams, including the exploit that caused a scandal during the 2016 U.S. presidential election. A look at some examples reveals how these attacks work.

▶ **What is phishing?** Phishing is an email scam that masquerades as a message from a trusted friend, legitimate company, or agency of authority, such as the IRS. The goal of a phishing scam is usually to obtain private information, including login passwords and bank card numbers.

Phishing scams often contain infected attachments or include links to fake Web sites infected with malware. Phishing email messages are typically the beginning of exploits that infect a device with malware, use keyloggers to collect personal information, set up a backdoor for intrusions, and link a device to a botnet.

Phishing messages are usually mass-mailed to millions of email addresses. A spear phishing attack is more targeted. It is typically sent only to members of a specific organization. The spear phishing email that caused such a scandal during the 2016 U.S. presidential election was sent to 100 of candidate Hillary Clinton's campaign workers. It contained a short URL that led to a hacker's site where additional exploits waited. Clinton's campaign manager clicked the link and unintentionally activated the spear phishing exploit, which gave hackers access to email messages and other files related to the campaign.

Some of the most common phishing attacks appear to originate from FedEx, UPS, DHL, or the U.S. Postal Service and pertain to package delivery services. Tax scams in messages headed with an official IRS seal are also prevalent, as are scams that use realistic logos of financial institutions, government agencies, and merchants (Figure 7-43).

Figure 7-43: Phishing attacks appear to originate from trusted businesses

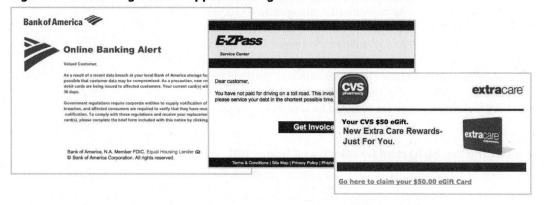

▶ **What is the best strategy for dealing with phishing attacks?** Phishing attacks are not always easy to identify. Their messages may appear to originate from trusted businesses. Although some phishing messages include misspellings and bad grammar, others contain no such errors. Phishing messages are more compelling than most spam, and the temptation to click the links they contain is strong.

Phishing exploits are a type of spam, and both require the same type of vigilance on the part of consumers: Take steps to keep your email address off mass-mailing lists, use spam filters, avoid opening attachments, and do not click links in email messages unless you are certain that they lead to a trusted source.

Try It!

Take another look at the contents of your junk email folder. How many of the messages would you classify as phishing attacks?

7

QuickCheck

Phishing attacks are a type of spam that _____.

a. appears to originate from a trusted business

b. is sent to undisclosed recipients

c. spoofs the target's email address

d. contains an infected dropper

Pharming

Email is not the only source of social engineering attacks. The Web is host to its share of fraudulent sites and other scams. Using screenshots and graphics tools, for example, one can construct Web sites that closely resemble those of trusted online retailers. But how are consumers tricked into visiting these sites? That's the purpose of pharming exploits.

▶ **What is pharming?** **Pharming** redirects Web site traffic to fraudulent Web sites that distribute malware, collect personal data, sell counterfeit products, and perpetrate other scams. Fraudulent Web sites often have URLs that are similar to the legitimate sites they imitate. A basic exploit is to establish a look-alike site at a URL, such as *www.amzon.com*, that is a common misspelling of a legitimate online storefront. Careless consumers who leave out the "a" end up at the look-alike Web site.

Another pharming strategy is to use a URL that sounds like a legitimate merchant. For example, a gang of offshore scammers selling counterfeit Louis Vuitton handbags hoped consumers would think the URL *www.nordstrom-louisvuitton.net* was affiliated with Nordstrom department stores.

▶ **How is pharming related to the domain name system?** The most insidious pharming attacks are implemented by DNS spoofing, which was explained in Module 3. Hackers infiltrate a domain name system server to alter the IP address of a legitimate site and send visitors to a fraudulent site instead. Past pharming attacks have redirected URLs for Web sites such as The New York Times, Google Malaysia, American Express, and The Huffington Post.

Pharming attacks carried out by DNS spoofing cannot be detected by antivirus software or spyware removal software. DNS spoofing is eventually detected and corrected by domain registrars. Until corrections are in place, consumers have little defense against such attacks except to remain alert to any details that don't look quite right when visiting familiar Web sites.

Pharming attacks can also be carried out by malware that changes an IP address in a file called Hosts. This file contains URLs and their corresponding IP addresses, which override the mapping accessed from a domain name server. Malware that enters a device, perhaps in a trojan, seeks out the Hosts file and inserts a bogus URL. For example, the entry 34.123.67.999 www.facebook.com sets the IP address of Facebook to a look-alike hacker's site (Figure 7-44). Because malware is used to carry out this pharming technique, it may be detected by antivirus software.

Figure 7-44: The hosts file can be hacked by injecting a bogus URL

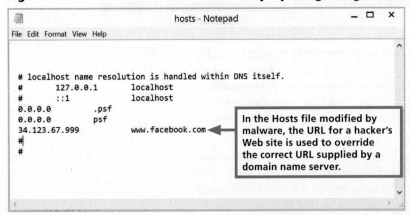

▶ **What is Safe Browsing?** Safe Browsing is a service offered by Google that checks URLs against a list of suspicious Web site URLs. The list is used to generate warnings like the one in Figure 7-45.

Figure 7-45: Warning generated by Google Safe Browsing

7

▶ **How can I activate Safe Browsing?** Chrome, Safari, and Firefox use Google's Safe Browsing service to alert users about sites to avoid. Microsoft offers a similar service called **SmartScreen**. Figure 7-46 illustrates how to activate safe browsing.

Figure 7-46: How to activate safe browsing

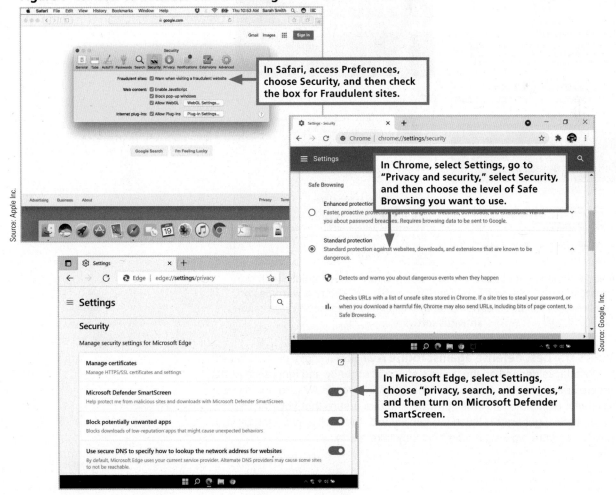

Rogue Antivirus

"WARNING! Your computer may be infected with spyware." When that window pops up, is it a warning generated by your antivirus software or a social engineering scam designed to prey on your desire to take precautions against malware? Knowing the difference between a real and a fake virus warning can prevent you from becoming a victim of fraud and identity theft.

❱ What is a rogue antivirus exploit? Most consumers who own digital devices know the dangers of malware. Seeing a notification that your device has a virus makes you want to take immediate action to eradicate it before further damage is done. Social engineers use fake virus notifications to prey on consumers' aversion to malware and their sense of urgency to eradicate it.

A **rogue antivirus exploit** usually begins with a virus warning and an offer to disinfect the infected device. The goal of this exploit is to trick consumers into clicking a link that downloads malware. Some of these fraudulent alerts offer a free virus scan or download, which often doesn't work or actually infects devices with the dangerous malware it is supposed to protect against. Other rogue antivirus exploits charge consumers for bogus software, obtain personal information, or carry out malware attacks.

Fake virus alerts commonly appear when browsing the Web at slightly sketchy Web sites. These alerts appear as pop-up windows. Can you tell which alerts in Figure 7-47 are real and which are fake?

Terminology

Rogue antivirus exploits are sometimes referred to as *rogue AV* or *rogue security software*.

Figure 7-47: Malware alerts: which are fake?

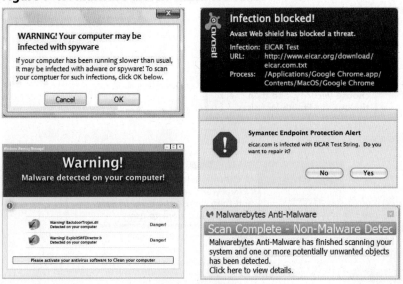

Fake virus alerts can look realistic, so it is important to be familiar with the legitimate alerts displayed by your antivirus software. The two warnings on the left are fake. The three warnings on the right were produced by legitimate antivirus software.

❱ What's the best defense against rogue AV? Social engineers who launch rogue AV attacks depend on the victim's sense of urgency and ignorance about legitimate antivirus alerts. Your best defense against rogue AV is to protect your devices with legitimate antivirus software and make sure that you can identify the virus alerts it generates. If you are familiar with the alerts generated by your legitimate software, you will not be fooled by fake alerts.

PUAs

Some software is not exactly malware, but it is a nuisance. It takes up residence on a digital device and seems impossible to disable or remove. What's up with that?

▶ **What is this stuff?** The acronym **PUP** stands for *potentially unwanted program*. A similar acronym, **PUA**, stands for *potentially unwanted application*. The terms are used interchangeably. The most common types of PUPs and PUAs are toolbars and alternative browsers. If you suddenly notice that an odd browser has become the default and your attempts to reset the default browser to Chrome, Edge, or Safari fail, your computer is likely to have a PUA.

▶ **How do PUAs end up on my devices?** PUAs are installed using social engineering techniques. Knowing that consumers often speed through the installation process, social engineers insert an option for accepting an application that "enriches" or "enhances" a function such as Web browsing. If you fail to read the fine print and accept the application, the PUA is installed along with the application you've downloaded (Figure 7-48).

QuickCheck

PUPs and PUAs are most similar to _____.

a. phishing scams

b. pharming attacks

c. pretexting

d. malware

7

Figure 7-48: When installing software, stay alert for PUAs

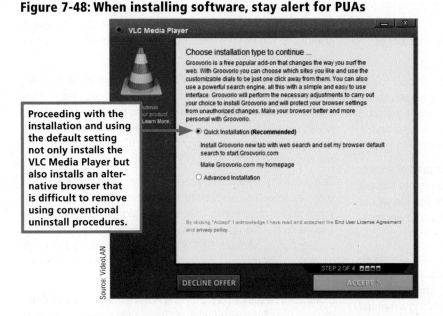

Proceeding with the installation and using the default setting not only installs the VLC Media Player but also installs an alternative browser that is difficult to remove using conventional uninstall procedures.

Source: VideoLAN

Try It!

Many antivirus utilities include PUP and PUA detection tools. Check the antivirus utility that you use to find out if it protects you from unwanted applications and make sure the detection feature is activated.

QuickQuiz   Section E

1. Advance [_____] fraud and stranded traveler scams are two social engineering exploits that are delivered in spam.

2. Blacklist spam [_____] block mail that originates from IP addresses of known spammers.

3. A(n) [_____] attack usually begins with a fraudulent email message that appears to be from a legitimate company.

4. Many [_____] attacks use DNS spoofing to send victims to a fraudulent Web site.

5. A(n) [_____] antivirus exploit displays a fake virus warning.

Issue: How Secure Is Democracy?

Russian hackers. The 2016 U.S. presidential election ended under a cloud of controversy with reports that Russian hackers influenced the vote. It was not the first time that election results were questioned, but it was the first time that a security breach was blamed.

The foundation of democracy is built upon the idea that "we the people" vote for our choice of candidates. In today's high-tech world, it might seem that touchscreen voting machines, ballot scanners, and even online voting might reduce the number of invalid ballots and fraudulent votes. Can technology assure free and fair elections? The track record so far has not been encouraging.

In the 1970s, when the country danced to disco music, cumbersome lever-operated voting booths began to be replaced by new technology. The new systems, based on IBM computer punch cards, required voters to use a stylus to punch through a card to select candidates.

For the 2000 presidential election, about one-third of all voters used these punch card voting systems. It was the closest election in the nation's history. The winner in Florida would become president, but the vote was too close to immediately call.

When a recount was conducted, the deficiencies of punched-card voting technology became clear. Some voters had failed to punch through the card, leaving "hanging chads." Those votes were rejected by the card reader, necessitating a manual recount. Teams of analysts examined each punched card, a process that stretched on for weeks. When the election results were finally certified, only 547 votes separated the winner from his opponent.

Determined to establish a voting system for subsequent elections that would be less prone to controversy, states adopted two emerging technology solutions: DRE voting machines and optical scan ballots.

DREs (direct recording electronic systems) are microprocessor-based voting machines that display candidates' names on a touchscreen. Votes are recorded on a memory card, which is later transferred to election headquarters where votes are tallied.

Optical scan technology requires voters to use a marker to fill in a circle next to the candidates of their choice. The paper ballots are tallied by an optical reader.

Unfortunately, DREs and optical scan ballots used in the 2004, 2008, and 2012 elections came with their own set of usability and security problems.

For the 2020 election, many states turned to yet another voting machine technology. Ballot marking devices (BMDs) provide a touchscreen for voters to select candidates, but that selection is not an actual vote. The BMD produces a printout of the voter's choices, which is fed into a scanner that records the vote.

Is it possible to hack voting machines? The answer is "yes," but not in the way you might think. To alter votes in standalone machines, each machine would need to be tampered with by someone who has physical access to the device. Pre-election testing procedures are designed to certify that each machine will accurately tally votes.

One weak link in the voting process is transmitting precinct-level vote tabulations to each state's secretary of state. For speed, some states accomplish that transmission via the Internet. A secure connection is critical for this process. But even if this connection is hacked, BMDs produce a paper trail of each person's vote that can be verified before a state certifies its election results.

Significant cases of voting machine tampering have not been discovered. Tampering with the vote tally requires physical access, so voting machines seem to be safe from remote intrusions by Russian, Chinese, or even U.S.-based hackers. Other aspects of the election process are less secure.

Voter registration data, campaign Web sites, email messages between campaign organizers, campaign files, fund-raising bank accounts, lists of campaign workers, and donor databases all flow over the Internet and are susceptible to attacks that steal, alter, or delete data. Security analysts warn that it is essential to reinforce security defenses to assure that future elections are accurate and fair.

Try It! Our intuition might tell us that technology offers improvements to just about every aspect of life. But when it comes to voting, technological innovations come with a cloud of suspicion about reliability and accuracy. Here is your chance to explore the emerging issues of election technology and security.

1 Permission to vote is essentially granted by voter registration databases. If your name is in a voter registration database, you are allowed to vote. Critics of every political affiliation have cast doubt on the accuracy and security of voter registration databases. Search online articles and news reports to discover if hackers have attempted to access the voter registration database in your state. Were they successful? If so, were the hackers caught and did their interference affect election results?

2 In the United States, each state is responsible for selecting the technology that is used to conduct elections. How reliable and secure is the technology used to collect and tabulate votes in your state? Do the majority of other states use similar technology? Check Ballotpedia to discover the voting technology used by each state and to see how your state compares to others.

3 Ballot marking devices (BMDs) were the technology of choice for the 2020 U.S. presidential election. Explore the technology to answer the following questions:

What is the cost of each BMD?

Exactly how does a voter use a BMD?

What is the configuration of a typical polling place that uses BMDs?

How do poll workers certify each machine before voting takes place?

How are results from each polling place transmitted to the state's secretary of state?

4 How secure was the most recent national election in your country? Search reliable online sources, such as the FBI Vault, National Intelligence Agency reports, and findings from congressional investigative committees, and then answer the following questions:

Was there hacking of voting machines, voter rolls, campaign communications, or other aspects of the election process?

If so, what type of attacks occurred and what was so damaging about the data that hackers collected?

What level of confidence do investigators attach to their findings?

How is the security of this election likely to affect the technology used in the next election?

What Do You Think?

Issue

1. Do you think that hacking is a top security threat facing the democratic process of free and fair elections?

2. Does it seem that technology has improved the electoral process?

3. Do you agree that paper ballots are the best defense against fraudulent elections?

Information Tools: Your Own Words

Plagiarism. Buying a term paper from a company or an individual and turning it in as your own. Copying words directly from someone else's print or online work. Paraphrasing without attribution. These are all forms of plagiarism.

Common knowledge. Whether you obtain information from an online or written source, to avoid plagiarism in your written work, you should include citations for any statements that are not common knowledge. Common knowledge includes ideas and facts that can be found in many places and are known by many people. Material that is based on the work, ideas, or statements of other people is not common knowledge and needs a citation for its source. Include a citation for:

- Any statement that refers to a research study or is based on its conclusions
- Any statement or graph that includes statistics
- Any word-for-word spoken or written quotations
- Any statement that restates or summarizes another person's original ideas

Paraphrasing. Citations are required even when you paraphrase. Changing the words of an original source is not sufficient. You must cite the source whenever you borrow ideas as well as words.

Acceptable paraphrasing should not be too similar to the original wording, yet you must be careful not to change the idea behind the original wording. Your paraphrase also requires a citation to the original source. Suppose you find this passage on Carla Charmer's blog that contains material you'd like to include in a mid-term report:

> A Michigan man who accessed his wife's email account while she was allegedly carrying on an affair faces up to five years in prison. He is being prosecuted for violating a state law typically used against hackers and identity thieves. It is shocking that a person could be charged with a felony for reading his spouse's email.

There are several ways in which you can use this material. Some ways are more ethical than others.

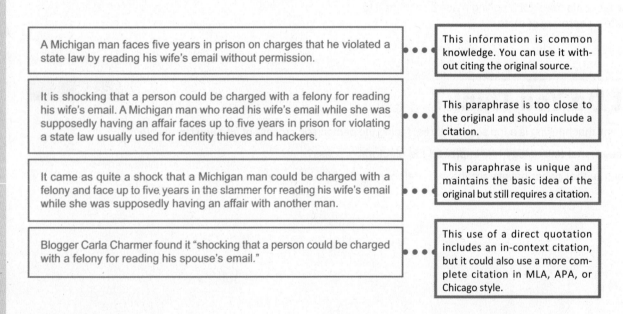

A Michigan man faces five years in prison on charges that he violated a state law by reading his wife's email without permission.

This information is common knowledge. You can use it without citing the original source.

It is shocking that a person could be charged with a felony for reading his wife's email. A Michigan man who read his wife's email while she was supposedly having an affair faces up to five years in prison for violating a state law usually used for identity thieves and hackers.

This paraphrase is too close to the original and should include a citation.

It came as quite a shock that a Michigan man could be charged with a felony and face up to five years in the slammer for reading his wife's email while she was supposedly having an affair with another man.

This paraphrase is unique and maintains the basic idea of the original but still requires a citation.

Blogger Carla Charmer found it "shocking that a person could be charged with a felony for reading his spouse's email."

This use of a direct quotation includes an in-context citation, but it could also use a more complete citation in MLA, APA, or Chicago style.

Try It! Explore the differences between original and plagiarized material by answering the following questions.

① Which of these statements would not need a citation because it is common knowledge?

a. While it is fairly uncomplicated to build a slow crawler that downloads one or a few pages per second for a short period of time, building a high-performance system that can download hundreds of millions of pages over several weeks presents a number of challenges in system design, I/O and network efficiency, and robustness and manageability.

b. Search engines, such as Google, include software called a Web crawler that visits Web sites and indexes the material it finds there. This material can later be accessed by entering keywords at a search engine site.

c. Experimental results show that a distributed Web crawler can more effectively visit Web pages than a single Web crawler.

② Which of these statements would need a citation because it refers to statements based on statistics?

a. The main problem search engines have to deal with is the size and rate of change of the Web, with no search engine indexing more than one-third of the publicly available Web.

b. Back in 2004, the average working day consisted of dealing with 46 phone calls, 15 internal memos, 19 items of snail mail, and 22 email messages.

c. Search engines deal with a vast amount of material. The process of collecting and organizing that material becomes ever greater as the Web expands.

③ Which of these statements should have citations because it refers to a research study or its conclusions?

a. We ran a crawl of more than 100 million Web pages on about 5 million hosts. The crawl was performed over a period of 18 days; however, the crawler was not continuously in operation during this time. Of the 138 million pages cataloged, more than 400,000 produced a 403 error, indicating that access was forbidden.

b. Given the current size of the Web, even large search engines cover only a portion of the publicly available part. A report from the Websonite Group indicates that large-scale search engines index no more than 40% to 70% of the indexable Web.

c. You can study the Web all you want, but there will still be more to learn.

④ Use a search engine to find the boxed quotation below, and then do the following:

> "Can ordinary Americans like you and me sue the government for illegally spying on them? When it comes to the NSA surveillance program, the government itself says the answer is no. After all, since it's a secret program you don't really know if you're being spied on. And if you don't know you're being spied on, you have no standing to sue."

a. Create an MLA citation for the original source.

b. Create an acceptable paraphrase for the quotation using an in-context citation.

c. Write at least two sentences on the same topic that would be common knowledge and not need a citation.

⑤ Plagiarism scanning services, such as Turnitin and Viper, make it easy for instructors to check the originality of your work. Before turning in a paper, you can make sure you've cited all relevant sources by running your document through the student version of Turnitin or a free plagiarism scanner such as Viper, Grammarly, Dustball, or Dupli Checker. Copy a page of text from one of your original documents and submit it to a plagiarism checker, and then do the same for a page that you copy out of Wikipedia. What are the results?

Technology in Context: Law Enforcement

Sirens wail. Blue lights flash. A speeding car slows and pulls off to the side of the road. It looks like a routine traffic stop, but the patrol car is outfitted with a mobile data computer. The police officers on this high-tech force have already checked the speeding car's license plate number and description against a database of stolen cars and vehicles allegedly used in kidnapping and other crimes.

Mounted in the dashboard of marked and unmarked police cars is a laptop computer with its flat-panel screen and compact keyboard. Unlike a consumer-grade laptop, however, the computers in police cruisers use hardened technology designed to withstand extreme conditions, such as high temperatures in parked vehicles. The dashboard-mounted computer communicates with an office-based server using a wireless link, such as short-range radio, mobile phone technology, or Wi-Fi. With this wireless link, police officers can access data from local, state, and national databases.

One national database, the National Crime Information Center (NCIC), is maintained by the FBI and can be accessed by authorized personnel in local, state, and federal law enforcement agencies. The system can process more than 12 million queries per day related to stolen vehicles, wanted criminals, missing persons, violent gang members, stolen guns, and members of terrorist organizations. The officers who pulled over the speeding car received information from the NCIC that the car was stolen, so they activate their body cameras and approach the vehicle with caution.

Technology for wearable body cameras has been available for several years, but police departments were slow to add these devices to officers' toolbelts. Costs and privacy concerns—for both the officers and the civilians they serve—prompted a wait-and-see attitude. In 2014, however, a disputed incident between a police officer and an unarmed civilian in Ferguson, Missouri, brought national attention to the need for documentary evidence of encounters between police and civilians.

Body cameras offered part of the solution to these disputes. A year-long pilot program in Rialto, California, showed a significant reduction in citizen complaints against police. The report concluded that filming improved the behavior of both the officers and the civilians they interacted with. Body cameras and the protocols that govern their use are still a work in progress to ensure that footage is not hacked, leaked, or tampered with.

Following protocol, the officers in our stolen car scenario arrest the car's occupant and take the suspect to the police station for booking.

At the police station, digital cameras flash and the suspect's mug shot is automatically entered into an automated warrants and booking system. The system stores the suspect's complete biographical and arrest information, such as name, aliases, addresses, Social Security number, charges, and arrest date. The system also checks for outstanding warrants against the suspect, such as warrants for other thefts. Booking agents can enter those charges into the system, assign a new inmate to a cell, log the perpetrator's personal items, and print a photo ID or wrist band.

Automated warrants and booking systems have been proven to increase police productivity. New York City's system handles more than 300,000 bookings per year, with gains in productivity that allow officers more time to investigate crimes and patrol neighborhoods.

As part of the booking process, suspects are fingerprinted. A standard fingerprint card, sometimes called a ten-print card, contains inked prints of the fingers on each hand, plus name, date of birth, and other arrest information. Now, however, instead of using ink, a biometric scanning device electronically captures fingerprints. Text information is entered using a keyboard and stored with digital fingerprint images.

The fingerprint information can be transmitted in digital format from local law enforcement agencies to the FBI's Next Generation Identification (NGI) system. This biometric identification system uses digital imaging technology and sophisticated algorithms to analyze fingerprints and other biometric data. Within an hour, NGI can match fingerprints with 99% accuracy from its database containing millions of records.

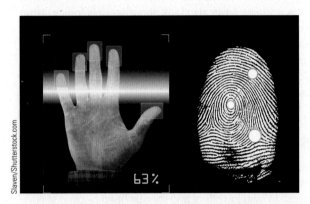

Conventional crimes, such as car theft, are often solved by using standard investigative techniques with information from computer databases. To solve cybercrimes, however, the special skills of computer forensic investigators are often required.

Computer forensics is the scientific examination and analysis of data located on computer storage media; it is conducted to offer evidence of computer crimes in court. Computer crimes can be separated into two categories. The first includes crimes that use computers, such as transmitting trade secrets to competitors, reproducing copyrighted material, and distributing child pornography. The second includes crimes targeted at computers, such as denial-of-service attacks on servers, Web site vandalism, data theft, and destructive viruses. Computer forensics can be applied to both categories.

Whether investigators suspect that a digital device is the origin of a cyber-attack or contains evidence, the first step in the forensic process is to use disk imaging software to make an exact replica of the information stored on the hard disk or SSD drive. The disk image is collected on a write-once medium that cannot be altered with planted evidence, and the forensic scientist begins analyzing the disk image data with basic search software that looks through files for keywords related to the crime.

In the case of the Gap-Toothed Bandit, who was twice convicted for robbing nine banks in Southern California, analysis of the disk image from his computer revealed word processing files containing notes he handed to tellers demanding money.

After a 2015 terrorist attack in San Bernardino, California, investigators were able to use data from the shooter's iPhone to track the activities of the shooter and his accomplice prior to the attack.

Criminals might attempt to delete files with incriminating evidence, but a good forensic scientist can retrieve data from deleted files with undelete software or data recovery software. Cloud storage, temporary Internet files, and cache files can also yield evidence that points law enforcement officers to Web sites the suspect visited that might be fronts for illegal activity.

When a network is the target of a cyber-attack, forensic investigators use three techniques to track the source. The first option is to make an immediate image of the server's hard disk and look through its log files for evidence of activity coming from unauthorized IP addresses. The second technique is to monitor the intruder by watching login attempts, changes to log files, and file access requests. Sophisticated intruders might be able to detect such monitoring, however, and cover their tracks. The third technique is to create a "honeypot"—an irresistible computer system or Web site containing fake information that allows investigators to monitor hackers until identification is possible.

Despite the many techniques and tools available to forensic investigators, they have three main constraints. First, they must adhere to privacy regulations and obtain warrants to set up wiretaps or gather information from ISPs about their customers. Second, investigators must scrupulously document their procedures so that the evidence they produce cannot be discredited in court as planted or fabricated. Third, forensic investigators must examine a wide range of alternatives pertaining to the crime, such as the chance that an IP address or email address used to commit a cybercrime might belong to an innocent bystander being spoofed by the real hacker.

Privacy, documentation, and evidentiary constraints cost forensic investigators time, and failure to adhere to strict standards can sometimes allow criminals to avoid conviction and penalties. But even within these constraints, careful forensic investigation is an important aspect of catching and convicting high-tech criminals.

Flipped Class Projects

Critical Thinking

What motivates hackers to create malware and launch cyber-attacks? Make a list of incentives, including financial and psychological, that might be the basis for attacks. Next, consider the types of cyber-attacks presented in Module 7. Classifying them according to severity may help you form some hypotheses about the incentives behind various attacks. Create a threat matrix with vertical headings for attack types and horizontal headings for incentives. When your matrix is complete, browse online to find out if your thoughts are in line with expert assessments.

Group Project

You see a similar scenario on television or in movies: a spy, hacker, or law enforcement agent needs to bypass a password. The password is cracked in three or four tries. How realistic is that? Work with a group of five classmates and try to guess one of the passwords used by a member of your group. You can ask questions such as "Is your password based on your dog's name? Your birthdate?" Does that sound risky? If someone can guess your password, it is very weak and you should change it immediately!

Cyberclassroom

One of the obstacles to distance education initiatives is securing the testing environment for students who are off-site in an unproctored environment. Several companies offer secure online testing products, but do they effectively prevent cheating? Work with a partner to brainstorm the requirements for exam security. Research an online exam monitoring product to determine its effectiveness. How could you defeat the security measures?

Multimedia Project

Envisioning how cybercrime exploits work can be difficult. YouTube contains several videos about security topics. What can they tell you? Choose a security topic from this module. You might choose a specific exploit, such as ransomware or IMSI catchers, or you might want to select a security product or a social engineering controversy. Describe the three best videos on the topic you selected.

Resume Builder

Job hunting can be stressful enough without worrying about scams, but con artists know that job seekers are particularly vulnerable to fake job offers and various head-hunting scams. When preparing for a job search, get your resume in order, but also get familiar with scams that circulate to job seekers. To begin, look for information on fake job phishing, reshipping, check-cashing, money laundering, and work-at-home scams. Next, locate guidelines on how to avoid job scams. Summarize what you find in a printed brochure, blog post, or Pinterest board.

Globalization

Because the Internet connects computers all over the globe, you might expect that malware and cybercrime exploits would be evenly spread among countries. That is far from the case. Search online for statistics about malware incidents by country. Which countries are hardest hit by malware? Also, examine the other side of the issue to gather statistics about which countries are the source of most malware attacks. You might be surprised by what you discover.

Key Terms

Interactive Summary

Section A:

[_____] transforms a message or data file in such a way that its contents are hidden from unauthorized readers. An original message or file that has not yet been encrypted is referred to as [_____] or cleartext. An encrypted message or file is referred to as [_____]. Data can be encrypted one file at a time, or an entire storage volume can be encrypted. User [_____] techniques, such as passwords, PINs, and fingerprint scanners, are the first line of defense against data thieves and snoopers. The single most effective security measure for digital devices is to password-protect access to them. A(n) [_____] password is quite secure because it is difficult to hack. Conventional wisdom tells us that a secure password is at least [_____]

characters in length and includes one or more uppercase letters, numbers, and symbols. A(n) [_____] force attack uses password-cracking software to generate every possible combination of letters, numerals, and symbols. A(n) [_____] attack helps hackers guess your password by stepping through a dictionary containing word lists in common languages. Password [_____] is a measure of a password's unpredictability. For example, the entropy of a four-digit iPhone passcode is 14 bits. The core function of a password [_____] (sometimes called a keychain) is to store user IDs with their corresponding passwords. Passwords can be stored in the [_____], locally, or on a USB drive.

Section B:

Malware refers to any computer program designed to surreptitiously enter a digital device. The action carried out by malware code is referred to as a(n) [_____] or payload. There are several types of malware. A computer [_____] is a set of self-replicating program instructions that surreptitiously attaches itself to a legitimate [_____] file on a host computer. This type of malware spreads when people exchange infected files on CDs, as email attachments, and via downloads. They can also be inadvertently obtained from unauthorized app stores. Through a process called side- [_____], an app from a source other than an official app store is installed on a device. Modern [_____] are used to hide malicious code by replacing parts of the operating system with modified code. A computer [_____] is a self-replicating, self-distributing program designed to carry

out unauthorized activity on a victim's device. They are usually [_____] executable programs that can spread themselves from one device to another without any assistance from victims. [_____] are a type of standalone malware that masquerades as useful utilities or applications, which victims download and install while unaware of their destructive nature. Antivirus software is a type of utility software that looks for and eradicates malware by watching for virus [_____] or through a(n) [_____] analysis that examines the behavior of suspicious files. When antivirus software detects malware, it can try to remove the infection, put the file into [_____], or simply delete the file. Antivirus software is an essential security tool. It should be installed, properly configured, and updated regularly.

Section C: An online intrusion takes place when an unauthorized person gains access to a digital device by using an Internet connection and exploiting vulnerabilities in hardware or software. A(n) [_____] Access Trojan is malware that arrives in a trojan, disguised as legitimate software, and then sets up a(n) [_____] that provides unauthorized access to a victim's device. An exploit known as [_____] locks a device and then requests payment for an unlocking code. Malware with [_____] control capability is programmed for off-site control of the camera or microphone on a victim's device. Hackers who gain control over several computers can organize them into a client-server network known as a(n) [_____]. Such networks are cloaked from the victims, who continue to use their devices as usual and are unaware of illicit activities that may be taking place behind the scenes. A(n) [_____]-day attack exploits previously unknown vulnerabilities in software applications, hardware, and operating system program code. To defend against these attacks, consumers can use an on-[_____] scanner. Defense against intrusions is also offered by personal [_____], which block unauthorized access through open [_____]. A network router can be deployed as a hardware-based firewall.

Section D: There are several types of [_____] exploits that surreptitiously capture data. Any software that secretly gathers personal information without the victim's knowledge is classified as [_____]. [_____] monitors Web browsing activity to supply ad-serving sites with data used to generate targeted ads. A(n) [_____] records keystrokes and sends them to a hacker. The objective of an MITM attack is for a third party to intercept communications between two entities without their knowledge. An MITM exploit executed at Wi-Fi hotspots is called a(n) [_____]. MITM attacks are also carried out by [_____] the addresses in email messages, IP packets, [_____] servers, and ARP routing tables. Data sent over encrypted channels also falls victim to MITM attacks that use fake digital [_____]. An MITM attack that targets cellular data can intercept conversations using a(n) [_____] catcher.

Section E: In the context of cyber security, social engineering (SE) is a deceptive practice that exploits human [_____] by inducing victims to interact with a digital device in a way that is not in their best interest. Many of these attacks begin with [_____], which is defined as unsolicited messages that are usually sent in massive numbers using electronic mail systems. A spam filter uses a set of [_____] to examine email messages and blocks those that appear to be spam. There are four common types of spam filters. [_____] filters examine the content within a message for certain words or phrases commonly used in spam emails. [_____] filters review the email header for falsified information, such as spoofed IP addresses. [_____] filters block mail that originates from IP addresses of known spammers. [_____] filters block or allow mail based on the sender's address. [_____] is an email scam that masquerades as a message from a legitimate company or agency of authority, such as the IRS. [_____] redirects Web site traffic to fraudulent Web sites that distribute malware, collect personal data, sell counterfeit products, and perpetrate other scams. A rogue [_____] exploit usually begins with a virus warning and an offer to disinfect the infected device. Some software is not exactly malware, but it is a nuisance. A(n) [_____] (Hint: Use the acronym) takes up residence on a digital device and seems impossible to disable or remove.

1. On your next vacation, you'll be traveling to India and taking your laptop. The device is protected by a login password, but for extra protection you decide to [_____] the entire storage volume.

2. An urgent security update arrives for Java. You have to assume that hackers have discovered a vulnerability and carried out a(n) [_____] -day attack, which the update is designed to fix.

3. You are fed up with receiving spam that offers free gift cards. To block such messages, you set up a(n) [_____] spam filter.

4. While browsing the Web, you suddenly see a virus alert. Oddly, it doesn't look like the alerts that usually appear while you are browsing and downloading email. You don't click the alert because you assume it is a(n) [_____] virus scam.

```
┌──────────────────────────────────────────┬───┐
│                                          │ X │
├──────────────────────────────────────────┴───┤
│  WARNING! Your computer may be                │
│  infected with spyware                        │
│                                               │
│  If your computer has been running slower than usual, │
│  it may be infected with adware or spyware! To scan   │
│  your comptuer for such infections, click OK below.   │
│                                               │
│         [ Cancel ]      [   OK   ]            │
└───────────────────────────────────────────────┘
```

5. One day you dash into the library to check your email. Before you can complete the login process, your phone chimes and you see a text message from your email provider. The text message contains a code for two-factor [_____] .

6. You're installing a new security suite that includes antivirus software and a personal firewall. Is it true that leaving Windows Firewall on in addition to using the firewall from the new security suite will beef up your digital security? [_____]

7. You are between flights at the airport, and you want to check your email. Your wireless settings show two options: a) a free, unsecured site called TerminalAir and b) a pay-by-the-hour site called Boingo. Which one is likely to be the most secure? [_____]

8. One of your former classmates has just returned from a visit to China. She complains that while she was there, some of her Google searches led to meaningless sites. Your friend was probably the victim of an MITM attack using fake digital [_____] .

9. You're in the process of downloading some email messages when your antivirus software displays an alert. You assume the software has discovered malware in a(n) [_____] , which will be moved to quarantine.

10. You just finished installing a new media converter that lets you download YouTube videos and run them when you are not connected to the Internet. Now, however, your default browser seems to have changed. You have a(n) [_____] , so you immediately fire up an on-demand scanner to eliminate the unwanted browser.

Lab: Chrome Lockdown

Every Web site is a potential risk. You know the exploits: malware, infected downloads, spyware, fraudulent Web sites, rogue JavaScripts...the list goes on. Antivirus software, firewalls, and other security software help to block some of these exploits, but they may leave cracks that allow exploits to slip into digital devices. In this lab, you'll find out how to lock down the Google Chrome browser to help defend against common online attacks.

Requirements:

For this lab, you'll need a desktop or laptop computer with Google Chrome installed. Chrome is a free browser. If it is not currently installed on your device, take a moment to do so before proceeding. (Note: The instructions for this lab apply to the version of Chrome that was available when this book went to print. If these instructions seem not to apply, check for updated instructions at *support.google.com/*.)

Assignment:

① Perform a safety check.

Log in to your Google account. Select the three dots in the upper-right corner of the browser window and choose Settings. Scroll down to the "Safety check" and select the button for "Check now." Note the status of Updates, Passwords, Safe browsing, Extensions, and Device software.

Select the "Safe browsing" option. Use the arrows to expand the explanations for "Enhanced protection" and "Standard protection." Select the one you want.

② Block third-party cookies and turn on Do Not Track.

Return to the Settings menu and scroll down to "Privacy and security." Select "Cookies and other site data." Selecting "Block third-party cookies in incognito" blocks those cookies only when you browse in incognito mode. Selecting "Block third-party cookies" blocks all third-party cookies.

The option for "Clear cookies and site data when you quit Chrome" should be On.

The option for "Send a Do Not Track request with your browsing traffic" should be On. If there are sites displayed under "Sites that can always use cookies," make sure that there are no sites listed that might serve malicious cookies.

③ Check Site Settings

Return to the "Privacy and security" menu and select "Site Settings." To ensure your privacy, make sure that Location, Camera, Microphone, and Notifications are set to "Ask before accessing" so that you will be alerted when a site wants to use these assets.

④ Manage JavaScripts, pop-ups, and redirects.

Scroll down the "Site Settings" menu and note that JavaScript can be allowed. It is sometimes used to deliver malware, but it is required for most dynamic Web pages.

The options for "Pop-ups and redirects" and for Ads should be set to Blocked.

⑤ Prevent download exploits.

Even trusted sites might get hacked so that malware is surreptitiously downloaded along with legitimate files.

From the main Settings menu, look in the Advanced section and select "Downloads." Activate the option "Ask where to save each file before downloading" so that you can verify that you want to accept each file to be downloaded.

⑥ Explore Privacy Sandbox settings.

When this book went to press, Google was introducing a technology called Privacy Sandbox, which is designed to prevent sites from tracking you but provides marketers with advertising opportunities. Determine the current status of the Privacy Sandbox feature. If you have options for settings, configure the feature to provide the security and privacy that you desire.

⑦ Screenshot and save your security settings.

Take a screenshot of the current content settings.

Select the Done button to complete the content Settings configuration.

Close the Settings tab at the top of the Chrome window.

8 The ICT Industry

Module Contents

The Victorian Internet. A steam-powered computer. Dot-com bubbles. Today's computers and telecommunications didn't spring out of thin air. They are a product of a sometimes quirky economic sector called ICT.

⬤ Try It! Apply what you learn.

- Find information on current stock market trends in the ICT industry.
- Recognize the global nature of the ICT industry in the context of economics, products, and jobs.
- Watch to see if Moore's law continues to be a factor associated with innovation in the ICT industry.
- Evaluate tech products and trends based on product life cycles, Rogers' bell curve, and the Gartner Hype Cycle.
- Identify and anticipate disruptive technologies.
- Remember the general timeline for technology developments, such as prototype computers, telegraphs, radios, telephones, cell phones, and televisions.
- Use a CPI calculator to compare historical prices with current-day values.
- Tap out SOS in Morse code.
- Access a streaming radio broadcast online.
- Get acquainted with some historic radio and television broadcasts.
- Find current wage levels for tech sector occupations.
- Locate information about corporate cultures at various tech companies.
- Evaluate certification opportunities that could improve your resume.
- Create a resume in formats for print, email, social media sites, online job services, and Web portfolios.
- Be prepared to make workplace decisions based on applicable laws and ethical guidelines.
- Consider the consequences of whistleblowing.

● Pre-Check

Gauge your level of expertise. The answers are in the module.

This chart shows a dot-com

_____.

_____ code

33%

Percentage of _____
with an advanced degree

This can help to augment
your technical resume

_____

Gartner _____ Cycle

LTE

1G
2G
3G
4G
5G

1986

The Electronic Communications
_____ Act extends
wiretap laws to data transmissions.

Jobs in the technology sector
estimated to grow by
_____ % by 2029?

4004

The first _____

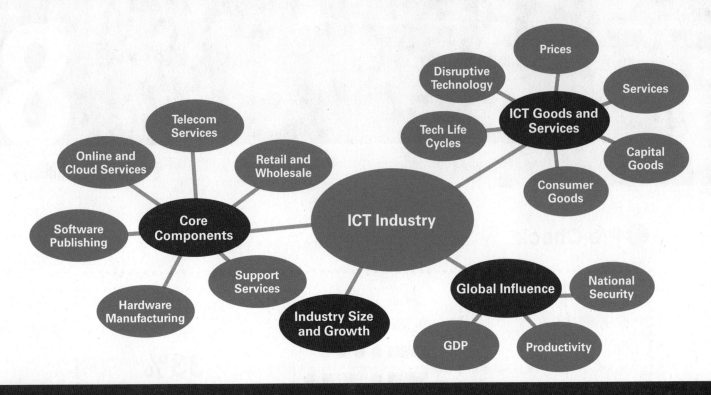

ICT Industry

- Core Components
  - Telecom Services
  - Online and Cloud Services
  - Retail and Wholesale
  - Software Publishing
  - Support Services
  - Hardware Manufacturing
- Industry Size and Growth
- ICT Goods and Services
  - Prices
  - Disruptive Technology
  - Services
  - Tech Life Cycles
  - Capital Goods
  - Consumer Goods
- Global Influence
  - National Security
  - GDP
  - Productivity

Objectives

▶ Provide examples of the businesses in each of six core ICT industry components.

▶ List four reasons why the ICT industry is one of the world's largest economic sectors.

▶ Draw a timeline showing stock market trends for the ICT industry through boom and bust cycles between 1991 and the present year.

▶ Give at least three examples of ICT consumer goods and three examples of ICT capital goods.

▶ Distinguish between outsourcing and offshoring.

▶ Explain how Moore's law is related to the declining price of ICT products.

▶ Draw diagrams representing the product life cycle, Rogers' bell curve, and the Gartner Hype Cycle.

▶ Provide at least three examples of disruptive technologies and explain their benefits as well as their drawbacks.

▶ Explain the relationship between ICT and productivity.

▶ List four of the six national security functions provided by the ICT industry.

▶ Explain the connection between cyberwarfare and the Tallinn Manual.

Apple, Facebook, and Verizon are all

part of the ICT industry, which supplies consumers with digital devices and all of those can't-live-without services, such as text messaging and streaming video. This industry affects the prosperity of emerging nations, as well as those with a sophisticated technology infrastructure. And as technology becomes more and more central to a smoothly functioning society, the ICT industry is increasingly a national security concern.

Terminology

economic sectors	goods	offshoring	disruptive technology
information industry	services	Moore's law	productivity
ICT industry	consumer goods	product life cycle	GDP
stock market bubble	capital goods	Rogers' bell curve	cyberwarfare
dot-coms	outsourcing	Gartner Hype Cycle	Tallinn Manual

ICT Core Industries

Companies such as IBM and Sperry Rand launched the computer industry when they brought the first mainframes to market in the 1960s. As the function of these machines expanded beyond number crunching to data storage and decision support, the IT (information technology) industry evolved. In the 21st century, the importance of accessing data over the Internet and other communications links instigated a convergence between the IT industry and the telecommunications industry. The result: today's ICT (information and communications technology) industry.

▶ **What is the ICT industry?** Companies and businesses create jobs, develop products, and offer services that drive the economy. These companies are classified into **economic sectors** according to the types of goods and services they provide. The largest economic sectors include retail, health care, manufacturing, energy, and information technology.

The **information industry** has three major facets: content, computers, and telecommunications. Information content includes books, magazines, newspapers, sound recordings, television and radio broadcasts, motion pictures, user-generated media, Web content, and other data. The technology used to generate, manipulate, and view this data includes equipment such as computers and peripheral devices. The infrastructure and services used to distribute content are handled by telecommunications technology.

The focus of Module 8 is the **ICT industry**, which is made up of businesses that focus on digital equipment, software, communications technologies, and related services. This industry creates and maintains the devices and infrastructure used to create content, store it, move it, manipulate it, and display it. Figure 8-1 lists the core components of the ICT industry. Do you recognize the logos for prominent companies in each of the core ICT industry components?

8

Figure 8-1: ICT industry core components

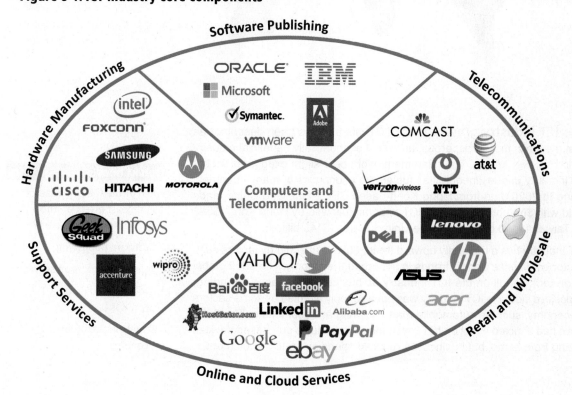

▶ **What is the size of the ICT industry?** ICT is one of the world's largest economic sectors. It is several times larger than the aerospace and defense industry. Its revenues exceed those of the oil and gas industry and the world's airlines.

Worldwide, the ICT industry directly employs about 4% of the total workforce in jobs such as computer manufacturing, programming, and data security. In the United States alone, there are more than 400,000 software and ICT service companies, which employ more than 10 million skilled workers.

In addition to jobs within the ICT industry, a broader group of careers require ICT skills. In developed countries, it is a rare job that does not require familiarity with digital devices or some degree of technology skill.

Global spending on ICT products and services exceeds $4 trillion every year, according to analysts at the International Data Corporation (IDC). Figure 8-2 depicts the percentage of ICT expenditures for each region and shows the United States as the world's largest consumer of ICT products and services.

Figure 8-2: Comparative ICT expenditures by region

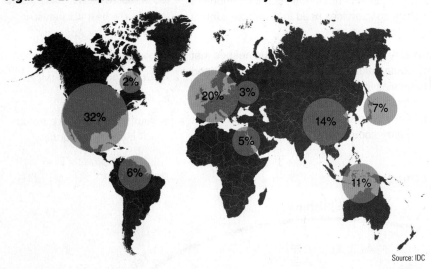

Source: IDC

▶ **Is the ICT industry growing?** The ICT industry has been described as the most dynamic, most prosperous, and most economically beneficial industry the world has ever known. That statement might be a slight exaggeration, but the ICT industry unquestionably has fueled the economies of many countries. According to 2020 data from Hong Kong-based CEIC, mainland China leads the world with $660 billion worth of ICT exports, followed by Hong Kong ($303 billion), Taiwan ($150 billion), and the United States ($145 billion).

The ICT industry has a generally upward trend, but it is affected by factors such as investor confidence and by trends in the broader economy. The 2009 global recession took its toll on the ICT industry as businesses reduced spending. On the positive side, the ICT industry was not as deeply affected as some sectors of the economy, such as automobile manufacturing and real estate. The 2020 pandemic had a mixed effect on ICT revenues as individuals purchased devices for working from home, but businesses reduced spending on ICT equipment.

QuickCheck

Which of the following factors has the least effect on the success of the ICT industry?

a. Software publishing

b. Telecommunication services

c. Global spending on ICT products

d. Trends in the broader economy

The 2009 recession was not the first downturn for the ICT industry. An economic boom in the form of a "dot-com bubble" began in the late 1990s and then burst in 1999 with devastating effects on ICT stock values. A **stock market bubble** refers to a sharp rise in stock values that is later followed by a sudden decline.

The dot-com bubble was fueled by a frenzy of online business startups called **dot-coms**. Entrepreneurs seemed certain that any Internet-based business was destined for success. Investors believed that dot-coms were the key to quick profits, which contributed to an unprecedented rise in the value of stocks on the technology-specialized NASDAQ stock exchange.

Unfortunately, many dot-coms lacked experienced management teams, failed to develop realistic business plans, burned through startup capital without making a profit, and then went bankrupt.

The high rate of dot-com business failures during 2001 and 2002 was a tough jolt of reality for many stockholders. It also affected a wide swath of the economy. The end of the dot-com bubble meant a temporary decline in equipment orders, Web site hosting contracts, and IT sector job openings.

The technology sector eventually recovered from the dot-com fiasco. Figure 8-3 shows the two major declines in ICT stock values and traces the trajectory of the sector's recovery.

Try It!

Are ICT stocks currently on an upward swing, or are they in decline? Connect to Fidelity's Information Technology Snapshot or to BigCharts to find out.

8

Figure 8-3: NASDAQ stock market trends for the ICT industry, 1991–2021

Source: BigCharts

❶ May 1997: The Amazon.com stock initial public offering (IPO) kicks off the dot-com frenzy.

❷ March 2000: The NASDAQ reaches a high of 5,048, and stocks are trading for an average of $55.92 per share.

❸ June 2001: The number of dot-coms that have closed their doors or filed for bankruptcy reaches 345.

❹ September 2002: The NASDAQ bottoms out at 1,184, and the average price per share drops to a dismal $14.07.

❺ March 2009: The NASDAQ hits a six-year low of 1,265 as world financial markets tumble.

❻ November 2013: The NASDAQ closes above 4,000 for the first time since 2000, in part because investors continue to see the stock market as the only positive economic indicator.

❼ March 2020: The COVID-19 pandemic caused a temporary drop in the NASDAQ amidst widespread economic uncertainty.

ICT Goods and Services

A computer for $250? In 1969, that price would have been unimaginable. Somehow, technology prices just keep falling, making ICT goods and services increasingly affordable to consumers in all economic brackets.

▶ **Are digital items, such as software, considered goods or services?** In economics, **goods** are things that can be used or consumed, whereas **services** are intangible actions performed for a consumer. Goods can be physical objects or digital intangibles. The ICT industry produces a variety of goods, such as computers, smartphones, software, circuit boards, integrated circuits, and industrial 3D printers. Most economists regard goods and services as a continuum, with intangible goods, such as software, in the middle of the continuum (Figure 8-4).

Figure 8-4: The continuum of goods and services

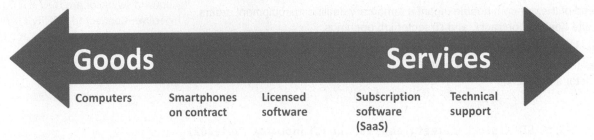

| Computers | Smartphones on contract | Licensed software | Subscription software (SaaS) | Technical support |

▶ **Who are the customers for ICT products?** ICT goods and services can be distributed locally, nationally, or internationally. They are purchased by individual consumers and by corporations. **Consumer goods** are items such as laptops, music downloads, productivity software, and flash drives that are purchased and used by individuals. **Capital goods** are raw materials, tools, and machinery used by businesses to make consumer goods.

The ICT industry produces both consumer goods and capital goods, and it offers services such as technical support, Web site hosting, Internet connections, and information access. Consumers might not pay much attention to capital goods that are used to produce digital devices, but circuit boards, chips, and fabrication machinery are a hugely profitable segment of the ICT industry.

The Internet has expanded the market for physical and digital ICT products, as it has also expanded the markets for apparel, books, sports equipment, and products in other industries. Consumers and businesses can shop at ecommerce sites to purchase all types of goods and services from local merchants or from businesses located all around the globe.

For many countries, imports and exports account for a high percentage of ICT revenues. Though China may be the world's top exporter of ICT goods, India and Ireland far outstrip the rest of the world for exports of ICT services. Ireland is home to regional headquarters, manufacturing facilities, or offices for big tech companies such as Google, Yahoo, Twitter, IBM, Microsoft, Oracle, and Adobe. India is known for its outsourcing and offshoring services, such as customer support centers, data analytics, and cybersecurity.

QuickCheck

ICT customers searching online for the best deal on a laptop computer would be looking for

_____.

a. exports

b. capital goods

c. consumer goods

d. ICT services

▶ **What are the advantages of outsourcing and offshoring?** The terms *outsourcing* and *offshoring* are often used interchangeably, but they are slightly different. **Outsourcing** is the use of components or labor from outside suppliers. Those suppliers could be nearby or remote. **Offshoring** relocates business processes, such as development, manufacturing, and customer support, to lower-cost locations in other countries.

Outsourcing enables businesses to obtain expertise, manufacturing capability, and labor without the financial outlay required to bring those resources in-house. When Dell outsources microprocessors from Intel, it doesn't have to have its own team of chip designers and chip fabrication facilities.

Offshoring reduces the cost of goods and services by using workers and manufacturing facilities in countries with inexpensive labor. For example, Apple uses offshoring to cost-effectively manufacture products at Foxconn's 1.16-square-mile facility in Longhua, China.

New ICT product development evolves through several phases, each requiring a set of skilled workers and high-tech facilities. In 1990, most new ICT product development took place in the United States at large companies, such as IBM, Hewlett-Packard, and Apple. Parallel development also took place in Japan at companies such as Sony, Epson, and Panasonic. By 2000, U.S. companies had outsourced all but the design process to Taiwan. Another shift took place in 2006, when mass production shifted to China (Figure 8-5).

QuickCheck

A U.S. company is developing an innovative product that will allow consumers to create their own Internets of Things. The company contracts with a firm in a neighboring state to produce the IoT sensors. This is an example of _____.

a. offshoring

b. outsourcing

c. prototyping

d. ecommerce

Figure 8-5: ICT product development cycle locations

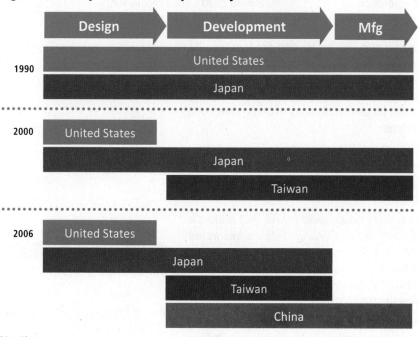

Adapted from
Dedrick and Kraemer, Globalization of Innovation

Through the 1990s, ICT companies performed all phases of product development in-house. Prototyping and mass production moved to Taiwan, and then to China. Outsourcing and manufacturing efficiencies contributed to falling prices of ICT goods and services.

▶ **What accounts for declining ICT prices?** While the prices of food, education, and health care continue to skyrocket, the prices of ICT products, which require massive investment in research and development, have generally dropped while providing increasing value in terms of processing power and performance.

Although the prices for cutting-edge smartphones have escalated, prices for laptop and desktop computers have tumbled. Whereas the average price of a computer in 1995 was $1,800, in 2020 consumers paid an average of $600 for a device that is far more powerful. Figure 8-6 compares the features and prices of the average computer in 1995 and 2020.

Figure 8-6: Price and performance of digital devices, 1995 and 2020

In 1995, $1,800 purchased a desktop computer with a 33 MHz processor, 8 MB of RAM, a 200 MB hard disk, a CD drive, and a bulky CRT monitor with a maximum 1024 x 768 resolution.

In 2020, $600 paid for a laptop computer with a 3.7 GHz 4-core processor, 8 GB of RAM, a 1 TB hard disk, and an integrated 15" screen with a maximum 1920 x 1080 resolution.

Factors that contribute to the declining cost of digital goods and services include strategies such as outsourcing and offshoring that reduce labor costs. Competition plays a part, too, as companies attempt to undercut their rivals by offering lower prices. Technological innovation is also an important factor in controlling the production costs of ICT products. Economists and technology experts often point to Moore's law to explain falling ICT prices.

▶ **What is Moore's law?** In 1965, Gordon Moore, co-founder of Intel Corporation, predicted that technological innovation would double the number of transistors in an integrated circuit every two years without raising its cost. This idea become known as **Moore's law**.

Increasing the number of transistors boosts processing power and makes it possible to build more sophisticated devices without raising costs. As integrated circuits grew in sophistication, fewer of them were required. Where once banks of RAM chips were required to supply four gigabytes of memory, today one low-cost chip will suffice. Not only is the cost of chips reduced, but with fewer chips required, the cost to assemble a device decreases.

Amazingly, Moore's law accurately described the rate of chip innovation for 50 years. Intel hopes to continue this rate of innovation, but industry experts are skeptical. Several technical and economic factors point to the end of Moore's law and the culture of "faster and cheaper." However, for consumers who are chiefly interested in watching YouTube videos, and for innovators who are developing low-capacity chips for the Internet of Things, the death of Moore's law and a leveling off of ICT prices might not be a concern.

At some point, the price of goods will reach a hard bottom. Many digital devices may be near that point now. It is unlikely that $20 smartphones are on the horizon, but with technology, the future can be surprising.

QuickCheck

The core idea of Moore's law is
_____.

a. the price of ICT goods will level off in 2020

b. $20 smartphones are on the horizon

c. the number of transistors on an integrated circuit will double every two years

d. technology innovation in RAM chips will cause ICT prices to decline for 50 years

Technology Life Cycles

Understanding technology life cycles is useful, whether you are purchasing digital products and services, investing in a technology company, or preparing for a career in the ICT industry. Let's take a look at three technology life cycles that affect consumers: the product life cycle, Rogers' bell curve, and the Gartner Hype Cycle.

▶ **What is the digital product life cycle?** From the perspective of a business that creates and sells a technology product, the **product life cycle** (PLC) maps the expected profitability of a product from its inception to its demise. A graph of the PLC begins with negative profitability during research and development, rises to a peak as sales increase, and then declines as the product is gradually replaced (Figure 8-7).

Figure 8-7: Product life cycle

▶ **What is Rogers' bell curve?** A team of sociologists including Everett M. Rogers developed a model to explain how products diffuse through the market-place and the way in which such diffusion affects commodity prices. This model, called **Rogers' bell curve**, is frequently used to describe patterns in the way consumers adopt technology products.

Rogers' bell curve shows that a small group of innovators initially experiment with a product, which then is picked up by early adopters before spreading to a majority of the population. The price of products begins to decline in the Late Majority phase. Later, laggards adopt the product, and eventually the product is no longer of interest to consumers (Figure 8-8).

Figure 8-8: Technology adoption life cycle

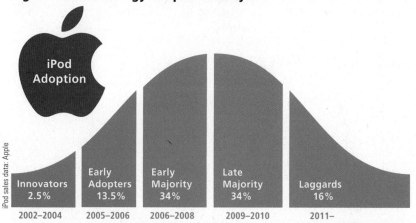

The percentage of consumers who participate in each phase of Rogers' bell curve indicates how much a product has spread. For example, at the end of the Early Adopters phase, about 16% of consumers have obtained the product.

▶ What is the Gartner Hype Cycle? Analysts at Gartner, Inc., have been tracking technology trends for decades. They devised a proprietary model called the **Gartner Hype Cycle** that represents the position of a product during its life cycle of publicity or "hype."

The curve of the Gartner Hype Cycle is quite different from that of Rogers' bell curve. Publicity about new products reaches a peak long before its mainstream adoption. This peak of inflated expectation gives way to disillusionment before consumers form a realistic understanding of a product's potential and put it to use productively (Figure 8-9).

QuickCheck

Which life cycle best helps consumers evaluate the most cost-effective time to purchase a product?

a. Digital product life cycle

b. Rogers' bell curve

c. Gartner Hype Cycle

Figure 8-9: Illustrative hype cycle for 2022

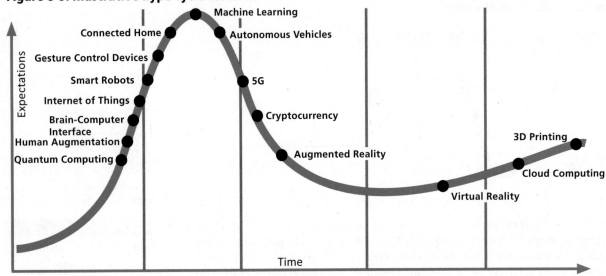

Technology Trigger	Peak of Inflated Expectations	Trough of Disillusionment	Slope of Enlightenment	Plateau of Productivity
Early announcements regarding a technology breakthrough trigger publicity and speculation about potential products and applications.	Success stories for early prototypes are highly publicized, leading to increasing speculation, much of which is unrealistic.	The technology does not fulfill inflated expectations. In this crucial phase, the technology may be abandoned or mutate into an unintended form.	The realistic potential of the technology becomes understood, and refinements of earlier developments begin to show stable benefits.	The technology spreads into the mainstream, based on demonstrated benefits.

Disruptive Technology

The ICT industry produces goods and services that are used in education, finance, manufacturing, health care, and just about every sector of the economy. These products improve people's lives and pave the way for new enterprises, but they can disrupt entire industries and put people out of work.

▶ How does technology become a disruptive influence? Disruptive technology displaces an existing business process, market, industry, or product. According to Harvard business professor Clayton Christensen, disruptive technologies overthrow established industries by introducing innovations that are simpler and less costly, though these new systems might not initially be as good as the old ones.

Examples of disruptive technologies are numerous. Their effects have an impact at many levels. They affect the people who use the original technology, the businesses that provide the original technology, the workers who make the original technology, and the entire support network associated with the original technology. Think about the disruptive technologies in Figure 8-10 and the scope of entities that they affect.

8

Figure 8-10: Disruptive technologies

 Flat-screen LCD technology replaced CRT displays, which affected manufacturers.

 Digital photography replaced film photography, which affected camera manufacturers, film manufacturers, and photo processing shops.

 Computers with word processors replaced typewriters.

 Digital publishing and Web-based access to information had a devastating effect on newspapers.

 Movies replaced radio as a form of entertainment. Movies were then disrupted by television, which in turn has been disrupted by download and streaming technology.

 The telegraph was disrupted by the telephone system, long distance by VoIP, and landline service by cellular service.

 Smartphones have replaced devices such as MP3 players, portable game consoles, point-and-shoot cameras, personal video players, voice recorders, handheld GPS devices, wristwatches, paper maps, and handheld calculators.

▶ Are disruptive technologies good or bad? New technologies are beneficial for businesses when they produce cost savings, improve service, save time, and increase productivity. They may also benefit national economies when they stimulate spending on new products.

Disruptive technologies often have negative effects, however. Employees in legacy businesses may be displaced. Workers may not have skills needed to use new technologies, they may become irrelevant to automated processes, or they may lose their jobs if their employer is put out of business by disruptive technology.

Disruptive technologies can also prove to be detrimental if they sweep away effective legacy business practices and replace them with substitute practices that turn out to be unsustainable. When profitable businesses are displaced by businesses with no clear financial model, an entire sector of the economy can suffer. Free Internet-based services, for example, could displace profit-earning businesses only to later fail and leave consumers without any services whatsoever.

QuickCheck

In the term **disruptive technology**, the meaning of **disruptive** is most closely associated with _____.

a. destruction

b. change

c. progress

d. benefits

ICT and Productivity

In theory, ICT products increase productivity, which in turn leads to economic growth and a better standard of living. If this theory is true, ICT products become a key technology for improving the general welfare of people in developed countries and emerging nations.

▶ **What is the importance of productivity?** In the context of economics, **productivity** is a measurement of the amount of output that is produced per unit of input. For example, the productivity of a computer game programmer is the number of lines of code (output) that the programmer can write in a day (unit of input).

Many businesses have found that technology and computerization can significantly increase productivity. As an example, consider telephone service. In 1970, approximately 400,000 switchboard operators manually handled more than 9 billion long-distance calls. Operator productivity was 64 calls per day. Thirty years later, new switching technology made long-distance calling less labor intensive. Only 150,000 operators were needed to handle more than 100 billion calls. Productivity rose to 1,861 calls per day, which increased system efficiency 30 times over.

▶ **Globally, how widespread is the use of ICT?** Societies benefit from ICT technology only to the extent that it is available and used by individuals and businesses. To measure and track ICT use, the United Nations Statistical Commission uses a set of core ICT indicators, which include cell phone subscriptions, Internet users, fixed telephone subscriptions, mobile-broadband subscriptions, and fixed broadband subscriptions. Between 2005 and 2020, significant gains were made in global ICT use, with the highest gains in cell phone and mobile broadband subscriptions (Figure 8-11).

> **QuickCheck**
>
> Which one of the core ICT indicators has declined rather than increased?
>
> a. Mobile telephone subscriptions
>
> b. Internet use
>
> c. Fixed broadband subscriptions
>
> d. Landline telephone subscriptions

Figure 8-11: Global use of ICT technology (millions)

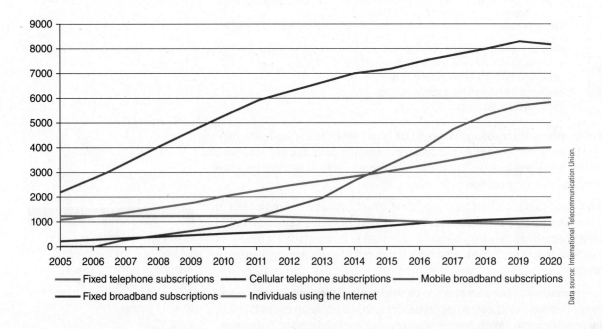

Data source: International Telecommunication Union.

❱ **How does ICT use in emerging nations compare to its use in developed nations?** As expected, ICT use in emerging nations lags behind its use in developed nations. The graph in Figure 8-12 shows the percentage of households with Internet access. Notice that use has been trending upward at about the same pace for both emerging and developing nations.

Figure 8-12: Percentage of households with Internet access

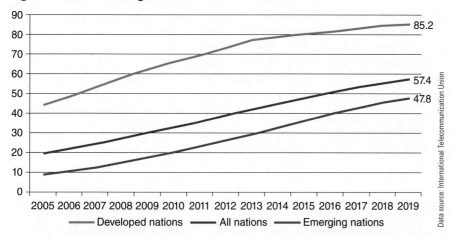

8

Data source: International Telecommunication Union

❱ **Can ICT technology improve the economies of emerging nations?**
Economists use indicators such as **GDP** to measure the total output of a nation. GDP (gross domestic product) is the monetary value of all the goods and services produced by a nation's workforce on an annual basis. GDP is one of the primary indicators used to gauge the strength of a nation's economy. When a nation's GDP increases from year to year, its economy is improving. Decreases in GDP indicate a declining economy.

Analysts at Strategy& suggest that if emerging nations could double their investment in technology over the next 10 years, the result would be a $4.4 trillion gain in GDP, an extra $930 billion in cumulative household income for families below the poverty line, and 64 million new jobs for today's socially and economically disadvantaged groups. These factors are a compelling argument for national investment in digital technologies.

The World Economic Forum produces an annual report on the global influence of the products and services produced by the ICT industry and identifies how well countries leverage ICT technologies (Figure 8-13).

Figure 8-13: ICT use across the globe

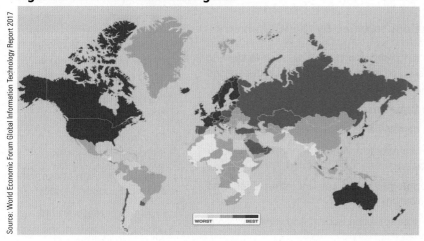

Source: World Economic Forum Global Information Technology Report 2017

ICT and National Security

In the 1960s, the United States and the Soviet Union faced off in what was called the Cold War. No shots were fired, but the two rival nations engaged in an extensive program of surveillance, espionage, and sabotage. Today, nations and non-state insurgents carry out these kinds of activities using cyberwarfare hacking tools, and the ICT industry now plays a major role in national security for countries throughout the world.

▶ **What are technology-based national security dangers?** Computers control industrial devices. They store sensitive corporate, government, and military data. They process banking records and commercial transactions. They track and monitor people and objects. All of these systems can be disabled by malware or infiltrated by intrusions. And to compound the danger, most of these systems are connected to the Internet, which makes remote infiltration relatively easy.

Infiltrating and disabling one or more of these important systems could create chaos and temporarily weaken military defenses. Exploits that particularly worry security officials are listed in Figure 8-14.

Terminology

SCADA (system control and data acquisition) automates many industrial tasks by receiving digital commands and converting them into real-world actions such as shutting down a power grid or opening a valve in a fuel pipeline. Many SCADA devices use off-the-shelf software, such as Microsoft Windows, that is vulnerable to hacking.

Figure 8-14: Targets and threats

Jam communications satellites	Pilots, ship captains, and military units rely on satellite-based GPS, communications, surveillance, navigation, and missile warning.
Shut down power grids, including nuclear generators	Massive power outages can disrupt military defense operations and cause civilian chaos.
Disrupt air traffic control	Without air traffic control systems, flights are grounded.
Shut down water and fuel pipelines	A lack of water and fuel creates chaos, especially in major cities.
Disrupt financial assets such as banking networks and the stock market	Without banking networks, consumers cannot obtain cash or make credit card purchases.
Cut off Internet access with DDoS attacks	Both civilian and military communications can be cut off during a massive DDoS attack.
Industrial espionage	Cyber break-ins at companies that develop military weaponry are especially dangerous.
Interfere with SCADA control devices	Malware that randomly targets SCADA devices can shut down power plants, dams, and manufacturing facilities.

▶ **What role does the ICT industry play in national security?** In addition to digital devices, the ICT industry provides many services that affect national security. The U.S. Department of Homeland Security identifies six national security functions supplied by the ICT sector (Figure 8-15).

Figure 8-15: National security functions supplied by the ICT industry

Source: DHS Information Technology Sector-Specific Plan 2016

Information Technology
Sector-Specific Plan
An Annex to the NIPP 2013
2016
Homeland Security

🛡 Provide ICT products and services, such as servers, computers, and routers, that are used in military and civilian installations

🛡 Provide incident management capabilities

🛡 Provide domain name resolution services

🛡 Provide identity management and trust support services

🛡 Provide Internet-based content, information, and communications services

🛡 Provide Internet routing, access, and communications services

QuickCheck

The existence and use of digital certificates would fall into which category from Figure 8-15?

a. Provide ICT products and services

b. Provide incident management capabilities

c. Provide identity management and trust support services

d. Provide Internet routing, access, and connections

8

▶ **How likely is cyberwarfare?** **Cyberwarfare** is the use of ICT technology to carry out politically motivated attacks designed to infiltrate, sabotage, or damage an opponent's information systems and defensive capabilities.

The evidence of cyberwarfare escalation is becoming quite clear. Examples include the Stuxnet virus that disabled Iranian nuclear centrifuges, an espionage campaign linked to hackers associated with the Chinese military that targeted defense agencies in Southeast Asian countries, and cyberattacks on Ukrainian critical infrastructure carried out by Russian GRU officials. North Korean hackers infiltrated several defense firms in the EU, while unknown state-sponsored hackers compromised military organizations in Nepal and Sri Lanka.

Cyberwars begin unannounced. There is no declaration of war. Instead, cyber soldiers carry out a few online attacks to test the enemy's defenses. The source of a cyberattack is seldom easy to identify. Perpetrators may be state-sponsored or members of independent groups.

National governments both large and small are acutely aware of cyber threats. Most have cyber security teams in place to monitor and respond to activities that threaten the ICT sector. In the United States, the Department of Homeland Security operates CISA, the Cybersecurity and Infrastructure Security Agency. Its mission is to "lead the national effort to understand and manage cyber and physical risk to our critical infrastructure."

Internationally, the **Tallinn Manual** is a non-binding document that is the cyber equivalent of the Geneva Convention. Based on existing laws governing international conflict, the Tallinn Manual sets out rules for conducting and responding to cyberwarfare.

Try It!

Exactly what does the U.S. Cybersecurity and Infrastructure Security Agency (CISA) do? Connect to the CISA Web site and take a look. How valuable is the information for individuals who use digital devices?

QuickCheck

Who is most likely to refer to the Tallinn Manual?

a. Terrorists

b. Police

c. Soldiers

d. Legal experts

QuickQuiz   Section A

1. The term Information and ⬚ Technology industry encompasses companies such as IBM, Verizon, Google, and Apple.

2. The ICT industry experienced a stock market bubble fueled by online startup businesses called ⬚ .

3. ⬚ goods are raw materials, tools, and machinery used to manufacture consumer goods, such as computers and mobile phones.

4. ⬚ relocates business processes in countries where labor costs are low.

5. The Stuxnet virus is a notable example of ⬚ , the use of technology to carry out politically motivated attacks designed to infiltrate, sabotage, or damage an opponent's information systems.

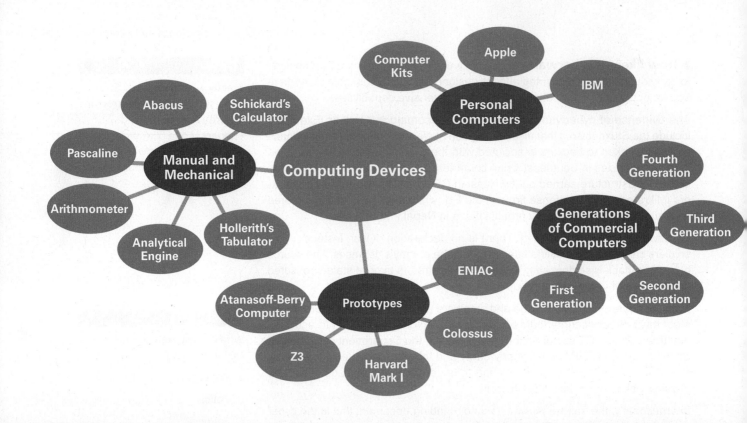

Objectives

▶ Explain how algorithms apply to manual and mechanical calculators.

▶ Name five mechanical calculators that were significant innovations leading to the first computer technology.

▶ Describe how five prototype computers contributed to the technology used in modern-day computers.

▶ Define von Neumann architecture.

▶ List the key hardware and software developments during the first, second, third, and fourth computer generations.

▶ Describe the hobbyist phase of the personal computer era.

▶ List key hardware devices in the emerging personal computer era.

Steampunk. It is the dark and industrial underbelly of sci-fi. It is a world of hulking machinery and intricate gears—and a world that might have been a reality if an audacious 19th-century inventor had just managed to cobble together a few more government grants. The evolution of modern computing devices and the ICT industry follows a path from ancient China, through pre-Victorian England, and along a deserted highway in rural Iowa. It then stops briefly in Nazi Germany before shifting from the East Coast to the West Coast and then breaking out internationally.

Terminology

manual calculator	Z3	second-generation	MITS Altair
abacus	Harvard Mark I	computers	Apple I
mechanical	Colossus	transistors	Apple II
calculator	ENIAC	third-generation	VisiCalc
Schickard's Calculator	von Neumann	computers	IBM PC
Pascaline	architecture	IBM 360	Apple Lisa
Arithmometer	UNIVAC	DEC PDP-8	Xerox Alto
Analytical Engine	first-generation	fourth-generation	Apple Macintosh
Atanasoff-Berry	computers	computers	
Computer	vacuum tube	Mark-8	

Manual Calculators

The origin of the computer industry traces far back to ancient times when simple calculators were used by merchants, engineers, and tax collectors. At inception, the computer industry was all about numbers. The notion that computers could also be used to manipulate text, images, and sound was a relatively late development in the timeline of events.

◗ **What came before computers?** Even before recorded history, humans used counting aids, such as pebbles and notched sticks, to keep track of quantities—the number of sheep in a flock, for example, or the number of oil jars purchased from a merchant. Many transactions, however, required calculations.

A calculation is based on an algorithm—the step-by-step process by which numbers are manipulated. Even basic paper-and-pencil addition requires an algorithm. The steps include adding the rightmost digits first, carrying a 1 if necessary, and then moving left to any remaining digits, where the process is repeated. A **manual calculator** is a device that assists in the process of numeric calculations but requires the human operator to keep track of the algorithm.

A manual calculator called an **abacus** was used in ancient Rome, Greece, India, China, and Japan. Only as the last century came to a close was the abacus replaced by handheld digital calculators. In a 1946 contest between a Japanese abacus expert and an American accountant using an adding machine, the abacus expert won! The same outcome is unlikely with today's technology, but abacus use is still taught to millions of children around the world as a foundation for basic numeracy.

An abacus, like the one in Figure 8-16, consists of beads mounted on rods within a rectangular frame. Each bead represents a quantity—1, 5, 10, 50, and so on. To use an abacus, you must learn the algorithm for manipulating the beads.

QuickCheck

The algorithms used to perform calculations with manual calculators are _____.

a. stored within the device

b. applied by the user

c. powered by steam

d. input from a peripheral storage device

Figure 8-16: An abacus—manual but surprisingly quick

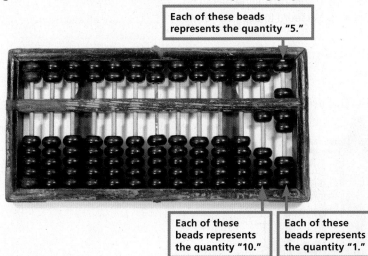

Each of these beads represents the quantity "5."

Each of these beads represents the quantity "10."

Each of these beads represents the quantity "1."

An abacus uses beads to represent numbers. This abacus shows the number 17. Using an algorithm, the beads on an abacus can be manipulated to perform arithmetic operations.

Mechanical Calculators

Manual calculators require the operator to apply algorithms to perform calculations. In contrast, a **mechanical calculator** implements algorithms autonomously. With a mechanical calculator, the operator simply enters the numbers for a calculation, and then pulls a lever or turns a wheel to carry out the calculation. No thinking—or at least very little—is required.

▶ **When did machines begin to perform calculations?** Mechanical calculators were developed as early as 1623. **Schickard's Calculator** had a series of interlocking gears. Each of the ten spokes on a gear represented a digit. Every time a gear completed a full circle, it moved the next gear one notch to the left to "carry the 1." A similar mechanism is used to advance the mileage on the odometers of vintage cars.

In 1642, a Frenchman named Blaise Pascal developed the **Pascaline**, a mechanical device that could be used to perform basic arithmetic. It was not until 1820, however, that Thomas de Colmar's **Arithmometer** became the first mass-produced mechanical calculator.

▶ **Did mechanical calculators require human power?** Between 1822 and 1833, as the Victorian Age was about to begin, an English mathematician named Charles Babbage drew plans for several calculating devices driven by steam power, which was cutting-edge technology during that time period.

Babbage might be considered the great-grandfather of steampunk. He called his devices "engines," and their hulking design—eleven feet long and seven feet high—called for thousands of precision-engineered levers, gears, and wheels. Babbage's **Analytical Engine** was an all-purpose computing device. Computer historians believe that its design embodies many of the concepts that define modern computers, including memory, a programmable processor, an output device, and user-definable input of programs and data.

Unfortunately for Babbage, he was unable to marshal financial and engineering resources to complete any of his engines. He did manage to construct a small prototype (Figure 8-17), but it was not until 1991 that a working engine based on his prototype was completed by the London Science Museum to commemorate the bicentennial year of Babbage's birth.

Try It!

Ada Lovelace is considered to be the first person to create an algorithm designed to be carried out by a computing machine. Search Wikipedia to learn about this extraordinary woman and her contributions to computer science. What was her relationship to fellow mathematician Charles Babbage and what role did she play in his creation of the Analytical Engine?

QuickCheck

How are mechanical calculators similar to the calculator app on an iPhone?

a. They all use binary representation.

b. They cannot do division.

c. The user does not need to know the algorithm.

d. They are all electronic devices.

Figure 8-17: Babbage's engine prototype—the original steampunk

Photos 12 / Alamy stock photo

▶ **When did calculators become electronic?** A world in which calculators and computers operate on steam power is the subject of several intriguing alternate-reality sci-fi books, but technology did not evolve in that direction—thanks to the U.S. Census Bureau and a man named Herman Hollerith.

The process of compiling data from the 1880 census dragged on until 1887—just three years before the next census was to begin. With a surge in population, Census Bureau administrators feared that the 1890 census could not be completed before the 1900 census would begin. A faster method of tabulating census results was required.

The U.S. Census Bureau held a competition to find a way to tabulate the 1890 census. Herman Hollerith won the competition with a design for an electronic punched-card tabulating device (Figure 8-18).

8

Figure 8-18: Hollerith's tabulating machine

Source: American Memory archives of the Library of Congress

Source: Computer History Museum

▶ **How did Hollerith's tabulator work?** Hollerith's device used cards with designated areas representing data fields, such as "nationality." Once punched, the cards were fed into a card reader that used an array of metal rods to electronically read data from the cards, tabulate the results, and display them on a series of dials.

The Hollerith Tabulating Machine was effective. The 1890 census was tallied in six months, and only two additional years were required to complete all statistical calculations. Hollerith incorporated the Tabulating Machine Company in 1896. In 1924, the name of the company was changed to International Business Machines, better known today as IBM.

▶ **Was this the beginning of the computer industry?** Not yet. IBM first gained prominence in the business machine industry, which predated the computer industry by about 50 years. In addition to IBM, the business machine industry included companies such as Burroughs, National Cash Register (NCR), and Remington. These companies mass-produced typewriters and calculating machines—sometimes called tabulators. Between 1930 and 1960, use of these machines became widespread in businesses, corporations, and government agencies. Business machines were in high demand because they introduced efficiencies and increased productivity.

Computer technology later caused major disruption to the business machine industry. Though several of the biggest business machine firms attempted to evolve with emerging digital technologies, IBM was one of the few companies that successfully managed the transition.

Computer Prototypes

The question "Who invented the computer?" doesn't have a simple answer because modern digital computers evolved from prototypes developed between 1936 and 1946 by various individuals and research teams. Computer prototypes popped up in surprising places, beginning with a device called the ABC.

▶ **What's the story behind the ABC?** Iowa seems like an odd birthplace for the computer. But in 1936, Iowa State College professor John V. Atanasoff began to seriously consider how to construct a digital device that would produce more accurate calculations than available analog devices. One night, after a long drive past endless Iowa cornfields, professor Atanasoff stopped at a roadside tavern. While sipping a drink, he scribbled the basic plan for a digital computer on a cocktail napkin.

In the ensuing months, Atanasoff and a graduate student, Clifford E. Berry, created the **Atanasoff-Berry Computer** (ABC). It was the first computing device to use vacuum tubes instead of mechanical switches as processing circuitry. Its design also incorporated the idea of basing calculations on the binary number system.

The ABC, shown in Figure 8-19, is often considered the first electronic digital computer. According to physicist Allan Mackintosh, the ABC may not have been much of a computer, just as the Wrights' model was not much of an airplane, but it demonstrated the feasibility of digital computing.

Figure 8-19: The Atanasoff-Berry Computer

AP Images/Frederick News-Post

Try It!

In 1997, a team of researchers at Iowa State University completed a replica of the ABC. You can see this replica in action by searching YouTube for **The Atanasoff-Berry Computer in Operation.**

QuickCheck

What aspect of the ABC is still used by modern computers?

a. Transistors

b. Binary

c. Microprocessors

d. Vacuum tubes

▶ **Did the ABC become the basis for modern computers?** Not exactly. The work of Atanasoff and Berry was largely ignored. In Germany, a similar fate awaited the work of Konrad Zuse, who developed a computer called the **Z3**. Like the ABC, Zuse's device used vacuum tubes and was designed to work with binary numbers. Built in Nazi Germany during World War II, the Z3 was cloaked in secrecy, even though Hitler believed that computers had no strategic use in the war effort. Information on Zuse's invention did not surface until long after the war ended. So although Zuse was on the trail of modern computer architecture, his work had little effect on the development of computers in other areas of the world.

Even with the work of Atanasoff, Berry, and Zuse, it was not clear that computers were destined to be binary electronic devices. IBM pursued an entirely different computer architecture by sponsoring an engineer named Howard Aiken, who embarked on an audacious plan to integrate 73 IBM Automatic Accounting Machines into a single unified computing unit.

▶ **Did Aiken succeed?** The collaboration between Aiken and IBM produced a mechanical computer officially named the IBM Automatic Sequence Controlled Calculator, but now usually referred to as the **Harvard Mark I** because it was moved to Harvard University shortly after completion.

The Harvard Mark I strayed considerably from the path of development leading to modern computers. The device was digital but used decimal rather than binary representation, which is used by today's computers. Constructed of relay switches, rotating shafts, and clutches, the Harvard Mark I sounded like a "roomful of ladies knitting," according to physicist Jeremy Bernstein. The device was 51 feet long and 8 feet tall and weighed about 5 tons (Figure 8-20).

Figure 8-20: The Harvard Mark I

akg-images/Newscom

▶ **Were prototypes able to perform any real computing?** Some computer prototypes were pressed into service barely before they were completed. In 1943, a team of British engineers created **Colossus**, an electronic device designed to decode intercepted messages sent from the Nazi High Command to field officers.

Colossus contained 1,800 vacuum tubes, used binary arithmetic, and was capable of reading input at the rate of 5,000 characters per second. It was a programmable device and has the distinction of being the world's first electronic digital programmable computer. The British manufactured ten Colossus machines during World War II, but their existence was a tightly kept secret.

When the war ended, Winston Churchill directed that all equipment and documentation about Colossus machines be destroyed. Only in 1976 was the veil of secrecy lifted, allowing Colossus designers and programmers to discuss their work. Unfortunately, the long period of secrecy prevented Colossus technology from making a significant contribution to developments in the post-war computer industry.

QuickCheck

Who produced the world's first operational electronic, digital, programmable computer?

a. IBM

b. German spies

c. British engineers

d. The U.S. Census Bureau

❯ Did the United States use computers during World War II? In 1943, a team headed by John W. Mauchly and J. Presper Eckert started work on ENIAC, a general-purpose electronic computer. **ENIAC** (Electronic Numerical Integrator and Computer) was designed to calculate artillery trajectory tables for the U.S. Army, but it wasn't finished until November 1945—three months after World War II ended.

ENIAC was over 100 feet long and 10 feet high and weighed 30 tons! This gigantic machine contained over 18,000 vacuum tubes and consumed 174,000 watts of power. ENIAC was programmed by manually connecting cables and setting 6,000 switches—a process that generally took two days to complete. It could perform 5,000 additions per second, which was astonishingly fast at the time, but seems pitifully slow compared to today's personal computers that easily perform billions of additions per second.

ENIAC's memory held both programs and data. This feature became known as **von Neumann architecture** after the mathematician, John von Neumann, who first described it. Module 2 explained how memory in modern computing devices works, and you know that program instructions and data are all loaded into the same memory space. That concept dates back to the 1940s and ENIAC's von Neumann architecture.

ENIAC was formally dedicated at the University of Pennsylvania Moore School of Electrical Engineering on February 15, 1946, and it was immediately pressed into service making atomic energy calculations and computing trajectories for new missile technologies (Figure 8-21). ENIAC received several upgrades and remained in service until 1955.

QuickCheck

What is significant about von Neumann architecture?

a. It is binary.

b. Programs and data reside in the same memory space.

c. It requires no coding.

d. It is based on microprocessor technology.

Figure 8-21: ENIAC

Bettmann/Getty Images

ENIAC's first programmers were a team of six women. Two of these women, Jean Jennings and Frances Bilas, are shown in this photo from 1946 at the Moore School of Electrical Engineering.

Try It!

Before computers were machines, they were humans who carried out calculations. Many human "computers," especially during World War II, were women. Some of them put their computing skills to use working with ENIAC. Their story is told in a documentary called **The Computers**. The YouTube video **Jean Bartik and the ENIAC Women** contains historic footage of these women at work.

Commercial Computers

After World War II, companies such as IBM, Remington Rand, and Sperry refocused on the business sector. They were successful in transforming the market for calculators into a dynamic computer industry. This transformation took place in four phases, now referred to as the four generations of computers.

◗ **What was the first commercially successful computer?** A computer called **UNIVAC** is considered by most historians to be the first commercially successful digital computer. The first UNIVAC computer was constructed under the auspices of the Eckert-Mauchly Computer Corp., a company hastily cobbled together by John Mauchly and J. Presper Eckert. This event marks the birth of the computer industry.

Eckert and Mauchly completed the first UNIVAC in 1951, but their company was in financial distress. The company, along with the UNIVAC schematics, was acquired by Remington Rand, one of IBM's chief rivals in the business machine industry. Forty-six UNIVAC computers were delivered to Remington Rand's customers between 1951 and 1958.

At 14.5 feet long, 7.5 feet high, and 9 feet wide, UNIVAC was physically smaller than ENIAC, but more powerful. UNIVAC could read data at the rate of 7,200 characters per second and complete 2.25 million instruction cycles per second (Figure 8-22).

Figure 8-22: UNIVAC

Keystone-France/Gamma-Keystone/Getty Images

The American public first saw a computer in action during the 1952 presidential election. CBS reporters Walter Cronkite and Charles Collingwood could not believe UNIVAC's prediction. The election was supposed to be close. But based on only 3 million votes, the computer correctly predicted that Eisenhower would win.

◗ **How did computers progress from room-sized behemoths to modern personal computers?** Early computers, such as the Harvard Mark I, ENIAC, and UNIVAC, used technology that required lots of space and electrical power. As technology evolved, relay switches and **vacuum tubes** were replaced with smaller, less power-hungry components. Each generation of computers became smaller, faster, more dependable, and less expensive to operate.

❱ **What characterized the first generation of computers?** First-generation computers, such as UNIVAC, can be characterized by their use of vacuum tubes to store individual bits of data. A vacuum tube is an electronic device that controls the flow of electrons in a vacuum (Figure 8-23). Each tube can be set to one of two states. One state is assigned a value of 0 and the other a value of 1.

Figure 8-23: Vacuum tubes used to store and process data

Courtesy of vintchip.com

Vacuum tubes respond more quickly than mechanical relays, resulting in faster computations, but they also have several disadvantages. They consume a lot of power, much of which is wasted as heat. They also tend to burn out quickly.

In addition to vacuum tube technology, first-generation computers were characterized by custom application programs made to order for the specific task the computer was to perform. Programming first-generation computers was difficult. As the computer era dawned, programmers were forced to think in 1s and 0s to write instructions in machine language.

Before the first generation ended, programmers had devised rudimentary compilers that allowed them to write instructions using assembly language op codes, such as LDA and JNZ. Assembly language was a small step forward; but like machine language, it was machine specific and required programmers to learn a different set of instructions for each computer.

❱ **What about second-generation computers?** Second-generation computers used transistors instead of vacuum tubes. First demonstrated in 1947 by AT&T's Bell Laboratories, **transistors** regulate current or voltage flow and act as a switch for electronic signals.

Transistors performed functions similar to vacuum tubes, but they were much smaller, cheaper, less power hungry, and more reliable. By the late 1950s, transistors such as those in portable radios (Figure 8-24) had replaced vacuum tubes as the processing and memory technology for most computers.

QuickCheck

Which of the following was not a characteristic of first-generation computers?

a. They used vacuum tubes.

b. They were digital.

c. They could be programmed using assembly language.

d. They were transistorized.

Figure 8-24: Transistors

Several successful transistor-based computers were manufactured by companies such as IBM, Burroughs, Control Data Corp., Honeywell, and Sperry Rand (which was the new name given to Remington Rand after its merger with Sperry Corp.). These computers served businesses and even played a major role in the U.S. space program (Figure 8-25).

Figure 8-25: Transistor-based computers were smaller, but not portable

Bettmann/Getty Images

In addition to the hardware breakthrough provided by transistors, an equally important development in software differentiated second-generation computers from their first-generation ancestors.

First-generation computers didn't have operating systems as we know them today. Instead, each software application included the instructions necessary for every aspect of the computing job, such as input, output, and processing activities.

Programmers were quick to realize that this style of programming was terribly inefficient. For example, although virtually every program sent results to a printer, every program was also required to have its own print routine.

Computer manufacturers such as IBM developed operating systems that provided standardized routines for input, output, memory management, storage, and other resource management activities.

Early operating systems were a step in the right direction; but unfortunately, learning to use each one was like learning a new and unique programming language. It was not until the third generation of computers that portable operating systems, such as CP/M and UNIX, provided programmers with similar operating system commands across hardware platforms.

In addition to operating systems, second-generation computers also ran programming language compilers that allowed programmers to write instructions using English-like commands rather than machine language 1s and 0s or cryptic assembly language commands.

High-level programming languages, such as COBOL (Common Business-Oriented Language) and Fortran (Formula Translator), were available for use on second-generation computers and remain in use on some legacy computer systems. The availability of high-level languages made it possible for third parties to develop software, and that capability was instrumental in the birth of the software industry.

Try It!

In 1969, Apollo astronauts landed on the moon. The mission was conducted with astonishingly primitive technology. By watching the YouTube video **Computer for Apollo**, you can get a sense of the mission and the rudimentary computer technology that was used.

8

QuickCheck

Which of the following innovations is not associated with second-generation computers?

a. Operating systems

b. Vacuum tubes

c. Transistors

d. High-level programming languages

> **What are the characteristics of third-generation computers?** Third-generation computers became possible in 1958, when Jack Kilby at Texas Instruments and Robert Noyce at Fairchild Semiconductor independently developed integrated circuits (Figure 8-26).

Figure 8-26: The original integrated circuit

© Texas Instruments (TI)

Integrated circuit technology made it possible to pack the equivalent of thousands of vacuum tubes or transistors onto a single miniature chip, vastly reducing the physical size, weight, and power requirements for devices such as computers.

IBM offered integrated circuit technology in its wildly successful **IBM 360**. The first orders for these computers were filled in 1965—a date regarded by many historians as the beginning of third-generation computing.

In 1965, Digital Equipment Corp. (DEC) introduced the **DEC PDP-8**, the first commercially successful minicomputer. Minicomputers were designed to be smaller and less powerful than mainframe computers, while maintaining the capability to simultaneously run multiple programs for multiple users. Thousands of manufacturing plants, small businesses, and scientific laboratories were attracted to the speed, small size, and reasonable cost of the PDP-8.

DEC introduced a succession of minicomputers that stole a share of the mainframe market. Eventually, IBM and other mainframe makers also produced these devices, but the star for minicomputers faded as a new technology—microcomputers—gradually gained popularity. DEC was purchased by Compaq in 1998. Compaq was later purchased by Hewlett-Packard (HP).

> **When did the fourth generation of computers emerge?** The technology for **fourth-generation computers** appeared in 1971, when Ted Hoff developed the first general-purpose microprocessor. Called the Intel 4004, this microprocessor dramatically changed the computer industry, resulting in fourth-generation microprocessor-based computer systems that were faster, smaller, and less expensive than third-generation computers.

Intel's 4004 microprocessor (Figure 8-27) was smaller than a cornflake but matched the computing power of ENIAC. The 4004 packed the equivalent of 2,300 transistors or vacuum tubes on a single chip and was able to perform 60,000 instructions per second.

Figure 8-27: The Intel 4004 chip

CC BY LLeslie

QuickCheck

Third-generation computers are associated with all of the following innovations except _____.

a. portable operating systems

b. integrated circuits

c. minicomputers

d. microprocessors

Try It!

The 4004 replaced a snaggle of circuitry and matched the processing power of ENIAC. There's a quick overview of its origins on YouTube. Search for **3 Minutes On... The Intel 4004 Microprocessor**.

As the fourth generation of computers emerged, microprocessor manufacturers soon flourished. Early industry leaders included Intel, Zilog, Motorola, and Texas Instruments. Today, microprocessors are a key component of all types of computers ranging from smartphones to supercomputers. Intel reigns as the world's leading microprocessor manufacturer, although microprocessors are also produced by companies such as Qualcomm, Texas Instruments, Taiwan Semiconductor, and AMD.

Personal Computers

The 1980s were a decade of big hair, leg warmers, and boom boxes. Ferris Bueller took his famous day off, and a DeLorean time machine starred in *Back to the Future*. The computer industry was changing its future, too, by transitioning into an information technology industry whose core business included data in addition to hardware. During this period, the industry shifted from the East Coast to the West Coast and began to focus on a vast new market: consumers. The era of personal computers was beginning.

▶ **Who invented the personal computer?** In the early 1970s, many hobbyists built their own computer systems based on integrated circuit and microprocessor technologies. One such system, the **Mark-8**, was developed by Jonathan A. Titus and featured in the July 1974 issue of *Radio-Electronics*. These early personal computers were not commercially produced or widely available, but they are often considered forerunners of today's personal computer.

In 1975, Ed Roberts and the MITS (Micro Instrumentation and Telemetry Systems) company announced the **MITS Altair**, which many historians believe to be the first commercial microcomputer.

The Altair was based on the Intel 8080 processor and sold as a kit for $395 or fully assembled for $650—about one-fourth the price of a 1975 Volkswagen Beetle. The Altair was a computer for the hobbyist. The kit came unassembled in a box containing a processor and 256 bytes of memory—not 256 KB, just 256 bytes. It had no keyboard, no monitor, and no permanent storage device (Figure 8-28).

Figure 8-28: Altair computer kits were snapped up by hobbyists

▶ **What were the first personal computers?** In 1976, Steve Jobs and Steve Wozniak founded Apple Computer Co., and released the **Apple I**, a kit containing a system board with 4 KB of RAM that sold for $666.66. Other companies, such as Commodore, Atari, and RadioShack, also pursued the hobbyist market, but with preassembled computers.

QuickCheck

The first personal computers were not_____.

a. available as kits

b. expensive

c. mostly purchased by hobbyists

d. easy to use

Try It!

A computer for $666 doesn't sound very expensive, but that price is in 1976 dollars. What is the price equivalent in today's dollars? Search online for the **CPI Inflation Calculator** to find out.

In 1978, Apple introduced a preassembled computer called the Apple II, which featured color graphics, expansion slots, a disk drive, a 1.07 MHz 6502 processor, and 16 KB of RAM for $1,195. The Apple II, shown in Figure 8-29, was the first desktop computer superstar. One of the main reasons behind its success was a commercial software program called VisiCalc—the first electronic spreadsheet. This program landed computers on the radar screen of business users and clearly marked a turning point where personal computers began to appeal to an audience beyond hobbyists.

▶ **When did the IBM PC hit store shelves?** In 1981, IBM began marketing what it called a personal computer or PC, based on the Intel 8088 processor. When the PC version of VisiCalc became available, the IBM PC quickly became the top-selling personal computer, far surpassing IBM's expectations.

The $3,000 IBM PC, shown in Figure 8-29, shipped with a 4.77 MHz Intel 8088 processor, 16 KB of RAM, and single-sided 160 KB floppy disk drives. The IBM PC was soon followed by the IBM PC XT, which featured RAM upgradable to 640 KB and a 10 MB hard disk drive.

IBM PCs were constructed with off-the-shelf parts that could be easily obtained from many electronics wholesalers. Within months, dozens of companies used these parts to produce clones of IBM-compatible computers that could run the same software and use the same expansion cards as the IBM PC and PC XT. These companies were also able to obtain essentially the same operating system used by IBM. The operating system was called PC-DOS and was marketed by a young entrepreneur named Bill Gates, founder of a fledgling software company called Microsoft.

▶ **How did personal computers become so successful?** Although hobbyists and the business community had embraced computers, these machines were still considered difficult for the average person to use. That perception began to change in 1983, when Apple introduced a product called the Apple Lisa. A key feature of the Lisa was its graphical user interface—an idea borrowed from the Xerox Alto computer.

At $10,000, the Lisa proved too expensive for most consumers. Apple remained committed to graphical user interfaces, however, and in 1984 released the first Apple Macintosh. The $2,495 Macintosh featured a graphical user interface that made programs easier to use than those on the command line–based IBM PC. The Macintosh became the computer of choice for graphical applications such as desktop publishing.

By the late 1980s, the computer industry had begun to consolidate around two primary platforms—the MS-DOS–based IBM-compatible platform and the Apple Macintosh. With the introduction of Microsoft Windows, IBM-compatible computer systems gained a graphical user interface and accounted for more than 90% of all personal computer sales by the mid-1990s. The Apple Macintosh accounted for most of the remainder, with other proprietary platforms accounting for a very small percentage of new computer sales.

▶ **How have personal computers evolved?** Desktop computers had their day. Although they are still available, the trend now is toward portable digital devices.

The first portable computers appeared in the early 1970s, but they were the size of a carry-on bag and weighed just as much! Throughout the 1980s and 1990s, portable computers became smaller, lighter, and more popular until sometime around 2005, when they outsold desktop computers.

Figure 8-29: Personal computers

The Apple II was the most popular computer of its time.

The IBM PC was launched in 1981 and evolved into today's popular Windows-based PCs.

The Apple Macintosh computer popularized graphical user interfaces.

The Apple iPhone ushered in the era of handheld computing devices. With a full-color graphical user interface, a touchscreen, a 412 MHz processor, 4 GB of RAM, a built-in camera, and easy-to-use apps, the iPhone offered features undreamed of when computers first became portable. A computer industry milestone occurred in 2011 when, for the first time, smartphones outsold desktop and laptop computers.

Apple set another hardware milestone when it introduced the iPad in 2010. Its sleek form factor enclosed a 1 GHz processor, 256 MB of RAM, 16 GB of storage, a full-color touchscreen, and cellular or Wi-Fi connectivity. The popularity of smartphones and tablet computers signaled yet another phase of the computer industry.

▶ **Is the computer industry still in transition?** The core business of the computer industry is hardware, and devices are continuing to evolve. Computers originated as tools for big business and government agencies. Later, desktop and laptop devices were deployed in businesses, and the same devices were used by individuals. This trend is changing, however, as consumer devices and their simplified software diverge from the more powerful devices and full-featured software used by business professionals (Figure 8-30).

QuickCheck

Which of the following technologies is not associated with the emerging personal computer market of the 1980s?

a. VisiCalc

b. IBM PC XT

c. Intel 4004

d. ABC computer

8

Figure 8-30: The ICT industry in transition

1950–1980

Big computers for big business

1980–2010

Big computers for big business	Desktops and laptops for business and personal use

2010–Future

Big computers for big business	Desktops and laptops for professional use	Handheld devices for personal use

QuickQuiz   Section B

1. Mechanical calculators and electronic computers have built-in [_____]—the step-by-step processes by which numbers are manipulated.

2. ENIAC's von Neumann [_____] placed program instructions and data in the same memory space.

3. The core technology for second-generation computer hardware was [_____].

4. Fourth-generation technology is characterized by construction based on [_____], such as the Intel 4004.

5. IBM PC sales skyrocketed when electronic [_____] software named VisiCalc became available.

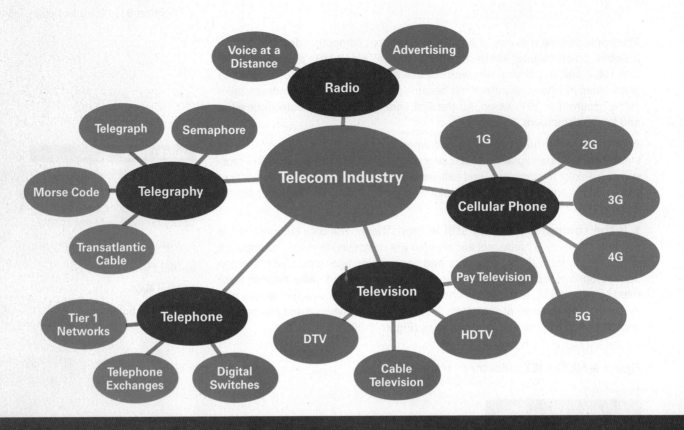

Section C The Telecom Industry

Objectives

▶ List six technologies in the telecommunications sector in the order they were invented.

▶ Sketch a timeline of key events in the evolution of the telegraph and show how they relate to the Gartner Hype Cycle.

▶ Explain the concept of common carrier, and list the communications industries that are included in this classification.

▶ Explain how the telephone industry evolved into a significant component of the Internet backbone.

▶ Describe at least two contributions that the radio industry made to modern telecommunications.

▶ List the major characteristics that differentiate 1G, 2G, 3G, 4G, and 5G cellular service.

▶ Sketch a timeline of key events in the television industry and explain how they affect modern Internet access.

In ancient times, news and information were carried along vast trade routes spread throughout Asia and the Middle East. The speed of communication was measured by the swiftness of messengers on foot, on horseback, or on wind-driven sailing ships. Messages might have taken days, weeks, or months to reach their destinations. That situation changed significantly in the 19th century, as one telecommunications technology after another emerged from inventors' workshops.

Terminology

telegraphy	gutta-percha	telephone exchange	cellular telephone
semaphores	telephone	common carrier	television
telegraph	rotary dialers	last mile	digital television
Morse code	touchtone	radio	pay television

Telegraph

You may recall the epic scene in the film *The Lord of the Rings: The Return of the King*, when Pippin lights a beacon in Minas Tirith and, one by one, signal fires on nearby mountain tops dramatically ignite into pillars of flame. Such communications were historically used by nation-states as warning signals, and they are a form of telecommunications called telegraphy.

▶ **What is telegraphy?** Telegraphy refers to transmitting text or symbolic information over long distances without the use of a living carrier, such as a courier or a carrier pigeon. Primitive forms of optical telegraphy used in ancient times included smoke signals, light beacons, and signal flags.

Flags and other visual signals were used on battlefields to help commanders communicate instructions to troops. These forms of telegraphic communications were limited to line-of-sight distances and were able to convey a very limited set of data. They became known as semaphores to differentiate them from a technology called the telegraph.

▶ **Who invented the telegraph?** The account of Benjamin Franklin flying a kite during a thunderstorm in 1752 represents the time period when scientists began to seriously study electricity. Until the concept of electricity was understood, semaphores, hand-delivered mail, and horseback riders of the Pony Express remained the primary telecommunications channels.

In the early 1800s—about the time Charles Babbage was designing his Analytical Engine—inventors began to experiment with electrical telegraphy, or what we now generally refer to as the telegraph. Francis Ronalds, a British inventor, built the first rudimentary telegraph in 1816 using a cable connected at either end to dials marked with the letters of the alphabet. It was a cumbersome apparatus, but it demonstrated that sending messages electronically at a distance was possible.

Carl Friedrich Gauss and Wilhelm Weber built an early prototype of a telegraph system that sent messages encoded as positive and negative currents—essentially a binary encoding system. As a two-way communication system, each node required a transmitter for sending messages and a receiver for collecting them.

The first commercial telegraph was co-developed by Sir William Cooke and Charles Wheatstone. Their device, patented in 1837, was composed of several compass-like needles that pointed to letters of the alphabet according to received electrical signals (Figure 8-31).

8

Figure 8-31: The Cooke and Wheatstone telegraph

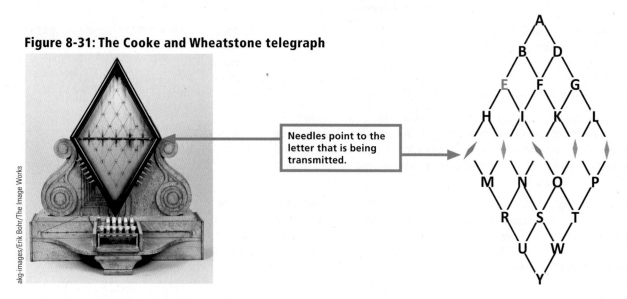

Needles point to the letter that is being transmitted.

▶ **When was Morse code introduced?** In 1837, U.S. inventor Samuel Morse developed and patented a telegraph system. His system transmitted data using the Morse code alphabet, a binary encoding system based on dots and dashes. Skilled telegraph operators listened to the dots and dashes through a headset and transcribed them into letters of the alphabet. Messages were encoded using a telegraph key (Figure 8-32).

Figure 8-32: Morse code

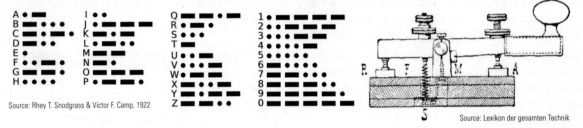

Source: Rhey T. Snodgrass & Victor F. Camp, 1922

Source: Lexikon der gesamten Technik

▶ **What was the significance of the telegraph?** Author Tom Standage refers to the telegraph as the Victorian Internet because "it revolutionized business practices, gave rise to new forms of crime, and inundated its users with a deluge of information. Romances blossomed over the wires. Secret codes were devised by some users and cracked by others...a technological subculture with its own customs and vocabulary was establishing itself."

As with technologies that developed in later years, the telegraph experienced a cycle of invention and prototyping, followed by a peak of expectations like those tracked by the Gartner Hype Cycle. That peak was followed by a period of disillusionment when the technical going got tough and it became apparent that the technology would not solve all the world's problems. Finally, the telegraph reached its plateau of productivity and became, for a time, the primary means of worldwide telecommunications.

▶ **How did the telegraph shape world events?** Thomas Edison was a telegraph operator when he was a teenager. He invented the stock ticker and went on to create many more devices that became part of mainstream life, including the phonograph and the motion picture camera. His early analog devices were the foundation for the film and recording industries that today provide digital audio and video content that streams over the Internet.

The telegraph served governments and individuals alike. It carried momentous dispatches as well as simple greetings. During the U.S. Civil War, for example, Abraham Lincoln nervously paced the floor of the War Department Telegraph Office throughout the day. He wanted to be in the same room as the telegraph apparatus when messages arrived from commanders on the front lines.

By 1861, commercial telegraph lines linked major cities in the United States, and the Pony Express was discontinued. All the capitals of Europe were connected, and news flowed over the wires in a never-ending stream. Optimists viewed the telegraph as a great uniting force among nations with the potential for establishing world peace.

But if the telegraph had any chance of becoming the instrument of world peace, it would first have to connect the continents, and that required some way to transmit messages across oceans. The technology used to lay transoceanic cables was essential for the telegraph industry and all the other communications industries that followed.

Try It!

What was it like to be a telegraph operator? Search online for **Morse Code Translator** and enter a few sentences. Then listen to them played back in Morse code. How do you tap out SOS in Morse code?

QuickCheck

The telegraph is sometimes called _____ because of its effect on society and the technical community.

a. steampunk

b. a hype cycle

c. telegraphy

d. the Victorian Internet

▶ **How did the telegraph span oceans?** The danger of submerging electrical devices in water is well known. Salt water conducts electricity, and that means a current sent over a bare wire would disperse into the ocean water, diverting the signal from its destination. The success of an underwater cable depended on the discovery of **gutta-percha**, a rubber-like substance derived from the sap of a tree grown in Malaysia.

A thick coat of gutta-percha was used to insulate the exterior surface of telegraph wires, which were then covered with a flexible mesh of protective steel. A spool of cable weighed about one ton for each nautical mile. In 1857, the Atlantic Telegraph Company deployed two converted warships on loan from the British and U.S. governments. Loaded with cables, these ships began the delicate process of spooling out cable and letting it sink to the ocean floor.

The cable broke on the first day, but it was retrieved with grappling hooks and repaired. A second break occurred in an area of the ocean more than a mile deep, and the mission was abandoned. The next year, a second expedition set out. Despite several additional mishaps, the cable successfully connected Europe to North America. On August 16, 1858, the transatlantic telegraph carried its first cable. It began, "Europe and America are united by telegraphy..." The 70-character message took over 17 hours to transmit. The reception was terrible. A month later, the cable failed.

It was not until 1866 that transatlantic telegraphy was reestablished. The new cable was much faster than the old one, with speeds reaching eight words per minute. Telegraphy remained the major technology for intercontinental communication well into the 1950s, but it was then surpassed by telephone communications and later by the Internet. British Telecom sold its telegraph division in 2003. Western Union sent its final telegram in 2006. But before its demise, telegraph cables stretched from continent to continent, marking out the routes for digital data that would come decades later (Figure 8-33).

8

QuickCheck

What is the major legacy of the telegraph for the current Information Age?

a. Morse code

b. Transoceanic communication

c. Telegraphic keys

d. Text messages

Figure 8-33: Major telegraph trunk lines in 1891

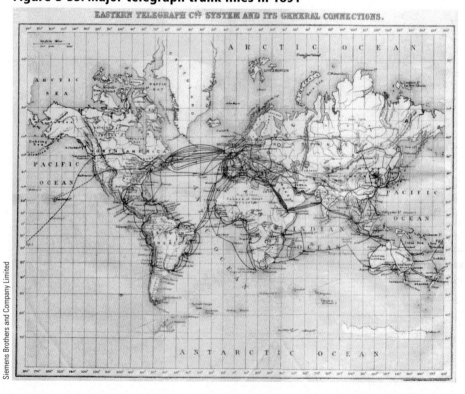

Telephone

There are some visionaries who make astoundingly accurate predictions. In 1878—more than 125 years before Skype and the iPhone—journalist Kate Field wrote, "I've just read of the electroscope, the province of which is to transmit waves of light by electricity. Combine it with the telephone, and while two persons, hundreds of miles apart, are talking together, they will actually see each other. Won't this be fun?"

▶ **How did the telephone industry get its start?** A **telephone** is, very simply, a device that transmits human voices over a distance using cables or airborne signals. The first telephone was invented and patented by Alexander Graham Bell in 1876. The telephone arrived after the telegraph and was based on technical discoveries related to sending multiple messages along a single wire using different frequencies.

Shortly after filing his telephone patents, Bell and several investors founded the Bell Telephone Company, which—after a long road of many twists and turns—became what is now AT&T.

▶ **How did early telephones differ from modern phones?** By definition, a telephone contains a microphone/transmitter and a speaker/receiver. Early telephones were primitive devices—not much more sophisticated than connecting two tin cans with a string. Like tin can phones, the first telephones had a transmitter and a receiver in the same port, so callers had to alternately shout into the port and then put it to their ear.

Telephones evolved through several design form factors, including box phones, candlesticks, phones with **rotary dialers**, and Trimline phones with **touchtone** keypads (Figure 8-34).

Figure 8-34: Telephone form factors

Chuck Rausin/Shutterstock.com

Adrio Communications Ltd/Shutterstock.com

Hemmarat/Shutterstock.com

Mikeledray/Shutterstock.com

1890–1910

Early box phones had no dialing mechanism. Turning the crank alerted the operator, who would ask for the number.

1890–1930

Candlestick telephones separated the microphone/transmitter from the speaker/receiver.

1940–1970

Rotary telephones included a rotary dialer; the handset included both a speaker and a microphone.

1960–2010

Trimline telephones introduced touchtone dialing in 1963.

▶ **Did the telephone network use the same infrastructure as the telegraph network?** The first telephones were connected by point-to-point networks, similar to those used by the telegraph system. This method meant that one phone was hard-wired to one destination. Speaking to people at several locations required a set of phones for each location. That scheme was unworkable, so a more practical network topology for the telephone system soon emerged.

Telephone networks are based on a hierarchy of interconnected stars. At the center of the star is a **telephone exchange** that manages connections between callers. The world's first commercial telephone exchange opened on November 12, 1877, in Germany. Its manual switchboard was controlled by a switchboard operator (Figure 8-35).

Figure 8-35: How a telephone switchboard works

Everett Collection/Shutterstock.com

When a subscriber cranked the handle of a box-style telephone or lifted a handset, the port for the subscriber's line would light up on the operator's panel. The operator plugged one end of a cable into the subscriber's port. That completed a circuit to the central office, and the operator could ask for the number by saying "Number please?" The operator would then plug the other end of the patch cable into the port for the call's destination.

▶ **What happened to switchboard operator jobs?** Automated exchanges, which eliminated the need for human operators, appeared as early as 1900. Telephones equipped with dials were able to directly interact with equipment at the telephone exchange, so switchboard operators were no longer needed to connect patch cables for local calls. For a time, operators were still required for long-distance calls and directory assistance, but eventually those jobs also became unnecessary.

▶ **What is a common carrier?** A **common carrier** is any person or company that transports goods, passengers, or electronic signals over regular routes at set rates. Common carriers are subject to a set of government regulations. They are legally required to provide services as long as there is enough space or capacity, requisite fees are paid, and no reasonable grounds exist to refuse carriage. Telegraph, telephone, and cellular phone services are classified as common carriers. Radio and television are not considered common carriers.

In 2015, Internet service providers were classified by the Federal Communications Commission as common carriers. This designation, which was straightforward for telephone services, eventually sparked controversy for Internet service providers and social media platforms.

QuickCheck

Why did the telephone system not use the same infrastructure as the telegraph?

a. There was too much traffic on the telegraph system.

b. There was not enough gutta-percha.

c. Telegraph lines were point-to-point connections.

d. Telegraph operators weren't trained to use a switchboard.

Try It!

New technologies require instructional videos, and the move from switchboards to operator-assisted dialing was no exception. Search online for **Instructional Videos for Rotary Phone** and browse the videos to see original footage presented to consumers in the 1930s.

QuickCheck

Telephone and telegraph services are _____.

a. classified as common carriers

b. regulated broadcast services

c. exempt from taxation

d. in a period of revival

8

▶ **When did the telephone system go digital?** The telephone system was initially analog. In 1976, AT&T installed the world's first electronic digital switchboard, or "switch." It handled 500,000 calls per hour. Digital switches digitize incoming speech using a process similar to music digitization, which you learned about in Module 1. The digitized voice is reconstructed as analog sound when it arrives at the recipient's local exchange. Although the switches worked with digital voice, the **last mile** from customer equipment to the switch remained analog.

End-to-end digital telephone service is now available using VoIP protocols. For example, Xfinity Voice customers make and receive calls over a high-speed Internet connection using a standard telephone handset.

▶ **How does the telephone system relate to ICT?** As the era of commercial Internet access began in 1995, the telephone system had an extensive worldwide network, including undersea cables and communications satellites for long-distance calls. The telephone system infrastructure became a key element of the Internet backbone and one of a few ways for consumers to gain Internet access. Not only was local telephone equipment used to dial in to local ISPs, but transcontinental lines were used to transport data between service providers.

Of today's Tier 1 Internet service providers, more than half began as telephone companies. Which of the company logos in Figure 8-36 are familiar to consumers today?

QuickCheck

Which statement is true about the telephone system's last mile?

a. It was used for dial-up Internet connections.

b. It stretched between two or more local exchanges.

c. It was the first segment of the telephone network to go digital.

d. It was the main technology for Tier 1 Internet service providers.

Figure 8-36: Telephone companies were early backbone providers

AT&T was a Bell Telephone Company subsidiary, but it acquired its parent company in 1899. In 1984, U.S. regulators required AT&T to divest its subsidiaries and make them separate entities, known as the Baby Bells. One of these subsidiaries, Southwestern Bell (SBC), eventually purchased AT&T.

Verizon traces its roots back to Bell Atlantic, one of the Baby Bells. After merging with GTE in 2000, the combined company was rebranded as Verizon.

Sprint Corporation originated as the Brown Telephone Company, founded in 1899. It has since done business as United Telephone and Electric, United Telecom, Southern Pacific Communications Company, GTE Sprint, and Sprint Nextel Corporation.

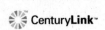

CenturyLink traces its heritage to the Oak Ridge Telephone Company, which acquired several smaller companies and in 1999 was renamed CenturyTel, Inc. In 2010, the company acquired Qwest and overnight became the third largest telecommunications company in the United States.

Qwest can be described as a digital native. Founded in 1996, it began by building an all-digital fiber-optic network along the Southern Pacific Railroad tracks. Qwest became one of the United States' largest Internet backbone providers.

TATA Communication was started by the government of India, and then acquired by the TATA group conglomerate based in Mumbai. The company operates an extensive undersea communications cable infrastructure spanning every continent.

Comcast is the only outlier in this roster of early Tier 1 ISPs. It originated as a cable television company, with a network unrelated to the telephone system. The company primarily serves U.S. customers.

Radio

It may seem like radio has been around since the Stone Age, but it was developed after the telegraph and telephone. Its contribution to modern technology is extensive. Without radio, we would have no cell phones and no Wi-Fi.

▶ **How did the radio industry get its start?** Guglielmo Marconi is credited as the person who invented the radio, a device that sends and receives sound as electromagnetic waves. Surprisingly, his 1895 invention was not intended to broadcast news and music, but rather to transmit wireless telegraph messages.

It was not until 1906 that a Canadian physicist, Reginald Fessenden, managed to broadcast voice and music over a long distance. News of Fessenden's accomplishment set off worldwide interest in radio technology.

The availability of radio kits marked the beginning of radio's Technology Trigger phase. Radios and computers had this development phase in common. Both were embraced by hobbyists who swapped tips, formed clubs, and eagerly awaited the publication of special-interest magazines. Radio enthusiasts looked forward to the latest issue of *Radio News* and *Wireless Age*. Years later, computer enthusiasts couldn't wait to get their hands on *Dr. Dobb's Journal* and *Byte* magazine.

Like computer enthusiasts 50 years later, radio hobbyists built their own devices using kits or off-the-shelf parts. Hobbyist radios, referred to as "radio sets," could both transmit and receive. Consequently, radio operators spent as much time talking to other radio enthusiasts as they spent receiving broadcasts. We now think of radios as one-way devices to pick up broadcasts, but early radio culture viewed these devices as two-way communications platforms similar to CB radios or cell phones.

Prior to 1912, there were no laws or regulations restricting amateur radio transmission in the United States. Radio stations popped up everywhere, sometimes broadcasting on the same frequencies as neighboring stations, creating a muddle on the airwaves. During World War I, the U.S. government took control of radio equipment as a national security precaution. Hundreds of independent radio stations were ordered shut down.

After the war, civilians were again allowed to use radio technology, and radio entered a phase of mass diffusion to mainstream consumers (Figure 8-37).

Figure 8-37: In the 1930s, radios became a major source of entertainment

National Archives, Records of the Extension Service

8

QuickCheck

Inventors who developed the first telephones and radios were attempting to improve _____.

a. voice communications

b. telegraphy

c. undersea cables

d. entertainment

Try It!

Did you know that National Public Radio is available online as a live audio stream? You can listen at **www.npr.org**.

▶ How did the radio affect mainstream consumers? The years between 1920 and 1960 are considered the Golden Age of Radio. During this time period, consumers snapped up millions of radios and spent hours listening to music, news, and variety shows.

Modern *Downton Abbey* viewers saw a reenactment of the king of England's first radio broadcast. The king's 1924 broadcast generated so much anticipation that loudspeakers were set up outside many retail establishments so customers and passersby could gather and listen.

On the other side of the Atlantic in 1933, President Franklin Roosevelt inaugurated his weekly fireside chats as a way of connecting "in person" to the American people (Figure 8-38).

Figure 8-38: President Roosevelt's fireside chats, 1933–1944

Source: National Archives and Records Administration

In the 1920s and 1930s, radios used vacuum tubes—a technology later used in first-generation computers such as ENIAC and UNIVAC. Radios were housed in desktops or freestanding units and usually constructed from ornately carved wood. In 1929, the average price of a radio was $139, equivalent to about $1,700 in today's currency. Just four years later in the aftermath of the Great Depression, the price tumbled to only $47. Americans continued to purchase radios, and by 1933 about 60% of U.S. households owned one.

Following the trajectory of other new technologies, radio technology changed with the invention of the transistor. By substituting transistors for bulky and power-hungry vacuum tubes, transistor radios became portable and battery operated. Post–World War II baby boomers were just reaching their teen years when portable radios hit store shelves and became the cool way to listen to Elvis Presley and other icons of pop music.

Mass-market television signaled the end of radio's Golden Age. Today, radio stations struggle to find a niche in the digital world through satellite radio, streaming Internet radio, and podcasts.

▶ **Was the radio industry profitable?** The radio industry includes companies that broadcast radio programs and that manufacture devices, such as radios and broadcast transmitters. Many early radio stations were operated by radio manufacturers whose primary interest was encouraging consumers to purchase radios. This strategy was successful until the market was saturated. Looking around for a new profit model, station operators began selling advertising time to offset the cost of producing news and variety shows.

Radio shows sponsored by companies advertising Ivory soap, Oxydol, and other cleaning products came to be known as soap operas. Advertising became the profit model for several modern technologies, including television and the Web. And as consumers are well aware, today's advertising technology is extremely sophisticated in its ability to collect and aggregate personal data for targeted ads on Web pages and in spam. By 2013, advertising revenue generated on the Internet surpassed that of advertising on television, radio, and other platforms (Figure 8-39).

Figure 8-39: Advertising by platform, 2020 (billions)

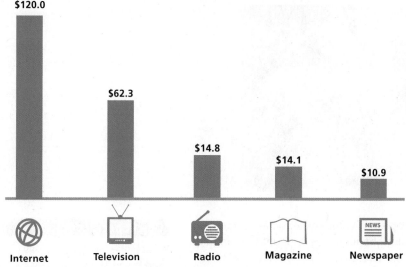

Sources: IAB/PricewaterhouseCoopers Internet Advertising Revenue Report, 2020

▶ **What did the radio industry contribute to today's technology?** Radio technology is the basis for cell phones, Wi-Fi, Bluetooth, and near-field communications (NFC), all indispensable tools of the digital age. But it is the underlying technology of radio, not the broadcasting industry itself, that provides these high-tech amenities. Neither the cellular phone system nor Wi-Fi utilizes radio broadcast facilities. At most, cellular service providers might share towers with radio stations. The technology contribution provided by radio is the means to transmit voice over long distances, and from that simple technology sprang the cellular telephone industry.

QuickCheck

Which one of the following does not use radio technology?

a. Cell phones

b. Wi-Fi

c. NFC

d. Landlines

Cellular Phones

There's a viral video on YouTube that appears to show a young woman walking among a group of people during the 1930s and using a cell phone. She holds it to her ear, smiles, and after a few seconds she seems to sign off and lower the phone. Was this woman a time traveler carrying a cell phone?

▶ **What was the role of radio technology in the development of cellular phones?** A cellular telephone is a device that uses a low-power radio transmitter to carry out two-way voice communications. Cellular telephones were initially developed for military and law enforcement.

Two-way radio technology went portable during World War II. Devices such as the 35-pound Radio Set SCR-300 were called "walkie-talkies" because their portability allowed a soldier to walk with the device and talk at the same time. As a backpack unit, however, the SCR-300 was typically operated by two soldiers: one to carry the device and one to tune in the call. As the war progressed, technological advancements produced the SCR-536, a large handheld unit (Figure 8-40).

Try It!

You can watch the video referenced at left by searching YouTube for **Time Traveler 1938**.

Figure 8-40: These bulky devices are the ancestors of today's cell phones

U.S. military Department of Defense

Australian War Memorial

▶ **When did modern cell phones appear?** A Motorola engineer is credited with developing the first handheld cellular phone. It was brought to market in 1984 under the impressive model name Motorola DynaTAC 8000X. The phone weighed almost two pounds, was more than 12 inches long, and contained a battery that lasted for only one hour of talk time. In the following 30 years, the cellular industry flourished. Devices became smaller, picked up a constellation of features, evolved through several "G" generations, and eventually went digital, culminating in the introduction of the iPhone in 2007 and the first Android phone in 2008 (Figure 8-41).

QuickCheck

What is the basic technology used by cellular telephones?

a. Direct dialing

b. Radio

c. Telegraphy

d. Walkie-talkie

Figure 8-41: Cell phone handset evolution

DynaTAC 8000X
1984

Flip Phone
1996

Smartphone
2007

▶ **What is the significance of the "G" generations?** Mobile phone signaling technology evolved through four generations. These generations refer to the way signals are transmitted from a handset to a cell tower. For example, the signals used for 1G mobile communications were analog, whereas 2G signals were digital, and 3G systems used different frequency bands and spread spectrum transmission to increase bandwidth (Figure 8-42).

Figure 8-42: Cell phone generations

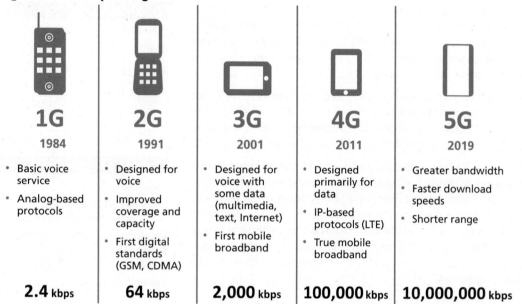

▶ **How does the cellular phone industry contribute to modern lifestyles?** Cell phones became smartphones when they converged with computing devices and became capable of executing programs, manipulating data, and accessing the Internet. Mobile phone services are offered around the globe from telecommunications giants, such as China Mobile, Vodafone, Airtel, T-Mobile, AT&T, and Verizon. About half of the top 30 service providers are government owned, while the rest are private-sector corporations.

Cellular providers have played a major role in placing computer power into the hands of consumers. Worldwide there were approximately 8 billion wireless service subscriptions in 2020, and about 5 billion of those subscribers used smartphones, according to the International Telecommunication Union (ITU).

The first cellular phones to access the Internet and the Web were available in 1996. These phones were not exactly "smart" and used WAP (Wireless Application Protocol) to provide access to Web sites specially designed for the small screens and slow data transfer rates of early 3G feature phones.

It is clear that smartphone use is booming, but do these devices produce lifestyle and economic benefits? A report from the European mobile telecommunications organization GSMA optimistically states, "In the hands of consumers, these devices are improving living standards and changing lives, especially in developing markets, while contributing to growing economies by stimulating entrepreneurship." Yes, an economy can benefit from revenues created when consumers purchase smartphones, but after the market is saturated, will those devices provide educational, career, and health benefits? That question is yet to be answered.

QuickCheck

Which generation of mobile phones first supplied mobile broadband?

a. 1G

b. 2G

c. 3G

d. 4G

Television

On March 25, 1925, Scottish inventor John Logie Baird wowed customers at Selfridges department store in London with the first public demonstration of televised images. The image quality produced by Baird's device was terrible compared to that of film-based motion pictures of the time, but observers who understood that Baird's images were "live" on the air must have been suitably impressed.

▶ **When was television available to consumers?** The 1930s can be characterized as a phase of innovation for **television**, a technology designed to send moving images over a distance. During that phase of innovation, a limited number of televisions were manufactured, broadcasting stations were few, and those stations were not on the air 24 hours a day.

The first mass-produced televisions were available to consumers in 1946. These devices contained a heavy and awkward cathode ray tube (CRT), which used an electron "gun" to essentially spray an image onto a fluorescent screen. This technology was later used in monitors for the first generations of personal computers.

Television reception required two elements: a screen and an antenna. Initially, the two components were separate. The screen was housed in a cabinet, and the antenna was connected to the cabinet by a cable. Consumers could purchase the console and the antenna as a set, hence the commonly used term *television set*. Unlike "radio sets," a television set did not include a transmitter; but like so many technologies at the beginning of their lifetime—including computers— televisions were supplied to consumers as several components rather than as a tidy, one-piece unit (Figure 8-43).

Figure 8-43: A television "set" from the 1960s

Palo_ok/Shutterstock.com

▶ **How did television technology evolve?** The first color television broadcast was in 1954, but the cost of color sets was out of reach for most consumers. Well into the 1960s, programming remained in black and white. In 1965, however, after most consumers had purchased black-and-white televisions, the networks transitioned to color programming. By 1972, programming was in full color on all networks, and consumers began to retire their black-and-white sets and—much to the joy of the television industry—purchase new color televisions.

The transition to **digital television** (DTV) did not proceed as smoothly as the transition from black and white to color. Analog televisions cannot receive digital signals without the use of a converter box, so when stations switched to digital broadcasts, consumers required either a new digital television or a converter box for legacy equipment. The FCC mandated the switch to DTV, and in 2009, U.S. consumers entered the brave new world of digital television.

The television industry began as a broadcast service, using the airwaves as a transmission medium much like its sister technology in the radio industry. Signals were broadcast from local towers and could be freely picked up by any set-top or rooftop antenna deployed by consumers. Television was a free service, supported solely by product advertisements—that is, until pay TV appeared.

▶ **What is the origin of pay TV?** **Pay television** is a subscription service in which consumers pay to receive a selection of television channels. It offers a profitable way to monetize broadcast content using a subscription model similar to that used by the telephone industry.

Pay television is essentially an offshoot of cable television, an innovation that began quite by accident in the 1940s when a television salesman strung a cable to a local hilltop to improve the reception and picture quality of the televisions for sale in the store. Customers wanted similar reception and signed up to be connected for $2 a month. The era of cable television and pay TV had begun, and by 2004, more U.S. households were watching cable television than broadcast television (Figure 8-44).

8

Figure 8-44: U.S. cable television evolution

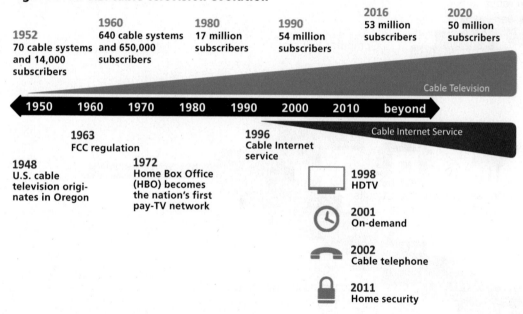

▶ **How did the cable television industry become part of the Internet backbone?** The use of cable television for Internet access varies substantially throughout the world. It is especially rare in emerging nations, where low-income demographics make it difficult to recover the high cost of building necessary infrastructure. The United States is somewhat unusual because it is one of the few countries in which cable television played a prominent role in supplying Internet service.

The U.S. cable television industry includes giant corporations such as Comcast, Cox Communications, and Charter Communications. These companies deployed hundreds of thousands of miles of high-capacity coaxial and optical fiber cables directly to homes. This infrastructure became a logical communications pathway for Internet service because it was already in place and offered higher capacity than the telephone company's analog dial-up service.

QuickCheck

According to Figure 8-44, in what decade did cable television providers emerge as large telecommunications companies?

a. 1960s

b. 1990s

c. 2000s

d. 2010s

Cable Internet service made its debut in 1996. Time Warner Cable offered Road Runner service, and Comcast partnered with Excite@Home. Through a series of acquisitions and peering agreements with Tier 1 ISPs, Comcast had emerged by 2001 as the largest U.S. Internet service provider and soon became a significant part of the Internet backbone.

At the same time, however, cable Internet subscriptions were beginning to decline as consumers began migrating to mobile wireless services. It appears that the Internet access story is yet unfinished and there are more changes ahead for the telecommunications industry.

▶ **What might lie ahead?** The future is difficult to predict, except to say that it is likely to be different. In retrospect, convergence between the computer industry and the telecommunications industry was inevitable. By examining the trend lines in Figure 8-45, you may be able to look ahead and make your own predictions.

Figure 8-45: The telecommunications and computer industries converge

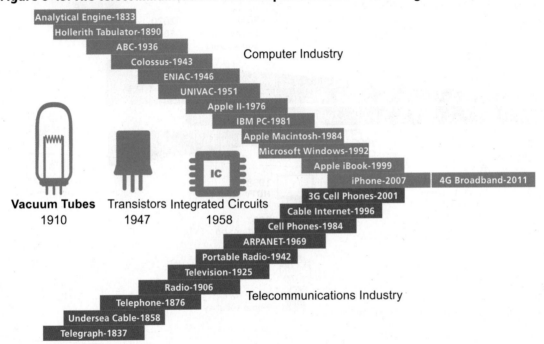

1. At about the same time as Charles Babbage was designing his Analytical Engine, inventors Gauss and Cooke were working on the _____.

2. Telephone, cellular services, and ISPs are classified as common _____.

3. Which telecommunications technology was prohibited by the U.S. government during World War I? _____

4. LTE is a _____ G technology.

5. The FCC mandated a switch to which television technology in 2009? _____ (Hint: Use the acronym.)

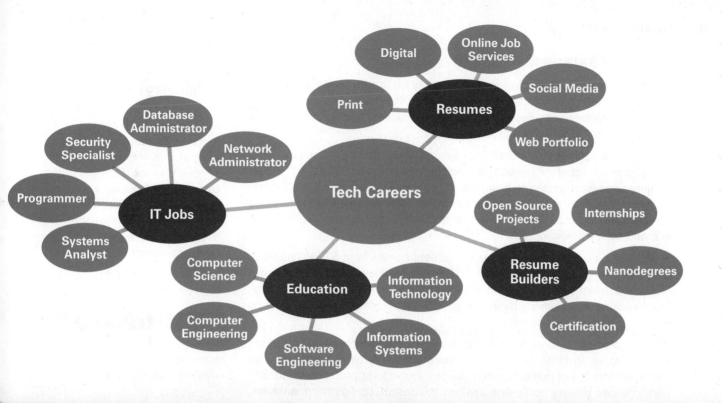

Objectives

▶ Differentiate between tech sector, STEM, and computer industry careers.

▶ List at least seven occupations within a typical IT department.

▶ Give an example of the titles used for various levels of career advancement in a tech job.

▶ Explain how contract workers differ from employees.

▶ List the five computing disciplines recognized by the ACM.

▶ Explain the relative merits of a college degree compared to certification, internships, badges, open source projects, and nanodegrees.

▶ List six resume formats, and describe when they are best used.

Digital devices are everywhere. But who designs all those computers, smartphones, and wearables? Who writes the software? Who are the search engine gurus and the cloud app wizards? Who designs all those Web sites? And who maintains the corporate safety nets that keep hackers at bay? The answer is tech professionals. If you're looking for a career field with high salaries and low unemployment rates, read on.

Terminology

technology workers	computer	technical support	computer engineering
STEM	programmer	specialist	computer science
computer professional	security specialist	Web site developer	information systems
IT department	database administrator	social networking analyst	information technology
chief information officer	network administrator	contract worker	software engineering
systems analyst	computer operator	telecommuters	Web portfolio

Jobs and Salaries

Computing devices are everywhere, but not every job that involves a computer is considered a technical occupation. Not surprisingly, the boundaries that delineate tech sector careers are subject to various classifications, perhaps because the tech sector itself is still evolving.

▶ **What are tech sector jobs?** Tech sector careers can be defined as being part of a broad set of information, technology, and communications industries, or more narrowly regarded as being part of the computer industry. A broad classification of **technology workers** encompasses jobs such as telephone cable installers and technical writers, as well as computer programmers, Web designers, and software developers.

A different classification of tech sector careers comes from **STEM** (science, technology, engineering, and math). STEM was originally used to describe a group of academic disciplines, but it is increasingly used to define an employment sector that includes jobs in biology, chemistry, information technology, engineering, math, and physics.

A third, more narrow, classification of tech sector careers focuses on **computer professionals**. In 1999, the U.S. Congress crafted an amendment to the Fair Labor Standards Act that essentially defines a computer professional as any person whose primary occupation involves the design, configuration, analysis, development, modification, testing, or security of computer hardware or software. We'll focus on those careers in this section.

▶ **What kinds of jobs are available to computer professionals?** Many computer professionals work in an **IT department**—the wing of a business or an organization responsible for computer, data, software, and support services. An IT department is also responsible for prioritizing an organization's information needs, modifying old information systems as necessary, and creating new systems.

Historically, IT departments were part of an organization's finance department because computers were initially deployed for accounting and inventory management functions. As computers began to assist with a wider variety of business tasks, some organizations changed their organizational charts to make the IT department a separate entity headed by a **chief information officer** (CIO), who reports directly to the chief executive officer or president. Figure 8-46 illustrates the organization of a typical IT department.

Terminology

With the wide variety of digital devices in use today and the pervasive digitization of so many aspects of the private and public sector, the term **computer professional** is beginning to seem outdated. This term may be in transition to **STEM worker**, **tech worker**, or **IT professional**.

QuickCheck

Which one of the following encompasses the narrowest variety of jobs related to ICT?

a. Tech sector

b. Computer professionals

c. STEM

Terminology

A **CIO** (chief information officer) is sometimes called a **CTO** (chief technology officer).

Figure 8-46: Basic IT department hierarchy chart

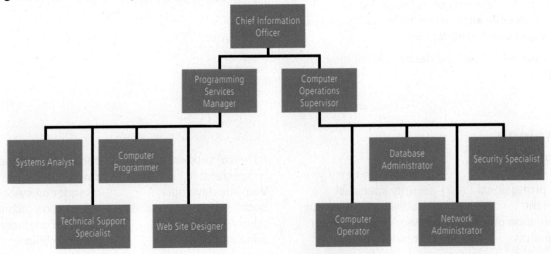

▶ **What are typical IT jobs?** IT jobs revolve around computers and networks that help an organization carry out its mission. There are hundreds of IT jobs, but the majority of entry-level positions tend to be similar to those listed in Figure 8-47.

Figure 8-47: Tech sector occupations

A **systems analyst** investigates the requirements of a business or an organization, its employees, and its customers in order to plan and implement new or improved computer services. This job requires the ability to identify problems and research technical solutions. Good communication skills are essential for interacting with managers and other employees.

A **computer programmer** (sometimes described as a programmer/analyst) designs, codes, and tests computer programs. In addition, programmers modify existing programs to meet new requirements or eliminate bugs. Computer programming requires concentration and a good memory for the countless details that pertain to a programming project. Programming projects range from entertainment and games to business and productivity applications. Programmers get satisfaction from devising efficient ways to make a computer perform specific jobs, tasks, and routines.

A **security specialist** analyzes a computer system's vulnerability to threats from viruses, worms, unauthorized access, and physical damage. Security specialists install and configure firewalls and antivirus software. They also work with management and employees to develop policies and procedures to protect computer equipment and data. Computer security jobs are punctuated by crises when a virus hits or a security breach is discovered. A security specialist needs a wide-ranging knowledge of computers and communication protocols that can be applied for a quick resolution to any crisis that occurs.

A **database administrator** analyzes a company's data to determine the most effective way to collect and store it. Database administrators create databases, data entry forms, and reports. They also define backup procedures, provide access to authorized users, and supervise the day-to-day use of databases.

A **network administrator** plans, installs, and maintains one or more local area networks and may also manage cloud resources. These specialists provide network accounts and access rights to approved users. They troubleshoot connectivity problems and respond to requests from network users for new software. Network administrators might be responsible for maintaining the security of a network, and they often pick up Web master duties to maintain an organization's Web site.

A **computer operator** works with system software for network servers, mainframes, and supercomputers. Computer operators monitor computer performance, install software patches and upgrades, perform backups, and restore data as necessary.

A **technical support specialist** troubleshoots hardware and software problems. Good interpersonal skills and patience are required for this job.

A **Web site developer** creates, tests, posts, and modifies Web pages. A good sense of design and artistic talent are required for this job, along with an understanding of how people use graphical user interfaces. Familiarity with Web tools, such as HTML and JavaScript, is becoming more important for this job, as is a knowledge of computer programming and database management.

 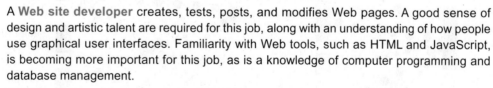

A **social networking analyst** manages an organization's online reputation by establishing and maintaining social media sites and evaluating analytics to support its mission. This occupation requires familiarity with social networking sites and an ability to interpret statistical metrics obtained from analytical tools.

8

❱ **What's the outlook for IT careers?** According to an Information Technology Association of America study, the U.S.-based IT workforce totaled about 10.4 million in 2000, but lost 500,000 jobs in 2001 as the dot-com bubble burst. A small but steady upswing from 2002 through 2006 brought the IT workforce close to its year 2000 peak, but the workforce again suffered cutbacks during the economic recession that began in 2008.

In coming years, the highest demand may be for network, technical support, and security specialists. The U.S. Bureau of Labor Statistics predicts that in the current decade, employment in the information and technology sector could grow by 11%, generating 500,000 new jobs. An unknown percentage of these jobs will be outsourced, which may negatively affect U.S. workers but will benefit offshore workers.

As in the past, economic trends could cause significant changes in the job market. In preparing for an IT career, flexibility is the key. As an IT professional, you should be willing to train and then retrain as new skills are needed to work with emerging technologies.

❱ **What are typical starting salaries in IT?** Web sites such as *www.bls. gov* provide salary data for various IT industry jobs. In addition to data from the Bureau of Labor Statistics, you can find comparative IT industry salary averages using a standard Web search engine.

As with almost every industry, the compensation rates for jobs in the IT industry vary. Jobs that require college degrees and certification tend to pay more than jobs that require a high school diploma and some on-the-job training. IT industry salaries also vary by geographic location. In the United States, the highest salaries tend to be offered in the Northeast and on the West Coast—two regions where the cost of living is relatively high.

❱ **Do IT jobs offer good advancement opportunities?** Workers in the IT industry have a fair amount of career mobility. Companies with large IT departments can offer in-house advancement, while workers in smaller firms might have to move up the career ladder by shifting to a different company. An entry-level worker could, for example, begin as an associate programmer, then advance to programmer status, then to senior programmer, and finally to lead programmer. Figure 8-48 illustrates additional advancement paths.

Try It!

The U.S. Bureau of Labor Statistics (BLS) publishes annual reports containing salary data for tech sector jobs. You can also find data at Web sites such as Salary.com or Payscale.com. Can you find the median pay for an information security analyst?

QuickCheck

Entry-level positions in an IT department are typically designated as

_____.

a. associate

b. analyst

c. lead

d. senior

Figure 8-48: Career advancement paths

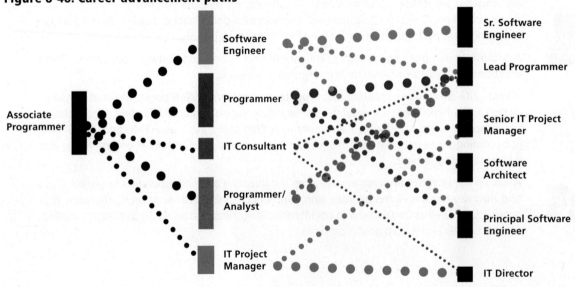
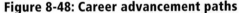

8

▶ **What are the advantages of working in the IT industry?** Many technology companies offer employee-friendly working conditions that include child care, flexible hours, and the opportunity to work from home. As in any industry, the exact nature of a job depends on the company and the particular projects that are in the works. Jobs and projects in some companies are more interesting than others (Figure 8-49).

Figure 8-49: IT workplaces reflect corporate cultures

IBM London   Google Dublin

▶ **What are the demographics of tech workers?** A disproportionate percentage of U.S. tech professionals self-identify as White, Asian, and Asian-Indian men, but tech companies are committed to increasing the number of workers from under-represented racial, gender, and ethnic groups.

Worker demographics vary significantly by occupation even within tech sector jobs. For example, a well-known tech company may claim that women are 40% of its workforce, but a closer look reveals that women are only 25% of its technical workforce, which means that a significant number of female employees hold non-technical sales, clerical, or service jobs.

Workplace demographics have become a complex and controversial issue. Although most tech companies are committed to a diverse workforce, qualified applicants from under-represented groups are sometimes difficult to find. Women earn fewer than 20% of computer science degrees. Less than 10% of computer science graduates are African American or Latinos. Both tech sector businesses and educational institutions are seeking ways to boost participation of under-represented groups.

▶ **What about part-time or contract work?** As with other industries, IT employs full-time, part-time, and contract workers. A **contract worker** is hired as a consultant. Contract workers are not official employees of a company. They might be paid by the job, rather than by the hour; they are not eligible for a company's health insurance benefits or retirement plan, and they must pay self-employment taxes.

IT businesses benefit from the ability to hire contract workers. The pool of IT contract workers offers a selection of people with specialized skills. Contract workers can be added to a company's staff when needed, instead of hiring full-time workers who might later be laid off if the company is forced to downsize.

Try It!

In movies, workplaces at tech companies such as Facebook and Apple are depicted as gadget-filled play areas. Is that reality? Search online for **recruitment videos tech companies** to see how these companies present their corporate cultures.

QuickCheck

As a contract worker, you would be _____.

a. an employee of the contracting company

b. responsible for your own healthcare insurance

c. exempt from employment taxes

d. laid off if the company downsizes

▶ Can I work at an IT job from home? Workers in many industries are interested in becoming **telecommuters** who use available technology to work from home or an off-site location. Telecommuters tend to be more productive and work longer hours because they have no commute time and they are not interrupted by routine office chatter. When fuel prices are high, telecommuting looks even more attractive to workers who can save money by avoiding long commutes.

Telecommuting does have its disadvantages. Some workers need supervision or they procrastinate. The home environment can be distracting, which reduces productivity. Security is also a concern—especially the security of data transmitted from home-based workers to corporate networks. Virtual private networks, encryption, and secure connections are essential for protecting business data transmitted over the Internet.

The Internet and telecommunications technologies have made an impact on the availability of telecommuting opportunities for workers. It has become common for employees to collaborate through email, fax, groupware, and videoconferencing. Although the majority of IT workers still commute to work, the success of remote work during the 2020 pandemic encouraged many employers to consider alternatives to in-office work.

▶ How do I find an IT job? Finding a job in the IT industry is similar to finding a job in most other industries. Effective job seekers begin by taking stock of their qualifications, identifying job titles relevant to their skills, identifying potential employers, and considering the geographic area in which they want to work.

Networking, both in person and online, is important. Job seekers should maximize their use of LinkedIn and similar social networking tools. In addition to mega job sites, such as Monster and Indeed, several smaller sites that specialize in tech job listings include Dice, Stack Overflow, GitHub Jobs, and CrunchBoard (Figure 8-50).

Figure 8-50: IT job listings online

Source: Dice.com

Education

Michael Dell, founder of Dell Computer Corporation. Bill Gates, founder of Microsoft. Larry Ellison, founder of database giant Oracle. Mark Zuckerberg, founder of Facebook. Steve Jobs, co-founder of Apple Computer Co. All of these successful entrepreneurs dropped out of college—but matching their achievements would require a huge helping of talent and a lot of luck. In case your great idea for an app doesn't take off, it is best to have some educational credentials that will impress recruiters.

▶ **Do I need a computer science degree?** Computer science is only one of many computer-related degrees that colleges and universities offer. According to the Association for Computing Machinery (ACM), there are five major computing disciplines, as described in Figure 8-51.

QuickCheck

If you are interested in working for a law enforcement agency performing computer forensics, which computing discipline would offer the best preparation?

a. Software engineering

b. Computer engineering

c. Information technology

d. Information systems

8

Figure 8-51: ACM computing disciplines

Degree	Curriculum	Careers
Computer engineering focuses on the design of computer hardware and peripheral devices, often at the chip level.	This degree involves basic studies in calculus, chemistry, engineering, physics, computer organization, logic design, computer architecture, microprocessor design, and signal processing. Students learn how to design new computer circuits, microchips, and other electronic components, plus they learn how to design new computer instruction sets and combine electronic or optical components to provide powerful, cost-effective computing.	Working at a chip manufacturer, such as Intel, Motorola, IBM, AMD, or Texas Instruments.
Computer science focuses on computer architecture and how to program computers to make them work effectively and efficiently.	This degree involves courses in programming, algorithms, software development, computer architecture, data representation, logic design, calculus, discrete math, and physics. Students investigate the fundamental theories of how computers solve problems, and they learn how to write application programs, system software, computer languages, and device drivers.	Computer programmers, with good possibilities for advancement to software engineers, object-oriented/GUI developers, and project managers in technical applications development. Also, theorists, inventors, and researchers in fields as diverse as artificial intelligence, virtual reality, and computer games.
Information systems degree programs, typically offered by a university's college of business, focus on applying computers to business problems.	This degree involves coursework in business, accounting, computer programming, communications, systems analysis, and human psychology. This degree is recommended for students who want to become computer professionals but lack strong math aptitude.	Programming or technical support jobs, with good possibilities for advancement to systems analyst, project manager, database administrator, network manager, or other management positions.
Information technology degree programs focus on computer equipment and software used by businesses.	This degree involves hands-on coursework with hardware, networks, Web pages, multimedia, email systems, and security.	Network specialists and administrators, systems analysts, forensic technicians, and help desk technicians.
Software engineering takes a disciplined approach to developing software that is reliable, efficient, affordable, user-friendly, and scalable.	This degree involves studying statistics, software design, programming, systems analysis, and courses from information systems and computer science curricula.	Programmers, analysts, or managers on large-scale, safety-critical applications.

▶ What are the basic qualifications for IT industry jobs? Qualifications for most IT industry jobs include some type of higher education, certification, and computer experience. A bachelor's degree in a computer-related discipline is the most prevalent requirement, but some employers accept a two-year associate's degree.

▶ What kinds of computer jobs require only an associate's degree? Colleges, community colleges, and technical schools offer computer-related associate's degrees ranging from computer programming to computer graphics, networking, and telecommunications.

The curriculum for these programs varies from one degree program to another, but all tend to require intensive course work. Graduates of two-year programs commonly find employment as entry-level technicians, programmers, and support personnel. Advancement opportunities might be limited, however, without additional education or certification.

▶ Do I need a graduate degree? A master's degree in computer science is available at most colleges and universities that offer graduate degrees. Another option at the graduate level is to pursue a master's degree in information systems or a master's degree in business administration (MBA). Any of these graduate degrees would help you get a management position in the computer industry.

Doctoral degrees are available in software engineering, applications software engineering, systems software development, and management information systems. A doctoral degree in any of these areas would qualify you for advanced technical research or for a position as a college professor. The graph in Figure 8-52 shows which IT professions tend to require higher levels of educational attainment.

Figure 8-52: Educational attainment in IT professions

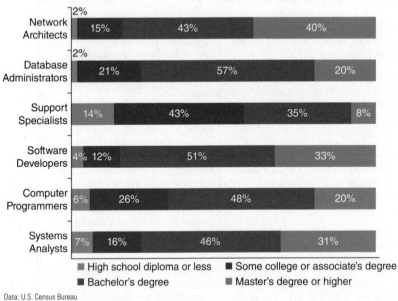

Data: U.S. Census Bureau

QuickCheck

In Figure 8-52, which computing profession has the highest number of employees with advanced degrees?

a. Systems analysts

b. Support specialists

c. Database administrators

d. Network architects

Certification

According to a study by resume specialists, recruiters spend an average of six seconds looking at a resume before deciding to reject it or save it for further consideration. That gives applicants little time to make an impression. By adding computer-related certifications to solid educational credentials, some job seekers hope to make the cut.

▶ **How important is certification?** Certification alone is rarely sufficient to qualify for a job in the IT industry. However, several studies suggest that certification paired with a college degree or extensive experience can improve your chances for employment, increase your credibility in the workplace, and lead to higher salaries.

Many employers view certification with some degree of skepticism, however, so the value of a certificate depends on where, when, and how it is obtained. Critics of certification exams, for example, maintain that a multiple-choice test cannot accurately measure a person's ability to deal with real-world equipment and software. Bottom line: Certification is only part of your total package of qualifications.

▶ **How do I get certified?** Certificates are awarded based on successful completion of an exam that verifies your level of knowledge about a particular technology or subject. Most of these exams use multiple-choice format, last several hours, and require substantial testing fees. Some certification exams also have a practical component that requires candidates to demonstrate skills.

▶ **How do I prepare?** You can prepare for a certification exam with independent study materials, an exam preparation class, or online tutorials such as those from CompTIA (Figure 8-53).

8

QuickCheck

Which of the following is the best all-around qualification for a tech sector job?

a. Bachelor's degree in computer science

b. Code Academy certificate

c. Microsoft network certification

d. Associate's degree in information technology

Figure 8-53: Prepare for certification online

Source: CompTIA, Inc.

What kind of certification is available? Hundreds of computer-related certification exams are offered in areas of specialty that range from desktop publishing to network installation. Certification exams can be divided into several categories, including the following:

General computer knowledge. IC3 certification, offered by Certiport, covers basic computing knowledge and skills. A general assessment of basic programming skills is also offered by the College Board's Accuplacer Computer Skills Placement (CSP).

The Institute for the Certification of Computing Professionals (ICCP) offers generalized certification exams, such as the Information Systems Core, leading to Certified Computing Professional certification. The organization also offers certification for computer scientists, application developers, IT consultants, and systems analysts.

Software applications. Many certification exams allow you to demonstrate your prowess with a specific software application. The Microsoft Office Specialist (MOS) certification is perhaps the most popular, but of limited value to most computer professionals who are expected to be able to quickly learn such applications on their own. Certification in productivity applications is most valuable for entry-level secretarial and clerical positions as well as help desk personnel.

Certiport offers the AutoCAD Certified User exam on the use of Autodesk 3D design software. Certification is also available for popular Adobe software applications, such as Illustrator, InDesign, Photoshop, Dreamweaver, and Premiere Pro.

Database administration. Databases require a high level of expertise, not only in the use of database software, but also in the conception and design of database structures. Many computer professionals have sought certification in database systems, such as Oracle, Access, SQL, Sybase, and DB2.

Networking and cloud. Among computer professionals, network and cloud certification might be the most useful. Network hardware certification includes the Cisco Certified Network Professional (CCNP), offered by network equipment supplier Cisco Systems. Cloud certification includes Amazon Web Services Certified Solutions Architect, CompTIA Cloud Essentials+, and Microsoft's Azure certification suite.

Computer hardware. One of the most popular computer hardware certifications is CompTIA's A+ Certification. This certification process is designed to measure the competency of entry-level computer service technicians for installing, configuring, upgrading, troubleshooting, and repairing personal computer systems. A+ Certification provides good credentials for employment in a computer store or computer repair shop.

Computer security. With the proliferation of computer viruses and worms, computer security has become a hot niche for IT workers. The CompTIA Security+ Certification is well regarded. The (ISC)^2 and Microsoft offer several security and compliance certifications.

❽

◗ **Are there additional useful credentials?** Educational credentials are just the starting point. Every other graduate in your field will have similar credentials. With a little effort, a few extracurricular activities can help you build a set of unique qualifications. Figure 8-54 offers some ideas for developing your personal brand.

Figure 8-54: Beyond formal training and certification

AP Exam

Students who pass the AP Computer Science exam in high school have a head start on their college-level courses and may increase their chances of acceptance into an elite computer science program.

Open Source Projects

Participants in open source community projects get experience and make connections with other professionals that can be valuable resources during a job hunt. You can find projects at GitHub, SourceForge, OpenHatch, and Open Hub.

Internships

Internships are resume builders. Look for opportunities during summer break or for an after-school job. Working in the field before graduating adds relevant work experience to your list of qualifications.

Badges

Badges are inspired by videogame awards and achievement patches earned by participating in scouting organizations. Online education providers, such as Khan Academy and OpenStudy, offer badges to students who complete various milestones.

Nanodegrees

Nanodegrees are awarded upon completion of one or more targeted online courses. These offshoots of MOOCs (massive open online courses) offer self-study training to career-minded individuals who might not have the time or means to complete a traditional degree program.

Try It!

How would you score on the AP Computer Science exam? Search for **AP Computer Science Practice test**. Varsity Tutors has a practice test that requires no sign-up. Have your binary calculator ready!

Resumes

Some large corporations use computer algorithms to sift through mountains of job applications and extract a select few that meet a set of exacting specifications. Recruiters cruise LinkedIn and other social media sites. And corporate computers link to online job databases to compile a short list of promising candidates. Job seekers have to cover a lot of bases these days.

▶ **What's the best format for an effective resume?** There is no "best" format for resumes in today's job market. Job seekers need to produce resumes in a variety of formats, including the following:

Print. You should save one version of your resume as a beautifully formatted word processing file. You might consider using desktop publishing software to put the finishing touches on your resume before printing it on high-quality paper. Make sure that you can output the file that holds your resume into a PDF that can be read on either a Mac or a PC in case a prospective employer asks you to send it as an email attachment.

Email. Before sending your resume as an attachment, try to discover the format that is easiest for your prospective employer to use. PDF is a universally accepted format. Microsoft's DOCX format is also widely used.

Some career counselors advise against the use of email attachments, suggesting that many employers never open attachments for fear of email viruses. Instead of attaching your resume, you can simply paste it into the body of an email message. To make sure it is formatted for maximum readability, consider creating an ASCII version of your resume, without fancy fonts, bullets, or symbols. This ASCII version might also be useful for online job posting sites that store your resume information in a searchable database.

HTML. You might consider creating an HTML version of your resume. You can paste the HTML version into an email message or post it on a Web site provided by your school or ISP.

LinkedIn. Your LinkedIn account can serve as a resume, so make sure that it is fully populated with your career data.

Online job service. Resume formats for online services vary. Some accept uploaded resumes in PDF or DOCX formats, while others store a job seeker's credentials in a series of database fields. When using an online service, take the time to learn about all the resume options it offers.

Web portfolio. A **Web portfolio** is a hypertext version of your resume, which might contain links to relevant Web sites, such as those from past employers, your alma mater, and sites that show samples of your work. For example, a programmer might include a link to one of her particularly well-documented and elegant programs, or a Web designer might provide links to sites that he designed.

You can post your Web portfolio on your personal Web site. As an alternative, you can create a blog with links to your work. By searching online, you can find tips and tools for creating your own effective online portfolio.

QuickCheck

Which resume format is most versatile?

a. HTML

b. ASCII

c. DOCX

d. PDF

> **Should an IT industry resume contain any special elements?**

Regardless of the industry in which you seek employment, an effective resume is clear, correct, and easy to read. Recruiters spend 80% of their time looking for the following resume items: applicant's name, current job title and company, previous job title and company, job start and end dates, and education. Make sure these items stand out on your resume so they are easy to find. Figure 8-55 shows a short checklist of resume writing guidelines.

Figure 8-55: Tips for effective resumes

Be clear and concise.

Eliminate unnecessary words, phrases, and sentences.

Be efficient with words when describing tasks, duties, titles, and accomplishments.

Be brief and to the point without selling yourself short.

Place the most important point first.

List your qualifications by importance and relevance to the job you seek.

Summarize skills at the top of the resume.

Use a bold font to emphasize skills and accomplishments that are required for the position you seek.

Include pertinent information about training, certification, and professional affiliations, but avoid personal information, such as religious affiliation and hobbies, that is not directly related to the job.

Use language effectively.

Target terms and wording to prospective employers.

Use industry jargon wherever appropriate.

Use action verbs to maintain the reader's interest.

Use past and present tenses consistently.

Double-check grammar and spelling.

When posting information in a database, use nouns that describe your skills.

Try It!

How do we know what recruiters look for in resumes? Researchers use eye-tracking heatmaps. Marketers also use this technology when designing advertising images. Search online for **eye-tracking heatmap** to see examples of this fascinating technology.

8

QuickQuiz   Section D

1. The term **computer professional** was defined in an amendment to the Fair Labor Standards Act of 1999. True or false? [   ]

2. [   ] workers are usually paid by the job, rather than by the hour, and are not officially employees of the company for which they work.

3. A student who wants to work with computers but does not have a strong aptitude for math might find a good fit by pursuing a(n) [   ] systems degree.

4. IC3 and CompTIA Cloud Essentials+ are examples of computer [   ] exams.

5. The job title for an entry-level programmer is likely to be [   ] programmer.

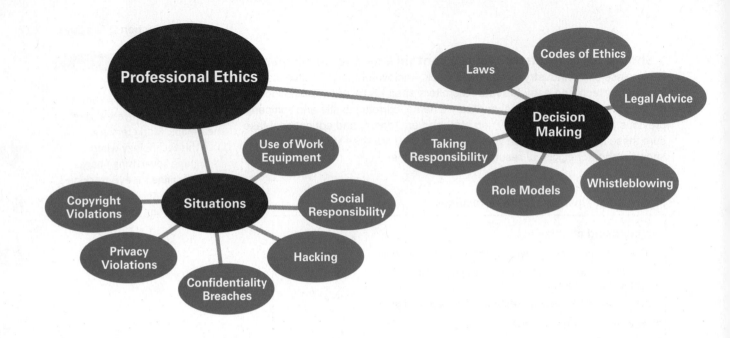

Objectives

▶ List at least five significant areas of information technology law.

▶ Explain the purpose of the following: Computer Fraud and Abuse Act, Electronic Communications Privacy Act, Communications Decency Act, Digital Millennium Copyright Act, and USA PATRIOT Act.

▶ Supply an example of an ethical dilemma that involves copyright.

▶ Supply examples of ethical dilemmas that involve privacy and confidentiality.

▶ Explain what technology professionals should consider before using resources at work for their personal projects.

▶ Explain the context in which technology professionals have social responsibility.

▶ List five resources for ethical decision making.

▶ Provide at least three examples of whistleblowing related to information technology.

▶ Explain the ethical dilemma faced by whistleblowers.

Decisions, decisions. Not all of them are easy, especially when confronted with a task on the job that doesn't seem completely legal or socially responsible. What should you do? Rock the boat and risk your job, or remain quiet and go with the flow? Section E gives you a heads up on some of the sticky problems that can arise in technology workplaces.

Terminology

information technology
   law

professional ethics
confidentiality

proprietary information
non-compete clause

code of ethics
whistleblowing

ICT Laws

Laws are legislated documentation of permissible behavior based on a community's ethics. As computers and digital technologies play a more central role in every aspect of daily life, laws have been created to deal with computer uses and abuses.

▶ What is information technology law? Information technology law is the legal framework that applies to the collection, storage, and distribution of digital information. Technology is governed by laws that existed long before computers were invented. Libel laws, for example, pertain to false and personally damaging statements regardless of whether they are published in print or online.

Laws and regulations have been specifically written to deal with problems generated by emerging digital technologies. For example, the Computer Fraud and Abuse Act, passed in 1996, makes it a crime to access a computer and the data it contains without authorization. This law was necessary because existing theft laws did not adequately cover theft of digital data that can be "stolen" yet still remain in the possession of the original owner.

Most technology laws attempt to sort out controversies by answering questions about what is allowed and what is not. Some of the most significant areas of information technology law include the following:

Copyright and intellectual property. Are mashups transformative or derivative works? Can libraries make copyrighted works available online?

Domain names. Who moderates domain name disputes? Is it legal to buy and sell domain names? Should domain names for trademarks be available to someone other than the trademark holder?

Patents. Are software patents socially beneficial, or should software be copyrighted instead? Can inventors obtain a patent for an idea such as one-click purchases?

Cybercrime. What is the legal definition of cyberbullying? Is it a crime to masquerade as someone else on social media sites? Are digital currencies, such as Bitcoin, legal or are they examples of counterfeiting?

Software and computer contracts. Are digital signatures legally binding? If consumers click "I agree" when installing software, have they entered into a legal contract?

Privacy. Is it constitutional for the National Security Agency (NSA) to collect private communications without a search warrant? Should privately controlled drones be allowed to take photographs through home and office windows? Under what circumstances can individuals be forced to reveal their passwords to law enforcement agents?

Communication. Can hotels use jamming devices to prevent guests from using their own Wi-Fi hotspots? Can a university block a student-run faculty evaluation Web site? Should government employees be fired for speaking out on social media? Should sexting be illegal?

Laws relating to technology vary from country to country. Figure 8-56 on the next page provides a brief overview of the most significant technology laws and court decisions in the United States.

Figure 8-56: Key U.S. information technology laws and legal decisions

United States Copyright Act (1976) extends copyright protection beyond print media to "original works of authorship fixed in any tangible medium of expression, now known or later developed, from which they can be perceived, reproduced, or otherwise communicated, either directly or with the aid of a machine or device."

Fair Use Doctrine, a part of the U.S. Copyright Act, generally allows copying if it is for educational or personal use, if only a portion of the original work is copied, and if it does not have a substantial effect on the market for the original work.

Sony Corp. v. Universal City Studios (1984) sets a precedent that companies are not liable for user infringements, such as using VCRs to make unauthorized copies of videotapes, so long as the technology has valid, non-infringing uses, such as copying personal home videos. In recent cases, the defense for peer-to-peer file sharing networks was based on this decision.

Computer Fraud and Abuse Act (1986, amended in 1994, 1996, 2001, and USA PATRIOT Act) makes it a criminal offense to knowingly access a computer without authorization; transmit a program, information, a code, or a command that causes damage; or distribute passwords that would enable unauthorized access.

Electronic Communications Privacy Act (1986) extends telephone wiretap laws by restricting government agents and unauthorized third parties from tapping into data transmissions without a search warrant. The law does not apply to data, such as email, transmitted on employer-owned equipment.

Health Insurance Portability and Accountability Act (1996) requires healthcare providers to take reasonable procedural and technical safeguards to insure the confidentiality of individually identifiable health information.

Communications Decency Act (1996) protects ISPs from liability for defamatory statements made by customers. Prohibits material deemed offensive by local community standards from being transmitted to minors. The latter section was overturned in 2002.

Digital Millennium Copyright Act (1998) makes it illegal to circumvent copy-protection technologies, such as those used to prevent unauthorized copying of software CDs, music CDs, and movie DVDs. In addition, it is illegal to distribute any type of software-cracking technology that would be used by others to circumvent copy protection. Protects ISPs against copyright infringement by subscribers if the ISP takes prompt action to block the infringement as soon as it discovers illegal activity.

Children's Online Privacy Protection Act (1998) regulates the types of data that can be collected and posted online with regard to children under the age of 13.

Gramm-Leach-Bliley Act (1999) requires financial institutions to protect the confidentiality and security of customers' personal information.

Children's Internet Protection Act (2000) requires schools and libraries that receive federal funds to implement filtering software that protects adults and minors from obscenity and pornography.

USA PATRIOT Act (2001) enhances the authority of law enforcement agents to preempt potential terrorist acts by various means, such as monitoring electronic communications without first obtaining a search warrant in situations where there is imminent danger. Offers safe harbor to ISPs that voluntarily disclose potentially threatening activities of users. Increases maximum penalties for hackers.

Homeland Security Act (2002) establishes a Department of Homeland Security with an agency to monitor threats to the communications infrastructure, including the Internet, and exempts from the Privacy Act any information about infrastructure vulnerabilities to terrorism submitted by individuals or non-federal agencies.

Sarbanes-Oxley Act (2002) establishes financial reporting regulations to prevent corporate fraud. Requires full disclosure in accounting systems and protects corporate whistleblowers.

CAN-SPAM Act (2003) establishes national standards for sending commercial email by requiring senders to use a valid subject line, include the sender's legitimate physical address, and provide an opt-out mechanism.

Green v. America Online (2003) interprets sections of the Communications Decency Act to mean that ISPs are not responsible for malicious software transmitted over their services by hackers.

MGM v. Grokster (2005) refines the precedent set in the 1984 **Sony Corp. v. Universal City Studios** case. Companies that actively encourage infringement, as seemed to be true of peer-to-peer file sharing networks such as Grokster, can be held accountable for user infringement.

Authors Guild v. HathiTrust (2014) allows Google and local libraries to copy and store millions of copyrighted works and display their contents in the context of search engine results.

ICT Ethics

Although most laws are designed to promote ethical behavior, laws and ethics are not necessarily the same. Some behaviors are legal, but not necessarily ethical. Some laws are not ethical or their ethics are controversial. An act isn't ethical simply because it is permissible or you can get away with it. An ethical person often chooses to do more than the law requires and less than the law allows.

▶ What are professional ethics? The term **professional ethics** refers to on-the-job choices and actions that reflect a person's values. Professional ethics are derived from principles of right and wrong. In most modern societies, the foundation for ethical decisions and actions is based on values such as impartiality, fairness, objectivity, honesty, regard for privacy, commitment to quality, and respect for others.

Professional ethics define standards of conduct that specify how workers should behave, particularly in situations where doing the right thing might not have short-term rewards, or when doing something of questionable legality seems to offer attractive benefits. Situations like the one in Figure 8-57, in which you ask yourself "What's the right thing to do?", often require ethical decisions.

▶ Why are professional ethics important for IT workers? Most computer professionals take pride in their work and strive to offer excellent products and services that benefit consumers. Sometimes, however, computer professionals have to cope with ethical dilemmas in which the right course of action is not entirely clear, or in which the right course of action is clear, but the consequences—such as getting fired—are not easy to face.

Ethical dilemmas in the workplace are more common than you might imagine. It is likely that you'll find yourself in an ethical quandary about some aspect of your job even before you've completed your first year. Some situations that call for an ethical decision don't require an immediate response, so you can take some time to think about what you'll do. Other situations require an immediate response. In those situations, you'll be less likely to take action that you'll later regret if you have considered potentially compromising situations ahead of time and have prepared some general guidelines you can use if necessary.

▶ What kinds of situations in an IT career might require ethical decisions? Situations that require computer professionals to make ethical decisions often involve software copyrights, privacy, conflict of interest, use of work computers, software quality, hacking, and social responsibility.

Sometimes, computer professionals are pressured to participate in activities that may be illegal or unethical. These marginal activities are sometimes justified with statements such as "Everyone does it," or "No one will know." Employees might be assured that "You won't be responsible," or "It's for the good of the company." However, such justifications are not always true or appropriate.

Outside of corporate IT departments, individual entrepreneurs sometimes get caught up in unethical activities because they make bad judgments or have not done their homework regarding applicable laws and regulations.

8

Figure 8-57: Copyright issues

Helen King/The Image Bank/Getty Images

❯ How would software copyrights become an ethical issue? Most computer professionals are familiar with the general principles of copyright law and the provisions of the Digital Millennium Copyright Act. They understand it is illegal to make unauthorized copies of software and other copyrighted media, such as commercial music and movies. Programmers, Web designers, and other creative professionals tend to respect intellectual property and try to adhere to copyright laws and license agreements. Tech workers are sometimes asked to install software or post copyrighted material that is not properly licensed.

Managers are not always familiar with current copyright restrictions or choose to ignore them. Computer professionals should stay up to date on current copyright law that applies to software and other digital media. Asking for a copy of a software license agreement is considered standard practice and can help resolve questions about the legality of copying software for use in multiple-user installations.

❯ What kinds of ethical issues pertain to privacy? It is ethical to respect the privacy of others, but business practices can clash with privacy rights. Network technicians occasionally see the content of email messages or files in the course of system maintenance or troubleshooting.

Most professionals simply try to forget what they see. However, computer professionals sometimes come across a file or an email message that's troubling. It might be a message from an employee who is corresponding with a competing company about a job offer. More seriously, a message might divulge proprietary information to the competitor, harass another employee, or describe plans for other illegal activities. If your employer has no guidelines for reporting suspicious activities, you'll have to make your own decision about what kinds of information are serious threats.

Computers are increasingly used to monitor employee activities. RFID chips embedded in ID badges can be used to track employee locations in an office or manufacturing facility. Keystroke monitors, random samples of active programs, Web browsing history, network logs, and email volume offer additional ways to monitor employee activities. Some surveillance is done with employee knowledge and consent, such as when it is clearly explained in an employment contract or company policy. Other surveillance is surreptitious.

Either way, surveillance is set up by someone, often a programmer or network administrator. How would you respond if you were asked to set up a remote monitoring system like the one in Figure 8-58?

Employees—particularly computer professionals—should be familiar with laws and company policy applicable to privacy. Privacy laws differ from one country to the next, and most companies have unique privacy policies. Rather than assume you know the rules, check applicable documents before you take action.

Figure 8-58: Privacy rights

Comstock Images/Alamy stock photo

Try It!

Imagine that you're a programmer for a local public school district that is distributing laptop computers to students. One day, the superintendent of schools calls you into her office and explains that the district needs some way to locate laptops that might be misplaced or stolen. She asks if you can write a utility that will remotely activate laptop cameras. You think it would be fairly easy for you to write such remote monitoring software. You realize, however, that the software could be used to secretly monitor students. You ask the superintendent if students and parents would be aware of the monitoring software, and she replies, "What they don't know won't hurt them." What would you do?

a. I would write the program.

b. I'd write the program, but start a rumor that monitoring software is being used to remotely activate cameras on laptops.

c. I'd pretend that it was technically impossible to write such software.

d. I would tell the superintendent that such a surveillance system would violate students' Fourth Amendment rights.

▶ How is confidentiality associated with ethical dilemmas?

Confidentiality is the obligation not to disclose willingly any information that should be kept private. Confidentiality rights apply to individuals and organizations. With respect to individuals, confidentiality means not disclosing names and associated data from databases or other information repositories.

Laws in most countries restrict the disclosure of an individual's medical or financial information. Marketers, however, currently take advantage of gray areas in these laws to use names, addresses, and phone numbers collected with consent on forms, applications, and Web sites. The ethics of such practices are doubtful.

With respect to organizations, confidentiality means protecting **proprietary information** about company finances, procedures, products, and research that competitors would find valuable. Computer professionals can find themselves in compromising situations where they are asked to disclose confidential information gathered while employed in previous jobs.

Job mobility is one of the perks of a hot career field. The skills you pick up on one job can increase your qualifications for other jobs. For example, you might learn about multimedia production while working for an educational software company, and those skills could provide you with qualifications to switch to a higher-paying and more challenging job working for an online game company.

Using your skills as a springboard to a new job is perfectly acceptable, but disclosing confidential information is not ethical in most situations, such as the one in Figure 8-59.

Figure 8-59: Confidentiality

Stephen Simpson/Stone/Getty Images

Try It!

Suppose you take a new job and then discover that your new employer—an online game company—wants you to lead the team that creates its first educational product, which sounds suspiciously like a rip-off of your old employer's best-selling software. What would you do?

a. I would risk my job by refusing to do it.

b. I would do it.

Many employment contracts contain a **non-compete clause** designed to prevent employees from divulging proprietary information to competitors or opening competing businesses. Non-compete clauses can extend beyond the period of employment and can remain in effect for a specified time after you leave a job. Most non-compete clauses, however, fail to delineate exactly what information cannot be divulged, so ex-employees are forced to make ethical decisions about competitive information.

To avoid compromising situations, you can check the business plans of prospective employers so that you won't be working on projects that compete directly with those at your previous place of employment. You can also have a frank discussion with your new boss to outline the boundaries of the knowledge you are able to share from your old job.

▶ **Can I get into trouble by using my work computer for personal activities?** When surveyed, a majority of computer professionals admit that they see no problem using their work computers for personal activities as long as it has no adverse effect on the employer.

It seems innocent enough to send and receive personal email over your account at work or place bids on an online auction, especially if you do so during your lunch hour. Maybe it also seems okay to use your corporate email server to send bulk mail to raise money for a private, nonprofit relief organization. Your employer might not agree, however.

There is a temptation to use computers, copiers, and network connections at work for personal activities; the equipment is convenient and usually cutting edge. Most companies have explicit policies about what is and what is not acceptable use. Some policies are strict, but designed to prevent conflicts like the one in Figure 8-60.

It is never a good idea to use facilities at work for personal activities unless you have a specific agreement with your employer and your activities do not breach your employment contract. Some employment contracts have restrictions pertaining to intellectual property. In the most restrictive contracts, anything employees develop at work or at home using on-the-job equipment or knowledge gained during their tenure of employment belongs to the company.

If your contract does not limit outside development, you might still have to make an ethical decision about what rightfully belongs to your company and what you created outside of your company's sphere of influence.

▶ **Why would I get involved in hacking?** Computer professionals have to keep up with the latest threats from viruses and intrusion attempts, but this familiarity can be a double-edged sword.

Most computing students learning about virus and intrusion countermeasures become more than a little curious about these technologies. "Is it really so easy to design and launch viruses?" they wonder. "Are passwords easy to crack? Do I have the skill to do it?" Pursuing these questions can get students and computer professionals into sticky ethical situations like the one in Figure 8-61.

Figure 8-60: Personal use

David Ellis/Getty Images

Try It!

Suppose you spend lunch hours writing an iPhone app for a friend. You post the app and it becomes a bestseller, but your employer claims to own your software because you used company computers to develop it. What should you have done differently?

a. I should have read the employee computer use policy.

b. I should have pretended that I developed the app at home.

Figure 8-61: Legitimate hacking

Silvia Bukovac/Shutterstock.com

Try It!

In the course of your computing career, you might be tempted to try some passwords at a protected site. What if you get in?

a. I would poke around.

b. I would notify the system administrator that the network password is not secure, even if I have to admit to illegal hacking.

▶ **Am I responsible for software quality?** Most computer professionals believe that software should be thoroughly tested to produce the most reliable and accurate product possible. But what if you encounter a situation like the one in Figure 8-62?

Software development is an incredibly complex undertaking. Bugs are virtually impossible to completely eradicate, so most companies have policies that guide developers on the number, severity, and type of bugs that are acceptable when the software ships to customers. Although developers, managers, and marketers are supposed to be governed by these policies, software testing cycles are sometimes cut short when deadlines loom. Computer professionals working on such projects should speak out when serious risks to users might result.

▶ **Am I responsible for how my work is used?** Technology may be neutral in and of itself, but technology can be put to use in both positive and negative ways.

Some IT projects are not socially responsible. For example, society would be better off without spam and viruses. Filtering software and monitoring software can be misused. If you are assigned to a project of questionable social value like the one in Figure 8-63, you might have to make an ethical decision about whether to participate or look for another job.

Decisions pertaining to social responsibility are not always easy. Members of a project team might not be supplied with enough information to make value judgments about the projects to which they are assigned.

Laws and court decisions sometimes conflict with regard to whether programmers and members of software development teams are responsible for the way their software is used. In **Sony Corp. v. Universal City Studios**, the U.S. Supreme Court set a precedent that Sony was not responsible when individuals used Sony Betamax recording technology to make and distribute illegal copies of movies. When applied to the IT industry, the Sony case seemed to absolve software developers from any illegal actions taken by users.

However, the Digital Millennium Copyright Act explicitly states that it is illegal to produce any product that allows individuals to circumvent copyright law or copy protection methods. Therefore, a programmer who produces software to crack video copy protection can be held responsible when individuals use it to make illegal copies of movies.

Court decisions aside, technology professionals have an ethical responsibility to use their skills to benefit society, rather than create products that may cause harm.

Figure 8-62: Quality assurance

John Foxx/The Print Collector/Alamy stock photo

Try It!

Suppose your project team has spent the better part of a year developing a new software product. The project is scheduled for release in four weeks; but to meet the deadline, you'll have to cut testing time in half. The team leader tells you to pare down the testing plan to the bare minimum. What would you do?

a. I'd do it, but only if the software was not life critical.

b. I would refuse to do it.

Figure 8-63: Do no harm

PeopleImages/Getty Images

Try It!

You've been assigned to a project team working on automated garment production software. You have an uneasy feeling about its benefits. Would you continue working on the project if you learned that it would displace thousands of garment workers?

a. Yes.

b. Yes, but only if the workers were not in this country.

c. I'd refuse to work on the project if I was sure that I could easily get another job.

d. No, I'd refuse to work on this project.

8

Ethical Decision Making

Ethical decisions that you make on the job can have long-term consequences for your career and lifestyle, so it is important to approach these decisions seriously.

▶ **How do I make ethical decisions?** Take time to think about your situation before responding or taking action. As you examine the immediate situation, make sure you have a good handle on your long-term and short-term career goals. Gather the information needed for a decision, and make sure the facts are credible. Use Web resources and legal services, if necessary, to check applicable laws.

With the facts in hand, list your options and consider the advantages and disadvantages of each one. For help in defining and evaluating your options, you can use strategies such as those listed below.

Talk to people whose judgment you respect. Mentors and responsible friends might be willing to help you evaluate your options. Your workplace might provide access to an arbitrator or a human resources counselor. Remember, however, that after you've gathered opinions and advice, you are ultimately responsible for the outcome of your decision.

Consider what the most ethical person you know would decide to do. Use a real-life person or fictional character who has strong values and impeccable ethical judgment as your decision-making role model and ask yourself what that person would do in your situation.

Think about what you would do if your actions were made public. Ask yourself how you would feel if you made a particular decision and everyone found out about it. Would you be proud or uncomfortable? Decisions that look good only if no one knows are usually wrong. When you've made a good decision, you should feel comfortable talking about it as long as it doesn't violate confidentiality.

Look at the problem from the opposite perspective. Put yourself in the place of other stakeholders, such as your boss, your clients, or consumers. How would you want to be treated if you were them?

Consult a code of professional ethics. The guidelines contained in a code of professional ethics might offer a suitable path of action.

▶ **What is a code of ethics?** A **code of ethics** is a set of guidelines designed to help professionals thread their way through a sometimes tangled web of ethical on-the-job decisions. A code of ethics can provide guidelines, but it might not offer ready answers to every dilemma that arises in the course of your career. When confronted with a difficult ethical decision, you should consider ethical guidelines, but also consider the policies of your workplace and relevant laws.

QuickCheck

How does a code of ethics relate to laws that pertain to the use and abuse of information technology?

a. Laws are usually more strict than ethical codes.

b. Laws are usually easier to understand than ethical codes.

c. Both laws and ethical codes should be considered when making ethical decisions.

d. There is no need to check laws and regulations after consulting a code of ethics.

▶ What are the basic principles? Some codes of ethics are short and concise, whereas others are long and detailed. Most codes contain principles similar to those from the Computer Ethics Institute (CEI) (Figure 8-64).

Figure 8-64: Ethical principles from the Computer Ethics Institute

- Do not use a computer to harm other people.

- Do not interfere with other people's computer work.

- Do not snoop around in other people's files.

- Do not use a computer to steal.

- Do not use a computer to bear false witness.

- Do not use or copy software for which you have not paid.

- Do not use other people's computer resources without authorization.

- Do not appropriate other people's intellectual output.

- Think about the social consequences of the programs you write.

- Use a computer in ways that show consideration and respect.

8

▶ How useful are codes of ethics? Professional codes of ethics are not without controversy. For example, the code published by the Computer Ethics Institute has drawn fire from critics who suggest that it is too simplistic.

One of the last points in the CEI code states that you should "Think about the social consequences of the programs you write." That statement is valid, but what should you think about? This guideline does not offer helpful criteria for distinguishing between socially useful programs and those that might be damaging. When a code of ethics does not offer a complete solution, professionals might have to refer to other resources before making a decision.

Some codes of ethics attempt to offer more complete guidelines. Such a comprehensive approach can be useful, but it can sometimes add complexity to the decision-making process. For example, the Association for Computing Machinery Code of Ethics and Professional Conduct contains a guideline to know and respect rules that "include local, regional, national, and international laws and regulations, as well as any policies and procedures of the organizations to which the professional belongs."

The code goes on, however, to suggest that there are times when rules, laws, and policies might be justifiably violated: "Rules that are judged unethical should be challenged. A rule may be unethical when it has an inadequate moral basis or causes recognizable harm. A computing professional should consider challenging the rule through existing channels before violating the rule."

Ethical decisions can be difficult, and sometimes the results of those decisions—good or bad—are not apparent right away. A decision with immediate negative repercussions might have beneficial long-term advantages that you cannot foresee. Ultimately, a decision about the right course of action is yours, and you must be willing to take responsibility for the consequences of your decision.

QuickCheck

What does the ACM code of ethics say about the need to follow laws?

a. Technology professionals should always adhere to the letter of the law.

b. When technology professionals follow the ACM code of ethics, they don't have to study up on technology law.

c. Existing laws and rules are sometimes immoral and inappropriate and must be challenged.

d. Technology professionals do not bear responsibility as long as they follow the law.

Whistleblowing

Shawn Carpenter was a network security analyst working for Sandia National Laboratories. He stumbled upon a massive intrusion into U.S. government computer systems carried out by Chinese hackers. When Carpenter revealed his discovery, he was told to focus on his job. Ignoring the warning, Carpenter contacted Army Intelligence and then the FBI. Sandia fired Carpenter, and he became one more person in a long line of whistleblowers who act with the best of intentions, but are penalized for their efforts.

▶ **Should I blow the whistle on unethical practices?** A widely accepted definition of whistleblowing is the disclosure by an employee (or professional) of confidential information that relates to some danger, fraud, or other illegal or unethical conduct connected with the workplace, be it of the employer or of fellow employees.

A whistleblower is someone in an organization who decides to speak out against on-the-job activities that are contrary to the mission of the organization or threaten the public interest.

▶ **Is whistleblowing effective?**
Whistleblowers have focused public attention on corporate abuses at Enron and WorldCom. Edward Snowden made headlines in 2013 when he leaked information about covert government surveillance programs that violate the constitutional rights of citizens. Whistleblowers also revealed major problems in the way the FBI investigated potential terrorists prior to 9/11, and uncovered defects in the body armor supplied to the U.S. president and combat troops (Figure 8-65).

Figure 8-65: Defective vests

USAart studio/Shutterstock.com

▶ **Can whistleblowing be dangerous?**
Although whistleblowing might seem effective, the consequences of whistleblowing can be extreme. Even with strong legal protection under the 2002 Sarbanes-Oxley Act, whistleblowers are often fired or forced out of their jobs. If they keep their jobs, they might be excluded from promotions and shunned by coworkers. They are sometimes branded as tattletales and have difficulty finding other jobs in their career field.

In extreme cases, whistleblowers have been forced to seek refuge offered by sympathetic foreign governments. They also may be subject to arrest, especially if the information revealed pertains to national security.

▶ **Is there any way to safely blow the whistle on unethical practices?**
Whistleblowing is risky under any circumstances. For example, a computer system administrator working for a state agency noticed that a supervisor spent the majority of the workday playing solitaire on an office computer. After several email messages up the chain of command were ignored, the system administrator installed Win-Spy software, which grabbed incriminating screenshots of the supervisor's computer over a period of several months. When the system administrator showed this evidence to superiors, the admin was fired for violation of privacy. The supervisor received only a light reprimand.

QuickCheck

What is the major ethical dilemma associated with whistleblowing?

a. The information revealed is usually confidential.

b. The information is true and harmful.

c. The Sarbanes-Oxley Act makes whistleblowing a federal crime.

d. Most whistleblowers are rewarded.

As a whistleblower, the system administrator did some things right but missed some important measures that might have led to a more positive outcome. Employee advocates have the following suggestions for reducing the risk of career repercussions so often experienced by whistleblowers.

Examine your motives. Make sure your cause is significant. Don't act out of frustration or because you feel underappreciated or mistreated.

Try the normal chain of command. Before you blow the whistle, try to correct the problem by reporting up the normal chain of command. Consider every possible way to work within the system before you take your concerns public.

Collect evidence to back up your accusations. Gather documentary evidence that proves your case and keep it in a safe place. Do not break any laws while collecting evidence. Try to collect evidence before you draw attention to your concerns.

Record events as they unfold. Keep detailed, dated notes about events before and after you blow the whistle. Keep in mind that your notes might become public if they are used as evidence in a trial.

Act ethically. Do not embellish your case, and do not violate confidentiality agreements unless absolutely necessary. Engage in whistleblowing activities on your own time, not your employer's.

Be ready to accept repercussions. Think through the effect your actions might have on your family. Be prepared to be dismissed from your job and for the possibility that you might have difficulty finding another equivalent job in your field.

Establish a support network. Seek out potential allies, such as elected officials, journalists, and activists who can support your cause.

Consult a lawyer. Make sure you understand your rights as an employee.

Consider your strategy. You might reduce the risk of repercussions if you lodge your complaint anonymously or as part of a group.

As with other ethical decisions, your resolution to become a whistleblower can have a long-term effect on your career, family, and lifestyle. Think about your situation carefully and make use of whatever resources are available to you.

> **Try It!**
>
> Which one of the suggestions for whistleblowers do you think would be most difficult to follow?

8

QuickQuiz   Section E

1. Computer professionals sometimes have to make _____ decisions in situations where the right course of action is not clear.

2. Many aspects of law that pertain to computers, software, and intellectual property are included in the _____ Millennium Copyright Act.

3. Computer professionals know that it is important to maintain _____ and privacy for data that pertains to individuals.

4. Computer professionals sometimes have difficulty evaluating whether a project is socially _____ because project team members might not be given detailed information about a product's application.

5. A(n) _____ is someone in an organization who decides to speak out against on-the-job activities that are contrary to the mission of the organization or threaten the public interest.

Issue: Is Big Tech Too Big?

Amazon. Apple. Facebook. Google.

Microsoft. These are the companies most associated with Big Tech. Amazon accounts for more than one quarter of all online retail sales in the United States. Apple's market capitalization exceeds $2 trillion—more than Canada's GDP. Facebook has more users than the combined populations of the United States, China, and Brazil. Consumers turn to Google for more than 90% of online searches. Microsoft Windows is the operating system that powers more than 80% of computers.

There is growing sentiment from people of all political persuasions that Big Tech is just too big. Critics of Big Tech are concerned when companies monopolize a market. Critics are also concerned about the amount of data that is controlled by Big Tech, as well as the potential of these companies to control news and information that influence beliefs and actions.

Every Big Tech company has faced charges of violating antitrust laws using practices such as acquiring competitive companies, pre-installing apps, controlling app stores, and using third-party seller data to create house-branded competitive products.

For example, Facebook came under fire for acquiring WhatsApp and Instagram, two platforms that threatened to erode Facebook's dominance in social media.

Apple has been accused of pre-installing Apple apps, such as Apple Music on iPhones, a practice that might discourage users from downloading similar third-party apps, such as Spotify.

Google and Apple have both been charged with monopolistic practices based on their policies to take a cut of in-app purchases. Because the Apple App Store is essentially the only way for consumers to access iOS apps, app developers are forced to use that platform and have no choice but to follow Apple's policies. So, for example, you may download the Spotify app for free, but when you subscribe, Spotify must remit a percentage of your monthly payment to Apple.

> "Big Tech platforms engage in viewpoint discrimination at an unprecedented scale and scope ... determining what news, information and perspectives Americans are allowed to read, hear and access."
>
> Rachel Bovard writing in USA Today

Amazon faces antitrust allegations that it uses third-party seller data as the basis for creating competitive Amazon-branded products. For example, suppose that sales data indicates that lots of consumers are buying air fryers. Amazon may contract with a Chinese manufacturer to produce air fryers branded as Amazon Basics. Critics further allege that Amazon has monopoly power over its "partner" small and medium-sized businesses that do not have viable alternatives for reaching online customers.

Critics are wary of the tremendous amount of data that is under the control of Big Tech. Google, for example, holds exabytes of search-related data and has devised algorithms that track an individual's searching patterns to produce targeted advertising. Cloud services hold billions of files. Privacy advocates worry whether this data is adequately protected and how it might be misused.

It has become apparent that Big Tech is not averse to using its power to influence attitudes and beliefs. It has the power to silence disagreeable voices, to promote particular ideas, and to shut down bothersome viewpoints.

As evidenced by contributions to political campaigns, workers at tech companies are overwhelmingly Democrats, which has led some conservative advocacy groups to question whether algorithms for newsfeeds and similar information feeds might not present balanced viewpoints.

But it is not only conservatives who are concerned about the influence of Big Tech. A Pew Research study found that 72% of U.S. adults believe that social media companies have too much power and influence in politics, a belief that is shared by Republicans, independents, and Democrats.

The power of Big Tech to have a monopoly over ideas may be on a collision course with our democratic principles of free speech. It is a controversial topic that may not be easy to resolve, but one that should be on the radar of every person who uses online services.

Try It! The Internet and social media platforms have the potential to provide an inclusive channel for national debate. But, the freedom to engage in that debate has become controversial. As Big Tech consolidates its hold over social media platforms, free speech advocates are questioning practices that appear to discriminate against dissenting viewpoints.

1 Big Tech companies have been criticized for using their substantial financial resources to acquire businesses that pose potential competitive threats. Is this really the case? Wikipedia lists acquisitions for Google's parent company Alphabet, and for Twitter, Microsoft, Apple, and Facebook. Skim through those lists and summarize the types of acquisitions for each Big Tech company.

2 Legal challenges to perceived monopolistic practices of Big Tech companies are based on antitrust law. Use online resources to find the legal definitions of "monopoly" and "antitrust."

3 Social media platforms, such as Facebook and Twitter, have been accused of viewpoint discrimination through the use of algorithms that push certain viewpoints and suppress others. Critics claim that these practices violate the First Amendment right to free speech. To explore this controversy, do the following:

    a. Read the First Amendment to the U.S. Constitution to understand what it guarantees.

    b. Use online resources to list the limitations on freedom of speech.

    c. Read Section 230 of the 1996 Communications Decency Act. Does it hold social media platforms responsible for material that users post? Does it allow platforms to remove or restrict content that would otherwise be protected as free speech?

4 Cancel culture is a meme that emerged on social media during the Obama presidency and became prevalent during the Trump presidency. To explore this controversial practice, do the following:

    a. The Pew Research Center studied American attitudes toward cancel culture practices. Summarize the findings of Pew's study, which is titled "Americans and 'Cancel Culture': Where Some See Calls for Accountability, Others See Censorship, Punishment."

    b. In defense of free speech, a group of influencers in 2020 submitted an open letter to *Harper's Magazine* titled "A Letter on Justice and Open Debate" (often referred to as the "Harper's Letter").

    Summarize the main ideas of the letter. Describe the political viewpoints of the individuals who drafted the letter. Which of the 153 signatories do you recognize?

5 What is the current status of efforts to rein in Big Tech? Describe a recent law, regulation, or court decision that affects social media platforms.

What Do You Think?

Issue

1. Do you think that Big Tech is too big?

2. How do you respond to social media posts that don't correspond to your worldview?

3. Do you believe that cancel culture is an effective way to hold people accountable for their viewpoints and actions?

Information Tools: Provenance

If you've watched *Antiques Roadshow*, you know that the Beatles signed many album covers, which today are worth between $8,000 and $10,000. However, an album with the right provenance, such as the first American album cover signed by the Beatles before their debut on *The Ed Sullivan Show*, could be worth up to $150,000.

The term *provenance* refers to the origins of an object and its history. It is commonly used in the antique business, but it can also be applied to printed documents and to electronic information including Web sites, photos, videos, and posts on social networking pages.

In the context of information, provenance provides clues that help you evaluate accuracy and reliability. Provenance also helps you track down permission to use and reuse articles, quotes, photos, videos, and music. The questions below can help you establish the provenance of electronic information.

- **What is the top-level domain?** Recognizing .edu, .com, .org, and other top-level domains helps to classify the person, organization, or business that is responsible for the site.

- **What else can the URL tell you?** The Web page title or site name can help you identify whether the information is provided by a Web site, blog, tweet, forum, news aggregator, or social network post.

- **Who sponsors the site?** Check the site copyright or About page to determine who or what is the site sponsor.

- **What kind of resources are provided?** Take an inventory of the objects (text, images, animations, videos, ads, links, comments, ratings) included and note those that are most relevant.

- **Has the information been peer reviewed?** See the box below for a description of reviews.

- **Are there ads on the page?** Pay attention to peripheral objects, such as ads, because they might offer clues you'll later use to determine the validity of information.

- **Who produced the content?** Look for the names of authors, photographers, designers, and others who produced content. Check their credentials with Web searches of their names to link to their biographies, social pages, or other work.

- **Did the material originate at the site?** Was the material reposted, republished, or retweeted? Redistributed material might be altered; you can refer to the original material to ensure its accuracy.

- **Is the material a mashup or a derivative work?** Stay alert for doctored photos and parodies.

- **Is the material date-appropriate?** Check the date when the material was created or posted.

- **Is there a contact link?** Can you use it to get additional information or obtain permission to use content from the site?

- **Are there access restrictions?** Take note of the site's access policy. Does it require a login or a paid subscription?

Peer-reviewed information is usually found in scholarly sources, such as journals. Articles reviewed by topic experts before publication produce information that is typically accurate and backed by facts or research.

Public-reviewed information can be found in popular media, such as news magazines, blogs, and social network sites. Articles with comments made by readers after publication are often opinionated, but can be useful for understanding divergent viewpoints.

Ratings are found on blogs, social networks, and commercial sites. Likes, stars, and other anonymous ratings have little meaning in the context of evaluating information.

Try It! On November 29, 2010, the U.S. space agency NASA announced that it would hold a press conference the following Thursday "to discuss an astrobiology finding that will impact the search for evidence of extraterrestrial life." The announcement led to widespread speculation that NASA had discovered proof of extraterrestrial life.

At the press conference, microbiologist Felisa Wolfe-Simon explained that her research team had isolated bacteria that could subsist on arsenic instead of phosphorus, which was considered essential for all terrestrial life forms.

Although the announcement wasn't as spectacular as receiving a radio telescope message saying "Hello, earthlings," the idea that arsenic could sustain life rocked the scientific community and caused all manner of misunderstanding in the popular press. Had Wolfe-Simon's team found some weird form of alien life? Readers who wanted reliable information about the discovery had to carefully choose their news sources. Let's see how provenance can help separate reliable reports from sensationalized trash.

1 Use a search engine to find the original NASA press release by entering *NASA Wolfe-Simon press release*. Make sure you have the primary-source document by examining the URL. How does the press release define *astrobiology*?

2 The press conference was held on December 2, 2010. Search the Web and locate what you think is the most reliable source of the information that was presented at the press conference. Based on the provenance of the site you've chosen, explain why you selected it.

3 In the aftermath of the press conference, blogs, Twitter, and YouTube carried a full spectrum of commentary, from wacky "arsenic-eating" conjectures of amateur scientists to very technical critiques from mainstream researchers. Search YouTube for a video that relates to Wolfe-Simon's research. Watch the video, read the public comments, and check the provenance of the video itself. Based on the provenance, explain how comfortable you would be including the information presented in a term paper.

4 Wolfe-Simon's research was immediately criticized. An especially strong blog post from Rosie Redfield called it "Lots of flim-flam, but very little reliable information." Find Rosie's post and determine its provenance based on the criteria listed on the facing page. Would you characterize this blog as authoritative or wacky? Why?

5 On December 2, 2010, the Web site for *Science* magazine published a paper authored by Wolfe-Simon and members of her team. The article was later published in the print version of *Science* magazine. Find the article online and determine if Wolfe-Simon's paper was peer reviewed. What does the peer review or lack of it tell you about the validity of Wolfe-Simon's claim that arsenic rather than phosphorus can sustain life?

Alien Life on Earth?

Rick Whitacre/Shutterstock.com

Technology in Context: Banking

For most of history, banks used low-tech methods to track one of the world's most cherished commodities—wealth. Checking accounts were in widespread use as early as 1550, when Dutch traders began depositing money with cashiers for safekeeping. The use of printed checks became popular in England in the late 18th century—so popular that banks found it difficult to process a

steadily increasing stream of checks, including those drawn on accounts from other banks.

An unverified story that has become part of bank lore describes the origin of a solution to the check processing problem. As the story goes, a London bank messenger stopped for coffee and got to talking with a messenger from another bank. Realizing that they were delivering checks drawn on each other's banks, the two messengers decided to exchange checks there in the coffee house. This event evolved into a system of check clearinghouses where representatives from various banks met periodically to exchange checks and reconcile totals in cash. By 1839, British clearinghouses were annually processing in excess of £954 million of checks—equivalent to $250 billion in today's money.

Bank clearinghouses were described in an essay, "On the Economy of Machinery and Manufactures," written by computer pioneer Charles Babbage in 1832. He also included

a reference to the "possibility of performing arithmetical calculations by machinery" along with a description of the Difference Engine, then under construction in his workshop.

This dream of automated check clearing did not, however, become reality until more than a century later when S. Clark Beise, senior vice president at Bank of America, contracted with Stanford Research Institute (SRI) to develop a computer system to automate check processing. SRI completed a prototype in 1955 that used mechanical sorting equipment to queue up each check and MICR (Magnetic Ink Character Recognition) technology to read check numbers. In 1959, the first ERMA (Electronic Recording Machine-Accounting) system went into service. With ERMA handling calculations, nine employees could handle the job that once required 50 people. By 1966, 32 regional ERMA systems operated by Bank of America were processing more than 750 million checks per year. ERMA and similar check processing technologies quickly integrated with bank transaction processing systems to become the bedrock of today's banking technology.

Output from check sorting machines can be submitted to the Automated Clearing House (ACH) network, which offers a secure, batch-oriented data exchange system that can be accessed by financial institutions. On a daily basis, banks submit check data and receive a report of balances due to other banks. These balances can be reconciled by electronic funds transfer over the Federal Reserve's Fedwire telecommunications network.

An upswing in check fraud during the 1960s made it increasingly difficult to cash checks at local merchants. As an alternative to trying to cash checks at banks and local merchants, automated teller machines (ATMs) were first installed in the 1970s. Originally, ATMs were operated by banks and connected to the bank's front-end processor—a computer that maintains account balances for in-network customers and monitors suspicious activity. The front-end processor is separated from the bank's main computer system for security.

Today, many ATMs are operated by private retail businesses and connected to the Internet using standard cable or wireless connections, which may not be secure. ATMs that are located inside a bank or credit union are more likely to be secure than those located in shopping malls or gas stations.

Once a promising entry-level occupation, an average bank teller today earns less than $30,000 per year. Although tellers continue to accept deposits, process withdrawals, and cash payroll checks, they are increasingly pressed into customer service roles—opening new accounts, issuing ATM cards, resolving disputed transactions, and assisting customers who have lost bank cards or checkbooks. Despite this shift in job description, the number of bank teller jobs is expected to fall at least 15% in the next few years.

ATMs offer access to bank services from convenient locations where customers shop, eat, and hang out with friends. The Internet takes banking convenience one step further and provides around-the-clock account access from desktops, laptops, tablets, and smartphones. Today, most banks and credit unions offer some type of online banking (also called home banking, Internet banking, or electronic banking).

Basic online banking services allow customers to access checking account and bank card activity, transfer funds between checking and savings accounts, view electronic images of checks and deposit slips, download and print monthly statements, and reorder checks. Customers can also pay bills online by scheduling payment dates and amounts.

Smartphone apps from major banks allow customers to use their digital devices to snap a photo of a check and deposit it without going to the bank.

Many credit card and utility companies offer e-billing services that automatically forward electronic bills to customers' online banking accounts. For monthly fixed-amount bills, such as car loans, online banking offers automatic payment options that deduct funds from specified checking or savings accounts.

Innovations continue to enhance the convenience of dealing with money. Devices such as Square can attach to a tablet computer or smartphone to turn the device into a credit card reader. Small businesses and artisans can easily process credit cards at pop-up shops, fairs, and bazaars.

Digital wallet platforms, such as Apple Pay and Android Pay, turn a smartphone into a credit card. A short-range network technology called NFC (near field communication) transmits secure data between the phone and a point-of-sale terminal.

Consumers are also becoming familiar with cryptocurrencies, such as Bitcoin. Cryptocurrency is a digital medium of exchange for goods and services using virtual tokens. Ownership of these tokens is stored in a secured, encrypted database and remains anonymous as long as government regulators do not require disclosure. The value of a crypto coin can vary based on demand and the degree of faith that consumers place in their legitimacy. Cryptocurrencies are not guaranteed by a gold standard, backed by government assets, or protected by the Federal Deposit Insurance Corporation (FDIC).

As the footprint of banking expands to encompass new devices and technologies, the potential for security breaches increases. ATMs and point-of-sale terminals have to communicate with bank computer systems. Wireless signals pass between handheld devices and point-of-sale terminals. Bank account passwords pass over the Internet and are housed in digital databases. Every time data is transmitted or stored, there is the potential for a security breach.

Technologies such as chip-enhanced credit cards, HTTPS data exchange, and two-factor authentication help to enhance security, but every security measure is eventually breached.

The number of bank tellers may be dwindling, but the number of technical professionals needed for today's banking industry is increasing. A cadre of security specialists are now essential to combat emerging digital threats. Online customer support personnel are required to answer questions about Internet banking services. Web masters and network technicians are also part of the job corps as banking emerges into an era of cryptocurrency and virtual systems.

Flipped Class Projects

Critical Thinking

New technologies are on the horizon. Digital books, self-driving cars, the Internet of Things, and 3D printers are just a sampling of technologies that may have considerable effects on lifestyles, employment, and economics. Which technology do you think will cause the most disruption in the next five years? Make a list of its potentially disruptive effects.

Group Project

Technology life cycles can be monitored using the digital product life cycle, Rogers' bell curve, and the Gartner Hype Cycle. Work with a small group of students to select a technology—it could be a product, an innovation, or an idea—and then map it out on each of the three life cycle charts. Based on your mapping, what would you advise investors who might consider purchasing stock or participating in crowdsourced funding for the technology?

Cyberclassroom

Radio and television were once regarded as promising technologies for education. Can you find five innovative ways that educators proposed to use radio and television to enhance teaching and learning? Today, many educational innovations are based on Internet technology. Find five contemporary ideas for using the Internet within education. Can you identify characteristics that might make the Internet a more successful platform for educational initiatives?

Multimedia Project

Use the Web to locate information about an interesting technology company. Now, suppose you are a recruiter for that company. Create a 10- to 15-slide PowerPoint presentation to show to college students at a job fair. Make sure your slides contain substantive information presented in a quick-to-understand format for students who are moving from booth to booth at the fair. Use photos to make the slides interesting and, because you are trying to capture student interest in a busy atmosphere, you might want to consider music or other sound effects, too. Follow your instructor's guidelines for submitting your PowerPoint presentation.

Resume Builder

Successful job seekers strategize about how to get noticed by corporate recruiters. The direct approach is to send resumes in response to job postings and to establish a presence at online employment services. But do social media open additional opportunities? What can you discover about the way recruiters use social media? Do they frequent certain Web sites? Do they post publicly on Twitter? Do they search LinkedIn? Gather a bibliography of links that contain hard evidence that recruiters use social media to locate potential employees.

Globalization

With growing trends toward outsourcing, some economists are pointing to the emergence of "global professionals," who are developing qualifications necessary to succeed in the international job market. For this project, use Web resources to conduct research about global professionals and international careers. Pay particular attention to the way this concept relates to your chosen career field. Using the information you've found, write a one-page paper outlining your thoughts. If the idea of becoming a global professional appeals to you, describe how you might enhance your qualifications. If the idea does not appeal to you, explain why.

Key Terms

Interactive Summary

Section A: Companies and businesses that create jobs, develop products, and offer services are classified into economic [＿＿＿＿＿]. The [＿＿＿＿＿] industry encompasses those companies that focus on digital equipment, software, communications technologies, and related services. As in other industries, businesses in the information sector produce consumer goods and [＿＿＿＿＿] goods. These goods may be produced in-house or they may be [＿＿＿＿＿] to other companies. Businesses also make extensive use of [＿＿＿＿＿] when manufacturing, services, and product development are moved to other countries. These practices account in part for declining prices of digital products, but another factor is [＿＿＿＿＿] law, which predicted that the number of transistors in an integrated circuit would double every two years. The life of a technology product, innovation, or idea can be tracked using a product life cycle, Rogers' bell curve, or the Gartner [＿＿＿＿＿]. Some technologies have transformative effects on lifestyles, employment, and economics. These [＿＿＿＿＿] technologies include digital photography, the telephone, and smartphones. Technologies also have an effect on [＿＿＿＿＿], which is the amount of output that is produced per unit of input. In theory, increased use of ICT can raise a country's GDP. However, technology has also created national [＿＿＿＿＿] vulnerabilities, and the threat of cyberwarfare continues to grow.

Section B: Even before recorded history, humans used various [＿＿＿＿＿] aids, such as pebbles and notched sticks, to keep track of quantities. By 1200, a(n) [＿＿＿＿＿] calculator, called the abacus, had appeared in China. Devices such as the abacus require the operator to apply a(n) [＿＿＿＿＿] to perform calculations. In contrast, [＿＿＿＿＿] calculators, such as the Pascaline and de Colmar's Arithmometer, are designed to carry out calculations autonomously. In the 1800s, an English mathematician named Charles [＿＿＿＿＿] proposed to build a device, called the Analytical Engine, that would operate using steam power. The design for this device embodied many of the concepts that define the modern computer. In the 1930s and 1940s, several [＿＿＿＿＿] computers were developed, including the Atanasoff-Berry Computer, Z3, Harvard Mark I, Colossus, and ENIAC. Most of these early computers used [＿＿＿＿＿] tubes, which paved the way for the architecture of first-generation computers, such as UNIVAC. Second-generation computers were smaller and less power hungry because they used [＿＿＿＿＿]. Third-generation computers were even smaller because they used [＿＿＿＿＿] circuits. The key technology for fourth-generation computers, including personal computers, is the [＿＿＿＿＿].

Section C: The telecommunications industry initially used couriers to carry information from place to place. In the 1800s, inventors created the [_____], which used electricity to transmit data over a distance. Signals were usually sent using [_____] code. One of the biggest challenges for this technology was creating a worldwide network that linked continents. In 1858, this worldwide network became a possibility when the first undersea cable was laid across the [_____] Ocean. Another telecommunications invention soon followed when Alexander Graham Bell managed to transmit human voice over wires. The telephone industry grew rapidly and is now classified as a(n) [_____] carrier because it is similar to shippers that transport goods and passengers over regular routes at set rates. The telephone system infrastructure eventually became a key element of the Internet backbone. Radio technology emerged after the telephone. Its ability to transmit sound through the air was the basis for several later technologies, including cellular phones. The first cellular phones that were able to access the Internet were available in [_____]. Now, they are the most prevalent Internet access device, used in emerging nations as well as in developed countries. Television was an additional technology to emerge in the telecommunications industry. Its evolution into [_____] television provided another Internet access technology, especially popular in the United States.

Section D: Tech sector careers can be defined in terms of a broad set of information, technology, and communications industries, or more narrowly focused within the computer industry. A computer [_____] is defined as any person whose primary occupation involves the design, configuration, analysis, development, modification, testing, or security of computer hardware or software. The IT industry encompasses a wide variety of jobs for computer professionals, and the career outlook appears to be relatively positive. Salaries and working conditions are quite favorable. Computer professionals work in full-time or part-time jobs, and some are [_____] workers, who arrange to work for a company on a temporary basis, usually as consultants for particular projects. Although these workers are usually highly paid, they are not official employees of a company and are not eligible for company healthcare or retirement benefits. Education is important to most high-tech jobs. Computer [_____] degree programs focus on the design of computer hardware and peripheral devices. Computer [_____] degree programs focus on digital computer architecture and how to program computers to make them work effectively and efficiently. Information [_____] degree programs focus on applying computers to business problems. In addition to a college degree, [_____] provides job applicants with marketable credentials pertaining to skills and knowledge of specific software or hardware. Finding a job in the IT industry is similar to finding any job. Preparing a resume is essential, and it can be supplemented by a Web [_____] with links to relevant Web sites, such as past employers, your alma mater, and samples of your work.

Section E: Computer professionals sometimes encounter situations in which the right course of action requires a decision based on evaluating what's right and wrong. Professional [_____] refers to on-the-job choices and actions that reflect a person's values. Ethical decisions should take into account applicable [_____], such as the Digital Millennium Copyright Act. Laws and ethics are not the same thing, however, and sometimes following the letter of the law does not result in ethical behavior. Situations that require computer professionals to make ethical decisions often involve software copyrights, privacy, conflict of interest, use of work computers, software quality, hacking, and social [_____]. Ethical decisions made on the job can have long-term career effects. Many IT organizations have [_____] of ethics designed to help computer professionals make tough decisions. Additional help in making ethical decisions can also be obtained from knowledgeable friends, mentors, lawyers, and workplace counselors. Computer professionals who are compelled to become [_____] and speak out against on-the-job activities that threaten the public interest should understand the potential legal and career risks before they proceed.

Interactive Situation Questions

1. Suppose that you were an accountant in 1981, and you wanted to use a state-of-the-art personal computer and software for your work. You would probably have selected an IBM PC and [   ] software.

2. You work as a manufacturing technician in a chip fabrication plant. Your aunt asks if you're in the IT industry. Your response: [   ]

3. When you call your computer manufacturer for technical support, you aren't surprised by the accents of the technicians because many call centers operate in other countries, a practice called [   ].

4. Your cousin shows you a Google Cardboard virtual reality viewer that she got in 2014. You're amazed that she was a(n) [   ] adopter according to Rogers' bell curve.

5. After studying and gaining practical experience on how to analyze a computer system's vulnerability to threats from viruses, worms, unauthorized access, and physical damage, you are ready for a job as a(n) [   ] specialist.

6. You accepted a project with an IT company as a(n) [   ] worker, fully realizing that you will not be considered an official employee of the company, nor will you be eligible for the company's healthcare or retirement benefits.

7. Your friend is not strong in math, but he really wants to work with computers. You suggest that your friend consider pursuing a(n) [   ] systems degree.

8. To supplement your computer science degree, you decide to take a(n) [   ] exam to become a Microsoft Certified Solutions Expert.

9. As part of your job-hunting activities, you plan to create your resume in several different [   ], for use in the body of an email message, as a Web page, and as a printed document.

10. Your friend is using a virus to shut down hate sites on the Web. This project gives you an uneasy feeling. You'll have to make a(n) [   ] decision about what to do.

11. You've discovered your company's accounting system was intentionally modified to disguise certain expenses. You're contemplating what might happen if you become a(n) [   ] and expose this unethical practice.

12. Suppose you are talking to a recruiter who seems to be assessing your overall knowledge of the computer industry. The discussion turns to declining hardware prices. You impress the recruiter by mentioning [   ] law and the way doubling transistors every two years contributed to economies of production.

Lab: Perfect Your Profile

Your professional profile is a key element of your career. LinkedIn is like your professional billboard on the social media superhighway. Recruiters and potential employers will cruise by before inviting you for an interview. Colleagues can keep track of your status and offer endorsements. Your profile might even get you an invite to a talk show in need of your expertise on a trending topic. Here's a chance to hone your LinkedIn profile to showcase your talents.

Requirements:

For this lab, you'll need a computer with access to the Internet. You'll also need a LinkedIn account.

Assignment:

1 Take stock of your basic LinkedIn profile information.

Begin on your Profile page and check the following:

- Your full name includes your middle name or initial.

- Your photo looks professional. In it, you should be dressed professionally and smiling.

- The Contact Info should include your current email address.

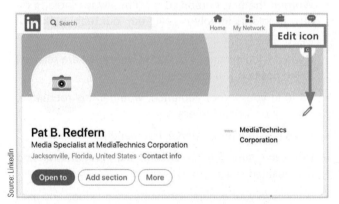

2 Use the Edit icon to access and verify your contact info:

Make sure your phone number, home address, and email address are correct.

Select your profile URL and request one that reflects your full name.

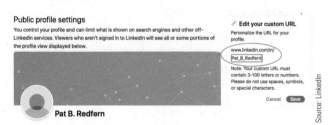

3 Refine your headline.

A LinkedIn headline is a short (120 character) description that highlights your talents. The words in your headline should be selected with care, keeping in mind that recruiters may use the headline as a search field.

There are two basic types of LinkedIn headlines: those with an occupational title and those that showcase your specialty. A specialty headline might be something like "Creative computer programmer | Java is my passion on screen or in a cup."

Job seekers—especially new entrants or career switchers—may have more success with a showcase-style headline. You might want to use external sources for advice on creating an effective headline.

Click the Edit icon next to your profile headline. Modify your headline to improve it.

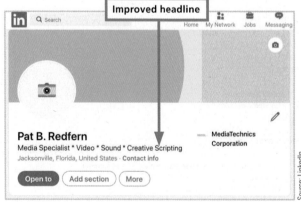

4 Polish your Experience section.

The Experience section is primarily used to list your current and previous jobs.

When entering work experience, be sure to correctly identify your job title, the name of the business, and the dates you were employed.

Try to phrase the job description in terms of PARS:

P - What was a problem or type of problem you worked to solve?

A - What action did you take?

R - What were the results? Did you succeed?

S - What skills did you develop in the process?

When you've worked for a business that is a LinkedIn member, its logo may automatically appear when you add the business to your experience list.

5 Add more sections to your profile.

In addition to work experience, LinkedIn offers other sections that you can add to your profile. These sections can be used to showcase volunteer efforts or membership in professional organizations.

For students and recent graduates, jobs, internships, and experiences that contribute to developing career skills are appropriate here.

Select the "Add section" button and expand the Experience option to display Education, Licenses & certifications, and Volunteer experience. Add your relevant experiences.

Source: LinkedIn

6 Add your educational credentials.

Add an Education section if your profile does not yet have one. Fill in the Education section for the school you are currently attending.

If your school is a LinkedIn member, the school's logo may automatically appear when you click the Save button.

7 Add pizzazz to your summary.

The Summary section is your professional bio. Aside from your headline, it is the most frequently read item on your LinkedIn page.

The Summary content is limited to 2,000 words, but you can add photos, videos, documents, and presentations.

Access your Summary from the About section and create a compelling introduction to yourself.

Consider these tips for an effective summary:

- Write in the first person (e.g., "I'm always looking for new problems to solve. Last year, our team tackled a complex...").

- If you are job hunting, include keywords that are relevant to the position you are seeking.

- Write to your target audience, whether it is recruiters, colleagues, or customers.

- Keep the tone professional, but friendly.

- Break the summary into several short paragraphs, and use bulleted lists for easy reading.

- Showcase your accomplishments, your values and passions, and things that make you stand out from your peers.

- Include statistics and other quantifiable information about your skills and accomplishments (e.g., "For three years, I managed a $40,000 budget for the local chapter of ACM.").

- Include testimonials from colleagues and supervisors, along with relevant awards.

- Add photos, icons, and other media. These can help draw attention to the Summary section and showcase additional accomplishments.

8 Choose skills so you can get endorsements.

Endorsements are similar to likes, but with a focus on career skills and accomplishments. You select your skill set, and then your LinkedIn connections can endorse your skills. Do the following:

Use the "Add section" button to select Skills.

Fill out the Skills template as shown below.

Add skills to your list.

Save the completed list.

You can request endorsements by emailing your instructors, friends, and classmates.

Endorse others. They will often reciprocate by endorsing you.

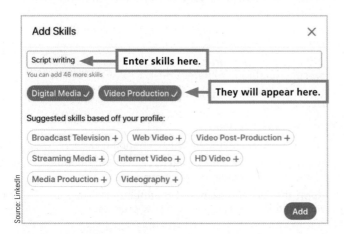
Source: LinkedIn

9 Get recommendations.

Letters of recommendation verify your skills, educational background, and work experience. You can request recommendations and link them to other items on your profile.

When asking someone for a recommendation, choose carefully to make sure the recommendation will be positive and well written.

For this lab, you can ask your instructor for a recommendation for your educational qualifications.

Select the "Add section" button and then expand the Additional information option to show Request a recommendation.

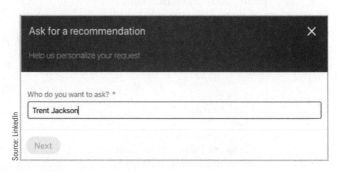
Source: LinkedIn

Begin entering the name of a LinkedIn member from whom you'd like a recommendation. When the list of your LinkedIn connections appears, choose that person from the list.

(You can request recommendations only from your first-level connections. If you don't have a relevant connection, you might want to Cancel for now and skip to activity #10.)

Complete the request form and then click the Send button.

10 Join groups and follow individuals.

Following industry groups, professional organizations, potential employers, and influencers in your career field is a fantastic way to keep up to date and extend your network.

To join a group, enter a keyword or group name in the Search bar at the top of your LinkedIn home page. Select the group you would like to join, then use the "Request to join" button.

To follow an individual, company, or organization, locate the one you would like to follow and select the Follow button. If you do not see a Follow button, that LinkedIn member does not allow followers.

11 Follow your instructor's guidelines for providing a link to your LinkedIn profile.

9 Information Systems

Module Contents

Behind every business, organization, and government agency is an information system that tracks operations and gathers data. In this module, you'll find out why some of these systems succeed while others fail.

⬤Try It! Apply what you learn.

- Find the mission statement for a nonprofit or for-profit organization.
- Recognize the differences among strategic, tactical, and operational planning.
- Differentiate structured problems from semi-structured and unstructured problems.
- Understand how commit or rollback affects your online transactions.
- Use an expert system.
- Locate cookies created by online shopping carts.
- Gauge the level of control you have over information collected by customer loyalty programs.
- Apply the Five Forces model to better understand how competition affects prices and new products.
- Identify problems and opportunities using PIECES.
- Select scheduling and management tools.
- Draw a basic data flow diagram.
- Draw basic use case and sequence diagrams.
- Create a decision support spreadsheet.
- Fill out a change request.
- Identify various types of testing that take place during the development of an information system.
- Find quality-of-service metrics for Web sites and social media sites.
- Understand the causes of corporate data breaches.
- Be aware of how identity thieves use stolen data.
- Locate authoritative information about data breaches that might affect your personally identifiable information.
- Set a fraud alert to reduce the possibility that an identity thief can carry out financial transactions using your name.

● Pre-Check

Gauge your level of expertise. The answers are in the module.

Ecommerce systems track shopping carts using

_____ .

A framework for classifying information system problems:

_____

What kind of diagram is this?

_____

An "information system in a box":

_____

The "central nervous system of an enterprise":

_____

Three components of CRM:

_____

_____

_____

Tracking products from supplier to consumer:

_____

After a data breach, consumers can set a(n)

_____ .

Lights-out management is used in

_____ .

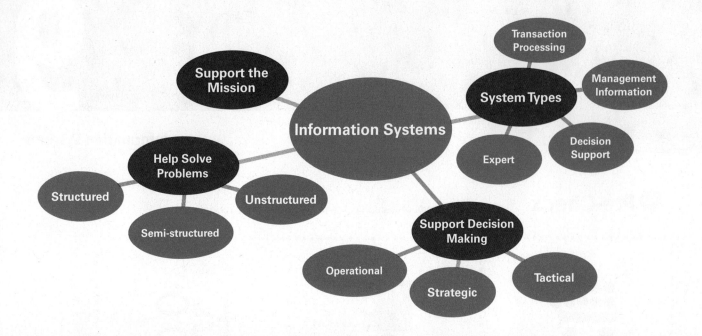

Information System Basics

Objectives

▶ Explain the relationship between an organization, its mission, and its information system.

▶ Provide examples of vertical and horizontal market applications.

▶ Match strategic, tactical, and operational planning needs to employees at each level of an organizational chart.

▶ Describe three classifications of problems.

▶ Describe the characteristics of TPS, MIS, DSS, and expert systems.

▶ Use the terms *decision model* and *decision query* in a sentence.

▶ Explain how fuzzy logic is used by expert systems.

"They have computers, and they may have other weapons of mass destruction." When former U.S. Attorney General Janet Reno made this statement in the late 1990s, she may not have meant that computers are weapons of mass destruction, but they are certainly powerful weapons used by businesses to keep competitors in check. Computer-based information systems have spread rapidly and are now an essential component of virtually every business, organization, and enterprise.

Terminology

information system
organization
enterprise
mission
mission statement
vertical market
horizontal market
organizational chart
workers
managers

strategic planning
tactical planning
operational planning
transaction
transaction processing
   system
batch processing
online processing
OLTP
commit or rollback

detail reports
management information
   system
summary report
exception report
decision support
   system
executive information
   system
decision model

decision query
expert system
knowledge base
inference engine
knowledge engineering
expert system shell
fuzzy logic

Enterprise Basics

The multibillion-dollar fast-food chain McDonald's has a mission to maintain its reputation as "our customers' favorite place and way to eat and drink." The scope of the company's enterprise is vast, and it can carry out its mission only with the assistance of a sophisticated information system.

▶ **What is an information system?** An **information system** collects, stores, and processes data to provide useful, accurate, and timely information, typically within the context of an organization. The scope of an information system includes computers, communications networks, and data, plus people, products, policies, and procedures (Figure 9-1).

Figure 9-1: Information system scope

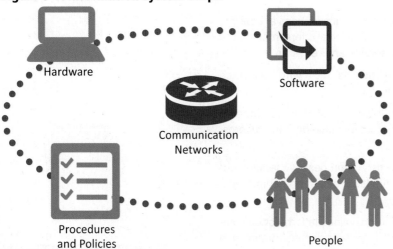

▶ **What's the official definition of organization?** An **organization** is a group of people working together to accomplish a goal. Organizations have accomplished amazing feats, such as sending astronauts into space, providing live television coverage of global events, and inventing the Happy Meal. They also accomplish all kinds of day-to-day, routine tasks, such as offering banking services, selling merchandise, improving the environment, and policing neighborhoods.

Any organization that seeks profit by providing goods and services is called a business or an **enterprise**. In contrast, organizations formed to accomplish political, social, or charitable goals that are not intended to accumulate profits are known as nonprofit organizations. Information systems can support the goals and missions of for-profit enterprises as well as nonprofit organizations.

▶ **What is a mission statement?** Every organization has a goal or plan that's referred to as its **mission**. All activities that take place in an organization, including those that involve computers, should contribute to this mission.

The written expression of an organization's mission is called a mission statement. A **mission statement** describes not only an organization's goals, but also the way in which those goals will be accomplished.

9

❱ **What kinds of enterprises can an information system serve?** Just about any type of enterprise can benefit from an information system, from a small startup to an established multinational corporation. Information systems designed for a specific industry or enterprise may use **vertical market** software. The software that controls touchscreen order entry at fast-food restaurants is an example of software designed for vertical markets. Figure 9-2 lists the ways in which information systems can help several kinds of enterprises monitor and improve their core business activities.

Figure 9-2: Vertical market applications

 Education. Manage student records, maintain data on instructors and staff, handle course registration, and schedule courses and facilities.

 Communications. Manage customer subscriptions and billing, track devices, contact customers with special offers, monitor the network for outages, and track service and repair crews.

 Health care. Manage patient records, deal with insurance claims, and schedule appointments.

 Local government. Manage local tax compliance, improve financial management and reporting, maintain property records, and store employee data.

 Manufacturing. Automate the design process; schedule suppliers; track orders; manage inventory, sales, and shipments; and monitor safety.

 Travel and hospitality. Provide an online platform for customers to make reservations, schedule facilities and equipment, and schedule employees.

 Retail. Operate point-of-sale systems in stores and online, process payments, and track inventory.

❱ **How about horizontal markets?** The core activities listed in the previous figure are unique to each industry. However, additional activities are common to many businesses. These common elements, which are the responsibility of **horizontal market** software, are listed in Figure 9-3.

Figure 9-3: Horizontal markets

 Customers or clients. Find, engage, profile, and entice them to buy products.

 Employees. Recruit, pay, verify compliance, evaluate, and track benefits.

 Management. Monitor productivity, improve profits, and plan for the future.

 Finances. Track income and expenses, monitor budgets, process customer transactions, interface with banks, and compute taxes.

 Products. Manufacture or procure, warehouse, monitor inventory, and ship.

 Communication. Collaborate among colleagues, communicate with employees, establish a social media presence, and interact with customers.

Who uses information systems? An information system is used by the people in an organization and its customers. You've used many information systems—for example, when registering for classes, getting cash from an ATM, and purchasing merchandise on the Web. You might even work for a business or nonprofit organization where you access an information system as part of your job.

Not everyone in an organization uses an information system in the same way. An information system must support the needs of people who engage in many different organizational activities.

To coordinate the activities of employees, most organizations use a hierarchical structure. An **organizational chart**, such as the one in Figure 9-4, depicts the hierarchy of employees in an organization.

Figure 9-4: An organizational chart depicts the hierarchy of employees

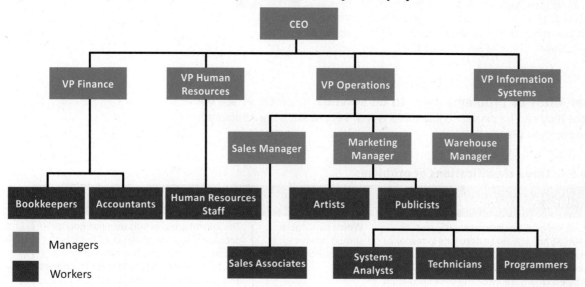

How are employees classified? In most businesses, employees can be classified as workers or managers. **Workers** are the people who directly carry out the organization's mission. For example, they flip burgers, assemble cars, write newspaper articles, sell merchandise, answer telephones, lay bricks, fix engines, or perform other types of labor. Workers routinely produce and collect data for information systems. For example, as checkout clerks ring up sales, their cash registers store each item in a database.

Managers determine organizational goals and plan how to achieve those goals. They approve new products, authorize new construction, and supervise workers. Executive managers plan an organization's long-range goals for profitability, market share, membership levels, and so on. This emphasis on long-range and future goals is referred to as **strategic planning**.

Mid-level managers are responsible for figuring out how to achieve long-range goals through sales, marketing, or new product development. To eventually accomplish long-range goals, these managers set incremental goals that can be achieved in a year or less—a process referred to as **tactical planning**.

Low-level managers are responsible for scheduling employees, ordering supplies, and other activities that make day-to-day operations run smoothly—a process referred to as **operational planning**. Information systems can provide some or all of the data needed for strategic, tactical, and operational planning.

QuickCheck

Which of the following is an example of tactical planning?

a. McDonald's opening new franchises in Qatar

b. Scheduling workers for New Year's Day

c. Adding McWraps to the McDonald's menu

d. Speeding up throughput at the drive-up window

❱ How do information systems help the people in an organization?
An information system can help employees perform their jobs more quickly and effectively by automating routine tasks, such as reordering inventory, taking customer orders, or sending out renewal notices. Information systems can also help employees solve business and organizational problems.

One of the major functions of an information system is to help people make decisions in response to problems. According to Herbert Simon, who was well known for his insights into organizational behavior, the decision-making process has three phases, shown in Figure 9-5.

Figure 9-5: The decision-making process

Reza Estakhrian/The Image Bank/Getty Images
Martin Barraud/Getty Images
Antonio Mo/PhotoDisc/Getty Images

Phase 1: Recognize a problem or a need to make a decision.

Phase 2: Devise and analyze possible solutions to the problem.

Phase 3: Select an action or a solution.

❱ What kinds of problems need to be solved? All problems are not alike, but they can be classified into three types: structured, semi-structured, and unstructured (Figure 9-6).

Figure 9-6: Three classifications of problems

Type of Problem	Example	Methodology
A *structured problem* is an everyday, routine problem. When you make decisions in response to structured problems, the procedure for obtaining the best solution is known, the objective is clearly defined, and the information necessary to make the decision is easier to identify.	Which customers should receive overdue notices?	The information for this overdue notice decision is usually stored in a file cabinet or computer system. The method for reaching a solution is to look for customers with outstanding balances, and then check whether the due dates for their payments fall before today's date.
A *semi-structured problem* has a known procedure for arriving at a solution; however, the process might involve some degree of subjective judgment. Also, some of the information regarding the problem might not be available, might lack precision, or might be uncertain.	How many mountain bikes should a store stock for the holidays?	The mountain bike decision can be based on the previous year's sales; but because future consumer spending is uncertain, determining the appropriate amount of holiday inventory might require some guesswork.
An *unstructured problem* requires human intuition as the basis for finding a solution. Information relevant to the problem might be missing, and few parts of the solution can be tackled using concrete models. If experts are presented with a problem but they disagree on a solution, it is likely an unstructured problem.	Should Saks Fifth Avenue stock Japanese-inspired evening gowns?	The purchasing agent for women's clothing makes this decision based on an intuitive sense of customer taste and fashion trends.

❱ Can an information system solve all three types of problems?
Traditionally, information systems contributed most to solving structured problems, but tools have emerged to tackle semi-structured and unstructured problems as well. Based on their approach to problem solving, information systems can be classified as transaction processing systems, management information systems, decision support systems, and expert systems. Let's look at each of these systems.

Transaction Processing Systems

Information systems deal with data, and one of the most common ways to accumulate data is by recording every transaction that takes place within an enterprise. The volume of transactions can be mind-boggling. Salesforce.com handles millions of transactions every day. Amazon processes about 66,000 orders per hour. PayPal processes more than 15 billion transactions every year.

▶ **What's a transaction?** In an information system context, a **transaction** is an exchange between two parties that is recorded and stored in a computer system. When you order a product at a Web site, buy merchandise in a store, search for a term on Google, or withdraw cash from an ATM, you are involved in a transaction.

▶ **What is a transaction processing system?** A **transaction processing system** (TPS) provides a way to collect, process, store, display, modify, or cancel transactions. Most transaction processing systems allow many transactions to be entered simultaneously.

The data collected by a TPS is usually stored in databases, and it can be used to produce a regularly scheduled set of reports, such as monthly bills, weekly paychecks, annual inventory summaries, and daily manufacturing schedules. Examples of transaction processing systems include payroll, accounting, inventory, point-of-sale, airline reservations, ecommerce, and billing.

▶ **How are transactions processed?** In the days before credit or debit cards, shoppers could write checks and then head to the bank to deposit enough cash to cover them. Check writers enjoyed this grace period because banks operated batch processing systems.

In the 1970s, early transaction processing systems, such as banking and payroll applications, used **batch processing** to collect and hold a group of transactions until the end of a day or pay period, when the entire batch was processed. Batch processing proceeds without human intervention, until all transactions are completed or until an error occurs.

In contrast to batch processing, most modern transaction processing systems use **online processing**—a real-time method in which each transaction is processed as it is entered. Such a system is often referred to as an **OLTP** (online transaction processing) system. Figure 9-7 illustrates these two types of systems.

9

QuickCheck

Which of the following could not be used to process payroll for a fast-food restaurant?

a. Batch

b. OLTP

c. TPS

d. Tactical app

Figure 9-7: Batch processing compared to OLTP

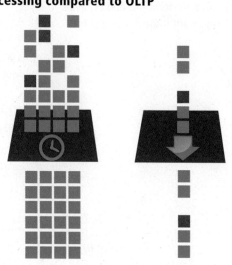

Batch processing collects and holds a series of transactions until a specified time or event, when all the transactions are then processed.

OLTP processes each transaction as it arrives.

How does OLTP work? OLTP uses a **commit or rollback** strategy to ensure that each transaction is processed correctly. This strategy is crucial because most transactions require a sequence of steps, and every step must succeed for the transaction to be completed.

Suppose you withdraw cash from an ATM. The bank's computer must make sure your account contains sufficient funds before it deducts the withdrawal from your account and allows the ATM to deliver cash. If the ATM is out of cash, however, the transaction fails, and the withdrawal should not be deducted from your account.

A TPS can commit to a transaction and permanently update database records only if every step of the transaction can be successfully processed. If even one step fails, however, the entire transaction fails and a rollback returns the records to their original state. The incomplete transaction will be recorded, along with data indicating where it failed. Figure 9-8 diagrams the processes that take place in a typical TPS.

Figure 9-8: Transaction processing systems

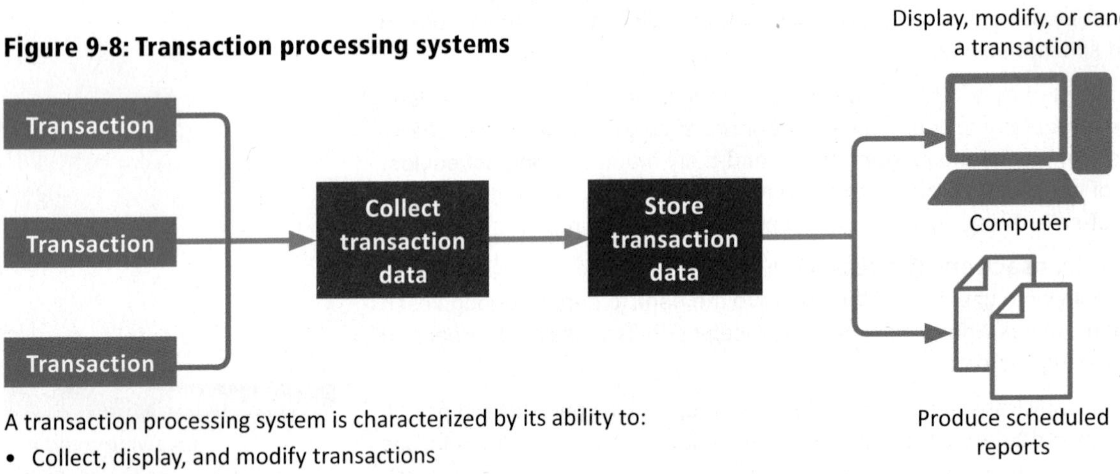

A transaction processing system is characterized by its ability to:

- Collect, display, and modify transactions
- Store transactions
- List transactions

What are the limitations of transaction processing systems? Although a TPS excels at maintaining transaction data entered by clerical personnel and online customers, its reporting capabilities are limited. A typical TPS generates **detail reports**, which provide a basic record of completed transactions. However, managers need more sophisticated reports to help them understand and analyze data. These reports are usually created by a management information system.

QuickCheck

When you make an online purchase, which of the following indicates a TPS rollback?

a. A sale price on the merchandise

b. A discount when you enter a coupon code

c. A message that you've exceeded your debit card balance

d. An offer to participate in a customer satisfaction survey

Management Information Systems

Transaction processing systems handle the details of an enterprise's core business. They record details such as airline bookings, point-of-sale purchases, or bank card transactions. However, the detailed data that these systems accumulate can be overwhelming unless it is summarized, aggregated, graphed, charted, or somehow formatted for human understanding. Early attempts to extract meaningful data from accumulated transactions produced management information systems.

▶ **What is a management information system?** The term *management information system* is sometimes used as a synonym for *information system*, basically referring to any computer system that processes data and provides information within a business setting. Today, this use of the term seems outdated.

There was a time, however, when a management information system (MIS, pronounced "em-eye-ess") was cutting-edge technology used to derive various reports from transaction data. Managers depend on these reports to make routine business decisions in response to structured problems. As Figure 9-9 shows, an MIS is characterized by the production of periodic reports that managers use for structured and routine tasks.

Figure 9-9: Management information systems

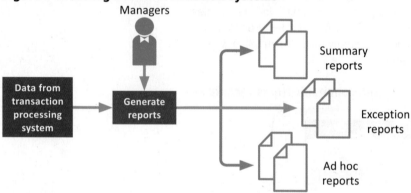

A management information system is characterized by its ability to:

- Produce routine and on-demand reports
- Provide useful information for managerial activities
- Increase managerial efficiency
- Provide information used for structured, routine decisions

▶ **What kinds of reports can an MIS produce?** An MIS typically produces a set of summary and exception reports. A summary report combines, groups, or totals data. For example, a summary report based on purchases at a McDonald's franchise might show the total annual sales for each of the past five years. Summary reports are useful in tactical and strategic planning.

An exception report contains information that is outside of normal or acceptable ranges. For example, a utility company's MIS might produce an exception report showing a list of customers with past-due electric bills.

MIS reports usually follow a fixed format. For example, the past-due report for a utility company would have the same number of columns with the same headings every month—just the names of the customers and their overdue amounts would differ from month to month.

9

Decision Support Systems

Some telecommunication companies have a horrible reputation when it comes to service and repair. Customers who've taken a day off from work to wait for a service technician are understandably aggravated when no one shows up. Or what about the technician who shows up without the necessary replacement parts? Or the new technician who doesn't have the expertise to fix the problem? IBM, Apple, and your telecom provider may have a solution, and it is based on decision support technology.

▶ **What's a decision support system?** A **decision support system** (DSS) helps people make decisions by directly manipulating data, accessing data from external sources, generating statistical projections, and creating data models of various scenarios. A DSS provides tools for routine decisions, non-routine decisions, structured problems, and even semi-structured problems in which a decision might be based on imprecise data or require guesstimates.

One type of decision support system, called an **executive information system** (EIS), is designed to provide senior managers with information relevant to strategic management activities—such as setting policies, planning, and preparing budgets—based on information from internal and external databases.

Decision support systems can also assist technical, professional, and clerical workers as they do their everyday jobs. Such systems can be useful for bankers, police officers, case workers, insurance agents, flight attendants, pilots, retail sales associates, telecom technicians, and workers in other occupations. For example, technicians working for a telecommunications company might be supplied with an iPad-based decision support app like the one in Figure 9-10.

Try It!

Visit the *Easy Decision Maker* and *80000 Hours* Web sites. Would you consider these examples of DSS?

Figure 9-10: A decision support app for telecommunications technicians

Copyright IBM Corporation 1994, 2017

Telecommunications repair technicians could use a mobile app to access work orders and load up their trucks with necessary repair parts. At the job site, they can connect to repair manuals or fire up FaceTime to interact with a supervisor.

❱ What are the components of a DSS? A decision support system derives its name from the fact that it *supports* the decision maker; that is, it provides the tools a decision maker needs to analyze data. A DSS might recommend a course of action, but the final choice remains the responsibility of the human decision maker.

DSSs contain various components, such as decision models, query engines, and statistical tools. A **decision model** is a numerical representation of a realistic situation, such as a cash-flow model of a business that shows how income adds to cash accounts and how expenses deplete those accounts. These models may be similar to spreadsheet "what-if" scenarios.

A **decision query** is a question or a set of instructions describing data that must be gathered to make a decision. Queries are handled by a query engine, similar to a search engine or the query module used to access data from a database.

DSS statistical tools help decision makers study trends by summarizing, comparing, and graphing data that is produced by queries.

DSS models, queries, and statistics can be based on data from an organization's transaction processing system and additional data gathered from external sources, such as stock market reports, as shown in Figure 9-11.

Figure 9-11: Decision support systems

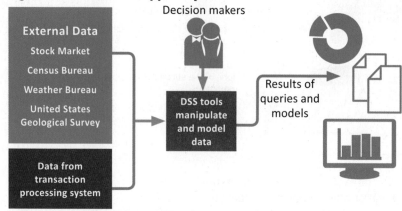

❱ What kinds of decisions can a DSS handle? A DSS can be used to tackle diverse problems because it contains a good selection of decision support tools. Directors of a disaster relief organization might use a DSS to set fund-raising targets based on internal data from its accounting system and previous donations recorded by its TPS.

A disaster relief DSS can also incorporate external information based on national fund-raising trends and current economic statistics pertaining to employment and disposable income. This data can be manipulated to examine what-if scenarios, such as "What if we are faced with a similar number of disasters as last year, but the country is dealing with a 5% rise in unemployment?"

❱ What are the limitations of a DSS? A DSS helps people manipulate the data needed to make a decision, but it does not actually make a decision. Instead, a person must analyze the data and reach a decision. A DSS is not a substitute for human judgment. When organizations want an information system to make decisions without direct guidance from an experienced decision maker, they turn to expert systems.

QuickCheck

Would a bank use a DSS to watch for fraudulent credit card use?

a. Yes, managers could be supplied with a DSS so they could monitor customer accounts.

b. Yes, tellers could use it to decide whether to permit a cash advance.

c. No, human decision makers cannot monitor every credit card transaction.

d. No, it isn't needed because credit cards have security numbers on the back.

Expert Systems

Spam filters manage to prevent lots of unwanted messages from landing in your inbox. The process of filtering out spam is based on an interlocking set of rules. Expert systems also use rules to evaluate data and make decisions. These systems can then be applied to consumer applications. They can also encompass the business logic underlying the decisions made within an enterprise.

▶ **What is an expert system?** An **expert system**, sometimes referred to as a knowledge-based system, is a computer system designed to analyze data and produce a recommendation, diagnosis, or decision based on a set of facts and rules, as shown in Figure 9-12.

Figure 9-12: Expert systems are based on a set of facts and rules

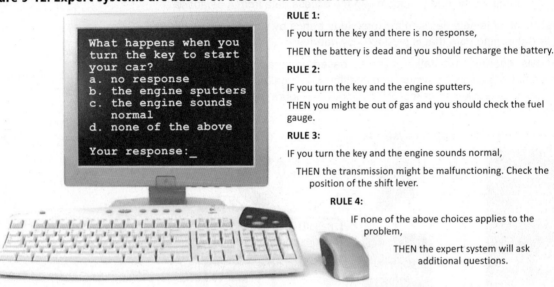

RULE 1:

IF you turn the key and there is no response,

THEN the battery is dead and you should recharge the battery.

RULE 2:

IF you turn the key and the engine sputters,

THEN you might be out of gas and you should check the fuel gauge.

RULE 3:

IF you turn the key and the engine sounds normal,

THEN the transmission might be malfunctioning. Check the position of the shift lever.

RULE 4:

IF none of the above choices applies to the problem,

THEN the expert system will ask additional questions.

▶ **Where do the rules come from?** The facts and rules for an expert system are usually derived by interviewing one or more experts. The facts and rules are then incorporated into a **knowledge base**. The knowledge base is stored in a computer file and can be manipulated by software called an **inference engine**. The process of designing, entering, and testing the rules in an expert system is referred to as **knowledge engineering**.

▶ **What kinds of decisions can an expert system make?** An expert system is not a general-purpose problem solver or decision maker. Each expert system is designed to make decisions in a particular area, referred to as a domain.

An expert system created for use at the Campbell Soup Company captured the knowledge of an expert cooking-vat operator to help less experienced employees troubleshoot problems that might arise during the cooking and canning process.

Other expert systems have been developed to watch for fraudulent credit card use, locate mineral deposits, diagnose blood diseases, underwrite complex insurance policies, order a customized personal computer, and recommend stock purchases.

Try It!

There are lots of expert systems online. You can go to the Animal Planet Web site and search for *Dog Breed Selector* (or *Cat Breed Selector*) to see how one works.

▶ **How are expert systems built?** Expert systems can be created with a computer programming language, an expert system shell, or tools included in business-oriented database applications. An **expert system shell** is a software tool containing an inference engine and a user interface that developers use to enter facts and rules for a knowledge base. An expert system shell also has tools for testing a knowledge base to make certain it produces accurate decisions.

▶ **Can an expert system deal with uncertainty?** Expert systems are designed to deal with data that is imprecise or with problems that have more than one solution. Using a technique called **fuzzy logic**, an expert system can deal with imprecise data by working with confidence levels.

Suppose an expert system is helping you identify a whale you spotted off the California coast. The expert system asks, "Did you see a dorsal fin?" You're not sure. You think you saw one, but it could have been a shadow. If the expert system is using fuzzy logic, it will let you respond with something like "I'm 85% certain I saw a dorsal fin." Based on the confidence level of your answer to this and other questions, the expert system might be able to tell you that it is 98% confident that you saw a gray whale.

▶ **How does an expert system work?** When it is time to make a decision, the inference engine begins analyzing the available data by following the rules in the knowledge base. If the expert system needs additional data, it checks external databases, looks for the data in a transaction processing system, or asks the user to answer questions. Figure 9-13 outlines the flow of information in an expert system and summarizes its capabilities.

QuickCheck   **9**

Which one of the following would not characterize an expert system?

a. Replicate the reasoning of a human expert.

b. Work with internal or external data.

c. Produce a recommendation or decision.

d. Produce routine and on-demand reports.

Figure 9-13: Expert systems

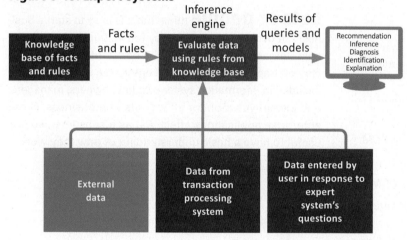

QuickQuiz   Section A

1. Effective information systems are designed to support goals that help an organization carry out its _____ statement.

2. Mid-level managers typically engage in _____ planning.

3. Batch processing was replaced by _____ transaction processing systems in which each transaction is processed when it is entered.

4. An executive information system is a type of decision _____ system.

5. The facts and rules for an expert system are stored in a(n) _____ base.

Objectives

▶ Provide at least two examples of businesses that engage in each of the following types of ecommerce: B2C, B2B, C2C, and B2G.

▶ List the cookie-related events that occur during an online shopping session.

▶ Explain how just-in-time inventory is related to SCM.

▶ Draw a diagram of a supply chain.

▶ Describe how loyalty programs are related to CRM.

▶ List the six major components of an ERP application.

▶ List at least five benefits of ERP systems.

Lots of people think that it is easy to start a business, sit back, and let the money roll in. But businesses are complex and risky. They require constant supervision to stay on track. A wide variety of enterprise software can be included in information systems to help owners, managers, and executives monitor all aspects of a business. These enterprise applications affect you as a consumer, so it is useful to have a basic understanding of how they work.

Terminology

ecommerce	B2B	payment gateway	CRM
B2C	B2G	supply chain	loyalty program
C2C	ecommerce application	SCM	ERP

Ecommerce

Customers can place an order for a pair of shoes on Zappos.com and have them delivered the next day. How is it possible for Zappos to process an order, validate the payment, transmit the order to a warehouse, locate the correct pair of shoes, box them up, get them on a truck, transport them halfway across the country, and place them on your doorstep all in the space of 24 hours? It is the modern miracle of ecommerce.

▶ **What is the scope of ecommerce?** Consumers usually think of ecommerce in terms of online storefronts such as Amazon and Zappos that sell various products to consumers, but the scope of ecommerce is much wider. **Ecommerce** refers to business transactions that are conducted electronically over a computer network. It encompasses all aspects of business and marketing enabled by Internet and Web technologies.

Ecommerce activities are classified as **B2C** (business-to-consumer), **C2C** (consumer-to-consumer), **B2B** (business-to-business), and **B2G** (business-to-government), as described in Figure 9-14.

Try It!

What kinds of goods and services are offered at B2B auction sites? Connect to Web sites such as *B-Stock* or *BlueLots* and browse the links to find out.

9

Figure 9-14: Ecommerce classifications

B2C

C2C

B2B and **B2G**

Online storefronts such as Zappos, Amazon, and Dell offer merchandise and services to consumers.	Consumers sell to each other at popular auction and list sites, such as eBay and Etsy.	Companies such as Oracle, B-Stock, and Ingram sell goods and services online to other businesses or to governments.

Ecommerce sites sell a variety of goods and services. Physical products offered at ecommerce sites include clothing, shoes, skateboards, and cars. Most of these products can be shipped to buyers through the postal service, a parcel delivery service, or a trucking company. This type of ecommerce—similar to mail order—is regarded as the traditional model. Zappos fits neatly into this niche.

Many ecommerce sites specialize in digital products, such as news, music, movies, databases, ebooks, and software. The unique feature of these products is that they can be transformed into bits and delivered over the Internet. Consumers get them immediately upon completing their orders, and there are no shipping costs. Amazon's Kindle store represents this type of ecommerce, as do the Apple Music store and Spotify.

Ecommerce merchants also peddle services, such as online medical consultation, distance education, and custom sewing. Some of these services can be carried out by computers. Others require human agents. Services can be delivered electronically, as in the case of a distance education course, or they might produce some physical product, such as a custom-fit boat cover.

Some online merchants sell across categories, providing digital products in addition to physical products. Some other merchants, such as Comcast, may even include services in their mix of online offerings. To manage their online storefronts, merchants use ecommerce applications.

QuickCheck

Craigslist would be classified as what kind of ecommerce business?

a. B2C

b. B2B

c. B2G

d. C2C

▶ What is an ecommerce application?
An **ecommerce application** is the software that handles ecommerce transactions. Any enterprise that intends to have an online storefront will include an ecommerce application as part of its information system. These applications help customers find products, make a selection, and submit payment. A key component of an ecommerce application is an online shopping cart.

▶ How does an online shopping cart work?
An online shopping cart uses cookies to store information about a customer's activities on an ecommerce site. Because HTTP is a stateless protocol, Web-based storefronts can't easily track the items a customer views or selects. That information has to be stored where it can be accessed during checkout.

The trend today is to assign an ID number to a customer, and then store that ID number in a cookie on the customer's computer. As the customer shops, items that the customer views are stored along with the customer ID on the ecommerce site's server. This enables the merchant to compile a profile of the kind of merchandise the customer is interested in.

Item numbers for the merchandise that a customer places in a shopping cart are also stored on the server. Even if the customer abandons the purchase, the items may remain in the cart. The next time the customer visits the site, the server can retrieve the ID cookie from the customer's computer and look up the customer's profile on the server. If it finds items in the cart, it can give the customer another chance to purchase them (Figure 9-15).

QuickCheck

How is it possible to leave an ecommerce site after putting items in a shopping cart, and then find those items still in the cart when you return to the site days later?

a. HTTP is a stateless protocol that saves session data for up to 10 days.

b. The dynamic HTML on a Web page is able to save the contents of a shopping cart for the next visit.

c. The ecommerce application running on the customer's local device stores a shopping cart number.

d. A cookie on the local device stores a shopping cart number that is matched to the ecommerce site database when the customer next visits the site.

Figure 9-15: How an ecommerce shopping cart works

❶ The customer arrives at the ecommerce site and is assigned a cookie containing a cart ID number.

❷ Item numbers are stored on the ecommerce site server under the customer's cart ID number.

Cart #209802
Item #B7655
Item #H050311

Cookie cart #209802

Customer's computer

buy it

Item #B7655

buy it

Item #H050311

❸ The next time this customer logs in, the site looks for any of its cookies. After finding a cookie with a cart ID number, the site can display the cart's contents to the customer.

Try It!

Go to an ecommerce site such as Amazon.com and place a few items in your shopping cart. (You won't have to buy them.) Now, check the cookies stored by your browser. Can you find the cookie that assigns you a shopping cart ID number?

How do online payments work? One factor that contributes to the amazingly fast order fulfillment at Zappos is a payment processing procedure that is virtually instantaneous. Zappos is not unique in its use of real-time transaction processing. Banking institutions make this service available to all ecommerce merchants.

Payment processing is based on an online **payment gateway** that authorizes credit and debit cards, PayPal, Venmo, and Apple Pay transactions. The payment gateway uses a secure connection to transmit customer payment data to a payment processor or financial institution where the payment can be verified. An authorization is sent back through the payment gateway to the merchant, which can then fulfill the order and submit a request for payment from the banking institution.

The merchant's ecommerce application carries out only the first and last stages of the payment process. It collects the customer's payment details on a secure form and then hands them off to the payment gateway. The approval process takes place outside of the ecommerce application, which then handles the last part of the transaction by confirming the customer's order and sending out a status email. The entire payment processing routine shown in Figure 9-16 takes just a few seconds.

Figure 9-16: Online order processing system using a payment gateway

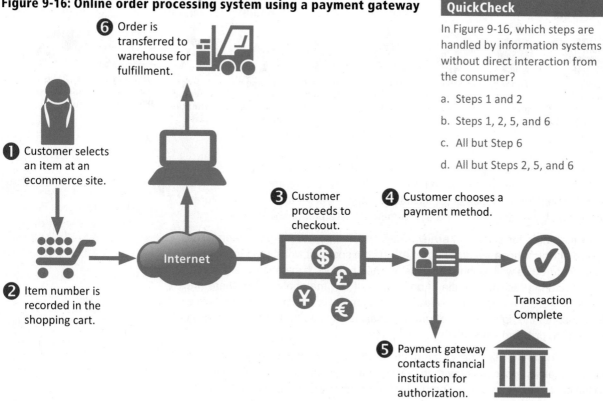

① Customer selects an item at an ecommerce site.

② Item number is recorded in the shopping cart.

⑥ Order is transferred to warehouse for fulfillment.

③ Customer proceeds to checkout.

④ Customer chooses a payment method.

⑤ Payment gateway contacts financial institution for authorization.

Transaction Complete

QuickCheck

In Figure 9-16, which steps are handled by information systems without direct interaction from the consumer?

a. Steps 1 and 2

b. Steps 1, 2, 5, and 6

c. All but Step 6

d. All but Steps 2, 5, and 6

Supply Chain Management

Every online business runs an ecommerce application. This factor does not differentiate Zappos from merchants that take almost a week to deliver orders. One of the keys to Zappos's speedy order fulfillment is the way it manages its supply chain.

▶ **What is a supply chain?** A **supply chain** is the sequence of organizations, people, activities, information, and resources involved in moving a product or service from supplier to customer.

For Zappos, the supply chain includes vendors such as Cole Haan and Nike, shipping companies such as UPS, and warehousing facilities—Zappos uses Amazon fulfillment centers, such as the one in Shepherdsville, Kentucky, just 18 miles from the Louisville airport.

Customer orders generated from the ecommerce system are transmitted to the fulfillment center, where robots gather boxes of shoes and carry them to packers. Packages are trucked to the airport, loaded on planes, transported to distant cities, unloaded at sorting centers, loaded on trucks, and delivered to customer doorsteps—all in fewer than 24 hours! (See Figure 9-17.)

Figure 9-17: The Zappos supply chain

Zappos Order Processing						UPS Delivery		
11:30am			2:30am			5:46am	6:30am	10:45am
Order placed	Order received at warehouse	Order picked and packed	Tracking number assigned	Package trucked to airport	Package departs Louisville airport	Package arrives at destination city	Package sorted at UPS shipping center	Package delivered to customer

▶ **What is the scope of a supply chain?** Technically, a supply chain stretches from raw materials and parts all the way to customer delivery. The supply chain for a Zappos order includes shipping leather to the manufacturer, storing that material, and eventually forming it into a pair of shoes.

Raw materials for a product are sourced and shipped to manufacturers. The speed at which those materials arrive affects the speed at which products can be manufactured as well as the cost of the finished product. If materials are delayed, manufacturing facilities sit idle. If an excess of raw materials arrive, there are costs for warehousing them. Inventory management is a business best practice that ensures the right amount of raw materials is on hand for the manufacturing process to proceed smoothly.

Zappos primarily sells finished products, so the manufacturing segment of the supply chain is a lower priority than the segment that stretches from the supplier to the customer. However, if a product sells out quickly and Zappos would like to sell more, the timeline for a manufacturing run becomes an important element in the supply chain. When Zappos customers see the message "Out of Stock, Notify me when this item is available," the manufacturing segment of the supply chain may swing into action to obtain more inventory.

QuickCheck

Which of the following factors is most likely to disrupt the supply chain for the next iPhone rollout?

a. A shortage of truck drivers

b. A lack of advertising

c. Competition from Samsung

d. The price of Apple stock

What is the role of an information system in the supply chain?

Supply chains are complex, so businesses use **SCM** (supply chain management) to maximize efficiency and profitability. SCM application software is a key aspect of information systems used by manufacturers and retailers. The goal of SCM is to supply customers with the right product at the right price. Time is of the essence, but the price of transport is also a factor that has to be monitored and controlled.

Data for SCM is supplied by computerized or manual systems such as warehouse inventories, shipper logs and billing, supplier inventories, and manufacturing schedules. Those elements define the supply side of SCM. The demand side is also important, and SCM must take into account customer demand for products.

Current demand can be quantified from customer orders, but astute managers understand that forecasting demand is also an essential part of having merchandise in stock and ready to ship. Data derived from demand planning and forecasting also plays a part in SCM.

How effective is SCM? Take a look at some case studies of well-known businesses to understand the effectiveness of SCM (Figure 9-18).

Terminology

Supply chain management is also referred to as *logistics*, though that term is somewhat less popular today.

9

Figure 9-18: SCM success stories

 H&M is an upscale fashion retailer that designs its own merchandise and sells to online and in-store customers. The company relies on a network of nearly 900 suppliers located in Asia and Europe. Merchandise is housed in a huge central warehouse in Germany, and from there it is shipped to local distribution centers in different countries. H&M's supply chain gets products to market in two to three weeks.

Home Depot, the DIY home improvement giant, uses 18 rapid deployment warehouses that make it possible to ship products to 90% of U.S. households within 48 hours.

BMW's 1,150-acre facility in South Carolina produces about 350,000 vehicles each year. The automated facility was originally controlled by a data center in South Africa. Its just-in-time supply chain management coordinates in such detail with suppliers that the steering wheel for a black X5, for example, arrives from a supplier just as that vehicle is rolling down the line, and the brown steering wheel that's next in the delivery van corresponds to the beige X3 that's next in line.

Walmart stocks products made in more than 70 countries and sells them online in more than 11,000 stores in 28 countries. A key element in Walmart's SCM is cross docking, in which products are transferred from one truck directly to another without passing through a warehouse. Walmart's information system handles the tracking of inventory on each truck and provides instructions for unloading and transferring it.

 Apple has been recognized as having the best supply chain in the world. Apple's strategy is to purchase component parts for computers, iPads, and iPhones from suppliers all over the globe. Those parts are then shipped to manufacturing facilities in China. From China, devices are shipped to Apple Stores and cell phone retailers as well as directly to customers. Products ordered online are made to order. The maximum time to manufacture and ship each made-to-order device is about 15 days. To deliver devices for product launches, Apple leases Boeing 777 air cargo planes, which can each carry 450,000 devices.

QuickCheck

In which case studies are suppliers featured as a key component of the supply chain?

a. H&M, BMW, and Apple

b. H&M, Walmart, and BMW

c. Home Depot and Apple

d. Walmart and Apple

Customer Relationship Management

Not every Zappos customer gets free next-day shipping. That perk is offered to VIP customers. To get free shipping and earn rewards, a customer can buy lots of shoes or apply for a VIP account. Customer loyalty programs such as Zappos VIP help attract and retain customers. In business circles, the galaxy of services that revolve around customers is called CRM.

❱ What is CRM? The acronym **CRM** stands for customer relationship management. It refers to practices and technologies that companies use to analyze and improve interactions with customers. The purpose of CRM is to attract new shoppers, convert those shoppers into buyers, and turn first-time buyers into repeat customers. Figure 9-19 illustrates this basic CRM strategy.

Figure 9-19: CRM helps turn shoppers into repeat buyers

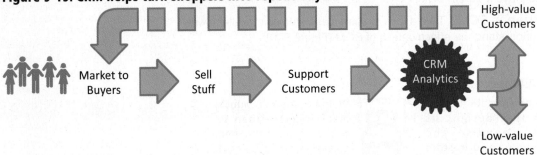

❱ What are the elements of CRM? Businesses use a variety of strategies to enhance CRM. Some strategies focus on human factors, such as training customer service representatives. Other strategies depend on data gathered by information systems and analyzed by CRM application software.

Consumers might not understand the full significance of loyalty programs, online chat, and other CRM techniques. Figure 9-20 provides a list that includes customer-facing CRM techniques and those that take place behind the scenes.

Terminology

The term *customer facing* is business jargon for systems that customers and clients interact with. The opposite of customer-facing systems are back-office systems, which customers do not see or use.

Figure 9-20: CRM supports customer-facing and back-office elements

Customer Facing

- Enhance the ecommerce site with a search function, recommendations, and reviews.
- Collect customer email addresses from loyalty programs and build profiles in a database.
- Target customers in the database with email marketing.
- Provide customer service through online chat and easy returns.
- Promote products in blogs and social media ads.

Back Office

- Provide analytics for back-office demand forecasting and online metrics, such as the number of visitors, mentions, and likes.

▶ **What is the point of loyalty programs?** A major source of data for CRM is produced by loyalty programs. A **loyalty program** or a rewards program is a marketing effort that provides customers with incentives for making purchases. Loyalty programs can offer rewards such as discounts, free shipping, notifications of sales, redeemable points, and airline miles.

Some loyalty programs use cards that get punched or stamped with each purchase. After filling out the card, a customer is entitled to a free or discounted product. Such uncomplicated programs were somewhat successful in encouraging repeat purchases, but businesses gained little else from them.

Computer-based loyalty programs store customer data in a database, which can be updated with customer preferences and can maintain a record of purchases. Incentives can be tailored to each customer's profile. Today, businesses are desperate for customer email addresses. Those addresses are used as customer IDs and provide a way to contact customers with information about sales and other incentives.

▶ **How does CRM fit into an enterprise information system?** In addition to data collected from loyalty programs, CRM applications gather data from several subsystems and deliver it to decision makers. For example, a technical support representative can be supplied with a customer's invoices from the sales subsystem to determine whether a product is under warranty.

CRM applications provide optimal information when they encompass customer support, marketing, and sales. Additional optimization can be gained when CRM applications mesh with ecommerce and payment platforms accessed by customers, as shown in Figure 9-21.

Figure 9-21: CRM systems interact with other information system modules

Try It!

Can you estimate the number of loyalty programs you are enrolled in? How many of them send you regular email messages? Can you stop participating in those loyalty programs and remove your name and email address from the CRM databases?

9

QuickCheck

What are the core cogs of a CRM system?

a. Customer support, marketing, sales

b. Marketing campaigns

c. Analytics

d. Ecommerce sites

Enterprise Resource Planning

From the perspective of consumers, businesses such as Zappos that offer an enjoyable ecommerce experience along with speedy delivery and world-class customer service seem to run smoothly. But ecommerce, CRM, and SCM are just one part of an enterprise software suite that includes financial management, human resources, inventory, planning, communication, collaboration, and keeping an eye on the competition. Sophisticated ERP systems can integrate all of these enterprise activities.

▶ **What is ERP?** The acronym **ERP** stands for enterprise resource planning. ERP is a suite of software modules that integrate major business activities. In addition to sales, CRM, and SCM, ERP modules support business activities such as product planning, manufacturing, purchasing, inventory control, distribution, accounting, marketing, finance, and human resources. ERP systems can run on in-house hardware or in the cloud. Cloud-based systems are usually deployed as SaaS (software as a service) with the business paying monthly or annual fees for its use.

All of the modules in an ERP system use a common interface and a common database. Having a common interface means that various modules use similar controls. This is the same principle as the interface for modules in an office suite, such as Microsoft Office, which use similar ribbon bars and other familiar controls. Standardizing the interface for all of the modules in an ERP system shortens the learning curve and lets workers easily switch between multiple modules.

The use of a common database is one of ERP's major advantages. Legacy information systems often had separate databases for each application module. For example, data from customer invoices would be stored in one database, while the data used by sales representatives to contact customers would be stored in a different database. Using a common ERP database allows workers and managers to access and analyze data from multiple business units.

Information system software vendors sometimes describe ERP as "the central nervous system of an enterprise." Figure 9-22 shows how ERP connects major business units to a central database.

Terminology

ERP is pronounced by using its initials: E. R. P.

Figure 9-22: ERP modules

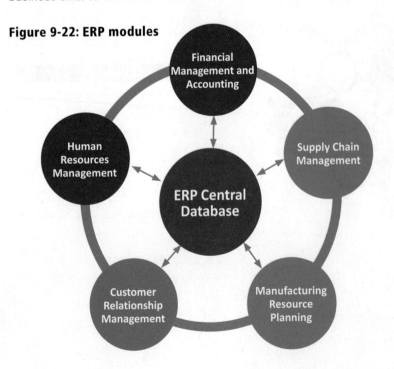

QuickCheck

What type of system uses a separate database for each module?

a. ERP

b. CRM

c. Legacy

d. Ecommerce

▶ **What is the cost benefit of ERP?** ERP systems can be costly, but a well-planned implementation can produce significant competitive advantages. The cost of software, planning, installation, and in-house hardware for a typical mid-sized business ranges between $50,000 and $750,000. Cloud-based ERP systems can be less costly.

Implementation may also require a company to change some of its basic processes to conform to the ERP system workflow. Although customization is possible, ERP software has a basic set of features that function according to accepted business practices. Businesses that deviate from those practices may have to restructure and retrain workers to effectively utilize an ERP system.

ERP streamlines processes and information across an entire enterprise. It allows employees to do their jobs more efficiently by providing them with tools to access data as necessary from across business units. Warehouse workers, for example, can access order data directly from the sales and invoicing module, and they can access shipping information from the procurement module.

Managers and executives access the same ERP modules, but rather than looking at order and inventory details, they may view analytics to gauge the profitability of products or measure the productivity of employees. In summary, ERP can provide the following benefits to an enterprise:

❶ Improved overall performance by standardizing business processes based on best practices

❷ Minimized technology overhead for managers and other workers who interact with a single, centralized, and integrated set of software modules

❸ Increased efficiency and productivity from streamlined workflows

❹ Improved access to information from a single database

❺ Enhanced customer satisfaction based on efficient sales and distribution

❻ Reduced costs and errors when transferring data between systems such as accounting and human resources

❼ Increased profitability from the ability to collect analytics for all aspects of business operations

❽ Reduced inventory costs resulting from better planning, forecasting, modeling, and tracking

QuickCheck

Which of the advantages listed at left would most benefit a business that is trying to compete with Zappos?

a. ❶

b. ❸

c. ❺

d. ❼

QuickQuiz   Section B

1. Online auction sites such as B-Stock and eBay are examples of B2G ecommerce. True or false? [   ]

2. An ecommerce system collects a customer's credit card number, which is handed off to a(n) [   ] gateway.

3. The application used by an information system to handle cross-docking logistics would be classified as [   ] management.

4. A major source of data for [   ] applications is gathered by loyalty programs. (Hint: Use the acronym.)

5. [   ] has been described as "the central nervous system of an enterprise." (Hint: Use the acronym.)

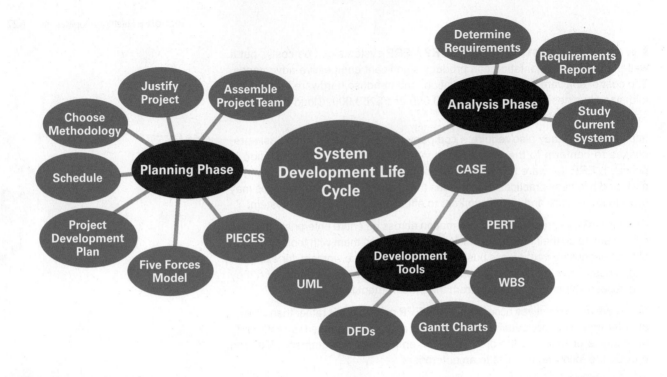

Objectives

▶ List the five phases of the SDLC.

▶ List five tasks that are completed during the planning phase.

▶ Draw a diagram of Michael Porter's Five Forces model.

▶ Define BI, BPM, JIT, MRP, and TQM.

▶ Use PIECES to classify problems and opportunities.

▶ Describe the three activities that take place during the analysis phase.

▶ Briefly describe at least six tools used by systems analysts.

$90+ billion. That is how much the United States federal government spends annually on information technology projects. Government watchdogs report that about half of these projects run over budget, fall behind schedule, or fail to deliver on their promises. How can technology project failures be avoided? There is a process for creating successful information systems. It is called systems analysis and design. Section C delves into analysis, and Section D introduces system design.

Terminology

system development life cycle
iterative SDLC
systems analysis and design
planning phase
project development plan
joint application design
BI
BPM
JIT

MRP
TQM
PIECES framework
structured methodology
information engineering methodology
object-oriented methodology
project management software
PERT

WBS
Gantt charts
critical path
analysis phase
system requirements
success factors
system requirements report
data flow diagram
external entity
data store

process
data flow
UML
use case diagram
actors
use case
class diagram
sequence diagram
CASE tool

System Development Life Cycles

If you're a fan of home remodeling shows on the HGTV network, you'll recall that the design team usually begins by looking at the house and asking the homeowners for a wish list. The designers then create a renovation plan and get approval from the homeowners before beginning construction. A similar process is used by IT teams that develop information systems. The overall process is called an SDLC.

▶ **What is an SDLC?** An information system progresses through several phases as it is developed, used, and finally retired. These phases encompass a **system development life cycle**, usually referred to as the SDLC. Figure 9-23 illustrates a typical sequence of SDLC phases.

Terminology

The standard SDLC, such as the one pictured in Figure 9-23, is sometimes referred to as a *waterfall SDLC* because one phase follows another like water falling from one level to the next.

9

Figure 9-23: SDLC phases

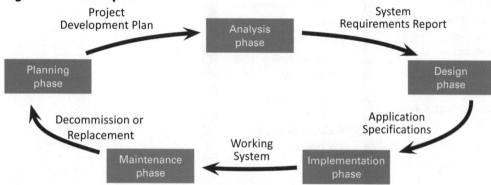

▶ **Which phase comes first?** A standard SDLC begins with the planning phase, and then it continues to analysis, design, implementation, and maintenance before the system is decommissioned and the planning for a new system begins.

The phases in an SDLC are not necessarily separate steps, however. An **iterative SDLC** can be used to create and implement a small subset of a system and then enhance it through a series of upgrades. Each subset has its own life cycle, which allows developers to focus on manageable parts of an information system, rather than tackle the entire system as one large project.

Iterative SDLCs are often referred to as "agile methods" because they allow flexibility as development progresses. Technically, agile methods are used for developing software, rather than entire information systems, but the two are intertwined. Using agile methods, a fully functional subset of an information system can be created, tested, and deployed. Then, with user feedback, additional modules and features can be added for subsequent versions.

▶ **How does the SDLC relate to systems analysis and design?** The SDLC provides a general outline of how an information system evolves. **Systems analysis and design** is a discipline that focuses on developing information systems according to the phases of an SDLC.

The scope of systems analysis and design encompasses the people, procedures, computers, communications networks, and software involved with handling information in an organization. It is much wider in scope than software engineering, which is only one of the tasks that takes place during the development process.

QuickCheck

Which of the following is most closely connected to agile methods?

a. Waterfall SDLC

b. Systems analysis and design

c. Iterative SDLC

d. HGTV

Planning Phase

On HGTV, each renovation episode begins with a homeowner consultation. Renovators don't just grab a hammer and start nailing pieces of wood together. It is important to have a plan. As with home renovations, initial plans for an information system are developed during a planning phase.

Figure 9-24: Planning phase

▶ **What does the planning phase entail?** The planning phase for an information system project includes the activities listed in Figure 9-24. The goal of these activities is to create a project development plan. Before the project proceeds beyond the planning phase, the project development plan is usually reviewed and approved by management. This planning document includes:

- A short description of the project, including its scope

- An estimate of the project costs and potential financial benefits

- A list of project team participants

- A schedule for the project, including an outline of its phases

▶ **Who supervises the project?** Depending on the scope of the problem and the expertise of the professional staff, an information systems project can be managed by an in-house information technology department or outsourced to a development firm.

A system development project team, or project team for short, is assigned to analyze and develop an information system. The project team has a leader, sometimes referred to as the project manager, who supervises the project team's workflow and output.

▶ **Who participates in the project?** The composition of a project team depends on the scope of the project. Large and complex projects tend to have sizeable project teams, whereas smaller projects tend to have fewer members on the project team. Having more team members doesn't necessarily lead to faster completion, however. Research seems to show that when the team size exceeds nine people, productivity drops. It is interesting to note that U.S. government standards stipulate at least 32 people who must participate in every system development project. That number may be one clue to the high failure rate for federally funded IT projects.

In addition to the project team, other members of an organization might be asked to participate in various phases of the project. A widely accepted technique called **joint application design** (JAD) is based on the idea that the best information systems are designed when end users and systems analysts work together on a project as equal partners.

JAD provides a structured methodology for planning and holding a series of meetings, called JAD sessions, in which users and analysts jointly identify problems and look for solutions.

QuickCheck

What is the extent of the planning that gets done in the planning phase?

a. Plans are completed for the entire information system.

b. A detailed budget is presented.

c. The software is selected.

d. The overall approach and justification are presented for approval.

▶ What motivates organizations to invest in information systems?

Information system projects may be designed to replace manual systems or replace obsolete computerized information systems. Information system projects do not necessarily reach across the entire enterprise. They may be undertaken to automate one department, such as when Zappos initiated a project to roboticize its warehouse operations.

Information system projects often result from changes to business practices and as a response to new government record keeping, reporting, and compliance regulations.

The justification for information system projects usually emerges from a serious problem with the current system, a threat to the organization's success, or an opportunity to improve an organization's products or services through technology.

▶ What kinds of threats and opportunities affect organizations?

Most organizations exist in a rapidly changing and competitive environment, where many opportunities and threats can be effectively handled only by using sophisticated information systems. A well-known business analyst, Michael Porter, created the Five Forces model, shown in Figure 9-25, to illustrate how opportunities and threats can affect an organization.

Figure 9-25: Michael Porter's Five Forces model

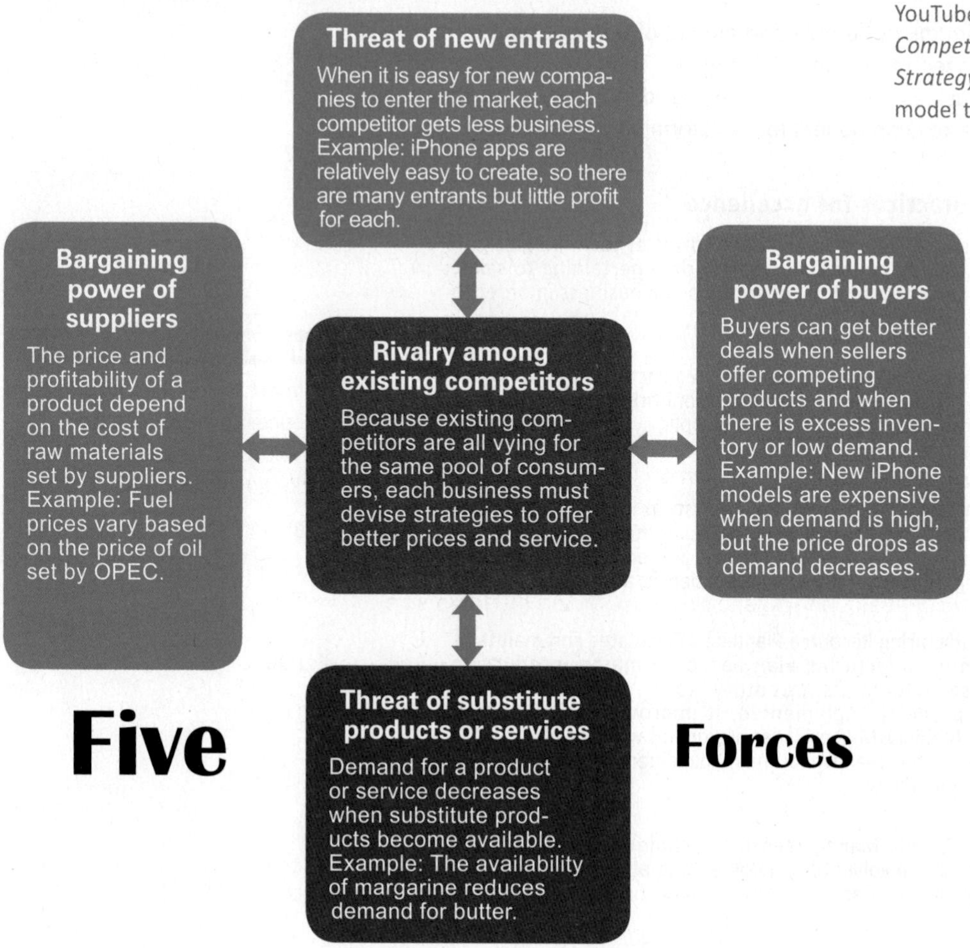

QuickCheck

Go online and check out sites such as eBay, Priceline, and AuctionZip. What do these sites have in common?

a. They are a potential threat from a new entrant.

b. They give customers more bargaining power.

c. They give suppliers more bargaining power.

d. They are a threat because they offer substitute products.

Try It!

Michael Porter talks about his Five Forces model in a YouTube video called *The Five Competitive Forces that Shape Strategy*. How does he apply the model to the airline industry?

Threat of new entrants
When it is easy for new companies to enter the market, each competitor gets less business. Example: iPhone apps are relatively easy to create, so there are many entrants but little profit for each.

Bargaining power of suppliers
The price and profitability of a product depend on the cost of raw materials set by suppliers. Example: Fuel prices vary based on the price of oil set by OPEC.

Rivalry among existing competitors
Because existing competitors are all vying for the same pool of consumers, each business must devise strategies to offer better prices and service.

Bargaining power of buyers
Buyers can get better deals when sellers offer competing products and when there is excess inventory or low demand. Example: New iPhone models are expensive when demand is high, but the price drops as demand decreases.

Threat of substitute products or services
Demand for a product or service decreases when substitute products become available. Example: The availability of margarine reduces demand for butter.

Five **Forces**

▶ How can an information system help an enterprise respond to threats and opportunities? To be successful in its mission, an enterprise must respond effectively to opportunities and threats. An enterprise has a choice of three fundamental responses:

- **Make improvements.** An enterprise can become better at what it does by cutting costs, lowering prices, improving its products, offering better customer service, and so on. Information systems often provide ways to make businesses run more efficiently, and they can supply timely information that helps improve customer service. For example, to better compete with other telecommunications companies, Comcast developed an information system and end-user app that allows consumers to track the estimated arrival time of installation and repair technicians.

- **Change the industry.** An enterprise can change the nature of an industry. Computers and communications technologies often make such changes possible. For example, Amazon pioneered the idea of selling books on the Web, which was a major change to an industry that sold books from mall-based stores.

- **Create new products.** An enterprise can create a new product, such as flavored potato chips, or a new service, such as overnight package delivery. Although creativity and invention usually spring from the minds of people, information systems can contribute to research and development efforts by collecting and analyzing data, helping inventors create models and explore simulations, and so on.

A new information system might be only one aspect of a larger plan to evolve an enterprise into a stronger, more competitive entity. The business community has embraced several business practices, summarized in Figure 9-26, that use information systems as a key component for transforming organizations.

Try It!

BMW takes just-in-time inventory seriously at its South Carolina factory. You can see the inventory arriving and being installed directly into vehicles in the YouTube video *BMW X3 Production*. Then watch the amazing assembly robots in the video called *New BMW 5 Series Sedan Assembly Line*.

Figure 9-26: Business practices for excellence

BI (Business Intelligence): An integrated set of technologies and procedures used to collect and analyze data pertaining to sales, production, and other internal operations of a business in order to make better business decisions.

BPM (Business Process Management): A structured methodology for improving business performance by monitoring, measuring, and modifying processes that support the people, systems, and goals in an enterprise.

JIT (Just In Time): A manufacturing system in which the parts needed to construct a finished product are produced or arrive at the assembly site just when they are needed. JIT tends to reduce costs by eliminating substantial warehousing expenses and obsolete parts.

MRP (Manufacturing Resource Planning): Calculates and maintains an optimum manufacturing plan based on master production schedules, sales forecasts, inventory status, open orders, and invoices. If properly implemented, it improves cash flow and increases profitability. MRP provides businesses with the ability to be proactive rather than reactive for the management of their inventory levels and material flow.

TQM (Total Quality Management): A technique initiated by top management that involves all employees and all departments, and focuses on quality assurance in every product and service offered to customers.

QuickCheck

Walmart once followed standard practices to store inventory in warehouses. Its shift to cross docking is an example of _____.

a. BI

b. BPM

c. JIT

d. TQM

❱ How does the project team identify problems and opportunities?

Justifying a project often involves identifying problems and opportunities within an organization's current information system. By eliminating problems and taking advantage of opportunities, an organization can become more competitive.

Project team members can identify problems and opportunities using a variety of techniques, such as interviews and data analysis. For example, James Wetherbe's **PIECES framework** helps classify problems in an information system. Each letter of *PIECES* stands for a potential problem, as shown in Figure 9-27.

Figure 9-27: PIECES framework

Performance

A performance problem means that an information system does not respond quickly enough to users or takes too long to complete processing tasks.

Economics

An economics problem means that the system costs too much to operate or use.

Efficiency

An efficiency problem means that too many resources are used to collect, process, store, and distribute information.

Information

An information problem means that users don't receive the right information at the right time in a usable format.

Control

A control problem means that information is available to unauthorized users or that authorized users are not given the authority to make decisions based on the information they receive.

Service

A service problem means that the system is too difficult or inconvenient to use.

QuickCheck

Which element of the PIECES framework would reveal a problem with an ecommerce site that does not tell customers when items are out of stock?

a. Performance

b. Information

c. Economics

d. Service

❱ What is a system development methodology?

As part of the planning phase, the project team selects one or more methodologies that provide structure for the development effort. Earlier, you learned that the SDLC delineates the phases of system development.

A system development methodology specifies what takes place in each phase; it encompasses the activities, procedures, methods, best practices, deliverables, and automated tools that system developers follow to complete the SDLC. In short, a system development methodology guides developers through the phases of system development.

There are many standard system development methodologies. **Structured methodology** focuses on the processes that take place within an information system. **Information engineering methodology** focuses on the data an information system collects before working out ways to process that data. **Object-oriented methodology** treats an information system as a collection of objects that interact to accomplish tasks.

QuickCheck

Suppose you are working with a team that is constructing a new information system to help researchers at a pharmaceutical company sift through vast quantities of patient data. What methodology would work best?

a. Structured

b. Information engineering

c. Object-oriented

How is the project schedule developed? Project management software is an effective tool for planning and scheduling. It helps managers track and visualize the complex interactions between tasks. Popular project management offerings include Asana, Trello, QuickBase, and Microsoft Project.

Project scheduling begins in the planning phase, but it stretches throughout the entire project. Project managers organize the work into tasks and milestones, which can be scheduled and assigned. As tasks are completed, the schedule is updated and adjusted. Industry standard tools for scheduling and project management include PERT, WBS, and Gantt charts (Figure 9-28).

Figure 9-28: Project management tools

PERT

PERT (Program Evaluation and Review Technique) is a method for analyzing the time needed to complete each project task and identify the minimum time needed to complete the total project. A PERT diagram uses arrows to map the sequence of tasks in a project. The **critical path** indicates the shortest time to complete all tasks.

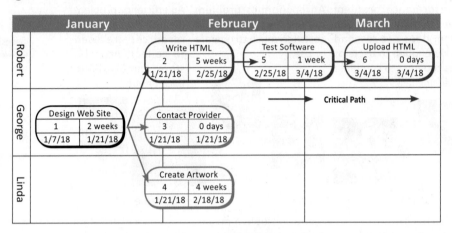

WBS

A WBS (work breakdown structure) breaks a complex task into a series of subtasks. The breakdown of tasks can be shown as a hierarchical diagram, but it can also be formatted as a simple outline. A WBS can be activity-oriented to list tasks or deliverable-oriented to list project milestones.

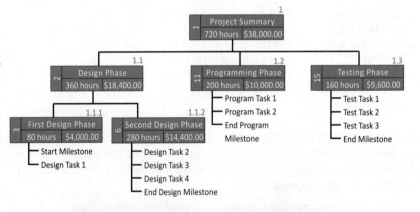

Gantt charts

A Gantt chart uses bars to show the duration of development tasks as they occur over time. Each bar on the chart represents a task; the length of a bar indicates the task's expected duration.

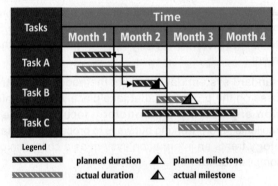

Analysis Phase

On HGTV, the planning phase ends after the homeowners reveal their wish list and budget. In the next segment of the show, the design team looks at the house to figure out how many items on the wish list are possible within time and budget limits. A similar routine takes place during the analysis phase of the SDLC.

▶ **What is the purpose of the analysis phase?** The planning phase of the SDLC ends after the project team selects a development methodology, draws up the project development plan, and receives permission from management to proceed. The goal of the **analysis phase** is to produce a list of requirements for a new or revised information system. Tasks for the analysis phase are listed in Figure 9-29.

Figure 9-29: Analysis phase

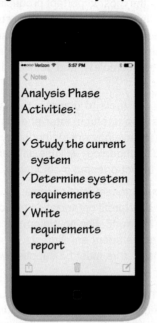

▶ **Why study the current system?** Most new information systems are designed to replace a system or process that is already in place. It is important to study the current system to understand its strengths and weaknesses before designing a new system.

▶ **How does the project team discover what happens in the current system?** Some members of the project team might have firsthand experience with the current system. They can often provide an overview of the system and identify key features, strengths, and weaknesses. To obtain additional information about the current system, project team members can observe the system in action and interview people who use it.

▶ **How does the project team determine what the new system should do?** System requirements are the criteria for successfully solving problems identified in an information system. These requirements guide the design and implementation for a new or updated information system. They also serve as an evaluation checklist at the end of the development project; because of this, they are sometimes called **success factors**. A new or updated information system should always meet requirements defined by the project team.

The project team determines requirements by interviewing users and studying successful information systems that solve problems similar to those in the current system. Another way to determine requirements is to construct a prototype as a trial version of an information system. Often the prototype is not a fully functioning system because it is designed to demonstrate only selected features that might be incorporated into a new information system. A systems analyst shows the prototype to users, who evaluate which features of the prototype are important for the new information system.

▶ **What does the project team do with system requirements?** After the project team studies the current system and then determines what the new system should do, system requirements are incorporated into a document called a **system requirements report** that describes the objectives for the information system.

QuickCheck

How does a system requirements report differ from a project development plan?

a. It contains estimated schedules.

b. It focuses on criteria for the system, rather than the planning process.

c. It focuses on the economic aspects of the new system.

d. It justifies the need to begin the SDLC.

9

Documentation Tools

A picture is worth a thousand words. That is the philosophy of systems analysts, who prefer to diagram the structure of an information system rather than describe it in words. Using diagrams is far more efficient than pages and pages of text, though clear narrative writing is also an important tool in the systems analyst's toolbox.

▶ **How does the project team document system requirements?** The system requirements report is one of the most important products of the SDLC. It documents key business practices in the current system and contains a list of success factors for a new or updated information system. If these factors have not been correctly identified, the information system will be a failure. The system requirements report must contain clear, complete, and detailed documentation, including diagrams and descriptions.

The project team can use a variety of tools to diagram the current system and produce documentation that is also useful in later phases of the SDLC. Documentation tools vary according to development methodology. For example, a project team following a structured methodology will use different documentation tools than a project team using object-oriented methodology.

To understand some of the most popular documentation tools, consider a project to develop an information system for a for-profit organization that offers business seminars and workshops throughout the world. The new information system must keep track of workshop schedules and student enrollments. Students have to be able to select workshops, and instructors must be supplied with a roster of students.

▶ **What are structured documentation tools?** The core documentation tool for project teams using structured methodology is the **data flow diagram** (DFD), which graphically illustrates how data moves through an information system.

You can think of a DFD as a map that traces the possible paths for data traveling from entities (such as students) to processes (such as enrolling in a workshop) or storage areas (such as databases). In DFD terminology, an **external entity** is a person, an organization, or a device outside the information system that originates or receives data. A **data store** is a filing cabinet, disk, or device that holds data. A **process** is a manual or computerized routine that changes data by performing a calculation, updating information, sorting a list, and so on. An arrow symbolizes a **data flow** and indicates how data travels from entities to processes and data stores. Each of these elements is represented on a DFD by a symbol, as shown in Figure 9-30.

QuickCheck

In an organization that offers business workshops, how would a workshop name be depicted on a DFD?

a. As an external entity

b. As a process

c. As a data store

d. As a data flow

Figure 9-30: Data flow diagram symbols

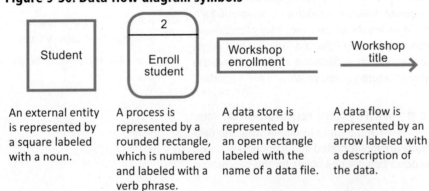

An external entity is represented by a square labeled with a noun.

A process is represented by a rounded rectangle, which is numbered and labeled with a verb phrase.

A data store is represented by an open rectangle labeled with the name of a data file.

A data flow is represented by an arrow labeled with a description of the data.

▶ **What does a DFD look like?** In a completed DFD, data flow arrows show the path of data to and from external entities, data stores, and processes. Figure 9-31 explains how to read a DFD.

Figure 9-31: How to read a DFD

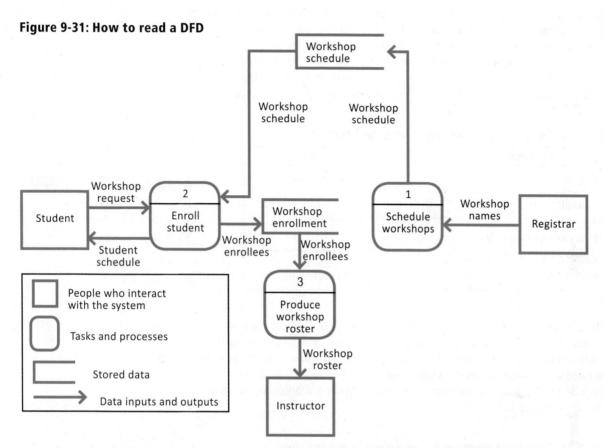

To read a DFD, begin at any one of the square entities and follow the arrows to trace the flow of data. The label on each data flow arrow identifies the data that moves through the system. Arrows moving into a process indicate input data. Arrows that emerge from a process show output. Rectangular data stores represent data that is stored in databases.

▶ **How do documentation tools differ for object-oriented analysis and design?** Structured documentation tools such as DFDs help analysts decide how to design databases and write applications that allow people to interact with those databases. In contrast, object-oriented design tools provide blueprints for creating data objects and the routines that allow people to interact with those objects. The current standard for object-oriented documentation is referred to as **UML** (Unified Modeling Language). Three of the most frequently used UML tools include use case diagrams, sequence diagrams, and class diagrams.

▶ **What is a use case diagram?** A **use case diagram** documents the users of an information system and the functions they perform. In object-oriented jargon, the people who use the system are called **actors**. Any task an actor performs is called a **use case**. Figure 9-32 shows a simple use case diagram for a workshop registration system.

Figure 9-32: Use case diagram

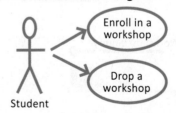

A use case diagram for a workshop registration system depicts two use cases—one in which a student (actor) enrolls in a workshop (use case 1), and one in which the student drops the workshop (use case 2).

▶ **What is the composition of an object?** A key element of object-oriented development is defining objects. In the registration example, a student interacts with two objects: a Workshop object and a Section object.

A **class diagram** provides the name of each object, a list of each object's attributes, a list of methods, and an indication of the associations between objects. An attribute is simply any data element that is stored as part of an object. A method is any behavior that an object is capable of performing. You'll find detailed definitions of object-oriented terms, such as classes, attributes, and methods, in Module 11. Figure 9-33 illustrates a class diagram for the workshop registration system.

Figure 9-33: Class diagram for workshops and sections

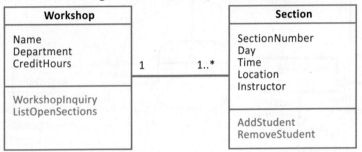

QuickCheck

In the class diagram shown in Figure 9-33, what is WorkshopInquiry?

a. A method

b. An attribute

c. An entity

d. A data store

▶ **What is a sequence diagram?** A **sequence diagram** depicts the detailed sequence of interactions that take place for a use case. For example, for the use case Enroll in a Workshop, a student might inquire which workshops are offered and then select a workshop based on a list of open workshop sections. Figure 9-34 shows a sequence diagram for the Enroll in a Workshop use case and explains how to interpret it.

Figure 9-34: Sequence diagram for enrolling in a workshop

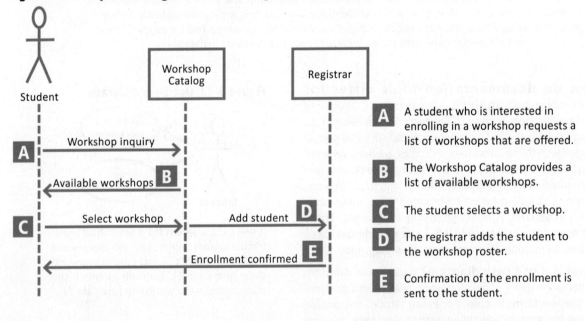

A   A student who is interested in enrolling in a workshop requests a list of workshops that are offered.

B   The Workshop Catalog provides a list of available workshops.

C   The student selects a workshop.

D   The registrar adds the student to the workshop roster.

E   Confirmation of the enrollment is sent to the student.

Are diagramming tools computerized? Maintaining documentation can become a complex task as the project progresses and system requirements are revised. A **CASE tool** (computer-aided software engineering tool) is a software application designed for documenting system requirements, diagramming current and proposed information systems, scheduling development tasks, and developing computer programs.

Commercial CASE tools such as Visible Analyst and PowerDesigner, and open source tools such as ArgoUML automate many of the routine housekeeping tasks required for systems analysis and design, such as changing the name of a data element on one diagram and making sure the change is reflected in other diagrams and program code. Figure 9-35 explains some of the features of CASE tools.

9

Figure 9-35: CASE software

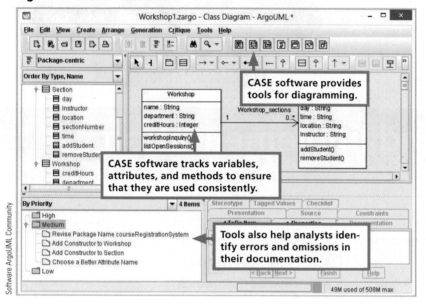

CASE software provides tools for diagramming.

CASE software tracks variables, attributes, and methods to ensure that they are used consistently.

Tools also help analysts identify errors and omissions in their documentation.

Software ArgoUML Community

QuickQuiz   Section C

1. In the planning phase, one of the main goals is to produce a project [＿＿＿＿] plan.

2. In Wetherbe's PIECES framework, the *S* represents a(n) [＿＿＿＿] problem that means the system is too difficult or inconvenient to use.

3. A(n) [＿＿＿＿] diagram shows the time needed to complete each project task and the critical path for the entire project. (Hint: Use the acronym.)

4. The project team fulfills the main objective of the [＿＿＿＿] phase by producing a system requirements report for a new or revised information system.

5. Data [＿＿＿＿] diagrams are used with structured methodology, whereas object-oriented methodology uses tools such as use cases, classes, and sequence diagrams.

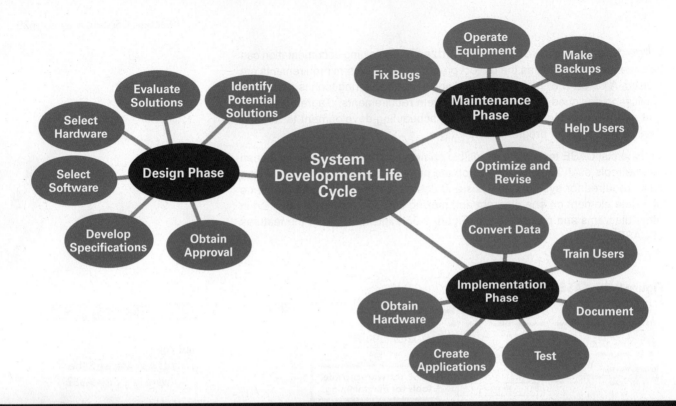

System Development Life Cycle

- **Design Phase**
  - Evaluate Solutions
  - Identify Potential Solutions
  - Select Hardware
  - Select Software
  - Develop Specifications
  - Obtain Approval
- **Maintenance Phase**
  - Fix Bugs
  - Operate Equipment
  - Make Backups
  - Help Users
  - Optimize and Revise
- **Implementation Phase**
  - Convert Data
  - Train Users
  - Obtain Hardware
  - Document
  - Create Applications
  - Test

Design and Implementation

Objectives

- List five activities that take place in the design phase of system development.
- Compare and contrast the four categories of software solutions that are available to the design team.
- List factors that affect the project team's choice of the best solution.
- Explain why some projects have a detailed design phase while other projects do not.
- Describe the significance of feature creep.
- List at least five activities that take place in the implementation phase.
- Describe five types of testing that take place in the implementation phase.
- Explain the purpose of system documentation and of user documentation.

- Describe four cutover methods.
- List tasks that occur during the maintenance phase.
- Describe six QoS metrics.

When things go wrong in a system development project, the trouble usually begins in the design phase. Attempting to implement a flawed information system only magnifies the trouble. What can go wrong, and how can the development team avoid design pitfalls? Section D examines successful approaches to system design and implementation.

Terminology

design phase
application development tool
turnkey system
decision support worksheet
application specifications

detailed design phase
feature creep
change requests
implementation phase
software customization
application testing
unit testing

integration testing
system testing
system documentation
user documentation
procedure handbook
system conversion
acceptance testing

maintenance phase
quality of service
quality-of-service metric
help desk

Design Phase

Let's look again at our HGTV example. After figuring out what the homeowners need and can afford, the designers get to work creating a blueprint and selecting materials for the new design. Their goal is to figure out the location for cabinets, closets, appliances, and structural elements, while ensuring that furniture can fit comfortably within the floor plan. As each element is placed in the floor plan, the design for the renovation begins to emerge. This process is a useful analogy for what happens during the design phase of the SDLC, as you will discover in this section.

▶ **What happens in the design phase?** In the analysis phase, the project team determines *what* the new information system must do. In the **design phase** of the SDLC, the project team must figure out *how* the new system will fulfill the requirements specified in the system requirements report. The activities that normally take place during the design phase for an information system are listed in Figure 9-36.

Figure 9-36: Design phase

●●○○○ Verizon 🛜   5:57 PM   ⁕ ◼▸
‹ Notes

Design Phase Activities:
✓ Identify potential
   solutions
✓ Evaluate solutions and
   select the best one
✓ Select hardware and
   software
✓ Develop application
   specifications
✓ Obtain approval

▶ **How does the project team come up with solutions?** There might be more than one way to solve the problems and meet the requirements identified in the analysis phase of the SDLC. Some potential solutions might be better than others. They might be more effective, less costly, or less complex. Therefore, it is typically not a good idea to proceed with the first solution that comes to mind. The project team should instead identify several potential hardware and software solutions by brainstorming and researching case studies.

▶ **What kinds of hardware solutions are available?** A myriad of hardware options are available for information systems. The project team has to consider the overall architecture based on device requirements, network technology, cloud hosting, and level of automation.

Device requirements. Servers and personal computers are the most commonly used components in information systems, but handheld devices, mainframes, and even supercomputers can also play a role. Systems analysts have to consider if users will be accessing the system at the office or in the field. How much mobility is required? How much processing power and storage are required? Will screen size be an issue? These are some of the hardware questions that will be answered in the design phase.

Network technology. An information system, by its very nature, is designed to serve an entire organization. That organization includes many people who work in different rooms, different buildings, and perhaps even different countries.

Virtually every information system requires a network, so the project team must examine network alternatives, such as LANs, extranets, intranets, and the Internet. Many information systems require a complex mixture of networks, such as a LAN in each branch office connected to a company intranet, with customers accessing selected data via the Internet.

Cloud hosting. The availability of cloud services offers yet another hardware option that can be addressed during the design phase. Rather than install an information system on costly in-house equipment, a viable alternative might be to install it in the cloud on equipment that is maintained by a cloud hosting company such as Amazon, Microsoft, or Google.

Level of automation. The project team should consider the pros and cons of different levels of automation because they affect all aspects of the planned information system. A point-of-sale system with a low level of automation might require the checkout clerk to enter credit card numbers from a keypad.

At a higher level of automation, a magnetic strip reader automates the process of entering a credit card number. A further level of automation is achieved by using a pressure-sensitive digitizing pad and stylus to collect customer signatures. Even more automation can be achieved with "tap-and-pay" systems, such as Apple Pay (Figure 9-37).

Figure 9-37: Tap and pay helps to automate point-of-sale systems

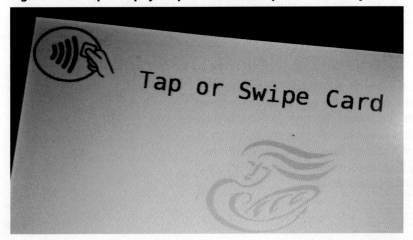

Try It!

The Amazon Elastic Compute Cloud offers hosting solutions to corporations of all sizes. What's it all about? Watch one of the Amazon EC2 videos on YouTube to find out.

QuickCheck

When the drugstore and pharmacy chain CVS decided to add tap-and-pay functionality, that automation was least likely to require a change to

_____.

a. the point-of-sale system

b. device requirements

c. system specifications

d. the planning phase

▶ **What kinds of software solutions are available?** The project team might consider software alternatives, such as whether to construct the system from scratch with programming tools, use an application development tool, purchase application software, or select a turnkey system (Figure 9-38).

Figure 9-38: Software solutions

Programming tools. Creating an information system from scratch using a programming language can take many months or even years. It is usually costly, but it offers the most flexibility for achieving the system requirements.

As an analogy, baking a cake from scratch allows you some flexibility in the ingredients you choose—margarine instead of butter, for example. However, baking from scratch requires a lot of time and work to sift the flour; mix the sugar, eggs, shortening, and milk; and so forth.

The project team can analyze the costs and benefits of developing an information system from scratch. If it appears to be a feasible solution, the team can also select a programming language to use.

Application development tools. An application development tool is essentially a software construction kit containing building blocks that can be assembled into a software product. Application development tools include expert system shells and database management systems.

An application development tool is the programmer's "cake mix," which contains many of the ingredients necessary for quickly developing the modules for an information system. Although application development tools usually speed up the development process, they might not offer the same level of flexibility as a programming language.

Application software. Application software for an information system is usually a series of preprogrammed software modules supplied by a software publisher.

Application software eliminates much of the design work required with programming languages or application development tools. However, application software requires extensive evaluation to determine how well it meets the system requirements. Following through with the cake analogy, application software is equivalent to buying a pre-made cake that you simply slice and serve.

Application software is available for standard business functions, such as human resources management, accounting, ecommerce, CRM, and SCM. It is also available for many vertical market businesses and organizations, such as law offices, schools, medical offices, libraries, churches, and charities.

Although most application software has some customization options, in many cases, it cannot be modified to exactly meet every system requirement, which necessitates adjustments in an organization's procedures. The project team must decide if the benefits of application software can offset the cost and inconvenience of procedural changes.

Turnkey systems. A turnkey system is essentially an "information system in a box," which consists of hardware and application software designed to offer a complete information system solution. These solutions may be designed for in-house installations or as cloud-based systems.

In terms of the cake analogy, a turnkey system is like going out to dinner and simply ordering your choice of cake for dessert.

A turnkey system might seem like a quick and easy solution, and it looks attractive to many project teams. Like application software, however, a turnkey system must be extensively evaluated to determine whether it can satisfy system requirements.

9

Evaluation and Selection

The drama depicted on HGTV inevitably involves a choice between designs—usually over a commercial break. There are also choices in an information system project, and there is a structured methodology for making those choices.

▶ **How does the team choose the best solution?** The project team devises a list of criteria for comparing each potential solution. This list includes general criteria related to costs, benefits, and development time. The list also includes technical criteria, such as the flexibility of the solution and its adaptability for future modifications and growth. Finally, the list includes functional criteria that indicate how well the solution satisfies the specified requirements. Using a **decision support worksheet**, the project team can assign scores to each criterion, weight them, and compare totals for all solutions (Figure 9-39).

Figure 9-39: Evaluating solutions with a decision support worksheet

A list of criteria includes features and factors that are important to the success of the information system.

The highest weights indicate the most important criteria.

Weighted scores are obtained by multiplying the weight by the raw score.

Raw scores indicate how well each solution meets each criterion.

		Solution 1: Custom Programming		Solution 2: Turnkey System	
Criterion	Weight	Raw Score	Weighted Score	Raw Score	Weighted Score
Satisfies requirements	10	10	100	6	60
Fast processing	9	8	72	8	72
Good security	10	8	80	8	80
Low construction cost	6	5	30	8	48
Low implementation cost	6	9	54	8	48
Low maintenance cost	9	7	63	7	63
Short development time	6	4	24	10	60
Good flexibility	7	9	63	6	42
Total			486		473

The solution with the highest total is the best choice.

QuickCheck

In Figure 9-39, which criteria are the most important?

a. Satisfies requirements and fast processing

b. Satisfies requirements and good security

c. Fast processing and good flexibility

d. Low maintenance cost and good security

▶ **How does the project team find the right hardware and software for the new information system?** After the project team selects a solution, the next task is to select the hardware and software needed to implement the solution. Sometimes more than one vendor sells the hardware and software necessary for the new system, so an organization might have a choice of vendors.

The method for selecting the hardware, software, and vendor depends on the project team's understanding of what is required for the solution. Sometimes the team knows exactly what brand, model, or version of hardware and software are required. At other times, the team has a general understanding but needs help from vendors to select specific products.

The project team should consider the vendor's reliability, expertise, and financial stability. Technical criteria for hardware might include processing speed, reliability, upgradability, maintenance costs, and warranty. Technical criteria for software might include reliability, compatibility, and the availability of patches to fix program errors.

Application Specifications

By selecting a solution, the design team has decided on a basic course of action, but there are details to be worked out before construction begins. On HGTV, this phase takes place behind the scenes as architects create detailed blueprints and contractors obtain permits. On an information system project, the team is now at a crossroad. It may proceed to a detailed design phase, or it may head to the next phase of the SDLC.

▶ **What happens after the project team selects a solution?** Exactly what happens next in the system design phase depends on the type of solution selected. If a turnkey solution is selected, the next step might be to get approval to move into the implementation phase of the SDLC.

In contrast, if the project team selects a solution that requires custom programming, the team's systems analysts will create a set of **application specifications** that describe the way the information system's software should interact with users, store data, process data, and format reports.

Detailed application specifications can be developed only after selecting the hardware and software for an information system. For example, the specifications for a program that runs on a Windows-based LAN might require a very different user interface and processing model than a program that runs on an application server that is accessed via the Internet.

This part of the SDLC is sometimes referred to as the **detailed design phase** because its goal is to create very detailed specifications for the completed information system, such as a detailed description of the process for discontinuing an inventory item (Figure 9-40).

Figure 9-40: Application specifications describe processes in detail

```
BEGIN

FIND item in INVENTORY with matching inventory-ID

IF record cannot be found

  DISPLAY "No inventory item matches the Inventory ID."

ELSE

  READ item record

  SET discontinued-item to YES

  WRITE item record

  DISPLAY "Item [inventory-ID] is now marked as
  discontinued."

ENDIF

END
```

Application specifications might look like program code, but they are written in a step-by-step style that reflects each part of a process that the information system is to perform. Read through the steps above and try to visualize what happens when a manager decides to mark an inventory item as discontinued.

Try It!

Suppose you're on the project team tasked with replacing your school's library management system. The most important criterion is to keep the initial cost low. Go online and decide which one of the following options is best:

Blackboard

LibLime Koha

Moodle

LibraryWorld

9

QuickCheck

If you join a project development team and are asked to write specifications such as those in Figure 9-40, it is likely that the project is in the _____ phase.

a. planning

b. analysis

c. detailed design

d. final

▶ **What is the importance of application specifications?** Application specifications are a key element in developing an effective information system. Not only do these specifications serve as a blueprint for the new system, but they play a critical role in ensuring that the development process is executed efficiently.

Some projects fail because of constant, unmanaged demand for changes, even before the system is implemented. This failure to constrain change is often referred to as **feature creep** because new features tend to creep into the development process with a snowball effect that leads to other features, higher costs, and longer schedules.

It might be important to change some specifications during the development process because of changes in business needs, laws, or regulations. Proposed changes should be managed within a formal process that includes written **change requests**, which detail the scope of a proposed change and can be evaluated by project team members (Figure 9-41).

Figure 9-41: Change request form

SOFTWARE CHANGE REQUEST

CHANGE REQUEST INITIATION: Originator: _____

Date Submitted: ____/____/____ System Name: _____

CONFIGURATION ITEM: Software: _____ Documentation: _____

CHANGE TYPE: New Requirement: _____ Requirement Change: _____

Design Change: _____ Other: _____

REASON: Legal: _____ Business: _____ Performance: _____ Defect: _____

PRIORITY: Emergency: _____ Urgent: _____ Routine: _____

CHANGE DESCRIPTION: (Detail functional and/or technical information. Use attachment if necessary.)

QuickCheck

The purpose of a document such as the one in Figure 9-41 is to

_____.

a. prevent users from changing the design plan

b. manage feature creep

c. collect bug reports from users

d. initialize a turnkey system

▶ **What happens to the completed specifications?** Application specifications are similar to the pages of an architectural blueprint that show the detailed plan for electrical wiring or plumbing. The specifications are given to a programming team or an application developer who creates the software.

▶ **When can the project team actually begin to build the new information system?** In the design phase of the SDLC, the project team chooses a solution, selects hardware and software, and designs detailed application specifications. Before the solution is implemented, the project team typically must seek approval from management.

The approval process might be fairly informal, simply involving a discussion with the CIO. In contrast, some organizations require a much more formal process for obtaining approval in which the project team submits a written proposal that is supplemented by presentations to management and user groups. After the project team's proposal is approved, the project can move to the next phase of development.

Implementation Phase

After the plan for an information system is approved, it's time to start building the system. During the implementation phase of the SDLC, an organization puts together the hardware, software, and operational components for the new information system.

▶ **What happens during the implementation phase?** During the imple-mentation phase of the SDLC, the project team supervises the tasks necessary to construct the new information system. The tasks that take place during the implementation phase can include any of those listed in Figure 9-42.

Figure 9-42: Implementation phase

▶ **How does the team acquire software and hardware?** As the imple-mentation phase begins, programming languages, development tools, and application software needed for the new information system are purchased, installed, and tested to ensure that they work correctly.

Software testing can reveal problems that result from incompatibilities with exist-ing hardware and software. These problems must be corrected before continuing with system development. Testing might also reveal bugs (errors) in the software, which must be corrected by the software developer.

In addition to new software, the specifications for many information systems require new hardware, which can either replace old equipment or supplement existing equipment. During the implementation phase, new hardware is pur-chased, installed, and tested to ensure that it operates correctly.

When an information system will be cloud-based, there may be connectivity and security requirements that have to be implemented locally. In addition, cloud applications will have to be configured and thoroughly tested.

▶ What's the next step in the implementation phase? After hardware and software are set up and tested, the next step in the implementation phase depends on the software tools selected for the project.

When the software for an information system is created by using a programming language or an application development tool, programmers must create and test all the new software modules. Module 11 provides more information about the programming process.

When an information system is constructed using application software, the software sometimes must be customized. **Software customization** is the process of modifying a commercial application to reflect an organization's needs. Customization might include modifying the user interface, enabling various security settings, selecting the menus that appear on the screen, and designing forms or reports.

▶ How can the team ensure that a new information system works? A rigorous testing process is the only way to make sure a new information system works correctly. Different types of testing during the implementation phase help identify and fix problems before the information system is incorporated into day-to-day business activities.

Application testing is the process of trying out various sequences of input values and checking the results to verify that the application works as it was designed. Application testing is performed in three ways: unit testing, integration testing, and system testing.

As each application module is completed, it undergoes **unit testing** to ensure that it operates reliably and correctly. When all modules have been completed and tested, **integration testing** is performed to ensure that the modules operate together correctly.

After unit and integration testing are completed, **system testing** ensures that all hardware and software components work together. Figure 9-43 summarizes the three stages of application testing.

Figure 9-43: Application testing

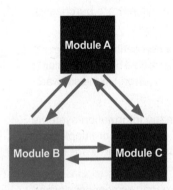
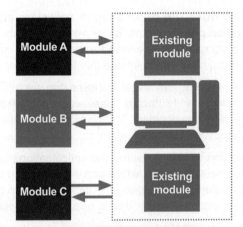

Unit testing ensures that each module of the application software works correctly.

Integration testing ensures that all the modules work together correctly.

System testing ensures that new modules work with the rest of the system hardware and software.

Documentation and Training

One of the most important tasks during the implementation phase is to make sure the information system is completely documented so that it can be used effectively and modified easily.

▶ **What kinds of documentation are required?** The documentation for an information system can be broadly categorized as system documentation or user documentation (Figure 9-44).

Figure 9-44: Documentation categories

System
Documentation

Target audience:

Programmers, designers, systems analysts

User
Documentation

Target audience:

Workers, employees, managers

System documentation describes a system's features, hardware architecture, and programming. The target audiences for system documentation are programmers, designers, and analysts who might maintain the system on a day-to-day basis and implement modifications.

Much of the information required for system documentation is generated in the analysis and design phases of the SDLC. At the end of the implementation phase, these documents should be reviewed for accuracy because features sometimes change as a result of problems or opportunities encountered during implementation.

For system documentation, many project teams turn to automated applications that produce documentation from completed source code. These tools help the team retrofit the documentation to the actual system, which might differ somewhat from the original system specifications.

User documentation describes how to interact with the system to accomplish specific tasks. It includes a list of features and instructions for using them. It might also include tutorials that demonstrate how to get started and how to accomplish specific tasks.

▶ **How do employees learn how to use a new information system?** In preparation for using a new information system, employees generally need training on software use and data entry. Some employees might also need training in hardware operation and backup procedures.

During training sessions, employees learn how to interact with the interface, use the new system to perform day-to-day tasks, and find additional information in user manuals, procedure handbooks, or video tutorials.

A **procedure handbook** is a type of user documentation that contains step-by-step instructions for performing specific tasks. It often takes the place of a lengthy user manual because in a large organization, an employee in a particular department usually performs specific tasks and does not need to know how all features of the system work.

9

Conversion and Cutover

People who remember the disorganized rollout of remote learning during the COVID-19 pandemic will understand the importance of a well-orchestrated system launch. Planning is crucial for a successful transition to a new information system.

▸ **What happens to data from the old system?** The data for a new information system might exist in card files, file folders, or an old information system. This data must be loaded into the new system—a process called data conversion. A programmer can write conversion software to convert existing data into a format that is usable by the new system. Without such software, users would be forced to manually re-enter data from the old system into the new system.

▸ **What are the "go live" options?** System conversion refers to the process of deactivating an old information system and activating a new one. It is also referred to as a "cutover" or "to go live." The strategies for converting to a new system are described in Figure 9-45.

Figure 9-45: Cutover options

■ ■ **Direct conversion** is a cutover method that completely deactivates the old system and immediately activates the new system. Direct conversion is risky. If the new system does not work correctly, it might have to be deactivated and undergo further development or testing. In the meantime, the old system is reactivated, and transactions that were entered into the new system must be re-entered into the old system.

■ ■
■ ■ **Parallel conversion** avoids some of the risk of direct conversion because the old system remains in service while some or all of the new system is activated. Both the old and new systems operate in parallel until the project team can determine whether the new system is performing correctly. Parallel conversion often requires that all entries be made in both the new and old systems, which is costly in terms of time, computer resources, and personnel.

■ ■
■ ■ **Phased conversion** works well with large, modularized information systems because the new system is activated one module at a time. After the project team determines that one module is working correctly, the next module is activated, and so on, until the entire new system is operational. In a phased conversion, however, each module of the new system must work with both the old and new systems, which greatly increases the complexity and cost of application development.

■ ■
■ ■ ■ **Pilot conversion** works well in organizations with several branches that have independent information processing systems because the new information system is activated one branch at a time. If the new system works correctly at one branch, it is activated at the next branch. To prepare for a pilot conversion, system developers must devise methods to integrate information from branches using the new system with information from branches still using the old system.

▸ **When is the new information system formally "live"?** A new or upgraded information system undergoes a final test called acceptance testing. Acceptance testing is designed to verify that the new information system works as required.

Procedures for acceptance testing are designed by users and systems analysts, and they often include the use of real data to demonstrate that the system operates correctly under normal and peak data loads. Acceptance testing usually marks the completion of the implementation phase.

QuickCheck

Could a school successfully implement a pilot conversion for its library management system?

a. Yes, it would be relatively easy to install the new system online as a pilot to see how it works.

b. Yes, but it could only be done if the conversion happens over the summer.

c. No, a phased conversion that implements a new patron module, then a new circulation module, and so on would work better.

d. No, if the new system does not work correctly, the students and instructors will not have access to any library management system.

Maintenance Phase

In 1962, the U.S. Internal Revenue Service launched an information system called Individual Master File (IMF) to store and access tax records. That system ran for 50 years before a failed attempt to replace it was discontinued in 2009. A second attempt was ongoing when this book went to press. A system such as IMF that remains in service for more than 60 years is rare, but information systems can have unexpectedly long life spans with a maintenance phase that outlasts the system developers.

▶ **What happens during the maintenance phase?** The maintenance phase of the SDLC involves the day-to-day operation of the system, making modifications to improve performance, and correcting problems. After an information system is implemented, it remains in operation for a period of time. During this time, maintenance activities ensure that the system functions as well as possible. Figure 9-46 lists the major maintenance activities for a typical information system.

Figure 9-46: Maintenance phase

The term *maintenance phase* is a little misleading because it seems to imply that the information system is maintained in a static state. On the contrary, during the maintenance phase, an information system is likely to undergo many changes to meet an organization's needs. Changes during the maintenance phase can include the following:

- Updates to the operating system and application software

- User interface revisions to make the system easier to use

- Hardware replacements necessary to retire defective equipment or enhance performance

- Security upgrades

- Quality-of-service enhancements

▶ **What is quality of service?** The term quality of service (QoS) refers to the level of performance a computer system provides. When quality of service is good, data flows swiftly through the system, software is easier and more intuitive to use, and work is completed quickly and without error. When quality of service is poor, users experience long waits, software is clumsy to use, and information is difficult to find.

Three key concepts ensure good quality of service: reliability, availability, and serviceability. Computer systems are reliable when they can be counted on to function correctly. Availability refers to the ability of the system to be continuously accessible to all the people who use it. Systems exhibit serviceability when they are easily upgraded or repaired.

❱ **What are quality-of-service metrics?** A quality-of-service metric is a technique used for measuring a specific QoS characteristic. Data for these metrics can be gathered by monitoring system performance and analyzing responses to user satisfaction surveys. Businesses use several QoS metrics, such as those described in Figure 9-47.

Figure 9-47: Quality-of-service metrics

QoS Metric	Description
Throughput	Amount of data processed in a particular time interval
Accuracy	Number of errors occurring in a particular time interval for a particular function
Downtime	Amount of time a system is not available for processing
Capacity	Available storage space, number of users, number of connections, or number of packets
User levels	Number of users at peak, average, and low times
Response time	Time period between when a user initiates a request for information and when the request is fulfilled

QuickCheck

When Microsoft OneDrive is out of service for a few hours, which QoS metric increases?

a. Throughput

b. Downtime

c. Capacity

d. Response time

❱ **How important is user support?** Even after in-depth training, employees sometimes forget procedures or have difficulty when they encounter a new set of circumstances. These employees turn to the IT department for help.

Many organizations establish a help desk to handle end-user problems. The help desk is staffed by technical support specialists who are familiar with the information system's software. Support specialists keep records of problems and solutions.

Users with questions are usually encouraged to access online help, user manuals, or procedure handbooks. When those sources don't provide solutions, users may be able to turn to the help desk.

Users' questions can often promote much-needed modifications in the information system. For example, suppose a Zappos customer service representative encounters a problem with an update procedure and contacts the help desk. The help desk technician begins to troubleshoot the problem and soon realizes that it was caused by a programming error not caught during system testing. This bug is recorded in a bug report that is routed to the programming group, which can determine the bug's severity and take steps to fix it.

Try It!

Quality-of-service metrics are available to consumers. Connect to the Web site *Downrightnow. com* or *social.downornot.com*. What kinds of metrics can you find for Facebook performance during the past 24 hours?

▶ **How long does the maintenance phase last?** The maintenance phase is the longest SDLC phase, and it lasts until the system is retired. Although the analysis, design, and implementation phases of the SDLC are costly, for many organizations, the maintenance phase is the most expensive because it is the longest.

The maintenance phase often accounts for 70% of the total cost of an information system. As shown in Figure 9-48, maintenance costs follow a U-shaped curve—an information system requires the most maintenance at the beginning and end of its life cycle.

Figure 9-48: Maintenance phase costs

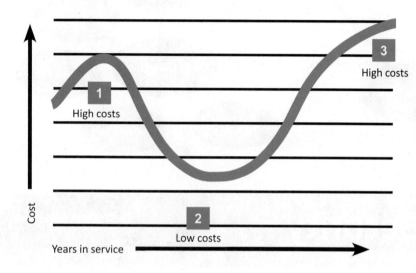

1 When a new information system first goes live, maintenance costs are high while programmers work out bugs and users clamor for support.

2 After most of the bugs are fixed and users become familiar with the information system, maintenance costs decrease.

3 As an information system nears the end of its useful life, repair costs rise, and changing business practices begin to require modifications that are time-consuming and expensive to implement.

▶ **When does the maintenance phase end?** The maintenance phase continues until an information system is no longer cost-effective or until changes in the organization make the information system obsolete. When an information system's useful or cost-effective life nears a close, it is then time to begin the system development life cycle again.

QuickQuiz   Section D

1. In the [_____] phase of the SDLC, a project team identifies several potential solutions and then selects the one that offers the most benefits at the lowest cost.

2. A(n) [_____] development tool is essentially a software construction kit containing building blocks that can be assembled into the software for an information system.

3. System development can get sidetracked by feature [_____].

4. At the end of the implementation phase of the SDLC, users verify that the entire system works as specified during a process called [_____] testing.

5. During the maintenance phase, three key concepts ensure good [_____] of service: reliability, availability, and serviceability.

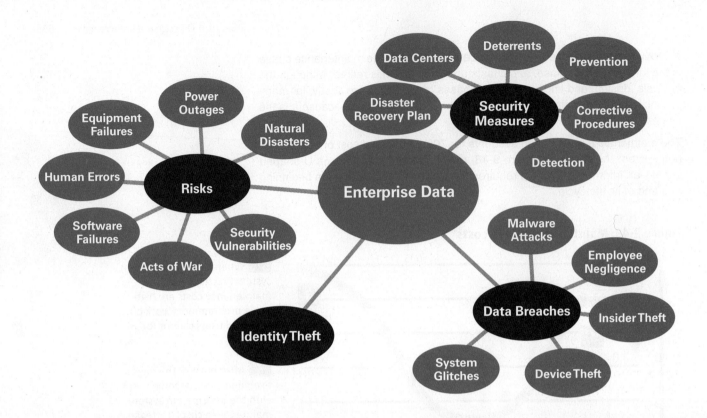

System Security

Objectives

- List at least five kinds of disasters that put information systems at risk.

- Explain three ways that a data center can reduce the risk of disasters that destroy data.

- Describe the elements of a disaster recovery plan.

- Name five things that can trigger a data breach.

- Describe how identity thieves use stolen data.

- Explain four security measures that protect data from breaches.

- Describe consumer notification laws in education, health care, and banking.

- List five steps that data breach victims should follow.

Threats against information systems are increasing. Corporations, government agencies, and other organizations are constantly shoring up their defenses to protect data and the people to whom it refers. In this section, you'll learn about threats to corporate data and methods for protecting that data. You can then draw some informed conclusions about the risks you might face when data about you is stored in information systems and when you depend on information systems for key aspects of your lifestyle.

Terminology

MTBF	disaster recovery plan	preventive	fraud alert
data center	data breach	countermeasures	
colocation center	identity theft	corrective procedures	
lights-out management	deterrents	detection activities	

Systems at Risk

When disaster strikes your PC, it is a major inconvenience—but just for one person. In contrast, threats to a corporate information system can affect millions of people. They can be life threatening. They cost companies billions of dollars in equipment, time, and restitution. And individuals may spend countless hours dealing with the aftereffects.

▶ **What kinds of disasters put information systems at risk?** Common threats to corporate information systems include natural disasters, power outages, equipment failures, human errors, software failures, acts of war, and security vulnerabilities.

Natural disasters can completely shut down a computer system, cut off service to customers, and potentially destroy the system completely. For example, when Hurricane Katrina tore through Louisiana, it left a swath of destruction in its wake. In many businesses, computer systems were drenched with rain and floodwaters. During the storm, power outages knocked down several major Internet hosting services. Power remained out for weeks in some places, and businesses without generators scrambled to continue operating.

Power outages can be caused by natural disasters, overloaded power grids, planned brownouts, and rolling blackouts. When power outages shut down information systems, the data is not accessible to carry out business operations nor is it available to clients and consumers.

Equipment failures can occur in any hardware component of an information system. The risk of failures increases as a hardware component ages, but they can also occur in new hardware. Many device specifications include an **MTBF** (mean time between failures) rating. For example, an MTBF rating of 125,000 hours means that, on average, a device could function for 125,000 hours before failing. MTBF ratings are averages, however, so a server with a 125,000 MTBF rating might operate for only 10 hours before it fails, for example.

Human errors are mistakes made by computer operators. Common errors within an information system include entering inaccurate data and failing to follow required procedures. Poorly trained computer operators were blamed for the biggest North American blackout in history, which left more than 50 million people without power in the summer of 2003.

Software failures can be caused by bugs or flawed software design. Flaws in critical software that controls air traffic or nuclear power plants can be deadly. Other bugs may cause security leaks that allow unauthorized access to corporate servers.

Acts of war once affected only computer systems located on battlefronts. With a recent increase in terrorist incidents, however, civilian areas have become targets. Acts of war can cause physical damage to computer systems. Cyberterrorism can also cause damage, using viruses and worms to destroy data and otherwise disrupt computer-based operations, which now include critical national infrastructures such as power grids and telecommunications systems.

Security vulnerabilities may be exploited by hackers, disgruntled employees, protesters, activists, or enemy combatants. Not limited to physical damage, these exploits also include defacing Web sites, launching denial-of-service attacks, and holding information systems for ransom.

9

QuickCheck

Which one of the following would not usually be responsible for destroying system equipment and the data it contains?

a. Natural disasters

b. Equipment failures

c. Acts of war

d. Human errors

Data Centers

When you are using a handheld device, such as an iPhone, have you ever wondered where Apple stores all those music tracks and apps? Where are the information systems that run Siri? Where is the storage facility that holds iCloud data? You might envision all these activities taking place on computers in the basement of Apple's Cupertino headquarters, but most Apple music and iCloud services are housed in massive data centers in California, Oregon, and North Carolina.

▶ **What does a data center contain?** A **data center** is a specialized facility designed to hold and protect computer systems and data. These centers may be dedicated to information systems for a single company, or they may be a **colocation center** in which several corporations lease space and equipment. The contents of a data center include computers, storage devices, telecommunications devices, and backup power supplies. In addition, data centers typically contain security equipment to restrict unauthorized access and environmental controls that protect all the equipment (Figure 9-49).

Figure 9-49: Data center components

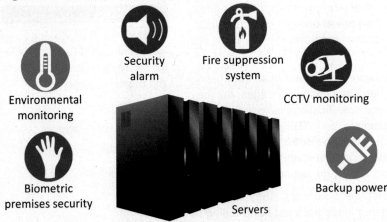

Environmental monitoring

Security alarm

Fire suppression system

CCTV monitoring

Biometric premises security

Servers

Backup power

▶ **How does a data center help minimize risks?** Data centers are designed to proactively reduce the risk of data loss that might occur as a result of a disaster. The best way to protect against risk is to avoid it altogether, and data centers can reduce or negate the effects of some types of disasters.

Most areas experience occasional power failures or blackouts, which can be costly to organizations whose goal is to offer 24/7 coverage. To avoid downtime, one of the most basic requirements for a data center is a supply of uninterrupted power from high-capacity backup batteries and power generators.

Physical security is critical to data centers. Most data centers limit physical access using fingerprint identification systems, badges, or security guards. Steel doors divide the centers into secure areas. Motion detectors and automated alarm systems prevent unauthorized movement through the building.

Environmental conditions in a data center must be monitored at all times. Computerized sensing devices track temperature, humidity, water, smoke, fire, air flow, power levels, security systems, and many other metrics. Cameras can be placed in air ducts, under raised floors, and in computer system units to detect intruders, pests, or chemical leaks.

QuickCheck

Which one of the following is not typically supplied by a data center?

a. Backup power supply

b. Antivirus software

c. Access security

d. Environmental monitoring

▶ **What is the most secure location for a data center?** Data centers can be located on-site or in specially selected off-site locations. In-house data centers are often located in basements where equipment and wires are out of sight and where server racks and battery backups are not adding excessive weight loads to aboveground floors. Basements are not an ideal location, however. They are susceptible to floods and plumbing leaks from floors above. Other locations that are not suitable for data centers include those listed in Figure 9-50.

Figure 9-50: Where not to put a data center

 Below sea level or in a floodplain

 In a location that is prone to hurricanes, tornadoes, or earthquakes

 Near facilities where hazardous materials are manufactured, stored, or transported

 In an area without world-class telecommunications infrastructure

 In any location where accidents and violence put people and equipment at risk

 Near an airport flight path

 In locations where power is expensive or unreliable

9

A data center might be a small room containing a single server with battery backup, or it can be an elaborate facility that stretches over many acres of land and requires a dedicated power-generating system. Apple built one of the world's largest data centers in Maiden, NC. The main building contains 505,000 square feet and is powered by a 55,000-panel solar array that generates enough electricity to supply more than 13,500 homes.

Data centers may be staffed, or they may be controlled and monitored remotely. A so-called dark data center requires no permanent staff. Technicians enter the facility only when equipment needs to be repaired or replaced. These dark data centers are an extension of **lights-out management** (LOM), which allows system administrators to monitor and manage servers using remote control software.

Off-site data centers are housed in specially constructed buildings or in refurbished facilities, such as former military bunkers, abandoned mines, or limestone caves. Some of the world's most secure data centers are listed in Figure 9-51.

Figure 9-51: World's most secure data centers

Jonathan Nackstrand/Afp/Getty Images

Bahnhof Pionen is located 100 feet beneath Stockholm, Sweden, and sometimes called the "James Bond" data center.

Iron Mountain is located 220 feet underground in a limestone cave near Pittsburgh.

Swiss Fort Knox is embedded deep within a mountain in the Swiss Alps and hermetically sealed.

InfoBunker is a 65,000-square-foot data center built in a decommissioned Air Force bunker designed to survive a 20-megaton nuclear blast.

Disaster Recovery Planning

It seemed like an ordinary Friday when a contract employee walked into a Chicago-area Federal Aviation Administration facility carrying a suitcase. But the suitcase contained gasoline, and minutes later, the facility's computers were in flames. Pilots lost radio links to the control tower, and air-traffic controllers' screens went black. Planes that were in the air managed to land without incident, but in the days and weeks that followed, thousands of flights were canceled and many more delayed at Chicago O'Hare International and Chicago Midway International airports. Data centers can't offer 100% protection, so savvy system administrators have disaster recovery plans.

▶ **What's included in a disaster recovery plan?** A **disaster recovery plan** is a step-by-step description of the methods used to secure data against disaster and a set of guidelines for how an organization will recover lost data and resume operations if and when a disaster occurs.

Disaster recovery plans not only must deal with calamities such as the 2014 FAA air-traffic control fire or the 2021 fire that destroyed a major data center in France, they also must take into account day-to-day events that could potentially disrupt operations. Backup tapes can become corrupted, an employee might spill coffee onto the most critical storage device in the building, or a virus can slow down the network to the point that it's unusable.

A well-formulated disaster recovery plan should account for all kinds of trouble, from the most minor glitch to the most destructive disaster. Specifically, an enterprise-wide disaster recovery plan should:

- Ensure the safety of people on the premises at the time of a disaster.
- Continue critical business operations.
- Minimize the duration of a serious disruption to operations.
- Minimize immediate damage and prevent additional losses.
- Establish management succession and emergency powers.
- Facilitate effective coordination of recovery tasks.

A disaster recovery plan can mean the difference between an organization rebounding after a disaster or simply ceasing to exist. Disaster recovery plans are as critical to data security as data backups, firewalls, and password protection.

▶ **Is a cloud-based information system more secure than a local one?** Today, many disaster recovery plans incorporate cloud facilities as off-site backup that will be available in case of a major incident at an in-house data center. Some companies operate mirror systems at cloud sites or depend on multiple colocation centers for processing data as well as storing it. Figure 9-52 lists the advantages of cloud facilities.

Try It!

In 2021, the OVH data center was destroyed. What can you discover about this event? What was the cause of the disaster? Who was affected by it? Did OVH have a disaster recovery plan?

Figure 9-52: Advantages of hosted cloud services

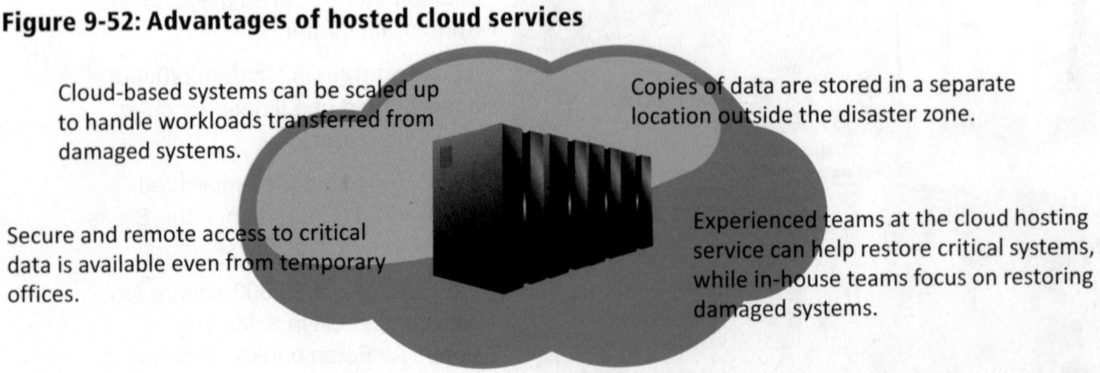

Cloud-based systems can be scaled up to handle workloads transferred from damaged systems.

Copies of data are stored in a separate location outside the disaster zone.

Secure and remote access to critical data is available even from temporary offices.

Experienced teams at the cloud hosting service can help restore critical systems, while in-house teams focus on restoring damaged systems.

Data Breaches

Zappos: 24 million. Facebook: 553 million. Target: 70 million. Home Depot: 56 million. IRS: 700,000. Yahoo: 1 billion. Those figures are not corporate profits, but the number of customer records that were subject to unauthorized access in the course of massive data breaches. In the United States, data breaches are on a steady upward swing, with more than 1,000 companies per year discovering that their information systems have been attacked.

▶ **What triggers a data breach?** A **data breach** is an incident in which personal data is viewed, accessed, or retrieved without authorization. Massive data breaches that expose personal data stored in an information system can be triggered by malware, human factors, and system glitches.

Malware attacks. Data breaches can occur over an extended period of weeks or months while hackers probe system weaknesses, plant malware, open backdoors, and try to crack administrator-level passwords. Malware can be inserted into the information systems that control credit card machines in physical locations. Hackers also use malware to capture data from Web applications that process payments. Increasingly, ransomware attacks steal data before encrypting it, creating a data breach in addition to denying access to that data.

Employee negligence. Access to data in information systems is controlled by login credentials, such as passwords. If these credentials fall into the wrong hands, data is vulnerable to access by unauthorized persons. Identity thieves acquire login credentials by scooping up passwords written on Post-it Notes, and using social engineering attacks to extract passwords from careless employees. During the COVID-19 pandemic, work-at-home employees using unsecured networks were the source of several data breaches.

Insider theft. Some employees are dishonest and use their legitimate access to information systems as a chance to skim data for illegal purposes. In 2015, financial services giant Morgan Stanley announced that an employee had stolen personal data for more than 900 wealthy clients. The employee allegedly posted the data on the Pastebin Web site and was trying to sell it to criminals who peddle in identity theft.

Device theft. Employees sometimes have legitimate reasons to carry devices loaded with consumer data or applications that provide remote access to corporate information systems. When these devices are stolen, the data they contain may fall into unauthorized hands. For example, in 2014, a home healthcare nurse's laptop bag was stolen. According to company policy, the laptop was password protected and its data was encrypted. However, the encryption key was on a slip of paper in the bag, giving the thief unencrypted access to all the patient data stored on the device.

System glitches. Poorly configured servers, networks that lack adequate security, and databases without proper access controls are the cause of many data breaches. In 2014, a misconfigured server at a U.S. financial institution allowed Google search crawlers to access and index information from the company's client databases. The exposed information, which appeared in Google searches, included client account statements with account holder names, routing numbers, and balances. Additional documents exposed by the data breach contained instructions on how to authorize new accounts and the passwords necessary to gain access to corporate servers.

Try It!

9

How big is the most recent data breach? The Identity Theft Resource Center has been tracking data breaches since 2005. On the ITRC Web site, you can link to a list of current incidents. At the Information is Beautiful site, you can see a motion graph of data breaches.

QuickCheck

In what sense is a data breach different from threats such as natural disasters and equipment failures?

a. As a result of a data breach, data is not usually destroyed.

b. A data breach is less serious.

c. The cause of a data breach can be quickly discovered and remedied.

d. Data breaches are not the concern of system developers.

▶ **How do security breaches affect individuals?** Just about every person in America has personal information stored in at least one digital information system. Every time you fill out a survey, register to use a Web site, visit your doctor, use your credit card, or make a phone call, personal information is stored in an information system. When that personal information falls into the wrong hands, the risk of identity theft increases.

Identity theft is the fraudulent use of someone's personal information to carry out transactions, such as applying for loans, making purchases, collecting tax refunds, or obtaining false identity documents. Identity thieves especially covet Social Security numbers, bank card numbers, and login passwords for financial accounts. Other personally identifiable information (PII), such as mother's maiden name, place of birth, driver's license number, and passport number, also opens doors for identity thieves.

▶ **How do identity thieves use the data they steal?** There are countless ways in which stolen personal information is fraudulently used. Figure 9-53 lists some of the most prevalent scams.

Figure 9-53: How identity thieves use stolen identities

Take out a loan in the victim's name and not pay off the debt. The **bad debt** becomes part of the victim's credit report and lowers the credit score. Identity thieves may even file for bankruptcy to cover the debts, further ruining the victim's credit score.

Open a **bank account** using the victim's name, and then write bad checks.

Cash **forged checks** to empty a victim's bank account.

Subscribe to cellular phone service, cable Internet service, or utilities using the victim's name, but never pay the bills.

Change the billing address for a victim's credit card, and then make purchases.

Produce **fake credit or debit cards** using the victim's card numbers, and then make electronic withdrawals.

Apply for a **tax refund** in the victim's name. The victim's legitimate return might be flagged as fraudulent or inaccurate and lead to an audit or tax fraud charges.

Use a stolen Social Security number to apply for **retirement benefits**, which will be sent to the identity thief. When the victim later applies for benefits, they will already have been distributed.

Sell the victim's data to other criminals who consolidate it with data gathered from different sources. Profiles that are detailed enough can supply an entire identity that criminals use when trying to evade police, work illegally, board planes, or carry out other illicit activities.

Security Measures

No computer system can be completely risk-free, but several proactive measures can protect enterprise information systems from threats.

▶ **How?** Measures that protect information systems can be grouped into four categories: deterrents, preventive countermeasures, corrective procedures, and detection activities.

- **Deterrents** reduce the likelihood of a deliberate attack. Physical deterrents, such as limiting access to critical servers, fall under this category. Common deterrents also include security features such as multi-level authentication, password protection, and biometric identification.

- **Preventive countermeasures** shield vulnerabilities to render an attack unsuccessful or reduce its impact. Firewalls that prevent unauthorized access to a system and encryption that makes stolen data indecipherable are examples of preventive countermeasures.

- **Corrective procedures** reduce the effect of an attack. Data backups, disaster recovery plans, and the availability of redundant hardware devices all are examples of corrective procedures.

- **Detection activities** recognize attacks and trigger preventive countermeasures or corrective procedures. For example, antivirus software detects viruses entering a system and can be configured to perform corrective procedures such as removing the virus and quarantining infected files. Theft or vandalism can be detected by periodic hardware inventories. The use of monitoring software to track users, file updates, and changes to critical systems can also help detect anomalies that indicate an intrusion or a threat.

▶ **How quickly are data breaches discovered?** Although most enterprises monitor their information systems, most data breaches are discovered by third parties, such as law enforcement agencies, ISPs, and security firms, which report suspicious activity to system administrators. Fraud detection systems designed to catch unauthorized credit card activity account for about 24% of the discoveries. Surprisingly, customer complaints lead to about 10% of data breach discoveries. What is somewhat disheartening is the length of time data breaches remain undiscovered and the time required to contain the breach after discovery (Figure 9-54).

9

Figure 9-54: Average data breach discovery and containment times

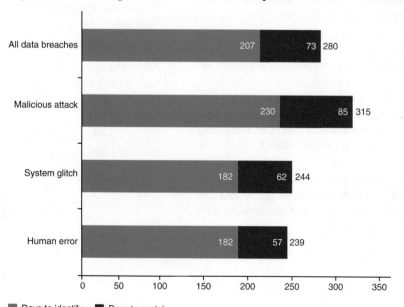

Source: IBM Cost of a Data Breach Report, 2020

▶ Are there laws that protect personal data? State governments have data breach notification statutes that require corporations to take specific steps if a data breach exposes personally identifiable information. There are also several federal data breach laws that apply to certain business sectors, such as education, health care, and banking (Figure 9-55).

Figure 9-55: Consumer notification laws

Education The Family Educational Rights and Privacy Act (FERPA) is designed to protect student records by allowing them to be distributed only to students, their parents, school officials, financial aid institutions, and accrediting agencies.

Health Care The Health Information Technology for Economic and Clinical Health (HITECH) Act requires any institution that handles personally identifiable health information to notify individuals of data breaches within 60 days.

Banking The Gramm-Leach-Bliley Act provides guidelines to financial institutions for notifying consumers of a data breach. The Red Flags Rule issued in 2007 requires financial institutions to implement identity theft programs.

▶ What can consumers do to minimize their vulnerability to security breaches? Even if businesses adhere to applicable disclosure laws, those laws apply to data that has already been breached. Although the laws also contain guidelines for securing data, the continuing succession of data breaches demonstrate that laws are not sufficient protection for personal data.

Consumers are dependent on corporate policies and security procedures to safeguard personal data stored on information systems. Once you've released data to an information system, you no longer have control of its distribution or its security. To minimize the risk of identity theft and other mishaps that arise from data breaches, consumers should be vigilant about the information they divulge.

- **Know when data is being collected.** Be aware of activities—both online and offline—that can possibly collect personal information, such as registering to use a Web site, participating in a survey, submitting your resume to an online employment service, requesting a product rebate, participating in online discussion groups, clicking pop-up ads, and so on. When asked for information, supply only what's required. Never divulge your Social Security number, and be cautious about sharing other personal information, such as your telephone number or address. When in doubt, you might consider using phony data.

- **Find out how data is being used.** Look at the organization's privacy policy. Is the data being used internally? Is it being shared with other organizations and aggregated with other data? If so, will that third party protect your data with an adequate level of security?

- **Find out what data is retained.** Some organizations anonymize data by removing names, Social Security numbers, credit card numbers, and other data that identifies a specific person. Consumers should realize that in an age of big data, even anonymized data can be relinked to your personal data through data mining techniques discussed in Module 10.

- **Don't trade your privacy.** Be wary of offers for free services in exchange for personal information or permission to track your online footprints. Such data can be especially useful for identity thieves assembling a profile to substantiate their use of your Social Security number and other personal data.

QuickCheck

What is the significance of anonymized data in the context of identity theft?

a. It is useless to identity thieves.

b. It is collected secretly.

c. When aggregated with other data, it can be relinked to a person's PII.

d. It is a result of trading private information for free access to Web sites and social media.

▶ **What should data breach victims do?** You might see it in a news report or receive an email alert: An information system that holds your medical, educational, or financial information has been breached. Your personal data may be in the hands of identity thieves. They might use it or they might not, but don't take a chance. Treat every breach seriously by following the steps in Figure 9-56.

9

Figure 9-56: Steps for data breach victims

① Change your passwords. Immediately change the password you used for the system that was breached. If you used the same password at any other site, change it there, too.

② Get informed. Do not take a "wait-and-see" approach to any data breach that involves Social Security numbers. Go to the company's Web site and carefully read information about the breach. Pay close attention to the scope of data that is exposed. Does it include other authentication data such as mother's maiden name and bank card security numbers?

③ Activate a fraud alert. If you suspect that your Social Security number has been compromised, place a fraud alert on your credit reports. A **fraud alert** informs potential lenders that they must verify the identity of anyone attempting to open an account in your name. Fraud alerts are free and don't interfere with your ability to receive instant credit. Fraud alerts are temporary, however, so they must be renewed every 90 days in most cases.

④ Remain vigilant. Regularly check your credit reports to make sure there are no unauthorized charges or other signs of fraud.

⑤ Ignore phishing emails. Scammers try to take advantage of victims with fraudulent offers to shield data or provide credit reports. Do not click on links in email, text messages, or social media sites about any data breaches. For information about a data breach, connect only to the company's legitimate Web site directly from your browser.

QuickQuiz   Section E

1. A(n) ⬚ rating of 125,000 hours means that, on average, a device could function for 125,000 hours before failing. (Hint: Use the acronym.)

2. A disaster ⬚ plan describes methods for securing data against disasters and sets guidelines for reconstructing lost data.

3. ⬚ procedures, such as data backups, can reduce the effect of a virus that spreads throughout corporate computers.

4. Some of the most secure ⬚ centers are located in old military bunkers.

5. When a data breach occurs, affected consumers can initiate a(n) ⬚ alert.

Open Enrollment is over. See if you can still get coverage

You can still enroll if you have a life change that gives you a Special Enrollment Period, or if you qualify for Medicaid or CHIP

★

IMPORTANT:

If you tried to enroll by 2/15, but couldn't finish, you may still be able to get 2015 coverage.

HealthCare.gov

Issue: What Can Go Wrong?

On a crisp autumn day in 2013, Americans eagerly began to access the federal government's new health insurance Web site, HealthCare.gov. Within minutes, response time slowed to a crawl, screens froze, and the site went offline, leaving consumers frustrated and confused.

HealthCare.gov is a product of the Patient Protection and Affordable Care Act or PPACA, which was enacted to lower the cost of health insurance and decrease the number of uninsured Americans. The PPACA established insurance exchanges where consumers can purchase health insurance. Exchanges are run by state governments and by the federal government. HealthCare.gov is a Web site that offers health insurance through the federal exchange.

Developing HealthCare.gov was an ambitious project. Its scope and complexity required top-notch communication, transparency, accountability, collaboration, design, and testing.

What went wrong? Who was at fault? The blame might be placed on the developers, the White House, or the oversight agency.

The developers. Fifty-five companies were contracted to participate in the development effort. Canadian firm CGI Federal was the primary contractor, and it was responsible for integrating the Web site with health insurer databases and Oracle identity management modules. Although in charge of integration, CGI was not responsible for oversight of the project. Within its designated scope of system requirements, CGI programmers may have produced sloppy code in order to meet unrealistic deadlines.

The White House. System requirements for HealthCare.gov depended on a set of regulations that outlined how the federal exchange would work, such as the list of services that were required for qualified health plans. The administration may have deliberately held up controversial rules to limit bad press

> "The real problems with HealthCare.gov are related to the 'worst practices' that went into the project nearly from the beginning. Each of these missteps, combined with the generally hostile atmosphere in Washington surrounding the Affordable Care Act, nearly guaranteed HealthCare.gov would be late, broken, or both."
>
> Columnist Sean Gallagher writing for *Ars Technica*

until after the 2012 elections. Final rules were not issued until February 2013. Developers then had fewer than eight months to develop and test the system before the October 2013 go-live date. The project was further politicized by the administration's desire to see its signature piece of legislation come to fruition before critics were able to block it.

The oversight agency. HealthCare.gov development was assigned to the Centers for Medicare and Medicaid Services (CMS) and under the oversight of the U.S. Department of Health and Human Services (HHS). These agencies lacked expertise in IT system development and were unable to manage the project's schedule. By June 2013, it was apparent that the project was headed for failure. A CMS email showed growing concern: "The build appears to be way off track and getting worse....We are one week out from production deployment, and we are being told already that it doesn't work."

Then in July, the U.S. Government Accountability Office voiced concern that final integration testing for all the agency systems would not be completed before the start of the enrollment period in October. And just a few days before the go-live date, a top official at CMS stated, "The facts are that we have not successfully handled more than 500 concurrent users."

Insiders at CMS had reasons to delay the launch date. In addition to lack of testing and inability to handle the anticipated load of users, the top CMS security officer recommended against signing the Authority to Operate needed to go live, noting that 40% of security controls were not tested, so it was unknown if the Web site would protect personally identifiable information.

Despite all the warning signs, CMS and HHS officials stated repeatedly that HealthCare.gov would be ready for launch in October. The system launched on the target date. It was not ready.

Try It!

The botched HealthCare.gov rollout is a classic "what can go wrong" case study in systems analysis and design. It was a high-stakes development effort that was besieged with problems. You can get a handle on the facts as the U.S. healthcare story continues to unfold.

1 Technology does not exist in a world of its own. It is designed and deployed within the context of societies and economies. HealthCare.gov was affected by political divisions over the Affordable Care Act. What was the stated purpose of the PPACA? How many people was it expected to serve? Which political party supported the bill? Why? Which political party opposed the bill? Why?

2 After the failure of the original HealthCare.gov rollout, a team of private sector IT professionals was hired to create HealthCare.gov 2.0. What can you learn about this development project? Can you identify various stages of the SDLC that they followed? Take a look at the current HealthCare.gov Web site. Can you identify five ways in which it resembles other popular ecommerce sites?

3 Open your browser and go to YouTube to view two videos: Dickerson Velocity NY Keynote (*7Vc8sxhy2I4*) and Kennedy dotScale Life in the Trenches (*GLQyjkBRdo*),

featuring speakers from IT firms that were called in to help identify and fix the major problems that HealthCare.gov version 1.0 experienced. Briefly outline the similarities between the two presentations. List the three top problems these developers identified in the first development attempt.

4 Looking back at the development effort for HealthCare.gov 1.0, some analysts have suggested that agile development methodology would have led to a more successful outcome. Although this would seem like a technical discussion, in today's Information Age, understanding the difference between agile methodology and waterfall methodology becomes a key part of making an informed decision on how the government spent more than $1 billion of taxpayer money. Write at least two paragraphs comparing agile methodology with waterfall methodology, and then explain which one you think would have been most successful for a system development project such as HealthCare.gov.

What Do You Think?

1. Would you enroll in a health insurance plan from HealthCare.gov?

2. Do you think that HealthCare.gov is a good use of tax dollars?

3. Do you think that the problems that were experienced during HealthCare.gov 1.0 will lead to better development methodology practices being adopted by future large government IT projects?

Information Tools: Recognizing Viewpoint

Information in newspapers, Web sites, blogs, and other sources is rarely 100% objective. No matter what the source, information is rarely presented in a way that is fair and balanced.

Rather than searching fruitlessly for unbiased information, it can be more practical to recognize the viewpoints of information at hand and sift through it for ideas and facts that can be corroborated as correct from other sources.

Biased material is not necessarily useless. For some projects, you might actively seek material that presents strong viewpoints. For example, when you want to compare and contrast divergent political viewpoints, you might actively look for biased material.

Information that is skewed toward a particular viewpoint can be classified as propaganda, misinformation, disinformation, or parody.

Propaganda

Information that is true but selectively represented in a way that encourages recipients to form certain opinions. In the old days, it was called "flim flam." Today, it is called "spin."

Disinformation

False information that is disseminated with the deliberate intention of influencing policies or opinions. Examples include spam, fake viruses, and hoaxes. It is also referred to as fake news.

Misinformation

Information that is unintentionally not true, such as a misstatement, gaffe, or error that isn't deliberate. Many urban legends fall into this category.

Parody

Humorous or satirical information that imitates or mimics a real event or an original work and is often disseminated to make fun of the subject.

Identifying biased information is not always easy. Viewpoints are sometimes subtle; and if they match your own views, you might not recognize them as biased. Here are some tips to help you detect viewpoint:

- Look for loaded words that evoke strong emotions, exaggerate, sensationalize, or vilify. Loaded words can help you uncover subtle viewpoints; positive words point to viewpoints that are supported.

- Look for evidence that the author is affiliated with a business or an organization that might affect the author's viewpoint. Skim the author's other publications (articles, blogs, Web site) and biographical information (Facebook, Wikipedia) for clues about the author's views.

- Consider if only one side of an issue is presented.

- Consider if a Web site's sponsor has a commercial, social, political, or other agenda that would affect the viewpoint of information presented at the site.

- Look at other articles on the site. Sites tend to carry articles of similar viewpoints, and some might more blatantly show their bias.

Try It!

How is your "spin" radar? Can you spot viewpoints? Can you identify misinformation and distinguish it from propaganda and disinformation? Let's see if you can.

1 Watch each of the following YouTube videos and indicate whether it is propaganda, disinformation, misinformation, or parody.

    a. Medieval help desk with English subtitles

    b. Jeep, The Middle (Super Bowl Commercial)

    c. Mac vs. PC (Viruses)

    d. iPhone App makes popcorn!

2 Richard Stallman and the Software & Information Industry Association (SIIA) are at odds about an important digital issue. What is the issue, and what are the two divergent viewpoints?

3 *HuffPost* has been labeled as a liberal-leaning news outlet. Many technology enthusiasts read its technology section, however, for information about the latest products and gadgets. Connect to the *HuffPost* Web site and read a technology article. Can you detect any evidence of bias in the article, and do any other elements on the page, such as advertising or links to other articles, reveal the site's bias?

4 How does Google's ranking system work? Use any search engine to look up *PigeonRank*. How would you classify the information at this site?

5 Many people are not aware of their own bias, and when gathering facts, they tend to accept information that supports their biases and look for ways to refute data that doesn't. To find out if you have a bias that you're not aware of, go to the Project Implicit site and take the Implicit Association Test. Were the results what you expected?

6 Today, rather than access news from a single outlet, many people turn to Internet news aggregators, such as Google News, Apple News, and Facebook. Do these aggregators supply a good balance of news? Connect to one of these news aggregators and count the links to articles from conservative and liberal outlets, using the table below as a basis for your classifications. Also, look at the categorization of these articles to determine if political articles tend to originate from liberal outlets, whereas science articles tend to originate from conservative sources. Describe your findings.

Ideological trends associated with news outlets

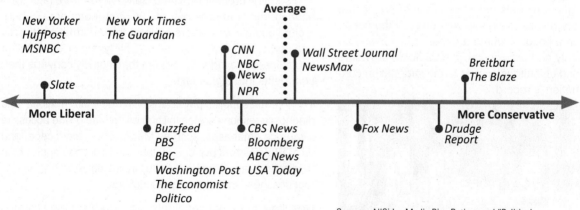

Sources: AllSides Media Bias Ratings and "Political Polarization & Media Habits." Pew Research Center 2014 survey of ideological views of those who got news from various sources.

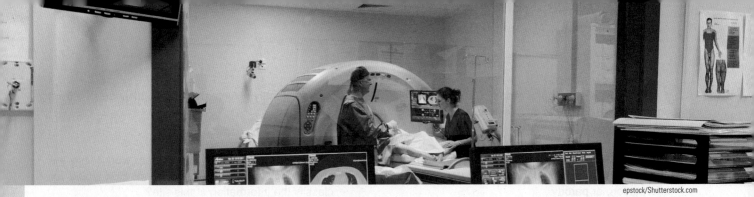

Technology in Context: Medicine

The healthcare industry was an early adopter of computer technology for traditional data processing applications, such as client billing and employee payroll. A computer's ability to process and store thousands of records helps reduce hospital administrative costs. Linking hospital billing to health insurance companies streamlines cumbersome manual procedures for submitting insurance claims. These behind-the-scenes applications do not, however, directly affect the quality of health care, where computer technology and information systems have made a significant contribution.

Until recent years, paper charts dangled from the foot of every hospital bed and additional information was stored in thick file folders in nursing stations or the hospital's medical records department. Patient records include doctors' diagnoses, laboratory test results, medication schedules, and charts depicting a patient's vital signs.

The process of maintaining these paper-based records is time-consuming and prone to errors. Effective treatments might be dangerously delayed while a slip of paper that holds laboratory results makes its way through the hospital corridors. In a hospital where a patient's condition can change suddenly and unexpectedly, healthcare providers need instant and ubiquitous access to the information contained in the patient's record.

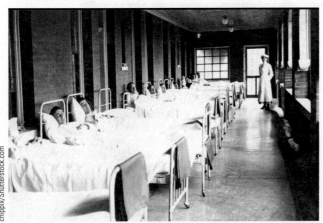

Today, technology allows hospitals to store patient records in information systems that are instantly accessible to doctors, nurses, and other healthcare workers. A nurse can access a patient's record from a computer in the nursing station to check care instructions and enter vital statistics. Doctors can access a patient's record from an office or home computer to check progress, order tests, and make decisions when minutes count. Lab technicians can enter test results immediately into a patient's record.

Patient records tie into a comprehensive hospital information system (HIS) that integrates just about every aspect of hospital management. Even the hospital dietitian can access relevant parts of a patient's record to work out menus that fit each patient's dietary needs, while avoiding allergies.

According to technology pioneer Ray Kurzweil, "Medicine is among the most knowledge-intensive professions." Most doctors agree that medicine has grown too complex to have all the answers "in their heads." Today, in just about every aspect of their practices, healthcare workers use computer applications and Internet technologies.

At one time, doctors dictated the results of an examination or a surgical procedure. The dictated notes were later transcribed into computer records by staff members. Today's technology allows doctors to enter this information directly into computerized patient records by typing or by dictating into a speech recognition system that digitally converts their comments into digital text.

The Internet supplies physicians with many informational and diagnostic resources. Health libraries provide online access to reference databases, such as MedlinePlus, Medscape, and STAT!Ref. Doctors use drug databases to choose appropriate medications, avoid dangerous drug interactions, determine correct dosages, and print out prescriptions.

Hospitals are ideal candidates for wireless technologies because just about everything and everyone is on the move, including doctors, nurses, patients, and equipment. In today's wireless, paperless healthcare systems, a patient scheduled for a CT scan can check in at reception to receive a barcoded wristband, which serves as the patient ID. The results of the CT scan are transmitted to the radiologist who interprets the scan. The results are then transmitted to the patient's doctor. The patient can log in to a Web-based portal to see the CT scan results.

The Internet's ability to rapidly disseminate information worldwide makes it a crucial tool for tracking global health threats. During the COVID-19 pandemic, Web sites maintained by the World Health Organization (WHO) and Centers for Disease Control (CDC) provided statistics on the spread of infection. They also kept doctors, researchers, and reporters up to date on efforts to identify the virus, develop a vaccine, and devise treatment options.

The CDC also operates an online registry called ArboNET that collects information about confirmed cases of Zika and West Nile viruses in the continental United States and its island territories. The data is used to produce maps showing areas with high disease activity and to help gauge the results of insect control efforts.

Telemedicine uses communications links to supply medical services at a distance. It can be used to provide specialty medical services to rural patients and allow medical personnel from several locations to collaborate on patient diagnosis and treatment. Telemedicine became an important tool for doctors to diagnose and treat patients who were locked down as the COVID-19 pandemic spread.

Healthcare professionals take full advantage of the Internet to exchange electronic patient records, still images, and even full-motion video sequences. Images from diverse sources, such as X-rays, MRIs, and CT scans, stored in the standard DICOM (Digital Imaging and Communications in Medicine) format, can be easily transferred over the Internet and displayed using a single software package.

Computers have become an integral part of modern medical equipment. The use of X-rays was a huge medical breakthrough in the early 1900s, but X-rays capture only a two-dimensional image. A technology called CT (computed tomography) essentially assembles a series of X-ray images taken from slightly different angles. A computer works with the data to generate a three-dimensional image that can be rotated and viewed from any angle.

Computers, data, and telecommunications technology team up in a number of mobile medical devices that have revolutionized emergency medical services. An EMS worker describes a device used to monitor cardiac patients: "We can do a comprehensive 12-lead EKG at the scene, and the computer inside the LIFEPAK 12 tells us what kind of arrhythmia we may be dealing with and even gives us suggestions for treatments."

Today, most patients want to be informed participants in their health care. Patients use Web sites such as WebMD to find information on diseases, drugs, and treatment options. Doctors

frequently recommend health-related Web sites and support groups to patients. Patients can gather information from these sites at their own pace and refer back to it as necessary. The availability of information on the Web reduces the need for doctors to make lengthy explanations that patients often cannot absorb or remember during an office visit.

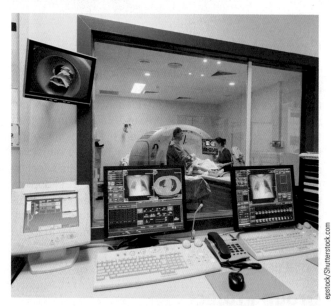

The use of information systems in medicine is not without potential pitfalls. Online patient records raise issues of confidentiality. Many patients are concerned about unauthorized access to their records by employers, human resources staff, and hackers.

The Health Insurance Portability and Accountability Act (HIPAA) requires healthcare providers and insurance companies to protect the privacy of their patients' and policy holders' information from inappropriate use or disclosure. Insurance company employees, for example, are allowed to look at clients' personal health information only in the course of administering claims.

Healthcare providers are not allowed to disclose personal health information without permission, unless requested by the government when a serious threat to public health and safety exists. HIPAA also gives patients the right to amend incorrect or missing information in their medical records, and it allows clients to request a list of the disclosures.

The next time you're in a hospital or doctor's office, look around for information systems. You're sure to find evidence of digital tools that improve the effectiveness of your health care.

Flipped Class Projects

Critical Thinking

The risk of identity theft continues to increase each year as it affects more and more consumers. Collect recent statistics for the number of people who are identity theft victims and the estimated annual financial losses it causes. In addition to the risk of identity theft, anyone who connects to the Internet is endangered by malware, unauthorized intrusions, and other exploits. How do you see these dangers affecting people's willingness to use online platforms for shopping, banking, and social interactions? Will these dangers eventually have a chilling effect on Internet use? Will people simply ignore the risk? Or will new technologies emerge that can dependably protect consumers? Explain your predictions.

Group Project

Form a group of two to five students to act as the project team for a system development project. Elect one person as the team leader, who will assign tasks to each group member. Your team's mission is to complete the planning phase for a system development project and produce a project development plan. The first task is to identify and briefly describe an information system at school, work, or a local business that needs improvement. The second task is to make a list of problems and opportunities that exist in that system by applying Porter's Five Forces Model and Wetherbe's PIECES framework. The third task is to make a list of actions your team would perform to design, construct, and implement a new information system. Finally, your team should incorporate all its findings into a document that would serve as the project development plan. Submit this plan to your instructor, who might provide additional directions for your group work and report format.

Cyberclassroom

Cybersecurity is important. Whether you're shopping online, using a social media site, or simply browsing the Web, the more you know, the safer you'll be. Search online for *test your security knowledge*. Find three interactive cybersecurity quizzes and take them. List each quiz and your scores. Did you learn anything new? Overall, how would you rate your cybersecurity knowledge?

Multimedia Project

One of the most fascinating aspects of Michael Porter's Five Forces model is the concept of substitute products and services. The classic case is the automobile industry replacing horse-drawn carriages and the widespread effects on associated industries. Find a unique example of a substitute product or service that changed an industry. Try to track its effects on at least ten suppliers or distributors. Locate photos to illustrate your examples.

Resume Builder

Create ten rules for an expert system that pertains to your career field. To complete the assignment, think of a set of simple decisions that someone on the job might be required to perform. For example, a loan officer might be required to make a quick evaluation of a borrower, an auto mechanic might be required to figure out what various tapping noises mean, or a fitness instructor might be required to recommend the best type of fitness class for clients. Make a list of ten rules that would help make the decision. The rules should be in the "If..., Then..." format. Submit your rules to your instructor.

Globalization

Many of the products we use every day have a surprisingly global supply chain. Connect to the Sourcemap Web site, *open.sourcemap.com*, where you can view supply chain maps. Choose one of the maps and track the chain from suppliers to consumers. Notice the significance of the color key that ranges from upstream (suppliers) to downstream (retailers). Now, draw your own source map for a product of your choice. Try something simple, such as lemonade or a pair of socks. To draw your map, you can register at the Sourcemap site, draw a map by hand, use graphics software, or superimpose your supply chain onto a Google map.

Key Terms

acceptance testing 650
actors 637
analysis phase 635
application development tool 643
application specifications 645
application testing 648
B2B 619
B2C 619
B2G 619
batch processing 611
BI 632
BPM 632
C2C 619
CASE tool 639
change requests 646
class diagram 638
colocation center 656
commit or rollback 612
corrective procedures 661
critical path 634
CRM 624
data breach 659
data center 656
data flow 636
data flow diagram 636
data store 636
decision model 615
decision query 615
decision support system 614
decision support worksheet 644
design phase 641
detail reports 612
detailed design phase 645
detection activities 661
deterrents 661
disaster recovery plan 658
ecommerce 619
ecommerce application 620
enterprise 607
ERP 626

exception report 613
executive information system 614
expert system 616
expert system shell 617
external entity 636
feature creep 646
fraud alert 663
fuzzy logic 617
Gantt charts 634
help desk 652
horizontal market 608
identity theft 660
implementation phase 647
inference engine 616
information engineering methodology 633
information system 607
integration testing 648
iterative SDLC 629
JIT 632
joint application design 630
knowledge base 616
knowledge engineering 616
lights-out management 657
loyalty program 625
maintenance phase 651
management information system 613
managers 609
mission 607
mission statement 607
MRP 632
MTBF 655
object-oriented methodology 633
OLTP 611
online processing 611
operational planning 609
organization 607
organizational chart 609
payment gateway 621
PERT 634

PIECES framework 633
planning phase 630
preventive countermeasures 661
procedure handbook 649
process 636
project development plan 630
project management software 634
quality of service 651
quality-of-service metric 652
SCM 623
sequence diagram 638
software customization 648
strategic planning 609
structured methodology 633
success factors 635
summary report 613
supply chain 622
system conversion 650
system development life cycle 629
system documentation 649
system requirements 635
system requirements report 635
system testing 648
systems analysis and design 629
tactical planning 609
TQM 632
transaction 611
transaction processing system 611
turnkey system 643
UML 637
unit testing 648
use case 637
use case diagram 637
user documentation 649
vertical market 608
WBS 634
workers 609

Interactive Summary

Section A: [_____] systems play a key role in helping organizations achieve goals, which are set forth in a(n) [_____] statement. Computers can be used by people at all levels of an organization. Workers use information systems to produce and manipulate information. Managers depend on information systems to supply data that is essential for long-term [_____] planning and short-term tactical planning. Transaction [_____] systems provide an organization with a way to collect, display, modify, or cancel transactions. These systems encompass activities such as general accounting, inventory tracking, and ecommerce. [_____] information systems typically build on the data collected by a TPS to produce reports that managers use to make the business decisions needed to solve routine, structured problems. A decision [_____] system helps workers and managers make non-routine decisions by constructing decision models that include data collected from internal and external sources. A(n) [_____] system is designed to analyze data and produce a recommendation or decision based on a set of facts and rules called a(n) [_____] base. These facts and rules can be written using an expert system shell or a programming language. A(n) [_____] engine evaluates the facts and rules to produce answers to questions posed to the system. Using a technique called [_____] logic, these systems can deal with imprecise data and problems that have more than one solution.

Section B: Enterprises use various kinds of software for core business operations. Ecommerce refers to business transactions that are conducted electronically over a computer network. Ecommerce activities are classified as B2C, C2C, B2G, and [_____]. When customers put items in their online shopping carts, the ecommerce site's server sends a(n) [_____] to the customer's computers containing the ID number of a shopping cart. The server also stores the ID number, along with a list of items purchased. Payment authorization is facilitated through a payment [_____]. Information systems are used to track and control the [_____] chain, which begins with raw materials shipped to a manufacturer, monitors finished goods shipped to distributors, and ends with merchandise delivered to customers. Enterprises also use [_____] applications to coordinate sales, marketing, and customer support. Data for these systems may originate from [_____] programs or from customer information collected during the sales cycle. [_____] is a suite of software modules that use a common database and a common user interface to integrate major business activities. These modules typically include applications for [_____] resources management, financial management, SCM, CRM, and manufacturing.

Section C: The process of planning and building an information system is referred to as systems [_____] and design, based on a system development [_____] cycle (SDLC), which consists of several phases. A project team can use one of several approaches to the system development process. For example, the [_____] methodology focuses on the processes that take place in an information system. The information [_____] methodology focuses on the data that an information system collects. The object-[_____] methodology treats an information system as a collection of interacting objects. A project begins with a(n) [_____] phase. In this phase, the project team is assembled and creates a project [_____] plan containing a justification of the project and an initial project schedule. The project team then proceeds to the [_____] phase, with the goal of producing a list of requirements for a new or revised information system. These requirements are sometimes called [_____] factors. The team uses documentation tools, such as data [_____] diagrams and [_____] case diagrams.

Section D: In the [_____] phase of the SDLC, the project team identifies potential software solutions, such as the use of programming languages, application [_____] tools, or application software. A(n) [_____] system might offer a complete hardware and software solution. When the solution requires custom programming, a(n) [_____] design phase produces specifications that describe the way the new information system should interact with users, store data, process data, and format reports. Development can be derailed by unmanaged [_____] creep, so the team should have a formal system of change requests. During the [_____] phase of the SDLC, the project team supervises the technicians who set up new hardware, install programming languages and other application [_____] tools, create and test applications, and customize software. The team also finalizes the system documentation and trains users. In this phase, three types of testing ensure that new software works correctly. [_____] testing is performed on each module, and then [_____] testing is performed to make sure that all the modules work together correctly. [_____] testing ensures that the software components work correctly on the hardware and with other, perhaps older, elements of the information system. Four types of information system go-live conversions are possible: direct, parallel, phased, or pilot. At the end of the conversion process, the information system undergoes a final test called [_____] testing, designed to assure the system's owner that the new system works as specified. After testing and installation, an information system enters the [_____] phase of its life cycle.

Section E: To protect data from being destroyed by natural disasters, human errors, and other factors, enterprises often house their information systems in private [_____] centers or shared [_____] centers. Enterprises also have [_____] recovery plans in place that contain step-by-step methods to secure data against threats, recover lost data, and resume operations after a disruption. Enterprises strive to prevent data [_____], in which personal data is viewed, accessed, or retrieved without authorization. [_____] reduce the likelihood of deliberate attack. [_____] countermeasures shield vulnerabilities to render an attack unsuccessful. [_____] procedures reduce the effect of an attack. [_____] activities recognize attacks and trigger a corrective response. Unauthorized access to corporate information systems is a primary source of [_____] theft. Although consumers have little control over data that is stored on corporate systems, they can take steps to protect their identity by placing a(n) [_____] alert on their credit reports.

Interactive Situation Questions

1. Suppose that you own a small bookstore located in a mall. Business seems to be declining, and you suspect that many of your former customers are now shopping at online bookstores. What can you do about declining sales? You realize that this situation falls into the category of a(n) [　　　　　] problem, and you might not be able to solve it by using the data supplied by your MIS.

2. Your friend just graduated and started working in a local pharmacy. She tells you about the pharmacy's computer system that warns of dangerous drug interactions by examining the patient's prescription record and sometimes asking the pharmacist to enter age and allergy information. The system that she has been describing sounds like a(n) [　　　　　] system.

3. The shelves in your local Target store are looking a little sparse because the dock workers' union is on strike. At Target's headquarters, managers are using [　　　　　] applications to plan the most efficient distribution logistics for when the strike ends.

4. As a member of the IT staff at a large corporation, you often hear about problems with the current information system. One recently discovered problem is that when an employee quits (or gets fired), sometimes the network manager is not notified, and the former employee continues to have access to company data over the Internet. Using the PIECES framework, you would classify this as a(n) [　　　　　] problem.

5. Your county provides online access to property records. You simply enter the address of the property or the owner's name into the site's search engine. However, each search seems to take longer than one minute. According to the PIECES framework, this delay would be classified as a(n) [　　　　　] problem.

6. You just received an email from Starbucks that reads: "Congratulations, you've achieved enough stars for Green level, so you now get free in-store refills." This message was likely sent from a(n) [　　　　　] application that tracks Starbucks customers. (Hint: Use the acronym.)

7. You just started working in the IT department at a very small company that's developing a new information system. Your coworkers are trying to track down a discrepancy that resulted from a change in the name of a data field. Although you don't say it, you realize that such a problem would not have occurred if the project team had used [　　　　　] tools. (Hint: Use the acronym.)

8. On your last job, you worked as an admitting clerk in a hospital. One day, you were told to begin using the hospital's new information system. The next day, you were told to go back to using the old system until further notice. You suspect that these events occurred as a result of a failed attempt at a(n) [　　　　　] conversion.

Levent Konuk/Shutterstock.com

Lab: Decisions, Decisions, Decisions

When you can't make up your mind, an organized approach to the problem might be in order. Whether you're making a career decision, selecting a new car, or wondering whether to take an extra course next semester, a decision worksheet can help you organize your thoughts and choose a course of action.

Requirements:

For this lab, you'll need a computer with spreadsheet software, such as Microsoft Excel, Apple Numbers, or Google Sheets. Although the steps specifically apply to Microsoft Excel, you can use them as general guidelines when working with other spreadsheet software.

Assignment:

1 Launch your spreadsheet software, enter a title and your name, and then save the worksheet as *YourName Decision Spreadsheet*.

Place the title in cell A1, and place your name in cell A2.

You can use your choice of font, font size, and color.

2 Add labels.

The decision spreadsheet will allow you to compare six options listed in cells A7 through A12.

The analysis will be based on four factors listed in cells B6 through E6.

Enter all of the labels shown in the screenshot below.

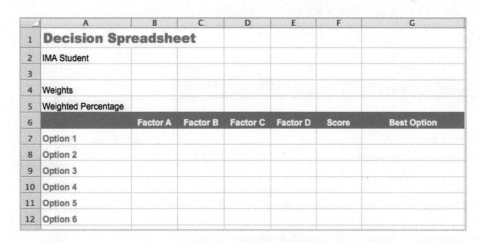

	A	B	C	D	E	F	G
1	**Decision Spreadsheet**						
2	IMA Student						
3							
4	Weights						
5	Weighted Percentage						
6		Factor A	Factor B	Factor C	Factor D	Score	Best Option
7	Option 1						
8	Option 2						
9	Option 3						
10	Option 4						
11	Option 5						
12	Option 6						

(Hint: Adjust the cell heights and widths as necessary to fit the text.)

③ Enter the weight formulas.

In cells B4 through E4, enter 1.

In cell F4, enter the formula =SUM(B4:E4).

In cells B5 through F5, enter the formulas in the screenshot below.

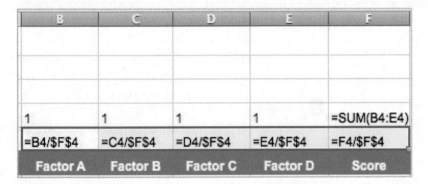

B	C	D	E	F
1	1	1	1	=SUM(B4:E4)
=B4/$F$4	=C4/$F$4	=D4/$F$4	=E4/$F$4	=F4/$F$4
Factor A	Factor B	Factor C	Factor D	Score

④ Use the Percentage format for cells B5 through F5.

Adjust the decimal places so the cells look like those in the following screenshot.

Weights	1	1	1	1	4
Weighted Percentage	25%	25%	25%	25%	100%
	Factor A	Factor B	Factor C	Factor D	Score

⑤ Enter the formulas for column F.

In cell F7, carefully enter this formula:

=($B$5*B7)+($C$5*C7)+($D$5*D7)+($E$5*E7)

After pressing Enter, copy the formula by dragging the small blue box down to cell F12.

	Factor A	Factor B	Factor C	Factor D	Score
Option 1					0
Option 2					
Option 3					
Option 4					
Option 5					
Option 6					

Drag this box down to cell F12.

6 Create a bar graph in column G to show a visual comparison of the options.

In cell G7, enter the formula =REPT("|",F7). Note: In Google Sheets and Apple Numbers, the formula is =REPT("|",F7).

The | symbol is the vertical bar, which is usually located on the same key as the backslash.

Copy the formula down to cells G8 through G12.

You'll not see any results yet.

7 Save the worksheet.

The worksheet is currently blank and can be used as a template for many different decisions. Each time you fill it in, use Save As to save it under a different name.

8 Fill in the worksheet with decision data.

Replace "Option 1," "Option 2," and so on with the options you're trying to evaluate. For example, you might be trying to decide among three elective courses for next semester. Enter the names of the courses in column A.

Replace "Factor A," "Factor B," and so on with the criteria you're using to make the decision, such as what time the class is offered and the topic.

Replace the 1s in row 4 with numbers to indicate the relative importance of each factor. Use a scale of 1–10, in which 1 indicates a factor that is not very important and 10 indicates a factor that is very important.

Fill in the grid with numbers between 1 and 10 to indicate the strength of each option. For example, if the Advanced Java class is offered at 8:00 in the morning and you are a night owl, give it a 1.

After you've filled in the grid, the best option will have the highest score.

9 Save your completed worksheet and submit it electronically or in printed format, as specified by your instructor.

	A	B	C	D	E	F	G
1	**Decision Spreadsheet**						
2	IMA Student						
3							
4	Weights	1	5	5	7	18	
5	Weighted Percentage	6%	28%	28%	39%	100%	
6		Time	Professor	Resume	Easy	Score	Best Option
7	Advanced Java	1	10	10	5	7.5555556	|||||||
8	Intro to Graphics	5	8	6	4	5.7222222	|||||
9	IPhone Programming	5	5	8	1	4.2777778	||||
10	Option 4					0	
11	Option 5					0	
12	Option 6					0	
13							

10 Databases

Module Contents

"Those who survive information overload will be those who search for information with broadband thinking but apply it with a single-minded focus." —Kathryn Alesandrini

 Try It! Apply what you learn.

- Draw an ERD diagram to represent database relationships.
- Draw the structure for hierarchical and graph database models.
- Sort lists of data using word processing software.
- Perform a mail merge.
- Use spreadsheet software to sort and filter data.
- Use local database clients, browsers, or apps to access databases.
- Define the fields for a database and use normalization techniques to minimize data redundancy.
- Identify the data types used by information systems that you interact with.
- Recognize real-world uses of field formatting and field validation at ecommerce and social media Web sites.
- Evaluate database user interfaces that you encounter online.
- Formulate SQL statements that can be used to query a database.
- Use Boolean operators when formulating queries for a database or search engine.
- Recognize how your personal data might be collected and used for big data marketing analytics.
- Experiment with Google Ngrams to get a glimpse of big data analytics.

● Pre-Check

Gauge your level of expertise. The answers are in the module.

What kind of diagram is this?

What kind of data model does this cube represent?

What kind of data model do these three tables represent?

Telephone Number:

( )   -

The database designer used a(n) _____ .

Bitcoin data is structured as a(n) _____ .

1024
exabytes

are equal to one _____ .

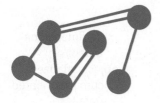

What kind of database model does this diagram represent?

Non-relational database tools are called _____ .

AND
OR
NOT

_____ operators

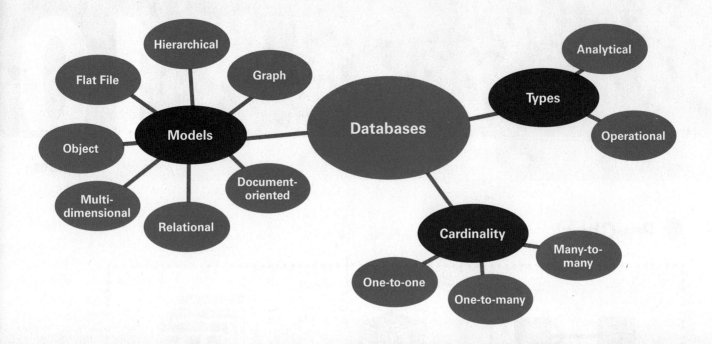

Objectives

▶ Describe the difference between an operational database and an analytical database.

▶ List seven activities associated with operational databases.

▶ Provide at least three examples of analytics applied to databases.

▶ Draw the data structure for a flat file and label each component.

▶ Draw ERDs and provide real-life examples of one-to-one, one-to-many, and many-to-many relationships.

▶ Diagram the data structure for hierarchical, graph, relational, multidimensional, and object database models.

A staggering 100 petabytes of data are stored in Uber's database. The telecommunications giant Sprint has databases that accumulate more than 800 million new call records every day. And then there's the National Security Agency, which may be collecting records of all voice and electronic communications that pass through ISPs in the United States. The job of collecting, storing, and retrieving such massive amounts of information is certainly daunting, and it requires the use of increasingly sophisticated database tools.

Terminology

operational database	structured file	record occurrence	multidimensional database
analytical database	database model	relationship	object database
data archive	flat file	cardinality	document-oriented database
executive dashboard	field	entity-relationship diagram	XML
data mining	field name	hierarchical database	
data warehouse	variable-length field	graph database	
predictive analytics	fixed-length field	relational database	
OLAP	record	table	
unstructured file	record type		

Operational and Analytical Databases

Databases are an essential aspect of modern life. Most businesses could not function without them, and they are the backbone of popular Internet services such as Apple Music, Facebook, Twitter, and eBay. Section A begins the module with an overview of databases and the many ways they are used today.

▶ **What is a database?** In its broadest definition, a database is a collection of information. Today, most databases are stored as computer files. A database can be a simple list of names and email addresses, or it can be a much more extensive compilation of data, such as Google's collection of user queries. Databases can even incorporate several lists. For example, the database for an ecommerce site, such as Amazon.com, includes inventory lists and customer lists.

Databases are created and managed by individuals and organizations. The tasks associated with creating, maintaining, and accessing the information in databases are referred to as data management, file management, or database management.

▶ **How are databases classified?** Databases are classified in several ways. They can be classified based on whether they are maintained by individuals or organizations. They can also be classified by their structure, which is a topic covered later in this section. One of the most basic ways to classify databases distinguishes whether they are used for everyday business operations or for analytical purposes.

Depending on their purpose and use, databases can be classified as operational databases or analytical databases. An **operational database** is used to collect, modify, and maintain data on a daily basis. An **analytical database** is used to collect data that will be used for spotting trends that offer insights for tactical and strategic business decisions. Figure 10-1 explains the differences between these two types of databases.

10

QuickCheck

An operational database is least likely to be used _____.

a. for a point of sale system

b. to store data collected by a TPS

c. to discover the average wait time for an Uber ride

d. for storing Zappos transactions

Figure 10-1: Operational and analytical databases

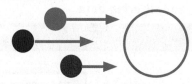

Operational Databases	**Analytical Databases**

Operational databases are commonly part of an enterprise's TPS, OLTP, CRM, SCM, or ERP information systems.

Analytical databases commonly hold historical data copied from one or more transaction processing systems.

They store data as it is collected from point-of-sale systems, customer loyalty programs, social media signups, and other transactions.

Unlike an operational database, the data in an analytical database is not being constantly updated. Therefore, it remains relatively static.

 The data is typically dynamic. It changes constantly and reflects up-to-the-minute information.

 Because the data is historical, the information that can be inferred is like a snapshot of a point in time.

▶ What are the main activities associated with operational databases? Operational databases collect and store data so that it can be viewed, updated, organized, and distributed. These activities are generally carried out by the organization that operates the database. Depending on the purpose of the information system that the database supports, consumers may also participate in these activities. In the following list of activities, the examples illustrate various entities that may have access to the data in an operational database.

Collect and store data. A database is a collection of data that grows as additional data is obtained. Data can be gathered by devices that process transactions and information systems that generate digital records to track inventory and similar physical objects. Data is added to a database when consumers carry out activities such as making purchases and subscribing to social media sites.

View data. Access to databases is usually limited to authorized users. Those users may be employees of the organization that maintains the database, but third parties may also be granted access. Usually, access rights include limitations. For example, consumers may be able to access their own bank account data, but they are not allowed to access data in other accounts. Even in-house workers may have limited access, as when a customer support technician is allowed access to information about a customer's device that is malfunctioning, but the technician is not allowed access to the customer's payment data.

Find data. Databases help you locate information. Library patrons can use an online public access catalog (OPAC) to find books. A pharmacist can check a pharmaceutical database for drug interactions before filling a prescription. A computer technician can check a manufacturer's database to find the part number for replacing your computer's fried hard drive. Searches can be used to find a specific piece of data, or they can be used as filters to view a subset of data that meets certain criteria. For example, a search for *Austin City Limits* at the Live Music Archive acts as a filter to list music from a specific live music event (Figure 10-2).

Try It!

Have you used the U.S. National Archives database? Connect to *www.archives.gov/research/search*. What kind of information is displayed when you search for *Marilyn Monroe*, the legendary actress who may have had a liaison with President Kennedy?

Figure 10-2: Searching, sorting, and filtering data

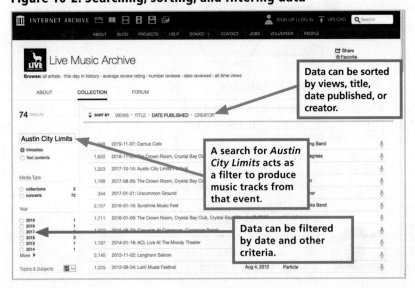

Source: Internet Archive Live Music Archive

Update data. One of the primary activities of database management is keeping data up to date by entering current addresses, inventory quantities, new account passwords, and so on. Data entry errors can produce database inaccuracies, which are not always easy to correct. Horror stories about data entry errors abound, including tales of individuals—very much alive—whose records were mistakenly marked "deceased." Data errors may originate within an information system or from external entities, such as consumers. To prevent errors, information systems include validation routines. You'll learn more about this topic later in the module.

Organize data. The data in a typical database is stored in no particular order. New data is appended to the end of the file because it is too cumbersome to insert the data in alphabetical order, for example, and then rearrange all the records that come after it. Reports created with this jumble of raw data would not be particularly useful. To turn data into a more suitable report, it can be organized in a variety of ways. It can be alphabetized, placed in numeric order, grouped, and subtotaled.

Distribute data. Databases—combined with mail merge and other computerized technologies—offer efficient ways to distribute information to customers, employees, the press, government agencies, and other companies. For example, your monthly electric bill is generated from the power company's database. That recall notice you received about the braking system in your six-month-old car, your monthly bank statement, and your class schedule for next semester all are generated from databases.

Unfortunately, databases also generate mountains of Publishers Clearing House mailings and an irritating amount of v1agr*a spam that lands in your email inbox. Today's digital databases are much more portable than old-fashioned paper-based databases, but the convenience of digital formats makes computer databases easier to misuse.

Spammers, junk mailers, and telemarketers pay only a fraction of a penny for each name on a mailing or call list. Millions of records can be easily copied, sent over the Internet, and stored on an external hard drive, a USB flash drive, or in the cloud. The U.S. legal system has yet to iron out details regarding database ownership and under what conditions it is allowable to share database data.

Move or remove data. Information can be removed from a database when it is no longer needed. Keeping a database lean can speed up searches and conserve storage space. Historical data can be valuable, however. Rather than deleting old data, it can be moved to a **data archive**. As a consumer, you should be aware that records can remain in databases and archives for years after transactions have been completed—even after your name has been "removed" or your records are designated as "inactive" (Figure 10-3).

> **QuickCheck**
>
> When records are added to a database, they are usually _____.
>
> a. appended to the end of the database file
>
> b. inserted into the file alphabetically
>
> c. monitored for the first query
>
> d. copied to a data archive

Figure 10-3: Unsubscribing does not remove personal data

> ⦿ Please unsubscribe me from future email messages, including sales events. If I place an order, however, and provide my email address, you may send me email pertaining to the status of my order.
>
> SUBMIT ▸

▶ **What are the main activities associated with analytical databases?**
Analytical databases store data that is used by corporate executives, strategic planners, and other workers to examine sales performance, inventory levels, and other business metrics. Although it is possible to extract analytical data from operational databases, analytical databases are structured to provide analytics more efficiently and flexibly.

Decision makers can access analytical databases using an **executive dashboard**, which includes tools for visually displaying query results. For example, city planners might be interested in information about city-wide employment. A dashboard can pull data from a database and display it in an easy-to-understand visual format. Tabs and other controls allow users to view data by criteria such as location or business type (Figure 10-4).

Figure 10-4: An executive dashboard visually displays data

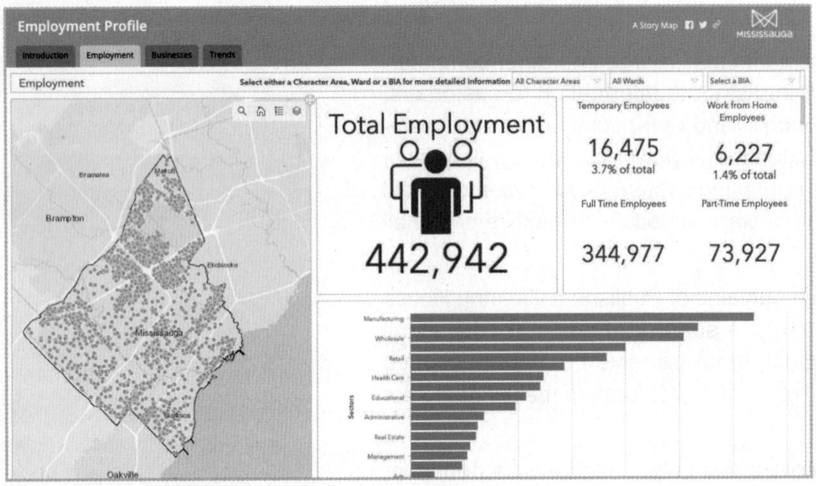

Source: ArcGIS Resources

Analytical databases contain data that is periodically copied from operational databases. For example, every month, data pertaining to sales of men's, women's, and children's shoes might be copied from a Zappos.com transaction processing system to an analytical database so executives can make inferences about customer gender, age, and buying habits.

Databases designed for analytical activities are generally used by in-house employees. Consequently, consumers rarely interact with analytical databases.

Analytical databases also differ from operational databases in that they are read-only. The data they contain is static and cannot typically be changed, modified, or deleted. For example, an executive would not be able to change a customer's order from within an analytical database. In some ways, it is similar to how Google works—you can query the Google database, but you cannot change the data it contains.

The data in an analytical database can be used for a variety of activities, such as data mining, predictive analytics, and OLAP.

QuickCheck

Which one of the following is not a characteristic of analytical databases?

a. Primarily used by in-house staff

b. Read-only

c. Contain data copied from transaction processing systems

d. Easy to update and change individual records

Find relationships and patterns. Data mining refers to computer algorithms that analyze information to discover previously unknown and potentially useful information, including relationships and patterns. The data accessed by data mining and other analysis techniques is often stored in a data warehouse, which can be a repository for data from more than one database. A repository for data mining is created by transferring data from operational databases to a data warehouse where it can be combined with data from other databases.

Data mining can reveal relationships that might not be expected or anticipated. For example, an analysis of over 10 million policies and accident claims in the Farmers Insurance Group data warehouse revealed that married baby boomers who owned a full-size car or minivan in addition to a sports car tended to make far fewer insurance claims than younger, unmarried sports car owners. As a result of the data analysis, lower insurance rates were offered to sports car owners who fit the low-risk profile.

Make predictions. Predictive analytics refers to a branch of data mining that analyzes current and historical data to predict future trends. It makes use of statistical algorithms and optimization research to discover patterns in data. For example, predictive analytics might help predict customer behavior, unmask terrorists, forecast storm paths, or determine genetic susceptibility to certain diseases. Like data mining, predictive analytics processes data autonomously, rather than under the direction of an operator who specifies what to look for.

Data mining and predictive analytics are sometimes criticized for finding relationships, patterns, and trends where none actually exist. The misuse of data mining is sometimes called data dredging or data fishing.

Examine multiple factors. OLAP (online analytical processing) is a data analysis technique used by decision makers to quickly get answers to complex queries that encompass multiple factors, such as locations, revenue, time periods, and employee status. Unlike data mining and predictive analytics, OLAP is an interactive process that allows decision makers to devise on-the-fly queries, enter them, and get an immediate response.

Suppose, for example, that a college administrator wants to keep track of student applications and admissions to see which departments are meeting enrollment goals based on the number of new students admitted and their test scores. An OLAP query can access information from the admissions office along with data from the college's student records database (Figure 10-5).

QuickCheck

What would a bank manager use to quickly find out how many fixed-rate and variable-rate mortgages were approved by the bank during each of the past four years?

a. A data mine

b. A CRM data warehouse

c. An OLAP executive dashboard

d. A TPS

Figure 10-5: OLAP produces analytics from multiple data sources

Database Models

Data can exist as a jumble of files, folders, images, and sounds, or it can be shaped and molded into a more structured format. Trying to fit diverse snippets of data into a uniform mold might increase access efficiency, but there can be costs and tradeoffs. Database designers always face a basic question: "What is the best structure for this data?"

▶ **What is the underlying structure of a database?** Computer databases evolved from manual filing systems. A filing cabinet full of folders and papers would be classified as an **unstructured file** because every document has a unique structure and contains different kinds of data.

In a box of unstructured documents, you could find old receipts, photos, product brochures, and handwritten letters. The electronic equivalent to this jumble of information might be the collection of documents and graphics stored at a social media Web site.

In contrast to a collection of dissimilar information, library card catalogs and address books would be classified as structured files. A **structured file** uses a uniform format to store data for each person or thing in the file. Many of the databases used in business, ecommerce, and government are stored as structured files.

The underlying structure of a database is referred to as a **database model**. There are several types of database models, each with a unique way of storing data. Database models such as flat files and relational tables are commonly used today, whereas hierarchical models are becoming obsolete. Other models such as graph and multidimensional databases are becoming more common. Let's see what these models are all about.

▶ **What's the simplest way to store data?** One of the simplest models for storing data is a **flat file** that consists of a single, two-dimensional table of data elements. Each row in the table is a record, and each column in the table is a field. Spreadsheets are stored as flat files displayed as rows and columns. Flat files are also the foundation for simple databases, such as an email address book, a music playlist, or a food nutrition table (Figure 10-6).

QuickCheck

Would the data stored in a spreadsheet be considered a structured file?

a. Yes

b. No

Figure 10-6: A flat file stores data in a two-dimensional table

Each column of the table represents a field.

Each row contains the data for one record.

FOOD ITEM	AMOUNT	CALORIES	CARBS	CHOLESTEROL	FIBER	PROTEIN	TOTAL FAT
BUTTER, SALTED	1 cup	717	0.06	215	0	0.85	81.11
CHEESE, CHEDDAR	1 cup, diced	403	1.28	105	0	24.9	33.14
COTTAGE CHEESE, LOWFAT	4 oz	98	3.38	17	0	11.12	4.3
CREAM CHEESE	1 cup	342	4.07	110	0	5.93	34.24
CHEESE, SWISS	1 cup, diced	380	5.38	92	0	26.93	27.8
HALF AND HALF	1 cup	130	4.3	37	0	2.96	11.5
WHIPPING CREAM	1 cup, whipped	292	2.96	111	0	2.17	30.91
SOUR CREAM	1 cup	135	4.26	39	0	2.94	12
EGGNOG	1 cup	135	13.54	59	0	3.81	7.48
BUTTERMILK	1 cup	40	4.79	4	0	3.31	0.88
MILK	1 cup	496	38.42	97	0	26.32	26.71
MILK SHAKE, CHOCOLATE	1 fl oz	119	21.15	11	0.3	3.05	2.7
MILK SHAKE, VANILLA	1 fl oz	112	17.75	12	0	3.86	3.03
YOGURT, PLAIN WHOLE MILK	1 cup	61	4.66	13	0	3.47	3.25
EGG, FRIED	1 large	196	0.88	457	0	13.63	15.31
EGG, HARD-BOILED	1 cup, chopped	155	1.12	424	0	12.58	10.61
EGG, SCRAMBLED	1 cup	167	2.2	352	0	11.09	12.21
BUTTER, UNSALTED	1 cup	717	0.06	215	0	0.85	81.11
APPLES	1 cup, quartered	52	13.81	0	2.4	0.26	0.17
APRICOTS	1 cup, halves	48	11.12	0	2.0	1.4	0.39
AVOCADOS	1 cup, cubes	160	8.53	0	6.7	2	14.66

Source: U.S. Department of Agriculture

10

▶ What are the basic elements of a flat file? A **field** contains the smallest unit of meaningful information, so you might call it the basic building block for a structured file or database. Each field has a unique **field name** that describes its contents. For example, in a music playlist, the field called Name could hold the name of a song, the Time field holds the song length, the Artist field holds the name of the performer, the Album field holds the name of the album that the song came from, and the Genre field holds the type of song.

A field can be variable length or fixed length. A **variable-length field** is like an accordion—it expands to fit the data you enter, up to some maximum number of characters. A **fixed-length field** contains a predetermined number of characters (bytes). The data you enter in a fixed-length field cannot exceed the allocated field length. Moreover, if the data you enter is shorter than the allocated length, blank spaces are automatically added to fill the field. The fields in Figure 10-7 are fixed length. The underscores indicate the number of characters allocated for each field.

Figure 10-7: Fixed-length fields hold a set amount of data

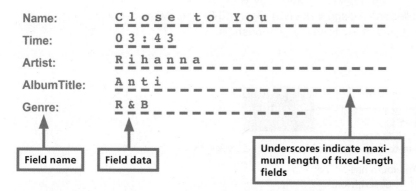

In the world of databases, a **record** refers to a collection of data fields. You're already familiar with several types of records, such as student records, medical records, and dental records. Each record stores data about one entity—a person, place, thing, or event. For example, a data record stored in a music playlist contains fields of data pertaining to a digital music track.

The template for a record is referred to as a **record type**. It contains field names, but no data. Creating record types is part of the design process that lets database designers specify the information needed to complete each record. A record type, similar to a blank form, is usually shown without any data in the fields. A record that contains data is referred to as a **record occurrence**, or simply a record (Figure 10-8).

Figure 10-8: A record type is different from a record occurrence

Record Type
NAME
TIME
ARTIST
ALBUMTITLE
GENRE

Record Occurrence	
Name	**Close to You**
Time	**03:43**
Artist	**Rihanna**
AlbumTitle	**Anti**
Genre	**R&B**

QuickCheck

In Figure 10-8, "R&B" is _____.

a. a record type

b. a record occurrence

c. a field

d. data

▶ Why would a database need to keep track of relationships? Each record in a flat file is an independent entity, and no relationships can be established between records. For example, you can't set up links between all of Rihanna's songs in your music playlist. If you are listening to *Close to You*, you can't automatically link to Rihanna's next-most-popular song.

In database jargon, a **relationship** is an association between data that's stored in different record types. Relationships are important because there are associations among the real-life things that database records represent. An online music service maintains a database with information about albums, tracks, and recording artists. Its database also contains information about customers. There are several important relationships within the database, such as the tracks that are related to each album and the customers related to albums they have purchased.

An important aspect of the relationship between record types is cardinality. **Cardinality** refers to the number of associations that can exist between two record types. For example, many albums can be classified as being part of the Rap genre. The reverse is not true, however. An album can have only one genre; it can't be classified as both Rap and Classical.

The relationship between record types can be depicted graphically with an **entity-relationship diagram** (sometimes called an ER diagram or ERD). Figure 10-9 shows ERDs for one-to-one, one-to-many, and many-to-many relationships.

QuickCheck

What type of relationship describes books and authors?

a. One-to-one

b. One-to-many

c. Many-to-many

Figure 10-9: ERDs

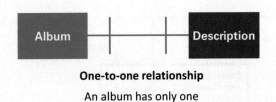

One-to-one relationship

An album has only one description.

One-to-many relationship

One genre can be assigned to many albums.

Many-to-many relationship

Albums contain many tracks, and tracks can be included on several different albums.

Key to ERD Symbols

The crossbar indicates exactly one occurrence.

The crossbar and crow's foot indicate one or more occurrences.

❱ What kinds of databases track relationships? Many database models keep track of relationships among data, but there are different techniques for doing so. For example, a **hierarchical database** allows one-to-one and one-to-many relationships, which are linked in a hierarchical structure (Figure 10-10).

Figure 10-10: The hierarchical database model

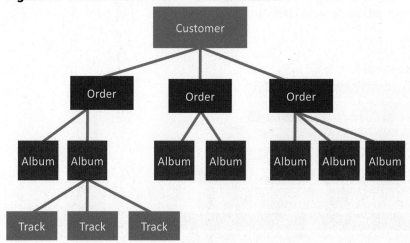

Although hierarchical databases offer lightning-quick searches and utilize a minimum amount of disk space for storage, they are rarely used today for business, consumer, and other mainstream database applications. Instead, they remain in use only for specialized applications. Windows uses a hierarchical database to store Registry data that keeps track of the software and hardware configuration of your PC.

A **graph database** offers an alternative way to track relationships. The structure of these databases resembles sociograms with their interlinked nodes. As you might expect, such databases are useful for storing data generated on Facebook, Twitter, and other social media platforms. A graph database includes nodes, edges, and properties, as shown in Figure 10-11.

Figure 10-11: The graph database model

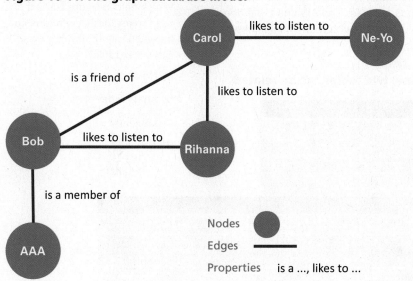

Try It!

How do graph databases relate to online dating? Do a quick Google search and see what you can discover.

QuickCheck

In Figure 10-11, Ne-Yo is a(n)

_____.

a. record type

b. node

c. edge

d. ERD

▶ **What's a relational database?** A **relational database** stores data in a collection of related tables. Each **table** is a sequence of records, similar to a flat file. All the records in a table are of the same record type. Each row of a table is equivalent to a record. Each column of a table is equivalent to a field.

Most relational databases contain several tables. For example, suppose a store called Vintage Music sells vinyl albums and singles both from a mall-based store and online. The store might use five tables to store data, as shown in Figure 10-12.

Figure 10-12: The relational database model

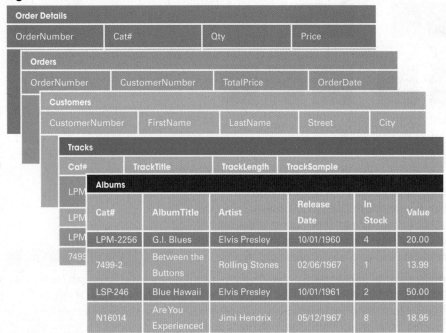

In a relational database, relationships are specified by joining common data stored in records from different tables. Suppose customers want to know which tracks are included in the Elvis Presley album *G.I. Blues*. The Albums table does not include this information. Figure 10-13 illustrates how a relationship links data in the Albums table with data in the Tracks table.

Figure 10-13: In a relational database, two tables can be related

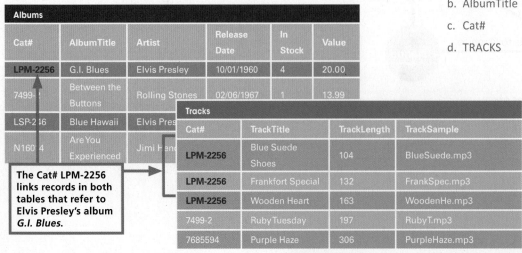

QuickCheck

Which field in Figure 10-13 is used to establish a relationship between the Albums table and the Tracks table?

a. LPM-2256

b. AlbumTitle

c. Cat#

d. TRACKS

❭ **What's a multidimensional database?** A **multidimensional database** organizes relationships over three or more dimensions. In the context of databases, a dimension is a layer based on a data element, such as a product, place, or customer, that can be used to categorize data.

Multidimensional databases can have any number of dimensions; but when there are more than seven dimensions, the models become difficult to work with. Multidimensional databases are often illustrated as a cube with three dimensions like the one in Figure 10-14, which has dimensions for age, location, and music preference.

Figure 10-14: The multidimensional database model

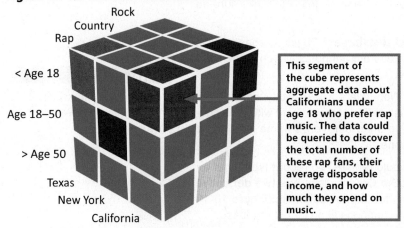

This segment of the cube represents aggregate data about Californians under age 18 who prefer rap music. The data could be queried to discover the total number of these rap fans, their average disposable income, and how much they spend on music.

A key element of multidimensional databases is their ability to support OLAP queries that make it possible to combine data, drill down to specifics, or slice and dice the data to view it from different perspectives. Each cube in the multi-dimensional model can produce multiple facts. So the red cube in Figure 10-14 not only could tell you how many young rap fans there are in California, but also could produce information about their disposable incomes and buying habits.

Multidimensional databases are used in data warehouses, where data from operational databases is aggregated and transformed to make it more useful for analytical queries. For example, suppose that the Vintage Music relational database does not include a field for a customer's musical preference. This miss-ing field could be added by moving data into the multidimensional database and generating data for a dimension called MusicPreference based on the kinds of music each customer has purchased in the past.

Try It!

The representation of multidimensional databases looks a lot like a Rubik's Cube. Although it might be slightly off-topic, several Web sites have virtual Rubik's Cubes that you can play with. When you've completed this section, take a break and give them a try.

▶ **What's an object database?** An object database, also referred to as an object-oriented database, stores data as objects, which can be grouped into classes and defined by attributes and methods. The Programming module in this text covers object-oriented terminology in detail; but in the context of object databases, a class defines a group of objects, such as customers or albums.

Classes are described by attributes and methods. The attributes for an object are equivalent to fields in a relational database. For example, a class called Orders might have attributes such as OrderNumber, OrderDate, CustomerNumber, and OrderedAlbums.

A method is any behavior that an object is capable of performing. A method called CheckInventory can be defined for this class. Its job is to make sure an album is in stock.

▶ **What are the advantages of object databases?** Object databases excel at representing objects that have slightly different attributes, which is the case in many real-world business applications.

Vintage Music accepts phone orders and Web orders. These two types of orders differ slightly because an email address is used to communicate with Web customers, whereas a telephone number and the order clerk's name need to be recorded for customers who order by phone.

In this scenario, a relational database would require two record types, but an object database can be set up so that the Orders class has two derivative classes: one for Web customers and one for phone customers. Figure 10-15 illustrates classes, derivative classes, and methods in an object database.

QuickCheck

In Figure 10-15, how many attributes does the Web Orders class inherit?

a. One

b. Two

c. Four

d. Five

Figure 10-15: The object database model

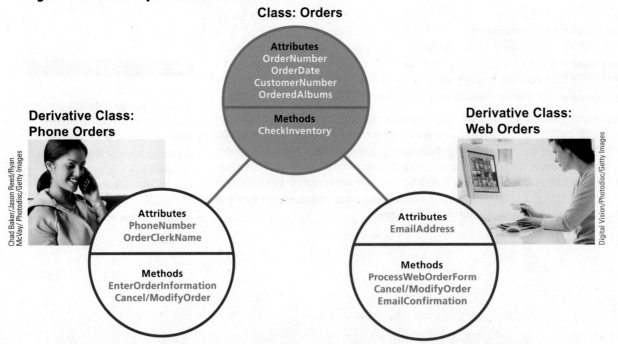

An object database can easily store data about different types of orders. A class called Orders holds data and methods common to all types of orders. A derivative class called Phone Orders inherits all the characteristics of Orders, but it has attributes and methods unique to orders placed by telephone. Web Orders is a derivative class that has attributes and methods unique to orders placed over the Web.

◗ **What is a document database?** A **document-oriented database** stores unstructured data, such as the text of a speech or a magazine article. Because these articles are of varying lengths and structure, it is not possible to mold them into a hierarchical, relational, or object structure. So, instead of molding the data to fit a database structure, document databases are created by inserting structural markups similar to HTML into the documents themselves. Two popular ways of formatting document databases are with XML and JSON, though XML offers more flexibility.

XML (eXtensible Markup Language) allows field tags, data, and tables to be incorporated into a document. It was developed in response to several deficiencies that became apparent as HTML gained widespread use. A database of historic speeches might be stored in XML format, allowing queries to locate speeches related to specific orators, dates, and places (Figure 10-16).

Figure 10-16: The document-oriented data model

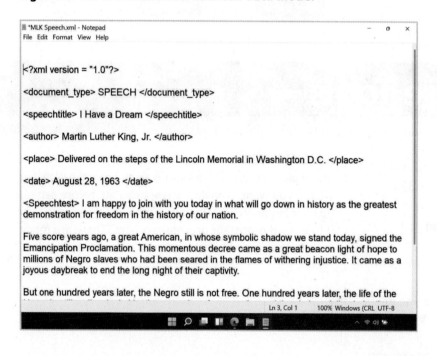

QuickQuiz   Section A

1. A(n) ☐ database commonly holds a snapshot of historical data, whereas an operational database reflects up-to-the minute transactions.

2. Data ☐ refers to computer algorithms that analyze information in databases to discover relationships and patterns.

3. A record ☐ is a template that consists of field names, but no data.

4. A(n) ☐ database resembles a sociogram with nodes linked by edges.

5. A(n) ☐ database stores data in a collection of related tables.

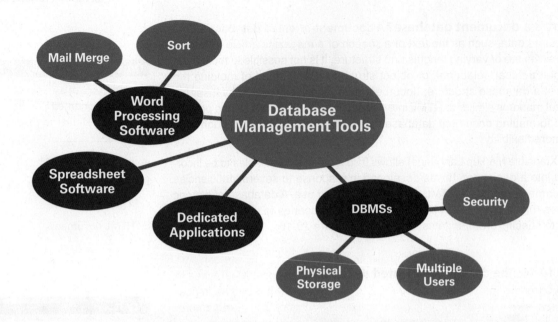

Objectives

▶ Explain why database designers try to avoid data dependence.

▶ Provide examples of at least five dedicated applications that are based on databases.

▶ Describe the data management features available in word processors.

▶ Provide three examples of the kinds of data you might successfully store and manipulate with spreadsheet software.

▶ Name two DBMSs that are relatively easy to use, and list four companies that produce an enterprise-level DBMS.

▶ Explain how the concept of serializability relates to databases.

▶ Describe the three categories of database clients.

▶ List at least four security measures that are important for database management.

Sports fans have an obsession with scores and player stats. Sure, you can look up anything on the Web, but what if you want to analyze a league's data before setting up your fantasy team? Do you want to pop the league data into a word processor or a spreadsheet? There are many tools for working with data. Section B provides an overview.

Terminology

data dependence	single-level sort	DBMS	database client software
data independence	multi-level sort	serializability	

Database Tool Basics

There's an old saying, "Don't use a sledgehammer to crack a nut," which means "Use the right tool for the job." Database tools range from enterprise-wide, multi-module information system suites to handy features tucked away in application software and social media apps. Section B will help you to determine which database tools are suitable for managing personal data and which are appropriate for enterprise tasks.

▶ **Is it easy to retrieve data from files?** Back when information systems emerged as important business tools, data was stored in ASCII files and programmers created custom software modules to access that data. It is still possible to create custom software to accommodate flat files and other database models. Today, however, custom software is rarely created to manage databases because a good variety of off-the-shelf tools are available. These tools are professionally designed to be efficient and avoid problems produced by data dependence.

Data dependence is a term that refers to data and program modules being so tightly interrelated that they become difficult to modify. Imagine a database in which program modules and data all exist in one large file! It would be impossible to access the data while editing any of the program modules. Furthermore, changing the file structure in any way might make the modules unusable.

Modern database tools support **data independence**, which entails separating data from the programs that manipulate data. As a result, a single data management tool can be used to maintain many different files and databases. In addition, standard search, sort, and print routines continue to function, regardless of changes to field names or record structure.

▶ **What kinds of database tools are available?** Simple tools for managing consumer-level databases, such as contact lists and research bibliographies, can be found in dedicated application software, word processing and spreadsheet software, and database management software. Database tools designed for enterprise-level tasks can be more expensive and more complex. The table in Figure 10-17 provides a quick classification of the database tools covered in the rest of this section.

QuickCheck

Which of the following is considered beneficial by database designers?

a. Data dependence

b. Data independence

c. Both

Figure 10-17: Database tools

Tool	Cost	Versatility	Ease of Use
Dedicated software, such as an address book	Shareware available for simple applications is inexpensive; dedicated software for business applications can be costly.	Normally, the software is dedicated to a single type of database.	Easy; minimal setup is required because fields are predefined.
Word processing software	Most consumers have word processing software.	The software is best for simple flat files, such as mailing lists.	Easy; the software uses an interface familiar to most users.
Spreadsheet software	Most consumers have spreadsheet software.	The software is best for simple flat files that involve calculations.	Easy; the software uses an interface familiar to most users.
Database software	Basic shareware database software is inexpensive; high-end database software can be expensive.	High-end packages provide excellent versatility.	High-end database software often has a steep learning curve.

Dedicated Applications

Individuals commonly have several personal databases, such as a contact list, a collection of photos, or a record of checkbook transactions. Enterprises tend to have more extensive databases containing terabytes or even petabytes of data. The tools required to manage small personal databases differ from enterprise data management tools.

▶ **Are simple data management tools available?** Yes. The simplest tools for managing data are dedicated applications for specific data management tasks, such as keeping track of appointments or maintaining an address book. To use one of these tools, simply enter your data. The software includes menus that allow you to manipulate the data after it is entered.

Although dedicated applications are fairly easy to use, they generally don't allow much flexibility because the record types are predefined. The apps shown in Figure 10-18 are handy, but they don't allow users to add fields or change field names.

Figure 10-18: Some dedicated apps access databases

Some dedicated tools do offer a choice of fields. As Figure 10-19 shows, users can select the fields they want to use for storing data in Apple's Contacts application.

Figure 10-19: Dedicated apps may have limited flexibility

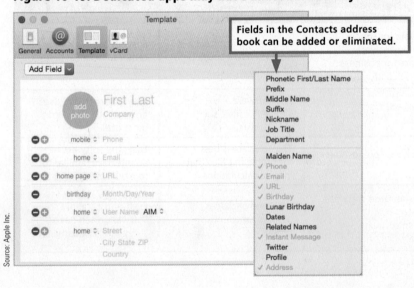

Fields in the Contacts address book can be added or eliminated.

▶ What kinds of dedicated data management tools are used in enterprise information systems? The previous module presented an overview of key enterprise applications, such as CRM, ERP, SCM, and ecommerce, that collect transactions in a database. These important business management tools are generally sold as application modules that include the structure to hold data and the routines to query, view, add, modify, delete, and analyze the data.

▶ How much flexibility do these enterprise tools offer? Like dedicated applications for managing personal databases, enterprise applications offer limited flexibility. The field types are predefined to coincide with the application. For example, an inventory application will have predefined fields such as Item Number, Description, Quantity on Hand, Reorder Level, Supplier, and Cost. In contrast, an SCM application might have fields such as CustomerID, MaterialsBill, CarrierID, Route, ArrivalTime, and TrackingNumber. The database tables set up for an inventory system are not suitable for SCM, so a unique data structure is required for each.

Enterprise applications tend to have some flexibility for customization, which allows field names to be modified to reflect business practices. For example, changing the MaterialsBill field name to OrderNumber might make more sense to workers. Such changes, however, are typically made only to the forms that are displayed on screens or printed.

Making core changes to a database can easily break the connections that form relationships between tables. For example, if the MaterialsBill field is used as a link between customers and shippers, renaming the field in only one table would sever the relationship to the other table.

The bottom line is that dedicated enterprise applications may allow cosmetic changes, but they generally do not encourage modifications of core data structures. There are exceptions. For example, the Microsoft Dynamics CRM online application allows modifications, including new fields and processes (Figure 10-20).

10

QuickCheck

Dedicated enterprise applications generally do not

_____.

a. offer limited flexibility

b. include enterprise-level and personal tools

c. allow changes to field names displayed on the screen or in reports

d. encourage modifications of core data structures

Figure 10-20: Microsoft Dynamics CRM

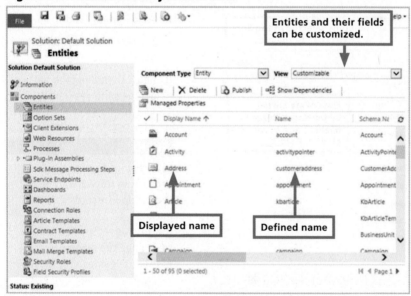

Microsoft Dynamics CRM allows its database to be customized by adding, deleting, and modifying entities and their attributes. For example, you can modify the display name for a field.

Word Processor Data Tools

Word processing software is designed to produce documents, but it also may include tools for working with unstructured or structured data. These tools can sort a simple list or create a file of data for mail merges.

▶ **What can a word processor sort?** Most word processing software includes a sort feature that can be used to arrange a simple list in alphabetical or numeric order. This feature is the most primitive data management tool, suitable for a limited amount of data.

Sorting can come in handy for alphabetizing a list of contacts or sorting the entries in a bibliography. Sorting tools can usually be applied to paragraphs of text, so they can be used to arrange glossaries and indexes. They can also be used to sort the contents of tables and text that is arranged in columns separated by tabs.

▶ **How does a sort work?** A sort rearranges information in a specified order, numerically or alphabetically. Sorts can be in ascending order (beginning with 1 or a) or in descending order. Multi-level sorts may also be possible.

A **single-level sort** uses only one field to arrange records. A **multi-level sort** arranges information by more than one field. For example, suppose that baseball player statistics are arranged in a tabular format with columns for players, teams, and batting statistics. A single-level sort can arrange the athletes by team, but a multi-level sort is required to arrange the data alphabetically so that within each team, the athletes' names are in alphabetical order. Figure 10-21 illustrates how to carry out a multi-level sort in Microsoft Word.

Figure 10-21: Microsoft Word has a sort feature

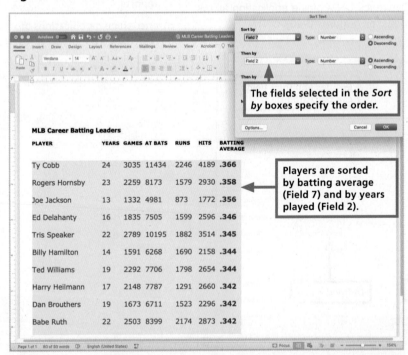

The fields selected in the *Sort by* boxes specify the order.

Players are sorted by batting average (Field 7) and by years played (Field 2).

MLB Career Batting Leaders						
PLAYER	YEARS	GAMES	AT BATS	RUNS	HITS	BATTING AVERAGE
Ty Cobb	24	3035	11434	2246	4189	.366
Rogers Hornsby	23	2259	8173	1579	2930	.358
Joe Jackson	13	1332	4981	873	1772	.356
Ed Delahanty	16	1835	7505	1599	2596	.346
Tris Speaker	22	2789	10195	1882	3514	.345
Billy Hamilton	14	1591	6268	1690	2158	.344
Ted Williams	19	2292	7706	1798	2654	.344
Harry Heilmann	17	2148	7787	1291	2660	.342
Dan Brouthers	19	1673	6711	1523	2296	.342
Babe Ruth	22	2503	8399	2174	2873	.342

Although a word processor can store data for a sports team and sort it in various ways, it is not a suitable tool for carrying out mathematical operations or statistical analysis. In this example, batting averages are entered manually.

What is mail merge? Mail merge creates customized documents by combining a template with a data source. Mail merge technology is used to produce mass mailings for sweepstakes and political campaigns. It can be useful for sending out employment query letters, personalized invitations, and customized holiday greetings.

Mail merge is a feature supplied by several word processors. What makes it a useful database tool is its associated data file. This file can be used as a mini-database for storing contacts, collectibles, or shipping labels—any list that is useful as a flat file and doesn't contain a huge number of items.

How does mail merge work? A mail merge requires two components. The first is a document that contains placeholders where custom data is to be inserted. The placeholders are field names such as SALUT and LAST. The second component is a list of data with corresponding fields, such as LAST: Moore and LAST: Diego. Microsoft Word combines these two components using the five-step mail merge routine shown in Figure 10-22.

10

Figure 10-22: The steps in a mail merge

1. Create the template document.

Dear   ,

As requested, my resume is attached.

2. Create a recipient list.

SALUT	FIRST	LAST	CHOICE
Mr.	Steve	Benton	2
Mr.	George	Moore	1
Mrs.	Shawnell	Nesbit	2
Ms.	Akiko	Sato	3
Mr.	**Luis**	Diego	1

3. Drag placeholders into the document to indicate where data from each field should be inserted.

Dear **<SALUT> <LAST>**,

As requested, my resume is attached.

4. Filter to select a subset of recipients—for example, to create a merge for only the top-choice employers.

SALUT	FIRST	LAST	CHOICE
Mr.	Steve	Benton	2
Mr.	**George**	**Moore**	**1** ←
Mrs.	Shawnell	Nesbit	2
Ms.	Akiko	Sato	3
Mr.	**Luis**	**Diego**	**1** ←

5. Complete the merge. The documents can be printed or sent out as email.

Dear Mr. Mo

As requ
my resu
attache

Dear Mr. Diego,

As requested, my resume is attached.

Spreadsheet Data Tools

Spreadsheets are organized in table format, so it makes sense that they can be used for storing data. They offer an easy-to-use starting point, and users who outgrow a spreadsheet's data-handling capabilities can transfer data to more sophisticated database software.

▶ **Can I use spreadsheet software for databases?** Most spreadsheet software also includes basic data management features. It does not require technical expertise to create simple flat files using a spreadsheet.

Depending on the spreadsheet software, it may be possible to sort records, validate data, search for records, perform simple statistical functions, and generate graphs based on the data. Figure 10-23 illustrates Microsoft Excel data management functions applied to national vaccination rates during the COVID-19 pandemic.

QuickCheck

Spreadsheets cannot be used to
_____ .

a. sort

b. filter

c. search

d. create relational databases

Figure 10-23: Spreadsheets have tools for sorting and searching

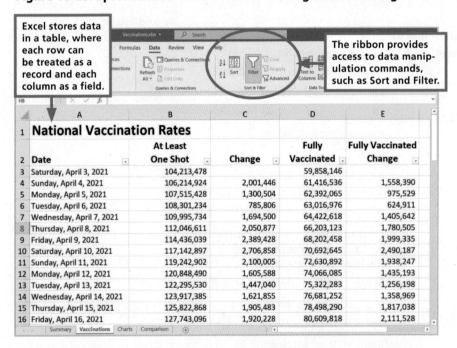

▶ **What are the limitations of using spreadsheets and word processors to manage data?** Simple file management tools provided by word processing and spreadsheet software are popular for individuals who want to maintain flat files that contain hundreds, not thousands, of records. These tools work well for a simple address book, an inventory of household goods, a record of healthcare costs, and a variety of other simple lists.

These basic tools do not, however, offer database capabilities for establishing relationships between different record types, and they are not powerful enough to maintain the large volume of records required for business information systems. As a guideline, use word processor data tools only for very simple lists and mail merges with fewer than 100 recipients. Use spreadsheets to manage data that may contain numeric quantities and hundreds, not thousands, of records. For larger collections of data, database software offers better management features.

Database Management Systems

There are situations in which a word processor or spreadsheet is not sufficient to handle a dataset, but a dedicated ERP, CRM, or SCM application is either too expensive or does not meet business needs. Designing a database from scratch and creating all the software necessary to access it is a complex and costly project. A DBMS offers a set of development tools for creating and accessing databases.

▶ **What is a DBMS?** The term **DBMS** (database management system) refers to software that manages data stored in a database. It includes routines to define the structure of a database, including its fields and relationships. A DBMS allows developers to set up applications that collect and process data from point-of-sale terminals, ecommerce Web sites, handheld data gathering devices, or the Internet of Things. It also offers routines for defining how data is displayed on the screen and in printed reports.

Developers can use a DBMS to create almost any application that revolves around a collection of data. It can be used for consumer-level applications, such as tracking player statistics for a local sports league or managing a nonprofit organization's fund-raising campaigns. Small businesses might use a DBMS to manage client billing or for scheduling projects. At the enterprise level, DBMSs are used to keep records pertaining to employees and compliance, sales leads, inventories, job costs, and just about every other aspect of business operations.

A variety of database management tools are available. Some of these tools are easy to use and require very little technical expertise, whereas others are designed for professional database developers.

▶ **Which DBMS tools are easiest to use?** Claris FileMaker and Microsoft Access are easy-to-use DBMSs that are a good fit for small businesses and individuals whose data can't be efficiently handled as a flat file spreadsheet. These DBMSs include all the tools necessary to manipulate data in a database, specify relationships, create data entry forms, query the database, and generate reports. They also have customizable starter templates for common types of databases (Figure 10-24).

10

Figure 10-24: Claris FileMaker starter templates

Projects

Event Management

Contacts

Assets

Content Management

Invoices

Inventory

Tasks

Estimates

Resource Scheduling

Meetings

Expense Reports

Product Catalog

Personnel Records

Time Billing

Research Notes

Source: Claris FileMaker

▶ **What about DBMS tools for professional developers?** Four DBMS vendors are the first stop for professional developers: IBM, Oracle, SAS, and SAP. All of these vendors offer a range of modules that can be assembled like LEGOs to accommodate most database structures and storage configurations. For example, snap the Database In-Memory module onto an existing Oracle Database module to build a lightning-fast transaction processing system. Or snap in the Oracle Advanced Analytics module to build applications for data mining.

Two open source DBMS products are also popular with database designers. MySQL is one of the world's most widely used DBMSs. SQLite is also popular. It is included with all Android devices, where it is used by various apps. On iPhones, SQLite is used to store text messages. It is also integrated into popular browsers.

▶ **What kinds of data can a DBMS work with?** Modern DBMSs work with many kinds of data, including text, numbers, images, PDFs, and audio files. The ability to work with many kinds of data is especially important in social media databases; but even in small businesses, the use of images, sound, and other data can be helpful. For example, a database for a commercial landscaping business might include photos of the customer premises, a map to the property, and a copy of the work contract in addition to the usual contact details. Figure 10-25 illustrates how the DBMS might display a customer's information on an iPad used by the landscapers on the job.

Figure 10-25: A modern DBMS works with a variety of data types

Source: MetroPlex

▶ **Do DBMSs work with different database models?** When building a database, one of the first design decisions is to determine which database model is the most appropriate. Although the relational database model is the most popular, for some applications an object database, a graph database, or some other model might be preferable.

Standard DBMSs offered by IBM, Oracle, SAP, and SAS are designed for relational databases. These tools are sometimes referred to as RDBMSs (relational DBMSs). They support the relational database model with data stored in tables that can be related to each other. Database tool vendors also offer products for other database models, such as document databases and graph databases. These alternative models and their associated development tools are generally used for enterprise-class database installations.

▶ **Does a DBMS take care of physical storage?** Today, databases might reside on an in-house server, on a cloud-based server, or on distributed servers scattered throughout the world. DBMSs handle the details of how to most efficiently arrange data on a storage medium for optimal access speed.

Physical storage is not a trivial design concern. Consider a relational database for an online music service that is too large to efficiently run on a single server, so it is distributed across multiple servers. The DBMS has to adjust to the way data is distributed. For example, if the data table containing cover art is housed on one server and the table of music tracks is housed on another server, the DBMS has to handle the data relationships across the two servers. It might do so by proactively fetching relationships in anticipation of their need, as shown in Figure 10-26.

Figure 10-26: Distributed databases

> **QuickCheck**
>
> In Figure 10-26, which table is the user querying?
>
> a. Music Tracks
>
> b. G.I. Blues
>
> c. Elvis
>
> d. Cover Art

▶ **How does a DBMS handle multiple users?** Consider this scenario. Paul, a landscaper, is on a job site and talking to a client who wants to change the lawn care day from Thursday to Friday. Paul attempts to enter this change into the database on his iPad. At the same time, Beth in the corporate office is on the phone with the client's partner, who wants to change the lawn care day to Monday. If both Paul and Beth attempt to enter these conflicting changes into the system at the same time, what will happen?

Or, suppose that a Zappos customer places a pair of to-die-for shoes in her shopping cart. It is the last pair in her size. If she continues to shop, can another customer swoop in, choose the same pair of shoes, and purchase them before the first customer checks out?

Enterprise-class DBMSs can handle thousands of simultaneous users, and some of those users may at times attempt to modify the same record but in different ways. A DBMS feature known as **serializability** ensures that transactions are updated in an orderly manner by establishing update rules. Depending on the situation, a DBMS might allow only one user at a time to access a record; other users are locked out until the record is closed. Alternatively, the DBMS could allow any number of users to access a record in view-only mode while it is being modified. A more sophisticated rule might lock only the field that is being modified, rather than the entire record.

> **Try It!**
>
> If you were a database and application designer for Zappos, how would you handle the situation when a customer places the last pair of shoes in a specific color and size in her shopping cart, but does not check out? Would you let another customer purchase them?

▶ Can a DBMS support multiple devices and operating systems?

Managers, workers, customers, and clients that access databases use a wide array of devices, including mainframes, laptops, tablets, smartphones, and data collection devices such as point-of-sale scanners. These devices may use consumer operating systems such as Windows, Android, macOS, and iOS, or enterprise operating systems such as Linux, UNIX, Solaris, and BSD.

A DBMS is installed on a specific in-house platform, such as Linux, or it runs as a cloud service hosted by the DBMS vendor. Once the DBMS is installed and set up, however, the database and applications can be extended to devices with other operating systems, allowing users to access the database using a client device such as a laptop, tablet, or smartphone.

Client devices require **database client software** to access the information in a database. There are three types of database clients: local software, browsers, and apps.

Local database clients are installed on a local storage device, such as a hard disk or a USB drive. The installation process can be manual, or it can take place behind the scenes without any action required on the part of a consumer.

Installing a local database client provides access to the database without installing the entire DBMS. As an added advantage, local clients are much simpler to use and less expensive than a full-blown DBMS. Local clients are developed or customized by database designers and programmers.

Browsers are the most commonly used database clients. They are used by consumers to access online databases and ecommerce sites. Because browsers are standard software on virtually every digital device, no additional installation is necessary.

A browser accesses databases using HTML forms and JavaScript embedded in Web pages. User queries are sent to the DBMS using HTTP calls. HTTP also returns query results, typically in the form of Web pages.

Apps are similar to local clients because they are installed locally. Their uniqueness is simply the fact that they are designed for mobile devices, which places restrictions on the user interface. Controls for entering queries and viewing data must be large enough to function with ease on a touchscreen. Screen size may also limit the amount of data that can be viewed, so creative ways of presenting data through images and graphs are often used.

Try It!

Look at the apps on your mobile device. How many of them would you classify as database clients?

QuickCheck

When searching Google from your laptop, what kind of database client are you using?

a. Local

b. Browser

c. App

d. Enterprise

What kind of security does a DBMS provide? DBMSs require security features to ensure data confidentiality, protect against insider threats, and block unauthorized access. Such features may be included in DBMS products, or they may be available as add-on modules. The suite of crucial database security features is explained in Figure 10-27.

Figure 10-27: Databases require security measures

Prevention

User rights management: Allows access to data on an as-needed basis

Encryption: Scrambles data that resides in storage, so that it is useless to thieves who acquire stolen devices containing databases

Database assessment: Identifies sensitive data and database vulnerabilities in order to secure them

Redaction: Masks confidential data such as credit card numbers

Intermediary servers: Prevent users from directly accessing the database, but instead allow users access only to a query processor

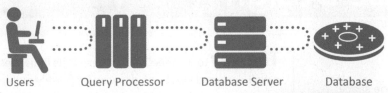

| Users | Query Processor | Database Server | Database |

Detection

Database activity monitoring: Tracks who accessed or changed data

QuickQuiz   Section B

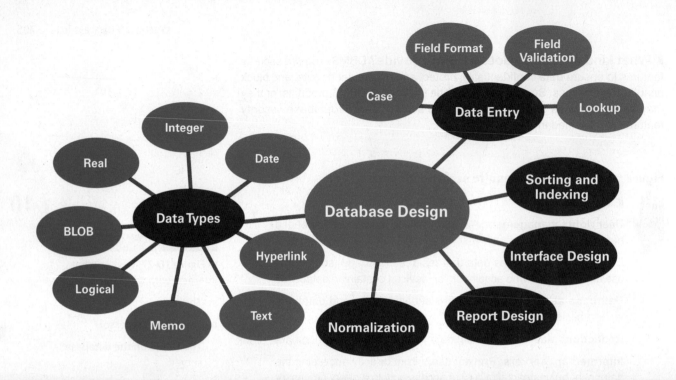

Objectives

▶ Explain how computed fields save storage space.

▶ Describe the function of a primary key.

▶ List three common data entry errors and the strategies that database designers use to reduce the number of them.

▶ List eight data types and provide a real-world example for each one.

▶ Explain why database designers normalize a database and how they do it.

▶ Distinguish the difference between a sort and an index.

▶ List at least three best principles for designing database interfaces.

▶ Explain the purpose of a report template.

The key to an effective database is its initial design. In a well-designed database, data can be flexibly manipulated to produce timely, meaningful, and accurate information for decision making. Bad database designs can lead to messy databases, lost records, and inaccurate data. Section C looks at databases from the perspective of the database designer and describes how you can create an efficient structure for a relational database.

Terminology

database structure	field format	normalization	database index
computed field	field validation rule	data redundancy	report generator
primary key	lookup routine	physical sort order	report template
case-sensitive database	data type	sort key	

Defining Fields

There are three core elements in a relational database: fields, tables, and relationships. These elements interlace to form the foundation of data that is used by operational and analytical information systems. If the database structure is designed correctly, information can be efficiently accessed and manipulated. A badly designed database can jeopardize an entire information system.

▶ **How does a database designer know what data to store?** The term **database structure** refers to the arrangement of fields, tables, and relationships in a database. The first step in structuring a relational database is to determine what data should be collected and stored. To do so, a database designer might begin by consulting users and studying the current system to compile a list of available data as well as any additional data necessary to produce screen-based output or printed reports.

Suppose that you are designing the database structure for Vintage Music, the business used in earlier examples. Initially, you would probably recognize that data, such as album titles and artist names, should be collected for each of the albums and singles in the store's inventory. Also, names, addresses, and order information should be collected for each customer. An initial list of the data to be collected might look something like Figure 10-28.

Figure 10-28: An initial list of data elements

Albums	Customers	
CatalogNumber	Name	OrderNumber
Title	Address	OrderDate
Artist	City	Customer
Price	State	Item
QuantityInStock	Zip	Quantity
Track Titles	Email	Price
	Phone	DiscountPrice
	VIPstatus	Total

Try It!

Can you think of at least four additional fields for the Albums table?

▶ **How much data goes in each field?** The Vintage Music database should store customer names, but should there be one field for first name and a separate field for last name? It is usually easy to break data into fields just by using common sense and considering how people might want to access the data. Any data that customers or store employees would want to search for, sort on, or use in a calculation should have its own field. By using a FirstName field and a LastName field, for example, it will be possible to search for customers by last name, use just the customer's first name in an email salutation, or combine the two fields for a shipping label (Figure 10-29).

QuickCheck

Is it good practice to use separate fields for the street number and street name?

a. Yes

b. No

Figure 10-29: Dividing data into fields

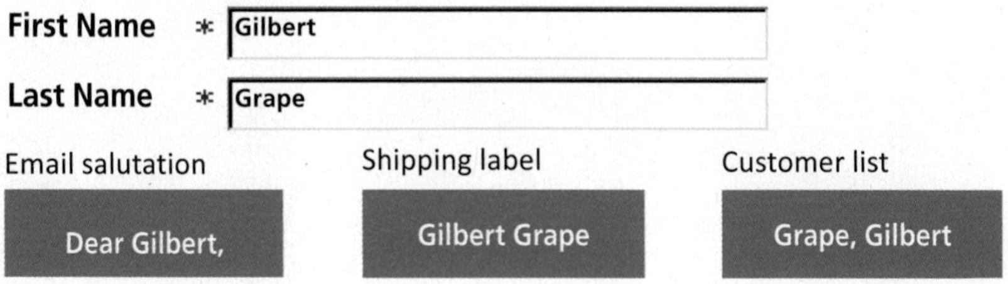

First Name * Gilbert

Last Name * Grape

Email salutation	Shipping label	Customer list
Dear Gilbert,	Gilbert Grape	Grape, Gilbert

▶ Is there any data that should be left out? DBMSs and associated applications may be able to generate some data on the fly, and that data would not need to be stored in the database. For example, suppose Vintage Music has a VIP program that gives members a 10% discount. When VIP customers shop for albums at Vintage Music's Web site, they see the regular price and the discounted price. The database, however, contains only one piece of pricing information: Price. The discounted price is not stored in the database. Instead, it is a computed field.

A **computed field** is a calculation that a DBMS performs, similar to the way a spreadsheet computes a formula. The computation can be stored in a permanent field or generated on the fly and then temporarily stored in a memory location. An efficiently designed database uses computed fields whenever possible because they do not require manual data entry. Figure 10-30 illustrates how a computed field produces the discounted price for a VIP customer.

Try It!

Can you think of a reason to use a computed field in the Albums database?

Figure 10-30: Computed fields are calculated on the fly

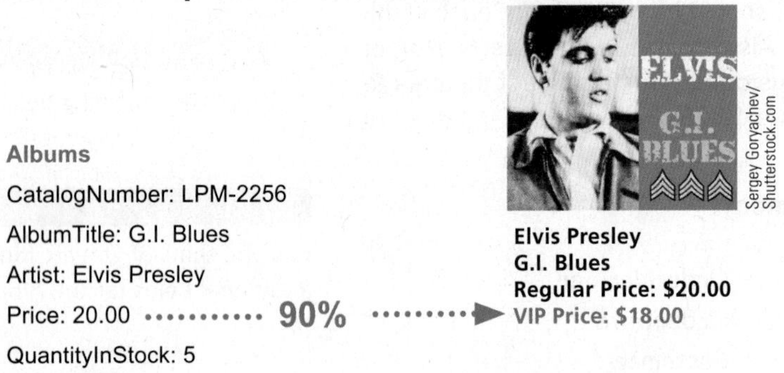

Albums
CatalogNumber: LPM-2256
AlbumTitle: G.I. Blues
Artist: Elvis Presley
Price: 20.00 ·········· **90%** ·········▶
QuantityInStock: 5

Elvis Presley
G.I. Blues
Regular Price: $20.00
VIP Price: $18.00

Sergey Goryachev/ Shutterstock.com

▶ What makes each record unique? Although two people might have the same name, or two paychecks might contain the same amount, a computer must have some way to differentiate between records. A **primary key** is a field that contains data unique to a record.

Database designers commonly designate fields such as CustomerNumber, AccountNumber, SocialSecurityNumber, TelephoneNumber, and PartNumber as primary keys.

As an alternative, the record number can be used as a primary key. A record number is assigned as each record is added. The first record in the database is record number 1; the second record is record number 2, and so on.

Although a record number is unique, it has no meaning in the context of the other data in a record. In contrast, a unique inventory number, for example, could correspond to an actual SKU or catalog number, so it has real-world meaning in the context of the data. In such a case, using the SKU or catalog number as the primary key would be preferable to using a record number.

QuickCheck

Which one of the following would be the best primary key for Vintage Music's Customer table?

a. LastName

b. FirstName

c. CustomerID

d. SocialSecurityNumber

10

▶ **Can a database designer prevent people from entering inaccurate data?** There's an old saying in the computer industry: "garbage in, garbage out." This adage is especially true when dealing with databases. The information produced by reports and processing routines is only as accurate as the information in the database. Unfortunately, data entry errors can compromise the accuracy and validity of a database.

When designing a database, it is important to think ahead and envision potential data entry errors. Most DBMSs provide tools that database designers can use to prevent some, but not all, data entry errors.

▶ **Do uppercase characters make a difference?** People who enter data into a database sometimes have difficulty deciding whether to use uppercase or lowercase characters. In a **case-sensitive database**, uppercase letters are not equivalent to their lowercase counterparts. For example, in a case-sensitive database, the artist name *Elvis* is not equivalent to *elvis*.

In a case-sensitive database, inconsistent use of case can lead to several problems. A search for *elvis* will not produce records for *Elvis* or *ELVIS*. Furthermore, in a sorted or indexed list, *elvis* and *ELVIS* might not be grouped together.

Most DBMSs give database designers an option to turn case sensitivity on or off. Designers may also have the option to force data to all uppercase or all lowercase as it is entered. These techniques are not infallible solutions to the inconsistent use of case, but they can help to keep the dataset more uniform.

▶ **How about entering numbers?** A customer or data-entry operator might enter a telephone number as 555-555-7777, (555) 555-7777, or 1-555-555-7777. When numbers are entered in different formats, it becomes difficult to produce properly formatted reports or locate a particular telephone number.

To prevent inconsistent formatting, a database designer can specify a field format. A **field format** is a template that adds the correct formatting as data is entered. If someone attempts to enter data in the wrong format, the database can be set up to reject that entry or correct it. For example, a telephone number field might use a field format such as the one shown in Figure 10-31.

QuickCheck

Which of the following fields in the Vintage Music database would most benefit from the use of a field format?

a. CustomerName

b. Price

c. City

d. Cat#

Figure 10-31: Field formats assist in data entry

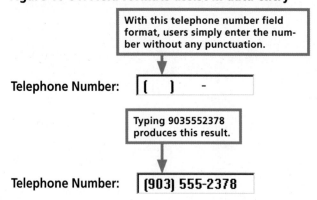

With this telephone number field format, users simply enter the number without any punctuation.

Telephone Number: [(   )   -   ]

Typing 9035552378 produces this result.

Telephone Number: [(903) 555-2378]

▶ **Can a database prevent typos?** People who enter data sometimes make a mistake and press the wrong keys. Preventing every typographical error is not possible. However, it is possible to catch some of these errors by using field validation rules, list boxes, or lookups.

A **field validation rule** is a specification that the database designer sets up to filter data entered into a particular field. For example, the price of albums in the Vintage Music database ranges from $0 (for promotions) to $800. No albums have a value greater than $1000. When attempting to enter $19.98 in the Value field, however, the omission of a decimal point could set the price of an album to $1998!

When designing the Vintage Music database, a database designer can use a field validation rule to limit entries in the Price field to numbers less than $1000. If the DBMS receives a number such as 1998 in the Price field, it displays a message requesting the correct price.

Another technique that prevents typographical and case-sensitivity errors is to limit data entry to the items on a specified list. For example, a customer living in Topeka might enter the state as Kansas, KANSAS, KS, Ks, or KA. However, most database software allows database designers to specify a list of acceptable entries for each field. You are probably familiar with clickable lists of states, such as the one in Figure 10-32.

Figure 10-32: Clickable lists reduce data entry errors

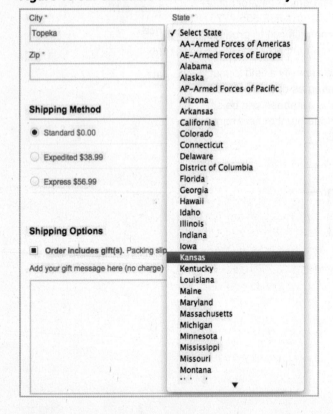

Database designers can also prevent entry errors by using lookup routines. A **lookup routine** validates an entry by checking data in an in-house or third-party database. For example, many ecommerce sites check the shipping address entered by customers against a list of valid addresses in the USPS database.

Data Types

In addition to naming each field, a database designer specifies what sort of data the field can hold. Many fields will hold text, but other fields might hold numbers, dates, or images. The type of data in a field defines whether it can be used for calculations or as a search key. It can also affect the validity of data that is entered into the database.

▶ **How does a database designer know what data types to use?**
The data that can be entered into a field depends on the field's data type. From a technical perspective, a **data type** specifies the way data is represented on physical storage media and in RAM. From a user perspective, the data type determines the way data can be manipulated. When designing a database, each field is assigned a data type. Most database management systems support a variety of data types, though some DBMSs may not support all of them.

Real. There are several numeric data types, including real, integer, and date. Database designers assign the real data type to fields that contain numbers with decimal places, such as prices and percentages.

Integer. The integer data type is used for fields that contain whole numbers—quantities, repetitions, rankings, and so on. Database designers use the integer data type unless the data requires decimal places because real numbers require more storage space.

Date. As you might expect, the date data type is used to store dates in a format that allows them to be manipulated, such as when you want to calculate the number of days between two dates.

Text. The text data type is normally assigned to fixed-length fields that hold character data—people's names, album titles, and so on. Text fields sometimes hold data that looks like numbers but won't be mathematically manipulated. Telephone numbers, Social Security numbers, ZIP codes, and item numbers are examples of data that looks numeric but is normally stored in text fields.

Memo. A memo data type usually provides a variable-length field into which users can enter comments. For example, the Vintage Music database might contain a memo field for storing comments about a particular album, such as "Where Did Our Love Go was The Supremes' first hit album."

Logical. The logical data type (sometimes called a Boolean or yes/no data type) is used for true/false and yes/no data, which requires minimal storage space. For example, a database designer might define a logical field called VIP, which would contain a Y if a customer has attained VIP status and is entitled to discounts.

BLOB. Some file and database management systems also include additional data types, such as BLOBs and hyperlinks. A BLOB (binary large object) is a collection of binary data stored in a single field of a database. BLOBs can be just about any kind of data you would store as a file, such as an MP3 music track or an image of an album cover.

Hyperlink. The hyperlink data type stores URLs used to link directly from a database to a Web page. For example, data stored in a hyperlink field of the Vintage Music database could provide a link to a musician's Web site.

QuickCheck

Which of the following would be the best field type to use for album covers in the Vintage Music database?

a. Real

b. Text

c. Logical

d. BLOB

10

Normalization

When the design process begins, a database designer roughly groups fields representing customers, inventory items, and other entities. These groupings, however, may not be optimal for fast access, analytics, or security. A challenging part of database design is to arrive at just the right group of fields for each database table.

▶ How does a database designer determine the best data groupings? A process called **normalization** helps database designers create a database structure that minimizes storage space and increases processing efficiency. The goal of normalization is to minimize **data redundancy**—the amount of data that is duplicated in a database.

Groupings usually correspond to the physical items or entities that are tracked in the database. Each normalized group becomes a table in the final database design.

An initial examination of Vintage Music data reveals two groups: albums and customers. The albums group contains data about album titles, artists, and tracks. The customers group contains data about each customer and the orders they place. But is this the best grouping? To answer this question, first take a look at a sample customer order in Figure 10-33.

Figure 10-33: A Vintage Music customer order

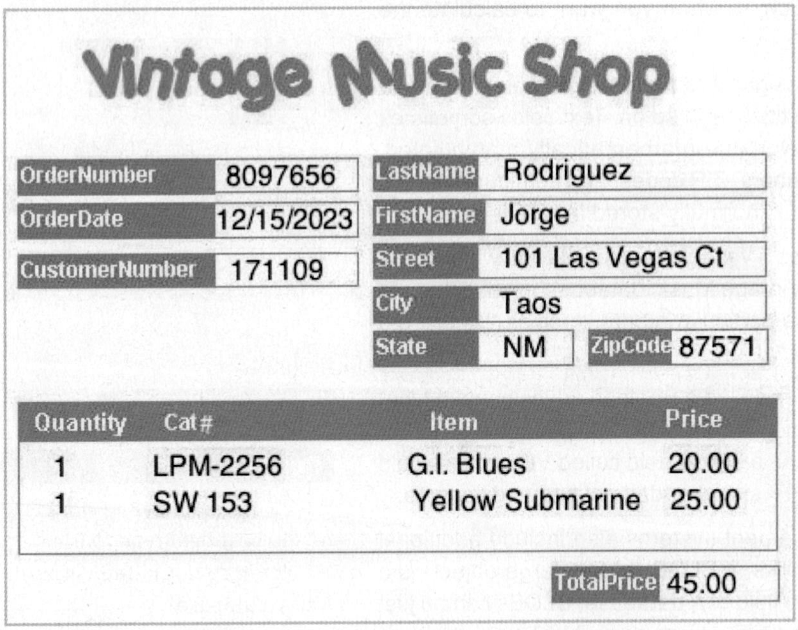
Vintage Music Shop

OrderNumber	8097656
OrderDate	12/15/2023
CustomerNumber	171109
LastName	Rodriguez
FirstName	Jorge
Street	101 Las Vegas Ct
City	Taos
State	NM
ZipCode	87571

Quantity	Cat#	Item	Price
1	LPM-2256	G.I. Blues	20.00
1	SW 153	Yellow Submarine	25.00

TotalPrice 45.00

▶ What's the problem? If customer information and order information are grouped in the same table, each time Jorge Rodriguez places an order, his name, shipping address, billing address, telephone number, and email address must be entered and stored. This data redundancy not only requires extra storage space, but it also could lead to storing inconsistent or inaccurate data. The solution is

QuickCheck

Which of the following data items would become redundant when Jorge places another order?

a. Order Number

b. Order Date

c. First Name

d. Cat#

to create separate tables for Orders and Customers, which can be related by including a CustomerNumber field in both tables, as shown in Figure 10-34.

Figure 10-34: Normalizing the data

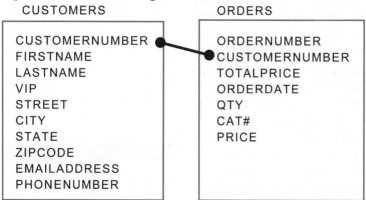

10

▶ **Is the problem solved?** Even after separating customer data from order data, the structure of the Vintage Music database can be further normalized. The Orders table in the figure above allows customers to purchase only one album per order because the fields Cat# and Price occur only once. Of course, the Vintage Music database should be able to handle orders for more than one album.

It might seem reasonable to provide several fields for the albums in an order. Perhaps they could be named AlbumNumber1, AlbumNumber2, AlbumNumber3, and so on. But how many of those fields should the database designer provide? If the designer provides fields for ordering ten albums, the database still cannot handle large orders for more than ten albums. Furthermore, if a customer orders fewer than ten albums, space is wasted by having empty fields in each record.

You might recognize that a one-to-many relationship exists between an order and the ordered items. That clue indicates that the database designer should separate the data into two tables, such as Orders and Order Details. These two tables are related by the OrderNumber field. Figure 10-35 illustrates how the Orders table is further normalized into two tables to store data more efficiently.

Figure 10-35: Additional normalization

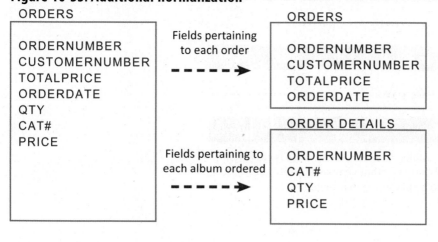

QuickCheck

In Figure 10-35, dividing Orders into two tables _____.

a. reduces redundancy

b. increases security

c. reduces the normalization

d. creates a relationship

Sorting and Indexing

Records can be organized in different ways depending on how people want to use them. For example, Vintage Music customers will most often view the information in the Albums table by album title or artist name. The inventory manager usually wants the data sorted by the quantity in stock to easily see which albums are overstocked. No single way of organizing the data accommodates everyone's needs, but the good news is that tables can be sorted or indexed in multiple ways.

▶ **What happens when the data in a table is sorted?** A table's **physical sort order** is the order in which records are arranged on storage devices. A **sort key** is the column of data that is used as the basis for arranging the data. Sorted tables produce faster queries and updates because they take advantage of clever algorithms that quickly pinpoint records. In a sorted table, new records are inserted to maintain the order.

When no sort order is specified, new records are appended to the end of the file, resulting in a file that is not arranged in any particular order. Queries and updates within an unsorted database are slow because the only algorithm for searching an unsorted table requires a sequential look at each record.

Some DBMSs store records on a physical storage medium according to a predetermined sort order. The database designer usually specifies this order for each table at the time the database structure is created. Each table can have only one sort order at a time, but the order can be changed. However, changing the sort order can take a long time because the process physically rearranges records. In Figure 10-36, you can see how records might be arranged sequentially on a storage device.

QuickCheck

If a record with Cat# LPM-5988 is added to the data stored in Figure 10-36, how many records would have to be physically moved?

a. One

b. Two

c. All

d. None

Figure 10-36: Sorting physically rearranges records on a storage device

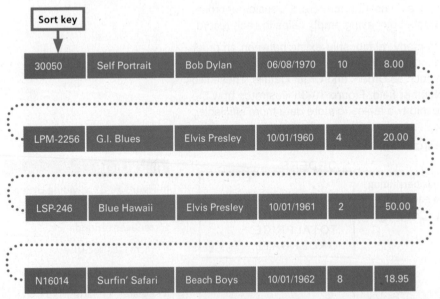

The sort key for this data is the Catalog Number (Cat#). Data is stored on the disk as a continuous stream, which means that changing the sort key requires all the data to be physically rearranged.

▶ How is indexing different from sorting? A database index can be used to organize data in alphabetical or numerical order. It is very similar to an index in a book that contains a list of keywords and pointers to the pages where they can be found. A **database index** contains a list of keys, and each key provides a pointer to the record that contains the rest of the fields related to that key.

Unlike a sort order, an index has no bearing on the physical sequence of records on a storage device. An index simply points to the record where the data can be found. The advantage of an index over a sort is that a table can have multiple indexes but only one sort order. For example, the Albums table could be indexed by AlbumTitle to facilitate searches for specific albums. The same table could also be indexed by Artist to facilitate searches using artist names.

Database tables should be indexed by any fields that are commonly used to organize or locate data. The database designer normally creates indexes at the time the database structure is designed. Indexes can also be created at a later date, as needed. Figure 10-37 illustrates how an index works.

Figure 10-37: Indexing

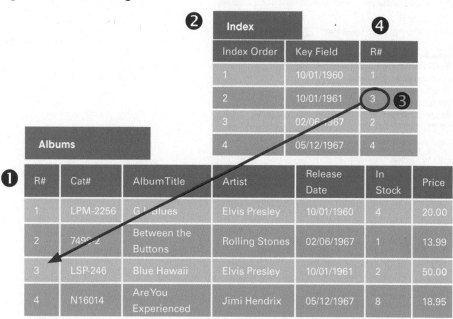

❶ These records are sorted and stored by R# (Record Number), which is simply the order in which they were added to the database.

❷ An index is created that will display the records in order by release date. The index contains only three fields, so it does not require much storage space.

❸ The R# field is the pointer that connects each record in the Albums table with the index.

❹ The order of records listed in the R# column of the index indicates the order for displaying the records by release date. The first record in the table where R# is 1 will be the first record displayed because it has the earliest release date. The third record in the table will be displayed next, followed by the second record and the fourth record.

QuickCheck

In Figure 10-37, if the red circle moved down one row, the end of the arrow would point to Record Number _____ .

a. 1

b. 2

c. 3

d. 4

10

Designing the Interface

The way that users interact with a database depends on the user interface. An operating system provides some conventions for elements of the user interface, such as dialog box and button styles, but additional design decisions must be made about how information is presented to users.

▶ **Doesn't the DBMS simply generate the user interface?** DBMSs used by consumers and small businesses generally include tools to create database interfaces. Some enterprise-class DBMSs require separate tools for this task. Either way, user interfaces are very unique to each application and to each business, so it is the responsibility of the database designer to map out which fields are displayed, the order in which they appear, and the way they are named. Figure 10-38 illustrates the process of designing a screen-based form for a database created with Microsoft Access.

Figure 10-38: Designing a form with Microsoft Access

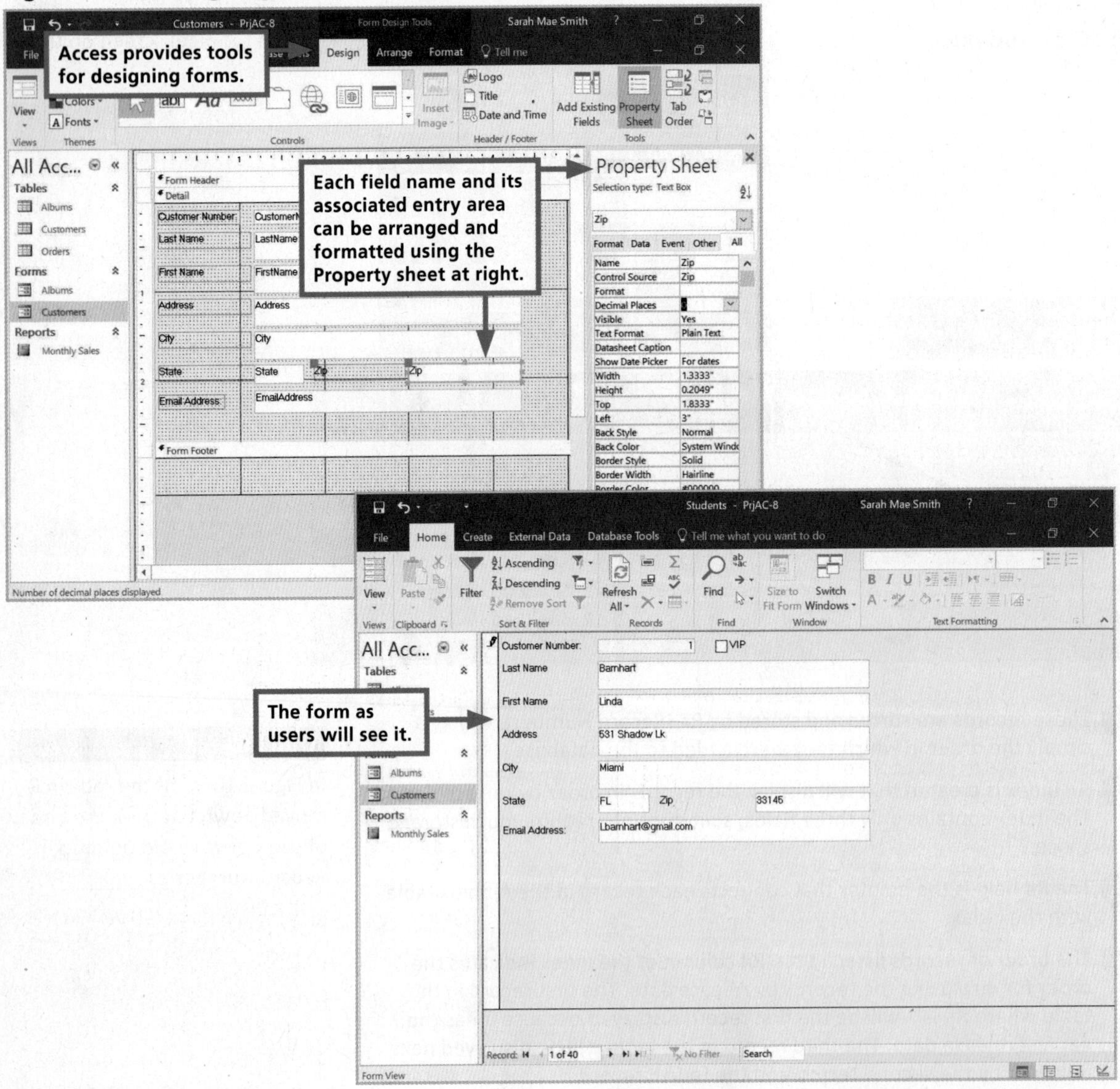

▶ **What are the challenges?** Today, a major challenge is to design interfaces that are effective on a variety of devices and platforms. As shown in Figure 10-39, more than one design might be required for an optimal user experience on diverse platforms such as terminals, laptops, and touchscreen devices.

Figure 10-39: Different devices require different database interfaces

Source: Sabre Native

Source: Expedia

Source: Expedia

Terminals (far left) primarily display text. Desktop and laptop computers (center) offer the user interface designer the option of using lots of screen space and colorful graphics. Mobile devices (right) have limited screen space and require large control buttons.

QuickCheck

In Figure 10-39, which screen shows the most data?

a. The terminal screen on the far left

b. The laptop screen in the middle

c. The smartphone screen on the right

d. All of the screens show the same amount of data

▶ **What are the elements of a well-designed database interface?** A well-defined user interface for a database should be clear, intuitive, and efficient. The following guidelines list strategies for producing well-designed database interfaces:

● Arrange fields in a logical order beginning at the upper-left corner of the screen. The first fields should be those used most often or those that come first in the data entry sequence.

● Provide visual clues to the entry areas. A box, a line, or shading can delineate data entry areas.

● Entry areas should appear in a consistent position relative to their labels. By convention, labels are placed to the left of the entry areas or above them.

● Provide a quick way to move through the fields in order. By convention, the Tab key performs this function on desktop and laptop computers.

● If all fields do not fit on a single screen, use scrolling or create a second screen.

● Provide buttons or other easy-to-use controls for moving from one record to another.

● Stay aware of the platform; controls for a touchscreen device have to be large, well spaced, and easy to operate.

● Supply on-screen instructions to help ensure that data is entered correctly. Web databases can benefit from links to help pages.

Try It!

Have you encountered any annoying user interfaces recently? Did they violate the principles listed here, or are additional guidelines necessary?

Designing Report Templates

A report is a printed or screen-based list of some or all of the data in a database. Reports can be used to display the results of queries, such as when a Vintage Music customer makes a query for all albums by The Rolling Stones. Reports can also be used by managers to view transaction details or summaries. They may also be used to list the contents of a customer's shopping cart or order form.

▶ **How are reports created?** Most DBMSs include a **report generator**, which is a software tool for specifying the content and format for a database report. Reports are based on report templates.

A **report template** contains the outline or general specifications for a report, including such elements as the report title, fields to include, fields to subtotal or total, and report format specifications. The template does not, however, contain data from the database. Data is merged into the template when the report is generated.

As an example, suppose that a manager at Vintage Music wants to create a report that lists albums arranged by price. The manager can create a report template called AlbumPriceGroup that specifies the following:

- The title of the report is Vintage Music Albums by Price.
- The report contains data from the Albums table, arranged in four columns, with data from the Price, AlbumTitle, Artist, and InStock fields.
- The headings for the columns are Price, Album Title, Artist, and Qty in Stock.
- The report is grouped by price.

These specifications would be used to produce a report similar to the one shown in Figure 10-40.

QuickCheck

A report template contains
_____.

a. no data

b. sample data

c. current data

d. current and future data

Figure 10-40: A report produced from a template

Report Date: 8/21/2022

Vintage Music Albums by Price

Price	Album Title	Artist	Qty in Stock
$9.00	Magical Mystery Tour	Beatles	3
$10.00	Surfin' Safari	Beach Boys	3
	Cheap Thrills	Janis Joplin	12
	Surrealistic Pillow	Jefferson Airplane	1
	One Day at a Time	Joan Baez	2
$14.00	Between the Buttons	Rolling Stones	1
$15.00	Let It Be	Beatles	2
	Abbey Road	Beatles	4
	Joan Baez	Joan Baez	1
$18.00	Chuck Berry's Golden Hits	Chuck Berry	1
	Strange Days	Doors	9

▶ **What happens when a report is generated?** When a report is actually produced, it is based on the data currently contained in the database table. For example, the report shown in Figure 10-40 was produced on August 21st and includes albums that were stored in the database as of that date.

Now suppose that at the beginning of October, Vintage Music receives a new shipment of albums. The AlbumPriceGroup report template is used again to print a report on October 12th. This report, shown in Figure 10-41, follows the same format as that of the previous report, but includes the new albums.

Figure 10-41: An updated report

Report Date: 10/12/2022

Vintage Music Albums by Price

Price	Album Title	Artist	Qty in Stock
$9.00	Magical Mystery Tour	Beatles	3
	The Kingsmen in Person	Kingsmen	1
$10.00	Cheap Thrills	Janis Joplin	8
	About This Thing Called Love	Fabian	2
	One Day at a Time	Joan Baez	2
$14.00	Between the Butt...	Rolling Stones	1

QuickQuiz   Section C

1. A primary _____ , such as Social Security number, contains data unique to a record.

2. A computed field is similar to a mail merge. True or false? _____

3. To filter data as it is entered into a field, the database designer can set up a field _____ rule.

4. Database designers use a process called _____ to minimize data redundancy in a database.

5. As an alternative to storing data in sorted order, a database can be _____ to produce a list of keys that can be used to alphabetize or otherwise organize the records.

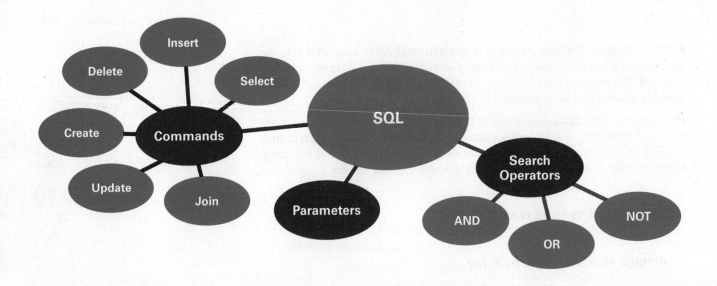

Objectives

▶ Explain how SQL relates to databases.

▶ List at least five SQL command words and describe what each one does.

▶ Formulate a valid SQL query to add a record to a database.

▶ Use Boolean operators in an SQL search query.

▶ Provide an example in which a global update is used efficiently.

▶ Illustrate how SQL can be used to join two tables using dot notation.

▶ Describe how SQL injection works.

SQL is the universal language of relational databases. It allows customers to search for products at ecommerce Web sites. It collects new subscriber information for social media signups. And it can be deployed to collect transaction data at ATMs or from point-of-sale systems. SQL also presents a potential security vulnerability for databases because it is susceptible to code injection attacks. Section D reveals what you need to know about SQL.

Terminology

query languages	SQL keywords	INSERT	global update
SQL	CREATE	SELECT	joining tables
SQL query	DELETE	Boolean operators	JOIN
SQL injection	parameters	UPDATE	dot notation

SQL Basics

The data in a database will change as new records are added, existing records are updated, and unneeded records are deleted. These changes are based on commands that are sent to the DBMS. The commands are issued using computer programming languages designed for databases. These languages are sometimes called **query languages** because one of their main capabilities is to request data from a database, such as when a customer searches Amazon.com for a specific product. SQL is the world's most popular query language.

▶ **How does a query language like SQL work?** Query languages like **SQL** (Structured Query Language) work behind the scenes as an intermediary between the database client software provided to users and the database itself.

Database client software provides an easy-to-use interface for entering search specifications, new records, data updates, and so on. The client software collects your input and then converts it into an **SQL query**, which can operate directly on the database to carry out your instructions, as shown in Figure 10-42.

10

Figure 10-42: SQL is used to query a database

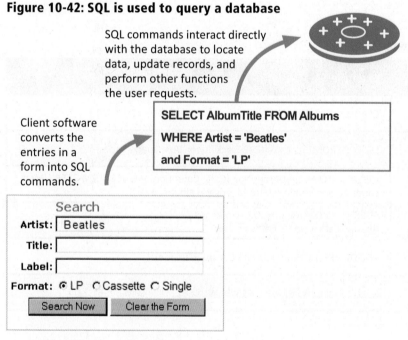

SQL commands interact directly with the database to locate data, update records, and perform other functions the user requests.

Client software converts the entries in a form into SQL commands.

SELECT AlbumTitle FROM Albums

WHERE Artist = 'Beatles'

and Format = 'LP'

Form-based user interface

QuickCheck

SQL is similar to _____.

a. HTML

b. a programming language

c. XML

d. CRM

▶ **Why does SQL pose a security risk?** SQL statements contain command words and data. These statements are executed by the DBMS. For example, in a typical ecommerce database, SQL statements normally allow users to search for products, make purchases, and update their own accounts. Under some circumstances, however, users can be the source of malicious SQL statements that manipulate the database in unauthorized ways. Exploits that use malicious SQL statements to gain unauthorized access to a database are called **SQL injection**. To understand what makes SQL vulnerable, you need some additional information about the structure of SQL queries.

▶ **What does a basic SQL query look like?** An SQL query is a sequence of words, much like a sentence. For example, an SQL query that searches for the song *Ruby Tuesday* in Vintage Music's database might look like this:

SELECT TrackTitle FROM Tracks WHERE TrackTitle = 'Ruby Tuesday'

The SQL query language provides a collection of special command words called **SQL keywords**, such as SELECT, FROM, INSERT, and WHERE, which issue instructions to the database. Although the SQL examples in this section of the module use uppercase letters for keywords, most implementations of SQL accept either uppercase or lowercase keywords.

Most SQL queries can be divided into three basic elements that specify an action, the name of a database table, and a set of parameters. Let's look at each of these elements.

▶ **How does SQL specify the action that I want carried out in the database?** An SQL query begins with an action keyword, or command, which specifies the operation you want carried out. For example, the command word **CREATE** produces a new table in a database. Figure 10-43 lists some of the most commonly used SQL command words.

Figure 10-43: Commonly used SQL commands

Command	Description	Example
CREATE	Create a database or table.	CREATE TABLE Albums
DELETE	Remove a record from a table.	DELETE FROM Tracks WHERE TrackTitle = 'Blue Suede Shoes'
INSERT	Add a record.	INSERT INTO AlbumDescription (Cat#, Condition) VALUES ('LPM-2256', 'Mint condition; no visible scratches; original album cover')
JOIN	Use the data from two tables.	SELECT * FROM Albums JOIN Tracks ON Albums.Cat# = Tracks.Cat#
SELECT	Search for records.	SELECT * FROM Albums WHERE Artist = 'Beatles'
UPDATE	Change data in a field.	UPDATE Albums SET Price = 15.95 WHERE Cat# = 'LPM-2256'

▶ **How does SQL specify which table to use?** SQL keywords such as USE, FROM, or INTO can be used to construct a clause specifying the table you want to access. The clause consists of a keyword followed by the name of the table. For example, the clause **FROM Tracks** indicates that you want to use the Tracks table from Vintage Music's database.

The command word **DELETE** removes a record from a table. An SQL query that begins with **DELETE FROM Tracks** means that you want to delete something from the Tracks table. To complete the query, you provide parameters that specify which record you want to delete.

QuickCheck

How would you complete the query below to delete the order for customer number 50?

a. Customer, Number

b. FROM, WHERE

c. TOTALS, Jorge

d. INTO, 50

DELETE ⬚ Orders ⬚ CustomerID ='50'

▶ **How does SQL specify parameters?** Parameters are detailed specifications for a command. Keywords such as WHERE usually begin an SQL clause containing the parameters for a command. Suppose that Vintage Music's inventory manager wants to delete all the albums recorded by Bob Marley. The parameter for the WHERE clause is Artist = 'Bob Marley'.

DELETE FROM Albums WHERE Artist = 'Bob Marley'

| SQL command word | FROM clause specifies the table to use | WHERE clause specifies the field name and its contents |

10

Now that you've learned the basic structure of an SQL query, take a closer look at the SQL for specific database tasks, such as adding records, searching for information, updating fields, organizing records, and joining tables.

Adding Records

A database record contains information about an entity, such as a customer, an online purchase, an ATM withdrawal, or a social media post. The data for a new record may be entered by employees, supplied by customers, or collected from digital devices. Regardless of the source, the data is bundled into an SQL statement that is handled by the DBMS.

▶ **How are records added to a database?** Suppose a customer wants to purchase an album from Vintage Music's Web site. The customer fills in fields for name, address, and so on. The client software that the customer uses collects the data entered in the form and generates an SQL statement using the INSERT command. The INSERT statement adds the customer's data to the Customers table. Figure 10-44 shows the Customer form, the SQL statement that adds the customer data to the database, and the data that is added to the Customers table.

QuickCheck

In Figure 10-44, which table is being used?

a. Customers

b. VALUES

c. Form

d. Rodriguez

Figure 10-44: How the INSERT command works

CUSTOMER FORM

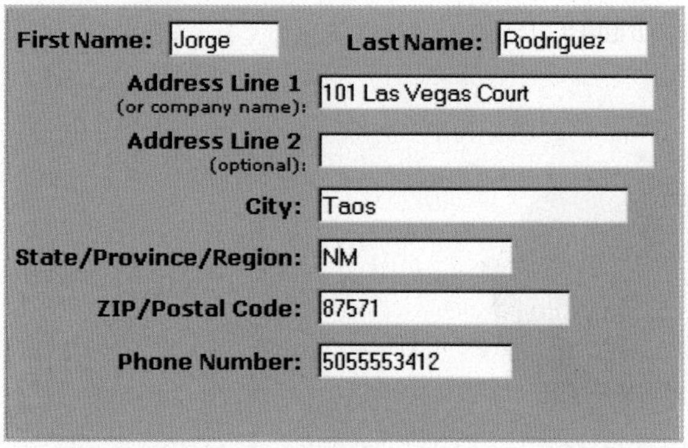

First Name:	Jorge
Last Name:	Rodriguez
Address Line 1 (or company name):	101 Las Vegas Court
Address Line 2 (optional):	
City:	Taos
State/Province/Region:	NM
ZIP/Postal Code:	87571
Phone Number:	5055553412

SQL STATEMENT

INSERT INTO Customers (LastName, FirstName, Street, City, State, ZipCode, PhoneNumber) VALUES ('Rodriguez', 'Jorge', '101 Las Vegas Court', 'Taos', 'NM', '87571', '5055553412')

CUSTOMERS TABLE

LastName	FirstName	Street	City	State	ZipCode	PhoneNumber
Rodriguez	Jorge	101 Las Vegas Court	Taos	NM	87571	505-555-3412
Bleuman	Jonathan	5822 Lake St.	Negaunee	MI	49866	906-555-2131
Wincheta	Daisy	499 Table Mesa	Boulder	CO	80301	303-555-6902
Venkata	Patel	872 Old York Way	Durango	CO	81301	970-555-4438
Wong	Joy	822 Park Place	New York	NY	10023	212-555-9903
Helwig	Nathaniel	5 Winsome Drive	Cheyenne	WY	82003	303-555-3223
Chen	Lu-Chi	2235 Overview Trail	San Francisco	CA	94118	415-555-9001
Walton	William	500 Vista Mesa Blvd	Santa Fe	NM	87504	505-555-1111
Bolduc	Luc	41 Rue Ste. Ca___ine	Detroit	MI	48210	313-555-6487
Stavros	Kal__				55411	612-555-087_

Searching for Information

A database can contain millions of records. Imagine, for example, all the products in Amazon's database or all the subscribers stored by Facebook. Sifting through such vast storehouses of data requires the use of queries that carry out searches.

▶ **How do SQL queries perform searches?** One of the most common database operations is to query for a particular record or group of records by using the **SELECT** command. To view all the records, you could use the * parameter, which means "all." The query **SELECT * FROM Albums** would display all of the records contained in the Albums table.

A customer who is looking for Jefferson Airplane albums can find them by using a form at the Vintage Music Web site, as shown in Figure 10-45.

Figure 10-45: An online form used to generate a SELECT statement

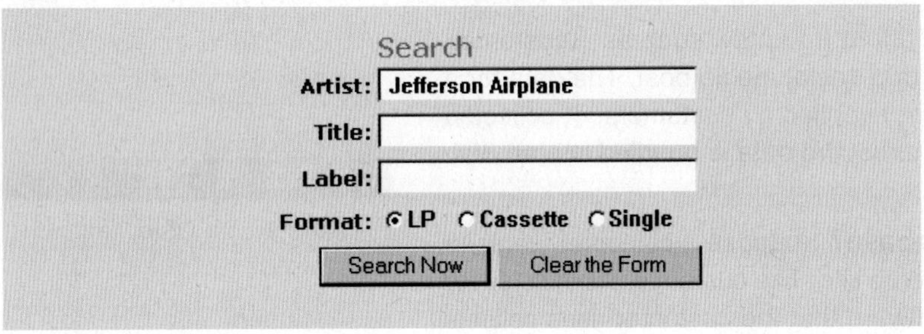

> Search
>
> Artist: | Jefferson Airplane |
>
> Title: | |
>
> Label: | |
>
> Format: ⦿ LP   ○ Cassette   ○ Single
>
> [Search Now]   [Clear the Form]

The database client software uses the search specification to create the following SQL query:

SELECT AlbumTitle, AlbumCover FROM Albums WHERE Artist = 'Jefferson Airplane'

As a result of this query, the Vintage Music Web page displays a list beginning with *Jefferson Airplane Takes Off*—the band's first album—and a photo of the album cover. Take a closer look at the parts of this query shown in Figure 10-46.

Figure 10-46: Anatomy of a SELECT statement

The DBMS should produce only the album title and cover.

Search the Albums table.

Look in the Artist field for *Jefferson Airplane*.

SELECT AlbumTitle, AlbumCover FROM Albums WHERE Artist = 'Jefferson Airplane'

▶ **Can SQL perform complex searches?** Yes. SQL uses **Boolean operators** such as AND, OR, and NOT to form complex queries. You might have used these operators to formulate Google searches. To discover how Boolean operators work in the context of SQL queries, let's use the small Albums database in Figure 10-47. Just remember that most operational databases are far larger, so the data they contain won't all be visible as in this tiny example!

Terminology

Boolean operators are named after mathematician George Boole, who originated the idea in the 1800s.

10

Figure 10-47: A sample of the Vintage Music Albums table

Cat#	AlbumTitle	Artist	Price
LSP-4058	Crown of Creation	Jefferson Airplane	9.00
LK 4955	Beggars Banquet	The Rolling Stones	25.00
BFL1-0717	Dragon Fly	Jefferson Starship	9.00
LPM-2256	G.I. Blues	Elvis Presley	23.00
LSP-3766	Surrealistic Pillow	Jefferson Airplane	8.00
LSP-4238	Volunteers	Jefferson Airplane	12.00
COC 39108	Some Girls	The Rolling Stones	8.00
7243-8-44909-2-8	Bridges to Babylon	The Rolling Stones	9.00
LPM-2426	Blue Hawaii	Elvis Presley	8.00
SO 383	Are You Experienced	Jimi Hendrix	15.00

▶ **How does AND work in an SQL query?** AND (sometimes indicated by a + sign) is used to retrieve records that meet more than one criterion. For example, suppose a customer wants to find all the albums by Jefferson Airplane, but wants to display only albums that are on sale for less than $10.00. The customer might enter something like **Jefferson Airplane <$10.00** in the Vintage Music Web site's search box. The database client creates an SQL query like this:

SELECT AlbumTitle FROM Albums WHERE Artist = 'Jefferson Airplane' AND Price < 10.00

You can perform the search manually using the records in Figure 10-47. How many records did you find that match the SQL statement? In this example, a record is selected only if the Artist field contains *Jefferson Airplane* and the value in the Price field is less than $10.00. If the price is $10.00 or more, the record is not selected. The AND operator specifies that both of the search criteria must be true for the record to be selected. There are two matching records in the database.

▶ **How does OR differ from AND?** Two variations of the OR operator exist. One variation, the inclusive OR, designates records that meet one criterion or both. The other variation, called the exclusive OR, designates records that meet one criterion or the other, but not both.

SQL uses the inclusive OR. A query such as

SELECT AlbumTitle FROM Albums WHERE Artist = 'Jefferson Airplane' OR Price < 10.00

produces all the Jefferson Airplane albums, regardless of price. It also produces any albums that are less than $10.00, regardless of the artist. Look back at Figure 10-47. How many records match this search query?

QuickCheck

If you perform the OR search manually using the data in Figure 10-47, how many records match?

a. Zero

b. Two

c. Four

d. Seven

▶ **Can OR be combined with AND?** Yes. AND and OR clauses can be combined to formulate complex queries. For example, Jefferson Airplane became Jefferson Starship in 1974. For a list of Jefferson Airplane or Jefferson Starship albums that cost less than $10.00, use a query like the following:

SELECT AlbumTitle FROM Albums WHERE (Artist = 'Jefferson Airplane' OR Artist = 'Jefferson Starship') AND Price < 10.00

Note the use of parentheses around the OR clause. Parentheses tell the DBMS to process this part of the query first. How many records does the above query find in Figure 10-48?

Figure 10-48: A sample of the Vintage Music Albums table

Cat#	AlbumTitle	Artist	Price
LSP-4058	Crown of Creation	Jefferson Airplane	9.00
LK 4955	Beggars Banquet	The Rolling Stones	25.00
BFL1-0717	Dragon Fly	Jefferson Starship	9.00
LPM-2256	G.I. Blues	Elvis Presley	23.00
LSP-3766	Surrealistic Pillow	Jefferson Airplane	8.00
LSP-4238	Volunteers	Jefferson Airplane	12.00
COC 39108	Some Girls	The Rolling Stones	8.00
7243-8-44909-2-8	Bridges to Babylon	The Rolling Stones	9.00
LPM-2426	Blue Hawaii	Elvis Presley	8.00
SO 383	Are You Experienced	Jimi Hendrix	15.00

▶ **Are the parentheses important?** The placement of parentheses can change the results of a query, sometimes drastically. Compare the previous query to the following query:

SELECT AlbumTitle FROM Albums WHERE Artist = 'Jefferson Airplane' OR (Artist = 'Jefferson Starship' AND Price < 10.00)

The query with parentheses around the AND clause returns all albums by Jefferson Airplane, regardless of price, and any albums by Jefferson Starship that cost less than $10.00.

▶ **How does NOT work in an SQL query?** The NOT operator can be used to omit records from a search by specifying a not-equal relationship. For example, the following query returns all records in the Albums table where the Artist is not equal to *Jefferson Airplane*:

SELECT AlbumTitle FROM Albums WHERE NOT (Artist = 'Jefferson Airplane')

Sometimes NOT relationships are specified with a not-equal operator, such as <> or !=, depending on the specifications of the query language. For example, the following query returns the same records as one that uses the NOT operator:

SELECT AlbumTitle FROM Albums WHERE Artist <> 'Jefferson Airplane'

QuickCheck

If you manually perform the search with OR in parentheses using the data in Figure 10-48, how many records match?

a. Zero

b. One

c. Two

d. Three

QuickCheck

If you manually perform the search with AND in parentheses using the data in Figure 10-48, how many records match?

a. Zero

b. Two

c. Four

d. Six

QuickCheck

If you manually perform the NOT search using the data in Figure 10-48, how many records match?

a. Zero

b. Three

c. Six

d. Seven

Updating Fields

Database records can be changed only by authorized users. At Vintage Music's ecommerce site, for example, customers do not have authorization to change album prices or alter the name of the songs on an album. Those activities are reserved for the inventory manager. When a customer purchases an album, however, an SQL routine reduces the number in the InStock field by one.

▶ **What SQL command changes the contents of a record?** Updates and modifications to the contents of a database field are made by using the SQL UPDATE command. The following command reduces the number of *G.I. Blues* albums by one:

UPDATE Albums SET InStock = InStock - 1 WHERE AlbumTitle = 'G.I. Blues'

▶ **Is it possible to update a group of records?** In addition to changing the data in a single record, SQL can perform a global update that changes the data in more than one record at a time.

Suppose you're Vintage Music's marketing manager and you want to put all Rolling Stones albums on sale by reducing the price to $5.95. You could do it the hard way by searching for an Artist field that contains *The Rolling Stones*, adjusting the Price field for that record, and then looking for the next Rolling Stones album. However, it would be easier to change all the records with a single command using this SQL statement:

UPDATE Albums SET Price = 5.95 WHERE Artist = 'The Rolling Stones'

Let's see how this command performs a global update. The UPDATE command means you want to change the data in some or all of the records. *Albums* is the name of the table containing the data you want to change. **SET Price = 5.95** tells the DBMS to change the data in the Price field to $5.95. **WHERE Artist = 'The Rolling Stones'** tells the DBMS to change only those records where the artist name is *The Rolling Stones*.

▶ **What are the limitations of the global UPDATE command?** Although the global UPDATE function is powerful, it works only for records that have similar characteristics—for example, all albums by The Rolling Stones or all albums produced in 1955. Custom programming is required to perform global operations on information that does not have any similar characteristics. Figure 10-49 provides an example.

10

Figure 10-49: Custom programming as an alternative to global updates

Hard Day's Night
Blue Hawaii
Strange Days
Cheap Thrills
Yellow Submarine
Surfin' Safari
Blonde on Blonde
Dragon Fly
Rubber Soul
Anthem of the Sun

Vintage Music's marketing manager picks ten albums each week to place on a special promotional sale. These albums have no common data that can be used to formulate a global UPDATE command.

Custom programming allows the marketing manager to simply submit a list of ten albums as a document. The module "reads" the document and issues an UPDATE command for each of the chosen albums.

Joining Tables

Suppose you want to see a list of songs on Elvis Presley's *G.I. Blues* album. The songs, however, are not stored in the same table as the rest of the album data. SQL is designed for relational databases, so it is adept at retrieving data from multiple tables.

▶ **How is data retrieved from more than one table at a time?** Recall that the process of normalization creates tables that can be related by fields that exist in both tables. In SQL terminology, creating a relationship between tables is referred to as joining tables.

The Albums table holds the album title, the artist's name, the release date, and other data about the album. The Tracks table holds the name of each song track, the track length, and an MP3 sample of the track. Both tables also contain a Cat# field.

Earlier in the module, you learned that a relationship can exist between Vintage Music's Albums table and Tracks table based on the data in the Cat# field, as shown in Figure 10-50.

Figure 10-50: Joining the Albums and Tracks tables

To take advantage of the relationship between these two tables, you first have to join the tables. Why? Remember that in a relational database, the tables are essentially independent unless you join them together. The SQL JOIN command allows you to temporarily join and simultaneously access the data in more than one table.

▶ **How does the JOIN command work?** A single SQL query can retrieve data for the *G.I. Blues* album from the Albums table and the Tracks table. To do so, however, requires some way to distinguish the data contained in each table. In the example, both tables contain a field called Cat#. How can you differentiate the Cat# field that belongs to the Albums table from the Cat# field in the Tracks table?

SQL uses dot notation to make this distinction. **Albums.Cat#** is the full specification for the Cat# field in the Albums table. **Tracks.Cat#** specifies its counterpart in the Tracks table.

QuickCheck

What is the dot notation for the field that holds the Price?

a. Price...

b. Price.Cat#

c. 20.00

d. Albums.Price

When joining two tables, the convention is to use dot notation for field names. Figure 10-51 dissects an SQL query that joins two Vintage Music database tables.

Figure 10-51: Using dot notation to join tables

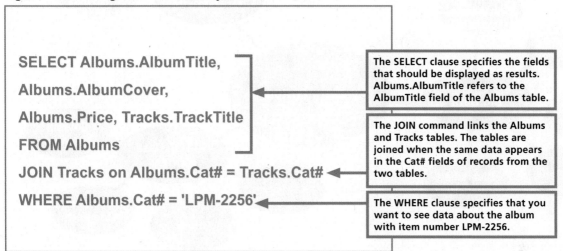

SELECT Albums.AlbumTitle,

Albums.AlbumCover,

Albums.Price, Tracks.TrackTitle

FROM Albums

JOIN Tracks on Albums.Cat# = Tracks.Cat#

WHERE Albums.Cat# = 'LPM-2256'

The SELECT clause specifies the fields that should be displayed as results. Albums.AlbumTitle refers to the AlbumTitle field of the Albums table.

The JOIN command links the Albums and Tracks tables. The tables are joined when the same data appears in the Cat# fields of records from the two tables.

The WHERE clause specifies that you want to see data about the album with item number LPM-2256.

10

▶ **So how does SQL injection work?** A malicious SQL command contains conventional command words, such as SELECT and UPDATE, but the parameters for the command contain unusual text that either provides the attacker with elevated privileges or overruns a buffer to inject malicious code in memory. The following command has the potential to delete an entire table from a database:

SELECT AlbumTitle, Artist, Price FROM Albums WHERE name = '\"; DROP TABLE Albums; --';

With a slight modification, the malicious SQL statement could copy the entire contents of a table to a hacker's computer. To prevent SQL injection, database designers construct DBMS applications with plenty of protective measures to screen out potentially harmful SQL statements. Hackers, however, continue to devise new attack vectors, so consumers do need to take precautions to monitor their personal data for identity theft.

QuickQuiz   Section D

1. In search specifications, AND, OR, and NOT are examples of search operators, which are also called _____ operators.

2. In SQL, the DATA command adds fields to a database. True or false? _____

3. To search for data in a specific field, you can use the SQL command _____ .

4. The SQL _____ command can change the data in a specified field in one or more records.

5. In SQL, the JOIN command allows you to add fields to a database. True or false? _____

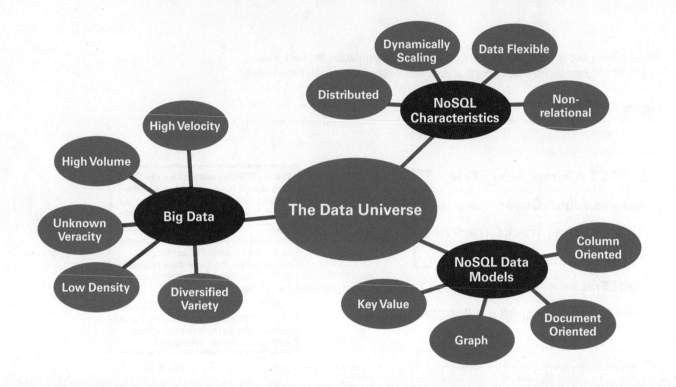

Section E Big Data

Objectives

- List the elements that define the 3rd platform of computing.
- List the five Vs that characterize big data.
- Describe at least three examples of datasets that would be considered big data.
- List the four characteristics of NoSQL.
- Explain the difference between scaling up and scaling out.
- Explain how dynamic scaling works and how it relates to big data.
- Support or refute the statement that NoSQL tools are schema-less.
- Draw a diagram representing an example of a key-value data model.

- Demonstrate the different retrieval strategies for data stored in a relational database and data stored in a column-oriented database.
- Give at least three examples of large datasets that would be best handled by a graph schema.
- Describe blockchain technology.

The number of stars in the sky. The number of sand grains on Earth. The number of data bits stored by the world's computers. Which is the biggest? We interact with vast, massive, and seemingly boundless amounts of information every day. In this section, you'll explore where this "big data" originates, how it is stored, and the tools that are used to manage it.

Terminology

big data	high-density data	shard	key-value data model
3rd platform	NoSQL	dynamic scaling	column-oriented data
data lake	scale up	schema	model
low-density data	scale out	schema-less databases	blockchain

Big Data Basics

Astronomers estimate that the universe contains 70 billion trillion stars. The digital universe is likely to soon contain as many digital bits as there are stars in the physical universe. Such a massive amount of data is almost impossible to visualize, let alone process and analyze. Dealing with a universe of data has become one of the top challenges of the Information Age.

▶ **What is big data?** The term *big data* seems oddly non-technical, but it has a specific meaning in the world of databases. **Big data** refers to huge collections of data that are difficult to process, analyze, and manage using conventional database tools.

An example of big data is the 1 million transactions generated by Walmart sales registers every hour. Other examples of big data include user profiles stored on social network sites, the archive of Google searches, medical records, astronomical data, and military surveillance data.

Analysts at International Data Corporation describe big data as a core component of an emerging computing platform that is likely to drive innovation and disruption through the next decade. This **3rd platform** is based on cloud computing, mobile devices, social networking, and big data. The 3rd platform has massive scale, not only in cloud-based hardware technology, but also in the vast amount of data that will be generated, consumed, and analyzed. Figure 10-52 offers hints about the volume of users and data that is produced by the 3rd platform.

10

QuickCheck

Which one of the following is not a component of the 3rd platform of computing?

a. Storing data in the cloud

b. Handling big data

c. Using SQL

d. Social networking

Figure 10-52: The big data universe

**32 Billion**
Number of things that were connected to the Internet in 2020

180 zettabytes
Estimated amount of data that will exist in the year 2025

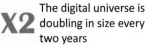**4 Billion**
Smartphone users

8 Billion
Global online population

**250+Billion**
Photos stored on Facebook

BIG DATA

2.5 Exabytes
Amount of data created per day

X2 The digital universe is doubling in size every two years

**1,782,579 Bytes**
The amount of data created each year for every person on Earth

500 Million
Tweets per day

 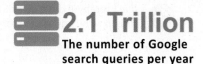**2.1 Trillion**
The number of Google search queries per year

▶ **How big are we talking?** The statement that the digital universe will grow to 180 zettabytes of data in 2025 is interesting—but only to those people who understand the magnitude of a zettabyte. It is easy to toss around terms like *petabyte*, *exabyte*, and *zettabyte*, but they are just words with little meaning unless compared to things we deal with every day. A few comparisons in Figure 10-53 can help convey the enormous size of these numbers.

Figure 10-53: That's a lot of data!

1024 Gigabytes = 1 Terabyte
1024 Terabytes = 1 Petabyte
1024 Petabytes = 1 Exabyte
1024 Exabytes = 1 Zettabyte
1024 Zettabytes = 1 Yottabyte
1024 Yottabytes = 1 Brontobyte
1024 Brontobytes = 1 Geopbyte

 Ten terabytes offer enough storage capacity to hold the printed collection of the Library of Congress.

 According to futurist and inventor Raymond Kurzweil, the capacity of a human being's functional memory is estimated to be **1.25 terabytes**. Based on this estimate, one petabyte can hold the memories of 800 human beings.

 If the average music track requires 1 megabyte per minute, and the average song lasts about four minutes, then a **petabyte of songs** would last over 2,000 years playing continuously.

 A single high-res photo is about 3 megabytes in size. Suppose you took a **petabyte's worth of photos** and printed each one on four-inch photo paper. The assembled photos placed side by side would be more than 48,000 miles long and would stretch around Earth's equator twice.

 One petabyte is enough to store the DNA of the entire population of the United States and the European Union.

 62 billion iPhones stacked on top of each other would reach from the Earth to the moon. If each iPhone has 64 GB of storage capacity, that stack of phones would store about **3 zettabytes of data**.

 Storing a **trillion gigabytes** would require 600,000,000,000 smartphones—enough to lay end to end over every road in America.

 If a 1 terabyte drive costs $100, it would cost $100 trillion to buy drives to store a **yottabyte** of data.

QuickCheck

Which of the following is the most accurate visualization of a zettabyte?

a. The memories of 800,000 human beings

b. The storage capacity of about 20 billion iPhones

c. All the data on the Internet

d. All the data indexed by Google

▶ **Why is big data a challenge?** Big data is quickly becoming a part of big business. Retailers, financial institutions, manufacturers, and other business sectors are investing in tools to collect, store, and analyze big data sets. Deploying these tools to produce meaningful information, however, is challenging.

The sheer volume of big data is difficult to handle, but additional factors further complicate its use. Big data was originally defined as having three Vs: volume, velocity, and variety. As big data evolved, however, additional V factors emerged. Today, big data is characterized as having high volume, high velocity, diversified variety, unknown veracity, and low-density value.

Volume. Big data is high volume. It is measured in petabytes, exabytes, and even higher volumes. Storing such high volumes of data can be a challenge, as is making backups of that data. Big data is typically distributed across many storage devices. For example, Walmart stores data across six huge data centers, each containing thousands of servers.

Velocity. Big data often needs to be handled quickly in order to be useful. As with Internet "speed," the velocity of big data is actually a measure of capacity and may be quantified in terabits per second (Tbps) or even petabits per second (Pbps). Although a single Internet connection cannot handle such speeds, data may arrive simultaneously over multiple connections. The challenge is to organize the data as it arrives, process it if necessary, and store it where it can be easily retrieved.

Variety. Big data commonly consists of multiple data types such as text, images, video, numbers, and audio that are generated from transaction processing systems, sensors, social media, smartphones, and other sources. Some data may be structured, while other data is unstructured. Organizing this mix of data is challenging and may require database designers to seek solutions other than the rigid structures of relational databases. The challenge of storing and mining a variety of data produced the idea of a **data lake**, which can store both unstructured and structured data.

Veracity. Big data can contain an unknown amount of inaccurate data that is counterproductive to accurate analytics and decision making. Data verification can require cross checks, which in turn depend on even more data.

Value. In the context of big data, value does not necessarily equate to money, but rather to the usefulness of data. Big data typically includes a high proportion of low-density data that is not relevant to processing or analysis. **Low-density data** refers to large volumes of very detailed data in which many of the details are not important. The opposite is **high-density data**, which is packed with lots of useful information.

10

Terminology

A *data lake* stores both structured and unstructured data, whereas a *data warehouse* typically stores only structured data.

QuickCheck

A week's worth of tweets by all Twitter users would be considered _____ by a Coca-Cola market researcher.

a. a zettabyte

b. low-density data

c. an archive

d. high-velocity data

Big Data Analytics

The 1970s rock band Led Zeppelin was accused of stealing a riff for its hit song *Stairway to Heaven* from a lesser-known band called Spirit. Unlike other cases of wholesale appropriation, such as when The Beach Boys based the entire melody for *Surfin' Safari* on an earlier Chuck Berry song called *Sweet Little Sixteen*, the Led Zeppelin case involves a short, 10-second riff. *Stairway to Heaven* begins with a melodic acoustic guitar sequence that is similar to a sequence of notes about 44 seconds into the Spirit song.

Suppose you were defending Led Zeppelin in court and wanted to find a similar melodic phrase in an even earlier piece of music. MusicHype CEO Kevin King estimates that there are about 97 million recorded songs. That's about 276 terabytes of data—more than 4.8 million hours of music. This is big data, and some sort of analytical tool is required to sift through it in time for it to be useful.

▶ **How useful are big data analytics?** Searching through all of the world's recorded music may be a very specialized use of big data. There are other interesting, but specialized, large datasets that are available for exploration.

Basketball fans can explore NBA player statistics to predict playoff winners and point spreads. For teams, there is a service called SportVU that uses strategically placed cameras to collect about 1 million data points during a typical professional basketball game. Reports from this data, processed within 90 seconds of each play, are routed to coaches' digital devices. Heat maps generated from the data can show where most of the action takes place on the court, and can then be used to adjust defensive strategies.

Another offbeat use of big data is searching through Google Books Ngram datasets. Google has stored the words from every book it has scanned as ngrams, which depict word sequences. Using Google Books Ngram Viewer, it is possible to extract word sequences, such as "Royal Wedding," from a vast collection containing more than 500 billion words derived from more than 8 million written works dating back to the 1800s. Practical applications of such data mining include finding the first use of terms and determining how long after world events occur that references to them appear in literature.

Mainstream big data exploration produces commercial benefits. A high percentage of today's expenditures on big data are for technologies that enhance the customer experience and provide targeted marketing solutions. Real-time analysis and decision making are also popular reasons to invest in big data technologies. Figure 10-54 provides an overview of business sectors that are making big investments in big data.

Terminology

An *ngram* is a sequence of items that are derived from a segment of text or speech. They are essentially phrases containing one or more words. Ngrams are an important tool in text and speech analysis.

Try It!

When was there the most buzz about royal weddings? Connect to the Google Books Ngram Viewer and enter the phrase *royal wedding* to find out. While there, enter a few additional phrases to see how their usage varies over time.

Figure 10-54: Big data across industries

Government

- Threat prediction
- Cybersecurity
- Compliance and regulatory analysis

Retail

- Shopper behavior analysis
- Loyalty program management
- Supply chain optimization

Health care

- Track infectious diseases
- Genetic analysis
- Design proactive care plans

Communications

- Retain customers
- Call record analysis
- Infrastructure optimization

▶ **How is big data used in marketing?** The vision for big data marketing analytics is to maximize profit from every item of merchandise and service that is offered by a business. Achieving this vision is a multifaceted task. Figure 10-55 presents a step-by-step example showing how a national superstore chain might use big data analytics to squeeze out the maximum profit from videogame sales in the upcoming holiday season.

Figure 10-55: Using big data analytics to sell videogames

STEP 1: Collect data from many sources and analyze it using a predictive model. This step can take place months before the holiday season.

Movie
releases

Web
browsing
patterns

Social media
comments

Gaming industry
advertising
expenditures

Previous season's
hot-selling games

STEP 2: Determine where demand will be greatest, and then plan to stock more games in those stores. Data for this step can come from many sources.

Transaction volume
for stores and
ecommerce site

Demographic
data

Localized social
media buzz

STEP 3: Use online analytical processing to produce on-the-fly price guidance for changing prices as demand grows or inventory shrinks.

Customer
demand

Competitor
pricing

Inventory
levels

STEP 4: Find and target customers by sifting through big data from in-house databases and external datasets.

Social
media

Purchase
history

Browsing
patterns

Gaming
forums

Loyalty
programs

STEP 5: Customize online and in-store promotions to entice consumers to purchase a videogame and as many additional items as possible.

Identify consumers who
pre-order, are early
adopters, or are
stand-in-liners.

Contact them using
social media, texting,
email, or sponsored ads.

Offer them
discounts, gift
cards, or loyalty
points.

Use their buying
history to offer
additional products.

10

NoSQL

What is the connection between 1960s rock star Jimi Hendrix, modern pop star Alicia Keys, and an amateur American poet named Francis Scott Key who was born in 1779? Musicologists would like to easily pull such arcane facts out of a massive pool of music trivia. Similarly, corporate executives would like to analyze connections and trends from data collected by operational and analytical databases. Relational databases and SQL might not be the best tools for this type of foray into big data, but alternative tools are available from NoSQL.

▶ **What is NoSQL?** The term **NoSQL** is used to refer to a group of technologies for managing databases that do not adhere to the relational model and standard SQL query language. SQL is not totally banned from the NoSQL toolbox, however, leading some jargon experts to suggest that *NoSQL* actually means "not only SQL." Other terminology authorities would prefer that the term was *NoREL*, meaning "not relational," which is a more accurate description. NoSQL is a fixed part of the technical vocabulary, however, so practitioners generally use it when referring to databases and database tools that are not relational.

NoSQL technologies are effective for building and managing non-relational databases containing big data that may be unstructured and may be distributed across multiple servers with dynamically scaling capabilities. When visualizing NoSQL, keep in mind the four characteristics in Figure 10-56.

Figure 10-56: Characteristics of NoSQL

 Distributed. Handles data that is stored across many devices

 Dynamically scaling. Easy to add storage devices as the database grows or as the velocity of incoming data accelerates

 Flexible data. Handles a variety of data types, as well as data that is structured, semi-structured, and unstructured

 Non-relational. Uses data models other than the standard relational models and SQL

▶ **Why is distributed data a challenge?** Picture your own computer, and consider if you were working on an astronomy project and you wanted to analyze data from the Sloan Digital Sky Survey. The dataset is about 116 TB, which is too big to fit on your 4 TB hard drive. You could scale up and purchase an industrial-size 160 TB drive, or you could scale out and distribute the data among several smaller drives.

A **scale up** (or scale vertically) solution adds resources to a single device. The advantage of scaling up is that the dataset remains as one unit. You can use standard relational database tools to perform queries, joins, and updates. Businesses use this scale-up strategy as their databases grow in size. They purchase ever larger storage devices and newer, faster computers to process database queries. Eventually, however, a single machine reaches a performance ceiling where additional users and their queries become entangled in processor bottlenecks. Regaining performance requires a solution other than scaling up.

A **scale out** (or scale horizontally) solution adds more devices to a system, typically by adding nodes on a LAN or in an Internet cloud. To scale out to accommodate the Sloan Digital Sky Survey data, you could distribute the data to other devices on your home network or cloud storage devices.

Distributing a database requires that it be divided into smaller units, much like breaking up a block of ice. The process of dividing a database into distributed subsets is called sharding, and each subset of data is called a **shard**. Distributing a database brings up the problem of how to divide it and then how to send a query across all of the devices that hold the data.

You can probably see how this scenario relates to businesses, Web sites, and social media platforms with big data collections. Information systems that work with big data can scale up to a point, but then they are forced to scale out and require a new set of tools for managing the database. Those tools are provided by NoSQL technologies.

▶ **What is significant about dynamic scaling?** Many years ago when ecommerce was an emerging technology, Victoria's Secret devised a sure-fire marketing plan that revolved around a live runway show video-cast over the Internet. Interest in the event was so high that within the first minute of the show, the number of users trying to connect overwhelmed the Victoria's Secret server.

Today, Victoria's Secret could use a dynamic cloud solution to add capacity on demand and then release the extra capacity when it is no longer needed. **Dynamic scaling** (or autoscaling) ensures acceptable database throughput by scaling out as necessary to handle peak loads. Dynamic scaling is desirable in situations such as when a newly launched Web site goes viral and generates a high volume of user traffic or when an ecommerce business expects seasonal peaks during holidays.

Dynamic scaling can be applied to database servers and to communications servers. Communications servers handle the number of users that are able to connect, whereas database servers handle the number of data records that are stored and available for access. Dynamic scaling for database servers can be a challenge because the additional sharding has to be handled on the fly by the DBMS. Once again, NoSQL tools have advantages over SQL for such adaptations (Figure 10-57).

Figure 10-57: How dynamic scaling works

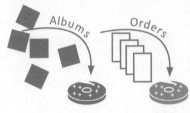
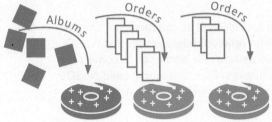

Initially, the information system stores album data on one storage device and order data on a second device. As the volume of orders spikes, a third storage device is dynamically allocated to handle the load.

▶ **Why is unstructured data such a challenge?** Relational databases store structured data, and that data has two important characteristics. First, the data easily breaks down into discrete fields that fit into a table format of rows and columns. Second, the data for multiple entities can be stored within a defined structure, such as a customer record type or an inventory item record type. Much of the data of interest to organizations is structured, but a surprising amount of data is semi-structured or unstructured, as shown in Figure 10-58.

Figure 10-58: Structured, semi-structured, and unstructured data

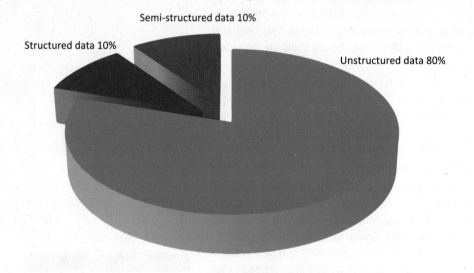

Semi-structured data 10%

Structured data 10%

Unstructured data 80%

Unstructured and semi-structured data—such as tweets, email messages, blog posts, Facebook posts, images, and videos—are difficult to mold into fixed structures. The effort to do so can be costly and time intensive. The results can be unsatisfactory because as the data is transformed, much of the context may be lost.

Tweets, for example, have a rich underpinning of associated data, such as the tweeter's number of followers. That data, if needed, could be placed in a table that is separate from the table that holds the body of the tweet. Pursuing the relationships between followers, tweets, hashtags, and @mentions, however, quickly produces a set of relationships that resembles a plate of spaghetti and becomes unmanageable.

A relational database is organized according to a **schema**, which is the blueprint for its structure. The rows, columns, and tables of a relational database are part of its schema. The schema is defined when the database is designed and remains essentially fixed for the duration of its life cycle.

NoSQL tools create what are often characterized as **schema-less databases**, allowing data structures such as fields to be added, modified, or distributed while the database is operational.

The concept of schema-less databases is something of an exaggeration. Schema changes are possible to some extent with relational databases, and NoSQL databases actually have structures. *Schema-less* is a term used to convey the idea of less formal and more flexible structures. Four commonly used NoSQL data models are key value, column oriented, document oriented, and graph.

QuickCheck

Which of the following terms is the best synonym for *schema* in the context of databases?

a. Structure

b. Relational

c. High density

d. Unreliable

NoSQL Data Structures

NoSQL databases typically have a flexible and simple data structure based on key-value pairs, columns, XML markup, graphs, or blocks.

▶ **What is the structure for the key-value database model?** The simplest structure for storing data in a NoSQL database is the **key-value data model**. Envision a big fish bowl filled with items. Each item is stamped with a unique ID, so you can pull out a specified item at any time.

In a key-value database, each data item has a key that is a unique identifier similar to a relational database key such as CustomerID or LicensePlateNumber. The value associated with each key can be any chunk of data, such as a tweet, an image, a video, an email message, a PDF, a hypertext link, or a sound recording. Figure 10-59 illustrates the key-value schema.

10

QuickCheck

How many key-value pairs are shown in Figure 10-59?

a. One

b. Three

c. Five

d. Seven

Figure 10-59: The key-value database model

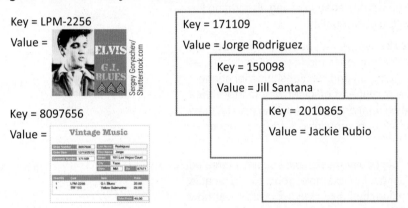

▶ **What is the structure for the column-oriented database model?** Suppose you are interested in finding all the tweets that include #pressplay. If tweets were somehow stored in a relational database, each one would begin with an ID that linked it to a user, and there would be a date field, a time field, and perhaps a field indicating retweets. Why read through all the irrelevant relational fields when a column-oriented database could help you reach the data faster?

The **column-oriented data model** stores data in columns, rather than in rows, so it works well in situations where the focus is on analysis of chunks of data, rather than delving into individual records. Figure 10-60 illustrates the column-oriented schema, which makes it easy to search through all the data in a column, such as Tweets.

Figure 10-60: The column-oriented data model

Name	@ UserName	Tweets
Jill Santana	@JillSantana	#pressplay One final giveaway!
Jan Kovack	@GroupieJ	#pressplay Singing my favorite song
Jill Santana	@JillSantana	#pressplay Love it!
Jackie Redmond	@JackieR	#PRESSPLAY Sasay Lobby Party
Ben Simons	@BeenBen	#Pressplay Next concert Chicago
Jorge Rodriguez	@JorgeAtlanta	#pressplay Breaking up
Jackie Redmond	@JackieR	#PRESSPLAY No!

Try It!

If the data in Figure 10-60 were structured as a relational database, you'd have to search through each record to find a specific tweet. Because this is a column-oriented database, however, you can just go to the Tweets column and quickly scan all the data it contains.

▶ How about the document model? Document-oriented databases were illustrated earlier in the module by a document marked up with XML tags to allow efficient searches within the text content. Documents are sometimes classified as unstructured data, but they can also be regarded as complexly structured data because different documents can exhibit extreme variations in their length and the sequence of elements they contain. For example, a CNN news article might feature the author's name at the top of the page, whereas an Association for Computing Machinery article displays the author's name and a short biography at the end.

The intriguing aspect of document-oriented databases is that the specific schema for each document is not planned when the database is built, nor is it maintained by the DBMS. Instead, each document essentially carries its own schema in the form of its markup.

With each document carrying its own schema, the placement of the <author> tag is unimportant. And if there is no author tag, that is fine, too. It is even acceptable for some future document to show up with a <coauthor> tag, illustrating the flexibility of this approach for content with high variability.

▶ How does the graph model work? Graph databases were introduced earlier as a flexible alternative to hierarchical database models. These databases are organized around nodes that have attributes and relationships that connect nodes. Graph database schemas are a useful and efficient way to store data that will be retrieved or organized based on relationships. They can also be used for social media applications to keep track of a subscriber's friends, friends of friends, and activities.

Suppose you are researching the history of popular music, and you are interested in tracing links between musicians and songs. For example, you'd like to be able to trace the musicians and bands that influenced Jimi Hendrix or discover how many modern artists have performed "The Star-Spangled Banner." You'd like to be able to pull any item from the database and unravel all its connections.

Consider how you might set up a relational database to reveal all these musical relationships. It is difficult unless you use a graph database. Figure 10-61 illustrates a small segment of a graph database where musicians, songs, and bands are nodes and their relationships are tracked by edges.

Figure 10-61: The graph data model

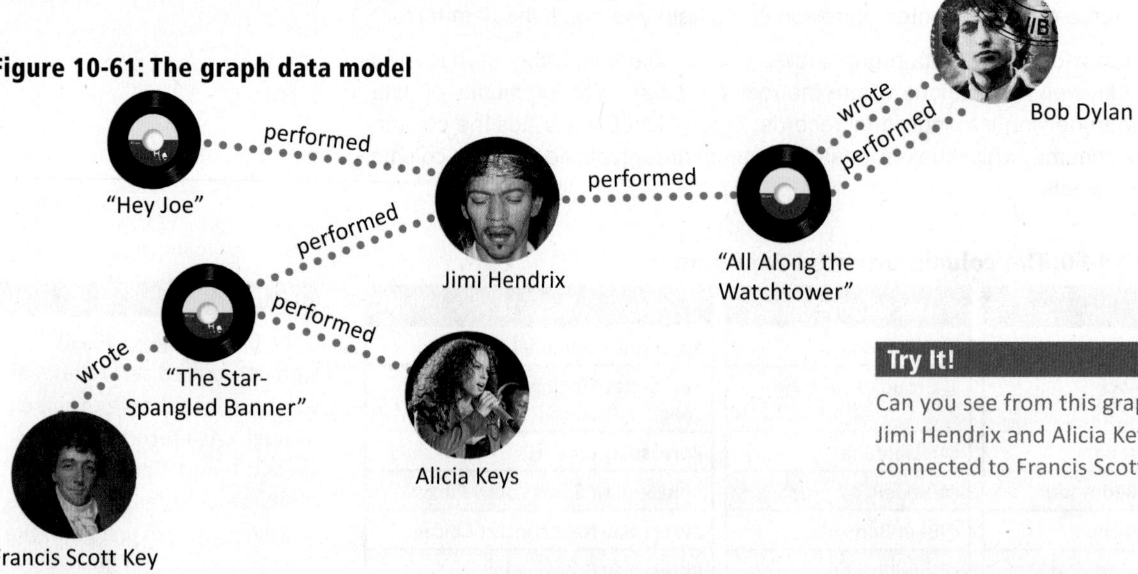

Courtesy Smithsonian
Brandonht/Shutterstock.com
Tom Begasse/Shutterstock.com
JStone/Shutterstock.com

Try It!

Can you see from this graph how Jimi Hendrix and Alicia Keys are connected to Francis Scott Key?

▶ **Is blockchain a database?** Blockchain is a distributed ledger database that operates using a distributed peer-to-peer network. It is the technology that is the foundation for digital currencies such as Bitcoin, because once data has been recorded in a blockchain, it becomes very difficult to change the data's value. As you accumulate Bitcoins, new blocks are added. Previous blocks remain unchanged to create a transaction trail.

A blockchain contains a series of records called blocks. Each block contains data, a unique ID, and the unique ID of the previous block (PB). A Bitcoin block, for example, contains data that includes the owner and the amount.

The unique ID is derived based on the contents of the block. If the data in a block is changed, or if the ID is changed, the block becomes invalid and the chain is broken, as shown in Figure 10-62.

Terminology

The unique IDs in a blockchain are usually referred to as a *hash*. A hash value is produced by applying some type of mathematical formula to the ASCII or binary value of data. Every time you apply the formula to the data, it should produce the same hash. If it does not, the data has been changed.

10

Figure 10-62: The validity of a blockchain depends on the IDs

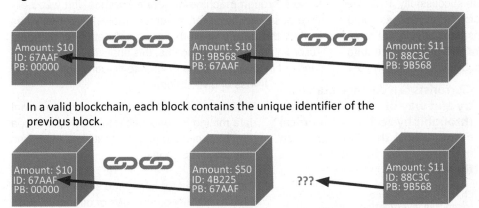

In a valid blockchain, each block contains the unique identifier of the previous block.

If the ID for a block is changed, the chain is broken and becomes invalid.

Blockchains are protected from tampering in additional ways. Adding a new block requires a process called Proof of Work that takes about 10 minutes per block. If a hacker attempts to change the data in a block and then regenerate all the subsequent blocks—and there could be thousands of blocks in a chain—the time lag would discourage that attempt.

Blockchains also take advantage of their distributed peer-to-peer topology. Each user in the blockchain network has the full chain. New blocks are sent to all the nodes on the network, where they must be verified by at least 51% of the nodes. Blocks that are tampered with will be rejected, so it is not possible for an individual to make a fraudulent change to a blockchain.

QuickQuiz   Section E

1. Big data needs to be handled quickly as it pours into a database. Therefore, it is characterized as high ☐ .

2. When analysts have to sort through large volumes of data to gather relevant information, the dataset is said to contain ☐ -density data.

3. Popular non-relational tools for managing big data are referred to as ☐ .

4. The simplest structure for storing data uses ☐ -value pairs.

5. ☐ is a distributed ledger database that is the basis for Bitcoin.

N.Andersen/Wikipedia

Issue: Can Data Mining Catch Terrorists?

Smoke rises over the skyline. It could be New York, Oslo, Moscow, Paris, Mumbai, or any major city. The cause: a terrorist attack. As the survivors mourn the dead, they inevitably ask: Could this attack have been prevented?

Modern data analysis techniques are successfully deployed in the private sector to detect consumer fraud, assess home loan applications, and predict consumer buying patterns. If direct marketers can easily aggregate and analyze data from Web sites that you visit and public information in your Facebook profile, wouldn't it be just as easy to mine existing databases to uncover patterns in terrorist behavior, identify individuals who fit the pattern, and prevent them from carrying out terrorist activities?

Governments maintain vast databases. Surely a proper search of this data, combined with public sector data, such as Web site access, credit card use, travel history, email messages, and telephone records, could produce a manageable list of potential terrorists.

This theory was put to the test when the founder of a data mining company trolled through a collection of data looking for people likely to commit acts of terror. His algorithm produced 1,200 names; five of them were hijackers in the 2001 September 11th attacks.

What seems like a remarkable feat of predictive analysis, however, reveals several problems with data mining methodology. The analysis identified 1,200 potential terrorists, but only five of those individuals actually participated in a terrorist operation. The remaining 1,195 people did not carry out attacks. Nineteen terrorists were involved in the attacks; data mining did not identify even a third of them.

Further, this data mining analysis was carried out after September 11th, using hindsight information available about the attackers. Predicting who will carry out future attacks is more difficult because the targets and methods are unknown.

> "Terrorists can damage our country and way of life in two ways: through physical, psychological damage and through our own inappropriate response to that threat."
>
> Charles Vest, former co-chair of the committee investigating the role of technology in preventing terrorism

An algorithmic search for patterns in a collection of databases is an example of an attempt to automate terrorist identification. Some degree of privacy is maintained because a machine, rather than a human analyst, searches the data.

To sort through machine-generated results and weed out false positives, however, a human analyst eventually has to view the data and all the personal details it includes. According to privacy advocates, this analysis subjects thousands of innocent civilians to intense scrutiny and potential loss of civil liberties.

Privacy advocates also fear that government data mining is susceptible to mission creep, a term that refers to projects that expand beyond their intended scope.

Data collected for homeland security might be used to identify other types of offenders, such as tax evaders, digital music pirates, or parents who are late on child support payments. Catching such individuals might be a worthy social goal, but it requires a considerable amount of government scrutiny into the lives of ordinary people.

Data mining could also be used to profile ethnic groups or harass individuals who contribute to organizations that oppose the policies of the dominant political party.

According to civil liberties advocates, government data mining is more dangerous than private sector analytics because the repercussions can be extreme. Government investigations can trigger IRS harassment, airport pat-downs, and wiretaps, rather than a few irritating ads that pop up based on your profile in an online marketing aggregator's data warehouse.

Governments have a responsibility for the safety of their citizens, but what is the correct balance between civil liberties and security? The answer to this question requires citizens to understand the potential as well as the limits of data mining technology.

Try It!

Data mining is controversial, but it is an evolving technology that might have the potential to increase civilian security. Explore data mining firsthand to understand the issues.

❶ As yet, there is not a fail-proof method for automatic terrorist identification. Suppose that a researcher devises an algorithm that is correct 99% of the time. For every 100 names it produces, one will be a false positive—someone who is not a terrorist. It will also miss one person who is a terrorist. If this algorithm is used to analyze the 324 million people in the United States, how many innocent people would be falsely identified as terrorists, and how many real terrorists would go undiscovered?

❷ People leave personal digital tracks whenever they make a purchase, take a trip, access their bank account, make a phone call, file an income tax return, stroll past a security camera, obtain a prescription, mail a package, apply for a loan, email a friend, rent a video, or download music. Create a fictitious person and provide five examples of online activities that person might perform that would look suspicious to a data mining algorithm but are actually perfectly innocent activities.

❸ To find out how extensively your government is using data mining, you can go directly to the source. For example, in the United States, the Department of Homeland Security Privacy Office issues an annual Data Mining Report to Congress. Read the most recent report. List and briefly describe the data mining projects that are operational. Also, do a Web search for *Signals Intelligence Presidential Policy Directive*. Summarize what that document says about data collection and data mining.

❹ The man walking down the jetway is sweating as his eyes flick nervously left and right. Is he planning to blow up a plane? The desire to identify terrorists before they carry out acts of destruction has revived a field of research called physiognomy: the art of judging character from facial features. In 2011, the U.S. Department of Homeland Security initiated a project called FAST (Future Attribute Screening Technology) to develop physiological and behavioral screening technologies designed to identify suspicious individuals. More recently, a Tel Aviv company developed software called Faception that classifies people based on facial images. How effective are these physiological analysis technologies? How do they relate to "pre-crime" and the movie *Minority Report*? Research these ideas online and assemble an executive briefing for a member of Congress who may be asked to approve funding for deploying a system similar to Faception.

❺ In 2016, the White House convened a counterterrorism summit for technology thought leaders. The summit produced a briefing document, *White House Briefing Document for Jan. 12 Counterterrorism Summit with Tech Leaders,* which is available at *http://bit.ly/1o3aOhg*. What were the four questions addressed in the briefing document? How do these questions relate to big data analytics?

FACE
RECOGNITION

Artem Oleshko/Shutterstock.com

What Do You Think?

Issue

1. Should your government continue to develop and deploy data mining techniques designed to identify terrorists?

2. Are you concerned about your personal data being included in government data mining operations?

3. Do you think that governments should apologize to and compensate individuals who are inappropriately harmed by data mining operations?

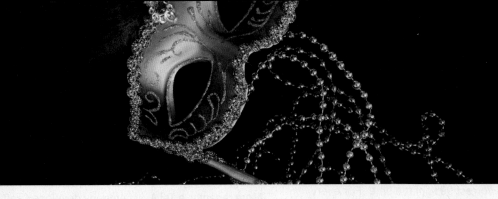

Information Tools: Vetting Anonymous Sources

Tweets, forum postings, and comments attached to online articles can be a gold mine of information. When you have a problem with a digital device, an online forum might offer advice on a quick "fix." When you want breaking eyewitness news as events unfold, there's no source like Twitter. And if you're interested in the other side of a story, look no further than the comments at the end of an online blog post or article.

The information from these sources is often difficult to verify. Many participants use pseudonyms, effectively making them anonymous. Let's take a look at the pros and cons of using these sources.

> You should be particularly careful about information on which you base personal activities, such as treating illness, dieting, filing taxes, and troubleshooting digital or automotive equipment.

Forums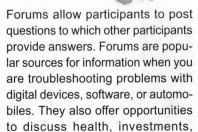

Forums allow participants to post questions to which other participants provide answers. Forums are popular sources for information when you are troubleshooting problems with digital devices, software, or automobiles. They also offer opportunities to discuss health, investments, diets, and a variety of other topics.

On technology topics, third-party forums sometimes address issues that are not acknowledged by technical support sites operated by equipment manufacturers and vendors.

When using information from forums to troubleshoot software, hardware, and connection problems, beware of misleading statements that could make problems worse.

Before you follow a complex set of instructions to tackle a technical problem, make sure the source is reliable and the solution seems technically plausible. Read comments and follow the discussion threads pertaining to suggested solutions; they can help you determine if the solution might work.

Twitter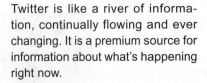

Twitter is like a river of information, continually flowing and ever changing. It is a premium source for information about what's happening right now.

Twitter posts broke the news of the Continental Airlines crash that became known as the Miracle on the Hudson, the Boston Marathon bombing, and Osama bin Laden's death.

But not everything on Twitter is legitimate. A group called Script Kiddies managed to hack into several legitimate Twitter accounts and post false tweets about an attack on Ground Zero just before the tenth anniversary of 9/11 and a false report that President Obama had been assassinated in 2010.

These tweets originating from NBC News and FOX News appeared legitimate, but they weren't—a reminder that even information with a source that seems genuine may not be true.

Tweets often provide links to blog posts or Web sites containing more detailed information on an issue or a topic. You can use standard techniques to check the provenance of those sites.

Comments

Provocative articles spawn commentary. That commentary is sometimes useful to readers and researchers because it reveals the scope of an issue and provides glimpses of its many facets.

Most sites that accept comments require participants to register and provide a valid email address. However, that requirement does not prevent people from using screen names and throwaway email accounts.

Commenters may have valid reasons for cloaking their identities, and their comments might be informative. Unless you can verify and cross-check the information, however, you should not accept it as authoritative.

Anonymous comments or comments from sources that can't be properly verified should not be used as the basis for factual citations, but they can give you ideas and viewpoints that help expand your research to encompass the full scope of a topic.

Try It!

So what should you do with information that comes from an anonymous source or one cloaked in the secrecy of a screen name? Here's a chance to work with a few verification techniques.

1 Verifying tweets requires a twofold approach: gathering information on the tweeter, and triangulating the location and timing of the content. To see how it works, check out a technology Twitter feed. You can access tweets even without a Twitter account by entering *twitter search* in a search engine and then using the Search box at the top of the screen. Enter *XBox* to find information about Microsoft's videogame device. Select a tweet that appears to come from an individual, and then answer the following questions:

   a. Does the tweeter provide a name, picture, and biography?

   b. If you search for the tweeter's name in Google, do you find further clues to the person's identity?

   c. What is the person's track record of blog posts, forum responses, or tweets?

   d. Does the source have a large following on Twitter or an extensive network of friends on Facebook or LinkedIn?

   e. Can you determine where the source is located and if the location might be relevant to verifying the information (as in an eyewitness account)?

   f. Are other sources reporting similar information?

   g. If the information is a link or retweet, can you identify the original source?

   h. Does the language of the message sound appropriate for the source?

2 Although forums are sometimes billed as "advice and recommendations from a community of experts," participants are not always experts, and the advice offered is not always accurate. The first step to identifying the source of information is to click any links available to the user's profile. Select an article from a technology news source, such as Engadget, Reddit, or TechRepublic, that includes lots of comments. Click the picture and name links for three commenters, and then fill in the following table, entering *NA* if the information is not available.

3 When you're looking for a solution to a technical problem and you come across forum postings such as "I don't know" or "I've never tried this but...," you probably wonder why anyone would waste your time with information that is totally useless. Connect to Reddit and search for *keyboard not responding*. Read at least ten posts on this topic. Select what you think are the best and the worst posts, and then briefly explain your selections.

	Commenter 1	Commenter 2	Commenter 3
Commenter "Handle"			
Commenter Real Name			
Number of Posts			
General Quality of Posts			

Orlando Sentinel/Tribune News Service/Getty Images

Technology in Context: Politics

Impassioned campaign rallies. Massive mailing campaigns. Saturation television ads. These remain part of today's political campaigns, but politicians increasingly depend on digital databases and social media to sway voters and get them to the polls. Modern campaign strategies illustrate the power of data mining, but also shed light on the associated privacy concerns.

The 2020 presidential election was a contest between the incumbent Republican President, Donald Trump, and former Vice President and Democrat Joe Biden. The candidates took advantage of every digital option to mine the data necessary to win this hotly contested election.

Biden's "relational organizing" strategy, pioneered by Barack Obama's 2008 campaign, encouraged supporters to network friends and family into a database of donors and voters. This strategy was based on the idea that the best way to sway a person's political opinion is with information provided by a trusted friend or relative.

A key component in Biden's relational organizing strategy was the Vote Joe app. Available from the Google Play Store or Apple's App Store, the app's signup required users to provide a name, email address, zip code, and phone number.

The Vote Joe app also required users to sync their phone and email contacts. Users were encouraged to text their friends to vote for Biden. Reportedly, more than 500,000 text messages were sent by Vote Joe users in battleground states, garnering as many as 40,000 extra votes that may have been instrumental in a Biden victory.

Although the campaign did not directly contact the individuals harvested from a user's contact list, the app supplied users with the political affiliations of each contact and a list of elections in which they voted. If you had downloaded the Vote Joe app, you would have been able to see the party affiliation for each of your contacts! Voter names and party affiliations are public information, but normally this data is not easily accessible by individuals.

The Vote Joe app, however, revealed political affiliations of individuals without their explicit knowledge or consent. Individuals who prefer not to broadcast their political philosophies may be troubled by these revelations.

Database purveyors such as Target Smart are able to aggregate data across databases to pull in additional information and map trends based on religion, ethnicity, gender, education, location, occupation, and issues. This data is highly valuable to political campaigns as they plan their targeting strategies. For example, declining support among women might compel a campaign to modify its messaging about issues important to that demographic.

The Trump campaign rolled out an app called Trump 2020. Its focus was energizing supporters and encouraging them to vote. Unlike Vote Joe, the Trump 2020 app did not focus on person-to-person outreach. Subscribers were asked to allow location sharing via GPS and Bluetooth. Using this data, the campaign supplied subscribers with information on nearby rallies and campaign events. It pushed notifications to subscribers' phones that solicited donations and broadcast the candidate's talking points. It included channels with messaging aimed at specific groups such as Black Votes for Trump, Latino Votes for Trump, and Women for Trump.

The Trump 2020 app was "gamified." Users accumulated points by getting friends to download the app, signing up to make calls for the campaign, registering voters, participating as a poll watcher, and attending campaign events. Accumulated points could be used to get discounts on Trump gear, such as hats and t-shirts. Only a month after its launch, the app had been downloaded more than 780,000 times.

In a *New Yorker* magazine article that demonstrates the wide reach of database aggregation during the 2020 election, Sue Halpern described purchasing a burner phone and signing up for one of the candidate's campaign apps using an alias and throw-away email address. The messages she received via the app "were sent not only to the name and address I'd used to access the app. They were also sent to the email address and name associated with the credit card I'd used to buy the phone and its sim card, neither of which I had shared with the campaign." Somehow, the app managed to aggregate the data across third-party databases to discover Halpern's real identity.

Voter databases and contacts gathered from campaign apps can be aggregated and used for targeted email campaigns.

On the eve of the election, the Trump campaign was reportedly sending supporters 26 messages a day.

In addition to apps and email, political campaigns marshal the full force of data science analytics to predict voter behavior and manipulate it with targeted advertising.

Machine learning algorithms help to determine what kinds of ads can sway undecided voters. Microtargeting can tailor ads to voters in specific battleground areas based on data gathered about their concerns, habits, and preferences.

If you were a blue-collar worker in Toledo or Youngstown, Ohio during the 2020 election, your vote might have been influenced by a "Build Back Better" ad campaign crafted to emphasize issues identified by data analytics as important to middle Americans living in those cities and surrounding areas.

Political campaigns also use analytics to monitor trending hashtags and posts on social media. Campaigns can then respond to these trends and use additional analytics to gauge which responses are most successful.

And then there is the role of social media in political campaigns. Biden became the Democratic Party's nominee for president in August 2020. At that time, Trump had ten times the Twitter followers and Facebook fans as Biden.

Although it appeared that Trump had won the social media war, a raw count of followers was only half the story. Trump used his social media platform to push *his* message to followers, but in another example of relational organizing, Biden made extensive use of social media influencers to spread *their* endorsements.

The Democrats used social media influencers to host online interviews with their candidate and surrogates; these interviews were then streamed live on Instagram and uploaded to YouTube and Facebook. Biden's messaging was intended to reach the influencers' audiences. Influencers included Elle Walker, with 3 million subscribers to her WhatsUpMoms YouTube channel, and Instagram maven Bethany Mota, with more than 4 million subscribers.

Some influencers are paid by campaigns for their endorsements. According to election watchdogs, this practice is not federally regulated and skirts the policies of many social media sites. Although sites such as Facebook and Twitter have banned or limited paid political ads, during the 2020 election they had not curtailed endorsements from paid influencers.

Biden's victory seems to confirm the success of relational organizing with person-to-person outreach. But analytics and artificial intelligence algorithms are increasingly used to imitate posts from friends and push connections to social media influencers. A CNBC article points out, "As this outreach strategy becomes less personal and more automated, the potential for manipulation grows." The people who shape your opinions are no longer limited to friends and family; they are influencers on Facebook and Twitter whose posts appear in your personal stream along with posts from your actual friends.

Political campaigns take place on a fast-paced and intense battlefield. Today, digital warriors are increasingly called into action. This digital emphasis provides career opportunities for programmers, social media experts, and data scientists who specialize in big data analytics.

The challenging job of a data scientist involves asking pertinent questions, gathering relevant data, modeling the data, and communicating the results in written, numeric, or visual formats. In addition to predictive analytics used in political campaigns, data scientists tackle recommendations based on business analytics and social network activity.

Data science combines computer science, statistical analysis, and communication skills. The Python programming language is a popular tool for applying statistical procedures to large datasets, and familiarity with SQL, NoSQL, and data analytics is essential. With coursework and experience in the realm of data science, you could find yourself helping the next president-elect to achieve victory.

Flipped Class Projects

Critical Thinking

A key component of the databases used by political campaigns for voter analytics is data about past voting. That data includes voter names, addresses, and voting history. The data does not include who you voted for, but in some states the data includes your race and whether you are a registered Democrat or Republican. Most states and several commercial Web sites provide this data for use in local, state, or national political campaigns. Did you know that your voting record is public information? What are the advantages and disadvantages of making that information public?

Group Project

Form a group of four to five students. Suppose you must design the record structure for a new information system that holds driver's license data. Using your own driver's licenses, design an effective record structure, indicating record types, field names, field lengths, and data types. Where appropriate, indicate ways that you could minimize data entry errors. Submit your record structure to your instructor.

Cyberclassroom

How do student demographics compare throughout the world? The Organisation for Economic Co-operation and Development has gathered statistics in interactive databases at *www.oecd.org/education/database.htm*.

Working alone or in a small group, link to any of the datasets that look interesting. Notice that you can create custom queries by selecting variables in the control panel above the data tables. After exploring the data, formulate three specific queries for extracting information. For example, you might be interested in which country has the highest number of non-resident students or the number of students who graduated with a degree in computing from U.S. colleges in the past ten years. If you are working in a small group, challenge the other students to predict what they think the data might produce. Can you surprise them with facts that run counter to commonly held assumptions about students around the world?

Multimedia Project

Today, Web-based videos are a viable way of learning about products and picking up technical skills. Locate an instructional video about a DBMS such as FileMaker, Oracle, or SAP. After viewing the video, write five short paragraphs describing five concepts or skills you learned. As an alternative to a written summary, your instructor could change up the assignment by asking you to mark five key concepts in the video and then present them to a partner in class.

Resume Builder

When you look for a job, you might have to send query letters and resumes to several employers. To track the status of each, you can use a database. Use word processing, spreadsheet, or database software to create a job-hunting database that includes company contact information plus fields to indicate the status of your inquiry. Load the database with at least five sample contacts. Make sure you can use the database to generate mailing labels. You should also be able to make queries to determine which job prospects are still "active" possibilities. Follow your instructor's guidelines for submitting your database and mailing labels.

Globalization

Computer databases often store personal information about the citizens of more than one country, yet privacy expectations and laws differ. For this project, explore the differences in privacy laws around the globe. Which countries have the strongest privacy laws and which have the weakest? Which laws would govern the data stored by multinational companies? As a global consumer, which databases would concern you the most for potential privacy violations? Consolidate your thoughts into a one- to two-page paper and submit it to your instructor.

Key Terms

3rd platform 731
analytical database 681
big data 731
blockchain 741
Boolean operators 725
cardinality 688
case-sensitive database 709
column-oriented data model 739
computed field 708
CREATE 722
data archive 683
data dependence 695
data independence 695
data lake 733
data mining 685
data redundancy 712
data type 711
data warehouse 685
database client software 704
database index 715
database model 686
database structure 707
DBMS 701
DELETE 722
document-oriented database 693
dot notation 728
dynamic scaling 737
entity-relationship diagram 688

executive dashboard 684
field 687
field format 709
field name 687
field validation rule 710
fixed-length field 687
flat file 686
global update 727
graph database 689
hierarchical database 689
high-density data 733
INSERT 723
JOIN 728
joining tables 728
key-value data model 739
lookup routine 710
low-density data 733
multidimensional database 691
multi-level sort 698
normalization 712
NoSQL 736
object database 692
OLAP 685
operational database 681
parameters 723
physical sort order 714
predictive analytics 685
primary key 708

query languages 721
record 687
record occurrence 687
record type 687
relational database 690
relationship 688
report generator 718
report template 718
scale out 737
scale up 736
schema 738
schema-less databases 738
SELECT 724
serializability 703
shard 737
single-level sort 698
sort key 714
SQL 721
SQL injection 721
SQL keywords 722
SQL query 721
structured file 686
table 690
unstructured file 686
UPDATE 727
variable-length field 687
XML 693

Interactive Summary

Section A: A(n) [_____] is a collection of information, generally stored as computer files. The information it contains can be stored, updated, organized, output, distributed, searched, and analyzed. A filing cabinet full of folders and papers would be classified as a(n) [_____] file. A(n) [_____] file uses a uniform format to store data for each person or thing in the file. One of the simplest models for storing data is a(n) [_____] file that consists of a single, two-dimensional table of data elements. Each row in the table is a(n) [_____], and each column of the table is a(n) [_____]. Each kind of record is referred to as a record [_____]. A record that contains data is sometimes referred to as a record [_____]. In databases, records can be related by one-to- [_____] relationships, one-to-many relationships, or many-to-many relationships. The number of associations that can exist between two record types is referred to as [_____]. Relationships can be depicted graphically by using [_____] -relationship diagrams. [_____] databases allow only one-to-many relationships. [_____] databases connect nodes much like a sociogram. [_____] databases exist as a series of tables that can be related by common fields. A(n) [_____] database organizes relationships over three or more dimensions. A(n) [_____] database stores data grouped into classes and defined by attributes and methods. Document-related databases store text in JSON format or marked up with [_____].

Section B: Modern database tools support data [_____], which means separating data from the programs that manipulate data. As a result, a single data management tool can be used to maintain many different files and databases. Many [_____] applications, from consumer apps to enterprise-level ERP systems, have a database at their core. [_____] files can be created and manipulated by using a variety of tools, including word processing and spreadsheet software. For databases composed of more than one record type, however, it is best to use a database management system, which is abbreviated as [_____]. Most of these systems support [_____] databases with data stored in tables, but database tool vendors also offer products for other database models. Database tools handle the way data is physically stored, including the process of [_____] data across multiple servers. Database tools also support multiple users and use a technique called [_____] to handle situations in which more than one user attempts to update the same record. A database and the DBMS used to create it are installed on a specific in-house computing platform, such as Linux, or are hosted as a(n) [_____] service. The data can be accessed by devices using other platforms through the use of database [_____] software.

Section C:
The first step in designing a relational database is to define its fields by specifying a field name and a data type. Integer, date, and [_____] data types are used for fields containing data that might be mathematically manipulated. The [_____] data type is used for fixed-length fields containing text that is not intended to be mathematically manipulated. The [_____] data type is a variable-length field for entering text. The [_____] data type is used to store true/false and yes/no data. The [_____] data type can be used to store URLs. The [_____] data type is used to store binary data, such as MP3 files and graphics. When designing fields, a database designer can also include field formats, field [_____] rules, and lookup routines to reduce data entry errors. The number of tables in a database can be determined by a process called [_____], which helps a database designer group fields into record types and avoid data redundancy. A database designer must also consider how to sort or index records. The [_____] key for a table specifies the order in which records are stored and indicates where new records are inserted in a table. Indexing provides an alternative way to organize records, using a series of keys and pointers to temporarily arrange data without affecting the physical sequence of records specified by the sort order.

Section D:
SQL is a database [_____] language that generally works behind the scenes as an intermediary between the database [_____] software provided to users and the database itself. Although the specifications for searches and other database tasks are collected by easy-to-use graphical user interfaces, those specifications are converted into SQL [_____], which can communicate directly with the database. An SQL query contains SQL [_____], such as SELECT, FROM, INSERT, JOIN, and WHERE, plus [_____] that specify the details of the command. Records can be removed from a database using the SQL [_____] command. Records can be added to a table using the SQL [_____] command. To search for data, you can use the SQL [_____] command. Changing or replacing the data in a field requires the SQL [_____] command. SQL also provides a(n) [_____] command that can be used to temporarily consolidate two tables so that data can be accessed simultaneously from both of them.

Section E:
Big data refers to huge collections of data that are difficult to process, analyze, and manage using conventional data tools. It is a core component of the [_____] platform, which also includes cloud computing, [_____] devices, and social networking. The five Vs of big data are high volume, high [_____], diversified variety, unknown veracity, and low-[_____] value. Although SQL and relational databases can be used for big datasets, a collection of alternative tools referred to as [_____] has become popular. These tools work well when databases scale [_____] (horizontally) and when databases are broken into subsets called [_____]. Modern database tools also handle [_____] scaling as devices are added when additional capacity is required. NoSQL tools are sometimes said to create [_____] databases, but they usually have some type of structure, though it may be more flexible than the relational model. A key-[_____] data model provides each data element with a key. A(n) [_____]-oriented data model makes it easy to access data stored in similar fields, rather than in individual records. [_____] is a distributed ledger database that operates using a distributed peer-to-peer network deployed for applications such as digital currency.

Interactive Situation Questions

1. You're working for a company that's just getting started with a database project. Your supervisor wants "the most standard kind of database," so you recommend using [_____] database management software.

2. You are analyzing a company's customer and order information. Because each customer can place multiple orders, you know this is a(n) [_____] -to-many relationship.

3. You are designing a record type that holds customer information. You should use a(n) [_____] data type for the fields that hold information such as telephone numbers and Social Security numbers because although this data looks like numbers, you'll never need to use it to perform mathematical calculations.

4. You are creating a movie review database, and one field stores the "star rating" that a popular reviewer gave each movie. Movies are rated from one to four stars, so the Stars field is valid only if the number is between 1 and 4. To ensure that nobody enters a value below 1 or above 4, you can use a field [_____] rule to filter the data as it's entered into the table.

5. You want to print a professionally designed list of all the records in your database. To organize and format the list, you use a report generator to create a reusable report [_____].

6. You own a fly-fishing shop and maintain an inventory database that, along with inventory data, stores the names of the wholesalers from which you buy each item. Hot Rod Wholesalers just changed its name to Northern Rod and Reel, so you need to update your database. The best way to accomplish this task would be to perform a(n) [_____] update that changes every instance of "Hot Rod Wholesalers" to "Northern Rod and Reel."

7. You are designing the database structure for a mail-order catalog company. You recognize that a many-to-many relationship exists between an order and the items listed on the order. This clue indicates that you should separate the data into two [_____] : one called Orders and the other called Order Details.

8. You've retrieved some documents from a database, and you notice that they contain tags such as <editor>Ella Ellison</editor> and <born>1960/05/26</born>. You surmise that this is a document-oriented database in which each document has been marked up using [_____].

9. Imagine that you just started working for a political campaign. The campaign manager obtained a database with 190 million voter records, which are now stored on one of the campaign's laptops. The campaign manager has heard all about big data. Should he use NoSQL or SQL to pull records for local voters from the dataset? [_____]

Lab: SQL

Google makes it too easy. Although Google queries search an amazing amount of data, Google's free-form query capability does not convey what it is like to query a relational database with a tool such as SQL. To get a more accurate idea about how business, ecommerce, and political databases work behind the scenes, you can experiment with SQL queries using a sample database.

Requirements:

For this lab, you'll need a computer with Internet access. Please use Google Chrome or Safari as your browser. The instructions are generalized; they provide helpful guidelines but not specific steps.

Assignment:

1 Connect to the W3Schools SQL Tryit Editor.

Open a browser, connect to *www.w3schools.com/sql,* and then click the button labeled "Try it yourself."

Click the Restore Database button, and then click OK when the small dialog box appears.

You should now see a list of database tables, such as Customers, Categories, and Employees, as shown below:

Tablename	Records
Customers	91
Categories	8
Employees	10
OrderDetails	518
Orders	196
Products	77
Shippers	3
Suppliers	29

2 Record the structure for the Customers, Orders, OrderDetails, and Products tables.

To do so, open a blank word processing document and name it *[Your Name] Module 10 Lab.*

Begin by selecting the Customers table. Highlight the field names at the top of the table, as shown at right. Copy the fields (use Ctrl-C for PCs, Command-C for Macs). Paste the field names into your word processor (use Ctrl-V for PCs, Command-V for Macs). Do the same with the Orders, OrderDetails, and Products tables.

3 List all the customers in Germany.

To display the Customers table, click the Customers link.

The window at the top of the screen shows the SQL for displaying all the customers:

SELECT * FROM [Customers].

Modify this SQL statement so that it reads:

SELECT * FROM [Customers] WHERE Country = 'Germany'

Click the Run SQL button to see the results. If you receive an error message, check your spelling and punctuation, and then run the query again.

4 Use SQL to find and record in your lab document how many records match each of the following queries:

How many customers are in London?

How many orders did customer 69 place?

What is the PRICE of Tofu? (Hint: Replace the * with Price in the SQL query.)

How many UNITS of Pavlova are in stock?

Number of Records: 92

CustomerID	CustomerName	ContactName	Address	City	PostalCode	Country
1	Alfreds Futterkiste	Maria Anders	Obere Str. 57	Berlin	12209	Germany
2	Ana Trujillo Emparedados y helados	Ana Trujillo	Avda. de la Constitución 2222	México D.F.	05021	Mexico
3	Antonio Moreno Taquería	Antonio Moreno	Mataderos 2312	México D.F.	05023	Mexico

5 Let SQL do the counting.

Suppose you want to know how many orders contained line items with quantities of 20 or more. Enter the following SQL, all on one line:

SELECT * FROM [OrderDetails] WHERE Quantity >=20

Scrolling down, you see there are many matches to this query. SQL can count these records for you when you enter the following, all on one line:

SELECT count(quantity) FROM [OrderDetails] WHERE Quantity >=20

Using this basic type of query, find out how many products were ordered in quantities fewer than 5.

Copy your query and paste it into your lab document.

6 Join two tables.

You may have noticed that when you counted the products that were ordered in large and small quantities, you only had access to the product numbers. The OrderDetails table does not contain any product names.

To see the names of products that have been ordered, you have to join the OrderDetails table and the Products table.

Remember the dot notation? OrderDetails.ProductID and Products.ProductID are the fields that will create the join.

Enter this SQL query all on one line:

SELECT ProductName, Quantity FROM Products JOIN OrderDetails on OrderDetails.ProductID = Products. ProductID WHERE Quantity <5

Can you modify the SQL so that the results also display the price of each item?

Copy all the records shown as results and paste them into your lab document.

7 Try another join.

Take a look at the Orders table. It contains five fields: OrderID, CustomerID, EmployeeID, OrderDate, and ShipperID. You can see when the order was placed, but the table does not contain the name of the customer.

Can you create a join that displays the OrderID, CustomerID, CustomerName, and OrderDate?

(Hint: You have to SELECT the four fields listed in the previous paragraph, and you have to join the Orders and Customers tables based on CustomerID.)

Copy your SQL query and the first five records shown as results, and then paste them into your lab document.

8 Use the INSERT command to add your name to the Customers table.

This is a long one, so enter it carefully! (Hint: It is all on one line.)

INSERT INTO Customers (CustomerID, CustomerName, Address, City, PostalCode, Country) VALUES ('100', 'Your Name', 'Your Address', 'Your City', 'Your ZIP Code', 'Your Country')

To discover if your name was inserted, select the Customers table and scroll to the end. Your name should be the last record in the table. (Note: Your name will not remain in the database after you exit the Web page.)

Copy the record containing your name plus the three records above it, and then paste them into your lab document.

Tom Gowanlock/Shutterstock.com

9 Add the following item to the Products table:

ProductID	ProductName	SupplierID	CategoryID	Unit	Price
78	Silver Sprinkles	17	3	6 - 1 oz jar	6.79

10 Find all the products that are listed in Category 3.

Join the Categories table with the Products table on the CategoryID field, select only records that are in Category 3, and then list the CategoryName, ProductID, ProductName, Unit, and Price for each item.

The first three results might look something like this (but you will have more than three records!):

CategoryName	ProductID	ProductName	Unit	Price
Confections	16	Pavlova	32 - 500 g boxes	17.45
Confections	19	Teatime Chocolate Biscuits	10 boxes x 12 pieces	9.2
Confections	20	Sir Rodney's Marmalade	30 gift boxes	81

Copy your SQL query and all the records shown as results and then paste them into your word processor.

11 Whew! Now you have some idea about the detailed commands required to query a database using SQL. No wonder executives use dashboards instead of SQL to query databases!

Save your lab document and submit it as a printout, an email attachment, or a Dropbox file according to your instructor's guidelines.

AnjelikaGr/Shutterstock.com

11 Programming

Module Contents

In the film, *Steve Jobs: The Lost Interview,* Apple's co-founder said, "I think everybody in this country should learn how to program a computer—should learn a computer language—because it teaches you how to think." Really?

 Try It!   Apply what you learn.

- Read a simple computer program to understand the task it is designed to accomplish.
- Write a problem statement that expresses the assumptions, known information, and termination condition for a programming project.
- Define the variables and constants for a computer program.
- Locate a text editor on your computer that could be used to write a computer program.
- Collect the necessary programming tools to write apps for an iPhone or Android device.
- Use a compiler or an interpreter in the process of developing a computer program.
- Select a programming language based on its intended use.
- Take an introductory Python tutorial.
- Develop an algorithm for a simple procedural program that includes flow controls for branching and looping.
- Walk through a Python program to determine its output.
- Draw a UML diagram that illustrates classes, subclasses, attributes, methods, and inheritance.
- Identify objects within an object-oriented program.
- Write simple facts using the Prolog programming language.
- Formulate Prolog queries that use variables.
- Identify rules within a Prolog program.
- Create a decision table to specify the conditions and actions that would be the basis for rules in a Prolog program.

● **Pre-Check**   Gauge your level of expertise. The answers are in the module.

2

SDKs for mobile development:

_____

_____

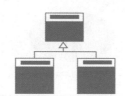

A(n) _____ diagram

What is the level of abstraction for assembly language?

LOW

HIGH

MOV eax 5h

MOV is a(n) _____ code.

A flowchart is used to visually depict a(n) _____ .

PIRNT

A(n) _____ error

shapeof(pizza,round).

Which programming language?

_____

getArea()

An OO _____

In OO programs, _____ creates a "black box."

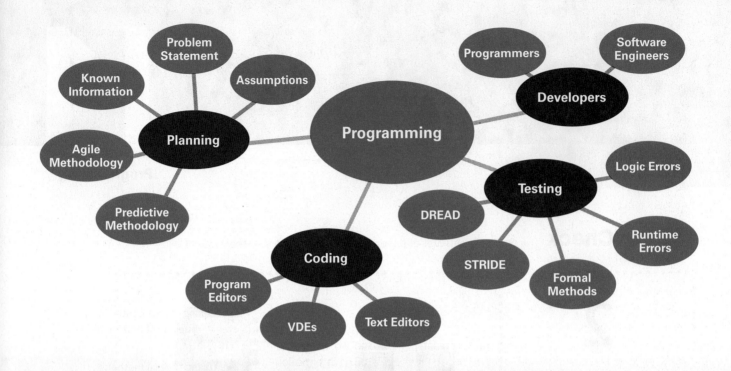

Objectives

▶ Describe the difference between programming and software engineering.

▶ List the three core elements of a problem statement and provide an example of each.

▶ Supply at least three examples of projects that would be best tackled using predictive methodology and three projects best tackled using agile methodology.

▶ Identify keywords and parameters in program statements.

▶ Describe the difference between constants and variables.

▶ Provide an example of how a constant and a variable would be used in a program.

▶ Describe three types of tools that can be used for composing computer programs.

▶ List three types of errors that might be encountered during program testing.

▶ Explain the significance of formal methods.

▶ Explain the purpose of STRIDE and DREAD.

▶ Explain the significance of defensive programming.

Hello World!
Writing a short program that displays "Hello World!" on the screen is typically how students are introduced to programming. This module starts differently. You'll be taking a high-level, executive overview of the programming process that is applicable to any programming language and to software that runs on a variety of devices, including smartphones, personal computers, and enterprise information systems.

Terminology

computer programming	agile methodology	program editor	debugging
software engineering	sprint	VDE	remarks
application programmers	program statement	storyboard	formal methods
systems programmers	keyword	control	threat modeling
problem statement	parameters	properties	defensive programming
assumption	variable	runtime error	
known information	constant	logic error	
predictive methodology	syntax	syntax error	

Programming Basics

Smartphone apps. Productivity software. Games. All the goodies on digital devices are powered by computer programs. What is programming all about? Section A introduces you to the programmer's world.

▶ **What's the scope of computer programming?** Computer programming encompasses a broad set of activities that include planning, writing, testing, and documenting. Most computer programmers participate to some extent in all of these phases of program development, but they focus on writing statements that computers follow to perform tasks.

A related activity, **software engineering**, is a development process that uses mathematical, engineering, and management techniques to reduce the cost and complexity of a computer program while increasing its reliability and modifiability. Software engineering can be characterized as more formalized and rigorous than computer programming. It is used on large software projects where cost overruns and software errors might have disastrous consequences.

Some software engineering activities overlap with the systems analysis and design activities presented in Module 9. To distinguish between the two, remember that systems analysis and design encompasses all aspects of an information system, including hardware, software, people, and procedures. In contrast, software engineering tends to focus on software development.

▶ **What does a computer program look like?** As you learned in earlier modules, a computer program is a set of step-by-step instructions that tell a computer how to carry out a task. A typical program contains familiar English-like words. Figure 11-1 illustrates a short program that converts inches into centimeters.

11

Figure 11-1: A program written using the Python programming language

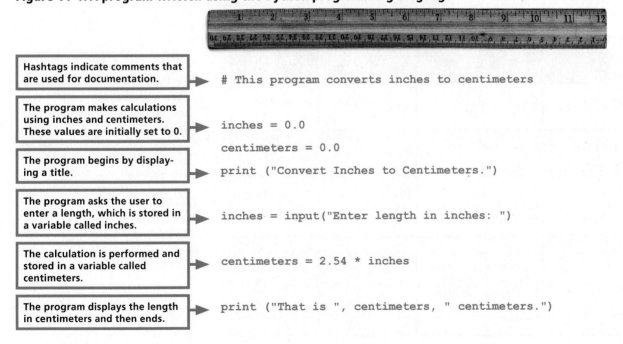

Hashtags indicate comments that are used for documentation.
```
# This program converts inches to centimeters
```

The program makes calculations using inches and centimeters. These values are initially set to 0.
```
inches = 0.0

centimeters = 0.0
```

The program begins by displaying a title.
```
print ("Convert Inches to Centimeters.")
```

The program asks the user to enter a length, which is stored in a variable called inches.
```
inches = input("Enter length in inches: ")
```

The calculation is performed and stored in a variable called centimeters.
```
centimeters = 2.54 * inches
```

The program displays the length in centimeters and then ends.
```
print ("That is ", centimeters, " centimeters.")
```

▶ **How big is a typical computer program?** Compared to commercial application software, the programs that you'll work with in this module are relatively tiny. The program for your computer's operating system consists of more than 50 million instructions. Even "small" iPhone apps can exceed 40,000 instructions. Research has shown that, on average, one person can write, test, and document only 20 instructions per day. It is not surprising, then, that most commercial programs are written by programming teams and take many months or years to complete.

▶ **Are there different types of programmers?** Programmers typically specialize in either application programming or system development.

Application programmers create productivity applications such as Microsoft Office, as well as enterprise applications such as CRM and ERP. They also create apps for mobile phones and develop Web applications that run in the cloud.

Systems programmers specialize in developing system software such as operating systems, device drivers, security modules, and communications software. Some systems programmers work on a team to create new system software. Other systems programmers may be responsible for ensuring that mainframes and servers perform at peak efficiency by adjusting various operating system and communication settings and writing small custom utilities to monitor performance.

▶ **How much time does it take to develop an iPhone or Android app?** Apps vary in complexity from simple MVP apps to more full-featured apps that interact with enterprise systems. As you might expect, complex apps tend to take longer to develop than simple apps. They are also more expensive.

The simplest mobile app generally requires several weeks of full-time programming effort. More complex apps may take a programming team more than a year to complete at a cost that could exceed $250,000. Figure 11-2 breaks down development times based on complexity.

Figure 11-2: Mobile app development time and cost

Complexity	Features	Cost	Time to Completion
Simple	Local app with no server-side interaction	$1,000–$30,000	2–4 weeks
Medium	Static data and server-side interaction	$8,000–$50,000	4–8 weeks
Complex	Dynamic data, server-side interaction, and social media integration	$9,000–$60,000	8–12 weeks
Enterprise	All the characteristics of a complex app, plus integration with CRM, ecommerce, and other enterprise information systems	$50,000–$500,000	12–52 weeks

Try It!

You can get an estimate of the time and cost to build an app by connecting to an app development cost calculator such as Cleveroad, Buildfire, or OOZOO.

Terminology

In the context of mobile apps, *MVP* stands for *minimum viable product*. These apps contain the basic features an app needs to perform its task. MVPs are essentially prototypes that are released as a first iteration of an app.

QuickCheck

In Figure 11-2, which category best describes the complexity of the Facebook app on your mobile phone?

a. Simple

b. Medium

c. Complex

d. Enterprise

Program Planning

Suppose a group of market analysts—or even a group of hungry students—wants to determine which pizza restaurants offer the best deals. You and a small group of friends decide to create a free app that helps users find the best deal from local pizzerias. Eventually, your team hopes to monetize the app by selling ads to restaurant owners. Initially, however, you plan to create a simple MVP app that can run on iPhones.

▶ How does a programmer plan a computer program? Problems you might try to solve using a computer often begin as questions—for example, "Which pizza place has the best deal?" But such questions might not be stated in a way that helps devise a method for a computer to arrive at an answer.

A question such as "Which pizza place has the best deal?" is vague. It does not specify what information is available or how to determine the best deal. What do you know about the pizzas? Prices? Toppings? Sizes? What does "best deal" mean? Is it the cheapest pizza? Is it the pizza that gives you the most toppings for the dollar? Is it the biggest pizza you can get for the $24.63 that you and your friends managed to scrape together?

The process of planning a computer program begins with a problem statement that clearly defines the program's purpose.

▶ What is a problem statement? In the context of programming, a **problem statement** defines certain elements that must be manipulated to achieve a result or goal. A good problem statement for a computer program has three characteristics:

- It specifies any assumptions that define the scope of the problem.
- It clearly specifies the known information.
- It specifies when the problem has been solved.

Study Figure 11-3 and see if you can formulate a problem statement that is better than the initial vague question "Which pizza place has the best deal?"

Figure 11-3: Can you formulate a problem statement for the "best deal"?

◗ **What is an assumption?** In a problem statement, an **assumption** is something you accept as true in order to proceed with program planning. Assumptions can be used to define the scope of a problem so that it does not become too complex. Programmers sometimes start with a set of assumptions that simplify a problem. After a simplified version of the problem is solved, subsequent versions can tackle more complex aspects of the problem. For example, with the pizza problem, you can limit its complexity by making the assumptions listed in Figure 11-4.

Figure 11-4: Assumptions for the pizza program

The program will compare two pizzas at a time. A later version of the program might allow users to compare any number of pizzas.

Some pizzas are round and others are square, but none of the pizzas are rectangular. This assumption simplifies the problem because you need to deal only with the size of a pizza, rather than the length and width of a pizza. Eventually, you can modify this aspect of the program to deal with rectangular pizzas.

Red Hot Deal

The pizzas have the same toppings, so the program will not have to deal with comparing one pizza with five meat toppings to a mushroom and cheese pizza with only two toppings.

The pizza with the lowest cost per square inch is the best buy.

Mike Flippo/
Shutterstock.com

◗ **How does known information apply to a problem statement?** The **known information** in a problem statement is the information that is supplied to the computer to help it solve a problem. For the pizza problem, the known information includes the prices, shapes, and sizes of pizzas from two pizzerias.

The known information is often included in the problem statement as *givens*. For example, a problem statement might include the phrase, "given the prices, shapes, and sizes of two pizzas...."

◗ **How can a problem statement specify when a problem is solved?** After identifying the known information, a programmer must specify how to determine when the problem has been solved. Usually this step means specifying the output that is expected. You cannot specify the actual solution in the problem statement. You won't know, for example, whether VanGo's Pizzeria or The Venice has the best deal before you run the program, but you can specify that the computer should output which pizza is the best deal.

Suppose you assume that the best deal is the pizza with the lowest price per square inch. For example, a pizza that costs 5¢ per square inch is a better deal than a pizza that costs 7¢ per square inch. The problem is solved, therefore, when the computer has calculated the price per square inch for both pizzas, compared the prices, and printed a message indicating which one has the lower price per square inch.

You could write this part of the problem statement as "The computer will calculate each pizza's price per square inch, compare the prices, and then print a message indicating which pizza has the lower price per square inch."

▶ **What's the problem statement for the pizza program?** You can incorporate your assumptions, known information, and expected output into a problem statement, such as the following:

> Assuming that there are two pizzas to compare, that both pizzas contain the same toppings, and that the pizzas could be round or square, and given the prices, shapes, and sizes of the two pizzas, the computer will print a message indicating which pizza has the lower price per square inch.

▶ **Does the problem statement provide sufficient planning to begin writing a program?** Formulating a problem statement provides a minimal amount of planning, which is sufficient for only the simplest programs. A typical commercial application or a non-MVP app requires far more extensive planning, which includes detailed program outlines, job assignments, and schedules. Several software development methodologies exist to help programmers plan, execute, and test software. Methodologies can be classified as predictive or agile.

Predictive methodology. A **predictive methodology** requires extensive planning and documentation up front. It is the type of methodology used to construct buildings and assemble cars—tasks that are well defined and predictable. Predictive methodologies work well for software development projects that are well defined and can be patterned after other similar projects.

Predictive methodologies tend to be used for large software development projects involving more than ten developers, geographically dispersed development teams, and life-critical applications. Creating the software for air-traffic control or a point-of-sale system might be successfully approached by using predictive methodology.

Agile methodology. Many software development projects are unique, however, and are not well defined. In contrast to predictive methodologies, an **agile methodology** focuses on flexible development and specifications that evolve as a project progresses. Agile methods seem best for projects with a small core of developers working at a single location.

In an agile-driven project, for example, programmers might produce a subset of the entire project, show it to users, and then plan the next phase of development based on the feedback received. Unlike predictive methodologies, agile development expects and welcomes feature creep, which pushes developers to produce a final product that better meets user needs.

Within the agile development framework, the process of developing each iteration of a program is called a **sprint**. Each sprint produces a fully functional and tested program. Subsequent sprints produce enhanced versions based on user feedback that may modify features or even expand the project's scope.

The pizza project is a small app being built by a small team, so it lends itself well to agile methodology. The first sprint as defined by the problem statement is to build an MVP app that asks for pizza prices, sizes, and shapes, and then calculates which pizza has the lowest price per square inch.

11

QuickCheck

Suppose you are part of a small team developing a mobile app to guide visitors through a museum. Your team can use a(n) _____ methodology and a series of sprints.

a. predictive

b. SDLC

c. agile

d. enterprise

Writing Programs

The cool thing about computer programming is that the instructions you supply to the computer are followed with precision and without question or complaint. Your program is a small universe over which you have complete control. You begin with a clean slate that is ready and waiting for your commands.

▶ **How do I create a computer program?** The core of a computer program is a sequence of instructions. These instructions are sometimes referred to as program statements. A **program statement** (sometimes simply called a statement) is the smallest unit of a computer program that directs a computer to carry out an action or operation.

Just as an English sentence is constructed from various words and punctuation marks that follow a set of grammar rules, a program statement consists of keywords and parameters that are held together by a set of rules.

For example, suppose you would like the pizza program to conclude with a message such as "Pizza at VanGo's Pizzeria is the best deal!" The statement to display that message looks like this when written in the Python programming language:

```
print ("Pizza at ", restaurant, " is the best deal!")
```

▶ **What keywords do I need to know?** A **keyword**, or command, is a word with a predefined meaning. Keywords differ depending on the programming language. As with human languages, however, there is a basic vocabulary that covers most necessary tasks. Figure 11-5 lists some keywords used in the Python programming language.

Figure 11-5: Keywords for the Python programming language

input	Collect information from the program's users.
print	Display information on the screen.
while	Begin a series of commands that will be repeated in a loop.
break	Terminate a loop.
if	Execute one or more statements only if a specified condition is true.
else	Add more options to extend the If command.
def	Define a series of statements that become a unit called a function.
return	Transfer data from a function to some other part of the program.
class	Define an object as a set of attributes and methods.

QuickCheck

Which Python keyword seems best for collecting the shape of a pizza from a user?

a. input

b. while

c. if

d. class

▶ **What comes after the keyword in a program statement?** Keywords can be combined with specific **parameters**, which provide more details about the actions the computer is supposed to carry out. These parameters include variables and constants.

▶ **How do programmers use variables?** Factors such as price, shape, and size are often treated as variables in computer programs. A **variable** represents a value that can change. For example, the price of a pizza can vary or change depending on the pizza shop from which it is purchased, so pizzaPrice could become a variable in the pizza program.

In contrast, a **constant** is a factor that remains the same throughout a program. For example, the mathematical constant *pi* always has a value of 3.142.

Computer programmers think of variables and constants as named memory locations, which are equivalent to empty boxes where data can be temporarily stored while being manipulated by a computer program (Figure 11-6).

11

Figure 11-6: The values for variables are stored in memory

pizzaShape	pizzaSize	pizzaPrice
round	**12**	**10.00**
pizzaArea	squareInchPrice	pizzeria
113.112	**.088**	**VanGos**

▶ **What is the significance of syntax?** Programming requires attention to details, such as the sequence of keywords and the placement of punctuation. Whereas humans can usually understand statements that are somewhat vague, computer languages are not flexible—every period, colon, semicolon, and space have to be accounted for.

The set of rules that specify the sequence of keywords, parameters, and punctuation in a program statement is referred to as **syntax**. Syntax is similar to the grammar of human languages. Figure 11-7 illustrates some syntax rules for Python.

Figure 11-7: Syntax rules govern punctuation and indentation

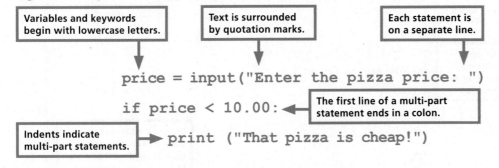

▶ **What can I use to compose computer programs?** The process of composing a computer program is sometimes called coding. You may be able to use a text editor, program editor, or graphical user interface to code computer programs. Your choice depends on your programming language and the distribution platform. Tools for developing Android apps differ from those used to develop apps for the iPhone. Yet another set of programming tools might be required for desktop and laptop computers. You'll explore programming languages and tools in more depth later in this module, but take a look at the three basic options for writing programs: text editors, program editors, and visual development environments.

▶ **What is a text editor?** A text editor is any word processor that can be used for basic text editing tasks, such as writing email, creating documents, and writing computer programs. Notepad, the accessory program supplied with Microsoft Windows, is one of the most popular text editors used for programming PCs. Text editors such as TextWrangler and TextEdit are popular on Macs.

When using a text editor to write a computer program, you simply type in each program statement. The statements are stored in a file, which can be opened and modified using the usual editing keys.

▶ **What is a program editor?** A **program editor** is a type of text editor specially designed for writing computer programs. These editors are available from several commercial and freeware sources. Features vary but can include helpful programming aids, such as keyword colorizing, word completion, keyboard macros, and search/replace. Figure 11-8 illustrates the difference between a text editor and a program editor.

Terminology

Programmers can use a text editor, but not a word processor, to write program statements. ASCII files produced with a text editor contain no embedded tags for centering, bold, and other formatting attributes, which are not allowed in program statements.

Try It!

Check your computer for a text editor, such as Notepad or TextEdit. Do you have software that could be used to write a program?

Figure 11-8: Text editors and program editors

A text editor such as Notepad allows programmers to enter program statements using a familiar word processing interface.

In a program editor, text colors help programmers easily recognize commands, comments, and variables.

Program editors also keep track of variable names, objects, and methods, so programmers can easily locate them.

▶ **What is a VDE?** A **VDE** (visual development environment) provides programmers with tools to build substantial sections of a program by pointing and clicking rather than typing each statement. VDEs for mobile devices are based on a **storyboard** that a programmer manipulates to design the user interface for an app.

Using tools provided by the VDE, a programmer can add objects, such as controls and graphics, to the storyboard. In the context of a VDE, a **control** is a screen-based object whose behavior can be defined by a programmer. Frequently used controls include labels, menus, toolbars, list boxes, text boxes, option buttons, check boxes, and graphical boxes.

A control can be customized by specifying values for a set of built-in **properties**. For example, a button control can be customized for the pizza program by selecting values for properties such as shape, color, font, and title (Figure 11-9).

11

Figure 11-9: Using the Xcode VDE to build an iPhone app

The Navigator Area lists the files used in the project. Currently, an element called Main.storyboard is selected.

The Main.storyboard lists controls and graphics that appear in the user interface.

A storyboard is used to lay out the controls and graphics that will appear on the screen when the app runs.

The Attributes Inspector lists properties for the selected element. To change the title of the Calculate button, enter the new title here.

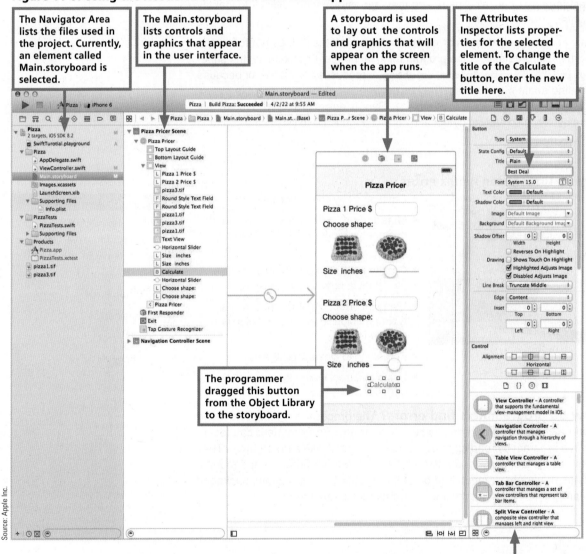

The programmer dragged this button from the Object Library to the storyboard.

The Object Library lists elements that can be added to the user interface.

Program Testing and Documentation

A computer program must be tested to ensure that it works correctly. Testing often consists of running the program and entering test data to see whether it produces the correct results. If testing does not produce the expected results, the program contains an error, sometimes called a bug. This error must be corrected, and then the program can be tested again and again until it runs error free.

▶ **What can cause program errors?** Programs that don't work correctly might crash, run forever, or provide inaccurate results. When a program doesn't work correctly, it is usually the result of a runtime, logic, or syntax error.

Runtime errors. A runtime error occurs as a program runs. Some runtime errors result from statements that the computer can't execute. The statement `discountPrice = regularPrice/0` produces a runtime error because dividing by 0 is a mathematically impossible operation that the computer cannot perform.

Logic errors. A logic error is a type of runtime error in the logic or design of a program, such as using the wrong formula to calculate the area of a round pizza. Logic errors can be caused by an inadequate definition of the problem or an incorrect formula for a calculation, and they are usually more difficult to identify than syntax errors.

Syntax errors. A syntax error occurs when a statement does not follow the syntax rules, or grammar, of the programming language. For example, the statement `print "A " price "pizza is cheap."` produces a syntax error because it is missing some punctuation. The correct version of the statement is `print ("A ", price, " pizza is cheap.")`. Syntax errors are easy to make, but they are usually also easy to detect and correct. Figure 11-10 lists some common syntax errors.

Figure 11-10: Common syntax errors

BalanceFormCreative/Shutterstock.com

- Omitting a keyword, such as ELSE
- Misspelling a keyword, such as mistakenly typing PIRNT instead of PRINT
- Omitting required punctuation, such as a period, comma, or bracket
- Using incorrect punctuation, such as typing a colon where a semicolon is required
- Forgetting to close parentheses
- Using incorrect indentation

▶ **How do programmers find errors?** The process of finding and fixing errors in a computer program is called debugging. Programmers can locate errors in a program by reading through each line, much like a proofreader. They can also use a tool called a debugger to step through a program and monitor the status of variables, input, and output. A debugger is sometimes packaged with a programming language or can be obtained as an add-on.

Do computer programs contain any special documentation? Programmers insert **remarks** (or comments) into programs to document and annotate their work. Remarks are identified by language-specific symbols, such as # in Python, or keywords, such as REM in BASIC.

Remarks make it easier for members of a programming team to read through a program and understand it. They are also helpful for programmers who want to understand how a program works before modifying it. For example, suppose you are assigned to make some modifications to a 50,000-line program that calculates income tax. Your task would be simplified if the original programmer included remarks that identify the purpose of each section of the program and explain the basis for any formulas used to perform tax calculations.

A well-documented program contains initial remarks that explain its purpose and additional remarks in any sections of a program where the purpose of a statement is not immediately clear. For example, in the pizza program, the purpose of the expression `3.142 * (radius * radius)` might not be immediately obvious. Therefore, it would be helpful to have a remark preceding the expression, as shown in Figure 11-11.

Figure 11-11: Remarks are used to document a program

```
# For a round pizza, calculate area using pi (3.142)
# multiplied by size1 / 2 **2, which is the radius
# squared.
if shape1 == "round":
    squareInches1 = 3.142 * (size1 / 2) **2
squareInchPrice1 = price1 / squareInches1
```

When is a program ready for release? Creating a program that runs without error is not the final goal of the software development process. Programs should also meet performance, usability, and security standards.

Performance. Users don't like to wait for a program to load. They don't like to pause while a program accesses Web-based resources. The attention span of users is about two seconds, which means that software has to respond to commands and input within that time span. Bottlenecks on a local device, on computer networks, or in the cloud can reduce response times to unacceptable levels, especially within enterprise information systems. To make sure performance is acceptable, programmers may need to carry out real-world tests or use simulation utilities that model thousands of virtual users, multiple devices, and variable network conditions.

Usability. Programs should be easy to learn and use. The process of learning how to use a program can be simplified if buttons and input areas are clearly labeled and similar to well-known standards. Using colors and graphics to make the program visually attractive can also improve usability and marketability. Usability is also enhanced when a program is efficient; users should be able to perform tasks in as few steps as possible.

Security. Software security begins when program specifications are formulated. Techniques such as formal methods, threat modeling, and defensive programming help programmers remain aware of security throughout the software development life cycle.

QuickCheck

Suppose you're looking at a Python program and you see # symbols. What does that tell you?

a. The text that follows the symbol is a remark that documents the program.

b. The program was developed using an SDK or an IDE.

c. The program was written as a sprint.

d. There is a syntax error in the program that was found by a debugger.

11

Terminology

The double equals signs in the if statement are not a mistake. They mean "check if the values are equal." In contrast, a single equals sign like the one in the squareInchPrice1 line means to change the value of the variable to make it equal.

QuickCheck

What is the attention span of a typical app user in the context of response time?

a. One minute

b. 15 seconds

c. Two seconds

d. Ten minutes

▶ What are formal methods? **Formal methods** help programmers apply rigorous logical and mathematical models to software design, composition, testing, and verification. According to security experts, most software security problems can be traced back to defects that programmers unintentionally introduce in software during design and development. The general nature of the defects that create security holes is widely known. One way to avoid these defects is to use formal methods.

Organizations that use formal methods tend to produce more secure software. Formal methods, however, add to the cost and time of software development, so they tend to be used primarily for systems, such as air-traffic control and nuclear reactor monitoring, where security and safety are crucial.

▶ What is threat modeling? **Threat modeling** (also called risk analysis) is a technique that can be used to identify potential vulnerabilities by listing the key assets of an application, categorizing the threats to each asset, ranking the threats, and developing threat mitigation strategies that can be implemented during programming. Threats can be categorized using a model such as STRIDE, as described in Figure 11-12.

Figure 11-12: Categorizing threats

 Spoofing: Pretending to be someone else

 Tampering: Changing, adding, or deleting data

 Repudiation: Covering tracks to make attacks difficult to trace

 Information disclosure: Gaining unauthorized access to information

 Denial of service: Making a system unavailable to legitimate users

 Elevation of privilege: Modifying user rights to gain access to data

Some threats are more likely to occur than others, and some threats have the potential to cause more damage than others. As part of the threat modeling process, software designers can rank threats using the DREAD categories in Figure 11-13.

Figure 11-13: Assessing threat severity

 Damage: How much damage can a particular attack cause?

 Reproduce: Is this attack easy to reproduce?

 Exploit: How much skill is needed to launch the attack?

 Affected: How many users would be affected by an attack?

 Discovered: How likely is it that this attack would be discovered?

▶ What is defensive programming? Defensive programming (also referred to as secure programming) is an approach to software development in which programmers anticipate what might go wrong as their programs run and take steps to smoothly handle those situations. It is analogous to defensive driving, which requires drivers to anticipate dangerous situations arising from adverse conditions or the mistakes of other drivers.

Defensive programmers anticipate ways in which their programs could be compromised by legitimate users, intruders, other applications, the operating system, or third-party software. Techniques associated with defensive programming include:

- **Walkthroughs.** Open source software goes through extensive public scrutiny that can identify security holes, but proprietary software can also benefit from a walkthrough with other in-house programmers.

- **Simplification.** Complex programs are more difficult to debug than simpler ones. Simplifying complex sections can sometimes reduce a program's vulnerability to attacks.

- **Filtering input.** It is dangerous to assume that users will enter valid input. Attackers have become experts at concocting input that causes buffer overflows and runs rogue HTML scripts. Programmers should use a tight set of filters on all input fields.

▶ Bottom line: Is programming really difficult? Programming is an activity that requires attention to detail and logical thinking. But it also requires a good dose of creativity and thinking outside of the box.

As you have discovered in this section, a handful of concepts for planning programs, entering program statements, testing programs, and securing them from threats apply to the programming process regardless of the programming language or the device on which the program will run. Whether creating a simple mobile app or tying together modules for a complex information system, these are the underlying concepts of the programmer's world.

11

QuickQuiz   Section A

1. _____ programmers specialize in developing software used for productivity and entertainment.

2. A(n) _____ methodology focuses on flexible program development and specifications that evolve as a project progresses.

3. Program elements such as pizzaSize and price are examples of _____ because their values can change.

4. A program _____ is the smallest unit of a computer program that directs a computer to carry out an action or operation.

5. _____ methods are mathematically based techniques for specifying and verifying that a computer program works correctly.

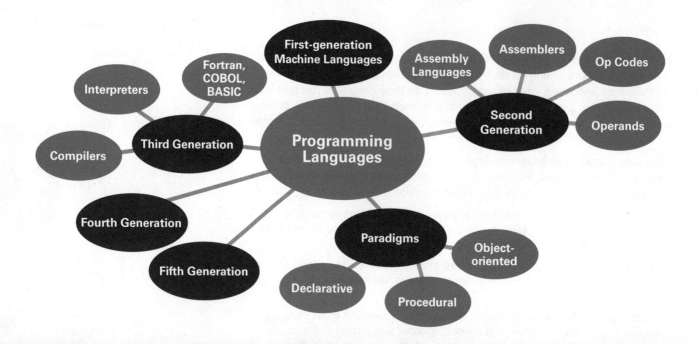

Objectives

▶ Explain how the concept of abstraction applies to programming languages.

▶ Provide two examples of low-level languages and five examples of high-level languages.

▶ Explain how assemblers are related to compilers.

▶ Describe the difference between compiling a program and using an interpreter.

▶ Describe three popular programming paradigms.

▶ List at least three legacy programming languages.

▶ List two programming languages used to program mobile apps.

▶ List three programming languages that are popular for developing dynamic Web sites.

▶ Explain how programmers use IDEs, SDKs, and APIs.

Human languages originated in the distant past, and linguists have only scant evidence of their roots and early evolution. In contrast, programming languages emerged fewer than 100 years ago, and their evolution is well documented. How did these essential programming tools evolve? Do they have similarities to human languages? Section B delves into these questions.

Terminology

abstraction	op code	fifth-generation	programming paradigm
low-level language	operand	languages	multiparadigm languages
high-level language	assembler	source code	SDK
first-generation	third-generation	compiler	IDE
languages	languages	object code	API
second-generation	fourth-generation	interpreter	
languages	languages	scripting languages	
assembly language			

Language Evolution

Programming languages may seem detailed and complex. Programs often appear to be a messy jumble of brackets, parentheses, and semicolons interspersed with unintelligible formulas and commands such as System.out.println. The languages that programmers use today evolved through several generations of increasing sophistication. Taking time to understand this evolution will help clear up some basic programming concepts that may otherwise seem mysterious.

▶ Why are some programming languages more sophisticated than others? *Sophistication* is not a technical term. Computer scientists instead use the term *abstraction*, which in a broad sense removes detail and theoretically reduces complexity. When applied to programming languages, **abstraction** inserts a buffer between programmers and the chip-level details of instruction sets and binary data representation.

As an analogy, think about driving a car with a manual transmission that requires you to shift gears using a clutch and a stick shift. Compare that to a car with an automatic transmission that does not require the driver to deal with shifting gears. The car with an automatic transmission has a higher level of abstraction because the driver does not need to be concerned with the mechanics and gears of the car's hardware.

For programming languages, abstraction automates hardware-level details, such as how to move data from memory to the processor or how to determine which button a user selects on a touchscreen. Programming languages evolved from low-level languages to languages with increasingly higher levels of abstraction (Figure 11-14).

Figure 11-14: High-level languages simplify using abstraction

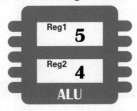

Programmers using low-level languages have to deal with hardware-level tasks. The following low-level statements load values into registers and then add them:

MOV REG1, 5

MOV REG2, 4

ADD REG1, REG2

Programmers using high-level languages are buffered from the hardware details by levels of abstraction. Loading two values and adding them requires only one high-level statement.

▶ What is a low-level language? A **low-level language** has a low level of abstraction because it includes commands specific to a particular CPU or microprocessor family. Low-level languages include machine languages and assembly languages. Programmers rarely use low-level languages today. The syntax is excruciatingly detailed and symbolic, which makes it difficult to write, debug, and maintain.

▶ What is a high-level language? A high-level language uses command words and grammar based on human languages to provide a level of abstraction that hides the underlying low-level assembly or machine language. High-level languages are used to develop applications, games, and most other software.

High-level languages, such as BASIC, Python, Java, Prolog, and C++, make the programming process easier by replacing unintelligible strings of 1s and 0s or cryptic assembly commands with understandable commands, such as PRINT and WRITE. Using a high-level language simplifies the programming process and produces programs that are easier to debug and maintain than programs written in low-level languages.

▶ How did programming evolve from low-level to high-level languages? The first computers were programmed without programming languages. Technicians rewired a computer's circuitry to prepare it for various processing tasks. Programming languages were very primitive at first, but they evolved through many generations into the computer languages of today.

▶ What was the first generation of programming languages? Initially, programmers used machine languages for programming computers, and these languages are sometimes referred to as first-generation languages. In Module 2, you learned that a machine language consists of a set of commands, represented as a series of 1s and 0s, corresponding to the instruction set that is hard-wired into the circuitry of a microprocessor.

Machine language programming is prone to errors. A zero out of place can cause a fatal error that is difficult to debug. Programmers quickly realized that alternative programming tools were essential, which led to the development of second-generation languages.

▶ What is a second-generation language? Second-generation languages added a level of abstraction to machine languages by substituting abbreviated command words for the strings of 1s and 0s used in machine languages. Languages in this new generation were called assembly languages.

Like a machine language, an assembly language is classified as a low-level language because it is machine specific—each assembly language command corresponds on a one-to-one basis to a machine language instruction.

An assembly language instruction has two parts: the op code and the operands. An op code, which is short for *operation code*, is a command word that specifies an operation such as add, compare, or jump. The operand for an instruction specifies the data, or the address of the data, for the operation. As you look at the parts of an assembly language statement in Figure 11-15, consider how tedious it would be to write a program consisting of thousands of these concise, but cryptic, op codes and operands.

QuickCheck

Assembly language is classified as _____.

a. a machine language

b. a low-level language

c. a third-generation language

d. a VDE

Figure 11-15: Assembly language statement to place 5 in register eax

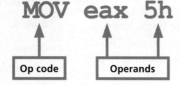

11

▶ **Can a processor directly execute assembly language statements?** Microprocessors only understand machine language, so there has to be some way to convert assembly language statements into 1s and 0s. That task is performed by a utility program called an assembler. An **assembler** typically reads a program written in an assembly language, translates the program into machine language, and then submits the machine language program to the processor for execution.

Programs written in assembly languages cannot run until they are translated. This extra step is the cost of abstraction. But as computer capacity and speed increased, this cost became less and less significant. In a moment you'll discover how assemblers paved the way for compilers and interpreters that emerged with third-generation programming languages.

▶ **What is a third-generation language?** When high-level languages were originally conceived in the 1950s, they were dubbed **third-generation languages** because they seemed to be a major improvement over machine and assembly languages. Third-generation languages used easy-to-remember command words, such as PRINT and INPUT, to take the place of several lines of assembly language op codes or lengthy strings of machine language 0s and 1s.

Third-generation languages, such as COBOL and Fortran, were used extensively for business and scientific applications. Pascal and BASIC were popular teaching languages. C and C++ remain popular today for system and application software development—for example, to develop Microsoft Windows and Linux. Recently developed third-generation languages are important for modern apps. Objective-C and Swift are programming languages used to develop iPhone and iPad apps. Java is used for Android apps.

An important characteristic of third-generation programming languages is that the program can be written with simple tools, such as a text editor, and the program statements can be easily understood by programmers. Read through the program in Figure 11-16. Can you guess what it does?

Figure 11-16: Can you guess what this program does?

```
1   import random
2   min = 1
3   max = 6
4
5   rollAgain = "yes"
6
7   while rollAgain == "yes" or rollAgain == "y":
8       print ("Rolling...")
9       print ("The values are ...")
10      print (random.randint(min,max))
11      print (random.randint(min,max))
12
13      rollAgain = input("Roll again? ")
```

QuickCheck

What does the program in Figure 11-16 do?

a. It compares two pizzas.

b. It calculates the area of a pizza.

c. It counts dinner rolls.

d. It simulates a pair of dice.

▶ What is a fourth-generation language? Many computer scientists believed that third-generation languages would eliminate programming errors. Programmers using third-generation languages still made a variety of errors, however, so computer language development continued to progress.

In 1969, computer scientists began to develop high-level languages, called **fourth-generation languages**, which more closely resembled human languages than did third-generation languages. Fourth-generation languages, such as SQL and RPG, eliminate many of the strict punctuation and grammar rules that complicate third-generation languages.

Today, fourth-generation languages are primarily used for database applications. A single SQL command, such as SORT TABLE Kids on Lastname, can replace many lines of a program written in a third-generation language, as shown in Figure 11-17.

Figure 11-17: Fourth-generation languages have simple syntax

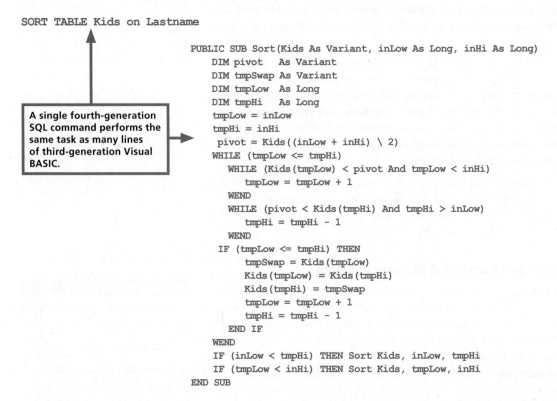

```
SORT TABLE Kids on Lastname

                    PUBLIC SUB Sort(Kids As Variant, inLow As Long, inHi As Long)
                        DIM pivot    As Variant
                        DIM tmpSwap As Variant
                        DIM tmpLow   As Long
                        DIM tmpHi    As Long
                        tmpLow = inLow
                        tmpHi = inHi
                        pivot = Kids((inLow + inHi) \ 2)
                        WHILE (tmpLow <= tmpHi)
                           WHILE (Kids(tmpLow) < pivot And tmpLow < inHi)
                              tmpLow = tmpLow + 1
                           WEND
                           WHILE (pivot < Kids(tmpHi) And tmpHi > inLow)
                              tmpHi = tmpHi - 1
                           WEND
                           IF (tmpLow <= tmpHi) THEN
                              tmpSwap = Kids(tmpLow)
                              Kids(tmpLow) = Kids(tmpHi)
                              Kids(tmpHi) = tmpSwap
                              tmpLow = tmpLow + 1
                              tmpHi = tmpHi - 1
                           END IF
                        WEND
                        IF (inLow < tmpHi) THEN Sort Kids, inLow, tmpHi
                        IF (tmpLow < inHi) THEN Sort Kids, tmpLow, inHi
                    END SUB
```

A single fourth-generation SQL command performs the same task as many lines of third-generation Visual BASIC.

▶ What about fifth-generation languages? In 1982, a group of Japanese researchers began work on a fifth-generation computer project that used Prolog—a computer programming language based on a declarative programming paradigm, which is described in detail in Section E. Prolog and other declarative languages became closely identified with the fifth-generation project and were classified as **fifth-generation languages**.

Some experts disagree with this classification, however, and instead define fifth-generation languages as those that allow programmers to use graphical or visual tools to construct programs rather than typing lines of statements.

QuickCheck

Which generation of programming languages is used to develop apps for iPhone and Android devices?

a. First generation

b. Second generation

c. Third generation

d. Fourth generation

Compilers and Interpreters

Have you ever tried to look at the contents of a software application? If you peer inside a file such as Excel.exe, all you'd see is a bunch of numbers and symbols. What happened to the human-readable program that the programmer created using a high-level programming language? Most likely, the programmer's source code got compiled.

▶ **What is source code?** The human-readable version of a program created in a high-level language by a programmer is called **source code**. Just as with an assembly language program, source code cannot be directly executed by a microprocessor. It must first be translated into machine language. This translation can be accomplished by a compiler or an interpreter.

▶ **How does a compiler work?** A **compiler** converts all the statements in a program in a single batch, and the resulting collection of statements, called **object code**, is placed in a new file. Software supplied at download sites and apps distributed for mobile devices are files containing object code that is ready for the processor to execute. Figure 11-18 illustrates how a compiler works.

Figure 11-18: A compiler converts source code into object code

NewYear.py
```
print ("Happy")
year = 2024
newYear = year + 1
print (newYear)
```
Source code

NewYear.exe
```
0001000101011101
1010010101000101
1011010100010100
1010100010100100
```
Object code

All statements are compiled into a new
file that contains machine code.

▶ **How does an interpreter work?** As an alternative to a compiler, an **interpreter** converts and executes one statement at a time while the program is running. After a statement is executed, the interpreter converts and executes the next statement, and so on. There are two major differences between a compiler and an interpreter. First, a compiler creates a standalone file of machine code, whereas an interpreter does not create any new files. Second, a compiler does not carry out any instructions, but an interpreter does. Figure 11-19 illustrates how an interpreter works.

Figure 11-19: An interpreter converts and executes each statement

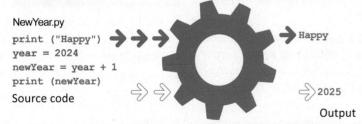

NewYear.py
```
print ("Happy")
year = 2024
newYear = year + 1
print (newYear)
```
Source code

Happy

2025

Output

Each statement is converted into machine
code and immediately executed.

QuickCheck

A compiler creates _____.

a. object code

b. source code

c. op code

d. interpreted code

▶ **Why do programmers care about compilers and interpreters?** When writing and testing a program, the extra step for compiling takes a few seconds, so it slows down the programming process. In addition, a program must compile without any errors before it can be run, which forces programmers to fix little bugs before viewing the "big picture" as the program executes.

As an analogy, imagine a new car with a diagnostic system that wouldn't start the engine unless the tire pressure, oil level, and other mechanics were in perfect order. You might have to make lots of adjustments before you could take the car for a test drive. As shown in Figure 11-20, a compiler requires programmers to fix all the syntax errors before they can see the program running.

Try It!

Connect to Tutorialspoint, where you can write a sample program. Select the link for CODING GROUND, and then select Java. A sample "Hello World!" program is displayed. Change "public" to "publix". Click the Execute tab to compile the program. A message in the green area displays the error found by the compiler.

Figure 11-20: Compilers do not create object code until the syntax is correct

```
1    import random

2    min = 1

3    max = 6

4

5    rollAgain = "yes"

6

7    while rollAgain == "yes" or rollAgain == "y":

8        print ("Rolling...")

9        print ("The values are ...")

10       print (random.randint(man,max))

11       print (random.randint(min,max))

12

13       rollAgain = input("Roll again? ")
```

Compile Error!
Traceback (most recent call last):
File "python", line 10, in <module>
NameError: name 'man' is not defined

This program contains an error in line 10. Even though lines 1 through 9 contain no errors, their output is not displayed because the program did not compile without errors.

An interpreter executes as many statements as possible until an error is encountered, allowing programmers to test the program and easily locate errors. One problem with interpreters is that they leave the source code exposed. Software applications distributed as source code can easily be copied and modified by users. Another problem with interpreters is that they operate more slowly than a compiled program, which decreases efficiency and negatively affects the user experience.

▶ **How do programmers choose which to use?** Many programming languages have both compilers and interpreters. Programmers may choose to use an interpreter for the initial phases of entering and testing statements, and then use a compiler to create the object code for distribution.

Some languages, such as C++ and Java, are traditionally run using compilers. Programmers just get accustomed to the process of debugging syntax errors before seeing any iteration of their programs running. Compiled languages may also be configured to compile and execute in a single pass. If the program compiles correctly, it is automatically executed.

Some languages do not generally use compilers. These **scripting languages** are distributed as human-readable source code, not as object code. Programmers select scripting languages such as Perl, PHP, Ruby, and JavaScript for Web development because they can be incorporated in HTML documents or installed as server-side scripts.

QuickCheck

Scripting languages, such as JavaScript and PHP, are _____.

a. interpreted

b. second generation

c. object code

d. op codes

Paradigms and Languages

Just how many programming languages are there? Estimates vary, but some researchers suggest that there are about as many programming languages as human languages—more than 8,000. The number of well-established programming languages is about 600. With so many languages to choose from, which programming languages should a programmer know? How do programmers select the best language for a project? Let's find the answers to these questions.

▶ How do programmers choose a language? The choice of a programming language is not random. When learning how to program computers, entering the job market, or embarking upon a software development project, programming language choices can contribute to success or to failure.

Because there are so many programming languages, it is handy to classify them. You have already seen how programming languages can be classified into five generations, beginning with first-generation machine languages. Historical classifications indicate when languages emerged, how they developed, and which languages are newest.

Many other classification schemes exist. Classifying languages by their popularity is helpful for gauging which languages are trending and might be useful for job seekers. Programming languages can also be categorized by their complexity, by their security vulnerabilities, and by their syntax. Believe it or not, there is an entire category of curly bracket programming languages that use { and } to group statements into blocks similar to paragraphs. Another approach to classifying programming languages is based on programming paradigms.

▶ What is a programming paradigm? The phrase **programming paradigm** refers to a way of conceptualizing and structuring the tasks a computer performs. Whereas some programming tasks can be best approached by focusing on the steps required to complete a specific computation, other tasks might be approached by focusing on the data that forms the basis for the computation.

Once a programmer has evaluated the best paradigm for a project, a programming language that supports the paradigm can be selected. Some programming languages support a single paradigm. Other programming languages—referred to as **multiparadigm languages**—support more than one paradigm. Figure 11-21 provides a brief description of today's three most popular programming paradigms.

Try It!

Would you like to find out which programming languages are currently most popular? Head over to the TIOBE Web site and check out the Tiobe Index. Scroll down to the graph to see how languages trend in popularity.

Figure 11-21: Programming paradigms

Paradigm	Description
Procedural	Emphasizes linear steps that provide the computer with instructions on how to solve a problem or carry out a task
Object-oriented	Formulates programs as a series of objects and methods that interact to perform a specific task
Declarative	Focuses on the use of facts and rules to describe a problem

❱ What is the most practical approach to programming language classification? Programmers generally find it useful to classify languages based on the types of projects for which they are used. Some languages tend to be used for Web programming, while others tend to be used for mobile apps, games, and enterprise applications. An additional group of older programming languages tend to be used for programming legacy systems. Figure 11-22, which continues to the next page, describes the most commonly used programming languages based on their use for specific types of projects.

Figure 11-22: Programming language roundup

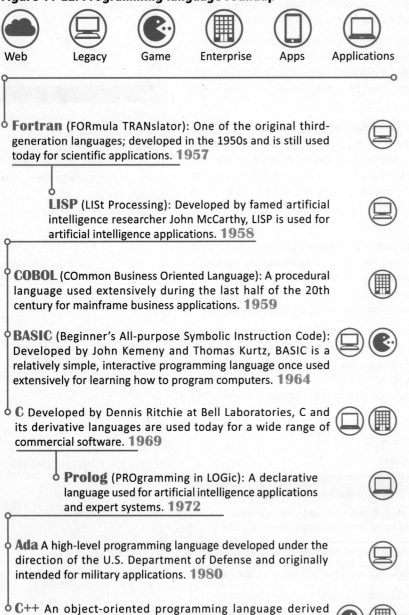

Web   Legacy   Game   Enterprise   Apps   Applications

Fortran (FORmula TRANslator): One of the original third-generation languages; developed in the 1950s and is still used today for scientific applications. 1957

LISP (LISt Processing): Developed by famed artificial intelligence researcher John McCarthy, LISP is used for artificial intelligence applications. 1958

COBOL (COmmon Business Oriented Language): A procedural language used extensively during the last half of the 20th century for mainframe business applications. 1959

BASIC (Beginner's All-purpose Symbolic Instruction Code): Developed by John Kemeny and Thomas Kurtz, BASIC is a relatively simple, interactive programming language once used extensively for learning how to program computers. 1964

C Developed by Dennis Ritchie at Bell Laboratories, C and its derivative languages are used today for a wide range of commercial software. 1969

Prolog (PROgramming in LOGic): A declarative language used for artificial intelligence applications and expert systems. 1972

Ada A high-level programming language developed under the direction of the U.S. Department of Defense and originally intended for military applications. 1980

C++ An object-oriented programming language derived from C, C++ is used extensively for many types of modern programming projects. 1983

Figure 11-22 (Continued)

Objective-C A general-purpose object-oriented programming language used to develop programs for macOS and iOS, including apps created for the Apple App Store. **1983**

Perl Originally developed as a scripting language for UNIX, Perl is an interpreted language that is used extensively for Web sites such as Ticketmaster, craigslist, and Priceline. **1987**

Python Named after the British comedy series *Monty Python's Flying Circus*, this language has a relatively simple syntax, which makes it fairly easy to learn. It supports procedural and object-oriented paradigms and is used for Google and YouTube. **1991**

Visual Basic (VB) Created by Microsoft and derived from BASIC, VB was one of the first languages with an easy-to-use visual development environment. After many versions, VB evolved into Microsoft's .NET development framework. **1991**

Ruby An interpreted language that is the core for a framework called Ruby on Rails, which is used at Web sites such as Twitter, Hulu, and Groupon. **1995**

Java A C++ derivative developed by Sun Microsystems and used extensively for Web-based programming. Web apps written in Java run in a Java virtual machine (JVM), which is why you might periodically see messages on your computer to update Java. Java is also used for mobile app development. **1995**

JavaScript Not to be confused with Java, JavaScript is an interpreted language most commonly used for client-side Web scripting, such as animating page elements and validating input on HTML forms. **1995**

PHP Currently used on millions of Web sites including Udemy, Wikipedia, and Facebook, PHP is an interpreted language that works well for server-side scripting. **1995**

C# Pronounced "C sharp," this language was developed by Microsoft and is more closely related to Java than to C. It is primarily used by developers working within the Windows platform. **2001**

Swift The newest language in this roster, Swift was created by Apple and is intended to replace Objective-C for macOS and iOS software development. **2014**

QuickCheck

Which of the following languages is generally used for legacy programming projects?

a. C++

b. Java

c. Swift

d. COBOL

11

Toolsets

Programming languages can be downloaded and installed just like any software application. Interactive programming environments are also available online as Web apps that don't require installation. Serious programmers typically download and install programming tools for local use, however, and the language is just one component of their toolset.

▶ **What tools do programmers use?** In addition to a programming language, the programmer's toolbox may include a compiler, a debugger, and an editor. Some programmers like to obtain programming tools à la carte by picking up a compiler from one vendor, selecting an interactive debugger from another vendor, and using any handy editor, such as Notepad. More typically, programmers download or purchase an SDK or IDE that contains a collection of programming tools.

▶ **What is an SDK?** An **SDK** (software development kit) is a collection of language-specific programming tools that enables a programmer to develop applications for a specific computer platform, such as Windows PCs. A basic SDK includes a compiler, documentation about the language and syntax, and sample programs. More sophisticated SDKs might also include an editor, a debugger, a visual user interface design module, and APIs.

The components of an SDK are sometimes a hodgepodge of tools without consistent user interfaces for the programmer. For a more polished development environment, programmers turn to IDEs.

▶ **What is an IDE?** An **IDE** (integrated development environment) is a type of SDK that packages a set of development tools into a sleek programming application. The modules in the application—editor, compiler, debugger, and user interface development tool—have a uniform set of menus and controls, which simplifies the programming process. Xcode is an example of an IDE. It is used for developing software for Macs, iPads, and iPhones. Android Studio is also an IDE. It is used to create apps for Android devices (Figure 11-23).

Figure 11-23: The Android Studio IDE

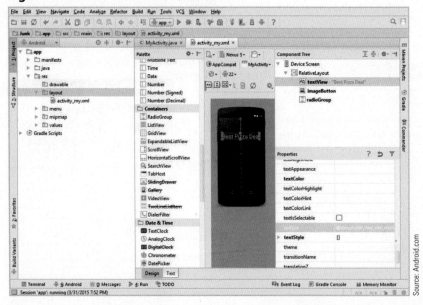

Source: Android.com

▶ **What's an API?** In the context of computer programming, **API** is an abbreviation for *application program interface* or *application programming interface*. An API is a set of application or operating system functions that programmers can add to the programs they create.

The Windows API, for example, includes routines for an assortment of dialog box controls familiar to most PC users. The ability to browse through file folders is another element of the Windows API that might be useful in any application program that allows users to open or save files. APIs are usually supplied as part of an SDK.

▶ **Do programmers use standard programming tools to develop computer games?** At the core of every computer game is a program that ties together the virtual game world, characters, weapons, and other objects. Most of these programs are written using standard SDK and IDE programming tools. Additional tools such as those in Figure 11-24 are also useful.

11

Figure 11-24: Programming tools for computer games

Graphics Tools	On commercial game projects, artists usually create, render, and animate game objects using bitmap, vector, 3D, and animation graphics software. For developers without artistic talent, 3D animated characters can be obtained from freelance artists who peddle their creations on the Web at sites such as Animation Central. A type of special effects software called a particle renderer helps developers create explosions, flares, fog, and fairy dust.
Motion Tools	Pathfinder algorithms distributed as APIs map character routes, limiting them to valid paths and preventing them from walking through walls (unless they are magic users).
Audio Tools	Developers also use a variety of audio software to record, edit, and mix sound effects for gunshots, explosions, footsteps, and so on. Even non-musicians can generate upbeat background music by using MIDI sequencers, sound effect engines, audio APIs, and ready-to-use audio clips.
Game Play Tools	Commercially available artificial intelligence APIs and components can plug into programs to control the actions of autonomous, non-player-controlled monsters and foes. Physics APIs can tie into objects to make them respond with lifelike realism to gravity, momentum, and collisions. Digital rights management (DRM) tools are also available to help game developers protect their creations from piracy and illegal copying.
Game Engines	Microsoft's DirectX SDK contains APIs that are popular tools for game developers. Popular cross-platform game engines such as Unity, Unreal Engine, CryEngine, and GameMaker Studio provide a variety of tools for 2D and 3D game development.

QuickQuiz   Section B

1. _____ -generation programming languages, such as C, COBOL, and Fortran, use easy-to-remember command words.

2. Computer programming _____ include procedural, object-oriented, and declarative.

3. _____ languages, such as JavaScript and PHP, are interpreted, not compiled.

4. A compiler creates _____ code.

5. A(n) _____ is a set of application program or operating system functions that programmers can add to the programs they create.

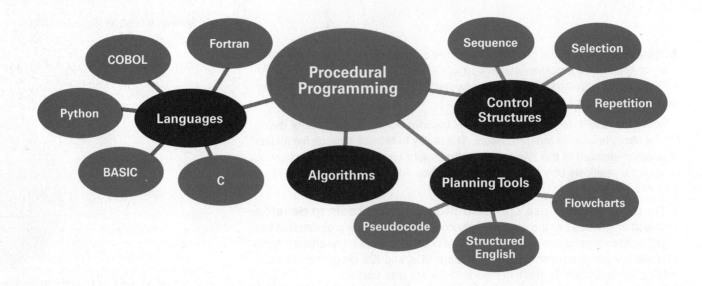

Objectives

▶ Explain how algorithms relate to procedural programming.

▶ List three tools that can be used to express an algorithm during the planning phase of program development.

▶ Draw a diagram that illustrates how a function controls program flow.

▶ Draw a diagram that illustrates how a selection control structure affects program flow.

▶ Draw a diagram that illustrates how a repetition control structure affects program flow.

▶ Describe at least two programming projects that are well suited for the procedural approach.

▶ Explain the advantages and disadvantages of the procedural paradigm.

Cooking mac and cheese. Solving a math problem. Assembling a bicycle. So many activities in everyday life are carried out as a series of steps. It should not be surprising that the first computer programmers also took a step-by-step approach to solving problems using computers. Today, this procedural approach is the basis for much of the software produced by programmers for videogames, mobile apps, and enterprise applications.

Terminology

procedural paradigm	flowchart	sequence control	repetition control
procedural language	walkthrough	structure	structure
algorithm	flow control	function	loop
structured English	sequential execution	selection control	iteration
pseudocode	control structures	structure	

Algorithms

Early approaches to computer programming were based on writing step-by-step instructions for the computer to follow. This technique is still in widespread use today and provides a useful starting point for learning what programming is all about. In this section, the examples are written in Python because it is one of the easiest programming languages to grasp.

▶ **What is procedural programming?** The traditional approach to programming uses a **procedural paradigm** (sometimes called an imperative paradigm) to conceptualize the solution to a problem as a sequence of steps. A program written in a procedural language consists of self-contained statements in a sequence that indicates how a task is to be performed or a problem is to be solved.

A programming language that supports the procedural paradigm is called a **procedural language**. Machine languages, assembly languages, BASIC, COBOL, Fortran, C, and many other third-generation languages are classified as procedural languages.

Procedural languages are well suited for problems that can be easily solved with a linear, step-by-step algorithm. Programs created with procedural languages have a starting point and an ending point. The flow of execution from the beginning to the end of a program is essentially linear—that is, the computer begins at the first statement and carries out the prescribed series of statements until it reaches the end of the program.

▶ **What is an algorithm?** An **algorithm** is a set of steps for carrying out a task that can be written down and implemented. For example, the algorithm for making a batch of macaroni and cheese is a set of steps that includes boiling water, cooking the macaroni in the water, and making a cheese sauce (Figure 11-25).

11

QuickCheck

What is the core characteristic of procedural programming languages?

a. A compiler

b. A step-by-step algorithm

c. A VDE

d. A paradigm

Figure 11-25: An algorithm is a series of steps similar to a recipe

An important characteristic of a correctly formulated algorithm is that carefully following the steps guarantees that you can accomplish the task for which the algorithm was designed. If the recipe on a macaroni and cheese package is a correctly formulated algorithm, following the recipe should guarantee a successful batch of macaroni and cheese.

▶ **How do I write an algorithm?** An algorithm for a computer program is a set of steps that explains how to begin with known information specified in a problem statement and how to manipulate that information to arrive at a solution.

Algorithms are usually written in a format that is not specific to a particular programming language. This approach allows programmers to focus on formulating a correct algorithm without becoming distracted by the detailed syntax of a computer programming language. In a later phase of the software development process, the algorithm is converted into statements written in a programming language so that a computer can implement it.

▶ **How do I figure out an algorithm?** To design an algorithm, you might begin by recording the steps required to solve the problem manually. If you take this route with the pizza problem, you must obtain initial information about the cost, size, and shape of each pizza. When the pizza program runs, it should ask the user to enter the initial information needed to solve the problem. Your algorithm might begin like this:

> **Ask the user for the shape of the first pizza and hold it in RAM as shape1.**
>
> **Ask the user for the price of the first pizza and hold it in RAM as price1.**
>
> **Ask the user for the size of the first pizza and hold it in RAM as size1.**

Next, your algorithm should specify how to manipulate this information. You want the computer to calculate the price per square inch. However, a statement like "Calculate the price per square inch" neither specifies how to do the calculation nor deals with the fact that you must perform different calculations for square and round pizzas. A more appropriate set of statements for the algorithm is shown in Figure 11-26.

Terminology

Remember variables from Section A? In most modern programming languages, variable names begin with lowercase letters. When a variable is composed of multiple words, such as *pizzaShape*, the second word begins with an uppercase letter.

Figure 11-26: The algorithm for calculating the area of pizzas

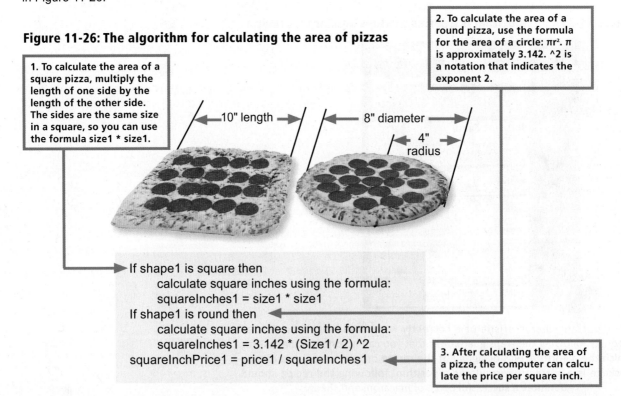

1. To calculate the area of a square pizza, multiply the length of one side by the length of the other side. The sides are the same size in a square, so you can use the formula size1 * size1.

2. To calculate the area of a round pizza, use the formula for the area of a circle: πr². π is approximately 3.142. ^2 is a notation that indicates the exponent 2.

3. After calculating the area of a pizza, the computer can calculate the price per square inch.

10" length   8" diameter   4" radius

```
If shape1 is square then
    calculate square inches using the formula:
    squareInches1 = size1 * size1
If shape1 is round then
    calculate square inches using the formula:
    squareInches1 = 3.142 * (Size1 / 2) ^2
squareInchPrice1 = price1 / squareInches1
```

▶ **What's next?** So far, the algorithm describes how to calculate the price per square inch of one pizza. It should specify a similar process for calculating the price per square inch of the second pizza.

Finally, the algorithm should specify how the computer decides what to display as the solution. You want the computer to display a message indicating which pizza has the lowest square-inch cost, so your algorithm should include steps like the following:

> **If squareInchPrice1 is less than squareInchPrice2 then display the message "Pizza 1 is the best deal."**

> **If squareInchPrice2 is less than squareInchPrice1 then display the message "Pizza 2 is the best deal."**

But don't forget to indicate what you want the computer to do if the price per square inch is the same for both pizzas:

> **If squareInchPrice1 equals squareInchPrice2 then display the message "Both pizzas are the same deal."**

The complete algorithm for the pizza problem is shown in Figure 11-27.

QuickCheck

In Figure 11-27, which section specifies the output?

a. Section 1

b. Section 3

c. Section 4

d. Section 5

11

Figure 11-27: The complete algorithm for comparing two pizzas

1. Get initial information for the first pizza.

Ask the user for the shape of the first pizza and hold it in RAM as shape1.
Ask the user for the price of the first pizza and hold it in RAM as price1.
Ask the user for the size of the first pizza and hold it in RAM as size1.

2. Calculate the price per square inch for the first pizza.

If shape1 is square then
    calculate the square inches using the formula:
    squareInches1 = size1 * size1
If shape1 is round then
    calculate the square inches using the formula:
    squareInches1 = 3.142 * (size1 / 2) ^2
squareInchPrice1 = price1 / squareInches1

3. Get initial information for the second pizza.

Ask the user for the shape of the second pizza and hold it in RAM as shape2.
Ask the user for the price of the second pizza and hold it in RAM as price2.
Ask the user for the size of the second pizza and hold it in RAM as size2.

4. Calculate the price per square inch for the second pizza.

If shape2 is square then
    calculate the square inches using the formula:
    squareInches2 = size2 * size2
If shape2 is round then
    calculate the square inches using the formula:
    squareInches2 = 3.142 * (size2 / 2) ^2
squareInchPrice2 = price2 / squareInches2

5. Compare the prices per square inch, and then output the results.

If squareInchPrice1 < squareInchPrice2 then
    display the message "Pizza 1 is the best deal."
If squareInchPrice2 < squareInchPrice1 then
    display the message "Pizza 2 is the best deal."
If squareInchPrice1 = squareInchPrice2 then
    display the message "Both pizzas are the same deal."

Pseudocode and Flowcharts

You can express an algorithm in several different ways, including structured English, pseudocode, and flowcharts. These tools are not programming languages, and they cannot be processed by a computer. Their purpose is to give programmers a way to document their ideas for program design.

▶ **What's structured English?** Structured English is a subset of the English language with a limited selection of sentence structures that reflect processing activities. Refer to Figure 11-27 on the previous page to see how structured English is used to express the algorithm for the pizza program.

▶ **What's pseudocode?** Another way to express an algorithm is with pseudocode. Pseudocode is a notational system for algorithms that is less formal than a programming language, but more formal than structured English. When writing pseudocode, programmers may incorporate command words and syntax from the computer language they intend to use for the actual program. Compare Figure 11-27 with Figure 11-28 and see if you can identify some of the differences between structured English and pseudocode.

Terminology

When writing pseudocode, an arrow is used for an assignment statement that assigns a value to a variable. You can make an arrow using the less than symbol and a dash, as in <-.

Figure 11-28: Pseudocode for a program to compare two pizzas

```
display prompts for entering shape, price, and size
input shape1, price1, size1
if shape1 = square then
     squareInches1 ← size1 * size1
if shape1 = round then
     squareInches1 ← 3.142 * (size1 / 2) ^2
squareInchPrice1 ← price1 / squareInches1
display prompts for entering shape, price, and size
input shape2, price2, size2
if shape2 = square then
     squareInches2 ← size2 * size2
if shape2 = round then
     squareInches2 ← 3.142 * (size2 / 2) ^2
squareInchPrice2 ← price2 / squareInches2
if squareInchPrice1 < squareInchPrice2 then
     output "Pizza 1 is the best deal."
if squareInchPrice2 < squareInchPrice1 then
     output "Pizza 2 is the best deal."
if squareInchPrice1 = squareInchPrice2 then
     output "Both pizzas are the same deal."
```

QuickCheck

In the pseudocode at left, what is the purpose of the following statement?

squareInches1 ← size1 * size1

a. It defines the squareInches variable.

b. It calculates the area of a square pizza.

c. It calculates the radius of a round pizza.

d. It determines which pizza is the best deal.

▶ **What is a flowchart?** A third way to express an algorithm is to use a flowchart. A flowchart is a graphical representation of the way a computer should progress from one statement to the next when it performs a task. The flowchart for the pizza program is shown in Figure 11-29 on the next page.

QuickCheck

Which of the following is not considered a way to express an algorithm?

a. Structured English

b. Flowchart

c. Compiler

d. Pseudocode

Figure 11-29: Flowchart for the pizza program

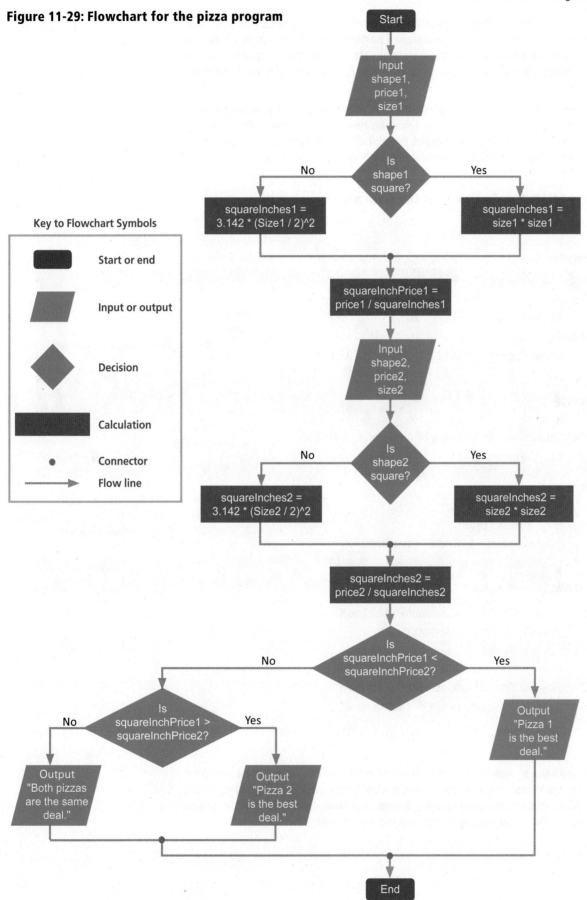

Key to Flowchart Symbols

▬	Start or end
▱	Input or output
◆	Decision
▬	Calculation
●	Connector
→	Flow line

11

▶ How do I know if my algorithm is correct? Before finalizing the algorithm for a computer program, you should perform a **walkthrough** to verify that your algorithm works. To perform a walkthrough for a simple program, you can use a calculator, paper, and pencil to step through the algorithm using realistic test data.

For more complex programs, a walkthrough might consist of a verbal presentation to a group of programmers who can help identify logical errors in the algorithm and suggest ways to make the algorithm more efficient. Figure 11-30 illustrates how to check the pseudocode for the pizza program.

Figure 11-30: A walkthrough of the pizza program algorithm

display prompts for entering shape, price, and size	User is asked to enter the first pizza's shape, price, and size
input shape1, price1, size1	User enters square, $10.00, 12

if shape1 = square **then**
    squareInches1 ← size1 * size1
if shape1 = round **then**
    squareInches1 ← 3.142 * (size1 / 2) ^2
	The first pizza is square, so the computer should calculate:
	12 * 12 = 144 for squareInches1

squareInchPrice1 ← price1 / squareInches1	The computer also calculates: $10.00 / 144 = .069 for squareInchPrice1
display prompts for entering shape, price, and size	User is asked to enter the second pizza's shape, price, and size
input shape2, price2, size2	User enters round, $10.00, 12

if shape2 = square **then**
    squareInches2 ← size2 * size2
if shape2 = round **then**
    squareInches2 ← 3.142 * (size2 / 2) ^2
	The second pizza is round, so the computer should calculate:
	$3.142 * (12 / 2)^2 = 113.112$ for squareInches2

squareInchPrice2 ← price2 / squareInches2	The computer should also calculate $10.00 / 113.112 = .088 for squareInchPrice2

if squareInchPrice1 < squareInchPrice2 **then**
    output "Pizza 1 is the best deal."
if squareInchPrice2 < squareInchPrice1 **then**
    output "Pizza 2 is the best deal."
if squareInchPrice1 = squareInchPrice2 **then**
    output "Both pizzas are the same deal."
	.069 < .088 so pizza 1 is the best deal

You may have to walk through a program several times to check that it works for all possible conditions. A second walkthrough for the pizza program should use input data that would result in pizza 2 being the best deal. A third walkthrough would use data making the two pizzas the same deal.

Flow Control

Have you ever wondered why computers seem so versatile and why they are able to adjust to so many situations? A key to this versatility is the programmer's ability to control the flow of a program. Let's see what that means.

▶ **What is flow control?** **Flow control** refers to the sequence in which a computer executes program statements. During **sequential execution**, the first statement in the program is executed first, then the second statement, and so on, to the last statement in the program. Here is a simple program written in the Python programming language that outputs `This is the first line.` and then outputs `This is the next line.`:

```
print("This is the first line.")
print("This is the next line.")
```

▶ **Is there an alternative to sequential execution?** Some algorithms specify that a program must execute statements in an order different from the sequence in which they are listed, skip some statements under certain circumstances, or repeat statements. **Control structures** are statements that specify the sequence in which a program is executed. Most procedural languages have three types of control structures: sequence controls, selection controls, and repetition controls.

A **sequence control structure** changes the order in which statements are carried out by directing the computer to execute a statement elsewhere in the program. In the following simple program, a `goto` command tells the computer to jump directly to the statement labeled "Widget":

```
print("This is the first line.")
goto Widget
print("This is the next line.")
Widget: print("All done!")
```

Follow the flowchart in Figure 11-31 to see how the `goto` statement affects the output.

QuickCheck

What is the output of the following program?

```
print("Hi!")
goto Greeting
print("Goodbye")
greeting
end
```

a. Hi!

b. Greeting

c. Goodbye

d. Hi!
   Goodbye

Figure 11-31: A goto flowchart

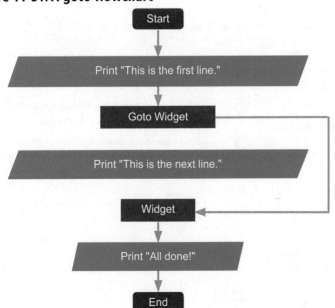

QuickCheck

How many lines of output would be produced by the program depicted by the flowchart in Figure 11-31?

a. One

b. Two

c. Three

d. Four

▶ **When do programmers use goto?** Never! Although it is the simplest control structure, the `goto` command is rarely used by skilled programmers because it can lead to programs that are difficult to understand and maintain.

In 1968, the journal *Communications of the ACM* published a now-famous letter from the Dutch computer scientist Edsger Dijkstra, called "Go To Statement Considered Harmful." In his letter, Dijkstra explained that injudicious use of the `goto` statement in programs makes it difficult for other programmers to understand the underlying algorithm, which in turn means that such programs are difficult to correct, improve, or revise.

▶ **So what is the alternative to goto?** Experienced programmers prefer to use sequence controls other than `goto` to transfer program execution to a subroutine, procedure, or function. A **function** is a section of a program that is not included in the main sequential execution path.

A sequence control structure directs the computer to the statements contained in a function; but when these statements have been executed, the computer neatly returns to the main program. Figure 11-32 shows the execution path of a program that transfers execution to a function.

QuickCheck

What characteristic of the goto command makes it undesirable?

a. Goto filters out unwanted commands.

b. Goto jumps to another part of the program without a way to return.

c. Goto simplifies program logic.

d. Goto does not execute.

Figure 11-32: How a function works

```
#This program calculates the square of any number
#between 1 and 10 that is entered.

❶ number = input("Pick a number between 1 and 10: ")
                        ❷
  number = checkinput(number)
❹ numberSquared = number * number
  print (str(number), " squared is ", str(numberSquared))



❸
  def checkinput(number):
      while number < 1 or number > 10:
          number = int(input("You must enter a number between 1 and 10: "))
      return number
```

❶ The program asks the user to enter a number.

❷ Next, the program takes the number and jumps to the checkinput function.

❸ In the checkinput function, the program makes sure the number is between 1 and 10.

❹ A valid number between 1 and 10 is returned to the main program, where the number is squared and displayed.

▶ Can the computer make decisions while it executes a program?
A **selection control structure** tells a computer what to do based on whether a condition is true or false. A simple example of a selection control structure is the `if...else` command.

The following program uses this command to decide whether a number entered is greater than 18. If the number is greater than or equal to 18, the computer prints `You can vote!` If the number is less than 18, the program performs the `else` statement and prints `You are not old enough to vote.`

```
age = input("Enter your age: ")
if age >= 18:
        print("You can vote!")
else: print("You are not old enough to vote.")
```

Figure 11-33 uses a flowchart to illustrate how a computer performs the statements in a decision structure.

Figure 11-33: A selection control flowchart

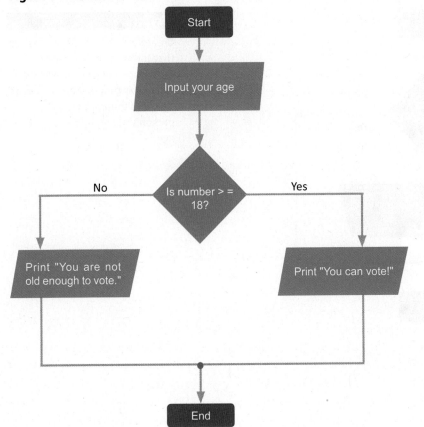

Terminology

Selection control structures are also referred to as *decision structures* or *branches*.

11

QuickCheck

When the number 8 is input for the flowchart in Figure 11-33, does it use the right fork or the left fork?

a. Right

b. Left

Try It!

Draw a flowchart for a program that asks for a user ID and password. If the password and ID are equal to a stored ID and its associated password, the program connects to the user's Twitter feed. If the password is not correct, the program displays "There was a problem with that password and User ID. Try again."

▶ **Can a computer automatically repeat a series of statements?** A **repetition control structure** directs the computer to repeat one or more statements until a certain condition is met. The section of a program that repeats is usually referred to as a **loop** or an **iteration**. There are several styles of loops, and in various languages the loop command words vary. For example, a loop that begins with `for` may function differently than a loop that beings with `while` or `do`.

In *The Wizard of Oz*, Dorothy has to click the heels of her ruby slippers three times and recite "There's no place like home." The following short Python program outputs the magic words three times.

```
for x in range(1, 4):

    print("There's no place like home.")
```

Follow the path of program execution in Figure 11-34 to see how a computer executes a series of statements in a repetition structure.

Figure 11-34: A repetition control flowchart

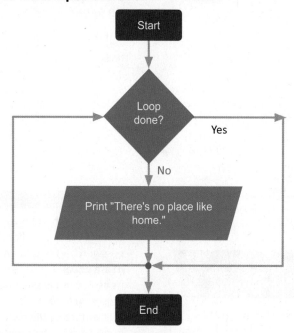

Try It!

Create a flowchart for a program that looks at each person's birth date in your contacts list, calculates that person's current age, and then prints each person's name, birth date, and age.

Try It!

To get a better idea of how a **for** loop works, pretend that you're the computer executing the short set of statements below. You can use the box labeled x in the margin as a RAM location. The computer would also have a screen on which to display output. You can use the Output box in the margin for that purpose. Now, walk through the loop.

```
for x in range(1, 4):
    print("There's no place like home.")
print("The end.")
```

1. As the computer, the first time you see the statement **for x in range(1, 4):**, you set x equal to 1. To do so, write the number 1 in the x box in the margin.

2. Now, execute the next statement, **print("There's no place like home.")**. To do so, write the phrase "There's no place like home." in the Output box. (Hint: Write small; there's more to go in the Output box.)

3. The statement **print("The end.")** is not in the loop. How do you know? Because it is not indented. You have to finish looping before you can execute that statement.

4. Go back to the statement **for x in range(1, 4):**. Because this is the second time you have executed this statement, put a 2 in the x box in the margin. (Hint: You can erase the 1 that was there previously.)

5. You must check whether the value in the x box is 4. Why? Because the statement **for x in range(1, 4):** means you can continue to loop only if x is less than 4. Now, x is only 2, so you can proceed.

6. Go to the next statement, which is **print("There's no place like home.")**. Write this sentence again in the Output box.

7. Moving on, loop back to the **for** statement.

8. Continue by changing the value in the x box to 3. Check the x box to make sure it does not contain 4 yet. It doesn't, so continue.

9. The next line instructs you to **print("There's no place like home.")**. Write this sentence again in the Output box. Increase the value in the x box to 4. Go back once again to the **for** statement.

10. This time, when you check whether the value in x is 4, it is. That means the loop is complete, and you should jump to the statement past the end of the loop.

11. The next statement is **print("The end.")**. Do that, and you've completed the program.

12. When your program is complete, the variable x should contain the number 4, and the Output box should contain:

There's no place like home.

There's no place like home.

There's no place like home.

The end.

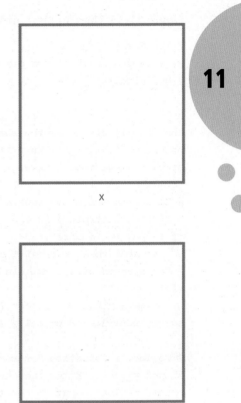

x

Output

11

▶ How do programmers use control structures to write a program?

The pizza program includes control structures, keywords, and syntax provided by the programming language. The completed pizza program, written in Python, is provided in Figure 11-35.

Figure 11-35: The complete pizza program

```
# The Pizza Program
# Tells you which of two pizzas is the best deal
# by calculating the price per square inch of each pizza.

# Collect information for first pizza.
shape1 = input("Enter the shape of pizza 1: ")
price1 = float(input("Enter the price of pizza 1: "))
size1 = float(input("Enter the size of pizza 1: "))

# Calculate price per square inch for first pizza.
# If the first pizza is square, multiply side1 by side2.
if shape1 == "square":
    squareInches1 = size1 * size1
# For a round pizza, calculate area using pi (3.142).
else:
    squareInches1 = 3.142 * (size1 / 2) **2
squareInchPrice1 = price1 / squareInches1

# Collect information for second pizza.
shape2 = input("Enter the shape of pizza 2: ")
price2 = float(input("Enter the price of pizza 2: "))
size2 = float(input("Enter the size of pizza 2: "))

# Calculate price per square inch for second pizza.
if shape2 == "square":
    squareInches2 = size2 * size2
else:
    squareInches2 = 3.142 * (size2 / 2) **2
squareInchPrice2 = price2 / squareInches2

# Decide which pizza is the best deal
# and display results.
if squareInchPrice1 < squareInchPrice2:
    print("Pizza 1 is the best deal.")
if squareInchPrice2 < squareInchPrice1:
    print("Pizza 2 is the best deal.")
if squareInchPrice1 == squareInchPrice2:
    print("Both pizzas are the same deal.")
```

QuickCheck

How many lines in the pizza program are designed to collect input?

a. Two

b. Four

c. Six

d. Eight

Procedural Applications

Procedural languages encourage programmers to approach problems by breaking the solution down into a series of steps. This approach has certain advantages, but it has disadvantages as well.

▶ **What are the most popular procedural languages?** The earliest programming languages were procedural. Fortran, developed by IBM in 1954, was the first widely used standardized computer language. Its implementation of the procedural paradigm set the pattern for other popular procedural languages, such as COBOL, Forth, APL, ALGOL, PL/1, Pascal, C, Ada, and BASIC. Python, used for the examples in this section, is a multiparadigm language suitable for procedural programming.

▶ **What kinds of problems are best suited to the procedural approach?** The procedural approach is best used for problems that can be solved by following a step-by-step algorithm. It is widely used for transaction processing, which is characterized by the use of a single algorithm applied to many different sets of data. For example, in the banking industry, the algorithm for calculating account balances is the same, regardless of the amounts deposited and withdrawn. Many problems in math and science also lend themselves to the procedural approach.

▶ **What are the advantages and disadvantages of the procedural paradigm?** The procedural approach and procedural languages tend to produce programs that run quickly and use system resources efficiently. It is a classic approach understood by many programmers, software engineers, and systems analysts.

The procedural paradigm is quite flexible and powerful, which allows programmers to apply it to many types of problems. For example, although the programming example in this section worked only for round and square pizzas, it could be modified to handle rectangular pizzas, too.

The downside of the procedural paradigm is that it does not fit gracefully with certain types of problems—those that are unstructured or those with very complex algorithms. The procedural paradigm has also been criticized because it forces programmers to view problems as a series of steps, whereas some problems might be better visualized as interacting objects or as interrelated words, concepts, and ideas.

11

QuickCheck

Would a procedural language be the best choice for a program that translates Russian into English?

a. Yes, because translation is a step-by-step process.

b. Yes, because Russian grammar has a simple syntax.

c. No, because Russian uses a different alphabet.

d. No, because translating languages is an unstructured problem.

QuickQuiz   Section C

1. A(n) _____ is a set of steps for carrying out a task that programmers express in structured English, pseudocode, or flowcharts.

2. COBOL, Fortran, and C are examples of programming languages used when working with the _____ paradigm.

3. A selection control structure tells a computer what to do based on whether a condition is true or false, whereas a(n) _____ control structure can change the order in which program statements are executed.

4. A function is a series of program statements that is part of a program, but is not included in the main execution path. True or false? _____

5. The section of a program that contains a repetition control is sometimes referred to as an iteration or a(n) _____ .

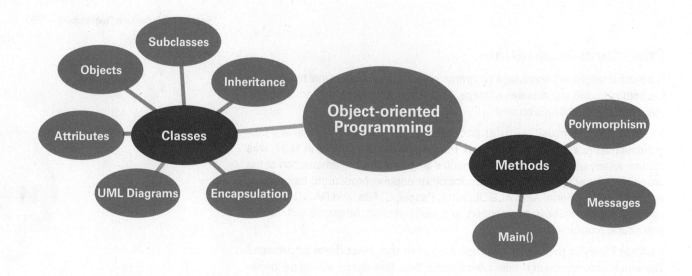

Object-Oriented Programs

Objectives

▶ Explain the significance of objects and classes within the object-oriented paradigm.

▶ Define an example class called People with at least four attributes.

▶ Create two subclasses of People called Students and Instructors that inherit at least two attributes from the superclass.

▶ Draw a UML diagram that illustrates the concept of inheritance.

▶ Explain the relationship between methods and messages in an object-oriented program.

▶ Provide an example of polymorphism that relates to classes called People, Students, and Instructors.

▶ Identify classes and methods while tracing through an object-oriented program.

▶ List at least three object-oriented programming languages.

▶ Explain how the concept of encapsulation relates to abstraction.

The real world is populated by objects that have specific attributes and behaviors. The interactions among these objects can't always be organized into a series of neat steps that can be specified as an algorithm for a procedural program. In this section, you'll discover the object-oriented world view and how it translates into computer programs.

Terminology

object-oriented paradigm	public attribute	superclass	polymorphism
object	private attribute	subclass	encapsulation
class	inheritance	method	
attribute	class hierarchy	message	

Objects and Classes

The object-oriented paradigm is based on objects and classes that can be defined and manipulated by a program's algorithms. The Java programming language is used for the examples in this section because it is a popular language for implementing object-oriented programs.

▶ **What is the basic focus of the object-oriented paradigm?** The object-oriented paradigm is based on the idea that the solution for a problem can be visualized in terms of objects that interact with each other. Rather than envisioning a program as a list of steps, programmers who work within the object-oriented paradigm envision a program as a collection of objects that essentially network with each other to exchange data (Figure 11-36).

Terminology

OO is sometimes used as an abbreviation for *object-oriented.*

11

Figure 11-36: Object-oriented paradigm vs. procedural paradigm

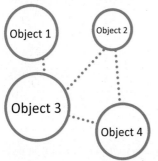

Object-Oriented Paradigm

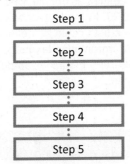

Procedural Paradigm

▶ **What is an object?** In the context of the OO paradigm, an **object** is a unit of data that represents an abstract or real-world entity, such as a person, place, or thing. An object can represent a $10.99 small round pizza. Another object can represent a person named Robin who delivers pizza. Yet another object can represent a customer who lives at 22 W. Pointe Rd.

▶ **What's the difference between an object and a class?** The real world contains lots of pizzas, customers, and delivery persons. These objects can be defined in a general way by using classes. Whereas an object is a single instance of an entity, a **class** is a template for a group of objects with similar characteristics.

For example, a Pizza class defines a group of gooey Italian snacks that are made in a variety of sizes, crafted into rectangular or round shapes, and sold for various prices. A class can produce any number of unique objects, as shown in Figure 11-37.

Figure 11-37: A pizza class can include several pizza objects

CLASS: Pizza

Pizza objects

▶ **How are objects and classes used to solve problems?** Certain characteristics of pizzas provide information necessary to solve the best-deal problem. This information—the price, size, and shape of a pizza—provides the structure for the Pizza class.

A class is defined by attributes and methods. An **attribute** defines a characteristic, such as pizza price, for objects in a class. You will learn about methods, which define actions, later in this section.

Each attribute generally has a name, scope, and data type. One attribute of the Pizza class might be named pizzaPrice. Its scope can be defined as public or private:

• A **public attribute** is available for use by any routine in the program.

• A **private attribute** can be accessed only from the routine in which it is defined.

The pizzaPrice attribute's data type can be defined as double, which means that it can be any decimal number, such as 12.99. In the Databases module, you encountered the idea of data types, where a field could be defined as text, an integer, a real number, a date, and so on. Programming languages use similar data types, but the terminology may be different. Figure 11-38 describes data types used by Java to specify class attributes.

Figure 11-38: Java data types

Data Type	Description	Example
Int	Integer whole numbers	10
Double	Numbers with decimal places	12.99
String	Multiple characters, symbols, and numerals	Square
Boolean	Limited to two values	T or F

Object-oriented programmers often use UML (Unified Modeling Language) diagrams to plan the classes for a program. The UML diagram in Figure 11-39 shows one possible way to envision the Pizza class.

Figure 11-39: UML diagram of the Pizza class

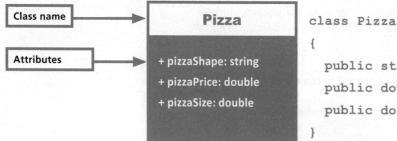

```
class Pizza
{
    public string pizzaShape;
    public double pizzaPrice;
    public double pizzaSize;
}
```

Attributes that begin with a + sign are public, which means they can be referenced by any methods or classes.

The Java statements for the Pizza class begin with the class name. The attributes are enclosed in brackets. Each statement ends with a semicolon. The attributes are indented for readability.

Inheritance

The object-oriented paradigm endows classes with quite a bit of flexibility. For the pizza program, objects and classes make it fairly easy to compare round pizzas to rectangular pizzas rather than just to square pizzas.

▶ **How flexible are classes?** Suppose you want to compare a 10-inch round pizza to a rectangular pizza that has a length of 11 inches and a width of 8 inches. The Pizza class in Figure 11-39 on the previous page holds only one measurement for each pizza: pizzaSize. This single attribute won't work for rectangular pizzas, which might have a different length and width.

Should you modify the class definition to add attributes for pizzaLength and pizzaWidth? No, because these attributes are necessary only for rectangular pizzas, not for round pizzas. An OO feature called inheritance provides flexibility to deal with objects' unique characteristics.

▶ **What is inheritance?** In object-oriented jargon, inheritance refers to passing certain characteristics from one class to other classes. For example, to solve the pizza problem, a programmer might decide to use a RoundPizza class and a RectanglePizza class. These two new classes can inherit attributes from the Pizza class, such as pizzaShape and pizzaPrice.

You can add specialized characteristics to the new classes. The RectanglePizza class can have attributes for length and width, and the RoundPizza class can have an attribute for diameter.

The process of producing new classes with inherited attributes creates a **class hierarchy** that includes a superclass and subclasses. A **superclass**, such as Pizza, is any class from which attributes can be inherited. A **subclass** (or derived class), such as RoundPizza or RectanglePizza, is any class that inherits attributes from a superclass (Figure 11-40).

Figure 11-40: Subclasses inherit attributes from a superclass

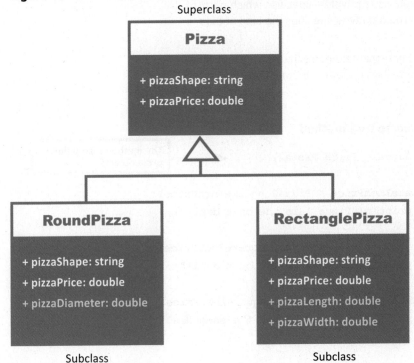

QuickCheck

Which attribute from the original Pizza class in Figure 11-39 (on the previous page) is no longer needed when the subclasses for round and rectangular pizzas are created?

a. Pizza

b. pizzaShape

c. pizzaPrice

d. pizzaSize

Try It!

Create a UML diagram that contains the following:

Classes: Person, Student, Instructor

Attributes: name, birthDate, studentID, instructorDepartment, gradePointAverage

What's the syntax for a subclass? Java uses the `extends` command to link a subclass to a superclass. The statement `class RectanglePizza extends Pizza` means "create a class called RectanglePizza that's derived from the superclass called Pizza." Figure 11-41 contains the Java syntax that creates attributes for the RectanglePizza class.

QuickCheck

The extends command is associated with _____.

a. inheritance

b. attributes

c. data types

d. an object

Figure 11-41: Java syntax for a RectanglePizza subclass

```
class RectanglePizza extends Pizza
{
        double pizzaLength;
        double pizzaWidth;
}
```

Methods and Messages

In an object-oriented program, objects can act and interact. Programmers specify how this action takes place by creating methods and messages.

What is a method? A **method** is one or more statements that define an action. The names of methods end in a set of parentheses—for example, compare() or getArea(). The statements that are contained in a method may be a series of steps similar to statements in procedural programs.

What can a method do? A method can perform a variety of tasks, such as collecting input, performing calculations, making comparisons, executing decisions, and producing output. For example, the pizza program can use a method named compare() to compare the square-inch prices of two pizzas and display a message indicating which pizza is the best deal.

What are the Java statements for the compare() method? A method begins with a statement that names the method and can include a description of its scope and data type. The scope—public or private—specifies which parts of the program can access the method. The data type specifies the kind of data, if any, that the method produces.

The initial statement is followed by one or more statements that specify the calculation, comparison, or routine that the method performs. Figure 11-42 illustrates the syntax for the compare() method.

Figure 11-42: Java syntax for the compare() method

```
public compare(Pizza Pizza1, Pizza Pizza2)
{
    if (Pizza1.squareInchPrice < Pizza2.squareInchPrice)
        System.out.println("Pizza 1 is the best deal!");

    if (Pizza1.squareInchPrice > Pizza2.squareInchPrice)
        System.out.println("Pizza 2 is the best deal!");

    if (Pizza1.squareInchPrice == Pizza2.squareInchPrice
        System.out.println("The pizzas are the same deal!");
}
```

The method manipulates pizza objects.

The method title includes its scope and name.

The body of the method contains statements to determine which pizza is the best deal.

> **What activates a method?** A method is activated by a **message**, which is included as a program statement that is sometimes referred to as a call. For example, in a Java program, a statement such as `compare(Pizza1, Pizza2)` produces a message used to activate or call the compare() method.

In the object-oriented world, objects often interact to solve a problem by sending and receiving messages. For example, a pizza object might receive a message asking for the pizza's area or price per square inch (Figure 11-43).

Figure 11-43: A method may ask an object for data

compare() Method   Pizza1 Object

> **How do methods relate to classes?** Methods can be defined along with the class they affect. The getSquareInchPrice() method pertains to pizzas of any shape, so it can be defined as part of the Pizza class. To calculate the square-inch price, however, it is necessary to know the area of a pizza. That calculation can be achieved by defining a getArea() method.

The area calculation for round pizzas is different from the calculation for rectangular pizzas, so the getArea() method should become part of the RoundPizza and RectanglePizza subclasses, as indicated by the UML diagram in Figure 11-44.

Figure 11-44: Different getArea() calculations are needed for pizza subclasses

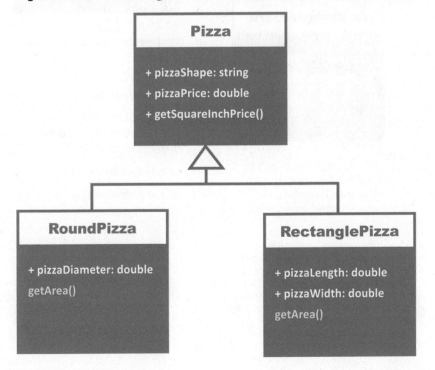

QuickCheck

What are the names of the methods in Figure 11-44?

a. getSquareInchPrice and getArea

b. pizzaShape and pizzaPrice

c. RoundPizza and RectanglePizza

d. string and double

11

▶ How does the getArea() method work? If you have been thinking ahead a bit, you might wonder how a programmer can define the getArea() method to perform two different calculations: one that calculates the area of a rectangle by multiplying its length times its width, and another that calculates the area of a circle using the formula πr². An object-oriented concept called polymorphism makes it possible to assign more than one formula to the getArea() method.

▶ What is polymorphism? Polymorphism, sometimes called overloading, is the ability to redefine a method in a subclass. It allows programmers to create a single, generic name for a procedure that behaves in unique ways for different classes.

In the pizza program, for example, both the RectanglePizza and RoundPizza classes can have a getArea() method. The calculation that getArea() performs is defined one way for the RectanglePizza class and another way for the RoundPizza class. Figure 11-45 illustrates how polymorphism allows subclasses to tailor methods to fit their unique requirements.

Try It!

Extend the UML diagram you created on page 801 to include the following methods:

calculateAge()

getTuition()

getClassSchedule()

Figure 11-45: Different getArea() methods for round and rectangular pizzas

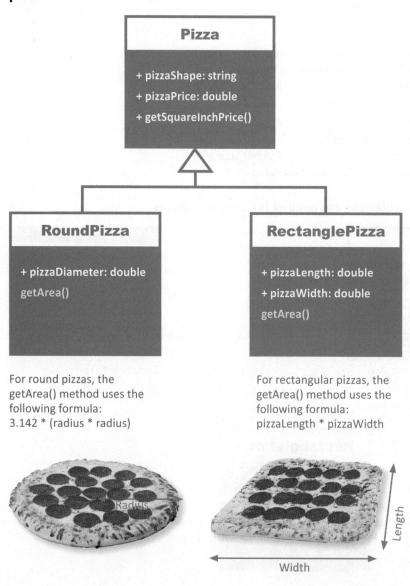

For round pizzas, the getArea() method uses the following formula:
3.142 * (radius * radius)

For rectangular pizzas, the getArea() method uses the following formula:
pizzaLength * pizzaWidth

QuickCheck

Which of the following statements is true about getArea()?

a. It is an example of polymorphism.

b. It carries out the same calculation for round and rectangular pizzas.

c. It is a message.

d. It is a variable.

11

❱ **How does the round getArea() method differ from the rectangle getArea() method?** The getArea() method defined in the RoundPizza class asks users to key in, or enter, the pizza's diameter. The method then divides the diameter by 2 to arrive at the radius. The value for the radius is used in the πr^2 calculation—3.142 * (radius * radius)—for the area of a circle.

The getArea() method defined in the RectanglePizza class asks users to key in the length of the pizza and then its width. This data is used in the calculation that multiplies length times width to produce the area of a rectangular pizza. Figure 11-46 illustrates the Java program segments for the getArea() methods. The lines that begin with // are remarks.

Figure 11-46: Java segments for two getArea() methods

```
getArea()

//Method to calculate the area of a round pizza
{
    pizzaDiameter = Keyin.inDouble("Enter the
    diameter of the pizza: ");

    radius = pizzaDiameter / 2;

    pizzaArea = 3.142 * (radius * radius);

}
```

```
getArea()

//Method to calculate the area of a rectangular pizza
{
    pizzaLength = Keyin.inDouble("Enter the length
    of the pizza: ");

    pizzaWidth = Keyin.inDouble("Enter the width of
    the pizza: ");

    pizzaArea = pizzaLength * pizzaWidth;
}
```

QuickCheck

The two methods in Figure 11-46 are different, but they both produce _____.

a. a value for pizzaArea

b. the value for the best pizza

c. the sizes and shapes of two pizzas

d. polymorphism

❱ **What are the advantages of polymorphism?** Polymorphism provides OO programs with easy extensibility and can help simplify program control structures. For example, if one of the pizzerias decides to get creative with pizza shapes, it would be fairly easy to extend the pizza program to work with triangular pizzas. To extend the program, simply define a TrianglePizza class that includes attributes for pizzaWidth and pizzaHeight and tailor its getArea() method for calculating the area of a triangle.

The ability to tailor the getArea() method for round and square pizzas allows programmers to simplify programs. As you can imagine, creating separate methods with unique names, such as getAreaRoundPizza(), getAreaRectanglePizza(), and getAreaTrianglePizza(), would add to the program's complexity and make it more difficult to extend the program for other pizza shapes.

OO Program Structure

So far in this section, you have learned how objects and methods interact to solve the pizza problem. You know that the pizza program uses a Pizza class and two subclasses: RectanglePizza and RoundPizza.

You also know that these classes include the getSquareInchPrice() and getArea() methods to perform calculations that supply data for solving the problem. You should also remember that the compare() method is used to manipulate pizza objects to determine which is the best deal.

▶ **How do the classes and methods fit together?** The classes and methods defined for the pizza program must be placed within the structure of a Java program, which contains class definitions, defines methods, initiates the comparison, and outputs results. Figure 11-47 provides an overview of the program structure.

Figure 11-47: Pizza program modules

Pizza Class Definition
- Define Pizza as a class with attributes for shape and price.
- Define the getSquareInchPrice() method that collects input for the pizza price.
- Calculate a pizza's square-inch price.

RectanglePizza Class Definition
- Define RectanglePizza as a subclass of Pizza with attributes for length and width.
- Define the getArea() method that collects input for the pizza length and width to calculate area.

RoundPizza Class Definition
- Define RoundPizza as a subclass of Pizza with an attribute for diameter.
- Define a getArea() method that collects input for the pizza diameter and then calculates area.

Compare() Method
- Compare the square-inch price of two pizzas and output the results.

Main Module
- Set up variables, and then create objects for Pizza1 and Pizza2.
- Activate the getArea(), getSquareInchPrice(), and compare() methods.

QuickCheck

Which module in Figure 11-47 would contain the call that activates the getArea() method?

a. Pizza class definition

b. RoundPizza and RectanglePizza class definitions

c. Compare() method

d. Main module

❯ **How does a Java program work?** The computer begins executing a Java program by locating a standard method called main(), which contains statements to send messages to objects by calling methods.

For the pizza program, the main() method includes statements that define a few variables and then asks the user to enter the shape of the first pizza. If the shape entered is Round, the program creates an object called Pizza1 that is a member of the RoundPizza class. If the shape entered is Rectangle, the program creates an object called Pizza1 that is a member of the RectanglePizza class.

After the pizza object is created, the program uses the getArea() method to calculate the pizza's area. The program then uses the getSquareInchPrice() method to calculate the pizza's square-inch price.

When the calculations are complete for the first pizza, the program performs the same process for the second pizza. Finally, the program uses the compare() method to compare the square-inch prices of the two pizzas and output a statement about which one is the best deal.

Because it is not the goal of this section to teach you the particulars of Java programming, don't worry about the detailed syntax of Java statements. Instead, refer to Figure 11-48 to get an overview of the activity that takes place in the main() method for the pizza program.

QuickCheck

In the program segment shown in Figure 11-48, which of the following activities happens first?

a. Creating pizza objects

b. Defining the Pizza class

c. Collecting input

d. Defining variables

11

Figure 11-48: The main() method of the pizza program

```
public static void main(String[] args)
   {

      Pizza Pizza1;
      Pizza Pizza2;
      String pizzaShape;

      pizzaShape = Keyin.inString("Enter the shape of the first pizza: ");
      if (pizzaShape.equals("Round"))
         {
         Pizza1 = new RoundPizza();
         }
      else
         Pizza1 = new RectanglePizza();

      Pizza1.getArea();
      Pizza1.getSquareInchPrice();

      pizzaShape = Keyin.inString("Enter the shape of the second pizza: ");
      if (pizzaShape.equals("Round"))
         Pizza2 = new RoundPizza();
      else
         Pizza2 = new RectanglePizza();

      Pizza2.getArea();
      Pizza2.getSquareInchPrice();

      compare(Pizza1, Pizza2);
   }
```

1. Define arguments for the main() method.

2. Define variables used in the main() method.

3. Collect input for the shape of the first pizza, and then create an object called Pizza1 that belongs to the RoundPizza or RectanglePizza class.

4. Use the getArea() and getSquareInchPrice() methods to calculate the area and square-inch price for the first pizza.

5. Collect input for the shape of the second pizza, and then create an object called Pizza2 that belongs to the RoundPizza or RectanglePizza class.

6. Use the getArea() and getSquareInchPrice() methods to calculate the area and square-inch price for the second pizza.

7. Use the compare() method to determine which pizza is the best deal, and then print the results.

▶ **What happens when the completed pizza program runs?** When you run the pizza program, it looks for the main() method. This method displays an on-screen prompt that asks for the pizza's shape. The getArea() method displays a prompt for the pizza's diameter (for a round pizza) or the pizza's length and width (for a rectangular pizza).

A similar series of prompts appears for the second pizza. The program concludes when the compare() method displays a statement about which pizza is the best deal. Figure 11-49 illustrates the output of the Java object-oriented pizza program.

Figure 11-49: Output for the pizza program written in Java

```
Command Prompt                                     —    □    ✕

C:\java>java PizzaProgram
Enter the shape of the first pizza: Round
Enter the diameter of the first pizza: 14
Enter the price of the first pizza: 12

Enter the shape of the second pizza: Rectangle
Enter the length of the second pizza: 11
Enter the width of the second pizza: 15
Enter the price of the second pizza: 13

Pizza 1 is the best deal!
```

QuickCheck

In Figure 11-49, why are there three entries for the first pizza, but four entries for the second pizza?

a. The second pizza is larger.

b. The second pizza is rectangular, so it has a length and a width.

c. The second pizza uses π, which requires an additional entry.

d. The second pizza uses the getSides() method rather than the getArea() method.

OO Applications

Computer historians believe that SIMULA (SIMUlation LAnguage) was the first programming language to work with objects, classes, inheritance, and methods. SIMULA was developed in 1962 by two Norwegian computer scientists for the purpose of programming simulations and models. SIMULA laid the foundation for the object-oriented paradigm.

▶ **How did object-oriented languages evolve?** The second major development in object-oriented languages came in 1972, when Alan Kay began work on the Dynabook project at the Xerox Palo Alto Research Center (PARC). Kay developed an easy-to-use programming language called Smalltalk that could be used to create programs based on real-world objects.

In 1983, object-oriented features were added to the C programming language, and C++ emerged as a popular tool for programming games and applications.

Java was originally planned as a programming language for consumer electronics, such as interactive cable television boxes, but it evolved into an object-oriented programming platform for developing Web applications. Java was officially launched in 1995 and has many of the characteristics of C++, from which it derives much of its syntax.

▶ **Which object-oriented languages are popular today?** Most of today's popular programming languages include object-oriented features. Whether a programmer is using Java, C++, Swift, Python, Objective-C, or C#, the language can define classes, objects, and methods.

▶ **What are the advantages of OO?** The object-oriented paradigm is cognitively similar to the way human beings perceive the real world. Using the OO approach, programmers might be able to visualize the solutions to problems more easily.

Facets of the object-oriented paradigm can also increase a programmer's efficiency because encapsulation allows objects to be adapted and reused in a variety of different programs. **Encapsulation** refers to the process of hiding the internal details of objects and their methods.

After an object is defined, it becomes a "black box," which hides its details from other objects and allows the data to be accessed using methods. Encapsulated objects can be easily reused and modified (Figure 11-50).

Figure 11-50: Encapsulation creates "black boxes"

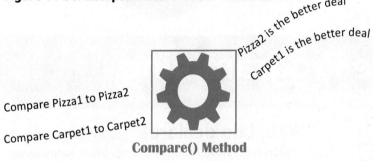

Compare Pizza1 to Pizza2

Compare Carpet1 to Carpet2

Pizza2 is the better deal

Carpet1 is the better deal

Compare() Method

Encapsulated methods have the potential to be reused for similar calculations. Here, a generalized version of the compare() method has become a "black box." Without knowing the details it contains, programmers can send it the names of two objects to see which one is the best deal.

▶ **What are the disadvantages of OO?** A potential disadvantage of object-oriented programs is runtime efficiency. Object-oriented programs tend to require more memory and processing resources than procedural programs. Programmers, software engineers, and systems analysts can work together to weigh the tradeoffs between the OO approach and runtime efficiency.

QuickQuiz   Section D

1. In OO programming, a class is a template for a group of [_____] with similar characteristics.

2. OO programmers often use [_____] diagrams to plan the classes for a program. (Hint: Use the abbreviation.)

3. In an OO program, getArea() would be called a(n) [_____].

4. The process of passing characteristics from a superclass to a subclass is referred to as [_____].

5. The object-oriented pizza program in this section of the module was written using the [_____] programming language.

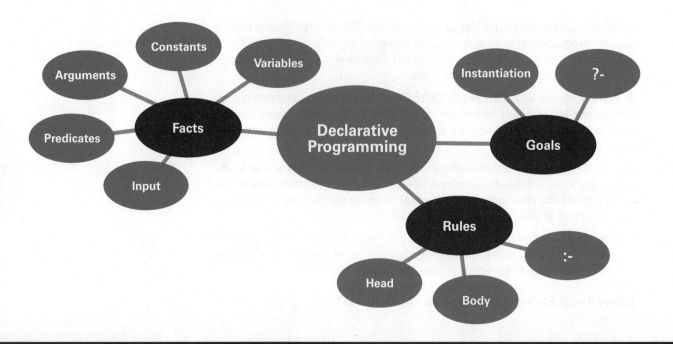

Objectives

▶ Describe how the declarative paradigm differs from the procedural and object-oriented paradigms.

▶ Identify the predicate and arguments in a Prolog statement.

▶ Identify constants and variables in a Prolog statement.

▶ Explain how Prolog uses goals.

▶ Draw a diagram to illustrate the concept of instantiation.

▶ Explain the difference between a Prolog fact and Prolog rule.

▶ Interpret Prolog rules.

▶ Identify Prolog statements that ask for user input.

▶ Interpret a decision table used to specify rules for a declarative program.

▶ List two types of projects, other than those mentioned in the text, that would be good candidates for a declarative language such as Prolog.

"Well, I do declare!" It is a characteristically Southern expression of surprise rarely heard today except in classic movies. Section E explains how this old expression relates to newfangled programming languages.

Terminology

declarative paradigm	rule	predicate	instantiation
fact	argument	goal	decision table

The Declarative Paradigm

Although procedural and object-oriented programming languages can deal with decisions and textual data, they begin to stumble when applied to problems with complex sequences of interrelated if...then branches. When dealing with problems that involve a spiderweb of logic, programmers can turn to declarative programming languages. This section focuses on the declarative paradigm by offering a little taste of the Prolog language.

▶ **What is the declarative paradigm?** In earlier sections of this module, you learned that procedural programming focuses on a step-by-step algorithm, which instructs the computer how to arrive at a solution. You also learned that the object-oriented approach emphasizes classes and methods that form objects. In contrast, the declarative paradigm describes aspects of a problem that lead to a solution. As in the expression "Well, I do declare!," programmers using declarative languages write statements that declare, or state, facts pertaining to a program.

The declarative paradigm might sound similar to the procedural paradigm, but it is fundamentally different. Whereas the procedural paradigm focuses on an algorithm that describes a solution, the declarative paradigm focuses on describing the problem. The procedural paradigm focuses on *how*; the declarative paradigm focuses on *what*. Figure 11-51 summarizes these differences.

Figure 11-51: Programming paradigms take different approaches

Procedural paradigm	Object-oriented paradigm	Declarative paradigm
Programs detail how to solve a problem	Programs define objects, classes, and methods	Programs describe the problem
Very efficient for number-crunching tasks	Efficient for problems that involve real-world objects	Efficient for processing words and language

▶ **What are the building blocks for the declarative paradigm?** Many declarative programming languages, such as Prolog, use a collection of facts and rules to describe a problem. In the context of a Prolog program, a **fact** is a statement that provides the computer with basic information for solving a problem. In the pizza problem, for example, these facts might include:

A pizza has a price of $10.99, a size of 12 inches, and a round shape.

Another pizza has a price of $12.00, a size of 11 inches, and a square shape.

In the context of a Prolog program, a **rule** is a general statement about the relationship between facts. For example, the following rule is useful for solving the problem of which pizza is a better deal:

A pizza is a better deal if its square-inch price is less than the square-inch price of another pizza.

Prolog Facts

Prolog programming is fun. The language does not have lots of maddening syntax rules or a long list of command words to memorize. The punctuation mainly consists of periods, commas, and parentheses, so programmers don't have to track levels and levels of curly brackets as when programming in languages such as C++ or Java. Prolog programming is all about facts and rules.

▶ **How does a programmer write facts?** Return to the simple problem of deciding which of two round or square pizzas is the best deal based on price per square inch. The first step in writing the program using Prolog is to enter facts that describe the prices, shapes, and sizes of two pizzas. The fact "The shape of a pizza is round." can be written this way:

    shapeof(pizza,round).

The words in parentheses are called arguments. An **argument** represents one of the main subjects that a fact describes. The word outside the parentheses, called the **predicate**, describes the relationship between the arguments. For example, the predicate shapeof describes the relationship between pizza and round. Figure 11-52 points out the simple syntax details pertaining to capitalization and punctuation for Prolog facts.

Figure 11-52: Prolog syntax

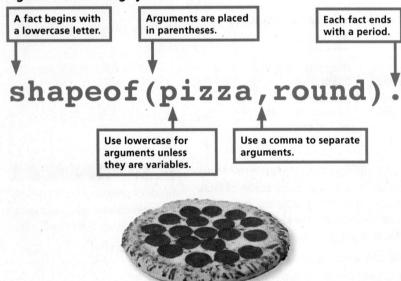

A fact begins with a lowercase letter.

Arguments are placed in parentheses.

Each fact ends with a period.

```
shapeof(pizza,round).
```

Use lowercase for arguments unless they are variables.

Use a comma to separate arguments.

▶ **What is the purpose of the predicate?** Although it might seem clear that round describes the shape of a pizza, the predicate must not be omitted. The predicate can drastically change the meaning of a fact. For example, the facts in Figure 11-53 have the same arguments, (joe,fish), but the predicates give the facts very different meanings.

Figure 11-53: Predicates are important

| `hates(joe,fish).` | `playscardgame(joe,fish).` | `name(joe,fish).` |
| Joe hates fish. | Joe plays a card game called fish. | Joe is the name of a fish. |

For the pizza program, a series of facts can be used to describe a pizza:

```
priceof(pizza1,10).
sizeof(pizza1,12).
shapeof(pizza1,square).
```

Another set of similar facts can be used to describe a second pizza:

```
priceof(pizza2,12).
sizeof(pizza2,14).
shapeof(pizza2,round).
```

Facts can have more than two arguments. For example, a single fact can be used to fully describe a pizza:

```
pricesizeshape(pizza1,10,12,square).
```

Using a series of facts to describe a pizza has some advantages and some disadvantages over using a single fact. A single fact tends to make a program more compact, whereas multiple facts might provide more flexibility. The structure of a fact also affects the syntax for goals that produce information.

▶ **What is a goal?** The facts in a Prolog program are useful even without any rules. Prolog can manipulate facts in several ways without explicit programming. Each fact in a Prolog program is similar to a record in a database, but you can query a Prolog program's database by asking a question, called a **goal** in Prolog jargon. As an example, the following facts can easily be queried by entering goals:

```
priceof(pizza1,10).
sizeof(pizza1,12).
shapeof(pizza1,square).
priceof(pizza2,12).
sizeof(pizza2,14).
shapeof(pizza2,round).
```

QuickCheck

Given the set of facts to the left, which pizza is square?

a. The most expensive pizza

b. The biggest pizza

c. pizza1

d. pizza2

▶ **How are goals entered?** You can ask questions by entering goals from the ?- prompt. For example, the goal `?- shapeof(pizza1,square)` means "Is the shape of pizza1 square?" Prolog searches through the facts to see if it can satisfy the goal by finding a match. If a match is found, Prolog responds with true; otherwise, it responds with false.

This goal might seem trivial if you are working with a small set of facts, which are all visible on the screen. Many programs, however, contain hundreds of facts, which cannot be displayed on a single screen or easily remembered by a programmer.

▶ **What about more creative questions?** Prolog allows you to ask open-ended questions by replacing constants with variables. A Prolog variable is like a placeholder or an empty box, into which Prolog can put information gleaned from a fact. A Prolog variable begins with an uppercase letter to distinguish it from a constant. The argument Pizza is a variable, whereas pizza1 is a constant. The argument Inches is a variable, whereas 14 is a constant.

Prolog variables are handy tools for formulating open-ended goals. As an example, suppose you want to find the size of pizza2. You can obtain this information by using the variable Inches in the goal:

```
?- sizeof(pizza2,Inches).
```

Prolog looks for any facts that have sizeof as a predicate and pizza2 as the first argument. It responds with the actual value of the second argument:

```
Inches = 14
```

Much of the power and flexibility of the Prolog language stems from its ability to query facts by matching predicates, comparing constants, and instantiating variables. Figure 11-54 illustrates how to query a set of Prolog facts.

Figure 11-54: A Prolog goal is similar to a database query

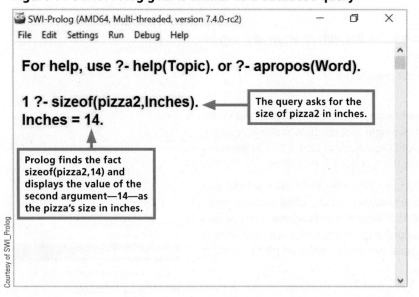

Courtesy of SWI_Prolog

The ?- prompt allows you to work with a knowledge base by entering facts, rules, and goals. Suppose you have opened a knowledge base containing facts about two pizzas. You can enter goals to find their prices, sizes, and shapes.

▶ **What is instantiation?** Finding a value for a variable is referred to as **instantiation**. To solve the goal `?- sizeof(pizza2,Inches)`, a Prolog program looks for a fact that begins with `sizeof(pizza2....`

When Prolog finds the rule `sizeof(pizza2,14)`, the program instantiates, or assigns, the value 14 to the variable Inches (Figure 11-55).

Figure 11-55: Instantiation replaces a variable with a constant

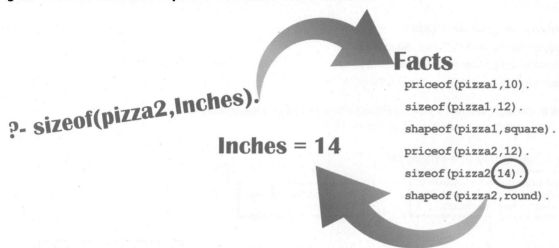

▶ **How do programmers use instantiation?** Instantiation can be used to produce information that is not implicitly stored in the database. Suppose you want to know the size of the round pizza. The knowledge base does not contain a fact like `sizeof(roundpizza,14)`; however, you can use a conjunction of two goals, as shown in Figure 11-56, to obtain the size of the round pizza.

Figure 11-56: Instantiation in action

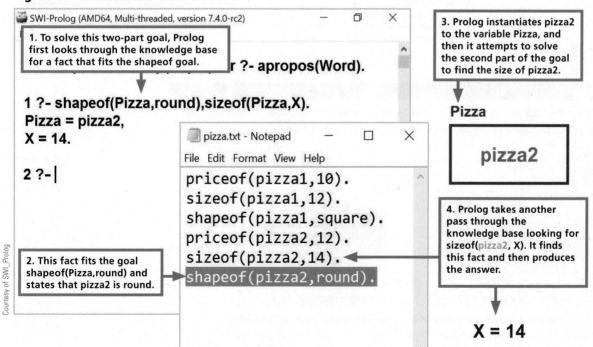

Prolog Rules

With just facts and goals, Prolog would be nothing more than a database. But the addition of rules gives programmers a set of tools to manipulate the facts.

▶ **How does a programmer write Prolog rules?** The pizza program requires a rule that states, "A pizza is a better deal if its price per square inch is less than the price per square inch of the other pizza." Translated into Prolog, this rule becomes:

```
betterdeal(PizzaX,PizzaY) :-
squareinchprice(PizzaX,AmountX),
squareinchprice(PizzaY,AmountY),
AmountX < AmountY.
```

Take a look at the logic behind this rule. A Prolog rule consists of a head, a body, and a connecting symbol, as described in Figure 11-57.

Figure 11-57: Anatomy of a Prolog rule

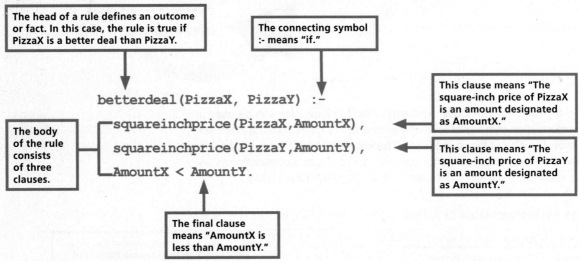

The head of a rule defines an outcome or fact. In this case, the rule is true if PizzaX is a better deal than PizzaY.

The connecting symbol :- means "if."

This clause means "The square-inch price of PizzaX is an amount designated as AmountX."

This clause means "The square-inch price of PizzaY is an amount designated as AmountY."

```
betterdeal(PizzaX, PizzaY) :-
    squareinchprice(PizzaX,AmountX),
    squareinchprice(PizzaY,AmountY),
    AmountX < AmountY.
```

The body of the rule consists of three clauses.

The final clause means "AmountX is less than AmountY."

QuickCheck

Think about the rule in Figure 11-57. Given the facts shown below, what is the result of the query **betterdeal(vangos,venice).**? (Hint: Think carefully!)

a. PizzaX

b. pizza1

c. vangos

d. true

Vango's Pizzeria
12" square pizza: $10
Price per square inch: $0.0694

The Venice
14" round pizza: $12
Price per square inch: $0.0779

▶ **How do Prolog rules work?** To understand how the betterdeal rule works, we'll have to perform a little bit of magic. In the completed pizza program, there would be a rule that calculates the square-inch price.

Because you don't yet have such a rule, temporarily assume that the square-inch price of the first pizza is .0694 (6.94 cents) and the square-inch price of the second pizza is .0779 (7.79 cents). These facts can be stated as follows:

```
squareinchprice(pizza1,.0694).
squareinchprice(pizza2,.0779).
```

Now, suppose you enter the query `?- betterdeal(pizza1,pizza2)`, which translates to "Is pizza1 a better deal than pizza2?" Figure 11-58 illustrates how Prolog uses the betterdeal rule to answer your query.

Figure 11-58: The betterdeal rule in action

Facts

```
priceof(pizza1,10).

sizeof(pizza1,12).

shapeof(pizza1,square).

priceof(pizza2,12).

sizeof(pizza2,14).

shapeof(pizza2,round).

squareinchprice(pizza1,.0694).

squareinchprice(pizza2,.0779).
```

Betterdeal Rule

```
betterdeal(PizzaX,PizzaY) :-

    squareinchprice(PizzaX,AmountX),

    squareinchprice(PizzaY,AmountY),

    AmountX < AmountY.
```

Query

```
?- betterdeal(pizza1,pizza2).
```

❶ Prolog instantiates pizza1 to PizzaX and pizza2 to PizzaY.

```
betterdeal(pizza1,pizza2) :-

    squareinchprice(pizza1,AmountX),

    squareinchprice(pizza2,AmountY),

    AmountX < AmountY.
```

❷ Prolog looks through the facts to find the squareinchprice for pizza1 and pizza2. These prices are instantiated to AmountX and AmountY, respectively.

```
betterdeal(pizza1,pizza2) :-

    squareinchprice(pizza1,.0694),

    squareinchprice(pizza2,.0779),

    .0694 < .0779.
```

❸ The last line now contains a statement that is true—.0694 < .0779—which validates the rule and produces "true" as a response to your query, "Is pizza1 a better deal than pizza2?"

▶ Does the order of rules affect the way a Prolog program runs?
When writing programs in a procedural language, such as C, Visual Basic, or Python, the order of program statements is critically important. For example, if you place input statements for pizza size and price after the IF statements that compare the square-inch prices, the program produces an error because it has no numbers to use for the comparison. In contrast, the order or sequence of rules in a Prolog program is usually not critical.

▶ What does the complete pizza program look like in Prolog? The complete pizza program includes the facts that describe two pizzas and rules that describe the better deal, square-inch price, and area. Figure 11-59 contains the entire pizza program.

Figure 11-59: The pizza program written in Prolog

```
priceof(pizza1,10).

sizeof(pizza1,12).

shapeof(pizza1,square).

priceof(pizza2,12).

sizeof(pizza2,14).

shapeof(pizza2,round).

betterdeal(PizzaX,PizzaY) :-

    squareinchprice(PizzaX,AmountX),

    squareinchprice(PizzaY,AmountY),

    AmountX < AmountY.

area(Pizza,Squareinches) :-

    sizeof(Pizza,Side),

    shapeof(Pizza,square),

    Squareinches is Side * Side.

area(Pizza,Squareinches) :-

    sizeof(Pizza,Diameter),

    shapeof(Pizza,round),

    Radius is Diameter / 2,

    Squareinches is 3.142 * (Radius * Radius).

squareinchprice(Pizza,Amount) :-

    area(Pizza,Squareinches),

    priceof(Pizza,Dollars),

    Amount is Dollars / Squareinches.
```

QuickCheck

Using the knowledge base in Figure 11-59, suppose you make the query **betterdeal(pizza1,pizza2).** What is instantiated to the variable PizzaX?

a. priceof

b. shapeof

c. sizeof

d. pizza1

Interactive Input

The pizza program on the previous page contains the size, price, and shape information for both pizzas. Such a program is not very versatile. Because the program contains facts, such as `priceof(pizza1,10)` and `priceof(pizza2,12)`, it is limited to specific pizzas that cost $10.00 and $12.00. The program can be generalized by collecting input from the user and storing it in variables or by asserting new facts at runtime.

▶ **How do programmers collect input from the user?** To collect input, programmers can use read and write statements. Examine the program in Figure 11-60 to see how `read` and `write` predicates collect user input, and then look at the output screen to see how the program interacts with users when it is run.

Figure 11-60: Prolog input

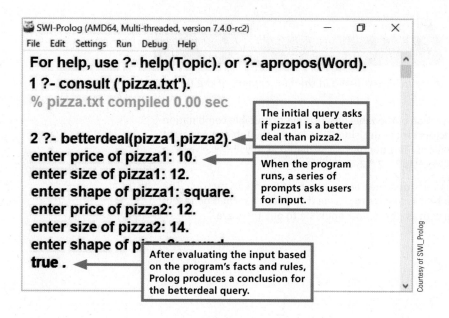

Prolog uses the write predicate to display a prompt for input.	`write(user,'enter price of pizza1: '),`
	`read(user,Price1), assertz(priceof(pizza1,Price1)),`
The read predicate gathers input entered by the user, and then the assertz predicate creates a fact, such as priceof(pizza1,12).	`write(user,'enter size of pizza1: '),`
	`read(user,Size1), assertz(sizeof(pizza1,Size1)),`
	`write(user,'enter shape of pizza1: '),`
	`read(user,Shape1), assertz(shapeof(pizza1,Shape1)),`
	`write(user,'enter price of pizza2: '),`
	`read(user,Price2), assertz(priceof(pizza2,Price2)),`
	`write(user,'enter size of pizza2: '),`
	`read(user,Size2), assertz(sizeof(pizza2,Size2)),`
	`write(user,'enter shape of pizza2: '),`
	`read(user,Shape2), assertz(shapeof(pizza2,Shape2)),`

SWI-Prolog (AMD64, Multi-threaded, version 7.4.0-rc2)

File Edit Settings Run Debug Help

For help, use ?- help(Topic). or ?- apropos(Word).
1 ?- consult ('pizza.txt').
% pizza.txt compiled 0.00 sec

2 ?- betterdeal(pizza1,pizza2).
enter price of pizza1: 10.
enter size of pizza1: 12.
enter shape of pizza1: square.
enter price of pizza2: 12.
enter size of pizza2: 14.
enter shape of pizza2: round.
true .

The initial query asks if pizza1 is a better deal than pizza2.

When the program runs, a series of prompts asks users for input.

After evaluating the input based on the program's facts and rules, Prolog produces a conclusion for the betterdeal query.

Courtesy of SWI_Prolog

Declarative Logic

Suppose we extend the pizza problem to include several more conditions. What if the decision to buy a pizza depends not just on its price, but on how quickly the pizza can be baked and whether the pizzeria offers delivery service. Suddenly the problem involves many more factors. Just how many factors is something a programmer would need to determine before starting to write facts and rules.

▶ **How does a programmer plan a declarative program?** The logic underlying the original pizza program was pretty simple: The pizza with the best square-inch price is the best deal. That logic required only one rule. In contrast, most real-world problems involve logic that is much more complex. Programmers need tools to help organize their thoughts and make provisions for all of the conditions that might exist in the real world.

A **decision table** is a tabular method for visualizing and specifying rules based on multiple factors. When the decision to buy a pizza depends on its price, whether it can be delivered, and how soon it is ready, these three factors produce eight possible situations.

In which of the eight situations would you purchase a pizza? What if the best-priced pizza is ready in less than 30 minutes, but it can't be delivered? What if the best-priced pizza won't be ready for an hour? Try to envision how you might implement this logic as a series of IF statements in a procedural or OO program. Figure 11-61 illustrates how a programmer might construct a decision table that describes all the rules pertaining to pizza prices, delivery, and time.

QuickCheck

In Figure 11-61, what's the decision for a pizza with the lowest price that's ready in less than 30 minutes, but can't be delivered?

a. Buy it.

b. Don't buy it.

c. Toss a coin.

d. There is no rule for this decision.

Figure 11-61: A decision table lays out the logic for factors and actions

❶ **❷**

Lowest price?	Y	N	Y	N	Y	N	Y	N
Delivery available?	Y	Y	N	N	Y	Y	N	N
Ready in less than 30 minutes?	Y	Y	Y	Y	N	N	N	N
❸ Buy it?	✓	✓	✗	✗	✓	✗	✗	✗

❶ Each factor that relates to the pizza purchase is listed in the first column of the upper part of the table.

❷ The remaining cells in the upper section of the table describe every possible combination of factors. This table has three factors for the decision. That means the table needs eight columns to cover all the combinations. This number is calculated as $2^{\text{number of factors}}$. In this case, there are three factors, so 2^3 is 2 * 2 * 2, or 8.

❸ The lower part of the table lists actions that are taken based on the factors. The programmer looks at each column of Ys and Ns to decide if the action should be taken. For example, in the column filled with Ys, the action would be to buy the pizza.

Declarative Applications

As you have seen from the pizza example, it is possible to use a declarative language to solve a problem that involves calculations. However, problems that require intensive computation are not usually best suited for the declarative paradigm. As a general rule, declarative programming languages are most suitable for problems that pertain to words, concepts, and complex logic rather than to numbers.

▶ **What are the advantages of declarative languages?** As you learned in this module, declarative languages offer a great deal of flexibility for querying a set of facts and rules. These languages also allow programmers to describe problems using words rather than the abstract structures required by procedural and object-oriented languages.

Although not in widespread use, declarative programming is popular in several niche markets. The U.S. Forest Service uses Prolog programs for resource management. Prolog programs are also used extensively in scientific research. The U.S. Department of Homeland Security experimented with a Prolog application developed to comb through social networking sites for terrorist activities. Finally, a growing trend is to incorporate Prolog modules with procedural and object-oriented programs to handle concept and language processing.

▶ **What are the disadvantages of declarative languages?** Currently, declarative languages are not commonly used for production applications. To some extent, today's emphasis on the object-oriented paradigm has pushed declarative languages out of the mainstream, both in education and in the job market. Many aspiring programmers are never introduced to declarative languages, so they are not included among the languages evaluated for a specific project.

Declarative languages have a reputation for providing minimal input and output capabilities. Although many of today's Prolog compilers provide access to Windows and Mac user interface components, programmers are often unaware of this capability. Despite their lack of popularity, declarative languages help to round out a programmer's repertoire and may offer employment opportunities in interesting niche projects.

> **Try It!**
>
> Suppose you're an NCIS detective trying to solve a case in which Tom is murdered with a revolver: The time of death is 10 am. One of the suspects, Mr. Plum, owns a revolver, but he has an alibi for the time of death. Miss Scarlett does not own a gun, but she has no alibi. However, Miss Scarlett has a brother, Greg, who owns a gun. Can you write a series of Prolog rules to describe these clues?

11

QuickQuiz   Section E

1. The declarative programming paradigm focuses on describing a(n) [_____], whereas the procedural paradigm focuses on algorithms that describe a(n) [_____].

2. In the Prolog fact `location(balcony,H1)`, balcony and H1 are [_____], whereas location is referred to as the [_____].

3. A Prolog attribute can be a(n) [_____], such as round (with a lowercase *r*), or it can be a(n) [_____], such as Shape (with an uppercase *S*).

4. Finding the value for a variable while solving a Prolog goal is called [_____].

5. In a Prolog rule, the :- connecting symbol means [_____].

Issue: Can Computers Think?

Today, we regard computers mostly in the context of connecting on Facebook, streaming music and video from the Web, and playing amusing little games like *Among Us*. But behind the scenes, there are computers doing some really heavy lifting, such as estimating climate change, piecing together the human genome, and researching the beginning of the universe.

The computers that delve into these problems are the descendants of room-sized machines constructed in the 1940s and 1950s that laboriously calculated ballistic tables and deciphered Nazi coded messages.

In the era when only a handful of computers existed, some visionary scientists looked toward the future and speculated that computers might rival humans in their capacity to think.

In 1950, the well-respected British mathematician Alan Turing wrote, "I believe that at the end of the century, the use of words and general educated opinion will have altered so much that one will be able to speak of machines thinking without expecting to be contradicted."

His prediction did not turn out to be correct, but it sparked a controversy that continues today: Can computers think, and how would we know if they do?

Turing described a test of machine intelligence in a 1950 paper called *Computing Machinery and Intelligence*. The "Turing Test," as it is now called, is somewhat like a TV game show. In a simplified version, it pits a judge against two backstage contestants: a computer and a human. The judge asks each contestant a series of questions, which are answered in written format or displayed on a screen.

A computer passes the Turing Test if the judge is unable to determine which contestant is the computer and which contestant is human. According to Turing, a computer that can respond as intelligently as a human must be intelligent and must be able to think.

> **"By the time the controversy dies down...AIs will already be thousands of times smarter than us."**
>
> Ray Kurzweil commenting on IBM's *Jeopardy!* victory

Turing's test of machine intelligence launched the study of artificial intelligence (AI), which is now a mainstream discipline of computer science. An idea that previously existed only in the fantasy worlds of science fiction writers, such as Karel Capek, L. Frank Baum, and Isaac Asimov, became a legitimate field of scientific inquiry.

Computers have competed with humans in domain-specific showdowns. An IBM computer named Deep Blue beat grand master Garry Kasparov in a 1997 chess match. Then in 2011, an AI computer named Watson won a combined-point *Jeopardy!* game, beating two of the quiz show's biggest all-time winners.

Watson had access to four terabytes of data, including the entire content of Wikipedia.

IBM's Web site describes Watson's technology as "an application of advanced Natural Language Processing, Information Retrieval, Knowledge Representation and Reasoning, and Machine Learning technologies..." The description continues, "At its core, Watson is built on IBM's DeepQA technology for hypothesis generation, massive evidence gathering, analysis, and scoring."

Beating two *Jeopardy!* experts does not make Watson intelligent, however. *Jeopardy!* requires contestants to answer questions in the form of "Who is..." or "What is...." Carrying out a sustained conversation, staying on topic, and responding sensibly require more sophistication; but that is not to say that Watson could not acquire those abilities through additional programming and learning.

Whether or not you believe that computers might eventually be able to think, consider Ray Kurzweil's prediction: "By the time the controversy dies down and it becomes unambiguous that nonbiological intelligence is equal to biological human intelligence, the AIs will already be thousands of times smarter than us." But not to worry. Kurzweil continues, "Ultimately, we will vastly extend and expand our own intelligence by merging with these tools of our own creation."

Try It! From science fiction to real life, artificial intelligence is fascinating. Yes, you can talk to an AI today! Have fun exploring while you compile your findings in a document called AI Project.

1 The 2014 film *The Imitation Game* features actor Benedict Cumberbatch as Alan Turing and recounts his attempts to build a computer that could crack the Nazi Enigma code machine. In the film, his description of the "game" was severely simplified for non-technical viewers. How was Turing's game really supposed to work? Use the Web to locate a PDF file of Turing's original paper, *Computing Machinery and Intelligence*. Find out how Turing described each of the three players and how he described the purpose of the original game. How did Turing propose to change this game to determine if a computer could be considered intelligent?

2 You can usually spot artificial intelligence programs because they tend to offer vague answers and sometimes try to change the subject when they don't understand a question. These programs are called chatbots. Online chatbots include Jabberwacky, ELIZA, and Rose. Digital assistants such as Siri, Alexa, and Google Assistant can also be classified as chatbots. Have a chat with a chatbot and write a short paragraph of your impressions. What did you ask that it answered intelligently? Give an example of a question for which you received a weird answer.

3 CAPTCHA technology turned the Turing Test inside out and is sometimes classified as a reverse Turing Test. What is the main goal of CAPTCHA, and is it really a reverse Turing Test? Use search terms such as *captcha*, *reverse turing test*, and *cracked* to find out.

4 Even if a computer can eventually pass the Turing Test, not everyone would agree that it can think. Philosopher John Searle, for example, attempted to refute the Turing Test

using the now-famous Chinese Room thought experiment. What can you find out about Searle's Chinese Room and how it applies to machine intelligence?

5 Recently, there has been a resurgence of concern about a future in which computers and AI begin to drastically change human society. Search online for the interview with Nick Bostrom entitled "AI Doomsayer Says His Ideas Are Catching On." Also check out the YouTube video "Building Mechanical Gods: Sam Harris on the Dangers of AI." Locate quotations that summarize what Ray Kurzweil, Daniela Rus, and Bill Gates have said about the future of AI. In what ways do your views about AI align with the viewpoints of these thought leaders?

Thomas Watson was the founder of IBM and namesake for the computer that bested human opponents in *Jeopardy!*. Notice the THINK sign—an intriguing motto for a computer company.

What Do You Think?   Issue

1. Does the Turing Test of machine intelligence make sense to you?

2. If a computer can beat human contestants in *Jeopardy!*, is it showing signs of intelligence?

3. Do you believe that computers might someday have the capacity to think?

Information Tools: Making the Cut

Searching Bing, Google Scholar, or academic databases produces mountains of links. How do you select and save the most relevant bits of information? The first step is to decide which information is relevant enough to make the cut. To decide, ask yourself the following three questions:

1. Is it relevant? Read the search engine synopsis carefully. With Google and other search engines, the synopsis shows your search terms in the context of the article. Academic databases display a standard synopsis. Don't waste your time linking to articles that are not relevant to your research topic.

Human-centered artificial intelligence: Reliable, safe & trustworthy

B Shneiderman - International Journal of Human-Computer ... 2020 - Taylor & Francis

Well-designed technologies that offer high levels of human control and high levels of computer automation can increase human performance, leading to wider adoption. The Human-Centered Artificial Intelligence (HCAI) framework clarifies how to (1) design for high...

☆ ⯈⯈ Cited by 82   Related articles   All 4 versions ≫

> In Google Scholar, select the Cite link to view and copy the bibliographic citation.

2. Is it reliable? An increasing number of so-called predatory publishers are stuffing search results with articles published in less-than-reputable scholarly journals that charge authors to publish their work. When in doubt about the pedigree of a scholarly article, check the Publons list of journals and publications.

3. Are there links to additional material? The first part of a full-text journal article summarizes historical research and may include lots of citations. Some of these ideas might be worth tracking down for your own research. The bibliography can help you locate specific material mentioned in the article.

Some people do not understand AI, hence the field of research known as explainable AI, or XAI, which attempts to build human-comprehensible and interpretable systems that can explain their decisions (Samek, Montavon, Vedaldi, Hansen, & Müller, 2019).

Bibliography
W. Samek, G. Montavon, A. Vedaldi, L.K. Hansen, Müller Explainable AI: interpreting, explaining and visualizing deep learning, 11700, Springer Nature (2019).

> For more sources, jump to resources mentioned in the bibliography.

NOTE-TAKING TIPS

○ Use a word processor or a citation/reference management application.

○ Be sure to identify information that is not your own. One technique is to put it inside quotation marks; another technique is to apply a highlight color.

○ Always capture the URL of a source document so that you can return to it if you eventually include it in your paper and need a full citation.

○ Make sure that you add your own identifier to each piece of information; use your notes as topic headers, which will help you group and organize the information.

○ Articles most relevant to your research topic require careful reading and note taking. For less relevant articles, simply make a note of the main idea and URL, just in case it becomes relevant later in your research process.

Try It!
As you find information that is relevant to your research topic, you need a way to record it and keep track of it. Note-taking tools help you record important ideas; the trick is to keep your notes in good order. Many students use word processors to take notes. Citation/reference management tools offer another option. Here's a chance to explore these tools and make a word cloud.

1 Use your favorite word processing software to create a blank document called Project [Your Name] Module 11, and then complete the rest of the steps.

2 Use an academic database to search for a journal article about artificial intelligence. Read the conclusion, highlight the most important idea, and copy it to your Project document using quotation marks to show that it is copied material. Capture the Web address (URL) in your Project document. Add a phrase in your own words that summarizes the main idea.

3 Find three pieces of information that support the idea you selected in Step 2. This information can be found in the journal article or another source. Copy the passages into your Project document (don't forget the quotation marks) along with the corresponding URLs.

4 Use a search engine, such as Google or Bing, to locate two images and one video pertaining to artificial intelligence. Copy the images into your Project document, along with their URLs. How will you reference the video?

5 Search for *artificial intelligence* in Wikipedia. Highlight one of the main ideas. Copy the text, add quotation marks, and capture the URL in your Project document.

6 Register for a free account on a reference management site such as Mendeley or Zotero. Use tools provided by the site to capture the same information you collected in Steps 2–5. Don't forget to add your own tags that summarize each idea. Export your bibliographic data and related research materials if the tool offers a way to do so, and then import the information into your Project document. If you can't import or export, then instead take a screenshot of your information and paste it into your document.

7 Search Wikipedia for the article about artificial intelligence. Copy the entire article, and then go to a word cloud Web site such as *WordClouds.com* and paste the text to create a word cloud. Take a screenshot of your word cloud and paste it into your Project document.

8 Some students prefer to use presentation software such as PowerPoint or Keynote to maintain research notes. Each slide represents a note, such as a quote, image, or video with its corresponding citation, as shown below. Organizational tools in the presentation software help you arrange your notes. You can even create a set of slides to serve as an outline for your topic, then arrange the slides containing your notes under appropriate outline headings. Copy and paste your notes about artificial intelligence to the slides provided by the presentation software.

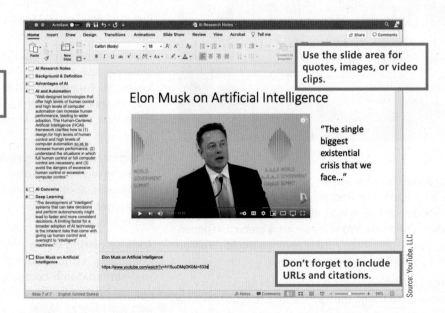

Each slide is a card in your stack of research notes.

Use the slide area for quotes, images, or video clips.

Don't forget to include URLs and citations.

Source: YouTube, LLC

Technology in Context: Computer Games

The lone programmer who develops a blockbuster videogame has become a cultural meme. But can an indie programmer expect to author the next *PUBG Mobile* or *Minecraft*? Do big corporations such as Sony, Activision, and EA have a monopoly on the market, or can independent developers keep a foot in the door of opportunity?

The computer game industry is on a roll. From arcade games to videogames, from PCs to mobile apps, worlds of colorful candy, blazing weaponry, and interstellar travel captivate gamers worldwide. Global revenue from computer and console games totals more than $100 billion each year. Sony, one of the largest video console manufacturers, generates billions in revenues each year from its PlayStation sales.

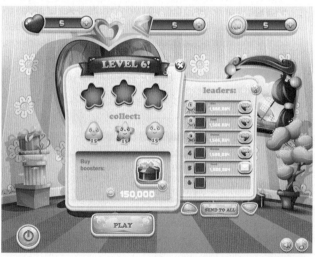

nearbirds/Shutterstock.com

As this book went to press, mobile gaming revenue accounted for $77 billion worldwide. Fortnite was earning $2.75 million per day, Roblox was raking in $2.40 million, and Pokemon Go $1.86 million. Every day. Wow! Producing a game that generates even a small percentage of that revenue would surely be a windfall for an enterprising programmer.

The outlook for earning revenue from mobile apps is not very bright, however. Although the Apple App Store carries some 100 million gaming apps, many of those games are distributed as freebies or under a "freemium" business model.

Forbes magazine reported that the average app developer offers five apps and earns less than $4,000 per year, total.

According to MIDiA Research, nearly 85% of the 700 top-grossing iPhone and Android apps are games, and 81% of the top-grossing apps originated from just 50 companies. As you may know, independent game developers have a difficult time breaking into the revenue brackets that rival a day job.

Back in the 1990s, when videogames such as *Mortal Kombat*, *EverQuest*, and *Unreal Tournament* hit the big time, a typical development budget hovered around $3 million. That may seem expensive, but the cost of today's mega games can exceed the annual budget for some small countries.

The *Wall Street Journal* reported that Disney's game development and toy production budget for *Infinity* was about $100 million. *Cyberpunk 2077,* a first-person role-playing game developed by CD Projekt, reportedly had a budget of $316 million.

Development budgets include a team of programmers and graphic designers, audio technicians, and project managers. In addition, budgets encompass marketing costs. Games that are based on books or movies have to be licensed, and those fees can be substantial.

Some independent developers have successfully used crowdsourcing at Web sites such as Kickstarter to raise funds. Yu Suzuki raised $6 million to develop the third installment of the Shenmue series. Isaac Childres received more than $12 million in pledges from more than 83,000 Kickstarter investors.

As with other genres of new media, opportunities afforded by emerging technologies open the gates to a flood of wannabe developers. Getting noticed without a substantial marketing budget requires the kind of luck that leads to picking a winning lottery ticket.

Today, aspiring game developers generally collect the necessary educational credentials to get hired at a well-staffed game company. There are several paths to pursue because game projects require team members with a variety of skills.

The terms *game developer* and *game designer* are sometimes used interchangeably, but within the industry they have distinct meanings. Game developers have a technical orientation, so their focus is on writing and testing programs. They decide how a game is built and programmed. In contrast, game designers focus on the game storyboard, character development, and soundscaping.

In major game studios, developers and designers work in specialized teams to fill these roles. For example, a game designer working at a major studio might be responsible just for the clothing of the main characters. A developer at the same studio might spend every day creating and testing the logic that assigns point totals to characters.

An alternative development strategy echoes the small-team approach used to create early computer games. Supercell, a 350-employee mobile game company based in Finland, organizes developers in autonomous groups of five to seven people. Each group generates game ideas and develops prototypes that are play-tested by other groups in the company. Games that pass the play-test will first debut in limited markets. Games that are successful in these test markets are released globally.

So how are blockbuster videogames developed? The process begins with months of planning and preparation. Every game has an underlying story that emerges from the creative mind of a writer or filmmaker. Games may be based on books, movies, or real-world events. Many games are spin-offs or sequels of already popular games.

From the story, artists and writers develop a storyboard using sketches and narratives to describe key aspects of the game, including characters, worlds, scoring, and play levels. Characters emerge from rough sketches that are refined by artists using digital drawing tools.

Two-dimensional concept drawings are rendered into three-dimensional characters beginning with a wireframe that gives each character its physique. Muscles, skin, clothing, and other features are added along with animation points supplied by models wearing motion capture suits.

While characters are being developed, other designers are working on the setting. Today's immersive games take place in environments that are rich in both visual and auditory details. Game worlds are drawn by artists and then rendered into three dimensions by programmers.

Programmers are also responsible for knitting together all the game elements. Characters controlled by gamers are programmed to be responsive and realistic as they move within the game environment. Weapons and objects are programmed to obey the laws of physics. Computer-controlled opponents have to be guided by artificial intelligence that is just smart enough to be challenging, but not too smart to be invincible.

Jobs for game developers typically require a minimum of a bachelor's degree, but some employers may accept an associate's degree. Internships help prospective developers gain experience that is usually a requirement for most programming positions.

For aspiring team members who want to work on creative rather than technical components of games, a Bachelor of Fine Arts degree with a focus on computer game design is an excellent resume builder.

Bardocz Peter/Shutterstock.com

Today, there are dedicated courses in computer game design that focus on tools and techniques for creating games for arcades, computers, and mobile devices. The Princeton Review ranked the University of Southern California, Becker College, and New York University as the top three undergraduate game development schools based on curriculum, faculty, and facilities.

These schools have studios equipped with virtual reality gear. They also have ADR (automatic dialog replacement) rooms for recording voice-overs and Foley studios for recording sound effects. Working with motion capture suits against a green screen, graphic arts students can collect data points for animating game characters—a technique used by most game companies to speed up development. If you're a student who wants to work in the game industry, get started on your career path with a degree in game design!

Flipped Class Projects

Critical Thinking

Think like a programmer and write a detailed description of making a peanut butter sandwich. Next, look at your detailed instructions and circle any looping or branching activities. If you don't have any, your description wasn't detailed enough and you should rework it. When you've completed the description, submit it to your instructor, who might compare the most and least detailed descriptions submitted by all students in your class.

Group Project

In a group of three students, create the specifications for a program to operate a gas pump. Make sure you create a problem statement, complete with assumptions and known information. Design the algorithm, making sure it dispenses the customer's choice of Regular, Mid-grade, or Premium gas. Assume that all customers will pay cash (credit cards are not accepted). Create mockups of the input/output displays shown to the customer. Create a test plan with a comprehensive set of inputs and outputs that could be used to check the accuracy of your finished program. You can collaborate on each aspect of the specifications or assign one student to each. Consolidate your completed specifications into a single document to submit to your instructor.

Cyberclassroom

Apple co-founder Steve Jobs famously said that everyone should learn to program "because it teaches you how to think." Discuss this idea with a group of your classmates. Do your experiences with programming and digital devices validate Jobs' statement? Assuming his idea has merit, should programming be a required part of the curriculum for elementary school, high school, or college students?

Multimedia Project

To appreciate the complexity of game programming, play a computer game. Make a list of the objects you encounter during the first five minutes of the game. You might have to stop and restart the game several times to complete your list. Don't forget to include the title screen, introductory music, video, and so on. Expand your list of objects by adding descriptions of what happens to the objects. For example, the background scenery object might move when the game character reaches a certain point on the screen, or a sound might be emitted by a character that gets struck by a weapon. Take a screenshot of the game during your observation period. Submit your list and screenshot. Indicate the name of the game you observed on the screenshot.

Resume Builder

The computer game industry is hot and employs professionals from a wide variety of career fields. How would a professional in your career field fit into a computer game development team? Even accountants can play a role! What aspect of the game would a professional from your field work on? Jot down your thoughts, and then go online and search for information about computer game development. What can you learn about jobs in the computer game industry for people with skills in your career field? Submit your findings in the format of your choice. You can write a one-page summary or get creative and develop a brochure or a 30-second radio spot.

Globalization

There is a growing trend to develop software that can be used globally. Suppose you are supervising a programming team, and you have directed them to internationalize a software application and make sure it can be easily converted into a variety of languages. After conducting research on the Web, create a list of best practices for software globalization that you would distribute to your programming team.

Key Terms

abstraction 773
agile methodology 763
algorithm 785
API 783
application programmers 760
argument 812
assembler 775
assembly language 774
assumption 762
attribute 800
class 799
class hierarchy 801
compiler 777
computer programming 759
constant 765
control 767
control structures 791
debugging 768
decision table 820
declarative paradigm 811
defensive programming 771
encapsulation 809
fact 811
fifth-generation languages 776
first-generation languages 774
flow control 791
flowchart 788
formal methods 770
fourth-generation languages 776
function 792

goal 813
high-level language 774
IDE 782
inheritance 801
instantiation 815
interpreter 777
iteration 794
keyword 764
known information 762
logic error 768
loop 794
low-level language 773
message 803
method 802
multiparadigm languages 779
object 799
object code 777
object-oriented paradigm 799
op code 774
operand 774
parameters 765
polymorphism 804
predicate 812
predictive methodology 763
private attribute 800
problem statement 761
procedural language 785
procedural paradigm 785
program editor 766
program statement 764

programming paradigm 779
properties 767
pseudocode 788
public attribute 800
remarks 769
repetition control structure 794
rule 811
runtime error 768
scripting languages 778
SDK 782
second-generation languages 774
selection control structure 793
sequence control structure 791
sequential execution 791
software engineering 759
source code 777
sprint 763
storyboard 767
structured English 788
subclass 801
superclass 801
syntax 765
syntax error 768
systems programmers 760
third-generation languages 775
threat modeling 770
variable 765
VDE 767
walkthrough 790

Interactive Summary

Section A: The instructions for a computer program are sometimes referred to as program [_____] . Computer programmers focus on [_____] computer programs, but they also plan, test, and document computer programs. In contrast, software [_____] apply formalized techniques to reduce the cost and complexity of software while increasing reliability. Before a program can be written, a programmer needs a clear problem [_____], which includes a list of assumptions, a description of known information, and a specification for what constitutes a solution. Programming projects can be approached using a(n) [_____] methodology, which requires extensive planning and documentation up front. An alternative approach is to use the [_____] methodology in which programs are developed in iterations called [_____] . With a clear plan, a programmer can begin composing using a text editor, program editor, or [_____]

development environment. Programs are composed of a series of statements that include a(n) [_____] such as input or print and parameters. Those parameters may include [_____] that represent values that can change, or [_____] that represent unchanging values. All computer programs should include internal documentation in the form of [_____], which are explanatory comments inserted into a computer program following language-specific symbols, such as #, or keywords such as REM. A program is not complete until it has been tested to ensure that it contains no [_____] errors, logic errors, or runtime errors. Programmers can use [_____] methods based on rigorous logical and mathematical models to reduce the number of defects in a software product. Additional techniques for producing high-quality, secure programs include threat modeling and [_____] programming.

Section B: A computer programming language is a set of grammar rules and [_____] for creating statements that can ultimately be processed by a computer. The first programming languages were low-level [_____] languages. Second-generation languages, called [_____] languages, allowed programmers to write programs consisting of abbreviated op codes instead of 1s and 0s. Third-generation languages provided programmers with easy-to-remember command words, such as PRINT and INPUT. Fourth-generation languages were designed to eliminate many of the strict punctuation and [_____] rules that complicated third-generation languages. Each generation of languages has a higher level of [_____] that removes or hides low-level details. Program statements ultimately must be converted into machine language so that they can be executed by the processor. That conversion can be performed by a(n)

[_____] that converts [_____] code into [_____] code. Alternatively, a(n) [_____] converts and executes one line at a time. [_____] languages, such as JavaScript and Perl, are executed one line at a time. Programming [_____] , such as procedural, object-oriented, and declarative, are methodologies that affect the way programmers conceptualize and approach computer programming. Programming languages such as Java, C++, Swift, and Python support one or more programming approaches. Programming languages can be obtained à la carte or in a package of tools such as an SDK or [_____] development environment. APIs also come in handy for adding standard user interface elements such as menu bars and functional elements such as print routines.

Section C:
Languages such as COBOL and Fortran support a traditional approach to programming called the [_____] paradigm, which is based on a step-by-step [_____]. Various planning tools, such as structured English, [_____], and flowcharts, help programmers plan the steps for a procedural program. Procedural languages provide programmers with a variety of [_____] control structures for specifying the order of program execution. A(n) [_____] directs the computer to execute one or more instructions not included as part of the main execution path of a program. A(n) [_____] control provides a choice of paths based on whether a condition is true or false. A(n) [_____] control, or loop, repeats one or more instructions until a certain condition is met. The procedural paradigm provides a solid approach to problems that can be solved by following a set of steps. Procedural languages tend to produce programs that run quickly and use system resources efficiently.

Section D:
The object-oriented paradigm is based on the idea that the solution to a problem can be visualized in terms of objects that [_____] with each other. An object is a single instance of an entity. Programmers can use a class as a template for a group of [_____] with similar characteristics. Classes can be derived from other classes through a process called [_____]. The set of superclasses and subclasses that are related to each other is referred to as a class [_____]. OO programmers often use [_____] Modeling Language diagrams to plan the classes for a program.

Objects interact with each other to solve problems by exchanging [_____], which initiate an action, a process, or a procedure. OO programmers can create [_____] to define what happens once an action is initiated. For flexibility, a concept called [_____], or overloading, allows programmers to create a single, generic name for a procedure that behaves in unique ways for different classes. The OO paradigm allows programmers to hide the internal details of objects and their methods. This process, called [_____], allows objects to be easily reused, modified, and repurposed.

Section E:
Programming languages such as Prolog support the [_____] programming paradigm because they encourage programmers to describe a(n) [_____] rather than its solution. Prolog programs are typically based upon a collection of facts and rules. A Prolog fact begins with a(n) [_____], such as shapeof, followed by a series of [_____] within parentheses, such as (pizza,round). Each Prolog rule has a(n) [_____], which defines an outcome or fact, followed by the notation :-, which means "if." The body of the rule consists of one or more clauses that define conditions that must be satisfied to validate the head of the rule. Prolog uses a process called [_____] to evaluate facts and rules to determine whether they are true. In Prolog jargon, a question or query to a program's database is called a(n) [_____]. Declarative languages such as Prolog can be used for problems that require calculations, but those problems are typically better suited to [_____] languages. As a general rule, declarative languages are best suited for problems that pertain to words, concepts, and complex logic rather than numbers.

1. A friend asks you for help writing a computer program to calculate the square yards of carpet needed for a dorm room. The statement "the dorm room floor is rectangular" is an example of a(n) [＿＿＿＿＿＿]. The length and width of the room are examples of [＿＿＿＿＿＿] information, which you can obtain as [＿＿＿＿＿＿] from the user.

2. Continuing with the carpet example, you devise a set of steps, or a(n) [＿＿＿＿＿＿], to solve the problem. You then use a programming language to write the [＿＿＿＿＿＿] shown below, which expresses the algorithm.

   ```
   width = input("Enter the width of the room
   in feet: ")

   length = input("Enter the length of the
   room in feet: ")

   areaInFeet = width * length

   areaInYards = areaInFeet/9

   print("The area is ", str(areaInFeet),
   " square feet")

   print("or approximately ",
   str(areaInYards), " square yards.")
   ```

3. Examine the statements shown below. This program prints [＿＿＿＿＿＿] lines of text.

   ```
   for x in range(1, 5):
       print("I got my mind set on you.")
   ```

4. You've just joined a programming team that is developing a Java program for an earth-moving equipment vendor. The lead programmer shows you a UML diagram containing labels such as Cranes, Trucks, and Front-end Loaders. With your background in object-oriented programming, you can tell immediately that these are [＿＿＿＿＿＿].

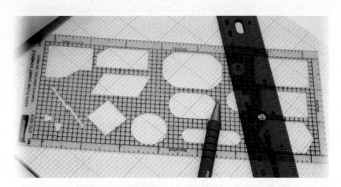

5. While browsing through several programs posted online, you come across the following program segment and realize it is written using the [＿＿＿＿＿＿] programming language:

   ```
   male(frodo).
   male(mungo).
   male(largo).
   male(balbo).
   female(berylla).
   female(belladonna).
   female(primula).
   female(sella).
   parents(mungo,berylla,balbo).
   parents(frodo,primula,drogo).
   parents(largo,berylla,balbo).
   parents(sella,berylla,balbo).
   brother_of(X,Y):-
       male(Y),
       parents(X,Mother,Father),
       parents(Y,Mother,Father).
   ```

6. Trace through the following program statements. Do they correctly output the chorus to the Beatles song *All You Need Is Love*? [＿＿＿＿＿＿]

   ```
   for x in range(1, 3):
       print ("All you need is love ")
   print("love")
   print("love is all you need")
   ```

Lab: Tunnels and Dragons

The original adventure game was text based. Gamers spent hours and hours immersed in a world of caves, treasure, riddles, and dangers. In this lab, you'll get into that retro vibe while designing the gateway to an adventure game. It is a fun way to learn some programming basics and gain appreciation for the programmer's mindset.

Requirements:

For this lab, you'll need a Windows or Apple computer with access to the Internet. The lab requires a Python development environment. You can use a locally installed Python IDE, or you can follow the instructions in Step 1 to access a free Web-based IDE. The lab instructions are generalized; they provide helpful guidelines, but not specific steps. Work carefully; programming requires precision, so type program statements exactly as they are printed. If you encounter syntax or runtime errors, look carefully at each line to find the errors.

Assignment:

1 Search the Web for *Python online* to locate an interactive Python programming environment, such as Replit. If the site requires registration, go ahead and register. (Hint: Be sure to use Python 3.0 or above. The syntax is slightly different from that of Python 1.0 and 2.0.)

2 Enter a comment and a command to output a message:

Type `# Adventure Game YourName` on line 1, substituting your full name for "YourName."

Press the Enter key to move down to line 2, and then type the following all on one line:

```
print("You are lost underground in a maze of tunnels.")
```

Run your program. (Hint: For Replit, select the Run button.)

If you receive an error message, make sure you've included the parentheses and quotation marks, and then try to run the program again.

3 Generate a random number.

Your Adventure program must generate a random number between 1 and 2. The number will not be displayed to players, but it will be used to secretly set up the game world and put a dragon in one of the tunnels.

The secret number will be stored in a variable that is called dangerTunnel.

Add the following statements to your program:

```
import random
dangerTunnel = random.randint(1,2)
```

Test your program to make sure you don't get an error message. The output should be "You are lost underground in a maze of tunnels." The screenshot below shows the program and output for this step.

```
1 # Adventure Game Sarah Smith
2 print ("You are lost underground in a maze of tunnels.")
3 import random
4 dangerTunnel = random.randint(1,2)
```

```
You are lost underground in a maze of tunnels.
>
```

After Step 3, the program and output of the Adventure game should look like this.

4 Ask players to choose a tunnel.

The next program segment asks players to select tunnel 1 or tunnel 2. The use of `int` in this statement ensures that the numbers entered by players are stored as integers.

Enter the following all on one line:

```
tunnelChoice = int(input("Choose tunnel 1 or tunnel 2: "))
```

5 Compare the chosen tunnel to the tunnel that contains a dragon, and then tell players if they are safe.

Enter the following, making sure to indent the two print statements as shown:

```
print("You chose tunnel ", tunnelChoice)
if tunnelChoice == dangerTunnel:
    print("You entered a tunnel with a dragon. Watch out.")
else:
    print("You entered an empty tunnel. You are safe for now.")
```

Run the program and debug any syntax errors that might result from missing punctuation. When you run the program and enter 1, the output should look like the screenshot below.

```
You are lost underground in a maze of tunnels.
Choose tunnel 1 or tunnel 2: 1
You chose tunnel 1
You entered an empty tunnel. You are safe for now.
>
```

6 Make sure the program does not contain any logic errors.

The program should display the "watch out" message when players select the number of the tunnel that contains a dragon. But how do you know if the program is doing that? To find out, you can print the number of the dangerTunnel just as a test. You can comment it out later if the program is working correctly.

Insert a print statement as line 5, so the program contains the following statements:

```
1 # Adventure Game Sarah Smith
2 print("You are lost underground in a maze of tunnels.")
3 import random
4 dangerTunnel = random.randint(1,2)
5 print("Dragon in tunnel ", dangerTunnel)          ◄———  Add this line.
6 tunnelChoice = int(input("Choose tunnel 1 or tunnel 2: "))
7 print("You chose tunnel ", tunnelChoice)
8 if tunnelChoice == dangerTunnel:
```

```
9       print("You entered a tunnel with a dragon. Watch out.")
10 else:
11      print("You entered an empty tunnel. You are safe for now.")
```

7 Test all conditions.

Run the program several times and test each of these conditions:

a. When the dragon is in tunnel 1, do players who enter 1 get the "watch out" message?

b. When the dragon is in tunnel 1, do players who enter 2 get the "safe" message?

c. When players enter a number that is not 1 or 2, what happens?

8 Trap the input so players must enter 1 or 2.

You can use a while loop to check player input. The loop will continue to ask for a number until the player enters a 1 or a 2. Insert the following statements as lines 6 and 7, and indent line 8 so your program looks like this:

```
1  # Adventure Game Sarah Smith
2   print("You are lost underground in a maze of tunnels.")
3  import random
4  dangerTunnel = random.randint(1,2)
5  print("Dragon in tunnel ", dangerTunnel)
6  tunnelChoice = 0                              ◀── Add these lines.
7  while tunnelChoice < 1 or tunnelChoice > 2: ◀──
8       tunnelChoice = int(input("Choose tunnel 1 or tunnel 2: ")) ◀── Indent this line.
9  print("You chose tunnel ", tunnelChoice)
10 if tunnelChoice == dangerTunnel:
11      print("You entered a tunnel with a dragon. Watch out.")
12 else:
13     print("You entered an empty tunnel. You are safe for now.")
```

Test your program by entering 5 as the tunnel number. You should be prompted to "Choose tunnel 1 or tunnel 2."

(Hint: If your program goes into an endless loop, use Ctrl-C to stop it.)

9 Comment out the print statement that you added for testing by adding a hashtag in front of it, like this:

```
5 # print("Dragon in tunnel ", dangerTunnel)
```

10 Now, get creative and modify the program to make it your own. You can modify the descriptions, add tunnels, allow players to collect treasure, or change the dragon into some other form of danger. After testing your adventure game to make sure it runs without error, save it or print it out so that you can submit it to your instructor.

Patrik Ruzic/Shutterstock.com

PY Coding with Python

Writing computer code is increasingly a core competency for 21st-century workers. If you want to get on the career fast track, programming proficiency could be just the ticket. Get started coding today by following the step-by-step tutorials presented in this module.

● Try It! Apply what you learn.

- Write, run, and save simple programs in Python.
- Use the Python debugger to find and correct errors in a program.
- Work with text strings to display user prompts and program output.
- Assign a value to a variable and then modify the contents of the variable.
- Use commands such as int() and str() to change data types.
- Create a Wacky Word Game program that uses variables, strings, and input.
- Set up calculations by loading values into variables to create formulas in your programs.
- Write the code for an airport kiosk that calculates airline baggage fees.
- Use *if* statements along with Boolean operators and the <, >, and == comparison operators to specify program logic.
- Manipulate input using the upper() and lower() methods.
- Use for-loops and while-loops to set up blocks of code that run multiple times.
- Use an import-random statement and the random.randint() command to generate random numbers.
- Write a program to pick lottery numbers.
- Work with Python lists to efficiently process key locations in an adventure game.
- Create an Ask the Fortune Teller program.
- Use the def command to create programmer-defined functions.
- Use object-oriented programming techniques, such as instantiation, methods, and polymorphism.

● Pre-Check

Gauge your level of expertise. The answers are in the module.

"Pizza"

"Pizza" is a(n) _____ .

==

>

!=

_____ operators

["Eva", "Mateo", "Jay"]

In Python, a(n) _____ is enclosed in square brackets.

def printme(str):

printme() is a(n) _____ .

"Hello" + "World!"

The + sign is used here as a(n) _____ operator.

class Dog(Pet):

Dog is a(n) _____ class.

sum = sum + number

The variable "sum" is used here as a(n) _____ .

Print()

A(n) _____ error

1.5, 5.0, -2.4

_____ numbers

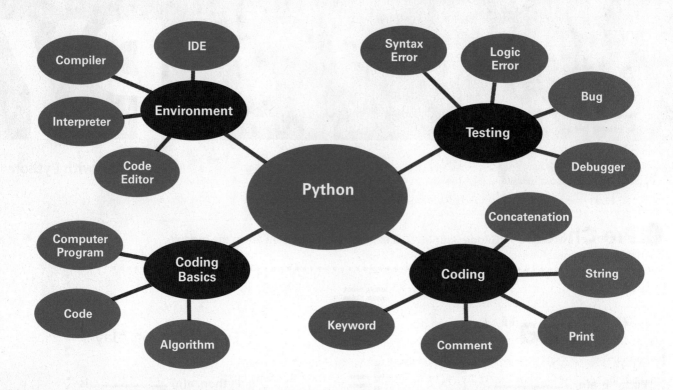

Objectives

▶ Identify the elements of a Python integrated development environment (IDE).

▶ Write a simple program using the Python programming language.

▶ Save a program you have written.

▶ Use the correct syntax for the print keyword.

▶ Use program comments effectively.

▶ Concatenate strings.

▶ Describe the vocabulary of Python keywords.

▶ Identify syntax and logic errors in a Python program.

Have you ever thought

you could create your own computer programs? One of the great things about programming is that it is open to everyone who wants to try it. All you need is access to a computer. Even the programmers of the popular Subway Surfer game had to start somewhere. You will start by writing a simple program in this section and build up to creating more advanced programs as you work through the module.

Terminology

code	interpreter	string	syntax error
coding	compiler	concatenation	logic error
algorithm	IDE	concatenation operator	
code editor	syntax	bug	
debugger	comment	debugging	

Python Basics

In today's digital age, almost everyone uses some type of computer program. You have probably used word processing software for school or played computer games at home. But do you know how to *write* a computer program? For writing code, you follow a set of rules and use logic to solve a problem. Section A is designed to get you coding quickly without requiring any prior experience.

▶ **What is a computer program?** A computer program is a set of step-by-step instructions that tells the computer what to do. These instructions are sometimes referred to as **code**, and the process of writing the instructions is referred to as **coding**.

The code for a computer program is based on an **algorithm**, which is simply a sequence of steps for solving a problem or performing a task. You use algorithms every day. For example, you bake a cake by following the algorithm for a recipe.

Just as there are many spoken languages that people use to communicate with each other, there are also many programming languages that people can use to communicate with a computer. Some of these languages—such as C, C++, Java, C#, JavaScript, and Python—you may have heard of before.

▶ **What is Python?** In this module, you will learn to use the Python programming language. Python was first released by its designer, Guido Van Rossum, in 1991. It was named not after a large snake, but after the British comedy television series *Monty Python's Flying Circus*.

Python is excellent for beginners, yet outstanding for experts. It is a language that is relatively easy to learn, but still powerful enough to be useful for solving real-life problems. There are several versions of Python, including versions 2 and 3. You will be using version 3 in this module.

▶ **How do I start writing code in Python?** To write code using Python, you will need a code editor, a debugger, and an interpreter or a compiler.

- A **code editor** is a place to enter source code for a computer program.
- A **debugger** is a computer program that is used to find errors that may exist in a program.
- An **interpreter** is a program that reads your code in text form and translates the code, instruction by instruction, into a machine language the computer can understand.
- A **compiler** is a program that reads your source code and translates all of the code to a machine language before sending it to the computer to run. Some compilers are Web apps that can be accessed online using a browser.

An **IDE** (integrated development environment) provides an editor, debugger, and interpreter. Several IDEs are available for Python programming. Some IDEs—such as PyCharm, Wing IDE, IDLE, and PyDev—are local software that you install onto your computer's hard disk. Python online IDEs include Replit, Python Fiddle, Pynative, and Ideone.

Terminology

Writing instructions or code for computers can be called programming or coding. Typically, *coding* is a term used for less formal programming. *Coding* is also a less intimidating term used for easy, basic, or fun programming tasks.

PY

Terminology

Programmers can use a text editor, but not a word processor, to write program code. Program code cannot contain the formatting codes that a word processor embeds.

QuickCheck

Where is the best place to enter program code?

a. A code editor

b. A Word document

c. A browser

d. A debugger

Setting Up Your Python Environment

To create the programs in this module, you can use a local or online Python IDE. To get started:

1 Access the Python IDE of your choice or the one specified by your instructor.

2 To use some IDEs, you are required to sign up for an account by providing your name, entering your email address, and creating a password.

3 If your IDE gives you a choice of languages, select Python 3. If you are prompted to name your program, enter **Hello**.

4 A typical online IDE provides two programming panels. Figure PY-1 and other screenshots in this module illustrate the panels displayed by the Replit IDE.

Figure PY-1: The Replit IDE for Python programs

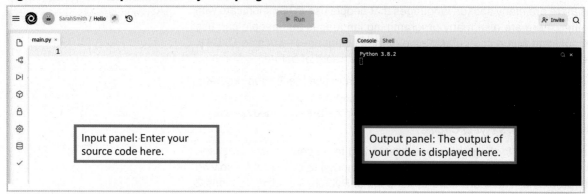

Source: Replit

Let's Start Coding

The most famous program in the world is a single line of code that prints "Hello World!" on the screen. It has been written millions of times in every programming language that exists and is frequently used to illustrate basic command structure.

▶ **Is it difficult to learn?** Learning how to write code can be exciting and challenging. It is certainly an important skill to have in today's digital world, and it is fun to do. This could be the beginning of a new adventure for you, so let's get started!

Writing a "Hello World!" Program in Python

While viewing the input and output panels of your IDE, follow these steps to start writing your program:

1 Select the Clear option to delete any sample code that might appear in the input panel.

2 Select line 1.

3 Type the following code on line 1. (Hint: You can use the Backspace and Delete keys to correct typing errors.)

```
# My first program
```

4 Press the Enter key to move down to line 2, and then type the following code all on one line. (Hint: Be sure to include the spaces and punctuation marks exactly as they appear in the example.)

```
print("Hello World! This is my first Python program.")
```

5 Select the button that will run your program. Compare your program and output to Figure PY-2.

Figure PY-2: First "Hello World!" program

```
1   # My first program
2   print("Hello World! This is my first Python program.")
3
4
```
```
Hello World! This is my first Python program.
>
```

Source: Replit

(Hint: If you receive an error message, make sure you have included the parentheses and quotation marks, and that the word *print* is in lowercase. Clear the output panel by selecting the Clear button, and then try to run the program again.)

6 When your program is running correctly, congratulations! You have just written your first program.

7 Some IDEs, such as Replit, automatically save your code. Other IDEs have a Save option. If your IDE does not provide a way to save your code, you can select it, copy it (with Ctrl+C), and then paste it into a text file, which you can then save.

Modifying a Saved Program

You can modify any of your saved code in the editor. Follow these steps to modify your first program:

1 Retrieve your saved code. To do this with Replit:

a. Select your user name in the upper-right corner of the screen to display a list of repls. (A "repl" is Replit jargon for your program code.)

b. Select Hello as the repl you want to open. Any code in the input panel will be replaced with code from your saved repl.

2 In the input panel, line 2, select the word "first" and then type **modified**.

The code for line 2 should now look like this:

```
print("Hello World! This is my modified Python program.")
```

3 Run your program and compare the output to Figure PY-3.

Figure PY-3: Modified "Hello World!" program

```
1   # My first program
2   print("Hello World! This is my modified Python program.")
3
```
```
Hello World! This is my modified Python program.
>
```

Source: Replit

Creating a Multi-Line Program

Most programs contain more than one line of code. The computer follows each line in the order it is written. For example, the code to display a "knock, knock" joke requires multiple lines. Let's try writing it.

1 Start a new program.

If you're using Replit, select the menu in the upper-left corner and then select the Create Repl option.

For other IDEs, be sure to clear the input and output panels.

2 Name your program **Joke**.

3 Type the following code on line 1:

```
# My second program
```

4 Press the Enter key to move down to line 2, and then type the following code on lines 2 through 6:

```
print("Knock, knock.")

print("Who's there?")

print("Tank.")

print("Tank who?")

print("You're welcome.")
```

5 Save and run the program. Compare your program and output to Figure PY-4.

Figure PY-4: Create a multi-line program

```
1   # My second program          Knock, knock.
2   print("Knock, knock.")        Who's there?
3   print("Who's there?")         Tank.
4   print("Tank.")                Tank who?
5   print("Tank who?")            You're welcome.
6   print("You're welcome.")      >
```

Source: Replit

▶ Are there rules for writing Python code? The Python programming language has its own **syntax**, which is a set of rules that defines how it can be written. You will start by using a few of these rules in this section and expand on them as you learn more of the language.

▶ What is the rule for using a comment? A **comment** in Python is used by programmers to explain what the code does. Comments do not show up when the program runs. Adding comments generally makes the code easier to understand and maintain.

An important rule to remember when coding in Python is that a comment must begin with the # character and end with the physical line on which the # character has been typed—that is, a comment ends when you move to the next line. If you need to include more than one line of comments, you must start each line with #.

For example, in your first program, line 1 contains this comment:

```
# My first program
```

Working with Strings

The first computers functioned without any programming languages. Instead, computers were rewired for each task they processed. Developers later created languages to process tasks more efficiently.

Python is considered a high-level programming language because it works by using command words and grammar based on human languages. This makes it easier for novice programmers to create code because it is similar to writing in their own language.

▶ What is a string? When you write a sentence, you create a sequence of words that your reader will understand. Similarly, when writing code, you create a sequence of characters called a string. A **string** can contain words, letters, punctuation marks, and numerals.

For example, in your first program, line 2 contains this string:

```
"Hello World! This is my first Python program."
```

▶ What is concatenation? The term **concatenation** is used by programmers any time two or more characters are connected. Several strings can be connected using a symbol, such as the + symbol, as a **concatenation operator**. Let's see how it works.

Concatenating a Simple String

You will concatenate two strings using the + symbol as the concatenation operator.

1 Start a new program. Enter **Strings** as the title for your program.

2 Type the following code in line 1:

```
# My first program
```

3 Type the following code in line 2, all on one line:

```
print("Hello World! " + "This is my first Python program.")
```

4 Save and run the program. The output should look exactly like the first program you created, which is shown in Figure PY-2. `"Hello World!"` is concatenated by the + symbol to `"This is my first Python program."`

Try It!

When concatenating strings, you must be careful about positioning spaces to separate words. Enter the following code and notice the different methods used to separate words:

```
# Add a space at the end
of a word.
```

```
print("I'm " + "glad to
see you.")
```

```
# Add a space between
two quotation marks
```

```
print("This" + " " +
"is" + " " + "fun.")
```

```
# Without a space,
```

```
# The strings combine
without a space.
```

```
print("Me" + "ow!")
```

Your output should look like this:

I'm glad to see you.

This is fun.

Meow!

Duplicating a String

Python gives programmers a shortcut for working with repeated strings. To print the same word to the screen more than once, just use the * symbol and the number of times you want it duplicated. Let's try it.

1 Start a new program.

2 Enter Judy as the program name.

3 Type the following code as line 1:

```
# Duplicate one word
```

4 Type the following code on lines 2 through 6:

```
print("Judy" * 4)

# Duplicate a sentence

print("There's no place like home. " * 3)

# Duplication and concatenation

print("very,  " * 3 + "hot")
```

5 Save and run the program. Compare your program and output to Figure PY-5.

Try It!

Using duplication, write a Python program that results in the following output:

****

****

****

****

Figure PY-5: Duplication examples

```
1    # Duplicate one word
2    print("Judy" * 4)
3    # Duplicate a sentence
4    print("There's no place like home. " * 3)
5    # Duplication and concatenation
6    print("very, " * 3 + "hot")
```

```
JudyJudyJudyJudy
There's no place like home. There's no place like home. There's no
place like home.
very, very, very, hot
>
```

Source: Replit

Using Python Keywords

All programming languages have their own vocabulary, which is based on a set of keywords. The Python programming language has a small vocabulary of only 34 keywords. Of these, only about ten are frequently used.

▶ **How do programmers use keywords?** In Python and other programming languages, each keyword has a predefined meaning. For example, you have already worked with the keyword *print*. In Python, using *print* means you want the computer to display something on the screen. You will work with many of the keywords listed in Figure PY-6 throughout this module.

Figure PY-6: Python keywords

False	class	finally	is	return
None	continue	for	lambda	try
True	def	from	nonlocal	while
and	del	global	not	with
as	elif	if	or	yield
assert	else	import	pass	print
break	except	in	raise	

Debugging

Programs must be tested to see if they work correctly. A coding error is called a **bug**, and the process of tracking down bugs and correcting them is called **debugging**.

▶ **My program does not work—what now?** A computer cannot read your mind. When running a program, the computer will only do exactly what you tell it to do—no more, no less. Any errors in the code that produce incorrect results are introduced by the programmer—you. This may seem to be a simple concept, but it is very important to keep in mind when devising algorithms for your programs.

▶ **What are coding errors?** Several kinds of errors can occur in a program. Syntax errors and logic errors are the two most frequently encountered. It is useful to distinguish between them so you can track them down more quickly.

▶ **What are typical syntax errors?** Python can only execute a program if the syntax is correct; otherwise, the process fails and the computer returns an error message. A **syntax error** occurs when an instruction does not follow the rules of the programming language.

The rules for coding syntax can be compared to the rules for English grammar. For example, in English, capitalization, word order, and punctuation are all important grammar elements. In Python, these elements are also important aspects of syntax. To avoid syntax errors, it is essential to follow the Python rules. You have already learned some of Python's syntax rules, including the following:

- Comments always start with a #.
- Python is case sensitive.
- Strings are delineated by quotation marks.
- Keywords can only be used for their intended purpose.

Debugging Syntax Errors

Let's introduce an error into a program and see how the Python debugger works.

1 Start a new program and use **Error** as the program name.

2 On line 1, type the following line of code, in which *Print* is incorrectly capitalized:

```python
Print("Hello World! This is my first Python program.")
```

3 Run the program. Notice the error message in Figure PY-7, which indicates that *Print* (with a capital *P*) is not defined.

Figure PY-7: Syntax error output

```
Traceback (most recent call last):
  File "main.py", line 1, in <module>
    Print("Hello World! This is my first Python
program.")
NameError: name 'Print' is not defined
>
```

Source: Replit

❱ **How can I fix a syntax error?** If there is a single syntax error anywhere in your program, Python prints an error message and quits. The error message displays the number of the last line the program was able to execute. Sometimes, however, the error occurs prior to that line, in which case you might have to look back a line or two to find the error.

To fix a syntax error, check the line carefully. If you are copying code from an example, start by comparing your code to the example's code very carefully. Be sure to check every character, space, and punctuation mark. When you find the error, you can modify the code and rerun your program.

❱ **How can I identify a logic error?** Another type of error is a logic error. A program containing a **logic error** will run without displaying an error message, but it will not produce the expected result. The problem is that the program you wrote is not the program you intended to write because the logic of the program is incorrect.

Identifying logic errors can be tricky because it requires you to work backward by looking at the output of the program and trying to figure out what it is doing. An example of a logic error would be to enter the following code:

```
print("Hello World! + This is my first Python program.")
```

These are the results you wanted:

```
Hello World! This is my first Python program.
```

The program runs without error, but you do not get the expected results. These are the results you get:

```
Hello World! + This is my first Python program.
```

What happened? The program needs more matching quotation marks to produce the expected results. The code should be:

```
print("Hello World! " + "This is my first Python program.")
```

❱ **How do I find the program errors?** One of the most important coding skills you can acquire is debugging. Debugging is like detective work. You are confronted with clues, and you have to figure out what led to the results you see. Once you have an idea of what is going wrong, you can modify your program and try again. Most coding errors are spelling mistakes and typos. Although it is sometimes frustrating, debugging is one of the most challenging and interesting parts of coding.

QuickCheck

A program that calculates the price for a store's sale produces the wrong amount. What kind of error did the programmer make?

a. A syntax error

b. A Python error

c. A logic error

d. An input error

QuickQuiz   Section A

1. The Python IDE provides an editor, a debugger, and a(n) [_____] that translates the code into machine language.

2. Python comments begin with a(n) [_____] symbol.

3. Programmers use the term [_____] to describe a sequence of letters, punctuation marks, and numerals.

4. In Python, using an uppercase keyword produces a(n) [_____] error.

5. The process of tracking down program errors and correcting them is called [_____].

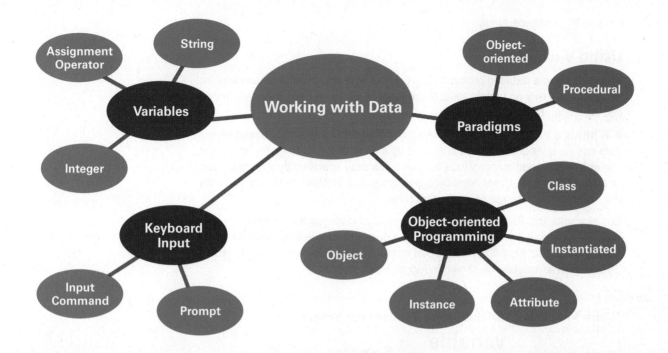

The Wacky Word Game

Objectives

▶ Create variables using an assignment statement.

▶ List four rules for naming variables in Python.

▶ Provide examples of three data types commonly used in Python programs.

▶ Explain the significance of a data type error.

▶ Convert numbers to strings.

▶ Distinguish the difference between classes and objects.

▶ Instantiate an object from a class.

▶ Use the correct Python syntax to collect user input.

▶ Code the Wacky Word Game.

▶ Share your programs using a Share link, file, or screenshot.

You are off to a great start! You now have some basic coding experience. In this section, you will learn how to use variables to make your programs more efficient and easier to code. You'll also learn how to collect input from users as your programs run. You can then use this skill to build interactive programs such as the Wacky Word Game, which is based on word games such as Mad Libs.

Terminology

variable	object-oriented	attribute	prompt
assignment operator	programming	instance	
data type	object	instantiated	
object-oriented paradigm	class	input command	

Using Variables

Writing code is a detailed process that requires time and careful concentration. Programmers rely on certain tools of the trade, such as variables, to help make coding easier, faster, and more enjoyable.

▶ **What is a variable?** Programmers think of variables as empty boxes where data can be temporarily stored and used by a computer program. Technically, a **variable** is a named memory location that holds data specified by a programmer or entered by an end user. Variables give programs flexibility because the data they contain can change as a program runs.

For example, the "Hello World!" program always displays the message "Hello World!"—but what if you wanted to display a customized greeting, such as "Hello Sarah!" or "Hello Khalil!"? This type of customization is possible by replacing "World" with a variable, as shown in Figure PY-8.

Figure PY-8: Using variables to customize your program

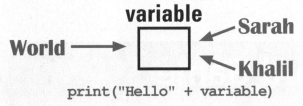

```
print("Hello" + variable)
```

▶ **Are there rules for naming variables?** A variable name should describe the information the variable is designed to store. For example, a good name for a variable that will contain a person's first name might be "firstname" or "first_name".

Here are some specific rules for naming variables in Python:

- The name must begin with a letter or an underscore character "_".
- The name can contain only letters, numbers, and the underscore character; no punctuation characters, special characters, or spaces are allowed.
- Python keywords, such as `print` and `class`, are not allowed as variable names.
- Every variable should have a unique name.

If you violate any one of the rules listed above, you will get a syntax error. Figure PY-9 shows some examples of invalid variable names.

Figure PY-9: Invalid variable names in Python

Invalid Name	Problem
76trombones	The name does not begin with a letter or an underscore.
more$	The name cannot contain a special character.
last name	The name cannot contain a space.
class	The name cannot be a Python keyword.

Terminology

In some programming languages, camel case or Pascal case is used when naming variables. *Camel case* capitalizes the second word of a two-word variable name: firstName. *Pascal case* capitalizes both words of a two-word variable name: FirstName. Camel case and Pascal case are used in Python programs, though they are not the standard.

Try It!

Type these lines in your Python IDE and run them to see what happens:

```
76trombones = "big parade"
more$ = 10000
class = "Computers 100"
```

▶ **How do I create a variable?** The process of creating a variable is sometimes referred to as *declaring a variable*. Putting data in a variable is referred to as *assigning a value* to it. Although the term *value* is used, the data that is assigned can be a string, such as "Joe," or a numeric value, such as 145, as shown in Figure PY-10.

Figure PY-10: Assigning a value to a variable

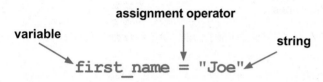

In Python, programmers can declare a variable and assign it a value using only one line of code. To store data in a variable, programmers use the = symbol, called the **assignment operator**.

Assigning a Value to a Variable

Let's assign the value `"Joe"` to the variable `first_name`.

1 Start a new program. Name it **Joe** and enter the following:

```
first_name = "Joe"
print(first_name)
```

2 Save and run the program. Compare your program and output to Figure PY-11.

Figure PY-11: Assigning the first_name variable

```
1    first_name = "Joe"
2    print(first_name)
```

```
Joe
> □
```

Source: Replit

PY

▶ **How do programmers use variables?** Programmers use variables to store data that might change when the program runs. Data can be changed by program code, by calculations that are carried out by a program, or by data entered by end users.

Changing a Variable While a Program Runs

Try modifying the program called Joe to see how the contents of the variable first_name can change as a program runs.

1 Modify the code so that it contains the following four lines:

```
first_name = "Joe"

print("Hello " + first_name)

first_name = "Mary"

print("Hello " + first_name)
```

2 Save and run the program. Compare your program and output to Figure PY-12.

Figure PY-12: Changing a variable

```
1    first_name = "Joe"
2    print("Hello " + first_name)
3    first_name = "Mary"
4    print("Hello " + first_name)
```

```
Hello Joe
Hello Mary
>
```

Source: Replit

▶ **Can I assign any value to a variable?** The type of data that a variable can hold is referred to as its **data type**. Every variable has a data type that limits the kind of data it can contain.

In Python, a variable automatically gets a data type based on the data stored in it by an assignment statement. If you assign a string such as "Joe" to a variable, its data type automatically becomes String. If you assign a number such as 20 to a variable, its data type automatically becomes Integer. The data types most frequently used in Python programs are listed in Figure PY-13.

Figure PY-13: Common data types

Data Type	Examples
Integers	-2, -1, 0, 1, 2, 3, 4, 5
Floating-point numbers	-1.0, -0.5, 0.0, 1.0, 1.25
Strings	"Joe", "Hello!", "11 cats"

▶ **What is the significance of data types?** Once a variable has a data type, it can only hold data of that type. If you begin a program and assign a string such as "Joe" to first_name, the variable first_name can only hold strings unless you later code a new assignment statement, such as first_name = 123. This second assignment statement would give first_name an integer data type and allow it to store numeric data instead of text data.

Variables with different data types must be treated carefully. For example, string variables cannot be concatenated directly with integer variables.

Encountering a Data Type Error

Let's see what happens if you try to combine string and integer data types.

1 Start a new program called **Age**, and then enter the following lines of code:

```
first_name = "Joe"

age = 22

info = first_name + age

print(info)
```

2 Save and run the program. The result is an error message, as shown in Figure PY-14. This message tells you that the string (str) variable first_name cannot be combined with the integer (int) variable age.

Figure PY-14: Data type error message

```
1    first_name = "Joe"
2    age = 22
3    info = first_name + age
4    print(info)
```

```
Traceback (most recent call last):
  File "main.py", line 3, in <module>
    info = first_name + age
TypeError: can only concatenate str (not "int") to str
>
```

Source: Replit

▶ **How can I avoid data type errors?** Because Python does not like to combine different types of data, you may have to convert some of your data. For example, when trying to combine a person's age and name in a variable, you can convert age into a string so it matches the data type for the person's name.

Converting a Number to a String

1 Revise line 3 of the previous program so that your code reads as follows:

```
first_name = "Joe"

age = 22

info = first_name + " " + str(age)

print(info)
```

2 Save and run the program. It should now run without an error and produce Joe 22 as the output.

When writing Python programs, keep in mind the data type for each variable. This requirement becomes more and more important as you write complex programs that combine variables and use them in calculations.

QuickCheck

In this code, what type of variable is zipcode?
```
zipcode = "60137"
```

a. Integer

b. Float

c. String

d. Number

Objects and Classes

Python is an object-oriented programming language, which is a language that enables you to use objects to accomplish a program's goals.

▶ **What is the object-oriented paradigm?** The object-oriented paradigm is based on objects and classes that can be defined and manipulated by program code. Object-oriented programming (OOP) is a style of programming that focuses on using objects to design and build applications.

▶ **What is an object?** An object is anything that can be seen, touched, or used. It can be a person, a place, or a thing, such as a car, a house, or a name.

▶ **What is a class?** Every object in an object-oriented program is created from a class, which is a description or template that the computer uses to create the object. A class is defined by attributes and methods. A class attribute defines the characteristics of a set of objects. You will learn more about methods in Section E.

▶ **What is the difference between an object and a class?** An object created from a class is called an instance of a class and is said to be instantiated (created) from the class. Think of a class as a cookie cutter. It is not a cookie itself—instead, it is a description or template of what a cookie looks like. The cookie cutter can be used to create many individual cookies. Each cookie can be thought of as an instance of the cookie cutter class. A cookie object can have different attributes, such as shape, color, and flavor. Figure PY-15 can help you visualize the difference between a class and objects.

Figure PY-15: Classes and objects

Class: Cookies

A class is similar to a template, mold, or cookie cutter.

Fortune cookie

Chocolate chip cookie

Frosted cookie

Objects

Objects are instances created by the template, mold, or cookie cutter.

Instantiating an Object from a Class

Consider the example of a dog object instantiated from the Pet class that has an attribute of having four legs. Let's instantiate an object of the Pet class. (Hint: Class names are generally capitalized in Python.)

1 Start a new program called **Fido**. Enter and run the following lines of code:

```
class Pet:
    number_of_legs = 0
dog = Pet()
dog.number_of_legs = 4
print("Dogs are pets with " + str(dog.number_of_legs) + " legs.")
```

> Be sure to indent this line using spaces or the Tab key.

2 Save this program. Compare your program and output to Figure PY-16.

Figure PY-16: Pet class

```
1.  class Pet:
2.      number_of_legs = 0
3.  dog = Pet()
4.  dog.number_of_legs = 4
5.  print("Dogs are pets with " + str
        (dog.number_of_legs) + " legs.")
```

```
Dogs are pets with 4 legs.
>
```

Source: Replit

The code `class Pet:` defines the Pet class. The Pet class has an attribute of the number of legs for the pet. The third line of code, `dog = Pet()`, instantiates a dog object of the Pet class. The fourth line, `dog.number_of_legs = 4`, assigns the number 4 to the number_of_legs attribute for a dog object in the Pet class.

▶ **Why use classes and objects?** Classes and objects help programmers develop programs modeled on the real world. Classes help programmers think about the characteristics and structure of the data that a program manipulates. In contrast to standalone variables, classes enable programmers to build objects with multiple attributes and define ways for objects to interact with each other.

Try It!

Now, add a parrot object, assign the correct number of legs to the parrot, and print your results.

PY

Input

Until now, you have only been able to assign strings and numbers to variables within your program. However, you might want a user to be able to interact with your program and enter input as it runs. This input can provide information that can be stored in your program's variables. Input can be accepted from a keyboard or a touchscreen.

▶ How does the computer accept input? Python uses the **input command** to get user input. The input command allows the program to display a message on the screen that asks a user to enter information. This message is often called a **prompt** because it prompts the user to enter something.

For example, suppose you want a program to gather the user's name. You could write the following code:

```
first_name = input("Please enter your name: ")
```

When this program runs, the prompt `Please enter your name:` is displayed on the screen. The program waits until the user enters a name and presses the Enter key. Whatever the user types after the prompt is stored as a string in the first_name variable.

Using the Input Command to Write Prompts

Writing prompts using the input command in Python is a great way to relay instructions to your program's user. These instructions help to make your program more user-friendly and accessible. The first step is to code the input command. Let's see how.

1 Start a new program called **Names**. Enter and run the following three lines of code:

```
# Getting keyboard input
first_name = input("What is your name? ")
print("Hi, " + first_name)
```

2 Run the program and enter your name when prompted.

3 Now, add the following code on lines 4 and 5:

```
answer = input("What did you have for breakfast? ")
print("You had " + answer + "! That sounds delicious!")
```

4 Save and run the program. Compare your program and output to Figure PY-17.

Figure PY-17: Using the input command

```
1  # Getting keyboard input
2  first_name = input("What is your name? ")
3  print("Hi, " + first_name)
4  answer = input("What did you have for
   breakfast? ")
5  print("You had " + answer + "! That
   sounds delicious!")
```

```
What is your name? Sasha
Hi, Sasha
What did you have for breakfast? eggs
You had eggs! That sounds delicious!
> 
```

Source: Replit

> **Try It!**
>
> Write a program that displays the prompt "Halt! Who goes there?" and waits for the user to enter a name. The program should produce the message "You may pass," plus the person's name, like this:
>
> Halt! Who goes there? Jenna
>
> You may pass, Jenna.

Wacky Word Game

You will now create a program that uses variables, strings, and input. This program produces a game that prompts a player for a list of words and then generates a nonsensical or comical story.

Creating the Wacky Word Game Program

1 Enter the following lines of code for a program called **Wacky**:

```
# Wacky Word Game program
# Part 1: request the input words
first_name = input("Type your name, and select enter. ")
print("")
print("Hello " + first_name + ". Let's play a game.")
print("")
adjective1 = input("Tell me an adjective, and select enter. ")
noun1 = input("Tell me a noun (plural), and select enter. ")
noun2 = input("Tell me another noun (plural), and select enter. ")
adjective2 = input("Tell me another adjective, and select enter. ")
# Part 2: print the poem
print(first_name + "'s Wacky Word Game")
print("")
print("Roses are " + adjective1)
print(noun1 + " are blue")
print(noun2 + " are " + adjective2)
print("And so are you!")
```

2 Save and run the program. Figure PY-18 shows a sample of output from the **Wacky Word Game** program.

Figure PY-18: Wacky Word Game

```
1   # Wacky Word Game program
2   # Part 1: request the input words
3   first_name = input("Type your name, and select enter. ")
4   print("")
5   print("Hello " + first_name + ". Let's play a game.")
6   print("")
7   adjective1 = input("Tell me an adjective, and select enter. ")
8   noun1 = input("Tell me a noun (plural), and select enter. ")
9   noun2 = input("Tell me another noun (plural), and select enter. ")
10  adjective2 = input("Tell me another adjective, and select enter. ")

11  # Part 2: print the poem
12  print(first_name + "'s Wacky Word Game")
13  print("")
14  print("Roses are " + adjective1)
15  print(noun1 + " are blue")
16  print(noun2 + " are " + adjective2)
17  print("and so are you!")
```

```
Type your name, and select enter. Annette

Hello Annette. Let's play a game.

Tell me an adjective, and select enter. smelly
Tell me a noun (plural), and select enter. dogs
Tell me another noun (plural), and select enter. cats
Tell me another adjective, and select enter. sleepy
Annette's Wacky Word Game

Roses are smelly
dogs are blue
cats are sleepy
and so are you!
>
```

Source: Replit

Sharing Your Programs

You may want to share your program code. The procedure depends on your IDE. Some IDEs provide a Share button that you can use to enter the recipient's email address. You might be able to copy the URL for your program and send it via email. If you've saved your program as a file, you can attach it to an email message.

If none of those options are available in your IDE, you can take a screenshot of your code using the following steps:

Making a Screenshot on a PC

1 Click the window containing your program.

2 While holding down the Windows key, press the Print Screen key.

3 Open a new blank Microsoft Word document. Right-click and choose Paste. Save your document as Wacky Word Game.

Making a Screenshot on a Mac

1 Press Command (⌘)-Shift-3.

2 Locate the new .png file on your desktop. You can change the name to Wacky Word Game.

Try It!

Here's your chance to get creative! Suppose you know a small child who loves bedtime stories. You're having a hard time coming up with plots. Create a program that generates stories. We've started one for you. Collect the input for the words in red and insert them into the story to view the output. Add at least two more lines to the story to collect input for the ending.

```
Once upon a time, there was a noun named name who lived in
place. name was very adjective and decided to explore place.
All of name's friends said "proverb." But name went anyway.
The journey to place was very adverb. "exclamation!" said
name. "I must have been adjective2 to think of going to
place." So, name turned around and headed back home. Then...
```

QuickQuiz   Section B

1. Programmers think of a(n) [_____] as a named memory location, which holds information that can change when a program is run.

2. In Python, the equal (=) symbol is known as the [_____] operator.

3. Every [_____] in an object-oriented program is created from a class.

4. A class [_____] defines the characteristics of a set of objects.

5. Python uses the input command to get user input from a(n) [_____] or a(n) [_____].

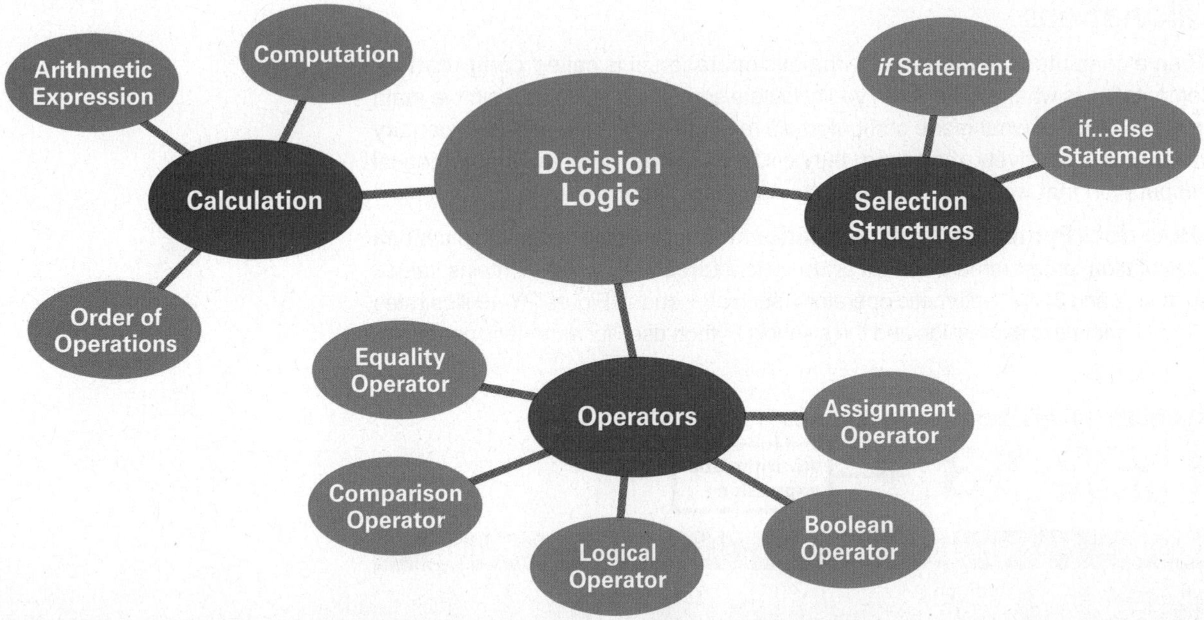

Section C Build Your Own Calculator

Objectives

- Identify the operators used in Python arithmetic expressions.
- Code calculations that store results in a variable.
- Collect user input to use in a calculation.
- Convert string input into integer values.
- Use the if and if...else commands along with comparison and logical operators to control program flow.
- List the comparison operators used in Python.
- Explain the difference between the = and == operators.
- Correctly use logical operators in Python statements.
- Convert strings to a known case.
- Code an interactive calculator program.

Computers are amazing machines. They can customize output based on user input and can even seem to make intelligent decisions. Programmers instruct computers to make decisions based on conditions that exist when a program runs. In this section, you will learn how to program calculations and how comparisons can help computers perform logical operations. Using these techniques, you will build a simple calculator program.

Terminology

computation
arithmetic expression
order of operations
selection control structure
comparison operator
equality operator
logical operators
Boolean operators

Calculations

When a computer calculates an arithmetic operation, it is called **computation**. Computation is what you do when you calculate something, such as a simple math problem. Much of what made computers so revolutionary in the mid-20th century was that in a relatively short time, they could perform a complex mathematical computation that would have taken a human many lifetimes to do.

▶ **How does Python perform calculations?** To instruct the computer to perform a calculation, programmers use an **arithmetic expression**, which contains values (such as 2 and 3) and arithmetic operators (such as + and -). Figure PY-19 illustrates a simple arithmetic expression and the symbols Python uses for arithmetic operators.

Figure PY-19: Arithmetic expressions

1 + 2 * 3 ← An arithmetic expression

Operator	Operation	Example	Output
+	Addition	4+3	7
-	Subtraction	7-5	2
*	Multiplication	4*5	20
/	Division	19/5	3
%	Modulus (Remainder)	19%5	4
**	Exponent	2**3	8

Coding a Simple Calculation

When coding Python programs, arithmetic expressions can be used in a variety of ways. Typically, they are assigned to variables or used in print statements.

1 Enter the following lines of code for a program called **Math**:

```
# Is the output 9 or 7?

result = 1+2*3

print("The result is ", result)
```

2 Before you run the program, try to guess what it will output.

3 Save and run the program.

▶ **Why wasn't the result 9?** The result of an arithmetic expression depends on the order in which Python performs the math. In this example, it performed the multiplication 2*3 before adding 1. Why? In mathematics, the **order of operations** is a collection of rules that dictate which procedures to perform first when calculating an arithmetic expression.

In Python, the order of operations follows these rules:

- Perform expressions in parentheses () first.
- Resolve exponential notations, such as 2**2, which means 2^2.
- Perform multiplication (*), division (/), and modulus (%) operations.
- Perform addition (+) and subtraction (-) last.

In your program, Python followed the order of operations and performed the multiplication before the addition. If you want the addition carried out before the multiplication, use parentheses to code the expression as `(1+2)*3`. Python will follow the order of operations and do the math in parentheses first.

Performing a Calculation

Programmers frequently set up calculations by loading values into variables and then writing formulas using variables instead of numbers. This technique allows you to modify the numbers used in a calculation or get the numbers as input when a program runs.

1 Enter the following lines of code for a program called **Discount** that uses the variables price and discount in an arithmetic expression:

```
price = 25
discount = 10
final_price = price - discount
print("Final price = ", final_price)
```

2 Save and run the program. Notice the code in line 4. You can print numbers and variables on the same line by using a comma to separate the string `"Final price = "` from the number represented by final_price.

3 Compare your program and output to Figure PY-20.

Figure PY-20: Variables in expressions

```
1   price = 25
2   discount = 10
3   final_price = price - discount
4   print("Final price = ", final_price)
```

```
Final price =  15
>
```

Source: Replit

❱ How do I get input values for calculations? Programs that perform calculations often use values that are input by the user as the program runs. For example, a bargain hunter might wonder if buying that supersized box of cereal or that gigantic package of chicken is really a better deal than buying the product in a smaller quantity. A program for a mobile app might ask shoppers to enter the number of ounces in the package and the price. It would then divide the price by the number of ounces to calculate the unit price.

Collecting Input for Calculations

1 Enter the following lines of code for a program called **Bargain Hunter**:

```
#Bargain Hunter
print("Enter the cost of the item: ")
cost = input()
print("Enter the quantity: ")
quantity = input()
print("The unit cost is ", cost/quantity)
```

2 Save and run the program, entering **20** as the item cost and **5** as the quantity.

3 It produces an error, as shown in Figure PY-21. Why?

QuickCheck

In the Bargain Hunter program, what are the names of the variables that collect input from the user?

a. input and cost

b. input and quantity

c. cost and quantity

d. input and input()

Figure PY-21: Output error

```
1   #Bargain Hunter
2   print("Enter the cost of the item: ")
3   cost = input()
4   print("Enter the quantity: ")
5   quantity = input()
6   print("The unit cost is ", cost/quantity)
```

```
Enter the cost of the item:
20
Enter the quantity:
5
Traceback (most recent call last):
  File "main.py", line 6, in <module>
    print("The unit cost is ", cost/quantity)
TypeError: unsupported operand type(s) for /: 'str
' and 'str'
>
```

Source: Replit

❱ What is the trick to collecting values with an input statement? When users enter numbers via the keyboard or touchscreen, Python treats the input as a string rather than a value. The string input cannot be used for calculations. To fix this problem, you can use the int() command to convert the input data to an integer, or you can use the float() command to convert the input to a floating point number with decimal places.

Converting String Input to Integer Values

To correct the syntax error in the Bargain Hunter program, you can add the int() command to the two lines of code that assign the input to variables.

1 Change line 3 of the Bargain Hunter program to the following:

```
cost = int(input())
```

2 Change line 5 of the program to the following:

```
quantity = int(input())
```

3 Save and run the program.

4 Enter **20** for the cost and **5** for the quantity.

5 Compare your program and output to Figure PY-22. The program should now run without a syntax error.

QuickCheck

To convert an input string into a floating point number, programmers can use which of the following commands?

a. float()

b. int()

c. str()

d. convert()

PY

Figure PY-22: Collecting input values

```
1    #Bargain Hunter
2    print("Enter the cost of the item: ")
3    cost = int(input())
4    print("Enter the quantity: ")
5    quantity = int(input())
6    print("The unit cost is ", cost/quantity)
```

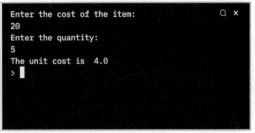

```
Enter the cost of the item:        Q  ×
20
Enter the quantity:
5
The unit cost is  4.0
>
```

Source: Replit

▶ **Can I simplify the input code?** Instead of using one line to display the input prompt and another line to convert the input to an integer, you can combine both tasks into one line of code, as shown in Figure PY-23.

Figure PY-23: Combined code for input, assignment, and integer conversion

Original Code
```
print("Enter the cost of the item: ")

cost = int(input())
```

Combined Code
```
cost = int(input("Enter the cost of the item: "))
```

An Alternative Method for Collecting Input Values

1 Modify the Bargain Hunter program to the following:

```
#Bargain Hunter

cost = int(input("Enter the cost of the item: "))

quantity = int(input("Enter the quantity: "))

print("The unit cost is ", cost/quantity)
```

2 Save and run the program to make sure that the revision works.

Selection Structures

So far, all the programs you've written have been executed line by line in sequence from beginning to end. Sometimes, however, programmers want parts of their code to be executed only when certain conditions are met. For example, an airport check-in kiosk might ask passengers to enter the number of bags they are checking. For passengers with more than one bag, the kiosk program would display a message indicating the charge for their baggage. For passengers without extra baggage, the program would not execute the lines that perform the calculation.

▶ **Can I design a program that handles different conditions?** Computer programs can be designed to execute sections of code based on specific conditions. These programs use selection control structures to determine which branch of code to execute. A **selection control structure** tells a computer what to do based on whether a condition is true or false. You can think of a selection control as one or more paths in a program. Figure PY-24 illustrates a simple branch.

Figure PY-24: A simple control structure creates two paths

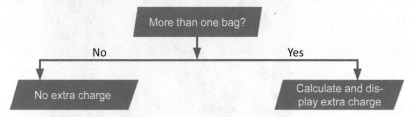

Using the *if* Command to Control Program Flow

An example of a selection control structure is the *if* command. You can use it to write the section of code for an airport check-in kiosk that calculates baggage fees.

1 Start a new program called **Airport Kiosk**.

2 Enter the following code. Use the Tab key, if necessary, to indent the last two lines.

```
#Airport Kiosk
print("How many bags are you checking?")
number_of_bags = int(input())
if number_of_bags >1:
    print("The first checked bag is free. Each
    additional bag is $25")
    print("Please pay $", (number_of_bags-1) * 25)
```

3 Save and run the program, entering **1** as the initial input. The program should end without displaying any charges.

4 Run the program again, entering **2** for the number of bags. The output should look like Figure PY-25 because this time, the *if* statement was true and the indented statements it contains were executed.

QuickCheck

In the Airport Kiosk program, why is -1 in the following calculation:

(number_of_bags-1) * 25?

a. Because the first bag is free

b. To designate the order of operations

c. To make the *if* statement true

d. Because it specified the end of the calculation

Figure PY-25: A simple if statement

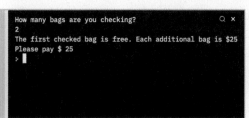

```
1   #Airport Kiosk
2   print("How many bags are you checking?")
3   number_of_bags = int(input())
4   if number_of_bags >1:
5       print("The first checked bag is free. Each
        additional bag is $25")
6       print("Please pay $", (number_of_bags-1) * 25)
```

Source: Replit

▶ Are there rules for creating *if* statements? Yes. The *if* command requires a colon as punctuation, and the statements in its execution path must be indented. It is standard in Python to use four spaces for indenting. You may also use the Tab key. To discontinue indents, simply press the Delete key or the left arrow key.

▶ What is an if…else statement? Frequently, programmers want one thing to happen when a condition is true and something else to happen when it is false. To accomplish this, they use the if…else statement.

PY

Using if…else Statements

1 Enter the following code for a program called **Weather**. (Hint: Include the colons in the if and else statements; be mindful of the indentation.)

```
temp = int(input("What is the outside temperature? "))

if temp > 70:

    print("Wear shorts ")

else:

    print("Wear jeans ")

print("when you go outside.")
```

2 Save and run the program, first using **50** as the input value and then using **80**. You should get different results depending on the input.

3 When you enter **80**, compare your program and output to Figure PY-26.

Figure PY-26: If…else statement

Source: Replit

▶ What happens if I need to use more than two conditions? Sometimes there are more than two possible conditions. You can code multiple conditions using elif statements. The keyword *elif* is an abbreviation of "else if." There must be a colon after the elif condition.

Coding Multiple Conditions

1 Enter the following lines of code for a program called **Compare** that uses elif statements to deal with three conditions:

```
x = 8

y = 4

if x < y:

    print("x is less than y")

elif x > y:

    print("x is greater than y")

else:

    print("x and y are equal")
```

2 Save and run the program.

3 Compare your program and output to Figure PY-27.

QuickCheck

In the program shown in Figure PY-26, why is the last line not indented?

a. It is never supposed to be executed.

b. It is part of the *if* statement.

c. It is part of the *else* statement.

d. It is part of the main program and is always executed.

Figure PY-27: Multiple conditions

```
1   x = 8
2   y = 4
3   if x < y:
4       print("x is less than y")
5   elif x > y:
6       print("x is greater than y")
7   else:
8       print("x and y are equal")
```

```
x is greater than y
>
```

Source: Replit

There is no limit on the number of elif statements that can follow an *if* statement. If there is an *else* clause, it must be at the end, but there doesn't have to be one.

Each condition is checked in order. If the first condition is false, the next is checked, and so on. If one of them is true, the code indented under the elif statement is executed, and then the sequence ends. Even if more than one condition is true, only the first true condition is executed.

Comparison and Logical Operators

In coding, an operator is a symbol that represents an action. You've used arithmetic operators (such as +, -, *, and /) to specify actions for calculations. Additional operators can be useful for a variety of coding tasks. When coding statements for control structures, it is handy to know the symbols for comparison and logical operators.

▸ **What is a comparison operator?** A comparison operator is used in an expression to compare two values. You have already used comparison operators, such as > and <, to write expressions such as `number_of_bags > 1` and `x < y`. Additional comparison operators are listed in Figure PY-28, where the example assumes that the variable x contains 10 and the variable y contains 20.

QuickCheck

If x = 7 and y = 9, which line in Figure PY-27 prints?

a. x is less than y

b. x is greater than y

c. x and y are equal

d. That input produces an error.

Figure PY-28: Comparison operators

Operator	Description	Example
==	If the values of two operands are equal, then the condition becomes true.	(x == y) is not true.
!=	If the values of two operands are not equal, then the condition becomes true.	(x != y) is true.
>	If the value of the left operand is greater than the value of the right operand, then the condition becomes true.	(x > y) is not true.
<	If the value of the left operand is less than the value of the right operand, then the condition becomes true.	(x < y) is true.
>=	If the value of the left operand is greater than or equal to the value of the right operand, then the condition becomes true.	(x >= y) is not true.
<=	If the value of the left operand is less than or equal to the value of the right operand, then the condition becomes true.	(x <= y) is true.

▶ How do comparison operators work? Typically, expressions with comparison operators are used with commands, such as *if*, that form control structures.

Using Comparison Operators

The most commonly used comparison operators are >, <, and ==. Let's see how they can be used in a program that might operate a "smart" thermostat.

① Enter the following lines of code for a program called **Temperature**:

```
room_temperature = 69

if room_temperature > 70:

    print("Turn on the fan!")

if room_temperature < 70:

    print("Turn on the heat!")

if room_temperature == 70:

    print("Perfect!")
```

② Save and run the program. The expression `room_temperature < 70` is evaluated as true based on the value assigned to room_temperature. Therefore, the *if* statement containing this expression is executed.

③ Modify the value assigned to room_temperature so that the expression `room_temperature > 70` is evaluated as true. What is the output?

④ Modify the program again so that the expression `room_temperature == 70` is evaluated as true.

▶ How does == differ from =? The == operator is the **equality operator**. It is used for comparisons such as `if room_temperature == 70`. The = symbol is the assignment operator. It is used to store values and strings in variables, as in `room_temperature = 70`.

▶ Are there other rules for using comparison operators? Two rules come in handy when using comparison operators.

- First rule: If an expression contains more than one comparison operator, the operators are evaluated from left to right in the expression.

- Second rule: Comparison operators are evaluated after any arithmetic operators in an expression. For example, in 3 + 6 < 16 / 2, the two arithmetic operators will be evaluated first, and then the two resulting numbers will be compared.

▶ What are logical operators? If...else statements can also contain **logical operators**. Python has three logical operators: AND, OR, and NOT. These are also known as **Boolean operators**, named after mathematician George Boole. You can use Boolean operators to formulate conditions, such as "if ticket is first class AND traveler is a frequent flyer then admit to airport lounge."

Expressions containing logical operators can be used in ways similar to expressions containing comparison operators. Python evaluates logical expressions as true or false, so they can be the basis for control structures that use *if* statements.

PY

QuickCheck

What is the result of this code?
```
num1 = 5

num2 = 10

num1 = num2

if num1 == num2:

    print("True")

else:

    print("False")
```

a. True

b. False

c. 15

d. 10

QuickCheck

What is the result of this code?
```
3 + 6 < 16 / 2
```

a. True

b. False

c. 17

d. Less than

Using Logical Operators

Python evaluates AND expressions differently than OR expressions. In the following program, can you understand why some statements evaluate to true, whereas others evaluate to false?

1 Enter the following lines of code for a program called **AndOr**:

```
print(1 < 2 and 4 > 2)
print(1 > 2 and 4 > 2)
print(1 < 2 or 4 > 2)
print(1 > 2 or 4 > 2)
print(not(1 > 2))
```

2 Save and run the program.

3 Can you change line 4 so that it evaluates to false?

Comparing Strings

When a program collects string input, such as a user's name, it can be used in expressions that become part of control structures. For example, a program might ask users if they know how to swim in order to enroll them in the appropriate swim class. This type of user interaction can make computers seem intelligent.

Strings in Python are case sensitive, which means the string "Yes" is not the same as either the string "YES" or the string "yes". However, programmers may not be able to anticipate whether users will enter upper- or lowercase strings.

How can you deal with case sensitivity? To avoid problems with case, you can use the upper() and lower() methods to convert string input to a known case.

Converting Strings to a Known Case

When converting input to a known case, programmers typically convert to uppercase. Let's see how that works.

1 Enter the following lines of code for a program called **Swim**:

```
answer = str(input("Can you swim? Enter Y for Yes or N for No. "))
if answer.upper() == "Y":
    print("Enroll in Swimming 2")
else:
    print("Enroll in Swimming for Beginners")
```

2 Save and run the program, entering a lowercase "n" as input.

3 Compare your program and output to Figure PY-29.

QuickCheck

Using the variables

  a = 1

  b = 2

which of the following statements will evaluate to false?

a. if a == 1 and b == 1:

b. if a == 1 or b == 1:

c. if a == 2 or b == 2:

d. if a == 1 or b == 2:

QuickCheck

In the swim class program, what prints if you enter **X**?

a. Enroll in Swimming 2

b. Enroll in Swimming for Beginners

c. Nothing

Figure PY-29: Comparing strings

```
1   answer = str(input("Can you swim? Enter Y for Yes or
    N for No. "))
2   if answer.upper() == "Y":
3     print("Enroll in Swimming 2")
4   else:
5     print("Enroll in Swimming for Beginners")
```

```
Can you swim? Enter Y for Yes or N for No. n
Enroll in Swimming for Beginners
>
```

Source: Replit

Building an Interactive Calculator Program

Let's use the coding techniques you learned in this section to write a program that takes two numbers as input and then performs the mathematical operation selected by the user. The boxes indicate lines that have been left out. You'll need to add the code for those lines yourself.

1 Enter the following code for a program called **Simple Calculator**:

```
# Simple Calculator

num1 = int(input("Enter a number: "))
[                                    ]

choice = input("Do you want to add, subtract, multiply, or divide?")
if choice.upper() == "ADD":
    answer = num1 + num2
    print(num1, "+", num2,"=",answer)
[                                    ]
    answer = num1 - num2
    print(num1, "-", num2,"=",answer)
elif choice.upper() == "MULTIPLY":
    [                                ]
    print(num1, "*", num2,"=",answer)
elif choice.upper() == "DIVIDE":
    answer = num1 / num2
    print(num1, "/", num2,"=",answer)
[                                    ]
    print("Invalid input. Sorry.")
```

2 Save and run the program.

3 Compare your output to Figure PY-30.

Figure PY-30: A simple calculator

```
>
Enter a number:  10
Enter another number:  25
Do you want to add, subtract, multiply, or divide? multiply
10 * 25 = 250

>
```

Source: Replit

QuickQuiz   Section C

1. An arithmetic expression contains [   ] and arithmetic operators.

2. The order of operations can be changed by using [   ] in an expression.

3. A(n) [   ] structure is a part of a computer program that tells the computer what to do, depending on whether a condition is true or false.

4. In Python, when you need to make multiple decisions in an *if* statement, use the [   ] keyword.

5. Logical operators are also known as [   ] operators.

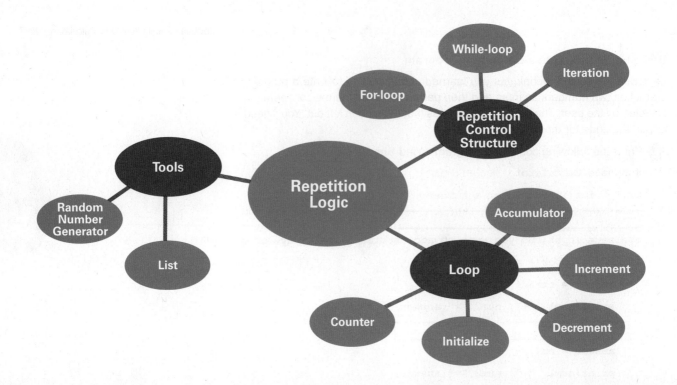

Objectives

▶ Code a basic for-loop.

▶ Determine the number of for-loop repetitions based on range parameters.

▶ Code a basic while-loop.

▶ Increment and decrement counters within loops.

▶ Use the import random command to generate random numbers.

▶ Incorporate random numbers in programs to roll dice, pick lottery numbers, and play a number guessing game.

▶ Use the correct Python syntax to create lists.

▶ Iterate through a list.

▶ Use an accumulator to combine the values in a list.

▶ Code the Fortune Teller program.

Repetition is part of your daily life. For example, you wash your clothes, dry them, and put them away—and then you repeat the cycle when your laundry basket fills up again. Computers can also perform repetitive tasks, such as calculating grades for every student in a college course. In this section, you will learn how to write a program that repeats multiple times. Using this new skill, you will create a number guessing game and a fun program that tells fortunes.

Terminology

repetition control structure	increment	random number generator	accumulator
loop	decrement	list	
iteration	counter		
	initialize		

Repetition Control Structures

Because applications often require the same tasks to be executed over and over again, all programming languages include repetition control structures. A **repetition control structure** allows programmers to write code that can repeatedly execute a statement or a series of statements.

The section of code that repeats is referred to as a loop or an iteration. Statements in the loop are executed repeatedly as long as a condition holds true. Python has two types of loops: the for-loop and the while-loop.

▶ **What is a for-loop?** When you know in advance the number of times you want to execute a statement or statements, use a for-loop. The for-loop is known as a counter-controlled loop because the loop will be repeated a certain number of times. It is best to illustrate how a loop works by using a simple Python example.

Coding a Basic For-Loop

Try entering this for-loop example that writes "Hello World!" four times.

1 Enter the following lines of code for a program called **Hello4**:

```
for repetitions in range(1,5):
    print(repetitions)
    print("Hello World!")
```

2 Save and run the program.

3 Compare your program and output to Figure PY-31.

Try It!

Modify the program in Figure PY-31 to produce the following output using a for-loop:

1

Go, fight, win!

2

Go, fight, win!

3

Go, fight, win!

Figure PY-31: For-loop

```
1  for repetitions in range(1,5):
2      print(repetitions)
3      print("Hello World!")
```

```
1
Hello World!
2
Hello World!
3
Hello World!
4
Hello World!
>
```

Source: Replit

▶ **What should I know about the syntax for a for-loop?** The control statement for a for-loop begins with the command word *for*, which is followed by a variable and a range. In the program you wrote, the variable is called "repetitions."

The function "range()" is used to indicate how many times the loop will be repeated. The structure of the range function is *range(start value, upto value)*. The *start value* is optional. If it is not present, the range starts with 0. The *upto value* must always be specified. It means "up to but not including" the value.

The range for your program is range(1,5). Here's what happens:

- When the loop begins, Python loads 1 into a variable called "repetitions" and performs the indented statements.

- Python then adds 1 to the value of "repetitions." As long as "repetitions" is not 5, Python will do the loop again. Although the range is (1,5), the loop repeats only four times.

- When the value of "repetitions" becomes 5, the loop ends without executing the indented statements a fifth time.

▶ **What is a while-loop?** When you do not know in advance the number of times you want to execute a statement or statements, use the while-loop. A while-loop repeats until a certain condition exists. You can specify the condition using many of the conditional expressions you learned in the previous section.

Using the While-Loop Control Structure

In a guess-the-number game, the programmer does not know how many times the program will have to loop before the user guesses the correct number. The following guessing game program uses a while-loop.

❶ Enter the following lines of code for a program called **Guess** that uses the while-loop control structure:

```
secret_number = 7

guess = 0

while guess != secret_number:

    print("I'm thinking of a number between 1 and 10.")

    print("Can you guess it?")

    guess = int(input())

    if guess == secret_number:

        print("That's it!")

    else:

        print("That's not the number. Try again")
```

❷ Save and run the program.

❸ Enter **5** as the input. Because that is not the secret number, the program loops and asks you to guess again. Enter a few more guesses before you enter the secret number. When you've guessed correctly, the program outputs "That's it!"

QuickCheck

What does this code print?
```
for y in range(4):

    print(y)
```

a. The letter "y" four times

b. The numbers 0 to 3

c. The numbers 0 to 4

d. The numbers 1 to 3

④ Compare your program and output to Figure PY-32.

Figure PY-32: While-loop

```
1   secret_number = 7
2   guess = 0
3   while guess != secret_number:
4     print("I'm thinking of a number between 1 and
      10.")
5     print("Can you guess it?")
6     guess = int(input())
7     if guess == secret_number:
8       print("That's it!")
9     else:
10      print("That's not the number. Try again")
```

```
I'm thinking of a number between 1 and 10. Q ×
Can you guess it?
5
That's not the number. Try again
I'm thinking of a number between 1 and 10.
Can you guess it?
7
That's it!
> █
```

Source: Replit

Manual Loop Controls

Although for-loops make it relatively easy to specify the number of repetitions in a loop, some programmers like to set up loop counters within a while-loop. These loops use techniques referred to as incrementing and decrementing, which update a variable—where the new value of the variable depends on the old one.

▶ **Can I set up manual loop controls?** To **increment** a variable means to add an amount to its current value. The statement `num = num + 1` takes the current value of num, adds 1, and then updates num with the new value. To **decrement** a variable, you subtract instead of add, as in `num = num - 1`.

In the above examples, the variable num is known as a counter. A **counter** is a numeric variable used for counting something, such as the total number of items purchased, the number of employees paid in a week, or the number of times to execute a loop.

Before you can increment or decrement a variable, you have to **initialize** it. To initialize a variable, you must give it a beginning value. This happens with a simple assignment:

`num = 0`

Controlling a Loop with a Counter

Here is a program that counts down from 5 and then prints "Blastoff!"

① Enter the following lines of code for a program called **Blastoff**:

```
counter = 5     # initialize counter
while counter > 0:
    print(counter)
    counter = counter - 1   # decrement counter
print("Blastoff!")
```

② Save and run the program.

③ Compare your program and output to Figure PY-33.

Figure PY-33: While-loop countdown

```
1   counter = 5     # initialize counter
2   while counter > 0:
3     print(counter)
4     counter = counter - 1   # decrement counter
5   print("Blastoff!")
```

```
5
4
3
2
1
Blastoff!
> █
```

Source: Replit

Try It!

Use a while-loop to print the following sentence three times: "There's no place like home."

Python's Random Number Generator

Most programming languages provide a **random number generator** to create the random numbers that are needed for certain programs, and Python is no exception. Python provides a tool called a random module that implements the random number generator. Here are a few situations where you would use random numbers:

- To play a game of chance where the computer needs to throw dice, pick a number, pick lottery numbers, or flip a coin
- To shuffle a deck of playing cards randomly
- To make an enemy spaceship appear at a random location in a game

▶ **How do I generate random numbers in Python?** To have access to the random number generator, you need to include an `import random` statement at the beginning of your program. Then you can use the `random.randint()` command to generate a random number and place it in a variable.

Generating a Random Number

This example generates a random integer in the range 1 to 10 inclusive.

1 Enter the following lines of code for a program called **Random1**:

```
import random

x = random.randint(1, 10)

print(x)
```

2 Save and run the program several times. Each time you run the program, it should output a random number.

Generating Multiple Random Numbers

The original Mega Millions lottery was based on selecting five winning numbers ranging from 1 to 56. You can create a Python program to randomly choose lottery numbers.

1 Enter the following lines of code for a program called **Random2**:

```
import random

count = 0

while count < 5:

    # Get random number in range 1 through 56.

    n = random.randint(1,56)

    print(n)

    count = count + 1
```

2 Save and run the program.

3 Compare your program and output to Figure PY-34.

Figure PY-34: Generate lottery numbers

```
1   import random
2   count = 0
3   while count < 5:
4       # Get random number in range 1 through 56.
5       n = random.randint(1,56)
6       print(n)
7       count = count + 1
```

```
21
37
2
15
16
>
```

Source: Replit

Using the Random Number Generator to Simulate Rolling Two Dice

Let's try using the random number generator to simulate rolling two dice.

1 Enter the following lines of code for a program called **Dice**:

```python
import random
roll_again = "y"
while roll_again.lower() == "y":
    print("Rolling the dice...")
    print("The first number is: ")
    print(random.randint(1, 6))
    print("The second number is: ")
    print(random.randint(1, 6))
    roll_again = input("Roll the dice again? y or n: ")
```

2 Save and run the program.

3 Compare your program and output to Figure PY-35. Your output should look similar to the figure.

Figure PY-35: Rolling dice simulation

```
1   import random
2   roll_again = "y"
3   while roll_again.lower() == "y":
4       print("Rolling the dice...")
5       print("The first number is: ")
6       print(random.randint(1, 6))
7       print("The second number is: ")
8       print(random.randint(1, 6))
9       roll_again = input("Roll the dice again? y or n: ")
```

```
Rolling the dice...
The first number is:
1
The second number is:
5
Roll the dice again? y or n: y
Rolling the dice...
The first number is:
3
The second number is:
5
Roll the dice again? y or n: n
>
```

Source: Replit

Revising the Guess the Number Game

You created a basic Guess the Number game earlier in this section. In that version, the secret number was hard-coded into the program. Now you can create the game using a random number, so each time the program runs, the secret number will be different. This more sophisticated program also limits users to five guesses.

1 Enter the following code for a program called **Secret Number** that asks the user's name, generates a random number, and starts the guessing game:

```python
import random
guesses_taken = 0
print("Hello! What is your name?")
myName = input()
secret_number = random.randint(1, 20)
print(myName + ", I am thinking of a number between 1 and 20.")
```

2 Enter the following while-loop that collects the user's guesses and provides hints when the number is too high or too low:

```
while guesses_taken < 6:

    print("Try to guess the number.")

    guess = input()

    guess = int(guess)

    guesses_taken = guesses_taken + 1

    if guess < secret_number:

        print("Your guess is too low.")

    if guess > secret_number:

        print("Your guess is too high.")

    if guess == secret_number:

        guesses_taken = 6  # force the while-loop to end
```

3 Enter the following lines of code that display the guessing game results. (Hint: These lines are outside the loop, so do not indent the two lines that begin with *if*.)

```
if guess == secret_number:

    guesses_taken = str(guesses_taken)

    print("Good job, " + myName + "! You guessed my number!")

if guess != secret_number:

    secret_number = str(secret_number)

    print("Nope. The number I was thinking of was" + secret_number)
```

4 Save and run the program several times. Each time it runs, the secret number should be selected at random.

5 Compare your program and output to Figure PY-36.

Figure PY-36: Guess the Number game

```
1  import random
2  guesses_taken = 0
3  print("Hello! What is your name?")
4  myName = input()
5  secret_number = random.randint(1, 20)
6  print(myName + ", I am thinking of a number between 1 and 20.")
7  while guesses_taken < 6:
8    print("Try to guess the number.")
9    guess = input()
10   guess = int(guess)
11   guesses_taken = guesses_taken + 1
12   if guess < secret_number:
13     print("Your guess is too low.")
14   if guess > secret_number:
15     print("Your guess is too high.")
16   if guess == secret_number:
17     guesses_taken = 6 # force the while-loop to end
18 if guess == secret_number:
19   guesses_taken = str(guesses_taken)
20   print("Good job, " + myName + "! You guessed my number!")
21 if guess != secret_number:
22   secret_number = str(secret_number)
23   print("Nope. The number I was thinking of was" + secret_number)
```

```
Hello! What is your name?
Carlotta
Carlotta, I am thinking of a number between 1 and 20.
Try to guess the number.
10
Your guess is too high.
Try to guess the number.
5
Your guess is too high.
Try to guess the number.
3
Good job, Carlotta! You guessed my number!
> 
```

Source: Replit

Python Lists

A list in Python is an ordered group of items that can be numbers or strings that are modifiable. Programs may need to hold a series of related values for various reasons, such as keeping a list of the days of the week, the months in a year, or the names of friends.

Creating a list is as simple as putting a series of comma-separated values between square brackets. The following are some examples of lists:

```python
my_list = [1, 2, 3, 4, 5]
some_names = ["Bob", "Kumar", "Jay"]
fruit_list = ["apple", "banana", "cantaloupe"]
```

▶ **Why would I use a list in a Python program?** Lists are tools that programmers use to make certain coding tasks straightforward when combined with repetition. For example, if you have a list of grocery items, you could use a loop to print the items or sort them into alphabetical order. Programmers can use a for-loop to process items in a list. The block of code in the for-loop is executed only once for each item in the list.

Printing the Items in a List

A very basic program for processing a list simply prints each item on a separate line.

1 Enter the following code for a program called **Basic List**:

```python
my_list = [1, 2, 3, 4, 5]
for item in my_list:
    print(item)
```

2 Run your program.

3 Compare your program and output to Figure PY-37.

Figure PY-37: Print the number list

```
1   my_list = [1, 2, 3, 4, 5]
2   for item in my_list:
3     print(item)
4
```

```
1
2
3
4
5
>
```

Source: Replit

Inserting List Items into Output Strings

List items can be inserted into print statements. Let's invite friends to a party by using one print() command.

1 Enter and run this code for a program called **Friends**:

```
friend_list = ["Jasmin","Zoe","Brad","Zuki",\
"Thandi","Amir"]

for name in friend_list:
    print("Hi " + name + ". Come to my party!")
```

2 Compare your program and output to Figure PY-38.

Terminology

The \ symbol tells Python that a line of code is continued on the next line. It is handy when creating long lists that exceed the width of your IDE's entry area.

Figure PY-38: List items in output

```
1   friend_list = ["Jasmin","Zoe","Brad","Zuki",\
2   "Thandi","Amir"]
3   for name in friend_list:
4     print("Hi " + name + ". Come to my party!")
```

```
Hi Jasmin. Come to my party!
Hi Zoe. Come to my party!
Hi Brad. Come to my party!
Hi Zuki. Come to my party!
Hi Thandi. Come to my party!
Hi Amir. Come to my party!
>
```

Source: Replit

▶ **Can list items be used for mathematical operations?** Yes. For example, you can total the items in a list and place the result in an accumulator. An **accumulator** is a numeric variable in which values are repetitively added. It works essentially like a hand calculator into which you enter a sequence of numbers.

Totaling the Numbers in a List

Let's see how you can use an accumulator to calculate the sum of the values in a list.

1 Enter the following code for a program called **Accumulator**:

```
num_list = [2,4,6,8]

sum = 0

for number in num_list:

    sum = sum + number

print("The sum is:", sum)
```

2 Save and run the program.

3 Compare your program and output to Figure PY-39.

QuickCheck

What is the value of sum after this code is run?

```
num_list = [1,3,-1,5]

sum = 0

for number in num_list:

    sum = sum + number

print("The sum is:", sum)
```

a. 9

b. 8

c. 5

d. 2

Figure PY-39: Print the sum of numbers in the list

```
1   num_list = [2,4,6,8]
2   sum = 0
3 ⊟ for number in num_list:
4     sum = sum + number
5   print("The sum is:", sum)
```

```
The sum is: 20
>
```

Source: Replit

Choosing Random Items from a List

The random number generator can be used to randomly choose items from a list. Using random.choice from the random module will pick a random item from a list.

1 Enter the following code for a program called **Pick**:

```
import random

# pick a random choice from a list

print(random.choice(["yes", "no", "maybe"]))
```

2 Save and run the program. Do you expect to get exactly the same results as in Figure PY-40?

Figure PY-40: Choose an item at random

```
1    import random
2    # pick a random choice from a list
3    print(random.choice(["yes", "no", "maybe"]))
```

```
maybe
> []
```

Source: Replit

Ask the Fortune Teller

Have you ever used the "fortune-telling" Magic 8 Ball toy? You can create a fortune-telling program that randomly produces a "fortune" in response to a question posed by a user. Your program will contain the following elements:

- A while-loop that allows the player to ask multiple questions
- A list to hold the "predictions"
- A random number generator to randomly select an answer from the list of predictions

Creating the Fortune Teller Program

1 Start a new program called **Fortune**. Enter the following code to begin the program and import the random module:

```
# The Fortune Teller

import random
```

2 Add the following code to populate a list with predictions. (Hint: Using a slash at the end of a line tells Python that the code continues on to the next line. So, you can press the Enter key after you type the slash.)

```
predictions = ["yes", "no", "maybe","certainly",\
"try again later", "my sources say no","very doubtful",\
"not now","outlook good","cannot predict now","most \
likely","reply hazy, try again","signs point to yes"]
```

3 Add the following code to display a message to the user and collect input in a variable called question.

```python
print("Welcome to Ask the Fortune Teller.")
print("Ask the Fortune Teller a question.")
question = input()
```

4 Add the following code to create a while-loop that randomly selects a prediction and displays it:

```python
# Loop that repeats until the user types "Quit"
while question.upper() != "QUIT":
    answer = random.choice(predictions)
    print("My answer is: " + answer + ".")
    print("Ask another question or type Quit to end!")
    question = input()
```

5 Save and run the program.

6 Compare your program and output to Figure PY-41.

Figure PY-41: Ask the Fortune Teller

```python
1   # The Fortune Teller
2   import random
3   predictions = ["yes", "no", "maybe","certainly",\
4   "try again later", "my sources say no","very doubtful",\
5   "not now","outlook good","cannot predict now","most \
6   likely","reply hazy, try again","signs point to yes"]
7   print("Welcome to Ask the Fortune Teller.")
8   print("Ask the Fortune Teller a question.")
9   question = input()
10  # Loop that repeats until the user types "Quit"
11  while question.upper() != "QUIT":
12      answer = random.choice(predictions)
13      print("My answer is: " + answer + ".")
14      print("Ask another question or type Quit to end!")
15      question = input()
```

```
Welcome to Ask the Fortune Teller.
Ask the Fortune Teller a question.
Will it rain today?
My answer is: outlook good.
Ask another question or type Quit to end!
Will I ace my math test?
My answer is: signs point to yes.
Ask another question or type Quit to end!
Quit
> █
```

Source: Replit

QuickQuiz   Section D

1. A(n) [_____] structure enables you to write code that can repeatedly execute a statement or a series of statements.

2. Another name for a loop is a(n) [_____].

3. Statements in a loop are executed repeatedly as long as a condition holds [_____].

4. If the number of times that you execute a loop varies, use the [_____] loop.

5. Use a(n) [_____] to store the names of the days of the week or the months of the year.

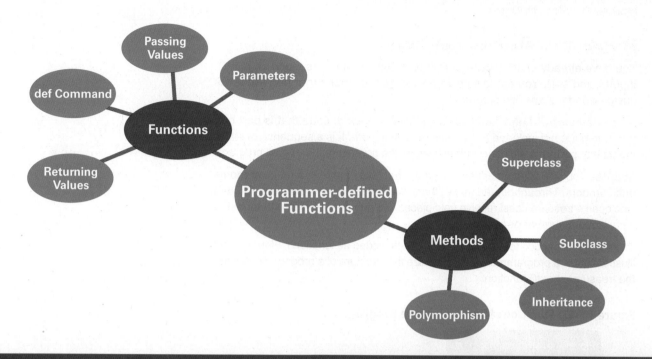

Dogs and Cats

Objectives

▶ Explain the advantages of using programmer-defined functions.

▶ Use the def command to code a function in a Python program.

▶ Pass values and strings to a function.

▶ Return values and strings from a function to the main program.

▶ Explain the purpose of a method used in an object-oriented program.

▶ Create methods for a class.

▶ Explain the efficiency of inheritance.

▶ Create a subclass that inherits attributes from a superclass.

▶ Describe the concept of polymorphism by providing an example in Python.

As you have worked through the sections in this module, the programs have become larger and more complex. Programmers use tools to make complex programs more manageable and understandable. In this section, you will learn how to use functions in an adventure game and how to use objects in a program about dogs and cats.

Terminology

programmer-defined function	parameters method	inheritance superclass	subclass polymorphism

Programmer-Defined Functions

You have already used several of Python's built-in functions, such as print(), input(), and str(). You can also define your own functions that perform tasks customized for a specific program.

A **programmer-defined function** is typically a block of code that is part of a program but is not included in the main execution path. It is a sequence of statements that performs a distinct subtask within the context of the overall program.

Suppose you're writing an adventure game that takes place in a maze of rooms and corridors. Throughout the maze, there are several treasure chests. Players who open a treasure chest receive gold pieces, the number of which is determined by a random number generator.

The segments of code for treasure chests can be coded as functions. Figure PY-42 illustrates how a programmer would visualize the structure of a program containing the treasure_chest() function.

Figure PY-42: Functions in an adventure program

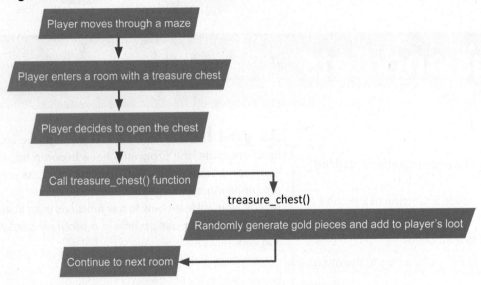

▶ **What's the advantage of using programmer-defined functions?** Once you've defined a function, it can be used over and over again, which saves you work. Functions eliminate the need to rewrite or copy code in order to reuse it. Using functions can also enhance the clarity and quality of a program by organizing subtasks into modules.

For the adventure game, the treasure_chest() function is written once, but it is used many times within the game whenever the player finds a treasure chest in the maze.

▶ **How do I define a function?** You can define functions in Python using the *def* command. The *def* command word is followed by the name of the function and a set of parentheses—for example, `def treasure_chest()`.

Coding Your First Function

Let's start with a basic function that generates a random amount of gold and prints a corresponding message.

1 Start a new program called **Treasure**. Enter the following lines of code for the treasure_chest() function:

```
def treasure_chest():
    amount = random.randint(1,10)
    print("The treasure chest contains", amount, "pieces
    of gold.")
```

2 Look back at the code you have just written. The first line defines the name of the function as treasure_chest(), and it ends with a colon. The indented lines are the body of the function.

3 A function cannot run on its own. It requires a function call within the main execution path of a program. The main program will begin on line 4. Enter the following code for lines 4 through 8. (Hint: Make sure these lines are not indented.)

```
# Main program begins here
import random
player_gold = 5
print("There is a treasure chest here.")
treasure_chest() # This statement calls the treasure_chest
function
```

4 Save your program and run it.

5 Compare your program and output to Figure PY-43.

Terminology

Parameters are also called *arguments*.

PY

Figure PY-43: A function that generates a random amount of gold

```
1  def treasure_chest():
2      amount = random.randint(1,10)
3      print("The treasure chest contains", amount, "pieces of gold.")
4  # Main program begins here
5  import random
6  player_gold = 5
7  print("There is a treasure chest here.")
8  treasure_chest() # This statement calls the treasure_chest function
```

```
There is a treasure chest here.
The treasure chest contains 9 pieces of gold.
>
```

Source: Replit

▶ **Can functions exchange values with the main program?** Yes. You can put a number or a variable in the parentheses of a function call. You can use a corresponding number or a variable in the function definition. The contents within parentheses that are passed to a function are called **parameters** (Figure PY-44).

Figure PY-44: Passing a parameter

```
def treasure_chest(max)
```
← The function definition contains one variable.

```
treasure_chest(20)
```
← The function call contains one number.

QuickCheck

In the code for Figure PY-43, what is the maximum amount of gold that can be in a treasure chest?

a. None

b. One piece

c. Five pieces

d. Ten pieces

Passing Data into a Function

Some treasure chests contain more than 10 pieces of gold. Let's add a "max" parameter to the treasure_chest() function so we can specify the maximum number produced by the random number generator. In the following program, the number 20 is passed from the function call to the treasure_chest() function, where it is the maximum number used to generate the number of gold pieces in the chest.

❶ Modify the Treasure program so it becomes the following:

```python
def treasure_chest(max):

    amount = random.randint(1,max)

    print("The treasure chest contains", amount, "pieces of
    gold.")

# Main program begins here

import random

player_gold = 5

print("There is a treasure chest here.")

treasure_chest(20) # This statement calls the treasure_chest
function
```

❷ Save the program and run it.

❸ Compare your program and output to Figure PY-45.

Figure PY-45: Passing a value to a function

```
1  def treasure_chest(max):
2    amount = random.randint(1,max)
3    print("The treasure chest contains", amount, "pieces of gold.")
4  # Main program begins here
5  import random
6  player_gold = 5
7  print("There is a treasure chest here.")
8  treasure_chest(20) # This statement calls the treasure_chest function
```

```
There is a treasure chest here.
The treasure chest contains 19 pieces of gold.
>
```

Source: Replit

❭ Is it possible to get a value out of a function and pass it to the main program? Yes. Here's the trick: Add a return command at the end of a function. When you do so, the function call takes on the value that was calculated in the function.

Using a Value Generated by a Function

Let's modify your program so that the gold generated by the treasure_chest() function is returned to the main program and placed in a variable called found_gold.

❶ Add the line `return amount` to the end of the function, like this:

```python
def treasure_chest(max):

    amount = random.randint(1,max)

    print("The treasure chest contains", amount, "pieces
    of gold.")

    return amount;
```

2 Modify the code in your main program to put the amount returned by the function call into a variable called found_gold, as follows:

```
# Main program begins here

import random

player_gold = 5

print("You are in a blue room. There is a treasure chest here.")
# The next statement calls the function and loads the result
into found_gold

found_gold = treasure_chest(20)
```

3 Now, add these two lines of code to the main program to add the found_gold to the amount of gold the player started with:

```
player_gold = found_gold + player_gold

print("Player gold =", player_gold)
```

4 Save and run the program.

5 Compare your program and output to Figure PY-46. Does the player now have the original five gold pieces plus the amount of gold in the treasure chest?

Figure PY-46: Returning a value from a function

```
1   def treasure_chest(max):
2       amount = random.randint(1,max)
3       print("The treasure chest contains", amount, "pieces of gold.")
4       return amount;
5   # Main program begins here
6   import random
7   player_gold = 5
8   print("You are in a blue room. There is a treasure chest here.")
9   # The next statement calls the function and loads the result
    into found_gold
10  found_gold = treasure_chest(20)
11  player_gold = found_gold + player_gold
12  print("Player gold =", player_gold)
```

```
You are in a blue room. There is a treasure chest here.
The treasure chest contains 13 pieces of gold.
Player gold = 18
>
```

Source: Replit

▶ **Can functions work with text strings?** Yes. Text strings can be used as parameters in function calls. As you would expect, strings need to be enclosed in quotation marks in the call. They can be represented by a variable in the function definition.

Using Text Strings in Functions

In the adventure game, some treasure chests contain gems in addition to gold. Let's add parameters to the treasure_chest function to hold the name of the gem ("ruby") and its value (8 gold pieces).

1 Modify the function call in the adventure game program to the following:

```
found_gold = treasure_chest("ruby",8,20)
```

QuickCheck

What is the output of this program?

```
def say_hello():

    print("Hello World!")

say_hello()

say_hello()
```

a. Hello World!
   Hello World!

b. "Hello World!"
   "Hello World!"

c. Hello
   Hello

d. say_hello
   say_hello

2 Modify the function definition as follows:

```
def treasure_chest(gem,value,max):

    amount = random.randint(1,max)

    print("The treasure chest contains", amount, "pieces of gold.")

    if gem != "none":

        print("The treasure chest contains a", gem, "worth ", value, "gold
        pieces.")

        amount = amount + value

    return amount;
```

3 Save and run the program. Calculate the contents of the treasure chest in your head and compare your results to Figure PY-47 to make sure the program is producing the correct results.

Try It!

What happens if the function call contains "none" instead of "ruby"? Modify the program and find out!

Figure PY-47: Passing a string value to a function

```
1   def treasure_chest(gem,value,max):
2       amount = random.randint(1,max)
3       print("The treasure chest contains", amount, "pieces of gold.")
4       if gem != "none":
5           print("The treasure chest contains a", gem, "worth",
            value, "gold pieces.")
6           amount = amount + value
7       return amount;
8   # Main program begins here
9   import random
10  player_gold = 5
11  print("You are in a blue room. There is a treasure chest here.")
12  # The next statement calls the function and loads the result
    into found_gold
13  found_gold = treasure_chest("ruby",8,20)
14  player_gold = found_gold + player_gold
15  print("Player gold =", player_gold)
```

```
You are in a blue room. There is a treasure chest here.
The treasure chest contains 13 pieces of gold.
The treasure chest contains a ruby worth 8 gold pieces.
Player gold = 26
>
```

Source: Replit

▶ **What should I remember about functions?** Now that you know how functions work, you can use them in your programs in place of blocks of code that perform specific repetitive tasks. Once a function is defined, it can be used over and over again. When using functions, keep the following rules in mind:

- Function blocks begin with the keyword def followed by the function name and parentheses ().
- The parentheses can hold parameters. Make sure that the function call and the function definition have the same number of parameters.
- The code block within every function starts with a colon (:) and is indented.
- The function terminates with the last indented line of code.
- The return statement passes data from the function to the main program.

Try It!

Add a red room to the maze. It contains a treasure chest with a diamond worth 50 pieces of gold.

Add a print statement and a second function call to the main program. The output should look similar to the following:

You are in a blue room.

There is a treasure chest here.

The treasure chest contains 10 pieces of gold.

The treasure chest contains a ruby worth 8 pieces of gold.

You are in a red room.

There is a treasure chest here.

The treasure chest contains 15 pieces of gold.

The treasure chest contains a diamond worth 50 pieces of gold.

Player gold = 88

Methods

In Section B, you were introduced to classes and objects. As a review, every object in an object-oriented program is created from a class. A class attribute defines the characteristics of a set of objects. Classes can also include methods.

▶ **What is a method?** A **method** is a segment of code that defines an action belonging to a class. In Python, methods are essentially functions, but they are defined slightly differently. A method must always have an argument called *self* within the parentheses.

When Python calls a method, it passes the current object to that method as the first parameter. Figure PY-48 explains how this works.

PY

Figure PY-48: A method for the Pet class

```
class Pet:  A
    number_of_legs = 0  B
    def sleep(self):  C
        print ("zzz")  D
    dog = Pet()  E
    dog.sleep()  F
```

A Class Pet: defines the Pet class.

B number_of_legs is an attribute of the Pet class. It is set to 0 when the program begins, but it can be changed according to the type of pet.

C The sleep() method is defined here. It must include (self) as the first parameter.

D print ("zzz") is the action the method performs.

E dog = Pet(): creates a dog object of the Pet class.

F dog.sleep: passes the dog object as an argument to the sleep() method, which prints out a message, "zzz".

Creating a Method in the Class

Let's create a Pet class with a method called sleep(), which prints "zzz" whenever it is called.

Try It!

Try running this program without the word *self* in line 3. What happens?

1 Start a new program called **Pets**. Enter the following:

```
class Pet:
    number_of_legs = 0
    def sleep(self):
        print("zzz")
```

2 Now, enter the following statement that creates a dog object:

```
dog = Pet()
```

3 Add the following statement that calls the sleep() method:

```
dog.sleep()
```

4 Save and run the program.

5 Compare your program and output to Figure PY-49.

Figure PY-49: The Pet class and its sleep() method

```
1  class Pet:
2      number_of_legs = 0
3      def sleep(self):
4          print("zzz")
5  dog = Pet()
6  dog.sleep()
```

```
zzz
> 
```

Source: Replit

▶ **Can a class have more than one method?** Yes. Each method begins with the def command and includes the word *self* as the parameter inside parentheses. Be sure to indent the code for each method and end the indent at the conclusion of the method.

Creating Another Method in the Class

Let's create a new method to print out how many legs a pet has. You will need to add the count_legs() method, an assignment statement that gives dogs four legs, and a statement that calls the count_legs() method.

1 Modify your program so that it contains the following lines of code:

```
class Pet:
    number_of_legs = 0
    def sleep(self):
        print("zzz")
    def count_legs(self):
        print("This pet has", self.number_of_legs, "legs.")
dog = Pet()
dog.sleep()
dog.number_of_legs = 4
dog.count_legs()
```

2 Save and run the program.

3 Compare your program and output to Figure PY-50.

Figure PY-50: Sleep() and count_legs() methods

```
1   class Pet:
2     number_of_legs = 0
3     def sleep(self):
4       print("zzz")
5     def count_legs(self):
6       print("This pet has", self.number_of_legs, "legs.")
7   dog = Pet()
8   dog.sleep()
9   dog.number_of_legs = 4
10  dog.count_legs()
```

```
zzz
This pet has 4 legs.
>
```

Source: Replit

Superclasses and Subclasses

A bark() method does not belong to the Pet class because not all pets bark. It makes sense, then, to create a Dog class that has a bark() method. But the Dog class also has other attributes common to all pets. You can combine attributes from the Pet class with special attributes for the Dog class using a technique called inheritance.

▶ **What is inheritance?** In object-oriented jargon, **inheritance** refers to passing certain characteristics from one class to other classes. For example, the Dog class can inherit attributes and methods of the Pet class and include methods that apply only to the Dog class.

The Pet class and the Dog class are related. The Pet class is known as the **superclass** because it is a class from which attributes and methods can be inherited. The Dog class is the **subclass** (or derived class) because it is a class that inherits attributes and methods from a superclass.

To designate that Dog is a subclass of Pet, you can define it using the statement `class Dog(Pet)`. That statement gives the Dog class all of the attributes of the Pet class, such as number_of_legs. For attributes specific to the Dog class, you can define methods. For example, you can add a bark() method, like this:

```
class Dog(Pet):

    def bark(self):

        print ("Woof")
```

Creating a Subclass from a Superclass

Let's modify the Pets program so that Dog is a subclass of Pet. The Dog class will have a bark() method that is unique for dogs.

1 Delete the last four lines of the previous program.

2 Add the following lines of code to define the Dog class:

```
class Dog(Pet):

    def bark(self):

        print("Woof")
```

3 Create an object in the Dog class called spike, as follows:

```
spike = Dog()
```

PY

④ Add this code to call the following methods that are defined in the Pet class and the Dog class:

```
spike.bark()

spike.sleep()

spike.number_of_legs = 4

spike.count_legs()
```

⑤ Save and run the program.

⑥ Compare your program and output to Figure PY-51. Notice that the spike object calls the bark(), sleep(), and count_legs() methods defined in the Dog class and inherited from the Pet class.

Figure PY-51: The Dog class inherits methods from the Pet class

```
1   class Pet:
2      number_of_legs = 0
3      def sleep(self):
4         print("zzz")
5      def count_legs(self):
6         print("This pet has", self.number_of_legs, "legs.")
7   class Dog(Pet):
8      def bark(self):
9         print("woof")
10  spike = Dog()
11  spike.bark()
12  spike.sleep()
13  spike.number_of_legs = 4
14  spike.count_legs()
```

```
woof
zzz
This pet has 4 legs.
>
```

Source: Replit

▶ **How would a Cat class fit in?** You can create a Cat subclass that inherits attributes from the Pet superclass. That should be easy.

Creating a Second Subclass

You can modify your program to add a Cat class and create a Cat object called Fluffy. While you're adding a Cat subclass, let's generalize the bark() method and rename it talk(). You'll find out why this is useful in a moment.

1 Modify your program to the following:

```python
class Pet:
    number_of_legs = 0
    def sleep(self):
        print("zzz")
    def count_legs(self):
        print("This pet has",self.number_of_legs, "legs.")
class Dog(Pet):
    def talk(self):
        print("woof")
class Cat(Pet):
    def talk(self):
        print("meow")
spike = Dog()
spike.talk()
fluffy = Cat()
fluffy.talk()
```

2 Save and run the program.

3 Compare your program and output to Figure PY-52. Spike "woofs" and Fluffy "meows."

QuickCheck

If the following statements are added to the Pets program, what is the output from the two statements?

```python
spot = Cat()
spot.talk()
```

a. woof

b. meow

c. zzz

d. Nothing

Figure PY-52: Two talk() methods perform different tasks

```python
1   class Pet:
2     number_of_legs = 0
3     def sleep(self):
4       print("zzz")
5     def count_legs(self):
6       print("This pet has",self.number_of_legs, "legs.")
7   class Dog(Pet):
8     def talk(self):
9       print("woof")
10  class Cat(Pet):
11    def talk(self):
12      print("meow")
13  spike = Dog()
14  spike.talk()
15  fluffy = Cat()
16  fluffy.talk()
```

```
woof
meow
>
```

Source: Replit

▶ **How can the Dog and Cat classes both have a talk() method?** An object-oriented concept called polymorphism makes it possible to assign more than one sound to the talk() method.

▶ **What is polymorphism?** Polymorphism, sometimes called overloading, is the ability to redefine a method in a subclass. It enables programmers to create a single, more generic name for a method that behaves in unique ways for different classes.

An object of the Dog class will print "Woof" when using the talk() method because this talk() method is a part of the Dog class. An object of the Cat class will print "Meow" when using the talk() method because this talk() method is a part of the Cat class. Through polymorphism, subclasses tailor methods to fit their unique requirements.

QuickQuiz   Section E

1. Python functions begin with the keyword [_____] followed by the function name and parentheses.

2. The contents between parentheses that are passed to a function are called [_____].

3. In Python, functions contained within a class are called [_____].

4. A(n) [_____] is a class from which attributes and methods can be inherited.

5. Passing certain characteristics from one class to other classes is referred to as [_____].

Flipped Class Projects

Critical Thinking

Think like a programmer and create a character that will perform a series of tasks in the videogame Minecraft. To get started, search online for *"minecraft hour of code"* at the code.org Web site. Select *Minecraft Voyage Aquatic* or the current project. Watch the video and then follow the instructions to select a character. Have your character follow the assigned tasks to complete each program. These assigned tasks will test your critical thinking with regard to how well you plan your moves so that your character successfully completes each mission. When you are finished going through all the tasks, answer the following questions: What coding techniques did you use to plan your character's actions? Was it easier to write programs using blocks of code? What difficulties, if any, did you experience?

Group Project

Working in a group of three students, develop a Python program that produces the average for a series of test scores using the steps below. The grading scale is 90–100 = A, 80–89 = B, 70–79 = C, 60–69 = D, <60 = F.

1 Use a loop to input a variable number of test scores.

2 Use a counter to keep track of how many scores are entered, and use an accumulator to store the test score total.

3 Calculate the average test score.

4 Print out the average test score.

5 After the program is running with no errors, add code to assign a letter grade to the grade average.

6 Print out the average test score and the letter grade.

7 Take a screenshot, print it out, and then submit the program and output to your instructor.

Cyberclassroom

There are a variety of free online classes to help you learn programming languages. Try at least three introductory Python tutorials, such as those you find at *Codecademy*, *W3Schools*, and *Coursera*. Write a short blog post comparing your experiences with the tutorials at each site.

Multimedia Project

Videos are a popular tutorial format. Search online for *MIT App Inventor*, scroll down the page to select *Tutorials*, and then select the *Talk To Me app* under *Beginner Tutorials*. Watch the videos and follow the instructions to create three starter apps. Were you able to build the apps based on the tutorial instructions? What are the apps used for? After completing this project, are you interested in trying to build your own app?

Resume Builder

In the job market of the 21st century, having the skills to perform technology-related tasks is essential. Make a list of careers you're interested in, and then search online to find out how coding skills might enhance your qualifications for each of these careers. Think outside of the box and into the future to come up with ideas about how coding might apply to the career fields you have selected.

Globalization

Which programming languages are used globally? Conduct research on the Web, and then create a list of the top ten most frequently used languages worldwide. Has this list changed since last year? Name your source(s) for this information. Most programming languages are written in English. Why do you think this is the case? Can you find three programming languages that are not written in English? List them and indicate what human language they are written in.

Key Terms

accumulator 876
algorithm 839
arithmetic expression 858
assignment operator 849
attribute 852
Boolean operators 865
bug 845
class 852
code 839
code editor 839
coding 839
comment 843
comparison operator 864
compiler 839
computation 858
concatenation 843
concatenation operator 843
counter 871
data type 850

debugger 839
debugging 845
decrement 871
equality operator 865
IDE 839
increment 871
inheritance 887
initialize 871
input command 854
instance 852
instantiated 852
interpreter 839
iteration 869
list 875
logic error 846
logical operators 865
loop 869
method 885
object 852

object-oriented paradigm 852
object-oriented programming 852
order of operations 859
parameters 881
polymorphism 890
programmer-defined function 880
prompt 854
random number generator 872
repetition control structure 869
selection control structure 862
string 843
subclass 887
superclass 887
syntax 843
syntax error 845
variable 848

Interactive Situation Questions

1. As an internship assignment, you are working with a team to modify a program that calculates employee wages. When employees work more than 40 hours per week, they get paid one and a half times their normal wages. The existing code shown below is supposed to calculate wages, but it is not working correctly:

```
1 if hours_worked > 40:
2     wages = (hours_worked - 40) * (pay_
      rate * 1.5) + (40 * pay_rate)
3 else:
4     wages = 40 * pay_rate
5 print(wages)
```

a. Based on the existing code, the input values for each employee are hours_worked and _____.

b. Which line of code should be changed so that it calculates wages for employees working 40 hours or less? _____

2. Your friend asks you for help with a coding assignment. She has written the following program:

```
1 def printMax(a, b):
2     if a > b:
3         print(a, "is maximum")
4     else if a == b:
5         print(a, "is greater than", b)
6     else
7         print(b, "is maximum")
8 printMax(3, 4)
```

a. What is the name of the function in your friend's program? _____

b. How many parameters are sent to the function? _____

c. There is a logic error in the program in line _____.

d. There is a syntax error in line _____.

3. Your internship team is also working on software for the company's accounting system. The team leader asks you to become familiar with the following code:

```
1 class Bank_account:
2     balance = 0
3     def withdraw(self, amount):
4         self.balance = self.balance -
          amount
5         print(self.balance)
6         return self.balance
7     def deposit(self, amount):
8         self.balance = self.balance +
          amount
9         print(self.balance)
10        return self.balance
11    def print_balance(self):
12        print("This account balance\
          is",self.balance)
13 acc101 = Bank_account()
14 acc101.deposit(100)
```

a. How many classes are defined in this segment of code? _____

b. In the program, withdraw(), deposit(), and print_balance() are _____.

c. What is the output of line 14 in the code shown above? _____

4. Skilled programmers are quite adept at visualizing program output. Walk through the three programs below to determine how many lines of text each one outputs.

```
x = 3

if x < 10:

    print ("Small")
```

a. The above program prints _____ line(s) of text.

```
food = "spam"

if food == "spam":

    print("Yummmm, my favorite!")

    print("food " *3)
```

b. The above program prints _____ line(s) of text.

```
food = "spam"

for x in range(1,5):

    print("food")
```

c. The above program prints _____ line(s) of text.

5. You are helping to develop a game that spins a wheel to determine how many times you can move your game piece. Review the following code:

```
1 import random

2 spin_again = "y"

3 while spin_again.upper() == "y":

4     print ("Spinning the wheel...")

5     print ("The number is: ")

6     print (random.randint(1, 5))

7     spin_again = input ("spin again? y or n: ")
```

a. There is a logic error in the program in line _____.

6. Review the following code:

```
1 value = "Car"

2 x = value.upper()

3 print(x)

4 # Lowercase the string.

5 y = value.lower()

6 print(y)
```

a. What is the output of line 3? _____

b. What is the output of line 6? _____

7. Review the following code:

```
1 import random

2 print (random.choice(["yesterday",\
   "today", "tomorrow"]))
```

a. In line 2, what is the term for (["yesterday", "today", "tomorrow"])? _____

b. In line 2, how many choices can print at one time? _____

8. Review the following code:

```
1 x ?? 8

2 if x ?? 8:

3     print ("It's 8!")

4 else:

5     print ("It's not 8!")
```

a. In the above program, what operator should be used in line 1 in place of the ?? (question marks)? _____

b. In the above program, what operator should be used in line 2 in place of the ?? (question marks)? _____

Lab: Adventure Game

The earliest computer games were text based. Using your Python knowledge, you can create your own text adventure game.

The game starts in a room of a house. The player wakes up in a locked room and must find the key to escape. The player must inspect items in the room to find the key and then use the key to open the door.

❶ Start a new program called **Adventure**. Begin by entering a comment, substituting your full name for "your_name":

```
#Adventure Game your_name
```

❷ Then enter the following commands to describe the start of the game:

```
print("Last night, you went to sleep in your own home.")
print("Now, you wake up in a locked room.")
print("Could there be a key hidden somewhere?")
print("In the room, you can see:")
```

❸ Create a function to print a menu of the items in the room that could contain the key to open the door. In a Python list, each item has an index number. The first item's index is 0, the second item's index is 1, and so on. The code `list.index(item)` produces the index number.

The first item in the items list, "backpack," has an index of 0. But when you display the list, the first item should be labeled 1, not 0. Therefore, you have to use the code `1 + list.index(item)` to display the number 1 in front of the backpack item.

The code `print(1 + list.index(item), item)` will print "1 backpack" when the program runs.

Enter the code for the menu() function:

```
#The menu function:
def menu(list, question):
    for item in list:
        print(1 + list.index(item), item)
    return int(input(question))
#This is a list of the items in the room:
items = ["backpack","painting","vase","bowl","door"]
```

Lab: Adventure Game (cont.)

4 Generate a random number for the location of the key among the first four items in the list. (The key is never located in the door.) Add the following statements to your program:

```
import random
keylocation = random.randint(1,4)
```

5 Now, add code that calls the menu() function using two parameters: items and the wording for a user prompt:

```
menu(items,"What do you want to inspect?")
```

6 Save the program and then test your code. Your program and output should look like this:

```
1   #Adventure Game
2   print("Last night, you went to sleep in your own
        home.")
3   print("Now, you wake up in a locked room.")
4   print("Could there be a key hidden somewhere?")
5   print("In the room, you can see:")
6   #The menu function:
7   def menu(list, question):
8       for item in list:
9           print(1 + list.index(item), item)
10      return int(input(question))
11  #This is a list of the items in the room:
12  items = ["backpack","painting","vase","bowl","door"]
13  import random
14  keylocation = random.randint(1,4)
15  menu(items,"What do you want to inspect? ")
```

```
Last night, you went to sleep in your own home.
Now, you wake up in a locked room.
Could there be a key hidden somewhere?
In the room, you can see:
1 backpack
2 painting
3 vase
4 bowl
5 door
What do you want to inspect?
```

Source: Replit

7 Once the first part of the program is working without errors, delete the last line. We will call the menu later from within a loop. Delete the following line of code:

```
menu(items,"What do you want to inspect?")
```

8 Before you create the loop, you first need to add the following code to initialize variables:

```
#The key is not found:
keyfound = "No"
loop = 1
```

9 You can use a loop to display the menu and collect the user's selection until the key is found. Add the following code:

```
#Display the menu until the key is found:

while loop == 1:

    choice = menu(items,"What do you want to inspect?")

    print("")

    if choice < 5:

        if choice == keylocation:

            print("You found a small key in the", items[choice -1])

            keyfound = "Yes"

        else:

            print("You found nothing in the", items[choice -1])
```

The code `print("You found a small key in the", items[choice -1])` prints the name of the item chosen from the menu, based on the item's index number. But remember that the items in the index are numbered beginning with 0, not 1. If the user's choice is 3 for the vase, the index number of the vase is actually 2. Therefore, the code subtracts 1 from the variable choice to get the correct index number.

10 Save your program and then test your code. Your program and output should look similar to this:

```
1   #Adventure Game
2   print("Last night, you went to sleep in your own home.")
3   print("Now, you wake up in a locked room.")
4   print("Could there be a key hidden somewhere?")
5   print("In the room, you can see:")
6   #The menu function:
7   def menu(list, question):
8     for item in list:
9       print(1 + list.index(item), item)
10    return int(input(question))
11  #This is a list of the items in the room:
12  items = ["backpack","painting","vase","bowl","door"]
13  import random
14  keylocation = random.randint(1,4)
15  #The key is not found:
16  keyfound = "No"
17  loop = 1
18  #Display the menu until the key is found:
19  while loop == 1:
20    choice = menu(items,"What do you want to inspect? ")
21    print("")
22    if choice < 5:
23      if choice == keylocation:
24        print("You found a small key in the", items[choice -1])
25        keyfound = "Yes"
26      else:
27        print("You found nothing in the", items[choice -1])
```

```
Last night, you went to sleep in your own home.
Now, you wake up in a locked room.
Could there be a key hidden somewhere?
In the room, you can see:
1 backpack
2 painting
3 vase
4 bowl
5 door
What do you want to inspect? 3

You found nothing in the vase
1 backpack
2 painting
3 vase
4 bowl
5 door
What do you want to inspect? 1

You found a small key in the backpack
1 backpack
2 painting
3 vase
4 bowl
5 door
What do you want to inspect? 
```

Source: Replit

11 What if the player chooses the door? Once the player has found the key, the door can be selected. The following code handles three conditions for when the player selects 5 from the menu. (Hint: Make sure elif is indented four spaces.)

```
elif choice == 5:
    if keyfound == "Yes":
        loop = 0
        print("You insert the key in the keyhole and turn it.")
    else:
        print("The door is locked. You need to find a key.")
else:
    print("Choose a number less than 6.")
```

12 Players can exit the room when they have found the key and opened the door. Add the following line of code. (Hint: The line should not be indented.)

```
print("You open the door to your freedom.")
```

13 Save your program and test your code. Your program and output should look like that in the figure on the following page.

14 Now, get creative and modify the code to make it your own. You can modify the names of the items in the room or add a few extra items to the list. You can also change the game to have the player collect a coin or gem instead of a key to get out of the room.

15 After testing your adventure game to make sure it runs without errors, you can save it and then submit it by making a screenshot of the program or sharing it, according to your instructor's preference.

Lab: Adventure Game (cont.)

```python
1   #Adventure Game
2   print("Last night, you went to sleep in your own home.")
3   print("Now, you wake up in a locked room.")
4   print("Could there be a key hidden somewhere?")
5   print("In the room, you can see:")
6   #The menu function:
7   def menu(list, question):
8       for item in list:
9           print(1 + list.index(item), item)
10      return int(input(question))
11  #This is a list of the items in the room:
12  items = ["backpack","painting","vase","bowl","door"]
13  import random
14  keylocation = random.randint(1,4)
15  #The key is not found:
16  keyfound = "No"
17  loop = 1
18  #Display the menu until the key is found:
19  while loop == 1:
20      choice = menu(items,"What do you want to inspect? ")
21      print("")
22      if choice < 5:
23          if choice == keylocation:
24              print("You found a small key in the", items[choice -1])
25              keyfound = "Yes"
26          else:
27              print("You found nothing in the", items[choice -1])
28      elif choice == 5:
29          if keyfound == "Yes":
30              loop = 0
31              print("You insert the key in the keyhole and turn it.")
32          else:
33              print("The door is locked. You need to find a key.")
34      else:
35          print("Choose a number less than 6.")
36  print("You open the door to your freedom.")
```

```
Last night, you went to sleep in your own home.
Now, you wake up in a locked room.
Could there be a key hidden somewhere?
In the room, you can see:
1 backpack
2 painting
3 vase
4 bowl
5 door
What do you want to inspect? 2

You found nothing in the painting
1 backpack
2 painting
3 vase
4 bowl
5 door
What do you want to inspect? 3

You found a small key in the vase
1 backpack
2 painting
3 vase
4 bowl
5 door
What do you want to inspect? 5

You insert the key in the keyhole and turn it.
You open the door to your freedom.
>
```

Source: Replit

Glossary

@mention On Twitter, a method for referring to any user within the body of a tweet. 339

@username On Twitter, a unique identifier for each user. 339

 # hashtag A hashtag such as #ipadgames specifies a keyword that can be used to find and group social media posts by topic, both in Twitter and across other social media. 339

2-in-1 A personal computer form factor that can be used as a tablet or with its attached keyboard. 97

3D graphics A digital graphics format that displays a three-dimensional image in a two-dimensional space. 56

3rd platform An Information Age platform that involves cloud computing, mobile devices, social networking, and big data. 731

AAC (Advanced Audio Coding) A file format that provides highly compressed audio files with very little loss of sound quality and is promoted by Apple on its iTunes Web site. 32

AAX (Audible Enhanced Audio) A popular digital audio format used by Amazon to distribute audio books. 32

Abacus A manual calculator that consists of beads mounted on sticks inside a frame with each bead representing a specific quantity. 537

Absolute reference In a worksheet formula, a cell reference (usually preceded by a $ symbol) that cannot change as a result of a move or copy operation. 422

Abstraction A concept that simplifies by masking details from a user or developer. In the context of computer programming, higher-level languages have greater levels of abstraction that shield programmers from having to deal with hardware details. 773

Accelerometer A device used in cell phones and other equipment to measure acceleration or g-force. 143

Acceptance testing The final phase of testing for a new information system, in which the system's new owner determines whether the system performs as required. 650

Access time The estimated time for a storage device to locate data on a disk, usually measured in milliseconds. 120

Accumulator In the context of computer programming, a variable used to hold the results of multiple arithmetic operations. 876

Actors Object-oriented jargon for people who use an information system. 637

Additive manufacturing An alternative term for 3D printing. 141

Address spoofing Using a fake IP or email address to conceal the origin of a packet or message. 491

Advance fee fraud A social engineering fraud that promises a large sum of money to a victim, but as an indication of good faith, the victim must first "forward" a small sum of money. 498

Adware Software that displays unwanted advertisements or analyzes user online behavior to create a profile used by advertisers. 489

AES (Advanced Encryption Standard) An encryption standard based on the Rijndael encryption algorithm that uses multiple steps to encrypt data. 455

Agile methodology A software development methodology that allows specifications to emerge as the project progresses through iterations called sprints. 763

AirDrop A built-in network utility for ad-hoc file sharing between devices using iOS and macOS. 202

Algorithm An abstract or general procedure for solving a problem, typically expressed as pseudocode, structured English, or a flowchart. 785, 839

Alpha blending The process of combining a foreground color with background colors, as when an image is pasted onto a background and the edges are blended to look more natural. 48

ALU (Arithmetic Logic Unit) The part of the CPU that performs arithmetic and logical operations on the numbers stored in its registers. 108

Anaglyph A method of achieving 3D effects using two differently colored images. 50

Analog data Data that is measured or represented on a continuously varying scale, such as a dimmer switch or a watch with a sweep second hand. 19

Analog-to-digital converter Any device, such as a sound card, that converts analog data into digital data. 30

Analysis phase Tasks performed by a project team whose goal is to produce a list of requirements for a new or revised information system. 635

Analytical database A collection of data that will be used for spotting trends that offer insights for tactical and strategic business decisions. 681

Analytical Engine A mechanical calculator designed by Charles Babbage that included memory and a programmable processor, and is widely regarded as the most important ancestor to modern computer design. 538

Android An open source operating system used primarily for tablet computers and smartphones. 401

Antivirus software A computer program used to identify, isolate, and eliminate viruses by scanning files as they arrive, leave, or are executed. 472

API (application program[ming] interface) A set of application programs or operating system functions that can be utilized by a program. 783

App Short for *application*; popularly used to refer to applications available for the iPhone, the iPad, and other mobile devices. 86

Apple I An unassembled computer kit released in 1976 by Apple Computer Inc. for computer hobbyists. 547

Apple II A complete microcomputer system, developed by Apple Computer Inc. and introduced in 1978, that helped broaden the personal computer market beyond hobbyists. 548

Apple Lisa A personal computer system, developed and manufactured by Apple Computer Inc., that featured one of the first graphical user interfaces. 548

Apple Macintosh First released in 1984, it was one of the first commercially successful personal computers sold with graphical user interface software. 548

Application development tool Software, such as 4GLs, expert system shells, and component objects, that can be assembled into the application software for an information system. 643

Application extensions Files, usually ending with .dll, containing program code that may be used by more than one software application. 409

Application programmers Software developers who specialize in developing application software rather than system software. 760

Application software Computer programs that help users perform a specific task such as word processing. Also called application programs, applications, or programs. 86

Application specifications A detailed description of the way that the software for an information system should interface with the user, store data, process data, and format reports. 645

Application testing The process of testing newly developed application software by running unit tests, integration tests, and system tests. 648

Argument In the context of Prolog programming, describes a predicate and is enclosed in parentheses in a Prolog fact. 812

Arithmetic expression A sequence, such as x + 5, that includes numbers, variables, and mathematical operators. 858

Arithmometer An early mechanical calculating device created by Thomas de Colmar in 1820. 538

ARM A RISC-based instruction set used as the basis for microprocessors in tablet computers and smartphones. 105

ARPANET (Advanced Research Projects Agency Network) One of the first packet switching computer networks using TCP/IP, and the prototype for the Internet. 173

ASCII (American Standard Code for Information Interchange) A code that represents characters as a series of 1s and 0s. Most computers use ASCII code to represent text, making it possible to transfer data between computers. 22

ASCII text Text files that contain no embedded formatting codes. 23

ASF (Advanced Systems Format) Microsoft's proprietary container format for streaming digital multimedia; typically holds WMV and WMA files. 67

Aspect ratio The ratio of the width and height of an image or display screen. 63

Assembler A utility that reads a program written in an assembly language, translates the program into machine language, and then submits the machine language program to the processor for execution. 775

Assembly language A low-level computer programming language that uses simple commands and is translated into machine language by an assembler. 774

Assignment operator The symbol (typically the equal sign =) used to place a value into a variable. 849

Assumption In the context of programming, a condition that you accept to be true, which often places limits on the scope of the programming problem. 762

Asymmetric connection A network connection in which the download capacity is different from (usually faster than) the upload capacity. 188

Asynchronous In the context of communications, such as email and text messaging, both parties need not be online at the same time. 345

Atanasoff-Berry Computer (ABC) An early electronic computer prototype that incorporated the use of vacuum tubes for data processing instead of mechanical switches. 540

Attribute In the context of computer programming, any characteristic assigned to an object or class. 852

Audio compression Techniques used to reduce the size of files that contain audio data. 32

Audio interface The hardware and software that accept input from a microphone and feed it into a digital device. 33

Automatic recalculation A feature found in spreadsheet software that automatically recalculates every formula after a user makes a change to any cell. 422

AVI (Audio Video Interleave) A video file format, developed by Microsoft, that was once the most common format for desktop video on the PC. 67

B2B (business-to-business) An ecommerce exchange of products, services, or information between businesses. 619

B2C (business-to-consumer) An ecommerce exchange of products, services, or information between businesses and consumers. 619

B2G (business-to-government) An ecommerce exchange of products, services, or information between businesses and governments. 619

Backdoor A method typically used by hackers for surreptitiously accessing computers. 480

Backup A duplicate copy of a file, disk, or tape. Also refers to a Windows utility that allows you to create and restore backups. 125

Bandwidth The data transmission capacity of a communications channel. Digital signals are measured in bits per second; analog signals in Hertz. 165

Bandwidth cap The maximum speed allowed by an Internet service provider, based on its system capacity or on the user's subscription plan. 188

Bandwidth throttling The process by which an Internet service provider intentionally slows service to regulate network traffic. 188

Batch processing A processing system that involves holding a group of transactions for processing until the end of a specified period of time. 611

BI (Business Intelligence) The process of collecting and analyzing past and present business data as the basis for operational and strategic decision making. 632

Bidirectional links In the context of the Web, links that allow two documents to refer to each other, rather than a link that contains only a one-way reference. 248

Big data Huge collections of data that are difficult to process, analyze, and manage using conventional database tools. 731

Binary The representation of data using two states, such as off-on or 1-0. 19

Binary adjacency matrix A representation in table format of the relationships among various people in a social network. 322

Binary number system A method for representing numbers using only two digits: 0 and 1. Contrast to the decimal number system, which uses ten digits: 0, 1, 2, 3, 4, 5, 6, 7, 8, and 9. 21

Bit The smallest unit of information handled by a computer. A bit is one of two values, either a 0 or a 1. Eight bits constitute a byte, which can represent a letter or a number. 20

Bit rate The number of bits that are transmitted or processed per unit of time; usually expressed as bps (bits per second). 65

Bitmap graphic An image, such as a digital photo, that is stored as a grid-work of colored dots. 39

BitTorrent A peer-to-peer technology in which pieces of files are distributed to and from a collection of networked computers; used for distributing music and movies over the Internet. 224

Blockchain A distributed ledger database that operates using a distributed peer-to-peer network; this technology is the foundation for digital currencies such as Bitcoin. 741

Blog (Web log) A publicly accessible series of posts on the Web. Blogs often reflect the views of the author and are periodically updated with new entries. 335

Blogging platform A platform that provides tools for creating blogs; it may also provide a Web site where blogs can be posted for access by the public. 336

Blogosphere The world of blogs and all their interconnections. 336

Bluetooth A short-range network technology, typically used to transmit data between a peripheral device and a computer or handheld digital device. 134

Bluetooth LE A low-power, short-range technology developed specifically for IoT networks. 212

BMP The native bitmap graphics file format of Microsoft Windows. 41

Bookmarks A feature of Web browsers that saves the URLs for selected Web sites. 259

Boolean operators Named after mathematician George Boole; AND, OR, and NOT are used to formulate database queries. 725, 865

Boot loader A program, usually stored in read-only memory, that starts the boot sequence, which loads the operating system into RAM. 114

Botnet A group of bots under the remote control of a botmaster; used to distribute spam and denial-of-service attacks. 482

BPM (Business process management) A systematic approach to improving the workflow of an organization, often through the use of information technology. 632

Broadband A term used to refer to communications channels that have bandwidth that equals or exceeds 25 Mbps. 165

Browser cache The collection of HTML pages and images that is stored locally by a browser and used to quickly load pages that have been previously viewed without waiting for them to be downloaded again. 262

Browser extension A module of computer code that adds capabilities to a browser, such as the ability to block ads on Web pages. 260

Browser home page The first page displayed when a browser starts. 258

Browser tabs Graphical controls near the top of a browser window that allow users to hold open multiple Web pages and switch back and forth between them. 259

Brute force attack A method of accessing encrypted data by trying all possible encryption keys. 460

BSD license (Berkeley Software Distribution license) An open source software license patterned on a license originally used by the University of California. 387

Buffers Memory that is temporarily used to store input or other data until the processor is ready to use it. 394

Bug In the context of programming, an error that must be found and corrected. 845

Bulletin board systems Early forms of online social networking in which user posts could be viewed asynchronously by other members of the bulletin board community. 326

Bus topology A network architecture in which devices connect sequentially to a main data link like birds on a telephone wire. 166

Byte An 8-bit unit of data that represents a single character. 25

C2C (consumer-to-consumer) An ecommerce exchange of products, services, or information between consumers; for example, online auctions. 619

Cable Internet service A type of Internet connection offered to subscribers by cable television companies. 192

CAN-SPAM Act The result of legislation passed by the U.S. Congress in 2003 to limit the dissemination of SPAM over email systems. 499

Capacitive technology A touchscreen technology coated with a thick layer of electrically conductive material; commonly used for smartphone screens. 138

Capacitors Electronic circuit components that store an electrical charge; in RAM, a charged capacitor represents an "on" bit, and a discharged one represents an "off" bit. 113

Capital goods Machinery, tools, and raw materials used to produce other goods. 526

Cardinality A description of the numeric relationship (one-to-one, one-to-many, or many-to-many) that exists between two record types. 688

Card reader A device that can be used to read and record data on solid state storage devices, such as flash memory cards. 122

Case-sensitive database A database in which uppercase letters are not equivalent to their lowercase counterparts. 709

CASE tool (computer-aided software engineering) Software that is used to summarize system requirements, diagram current and proposed information systems, schedule development tasks, prepare documentation, and develop computer programs. 639

CCD (charge-coupled device) One of the components in a digital camera that captures light from an image and converts it into color data. 40

CDs (compact discs) A useful method of archival storage for documents, music, and photos. 121

Cell In spreadsheet terminology, the intersection of a column and a row. 419

Cell references The column letter and row number that designate the location of a worksheet cell; for example, the cell reference C5 refers to a cell in column C, row 5. 421

Cell tower triangulation The process used to find the location of a cellular phone by gauging the strength of its signal from nearby cell towers. 320

Cellular telephone A handheld, battery-operated device that uses radio signals to transmit and receive voice and text messages, and may also offer data services for accessing the Internet. 560

Central processing unit (CPU) The main processing circuitry, or "chip," within a computer that contains the ALU, control unit, and registers. 84

CGI (Computer-generated imagery) The use of computer-based graphics to create realistic characters and scenery for films, videogames, and other motion graphics. 58

Change requests A formal, written request to add, delete, or change the features of an information system. 646

Character data Letters, symbols, or numerals that will not be used in arithmetic operations (name, Social Security number, etc.). 22

Chief information officer (CIO) The highest-ranking executive responsible for the information systems in an organization. 566

Chromebook A clamshell-style laptop computer that uses Chrome OS as an operating system and a thin client for Web access. 96

Chrome OS An operating system, developed by Google, that is used for Chromebooks. 402

Ciphertext An encrypted message. 455

Circuit switching The method used by the telephone network to temporarily connect one telephone with another for the duration of a call. 177

CISC (complex instruction set computer) A general-purpose microprocessor chip designed to handle a wider array of instructions than a RISC chip. 112

Class In object-oriented terminology, a group with specific characteristics to which an object belongs. 799, 852

Class diagram A diagram that provides the name of each object, a list of the object's attributes, a list of methods, and an indication of the cardinality between objects. 638

Class hierarchy Like a hierarchical diagram, a class hierarchy is a set of related superclasses and subclasses defined within the object-oriented paradigm. 801

Client-side scripts Program code that is executed by a client's browser, as opposed to being executed by a remote server. 274

Clickbait Eye-catching content with a teaser headline designed to entice people to click a provided link and satisfy their curiosity. 497

Clipping path The outline of an object in a digital image that can be used to cut out the object from its background. 48

Cloning In the context of digital graphics, the process of replicating a section of an image, often used to cover blemishes or fill in backgrounds. 47

Cloud storage A storage area that is located on a remote server, usually on the Internet, rather than on a local storage device. 123

Cluster A group of sectors on a storage medium that, when accessed as a group, speeds up data access. 436

Code One or more statements written as part of a computer program. 839

Codec Short for compressor/decompressor; a hardware or software routine that compresses and decompresses digital graphics, sound, and video files. 66

Code editor A software tool, similar to a word processor, that can be used to write computer programs. 839

Code injection A method used by hackers to insert malicious code into otherwise legitimate files or data transmissions. 468

Code of ethics A set of guidelines designed to help professionals make on-the-job ethical decisions. 586

Coding The process of writing statements using a computer programming language. 839

Colocation center A data center that contains servers for more than one business. 656

Color depth The number of bits that determines the range of possible colors that can be assigned to each pixel. For example, an 8-bit color depth can create 256 colors. 42

Colossus An early electronic computer prototype that used binary data representation and was operated during WWII to decode messages encrypted by the German ENIGMA device. 541

Column-oriented data model A database model in which data is accessed from columns, rather than from rows. 739

Comment In the context of computer programming, an annotation placed in the code by a programmer that is not executed at runtime. 843

Commercial software Copyrighted computer applications sold to consumers for profit. 385

Commit or rollback A procedure in transaction processing systems that will nullify, or roll back, a transaction if all the steps cannot be finalized or committed to. 612

Common carrier A person or company, such as Delta Airlines or AT&T, that transports goods or data for the general public. 555

Communication channel Any pathway between the sender and receiver; *channel* may refer to a physical medium or a frequency. 162

Communication network A collection of devices used to originate, send, route, and receive data transmissions. 161

Communication port In the context of computer networks, a virtual location for data that arrives or leaves the device; common ports include 21 for FTP, 110 for email, and 80 for Web data. 178

Communication protocol A set of rules that ensures the orderly and accurate transmission and reception of data. 170

Comparison operator A symbol, such as > <, ==, or =>, used in logical statements to determine equality or the difference between variables or values. 864

Compatible In the context of digital devices, the situation when two devices use interchangeable software and peripherals. 101

Compiler Software that translates a program written in a high-level language into low-level instructions before the program is executed. 777, 839

Compression ratio A ratio such as 5:1 indicating the amount of compression that has been applied to a file. High compression ratios such as 35:1 indicate more compression so data can be contained in smaller files. 66

Computation The process of mathematical calculation. 858

Computed field A calculation that a DBMS performs to arrive at values derived from one or more fields in a database. 708

Computer A device that accepts input, processes data, stores data, and produces output according to a stored program. 85

Computer engineering A career that focuses on the design and development of computer hardware and peripheral devices. 571

Computer graphics Images created using computers and stored in digital formats. 39

Computer operator A computer professional who works directly with and maintains mainframe computers or server arrays. 567

Computer professional Any person whose primary occupation involves one or more aspects of computer technology. 566

Computer program A detailed set of instructions that tells a computer how to solve a problem or carry out a task. 86

Computer programmer A person who designs, codes, and tests computer programs. 567

Computer programming The process of designing, coding, and testing computer programs. 759

Computer science A career field that focuses on developing fast and efficient computers, programming languages, operating systems, and software. 571

Computer virus A program designed to attach itself to a file, reproduce, destroy data, display an irritating message, or otherwise disrupt computer operations. 468

Computer worm A software program designed to enter a computer system, usually a network, through security "holes" and then replicate itself and spread to other devices. 470

Concatenation The process of combining two or more strings within a computer program. 843

Concatenation operator The symbol (typically a + sign) used to combine two or more strings in a computer program. 843

Confidentiality The obligation not to disclose willingly any information obtained in confidence. 583

Connection speed A common term for the capacity of an Internet connection, usually measured in Mbps or Gbps. 187

Constant In the context of programming, represents an unchanging value. In contrast, the data held in a variable can change. 757

Consumer goods Merchandise that is intended for sale to consumers. 526

Container formats The formats for files that hold multiple types of media files, such as video and audio. 66

Content aggregator A way to collect Web or media content and applications; it can be used to monitor blogs, collect current posts, and display them. 336

Content communities Social media sites where members post original content, such as stories, photos, music, or videos. 325

Contract worker A computer professional who does not work directly for one company and often is paid by the job instead of a salary. 569

Control In the context of graphical user interfaces and programming, a screen-based object whose behavior can be specified by a programmer. 767

Control structures Instructions that specify the sequence in which a program is to be executed: sequence, selection, and repetition controls. 791

Control unit The part of the microprocessor that directs and coordinates processing. 108

Cookie A message sent from a Web server to a browser and stored on a user's hard disk, usually containing information about the user. 281

Copyleft A modification of copyright practices; allows third-party copying and distribution as long as the copies have the same license as the original. 332

Copy protection The use of various technologies by music and video distributors to curtail unauthorized copying. 34

Copyright A form of legal protection that grants certain exclusive rights to the work's creator or the owner of the copyright. 330

Corrective procedures Strategies, typically outlined in disaster recovery plans, that reduce the effect of a data breach or natural disaster. 661

Counter In the context of computer programming, a variable that is used to keep track of the number of repetitions in a loop. 871

CPU cache Special high-speed memory providing the CPU with rapid access to data that would otherwise be accessed from disk or RAM. 112

CREATE An SQL command that produces a new table in a database. 722

Creative Commons license Licensing options that extend rights, such as creating derivatives, to someone other than the copyright owner. 331

Critical path In a PERT chart, the sequence of tasks that takes the shortest time to complete. 634

CRM (customer relationship management) A technique for increasing profitability by improving the relationship between a company and its customers. 624

Cross-site tracking A practice in which third-party cookies are often set by Web sites that have affiliations with wide-ranging ad-serving companies able to combine cookie data from multiple sites. 282

Crowdsourcing An activity in which a group of people contribute, usually online, to solving a problem or completing a task. 319

Cryptographic algorithm A specific procedure for encrypting and decrypting data. 455

Cryptographic key A specific word, number, or phrase that must be used to encrypt or decrypt data. 455

CSS (Cascading Style Sheets) Used in conjunction with HTML, a means of formatting the appearance of text and other elements of a Web page. 272

Cyberbullying The use of computers and online technology to harass others. 357

Cyberwarfare The use of hacking, computer viruses, bots, and other digital techniques to conduct politically motivated espionage or sabotage. 535

Dark Web A part of the deep Web accessible with special software that encrypts searches and anonymizes users; it has a reputation for illicit content and activities. 289

Data In the context of computing and data management, the symbols that a computer uses to represent facts and ideas. 19

Data archive A collection of infrequently used data that has been removed from an active database and stored in a secondary location. 683

Database A collection of information that might be stored in more than one file or in more than one record type. 423

Database administrator A person who supervises database design, development, testing, and maintenance. 567

Database client software Software that allows any remote computer or network workstation to access data in a database. 704

Database index A file of keys and pointers used to display a list of database records organized according to the data in one or more fields. 715

Database model The underlying structure or category of a database, such as relational, hierarchical, network, or object. 686

Database software Software designed for entering, finding, organizing, updating, and reporting information stored in a database. 423

Database structure The arrangement of the fields, tables, and relationships in a database. 707

Data breach A situation in which data is accessed by unauthorized parties. 659

Data bus An electronic pathway or circuit that connects electronic components (such as the processor and RAM) on a computer's system board. 131

Data center A specialized facility designed to house and protect computer systems and data. 656

Data compression The process of shrinking the size of a file by removing data or recoding it more efficiently. 26

Data dependence The undesirable situation in which data and program modules become so interrelated that modifications become difficult. 695

Data flow On a DFD, a line with an arrow on the end that indicates the direction in which data flows. 636

Data flow diagram (DFD) A diagram that illustrates how data moves through an information system. 636

Data independence The separation of data from the programs that manipulate the data. 695

Data lake A means of storing both unstructured and structured data. 733

Data mining Analyzing data to discover patterns and relationships that are important to decision making. 685

Data redundancy Repetition of data within a database. 712

Data representation The use of electronic signals, marks, or binary digits to represent character, numeric, visual, or audio data. 19

Data store A filing cabinet, disk, or tape that holds data. On a DFD, usually represented by an open-ended rectangle. 636

Data transfer rate The amount of data that a storage device can move from a storage medium to computer memory in one time unit, such as one second. 120

Data type The characteristics of data that can be entered into a field in a data file; data types include character, numeric, date, logical, and memo. 711, 850

Data warehouse A collection of information organized for analysis. 685

DBMS (database management system) Application software that assists the user in manipulating, storing, and maintaining database files. 701

DCE (data communication equipment) Devices, such as routers and hubs, that are used to manage data that flows over a communication network. 168

DDoS (Distributed Denial of Service) An attack in which a target system, such as a Web server, is deliberately flooded with data from a malicious source, denying service to legitimate customers. 482

Debugger A programming utility that helps programmers locate and correct syntax and logic errors. 839

Debugging The process of testing and correcting a computer program. 768, 845

Decision model A numerical representation of a realistic situation, such as a cash flow model of a business. 615

Decision query A question or set of instructions that describes the data that needs to be gathered to make a decision. 615

Decision support system (DSS) A computer system that allows decision makers to manipulate data directly, to incorporate data from external sources, and to create data models or "what-if" scenarios. 614

Decision support worksheet A comparison table used by a project team to evaluate solutions by assigning a score and a weight to each criterion. 644

Decision table A tabular method for listing rules and specifying the outcomes for various combinations of rules. 820

Declarative paradigm An approach to the programming process in which a programmer writes a program by specifying a set of statements and rules that define the conditions for solving a problem. 811

DEC PDP-8 Built by Digital Equipment Corp. and introduced in 1965; the first commercially successful minicomputer. 546

Decrement The process of decreasing the value of a variable, as in counter = counter−1. 871

Decryption The process of removing the encryption to produce clear text. 455

Dedicated graphics Circuitry for graphics that is supplied on an expansion card rather than integrated into the main system board of a digital device. 139

Deep Web Web pages that require password-protected logins and pages that are dynamically generated with server-side scripts; also called the "invisible Web." 289

Defamation The communication of false statements intended to harm the reputation of a person, business, product, religion, or organization. 357

Default application The software application that automatically runs when files of a particular file type are opened. 432

Default browser The browser that opens automatically when clicking links from email messages or other sources. 257

Defensive programming An approach to programming that attempts to identify possible threats and proactively create code to avoid them; also called secure programming. 771

DELETE An SQL keyword that removes a record from a table. 722

Delimiter A special character used to separate commands or formatting characters from the rest of the text in a file. 24

Demoware Software that is supplied for free, but is limited in some way until you pay for it. 386

Derivative work A work, such as a translation or adaptation, that contains major elements of a previously copyrighted work. 333

Design phase The process a project team uses to figure out how to implement a new system. This phase is undertaken after the analysis phase is complete. 641

Desktop computer A computer that is small enough to fit on a desk, runs from a wall outlet, and is built around a single microprocessor chip. 96

Desktop operating system An operating system, such as Microsoft Windows or macOS, specifically designed for use on personal computers. 391

Detailed design phase A phase of the SDLC in which systems analysts and designers generate precise specifications for an information system. 645

Detail reports Organized lists generated by a management information system (for example, an inventory list). 612

Detection activities Methodologies and software, such as antivirus utilities, used to discover attacks and trigger preventive countermeasures or corrective procedures. 661

Deterrents Procedures such as passwords and biometrics that reduce the likelihood of a data breach. 661

Development tools A software classification used to create software; examples include programming languages and scripting languages. 86

Device driver A type of system software that provides the computer with the means to control a peripheral device. 135

Device letter The letter of the alphabet, such as C:, used to label a storage device on a computer running Windows. 428

DHCP (Dynamic Host Configuration Protocol) A set of rules that allow network client computers to find and use the Internet address that corresponds to a domain name. 180

Dial-up A connection that uses a phone line to establish a temporary Internet connection. 193

Dictionary attack A method of discovering a password by trying every word in an electronic dictionary. 460

Digital audio Music or voice that has been digitized into files using sampling techniques; sometimes referred to as waveform audio. 30

Digital audio extraction The process of copying files from an audio CD and converting them into a format that can be stored and accessed from a computer storage device, such as a hard disk; sometimes referred to as ripping. 33

Digital certificate A file that verifies the identity of a device; usually used in the context of network-based servers sending an encryption key to a client device. 492

Digital compositing Assembling parts from multiple digital images into a single image. 48

Digital data Text, numbers, graphics, or sound represented by discrete digits, such as 1s and 0s. 19

Digital rights management The use of various technologies by music and video distributors to curtail unauthorized copying. 34

Digital television (DTV) The use of digital signals to transmit the audio and video for television shows; replaced analog television technology. 562

Digital-to-analog converter A device that converts digital data, such as 1s and 0s, in an audio file into continuous data, such as audio sounds. 30

Digital video A series of still frames stored sequentially in digital format by assigning values to each pixel in a frame. 61

Digitization Converting non-digital information or media to a digital format through the use of a scanner, sampler, or other input device. 20

Directory In the context of computer file management, a list of files contained on a computer storage device. 429

Disaster recovery plan A step-by-step plan that describes the methods used to secure equipment and data against disasters, and how to recover from fires, floods, and other such events. 658

Discharge rate In the context of battery life, the speed at which energy stored in the battery is released. 93

Disk image A bit-by-bit copy of the contents of a disk; created for backup, archiving, or duplication of data. 127

Disk partition An area of a hard disk created by dividing a large hard disk into several smaller virtual ones, such as when using two operating systems on a single computer. 428

Disruptive technology An invention that changes markets by replacing existing goods or services. 531

DM In the context of Twitter, messages similar to email that are sent directly to followers. 339

DMG A container format used to deliver software applications to Macs. 412

DNS spoofing A malicious attack on the domain name system in which the IP address corresponding to a Web site is changed in order to redirect users to different locations. 184

Document formatting The specifications applied to fonts, spacing, margins, and other elements in a document created with word processing software. 418

Document-oriented database Stores unstructured data, such as the text of a speech or newspaper article. 693

Domain name Short for *fully qualified domain name*; an identifying name by which host computers on the Internet are familiarly known (for example, nike.com). 182

Domain name servers Computers that host the Domain Name System database. 183

Domain name system (DNS) A large database of unique IP addresses that correspond to domain names. 182

Doppelgangers In the context of social media, two unrelated people whose online identities are so similar that they cause confusion. 357

Dot-coms A legacy term for companies formed mainly to offer goods and services online. 525

Dot notation The use of a period to specify the database table or data class that owns an attribute, such as Customers.CustomerID. 728

Dot pitch (dp) The diagonal distance between colored dots on a display screen. Measured in millimeters, dot pitch helps to determine the quality of an image displayed on screen. 137

Download The process of transferring a copy of a file from a remote computer to a local computer's storage device. 33

Dropper A type of malware with a small footprint that is "dropped" into a computer to pave the way for more extensive malware. 471

DSL (digital subscriber line) A high-speed Internet connection that uses existing telephone lines, requiring close proximity to a switching station. 194

DTE (data terminal equipment) Computers and other devices connected to a network to send or receive data. 168

Dual-band The capability of a communications device, such as a router, to use two communication frequencies. 206

DVDs (digital video discs) A useful method of archival storage for documents, music, and photos. 121

Dynamic IP addresses Temporarily assigned IP addresses usually provided by an ISP. 180

Dynamic RAM (DRAM) Random access memory that requires a power source to hold data; used as main memory on most computers. 113

Dynamic scaling The ability of an information system to expand by taking advantage of additional resources, such as storage space or communication channels. 737

Dynamic Web page A way of displaying customized content in response to keyboard or mouse actions, or based on information supplied directly or indirectly by the person viewing the page. 274

Ecommerce Short for *electronic commerce*; the business of buying and selling products online. 619

Ecommerce application The software that handles ecommerce transactions. 620

Economic sectors Groups of companies and industries, such as the computer industry, that provide similar types of goods and services. 523

Editorial newsletter platform A spin-off of blogs that offers tools for creating and sending content directly to subscribers' inboxes; examples are Substack and Review. 337

Email A system for sending messages from one digital device to another using protocols such as SMTP, POP, and IMAP. 346

Email message A computer file containing a letter or memo that is transmitted electronically via a communication network. 346

Email server A computer that uses special software to store and send email messages over the Internet. 346

Email system The collection of computers and software that works together to provide email services. 346

Encapsulation An object-oriented technique in which the internal details of an object are "hidden" in order to simplify their use and reuse. 809

Encryption The process of scrambling or hiding information so that it cannot be understood without the key necessary to change it back into its original form. 455

ENIAC (Electronic Numerical Integrator and Computer) An early electronic computer prototype that was designed for the U.S. Army for calculating trajectories and was completed in 1945. 542

Enterprise A synonym for business, company, or organization; used in the context of software to indicate applications that are designed for business use rather than personal use. 607

Entity-relationship diagram (ERD) A diagram that graphically depicts relationships between record types. 688

Equality operator A symbol (== in Python) used in statements that compare if two variables or values are equal. 865

ERP (enterprise resource planning) A suite of software modules that integrate major business activities such as sales, CRM, and SCM. 626

Error correction The method used by a digital communication system to identify transmission errors and correct them. 171

Ethernet A popular network technology in which network nodes are connected by coaxial cable or twisted-pair wire. 203

Ethernet adapter A type of network interface card designed to support Ethernet protocols. 204

EULAs (end-user license agreements) A type of software license that appears on the computer screen when software is being installed and prompts the user to accept or decline. 384

Evil Twin A malicious wireless network or hotspot designed to look legitimate and ensnare unwary users looking for a free Internet connection. 490

Exabyte One billion gigabytes. 174

Exception report A report generated by a management information system listing information that is outside normal or acceptable ranges, such as a reorder report showing low-stock inventory items. 613

Executable file A file, usually with an .exe extension, containing instructions that tell a computer how to perform a specific task. 382

Executive dashboard Software designed for managers that typically uses widgets to graphically display statistics relevant to business decisions. 684

Executive information system (EIS) A special type of decision support system that is designed to provide senior managers with information relevant to strategic management activities. 614

Expansion ports Sockets into which the user plugs a cable from a peripheral device, allowing data to pass between the computer and the peripheral device. 131

Expert system A computer system that incorporates knowledge from human experts, in order to analyze data and produce a recommendation or decision (also called a knowledge-based system). 616

Expert system shell A software tool used for developing expert system applications. 617

Extended ASCII Similar to ASCII but with 8-bit character representation instead of 7-bit, allowing for an additional 128 characters. 22

External CSS A Cascading Style Sheet that is stored in a file separate from the HTML source document for a Web page. 272

External entity A person, an organization, or a device that exists outside an information system, but provides it with input or receives output; on a DFD, usually represented by a square. 636

Fact In the context of Prolog programming, a statement incorporated into a program that provides basic information for solving a problem. 811

Fair use The concept that copyrighted materials can be legally used in some specifically defined instances such as for critical reviews and teaching. 333

False positives In the context of antivirus software, reports of a virus infection when in fact no infection exists. 473

Feature creep An undesirable occurrence during information system development when users, customers, or designers attempt to add features after the final specifications have been approved. 646

Field The smallest meaningful unit of information contained in a data file. 423, 687

Field format A specification for the way that data is displayed on the screen and printouts, usually using a series of Xs to indicate characters and 9s to indicate numbers. 709

Field name A name that identifies the contents of a field. 687

Field validation rule A specification that a database designer sets up to filter the data entered into a particular field. 710

Fifth-generation languages Either declarative languages, such as Prolog, or programming languages that allow programmers to use graphical or visual tools to construct programs. 776

File A named collection of data (such as a computer program, document, or graphic) that exists on a storage medium, such as a hard disk or flash drive. 20

File format The method of organization used to encode and store data in a computer. Text formats include DOCX and TXT. Graphics formats include BMP, TIFF, GIF, and PNG. 20

File hosting services A company that offers online space for a fee to companies and individuals who want to store files or establish a Web presence. 223

File management utilities Software, such as Finder and File Explorer, that helps users locate, rename, move, copy, and delete files. 430

File name extension The characters in a file name after the period, such as .exe and .txt. 20

File-naming conventions A set of rules, established by the operating system, that must be followed to create a valid file name. 427

File path The specification for a file's location that includes the device, folders, and file name (for example, C:\Documents\Homework\Assignment 1.DOCX). 429

File sharing The process of allowing access to document, photo, video, and other files from a computer other than the one on which they are stored. 215

File-sharing worm A type of malware that is distributed on file sharing networks, such as pirated music download sites. 470

File shredder software Software designed to overwrite sectors of a disk with a random series of 1s and 0s to ensure deletion of data. 437

File synchronization A method for backing up data by copying any additions, changes, or deletions made on one storage device to another storage device. 126

File system A method that is used by an operating system to keep track of the locations for all files stored on a device. 436

Firewall Software or hardware designed to analyze and control incoming and outgoing packets on a network; used to enhance security by filtering out potential intrusion attempts. 485

First-generation computers Computers, such as UNIVAC, that used vacuum tubes to process and store data. 544

First-generation languages Machine languages that were available for programming the earliest computers. 7774

First-party cookie A cookie generated by the Web page that is shown in the browser. 282

Fixed Internet access Any Internet access service designed to be used from a fixed, non-portable location (for example, dial-up, DSL, and cable Internet service). 191

Fixed-length field A field in a data file that has a predetermined number of characters. 687

Flat file A single file that is the electronic version of a box of index cards, in which all records use the same record format. 686

Flowchart In software engineering, a graphical representation of the way a computer should progress from one instruction to the next when it performs a task. 788

Flow control In the context of programming, the sequence in which a computer executes program instructions. 791

Folder The subdirectories, or subdivisions of a directory, that can contain files or other folders. 429

Follow A Twitter term that describes when people elect to see the tweets of another person. 339

Follow back The process of following someone who is following you on Twitter. 339

Follower A person who receives your tweets. 339

Font A typeface or style of lettering, such as Arial, Times New Roman, or Gothic. 418

Footer Text that appears in the bottom margin of each page of a document. 418

Forked In the context of open source programming, the process of deriving a new version of a software application from an already established version. 402

Formal methods Mathematically based techniques for specifying and developing reliable and robust software or hardware. 770

Formal tagging The process of adding tags to media files based on a standard set of identifiers. 328

Formatting The process of dividing a disk into sectors so that it can be used to store information. 436

Form factor The configuration of a computer's system unit; examples include tower, mini-tower, and cube. 89

Formula In spreadsheet terminology, a combination of numbers and symbols that tells the computer how to use the contents of cells in calculations. 420

Fourth-generation computers Computers, such as today's personal computers, servers, and mainframes, that use a general-purpose microprocessor for data processing. 546

Fourth-generation languages Programming and query languages, such as SQL and RPG, that more closely resemble human languages than did third-generation languages. 776

Frame In the context of digital video, one of the sequential images that are combined to produce video footage. 58

Frame rate The number of frames that are displayed in a video per second. 62

Fraud alert A means of notification when suspicious activity takes place on an individual's bank account or other secure information. 663

Freeware Copyrighted software that is given away by the author or copyright owner. 386

FTP (File Transfer Protocol) A set of rules for uploading and downloading files between a client computer and a remote server. 222

FTTH (fiber-to-the-home) A communication link that connects subscribers' homes using fiber-optic cable. 194

Fully justified The horizontal alignment of text where the text terminates exactly at both margins of the document. 418

Function (1) In the context of spreadsheet software, a built-in formula for making a calculation. 421 (2) In the context of programming, a section of code that manipulates data, but is not included in the main sequential execution path of a program. 792

Fuzzy logic A technique used within an expert system to deal with imprecise data by incorporating the probability that the input information is correct. 617

Game engine The software that controls the characters, background, and scoring for a computer game. 59

Gantt charts Horizontal bar charts that depict project schedules by showing each task as a bar on the chart. 634

Gartner Hype Cycle A graphical depiction of the phases of publicity pertaining to a technology product during its lifespan. 530

GDP A measure of the total economic performance of a country or municipality. 533

Generic profile image The photo or icon supplied to new subscribers by a social network service as a placeholder. 356

Geocoding Using informal information such as street addresses to derive more formal geolocational data, such as GPS coordinates. 320

Geosocial networking Social networking services, such as Yelp and Google Maps, that offer location-based interaction. 319

Geotagging Adding geographic data, such as GPS coordinates, to a file tag. 320

GIF (Graphics Interchange Format) A bitmap graphics file format, popularized by CompuServe, for use on the Web. 41

Gigabit (Gb or Gbit) Approximately 1 billion bits; exactly 1,024 megabits. 26

Gigabyte (GB) Approximately 1 billion bytes; exactly 1,024 megabytes (1,073,741,824 bytes). 26

Gigahertz (GHz) A measure of frequency equivalent to 1 billion cycles per second. 110

Global update In the context of databases, changing data in more than one record at a time (e.g., changing the due date in all the records). 727

Goal In the context of Prolog programming, a query that searches for an answer based on a set of Prolog facts and rules. 813

Goods Merchandise that is offered for sale to consumers. 526

GPL (General Public License) A software license often used for freeware that ensures software will be distributed freely whether in its original form or as a derivative work. 387

GPS trilateration The process of determining the location of a person or thing based on GPS signals. 320

Grammar checker A feature of word processing software that coaches the user on correct sentence structure and word usage. 417

Graph database A database model in which data is arranged as nodes and connected by lines (edges) that establish relationships. 689

Graphics processing unit (GPU) A microprocessor dedicated to rendering and displaying graphics on personal computers, workstations, and video-game consoles. 139

Guest network A wireless LAN that allows access to the Internet, but not to other devices on the network. 209

Gutta-percha A rubber-like waterproof substance previously used to coat undersea telegraph cables. 553

Gyro sensor A device used in smartphones and other equipment to determine spatial orientation and direction of movement. 143

Handshaking A process where a protocol helps two network devices communicate. 170

Hard disk drive A storage device that contains a large-capacity magnetic storage surface sealed inside a drive case. Typically used as the primary storage device in desktop and laptop computers. 119

Hard disk platter The component of a hard disk drive on which data is stored. It is a flat, rigid disk made of aluminum or glass and coated with magnetic oxide. 119

Harvard Mark I An early computer prototype also known as the ASCC (Automatic Sequence Controlled Calculator) developed by IBM that used decimal data representation rather than binary. 541

Hash value A number produced by a hash function to create a unique digital "fingerprint" that can be used to allow or deny access to a software application. 386

Head crash A collision between the read-write head and the surface of the hard disk platter, resulting in damage to some of the data on the disk. 120

Header Text that is placed in the top margin of each page of a document. 418

Help desk Part of the Information Systems department designated to assist users experiencing problems with their computers or applications. 652

Heuristic analysis In the context of antivirus software, the process of identifying malware based not on a signature, but on other factors, such as context and behavior. 472

Hierarchical database A database model in which record types are arranged as a hierarchy, or tree, of child nodes that can have only one parent node. 689

High-density data Database records that contain a lot of useful information per kilobyte. 733

High-level language A programming language that allows a programmer to write instructions using human-like language. 774

History list A file of recently visited Web sites maintained by a browser. 263

Horizontal market An opportunity for sales of a product (such as accounting software) or a service that meets the needs of a wide range of buyers. 608

Hot-plugging The ability of a component, such as a USB flash drive, to connect to or disconnect from a computer while it is running; also referred to as hot-swapping. 133

Hotspot triangulation The process of locating a device based on its distance from various hotspot servers. 320

HTML conversion utility Utility software that converts documents, spreadsheets, and databases into HTML files that can be posted on the Web. 269

HTML document A plain text or ASCII document with embedded HTML tags that dictate formatting and are interpreted by a browser. 267

HTML tags A set of instructions, such as <B>, inserted into an HTML document to provide formatting and display information to a Web browser. 267

HTML5 The current version of HTML. 267

HTTP (Hypertext Transfer Protocol) The communication protocol used to transmit Web pages. HTTP:// is an identifier that appears at the beginning of Web URLs (for example, *http://www .fooyong.com*). 279

HTTP methods A set of commands, such as GET and POST, that are transmitted between Web servers and clients using the HTTP protocol. 279

HTTPS (HTTP Secure) The protocol used to create secure connections for ecommerce by adding a layer of encryption. 284

HTTP session The connection between a Web server and a client that begins with an HTTP request and ends when the response is complete. 280

HTTP status code A code that is sent in reply to an HTTP command. For example, 404 is the status code for Page Not Found. 280

Hypertext A way of organizing a collection of documents by assigning an address to each and providing a way to link from one address to another. 244

Hypertext links Words, phrases, or images on a Web page that, when clicked, take you to designated URLs; also referred to simply as links. 247

IBM 360 An early third-generation computer that is widely regarded as the first general-purpose mainframe. 546

IBM PC An early, commercially successful personal computer system that featured a 4.77 MHz Intel 8088 processor, 64 KB RAM, and a floppy disk drive. An ancestor to today's PCs. 548

ICANN (Internet Corporation for Assigned Names and Numbers) A global organization that coordinates the management of the Internet's domain name system, IP addresses, and protocol parameters. 174

ICT industry (information and communications industry) Companies involved in the development, production, sales, and support of computers, software, and telecommunication networks. 523

IDE (integrated development environment) A set of programming tools, typically including an editor, a compiler, and a debugger, packaged into an application for creating programs. 782, 839

Identity theft An illegal practice in which a criminal obtains enough information to masquerade as someone. 660

IEEE 802.11 The IEEE (Institute of Electrical and Electronics Engineers) standard for wireless Wi-Fi networks. 205

IEEE 802.3 The IEEE standard for Ethernet networks. 203

Image compression Any technique that is used to reduce the size of a file that holds a graphic. 44

Image histogram An interactive graph that can be used to adjust the colors in a digital photo. 46

Image resolution The number of pixels in an image, usually expressed as horizontal pixels × vertical pixels. 43

Image stitching The process of combining two or more images together to produce a panoramic scene. 48

IMAP (Internet Message Access Protocol) A protocol similar to POP that is used to retrieve email messages from an email server, but offers additional features, such as choosing which emails to download from the server. 348

Impersonation Pretending to be someone you are not. 357

Implementation phase A set of tasks performed with the supervision of a system development project team in which a new information system is constructed. 647

IMSI (International Mobile Subscriber Identity) A unique identifier used on mobile networks and sometimes intercepted by IMSI catchers. 494

Increment The process of increasing the value of a variable, as in counter = counter + 1. 871

Inference engine Software that can analyze and manipulate a knowledge base or an expert system. 616

Information engineering methodology A method of developing an information system that focuses on data collected by an information system before finding ways to process that data. 633

Information industry An economic sector that focuses on distributing content, usually with the help of digital devices and communication networks. 523

Information system A computer system that collects, stores, and processes information, usually within the context of an organization. 607

Information systems (IS or CIS) The career field or academic major that focuses on developing computer systems and networks for businesses. 571

Information technology A degree program that focuses on the computer equipment and software used by businesses and organizations. 571

Information technology law The legal framework that applies to the collection, storage, and distribution of digital information. 579

Inheritance In object-oriented terminology, a method for defining new classes of objects based on the characteristics of existing classes. 801, 887

Initialize To assign a value or condition to a variable. 871

Ink jet printer A non-impact printer that creates characters or graphics by spraying liquid ink onto paper or other media. 140

Inline CSS A Cascading Style Sheet that is embedded among the lines of HTML in a source document. 272

Inpainting The process of reconstructing missing parts of digital images, usually by means of an algorithm built into graphics software. 47

Input As a noun, the information that is conveyed to a computer. As a verb, to enter data into a digital device. 85

Input command The Python keyword that collects input from a keyboard or touchscreen. 854

INSERT An SQL keyword that adds a record to a table. 723

Instance In object-oriented programming, a specific realization of an object. 852

Instantiated In programming, the creation of an instance of an abstraction or template, such as a class of objects or a computer process. 852

Instantiation A programming term that refers to the process of assigning a value to a variable. 815

Instant messaging (IM) A private chat in which users can communicate with each other in real time using electronically transmitted text messages. 351

Instruction cycle The steps followed by a computer to process a single instruction: fetch, interpret, execute, and then increment the instruction pointer. 108

Instruction pointer A component of the CPU that keeps track of sequential program execution. 109

Instruction set The collection of instructions that a CPU is designed to process. 107

Integrated circuit Electronic circuitry etched on a base of silicon to form a microchip. 87

Integrated graphics Circuitry for graphics processing that is integrated into the mainboard of a device rather than as an expansion card. 139

Integration testing The testing of completed modules of an application to ensure that they operate together correctly. 648

Intellectual property A legal concept that refers to ownership of intangible information, such as ideas. 329

Interframe compression Shrinking the size of a video by removing redundant data that is the same in two successive frames. 66

Interlaced scan The way a display device builds an image by showing every other row of pixels, and then going back and filling in the remaining rows. 63

Internal CSS A Cascading Style Sheet that is part of an HTML document, but located in a separate area (usually the head section). 272

Internet backbone The major communications links that form the core of the Internet. 175

Internet exchange points (IXPs) Nodes on the Internet where data from one service provider is transferred to a different service provider. 175

Internet governance The rules and standards that are the foundation for global operation of the Internet. 174

Internet infrastructure The communication channels and data communication equipment that are deployed as the foundation for the Internet. 175

Internet service providers (ISPs) Companies that provide Internet access to businesses, organizations, and individuals. 175

Internet worm A type of malware that spreads over the Internet, usually by sending itself to random IP addresses. 470

Interpreter A program that converts high-level instructions in a computer program into machine language instructions, one instruction at a time. 777, 839

Intraframe compression In a digital video, compression that takes place within a single frame, similar to the compression used for still images. 66

iOS The operating system used for iPhones, iPods, and iPads. 400

IP (Internet Protocol) One of the main protocols of TCP/IP; responsible for addressing packets so that they can be routed to their destinations. IPv4 offers 32-bit addresses, whereas IPv6 offers 128-bit addresses. 179

IP address lookup Finding an IP address using a service such as What's My IP. 320

IPv4 (Internet Protocol version 4) Internet addresses that are 32-bit IP addresses. 179

IPv6 (Internet Protocol version 6) Internet addresses that are 128 bits in length. 179

ISDN (Integrated Services Digital Network) A digital communications system used to access the Internet over the telephone system's copper wiring. 194

IT department The wing of a business or an organization responsible for computer, data, software, and support services. 566

Iteration In the context of computer programming, a section of code that is repeated; also called a loop. 794, 869

Iterative SDLC A system development methodology in which a subset of a system is developed, tested, and then used as the basis for each more full-featured development phase. 629

Jailbreak Making unauthorized changes to an iPod, iPhone, or iPad to get apps from a source other than the official iTunes App Store. 408

JIT (Just In Time) A manufacturing system in which the parts needed to construct a product are received at the assembly site only as needed. 632

Jitter Deviations in the timing of a digital signal that can interfere with communications, especially voice over IP. 189

JOIN An SQL command that temporarily joins data from more than one table in order to allow simultaneous access to both tables. 728

Joining tables In SQL terminology, the act of creating a relationship between tables. 728

Joint application design (JAD) A widely accepted design technique that is based on the idea that the best information systems are designed when end users and systems analysts work together on a project as equal partners. 630

JPEG (Joint Photographic Experts Group) A format that uses lossy compression to store bitmap images. JPEG (pronounced "JAY-peg") files have a .jpg extension. 41

Kernel The core module of an operating system that typically manages memory, processes, tasks, and storage devices. 391

Keyframe In animation and video, the beginning frame of a transition or movement sequence. 58

Keylogger A program, sometimes part of a trojan, that records a person's keystrokes, saves them, and then sends them to a system administrator or remote hacker. 489

Key-value data model A database model in which each value has a key that can be used as its locator. 739

Keyword (1) A word or term used as the basis for a Web page search. (2) A command word provided by a programming language. 764

Kilobit (Kbit or Kb) 1024 bits. 26

Kilobyte (KB) Approximately 1,000 bytes; exactly 1,024 bytes. 26

Knowledge base The collection of facts and rules obtained from experts that are incorporated into an expert system. 616

Knowledge engineering The process of designing rules, entering them into an expert system, and testing them. 616

Known information In a problem statement, information supplied to the computer to help it solve a problem. 762

Label In the context of spreadsheets, any text used to describe data. 419

LAN (local area network) An interconnected group of computers and peripherals located within a relatively limited area, such as a building or campus. 161

Laptop computer A small, lightweight, portable computer that usually runs on batteries. Sometimes called a notebook computer. 96

Laser printer A printer that uses laser-based technology, similar to that used by photocopiers, to produce text and graphics. 140

Last mile A term used in the telecommunication industry to describe the wiring segment that connects a home or business to the common carrier's system. 556

Latency The elapsed time it takes for a packet of data to arrive at its destination. 188

LCD (liquid crystal display) Technology used for flat panel computer screens typically found on laptop computers, tablets, and smartphones. 136

Leading Also called line spacing; the vertical spacing between lines of text. 418

Lidar A technique for measuring distance to a target using laser light; a key component of autonomous vehicles. 145

Lights-out management The process of remotely monitoring an unstaffed data center. 657

Link popularity A metric used by some search engines to rank the sites that are relevant to a query. 290

Linkrot Web page links that no longer connect to active sites. 251

Linux An open source operating system commonly used for servers, and also available for desktop computers. 403

Linux distribution Bundles of software, such as Ubuntu and Mint, that contain the Linux operating system, utilities and a graphical desktop; also called *distros*. 403

List In computer science, an abstract data type that represents an ordered sequence of values, where the same value may occur more than once. 875

Lithium ion The type of battery technology used in many of today's portable electronic devices. 92

Live stream Streaming data that carries an event happening in real time. 33

Local application Software that is stored on a local device and loaded from there into RAM when it runs. 409

Local email An email system that requires users to install email client software on their computer hard disk or flash drive; messages are held on a server until the client software downloads them to the local computer. 348

Local HTML editors Software stored on a local device that can be used for creating HTML pages. 269

Local storage Devices such as disk drives that store data within a computer or smartphone system unit, rather than on a network or in the cloud. 117

Logical storage model A metaphor for the representation of stored files as, for example, a file cabinet containing folders. 436

Logical operators AND, OR, and NOT. Included in program statements and evaluated at runtime as true or false. 865

Logic error A run-time error in the logic or design of a computer program. 768, 846

Lookup routine A validation process used by database designers to prevent data entry errors by searching for an entry such as a state abbreviation in a file or database table. 710

Loop The section of program code that is repeated because of a repetition control structure; also called an iteration. 794, 869

Lossless compression A compression technique that is able to reconstitute all of the data in the original file; hence, *lossless* means that this compression technique does not lose data. 26

Lossy compression Any data compression technique in which some of the data is sacrificed to obtain more compression. 26

Low-density data Database records that contain very little data per megabyte. 733

Low-level language A programming language that requires a programmer to write instructions for specific hardware elements such as the computer processor, registers, and RAM locations. 773

Loyalty program A scheme used by businesses to encourage customers to register for discounts and sale alerts. The information can also be used by CRM systems and OLAP systems to target customers with advertising based on their buying habits. 625

MAC address (Media Access Control address) A unique identifier similar to a serial number assigned to networking equipment at the time of manufacture. 202

Machine language A low-level language written in binary code that the computer can execute directly. 107

macOS An operating system used on Apple desktop and laptop computers; formerly *OS X.* 398

Magnetic storage A technology for recording data onto disks or tape by magnetizing particles of an oxide-based surface coating. 119

Magnetometer A device or component that measures magnetism and is used as a compass in mobile devices. 143

Mainframe A large, fast, and expensive computer generally used by businesses or government agencies to provide centralized storage, processing, and management for large amounts of data. 95

Maintenance phase The day-to-day operation of an information system, including making modifications and correcting problems to ensure correct operation. 651

Malware Programs such as viruses, worms, and bots designed to disrupt computer operations. 467

Malware exploit The actions carried out by malicious code supplied by viruses, worms, and bots. 467

Management information system (MIS) A type of information system that manipulates the data collected by a transaction processing system to generate reports that managers can use to make business decisions. 613

Managers People who make decisions about how an organization carries out its activities. 609

Man-in-the-middle A malicious exploit in which messages between two people are intercepted without their knowledge. 489

Manual calculator A device that helps solve mathematical calculations, but does not contain sophisticated built-in algorithms. 537

Mark-8 A microprocessor-based computer system, developed by Jonathan A. Titus in 1974, that helped lead to the development of personal computers. 547

Markup language A language that provides text and graphics formatting through the use of tags. Examples of markup languages include HTML, XML, and SGML. 267

Mass-mailing worm A worm that sends itself to every email address in the address book of an infected computer. 470

Mechanical calculator A machine capable of implementing algorithms used to solve mathematical calculations. 538

Megabit (Mb or Mbit) 1,048,576 bits. 26

Megabyte (MB) Approximately 1 million bytes; exactly 1,048,576 bytes. 26

Memory The computer circuitry that holds data waiting to be processed. 85

Memory card A small, flat, solid state storage medium; frequently used to store data on cameras and handheld devices. 122

Memory leak An undesirable state in which a program requests memory but never releases it, which can eventually prevent other programs from running. 393

Mesh topology A system for connecting nodes of a network in which devices connect to one another rather than to a central server. 166

Message In the context of object-oriented programming, input that is collected and sent to an object. 803

Message header The section of an email file that contains the address, subject, and file attachment information. 346

Metadata tag Data that contains information about other data; file tags are an example of metadata. 328

Method In the context of object-oriented programming, any action that an object can perform. 802, 885

Microblogging service A social media service for posting short asynchronous messages such as tweets. 338

Microcontrollers Special-purpose microprocessors that are built into the device they control. 98

Microprocessor An integrated circuit that contains the circuitry for processing data. It is a single-chip version of the central processing unit (CPU) found in all computers. 85

Microprocessor clock A timing signal that sets the pace for executing instructions in a microprocessor. 110

Microsoft Windows An operating system, developed by Microsoft Corporation, that provides a graphical interface. 395

Microwaves Electromagnetic waves with a frequency of at least 1 gigahertz; one type of channel for transmitting data over communications networks. 164

MIDI (Musical Instrument Digital Interface) A standardized way in which sound and music are encoded and transmitted between digital devices that play music. 34

MIDI messages The commands that create MIDI music by specifying the note to play, its duration, and the instrument that plays it. 34

Mission An organization's goal or plan, which is reflected by the organization's activities. 607

Mission statement The written expression of an organization's goals and how those goals will be accomplished. 607

MITS Altair The first commercial microcomputer. It was based on the Intel 8080 processor and sold primarily to computer hobbyists. 547

Mobile app An application designed to be downloaded to a handheld device, such as a smartphone or tablet computer. 408

Mobile broadband service High-bandwidth wireless technology that was developed for sending digital data over cell phone systems. 196

Mobile hotspot A wireless network with a server that gets its Internet connection from a mobile network. 197

Mobile Internet access Any service that allows subscribers to access the Internet while on the go. 191

Mobile operating systems Operating systems used by handheld devices, such as smartphones or tablet computers. 391

Modem A device that modulates and demodulates a signal; typically used to send data from a computer to the Internet over telephone, cable television, or satellite networks. 168

Module In the context of software, a component or part of a software program or an office suite (for example, a word processing module). 415

Moore's law Gordon Moore's prediction that technological innovation would double the number of transistors in an integrated circuit every two years without raising its cost. 528

Morse code A method of coding information into a series of dots and dashes. 552

Motion graphics Digital video and animation that create the illusion of motion; opposite of *still graphics*. 39

MOV A multimedia file format, popular for digital videos, that works with QuickTime software. 67

MP3 A file format that provides highly compressed audio files with very little loss of sound quality. 32

MPEG (Moving Picture Experts Group) A family of highly compressed container file formats and codecs for digital multimedia; MPEG-1, MPEG-2, and MPEG-4. 67

MRP (manufacturing resource planning) A business management technique in which an optimum manufacturing plan is generated based on a wide variety of data. 632

MTBF (mean time between failures) An estimate of the length of time a device will perform before it fails. 655

Multi-core processor A microprocessor that contains circuitry for more than one processing unit. 110

Multidimensional database A database often created for data analysis that has a more complex structure than a simple two-dimensional table. 691

Multi-level sort The process of arranging database records in alphabetical or numerical order based on the data contained in two or more fields. 698

Multiparadigm language A programming language that supports more than one paradigm, such as object-oriented and procedural paradigms. 779

Multiple-user license Legal permission for more than one person to use a particular software package. 385

Multiprocessing The ability of a computer or an operating system to support dual-core processors or multiple processors. 393

Multitasking The ability of a computer, a processor, or an operating system to run more than one program, job, or task at the same time. 393

Multithreading A technology that allows multiple parts, or threads, from a program to run simultaneously. 393

MU-MIMO (multiple-user, multiple-input multiple-output) A technology that transmits signals simultaneously to multiple devices that have one or more antennas. 206

Narrowband A term that refers to communication channels that have low bandwidth. 165

NAT (network address translation) A security technique that allows a LAN to use one set of IP address for intra-network data and another set of address for data traveling to and from the Internet. 181

Network administrator The person responsible for configuring and monitoring a computer network. 567

Network discovery A setting that when turned on allows a computer to see other computers on a network and to be seen by those other computers. 217

Network interface controller Circuitry, often on an expansion card mounted inside a computer, that transmits and receives data on a local area network. Also called a NIC, network card, or network adapter. 202

NFC (near field communication) A short-range wireless communication technology that allows two devices to exchange data by touching or being in very close proximity. 212

Node In a network, a connection point; in a hierarchical database, a segment or record type. 168

Non-compete clause A section of a contract that prohibits a worker from producing work that would compete in some way with the business while employed by the business or for a period time after leaving the business. 583

Non-volatile Any electronic component that does not require a constant supply of power to hold data. 122

NOR A Wikipedia policy that means "no original research." All material must be backed by references. 340

Normalization The process of analyzing data to create the most efficient database structure. 712

NoSQL A collection of technologies for efficiently working with very large data sets or big data. 736

NPOV A Wikipedia policy that means "neutral point of view." 340

Numeric data Numbers that represent quantities and can be used in arithmetic operations. 21

Object In an object database or OO programming language, a discrete piece of code describing a person, place, thing, event, or type of information. 799, 852

Object code The low-level instructions that result from compiling source code. 777, 852

Object database A database model that organizes data into classes of objects that can be manipulated by programmer-defined methods; also referred to as an object-oriented database. 692

Object-oriented methodology An approach to system development that regards the elements of a system as a collection of objects that interact with each other to accomplish tasks. 633

Object-oriented paradigm An approach to programming that focuses on the manipulation of objects rather than on the generation of procedure-based code. 799, 852

Object-oriented programming A programming language model organized around objects rather than "actions" and organized around data rather than control structures. 852

OCR (optical character recognition) The ability of a device or software to digitize text from printed sources. 25

Office suite A collection of productivity programs, typically word processing, spreadsheet, presentation, and database modules. 415

Offshoring The corporate practice of relocating production, manufacturing, or customer service to lower-cost overseas locations. 527

Ogg Theora A non-proprietary container format (Ogg) and video codec (Theora). 67

Ogg Vorbis An open source audio file format. 32

OLAP (online analytical processing) A system that consists of computer hardware, database software, and analytical tools that are optimized for analyzing and manipulating data. 685

Oleophobic The characteristic of smartphone screens that resists oils. 92

OLTP (online transaction processing) Interactive online transaction processing methods that use a "commit or rollback" strategy to ensure accurate transaction processing. 611

On-access scan Virus scanning that automatically takes place in the background while the device is turned on. 483

On-demand scan Virus scanning that is manually initiated by a user. 483

On-demand stream Streaming media that starts and stops when requested, as opposed to a live stream. 33

One-way edges In a sociogram, the lines between two entities that go only one way. 321

Online HTML editor A Web app that provides tools for creating HTML pages. 269

Online identity The aggregation of a person's social media presence online. 317

Online intrusion Unauthorized access to a digital device that originates from the Internet. 479

Online processing An interactive method of processing transactions in which each transaction is processed as it is entered. 611

Online reputation The perception formed by third parties of a person's online identity. 357

Online services A term used to describe pre-Internet social networking sites such as America Online, MySpace, and Prodigy. 316

Op code The part of a machine language instruction that specifies the operation that is to be performed by the processor. 774

Open source software Software that includes its source code, allowing programmers to modify and improve it. 387

Operand In the context of computer programming, the part of an instruction that specifies the data that is be manipulated. 774

Operating system The software that controls the computer's use of its hardware resources, such as memory and disk storage space. Also called an OS. 86

Operational database A type of database that is used in day-to-day business operations. (Contrast with *analytical database*.) 681

Operational planning The scheduling and monitoring of workers and processes. 609

Optical storage A technology that records data as light and dark spots on a CD, DVD, or other optical media. 121

Order of operations A standard order for calculations involving more than one arithmetic operation. 859

Organization A group of people working together to accomplish a goal. 607

Organizational chart A diagram showing the hierarchy of workers in an organization. 609

Output The results produced by a computer (for example, reports, graphs, and music). 85

Outsourcing The corporate practice of using third-party contractors to supply raw goods, manufacturing, or services. 527

Packet A small unit of data transmitted over a network. 176

Packet loss A situation in which data bits are lost in transit, requiring them to be re-sent, which significantly increases the time required for an intact message to arrive at its destination. 189

Packet switching A technology used by data communications networks, such as the Internet, where a message is divided into smaller units called packets for transmission. 177

Page layout The physical positions of elements on a document page such as headers, footers, page numbering, and graphics. 418

PAN (personal area network) An interconnected group of personal digital devices located within a range of about 30 feet. 161

Paragraph alignment The horizontal position (left, right, justified, centered, for example) of the text in a document. 418

Paragraph style A specification for the format of a paragraph that includes the alignment of text within the margins and line spacing. 418

Parallel processing The simultaneous use of more than one processor to execute a program. 111

Parameters (1) In the context of SQL, the specifications used to delineate a command by specifying a table or search keyword. 723 (2) In the context of programming, a keyword or variable used to specify variations of commands. 765, 881

Pascaline An early mechanical calculator capable of performing addition, subtraction, division, and multiplication. 538

Password entropy A measure of a password's unpredictability and resistance to discovery. 462

Password manager Software that keeps track of sites at which a user has registered and the password that corresponds to each site. 464

Payment gateway The part of an ecommerce system that connects a merchant Web site to the bank or credit card service provider to handle customer payments. 621

Pay television A service offered by cable television companies that provides a television connection for a monthly fee. 563

PDA (personal digital assistant) A device or software that helps track appointments, contacts, and notes. 97

Peripheral devices Components or equipment, such as printers, that expand a computer's input, output, or storage capability. 130

Permissions In the context of file sharing, the activities that third parties are allowed to perform when accessing shared files. 219

Persistent cookies Cookies that are stored on a local device and remain there when a session ends. 282

Personal computer A microcomputer designed for use by an individual user for applications such as Web browsing and word processing. 96

Personal firewall A device or software controlled by an end user that is designed to block unauthorized intrusions. 485

Personally identifiable information (PII) Data pertaining to a person that can be used for purposes of identification or tracking. 360

PERT (Program Evaluation and Review Technique) A project management technique that displays interconnected events and task milestones on a timeline. 634

Pharming An exploit that redirects users to fake Web sites. 504

Phishing An email-based scam that's designed to fool users into revealing confidential information. 503

Phoneme A unit of sound that is a basic component of words and is produced by speech synthesizers. 36

Photosites In digital photography, a single point on an image capture chip, equivalent to one pixel. 40

Physical sort order In a database table, the order in which records are stored on disk. 714

Physical storage model A representation of data as it is physically stored. 436

PIECES framework A concept developed by James Wetherbe to help identify problems in an information system. Each letter of *PIECES* stands for a potential problem (Performance, Information, Economics, Control, Efficiency, and Service). 633

Ping (Packet Internet Groper) A command on a TCP/IP network that sends a test packet to a specified IP address and waits for a reply. 188

Pipeline processing A technology that allows a processor to begin executing an instruction before completing the previous instruction. 111

Pirated software Software that is copied, sold, or distributed without permission from the copyright holder. 389

Pixel Short for *picture element*; the smallest unit in a graphic image. Computer display devices use a matrix of pixels to display text and graphics. 39

Pixelation Describes the effect of increasing the size of an image until smooth edges become jagged. 43

Pixel interpolation A process that is used by graphics software to average the color of adjacent pixels in an image, usually when the image is enlarged. 43

Plaintext An original, unencrypted message. 455

Planning phase The first phase of an information system development project with the goal of creating a project development plan. 630

PNG (Portable Network Graphics) A type of graphics file format similar to but newer than GIF and JPEG. 41

Point size A unit of measure (1/72 of an inch) used to specify the height of characters in a font. 418

Point-to-point topology A network link that directly connects two devices. 166

Polymorphism In the context of object-oriented programming, the ability to redefine a method for a subclass. Also called overloading. 804, 890

POP3 (Post Office Protocol version 3) A standard for retrieving email messages from an email server. 348

Portable computer A computer, such as a laptop, tablet, or smartphone, that runs on battery power. 96

Portable Internet access Any type of Internet service, such as portable satellite, that can be moved from one place to another. 191

Port scan An exploit used by hackers to locate computer ports that can be used for surreptitious access; also called a port probe. 484

Predicate In a Prolog fact, such as likes(John, Mary), the predicate *likes* describes the relationship between the arguments in parentheses, such as *(John, Mary)*. 812

Predictive analytics A branch of data mining that focuses on predicting future probabilities and trends using statistical algorithms, neural networks, and optimization research. 685

Predictive methodology The traditional approach to software development in which detailed specifications are created before coding begins. 763

Predictive services In the context of browsers, search engines, and the Web, the ability of software to better locate information using accumulated historical queries. 258

Pre-rendering The process of rendering an animated sequence and saving it prior to displaying it; opposite of *real-time rendering*. 58

Presentation software Software that provides tools to combine text, graphics, graphs, animation, and sound into a series of electronic slides that can be output on a projector, as overhead transparencies, or paper copies. 425

Pretexting The use of some false pretext to trick victims into participating in a scam. 500

Preventive countermeasures Firewalls and similar technologies that shield vulnerabilities in order to render an attack unsuccessful or reduce its impact. 661

Primary key A field in a database that contains data, such as a Social Security number, that is unique to a record. 708

Privacy The right to be let alone or at least control the dissemination of personally identifiable information. 360

Privacy policy A set of statements describing how collected data will and will not be used by a Web site or other entity that collects it. 360

Private attribute An attribute for an object, a class, or a record that can be accessed only from the program routine in which it is defined. 800

Private browsing A service offered by many browsers that deletes the browser cache and history list. 264

Private IP address An IP address that cannot be routed over the Internet. 180

Problem statement A description of the factors that must be addressed to devise a solution to a problem. 761

Procedural language Any programming language used to create programs composed of a series of statements that tell the computer how to perform a specific task. 785

Procedural paradigm An approach to programming in which a programmer defines the steps for solving a problem. 785

Procedure handbook Step-by-step instructions for performing a specific job or task. 649

Process In the context of an information system data flow diagram (DFD), a manual or computerized routine that changes data by performing a calculation, updating information, sorting a list, and so on. 636

Process data A systematic series of actions that a computer performs to manipulate data; typically represented on a DFD by a rounded rectangle. 85

Processes Activities that are performed by the microprocessor. 392

Product activation The process of becoming a registered user of a software product; the process might include entering a validation code to unlock the software. 386

Productivity A measurement of the amount of output that is produced per unit of input. 532

Productivity software Software that helps people work more efficiently; traditionally, word processing, spreadsheet, presentation, email, and database software. 415

Product life cycle The expected profitability of a product from its inception to its demise. 529

Professional ethics On-the-job actions and choices that reflect a person's values. 581

Program editor A programming tool, similar to a word processor, that provides specialized editing and formatting features to streamline the programming process. 766

Programmer-defined function A function that is named and defined as a block of code by the programmer. 880

Program statement An instruction written in a high-level programming language that specifies an action to be carried out by the processor. 764

Programming language A set of keywords and grammar (syntax) that allows a programmer to write instructions that a computer can execute. 107

Programming paradigm A programming methodology or approach, as in the object-oriented paradigm. 779

Progressive scan A method for displaying motion graphics in which the lines of pixels are drawn in sequence; opposite of *interlaced scan*. 63

Project development plan A planning document that is the final result of a planning phase and is reviewed and approved by management. 630

Project management software Software specifically designed as a tool for planning, scheduling, and tracking projects and their costs. 634

Promoted tweet Tweets purchased by advertisers. 339

Prompt One or more characters in a command line interface that indicate the computer is ready to accept typed input. 854

Properties The characteristics of an object in a program. 767

Proprietary information Financial and product data, procedures, or concepts created by an individual or an organization that are not made public because they would aid the competition. 583

Proprietary software Software that carries restrictions on its use that are delineated by copyright, patents, or license agreements. 385

Protocol stack The collection of protocols used by a network (for example, TCP and IP). 170

Pseudocode A notational system for algorithms that combines English and a programming language. 788

PUA (potentially unwanted application) A program that is installed surreptitiously and is sometimes difficult to remove. 507

Public attribute An attribute for an object, a class, or a record that can be accessed from any routine in a program. 800

Public domain Material that is not subject to copyright restrictions on its use and distribution. 330

Public domain software Software that is available for public use without restriction except that it cannot be copyrighted. 385

Public IP address IP addresses that can be routed over the Internet (as opposed to private IP addresses that cannot). 181

Public key encryption A method of encryption that uses one key to encrypt data, but a different key to decrypt it. 285

PUP (potentially unwanted program) See *PUA*. 507

Quality of service (QoS) The level of performance that is provided by a computer system and measured by factors such as response time, downtime, and capacity. 651

Quality-of-service metric A technique for measuring a particular quality-of-service characteristic, such as response time. 652

Quarantined file A file suspected to be infected with a virus that is moved to a special folder by antivirus software to prevent accidental access to it. 473

Query languages A set of command words that can be used to direct the computer to create databases, locate information, sort records, and change the data in those records. 721

Query processor The component of a search engine that examines keywords entered by users and fetches results that match the query. 290

Radio A technology invented by Guglielmo Marconi in 1895 that is a parent technology to today's mobile phones. 557

RAM (random access memory) Computer memory circuitry that holds data, program instructions, and the operating system while the computer is on. 113

Random number generator A routine that creates random numbers for use in computer programs. 872

Ransomware Malware that encrypts files as part of an exploit to extort money from victims who want to regain use of their files in unencrypted format. 481

Rasterization The process of superimposing a grid over a vector image and determining the color depth for each pixel. 56

RAT (Remote Access Trojan) Malware that creates a backdoor for unauthorized remote access. 480

RAW In the context of digital graphics, a file that contains unprocessed image data directly from a digital camera's sensors. 41

Ray tracing A technique by which light and shadows are added to a 3D image. 57

Readability formula A feature found in some word processing software that can estimate the reading level of a written document. 417

Read-only Storage media that can only be read from, but not recorded on. 121

Read-write head The mechanism in a disk drive that magnetizes particles on the storage disk surface to write data, or senses the bits that are present to read data. 119

Real-time rendering The process in which motion graphics are rendered as they are displayed; opposite of *pre-rendering*. 59

Record In the context of database management, the fields of data that pertain to a single entity in a database. 423, 687

Recordable The devices and standards that allow computers to write data permanently on CDs and DVDs, but do not allow that data to be changed once it has been recorded. 121

Record occurrence A record that has been filled with data for a particular entity. 687

Record type The structure of a record, including the names, length, and data types for each field. 687

Recovery drive A storage device containing all the operating system files and application software files necessary to restore a computer to its original state. 126

Registers A sort of "scratch pad" area of the microprocessor into which data or instructions are moved so that they can be processed. 108

Relational database A database structure that incorporates the use of tables that can establish relationships with other, similar tables. 690

Relationship In the context of databases, an association between entities that can be used to link records in more than one file. 688

Relative reference In a worksheet, a cell reference that can change if cells change position as a result of a move or copy operation. 422

Remarks Programmer notes or documentation included in a program, but preceded by a special symbol so they are not executed. Also called comments. 769

Remote storage Any storage device that is not directly connected to a computer, but rather is accessed over a network. 123

Rendering In graphics software, the process of creating a 3D solid image by covering a wireframe drawing and applying computer-generated highlights and shadows. 56

Repetition control structure A component of a computer program that repeats one or more instructions until a certain condition is met (also called loop or iteration). 794, 869

Report generator The component of a data management environment that provides a user with the ability to design reports. 718

Report template A predesigned pattern that provides the outline or general specifications for a report. 718

Resistive technology Touchscreen technology composed of multiple layers that when pressed contact each other and complete an electrical circuit. 138

Resolution dependent Graphics, such as bitmaps, in which the quality of the image is dependent on the number of pixels constituting the image. 43

Resource A component, either hardware or software, that is available for use by a computer's processor. 392

Response rate In the context of display technology, the time it takes for one pixel to change from black to white and then back to black. 136

Retweet A tweet that is forwarded by someone other than the original tweeter. 339

Rewritable The devices and standards that allow users to write data on a storage medium and then change that data. 121

RFID (radio-frequency identification) A short-range wireless network technology commonly used to track products containing RFID tags. 212

RF signals (radio frequency signals) Data that is broadcast and received via radio waves with a transceiver. 164

RGB color model The use of red, green, and blue light that can be combined to create the full spectrum of colors. 42

RISC (reduced instruction set computer) A microprocessor designed for rapid and efficient processing of a small set of simple instructions. 112

Rogers' bell curve A statistical and graphical depiction used to describe phases for product adoption, beginning with innovators and early adopters, followed by early majority, late majority, and laggards. 529

Rogue antivirus exploit Fake virus alerts that warn of virus infections and then offer to remove them. 506

ROM (read-only memory) Refers to one or more integrated circuits that contain permanent instructions that the computer uses during the boot process. 114

Root directory The main directory of a disk. 429

Rooting A process that enables users to gain root access to Android mobile devices with the purpose of overcoming limitations imposed by mobile service providers. 408

Rootkit Software that conceals running processes; used by hackers to disguise security breaches and break-ins. 469

Rotary dialers A rotating dial used on legacy telephones to enter a telephone number. 554

Router A device used to make wired or wireless connections and route data to its destination on a network. 168

Rule In the context of Prolog programming, a general statement about the relationship between facts. 811

Run-length encoding (RLE) A graphics file compression technique that looks for patterns of bytes and replaces them with messages that describe the patterns. 44

Runtime error An error that occurs when a computer program is run. 768

Safe Browsing A Google service that maintains a list of suspicious Web sites and warns users if they attempt to access those sites. 505

Sampling rate The number of times per second a sound is measured during the recording process. 31

SATA (Serial Advanced Technology Attachment) The interface that transfers data from a drive to the main circuit board. 120

Satellite Internet service A high-speed Internet service that uses a geosynchronous or low-earth orbit satellite to send data directly to satellite dishes owned by individuals. 195

Scale out The ability to increase the capacity of an information system by adding additional hardware components, such as more servers. 737

Scale up The ability to increase the capacity of an information system by increasing the processing or storage capacity of the current hardware. 736

Scanner A device that converts a printed image into a bitmap graphic. 40

Schema In the context of databases, a fairly rigid or inflexible underlying data structure, as in a relational database. 738

Schema-less databases Those databases that are not highly structured, such as those provided by NoSQL technologies. 738

Schickard's Calculator An early mechanical calculator consisting of a series of gears and spokes representing numerical values. 538

SCM (supply chain management) The process of monitoring products from manufacturers to distributors and then to customers, often with the aid of specialized software. 623

Screen resolution The density of the grid used to display text or graphics on a display device; the greater the horizontal and vertical density, the higher the resolution. 137

Scripting languages Programming languages, such as PHP, Perl, Ruby, and JavaScript, distributed as human-readable source code. 778

SDK (software development kit) A collection of language-specific programming tools. 782

Search and Replace A feature of document production software that allows the user to automatically locate all instances of a particular word or phrase and substitute another word or phrase. 416

Search engine indexer The component of a search engine that reviews the Web pages brought back by a crawler and creates pointers to them so that they can be quickly accessed. 289

Search engine optimization (SEO) Making modifications to a Web site to move it closer to the top of the list returned by search engines. 291

Search history A list of queries entered into a search engine and also stored by the search engine. 295

Search operator A logical operator such as AND, OR, and NOT used to formulate complex queries. 293

Search terms The words entered into a search engine or database to form a query. 292

Second-generation computers Computers that use transistors for data processing and storage instead of vacuum tubes. 544

Second-generation languages Assembly languages that followed machine languages. 774

Sectors Subdivisions of the tracks on a storage medium that provide storage areas for data. 436

Security specialist A computer professional who analyzes security threats, implements solutions, and develops policies and procedures to protect computer equipment and data. 567

SELECT An SQL keyword that queries for a particular record or group of records from a table. 724

Selection control structure A component of a computer program that tells a computer what to do, depending on whether a condition is true or false (also called decision structure or branch). 793, 862

Semaphores A way of conveying information at a distance using visual signals, such as flags or hand signals. 551

Semiconductors Substances, such as silicon or germanium, that can act as either a conductor or an insulator. Used in the manufacture of computer chips. 87

Sense-plan-act algorithms Artificial intelligence routines that make decisions and carry out activities in autonomous cars and other digital systems without human intervention. 144

Sequence control structure A programming construct that alters the order in which instructions are executed. 791

Sequence diagram A tool used by a project team that depicts the detailed interactions that take place within an information system. 638

Sequential execution The computer execution of program instructions performed in the sequence established by a programmer. 791

Serial processing Processing data one instruction at a time, completing one instruction before beginning another. 111

Serializability The ability of a database to handle multiple users who try to access the same record at the same time. 703

Server A computer or software on a network that supplies the network with data and storage. 95

Server operating system A type of operating system, sometimes called a network operating system, that provides management tools for distributed networks, email servers, and Web hosting sites. 391

Server-side scripts Program code that is executed by a Web server in response to client data. 275

Services In the context of economics, intangible actions performed for a consumer (contrast with *goods*.) 526

Session cookies Cookies that are deleted when the browser is closed. 282

Setup program A program module supplied with a software package for the purpose of installing the software. 410

Shard A portion of a database that is stored on a device and is different from the devices holding other portions of the database. 737

Short URLs Web site addresses that have been shortened by services such as Bitly; commonly used in tweets where there is a character limit. 252

Side-loading Installing a mobile app by some means other than downloading it from an official app store. 469

Single-level sort The process of organizing database records in alphabetical or numerical order based on only one sort criterion, such as Name. 698

Single-user license Legal permission for one person to use a particular software package. 385

Site license Legal permission for software to be used on any and all computers at a specific location (for example, within a corporate building or on a university campus). 385

Slate tablet A computer form factor in which the screen covers most of the system unit and there is no physical keyboard. 97

Smart sensors Sensors that include processing capabilities. 142

Smartphones Cellular phones that have a high-resolution color screen, a browser, and the ability to run apps. 97

SmartScreen A feature of Microsoft browsers that warns users of unsafe Web sites. 505

SMTP (Simple Mail Transfer Protocol) A communication protocol used to send email across a network or the Internet. 348

Social discovery Connecting with other nearby users on a geosocial network. 319

Social engineer Someone who uses psychology to encourage people to do something. 497

Social engineering Methods for tricking people into engaging in non-secure activities, such as clicking links and downloading infected files. 497

Social media Online Web sites and services, such as Facebook, Twitter, and LinkedIn, that help users create content and share it with others. 313

Social Media Honeycomb A model or taxonomy for classifying social networking services. 313

Social media profile The basic, publicly viewable information about an online persona. 317

Social networking analyst A person who is responsible for collecting data from social media sites, applying that data to business goals, and planning social media marketing. 567

Social networking service Web-based services, such as Facebook and LinkedIn, for connecting with other users. 316

Sociogram edges The lines that connect entities in a sociogram. 321

Sociogram nodes The entities in a sociogram. 321

Sociograms A visual model of the links between entities in a social network. 321

Sockpuppets Fake online personas often used to bolster someone's real online presence. 355

Software The instructions that direct a computer to perform a task, interact with a user, or process data. 86

Software customization The process of modifying a commercially available software application to meet the needs of a specific user or organization. 648

Software engineering The process of developing software using systematic mathematical, engineering, and management techniques. 571, 759

Software license A legal contract that defines the ways in which a user may use a computer program. 384

Software update A section of code or a program module designed to correct errors or enhance security on an already installed software product. 383

Software upgrade A version of a software product containing new features and designed to replace the entire earlier version of the product. 383

Solid state drive A data storage device that utilizes erasable, rewritable circuitry. 123

Solid state storage A technology that records data and stores it in a microscopic grid of cells on a non-volatile, erasable, low-power chip. 122

Sort key A field used to arrange records in order. 714

Source code Computer instructions written in a high-level language. 777

Source document A file containing the HTML tags or scripts for a Web page. 268

Spam Unsolicited email typically sent as a bulk or mass mailing and often used for fraudulent or deceptive marketing. 499

Spam filter Software that identifies unsolicited and unwanted email messages and blocks them from the recipient's inbox. 502

Spear phishing A social engineering exploit in which email with links to malware is sent to specific targets. 503

Speech recognition The process by which computers recognize voice patterns and words, and then convert them to digital data. 36

Speech synthesis The process by which computers produce sound that resembles spoken words. 36

Spelling checker A feature of document production software that checks each word in a document against an electronic dictionary of correctly spelled words and then presents a list of alternatives for possible misspellings. 417

Spelling dictionary A data module that is used by a spelling checker as a list of correctly spelled words. 417

Sponsored links Links displayed by a search engine that have paid placements. 291

Spreadsheet A numerical model or representation of a real situation, presented in the form of a table. 419

Spreadsheet software Software for creating electronic worksheets that hold data in cells and perform calculations based on that data. 419

Sprint In the context of computer programming, an iteration in the agile development process in which a working prototype of a product is created. 763

Spyware Any software that covertly gathers user information without the user's knowledge, usually for advertising purposes. 489

SQL A popular query language used by mainframes and microcomputers. 721

SQL injection A hacking technique that uses malicious SQL queries. 721

SQL keywords A collection of command words that issue instructions to an SQL database. 722

SQL query A command created using SQL database client software that operates directly on the records in a database. 721

SSID (service set identifier) A code that identifies a network containing wireless connections and is attached to every packet that travels on that network. 208

Star topology An arrangement of network devices in which they connect to a central device such as a router. 166

Stateless protocol A protocol, such as HTTP, that allows one request and response per session. 280

Static IP addresses Permanently assigned and unique IP addresses used by hosts or servers. 179

Static Web page A Web page that does not change once it is displayed on the screen by a browser. 274

STEM (science, technology, engineering, and mathematics) An acronym used to describe educational and career sectors that focus on hard sciences. 566

Stereo pair A set of two images that produce the sense of 3D when viewed one image per eye through a stereoscope. 49

Stereogram Two images from a stereo pair that are combined into a single slide. 49

Stereoscopic imaging A graphical technique used to produce the sense of three dimensions from the use of one or more 2D images. 49

Still images Photos and computer graphics that are not in motion. 39

Stock market bubble A situation in which the value of stocks rises rapidly until stocks are overvalued, which is followed by a sharp drop in stock prices. 525

Storage The area in a computer where data is retained on a permanent basis. 85

Store-and-forward A technology used by communication networks in which a message, such as an email, is temporarily held in storage on a server until it is requested by a client computer. 348

Stored program A set of program statements that resides on a storage device, such as a hard drive, and can be loaded into computer memory and executed. 86

Storyboard A screen-based graphical surface provided by a VDE for organizing the objects and methods used to create computer programs. 767

Strategic planning The process of developing long-range goals and plans for an organization. 609

Strength meter An indication of the strength of a password. 464

String In the context of computer programming, a sequence of characters, such as a word or a sentence, that can include letters, numerals, symbols, and punctuation marks. 843

Strong password A password that is difficult to guess or to discover using password-cracking software. 460

Structured English Vocabulary and syntax used by systems analysts to concisely and unambiguously explain the logic of a process. It is limited to words defined in a data dictionary and to specific logical terms such as IF... THEN. 788

Structured file A file that consists of a collection of data organized as a set of similarly structured records. 686

Structured methodology A method of developing an information system that focuses on the processes that take place within a business or organization. 633

Style A feature in many desktop publishing and word processing programs that allows the user to apply numerous format settings with a single command. 418

Style rules Specifications for styles that are compiled into Cascading Style Sheets (CSS). 272

Subclass In object-oriented programming, a class derived from a superclass inheriting its attributes and methods. 801, 887

Subdirectory Any directory found under the root directory. 429

Success factors System requirements that also serve as an evaluation checklist at the end of a development project. 635

Summary report A report generated by a management information system that combines or groups data and usually provides totals, such as a report of total annual sales for the past five years. 613

Superclass In object-oriented programming, a class that provides attributes and methods for subclasses. 801, 887

Supercomputer The fastest and most expensive type of computer, capable of processing trillions of instructions per second. 95

Supply chain All of the businesses, people, and vehicles that move products from suppliers to consumers. 622

SVG (Scalable Vector Graphics) A graphics format designed specifically for Web display that automatically resizes when displayed on different screens. 54

Symmetric connection Any connection to the Internet in which the upstream speed is the same as the downstream speed. 188

Synchronous A communication mode, such as VoIP, in which participants must be online at the same time. 345

Syntax In the context of programming languages, the grammar rules that create valid program statements. 765, 843

Syntax error An error that results when an instruction does not follow the syntax rules, or grammar, of the programming language. 768, 845

Synthesized sound Artificially created sound, usually found in MIDI music or synthesized speech. 34

System board The main circuit board in a computer that houses chips and other electronic components. 88

System conversion The process of deactivating an old information system and activating a new one. 650

System development life cycle (SDLC) The series of phases that outlines the development process of an information system. 629

System documentation A description of the features, hardware architecture, and programming of an information system written for programmers, designers, and analysts who maintain the system. 649

System programmers Computer programmers who specialize in developing operating systems and utilities rather than applications. 760

System requirements (1) The minimum hardware and operating system specifications required for a software application to operate correctly. 382 (2) Criteria for developing a successful information system, which are typically compiled into a system requirements report at the conclusion of the SDLC analysis phase. 635

System requirements report A report generated at the conclusion of the analysis phase of the SDLC by a project team that has studied a system and determined the system requirements. 635

Systems analysis and design The process of evaluating business needs and using that analysis as the basis for designing and building an information system. 629

Systems analyst A computer professional responsible for analyzing requirements, designing information systems, and supervising the implementation of new information systems. 567

System software Computer programs, such as an operating system or utility software, that help the computer carry out essential operating tasks. 86

System testing The process of testing an information system to ensure that all of the hardware and software components work together. 648

System unit The case or box that contains the computer's power supply, storage devices, main circuit board, processor, and memory. 89

Table A structure in a relational database in which records are rows and fields are columns. 690

Tablet computer A small, portable computer with a touch-sensitive screen configured in a slate form factor. 97

Tactical planning Short- or near-term decisions and goals that deploy the human, financial, and natural resources necessary to meet strategic goals. 609

Tagline In the context of social media, a short description of an online persona. 356

Tallinn Manual A non-binding document that is the cyber equivalent of the Geneva Convention, specifying the rules of cyberwarfare. 535

TCP (Transmission Control Protocol) The protocol within TCP/IP that is responsible for establishing a data connection between two hosts and breaking data into packets. 178

Technical support specialist A computer professional who provides phone or online help to customers of computer companies and software publishers. 567

Technology workers Employees who are directly involved with manufacturing, installing, and programming digital devices. 566

Telecommuters Worker who use available technologies, such as computers, telephones, and the Internet, to work from home or other off-site locations. 570

Telegraph A technology invented by Francis Ronalds in 1823, which transmits electrical signals that represent data. Pioneering work in the telegraph industry laid the groundwork for modern telecommunication networks. 551

Telegraphy The act of sending a signal at a distance. 551

Telephone A technology that transmits sound over a distance; also the device used to place and receive voice calls. 554

Telephone exchange A technology used to interconnect telephone lines as calls are placed; also the physical location where such circuitry is housed. 555

Television A technology that transmits voice and moving images at a distance; also the device for receiving such transmissions. 562

Tethering Connecting devices to a network server that has a mobile Internet connection. 197

Text-to-speech software Software that generates speech based on written text that is played back through a computer's sound card. 36

Thesaurus A feature of documentation software that provides synonyms. 417

Thin client A device or software that depends on software, storage, and other services provided by another device, such as a Web server. 402

Third-generation computers Computers characterized by using integrated circuits instead of transistors or vacuum tubes for data processing. 546

Third-generation languages Programming languages, such as Fortran, BASIC, and COBOL, that followed assembly languages and provided English-like keywords. 775

Third-party cookie A cookie that is generated by an ad or an entity other than the Web page that is shown in the browser. 282

Threat modeling A component of defensive programming that helps programmers identify ways in which their programs might be compromised; also called risk analysis. 770

TIFF (Tagged Image File Format) A bitmap image file format with the .tif extension that automatically compresses file data. 41

TLS (Transport Layer Security) An update of the Secure Sockets Layer (SSL) protocol for encrypting data before it is transmitted over a network. 492

Top-level domain A major domain category into which groups of computers on the Internet are divided, such as .com, .edu, .gov, .int, .mil, .net, and .org. 183

Topology The physical structure of a network including its devices and connections. 166

Touchscreen A display device that accepts input from being touched with a stylus or fingertip. 138

Touchtone A legacy technology for entering telephone numbers by pressing buttons. Also the name of a telephone with a touchtone keypad. 554

TQM (total quality management) The process by which an organization analyzes and implements ways to improve the quality of its products and/or services. 632

Traceroute A network utility that records a packet's path, the number of hops, and the time it takes for the packet to make each hop. 190

Tracks In the context of computer storage, a series of concentric or spiral storage areas created on a storage medium during the formatting process. 436

Trademark A logo, symbol, or word used to represent a business. 329

Transaction An exchange between two parties that can be recorded and stored in a computer system. 611

Transaction processing system (TPS) A system that keeps track of transactions for an organization by providing ways to collect, display, modify, and cancel transactions. 611

Transceiver A combination of a transmitter and a receiver used to send and receive data in the form of radio frequencies. 164

Transcoding The process of converting audio and video files from one digital format to another, such as converting an MOV file into an MP4 file. 67

Transformative work An image, a video, or music that is based on someone else's work, but has been sufficiently transformed so as not to be a derivative work. 333

Transistors A computer processing technology created by Bell Laboratories in 1947; a characteristic of second-generation computers, which replaced vacuum tubes. 544

Trending Becoming noticed or popular. 339

Trojan A computer program that appears to perform one function while actually doing something else, such as inserting a virus into a computer system or stealing a password. 471

True Color A color image with a color depth of 24 bits or 32 bits. Each pixel in a True Color image can be displayed using any of 16.7 million different colors. 42

Turnkey system A complete information system that consists of both hardware and commercial software. 643

Tweets Short messages, sometimes called microblogs, posted on Twitter. 338

Twitter stream/timeline The succession of tweets displayed by Twitter; also called a "feed." 339

Two-factor authentication The use of two identity validators, such as a password and a code sent to the user's cell phone. 456

Two-way edges In a sociogram, links between entities A and B that show relationships from A to B and from B to A. 321

UDP (User Datagram Protocol) A protocol used on the Internet as an alternative to TCP. 178

UML (Unified Modeling Language) A tool for diagramming a set of object classes. 637

Unicode A 16-bit character-representation code that can represent more than 65,000 characters. 22

Unidirectional links Links between Web pages that go in one direction only, linking A to B, but not linking B back to A. 248

Uninstall utility A program that removes software files, references, and registry entries from a computer's hard disk. 413

Unit testing The process of testing a completed application module to make sure that it operates reliably and correctly. 648

UNIVAC The first commercially successful digital computer. 543

Unstructured file A file that contains data, but that is not in a structured format of fields and records. 686

Upconverting Adding pixel data to video frames to increase the resolution. 62

UPDATE An SQL keyword used to alter the values in a database record. 727

URL (Uniform Resource Locator) The address of a Web page. 249

USB flash drive A portable solid state storage device nicknamed "pen drive" or "keychain drive" that plugs directly into a computer's USB port. 123

USB hub A device that provides several auxiliary USB ports. 133

Use case Tasks performed by an actor in an information system. 637

Use case diagram A diagram documenting the tasks performed by the users of an information system. 637

User authentication The process of verifying the identity of an entity that is attempting to access a device, network, or Web site. 456

User documentation Descriptions of how to interact with an information system or a program, including instructions on use, features, and troubleshooting. 649

User interface The software and hardware that enable people to interact with computers. 391

UTF-8 A variable-length coding scheme that uses seven bits for common ASCII characters, but uses 16-bit Unicode as necessary. 22

V A Wikipedia policy that requires information to be verifiable. 340

Vacuum tube An electronic device that controls the flow of electrons in a vacuum and represents binary data; used in the construction of first-generation computers. 544

Value A number used in a calculation. 419

Variable A named storage location that is capable of holding data that can be modified during program execution. 765, 848

Variable-length field A field in a data file that can expand to accept any number of characters up to a maximum limit. 687

VDE (visual development environment) Programming tools that allow programmers to build substantial parts of computer programs by pointing and clicking, rather than entering code. 767

Vector Lines and curves that form simple shapes. 52

Vector animation A series of vector images designed to be viewed sequentially to impart a vision of motion. 58

Vector graphic An image generated from descriptions that specify the position, length, and direction in which lines and shapes are drawn. 52

Vertical market In the context of software, applications designed to meet the needs of a specific market segment or industry, such as medical record-keeping software for use in hospitals. 608

VFX (visual effects) The integration of computer-generated imagery (CGI) with live-action footage. 58

Viral An image, a video, or other content that spreads rapidly on social media sites. 326

Virtual keyboard A keyboard that is displayed on a touchscreen and used for input on smartphones and tablet computers. 138

Virtual machine Software that creates an operating environment, which emulates another computer platform (for example, Parallels Desktop creates a virtual Windows PC on a macOS computer). 404

Virtual memory A computer's use of hard disk storage to simulate RAM. 114

Virus hoax A message, usually email, that makes claims about a virus problem that doesn't actually exist. 477

Virus signature The unique computer code contained in a virus that security software uses to identify it. 472

VisiCalc The first electronic spreadsheet software. 548

VOB (Video Object) An industry-standard video format for stand-alone DVD players. 67

Voiceband modem The type of modem typically used to connect a computer to a telephone line. 193

VoIP (Voice over Internet Protocol) Hardware, software, and protocols used to make telephone-style calls over the Internet. Also referred to as Internet telephony. 352

Volatile A term that describes data (usually in RAM) that can exist only with a constant supply of power. 113

Von Neumann architecture The concept that computer memory can hold both programs and data. 542

Walkthrough In the context of programming, a method of verifying that an algorithm functions properly when using realistic test data. 790

WAN (wide area network) An interconnected group of computers and peripherals that covers a large geographical area, such as multiple branches of a corporation. 161

WAN port A wired port on a router that is used to connect to an Internet modem. 207

WAV An audio file format with the .wav extension that was the original "native" sound format for Windows. 32

WBS (work breakdown structure) A project management tool based on a hierarchical structure of tasks and deliverables. 634

Wearable computers Computers that are designed to be worn as clothing rather than to be carried. 98

Web application Application software that is accessed and used from within a browser. 406

Web browser A program that communicates with a Web server and displays Web pages. 243

Web crawler The component of a search engine that autonomously visits Web sites collecting Web page data that will be indexed and available for searching. 288

Web hosting service A company that offers Web server space for people or businesses that want to create Web sites. 276

Web page Information displayed by a Web browser that's produced from an HTML document or generated on the fly from data in a database. 246

Web portfolio A hypertext version of a resume containing links to Web sites of former employers or schools. 576

Web search engine A program that uses keywords to find information on the Internet and returns a list of links to relevant documents. 287

Web server A computer that listens for HTTP queries from Web browsers and transmits HTML documents over the Internet. 246

Web site A group of Web pages accessible at a specific Web address that holds a collection of information identified by a common domain name, such as *www.cnn.com*. 246

Web site developer A computer professional who creates, tests, posts, and modifies HTML documents and other data for a Web site. 567

WebM A multimedia container format designed for HTML5 projects. 67

Webmail An email system that allows users to access email messages using a browser. 347

WEP (Wired Equivalent Privacy) An encryption algorithm used to protect data on Wi-Fi networks. 208

What-if analysis The process of setting up a model in a spreadsheet and experimenting to see what happens when different values are entered. 419

Whistleblowing The disclosure by an employee of confidential information that relates to some danger, fraud, or other illegal or unethical conduct connected with the workplace. 588

Wi-Fi An Ethernet-compatible wireless connection that uses 802.11a, b, g, and n standards. 205

Wi-Fi adapter A type of network interface card that includes a transmitter and a receiver using Wi-Fi protocols. 206

Wi-Fi hotspot The geographical area in which you can connect to a Wi-Fi signal, such as a Wi-Fi equipped campus or coffeehouse. 198

Wiki Software that allows users to collaborate to create, change, and link Web pages. Used for applications such as Wikipedia and open source project management. 340

Wired channels Communication pathways that use copper, coaxial, or fiber cables to carry data. 162

Wireframe A representation of a 3D object using vectors, which resemble wire, to create a model. 56

Wireless channels Communication pathways that travel through the air as radio frequencies or microwave signals. 162

Wireless encryption A security measure for networks containing wireless connections that scrambles data transmitted between network devices. 208

Wireless encryption key The basis for scrambling and unscrambling the data that travels over a wireless connection; sometimes called a network security key. 208

WMA (Windows Media Audio) A file format with the .wma extension that is promoted by Microsoft and provides highly compressed audio files with very little loss of sound quality. 32

Word processing software Productivity software that assists the user in producing documents, such as reports, letters, papers, and manuscripts. 416

Word size The number of bits that a CPU can manipulate at one time, which is dependent on the size of the registers in the CPU and the number of circuits in the data bus. 112

Word wrap The ability of word processing software to automatically sense the right margin and stream text to the next line. 416

Workers People who perform the tasks necessary to carry out an organization's mission. 609

Worksheet A computerized, or electronic, spreadsheet. 419

World Wide Web An Internet-based collection of linked HTML documents identified by URLs and accessed using browsers and the HTTP protocol; usually called *the Web*. 243

WPA (Wi-Fi Protected Access) A method for encrypting data transmitted over wireless connections. 208

WPS (Wi-Fi Protected Setup) A standard for the easy and secure establishment of a wireless network. 208

X86 A family of microprocessors manufactured by Intel Corporation that defines the PC platform. 105

Xerox Alto An early personal computer prototype developed by Xerox Corp. featuring, among other things, a graphical user interface that became influential in the development of the Apple Macintosh. 548

XML (eXtensible Markup Language) A document format similar to HTML, but that allows the Web page developer to define customized tags, generally for the purpose of creating more interactivity. 693

Z3 An early electronic computer prototype designed by Konrad Zuse that was the first to incorporate the use of binary numbers for data representation. 540

Z-Wave A short-range, low-power network technology used for the Internet of Things. 212

Zero-day attack A malicious attack that takes advantage of previously unknown vulnerabilities in a device, an operating system, or an application. 483

ZigBee A short-range, low-power network technology used for the Internet of Things. 212

Index

Answers

Introduction

QuickChecks
4. A
6. D
7a. B
7b. C
9. A
10. C
11. B
15. B

QuickQuiz
1. input
2. local
3. convergence
4. Internet
5. Cloud

Module 1

Pre-Check
1a. 110
1b. 00110110
2. sampling
3. Lossless
4. JPG, RAW, TIF, GIF, PNG, BMP
5. Phoneme
6. Violet
7. Vector
8. MPEG, VP8, DivX, H.264, Theora, WMV
9. Rendering

QuickChecks
19. D
20. C
21a. C
21b. B
22. 01001000, 01101001, 00100001
23a. B
23b. C
25. A
26a. C
26b. A
27. B
30. B
31. B
32. A
33. C
34. A
35. D
36. A
39. B
42. A
44a. C
44b. B
46. A
48. D
50. A
52a. D
52b. B
54. B
55. C
56. A
58. C
61. A
62. B

64. D
66a. A
66b. B

QuickQuizzes
Section A
1. bit
2. ASCII
3. delimiter
4. terabyte
5. lossy
Section B
1. Sampling
2. lossy
3. extraction
4. MIDI
5. concatenative
Section C
1. CCD
2. dependent
3. 24
4. stereogram
5. PNG
Section D
1. True
2. rasterization or rendering
3. SVG
4. wireframe
5. tracing
Section E
1. capture
2. codec
3. progressive
4. container
5. transcoding

Module 2

Pre-Check
1. Input, Process, Output, Storage
2. Lithium ion (Li-ion)
3. Processor (CPU), Video (Graphics) card
4. The smartphone
5. GHz (Gigahertz)
6. Boot loader
7. pipeline processing
8. USB 3.0
9. image

QuickChecks
85. B
86. C
87a. B
87b. A
89. C
90. C
91. C
92. A
93. B
99. C
100. B
101. B
102a. C
102b. B
105a. C
105b. B
107. B
108a. C
108b. A
109a. B
109b. D
110. D
111. A
112. B
113. B
114. A
119. C
120. A
121a. B
121b. D
122. D
123. A
124. A
126. A
127. B
130. A
131. C
132. A
133. B
134. B
135. D
136. A
137. D
138. A
140. B
143. A

QuickQuizzes
Section A
1. data
2. system
3. integrated
4. clamshell
5. oleophobic
Section B
1. servers
2. macOS
3. desktop
4. Smartphones
5. operating
Section C
1. GHz
2. x86
3. ALU
4. volatile
5. ROM
Section D
1. write
2. optical
3. remote
4. SSD
5. image
Section E
1. expansion
2. Bluetooth
3. GPU
4. capacitive
5. USB

Module 3

Pre-Check
1. Partial mesh
2. Packets
3. Latency
4. Cable, DSL, ISDN, Satellite, Fiber-to-the-home
5. WPA
6. LTE
7. .com
8. TCP/IP
9. file sharing

QuickChecks
161. D
162. B
163a. A
163b. B
164. A
165. C
166. B
168a. A
168b. C
169. C
170. C
173. B
174. C
175. B
176a. A
176b. A
177. C
178a. A
178b. B
179. B
180. A
181. C
182. B
183. C
184. A
185. D
187. B
188. B
189. C
190. B
191. B
192. C
193. D
194a. D
194b. B
195. B
196. B
197. C
198. A
199. C
201. C
202. D
203. A
204. A
205. B
206a. C
206b. C
208. C
209. C
212. C
213. A
216. D
217. C
218. A
219. A
220. C
221. D
222. B
224. A
225. D

QuickQuizzes
Section A
1. personal
2. channels
3. broadband
4. DCE
5. protocols
Section B
1. backbone
2. packet
3. TCP
4. IPv4
5. Private
Section C
1. capacity
2. jitter
3. Traceroute
4. latency
5. motion
Section D
1. router
2. MAC, media access control
3. Ethernet
4. encryption
5. IoT, Internet of Things
Section E
1. discovery
2. write
3. sharing
4. FTP
5. mesh

Module 4

Pre-Check
1. hyperlink, link, or hypertext link
2. refresh or reload
3. URL or Uniform Resource Locator
4. Cookies, HTTP cookies, or cookie
5. incognito or incognito mode
6. HTML, HTM
7. AND, OR, NOT
8. HTTPS
9. Public key encryption

QuickChecks
243. B
244. D
246. D
247. A
248. B
249. C
251. C
257. C
259. D
262. A
264. B
265. D
267. A
268. A
269. C
270. D
272a. A
272b. C
273. C
274. A
275. D
276. B
279a. B
279b. A
280. C
281a. A
281b. B
282. C
283. B
284. B
285. A
288. A
289. D
290. A
291. A
295. C
297. A

QuickQuizzes
Section A
1. Internet
2. hypertext
3. ? or question mark
4. domain
5. short
Section B
1. update
2. History
3. cache
4. Predictive, preload
5. extension
Section C
1. HTML or source
2. code, tags
3. links or hyperlinks
4. Style
5. scripts
Section D
1. stateless
2. third
3. session
4. status
5. public
Section E
1. indexer
2. query
3. operators
4. cookie
5. URL

Module 5

Pre-Check
1. profile or avatar
2. hashtag
3. sociogram or sociograph
4. POP3, IMAP, SMTP
5. trademark or registered trademark
6. Wikipedia
7. derivatives
8. doppelganger
9. Share Alike

QuickChecks
313. C
314. C
316. B
319a. A
319b. D
320. B
321. A
322. A
323. A
325. A
326. A
327. D
328. C
329. B
330. D
332. A
333. D
335. D
337a. A
337b. D
338. A
339. D
340. A
342. A
345. B
346. C
348. C
349. D
350. B
351. A
352. B
355. C
356. A
358. A
360. C
361. D
362. B

QuickQuizzes
Section A
1. Honeycomb
2. crowdsourcing
3. triangulation
4. sociogram
5. adjacency
Section B
1. viral
2. generated
3. tagging
4. trademark
5. ND
Section C
1. platforms
2. content
3. # or hashtag
4. wiki
5. research
Section D
1. asynchronous
2. header or message header
3. IMAP
4. IM or instant messaging
5. synchronous
Section E
1. sockpuppet
2. identities
3. cyberbullying
4. identifiable
5. service

Module 6

Pre-Check
1. kernel
2. multitasking
3. thin
4. virtual
5. DMG
6. absolute
7. 256 characters
8. root
9. Windows File Explorer, macOS Finder

QuickChecks
381. B
382. C
384. A
385. C
386. A
387. B
391. B
392. B
393. B
395. B
396. B
398. A
400. B
401. D
402. C
403. D
404. C
406. A
408. B
409. A
410. D
411. B
412. C
416. B
417. A
418. D
419. A
420. D
421. B
422. A
423. B
424a. A
424b. C
427. A
428. B
429. C
434. B
436. A
437. C

QuickQuizzes
Section A
1. system
2. exe
3. intellectual
4. freemium
5. activation

Section B
1. False
2. kernel
3. iOS
4. Android
5. virtual

Section C
1. Web
2. setup
3. Registry
4. .dmg
5. uninstall

Section D
1. paragraph
2. Spreadsheet
3. absolute
4. table
5. fields

Section E
1. conventions
2. partition
3. root
4. cluster or block
5. system or systems

Module 7

Pre-Check
1. AES
2. password entropy
3. signature
4. Trojan
5. Stuxnet
6. Zero-day attack
7. ports
8. MITM
9. botnet

QuickChecks
456. D
459. C
460. B
461. C
462. C
464. A
468. B
469. D
470. D
471. A
472. C
473. D
475. C
476. B
479. C
482. A
483. B
484. C
485. A
487. C
489. A
490. A
491. B
492. D
495. A
497. D
499. A
501. B
502. C
503. A
504. C
507. D

QuickQuizzes
Section A
1. encrypt
2. authentication
3. dictionary
4. entropy
5. browser

Section B
1. worm
2. dropper
3. heuristic
4. positive
5. hoax

Section C
1. remote
2. denial
3. zero
4. port
5. firewall

Section D
1. Wi-Fi or wireless
2. DNS
3. TLS
4. True
5. IMSI

Section E
1. fee
2. filters
3. phishing or spear phishing
4. pharming
5. rogue

Module 8

Pre-Check

1. bubble
2. Morse
3. software developers
4. certification
5. hype
6. 4G
7. Privacy
8. 11, eleven
9. general purpose microprocessor

QuickChecks

523. D
524. A
526. C
527. B
528. C
529. C
530. B
531. B
532. D
533. D
534. C
535. D
537. B
538. C
539. A
540. B
541. C
542. B
543. A
544. D
545. B
546. D
547. D
549. D
551. A
552. D
553. B
554. B
555a. C
555b. A
556. A
557. B
558. D
559. D
560. B
561. C
562. C
563. B
564. A
566. B
568. A
569. B
570. D
571. C
572. D
573. A

576. D
581. B
583. C
586. C
587. C
588. A

QuickQuizzes

Section A

1. Communications
2. dot-coms
3. Capital
4. Offshoring
5. cyberwarfare

Section B

1. algorithms
2. architecture
3. transistors
4. microprocessor (or microprocessors)
5. spreadsheet

Section C

1. telegraph
2. carriers
3. radio
4. 4
5. DTV

Section D

1. True
2. Contract
3. information
4. certification
5. associate

Section E

1. ethical
2. Digital
3. confidentiality
4. ethical (or responsible)
5. whistleblower

Module 9

Pre-Check

1. cookies
2. PIECES
3. use case
4. turnkey
5. ERP
6. customer support, marketing, sales
7. SCM
8. fraud alert
9. data centers

QuickChecks

607. C
608. A
609. C
610. A
611. D
612. C
615. C
617. D
619. D
620. D
621. D
622. A
623. A
624. C
625. A
626. C
627. C
629. C
630. D
631. B
632. B
633a. B
633b. B
635. B
636. D
638. A
639. C
641. A
642. D
644. B
645. C
646. B
647. B
648. C
650. C
652. B
655. D
656. B
659. A
661a. A
661b. D
662. C

QuickQuizzes

Section A

1. mission
2. tactical
3. online
4. support
5. knowledge

Section B

1. False
2. payment
3. supply chain
4. CRM
5. ERP

Section C

1. development
2. Service
3. PERT
4. analysis
5. flow

Section D

1. design
2. application
3. creep
4. acceptance
5. quality

Section E

1. MTBF
2. recovery
3. Corrective
4. data
5. fraud

Module 10

Pre-Check

1. entity-relationship diagram (or ERD)
2. multidimensional database model
3. column-oriented data model
4. field format
5. Blockchain
6. zettabyte
7. Graph data model
8. NoSQL
9. Boolean

QuickChecks

681. C
683. A
684. D
685. C
686. A
687. D
688. C
689. B
690. C
691. C
692. C
693. D
695. B
697. D
698. D
699. A
700. D
701. A
702. C
703. A
704. B
705. C
707. B
708. C
709. B
710. A
711. D
712. C
713. A
714. B
715. B
717. A
718. A
721. B
722. B
723. A
725. D
726a. D
726b. C
726c. D
727. A
728. D
731. C
732. B

733. B
736. D
737a. A
737b. C
738. A
739. C

QuickQuizzes

Section A
1. analytical
2. mining
3. type
4. graph
5. relational

Section B
1. True
2. independence
3. client
4. serializability or serialization
5. level

Section C
1. key
2. False
3. validation
4. normalization
5. indexed

Section D
1. Boolean
2. False
3. SELECT
4. UPDATE
5. False

Section E
1. velocity
2. low
3. NoSQL
4. key
5. Blockchain

Module 11

Pre-Check

1. Android Studio, Xcode
2. UML
3. low
4. op
5. algorithm
6. syntax
7. Prolog
8. method
9. encapsulation

QuickChecks

759. B
760. C
761. D
762. C
763. C
764. A
765. D
767. D
768. C
769a. A
769b. C
770. C
773. D
774. B
775. D
776. C
777. A
778. A
781. D
782. A
785. B
787. D
788a. B
788b. C
791a. A
791b. B
792. B
793. B
796. C
797. D
800. D
801. D
802. A
803. A
804. A
805. A
806. D
807. D
808. B
809. A
811. C
812. A
813. C
814. A
816. D
818. D
820. B

QuickQuizzes

Section A
1. application(s)
2. agile
3. variables
4. statement
5. Formal

Section B
1. Third
2. paradigms
3. Scripting
4. object
5. API

Section C
1. algorithm
2. procedural
3. sequence
4. True
5. loop

Section D
1. objects
2. UML
3. method
4. inheritance
5. Java

Section E
1a. problem
1b. solution
2a. arguments
2b. predicate
3a. constant
3b. variable
4. instantiation
5. if

Module PY

Pre-Check

1. string
2. comparison
3. list
4. function
5. concatenation
6. sub or derived
7. accumulator
8. syntax
9. floating point or floating-point

QuickChecks

839.	A
846.	C
851.	C
859.	C
860.	C
861.	A
862.	A
863.	D
864.	A
865a.	A
865b.	B
866a.	A
866b.	B
870.	B
872.	C
876.	B
881.	D
883.	A
889.	B

QuickQuizzes

Section A
1. interpreter
2. #, hashtag, or pound sign
3. string
4. syntax
5. debugging

Section B
1. variable
2. assignment
3. object
4. attribute
5. keyboard, touchscreen

Section C
1. values
2. parentheses
3. selection control
4. elif
5. Boolean

Section D
1. repetition control
2. iteration
3. True
4. while
5. list

Section E
1. def
2. parameters
3. methods
4. superclass
5. inheritance